State Information Directory
2000–2001

State
Information
Directory
2000–2001

A DIVISION OF CONGRESSIONAL QUARTERLY INC.
WASHINGTON, D.C.

State Information Directory, 2000-2001
Produced by Jankowski Associates, Inc.,
  Frederick, Maryland

CQ Press
A Division of Congressional Quarterly Inc.
1414 22nd Street, N.W.
Washington, D.C. 20037

(202) 822-1475; (800) 638-1710

www.cqpress.com

Printed in the United States of America

04 03 02 01 00   5 4 3 2 1

Library of Congress Cataloging-in-Publication Data:
In process

ISBN: 1-56802-516-5

Contents

Preface

CQ Press is pleased to introduce the first edition of the *State Information Directory 2000–2001*. This comprehensive, user-friendly guide to state government leaders is an indispensable resource for quickly identifying key individuals and agencies at all fifty states and the District of Columbia. Each state listing contains information on the executive, legislative, and judicial branches of government.

As power — both political and spending — continues to shift to states and localities from the federal government, it remains important for corporations, associations, and government managers, as well as librarians serving the public, to know who's who in state government. The *State Information Directory* provides this information in an easy-to-read, one-stop research tool.

The *State Information Directory* also reflects state governments' move to providing increasing amounts of information on the Internet. Throughout this first edition, users will find thousands of Internet resources, agency home pages, and ways to access people and data directly. More than 80 percent of the agencies profiled have home pages on the Internet and more than 70 percent of the profiles provide e-mail addresses for contacting individuals or agencies. Please see **How to Use This Directory** for more information on the contents of each listing.

In creating this directory, CQ editors and researchers wanted to provide important background information on each state, in addition to the critical government and agency data. Each state listing includes the official state seal, state facts, higher educational institutions, frequently called numbers, ways to access the important boards and licensing agencies, state laws, and legislative and political party information. Readers will find this information boxed out for quick reference. Two indexes, a functional index and a name index, also provide quick entry points to the detailed information contained in the *State Information Directory.*

Our goal is to produce the most comprehensive, useful, and authoritative directory of its kind. We encourage anyone with changes or corrections to forward them to us for inclusion in the next edition. As always, we welcome your comments and suggestions.

How to Use This Directory

The *State Information Directory 2000-2001* is designed to make your search for information fast and easy.

The directory is organized in state-by-state listings, with each state and the District of Columbia beginning on a new page. State headings contain the address for the state capital, general information telephone and fax numbers, and the URL for each state's home page on the Internet. The information within each state begins with the office of the governor and key administration officials such as the lieutenant governor and secretary of state. Agency data follow, listed in alphabetical order by agency name. Legislative and judicial information come after the agency listings. Detailed explanations of how information is presented in each section of a state profile follow.

Executive Branch

State listings begin with the executive branch. Offices of the governor, lieutenant governor, secretary of state, attorney general, treasurer, comptroller, and adjutant general are listed at the top of each state for which they are applicable. In addition to contact information, party information for elected officials follows each individual's name. Within the office of the governor, you also will find the governor's chief of staff, press secretary or communications contact, and a contact for constituent affairs.

Following these offices, you will find the main state agencies and departments, as well as key state boards. Agencies are listed alphabetically by name. In some instances when a key state function falls within a larger state agency, this office is hierarchically indented under the main state agency. Flush left under an agency's name you will find information useful for contacting the agency or finding out about it.

Each agency listing begins with the following data, as available: Internet home page, agency e-mail address, main telephone and fax numbers, in-state toll-free number, TTY number, and mailing address.

The name, title, and contact information for the agency head comes next. Contact information includes the following, as available: address, room number, direct phone number, direct fax number, and contact person's e-mail address. Some agencies do not have separate phone numbers for the agency head because of their size or structure. In these instances, we list the telephone number under the main agency contact information.

Legislative Branch

The legislative branch for each state begins with address information for the seat of the legislature and telephone numbers for the main switchboard and bill status. More than 98 percent of state legislatures have home pages on the Internet, and the URL can be found in each heading.

Background information is followed by listings for the two legislative chambers. The senate precedes the house of representatives or assembly. Leadership information includes, as available, the president of the senate and speaker of the house, president pro tempore and speaker pro tempore, majority leaders, majority whips, minority leaders, minority whips, and clerk or secretary. If the individual listed has his or her own home page on the Internet, we list this URL in addition to the other contact information.

Judicial Branch

The judicial branch for each state begins with the address for the state supreme court followed by the judicial branch's home page on the Internet, as applicable. The heading is followed by contact information for the supreme court. Every state listed has an Internet home page for either the judicial branch or the supreme court.

The court clerk is listed first, followed by brief information on the supreme court's composition, selection method, and length of term for justices. A list of justices comes next, including the names and telephone numbers for the chief justice followed by an alphabetical listing of the other justices.

The judicial branch profile also includes listings for each administrative office of the court and the state's law library or supreme court library.

Boxes

Throughout each state profile you will find boxes containing important information about each state as well as information that will help you quickly contact key offices and agencies.

State Facts

A state facts box begins each state's listing. Pulled together into one spot is useful information on the following: when the state was founded, statehood date, date the constitution was adopted, area and rank in terms of size, population and population rank, five largest cities, five largest counties, U.S. senators and the number of representatives in Congress, nicknames, motto, song, bird, tree, flower, state fair location, and former state capitals.

Higher Educational Institutions

This box contains the name, address, phone number, and Internet home page for state-affiliated institutions of higher education. Branch locations for large university systems also are referenced.

Frequently Called Numbers

This box contains a quick synopsis of the telephone numbers most frequently needed, including tourism, the state library, board of education, vital statistics, tax and revenue, motor vehicles, state police or highway patrol, unemployment, election information, consumer affairs, and hazardous materials.

Boards and Licensing

This box contains information on the major boards and licensing agencies at each state. If a single state agency coordinates or oversees this function, it is listed in the box's heading. In most cases, however, various agencies oversee licensing activities. Each state profile contains additional contact information for these boards, but we have pulled out the most frequently needed phone numbers and Internet addresses for quick reference. These include accountancy, architects, child care, contractors, cosmetology, engineers and land surveyors, medical examiners, nursing, pharmacy, and real estate appraisers.

Laws

Each state profile provides an overview of key laws and regulations within the state. We have attempted to simplify statutes so that they can be compared easily. However, state laws have many exceptions and are subject to change: this information is not intended as legal advice. Laws have been selected to answer basic questions that are frequently asked and to allow readers to see where the individual states currently stand on major controversies, such as access to guns, legalized gambling, gay rights, and mandatory sentencing for a third felony.

Here, as elsewhere in the directory, the District of Columbia is treated as the equivalent of a state.

The laws and regulations listed in the *State Information Directory 2000-2001* are defined as follows:

Sales tax: The percentage of tax on most retail sales to consumers. Many states exempt certain items, such as groceries, newspapers and magazines, and clothing.

Income tax: The highest personal income tax rate, by percentage of income, that was in effect in each state for income earned in 1998. For most states this rate applies only if the taxpayer's annual income exceeds $100,000.

State minimum wage: The dollar amount per hour for each state. States vary in terms of who is covered by the minimum wage; as noted, some states set a lower rate for small businesses. For comparison we include the federal minimum wage.

Marriage age: The age at which individuals may marry without parental consent. States permit younger people to marry with parental consent; the absolute minimum varies.

First-cousin marriage: Whether or not states permit marriage between first cousins. Some states make exceptions for older people; the restrictions are intended to reduce the likelihood of passing on genetic disorders.

Drinking age: The minimum age for consuming alcohol without parental consent.

State control of liquor sales: Whether or not a state controls the sale of hard liquor within its boundaries.

Blood alcohol for DWI: The percentage of alcohol in the blood at which a driver is considered legally drunk and can be charged with driving while intoxicated.

Driving age: The minimum age at which a person can hold an unrestricted license to operate an automobile. In all instances the age for a learner's permit is lower; some states have also implemented a restricted or probationary license following the learner's permit.

Speed limit: The maximum speed for passenger cars on rural interstates. Most states have lower maximum speeds in all other conditions: on urban interstates, on secondary roads and city streets, and for trucks and other commercial vehicles.

Permit to buy handguns: Whether states require a permit to own a handgun and the minimum waiting period for this permit, if any. Unless noted otherwise, there is no other waiting period to purchase subsequent handguns once an individual has a valid owner's permit.

Minimum age to possess handguns: The minimum age to possess a handgun without parental consent, if any.

Minimum age to possess rifles, shotguns: The minimum age to possess a sporting gun without parental consent, if any.

State lottery: Whether a state operates a lottery or participates in Powerball.

Casinos: Types of casinos, such as tribal or commercial, that operate legally within the state.

Pari-mutuel betting: Legal forms of betting in the state, including horse racing, dog racing, and jai alai.

Death penalty: Whether the state has legalized capital punishment.

3 strikes minimum sentence: The sentence for a third felony in states that have implemented "three strikes and you're out" laws.

Hate crimes law: Whether the state has outlawed certain crimes against minority groups. States vary in terms of which groups are protected.

Gay employment non-discrimination: Whether a state protects gay men and lesbians from workplace discrimination in the private sector.

Official language(s): Languages which a state has designated for the conduct of official business, if any.

Term limits: The number of years of service to which states restrict governors and state legislators.

Legislative and Political Party Information Resources

This box contains Internet resources for keeping track of each state legislature, including links for the Senate and House home pages, current session information, legislative information, and the legislative process. These links are followed by contact information for the state-level offices of the Democratic and Republican Parties.

Indexes

Functional Index

This index contains 163 functional subject areas ranging from administration to veterans affairs and the state offices responsible for these areas. Page number references help you find the office you are looking for quickly and easily.

Name Index

The name index lists the more than 4,700 individuals contained in the *State Information Directory 2000-2001.* Individuals are listed alphabetically by last name with state abbreviation, phone number, and page reference.

State Listings

Alabama

State Capitol
600 Dexter Ave.
Montgomery, AL 36130
Public information: (334) 242-8000
Fax: (334) 242-2700
http://www.state.al.us

Office of the Governor
http://www.governor.state.al.us
Main phone: (334) 242-7100
Main fax: (334) 242-0937

Don Siegelman (D), Governor
State Capitol, 600 Dexter Ave., #N-104, Montgomery,
AL 36130

Paul M. Hamrick, Chief of Staff
State Capitol, 600 Dexter Ave., #NB08, Montgomery,
AL 36130
(334) 242-4738; *Fax:* (334) 242-2766
E-mail: phamrick@governor.state.al.us

**Carrie Kurlander, Director, Press Relations, Public
Information and Communications**
State Capitol, 600 Dexter Ave., #NB06, Montgomery,
AL 36130
(334) 242-7150; *Fax:* (334) 242-4407

Josh Hayes, Special Assistant to the Governor
State Capitol, 600 Dexter Ave., #N-104, Montgomery,
AL 36130
(334) 242-7140; *Fax:* (334) 242-0937
E-mail: jhayes@governor.state.al.us

Office of the Lieutenant Governor
Main phone: (334) 242-7900
Main fax: (334) 242-4661

Steve Windom (R), Lieutenant Governor
Alabama State House, 11 S. Union St., #725,
Montgomery, AL 36130-6050

Office of the Secretary of State
http://www.sos.state.al.us/
Main phone: (334) 242-7200
Main fax: (334) 242-4993
Mailing address: P.O. Box 5616, Montgomery, AL
36103-5616

Jim Bennett (R), Secretary of State
State Capitol, 600 Dexter Ave., #S-105, Montgomery,
AL 36103-5616
(334) 242-7205; *Fax:* (334) 242-4993
E-mail: alsecst@alalinc.net

State of Alabama

Capital: Montgomery, since 1846
Founded: 1817, Alabama Territory created from Mississippi Territory
Statehood: December 14, 1819 (22nd state)
Constitution adopted: November 28, 1901
Area: 50,750 sq. mi. (ranks 28th)
Population: 4,351,999 (1998 est.; ranks 23rd)
Largest cities: (1998 est.) Birmingham (252,997); Mobile (202,181); Montgomery (197,014); Huntsville (175,979); Tuscaloosa (83,376)
Counties: 67, Most populous: (1998 est.) Jefferson (659,524); Mobile (399,429); Madison (278,187); Montgomery (217,693); Tuscaloosa (160,768)
U.S. Congress: Jeff Sessions (R), Richard C. Shelby (R); 7 Representatives
Nickname(s): Heart of Dixie, Cotton State, Yellowhammer State
Motto: We dare defend our rights
Song: "Alabama"
Bird: Yellowhammer
Tree: Southern longleaf pine
Flower: Camellia
State fair: at Montgomery and Mobile, late Oct.
Former capital(s): St. Stephens, Huntsville, Cahaba, Tuscaloosa

Office of the Attorney General
http://www.ago.state.al.us
Main phone: (334) 242-7300
Main fax: (334) 242-7458

William Holcombe Pryor Jr. (R), Attorney General
Alabama State House, 11 S. Union St., 3rd Fl.,
Montgomery, AL 36104-3760
(334) 242-7401

Office of the Treasurer
http://www.treasury.state.al.us
General e-mail: altreas@treasury.state.al.us
Main phone: (334) 242-7500
Main fax: (334) 242-7592
Mailing address: P.O. Box 302510, Montgomery,
AL 36130

Lucy Baxley (D), State Treasurer
State Capitol, 600 Dexter Ave., #S-106, Montgomery,
AL 36130-2751
(334) 242-7501

Office of the State Auditor
http://agencies.state.al.us/auditor
Main phone: (334) 242-7010
Main fax: (334) 242-7650
Mailing address: P.O. Box 300200, Montgomery,
AL 36130

Susan D. Parker (D), State Auditor
State Capitol, #S-101, Montgomery, AL 36130
E-mail: sparker@auditor.state.al.us

Military Dept.
http://www.alguard.com/
Main phone: (334) 271-7400
Main fax: (334) 213-7511
Mailing address: P.O. Box 3711, Montgomery, AL
36109-0711

Willie A. Alexander, Adjutant General
1720 Congressman William L. Dickinson Dr.,
Montgomery, AL 36109-0711
(334) 271-7200
E-mail: alexanderw@al-arng.ngb.army.mil

Agencies

Aeronautics Dept.
General e-mail: alada@aeronautics.state.al.us
Main phone: (334) 242-4480
Main fax: (334) 240-3274

John C. Eagerton, Director
770 Washington Ave., #544, Montgomery, AL 36130

Aging Commission
http://agencies.state.al.us/coa
General e-mail: ageline@coa.state.al.us
Main phone: (334) 242-5743
Main fax: (334) 242-5594
Toll free: (877) 425-2243
Mailing address: P.O. Box 301851, Montgomery,
AL 36130-1851

Melissa Mauser Galvin, Executive Director
770 Washington Ave., RSA Plaza, #470, Montgomery,
AL 36130
E-mail: mgalvin@coa.state.al.us

Agriculture and Industries Dept.
http://www.agri-ind.state.al.us
General e-mail: alagicom02@agri-ind.state.al.us
Main phone: (334) 240-7171
Main fax: (334) 240-7190
Toll free: (800) 642-7761

Mailing address: P.O. Box 3336, Montgomery, AL
36109-0336

Charles Bishop (D), Commissioner
Richard Beard Bldg., 1445 Federal Dr.,
Montgomery, AL 36107-0336
(334) 240-7100; *Fax:* (334) 240-7190

Alcoholic Beverage Control Board
http://www.abcboard.state.al.us/
General e-mail: admin@abcboard.state.al.us
Main phone: (334) 271-3840
Main fax: (334) 277-2150

Randall C. Smith, Administrator
2715 Gunter Park Dr. West, Montgomery, AL 36109-
1021

Architects Registration Board
http://www.alarchbd.state.al.us
Main phone: (334) 242-4179
Main fax: (334) 242-4531

Cindy J. Gainey, Administrator
770 Washington Ave., #150, Montgomery, AL
36130-4450
E-mail: cgainey@dsmd.dsmd.state.al.us

Archives and History Dept.
http://www.archives.state.al.us
Main phone: (334) 242-4363
Main fax: (334) 240-3433
TTY: (334) 242-4435, ext. 286
Mailing address: P.O. Box 300100, Montgomery,
AL 36130-0100

Edwin C. Bridges, Director
624 Washington Ave., Montgomery, AL 36130-0100
(334) 242-4441, ext. 248; *Fax:* (334) 240-3125
E-mail: ebridges@archives.state.al.us

Arts Council
http://www.arts.state.al.us
General e-mail: staff@arts.state.al.us
Main phone: (334) 242-4076
Main fax: (334) 240-3269

Albert B. Head, Executive Director
201 Monroe St., #110, Montgomery, AL 36130-1800
(334) 242-4076, ext. 245
E-mail: al@arts.state.al.us

Banking Dept.
Main phone: (334) 242-3452
Main fax: (334) 242-3500

Norman B. Davis Jr., Superintendent
401 Adams Ave., #680, Montgomery, AL 36130
(334) 242-3585

Conservation and Natural Resources Dept.
http://www.dcnr.state.al.us
Main phone: (334) 242-3846
Main fax: (334) 242-1880
Toll free: (800) 262-3151
TTY: (334) 242-3151
Mailing address: P.O. Box 301450, Montgomery,
AL 36130-1450

Riley Boykin Smith, Commissioner
64 N. Union St., #468, Montgomery, AL 36130-1450
Fax: (334) 242-3849
E-mail: commissioner@dcnr.state.al.us

Game and Fish Division
http://www.dcnr.state.al.us/agfd/index.html
General e-mail: twilson@dcnr.state.al.us
Main phone: (334) 242-3465
Main fax: (334) 242-3032
Mailing address: P.O. Box 301450,
Montgomery, AL 36130-1457

M. N. Corky Pugh, Assistant Director (Acting)
64 N. Union St., #567, Montgomery, AL 36130

State Parks Division
http://www.dcnr.state.al.us/parks/
state_parks_index_1a.html
General e-mail: vsmith@dcnr.state.al.us
Main phone: (334) 242-3334
Toll free: (800) ALAPARK

Don Cooley, Director
64 N. Union St., Montgomery, AL 36130

Consumer Assistance Division
Main phone: (334) 242-7335
Main fax: (334) 242-7458
Toll free: (800) 392-5658

Dennis M. Wright, Director
Alabama State House, 11 S. Union St., Montgomery,
AL 36130
(334) 242-7463; *Fax:* (334) 242-2433
E-mail: dwright@ago.state.al.us

Contractors Licensing Board
Main phone: (334) 272-5030
Main fax: (334) 240-3424

Cherie E. Colquett, Executive Secretary
400 S. Union St., #235, Montgomery, AL 36130

Corrections Dept.
http://agencies.state.al.us/doc
General e-mail: pio@doc.state.al.us
Main phone: (334) 261-3600
Main fax: (334) 353-3891
Mailing address: P.O. Box 301501, Montgomery,
AL 36130-1501

Higher Educational Institutions

Alabama A&M University
http://www.aamu.edu
4900 Meridian St., Normal, AL 35762
Main phone: (334) 851-5000

Alabama State University
http://www.alasu.edu
915 S. Jackson St., Montgomery, AL 36101-0271
Main phone: (334) 229-4100

Athens State College
http://www.athens.edu
302 Beaty St., Athens, AL 35611
Main phone: (205) 233-8100

Auburn University
http://www.auburn.edu
ETV Annex, Telecom Blvd., Auburn, AL 36849-5423
Main phone: (334) 844-4000
Branches: Montgomery

Jacksonville State University
http://www.jsu.edu
N. Pelham Rd., Jacksonville, AL 36265
Main phone: (205) 782-5781

Troy State University
http://www.troyst.edu
University Ave., Troy, AL 36082
Main phone: (334) 670-3100
Branches: Dothan, Montgomery

University of Alabama
http://www.ua.edu
401 Queen City Ave., Tuscaloosa, AL 35401
Main phone: (205) 348-5122
Branches: Birmingham, Huntsville, Montgomery

University of Montevallo
http://www.montevallo.edu
Station 6000, Montevallo, AL 35115
Main phone: (205) 665-6000

University of North Alabama
http://www.una.edu
Weslyan Ave., Florence, AL 35632
Main phone: (205) 765-4100

University of South Alabama
http://www.usa.edu
307 University Blvd., Mobile, AL 36688
Main phone: (334) 460-6101

University of West Alabama
http://www.westal.edu
Hwy. 11 North, Livingston, AL 35470
Main phone: (205) 652-3400

Michael W. Haley, Commissioner
101 S. Union St., Montgomery, AL 36130
(334) 353-3883; *Fax:* (334) 353-3891

Cosmetology Board
http://www.aboc.state.al.us
Main phone: (334) 242-1918
Main fax: (334) 242-1926

Keith E. Warren, Director
100 N. Union St., Montgomery, AL 36130

Criminal Justice Information Center
http://agencies.state.al.us/acjic/
General e-mail: acjic@acjic.state.al.us
Main phone: (334) 242-4900
Main fax: (334) 242-0577

Larry Wright, Director
770 Washington Ave., #350, Montgomery, AL 36130-0660

Development Office
http://www.ado.state.al.us/index.html
General e-mail: idinfo@www.ado.state.al.us
Main phone: (334) 242-0400
Main fax: (334) 242-5669
Toll free: (800) 248-0033
Mailing address: P.O. Box 304106, Montgomery, AL 36130-4106

Ken Funderburk, Director
401 Adams Ave., #670, Montgomery, AL 36130-4106
E-mail: ado_dir@www.ado.state.al.us

Education Dept.
http://www.alsde.edu
General e-mail: astarks@sdenet.alsde.edu
Main phone: (334) 242-9950
Main fax: (334) 353-4682

Ed Richardson, State Superintendent
Gordon Persons Bldg., 50 N. Ripley St., Montgomery, AL 36130-2101
(334) 242-9700; *Fax:* (334) 242-9708
E-mail: edrich@sdenet.alsde.edu

Board of Education
http://www.alsde.edu/boe/boe.html
Main phone: (334) 242-9950
Main fax: (334) 242-9708
TTY: (334) 242-8114
Mailing address: P.O. Box 302101, Montgomery, AL 36130-2101

Ed Richardson, Executive Officer/Secretary
Gordon Persons Bldg., 50 N. Ripley St., #5114, Montgomery, AL 36130
(334) 242-9700; *Fax:* (334) 242-9708
E-mail: edrich@sdenet.alsde.edu

Emergency Management Agency
http://www.aema.state.al.us
General e-mail: info@aema.state.al.us
Main phone: (205) 280-2200
Main fax: (205) 280-2495
Toll free: (800) 843-0699
TTY: (205) 280-0405
Mailing address: P.O. Box 2160, Clanton, AL 35046

Warren L. Helms, Director
5898 County Rd. 41, Clanton, AL 35046
(205) 280-2201; *Fax:* (205) 280-2410
E-mail: leeh@aema.state.al.us

Engineers and Land Surveyors Board of Licensure
General e-mail: engineer@dsmd.dsmd.state.al.us
Main phone: (334) 242-5568
Main fax: (334) 242-5105
Mailing address: P.O. Box 304451, Montgomery, AL 36130-4451

Regina A. Dinger, Executive Director
100 N. Union St., #382, Montgomery, AL 36104
(334) 242-5021
E-mail: rdinger@dsmd.dsmd.state.al.us

Environmental Management Dept.
http://www.adem.state.al.us
General e-mail: dcp@adem.state.al.us
Main phone: (334) 271-7700
Main fax: (334) 271-7950
Toll free: (800) 533-2336
Mailing address: P.O. Box 301463, Montgomery, AL 36130-1463

James W. Warr, Director
1400 Coliseum Blvd., Montgomery, AL 36110-2059
(334) 271-7710; *Fax:* (334) 279-3043

Ethics Commission
http://www.ethics.alalinc.net
General e-mail: ethics@alalinc.net
Main phone: (334) 242-2997
Main fax: (334) 242-0248
Mailing address: P.O. Box 4840, Montgomery, AL 36103-4840

James L. Sumner Jr., Director
100 N. Union St., #104, Montgomery, AL 36104
(334) 242-2806

Finance Dept.
General e-mail: ladams@governor.state.al.us
Main phone: (334) 242-7160
Main fax: (334) 353-3300

Henry C. Mabry III, Director
State Capitol, 600 Dexter Ave., #105-N, Montgomery, AL 36130

Forestry Commission
http://www.forestry.state.al.us
Main phone: (334) 240-9300
Main fax: (334) 240-9390
Mailing address: P.O. Box 302550, Montgomery,
AL 36130-2550

Timothy C. Boyce, State Forester
513 Madison Ave., Montgomery, AL 36130-2550
(334) 240-9304
E-mail: boycet@forestry.state.al.us

Funeral Services Board
Main phone: (334) 242-4049
Main fax: (334) 353-7988
Mailing address: P.O. Box 309522, Montgomery,
AL 36130-9522

Warren S. Higgins, Executive Secretary
11 S. Union St., #219, Montgomery, AL 36130-9522

Geological Survey of Alabama
http://www.gsa.state.al.us
General e-mail: info@gsa.state.al.us
Main phone: (205) 349-2852
Main fax: (205) 349-2861
Mailing address: P.O. Box 869999, Tuscaloosa, AL
35486-6999

Donald F. Oltz, State Geologist
420 Hackberry Lane, Tuscaloosa, AL 35486-6999
E-mail: doltz@gsa.state.al.us

Health Planning and Development Agency
Main phone: (334) 242-4103
Main fax: (334) 242-4113
Mailing address: P.O. Box 303025, Montgomery,
AL 36130-3025

Alva M. Lambert, Executive Director
100 N. Union St., #870, Montgomery, AL 36130-3025
E-mail: jlogan@dsmd.dsmd.state.al.us

Higher Education Commission
http://www.ache.state.al.us
Main phone: (334) 242-1998
Main fax: (334) 242-0268
Mailing address: P.O. Box 302000, Montgomery,
AL 36130-2000

Henry J. Hector, Executive Director
100 N. Union St., #724, Montgomery, AL 36130-2000
(334) 242-2123; *Fax:* (334) 242-0268
E-mail: hhector@ache.state.al.us

Historical Commission
http://www.preserveala.org
Main phone: (334) 242-3184
Main fax: (334) 240-3477

Lee Warner, Executive Director
468 Perry St., Montgomery, AL 36130-0900
E-mail: lwarner@preserveala.org

Frequently Called Numbers

Tourism: (334) 242-4169; 1-800-ALABAMA;
  http://www.touralabama.org
Library: (334) 213-3900;
  http://www.apls.state.al.us
Board of Education: (334) 242-9950;
  http://www.alsde.edu/boe/boe.html
Vital Statistics: (334) 206-5418; http://
  www.alapubhealth.org/vital/vitalrcd.htm
Tax/Revenue: (334) 242-1170;
  http://www.ador.state.al.us
Motor Vehicles: (334) 242-9000
State Police/Highway Patrol: (334) 242-4394
Unemployment: (334) 242-8800
General Election Information:
  (334) 242-7210; http://www.sos.state.al.us/
  election/election.htm
Consumer Affairs: (334) 242-7335
Hazardous Materials: (334) 242-4395;
  http://www.dps.state.al.us/MCSU.html

Housing Finance Authority
http://www.ahfa.com
Main phone: (334) 244-9200
Main fax: (334) 244-9214
Toll free: (800) 325-2432
TTY: (334) 271-6785
Mailing address: P.O. Box 230909, Montgomery,
AL 36123-0909

Robert Strickland, Executive Director
2000 Interstate Park Dr., Montgomery, AL 36109
E-mail: rstrickland@ahfa.com

Human Resources Dept.
Main phone: (334) 242-1160
Main fax: (334) 242-0198

Tony Petelos, Commissioner
Gordon Persons Bldg., 50 N. Ripley St., Montgomery,
AL 36130-4000

Industrial Relations Dept.
http://www.dir.state.al.us
General e-mail: hcornett@dir.state.al.us
Main phone: (334) 242-8618
Main fax: (334) 242-8843

Alice D. McKinney, Director
649 Monroe St., Montgomery, AL 36131
(334) 242-8990; *Fax:* (334) 242-3960

Institute for the Deaf and Blind
http://www.aidb.org
Main phone: (256) 761-3201

Main fax: (256) 761-3344
TTY: (256) 761-3200
Mailing address: P.O. Box 698, Montgomery, AL
35161

Joseph F. Busta Jr., President
205 E. South St., Talladega, AL 35160
(256) 761-3200
E-mail: jbust@aidb.state.al.us

Insurance Dept.
http://www.aldoi.org
General e-mail: insdept@insurance.state.al.us
Main phone: (334) 269-3350
Main fax: (334) 241-4192
Mailing address: P.O. Box 303351, Montgomery,
AL 36130-3351

D. David Parsons, Commissioner (Acting)
201 Monroe St., #1700, Montgomery, AL 36130-3351
(334) 241-4101

State Fire Marshal
http://www.aldoi.org/firemarshal/index.cfm
General e-mail:
firemarshal@insurance.state.al.us
Main phone: (334) 241-4166
Main fax: (334) 241-4158
Mailing address: P.O. Box 303352,
Montgomery, AL 36130-3352

John S. Robison, State Fire Marshal
201 Monroe St., #1780, Montgomery, AL 36104

Labor Dept.
Main phone: (334) 242-3460
Main fax: (334) 240-3417

Boards and Licensing

Accountancy, (334) 242-5700
Architects Registration, (334) 242-4179,
http://www.alarchbd.state.al.us
Child Care, (334) 242-1425
Contractors, (334) 272-5030
Cosmetology, (334) 242-1918,
http://www.aboc.state.al.us
Engineers and Land Surveyors,
(334) 242-5568
Medical Examiners, (334) 242-4116,
http://www.mindspring.com/~bmedixon/
Nursing, (334) 242-4060,
http://www.abn.state.al.us/
Pharmacy, (205) 967-0130,
http://www.albop.com/
Real Estate Appraisers, (334) 242-8747,
http://agencies.state.al.us/reab

Mailing address: P.O. Box 303500, Montgomery,
AL 36130-3500

James Barnhart, Commissioner (Acting)
100 N. Union St., #620, Montgomery, AL 36130-3500

Medicaid Agency
http://www.medicaid.state.al.us
General e-mail: almedicaid@medicaid.state.al.us
Main phone: (334) 242-5000
Main fax: (334) 242-0556
Toll free: (800) 362-1504
TTY: (800) 253-0799
Mailing address: P.O. Box 5624, Montgomery, AL
36103-5624

W. Dale Walley, Commissioner (Acting)
501 Dexter Ave., Montgomery, AL 36103-5624
Fax: (334) 242-5097

Medical Examiners Board
http://www.mindspring.com/~bmedixon/
Main phone: (334) 242-4116
Main fax: (334) 242-4155
Mailing address: P.O. Box 946, Montgomery, AL
36101-0946

Larry D. Dixon, Executive Director
848 Washington Ave., #100, Montgomery, AL 36101-
0946
E-mail: bmedixon@mindspring.com

Mental Health and Mental Retardation Dept.
General e-mail: cjohnson@mh.state.al.us
Main phone: (334) 242-3417
Main fax: (334) 242-0725
Mailing address: P.O. Box 301410, Montgomery,
AL 36130-1410

Kathy C. Sawyer, Commissioner
100 N. Union St., Montgomery, AL 36130
(334) 242-3107; *Fax:* (334) 242-0684
E-mail: ksawyer@mh.state.al.us

Developmental Disabilities Council
http://www.agencies.state.al.us/disabilities
General e-mail: addpc@mh.state.al.us
Main phone: (334) 242-3973
Main fax: (334) 242-0797
Toll free: (800) 232-2158
Mailing address: P.O. Box 301410,
Montgomery, AL 36130-1410

Sheryl R. Matney, Executive Director
RSA Union Bldg., 100 N. Union St., #498,
Montgomery, AL 36130
(334) 242-3972
E-mail: smatney@yahoo.com

Motor Vehicles Dept.
http://www.ador.state.al.us
Main phone: (334) 242-9056

Main fax: (334) 242-0312
Mailing address: P.O. Box 3711, Montgomery, AL 36109-0711

Terry Lane, Director
50 N. Ripley St., Montgomery, AL 36104
(334) 271-7200

Nursing Board
http://www.abn.state.al.us/
General e-mail: abn@abn.state.al.us
Main phone: (334) 242-4060
Main fax: (334) 242-4360
Mailing address: P.O. Box 303900, Montgomery, AL 36130-3900

Genell Lee, Executive Officer (Interim)
770 Washington Ave., #250, Montgomery, AL 36130-3900
(334) 242-4184
E-mail: glee@abn.state.al.us

Oil and Gas Board
http://www.ogb.state.al.us/
General e-mail: info@ogb.state.al.us
Main phone: (205) 349-2852
Main fax: (205) 349-2861
Mailing address: P.O. Box 869999, Tuscaloosa, AL 35846-6999

Donald F. Oltz, Oil and Gas Supervisor
420 Hackberry Lane, Tuscaloosa, AL 35486-6999
E-mail: doltz@ogb.state.al.us

Pardons and Parole Board
http://agencies.state.al.us/pardons/
General e-mail: cbarton@paroles.state.al.us
Main phone: (334) 242-8700
Main fax: (334) 242-1809
Mailing address: P.O. Box 302405, Montgomery, AL 36130-2405

Gladys R. Riddle, Chair
Lurleen B. Wallace Bldg., 500 Monroe St., 2nd Fl., Montgomery, AL 36130

Personnel Dept.
http://www.personnel.state.al.us/
Main phone: (334) 242-3389
Main fax: (334) 242-1110
Mailing address: P.O. Box 304100, Montgomery, AL 36130-4100

Thomas G. Flowers, Director
64 N. Union St., Montgomery, AL 36130-4100

Pharmacy Board
http://www.albop.com/
Main phone: (205) 967-0130
Main fax: (205) 967-1009

Jerry Moore, Executive Director
1 Perimeter Park South, #425-S, Birmingham, AL 35243
E-mail: JMOORERPH@worldnet.att.net

Postsecondary Education Dept.
http://www.acs.cc.al.us
General e-mail: hostmaster@acs.cc.al.us
Main phone: (334) 242-2900
Main fax: (334) 242-2888
Mailing address: P.O. 302130, Montgomery, AL 36130

Fred Gainous, Chancellor
401 Adams Ave., #280, Montgomery, AL 36104-4340
(334) 242-2927; *Fax:* (334) 242-0214
E-mail: fgainous@acs.cc.al.us

Prosecution Services Office
http://www.adaa-ops.org
General e-mail: dabercorombie@ops.state.al.us
Main phone: (334) 242-4191
Main fax: (334) 240-3186
Toll free: (800) 423-7658
Mailing address: P.O. Box 4780, Montgomery, AL 36103

Tom W. Sorrells, Executive Director
515 S. Perry St., Montgomery, AL 36104-4615
E-mail: tsorrells@ops.state.al.us

Public Accountancy Board
Main phone: (334) 242-5700
Main fax: (334) 242-2711
Toll free: (800) 435-9743
Mailing address: P.O. Box 300375, Montgomery, AL 36130-0375

J. Lamar Harris, Executive Director
770 Washington Ave., RSA Plaza, #236, Montgomery, AL 36130-0375

Public Health Dept.
http://www.alapubhealth.org/
General e-mail: adph@state.al.us
Main phone: (334) 206-5300
Main fax: (334) 206-5534
Mailing address: P.O. Box 303017, Montgomery, AL 36130-3017

Donald Ellis Williamson, State Health Officer
201 Monroe St., #1552, Montgomery, AL 36104
(334) 206-5200; *Fax:* (334) 206-2008

Public Library Service
http://www.apls.state.al.us
Main phone: (334) 213-3900
Main fax: (334) 213-3993
Toll free: (800) 723-8459

Lamar Veatch, Director
6030 Monticello Dr., Montgomery, AL 36130
(334) 213-3901; *Fax:* (334) 213-3993
E-mail: lveatch@apls.state.al.us

Public Safety Dept.
http://www.dps.state.al.us/
General e-mail: ashleya@gsiweb.net
Main phone: (334) 242-4371
Main fax: (334) 242-0512
Mailing address: P.O. Box 1511, Montgomery, AL 36102-1511

James H. Alexander, Director (Acting)
500 Dexter Ave., Montgomery, AL 36102-1511
(334) 242-4394

Public Television
http://www.aptv.org
Main phone: (205) 328-8756
Main fax: (205) 251-2192
Toll free: (800) 239-5233

Judy Stone, Executive Director
2112 11th Ave. South, #400, Birmingham, AL 35205-2884
(205) 328-8756, ext. 138
E-mail: jstone@aptv.org

Real Estate Appraisers Board
http://agencies.state.al.us/reab
General e-mail: jhenderson@email.state.al.us
Main phone: (334) 242-8747
Main fax: (334) 242-8749
Mailing address: P.O. Box 304355, Montgomery, AL 36130-4355

Jim W. Holland Jr., Executive Director
100 N. Union St., #370, Montgomery, AL 36104
(334) 242-8748

Retirement Systems
http://www.rsa.state.al.us/
General e-mail: info@rsa.state.al.us
Main phone: (334) 832-4140
Main fax: (334) 240-3230
Toll free: (800) 214-2158
Mailing address: P.O. Box 302150, Montgomery, AL 36130-2150

David G. Bronner, Chief Executive Officer
135 S. Union St., #570, Montgomery, AL 36104
(334) 832-4140, ext. 503
E-mail: dbronner@rsa.state.al.us

Revenue Dept.
http://www.ador.state.al.us
Main phone: (334) 242-1170
Main fax: (334) 242-0550

James P. Hayes Jr., Commissioner
Gordon Persons Bldg., 50 N. Ripley St., #4112, Montgomery, AL 36132
(334) 242-1175
E-mail: jhayes@revenue.state.al.us

Soil and Water Conservation Committee
Main phone: (334) 242-2620
Main fax: (334) 242-0551
Mailing address: P.O. Box 304800, Montgomery, AL 36130-4800

Stephen M. Cauthen, Executive Director
100 N. Union St., #334, Montgomery, AL 36130-4800
E-mail: scauthen@dsmd.dsmd.state.al.us

State Fair Facilities Management
Main phone: (205) 786-8100
Main fax: (205) 786-8222

Kenneth M. Blackledge, General Manager
2331 Bessemer Rd., Birmingham, AL 35208

State Troopers
Main phone: (334) 242-4394
Main fax: (334) 242-0512
Mailing address: P.O. Box 1511, Montgomery, AL 36102

Jim Alexander, Director, Central Operations
500 Washington Ave., Montgomery, AL 36102

Tourism and Travel Bureau
http://www.touralabama.org
General e-mail: admin@touralabama.org
Main phone: (334) 242-4169
Main fax: (334) 242-4534
Toll free: (800) 252-2262
TTY: (334) 242-4717
Mailing address: P.O. Box 4927, Montgomery, AL 36103-4927

Frances Smiley, Director (Acting)
401 Adams Ave., #126, Montgomery, AL 36103-4927
(334) 242-4413; *Fax:* (334) 242-1478

Transportation Dept.
http://www.dot.state.al.us
General e-mail: aldotinfo@dot.state.al.us
Main phone: (334) 242-6311
Main fax: (334) 242-8041
Mailing address: P.O. Box 303050, Montgomery, AL 36130-3050

G. Mack Roberts, Director
1409 Coliseum Blvd., #A-101, Montgomery, AL 36130

Veterans Affairs Dept.

http://agencies.state.al.us/va/
Main phone: (334) 242-5077
Main fax: (334) 242-5102
Mailing address: P.O. Box 1509, Montgomery, AL 36102-1509

Frank D. Wilkes, Director
770 Washington Ave., #530, Montgomery, AL 36102-1509
E-mail: fwilkes@va.state.al.us

Youth Services Dept.

Main phone: (334) 215-8100
Main fax: (334) 215-3011
Mailing address: P.O. Box 66, Mount Meigs, AL 36057-0066

J. Walter Wood Jr., Executive Director (Acting)
1000 Industrial School Rd., Mount Meigs, AL 36057-0066
(334) 215-3800; *Fax:* (334) 215-1453

Alabama Legislature

State House
11 S. Union St.
Montgomery, AL 36130
General information: (334) 242-7800
http://www.legislature.state.al.us

Senate

General information: (334) 242-7800
Fax: (334) 242-8819
Bill status: (334) 242-7826

Steve Windom (R), President and Presiding Officer
State House, 11 S. Union St., #725, Montgomery, AL 36130
(334) 242-7900; *Fax:* (334) 242-4661
E-mail: swindom@ltgov.state.al.us
http://www.legislature.state.al.us/senate/senators/senatebios/windom_s.html

Lowell R. Barron (D), President Pro Tempore
State House, 11 S. Union St., #726, Montgomery, AL 36130
(334) 242-7858
http://www.legislature.state.al.us/senate/senators/senatebios/sd008.html

Tom Butler (D), Majority Leader
State House, 11 S. Union St., #726, Montgomery, AL 36130
(334) 242-7854
E-mail: senbutler@aol.com
http://www.legislature.state.al.us/senate/senators/senatebios/sd002.html

J. T. Waggoner (R), Minority Leader
State House, 11 S. Union St., #737, Montgomery, AL 36130
(334) 242-7892
E-mail: senator.wag@internetmci.com
http://www.legislature.state.al.us/senate/senators/senatebios/sd016.html

Charles McDowell Lee, Secretary
State House, Senate Chamber, 11 S. Union St., Montgomery, AL 36130
(334) 242-7803
http://www.legislature.state.al.us/senate/senators/senatebios/lee_cm.html

House

General information: (334) 242-7600
Fax: (334) 242-2488
Bill status: (334) 242-7627
E-mail: house3@mindspring.com

Seth Hammett (D), Speaker of the House
State House, 11 S. Union St., #519-A, Montgomery, AL 36130
(334) 242-7668

Laws

Sales tax: 4%
Income tax: 3%
State minimum wage: None (Federal is $5.15)
Marriage age: 18
First-cousin marriage: Permitted
Drinking age: 21
State control of liquor sales: Yes
Blood alcohol for DWI: 0.08%
Driving age: 16
Speed limit: 70 mph
Permit to buy handguns: No, but 2-day wait
Minimum age to possess handguns: None
Minimum age to possess rifles, shotguns: None
State lottery: No
Casinos: No
Pari-mutuel betting: Horse and dog racing
Death penalty: Yes
3 strikes minimum sentence: None
Hate crimes law: Yes
Gay employment non-discrimination: No
Official language(s): English
Term limits: None

State laws are complex and subject to change; this information is not intended as legal advice. For an explanation of this information, see p. x.

E-mail: alaspkr@mindspring.com
http://www.legislature.state.al.us/house/
   representatives/housebios/hd092.html

Demetrius C. Newton (D), Speaker Pro Tempore
State House, 11 S. Union St., #516-B, Montgomery,
   AL 36130
(334) 242-7663
http://www.legislature.state.al.us/house/
   representatives/housebios/hd053.html

Ken Guin (D), Majority Leader
State House, 11 S. Union St., #526-D, Montgomery,
   AL 36130
(334) 242-7771
E-mail: repkenguin@aol.com
http://www.legislature.state.al.us/house/
   representatives/housebios/hd014.html

Mike Rogers (R), Minority Leader
State House, 11 S. Union St., #538-A, Montgomery,
   AL 36130
(334) 242-7749
http://www.legislature.state.al.us/house/
   representatives/housebios/hd036.html

Greg Pappas, Clerk
State House, 11 S. Union St., Montgomery, AL 36130
(334) 242-7600

Alabama Judiciary

300 Dexter Ave.
Montgomery, AL 36104
http://www.alalinc.net

Supreme Court
http://www.alalinc.net/apellate/supreme/index.cfm

Robert G. Esdale, Clerk
300 Dexter Ave., Montgomery, AL 36104
(334) 242-4609; *Fax:* (334) 242-0588

Justices
Composition: 9 justices
Selection Method: partisan election; vacancies
   filled by governor until new election is held
Length of term: 6 years
Perry O. Hooper Sr., Chief Justice, (334) 242-4599
Jean Williams Brown, Associate Justice,
   (334) 353-4244
Ralph D. Cook, Associate Justice, (334) 242-4585
John Henry England Jr., Associate Justice,
   (334) 242-4579
J. Gorman Houston Jr., Associate Justice,
   (334) 242-4587
Douglas Inge Johnstone, Associate Justice,
   (334) 242-4597
Champ Lyons Jr., Associate Justice, (334) 242-4351
Alva Hugh Maddox, Associate Justice, (334) 242-4593
Harold F. See, Associate Justice, (334) 242-1001

Administrative Office of Courts
http://www.alacourt.org
Main phone: (334) 242-0300
Main fax: (334) 242-2099
General e-mail: aoc@alalinc.net

Frank W. Gregory, Administrative Director
300 Dexter Ave., Montgomery, AL 36104-3741
(334) 242-0366
E-mail: frank.gregory@alalinc.net

State Law Library
http://www.alalinc.net/library/index.cfm
Main phone: (334) 242-4347
Main fax: (334) 242-4484
General e-mail: reference@alalinc.net

Timothy Lewis, Director and State Law Librarian
300 Dexter Ave., Montgomery, AL 36104
E-mail: director@alalinc.net

Legislative and Political Party Information Resources

Senate home page: http://www.legislature.state.al.us/senate/senate.html

House home page: http://www.legislature.state.al.us/house/house.html

Committees: Senate: http://www.legislature.state.al.us/senate/senatecommittees.html

Legislative information: http://www.legislature.state.al.us/ALISHome.html

Legislative process: http://www.legislature.state.al.us/misc/legislativeprocess/legislative process.html

Alabama Democratic Party: http://www.aladems.org
   290 21st St. North, Birmingham, AL 35203; *Phone:* (205) 326-3366; *Fax:* (202) 324-3320; *E-mail:*
   democrate@quicklink.net

Alabama Republican Party: http://www.algop.org
   3321 Lorna Rd., Birmingham, AL 35216; *Phone:* (205) 313-2000; *Fax:* (205) 313-2010

Alaska

State Capitol
Juneau, AK 99811-0001
Public information: (907) 465-2111
Fax: (907) 465-3532
http://www.state.ak.us

Office of the Governor
http://www.gov.state.ak.us
General e-mail: governor@gov.state.ak.us
Main phone: (907) 465-3500
Main fax: (907) 465-3532
Mailing address: P.O. Box 110001, Juneau, AK
99811-0001

Tony Knowles (D), Governor
State Capitol, Juneau, AK 99811-0001
Jim Ayers, Chief of Staff
State Capitol, Juneau, AK 99811-0001
(907) 465-3500; *Fax:* (907) 465-3532
Robert W. King, Press Secretary
State Capitol, Juneau, AK 99811-0001
(907) 465-3500; *Fax:* (907) 465-3533
E-mail: Bob_King@gov.state.ak.us
Susan Scudder, Director, Constituent Affairs
State Capitol, Juneau, AK 99811-0001
(907) 465-3500; *Fax:* (907) 465-3532
E-mail: susan_scudder@gov.state.ak.us
**John Katz, Special Counsel for State/Federal
Relations, Washington Office**
444 N. Capitol St. N.W., #336, Washington, DC
20001-1512
(202) 624-5858; *Fax:* (202) 624-5857

Office of the Lieutenant Governor
http://www.gov.state.ak.us/ltgov
Main phone: (907) 465-3520
Main fax: (907) 465-5400
Mailing address: P.O. Box 110015, Juneau, AK
99811-0015

Fran A. Ulmer (D), Lieutenant Governor
State Capitol, Juneau, AK 99811-0015
E-mail: fran_ulmer@gov.state.ak.us

Office of the Attorney General
http://www.law.state.ak.us
General e-mail: attorney_general@law.state.ak.us
Main phone: (907) 465-3600
Main fax: (907) 465-2075
TTY: (907) 465-6727

State of Alaska

Capital: Juneau, since 1906
Founded: 1867, Alaska Territory acquired from Russia
Statehood: January 3, 1959 (49th state)
Constitution adopted: January 3, 1959
Area: 570,374 sq. mi. (ranks 1st)
Population: 621,400 (1998 est.; ranks 48th)
Largest cities: (1998 est.) Anchorage (254,982); Fairbanks (33,295); Juneau (30,191); Sitka (8,338); Kenai (7,943)
Counties: 27, Most populous: (1998 est.) Anchorage Borough (254,982); Fairbanks North Star Borough (84,217); Matanuska-Susitina Borough (56,258); Kenai Peninsula Borough (48,008); Juneau Borough (30,191)
U.S. Congress: Frank H. Murkowski (R), Ted Stevens (R); 1 Representative
Nickname(s): Last Frontier, Land of the Midnight Sun
Motto: North to the future
Song: "Alaska's Flag"
Bird: Willow ptarmigan
Tree: Sitka spruce
Flower: Forget-Me-Not
State fair: at Palmer, late Aug.-early Sept.
Former capital(s): Sitka

Mailing address: P.O. Box 110300, Juneau, AK
99811-0300

Bruce M. Botelho, Attorney General
123 4th St., #450, Juneau, AK 99801
(907) 465-2133

Military and Veteran's Affairs Dept.
http://www.state.ak.us/local/akpages/military/
home.htm
Main phone: (907) 428-6003
Main fax: (907) 428-6019
Mailing address: P.O. Box 5800, Fort Richardson,
AK 99505-5800

Phillip E. Oates, Adjutant General
4900 Camp Denali, #C-222, Fort Richardson, AK
99505
E-mail: phillip_oates@ak-prepared.com

Agencies

Administration Dept.
http://www.state.ak.us/local/akpages/ADMIN/
home.htm
Main phone: (907) 465-2200
Main fax: (907) 465-2135
Mailing address: P.O. Box 110200, Juneau, AK
99811-0200

Robert Poe Jr., Commissioner
333 Willoughby Ave., State Office Bldg., 10th Fl.,
Juneau, AK 99801
(907) 465-5670
E-mail: bob_poe@admin.state.ak.us

Finance Division
http://www.state.ak.us/local/akpages/ADMIN/
dof/akfin.htm
General e-mail:
Finance_web@admin.state.ak.us
Main phone: (907) 465-2240
Main fax: (907) 465-2576
TTY: (907) 465-2242
Mailing address: P.O. Box 110204, Juneau, AK
99811-0204

Kim J. Garnero, Director, Finance
333 Willoughby Ave., State Office Bldg., 10th Fl.,
Juneau, AK 99801
Fax: (907) 465-2169
E-mail: kim_garnero@admin.state.ak.us

Motor Vehicles Division
http://www.state.ak.us/dmv
General e-mail:
dmv_webmaster@admin.state.ak.us
Main phone: (907) 269-5559
Main fax: (907) 269-6084

Mary Marshburn, Director
3300-B Fairbanks St., Anchorage, AK 99503

Personnel Division
http://www.state.ak.us/local/akpages/ADMIN/
dop/akpers.htm
Main phone: (907) 465-4430
Main fax: (907) 465-2576
TTY: (907) 465-2461
Mailing address: P.O. Box 110201, Juneau, AK
99811-0201

Sharon Barton, Director
333 Willoughby Ave., State Office Bldg., 10th Fl.,
Juneau, AK 99801
Fax: (907) 465-2269
E-mail: sharon_barton@admin.state.ak.us

Public Broadcasting Commission
http://www.state.ak.us/local/akpages/ADMIN/
apbc/akpbc.htm
Main phone: (907) 465-2220
Main fax: (907) 465-3450
Mailing address: P.O. Box 110206, Juneau, AK
99811-0206

Douglas Samimi-Moore, Coordinator (Interim)
State Office Bldg., 5th Fl., Juneau, AK 99811
E-mail: Douglas_Samimi-
Moore@admin.state.ak.us

Public Defender Agency
http://www.state.ak.us/local/akpages/ADMIN/pd/
homepd.htm
General e-mail:
carol_ausbahl@admin.state.ak.us
Main phone: (907) 264-4400
Main fax: (907) 269-5476
Toll free: (800) 478-4404
TTY: (907) 264-4455

Barbara Brink, Director
900 W. 5th Ave., #200, Anchorage, AK 99501-
2090
E-mail: barbara_brink@admin.state.ak.us

Retirement and Benefits Division
http://www.state.ak.us/local/akpages/ADMIN/
drb/home.htm
Main phone: (907) 465-4460
Main fax: (907) 465-3086
TTY: (907) 465-2805
Mailing address: P.O. Box 110203, Juneau, AK
99811

Guy Bell, Director
State Office Bldg., 333 Willoughby Ave., 6th Fl.,
Juneau, AK 99801-1755
(907) 465-4471
E-mail: guy_bell@admin.state.ak.us

Senior Services Division
http://www.state.ak.us/admin/dss/
Main phone: (907) 269-3666
Main fax: (907) 269-3689
Toll free: (800) 478-9996
TTY: (907) 269-3691

Kay L. Burrows, Director
3601 C St., #310, Anchorage, AK 99503-5984
(907) 269-3665; *Fax:* (907) 269-3688

Architects, Engineers, and Land Surveyors Occupational Licensing
http://www.dced.state.ak.us/occ/pael.htm
General e-mail: licence@dced.state.ak.us
Main phone: (907) 465-2534
Main fax: (907) 465-2974

Mailing address: P.O. Box 110806, Juneau, AK 99811-0806

Catherine Reardon, Director
333 Willoughby Ave., 9th Fl., Juneau, AK 99801
(907) 465-2538
E-mail: catherine_reardon@dced.state.ak.us

Certified Real Estate Appraisers Board
http://www.dced.state.ak.us/occ/papr.htm
General e-mail: license@dced.state.ak.us
Main phone: (907) 465-2542
Main fax: (907) 465-2974
TTY: (907) 465-2500
Mailing address: P.O. Box 110806, Juneau, AK 99811-0806

Jenny McElwain, Licensing Examiner
333 Willoughby Ave., 9th Fl., Juneau, AK 99801

Child Care Center Licensing Information
http://www.labor.state.ak.us/research/dlo/children.htm
Main phone: (907) 465-3207
Main fax: (907) 465-3397
Mailing address: P.O. Box 110630, Juneau, AK 99811-0630

Charles Knittel, Program Coordinator
350 Main St., #407, Juneau, AK 99801
(907) 465-2218; *Fax:* (907) 465-3380
E-mail: cknittel@health.state.ak.us

Community and Economic Development Dept.
http://www.dced.state.ak.us
General e-mail: questions@dced.state.ak.us
Main phone: (907) 465-2500
Main fax: (907) 465-5442
TTY: (907) 465-5437
Mailing address: P.O. Box 110800, Juneau, AK 99515-0800

Deborah B. Sedwick, Commissioner
State Office Bldg., 9th Fl., Juneau, AK 99811-0800

Banking, Securities, and Corporations Division
http://www.dced.state.ak.us/bsc/bsc.htm
General e-mail: dbsc@dced.state.ak.us
Main phone: (907) 465-2521
Main fax: (907) 465-2549
Mailing address: P.O. Box 110807, Juneau, AK 99811-0807

Franklin T. Elder, Director
150 3rd St., #217, Juneau, AK 99801
(907) 465-5448
E-mail: Terry_Elder@dced.state.ak.us

Insurance Division
http://www.dced.state.ak.us/insurance

General e-mail: insurance@dced.state.ak.us
Main phone: (907) 465-2515
Main fax: (907) 465-3422
TTY: (907) 465-5437
Mailing address: P.O. Box 110805, Juneau, AK 99811-0805

Robert A. Lohr, Director
State Office Bldg., 333 Willoughby Ave., 9th Fl., Juneau, AK 99801
(907) 465-7900; *Fax:* (907) 465-7910
E-mail: Robert_Lohr@dced.state.ak.us

Occupational Licensing Division
http://www.dced.state.ak.us/occ/
General e-mail: license@dced.state.ak.us
Main phone: (907) 465-2534
Main fax: (907) 465-2974
TTY: (907) 465-5437
Mailing address: P.O. Box 110806, Juneau, AK 99811-0806

Catherine A. Reardon, Director
State Office Bldg., 333 Willoughby Ave., 9th Fl., Juneau, AK 99801
(907) 465-2538
E-mail: catherine_reardon@dced.state.ak.us

Regulatory Commission
http://www.state.ak.us/rca
General e-mail: RCA_mail@rca.state.ak.us
Main phone: (907) 276-6222
Main fax: (907) 276-0160
Toll free: (800) 390-2782
TTY: (907) 276-4533

G. Nanette Thompson, Chair
1016 W. 6th Ave., #400, Anchorage, AK 99501-1963
E-mail: nan_thompson@rca.state.ak.us

Tourism Division
http://www.dced.state.ak.us/tourism/homenew.htm
General e-mail: GoNorth@dced.state.ak.us
Main phone: (907) 465-2012
Main fax: (907) 465-3767
Mailing address: P.O. Box 110801, Juneau, AK 99811-0801

Higher Educational Institutions

University of Alaska
http://www.alaska.edu/
3211 Providence Dr., Anchorage, AK 99508
Main phone: (907) 786-1480
Branches: Anchorage, Fairbanks, Southeast

Virginia Fay, Director
333 Willoughby Ave., State Office Bldg., 9th Fl.,
Juneau, AK 99801
E-mail: ginny_fay@dced.state.ak.us

Corrections Dept.
http://www.correct.state.ak.us
General e-mail: webmaster@correct.state.ak.us
Main phone: (907) 465-3376
Main fax: (907) 465-2006
TTY: (907) 465-3274
Mailing address: P.O. Box 112000, Juneau, AK
99811-2000

Margaret M. Pugh, Commissioner
240 Main St., #700, Juneau, AK 99801
(907) 465-4652; *Fax:* (907) 465-3390
E-mail: margaret_pugh@correct.state.ak.us

Parole Board
http://www.correct.state.ak.us/corrections/parole
Main phone: (907) 465-3384
Main fax: (907) 465-3110
Mailing address: P.O. Box 112000, Juneau, AK
99811-2000

Lawrence W. Jones, Executive Director
802 3rd St., Douglas, AK 99824
E-mail: lawrence_jones@correct.state.ak.us

Education and Early Development Dept.
http://www.eed.state.ak.us/stateboard/home.html
Main phone: (907) 465-2800
Main fax: (907) 465-3452

Barbara Thompson, Director
801 W. 10th St., #200, Juneau, AK 99801
E-mail: Barbara_Thompson@eed.state.ak.us

Arts Council
http://www.aksca.org
General e-mail: info@aksca.org
Main phone: (907) 269-6610
Main fax: (907) 269-6601
Toll free: (888) 278-7424
TTY: (800) 770-8973

Helen Howarth, Executive Director
411 W. 4th Ave., #1-E, Anchorage, AK 99501-2343
(907) 269-6607
E-mail: helen@aksca.org

Board of Education
http://www.eed.state.ak.us/stateboard/
home.html
Main phone: (907) 465-2801
Main fax: (907) 465-4156

Jesse Kiehl, Executive Secretary
801 W. 10th St., #300, Juneau, AK 99801
E-mail: Jesse_Kiehl@eed.state.ak.us

Libraries, Archives, and Museums: Archives and Records Management
http://www.educ.state.ak.us/lam/archives/
home.html
General e-mail: archives@eed.state.ak.us
Main phone: (907) 465-2270
Main fax: (907) 465-2465

John Stewart, State Archivist
141 Willoughby Ave., Juneau, AK 99801-1720
(907) 465-2275
E-mail: John_Stewart@eed.state.ak.us

Libraries, Archives, and Museums: State Library
http://www.eed.state.ak.us/lam/library.html
General e-mail: asl@eed.state.ak.us
Main phone: (907) 465-2910
Main fax: (907) 465-2665
Mailing address: P.O. Box 110571, Juneau, AK
99811-0571

Karen Crane, Director
State Office Bldg., 333 Willoughby Ave., 8th Fl.,
Juneau, AK 99801
(907) 465-2911; *Fax:* (907) 465-2151
E-mail: karen_crane@eed.state.ak.us

Postsecondary Education Commission
http://www.state.ak.us/acpe
General e-mail: custsvc@acpe.state.ak.us
Main phone: (907) 465-2962
Main fax: (907) 465-5316
Toll free: (800) 441-2962

Diane Barrans, Executive Director
3030 Vintage Blvd., Juneau, AK 99801-7109
(907) 465-6740; *Fax:* (907) 465-3293
E-mail: execdir@acpe.state.ak.us

Emergency Services Division
http://www.ak-prepared.com
General e-mail: emergency_svcs_(des)@ak-
prepared.com
Main phone: (907) 428-7000
Main fax: (907) 428-7009
Toll free: (800) 478-2337
Mailing address: P.O. Box 5750, Fort Richardson,
AK 99505-5750

David E. Liebersbach, Director
4900 Camp Denali, Fort Richardson, AK 99505
(907) 428-7058; *Fax:* (907) 428-7081
E-mail: david_liebersbach@ak-prepared.com

Environmental Conservation Dept.
http://www.state.ak.us/dec/home.htm
Main phone: (907) 465-5010
Main fax: (907) 465-5097
Report a spill: (800) 478-9300

Michele D. Brown, Commissioner
410 Willoughby Ave., #105, Juneau, AK 99801-1795
(907) 465-5065; *Fax:* (907) 465-5070
E-mail: commissioner@environ.state.ak.us

Fish and Game Dept.
http://www.state.ak.us/local/akpages/FISH.GAME/
 adfghome.htm
Main phone: (907) 465-4100
Main fax: (907) 465-2332
TTY: (800) 478-3648
Mailing address: P.O. Box 25526, Juneau, AK
 98802-5526

Frank Rue, Commissioner
Capital Office Park, 1255 W. 8th St., Juneau, AK
 99801
(907) 465-6141
E-mail: commfrue@fishgame.state.ak.us

Health and Social Services Dept.
http://www.hss.state.ak.us
Main phone: (907) 465-3030
Main fax: (907) 465-3068
TTY: (907) 586-4265
Mailing address: P.O. Box 110601, Juneau, AK
 99811-0601

Karen Perdue, Commissioner
Alaska Office Bldg., #229, Juneau, AK 99811-0601
E-mail: karen_perdue@health.state.ak.us

Family and Youth Services Division
http://www.hss.state.ak.us/DFYS/
General e-mail: dfys@health.state.ak.us
Main phone: (907) 465-3170
Main fax: (907) 465-3397
Mailing address: P.O. Box 110630, Juneau, AK
 99811-0630

Theresa Tanoury, Director
350 Main St., #404, Juneau, AK 99801
(907) 465-3191; *Fax:* (907) 465-3097

Medical Assistance Division
http://www.hss.state.ak.us/dma
Main phone: (907) 465-3355
Main fax: (907) 465-2204
Mailing address: P.O. Box 110660, Juneau, AK
 99811

Bob Labbe, Director
350 Main St., #412, Juneau, AK 99801
E-mail: blabbe@health.state.ak.us

Mental Health and Developmental Disabilities Division
http://www.hss.state.ak.us/dmhdd/

Frequently Called Numbers

Tourism: (907) 465-2012; http://
 www.dced.state.ak.us/tourism/homenew.htm
Library: (907) 465-2910;
 http://www.eed.state.ak.us/lam/library.html
Board of Education: (907) 465-2801; http://
 www.eed.state.ak.us/stateboard/home.html
Vital Statistics: (907) 465-3391; http://
 www.hhs.state.ak.us/dph/bvs/bvs_home.htm
Tax/Revenue: (907) 465-2300;
 http://www.revenue.state.ak.us/
Motor Vehicles: (907) 269-5559;
 http://www.state.ak.us/dmv
State Police/Highway Patrol: (907) 269-5641;
 http://www.dps.state.ak.us/ast
Unemployment: (907) 465-5552, 888-252-
 2557; http://www.labor.state.ak.us:5103/
 esd.unemploymentinsurance/ui.htm
General Election Information: (907)
 465-4611; http://www.gov.state.ak.us/ltgov/
 elections/homepage.html
Consumer Affairs: (907) 465-3520
Hazardous Materials: Central, (907)
 269-3063; Northern (907) 451-2121;
 Southeast, (907) 465-5340; http://
 www.state.ak.us/dec/dspar/dec_dspr.htm

General e-mail: director@health.state.ak.us
Main phone: (907) 465-3370
Main fax: (907) 465-2668
Toll free: (800) 465-4828
TTY: (907) 465-2225
Mailing address: P.O. Box 110620, Juneau, AK
 99811-0620

Karl Brimner, Director
350 Main St., #214, Juneau, AK 99811
(907) 465-3166
E-mail: karl_brimner@health.state.ak.us

Public Health Division
http://www.hss.state.ak.us/dph/dph_home.htm
Main phone: (907) 465-3090
Main fax: (907) 586-1877
Mailing address: P.O. Box 110610, Juneau, AK
 99811-0610

Peter Nakamura, Director
350 Main St., #503, Juneau, AK 99801
E-mail: petern@health.state.ak.us

Human Rights Commission
http://www.gov.state.ak.us/aschr/aschr.htm

Main phone: (907) 274-4692
Main fax: (907) 278-8588
Toll free: (800) 478-4692
TTY: (907) 276-3177

Paula Haley, Executive Director
800 A St., #204, Anchorage, AK 99501-3669
(907) 276-7474, ext. 241

Labor and Workforce Development Dept.
http://www.state.ak.us/local/akpages/LABOR/
home.htm
Main phone: (907) 465-2700
Main fax: (907) 465-2784
Mailing address: P.O. Box 21149, Juneau, AK
99802-1149

Ed Flanagan, Commissioner
1111 W. 8th St., #308, Juneau, AK 99802-1149
E-mail: ed_flanagan@labor.state.ak.us

Workers Compensation Division
http://www.labor.state.ak.us/wc/wc.htm
Main phone: (907) 465-2790
Main fax: (907) 465-2797
TTY: (907) 465-5952
Mailing address: P.O. Box 25512, Juneau, AK
99802-5512

Paul L. Grossi, Director
1111 W. 8th St., #307, Juneau, AK 99802
E-mail: Paul_Grossi@labor.state.ak.us

Natural Resources Dept.
http://www.dnr.state.ak.us
General e-mail: pic@dnr.state.ak.us
Main phone: (907) 269-8431

Boards and Licensing

Accountancy, (907) 465-2534, http://
www.dced.state.ak.us/occ/pcpa.htm
*Architects, Engineers, and Land Surveyors
Occupational Licensing,* (907) 465-2534,
http://www.dced.state.ak.us/occ/pael.htm
Child Care, (907) 465-3207, http://
www.labor.state.ak.us/research/dlo/
children.htm
Contractors, (907) 465-2546
Cosmetology, (907) 465-2547
Medical Examiners, (907) 465-2541
Nursing, (907) 269-8161, http://
www.dced.state.ak.us/occ/pnur.thm
Pharmacy, (907) 465-2589, http://
www.dced.state.ak.us/occ/ppha.htm
Real Estate Appraisers, (907) 465-2542,
http://www.dced.state.ak.us/occ/papr.htm

Main fax: (907) 269-8918
TTY: (907) 269-8411
Mailing address: 550 W. 7th St., #1400,
Anchorage, AK 99501-3557

John Shively, Commissioner
400 Willoughby Ave., 5th Fl., Juneau, AK 99801-1796
(907) 465-2400; Fax: (907) 465-3886
E-mail: john_shively@dnr.state.ak.us

Forestry Division
http://www.dnr.state.ak.us/forestry/
Main phone: (907) 465-3379
Main fax: (907) 465-3113
Mailing address: 550 W. 7th St., #1450,
Anchorage, AK 99501-3557

Jeff Jahnke, State Forester
400 Willoughby Ave., 3rd Fl., Juneau, AK 99801
(907) 269-8463; Fax: (904) 586-3113
E-mail: jeff_jahnke@dnr.state.ak.us

Geological and Geophysical Surveys Division
http://www.dggs.dnr.state.ak.us
General e-mail: dggspubs@dnr.state.ak.us
Main phone: (907) 451-5010
Main fax: (907) 451-5050

Milton A. Wiltse, Director and State Geologist
794 University Ave., #200, Fairbanks, AK 99709-
3645
(907) 451-5001
E-mail: milt_wiltse@dnr.state.ak.us

Oil and Gas Division
http://www.dnr.state.ak.us/oil/index.htm
Main phone: (907) 269-8800
Main fax: (907) 269-8938
TTY: (907) 269-8672

Kenneth A. Boyd, Director
550 W. 7th Ave., #800, Anchorage, AK 99501-
3560
E-mail: ken_boyd@dnr.state.ak.us

Parks and Outdoor Recreation Division: Historical Commission
http://www.dnr.state.ak.us/parks/oha_web/
ahc.htm
General e-mail: oha@alaska.net
Main phone: (907) 269-8721
Main fax: (907) 269-8908

Fran A. Ulmer, Chair
550 W. 7th St., #1310, Anchorage, AK 99501-3561

Parks and Outdoor Recreation Division: State Parks
http://www.dnr.state.ak.us/parks/parks.htm
Main phone: (907) 269-8700

Main fax: (907) 269-8907
TTY: (907) 269-8411

Jim Stratton, Director
550 W. 7th Ave., #1390, Anchorage, AK 99501-3561
(907) 269-8701
E-mail: jim_stratton@dnr.state.ak.us

Nursing Board
http://www.dced.state.ak.us/occ/pnur.thm
Main phone: (907) 269-8161
Main fax: (907) 269-8196

Dorothy Fulton, Executive Administrator
3601 C St., #722, Anchorage, AK 99503
E-mail: dorothy_fulton@dced.state.ak.us

Pharmacy Board
http://www.dced.state.ak.us/occ/ppha.htm
General e-mail: license@dced.state.ak.us
Main phone: (907) 465-2589
Mailing address: P.O. Box 110806, Juneau, AK 99811

Margaret Soden, President (Acting)
333 Willoughby Ave., 9th Fl., Juneau, AK 99811

Public Accountancy Board
http://www.dced.state.ak.us/occ/pcpa.htm
General e-mail: license@dced.state.ak.us
Main phone: (907) 465-2534
Main fax: (907) 465-2974
TTY: (907) 465-5437
Mailing address: P.O. Box 110806, Juneau, AK 99811

Steve Snyder, Licensing Examiner
333 Willoughby Ave., 9th Fl., Juneau, AK 99811
(907) 465-2580
E-mail: steve_snyder@dced.state.ak.us

Public Safety Dept.
http://www.dps.state.ak.us
Main phone: (907) 465-4322
Main fax: (907) 465-4362
Mailing address: P.O. Box 111200, Juneau, AK 99811-1200

Ronald L. Otte, Commissioner
450 Whittier St., #208, Juneau, AK 99811-1200
(907) 465-4323
E-mail: holly_carrier@dps.state.ak.us

Alaska State Troopers Division
http://www.dps.state.ak.us/ast
Main phone: (907) 269-5641

Glenn Godfrey, Director
5700 E. Tudor Rd., Anchorage, AK 99507

Fire Marshal's Office
http://www.dps.state.ak.us/fire/
Main phone: (907) 269-5491
Main fax: (907) 338-4375
TTY: (907) 269-5094

Gary L. Powell, State Fire Marshal
5700 E. Tudor Rd., Anchorage, AK 99507
E-mail: gary_powell@dps.state.ak.us

Revenue Dept.
http://www.revenue.state.ak.us/
Main phone: (907) 465-2300
Main fax: (907) 465-2389
TTY: (907) 465-3678
Mailing address: P.O. Box 110400, Juneau, AK 99811-0400

Wilson L. Condon, Commissioner
State Office Bldg., Juneau, AK 99811-0400
(907) 465-2301
E-mail: Wilson_Condon@revenue.state.ak.us

Alcoholic Beverage Control Board
http://www.revenue.state.ak.us/abc/abc.htm
Main phone: (907) 269-0350
Main fax: (907) 272-9412

Douglas B. Griffin, Director
550 W. 7th Ave., 5th Fl., Anchorage, AK 99501-3556
(907) 269-0351
E-mail: Doug_Griffin@revenue.state.ak.us

Housing Finance Corporation
http://www.ahfc.state.ak.us
Main phone: (907) 338-6100
Main fax: (907) 338-9218
Toll free: (800) 478-AHFC
TTY: (800) 478-5558
Mailing address: P.O. Box 101020, Anchorage, AK 99510-1020

Dan Fauske, Executive Director
4300 Boniface Pkwy., #130, Anchorage, AK 99504
E-mail: dfauske@ahfc.state.ak.us

State Fair
http://www.akstatefair.org/
Main phone: (907) 745-4827
Main fax: (907) 746-2699
Vacant, Director
2075 Glenn Hwy., Palmer, AK 99645-6799

Transportation and Public Facilities Dept.
http://www.dot.state.ak.us
General e-mail:
   commissioner_dotpf@dot.state.ak.us
Main phone: (907) 465-3900
Main fax: (907) 586-8365
TTY: (907) 465-3652

Joseph L. Perkins, Commissioner
3132 Channel Dr., #300, Juneau, AK 99801-7898
(907) 465-3901
E-mail: joe_perkins@dot.state.ak.us

Alaska Legislature

State Capitol
120 4th St.
Juneau, AK 99801-1182
General information: (907) 465-4648
Fax: (907) 465-2864
TTY: (907) 465-4980
http://www.legis.state.ak.us

Senate
General information: (907) 465-3701
Fax: (907) 465-2832

Drue Pearce (R), President
State Capitol, #107, Juneau, AK 99801-1182
(907) 465-4993; *Fax:* (907) 465-3872
E-mail: senator_drue_pearce@legis.state.ak.us
http://www.legis.state.ak.us/home/senate/pearce.htm

Jerry Mackie (R), Majority Leader
State Capitol, #427, Juneau, AK 99801-1182
(907) 465-4925; *Fax:* (907) 465-3517
E-mail: senator_jerry_mackie@legis.state.ak.us
http://www.legis.state.ak.us/home/senate/mackie.htm

Johnny Ellis (D), Minority Leader
State Capitol, #9, Juneau, AK 99801-1182
(907) 465-3704; *Fax:* (907) 465-2529
E-mail: senator_johnny_ellis@legis.state.ak.us
http://www.legis.state.ak.us/home/senate/ellis.htm

Nancy Quinto, Secretary
State Capitol, Juneau, AK 99801-1182
(907) 465-3701
E-mail: nancy_quinto@legis.state.ak.us

House
General information: (907) 465-3725
Fax: (907) 465-5334

Brian Porter (R), Speaker of the House
State Capitol, #208, Juneau, AK 99801-1182
(907) 465-4930; *Fax:* (907) 465-3834
E-mail: representative_brian_porter@legis.state.ak.us
http://www.legis.state.ak.us/home/house/porter.htm

Joe Green (R), Majority Leader
State Capitol, #214, Juneau, AK 99801-1182
(907) 465-4931; *Fax:* (907) 465-4316
E-mail: representative_joe_green@legis.state.ak.us
http://www.legis.state.ak.us/home/house/greenj.htm

Laws

Sales tax: None
Income tax: None
State minimum wage: $5.65 (Federal is $5.15)
Marriage age: 18
First-cousin marriage: Permitted
Drinking age: 21
State control of liquor sales: No
Blood alcohol for DWI: 0.10%
Driving age: 16
Speed limit: 65 mph
Permit to buy handguns: No
Minimum age to possess handguns: 16
Minimum age to possess rifles, shotguns: 16
State lottery: No
Casinos: No
Pari-mutuel betting: No
Death penalty: No
3 strikes minimum sentence: 40 yrs. (3rd serious felony)
Hate crimes law: Yes
Gay employment non-discrimination: No
Official language(s): English
Term limits: None

State laws are complex and subject to change; this information is not intended as legal advice. For an explanation of this information, see p. x.

Richard Foster (R), Majority Whip
State Capitol, #410, Juneau, AK 99801-1182
(907) 465-3789; *Fax:* (907) 465-3242
E-mail:
   representative_richard_foster@legis.state.ak.us
http://www.legis.state.ak.us/home/house/foster.htm

Ethan Berkowitz (D), Minority Leader
State Capitol, #404, Juneau, AK 99801-1182
(907) 465-4919; *Fax:* (907) 465-2137
E-mail:
   representative_ethan_berkowitz@legis.state.ak.us
http://www.legis.state.ak.us/home/house/berkowit.htm

Reggie Joule (D), Minority Whip
State Capitol, #405, Juneau, AK 99801-1182
(907) 465-4833; *Fax:* (907) 465-4586
E-mail: representative_reggie_joule@legis.state.ak.us
http://www.legis.state.ak.us/home/house/joule.htm

Suzanne Lowell, Chief Clerk
State Capitol, Juneau, AK 99801-1182
(907) 465-3725
E-mail: suzi_lowell@legis.state.ak.us

Alaska Judiciary

Boney Memorial Courthouse
303 K St.
Anchorage, AK 99501
http://www.alaska.net/~akctlib/
homepage.htm

Supreme Court

Marilyn May, Clerk
Boney Memorial Courthouse, 303 K Street,
Anchorage, AK 99501-2099
(907) 264-0618; *Fax:* (907) 264-0878
E-mail: mmay@appellate.courts.state.ak.us

Justices
Composition: 5 justices
Selection Method: appointed by governor;
retention vote held at first general election
more than 3 years after appointment
Length of term: 10 years if retention ballot is
successful

Warren W. Matthews, Chief Justice, (907) 264-0618
Walter L. Carpeneti, Justice, (907) 463-4771
Robert L. Eastaugh, Justice, (907) 264-0624
Dana Fabe, Justice, (907) 264-0768
Alexander O. Bryner, Justice, (907) 264-0632

Alaska Court System Administration
Main phone: (907) 264-0548
Main fax: (907) 264-0881

Stephanie Cole, Administrative Director
Boney Memorial Courthouse, 303 K St., Anchorage,
AK 99501-2099
E-mail: scole@courts.state.ak.us

State Law Library
http://www.alaska.net/~akctlib/libinfo.htm
Main phone: (907) 264-0580
Main fax: (907) 2640733
General e-mail: akctlib@alaska.net

Cynthia Fellows, State Law Librarian
Boney Memorial Courthouse, 303 K St., Anchorage,
AK 99501-2099
(907) 264-0583; *Fax:* (907) 264-8291
E-mail: cfellows@courts.state.ak.us

Alaska Legislative and Political Party Information Resources

Senate home page: http://www.legis.state.ak.us/senate/home.htm
House home page: http://www.legis.state.ak.us/house/home.htm
Legislative information: http://www.legis.state.ak.us/folhome.htm.htm
Budget: http://www.legfin.state.ak.us
Alaska Democratic Party: http://www.alaska.net/~adp/
   1441 W. Northern Lights, Suite C, P.O. Box 104119, Anchorage, AK 99510; *Phone:* (907) 258-3050;
   E-mail: adp@alaska.net
Alaska Republican Party: http://www.alaskarepublicans.com
   1001 W. Fireweed Ln., Anchorage, AK 99503; *Phone:* (907) 276-4467; *Fax:* (907) 276-0425; *E-mail:*
   cachberger@gci.net

Arizona

State Capitol
1700 W. Washington St.
Phoenix, AZ 85007
Public information: (602) 542-1318
Fax: (602) 542-7601
http://www.state.az.us

Office of the Governor

http://www.state.az.us/gv/
General e-mail: azgov@azgov.state.az.us
Main phone: (602) 542-4331
Main fax: (602) 542-7602
Toll free: (800) 253-0883

Jane Dee Hull (R), Governor
State Capitol, 1700 W. Washington St., 9th Fl.,
Phoenix, AZ 85007

Rick L. Collins, Chief of Staff
State Capitol, 1700 W. Washington St., 9th Fl.,
Phoenix, AZ 85007
(602) 542-1317; *Fax:* (602) 542-7602
E-mail: rcollins@azgov.state.az.us

Francie Noyes, Press Secretary
State Capitol, 1700 W. Washington St., 9th Fl.,
Phoenix, AZ 85007
(602) 542-1342; *Fax:* (602) 542-7602
E-mail: fnoyes@azgov.state.az.us

Cecilia Nelson, Director, Constituent Services
State Capitol, 1700 W. Washington St., 1st Fl.,
Phoenix, AZ 85007
(602) 542-1318; *Fax:* (602) 542-1381
E-mail: cnelson@azgov.state.al.us

Office of the Secretary of State

http://www.sosaz.com
Main phone: (602) 542-4285
Main fax: (602) 542-1575
TTY: (602) 255-8683

Betsey Bayless (R), Secretary of State
West Wing, State Capitol, 1700 W. Washington St., 7th
Fl., Phoenix, AZ 85007
(602) 542-3012; *Fax:* (602) 542-1575
E-mail: bbayless@mail.sosaz.com

Office of the Attorney General

http://www.ag.state.az.us/
General e-mail: aginquiries@ag.state.az.us
Main phone: (602) 542-5025
Main fax: (602) 542-1275

State of Arizona

Capital: Phoenix, since 1889
Founded: 1862, as Confederate Territory of Arizona; 1863, Arizona Territory created from New Mexico Territory
Statehood: February 14, 1912 (48th state)
Constitution adopted: February 14, 1912
Area: 113,642 sq. mi. (ranks 6th)
Population: 4,668,631 (1998 est.; ranks 21st)
Largest cities: (1998 est.) Phoenix (1,198,064); Tucson (460,466); Mesa (360,076); Scottsdale (195,394); Glendale (193,482)
Counties: 15, Most populous: (1998 est.) Maricopa (2,784,075); Pima (790,755); Yavapai (148, 511); Pinal (146,929); Yuma (132,259)
U.S. Congress: John Kyl (R), John McCain (R); 6 Representatives
Nickname(s): Grand Canyon State
Motto: God enriches
Song: "Arizona March Song"
Bird: Cactus wren
Tree: Palo verde
Flower: Saguaro cactus blossom
State fair: at Phoenix, mid-late Nov.
Former capital(s): Prescott

Toll free: (888) 377-6178
TTY: (602) 542-5002

Janet Napolitano (D), Attorney General
1275 W. Washington St., Phoenix, AZ 85007
(602) 542-4266; *Fax:* (602) 542-4085

Office of the Treasurer

http://www.state.az.us/tr/welcome.html
Main phone: (602) 542-5815
Main fax: (602) 542-7176

Carol Springer (R), State Treasurer
1700 W. Washington, 1st Fl., Phoenix, AZ 85007
(602) 542-1463
E-mail: carols@treasury.state.az.us

Office of the Auditor General

http://www.auditorgen.state.az.us/

General e-mail:
  webmaster@auditorgen.state.az.us
Main phone: (602) 553-0333
Main fax: (602) 553-0051

Debra K. Davenport, Auditor General
2910 N. 44th St., #410, Phoenix, AZ 85018

Army National Guard, Adjudant General's Office
http://www.azng.com
General e-mail: tagaz@az.ngb.army.mil
Main phone: (602) 267-2710
Main fax: (602) 267-2715

David P. Rataczak, Adjutant General
5636 E. McDowell Rd., Phoenix, AZ 85008-3495
(602) 267-2712
E-mail: rataczakd@az.ngb.army.mil

Agencies

Accountancy Board
http://www.accountancy.state.az.us/
General e-mail:
  info@mail.accountancy.state.az.us
Main phone: (602) 255-3648
Main fax: (602) 255-1283

Ruth R. Lee, Executive Director
3877 N. 7th St., #106, Phoenix, AZ 85014

Administration Dept.
http://www.adoa.state.az.us/
General e-mail: webmaster@state.az.us
Main phone: (602) 542-1500
Main fax: (602) 542-2199

J. Elliott Hibbs, Director
West Wing, State Capitol, 1700 W. Washington St.,
  #601, Phoenix, AZ 85007

Human Resources Division
http://www.hr.state.az.us
Main phone: (602) 542-3644
Main fax: (602) 542-2796

James Matthews, Director
1831 W. Jefferson, #117, Phoenix, AZ 85007
E-mail: jim_matthews@ad.state.az.us

Aging and Adult Administration
http://www.de.state.az.us/links/aaa.page1.html
Main phone: (602) 542-4446
Main fax: (602) 542-6575
Mailing address: P.O. Box 6123, Phoenix, AZ
  85005

Malena Albo, Assistant Director
1789 W. Jefferson, Site Code 950A-2SW, Phoenix, AZ
  85007
(602) 542-6572

Agriculture Dept.
http://www.agriculture.state.az.us
General e-mail:
  mark.hernandez@agric.state.az.us
Main phone: (602) 542-0998
Main fax: (602) 542-5420

Sheldon R. Jones, Director
1688 W. Adams St., Phoenix, AZ 85007
E-mail: sheldon.jones@agric.state.az.us

Arts Commission
http://az.arts.asu.edu/artscomm/
General e-mail: artscomm@primenet.com
Main phone: (602) 255-5882
Main fax: (602) 256-0282

Shelley M. Cohn, Executive Director
417 W. Roosevelt St., Phoenix, AZ 85003
E-mail: scohn@arizonaarts.org

Banking Dept.
http://www.azbanking.com/
General e-mail: mailbox@azbanking.com
Main phone: (602) 255-4421
Main fax: (602) 381-1225

Richard C. Houseworth, Superintendent
2910 N. 44th St., #310, Phoenix, AZ 85018
(602) 255-4421, ext. 113

Child Care Licensure Office
http://www.hs.state.az.us/als/childcare/index.html
Main phone: (602) 674-4220
Main fax: (602) 861-0674

Lourdes Ochoa, Program Manager
1647 E. Morten Ave., #230, Phoenix, AZ 85020

Commerce Dept.
http://www.azcommerce.com/
General e-mail: joanl@ep.state.az.us
Main phone: (602) 280-1300
Main fax: (602) 280-1305
TTY: (602) 280-1301

Jackie Vieh, Director
3800 N. Central Ave., #1500, Phoenix, AZ 85012
(602) 280-1306
E-mail: jackiev@azcommerce.com

Finance Division
http://www.azcommerce.com/finance.htm
General e-mail: fin@ep.state.az.us
Main phone: (602) 280-1369
Main fax: (602) 280-1358

Dale Sagebiel, Director (Acting)
3800 N. Central Ave., #1500, Phoenix, AZ 85012

Consumer Protection
http://www.ag.state.az.us/frames/default3x.html
General e-mail: webmaster@ag.state.az.us
Main phone: (602) 542-5025
Main fax: (602) 542-1275
Consumer complaint: (800) 952-8431

Janet Napolitano, Attorney General
1275 W. Washington St., Phoenix, AZ 85007-2926
(602) 542-4266; *Fax:* (602) 542-4085

Contractors Registrar
http://www.rc.state.az.us/
General e-mail: rocex1@roc1.rc.state.az.us
Main phone: (602) 542-1525
Main fax: (602) 542-1536
Toll free: (888) 271-9286
TTY: (602) 542-1588

Michael Goldwater, Director
800 W. Washington St., 6th Fl., Phoenix, AZ 85007
(602) 542-1525, ext. 7105

Corrections Dept.
http://www.adc.state.az.us
Main phone: (602) 542-5536
Main fax: (602) 542-2859

Terry L. Stewart, Director
1601 W. Jefferson St., Phoenix, AZ 85007
(602) 542-5497
E-mail: tstewart@adc.state.az.us

Cosmetology Board
Main phone: (480) 784-4539
Main fax: (602) 255-3680

Sue Sansom, Executive Director
1721 Broadway, Tempe, AZ 85282

Council for the Hearing Impaired
http://www.state.az.us/achi
Main phone: (602) 542-3323
Main fax: (602) 542-3380

Sherri L. Collins, Director
1400 W. Washington St., #126, Phoenix, AZ 85007

Developmental Disabilities Division
http://www.nau.edu/~ihd/ddd/
Main phone: (602) 542-0419
Main fax: (602) 542-6870
Mailing address: P.O. Box 6123, Phoenix, AZ
85005-6123

Roger Deshaies, Assistant Director
1789 W. Jefferson, Phoenix, AZ 85007
(602) 542-6853
E-mail: r.deshaies@worldnet.att.ent

Education Dept.
http://www.ade.state.az.us/
General e-mail: ade@mail1.ade.state.az.us
Main phone: (602) 542-4361
Main fax: (602) 542-5440
Toll free: (800) 352-8400

Lisa Graham Keegan (R), Superintendent of Public Instruction
1535 W. Jefferson St., Phoenix, AZ 85007
(602) 542-5460; *Fax:* (602) 542-5440
E-mail: lkeegan@mail1.ade.state.az.us

Board of Education
http://www.ade.state.az.us/
General e-mail: ADE@mail1.ade.state.az.us
Main phone: (602) 542-5057
Main fax: (602) 542-3046

Corinne L. Velasquez, Executive Director
1535 W. Jefferson St., Bin 11, Phoenix, AZ 85007
E-mail: cvelasq@mail1.ade.state.az.us

Emergency Management Division
http://www.state.az.us/es/director.htm
General e-mail: paulsenj@dem.state.az.us
Main phone: (602) 231-6219

Michael P. Austin, Director
5636 E. McDowell Rd., Phoenix, AZ 85008
E-mail: austinm@dem.state.az.us

Environmental Quality Dept.
http://www.adeq.state.az.us
Main phone: (602) 207-2300
Main fax: (602) 207-2218
Toll free: (800) 234-5677

Jacqueline E. Schafer, Director (Acting)
3033 N. Central Ave., Phoenix, AZ 85012
(602) 207-2203

Fire Marshal
Main phone: (602) 255-4964
Main fax: (602) 255-4961
TTY: (800) 367-8939

Duane Pell, Fire Marshal
99 E. Virginia, #100, Phoenix, AZ 85004

Game and Fish Dept.
http://www.gf.state.az.us
Main phone: (602) 942-3000
Main fax: (602) 789-3924

Duane L. Shroufe, Director
2221 W. Greenway Rd., Phoenix, AZ 85023-4399
(602) 789-3278; *Fax:* (602) 789-3299
E-mail: dshroufe@gf.state.az.us

Geological Survey
http://www.azgs.state.az.us
Main phone: (520) 770-3500
Main fax: (520) 770-3505

Larry D. Fellows, Director, State Geologist
416 W. Congress St., #100, Tucson, AZ 85701
E-mail: fellows_larry@pop.state.az.us

Oil and Gas Conservation Commission
http://www.azgs.state.az.us/azgs-ogc.htm
Main phone: (520) 770-3500

Steve Rauzi, Administrator
416 W. Congress St., #100, Tucson, AZ 85701
E-mail: rauzi_steve@pop.state.az.us

Health Care Cost Containment System
http://www.ahcccs.state.az.us/
General e-mail: flopez@ahcccs.state.az.us
Main phone: (602) 417-4000
Main fax: (602) 252-6536
Toll free: (800) 654-8731 x7000
TTY: (800) 826-5140
Mailing address: P.O. Box 25520, Phoenix, AZ 85002

Phyllis Biedess, Director
801 E. Jefferson St., #MD-4100, Phoenix, AZ 85034
(602) 417-4680
E-mail: pxbiedess@ahcccs.state.az.us

Health Services Dept.
http://www.hs.state.az.us/
Main phone: (602) 542-1000
Main fax: (602) 542-1062

James L. Schamadan, Director (Acting)
1740 W. Adams St., #407, Phoenix, AZ 85007
(602) 542-1025

Behavioral Health Services Division
http://www.hs.state.az.us/bhs

Frequently Called Numbers

Tourism: (602) 230-7733;
   http://www.arizonaguide.com/
Library: (602) 542-4035;
   http://www.dlapr.lib.az.us
Board of Education: (602) 542-5057;
   http://www.ade.state.az.us/
Vital Statistics: (602) 255-3260;
   http://www.hs.state.az.us/ohpes.htm
Tax/Revenue: (602) 255-3381;
   http://www.revenue.state.az.us
Motor Vehicles: (602) 255-0072;
   http://www.dot.state.az.us/MVD/mvd.htm
State Police/Highway Patrol: (602) 223-2000;
   http://www.dps.state.az.us/fy96-97/ms96-hp.htm
Unemployment: (602) 252-7771; http://
   www.de.state.az.us/links/esa/index.html
General Election Information: (877) 843-8683; http://www.sosaz.com/election/
Consumer Affairs: (602) 542-5025; http://
   www.ag.state.az.us/frames/default3x.html
Hazardous Materials: (602) 231-6309; http://
   www.state.az.us/es/azserc/Graphics/
   azserc.htm

Main phone: (602) 381-8999
Main fax: (602) 553-9140

Ronald Smith, Assistant Director
2122 E. Highland, #100, Phoenix, AZ 85016
E-mail: rsmith@hs.state.az.us

Historical Society
General e-mail: azhist@azstarnet.com
Main phone: (520) 628-5774
Main fax: (520) 628-5695

Joel Hiller, Executive Director (Interim)
949 E. 2nd St., Tucson, AZ 85719

Industrial Commission
http://www.ica.state.az.us/
General e-mail: webmaster@ica.state.az.us
Main phone: (602) 542-4411
Main fax: (602) 542-3104

Gay Conrad Kruglick, Chair
800 W. Washington St., Phoenix, AZ 85007

Insurance Dept.
http://www.state.az.us/id/
General e-mail: info@azdoi.e-mail.com
Main phone: (602) 912-8400
Main fax: (602) 912-8452

Charles R. Cohen, Director
2910 N. 44th St., #210, Phoenix, AZ 85018-7256

Juvenile Corrections Dept.
http://www.juvenile.state.az.us
General e-mail: stevem@dj.state.az.us
Main phone: (602) 542-3987
Main fax: (602) 542-5156

David A. Gaspar, Director
1624 W. Adams St., #306, Phoenix, AZ 85007
(602) 542-4302; *Fax:* (602) 542-5156
E-mail: Daveg@dj.state.az.us

Land Dept.
http://www.land.state.az.us/
General e-mail: kkudo@lnd.state.az.us
Main phone: (602) 542-4621
Main fax: (602) 542-2590

Michael E. Anable, Commissioner
1616 W. Adams, Phoenix, AZ 85007

Fire Management Division
http://www.land.state.az.us/asld/htmls/fire.html
Main phone: (602) 255-4059
Main fax: (602) 255-1781

Kirk Rowdabaugh, Director
2901 W. Pinnacle Peak Rd., Phoenix, AZ 85027-
1002
E-mail: krowdabaughaz@cybertrails.com

Forestry Management Division
http://www.land.state.az.us/asld/htmls/
forestry_97.html
Main phone: (602) 542-2518

Mike Hart, Director
1616 W. Adams, Phoenix, AZ 85007

Natural Resources Division
http://www.land.state.az.us/asld/htmls/
natural_97.html
Main phone: (602) 542-4625
Main fax: (602) 542-4668

William Dowdel, Director (Acting)
1616 W. Adams, #305, Phoenix, AZ 85007
(602) 542-2657

Library, Archives, and Public Records Dept.
http://www.dlapr.lib.az.us
General e-mail: services@dlapr.lib.az.us
Main phone: (602) 542-4035
Main fax: (602) 542-4972

Gladys Ann Wells, Director
State Capitol, 1700 W. Washington St., #200, Phoenix,
AZ 85007

History and Archives Division
http://www.dlapr.lib.state.az.us/archives/
index.html

General e-mail: archive@dlapr.lib.az.us
Main phone: (602) 542-4159
Main fax: (602) 542-4402

Melanie Sturgeon, Director
State Capitol, 1700 W. Washington St., #342,
Phoenix, AZ 85007
E-mail: msturgeo@dlapr.lib.az.us

Library Extension Division
http://www.lib.az.us/extension/index.html
General e-mail: webedits@dlapr.lib.az.us
Main phone: (602) 542-5841
Main fax: (602) 364-2257

Jane Kolbe, Director
J. M. Evans House, 1100 W. Washington, Phoenix,
AZ 85007
E-mail: jkolbe@dlapr.lib.az.us

Liquor Licences and Control Dept.
http://www.azll.com
General e-mail: liqr@azll.com
Main phone: (602) 542-5141
Main fax: (602) 542-5707
TTY: (602) 542-9069

Howard Adams, Director
800 W. Washington St., Phoenix, AZ 85007
(602) 542-9020

Lottery
http://www.arizonalottery.com
General e-mail: feedback@lottery.state.az.us
Main phone: (480) 921-4400
Main fax: (480) 921-4488

Geoffrey Gonsher, Executive Director
4740 E. University Dr., Phoenix, AZ 85034
(480) 921-4514; *Fax:* (480) 921-4488
E-mail: Geoffrey@lottery.state.az.us

Medical Examiners Board
http://www.docboard.org/bomex
Main phone: (602) 255-3751
Main fax: (602) 255-1848

Claudia Foutz, Executive Director
1651 E. Morten Ave., #210, Phoenix, AZ 85020
(602) 255-3751, ext. 2791
E-mail: cfoutz@bomex.org

Nursing Board
http://www.azboardofnursing.org
General e-mail: arizona@ncsbn.org
Main phone: (602) 331-8111
Main fax: (602) 906-9365

Joey Ridenour, Director
1651 E. Morten Ave., #150, Phoenix, AZ 85020
(602) 331-8111, ext. 125

Personnel Board
Main phone: (602) 542-3888
Main fax: (602) 542-3588

Judith L. Henkel, Executive Director
1400 W. Washington St., #280, Phoenix, AZ 85007
E-mail: henkel_judy@pop.state.az.us

Pharmacy Board
http://www.pharmacy.state.az.us/
General e-mail: info@azsbp.com
Main phone: (602) 255-5125 x123
Main fax: (602) 255-5740
TTY: (800) 367-8939

L. A. Lloyd, Executive Director
5060 N. 19th Ave., #101, Phoenix, AZ 85015
(602) 255-5125, ext. 129
E-mail: lalloyd@azsbp.com

Postsecondary Education Commission
http://www.acpe.asu.edu
General e-mail: toni@www.acpe.asu.edu
Main phone: (602) 229-2591
Main fax: (602) 229-2599

Verna L. Allen, Executive Director
2020 N. Central Ave., #275, Phoenix, AZ 85004-4503
(602) 229-2595
E-mail: vallen@www.acpe.asu.edu

Public Safety Dept.
http://www.dps.state.az.us/welcome2.htm
Main phone: (602) 223-2000
Main fax: (602) 223-2916
Mailing address: P.O. Box 6638, Phoenix, AZ 85005-6638

Joe Albo, Director
2102 W. Encanto Blvd., Phoenix, AZ 85005-6638
(602) 223-2359

Highway Patrol Bureau
http://www.dps.state.az.us/fy96-97/ms96-hp.htm
General e-mail: feedback@pr.state.az.us
Main phone: (602) 223-2000
Main fax: (602) 223-2919

C. R. Johnson, Bureau Chief
2102 W. Encanto Blvd., Phoenix, AZ 85009

Real Estate Education and Licensing Division
http://www.re.state.az.us/e&l.html
Main phone: (602) 468-1414 x345
Main fax: (602) 955-6284

John Bechtold, Director
2910 N. 44th St., #100, Phoenix, AZ 85018

Retirement System
http://www.asrs.state.az.us/
Main phone: (602) 240-2000

Main fax: (602) 264-6113
Toll free: (800) 621-3778
TTY: (602) 240-2023
Mailing address: P.O. Box 33910, Phoenix, AZ 85067

LeRoy Gilbertson, Director
3300 N. Central Ave., Phoenix, AZ 85010
(602) 240-2031
E-mail: gil_asrs@pop.state.az.us

Revenue Dept.
http://www.revenue.state.az.us
Main phone: (602) 255-3381
Main fax: (602) 542-4772
Toll free: (800) 352-4090
TTY: (602) 542-4021

Mark W. Killian, Director
1600 W. Monroe St., #911, Phoenix, AZ 85007
(602) 542-3572; *Fax:* (602) 542-4772

Schools for the Deaf and the Blind
http://www.asdb.org/
Main phone: (520) 770-3719
Main fax: (520) 770-3711
Mailing address: P.O. Box 88510, Tucson, AZ 85754

Kenneth D. Randall, Superintendent
1200 Speedway, Tucson, AZ 85745
(520) 770-3718
E-mail: kenr@asdb.state.az.us

Boards and Licensing

Accountancy, (602) 255-3648,
http://www.accountancy.state.az.us/

Child Care, (602) 674-4220, http://www.hs.state.az.us/als/childcare/index.html

Cosmetology, (480) 784-4539

Medical Examiners, (602) 255-3751,
http://www.docboard.org/bomex

Nursing, (602) 331-8111,
http://www.azboardofnursing.org

Pharmacy, (602) 255-5125, ext. 123,
http://www.pharmacy.state.az.us/

Real Estate Appraisers, (602) 468-1414, ext. 345, http://www.re.state.az.us/e&l.htm

Technical Registration Board, (602) 255-4053, http://www.btr.state.az.us/

State Fair and Exposition
http://www.azstatefair.com
Main phone: (602) 252-6771
Main fax: (602) 495-1302
Mailing address: P.O. Box 6728, Phoenix, AZ
85005-6728

Gary D. Montgomery, Executive Director
1826 McDowell Rd., Phoenix, AZ 85007
E-mail: garym@azstatefair.com

State Parks
http://www.pr.state.az.us/
General e-mail: feedback@pr.state.az.us
Main phone: (602) 542-4174
Main fax: (602) 542-4180
Toll free: (800) 285-3703
TTY: (602) 542-4174

Ken Travous, Executive Director
1300 W. Washington St., Phoenix, AZ 85007

Technical Registration Board
http://www.btr.state.az.us/
General e-mail: azbtrweb@yahoo.com
Main phone: (602) 255-4053
Main fax: (602) 255-4051
Toll free: (800) 252-3456

Gregory M. Tuttle, Chair
1990 W. Camelback Rd., #406, Phoenix, AZ 85015-
3465
(602) 263-3170; *Fax:* (602) 263-3175
E-mail: gmtuttle@srpnet.com

Tourism Office
http://www.arizonaguide.com/
Main phone: (602) 230-7733
Main fax: (602) 240-5475
Toll free: (888) 520-3434

Mark McDermott, Director
2702 N. 3rd St., Phoenix, AZ 85004
(602) 248-1490; *Fax:* (602) 255-4600

Transportation Dept.
http://www.dot.state.az.us
General e-mail: info@dot.state.az.us
Main phone: (602) 712-7011
Main fax: (602) 712-6941

Mary E. Peters, Director
206 S. 17th Ave., #MD-100A, Phoenix, AZ 85007
(602) 712-7227; *Fax:* (602) 712-6941
E-mail: director@dot.state.az.us

Aeronautics Division
http://www.dot.state.az.us/aero
Main phone: (602) 294-9144
Main fax: (602) 294-9141
Mailing address: P.O. Box 13588, Phoenix, AZ
85002-3588

Gary Adams, Director
255 E. Osborn Rd., #101, Phoenix, AZ 85012
(602) 712-7691

Motor Vehicles Division
http://www.dot.state.az.us/MVD/mvd.htm
General e-mail: mvdinfo@dot.state.az.us
Main phone: (602) 255-0072
TTY: (602) 407-3222
Mailing address: P.O. Box 2100, MD #500M,
Phoenix, AZ 85001

Stacey Stanton, Director
1801 W. Jefferson, Phoenix, AZ 85007
(602) 712-8152; *Fax:* (602) 712-6539

Veterans Service Commission
http://www.azvets.com/
Main phone: (602) 255-4183
Main fax: (602) 255-1038
Toll free: (800) 852VETS

Patrick F. Chorpenning, Director
3225 N. Central Ave., #910, Phoenix, AZ 85012
(602) 255-3373; *Fax:* (602) 255-1038
E-mail: director@avsc-phx.com

Water Resources Dept.
http://www.adwr.state.az.us
Main phone: (602) 417-2400
Main fax: (602) 417-2401

Rita P. Pearson, Director
500 N. 3rd St., Phoenix, AZ 85004
(602) 417-2410; *Fax:* (602) 417-2415
E-mail: rppearson@adwr.state.az.us

Women's Division
http://www.governor.state.az.us/women
Main phone: (602) 542-1739
Main fax: (602) 542-5804

Dana Campbell Saylor, Director
1700 W. Washington, #101-A, Phoenix, AZ 85007
E-mail: dsaylor@azgov.state.az.us

Arizona Legislature
Capitol Complex
1700 W. Washington
Phoenix, AZ 85007-2890
General information: (602) 542-4900
http://www.azleg.state.az.us

Senate
General information: (602) 542-3559
Fax: (602) 542-3429

Brenda Burns (R), President
Capitol Complex, 1700 W. Washington St., #204,
 Phoenix, AZ 85007-2890
(602) 542-3160
E-mail: bburns@azleg.state.az.us
http://www.azleg.state.az.us/members/bburns.htm

Russell (Rusty) Bowers (R), Majority Leader
Capitol Complex, 1700 W. Washington St., #212,
 Phoenix, AZ 85007-2890
(602) 542-5288
E-mail: rbowers@azleg.state.az.us
http://www.azleg.state.az.us/members/rbowers.htm

Ann Day (R), Majority Whip
Capitol Complex, 1700 W. Washington St., #212,
 Phoenix, AZ 85007-2890
(602) 542-4326
E-mail: aday@azleg.state.az.us
http://www.azleg.state.az.us/members/aday.htm

Jack Brown (D), Minority Leader
Capitol Complex, 1700 W. Washington St., #213,
 Phoenix, AZ 85007-2890
(602) 542-4129
E-mail: jbrown@azleg.state.az.us
http://www.azleg.state.az.us/members/jbrown.htm

Peter Rios (D), Minority Whip
Capitol Complex, 1700 W. Washington St., #316,
 Phoenix, AZ 85007-2890
(602) 542-5685
E-mail: prios@azleg.state.az.us
http://www.azleg.state.az.us/members/prios.htm

Charmion Billington, Secretary
Capitol Complex, 1700 W. Washington St., Phoenix,
 AZ 85007-2890
(602) 542-4231

House
General information: (602) 542-4221
Fax: (602) 542-4511

Jeff Groscost (R), Speaker of the House
Capitol Complex, 1700 W. Washington St., #221,
 Phoenix, AZ 85007-2890
(602) 542-5735
E-mail: groscost@azleg.state.az.us
http://www.azleg.state.az.us/members/jgroscos.htm

Lori S. Daniels (R), Majority Leader
Capitol Complex, 1700 W. Washington St., #206,
 Phoenix, AZ 85007-2890
(602) 542-5898
E-mail: ldaniels@azleg.state.az.us
http://www.azleg.state.az.us/members/ldaniels.htm

Jim Weiers (R), Majority Whip
Capitol Complex, 1700 W. Washington St., #217,
 Phoenix, AZ 85007-2890

Laws

Sales tax: 5%
Income tax: 5.2%
State minimum wage: None (Federal is $5.15)
Marriage age: 18
First-cousin marriage: Prohibited
Drinking age: 21
State control of liquor sales: No
Blood alcohol for DWI: 0.10%
Driving age: 16
Speed limit: 75 mph
Permit to buy handguns: No
Minimum age to possess handguns: 18
Minimum age to possess rifles, shotguns:
 None, with adult supervision
State lottery: Yes; also Powerball
Casinos: Yes (tribal)
Pari-mutuel betting: Horse and dog racing
Death penalty: Yes
3 strikes minimum sentence: None
Hate crimes law: Yes
Gay employment non-discrimination: No
Official language(s): None
Term limits: Governor (8 yrs.); state legislators
 (8 yrs.)

*State laws are complex and subject to
change; this information is not intended as
legal advice. For an explanation of this
information, see p. x.*

---

(602) 542-4639
E-mail: jweiers@azleg.state.az.us
http://www.azleg.state.az.us/members/jweiers.htm

Robert McLendon (D), Minority Leader
Capitol Complex, 1700 W. Washington St., #320,
 Phoenix, AZ 85007-2890
(602) 542-4430
E-mail: rmclendo@azleg.state.az.us
http://www.azleg.state.az.us/members/rmclendo.htm

John A. Loredo (D), Minority Whip
Capitol Complex, 1700 W. Washington St., #322,
 Phoenix, AZ 85007-2890
(602) 542-5830
E-mail: jloredo@azleg.state.az.us
http://www.azleg.state.az.us/members/jloredo.htm

Norman Moore, Chief Clerk
Capitol Complex, 1700 W. Washington St., Phoenix,
 AZ 85007-2890
(602) 542-3032

Arizona Judiciary

Arizona State Courts Bldg.
1501 W. Washington St.
Phoenix, AZ 85007-3231
http://www.supreme.state.az.us

Supreme Court
http://www.supreme.state.az.us/supreme

Noel K. Dessaint, Clerk
Arizona State Courts Bldg., 1501 W. Washington St.,
#402, Phoenix, AZ 85007-3231
(602) 542-9396

Justices
Composition: 5 justices
Selection Method: appointed by governor;
retention vote in first general election after 2
years

Length of term: 2-year appointment; 6 years if
retention ballot is successful

Thomas A. Zlaket, Chief Justice, (520) 628-6682
Charles E. Jones, Vice Chief Justice, (520) 542-4534
Stanley G. Feldman, Justice, (602) 542-4532
Frederick J. Martone, Justice, (602) 542-4535
Ruth V. McGregor, Justice, (602) 542-5789

State Law Library
http://www.lib.az.us/law/index.html
Main phone: (602) 542-5297
General e-mail: sll@dlapr.lib.az.us

David Melillo, State Law Librarian
Arizona State Courts Bldg., 1501 W. Washington St.,
#102, Phoenix, AZ 85007
E-mail: dmelillo@dlapr.lib.az.us

Arizona Legislative and Political Party Information Resources

Membership: http://www.azleg.state.az.us/members/members.htm
Committees: http://www.azleg.state.az.us/committes.htm
Legislative process: http://www.azleg.state.az.us/bill2law.htm
Current session information: http://www.azleg.state.az.us/calender/calender.htm
Budget: http://www.azleg.state.az.us/jlbc.htm
Arizona Democratic Party: http://www.azdem.org
    13610 N. Black Canyon Freeway, Phoenix, AZ 85029; *Phone:* (602) 298-4200; *Fax:* (602) 298-7117;*E-mail:* staff@azdem.org
Arizona Republican Party: http://www.azgop.org
    3501 N. 24th St., Phoenix, AZ 85016; *Phone:* (602) 957-7770; *E-mail:* info@azgop.org

Arkansas

250 State Capitol Bldg.
Little Rock, AR 72201
Public information: (501) 682-3000
Fax: (501) 682-1382
http://www.state.ar.us

Office of the Governor
http://www.state.ar.us/governor/governor.html
Main phone: (501) 682-2345
Main fax: (501) 682-1382
TTY: (501) 682-7515

Mike Huckabee (R), Governor
250 State Capitol Bldg., Little Rock, AR 72201
E-mail: mike.huckabee@state.ar.us

Brenda Turner, Chief of Staff
250 State Capitol Bldg., Little Rock, AR 72201
(501) 682-2345; *Fax:* (501) 682-1382
E-mail: brenda.turner@gov.state.ar.us

Rex Nelson, Executive Director, Communications
238 State Capitol Bldg., Little Rock, AR 72201
(501) 682-2345; *Fax:* (501) 682-2164
E-mail: rex.nelson@gov.state.ar.us

DeWayne Hayes, Director, Constituent Affairs Staff
250 State Capitol Bldg., Little Rock, AR 72201
(501) 682-2345; *Fax:* (501) 682-1382

Office of the Lieutenant Governor
http://www.state.ar.us/ltgov/
Main phone: (501) 682-2144
Main fax: (501) 682-2894

Winthrop P. Rockefeller (R), Lieutenant Governor
State Capitol Bldg., #270, Little Rock, AR 72201-1061
E-mail: winrock@state.ar.us

Office of the Secretary of State
http://www.sosweb.state.ar.us
Main phone: (501) 682-1010
Main fax: (501) 682-3510
Toll free: (800) 247-3312
TTY: (800) 262-4704

Sharon Priest (D), Secretary of State
State Capitol Bldg., #256, Little Rock, AR 72201
(501) 682-1216; *Fax:* (501) 682-3510
E-mail: spriest@sosmail.state.ar.us

Office of the Attorney General
http://www.ag.state.ar.us/
General e-mail: oag@ag.state.ar.us

State of Arkansas

Capital: Little Rock,
  since 1821
Founded: 1819, Arkansas
  Territory created from Missouri Territory
Statehood: June 15, 1836 (25th state)
Constitution adopted: 1874
Area: 52,075 sq. mi. (ranks 27th)
Population: 2,538,303 (1998 est.; ranks 33rd)
Largest cities: (1998 est.) Little Rock
  (175,303); Fort Smith (75,637); North Little
  Rock (59,184); Pine Bluff (52,968);
  Jonesboro (52,250)
Counties: 75, Most populous: (1998 est.)
  Pulaski (350,345); Washington (138,454);
  Benton (134,162); Sebastian (106,180);
  Garland (83,976)
U.S. Congress: Tim Hutchinson (R), Blanche
  Lambert Lincoln (D); 4 Representatives
Nickname(s): Natural State, Land of
  Opportunity
Motto: The people rule
Song: "Arkansas (You Run Deep in Me),"
  "Oh, Arkansas," "Arkansas Traveler"
Bird: Mockingbird
Tree: Pine tree
Flower: Apple blossom
State fair: at Little Rock, early Oct.
Former capital(s): Arkansas Post

Main phone: (501) 682-2007
Main fax: (501) 682-8084
Toll free: (800) 482-8982
TTY: (501) 682-6073

Mark Pryor (D), Attorney General
Tower Bldg., 323 Center St., #200, Little Rock, AR
  72201-2610

Office of the State Treasurer
Main phone: (501) 682-5888
Main fax: (501) 682-3842

Jimmie Lou Fisher (D), State Treasurer
State Capitol Bldg., #220, Little Rock, AR 72201
(501) 682-3835; *Fax:* (501) 682-3820
E-mail: jfisher@artreasury.state.ar.us

Office of the State Auditor

http://www.state.ar.us/auditor/auditor.html
General e-mail: aos@ipa.net
Main phone: (501) 682-6030
Main fax: (501) 682-2521

Gus Wingfield (D), Auditor of State
230 State Capitol Bldg., #230, Little Rock, AR 72201-1096

Military Dept.

http://www.arguard.org/
General e-mail: tag@ar-ngnet.army.mil
Main phone: (501) 212-5100
Main fax: (501) 212-5009

Don C. Morrow, Adjutant General
Camp J. T. Robinson, North Little Rock, AR 72199-9600
E-mail: morrowdc@ar-arng.ngb.army.mil

Agencies

Aeronautics Dept.

General e-mail: deptaero@ar.state.us
Main phone: (501) 376-6781
Main fax: (501) 378-0820

John Knight, Director
1 Airport Rd., 3rd Fl., Little Rock, AR 72202

Appraiser Licensing and Certification Board

http://www.state.ar.us/alcb
General e-mail: alcb@mail.state.ar.us
Main phone: (501) 296-1843
Main fax: (501) 296-1844

James B. Martin, Director
2725 Cantrell Rd., #202, Little Rock, AR 72202

Architects State Board

http://www.state.ar.us/arch/aboa1.html
General e-mail: arch@mail.state.ar.us
Main phone: (501) 682-3171
Main fax: (501) 682-3172
Toll free: (888) 800-3711

John Harris, Director
101 E. Capitol Ave., #208, Little Rock, AR 72201

Arts Council

http://www.arkansasarts.com
General e-mail: info@dah.state.ar.us
Main phone: (501) 324-9766
Main fax: (501) 324-9207

James E. Mitchell, Executive Director
1500 Tower Bldg., 323 Center St., Little Rock, AR 72201

Bank Dept.

http://www.state.ar.us/bank
General e-mail: asbd@banking.state.ar.us
Main phone: (501) 324-9019
Main fax: (501) 324-9028

Frank White, Commissioner
323 Center St., #500, Little Rock, AR 72201

Child Care and Early Childhood Education Division: Child Care Licensing

http://www.state.ar.us/childcare
Main phone: (501) 682-8590
Main fax: (501) 682-2317
Mailing address: P.O. Box 437, Slot 720, Little Rock, AR 72203

David Griffin, Administrator
101 E. Capitol Ave., #108, Little Rock, AR 72203-1437
E-mail: David.Griffin@mail.state.ar.us

Community Punishment Dept.

Main phone: (501) 682-9510
Main fax: (501) 682-9513

G. David Guntharp, Director
2 Union National Plaza, 105 W. Capitol Ave., Little Rock, AR 72201
(501) 682-9566; *Fax:* (501) 682-9539
E-mail: david.guntharp@mail.state.ar.us

Contractors Licensing Board

http://www.state.ar.us/clb
General e-mail: debi.archer@mail.state.ar.us
Main phone: (501) 372-4661
Main fax: (501) 372-2247

Howard Williams, Administrator
621 E. Capitol Ave., Little Rock, AR 72202
(501) 371-1500; *Fax:* (501) 372-2247
E-mail: howard.williams@mail.state.ar.us

Correction Dept.

http://www.state.ar.us/doc/
General e-mail: jack.carr@mail.state.ar.us
Main phone: (870) 267-6999
Main fax: (870) 267-6244
Mailing address: P.O. Box 8707, Pine Bluff, AR 71611

Larry Brown Norris, Director
6814 Princeton Pike, Pine Bluff, AR 71602
(870) 267-6200
E-mail: larry.norris@mail.state.ar.us

Cosmetology Board

General e-mail: cosmo@mail.state.ar.us
Main phone: (501) 682-2168
Main fax: (501) 682-5640

Debra Norton, Director
101 E. Capitol Ave., #108, Little Rock, AR 72201
(501) 682-5639; *Fax:* (501) 682-5640
E-mail: debra.norton@mail.state.ar.us

Crime Information Center
http://www.acic.org
Main phone: (501) 682-2222
Main fax: (501) 682-7444

David Eberdt, Director
1 Capitol Mall, #4D-200, Little Rock, AR 72201

Development Finance Authority
http://www.state.ar.us/adfa/
General e-mail: drose@adfa.state.ar.us
Main phone: (501) 682-5900
Main fax: (501) 682-5859
Mailing address: P.O. Box 8023, Little Rock, AR
72203-8023

Rush Deacon, President
100 Main St., #200, Little Rock, AR 72201
(501) 682-3839; *Fax:* (501) 682-5939
E-mail: rdeacon@adfa.state.ar.us

Economic Development Commission
http://www.1800arkansas.com
General e-mail: info@1800arkansas.com
Main phone: (501) 682-1121
Main fax: (501) 682-7394

Barbara I. Pardue, Executive Director
1 Capitol Mall, #4C-300, Little Rock, AR 72201
(501) 682-2052; *Fax:* (501) 682-7394
E-mail: bpardue@1800arkansas.com

Education Dept.
http://arkedu.state.ar.us/
General e-mail: gmorris@arkedu.k12.ar.us
Main phone: (501) 682-4475

Raymond Simon, Director
Arch Ford Education Bldg., 4 Capitol Mall, Little
Rock, AR 72201-1071
(501) 682-4204; *Fax:* (501) 682-1079
E-mail: rsimon@arkedu.k12.ar.us

Board of Education
http://arkedu.state.ar.us/arkansas1.htm
Main phone: (501) 682-4247
Main fax: (501) 682-9026

Luke Gordy, Chair
4 Capitol Mall, #403-A, Little Rock, AR 72201
E-mail: lgordy@arkedu.k12.ar.us

School for the Blind
http://www.asbhome.k12.ar.us
General e-mail: kenf@asb.k12.ar.us
Main phone: (501) 296-1810

Higher Educational Institutions

Arkansas State University
http://www.astate.edu
P.O. Box 1630, Jonesboro, AR 72467
Main phone: (870) 972-3024

Arkansas Tech University
http://www.atu.edu
Bryan Student Services Bldg., Russellville, AR
72801-2201
Main phone: (800) 582-6953

Henderson State University
http://www.hsu.edu
1100 Henderson St., Arkadelphia, AR 71999-0001
Main phone: (870) 230-5000

Southern Arkansas University
http://www.saumag.edu
100 E. University, Magnolia, AR 71753-5000
Main phone: (870) 235-4000

University of Arkansas
http://www.uark.edu
200 Silas H. Hunt Hall, Fayetteville, AR 72701
Main phone: (501) 575-5346
Branches: Little Rock, Monticello, Pine Bluff

University of Arkansas for Medical Sciences
http://www.uams.edu
4301 W. Markham, Little Rock, AR 72205
Main phone: (501) 686-5000

University of Central Arkansas
http://www.uca.edu
201 Donaghey Ave., Conway, AR 72035
Main phone: (501) 450-5000

Main fax: (501) 663-3536
Toll free: (800) 362-4451

Jim Hill, Superintendent
2600 W. Markham St., Little Rock, AR 72205
E-mail: hill@asb.k12.ar.us

School for the Deaf
http://www.state.ar.us/asd/
Main phone: (501) 324-9506
Main fax: (501) 324-9822
TTY: (501) 324-9800
Mailing address: P.O. Box 3811, Little Rock, AR
72203

Peter J. Seiler, Superintendent
2400 W. Markham St., Little Rock, AR 72205
E-mail: petes@asd.k12.ar.us

Educational Television Network
http://www.aetn.org

Main phone: (501) 682-2386
Main fax: (501) 682-4122
Toll free: (800) 662-2386
Mailing address: P.O. Box 1250, Conway, AR
72033

Susan Howarth, Executive Director
Sesame St. and Donaghey Ave., Conway, AR 72033

Emergency Management Dept.
http://www.adem.state.ar.us
Main phone: (501) 730-9751
Main fax: (501) 730-9754
Mailing address: P.O. Box 758, Conway, AR
72033-3278

W. R. (Bud) Harper, Director
1835 S. Donaghey Ave., Conway, AR 72032
(501) 730-9781; *Fax:* (501) 730-9754
E-mail: wharper@adem.state.ar.us

Ethics Commission
http://www.ArkansasEthics.com
General e-mail: contactus@ArkansasEthics.com
Main phone: (501) 324-9600
Main fax: (501) 324-9606
Toll free: (800) 422-7773
Mailing address: P.O. Box 1917, Little Rock, AR
72203-1917

Bob Brooks, Director
910 W. 2nd St., #100, Little Rock, AR 72201
(501) 324-9731; *Fax:* (501) 324-9602
E-mail: bob.brooks@mail.state.ar.us

Finance and Administration Dept.
http://www.state.ar.us/dfa/
Main phone: (501) 682-2242
Main fax: (501) 682-1086
TTY: (501) 682-5050
Mailing address: P.O. Box 3278, Little Rock, AR
72203-3278

Dick Barclay, Director
1509 W. 7th St., #401, Little Rock, AR 72203-3278
E-mail: dick.barclay@dfa.state.ar.us

Alcoholic Beverage Control Administration
http://www.state.ar.us/dfa/abcadministration/
index.html
Main phone: (501) 682-1105
Main fax: (501) 682-2221

Robert S. Moore Jr., Director
Technology Center, 100 Main St., #503, Little
Rock, AR 72201
E-mail: robert.moore@dfa.state.ar.us

Management Services Division: Personnel Management Office
http://www.state.ar.us/dfa/opm/index.html

Main phone: (501) 682-1823
Main fax: (501) 682-5104

Artee Williams, Administrator
201 DFA Bldg., 1509 W. 7th St., Little Rock, AR
72201
E-mail: artee.williams@dfa.state.ar.us

Motor Vehicles Office
Main phone: (501) 682-4692
Main fax: (501) 682-1116
Mailing address: P.O. Box 1272, Little Rock, AR
72203

Fred Porter, Administrator
7th and Battery Sts., #2042, Little Rock, AR 72203
(501) 682-4630
E-mail: fred.porter@rev.state.ar.us

Revenue Division
http://www.state.ar.us/dfa
Main phone: (501) 682-7025
Main fax: (501) 682-7900
Mailing address: P.O. Box 1272, Little Rock, AR
72203

Preston Means, Assistant Commissioner of Revenue for Operations and Administration
1908 Raglard Blvd., #2047, Little Rock, AR 72201
E-mail: preston.means@rev.state.ar.us

Forestry Commission
http://www.forestry.state.ar.us
General e-mail: forestry@mail.state.ar.us
Main phone: (501) 296-1940
Main fax: (501) 296-1949

John T. Shannon, Director
3821 W. Roosevelt Rd., Little Rock, AR 72204-6396
E-mail: john.shannon@mail.state.ar.us

Game and Fish Commission
http://www.agfc.state.ar.us/
General e-mail: algreen@agfc.state.ar.us
Main phone: (501) 223-6300
Main fax: (501) 223-6444
Toll free: (800) 364-4263

Steve N. Wilson, Director
2 Natural Resources Dr., #200, Little Rock, AR 72205
(501) 223-6305; *Fax:* (501) 223-6448
E-mail: snw001@agfc.state.ar.us

Geology Commission
http://www.state.ar.us/agc/agc.htm
General e-mail: agc@mail.state.ar.us
Main phone: (501) 296-1877
Main fax: (501) 663-7360

William V. Bush, Director and State Geologist
3815 W. Roosevelt Rd., Little Rock, AR 72204
Fax: (501) 663-7360
E-mail: bill.bush@mail.state.ar.us

Health Dept.
http://www.health.state.ar.us/
General e-mail: wbankson@mail.doh.state.ar.us
Main phone: (501) 661-2000

Fay W. Boozman, Director
4815 W. Markham St., Little Rock, AR 72205-3867
(501) 661-2400; *Fax:* (501) 671-1450
E-mail: dr.boozman@mail.doh.state.ar.us

Heritage Dept.
http://www.arkansasheritage.com
General e-mail: info@arkansasheritage.com
Main phone: (501) 324-9150
Main fax: (501) 324-9154
TTY: (501) 324-9811

Cathie Matthews, Director
Tower Bldg., 323 Center St., #1500, Little Rock, AR
72201
(501) 324-9162; *Fax:* (501) 324-9154

Higher Education Dept.
http://www.adhe.arknet.edu/
Main phone: (501) 371-2000
Main fax: (501) 371-2003

Lu Hardin, Director
114 E. Capitol Ave., Little Rock, AR 72201
E-mail: luh@adhe.arknet.edu

Highway and Transportation Dept.
http://www.ahtd.state.ar.us/
General e-mail: info@ahtd.state.ar.us
Main phone: (501) 569-2000
Main fax: (501) 569-2400
Mailing address: P.O. Box 2261, Little Rock, AR
72203-2261

Dan Flowers, Director
10324 Interstate 30, Little Rock, AR 72203-2261
(501) 569-2211; *Fax:* (501) 569-2698

Human Services Dept.
http://www.state.ar.us/dhs/
Main phone: (501) 682-1001
Main fax: (501) 682-6836
Toll free: (800) 285-1121
TTY: (501) 682-7958
Mailing address: P.O. Box 1437, Slot 3430, Little
Rock, AR 72203

Kurt Knickrehm, Director
Donaghey Plaza South, #329, Little Rock, AR 72203-
1437
(501) 682-8650; *Fax:* (501) 682-6836
E-mail: Kurt.Knickrehm@mail.state.ar.us

Aging and Adult Services Division
http://www.state.ar.us/dhs/aging/
Main phone: (501) 682-2441

Frequently Called Numbers

Tourism: (501) 682-7777; 1-800-NATURAL;
http://www.arkansas.com
Library: (501) 682-2053;
http://www.asl.lib.ar.us
Board of Education: (501) 682-4247;
http://arkedu.state.ar.us/arkansas1.htm
Vital Statistics: (501) 661-2336
Tax/Revenue: (501) 682-7025
Motor Vehicles: (501) 682-4692
State Police/Highway Patrol: (501) 618-8000;
http://www.state.ar.us/asp/asp.html
Unemployment: (501) 682-3200; http://
www.state.ar.us/esd/unemployment.htm
General Election Information: (501) 682-
5070; http://www.sosweb.state.ar.us/
elect.html
Consumer Affairs: (501) 682-6150
Hazardous Materials: (501) 569-2421

Main fax: (501) 682-8155
Toll free: (800) 981-4457
TTY: (501) 682-2443
Mailing address: P.O. Box 1437, Slot 1412,
Little Rock, AR 72203-1437

Herb Sanderson, Director
1417 Donaghey Plaza South, 7th. and Main, Little
Rock, AR 72203
E-mail: Herb.Sanderson@mail.state.ar.us

Developmental Disabilities Services Division
http://www.state.ar.us/dhs/ddds/index.html
Main phone: (501) 682-8665
Main fax: (501) 682-8380
TTY: (501) 682-1332
Mailing address: P.O. Box 1437, Slot 2510,
Little Rock, AR 72203-1437

David F. Fray, Assistant Director
Donaghey Plaza South, #207, Little Rock, AR
72203
(501) 682-8662; *Fax:* (501) 682-8380
E-mail: david.fray@mail.state.ar.us

Medical Services Division
http://www.medicaid.state.ar.us
Main phone: (501) 682-8292
Main fax: (501) 682-1197
TTY: (501) 682-2117
Mailing address: P.O. Box 1437, Slot 1100,
Little Rock, AR 72203-1437

Ray Hanley, Director
Donaghey Plaza South, #1100, Little Rock, AR
72203-1437
E-mail: ray.hanley@medicaid.state.ar.us

Mental Health Services Division
http://www.state.ar.us/dhs/dmhs
Main phone: (501) 686-9164
Main fax: (501) 686-9182
TTY: (501) 682-9176

Richard Hill, Director
4313 W. Markham, Slot 4313, Little Rock, AR 72205
(501) 686-9465; *Fax:* (501) 686-9182
E-mail: Richard.Hill@mail.state.ar.us

Youth Services Division
http://www.state.ar.us/dhs/dys/
Main phone: (501) 682-8654
Main fax: (501) 682-1339
TTY: (501) 682-1344
Mailing address: P.O. Box 1437, Slot 450, Little Rock, AR 72203-1437

Russell Rigsby, Director
Atkins Bldg., 105 W. Capitol Ave., 4th Fl., Little Rock, AR 72203
(501) 682-8755; *Fax:* (501) 682-8792
E-mail: Russell.Rigsby@mail.state.ar.us

Insurance Dept.
http://www.state.ar.us/insurance/
General e-mail:
  insurance.Administration@mail.state.ar.us
Main phone: (501) 371-2600
Main fax: (501) 371-2629
Toll free: (800) 282-9134

Boards and Licensing

Accountancy, (501) 682-1520,
  http://www.state.ar.us/asbpa/
Architects, (501) 682-3171,
  http://www.state.ar.us/arch/aboa1.html
Child Care, (501) 682-8590,
  http://www.state.ar.us/childcare
Contractors, (501) 372-4661,
  http://www.state.ar.us/clb
Cosmetology, (501) 682-2168
Engineers and Land Surveyors, (501) 682-2824, http://www.state.ar.us/pels/
Medical Licensing, (501) 296-1802
Nursing, (501) 686-2700,
  http://www.state.ar.us/nurse
Pharmacy, (501) 682-0190,
  http://www.state.ar.us/asbp
Real Estate Appraisers, (501) 296-1843,
  http://www.state.ar.us/alcb

Mike Pickens, Commissioner
1200 W. 3rd St., Little Rock, AR 72201-1904
(501) 371-2620; *Fax:* (501) 371-2629

Labor Dept.
http://www.state.ar.us/labor
Main phone: (501) 682-4500
Main fax: (501) 682-4535
TTY: (800) 285-1131

James L. Salkeld, Director
10421 W. Markham St., Little Rock, AR 72205
(501) 682-4541; *Fax:* (501) 682-4535

Liquefied Petroleum Gas Board
Main phone: (501) 324-9228
Main fax: (501) 324-9230

Sharon E. Coates, Director
1421 W. 6th St., Little Rock, AR 72201-2901
E-mail: scoates@cei.net

Medical Board
General e-mail: armb@mail.state.ar.us
Main phone: (501) 296-1802
Main fax: (501) 296-1805

Peggy Cryer, Executive Director
2100 Riverfront Dr., #200, Little Rock, AR 72202-1793

Nursing Board
http://www.state.ar.us/nurse
General e-mail: chad.calhoun@mail.state.ar.us
Main phone: (501) 686-2700
Main fax: (501) 686-2714

Faith A. Fields, Executive Director
University Tower Bldg., 1123 S. University Ave., #800, Little Rock, AR 72204
E-mail: Faith.Fields@mail.state.ar.us

Oil and Gas Commission
General e-mail: aogc@ipa.net
Main phone: (870) 862-4965
Main fax: (870) 862-8823
Mailing address: P.O. Box 1472, El Dorado, AR 71731-1472

Grant E. Black, Director
2215 W. Hillsboro St., El Dorado, AR 71730
E-mail: gblack@aogc.state.ar.us

Parks and Tourism Dept.
http://www.arkansas.com
General e-mail: info@arkansas.com
Main phone: (501) 682-7777
Main fax: (501) 682-1364
TTY: (501) 682-1191

Richard W. Davies, Executive Director
1 Capitol Mall, Little Rock, AR 72201
(501) 682-2535; *Fax:* (501) 682-2383

Pharmacy Board
http://www.state.ar.us/asbp
Main phone: (501) 682-0190
Main fax: (501) 682-0195

John Douglas, Executive Director
101 E. Capitol Ave., #218, Little Rock, AR 72201

Professional Engineers and Land Surveyors Board
http://www.state.ar.us/pels/
Main phone: (501) 682-2824
Main fax: (501) 682-2827
Mailing address: P.O. Box 3750, Little Rock, AR 72203

Joseph T. Clements Jr., Executive Director
410 W. 3rd St., #110, Little Rock, AR 72201
E-mail: josepht.clements@mail.state.ar.us

Public Accountancy Board
http://www.state.ar.us/asbpa/
Main phone: (501) 682-1520
Main fax: (501) 682-5538

James E. George, Executive Director
101 E. Capitol Ave., #430, Little Rock, AR 72201
(501) 682-2575

Public Defender Commission
Main phone: (501) 682-9070
Main fax: (501) 682-9073
Toll free: (800) 330-0630

Didi Sallings, Executive Director
101 E. Capitol Ave., #201, Little Rock, AR 72201
E-mail: Didi.Salling@mail.state.ar.us

Public Employees Retirement System
http://www.state.ar.us/apers/
Main phone: (501) 682-7800
Main fax: (501) 682-7825
Toll free: (800) 682-7377

Bill Van Cleve, Executive Director
1 Union National Plaza, 124 W. Capitol Ave., #400, Little Rock, AR 72201

Public Protection Division: Consumer Protection
General e-mail: consumer@ag.state.ar.us
Main phone: (501) 682-6150
Main fax: (501) 682-8118
Toll free: (800) 482-8982
TTY: (501) 682-6073

Sheila McDonald, Director
323 Center St., #200, Little Rock, AR 72201
E-mail: sheilam@ag.state.ar.us

Public Protection Division: Utilities and Environmental Section
http://www.aragstuff.com

Main phone: (501) 682-3649
Main fax: (501) 682-8118
Toll free: (800) 482-8482
TTY: (501) 682-6073

Sheila McDonald, Director
323 Center St., #200, Little Rock, AR 72201
E-mail: sheilam@ag.state.ar.us

Soil and Water Conservation Commission
http://www.state.ar.us/aswcc/
General e-mail: aswcc@aswcc.state.ar.us
Main phone: (501) 682-1611
Main fax: (501) 682-3991

J. Randy Young, Executive Director
101 E. Capitol Ave., #350, Little Rock, AR 72201
(501) 682-3986
E-mail: randy.young@aswcc.state.ar.us

State Fair
http://www.arkfairgrounds.com/
General e-mail: booking@arkfairgrounds.com
Main phone: (501) 372-8341
Main fax: (501) 372-4197
TTY: (501) 372-7055
Mailing address: P.O. Box 166660, Little Rock, AR 72216

Jeff Bowers, Assistant General Manager
2600 Howard, Little Rock, AR 72206

State Library
http://www.asl.lib.ar.us
Main phone: (501) 682-2053
Main fax: (501) 682-1529
TTY: (501) 682-2073

John A. "Pat" Murphy Jr., State Librarian
1 Capitol Mall, 5th Fl., Little Rock, AR 72201
(501) 682-1526; *Fax:* (501) 682-1899
E-mail: jmurphy@asl.lib.ar.us

State Police
http://www.state.ar.us/asp/asp.html
Main phone: (501) 618-8000
Main fax: (501) 618-8222

Thomas A. Mara, Director
1 State Police Plaza Dr., Little Rock, AR 72209
(501) 618-8200; *Fax:* (501) 618-8222

Regulatory Services: Fire Marshal
http://www.state.ar.us/asp/firem.html
Main phone: (501) 618-8624
Main fax: (501) 618-8621

Ray E. Carnahan, State Fire Marshal
1 State Police Plaza Dr., Little Rock, AR 72209
E-mail: rcarnahan@afp.state.ar.us

Veterans Affairs Dept.

Main phone: (501) 370-3820
Main fax: (501) 370-3829
TTY: (800) 285-1131
Mailing address: P.O. Box 1280, North Little Rock, AR 72115

Nick D. Bacon, Director
Bldg. 65, #114, North Little Rock, AR 72115
E-mail: nick.smith@mail.state.ar.us

Workers' Compensation Commission

http://www.awcc.state.ar.us
Main phone: (501) 682-2607
Main fax: (501) 682-2777
Toll free: (800) 622-4472
TTY: (800) 285-1131
Mailing address: P.O. Box 950, Little Rock, AR 72203-0950

Eldon Coffman, Chair
4th and Spring Sts., Little Rock, AR 72203-0950
(501) 324-9560; *Fax:* (501) 324-9564
E-mail: ecoffman@awcc.state.ar.us

Arkansas Legislature

State Capitol Bldg.
Little Rock, AR 72201
General information: (501) 682-1937
http://www.arkleg.state.ar.us

Senate

Address: 320 State Capitol Bldg., Little Rock, AR 72201
General information: (501) 682-2902
Fax: (501) 682-2917
Bill status: (501) 682-5951

Winthrop P. Rockefeller (R), President
State Capitol Bldg., Little Rock, AR 72201
(501) 682-2144; *Fax:* (501) 682-2894
E-mail: winrock@state.ar.us
http://www.state.ar.us/ltgov/

Jay Bradford (D), President Pro Tempore
State Capitol Bldg., Little Rock, AR 72201
(501) 682-5965; *Fax:* (870) 535-8318
http://www.arkleg.state.ar.us/scripts/ablr/members/members3b.idc?mcode=504

Stanley Russ (D), Majority Leader
State Capitol Bldg., Little Rock, AR 72201
(501) 682-5455
E-mail: sruss@arkleg.state.ar.us
http://www.arkleg.state.ar.us/scripts/ablr/members/members3b.idc?mcode=524

Laws
Sales tax: 4.5%
Income tax: 7%
State minimum wage: $5.15 (Federal is $5.15)
Marriage age: 18
First-cousin marriage: Prohibited
Drinking age: 21
State control of liquor sales: No
Blood alcohol for DWI: 0.10%
Driving age: 16
Speed limit: 70 mph
Permit to buy handguns: No
Minimum age to possess handguns: 18
Minimum age to possess rifles, shotguns: None
State lottery: No
Casinos: No
Pari-mutuel betting: Horse and dog racing
Death penalty: Yes
3 strikes minimum sentence: 40 yrs. (2nd serious violent felony)
Hate crimes law: No
Gay employment non-discrimination: No
Official language(s): English
Term limits: Governor (8 yrs.); state senate (8 yrs.), house (6 yrs.)
State laws are complex and subject to change; this information is not intended as legal advice. For an explanation of this information, see p. x.

Bill Walters (R), Minority Leader
State Capitol Bldg., Little Rock, AR 72201
(501) 682-6050; *Fax:* (501) 996-2565
E-mail: bwalters@arkleg.state.ar.us
http://www.arkleg.state.ar.us/scripts/ablr/members/members3b.idc?mcode=528

Ann Cornwell, Secretary and Fiscal Officer
State Capitol Bldg., Little Rock, AR 72201
(501) 682-5951
E-mail: annc@arkleg.state.ar.us

House

Address: 350 State Capitol Bldg., Little Rock, AR 72201
General information: (501) 682-7771

Bob Johnson (D), Speaker of the House
State Capitol Bldg., Little Rock, AR 72201
(501) 682-7771; *Fax:* (501) 354-6700
http://www.state.ar.us/house/speaker_99.html

Douglas C. Kidd (D), Speaker Pro Tempore
State Capitol Bldg., Little Rock, AR 72201
(501) 682-7771
http://www.arkleg.state.ar.us/scripts/ablr/members/
    members3b.idc?mcode=68

Steve Faris (D), Majority Leader
State Capitol Bldg., Little Rock, AR 72201
(501) 682-7771; *Fax:* (501) 865-2112
http://www.arkleg.state.ar.us/scripts/ablr/members/
    members3b.idc?mcode=23

James Paul Hendren (R), Minority Leader
State Capitol Bldg., Little Rock, AR 72201
(501) 682-7771; *Fax:* (501) 787-6116
http://www.arkleg.state.ar.us/scripts/ablr/members/
    members3b.idc?mcode=51

Jo Renshaw, Chief Clerk
State Capitol Bldg., Little Rock, AR 72201
(501) 682-7771

Arkansas Judiciary

Justice Bldg.
625 Marshall St.
Little Rock, AR 72201
http://courts.state.ar.us/

Supreme Court
http://courts.state.ar.us/arksct.htm

Leslie W. Steen, Clerk
Justice Bldg., 625 Marshall St., 1st Fl., Little Rock,
    AR 72201
(501) 682-6849; *Fax:* (501) 682-6877

Justices
Composition: 7 justices
Selection Method: partisan election; vacancies
    filled by governor on temporary basis
Length of term: 8 years
W. H. (Dub) Arnold, Chief Justice, (501) 682-6861
Robert L. Brown, Justice, (501) 682-6864
Donald L. Corbin, Justice, (501) 682-6838
Tom Glaze, Justice, (501) 682-6870
Annabelle Clinton Imber, Justice, (501) 682-6867
Lavenski R. Smith, Justice, (501) 682-6873
Ray Thornton, Justice, (501) 682-6876

Administrative Office of the Courts
http://courts.state.ar.us/admin.htm
Main phone: (501) 682-9400
Main fax: (501) 682-9410

James D. Gingerich, Director
Justice Bldg., 625 Marshall St., #110, Little Rock, AR
    72201

Supreme Court Library
http://courts.state.ar.us/sclib.htm
Main phone: (501) 682-2147
Main fax: (501) 682-6877
General e-mail: arsclib@mail.state.ar.us

Timothy N. Holthoff, Director
1310 Justice Bldg., 625 Marshall St., Little Rock, AR
    72201
E-mail: tim.holthoff@mail.state.ar.us

Arkansas Legislative and Political Party Information Resources

Senate home page: http://www.arkleg.state.ar.us/data/senate.htm
House home page: http://www.state.ar.us/house
Committees: http://www.arkleg.state.ar.us/scripts/ablr/committees/committee3.asp?
Legislative process: http://www.state.ar.us/house/bill_law.htm
Budget: http://www.arkleg.state.ar.us/data/revrepor/revrpt.htm
Arkansas Democratic Party: http://www.arkdems.org
    1300 W. Capitol Ave., Little Rock, AR 72201; *Phone:* (501) 374-2361; *Fax:* (501) 376-8049; *E-mail:*
    dpa@arkdems.org
Arkansas Republican Party: http://www.arkgop.org
    1201 W. 6th St., Little Rock, AR 72201; *Phone:* (501) 372-7301

California

State Capitol
Sacramento, CA 95814
Public information: (916) 322-9900
Fax: (916) 445-4633
http://www.state.ca.us

Office of the Governor
http://www.ca.gov/s/governor/
Main phone: (916) 445-2841
Main fax: (916) 445-4633

Gray Davis (D), Governor
State Capitol, Sacramento, CA 95814

Lynn Schenk, Chief of Staff
State Capitol, Sacramento, CA 95814
(916) 445-2841; *Fax:* (916) 445-4633

Michael Bustamante, Press Secretary
State Capitol, Sacramento, CA 95814
(916) 445-2841; *Fax:* (916) 445-4633

Celia Mata, Chief of Constituent Affairs
State Capitol, Sacramento, CA 95814
(916) 445-2841; *Fax:* (916) 445-4633

Olivia Morgan, Director, Washington Office
444 N. Capitol St. N.W., #134, Washington, DC 20001
(202) 624-5270; *Fax:* (202) 624-5280

Office of the Lieutenant Governor
http://www.ltg.ca.gov/
Main phone: (916) 445-8994
Main fax: (916) 323-4998

Cruz M. Bustamante (D), Lieutenant Governor
State Capitol, #1114, Sacramento, CA 95814

Office of the Secretary of State
http://www.ss.ca.gov
General e-mail: constituentaffairs@ss.ca.gov
Main phone: (916) 653-6814
Main fax: (916) 653-4620

Bill Jones (R), Secretary of State
1500 11th St., #600, Sacramento, CA 95814
(916) 653-7244; *Fax:* (916) 653-4795
E-mail: bjones@ss.ca.gov

Office of the Attorney General
http://caag.state.ca.us/
General e-mail: PIU@hdcdojnet.state.ca.us
Main phone: (916) 445-9555
Main fax: (916) 324-5205
Mailing address: P.O. Box 944255, Sacramento, CA 94244-2550

State of California

Capital: Sacramento, since 1854
Founded: 1848, province of Alta California included in Mexican Cession
Statehood: September 9, 1850 (31st state)
Constitution adopted: December 20, 1849
Area: 155,973 sq. mi. (ranks 3rd)
Population: 32,666,550 (1998 est.; ranks 1st)
Largest cities: (1998 est.) Los Angeles (3,597,556); San Diego (1,220,666); San Jose (861,284); San Francisco (745,774); Long Beach (430,095)
Counties: 58, Most populous: (1998 est.) Los Angeles (9,213,533); San Diego (2,780,592); Orange (2,721,701); Santa Clara (1,641,215); Riverside (1,478,838)
U.S. Congress: Barbara Boxer (D), Dianne Feinstein (D); 52 Representatives
Nickname(s): Golden State
Motto: Eureka!
Song: "I Love You, California"
Bird: California valley quail
Tree: California redwood
Flower: Golden poppy
State fair: at Sacramento, late Aug.-early Sept.
Former capital(s): Monterey, Vallejo, Benicia

Bill Lockyer (D), Attorney General
1300 I St., #1101, Sacramento, CA 94244-2550
(916) 324-5437

Office of the State Treasurer
http://www.treasurer.ca.gov/
General e-mail: treasurer@treasurer.ca.gov
Main phone: (916) 653-2995
Main fax: (916) 653-3125
Mailing address: P.O. Box 942809, Sacramento, CA 94209-0001

Philip Angelides (D), State Treasurer
915 Capitol Mall, #110, Sacramento, CA 94209-0001

Office of the State Controller
http://www.sco.ca.gov/
General e-mail: cogen@vmmail.teale.ca.gov
Main phone: (916) 445-3028
Main fax: (916) 445-6379

Kathleen M. Connell (D), Controller
300 Capitol Mall, 18th Fl., Sacramento, CA 95814
(916) 445-2636

Military Dept.
http://www.calguard.ca.gov/
Main phone: (916) 854-3000
Main fax: (916) 854-3671
Mailing address: P.O. Box 269101, Sacramento, CA 95826-9101

Paul D. Monroe Jr., Adjutant General
9800 Goethe Rd., Sacramento, CA 95826-9101
(916) 854-3500; *Fax:* (916) 854-3671
E-mail: paul.monroe@ca-arng.ngb.army.mil

Agencies

Accountancy Board
http://www.dca.ca.gov/cba/
Main phone: (916) 263-3680
Main fax: (916) 263-3675

Carol Sigman, Executive Officer
2000 Evergreen St., #250, Sacramento, CA 95815-3832
(916) 263-3692; *Fax:* (916) 263-3674

Administrative Law Office
http://www.oal.ca.gov/
General e-mail: staff@oal.ca.gov
Main phone: (916) 323-6225
Main fax: (916) 323-6826

Vacant, Director
555 Capitol Mall, #1290, Sacramento, CA 95814
(916) 323-6221

Aging Dept.
http://www.aging.state.ca.us/
Main phone: (916) 322-3887
Main fax: (916) 324-4989
Toll free: (800) 510-2020

Lynda Terry, Director
1600 K St., Sacramento, CA 95814

Alcoholic Beverage Control
http://www.abc.ca.gov/
General e-mail: webmaster@email.abc.ca.gov
Main phone: (916) 263-6900
Main fax: (916) 263-6843

Jay R. Stroh, Director
3810 Rosin Ct., #150, Sacramento, CA 95834

Architectural Examiners Board
http://www.cbae.cahwnet.gov/
General e-mail: cbae@dca.ca.gov
Main phone: (916) 445-3393
Main fax: (916) 445-8524

Kirk Miller, Secretary
400 R St., #4000, Sacramento, CA 95814

Archives
http://www.ss.ca.gov/archives/archives.htm
General e-mail: ArchivesWeb@ss.ca.gov
Main phone: (916) 653-7715
Main fax: (916) 653-7363

Walter P. Gray, Director
1020 O St., Sacramento, CA 95814

Arts Council
http://www.cac.ca.gov
General e-mail: cac@cwo.net
Main phone: (916) 322-6555
Main fax: (916) 322-6575
Toll free: (800) 201-6201
TTY: (916) 322-6569

Barbara Pieper, Director
1300 I St., #930, Sacramento, CA 95814

Business, Transportation, and Housing Agency
http://www.bth.ca.gov/
General e-mail: bth@bth.ca.gov
Main phone: (916) 323-5400
Main fax: (916) 323-5440

Maria Contreras-Sweet, Secretary
980 9th St., #2450, Sacramento, CA 95814-2719
(916) 323-5401
E-mail: secretary@bth.ca.gov

Highway Patrol
http://www.chp.ca.gov/
Main phone: (916) 657-7261
Main fax: (916) 657-7324
TTY: (800) 735-2929
Mailing address: P.O. Box 942898, Sacramento, CA 94298-0001

Dwight O. Helmick Jr., Commissioner
2555 1st Ave., Sacramento, CA 94298
(916) 657-7152

Housing and Community Development
http://www.hcd.ca.gov/
Main phone: (916) 445-4782
Mailing address: P.O. Box 952050, Sacramento, CA 94252-2050

Judy Nevis, Director (Acting)
1800 3rd St., Sacramento, CA 94252-2050

Housing Finance Agency
http://www.chfa.ca.gov/
General e-mail: drichardson@chfa.ca.gov
Main phone: (916) 322-3991
Main fax: (916) 322-1464
Mailing address: P.O. Box 952050, Sacramento, CA 94252-2050

Higher Educational Institutions

California State University
http://www.calstate.edu
401 Golden Shore, Long Beach, CA 90802-4210
Main phone: (562) 951-4000
Branches: Bakersfield, California Maritime Academy, Channel Islands, Chico, Coachella Valley, Dominguez Hills, Fresno, Fullerton, Hayward, Humboldt, Long Beach, Los Angeles, Monterey Bay, Northridge, Pomona, Sacramento, San Bernadino, San Diego, San Francisco, San Jose, San Luis Obispo, San Marcos, Sonoma, Stanislaus

University of California
http://www.ucop.edu
1111 Franklin St., Oakland, CA 94607-5200
Main phone: (510) 987-9074
Branches: Berkeley, Davis, Irvine, Los Angeles, Merced, Riverside, San Diego, San Francisco, Santa Barbara, Santa Cruz

Theresa A. Parker, Executive Director
1121 L St., 7th Fl., Sacramento, CA 95814
(916) 324-0801

Motor Vehicles Dept.
http://www.dmv.ca.gov/
General e-mail:
dmvwebmaster@smtp.dmv.ca.gov
Main phone: (916) 657-7669

Ed Snyder, Director (Acting)
2415 1st Ave., #MS-F101, Sacramento, CA 95818

Transportation Dept.
http://www.dot.ca.gov/
General e-mail: Web_Admin@dot.ca.gov
Main phone: (916) 654-5266
Main fax: (916) 654-6608
Mailing address: P.O. Box 942873, Sacramento, CA 94273-0001

Jose Medina, Director
1120 N St., Sacramento, CA 95814
E-mail: jose_medina@dot.ca.gov

Transportation Dept: Aeronautics Program
Main phone: (916) 654-4959
Main fax: (916) 653-9531
Mailing address: MS #40, P.O. Box 942874, Sacramento, CA 94274-0001

Marlin Beckwith, Program Manager
1120 N St., #3300, Sacramento, CA 95814
(916) 654-5470; *Fax:* (916) 653-9531
E-mail: marlin.beckwith@dot.ca.gov

Conservation Dept.
http://www.consrv.ca.gov/index.htm
General e-mail: webmaster@consrv.ca.gov
Main phone: (916) 322-1080
Main fax: (916) 445-0732
TTY: (916) 324-2555

Darryl Young, Director (Acting)
801 K St., #2400, Sacramento, CA 95814
E-mail: dyoung@consrv.ca.gov

Consumer Affairs Dept.
http://www.dca.ca.gov/
General e-mail: cic@dca.ca.gov
Main phone: (916) 445-1254
Main fax: (916) 445-3755
Toll free: (800) 952-5210
TTY: (916) 322-1700

Kathleen Hamilton, Director
400 R St., #3000, Sacramento, CA 95814
(916) 445-4465; *Fax:* (916) 323-6639

Contractors State License Board
http://www.cslb.ca.gov/
General e-mail: lbcslb@vmmail.teale.ca.gov
Main phone: (916) 255-3900
Main fax: (916) 366-9130
Toll free: (800) 321-CSLB

Joe Tavaglione, Chair
9835 Goethe Rd., Sacramento, CA 95826

Corrections Dept.
http://www.cdc.state.ca.us/
General e-mail:
correscont@adminsvcs.corr.ca.gov
Main phone: (916) 445-7688
Main fax: (916) 322-2877
Mailing address: P.O. Box 942883, Sacramento, CA 94283-0001

C. A. Terhune, Director
1515 S St., #351-N, Sacramento, CA 95814
(916) 445-7682

Criminal Justice Planning Office
http://www.ocjp.ca.gov/
General e-mail: bbenson@ocjp.ca.gov
Main phone: (916) 324-9100
Main fax: (916) 327-8711

Frank J. Grimes, Executive Director
1130 K St., #300, Sacramento, CA 95814
E-mail: frankgrimes@ocjp.ca.gov

Developmental Disabilities Council
http://www.scdd.ca.gov/
General e-mail: scdd@dss.ca.gov
Main phone: (916) 322-8481
Main fax: (916) 443-4957
TTY: (916) 324-8420

Judy McDonald, Executive Director
2000 O St., #100, Sacramento, CA 95814
(916) 322-5520; *Fax:* (916) 443-4957
E-mail: jmcdonal@dss.ca.gov

Education Dept.
http://www.cde.ca.gov/
Main phone: (916) 657-2451
Main fax: (916) 657-4975
Mailing address: P.O. Box 944272, Sacramento, CA 94244-2720

Delaine A. Eastin, State Superintendent of Public Instruction and Director of Education
721 Capitol Mall, Sacramento, CA 94244-2720
(916) 657-4766
E-mail: deastin@cde.ca.gov

Emergency Services Office
http://www.oes.ca.gov/
General e-mail: lennette_dease@oes.ca.gov
Main phone: (916) 262-1800
Main fax: (916) 262-1677

Dallas Jones, Director
2800 Meadowview Rd., #107, Sacramento, CA 95832
(916) 262-1816; *Fax:* (916) 262-1677

Engineers and Land Surveyors Board
http://www.dca.ca.gov/pels/
Main phone: (916) 263-2222
Main fax: (916) 263-2246
Mailing address: P.O. Box 349002, Sacramento, CA 95834-9002

Cindi Christenson, Executive Officer
2535 Capitol Oaks Dr., #300, Sacramento, CA 95833-2944

Environmental Protection Agency
http://www.calepa.ca.gov
General e-mail: cepacomm@calepa.ca.gov
Main phone: (916) 445-3846
Main fax: (916) 445-6401

Winston H. Hickox, Secretary
555 Capitol Mall, #525, Sacramento, CA 95814
E-mail: epasecty@calepa.ca.gov

Fair Political Practices Commission
http://www.fppc.ca.gov/
General e-mail: bulletin@fppc.ca.gov
Main phone: (916) 322-5660
Main fax: (916) 322-0886
Mailing address: P.O. Box 807, Sacramento, CA 95812

Robert Tribe, Executive Director
428 J St., #450, Sacramento, CA 95814
Fax: (916) 327-2026

Finance Dept.
http://www.dof.ca.gov/
Main phone: (916) 445-3878
Main fax: (916) 324-7311

B. Timothy Gage, Director
State Capitol, #1145, Sacramento, CA 95814
(916) 445-4141

Financial Institutions Dept.
http://www.dfi.ca.gov/
General e-mail: adelacruz@dfi.ca.gov
Main phone: (415) 263-8555
Main fax: (415) 989-5310
Toll free: (800) 622-0620

Jan Lynn Owen, Commissioner (Acting)
801 K St., #2124, Sacramento, CA 95814
(916) 322-0282; *Fax:* (916) 322-5976
E-mail: Jowen@dfi.ca.gov

Fire Marshal's Office
http://www.fire.ca.gov/office_sfm.html
Main phone: (916) 445-8200
Main fax: (916) 445-8509
Mailing address: P.O. Box 944246, Sacramento, CA 94244-2460

Nancy Wolfe, State Fire Marshal (Acting)
1131 S St., Sacramento, CA 95814
(916) 445-8174

Fish and Game Dept.
http://www.dfg.ca.gov/dfghome.html
Main phone: (916) 653-7664
Main fax: (916) 653-1856

Robert C. Hight, Director
1416 9th St., #1240, Sacramento, CA 95814
(916) 653-7667; *Fax:* (916) 653-7387
E-mail: rhight@dfg.ca.gov

Food and Agriculture Dept.
http://www.cdfa.ca.gov
Main phone: (916) 654-0466
Main fax: (916) 654-0542
Mailing address: P.O. Box 942871, Sacramento, CA 94271-0001

William Lyons, Secretary
1220 N St., Sacramento, CA 95814
(916) 654-0433; *Fax:* (916) 652-4723
E-mail: shessing@cdfa.ca.gov

Forestry and Fire Protection Dept.
http://www.fire.ca.gov/
Main phone: (916) 653-5123
Mailing address: P.O. Box 944246, Sacramento, CA 94244-2460

Andrea E. Tuttle, Director
1416 9th St., Sacramento, CA 95814
(916) 653-7772; *Fax:* (916) 653-4171
E-mail: andrea_tuttle@fire.ca.gov

General Services Dept.
http://www.dgs.ca.gov/
Main phone: (916) 657-9900
Main fax: (916) 323-6567
TTY: (916) 324-0940

Cliff Allenby, Director (Interim)
1325 J St., #1910, Sacramento, CA 95814-2928
(916) 445-3441

Human Resources Office
http://www.ohr.dgs.ca.gov/
Main phone: (916) 323-1701
Main fax: (916) 327-7145

Debra Bouler, Chief
1325 J St., #1714, Sacramento, CA 95814
(916) 322-5991; *Fax:* (916) 445-5438
E-mail: debra_bouler@dgs.ca.gov

Health and Welfare Agency
http://www.chhs.cahwnet.gov
Main phone: (916) 654-3454
Main fax: (916) 654-3343

Grantland Johnson, Secretary
1600 9th St., #460, Sacramento, CA 95814-6404
(916) 654-3345

Health Planning and Development Office
http://www.oshpd.cahwnet.gov/
General e-mail: oshpd@oshpd.cahwnet.gov

David Werdegar, Director
1600 9th St., #433, Sacramento, CA 95814
(916) 654-1606; *Fax:* (916) 653-1448
E-mail: dwerdega@oshpd.state.ca.us

Historic Preservation Office
http://ohp.cal-parks.ca.gov/
General e-mail: calshpo@ohp.parks.ca.gov
Main phone: (916) 653-6624
Main fax: (916) 653-9824
Mailing address: P.O. Box 942896, Sacramento,
CA 94296-0001

**Daniel Abeyta, State Historic Preservation Officer
(Acting)**
1416 9th St., #1442-7, Sacramento, CA 95814
E-mail: dabey@parks.ca.gov

Industrial Relations Dept.
http://www.dir.ca.gov
General e-mail: info@dir.ca.gov
Main phone: (415) 703-5050
Main fax: (415) 703-5058
Mailing address: P.O. Box 420603, San Francisco,
CA 94142

Stephen J. Smith, Director
455 Golden Gate Ave., #10515, San Francisco, CA
94102

Insurance Dept.
http://www.insurance.ca.gov/docs/index.html
Main phone: (916) 492-3500
Main fax: (916) 445-5280

Charles W. (Chuck) Quackenbush (R), Commissioner
300 Capitol Mall, #1500, Sacramento, CA 95814

Lottery Commission
http://www.calottery.com/
Main phone: (916) 323-7095
Main fax: (916) 327-1345
Toll free: (800) LOTTERY
TTY: (800) 345-4275

David Rosenberg, Chair
600 N. 10th St., Sacramento, CA 95814-0393

Medical Board
http://www.medbd.ca.gov/
Main phone: (916) 263-2389
Main fax: (916) 263-2387
Toll free: (800) 633-2322

Ron Joseph, Executive Director
1426 Howe Ave., #54, Sacramento, CA 95825
E-mail: rjoseph@smtp.medbd.dca.ca.gov

Mental Health Dept.
http://www.dmh.cahwnet.gov/
General e-mail: webmaster@dmhhq.state.ca.us
Main phone: (916) 654-2309
Main fax: (916) 654-3198

Stephen W. Mayberg, Director
1600 9th St., #151, Sacramento, CA 95814

Nursing Board
http://www.rn.ca.gov
Main phone: (916) 322-3350
Main fax: (916) 327-4402
Toll free: (800) 838-6828
TTY: (916) 322-1700

Ruth Ann Terry, Executive Officer
400 R St., #4030, Sacramento, CA 95814

Parks and Recreation
http://parks.ca.gov/
General e-mail: info@parks.ca.gov
Main phone: (916) 653-6995
Main fax: (916) 657-3903
Mailing address: P.O. Box 942896, Sacramento, CA 94296-0001

Rusty Areias, Director
1416 9th St., #1405, Sacramento, CA 95814
(916) 653-8380

Personnel Administration Dept.
http://www.dpa.ca.gov/
Main phone: (916) 324-0455
Main fax: (916) 322-8376

Marty Morgenstern, Director
North Bldg., 1515 J St., #400, Sacramento, CA 95814-7243
(916) 322-5193

Pharmacy Board
Main phone: (916) 324-2302
Main fax: (916) 327-6308

Patricia Harris, Executive Officer
400 R St., #4070, Sacramento, CA 95814

Postsecondary Education Commission
http://www.cpec.ca.gov
Main phone: (916) 445-7933
Main fax: (916) 327-4417

Warren H. Fox, Executive Director
1303 J St., #500, Sacramento, CA 95814-2983

Public Defender
http://www.ospd.ca.gov/

Main phone: (916) 322-2676
Main fax: (916) 327-0707

Jeffrey J. Gale, State Public Defender (Acting)
801 K St., 11th Fl., Sacramento, CA 95814
E-mail: gale@ospd.ca.gov

Public Employees Retirement System
http://www.calpers.ca.gov/
Main phone: (916) 326-3000
TTY: (916) 326-3240

James E. Burton, Chief Executive Officer
Lincoln Plaza, 400 P St., #3340, Sacramento, CA 95814
(916) 326-3825; *Fax:* (916) 326-3410

Public Utilities Commission
http://www.cpuc.ca.gov
General e-mail: webmaster@cpuc.ca.gov
Main phone: (415) 709-2782
Main fax: (415) 703-1758
Toll free: (800) 848-5580
TTY: (415) 703-2032

Richard A. Bilas, President
505 Van Ness Ave., San Francisco, CA 94102-3298
(415) 703-3703

Real Estate Appraisers Board
http://www.orea.ca.gov/
General e-mail: questions@smtp.orea.ca.gov
Main phone: (916) 263-0722

Jerry R. Jolly, Director (Acting)
1755 Creekside Dr., #190, Sacramento, CA 95833

Resources Agency
http://ceres.ca.gov/cra/
Main phone: (916) 653-5856

Mary D. Nichols, Secretary
1416 9th St., #1311, Sacramento, CA 96814

Mines and Geology Division
http://www.consrv.ca.gov/smgb/index.htm
General e-mail: dmglib@consrv.ca.gov
Main phone: (916) 445-1923
Main fax: (916) 327-1853

James F. Davis, State Geologist
801 K St., MS 24-01, Sacramento, CA 95814
(916) 445-1825

Oil and Gas Division
http://www.consrv.ca.gov/dog/index.htm
Main phone: (916) 323-1777
Main fax: (916) 323-0424

William F. Guerard Jr., State Oil and Gas Supervisor
801 K St., MS 20-20, Sacramento, CA 95814

Social Services Dept.

http://www.dss.cahwnet.gov/
General e-mail: piar@dss.ca.gov
Main phone: (916) 657-3667
Main fax: (916) 657-3173
Toll free: (800) 952-5253
TTY: (800) 952-8349

Rita Saenz, Director
744 P St., MS 17-11, Sacramento, CA 95814
(916) 657-2598; *Fax:* (916) 654-6012

State and Consumer Services Agency

http://www.scsa.ca.gov/
Main phone: (916) 653-3817
Main fax: (916) 653-3815

Aileen Adams, Secretary
915 Capitol Mall, #200, Sacramento, CA 95814
(916) 653-2636

State Library

http://www.library.ca.gov/
General e-mail: cls-adm@library.ca.gov
Main phone: (916) 654-0183
Main fax: (916) 654-0064
Mailing address: P.O. Box 942837, Sacramento, CA 94237-0001

Kevin Starr, State Librarian
Library and Court Bldg., #220, Sacramento, CA 94237-0001
(916) 654-0174; *Fax:* (916) 654-0064

Boards and Licensing

Accountancy, (916) 263-3680,
    http://www.dca.ca.gov/cba/
Architectural Examiners, (916) 445-3393,
    http://www.cbae.cahwnet.gov/
Contractors, (916) 255-3900,
    http://www.cslb.ca.gov/
Cosmetology, (916) 445-1254
Engineers and Land Surveyors, (916) 263-2222,
    http://www.dca.ca.gov/pels/
Medical Licensing, (916) 263-2389,
    http://www.medbd.ca.gov/
Nursing, (916) 322-3350,
    http://www.rn.ca.gov
Pharmacy, (916) 324-2302
Real Estate Appraisers, (916) 263-0722,
    http://www.orea.ca.gov/

Trade and Commerce Agency

http://www.commerce.ca.gov
Main phone: (916) 322-1394

Lon Hatamiya, Secretary
801 K St., #1918, Sacramento, CA 95814
(916) 322-3962; *Fax:* (916) 323-2887
E-mail: sperry@commerce.ca.gov

Tourism Office

http://gocalif.ca.gov/index2.html
General e-mail: caltour@commerce.ca.gov
Main phone: (916) 322-2881
Main fax: (916) 322-3402
Toll free: (800) 862-2543

Carolyn Beteta, Deputy Secretary
801 K St., #1600, Sacramento, CA 95814

Transportation Commission

http://www.catc.ca.gov/
General e-mail: Mary_Lea_Filbert@dot.ca.gov
Main phone: (916) 654-4245
Main fax: (916) 653-2134

Edward Sylvester, Chair
1120 N St., MS-52, #2221, Sacramento, CA 95814

Veterans Affairs Dept.

http://www.ns.net/cadva
Main phone: (916) 653-2573
Main fax: (916) 653-2456
Toll free: (800) 952-5626
TTY: (916) 653-1966
Mailing address: P.O. Box 942895, Sacramento, CA 94295-0001

Tomas Alvarado, Secretary
1227 O St., #300, Sacramento, CA 95814
(916) 653-2158; *Fax:* (916) 653-2611

Water Resources Control Board

http://www.swrcb.ca.gov/
General e-mail: webmaster@swrcb.ca.gov
Main phone: (916) 657-1247
Main fax: (916) 657-0932

Walt Pettit, Chair
Bonderson Bldg., 901 P St., Sacramento, CA 95814
(916) 657-0941
E-mail: wpettit.exec@swarcb.ca.gov

Women's Commission

http://www.statusofwomen.ca.gov
General e-mail: csw@sna.com
Main phone: (916) 445-3173
Main fax: (916) 322-9466

Iola Eliana Gold, Executive Director
1303 J St., #400, Sacramento, CA 95814-2900

Youth and Adult Correctional Agency
http://www.yaca.state.ca.us
Main phone: (916) 323-5565

Robert Presley, Secretary
1100 11th St., Sacramento, CA 95814

Prison Terms Board
http://www.bpt.ca.gov/
Main phone: (916) 445-4071
Main fax: (916) 445-5242

Louie DiNinni, Executive Officer
428 J St., 6th Fl., Sacramento, CA 95814
(916) 445-1539
E-mail: ldininni@bpt.ca.gov

Youth Authority Dept.
http://www.cya.ca.gov/
Main phone: (916) 262-1480
Main fax: (916) 262-1483

Greg S. Zermeno, Director
4241 Williamsbourgh Dr., Sacramento, CA 95823
(916) 262-1467

California Legislature
State Capitol
Sacramento, CA 95814
General information: (916) 657-9900

Senate
General information: (916) 445-4311
Fax: (916) 445-4450
Bill status: (916) 445-4251

Cruz M. Bustamante (D), President
State Capitol, Sacramento, CA 95814
(916) 445-8994; *Fax:* (916) 323-4998
http://www.ltg.ca.gov/

John Burton (D), President Pro Tempore
State Capitol, #205, Sacramento, CA 95814
(916) 445-1412
http://www.sen.ca.gov/burton

Richard G. Polanco (D), Majority Leader
State Capitol, #313, Sacramento, CA 95814
(916) 445-3456
E-mail: Senator.Polanco@sen.ca.gov
http://www.sen.ca.gov/majleader/

Richard Alarcon (D), Majority Whip
State Capitol, #4066, Sacramento, CA 95814
(916) 445-7928
E-mail: Senator.Alarcon@sen.ca.gov
http://www.sen.ca.gov/alarcon/

Ross Johnson (R), Republican Floor Leader
State Capitol, #305, Sacramento, CA 95814
(916) 445-4961
http://www.sen.ca.gov/johnson

Laws

Sales tax: 8.25%
Income tax: 9.3%
State minimum wage: $5.75 (Federal is $5.15)
Marriage age: 18
First-cousin marriage: Permitted
Drinking age: 21
State control of liquor sales: No
Blood alcohol for DWI: 0.08%
Driving age: 17
Speed limit: 70 mph
Permit to buy handguns: No, but 10-day wait
Minimum age to possess handguns: 18
Minimum age to possess rifles, shotguns:
  None
State lottery: Yes
Casinos: Yes (tribal)
Pari-mutuel betting: Horse racing
Death penalty: Yes
3 strikes minimum sentence: 25 yrs. (any 3rd
  felony)
Hate crimes law: Yes
Gay employment non-discrimination: Yes
Official language(s): English
Term limits: Governor (8 yrs.); state senate (8
  yrs.), house (6 yrs.)

*State laws are complex and subject to
change; this information is not intended as
legal advice. For an explanation of this
information, see p. x.*

Ray N. Haynes (R), Republican Whip
State Capitol, #2187, Sacramento, CA 95814
(916) 445-9781
E-mail: Senator.Haynes@sen.ca.gov
http://www.sen.ca.gov/haynes/

Gregory P. Schmidt, Secretary
State Capitol, Sacramento, CA 95814
(916) 445-4251

Assembly
General information: (916) 445-5873

Antonio R. Villaraigosa (D), Speaker of the State Assembly
State Capitol, P.O. Box 942849, Sacramento, CA 94249-0001
(916) 445-0703
E-mail: Speaker@assembly.ca.gov
http://democrats.assembly.ca.gov/members/a45/

Fred Keeley (D), Speaker Pro Tempore
State Capitol, P.O. Box 942849, #3152, Sacramento,
   CA 94249-0001
(916) 319-2027
E-mail: fred.keeley@assembly.ca.gov
http://democrats.assembly.ca.gov/members/a27/

Kevin Shelley (D), Majority Leader
State Capitol, P.O. Box 942849, #3160, Sacramento,
   CA 94249-0001
(916) 319-2012
E-mail: kevin.shelley@assembly.ca.gov
http://democrats.assembly.ca.gov/members/a12/

Gloria Romero (D), Majority Whip
State Capitol, P.O. Box 942849, Sacramento, CA
   94249-0001
(916) 319-2049; *Fax:* (916) 319-2149
E-mail: gloria.romero@assembly.ca.gov
http://democrats.assembly.ca.gov/members/a49/

Scott Baugh (R), Minority Leader
State Capitol, P.O. Box 942849, #3104, Sacramento,
   CA 94249-0001
(916) 319-2067
http://republican.assembly.ca.gov/members/67/

Mike Briggs (R), Minority Whip
State Capitol, #2111, Sacramento, CA 95814
(916) 319-2029
E-mail: assemblymember.briggs@assembly.ca.gov
http://republican.assembly.ca.gov/members/29/

E. Dotson Wilson, Chief Clerk
State Capitol, Sacramento, CA 95814
(916) 319-2856; *Fax:* (916) 319-2855

California Judiciary

350 McAllister St.
San Francisco, CA 94102-3600
http://www.courtinfo.ca.gov

Supreme Court
http://www.courtinfo.ca.gov/courts/supreme

Robert F. Wandruff, Clerk
350 McAllister St., #1295, San Francisco, CA 94102-
   3600
(415) 865-7000

Justices
Composition: 7 justices
Selection Method: appointed by governor with
   consent of Commission on Judicial
   Appointments; retention ballot held at next
   gubernatorial general election
Length of term: 12 years, after retention ballot

Ronald M. George, Chief Justice, (415) 865-7060
Marvin R. Baxter, Associate Justice, (415) 865-7080
Janice R. Brown, Associate Justice, (415) 865-7040
Ming W. Chin, Associate Justice, (415) 865-7050
Joyce L. Kennard, Associate Justice, (415) 865-7100
Stanley Mosk, Associate Justice, (415) 865-7090
Kathryn M. Werdegar, Associate Justice, (415) 865-
   7030

Administrative Office of the Courts
http://www.courtinfo.ca.gov/courtadmin/aoc/
Main phone: (415) 865-4200
Main fax: (415) 865-4205
General e-mail: pubinfo@courtinfo.ca.gov

William C. Vickrey, Administrative Director
455 Golden Gate Ave., San Francisco, CA 94102

State Law Library
Main phone: (916) 654-0185
Main fax: (916) 654-2029
General e-mail: csllaw@library.ca.gov

Mark Linneman, State Law Librarian
914 Capitol Mall, Sacramento, CA 95814
(916) 653-3883
E-mail: mlinnema@library.ca.gov

California Legislative and Political Party Information Resources

Senate home page: http://www.senate.ca.gov
Assembly home page: http://www.assembly.ca.gov
Committees: Senate: http://www.sen.ca.gov/~newsen/committees/committees.htp; *House:* http://
   www.assembly.ca.gov/acs/acsframeset8text.asp
Legislative information: http://www.leginfo.ca.gov
California Democratic Party: http://www.ca-dem.org
   911 20th St., Sacramento, CA 95814-3115; *Phone:* (916) 442-5707; *Fax:* (916) 442-5715; *E-mail:*
   info@ca-dem.org
California Republican Party: http://www.cagop.org
   1963 W. Magnolia Blvd., Burbank, CA 91506; *Phone:* (818) 841-5210; *Fax:* (916) 841-6668

Colorado

State Capitol Bldg.
Denver, CO 80203-1792
Public information: (303) 866-5000
Fax: (303) 866-2763
http://www.state.co.us

Office of the Governor
http://www.state.co.us/gov_dir/governor_office.html
Main phone: (303) 866-2471
Main fax: (303) 866-2003
Toll free: (800) 283-7215
TTY: (303) 866-5790

Bill Owens (R), Governor
State Capitol Bldg., #136, Denver, CO 80203-1792
E-mail: governorowens@state.co.us

Roy Palmer, Chief of Staff
State Capitol Bldg., #136, Denver, CO 80203-1792
(303) 866-2471; *Fax:* (303) 866-2003

Dick Wadhams, Press Secretary
State Capitol Bldg., #136, Denver, CO 80203-1792
(303) 866-6324; *Fax:* (303) 866-6326
E-mail: dick.wadhams@state.co.us

Office of the Lieutenant Governor
http://www.state.co.us/gov_dir/ltgov/index.html
Main phone: (303) 866-2087
Main fax: (303) 866-5469

Joe Rogers (R), Lieutenant Governor
State Capitol Bldg., #130, Denver, CO 80203
E-mail: ltgovrogers@state.co.us

Office of the Secretary of State
http://www.state.co.us/gov_dir/sos/index.html
General e-mail: sos.admin1@state.co.us
Main phone: (303) 894-2204
Main fax: (303) 894-2212

Donetta Davidson (R), Secretary of State
1560 Broadway, #200, Denver, CO 80202
(303) 894-2200, ext. 301

Office of the Attorney General
http://www.state.co.us/gov_dir/dol/index.htm
General e-mail: attorney.general@state.co.us
Main phone: (303) 866-3617
Main fax: (303) 866-5691

Ken Salazar (D), Attorney General
1525 Sherman St., 5th Fl., Denver, CO 80203
(303) 866-3557

State of Colorado

Capital: Denver, since 1867
Founded: 1859, Jefferson Territory created within Kansas Territory; 1861, separate Colorado Territory created
Statehood: August 1, 1876 (38th state)
Constitution adopted: 1876
Area: 103,729 sq. mi. (ranks 8th)
Population: 3,970,971 (1998 est.; ranks 24th)
Largest cities: (1998 est.) Denver (499,055); Colorado Springs (344,987); Aurora (250,604); Lakewood (136,883); Fort Collins (108,905)
Counties: 63, Most populous: (1998 est.) Jefferson (501,591); Denver (499,055); El Paso (490,378); Arapahoe (473,168); Adams (323,853)
U.S. Congress: Wayne A. Allard (R), Ben Nighthorse Campbell (R); 6 Representatives
Nickname(s): Centennial State
Motto: Nothing without providence
Song: "Where the Columbines Grow"
Bird: Lark bunting
Tree: Colorado blue spruce
Flower: Columbine
State fair: at Pueblo, late Aug.-early Sept.
Former capital(s): Colorado City, Golden

Office of the Treasurer
http://www.treasurer.state.co.us/
Main phone: (303) 866-2441
Main fax: (303) 866-2123

Mike Coffman (R), State Treasurer
State Capitol Bldg., #140, Denver, CO 80203
E-mail: mike.coffman@state.co.us

Military Affairs Dept.
http://www.coloradoguard.com
Main phone: (303) 397-3023
Main fax: (303) 397-3003

William A. Westerdahl, Adjutant General
6848 S. Revere Pkwy., Englewood, CO 80112-6703
(303) 397-3024; *Fax:* (303) 397-3281

Agencies

Accountancy Board
http://www.dora.state.co.us/accountants
General e-mail: accountants@dora.state.co.us
Main phone: (303) 894-7800
Main fax: (303) 894-7802
TTY: (303) 894-7880

Robert T. Longway, Program Administrator
1560 Broadway, #1340, Denver, CO 80202
(303) 894-7794
E-mail: Robert.Longway@dora.state.co.us

Agriculture Dept.
http://www.ag.state.co.us
Main phone: (303) 239-4100
Main fax: (303) 239-4125
TTY: (303) 866-5790

Don Ament, Commissioner
700 Kipling St., #4000, Lakewood, CO 80215-5894
(303) 239-4104; *Fax:* (303) 239-4176
E-mail: don.ament@ag.state.co.us

Archaeology and Historic Preservation
http://history.state.co.us/oahp/
General e-mail: oahp@chs.state.co.us
Main phone: (303) 866-3395
Main fax: (303) 866-2711

Georgianna Contiguglia, Historical Society President
1300 Broadway, Denver, CO 80203
(303) 866-3355
E-mail: Georgianna.Contiguglia@chs.state.co.us

Architects Board of Examiners
http://www.dora.state.co.us/architects
General e-mail: architects@dora.state.co.us
Main phone: (303) 894-7801
Main fax: (303) 894-7802
TTY: (303) 894-7880

Robert T. Longway, Program Administrator
1560 Broadway, #1340, Denver, CO 80202
(303) 894-7794
E-mail: Robert.Longway@dora.state.co.us

Archives
http://www.state.co.us/gov_dir/gss/archives/
index.html
General e-mail: archives@state.co.us
Main phone: (303) 866-2358
Main fax: (303) 866-2257

Terry Ketelsen, State Archivist
1313 Sherman St., #1-B-20, Denver, CO 80203
(303) 866-2055; *Fax:* (303) 866-2257

Arts Council
http://www.state.co.us/gov_dir/arts/
General e-mail: coloarts@artswire.org
Main phone: (303) 894-2617
Main fax: (303) 894-2615
Toll free: (800) 291-2787
TTY: (303) 894-2264

Fran Holden, Executive Director
750 Pennsylvania St., Denver, CO 80203
(303) 894-2617, ext. 11
E-mail: fran.holden@state.co.us

Banking Division
http://www.dora.state.co.us/Banking/
General e-mail: Banking@dora.state.co.us
Main phone: (303) 894-7575
Main fax: (303) 894-7570
TTY: (303) 894-7880

Richard J. Fulkerson, Commissioner
1560 Broadway, #1175, Denver, CO 80202

Barbers and Cosmetologists Board
http://www.dora.state.co.us/
  Barbers_Cosmetologists
General e-mail: Barber-
  Cosmetology@dora.state.co.us
Main phone: (303) 894-7772
Main fax: (303) 894-7802
TTY: (303) 894-2900 x833

Cathy Wells, Program Administrator
1560 Broadway, #1340, Denver, CO 80202

Civil Rights Commission
http://www.dora.state.co.us/Civil-Rights/
General e-mail: civil.rights@dora.state.co.us
Main phone: (303) 894-2997
Main fax: (303) 894-7830
Toll free: (800) 262-4845
TTY: (303) 894-7832

Jack Lang y Marquez, Director
1560 Broadway, #1050, Denver, CO 80202
E-mail: jack.langymarquez@dora.state.co.us

Corrections Dept.
http://www.state.co.us/gov_dir/DOC_dir/index.html
Main phone: (719) 579-9580
Main fax: (719) 226-4775

John W. Suthers, Executive Director
2862 S. Circle Dr., Colorado Springs, CO 80906
(719) 226-4701; *Fax:* (719) 226-4700
E-mail: John.Suthers@state.co.us

Criminal Justice Division
http://www.state.co.us/gov_dir/cdps/dcj/dcj.htm
General e-mail: Carol.Poole@cdps.state.co.us

Main phone: (303) 239-4442
Main fax: (303) 239-4491

Raymond T. Slaughter, Division Director
Division of Criminal Justice, 700 Kipling, #3000,
Denver, CO 80215

Developmental Disabilities Services
http://www.cdhs.state.co.us/ohr/dds/
DDS_center.html
Main phone: (303) 866-7450
Main fax: (303) 866-7470
TTY: (303) 866-7471

Charlie Allinson, Director
3824 W. Princeton Circle, Denver, CO 80236
(303) 866-7454
E-mail: Charlie.Allinson@state.co.us

Economic Development
http://www.state.co.us/gov_dir/oed.html
Main phone: (303) 892-3840
Main fax: (303) 892-3848

David M. Solin, Director
1625 Broadway, #1710, Denver, CO 80202
E-mail: david.solin@state.co.us

Education Dept.
http://www.cde.state.co.us
General e-mail: howerter_c@cde.state.co.us
Main phone: (303) 866-6600
Main fax: (303) 830-0793

William J. Moloney, Commissioner
201 E. Colfax Ave., Denver, CO 80203-1799
(303) 866-6806

School for the Deaf and Blind
http://www.csdb.org
General e-mail: csdbfupt@csdb.org
Main phone: (719) 578-2102
Main fax: (719) 578-2258
TTY: (719) 578-2101

Marilyn Jaitly, Superintendent
33 N. Institute St., Colorado Springs, CO
80903-3599

Educational and Cultural Facilities Authority
Main phone: (303) 297-2538
Main fax: (303) 297-2615
TTY: (303) 297-7305

Mark D. Gallegos, Executive Director
1981 Blake St., Denver, CO 80202-1272
(303) 297-7332

Emergency Management Office
Main phone: (303) 273-1622
Main fax: (303) 273-1795

Higher Educational Institutions

Adams State College
http://www.adams.edu
208 Edgemont Blvd., Alamosa, CO 81102
Main phone: (719) 587-7011

Colorado School of Mines
http://www.mines.edu
1500 Illinois St., Golden, CO 80401-1887
Main phone: (303) 273-3000

Colorado State University System
http://www.colostate.edu
Spruce Hall, Fort Collins, CO 80523-015
Main phone: (970) 491-6909
Branches: Fort Collins, Fort Lewis College,
University of Southern Colorado

Mesa State College
http://www2.mesastate.edu
P.O. Box 2647, Grand Junction, CO 81502
Main phone: (970) 248-1020

Metropolitan State College of Denver
http://www.mscd.edu
P.O. Box 173362, Denver, CO 80217
Main phone: (303) 556-2400

United States Air Force Academy
http://www.usafa.af.mil
HQ USAFA, Colorado Springs, CO 80840
Main phone: (719) 333-1110

University of Colorado System
http://www.cusys.edu
Campus Box 30, Boulder, CO 80309
Main phone: (303) 492-6301
Branches: Boulder, Colorado Springs, Denver, Health
Sciences

University of Northern Colorado
http://www.univnorthco.edu
501 20th St., Greeley, CO 80639
Main phone: (970) 351-1890

Western State College
http://www.western.edu
600 N. Adams, Gunnison, CO 81231
Main phone: (970) 943-0120

Tom Grier, Director
15075 S. Golden Rd., Golden, CO 80401
E-mail: tom.grier@state.co.us

Engineers and Land Surveyors Board of Registration
http://www.dora.state.co.us/Engineers_Surveyors/
Main phone: (303) 894-7788

Main fax: (303) 894-7790
TTY: (303) 894-7880

Angeline C. Kinnaird, Program Administrator
1560 Broadway, #1370, Denver, CO 80202

Financial Services Division
http://www.dora.state.co.us/financial_services/
General e-mail:
  edwina.mcdaniel@dora.state.co.us
Main phone: (303) 894-2336
Main fax: (303) 894-7886
TTY: (303) 894-2900

David L. Paul, Commissioner
1560 Broadway, #1520, Denver, CO 80202
E-mail: David.Paul@dora.state.co.us

Fire Safety Division
http://www.state.co.us/gov_dir/cdps/dfsgi.htm
Main phone: (303) 239-4463

Paul Cooke, Director
700 Kipling St., #1000, Denver, CO 80215
E-mail: paul.cooke@cdps.state.co.us

Forest Service
http://www.colostate.edu/depts/csfs
Main phone: (970) 491-6303
Main fax: (970) 491-7736

James Hubbard, State Forester
Colorado State University, 203 Forestry Bldg., Fort
  Collins, CO 80523-5060
E-mail: jhubbard@lamar.colostate.edu

Geological Survey
http://www.dnr.state.co.us/geosurvey/
General e-mail: cgspubs@state.co.us
Main phone: (303) 866-2611
Main fax: (303) 866-2461

Vicki Cowart, State Geologist and Director
1313 Sherman St., #715, Denver, CO 80203
E-mail: vicki.cowart@state.co.us

Health Care Policy and Financing Dept.
http://www.chcpf.state.co.us
Main phone: (303) 866-2993
Main fax: (303) 866-4411
Toll free: (800) 221-3943
TTY: (303) 866-3883

Jim Rizzuto, Executive Director
1575 Sherman St., Denver, CO 80203-1714
(303) 866-2868; *Fax:* (303) 866-2828

Medical Assistance Office
Main phone: (303) 866-2859
Main fax: (303) 866-4411
TTY: (303) 866-3883

Richard Allen, Director
1575 Sherman St., #415, Denver, CO 80203-1714
(303) 866-5401; *Fax:* (303) 866-2803
E-mail: richard.allen@state.co.us

Higher Education Commission
http://www.state.co.us/cche_dir/hecche.html
Main phone: (303) 866-2723
Main fax: (303) 860-9750

Timothy E. Foster, Executive Director
1300 Broadway, 2nd Fl., Denver, CO 80203
E-mail: tim.foster@state.co.us

Housing and Finance Authority
http://www.colohfa.org
Main phone: (303) 297-2432
Main fax: (303) 297-2615
TTY: (303) 297-7305

David W. Herlinger, Executive Director
1981 Blake St., Denver, CO 80202-1272
(303) 297-7302

Human Resource Services
http://www.state.co.us/gov_dir/gss/hr/index.html
Main phone: (303) 866-2431
Main fax: (303) 866-2021

Larry Trujillo, Director
1313 Sherman St., #110, Denver, CO 80203

Human Services Dept.
http://www.cdhs.state.co.us/
Main phone: (303) 866-5700
Main fax: (303) 866-4214
TTY: (303) 866-4740

Marva Livingston Hammons, Executive Director
1575 Sherman St., Denver, CO 80203-1714
(303) 866-5096
E-mail: marva.hammons@state.co.us

Aging Commission
Main phone: (303) 866-2800
Main fax: (303) 866-2696

Rita Barreras, Staff Director
1575 Sherman St., Ground Fl., Denver, CO 80203
E-mail: Rita.Barreras@state.co.us

Direct Services Office: Veterans Affairs
  Division
Main phone: (303) 894-7474
Main fax: (303) 894-7442

Richard Ceresko, Director
789 Sherman St., #260, Denver, CO 80203

Youth Corrections
Main phone: (303) 866-7980

Betty Marler, Director
4255 S. Knox Court, Denver, CO 80236

Labor and Employment Dept.

http://www.cdle.state.co.us/default.asp
Main phone: (303) 620-4701
Main fax: (303) 620-4714

Vickie Armstrong, Executive Director
1515 Arapahoe St., Tower 2, #400, Denver, CO 80202-2117
E-mail: vickie.armstrong@state.co.us

Liquor Enforcement Division

http://www.state.co.us/gov_dir/revenue_dir/
liquor_dir/liquor.htm
General e-mail: nhamby@spike.dor.state.co.us
Main phone: (303) 205-2300
Main fax: (303) 205-2341

David C. Reitz, Director
1375 Sherman St., Denver, CO 80261

Medical Examiners Board

http://www.dora.state.co.us/Medical/
Main phone: (303) 894-7960
Main fax: (303) 894-7962

Susan Miller, Director
1560 Broadway, #1300, Denver, CO 80202-5140
(303) 894-7714

Mental Health Services

http://www.cdhs.state.co.us/ohr/mhs/index.html
General e-mail: debra.kupfer@state.co.us
Main phone: (303) 866-7400
Main fax: (303) 866-7428
Toll free: (800) 290-4530
TTY: (303) 866-7471

Tom Barrett, Director
3824 W. Princeton Circle, Denver, CO 80236
E-mail: tom.barrett@state.co.us

Motor Vehicle Business Group

http://www.state.co.us/gov_dir/revenue_dir/MV_dir/
mv.html
General e-mail: mvadmin@spike.dor.state.co.us
Main phone: (303) 205-5600
Main fax: (303) 205-5975
TTY: (303) 205-5940

R. J. Hicks, Senior Director (Acting)
1881 Pierce St., #100, Lakewood, CO 80214

Natural Resources Dept.

http://www.dnr.state.co.us/index.asp
Main phone: (303) 866-3311
Main fax: (303) 866-2115
TTY: (303) 866-3543

Greg E. Walcher, Executive Director
1313 Sherman St., #718, Denver, CO 80203
(303) 866-4902
E-mail: greg.walcher@state.co.us

Frequently Called Numbers

Tourism: (303) 832-6171; 1-800-COLORADO; http://www.colorado.com
Library: (303) 866-6900; http://www.cde.state.co.us/index_library.htm
Board of Education: (303) 866-6817
Vital Statistics: (303) 756-4464; http://www.cdphe.state.co.us/hs/cshom.html
Tax/Revenue: (303) 866-3091; http://www.state.co.us/gov_dir/revenue_dir/home_rev.html
Motor Vehicles: (303) 205-5600; http://www.state.co.us/gov_dir/revenue_dir/MV_dir/mv.html
State Police/Highway Patrol: (303) 239-4500; http://www.state.co.us/gov_dir/cdps/csp.htm
Unemployment: (303) 861-5515, 800-388-5515; http://unempben.cdle.state.co.us
General Election Information: (303) 894-2680, ext. 1
Consumer Affairs: (303) 866-5189
Hazardous Materials: (303) 239-4546; http://www.hazmattran.state.co.us/public/section.htm

---

Parks and Outdoor Recreation Division

http://www.coloradoparks.org
Main phone: (303) 866-3437
Main fax: (303) 866-3206

Laurie Mathews, Director
1313 Sherman St., #618, Denver, CO 80203
(303) 866-2884

Soil Conservation Division

http://www.dnr.state.co.us/edo/soil.html
Main phone: (303) 866-3351
Main fax: (303) 832-8106

Vacant, Director
1313 Sherman St., #219, Denver, CO 80203

Water Conservation Division

Main phone: (303) 866-3441
Main fax: (303) 866-4474

Peter Evans, Director
1313 Sherman St., Denver, CO 80203

Wildlife Division

http://www.dnr.state.co.us/wildlife/
Main phone: (303) 291-7208
Main fax: (303) 294-0874

John Mumma, Director
6060 Broadway, Denver, CO 80216

Nursing Board
http://www.dora.state.co.us/Nursing/
Main phone: (303) 894-2430
Main fax: (303) 894-2821

Patricia Uris, Director
1560 Broadway, #880, Denver, CO 80202
(303) 894-2439, ext. 894
E-mail: patricia.uris@dora.state.co.us/nursing

Oil and Gas Conservation Commission
http://www.dnr.state.co.us/oil-gas/
General e-mail: dnr.ogcc@state.co.us
Main phone: (303) 894-2100
Main fax: (303) 894-2109

Rich Griebling, Director
1120 Lincoln St., #801, Denver, CO 80203

Parole Board
Main phone: (719) 583-5800
Main fax: (719) 583-5805

Kent A. Cottrell, Chair
1600 W. 24th St., Bldg. 54, Pueblo, CO 81003

Personnel/General Support Services Dept.
http://www.state.co.us/gov_dir/gss/index.html
Main phone: (303) 866-6566
Main fax: (303) 866-6569

Larry E. Trujillo Sr., Executive Director
1525 Sherman St., #200, Denver, CO 80203
(303) 866-6559
E-mail: larry.trujillo@state.co.us

Boards and Licensing

Accountancy, (303) 894-7800,
  http://www.dora.state.co.us/accountants
Architects, (303) 894-7801,
  http://www.dora.state.co.us/architects
Child Care, (303) 866-5958
Contractors, (303) 592-5920
Cosmetology, (303) 894-7772,
  http://www.dora.state.co.us/
  Barbers_Cosmetologists
Engineers and Land Surveyors, (303) 894-
  7788, http://www.dora.state.co.us/
  Engineers_Surveyors/
Medical Examiners, (303) 894-7960,
  http://www.dora.state.co.us/Medical/
Nursing, (303) 894-2430,
  http://www.dora.state.co.us/Nursing/
Pharmacy, (303) 894-7750,
  http://www.dora.state.co.us/Pharmacy/
Real Estate Appraisers, (303) 894-2166

Pharmacy Board
http://www.dora.state.co.us/Pharmacy/
General e-mail: Pharmacy@dora.state.co.us
Main phone: (303) 894-7750
Main fax: (303) 894-7764
TTY: (303) 894-7880

W. Kent Mount, Program Administrator
1560 Broadway, #1310, Denver, CO 80202
(303) 894-7753
E-mail: kent.mount@dora.state.co.us

Public Defender
http://www.state.co.us/gov_dir/pdef_dir/
Main phone: (303) 620-4888
Main fax: (303) 620-4931

David F. Vela, State Public Defender
110 16th St., #800, Denver, CO 80202
E-mail: pubdef@governor.state.co.us

Public Health and Environment Dept.
http://www.cdphe.state.co.us/cdphehom.asp
General e-mail: ken.mesch@state.co.us
Main phone: (303) 692-2000
Main fax: (303) 782-0095
TTY: (303) 691-7700

Jane E. Norton, Executive Director
4300 Cherry Creek Dr. South, Denver, CO 80246
(303) 692-2011; *Fax:* (303) 691-7702

Public Safety Dept.
http://www.state.co.us/gov_dir/cdps/cdps.htm
Main phone: (303) 239-4400
Main fax: (303) 231-9708
TTY: (303) 239-4499

Aristedes W. Zavaras, Executive Director
700 Kipling St., #1000, Denver, CO 80215-5865
(303) 239-4398
E-mail: aristedes.zavaras@cdps.state.co.us

State Patrol
http://www.state.co.us/gov_dir/cdps/csp.htm
General e-mail:
  raymond.fisher@cdps.state.co.us
Main phone: (303) 239-4500
Main fax: (303) 239-4481
TTY: (303) 239-4505

Lonnie J. Westphal, Chief
700 Kipling St., #3000, Denver, CO 80215-5865
(303) 239-4403
E-mail: lonnie.westphal@cdps.state.co.us

Public Utilities Commission
http://www.dora.state.co.us/PUC/
General e-mail: puc@dora.state.co.us
Main phone: (303) 894-2000
Main fax: (303) 894-2065

Bruce N. Smith, Director
1580 Logan St., OL2, Denver, CO 80203

Revenue Dept.
http://www.state.co.us/gov_dir/revenue_dir/
   home_rev.html
General e-mail: Questions@spike.dor.state.co.us
Main phone: (303) 866-3091
Main fax: (303) 866-2400

Fred Fisher, Executive Director
1375 Sherman St., #404, Denver, CO 80261

Lottery Division
http://www.coloradolottery.com
Main phone: (719) 546-2400
Main fax: (719) 546-5208
Mailing address: P.O. Box 7, Pueblo, CO 81002

Mark Zamarripa, Director
Norwest Bank Bldg., Pueblo, CO 81002
(719) 546-5206; *Fax:* (719) 546-5208
E-mail: mzamarripa@compuserve.com

Soil Conservation Board
http://www.dnr.state.co.us/edo/soil.html
Main phone: (303) 866-3351
Main fax: (303) 832-8106

Vacant, Director
1313 Sherman St., #219, Denver, CO 80203

State Fair and Industrial Exposition
www.coloradosfair.com
General e-mail: csf@ria.net
Main phone: (719) 561-8484
Main fax: (719) 561-0283
Toll free: (800) 444-3247

Ed Kruse, General Manager
1001 Beulah Ave., Pueblo, CO 81004
(719) 561-8484, ext. 2012
E-mail: e.kruse@ria.net

State Library
http://www.cde.state.co.us/index_library.htm
Main phone: (303) 866-6900
Main fax: (303) 866-6940

Nancy Bolt, Director
201 E. Colfax Ave., Denver, CO 80203
(303) 866-6733
E-mail: nbolt@csn.net

Tourism Office
http://www.colorado.com
Main phone: (303) 832-6171
Toll free: (800) 265-6723

Rick Wilder, Director
1127 Pennsylvania St., Denver, CO 80203

Transportation Dept.
http://www.dot.state.co.us/
General e-mail: info@dot.state.co.us
Main phone: (303) 757-9011
TTY: (303) 757-9087

Tom Norton, Executive Director
4201 E. Arkansas Ave., #262, Denver, CO 80222
(303) 757-9201; *Fax:* (303) 757-9656

Aeronautics Division
http://www.colorado-aeronautics.org
Main phone: (303) 261-4418
Main fax: (303) 261-9608

Travis Vallin, Director
5200 Front Range Pkwy., Watkins, CO 80137
(303) 261-7705; *Fax:* (303) 261-9608
E-mail: Travis.Vallin@dot.state.co.us

Water Resources and Power Development Authority
General e-mail: info@cwrpda.com
Main phone: (303) 830-1550
Main fax: (303) 832-8205

Daniel L. Law, Executive Director
1580 Logan St., #620, Denver, CO 80203
(303) 830-1550, ext. 14
E-mail: dlaw@cwrpda.com

Workmen's Compensation/Pinnacol Assurance
http://www.pinnacol.com
General e-mail: esther.connors@pinnacol.com
Main phone: (303) 782-4000
Main fax: (303) 782-4196
Mailing address: P.O. Box 80246, Denver, CO
   80224-9302

Gary J. Pon, President/General Manager
720 S. Colorado Blvd., #100-N, Denver, CO 80224-9302
(303) 782-4082; *Fax:* (303) 782-4031

Colorado Legislature

State Capitol
200 E. Colfax Ave.
Denver, CO 80203
General information: (303) 866-3521
Bill status: (303) 866-3055
http://www.state.co.us/gov_dir/stateleg.html

Senate
General information: (303) 866-2316
Toll free: (800) 473-8136

Laws

Sales tax: 3%
Income tax: 5%
State minimum wage: $5.15 (Federal is $5.15)
Marriage age: 18
First-cousin marriage: Permitted
Drinking age: 21
State control of liquor sales: No
Blood alcohol for DWI: 0.10%
Driving age: 17
Speed limit: 75 mph
Permit to buy handguns: No
Minimum age to possess handguns: 18
Minimum age to possess rifles, shotguns:
  None
State lottery: Yes
Casinos: Yes (commercial, tribal)
Pari-mutuel betting: Horse and dog racing
Death penalty: Yes
3 strikes minimum sentence: Life (3rd serious
  or violent felony)
Hate crimes law: Yes
Gay employment non-discrimination: No
Official language(s): English
Term limits: State legislators (8 yrs.)

*State laws are complex and subject to
change; this information is not intended as
legal advice. For an explanation of this
information, see p. x.*

Ray Powers (R), President
State Capitol, 200 E. Colfax Ave., #257, Denver, CO
  80203
(303) 866-3342
http://www.state.co.us/gov_dir/leg_dir/senate/
  members/powers.htm

Doug Lamborn (R), President Pro Tempore
State Capitol, 200 E. Colfax Ave., #259, Denver, CO
  80203
(303) 866-4835
http://www.state.co.us/gov_dir/leg_dir/senate/
  members/lamborn.htm

Tom Blickensderfer (R), Majority Leader
State Capitol, 200 E. Colfax Ave., #263, Denver, CO
  80203
(303) 866-3341
http://www.state.co.us/gov_dir/leg_dir/senate/
  members/blickensderfer.htm

Michael F. Feeley (D), Minority Leader
State Capitol, 200 E. Colfax Ave., #274, Denver, CO
  80203
(303) 866-2318
E-mail: mike.feeley@state.co.us
http://www.state.co.us/gov_dir/leg_dir/senate/
  members/feeley.htm

Patricia K. Dicks, Secretary
State Capitol, 200 E. Colfax Ave., Denver, CO 80203
(303) 866-2316; *Fax:* (303) 866-2443

House
General information: (303) 866-2331
Toll free: (800) 811-7647

Russell (Russ) George (R), Speaker of the House
State Capitol, 200 E. Colfax Ave., #246, Denver, CO
  80203
(303) 866-2346
E-mail: russgeor@sni.net
http://www.state.co.us/gov_dir/leg_dir/house/
  members/george.htm

William G. (Bill) Kaufman (R), Speaker Pro Tempore
State Capitol, 200 E. Colfax Ave., #212, Denver, CO
  80203
(303) 866-2947
E-mail: wkaufman@sni.net
http://www.state.co.us/gov_dir/leg_dir/house/
  members/kaufman.htm

Doug Dean (R), Majority Leader
State Capitol, 200 E. Colfax Ave., #246, Denver, CO
  80203
(303) 866-2348
http://www.state.co.us/gov_dir/leg_dir/house/
  members/dean.htm

Dorothy Gotlieb (R), Majority Whip
State Capitol, 200 E. Colfax Ave., #200, Denver, CO
  80203
(303) 866-2910
E-mail: fxfw49b@prodigy.com
http://www.state.co.us/gov_dir/leg_dir/house/
  members/gotlieb.htm

Ken Gordon (D), Minority Leader
State Capitol, 200 E. Colfax Ave., #222, Denver, CO
  80203
(303) 866-5523
http://www.state.co.us/gov_dir/leg_dir/house/
  members/gordon.htm

Frana Araujo Mace (D), Minority Whip
State Capitol, 200 E. Colfax Ave., #307, Denver, CO
  80203
(303) 866-2954
E-mail: fmace@sni.net
http://www.state.co.us/gov_dir/leg_dir/house/
  members/mace.htm

Judith M. (J.R.) Rodrigue, Chief Clerk
State Capitol, 200 E. Colfax Ave., Denver, CO 80203
(303) 866-2903; *Fax:* (303) 866-2218

Colorado Judiciary

1301 Pennsylvania St.
Denver, CO 80203-2416
http://www.courts.state.co.us

Supreme Court
http://www.courts.state.co.us/supct/supct.htm

Mac V. Danford, Clerk
1301 Pennsylvania St., 4th Fl., Denver, CO 80203-2416
(303) 861-1111, ext. 277

Justices
Composition: 7 justices
Selection Method: appointed by governor for 2-year term; subject to retention ballot in general election for 10-year term
Length of term: 2 years by appointment, 10 years by retention ballot

Mary J. Mullarkey, Chief Justice, (303) 861-1111, ext. 271

Michael L. Bender, Justice, (303) 861-1111, ext. 242
Gregory J. Hobbs Jr., Justice, (303) 861-1111, ext. 248
Rebecca Love Kourlis, Justice, (303) 861-1111, ext. 251
Alex J. Martinez, Justice, (303) 861-1111, ext. 261
Nancy E. Rice, Justice, (303) 861-1111, ext. 266
Gregory Kellam Scott, Justice, (303) 861-1111, ext. 256

State Court Administration
http://www.state.co.us/scao/scao.htm
Main phone: (303) 861-1111
Main fax: (303) 837-2340

Steven V. Berson, State Court Administrator
1301 Pennsylvania St., 3rd Fl., Denver, CO 80203-2416
(303) 837-3668
E-mail: steve.berson@judicial.state.co.us

State Law Library
http://www.state.co.us/courts/sctlib
Main phone: (303) 837-3720

Lois Calvert, Librarian
Colorado State Judicial Bldg., 2 E. 14th Ave., #B-12, Denver, CO 80203

Colorado Legislative and Political Party Information Resources

Committees: Senate: http://www.state.co.us/gov_dir/leg_dir/pinkbook/pbscom.htm; *House:* http://www.state.co.us/gov_dir/leg_dir/pinkbook/pbhcom.htm
Legislative information: http://www.leg.state.co.us/pubhome.nsf
Legislative process: http://www.state.co.us/gov_dir/leg_dir/process.htm
Colorado Democratic Party: http://www.coloradodems.org
770 Grant St., #200, Denver, CO 80203; *Phone:* (303) 830-8989; *Fax:* (303) 870-2743; *E-mail:* info@coloradodems.org
Colorado Republican Party: http://www.cologop.org
1776 S. Jackson St., #210, Denver, CO 80210; *Phone:* (303) 758-3333; *Fax:* (303) 753-4611

Connecticut

State Capitol
210 Capitol Ave.
Hartford, CT 06106
Public information: (860) 566-2211
Fax: (860) 524-7396
http://www.state.ct.us

Office of the Governor
http://www.state.ct.us/governor
Main phone: (860) 566-4840
Main fax: (860) 524-7396
Toll free: (800) 406-1527
TTY: (860) 524-7397

John G. Rowland (R), Governor
State Capitol, 210 Capitol Ave., #202, Hartford, CT 06106
E-mail: governor.rowland@po.state.ct.us

Peter N. Ellef, Co-Chief of Staff
State Capitol, 210 Capitol Ave., #200, Hartford, CT 06106
(860) 566-4840; *Fax:* (860) 524-7396
E-mail: peter.ellef@po.state.ct.us

Sidney J. Holbrook, Co-Chief of Staff
State Capitol, 210 Capitol Ave., #200, Hartfold, CT 06106
(860) 566-4840; *Fax:* (860) 524-7396

Dean Pagani, Press Secretary
State Capitol, 210 Capitol Ave., #208, Hartford, CT 06106
(860) 566-4840; *Fax:* (860) 524-7396
E-mail: dean.pagani@po.state.ct.us

Julie Cammarata, Director, Constituent Services
State Capitol, 210 Capitol Ave., #408, Hartford, CT 06106
(860) 566-8640; *Fax:* (860) 524-7396
E-mail: julie.cammarata@po.state.ct.us

Alison Kaufman, Director, Washington Office
444 N. Capitol St. N.W., #317, Washington, DC 20001
(202) 347-4535; *Fax:* (202) 347-7151
E-mail: akaufman@sso.org

Office of the Lieutenant Governor
http://www.state.ct.us/otlg/
Main phone: (860) 524-7384
Main fax: (860) 524-7304

State of Connecticut

Capital: Hartford, since 1633
Founded: 1633, as offshoot of Massachusetts Bay colony; 1638, separate New Haven colony; colonies merged 1662
Statehood: January 9, 1788 (5th state)
Constitution adopted: December 30, 1965
Area: 4,845 sq. mi. (ranks 48th)
Population: 3,274,069 (1998 est.; ranks 29th)
Largest cities: (1998 est.) Bridgeport (137,425); Hartford (131,523); New Haven (123,189); Stamford (110,056); Waterbury (106,412)
Counties: 8, Most populous: (1998 est.) Fairfield (838,362); Hartford (828,200); New Haven (793,504); New London (245,740); Litchfield (181,277)
U.S. Congress: Christopher J. Dodd (D), Joseph I. Lieberman (D); 6 Representatives
Nickname(s): Constitution State, Nutmeg State
Motto: He who transplanted still sustains
Song: "Yankee Doodle"
Bird: American robin
Tree: White oak
Flower: Mountain laurel
State fair: None
Former capital(s): New Haven (co-capital with Hartford)

M. Jodi Rell (R), Lieutenant Governor
State Capitol, 210 Capitol Ave., #304, Hartford, CT 06106
E-mail: jodi.rell@po.state.ct.us

Office of the Secretary of State
http://www.state.ct.us/sots
Main phone: (860) 509-6200
Main fax: (860) 509-6209
Mailing address: P.O. Box 150470, Hartford, CT 06115-0470

Susan Bysiewicz (D), Secretary of State
State Capitol, 210 Capitol Ave., #104, Hartford, CT 06106
E-mail: susan.bysiewicz@po.state.ct.us

Office of the Attorney General

http://www.cslib.org/attygenl/
General e-mail: attorney.general@po.state.ct.us
Main phone: (860) 808-5318
Main fax: (860) 808-5387

Richard Blumenthal (D), Attorney General
55 Elm St., Hartford, CT 06106

Office of the State Treasurer

http://www.state.ct.us/ott/
Main phone: (860) 702-3000
Main fax: (860) 702-3043
Toll free: (800) 618-3404

Denise L. Nappier (D), State Treasurer
55 Elm St., Hartford, CT 06106-1773
(860) 702-3001

Office of the Comptroller

http://www.osc.state.ct.us
General e-mail: kathleen.anderson@po.state.ct.us
Main phone: (860) 702-3300
Main fax: (860) 702-3319

Nancy Wyman (D), Comptroller
55 Elm St., Hartford, CT 06106-1775
(860) 702-3301
E-mail: nancy.wyman@po.state.ct.us

Auditors of Public Accounts Office

http://www.state.ct.us/apa
Main phone: (860) 240-8653
Main fax: (860) 240-8655
Toll free: (800) 797-1702

Robert G. Jackle, State Auditor
State Capitol, 210 Capitol Ave., Hartford, CT 06106-1568
E-mail: robert.jackle@po.state.ct.us

Kevin Johnston, State Auditor
State Capitol, 210 Capitol Ave., Hartford, CT 06106-1568
(860) 240-8651
E-mail: kevin.johnston@po.state.ct.us

Military Dept.

http://ctarng-web.ct.ngb.army.mil/
General e-mail: tagct@ct-ngnet.army.mil
Main phone: (860) 524-4991
Main fax: (860) 548-3247

William A. Cugno, Adjutant General
National Guard Armory, 360 Broad St., Hartford, CT 06105-3795

Agencies

Accountancy Board

Main phone: (860) 509-6179

Main fax: (860) 509-6230
Mailing address: P.O. Box 150470, Hartford, CT 06106-0470

David Guay, Executive Director
State Capitol, 210 Capitol Ave., Hartford, CT 06106
(860) 509-6182; *Fax:* (860) 509-6247

Administrative Services Dept.

http://www.das.state.ct.us/
General e-mail: b117@aol.com
Main phone: (860) 713-5000
Main fax: (860) 713-7481
Toll free: (800) 528-7442
TTY: (800) 713-7463

Barbara A. Waters, Commissioner
165 Capitol Ave., #G1, Hartford, CT 06106
(860) 713-5100
E-mail: barbara.waters@po.state.ct.us

Human Resources

http://www.das.state.ct.us/HR/HRhome.htm
Main phone: (860) 713-5205
Main fax: (860) 713-7470
Toll free: (800) 528-7442
TTY: (860) 713-7463

Vacant, Director
165 Capitol Ave., #G1, Hartford, CT 06106
(860) 713-5052; *Fax:* (860) 713-7486

Aging Commission

General e-mail: commission.aging@po.state.ct.us
Main phone: (860) 424-5360
Main fax: (860) 424-4985

A. Cynthia Matthews, Executive Director
25 Sigourney St., Hartford, CT 06106

Agriculture Dept.

http://www.state.ct.us/doag
General e-mail: ctdeptag@po.state.ct.us
Main phone: (860) 713-2503
Main fax: (860) 713-2514
Toll free: (800) 861-9939

Shirley Cole Ferris, Commissioner
765 Asylum Ave., Hartford, CT 06105

Arts Commission

http://www.ctarts.org/
Main phone: (860) 566-4770
Main fax: (860) 566-6462

John Ostrout, Executive Director
755 Main St., 1 Financial Plaza, Hartford, CT 06103
E-mail: jostrout@cslib.org

Banking Dept.

http://www.state.ct.us/dob/
Main phone: (860) 240-8299

Higher Educational Institutions

Charter Oak State College
http://www.cosc.edu
55 Paul Manafort Dr., New Britain, CT 6053
Main phone: (860) 832-3800

Connecticut State University System
http://www.csu.ctstateu.edu
39 Woodland St., Hartford, CT 06105-2337
Main phone: (860) 493-0000
Branches: Central, Eastern, Southern, Western

U.S. Coast Guard Academy
http://www.cga.edu
31 Mohegan Ave., New London, CT 6320
Main phone: (860) 444-8500

University of Connecticut
http://www.uconn.edu
2131 Hillside Rd., Box U-88, Storrs, CT 06269-3088
Main phone: (860) 486-3137

Main fax: (860) 240-8178
Toll free: (800) 831-7225

John P. Burke, Commissioner
260 Constitution Plaza, Hartford, CT 06103-1800
(860) 240-8100
E-mail: john.burke@po.state.ct.us

Children and Families Dept.
http://www.state.ct.us/dcf
Main phone: (860) 550-6497
Main fax: (860) 566-7947
Report child abuse: (800) 842-2288

Kristine D. Ragaglia, Commissioner
505 Hudson St., Hartford, CT 06106
E-mail: Commissioner.Dcf@po.state.ct.us

Juvenile Justice Bureau
http://www.state.ct.us/dcs
Main phone: (860) 550-6654
Main fax: (860) 566-6726
Toll free: (800) 624-5518

Rudolph Brooks, Chief
505 Hudson St., Hartford, CT 06106-7107
E-mail: rudolph.brooks@po.state.ct.us

Consumer Protection Dept.
http://www.state.ct.us/dcp/
Main phone: (860) 713-6300
Main fax: (860) 713-7239
Toll free: (800) 842-2649
TTY: (800) 713-7240

James T. Fleming, Commissioner
165 Capitol Ave., Hartford, CT 06106

(860) 713-6050; *Fax:* (860) 713-7244
E-mail: james.fleming@po.sate.ct.us

Liquor Control Division
http://www.state.ct.us/dcp/
Main phone: (860) 713-6210
Main fax: (860) 713-7235

Maria M. Delaney, Director
165 Capitol Ave., Hartford, CT 06106-1630

Correction Dept.
http://www.state.ct.us/doc
General e-mail: wlwheel@compuserve.com
Main phone: (860) 692-7780
Main fax: (860) 692-7783

John J. Armstrong, Commissioner
24 Wolcott Hill Rd., Wethersfield, CT 06109
(860) 692-7482; *Fax:* (860) 692-7483

Criminal Justice Division
http://www.state.ct.us/csao/
Main phone: (860) 692-5800
Main fax: (860) 258-5858

John M. Bailey, Chief States Attorney
300 Corporate Pl., Rocky Hill, CT 06067

Deaf and Hearing Impaired Commission
http://www.state.ct.us/cdhi/index.htm
General e-mail: cdhi@po.state.ct.us
Main phone: (860) 566-7414
Main fax: (860) 561-0162
Toll free: (800) 708-6796

Stacie J. Mawson, Executive Director
1245 Farmington Ave., West Hartford, CT 06107-2667
(860) 561-0196
E-mail: stacie.mawson@po.state.ct.us

Economic and Community Development Dept.
http://www.state.ct.us/ecd/
General e-mail: DECD@po.state.ct.us
Main phone: (860) 270-8000
Main fax: (860) 270-8188

James F. Abromaitis, Commissioner
505 Hudson St., Hartford, CT 06106-7106
(860) 270-8009

Business and Housing Development
Main phone: (860) 270-8053
Main fax: (860) 270-8055
Business startup: (800) 392-2122

Holly Dennehey, Executive Director (Acting)
505 Hudson St., Hartford, CT 06106-7106
(860) 270-8045
E-mail: holly.dennehey@po.state.ct.us

Tourism Office

http://www.tourism.state.ct.us/
General e-mail: robert.damroth@po.state.ct.us
Main phone: (860) 270-8080
Main fax: (860) 270-8077
Toll free: (800) 282-6863

Edward Dombroskas, Executive Director
505 Hudson St., 4th Fl., Hartford, CT 06106
(860) 270-8075; *Fax:* (860) 270-8077
E-mail: edward.dombroskas@po.state.ct.us

Education Dept.

http://www.state.ct.us/sde/
General e-mail: thomas.murphy@po.state.ct.us
Main phone: (860) 566-5677
Main fax: (860) 566-8964
TTY: (860) 807-2045
Mailing address: P.O. Box 2219, Hartford, CT
06145-2219

Theodore S. Sergi, Commissioner
165 Capitol Ave., Hartford, CT 06106
(860) 566-5061; *Fax:* (860) 566-1080
E-mail: theodore.sergi@po.state.ct.us

Board of Education

http://www.state.ct.us/sde
General e-mail: thomas.murphy@po.state.ct.us
Main phone: (860) 566-5371
Main fax: (860) 566-1723
TTY: (860) 566-9970
Mailing address: P.O. Box 2219, Hartford, CT
06145-2219

Theodore S. Sergi, Commissioner
165 Capitol Ave., Hartford, CT 06106
(860) 566-5061; *Fax:* (860) 566-1080
E-mail: theodore.sergi@po.state.ct.us

Emergency Management Office

http://www.state.ct.us/dps/DFEBS/OEM/ctoem.htm
Main phone: (860) 566-3180
Main fax: (860) 247-0664

John T. Wiltse, Director
360 Broad St., Hartford, CT 06105

Environmental Protection Dept.

http://dep.state.ct.us/
General e-mail: dep.webmaster@po.state.ct.us
Main phone: (860) 424-3000
Main fax: (860) 424-4053
TTY: (860) 424-3164

Arthur J. Rocque Jr., Commissioner
79 Elm St., Hartford, CT 06106-1527
(860) 424-3001; *Fax:* (860) 424-4051

Natural Resources Bureau

http://dep.state.ct.us/burnatr/index.htm

General e-mail:
dep.webmaster@po.state.co.us
Main phone: (860) 424-3010
Main fax: (860) 424-4078

Edward Parker, Chief
79 Elm St., Hartford, CT 06106
E-mail: karen.onofri@po.state.ct.us

Water Management Bureau

http://dep.state.ct.us/wtr/index.htm
Main phone: (860) 424-3704
Main fax: (860) 424-4067

Robert Smith, Chief
79 Elm St., Hartford, CT 06106
E-mail: robert.smith@po.state.ct.us

Ethics Commission

http://www.state.ct.us/eth
Main phone: (860) 566-4472
Main fax: (860) 566-3806

Alan S. Plofsky, Executive Director and General Counsel
20 Trinity St., Hartford, CT 06106-1660

Fire Prevention and Control Commission

http://www.state.ct.us/cfpc/
General e-mail: cfpc@po.state.ct.us
Main phone: (860) 627-6363
Main fax: (860) 654-1889
Toll free: (877) SCT-FIRE

Jeffrey J. Morrissette, State Fire Administrator
34 Perimeter Rd., Windsor Locks, CT 06096-1069
(860) 627-6363, ext. 230
E-mail: jeff.morrissette@po.state.ct.us

Health Care Access Office

http://www.state.ct.us/ohca/
General e-mail: Claudette.Carver@po.state.ct.us
Main phone: (860) 418-7001
Main fax: (860) 418-7053
Toll free: (800) 797-9688
TTY: (860) 418-7058
Mailing address: P.O. Box 340308, Hartford, CT
06134-0308

Raymond J. Gorman, Commissioner
410 Capitol Ave., MS 13HCA, Hartford, CT 06134-0308
E-mail: Raymond.Gorman@po.state.ct.us

Higher Education Dept.

http://ctdhe.commnet.edu/dheweb/default.htm
General e-mail: dhewebmaster@commnet.edu
Main phone: (860) 947-1800
Main fax: (860) 947-1310
Toll free: (800) 842-0229
TTY: (860) 566-3910

Valerie F. Lewis, Interim Commissioner
61 Woodland St., Hartford, CT 06105-2391
(860) 947-1801; *Fax:* (860) 947-1310
E-mail: vlewis@commnet.edu

Historical Commission
General e-mail: cthist@neca.com
Main phone: (860) 566-3005
Main fax: (860) 566-5078

John W. Shannahan, Director
59 S. Prospect St., Hartford, CT 06106

Human Rights and Opportunities Commission
http://www.state.ct.us/chro/
Main phone: (860) 541-3400
Main fax: (860) 246-5068
Toll free: (800) 477-5737
TTY: (860) 541-3459

Cynthia Watts-Elder, Executive Director
21 Grand St., Hartford, CT 06106
(860) 541-3451; *Fax:* (860) 246-5419
E-mail: cynthia.watts-elder@po.state.ct.us

Insurance Dept.
http://www.state.ct.us/cid/
General e-mail: Fred.Massa@po.state.ct.us
Main phone: (860) 297-3800
Main fax: (860) 566-7410

Toll free: (800) 203-3447
Mailing address: P.O. Box 816, Hartford, CT
06142-0816

George M. Reider Jr., Commissioner
153 Market St., 11th Fl., Hartford, CT 06103
(860) 297-3802
E-mail: george.reider@po.state.ct.us

Labor Dept.
http://www.ctdol.state.ct.us/
Main phone: (860) 263-6000
Main fax: (860) 263-6529

James P. Butler, Commissioner
200 Folly Brook Blvd., Wethersfield, CT 06109
(860) 263-6505
E-mail: james.butler@po.state.ct.us

Medical Examiner's Office
http://www.state.ct.us/ocme/
General e-mail: ocme.webmaster@po.state.ct.us
Main phone: (860) 679-3980
Main fax: (860) 679-1257
Toll free: (800) 842-8820

H. Wayne Carver II, Chief Medical Examiner
11 Shuttle Rd., Farmington, CT 06032
E-mail: H.Wayne.Carver@po.state.ct.us

Mental Health and Addiction Services Dept.
http://www.dmhas.state.ct.us/
General e-mail: thomas.gugliotti@po.state.ct.us
Main phone: (860) 418-7000
Main fax: (860) 418-6691
TTY: (860) 418-6999
Mailing address: P.O. Box 341431, Hartford, CT
06134

Albert J. Solnit, Commissioner
410 Capitol Ave., Hartford, CT 06134
(860) 418-6969

Mental Retardation Dept.
http://www.state.ct.us/dmr
Main phone: (860) 418-6000
Main fax: (860) 418-6001
TTY: (860) 418-6079

Peter H. O'Meara, Commissioner
460 Capitol Ave., Hartford, CT 06106
(860) 418-6011; *Fax:* (860) 418-6009
E-mail: peter.omeara@po.state.ct.us

Motor Vehicles Dept.
http://dmvct.org
General e-mail: mail@dmvct.org
Main phone: (860) 263-5700
Main fax: (860) 263-5550
Toll free: (800) 842-8222

Jose O. Salinas, Commissioner
60 State St., Wethersfield, CT 06161
(860) 263-5015; *Fax:* (860) 263-5550

Parole Board
http://www.state.ct.us/bop
General e-mail: kathy.diana@po.state.ct.us
Main phone: (860) 692-7400
Main fax: (860) 692-7437
Toll free: (800) 303-2884

Michael L. Mullen, Chair
21 Grand St., Hartford, CT 06106
(860) 692-7402

Public Health Dept.
http://www.state.ct.us/dph/
General e-mail: webmaster.dph@po.state.ct.us
Main phone: (860) 509-8000
Main fax: (860) 509-7111
TTY: (860) 509-7191
Mailing address: P.O. Box 340308, Hartford, CT 06134

Joxel Garcia, Commissioner
410 Capitol Ave., Hartford, CT 06134
(860) 509-7101

Public Safety Dept.
http://www.state.ct.us/dps/
General e-mail: DPS.Feedback@po.state.ct.us
Main phone: (860) 685-8000
Main fax: (860) 685-8354
TTY: (860) 685-8386
Mailing address: P.O. Box 2794, Middletown, CT 06457-9294

Henry C. Lee, Commissioner
1111 Country Club Rd., Middletown, CT 06457-9294
E-mail: dr.henry.lee@po.state.ct.us

State Police Division
http://www.state.ct.us/dps/CSP.htm
General e-mail: DPS.Feedback@po.state.ct.us
Main phone: (860) 685-8180
Main fax: (860) 685-8354
Toll free: (800) 842-0200
Mailing address: P.O. Box 2794, Middletown, CT 06457-9294

John F. Bardelli, Commanding Officer
1111 Country Club Rd., Middletown, CT 06457-9294
(860) 685-8000

Public Utility Control Dept.
http://www.state.ct.us/dpuc/
General e-mail: dpuc.information@po.state.ct.us
Main phone: (860) 827-1553
Main fax: (860) 827-2613

Consumer services: (800) 382-4586
TTY: (860) 827-2837

Donald W. Downes, Chair
10 Franklin Square, New Britain, CT 06051
(860) 827-2801; *Fax:* (860) 827-2806
E-mail: donald.downes@po.state.ct.us

Public Works Dept.
http://www.state.ct.us/dpw/
General e-mail: William.Andrews@po.state.ct.us
Main phone: (860) 566-7469
Main fax: (860) 566-1463

Theodore R. Anson, Commissioner
165 Capitol Ave., Hartford, CT 06106
(860) 713-5800; *Fax:* (860) 713-7253

Revenue Services Dept.
http://www.state.ct.us/drs
Main phone: (860) 297-5962
Main fax: (860) 297-5714
Toll free: (800) 382-9463
TTY: (860) 297-5742

Gene Gavin, Commissioner
25 Sigourney St., Hartford, CT 06106
(860) 297-5650

Retirement and Employee Benefits Services Division
Main phone: (860) 702-3481
Main fax: (860) 702-3489

Steven Weinberger, Director
55 Elm St., Hartford, CT 06106
E-mail: steve.weinberger@po.state.ct.us

Social Services Dept.
http://www.dss.state.ct.us/
General e-mail: pgr.dss@po.state.ct.us
Main phone: (860) 424-5026
Main fax: (860) 424-4960
Toll free: (800) 842-1508
TTY: (800) 842-4524

Boards and Licensing

Accountancy, (860) 509-6179
Architects, (860) 713-6135
Child Care, (860) 509-8045
Contractors, (860) 713-6135
Cosmetology, (860) 509-7569
Engineers and Land Surveyors, (860) 713-6135
Medical Examiners, (860) 679-3980
Nursing, (860) 509-7624
Pharmacy, (860) 713-6065
Real Estate Appraisers, (860) 713-6150

Patricia Wilson-Coker, Commissioner
25 Sigourney St., Hartford, CT 06106-5033
(860) 424-5008; *Fax:* (860) 424-5129
E-mail: pat.wilson.coker@po.state.ct.us

State Library
http://www.cslib.org/
General e-mail: isref@cslib.org
Main phone: (860) 566-4971
Main fax: (860) 566-8940
TTY: (860) 566-4971

Kendall F. Wiggin, State Librarian
231 Capitol Ave., Hartford, CT 06106
(860) 566-4301
E-mail: kwiggin@cslib.org

State Archivist
http://www.cslib.org/archives.htm
Main phone: (860) 566-5650
Main fax: (860) 566-1421

Mark Jones, State Archivist
231 Capitol Ave., Hartford, CT 06106
E-mail: MJones@cslib.org

Women's Commission
http://www.cga.state.ct.us/pcsw
General e-mail: pcsw@po.state.ct.us
Main phone: (860) 240-8300
Main fax: (860) 240-8314

Leslie Brett, Executive Director
18-20 Trinity St., Hartford, CT 06106
E-mail: leslie.brett@po.state.ct.us

Transportation Dept.
http://www.state.ct.us/dot
Main phone: (860) 594-2000
Main fax: (860) 594-3008
TTY: (860) 594-3090
Mailing address: P.O. Box 317546, Newington, CT
06131-7546

James F. Sullivan, Commissioner
2800 Berlin Turnpike, Newington, CT 06111
(860) 594-3000
E-mail: james.sullivan@po.state.ct.us

Aviation and Ports Bureau
Main phone: (860) 594-2575
Main fax: (860) 594-2706
TTY: (860) 594-3090
Mailing address: P.O. Box 317546, Newington,
CT 06131-7546

Louis S. Cutillo, Deputy Commissioner
2800 Berlin Turnpike, Newington, CT 06131-7546
E-mail: louis.cutillo@po.state.ct.us

Veterans Affairs Dept.
http://www.state.ct.us/ctva

Main phone: (860) 529-2571
Main fax: (860) 721-5904
Toll free: (800) 550-0000

Eugene A. Migliaro Jr., Commissioner
287 West St., Rocky Hill, CT 06067
(860) 721-5891
E-mail: eugene.migliaro@po.state.ct.us

Workers' Compensation Commission
http://wcc.state.ct.us/
Main phone: (860) 493-1500
Main fax: (860) 247-1361

John A. Mastropietro, Chair
21 Oak St., 4th Fl., Hartford, CT 06106

Connecticut Legislature
Legislative Office Bldg.
Hartford, CT 06106-1591
General information: (860) 240-0100
Bill status: (860) 240-0555
http://www.cga.state.ct.us

Senate
General information: Republican Caucus: (860)
240-8800; Democratic Caucus: (860) 240-8600
Toll free: Democrats: (800) 842-1420; Republicans:
(800) 242-1421
E-mail: Democrats: info@senatedems.state.ct.us

M. Jodi Rell (R), President
State Capitol, 210 Capitol Ave., #304, Hartford, CT
06106
(860) 524-7384; *Fax:* (860) 524-7304
E-mail: jodi.rell@po.state.ct.us
http://www.state.ct.us/otlg/

Kevin B. Sullivan (D), President Pro Tempore
Legislative Office Bldg., #3300, Hartford, CT 06106
(860) 240-8625
E-mail: Kevin.B.Sullivan@po.state.ct.us
http://www.senatedems.state.ct.us/Sullivan.html

George C. Jepsen (D), Majority Leader
Legislative Office Bldg., #3300, Hartford, CT 06106
(860) 240-8620
E-mail: Jepsen@senatedems.state.ct.us
http://www.senatedems.state.ct.us/Jepsen.html

Donald E. Williams (D), Majority Whip
Legislative Office Bldg., #3300, Hartford, CT 06106
(860) 240-0527
E-mail: Williams@senatedems.state.ct.us
http://www.senatedems.state.ct.us/Williams.html

M. Adela Eads (R), Minority Leader
Legislative Office Bldg., Senate Republican Office,
#3400, Hartford, CT 06106
(860) 240-8800

E-mail: Dell.Eads@po.state.ct.us
http://www.senatereps.state.ct.us/senainfo/
eadsinfo.htm

David Cappiello (R), Minority Whip
Legislative Office Bldg., Senate Republican Office,
#3400, Hartford, CT 06106
(860) 240-0474
E-mail: David.Cappiello@po.state.ct.us
http://www.senatereps.state.ct.us/senainfo/
cappiell.HTM

Thomas P. Sheridan, Clerk
Legislative Office Bldg., Hartford, CT 06106
(860) 240-0500; *Fax:* (860) 240-0586

House
General information: Republican Caucus: (860)
240-8700; (860) Democratic Caucus: 240-8500
Toll free: Democrats: (800) 842-1902; Republicans:
(800) 842-1423

Laws

Sales tax: 6%
Income tax: 4.5%
State minimum wage: $6.15 (Federal is $5.15)
Marriage age: 18
First-cousin marriage: Permitted
Drinking age: 21
State control of liquor sales: No
Blood alcohol for DWI: 0.10%
Driving age: 16, 4 mos.
Speed limit: 65 mph
Permit to buy handguns: Yes, 14 days to
acquire
Minimum age to possess handguns: 21
Minimum age to possess rifles, shotguns:
None
State lottery: Yes; also Powerball
Casinos: Yes (tribal)
Pari-mutuel betting: Dog racing; jai alai
Death penalty: Yes
3 strikes minimum sentence: Up to life (3rd
dangerous felony)
Hate crimes law: Yes
Gay employment non-discrimination: Yes
Official language(s): None
Term limits: None

*State laws are complex and subject to
change; this information is not intended as
legal advice. For an explanation of this
information, see p. x.*

Moira K. Lyons (D), Speaker of the House
Legislative Office Bldg., #4105, Hartford, CT
06106-1591
(860) 240-8500
http://www.cga.state.ct.us/hdo/HDO146.htm

Joan V. Hartley (D), Speaker Pro Tempore
Legislative Office Bldg., #4107, Hartford, CT
06106-1591
(860) 240-8500
E-mail: Joan.Hartley@po.state.ct.us
http://www.cga.state.ct.us/hdo/HDO073.htm

David B. Pudlin (D), Majority Leader
Legislative Office Bldg., #4106, Hartford, CT
06106-1591
(860) 240-8500
E-mail: David.Pudlin@po.state.ct.us
http://www.cga.state.ct.us/hdo/HDO024.htm

Richard D. Tulisano (D), Majority Whip-At-Large
Legislative Office Bldg., #4101, Hartford, CT 06106
(860) 240-8500
E-mail: Richard.Tulisano@po.state.ct.us
http://www.cga.state.ct.us/hdo/HDO029.htm

Robert M. Ward (R), Minority Leader
Legislative Office Bldg., Hartford, CT 06106
(860) 240-8700
E-mail: Robert.Ward@housegop.state.ct.us
http://www.housegop.state.ct.us/pages/Ward.htm

Raymond V. Collins (R), Minority Whip
Legislative Office Bldg., Hartford, CT 06106
(860) 240-8700
E-mail: Raymond.Collins@housegop.state.ct.us
http://www.housegop.state.ct.us/pages/Collins.htm

Garey E. Coleman, Clerk
Legislative Office Bldg., Hartford, CT 06106
(860) 240-0400; *Fax:* (860) 240-8405

Connecticut Judiciary

Supreme Court Bldg.
231 Capitol Ave.
Hartford, CT 06106
http://www.jud.state.ct.us

Supreme Court
http://www.jud.state.ct.us/external/supapp/
default.htm

Francis J. Drumm Jr., Chief Clerk
Supreme Court Bldg., 231 Capitol Ave., Hartford, CT
06106
(860) 566-8160; *Fax:* (860) 566-6731

Justices

Composition: 7 justices
Selection Method: nominated by governor; appointed by the general assembly
Length of term: 8 years

Francis M. McDonald Jr., Chief Justice, (860) 566-1102
David M. Borden, Associate Justice, (860) 566-5989
Joette Katz, Associate Justice, (860) 566-5641
Flemming L. Norcott Jr., Associate Justice, (860) 566-3586
Richard N. Palmer, Associate Justice, (860) 566-2665
William J. Sullivan, Associate Justice, (860) 566-2218
Christine Vertefeuille, Associate Justice, (860) 566-4104

Office of the Chief Court Administrator

Main phone: (860) 566-4461
Main fax: (860) 566-2130

Robert Leuba, Chief Court Administrator
Supreme Court Bldg., 231 Capitol Ave., Hartford, CT 06106

State Law Library

Main phone: (860) 566-4777
Main fax: (860) 566-3449

Maureen D. Well, Director
Supreme Court Bldg., 231 Capitol Ave., Hartford, CT 06106
(860) 566-7850

Legislative and Political Party Information Resources

Senate home page: http://www.cga.state.ct.us/senate.htm
House home page: http://www.cga.state.ct.us/house.htm
Committees: http://www.cga.state.ct.us/Committee.htm
Legislative process: http://www.cga.state.ct.us/Learning%20Center/RoadMap/btlintro.htm
Legislative information: http://www.cga.state.ct.us/GeneralInfo.htm
Budget: http://www.cga.state.ct.us/ofa
Connecticut Democratic Party: http://www.ctdems.org
   380 Franklin Ave., Hartford, CT 06114; *Phone:* (860) 296-1775
Connecticut Republican Party: http://www.ctgop.org
   97 Elm St., Rear, Hartford, CT 06106; *Phone:* (860) 547-0589; *Fax:* (860) 278-8568

Delaware

Carvel State Office Bldg.
820 N. French St.
Wilmington, DE 19801
Public information: (800) 464-4357
Fax: (302) 577-3118
http://www.state.de.us

Office of the Governor
http://www.state.de.us/govern/governor/
introgov.htm
General e-mail: ssnyder@state.de.us
Main phone: (302) 577-3210
Main fax: (302) 577-3118
Toll free: (800) 464-4357

Thomas R. Carper (D), Governor
Carvel State Office Bldg., 820 N. French St., 12th Fl.,
Wilmington, DE 19801

Jeff Bullock, Chief of Staff
Carvel State Office Bldg., 820 N. French St., 12th Fl.,
Wilmington, DE 19801
(302) 577-3210; *Fax:* (302) 577-3118
E-mail: JBullock.state.de.us

Anthony Farina, Press Secretary
Carvel State Office Bldg., 820 N. French St., 12th Fl.,
Wilmington, DE 19801
(302) 577-8711; *Fax:* (302) 577-3118
E-mail: afarina@state.de.us

Shawn Snyder, Constituent Affairs
Carvel State Office Bldg., 820 N. French St.,
Wilmington, DE 19801
(202) 577-3210; *Fax:* (202) 577-3118
E-mail: ssnyder@state.de.us

Jonathan Jones, Director, Washington Office
444 N. Capitol St. N.W., #230, Washington, DC 20001
(202) 624-7724; *Fax:* (202) 624-5495
E-mail: jjones@gov.state.de.us

Office of the Lieutenant Governor
http://www.state.de.us/ltgov/lgindex.htm
Main phone: (302) 739-4151
Main fax: (302) 739-6965

Ruth Ann Minner (D), Lieutenant Governor
Tatnall Bldg., 3rd Fl., Dover, DE 19901
E-mail: rminner@ltgov.state.de.us

Office of the Secretary of State
http://www.state.de.us/sos
General e-mail: ebaker@state.de.us
Main phone: (302) 739-4111

State of Delaware

Capital: Dover, since 1777
Founded: 1682, as British colony under William Penn; previously Swedish and Dutch
Statehood: December 7, 1787 (1st state)
Constitution adopted: 1897
Area: 1,955 sq. mi. (ranks 49th)
Population: 743,603 (1998 est.; ranks 45th)
Largest cities: (1998 est.) Wilmington (71,678); Dover (30,369); Newark (28,000); Milford (6,665); Seaford (6,600)
Counties: 3, Most populous: (1998 est.) New Castle (482,807); Sussex (136,707); Kent (124,089)
U.S. Congress: Joseph R. Biden Jr. (D), William V. Roth (R); 1 Representative
Nickname(s): Diamond State, First State
Motto: Liberty and independence
Song: "Our Delaware"
Bird: Blue hen chicken
Tree: American holly
Flower: Peach blossom
State fair: at Harrington, late July
Former capital(s): New Castle

Main fax: (302) 739-3811
Mailing address: P.O. Box 898, Dover, DE 19903

Edward J. Freel, Secretary of State
401 Federal St., #3, Dover, DE 19901

Office of the Attorney General
http://www.state.de.us/attgen/index.htm
Main phone: (302) 577-8500
Main fax: (302) 577-2610

M. Jane Brady (R), Attorney General
Carvel State Office Bldg., 820 N. French St.,
Wilmington, DE 19801
(302) 577-8338
E-mail: jbrady@state.de.us

Office of the Treasurer
http://www.state.de.us/treasure/index.html
Main phone: (302) 744-1000
Main fax: (302) 739-5635

Jack Markell (D), State Treasurer
Thomas Collins Bldg., 540 S. Dupont Hwy., #4,
    Dover, DE 19901-4516
(302) 744-1001
E-mail: jmarkell@state.de.us

Auditor of Accounts Office
http://www.state.de.us/auditor/htm
Main phone: (302) 739-4241
Main fax: (302) 739-2723

R. Thomas Wagner Jr. (R), State Auditor
Townsend Bldg., 401 Federal St., #1, Dover, DE
    19901
(302) 739-5055; *Fax:* (302) 739-6707
E-mail: wagner@state.de.us

National Guard
http://www.dearng.ngb.army.mil/
General e-mail: diane.chattius@de-
    arng.ngb.army.mil
Main phone: (302) 326-7000
Main fax: (302) 326-7029

Francis D. Vavala, Adjutant General
1st Regiment Rd., Wilmington, DE 19808-2191
(302) 326-7008

Agencies

Administrative Services Dept.
Main phone: (302) 739-3613
Main fax: (302) 739-6704
TTY: (302) 739-3699

Vincent P. Meconi, Secretary
Margaret M. O'Neill Bldg., 410 Federal St., #1, Dover,
    DE 19901
(302) 739-3611
E-mail: vmeconi@state.de.us

Professional Regulation Division
Main phone: (302) 739-4522
Main fax: (302) 739-2711

Carol H. Ellis, Director
Cannon Bldg., 861 Silver Lake Blvd., #203, Dover,
    DE 19904

Public Utilities Control Division
http://www.state.de.us/delpsc
Main phone: (302) 739-4247
Main fax: (302) 739-4849
Toll free: (800) 282-8574
TTY: (302) 739-4333

Bruce H. Burcat, Executive Director
Cannon Bldg., 861 Silver Lake Blvd., #100, Dover,
    DE 19904
E-mail: bburcat@state.de.us

Agriculture Dept.
http://www.state.de.us/deptagri/index.htm
Main phone: (302) 739-4811
Main fax: (302) 697-6287
Toll free: (800) 282-8685

Jack Tarburton, Secretary
2320 S. Dupont Hwy., Dover, DE 19901-5515
E-mail: jackt@smtp.dda.state.de.us

Forestry Administration
http://www.state.de.us/deptagri/dfs/forest.htm
Main phone: (302) 739-4811
Main fax: (302) 697-6245
Toll free: (800) 282-8685

E. Austin Short III, State Forester
2320 S. Dupont Hwy., Dover, DE 19901-5515
(302) 739-4811, ext. 225
E-mail: austin@smtp.dda.state.de.us

Arts Division
http://www.artsdel.org/
General e-mail: delarts@artswire.org
Main phone: (302) 739-5304
Main fax: (302) 577-6561

Peggy Amsterdam, Director
Carvel State Office Bldg., 820 N. French St.,
    Wilmington, DE 19801
(302) 577-8280
E-mail: pamsterdam@state.de.us

Bank Commissioner
http://www.state.de.us/bank/index.htm
General e-mail: scrump@state.de.us
Main phone: (302) 739-4235
Main fax: (302) 739-3609

Robert A. Glen, Commissioner
555 E. Loockerman St., #210, Dover, DE 19901

Correction Dept.
http://www.state.de.us/correct/ddoc/default.htm
General e-mail: gstallings@state.de.us
Main phone: (302) 739-5601
Main fax: (302) 739-8221

Stanley W. Taylor Jr., Commissioner
245 McKee Rd., Dover, DE 19904
Fax: (302) 739-8221

Criminal Justice Council
http://www.state.de.us/cjc/index.html
Main phone: (302) 577-5030
Main fax: (302) 577-3440

James Kane, Executive Director
Carvel State Office Bldg., 820 N. French St., 10th Fl.,
    Wilmington, DE 19801
E-mail: jkane@state.de.us

Developmental Disabilities Council
http://www.state.de.us/ddc/index.htm
Main phone: (302) 739-3333
Main fax: (302) 739-2015
TTY: (800) 232-5460

James F. Linehan, Administrator
821 Silver Lake Blvd., #108, Dover, DE 19904
E-mail: jlinehan@state.de.us

Economic Development Office
http://www.state.de.us/dedo/index.htm
General e-mail: mreardon@state.de.us
Main phone: (302) 739-4271
Main fax: (302) 739-5749
Toll free: (800) 441-8846
Mailing address: P.O. Box 1401, Dover, DE 19903-1401

Darrell Minott, Director
99 Kings Hwy., Dover, DE 19901

Tourism Office
http://www.state.de.us/tourism/
General e-mail: dporter@state.de.us
Main phone: (302) 739-4271 x131
Main fax: (302) 739-5749
Toll free: (800) 441-8846
Mailing address: P.O. Box 1401, Dover, DE 19903-1401

Keia Benefield, Director
99 Kings Hwy., Dover, DE 19901
(302) 672-6842
E-mail: kbenefield@state.de.us

Education Dept.
http://www.doe.state.de.us/
Main phone: (302) 739-4601
Main fax: (302) 739-4654
Mailing address: P.O. Box 1402, Dover, DE 19903-1402

Valerie A. Woodruff, Secretary of Education (Acting)
John G. Townsend Bldg., #2, Dover, DE 19903-1402
E-mail: vwoodruff@state.de.us

Emergency Management Agency
http://www.state.de.us/dema/index.htm
General e-mail: jgooding@state.de.us
Main phone: (302) 659-3362
Main fax: (302) 659-6855
Toll free: (877) 729-3362
Mailing address: P.O. Box 527, Delaware City, DE 19706

John P. Mulhern, Director
165 Brick Store Landing Rd., Smyrna, DE 19977
(302) 659-2240
E-mail: jmulhern@state.de.us

Higher Educational Institutions

Delaware State University
http://www.dsc.edu
1200 N. DuPont Hwy., Dover, DE 19901-2277
Main phone: (302) 739-4917

University of Delaware
http://www.udel.edu
Newark, DE 19716
Main phone: (302) 831-2000

Finance Dept.
http://www.state.de.us/finance/index.htm
Main phone: (302) 577-8979
Main fax: (302) 577-8982

John C. Carney Jr., Secretary of Finance
Carvel State Office Bldg., 820 N. French St., 8th Fl., Wilmington, DE 19801
(302) 577-8980
E-mail: jcarney@state.de.us

Revenue Division
http://www.state.de.us/revenue/index.htm
General e-mail: personaltax@state.de.us
Main phone: (302) 577-8200
Main fax: (302) 577-8202
Toll free: (800) 292-7826

William M. Remington, Director
Carvel State Office Bldg., 820 N. French St., 8th Fl., Wilmington, DE 19801
(302) 577-8686
E-mail: wremington@state.de.us

Fire Marshal Office
http://www.state.de.us/sfmo
Main phone: (302) 739-5665
Main fax: (302) 739-3696

Daniel R. Kiley, State Fire Marshal
1537 Chestnut Grove Rd., Dover, DE 19904-9610
E-mail: dkiley@state.de.us

Fire Prevention Commission
http://www.state.de.us/dvfa
General e-mail: slambertson@state.de.us
Main phone: (302) 739-3160
Main fax: (302) 739-4436

Carleton E. Carey Sr., Chair
Delaware Fire Service Center, 1463 Chestnut Grove Rd., Dover, DE 19904

Fraud and Consumer Protection Division
http://state.de.us/attgen/index.htm
Main phone: (302) 577-8600

Eugene M. Hall, Director
Carvel State Office Bldg., 820 N. French St., 5th Fl.,
Wilmington, DE 19801
E-mail: ehall@state.de.us

Geological Survey
http://www.udel.edu/dgs/dgs.html
General e-mail: delgeosurvey@udel.edu
Main phone: (302) 831-2833
Main fax: (302) 831-3579

Robert R. Jordan, State Geologist and Director
University of Delaware, DGS Bldg., Newark, DE
19716-7501

Health and Social Services
http://www.state.de.us/dhss/
General e-mail: dhssinfo@state.de.us
Main phone: (302) 739-5264
Main fax: (302) 739-6659

Gregg C. Sylvester, Secretary
1901 N. Dupont Hwy., Main Bldg., New Castle, DE
19720
(302) 577-4500; *Fax:* (302) 577-4510

Alcoholism, Substance Abuse, and Mental Health Division
http://www.state.de.us/dhss/irm/dadamh/
dmhhome.htm
General e-mail: dhssinfo@state.de.us
Main phone: (302) 577-4461
Main fax: (302) 577-4484
Toll free: (888) 889-6432
TTY: (888) 889-6432

Renata J. Henry, Director
1901 N. Dupont Hwy., Main Bldg., New Castle,
DE 19720

Mental Retardation Division
http://www.state.de.us/dhss/irm/dmr/
dmrhome.htm
General e-mail: dhssinfo@state.de.us
Main phone: (302) 739-4452
Main fax: (302) 739-3202

Marianne Smith, Director
417 Federal St., Jesse Cooper Bldg., Dover, DE
19901
E-mail: MA.Smith@state.de.us

Services for Aging and Adults with Physical Disabilities
http://www.state.de.us/dhss/irm/dsaapd/
doahome.htm
General e-mail: dhssinfo@state.de.us
Main phone: (302) 577-4791
Main fax: (302) 577-4793
Social worker: (800) 223-9074

Eleanor Cain, Director
1901 N. Dupont Hwy., Main Bldg., New Castle,
DE 19720

Social Services Division
http://www.state.de.us/dhss/irm/dss/
dsshome.htm
General e-mail: dhssinfo@state.de.us
Main phone: (302) 577-4900
Main fax: (302) 577-4405
Toll free: (800) 372-2022
TTY: (800) 924-3958
Mailing address: P.O. Box 906, New Castle, DE
19720

Elaine Archangelo, Director
1901 N. Dupont Hwy., Lewis Bldg., New Castle,
DE 19720
(302) 577-4400; *Fax:* (302) 577-4557
E-mail: earchangelo@state.de.us

Health Care Commission
http://www.state.de.us/dhcc/index.htm
Main phone: (302) 739-6906
Main fax: (302) 739-6927

Paula Roy, Executive Director
Tatnall Bldg., 150 William Penn St., Ground Fl.,
Dover, DE 19901

Higher Education Commission
http://www.doe.state.de.us/high-ed/index.htm
General e-mail: mlaffey@state.de.us
Main phone: (302) 577-3240
Main fax: (302) 577-6765
Toll free: (800) 292-7935

Marilyn B. Quinn, Executive Director
Carvel State Office Bldg., 820 N. French St.,
Wilmington, DE 19801
E-mail: mquinn@state.de.us

Historic Preservation Office
http://www.state.de.us/shpo/index.htm
General e-mail: aguerrant@state.de.us
Main phone: (302) 739-5313
Main fax: (302) 739-6711

Daniel R. Griffith, Director
Hall of Records, 121 Duke of York St., #2, Dover, DE
19901
E-mail: dgriffith@state.de.us

Housing Authority
Main phone: (302) 739-4263
Main fax: (302) 739-6122
TTY: (302) 739-4264
Mailing address: P.O. Box 1401, Dover, DE 19901

Susan A. Frank, Director
18 The Green, Dover, DE 19901

Insurance Dept.
Main phone: (302) 739-4251
Main fax: (302) 739-5280

Donna Lee H. Williams (R), Commissioner
841 Silver Lake Blvd., Dover, DE 19904

Labor Dept.
http://www.state.de.us/labor/index.shtml
General e-mail: dlabor@state.de.us
Main phone: (302) 761-8000
Main fax: (302) 761-6621
TTY: (302) 761-8275

Lisa Blunt-Bradley, Secretary
4425 N. Market St., Wilmington, DE 19802
(302) 761-8001
E-mail: lbradley@state.de.us

Industrial Affairs Division
http://www.delawareworks.com/divisions/
    industaffairs/diaindex.html
Main phone: (302) 761-8200
Main fax: (302) 761-6601

Karen E. Peterson, Director
4425 N. Market St., Wilmington, DE 19802

Women's Commission Office
http://www.state.de.us/labor/divisions/dcw/
    welcome.htm
General e-mail: cgomez@state.de.us
Main phone: (302) 761-8005
Main fax: (302) 761-6652

Romona S. Fullman, Executive Director
4425 Market St., Wilmington, DE 19802

Workers Compensation Administration
http://www.state.de.us/labor/divisions/
    industaffairs/workers.comp.htm
Main phone: (302) 761-8200
Main fax: (302) 761-6601

John F. Kirk III, Administrator
4425 Market St., Wilmington, DE 19802

Libraries Division
http://www.lib.de.us/
General e-mail: webmaster@www.lib.de.us
Main phone: (302) 739-4748
Main fax: (302) 739-6787

Tom Sloan, Director
43 S. Dupont Hwy., Dover, DE 19901

Lottery
http://lottery.state.de.us
General e-mail: webmaster@lottery.state.de.us
Main phone: (302) 739-5291
Main fax: (302) 739-6706

Frequently Called Numbers

Tourism: (302) 739-4271; 1-800-441-8846;
    http://www.state.de.us/tourism/
Library: (302) 739-4748; http://www.lib.de.us/
Board of Education: (302) 739-4602
Vital Statistics: (302) 739-4721; http://
    www.archives.lib.de.us/research/vital.htm
Tax/Revenue: (302) 577-8200;
    http://www.state.de.us/revenue/index.htm
Motor Vehicles: (302) 744-2500
State Police/Highway Patrol: (302) 739-5900;
    http://www.state.de.us/dsp/index.htm
Unemployment: (302) 761-6576, New Castle
    County residents; 800-744-30332, Kent and
    Sussex county residents;
    http://www.state.de.us/labor/divisions/
    unemployment/reghand/regs2.html
General Election Information:
    (302) 739-4277; http://www.state.de.us/
    election/index.htm
Consumer Affairs: (302) 577-8600;
    http://state.de.us/attgen/index.htm
Hazardous Materials: (302) 659-3362;
    http://www.state.de.us/dema/HazMats.htm

Wayne Lemons, Director
1575 McKee Rd., #102, Dover, DE 19904
(302) 774-1600; *Fax:* (302) 739-6706
E-mail: wlemons@lottery.state.us

Medical Board
Main phone: (302) 739-4522
Main fax: (302) 739-2711

Douglas J. Reed, Executive Director
Cannon Bldg., 861 Silver Lake Blvd., #203, Dover,
    DE 19904
(302) 739-4522, ext. 229

**Natural Resources and Environmental Control
Dept.**
http://www.dnrec.state.de.us/
General e-mail: mpolo@state.de.us
Main phone: (302) 739-4506
Main fax: (302) 739-6242

Nicholas A. Dipasquale, Secretary
89 Kings Hwy., Dover, DE 19901
(302) 739-4403

Fish and Wildlife Division
http://www.dnrec.state.de.us/fandw.htm
General e-mail: lherman@dnrec.state.de.us
Main phone: (302) 739-5295
Main fax: (302) 739-6157

Andrew T. Manus, Division Director
89 Kings Hwy., Dover, DE 19901
E-mail: amanus@dnrec.state.de.us

Parks and Recreation
http://www.dnrec.state.de.us
General e-mail: parkinfo@dnrec.state.de.us
Main phone: (302) 739-4401
Main fax: (302) 739-3817

Charles A. Salkin, Director
89 Kings Hwy., Dover, DE 19901

Soil and Water Conservation Division
http://www.dnrec.state.de.us/sandw.htm
Main phone: (302) 739-4411
Main fax: (302) 739-6724

John A. Hughes, Division Director
89 Kings Hwy., Dover, DE 19901
E-mail: jhughes@state.de.us

Water Resources Division
http://www.dnrec.state.de.us/water.htm
Main phone: (302) 739-4860

Kevin Donnelly, Division Director
89 Kings Hwy., Dover, DE 19901
E-mail: kdonnelly@dnrec.state.de.us

Nursing Board
Main phone: (302) 739-4522
Main fax: (302) 739-2711
Toll free: (800) 464-4357

Iva Boardman, Executive Director
Cannon Bldg., 861 Silver Lake Blvd., #203, Dover,
DE 19904

Parole Board
http://www.state.de.us/parole/index.htm
Main phone: (302) 577-5233
Main fax: (302) 577-3501

Professional Regulation
(302) 739-4522

Accountancy, (302) 739-4522
Architects, (302) 739-4522
Child Care, (302) 739-4522
Contractors, (302) 739-4522
Cosmetology, (302) 739-4522
Engineers and Land Surveyors,
   (302) 739-4522
Medical Examiners, (302) 739-4522
Nursing, (302) 739-4522
Pharmacy, (302) 739-4522
Real Estate Appraisers, (302) 739-4522

Marlene Lichtenstadter, Chair
Carvel State Office Bldg., 820 N. French St., 5th Fl.,
   Wilmington, DE 19801
E-mail: elichtensta@state.de.us

Personnel Office
http://www.state.de.us/spo/index.htm
Main phone: (302) 739-4195
Main fax: (302) 739-3000
Job hotline: (800) 345-1789

Harriet N. Smith Windsor, Director
Townsend Bldg., 401 Federal St., #5, Dover, DE
19901

Prosecution Office
Main phone: (302) 577-8801

Ferris Wharton, State Prosecuter
Carvel State Office Bldg., 820 N. French St.,
   Wilmington, DE 19801

Public Archives
http://www.archives.lib.de.us
Main phone: (302) 739-5318
Main fax: (302) 739-2578

Howard Lowell, State Archivist
Hall of Records, 121 Duke of York St., Dover, DE
19901
E-mail: hlowell@state.de.us

Public Defender
http://www.state.de.us/pubdefen/index.htm
Main phone: (302) 577-5200
Main fax: (302) 577-3995

Lawrence M. Sullivan, Public Defender
Carvel State Office Bldg., 820 N. French St., 3rd Fl.,
   Wilmington, DE 19801

Public Safety Dept.
http://www.state.de.us/pubsafe/index.htm
Main phone: (302) 744-2680
Main fax: (302) 739-4874
Mailing address: P.O. Box 818, Dover, DE 19903-
0818

Brian J. Bushweller, Secretary
Public Safety Bldg., 303 Transportation Circle, Dover,
DE 19901
E-mail: bbushweller@state.de.us

Alcoholic Beverage Control Division
Main phone: (302) 577-5202
Main fax: (302) 577-3204
Toll free: (800) 275-9500

Donald J. Bowman Sr., Director
Carvel State Office Bldg., 820 N. French St.,
   Wilmington, DE 19801
   (302) 577-5191
E-mail: dbowman@state.de.us

Motor Vehicles Division
Main phone: (302) 744-2500
Main fax: (302) 739-3152
Mailing address: P.O. Box 698, Dover, DE 19903

Michael D. Shahan, Director
303 Transportation Circle, Dover, DE 19901
(302) 744-2510
E-mail: mshahan@state.de.us

State Police
http://www.state.de.us/dsp/index.htm
Main phone: (302) 739-5900
Main fax: (302) 739-5966
Mailing address: P.O. Box 430, Dover, DE 19903

Gerald R. Pepper Jr., Superintendent
1441 N. Dupont Hwy., Dover, DE 19901
(302) 739-5911

State Fair
http://www.delawarestatefair.com/
Main phone: (302) 398-3269
Main fax: (302) 398-3050
Mailing address: P.O. Box 28, Harrington, DE 19952-0028

Dennis S. Hazzard, General Manager
S. Dupont Hwy., Harrington, DE 19952-0028
E-mail: dhazzard@delawarestatefair.com

Transportation Dept.
http://www.state.de.us/deldot/index.html
Main phone: (302) 760-2080
Main fax: (302) 739-4329
Toll free: (800) 652-5600
Mailing address: P.O. Box 778, Dover, DE 19903-0778

Anne P. Canby, Secretary
800 Bay Rd., Dover, DE 19903
(302) 760-2303

Aeronautics Office
Main phone: (302) 760-2155
Main fax: (302) 739-2251
Mailing address: P.O. Box 778, Dover, DE 19903

Anthony J. Amato, Director
Administration Center, Route 113, Dover, DE 19903
(302) 760-2160
E-mail: aamato@mail.dot.state.de.us

Veterans Affairs Commission
http://www.state.de.us/veteran/index.htm
Main phone: (302) 739-2792
Main fax: (302) 739-2794
Toll free: (800) 344-9900

Antonio Davila, Executive Director
Robbins Bldg., 802 Silver Lake Blvd., #100, Dover, DE 19904
E-mail: tony.davila@dol.net

Delaware Legislature
Legislative Hall
P.O. Box 1401
Dover, DE 19903
General information: (302) 739-4114
Fax: (302) 739-3895
http://www.state.de.us/research/assembly.htm

Senate
General information: (302) 739-4129

Ruth Ann Minner (D), President
Tatnall Bldg., Dover, DE 19901
(302) 739-4151; *Fax:* (302) 739-6965
E-mail: rminner@ltgov.state.de.us
http://www.state.de.us/ltgov/lgindex.htm

Thomas B. Sharp (D), President Pro Tempore
Legislative Hall, P.O. Box 1401, Dover, DE 19903
(302) 739-4163
http://www.state.de.us/research/senate/salpha/tbsharp.htm

Thurman Adams Jr. (D), Majority Leader
Legislative Hall, P.O. Box 1401, Dover, DE 19903
(302) 739-4117
http://www.state.de.us/research/senate/salpha/tadams.htm

Harris B. McDowell III (D), Majority Whip
Legislative Hall, P.O. Box 1401, Dover, DE 19903
(302) 739-4147
http://www.state.de.us/research/senate/salpha/mcdowell.htm

Steven H. Amick (R), Minority Leader
Legislative Hall, P.O. Box 1401, Dover, DE 19903
(302) 739-4138
http://www.state.de.us/research/senate/salpha/samick/htm

Myrna L. Bair (R), Minority Whip
Legislative Hall, P.O. Box 1401, Dover, DE 19903
(302) 739-4137
http://www.state.de.us/research/senate/salpha/mlbair.htm

Bernard J. Brady, Secretary
Legislative Hall, P.O. Box 1401, Dover, DE 19903
(302) 739-4129; *Fax:* (302) 739-6890

House
General information: (302) 739-4087

Terry R. Spence (R), Speaker of the House
Legislative Hall, P.O. Box 1401, Dover, DE 19903
(302) 739-4127
http://www.state.de.us/research/house/halpha/
trspence.htm

Wayne A. Smith (R), Majority Leader
Legislative Hall, P.O. Box 1401, Dover, DE 19903
(302) 739-4120
E-mail: wsmith@legis.state.de.us
http://www.state.de.us/research/house/halpha/
wasmith.htm

Charles W. Welch (R), Majority Whip
Legislative Hall, P.O. Box 1401, Dover, DE 19903
(302) 739-4175
http://www.state.de.us/research/house/halpha/
cwwelch.htm

Robert F. Gilligan (D), Minority Leader
Legislative Hall, P.O. Box 1401, Dover, DE 19903
(302) 739-4351
http://www.state.de.us/research/house/halpha/
gilligan.htm

John F. Van Sant (D), Minority Whip
Legislative Hall, P.O. Box 1401, Dover, DE 19903
(302) 739-4351
E-mail: jvansant@legis.state.de.us
http://www.state.de.us/research/house/halpha/
vansant.htm

JoAnn Helrick, Chief Clerk
Legislative Hall, P.O. Box 1401, Dover, DE 19903
(302) 739-4087; *Fax:* (302) 739-2773

Laws

Sales tax: None
Income tax: 6.9%
State minimum wage: $6.15, from Oct. 2000
  (Federal is $5.15)
Marriage age: 18
First-cousin marriage: Prohibited
Drinking age: 21
State control of liquor sales: No
Blood alcohol for DWI: 0.10%
Driving age: 16, 10 mos.
Speed limit: 65 mph
Permit to buy handguns: No
Minimum age to possess handguns: Illegal
  for juveniles
Minimum age to possess rifles, shotguns:
  None
State lottery: Yes; also Powerball
Casinos: No; but slot/video machines
Pari-mutuel betting: Horse racing
Death penalty: Yes
3 strikes minimum sentence: Life (3rd serious
  felony)
Hate crimes law: Yes
Gay employment non-discrimination: No
Official language(s): None
Term limits: None

*State laws are complex and subject to
change; this information is not intended as
legal advice. For an explanation of this
information, see p. x.*

Delaware Judiciary
55 The Green
Dover, DE 19901
http://courts.state.de.us

Supreme Court
http://courts.state.de.us/supreme

Cathy Howard, Clerk
Elbert N. Carvel State Office Bldg., 820 N. French St.,
  Wilmington, DE 19801
(302) 739-4155; *Fax:* (302) 739-3751

Justices
Composition: 5 justices
Selection Method: appointed by governor with
  consent of state senate
Length of term: 12 years

E. Norman Veasey, Chief Justice, (302) 577-8700
Carolyn Berger, Justice, (302) 577-8730
Maurice A. Hartnett III, Justice, (302) 739-4214
Randy J. Holland, Justice, (302) 856-5363
Joseph T. Walsh, Justice, (302) 577-8690

Administrative Office of the Courts
Main phone: (302) 577-2480
Main fax: (302) 577-3139

Lawrence P. Webster, Director
Elbert N. Carvel State Office Bldg., 820 N. French St.,
  Wilmington, DE 19801
(302) 577-8481
E-mail: lwebster@state.de.us

State Law Library
Main phone: (302) 577-2437
Main fax: (302) 577-2813
Jean D. Winstead, Law Librarian
1020 N. King St., 2nd Fl., Wilmington, DE 19801

Legislative and Political Party Information Resources

Senate home page: http://www.state.de.us/research/senate/senate.htm
House home page: http://www.state.de.us/research/house/house.htm
Committees: Senate: http://www.state.de.us/research/senate/sencomm.htm; *House:* http://
  www.state.de.us/research/house/hcomm.htm
Legislative process: http://www.state.de.us/research/dor/billlaw.htm
Legislative information: http://www.state.de.us/research/dor/lis.htm
Delaware Democratic Party: http://www.deldems.org
  P.O. Box 2065, Wilmington, DE 19805; *Phone:* (302) 996-9458; *Fax:* (302) 996-9405; *E-mail:*
  delaware@deldems.org
Delaware Republican Party: http://www.delawaregop.com
  2 Mill Rd., #108, Wilmington, DE 19806; *Phone:* (302) 651-0260; *Fax:* (302) 651-0270 *E-mail:*
  chairman@delawaregop.com

District of Columbia

1 Judiciary Square
441 4th St. N.W.
Washington, DC 20001
Public information: (202) 757-5011
Fax: (202) 757-2357
http://www.ci.washington.dc.us

Office of the Mayor
http://www.ci.washington.dc.us
Main phone: (202) 727-1000
Main fax: (202) 727-2357

Anthony Williams (D), Mayor
1 Judiciary Square, 441 4th St. N.W., Washington, DC 20001
(202) 727-2980
E-mail: mayor@dcgov.org

Abdusalem Omer, Chief of Staff (Acting)
1 Judiciary Square, 441 4th St. N.W., Washington, DC 20001
(202) 727-2643; *Fax:* (202) 727-2975
E-mail: aomer@dcgov.org

Peggy Armstrong, Press Secretary
1 Judiciary Square, 441 4th St. N.W., Washington, DC 20001
(202) 727-5011; *Fax:* (202) 727-9561
E-mail: parmstrong@dcgov.org

Office of the Secretary of the District of Columbia
Main phone: (202) 727-6306
Main fax: (202) 727-3582

Beverly D. Rivers, Secretary
1 Judiciary Square, 441 4th St. N.W., #1130, Washington, DC 20001
E-mail: brivers-eom@dcgov.org

Auditor
Main phone: (202) 727-3600
Main fax: (202) 724-8814

Deborah K. Nichols, Auditor
717 14th St. N.W., #900, Washington, DC 20005
E-mail: dksnick@aol.com

Agencies

Aging Office
http://www.ci.washington.dc.us/aging/aghome.htm

District of Columbia

Capital: U.S. Capital
Founded: 1790, from land ceded from Virginia and Maryland
Statehood: Not Applicable
Constitution adopted: Not Applicable
Area: 61 sq. mi. (ranks 51st)
Population: 523,124 (1998 est.; ranks 50th)
Largest cities: (1998 est.) Washington (523,124)
Counties: None
U.S. Congress: Not Applicable
Nickname(s): None
Motto: Justice for all
Song: None
Bird: Woodthrush
Tree: Scarlet oak
Flower: American beauty rose
State fair: None

Main phone: (202) 724-5622
Main fax: (202) 724-4979
TTY: (202) 724-8925

E. Veronica Pace, Executive Director
441 4th St. N.W., #900-S, Washington, DC 20001
(202) 724-5622

Alcohol and Beverage Control Board
http://www.dcra.org
Main phone: (202) 727-7375
Main fax: (202) 727-7388

Roderic L. Woodson, Chair
941 N. Capitol St. N.E., #807, Washington, DC 20002
(202) 442-4445

Archives and Public Records Office
Main phone: (202) 671-1113
Main fax: (202) 727-6076

Clarence Davis, Administrator
1300 Naylor Court N.W., Washington, DC 20001

Arts and Humanities Commission
http://www.capaccess.org/ane/dccah/
General e-mail: dccah@erols.com
Main phone: (202) 724-5613
Main fax: (202) 727-4135

Anthony Gittens Jr., Executive Director
410 8th St. N.W., 5th Fl., Washington, DC 20004
E-mail: filmfestdc@aol.com

Banking and Financial Institutions Office
http://www.obfi.dcgov.org
General e-mail: obfi@dcgov.org
Main phone: (202) 727-1563
Main fax: (202) 727-1588

S. Kathryn Allen, Superintendent
717 14th St. N.W., #1100, Washington, DC 20005

Board of Education
Main phone: (202) 442-4289
Main fax: (202) 442-5198

Wilma Harvey, President
825 N. Capitol St. N.E., #1205, Washington, DC 20002

City Administrator
http://www.ci.washington.dc.us
Main phone: (202) 727-6053
Main fax: (202) 727-9878

Vacant, City Administrator (Interim)
1 Judiciary Square, 441 4th St. N.W., #1120-S, Washington, DC 20001

Corrections Dept.
Main phone: (202) 673-2300
Main fax: (202) 332-1470

Odie Washington, Director
1923 Vermont Ave. N.W., #N-203, Washington, DC 20001
(202) 673-7316
E-mail: OWashington@dcgov.org

Human Services Dept.
http://www.dhs.washington.dc.us
General e-mail:
rhondastewart@dhs.washington.dc.us
Main phone: (202) 279-6002
Main fax: (202) 673-6014
Mailing address: P.O. Box 54047, Washington, DC 20032-0247

Jearline F. Williams, Director
2700 Martin Luther King Jr. Ave. S.E., 801 East Bldg., Washington, DC 20032
E-mail: jwilliams-dhs@dcgov.org

Metropolitan Police Dept.
http://www.mpdc.org
General e-mail: mpdc_org@excite.com
Main phone: (202) 727-4218
Main fax: (202) 727-9524
TTY: (202) 727-1010

Charles H. Ramsey, Chief of Police
300 Indiana Ave. N.W., #5080, Washington, DC 20001
E-mail: mpdcchief_org@excite.com

Recreation and Parks Dept.
http://www.dcrecreation.com
Main phone: (202) 673-7665
Main fax: (202) 673-2087

Robert P. Newman, Director
3149 16th St. N.W., Washington, DC 20010
E-mail: rpnewman@drpntz.dcgov.org

Contracting and Procurement Office
http://www.ocp.dcgov.org

Higher Educational Institutions

National Defense University
http://www.ndu.edu
300 5th Ave., Fort McNair, DC 20319-5066
Main phone: (202) 475-1844
Branches: Armed Forces Staff College, Center for Hemispheric Defense Studies, Industrial College of the Armed Forces, Information Resources Management College, Institute for National Strategic Studies, National War College

University of the District of Columbia
http://www.udc.edu
4200 Connecticut Ave. N.W., Washington, DC 20008
Main phone: (202) 832-4888

Main phone: (202) 727-0252
Main fax: (202) 727-3229

Elliott Branch, Director and Chief Procurement Officer
1 Judiciary Square, 441 4th St. N.W., #800-S, Washington, DC 20001

Elections and Ethics Board
Main phone: (202) 727-2525
Main fax: (202) 347-2648
TTY: (202) 639-8916

Benjamin F. Wilson, Chair
1 Judiciary Square, 441 4th St. N.W., #250, Washington, DC 20001-2745

Finance and Treasury Office
Main phone: (202) 727-6055
Main fax: (202) 727-6049

William Hall, Deputy Chief Financial Officer
1 Judiciary Square, 441 4th St. N.W., #360-N, Washington, DC 20001
Fax: (202) 727-0963

Financial Operations and Systems Office
Main phone: (202) 442-8200
Main fax: (202) 442-8201

Anthony F. Pompa, Deputy Chief Financial Officer (Interim)
410 1st St. N.W., #200, Washington, DC 20002

Fire and Emergency Medical Services Dept.
Main phone: (202) 673-3320
Main fax: (202) 462-0807

Thomas Tippett, Fire Chief
1923 Vermont Ave. N.W., Washington, DC 20001

Fire Prevention Bureau/Office of the Fire Marshal
Main phone: (202) 727-1614
Main fax: (202) 727-3238

Alvin Carter, Fire Marshal
1 Judiciary Square, 441 4th St. N.W., #370,
Washington, DC 20001

Health Dept.
http://www.dchealth.com/
Main phone: (202) 442-5999
Main fax: (202) 442-4788

Ivan C.A. Walks, Director
825 N. Capitol St. N.E., Washington, DC 20002

Medical Assistance Administration
Main phone: (202) 727-0735
Main fax: (202) 610-3209

Herbert H. Weldone Jr., Deputy Director
2100 Martin Luther King Jr. Ave. S.E., #302,
Washington, DC 20020

Housing Authority
http://www.dc-ha.org
Main phone: (202) 535-1000
Main fax: (202) 535-1740

David I. Gilmore, Receiver
1133 N. Capitol St. N.E., Washington, DC 20002
(202) 535-1500

Human Rights Commission
http://www.ci.washington.dc.us/dhr_lbd/ohr
General e-mail: COHR@hotmail.com
Main phone: (202) 727-0656
Main fax: (202) 727-3781

James M. Loots, Chair (Acting)
1 Judiciary Square, 441 4th St. N.W., #970-N,
Washington, DC 20001

Frequently Called Numbers

Tourism: (202) 789-7000
Library: (202) 727-1101;
   http://www.dclibrary.org
Board of Education: (202) 442-4289
Vital Statistics: (202) 442-9009;
   http://www.dchealth.com/schs/welcome.htm
Tax/Revenue: (202) 442-6200
Motor Vehicles: (202) 727-5000
State Police/Highway Patrol: (202) 727-4218;
   http://www.mpdc.org
Unemployment: (202) 724-7274;
   http://does.ci.washington.dc.us/ui.html
General Election Information:
   (202) 727-2525; http://www.dcboee.org
Consumer Affairs: (202) 442-4400;
   http://www.dcra.dc.gov.org
Hazardous Materials: (202) 645-7044

Insurance and Securites Regulation Dept.
Main phone: (202) 442-7770
Main fax: (202) 535-1196

Lawrence Mirel, Commissioner (Acting)
810 1st St. N.E., #710, Washington, DC 20002
(202) 727-8000
E-mail: lhmirel-dcia@dcgov.org

Library Trustees Board
http://www.dclibrary.org
Main phone: (202) 727-1101
Main fax: (202) 727-1129
TTY: (202) 727-2255

Marie Harris Aldridge, President
D.C. Public Library, 901 G St. N.W., #400,
Washington, DC 20001-4599

Lottery and Charitable Games Control Board
Main phone: (202) 645-8000
Main fax: (202) 645-3683

Anthony S. Cooper, Executive Director
2101 Martin L. King Ave. S.E., Washington, DC
20020
(202) 645-8010
E-mail: acooper@dclottery.com

Mental Retardation and Developmental Disabilities Administration
Main phone: (202) 673-7657
Main fax: (202) 671-1628
TTY: (202) 673-3580

Adrienne Buckner, Administrator (Acting)
429 O St. N.W., Washington, DC 20001

Occupational and Professional Licensing Administration
Main phone: (202) 442-4320
Main fax: (202) 442-4258

Clifford Cooks, Administrator (Acting)
941 N. Capitol St. N.E., #9500, Washington, DC
20002

Office of the Deputy City Administrator
Main phone: (202) 727-6053
Main fax: (202) 727-9878

Norman Dong, Deputy Mayor for Operations
1 Judiciary Square, 441 4th St. N.W., #1120-S,
Washington, DC 20001
E-mail: ndong-eom@dcgov.org

Committee to Promote Washington
Main phone: (202) 724-5644
Main fax: (202) 724-2445

V. Melanie Suggs, Executive Director
1212 New York Ave. N.W., #200, Washington, DC
20005
E-mail: melanie@promote-dc.org

Consumer and Regulatory Affairs Dept.
http://www.dcra.dc.gov.org
Main phone: (202) 442-4400

Main fax: (202) 442-9445
TTY: (202) 442-4526

Lloyd J. Jordan, Director
941 N. Capitol St. N.E., #9500, Washington, DC
20002
(202) 442-8947; *Fax:* (202) 442-9475

Housing Finance Authority
http://www.dchfa.com
General e-mail: dchfa@erols.com
Main phone: (202) 777-1600
Main fax: (202) 986-6705

Milton Bailey, Executive Director
815 Florida Ave. N.W., #600, Washington, DC
20001

Housing and Community Development Dept.
http://www.dhcd.dcgov.org
Main phone: (202) 442-7200
Main fax: (202) 442-8391

Othello Mahone, Director (Interim)
801 N. Capitol St. N.E., 8th Fl., Washington, DC
20002

Human Rights and Local Business Development Dept.
http://www.ci.washington.dc.us/dhr_lbd
Main phone: (202) 727-3900
Main fax: (202) 724-3786

Jacqueline Flowers, Director
1 Judiciary Square, 441 4th St. N.W., #970-N,
Washington, DC 20001

Parole Board
Main phone: (202) 220-5450
Main fax: (202) 220-5466

Margaret Quick, Chair
633 Indiana Ave. N.W., Washington, DC 20004

Boards and Licensing

Accountancy, (202) 442-4461
Architects, (202) 442-4461
Child Care, (202) 442-5929
Contractors, (202) 727-0252
Cosmetology, (202) 442-4459
Engineers and Land Surveyors,
  (202) 442-4464
Medical Examiners, (202) 442-9200
Nursing, (202) 442-9200
Occupational Licensing, (202) 442-4320
Pharmacy, (202) 442-9200
Real Estate Appraisers, (202) 442-4340

Personnel Dept.
Main phone: (202) 442-9700
Main fax: (202) 442-6542

Charles Meng, Administrative Director (Interim)
1 Judiciary Square, 441 4th St. N.W., #340-N,
Washington, DC 20001
(202) 442-9630

Public Defender Service
Main phone: (202) 628-1200
Main fax: (202) 626-8423

Vacant, Director
633 Indiana Ave. N.W., #248, Washington, DC 20004

Public Works Dept.
Main phone: (202) 673-6813
Main fax: (202) 939-8171

Vanessa Dale Burns, Director (Interim)
2000 14th St. N.W., 6th Fl., Washington, DC 20009
(202) 673-6812
E-mail: vburns-dcw@dcgov.org

Tax and Revenue Dept.
Main phone: (202) 442-6200
Main fax: (202) 442-6477

Natwar M. Gandhi, Deputy Chief Financial Officer
941 N. Capitol St. N.E., #800, Washington, DC 20002
(202) 442-6282

Workers' Compensation Office
http://does.ci.washington.dc.us
Main phone: (202) 576-6265
Main fax: (202) 541-3595

Charles L. Green, Assistant Director (Interim)
1200 Upshur St. N.W., Washington, DC 20011

Youth Services Administration
Main phone: (301) 497-8100
Main fax: (301) 497-8510

Gayle Turner, Administrator
8300 Riverton Ct., Laurel, MD 20707
(301) 497-8114; *Fax:* (301) 497-8510

District of Columbia Council
441 4th St. N.W.
Washington, DC 20001
General information: (202) 724-8000
Bill status: (202) 724-8050
http://www.dccouncil.washington.dc.us/

Linda W. Cropp (At Large), Chair
441 4th St. N.W., #704, Washington, DC 20001
(202) 724-8032; *Fax:* (202) 724-8085
E-mail: lcropp@dccouncil.washington.dc.us

Harold Brazil (At Large), Councilmember
441 4th St. N.W., #701, Washington, DC 20001
(202) 724-8174; *Fax:* (202) 724-8156
E-mail: hbrazil@dccouncil.washington.dc.us

David A. Catania (At Large), Councilmember
441 4th St. N.W., #712, Washington, DC 20001
(202) 724-7772; *Fax:* (202) 724-8087
E-mail: dcatania@dccouncil.washington.dc.us

Phil Mendelson (At Large), Councilmember
441 4th St. N.W., #720, Washington, DC 20001
(202) 724-8064; *Fax:* (202) 724-8099
E-mail: pmendelson@dccouncil.washington.dc.us

Carol Schwartz (At Large), Councilmember
441 4th St. N.W., #706, Washington, DC 20001
(202) 724-8105; *Fax:* (202) 724-8071
E-mail: schwartzc@dccouncil.washington.dc.us

Jim Graham (Ward 1), Councilmember
441 4th St. N.W., #718, Washington, DC 20001
(202) 724-8181; *Fax:* (202) 724-8109
E-mail: jgraham@dccouncil.washington.dc.us

Jack Evans (Ward 2), Councilmember
441 4th St. N.W., #703, Washington, DC 20001
(202) 724-8058; *Fax:* (202) 724-8023
E-mail: jackevans@dccouncil.washington.dc.us

Kathleen Patterson (Ward 3), Councilmember
441 4th St. N.W., #709, Washington, DC 20001
(202) 724-8062; *Fax:* (202) 724-8118
E-mail: kpatterson@dccouncil.washington.dc.us

Charlene Drew Jarvis (Ward 4), Chair Pro Tempore
441 4th St. N.W., #708, Washington, DC 20001
(202) 724-8052; *Fax:* (202) 724-8120
E-mail: cdjarvis@dccouncil.washington.dc.us

Vincent B. Orange, Sr. (Ward 5), Councilmember
441 4th St. N.W., #702, Washington, DC 20001
(202) 724-8028; *Fax:* (202) 724-8076

Sharon Ambrose (Ward 6), Councilmember
441 4th St. N.W., #710, Washington, DC 20001

Laws

Sales tax: 5.75%
Income tax: 9.5%
State minimum wage: $6.15 (Federal is $5.15)
Marriage age: 18
First-cousin marriage: Permitted
Drinking age: 21
State control of liquor sales: No
Blood alcohol for DWI: 0.10%
Driving age: 16
Speed limit: N/A
Permit to buy handguns: Sales prohibited
Minimum age to possess handguns: 21
Minimum age to possess rifles, shotguns: 21
State lottery: Yes; also Powerball
Casinos: No
Pari-mutuel betting: No
Death penalty: No
3 strikes minimum sentence: Up to life (3rd felony)
Hate crimes law: Yes
Gay employment non-discrimination: Yes
Official language(s): None
Term limits: None

(202) 724-8072; *Fax:* (202) 724-8054
E-mail: sambrose@dccouncil.washington.dc.us

Kevin P. Chavous (Ward 7), Councilmember
441 4th St. N.W., #705, Washington, DC 20001
(202) 724-8068; *Fax:* (202) 724-8097
E-mail: kpchavous@dccouncil.washington.dc.us

Sandy Allen (Ward 8), Councilmember
441 4th St. N.W., #707, Washington, DC 20001
(202) 724-8045; *Fax:* (202) 724-8055
E-mail: cmallen@dccouncil.washington.dc.us

Legislative and Political Party Information Resources

Committees: http://www.dccouncil.washington.dc.us/organization.html
Legislative information: http://www.dccouncil.washington.dc.us/status.html
Legislative process: http://www.dccouncil.washington.dc.us/how.html
Current session information: http://www.dccouncil.washington.dc.us/calendar.html
D.C. Democratic Party: 499 S. Capital St. S.W., #100, Washington, DC 20024; Phone:
    (202) 554-8790
D.C. Republican Party: http://www.dcrc.org
    600 Pennsylvania Ave. SE, #300, Washington, DC 20003; Phone: (202) 608-1407,
    E-mail: dcgop@aol.com

Florida

The Capitol
Tallahassee, FL 32399-0001
Public information: (850) 488-1234
Fax: (850) 487-0801
http://www.state.fl.us

Office of the Governor
http://www.eog.state.fl.us/
General e-mail: fl_governor@eog.state.fl.us
Main phone: (850) 488-4441
Main fax: (850) 487-0801

Jeb Bush (R), Governor
The Capitol, Tallahassee, FL 32399-0001

Sally Bradshaw, Chief of Staff
The Capitol, Tallahassee, FL 32399-0001
(850) 488-5603; *Fax:* (850) 922-4292
E-mail: bradshs@eog.state.fl.us

Elizabeth Hirst, Press Secretary
The Capitol, Tallahassee, FL 32399-0001
(850) 488-5394; *Fax:* (850) 487-4042
E-mail: HirstE@eog.state.fl.us

Nina Oviedo, Director, Washington Office
444 N. Capitol St. N.W., #349, Washington, DC 20001
(202) 624-5885; *Fax:* (202) 624-5886

Office of the Lieutenant Governor
Main phone: (850) 488-4711
Main fax: (850) 921-6114

Frank T. Brogan (R), Lieutenant Governor
The Capitol, #PL-05, Tallahassee, FL 32399-0001
E-mail: broganf@eog.state.fl.us

Office of the Secretary of State
http://www.dos.state.fl.us
General e-mail: secretary@mail.dos.state.fl.us
Main phone: (850) 488-3680
Main fax: (850) 487-2214

Katherine Harris (R), Secretary of State
The Capitol, PL-02, Tallahassee, FL 32399-0250
(850) 414-5500
E-mail: secretary@mail.dos.state.fl.us

Office of the Attorney General
http://legal.firn.edu/
Main phone: (850) 487-1963
Main fax: (850) 487-2564

Robert A. Butterworth (D), Attorney General
The Capitol, Tallahassee, FL 32399-1050

State of Florida

Capital: Tallahassee, since 1823
Founded: 1819, Florida Territory acquired from Spain; also previously British
Statehood: March 3, 1845 (27th state)
Constitution adopted: 1969
Area: 53,937 sq. mi. (ranks 26th)
Population: 14,915,980 (1998 est.; ranks 4th)
Largest cities: (1998 est.) Jacksonville (693,630); Miami (368,624); Tampa (289,156); St. Petersburg (236,029); Hialeah (211,392)
Counties: 67, Most populous: (1998 est.) Miami-Dade (2,152,437); Broward (1,503,407); Palm Beach (1,032,625); Hillsborough (925,277); Pinellas (878,231)
U.S. Congress: Bob Graham (D), Connie Mack III (R); 23 Representatives
Nickname(s): Sunshine State
Motto: In God we trust
Song: "The Suwanee River (Old Folks at Home)"
Bird: Mockingbird
Tree: Sabal palm
Flower: Orange Blossom
State fair: at Tampa, mid-Feb.
Former capital(s): Pensacola, St. Augustine

Office of the Treasurer
http://www.doi.state.fl.us
General e-mail: doi@doi.state.fl.us
Main phone: (850) 922-3100
Main fax: (850) 488-6581

Bill Nelson (D), Treasurer, Insurance Commissioner, and Fire Marshal
200 E. Gaines St., Tallahassee, FL 32301
(850) 922-3100, ext. 2850
E-mail: nelson@doi.state.fl.us

Office of the Auditor General
http://www.state.fl.us/audgen/
General e-mail: flaudgen@aud.st.fl.us
Main phone: (850) 488-5534
Main fax: (850) 488-6975

William O. Monroe, Auditor General
Pepper Bldg., 111 W. Madison St., #G-74, Tallahassee,
FL 32399-1450
(850) 487-9175

Military Affairs Dept.
http://www.dma.state.fl.us/
Main phone: (904) 823-0160
Main fax: (904) 823-0125
Mailing address: P.O. Box 1008, St. Augustine, FL
32085-1008

Ronald O. Harrison, Adjutant General
St. Francis Barracks, St. Augustine, FL 32085-1008
(904) 823-0100

Agencies

Administrative Services Division
Main phone: (850) 488-3963
Main fax: (850) 922-0312
Mailing address: P.O. Box 13300, Tallahassee, FL
32308

Hal Lench, Director
The Capitol, #1901, Tallahassee, FL 32399-0250

Agriculture and Consumer Services Dept.
Main phone: (850) 487-2785
Main fax: (850) 922-6967

Bob Crawford (D), Commissioner
The Capitol, Plaza Level, Tallahassee, FL 32399-0810
(850) 488-3022; *Fax:* (850) 488-7585

Forestry Division
http://www.fl-dof.com/
General e-mail: harbinl@doacs.state.fl.us
Main phone: (850) 488-4274
Main fax: (850) 488-0863

Earl Peterson, Director
3125 Conner Blvd., #228, Tallahassee, FL 32399-
1650
(850) 922-0135
E-mail: peterse@doacs.state.fl.us

Liquefied Petroleum Gas Inspections Bureau
http://doacs.state.fl.us/lpgas
Main phone: (850) 921-8001
Main fax: (850) 921-8079

Vicki O'Neil, Chief
3125 Conner Blvd., Tallahassee, FL 32399-1650
(301) 921-4944s

Alcoholic Beverages and Tobacco Divison
http://www.state.fl.us/dbpr/html/abt/abtpage.html
General e-mail: abt_all@mail.dbpr.state.fl.us
Main phone: (850) 488-3227
Main fax: (850) 922-5175

Joseph R. Martelli, Director
Northwood Center, 1940 N. Monroe St., Tallahassee,
FL 32399-1000

Archives and Records Management Bureau
http://www.dos.state.fl.us/dlis/barm/fsa.html
General e-mail: barm@mail.dos.state.fl.us
Main phone: (850) 487-2073
Main fax: (850) 488-4894

James Berberich, Chief
500 S. Burrough St., R. A. Gray Bldg., #101,
Tallahassee, FL 32399-0250
E-mail: jberberich@mail.dos.state.fl.us

Banking and Finance Dept.
http://www.dbf.state.fl.us/
General e-mail: dbf@mail.dbf.state.fl.us
Main phone: (850) 410-9286
Main fax: (850) 410-9026
Consumer hotline: (800) 848-3792
TTY: (850) 921-8377

Robert F. Milligan (R), Comptroller
101 E. Gaines St., Tallahassee, FL 32399-0350
(850) 410-9370; *Fax:* (850) 410-9620

Children and Families Dept.
http://www.state.fl.us/cf_web/
General e-mail: http://www.state.fl.us/cf_web/
contacts.html
Main phone: (850) 487-1111
Main fax: (850) 922-2993

Kathleen A. Kennedy, Secretary
1317 Winewood Blvd., Tallahassee, FL 32399-0700

Mental Health Division
http://www.state.fl.us/cf_web/adm/
Main phone: (850) 488-8304
Main fax: (850) 487-2239

John Bryant, Assistant Secretary
1317 Winewood Blvd., Tallahassee, FL 32399-
0700
(850) 413-0936

Civil Rights Division
Main phone: (954) 712-4600
Main fax: (954) 712-4826

Gregory Durden, Director
Autonation Tower, 110 S.E. 6th St., 10th Fl., Fort
Lauderdale, FL 33301-5000

Construction Industry Licensing Board
http://www.dbpr.state.fl.us
Main phone: (904) 727-6530
Main fax: (904) 727-3679

Rodney Hurst, Executive Director
7960 Arlington Expressway, Bldg. 3, #300,
  Jacksonville, FL 32311
(904) 727-3689; *Fax:* (904) 727-3677
E-mail: rhurst@mail.dbpr.state.fl.us

Corrections Dept.
http://www.dc.state.fl.us/
General e-mail:
  buchanan.debra@mail.dc.state.fl.us
Main phone: (850) 488-5021
Main fax: (850) 488-4534
Toll free: (877) 884-2846

Michael W. Moore, Secretary
2601 Blairstone Rd., Tallahassee, FL 32399-2500
(850) 488-7480; *Fax:* (850) 922-2848
E-mail: moore.michael@dc.state.fl.us

Cultural Affairs Division
http://www.dos.state.fl.us
Main phone: (850) 487-2980
Main fax: (850) 922-5259
TTY: (850) 488-5779

Peg Richardson, Director
The Capitol, 1001 Desoto Park Dr., Tallahassee, FL
  32399-0250
E-mail: PRichardson@mail.dos.state.fl.us

Education Dept.
http://www.firn.edu/doe
Main phone: (850) 487-1785
Main fax: (850) 413-0378

Tom Gallagher (R), Commissioner
The Capitol, PL-08, Tallahassee, FL 32399
E-mail: gallagt@mail.doe.state.fl.us

Postsecondary Education Planning Commission
Main phone: (850) 488-7894
Main fax: (850) 922-5388

William B. Proctor, Executive Director
325 W. Gaines, Tallahassee, FL 32399-0400
E-mail: proctob@mail.doe.state.fl.us

Elder Affairs Dept.
http://fcn.state.fl.us/doea/doea.html
General e-mail: information@elderaffairs.org
Main phone: (850) 414-2000
Main fax: (850) 414-2004
Toll free: (800) 963-5337
TTY: (850) 414-2001

Gema G. Hernandez, Secretary
4040 Esplanade Way, Tallahassee, FL 32399-7000
E-mail: hernandezg@elderaffairs.org

Emergency Management Office
http://www.floridadisaster.org
General e-mail: craig.fugate@dca.state.fl.us
Main phone: (850) 413-9900
Main fax: (850) 488-7841
Toll free: (800) 320-0519
TTY: (800) 226-4329

Joseph F. Myers, Director
2555 Shumard Oak Blvd., Tallahassee, FL 32399-2100
(850) 413-9969
E-mail: joe.myers@dca.state.fl.us

Environmental Protection Dept.
http://www.dep.state.fl.us
Main phone: (850) 488-1073
Main fax: (850) 921-6227

David B. Struhs, Secretary
3900 Commonwealth Blvd., MS 45, Tallahassee, FL
  32399-3000
(850) 488-1554; *Fax:* (850) 488-7093
E-mail: david.struhs@dep.state.fl.us

Recreation and Parks Division
http://www.dep.state.fl.us/parks
Main phone: (850) 488-6131
Main fax: (850) 488-8442

Fran Mainella, Director
3900 Commonwealth Blvd., Tallahassee, FL
  32399-3000

Water Resource Division
Main phone: (850) 487-1855
Main fax: (850) 487-3618

Mimi Drew, Director
2600 Blair Stone Rd., #272, Tallahassee, FL
  32399-2400

Ethics Commission
http://www.ethic.state.fl.us
Main phone: (850) 488-7864
Main fax: (850) 488-3077
Mailing address: P.O. Drawer 15709, Tallahassee,
  FL 32317-5709

Bonnie J. Williams, Executive Director
2822 Remington Green, #101, Tallahassee, FL 32308

Fire Marshal Division
Main phone: (850) 922-3170 x3601
Main fax: (850) 922-1235
Toll free: (800) 638-3473
Mailing address: 200 E. Gaines St., Tallahassee,
  FL 32399-0300

Charles Clark, Director
The Capitol PL-11, 325 John Knox Rd., Tallahassee,
  FL 32303
E-mail: clarkc@doi.state.fl.us

Game and Fresh Water Fish Commission

http://www.state.fl.us/fwc
General e-mail: gfcmail@gfc.state.fl.us
Main phone: (850) 488-4676
Main fax: (850) 488-6988
TTY: (850) 488-9542

Allan L. Egbert, Executive Director
620 S. Meridian St., Tallahassee, FL 32399-1600
(850) 487-3796

Health Care Administration Agency

http://www.fdhc.state.fl.us/
General e-mail: infocentral@fdhc.state.fl.us
Main phone: (850) 488-1295
Main fax: (850) 922-3802
Toll free: (888) 419-3456

Ruben J. King-Shaw Jr., Director
2727 Nahan Dr., Tallahassee, FL 32308-5403
(850) 922-3809; *Fax:* (850) 488-0043
E-mail: kingshaw@fdhc.state.fl.us

Health Dept.

http://www.doh.state.fl.us/
General e-mail: executive_office@doh.state.fl.us
Main phone: (850) 487-2945
Main fax: (850) 487-3729
Mailing address: 2020 Capital Circle S.E., Bin A07, Tallahassee, FL 32399-0700

Robert G. Brooks, Secretary
2585 Merchants Row Blvd., Tallahassee, FL 32399

Highway Safety and Motor Vehicles Dept.

http://www.hsmv.state.fl.us
Main phone: (850) 921-8961
Main fax: (850) 921-4476

Fred O. Dickinson III, Executive Director
Neil Kirkman Bldg., 2900 Apalachee Pkwy., MS 44, Tallahassee, FL 32399-0500
(850) 487-3112

Historical Resources Division

http://www.flheritage.com
Main phone: (850) 488-1480
Main fax: (850) 488-3353

James J. Miller, Director (Acting)
305 R. A. Gray Bldg., 500 S. Burrough St., Tallahassee, FL 32399-0250
E-mail: jmiller@mail.dos.state.fl.us

Insurance Dept.

http://www.doi.state.fl.us/
Main phone: (850) 413-4902
Main fax: (850) 488-7265

Bill Nelson, Insurance Commissioner
The Capitol, PL-11, Tallahassee, FL 32399-0301

Higher Educational Institutions

Florida A&M University
http://www.famu.edu
Tallahassee, FL 32307
Main phone: (850) 599-3796

Florida Atlantic University
http://www.fau.edu
777 Glades Rd., P.O. Box 3091, Boca Raton, FL 33431-0091
Main phone: (800) 299-4328

Florida Gulf Coast University
http://www.fgcu.edu
10501 FGCU Blvd. South, Fort Meyers, FL 33965-6565
Main phone: (941) 590-1000

Florida International University
http://www.fiu.edu
S.W. 8th St. and 107th Ave., Miami, FL 33199
Main phone: (305) 348-2000

Florida State University
http://www.fsu.edu
Tallahassee, FL 32306-2400
Main phone: (850) 644-6200
Branches: Panama City, Sarasota, Republic of Panama

Troy State University Florida Region
http://www.tsufl.edu
81 Beal Pkwy. S.E., Fort Walton Beach, FL 32549
Main phone: (850) 244-7414

University of Central Florida
http://www.ucf.edu
4000 Central Florida Blvd., Orlando, FL 32816
Main phone: (407) 823-2000

University of Florida
http://www.ufl.edu
P.O. Box 114000, Gainesville, FL 32611-4000
Main phone: (352) 392-3261

University of North Florida
http://www.unf.edu
4567 St. Johns Bluff Rd. South, Jacksonville, FL 32224
Main phone: (904) 620-1000

University of Sarasota
http://www.sarasota.edu
5250 17th St., Sarasota, FL 34235

---

(850) 488-2800; *Fax:* (850) 488-6581
E-mail: cabaff@doi.state.fl.us

Juvenile Justice Dept.

http://www.djj.state.fl.us/

Main phone: (850) 488-1850
Main fax: (850) 922-2992

William Bankhead, Secretary
Knight Bldg., 2737 Centerview Dr., Tallahassee, FL
32399-3100
(850) 921-0904

Labor and Employment Security Dept.
http://www.state.fl.us/dles
Main phone: (850) 488-4398
Main fax: (850) 488-8930

Mary B. Hooks, Secretary
303 Hartman Bldg., 2012 Capital Circle S.E.,
Tallahassee, FL 32399-2152
(850) 922-7021
E-mail: mary_b_hooks@fdles.state.fl.us

Workers Compensation Division
http://www.wc.les.state.fl.us/DWC/
Main phone: (850) 488-2514
Main fax: (850) 922-6779

Charles Williams, Director
300 Forrest Bldg., 2728 Centerview Dr.,
Tallahassee, FL 32399-0680
E-mail: WilliaC5@wcpost.fdles.state.fl.us

Law Enforcement Dept.
http://www.fdle.state.fl.us
Main phone: (850) 410-7000
Main fax: (850) 410-7022
TTY: (850) 488-6085
Mailing address: P.O. Box 1489, Tallahassee, FL
32302

James T. (Tim) Moore, Commissioner
2331 Phillips Rd., Tallahassee, FL 32308
(850) 410-7001

Criminal Justice Information Program
http://www.fdle.state.fl.us
Main phone: (850) 410-7100
Main fax: (850) 410-7125

Donna Uzzell, Director
2331 Phillips Rd., Tallahassee, FL 32308

Library and Information Services Division
http://dlis.dos.state.fl.us/fgils
Main phone: (850) 487-2651
Main fax: (850) 488-2746

Barratt Wilkins, Director
R. A. Gray Bldg., Tallahassee, FL 32399-0250

Lottery Dept.
http://www.flalottery.com
General e-mail: asklott@dol.state.fl.us
Main phone: (850) 487-7777
Main fax: (850) 487-4541

Frequently Called Numbers

Tourism: (850) 488-5607; 1-888-7FLA-USA;
http://www.fla.usa.com
Library: (850) 487-2651;
http://dlis.dos.state.fl.us/fgils
Vital Statistics: (904) 359-6911
Tax/Revenue: (850)488-5050; http://
sun6.dms.state.fl.us/dor/
Motor Vehicles: (850) 921-8961;
http://www.hsmv.state.fl.us
State Police/Highway Patrol: (850) 410-7000;
http://www.fdle.state.fl.us
Unemployment: (850) 921-3893;
http://www.fdles.state.fl.us/uc/
General Election Information: (850)
488-7690; http://election.dos.state.fl.us
Consumer Affairs: (850) 487-2785;
http://doacs.state.fl.us
Hazardous Materials: (850) 488-0300

Mailing address: Capitol Complex, Tallahassee, FL
32399-4002

David Griffin, Secretary (Interim)
250 Marriott Dr., Tallahassee, FL 32301
(850) 487-7728

Parole Commission
Main phone: (850) 488-3417
Main fax: (850) 414-1915
TTY: (800) 955-8771

Jimmie L. Henry, Chair
Bldg. C, 2601 Blairstone Rd., Tallahassee, FL 32399-
2450
(850) 487-1980
E-mail: jimmiehenry@fpc.state.fl.us

Prosecution Office
http://legal.firn.edu.swp
Main phone: (850) 414-3700
Main fax: (850) 922-6191
Mailing address: The Capitol, PL-01, Tallahassee,
FL 32399-1050

Melanie A. Hines, Statewide Prosecuter
107 W. Gaines St., Collins Bldg., #523, Tallahassee,
FL 32301
E-mail: melanie_hines@oag.state.fl.us

Public Counsel's Office
Main phone: (850) 488-9330
Main fax: (850) 488-4491
Toll free: (800) 342-0222

Jack Shreve, Public Counsel
111 W. Madison St., #812, Tallahassee, FL 32399-
6588
E-mail: shreve.jack@leg.state.fl.us

Public Service Commission
http://www.seri.net/psc
Main phone: (850) 413-6860
Main fax: (850) 413-6861
Toll free: (800) 342-3552

Bill Talbott, Executive Director
2540 Shumard Oak Blvd., Tallahassee, FL 32399-0850
(850) 413-6055
E-mail: btalbott@psc.state.fl.us

Real Estate Division
http://www.state.fl.us/dbpr/html/re
Main phone: (407) 245-0800
Main fax: (407) 317-7245

Herbert S. Fecker Jr., Director
400 W. Robinson St., #N-308, Orlando, FL 32801-
1772
(407) 481-5662

Retirement Division
http://www.dof.state.fl.us/fgill/retirement
General e-mail: Retired@frs.state.fl.us
Main phone: (850) 488-0294
Main fax: (850) 488-5290
Toll free: (800) 955-8771
TTY: (800) 955-8771

A. J. McMullian III, Director
Cedars Executive Center, 2639 N. Monroe St., Bldg.
C, Tallahassee, FL 32399-1560
(850) 488-5540
E-mail: mcmullian_a@frs.state.fl.us

Revenue Dept.
http://sun6.dms.state.fl.us/dor/
Main phone: (850) 488-5050
Main fax: (850) 488-0024
Toll free: (800) 622-5437

L. H. Fuchs, Executive Director
104 Carlton Bldg., 5050 W. Tennessee St., #104,
Tallahassee, FL 32399-0100

State Fair
http://www.fl-ag.com/statefair/
Main phone: (813) 627-FAIR
Main fax: (813) 740-3505
Toll free: (800) 345-FAIR
Mailing address: P.O. Box 11766, Tampa, FL
33680

Rick Vymlatil, Executive Director
4800 U.S. Hwy. 301 N., Tampa, FL 33610

Transportation Dept.
http://www.dot.state.fl.us/
General e-mail: olivia.chase@dot.state.fl.us
Main phone: (850) 414-5300
Main fax: (850) 488-5526

Thomas F. Barry Jr., Secretary
605 Suwannee St., #580, Tallahassee, FL 32399-0450
(850) 414-5205; *Fax:* (850) 410-5494

Aviation Office
http://www.dot.state.fl.us/aviation
Main phone: (850) 414-4500
Main fax: (850) 922-4942

Bill Ashbaker, State Aviation Manager
605 Suwannee St., #14S-46, Tallahassee, FL
32399-0450
E-mail: bj.ashbaker@dot.state.fl.us

Veterans Affairs Dept.
http://www.state.fl.us/fdva/
General e-mail: fdvamcohe@vba.va.gov
Main phone: (727) 319-7400
Main fax: (727) 319-7780
Toll free: (800) 827-1000 x7440
Mailing address: P.O. Box 31003, St. Petersburg,
FL 33731

Robin L. Higgins, Executive Director
Kroger Center 2540, Executive Center West, Douglas
Bldg., #100, St. Petersburg, FL 32301
(850) 487-1533; *Fax:* (850) 488-5698
E-mail: higginsr@fdva.state.fl.us

Visit Florida
http://www.fla.usa.com
Main phone: (850) 488-5607
Main fax: (850) 224-9589
Travel information: (888) 7FLAUSA

Boards and Licensing

Accountancy, (352) 955-2165
Architects, (850) 488-6685
Child Care, (850) 488-4900
Contractors, (904) 727-6530,
http://www.dbpr.state.fl.us
Cosmetology, (850) 488-5702
Business and Professional Regulation Dept.,
(850) 487-2252
Medical Examiners, (850)
Nursing, (850) 858-6940
Pharmacy, (850) 488-0595
Real Estate Appraisers, (850) 245-0800

Mailing address: P.O. Box 31003, St. Petersburg, FL 33731

Austin Mott, President
661 E. Jefferson St., #300, Tallahassee, FL 32301

Florida Legislature
The Capitol
Tallahassee, FL 32399
General information: (850) 488-4371
Bill status: (850) 488-4371
http://www.leg.state.fl.us

Senate
Address: 404 S. Monroe St., Tallahassee, FL 32399-1100
General information: (850) 487-5270
Fax: (850) 487-5174

Toni Jennings (R), President
Senate Office Bldg., 404 S. Monroe St., #409, Tallahassee, FL 32399-1100
(850) 487-5229
E-mail: jennings.toni.web@leg.state.fl.us
http://www.leg.state.fl.us/senate/members/s09/index.html

William G. (Doc) Myers (R), President Pro Tempore
Senate Office Bldg., 404 S. Monroe St., #402, Tallahassee, FL 32399-1100
(850) 487-5088
E-mail: myers.william.web@leg.state.fl.us
http://www.leg.state.fl.us/senate/members/s27/index.html

Jack Latvala (R), Republican Leader
Senate Office Bldg., 404 S. Monroe St., #300, Tallahassee, FL 32399-1100
(850) 487-5062
E-mail: latvala.jack.web@leg.state.fl.us
http://www.leg.state.fl.us/senate/members/s19/index.html

Buddy Dyer (D), Democratic Leader
Senate Office Bldg., 404 S. Monroe St., #200, Tallahassee, FL 32399-1100
(850) 487-5190
E-mail: dyer.buddy.web@leg.state.fl.us
http://www.leg.state.fl.us/senate/members/s14/index.html

Faye W. Blanton, Secretary
Senate Office Bldg., 404 S. Monroe St., Tallahassee, FL 32399-1100
(850) 487-5270; *Fax:* (850) 487-5174

Laws
Sales tax: 6%
Income tax: None
State minimum wage: None (Federal is $5.15)
Marriage age: 18
First-cousin marriage: Permitted
Drinking age: 21
State control of liquor sales: No
Blood alcohol for DWI: 0.08%
Driving age: 18
Speed limit: 70 mph
Permit to buy handguns: No, but 3-day wait
Minimum age to possess handguns: 18
Minimum age to possess rifles, shotguns: 16
State lottery: Yes
Casinos: No
Pari-mutuel betting: Horse and dog racing; jai alai
Death penalty: Yes
3 strikes minimum sentence: Life (3rd serious felony)
Hate crimes law: Yes
Gay employment non-discrimination: No
Official language(s): English
Term limits: Governor (8 yrs.); state legislators (8 yrs.)
State laws are complex and subject to change; this information is not intended as legal advice. For an explanation of this information, see p. x.

House
Address: Florida Capitol, 402 S. Monroe St., Tallahassee, FL 32399-1300
General information: (850) 488-2812 (Library)

John Thrasher (R), Speaker of the House
Florida Capitol, 402 S. Monroe St., #420, Tallahassee, FL 32399-1300
(850) 488-1450
E-mail: thrasher.john@leg.state.fl.us
http://www.leg.state.fl.us/house/members/h19.htm

Dennis L. Jones (R), Speaker Pro Tempore
Florida Capitol, 402 S. Monroe St., #319, Tallahassee, FL 32399-1300
(850) 488-9960
E-mail: jones.dennis@leg.state.fl.us
http://www.leg.state.fl.us/house/members/h54.html

Jerry Louis Maygarden (R), Majority Leader
Florida Capitol, 402 S. Monroe St., #322, Tallahassee, FL 32399-1300
(850) 488-8278

E-mail: JMaygarden@aol.com
http://www.leg.state.fl.us/house/members/h2.html

Lesley (Les) Miller Jr. (D), Democratic Leader
Florida Capitol, 402 S. Monroe St., #316, Tallahassee,
FL 32399-1300
(850) 488-5432
E-mail: miller.lesley.web@leg.state.fl.us
http://www.leg.state.fl.us/house/members/h59.html

John B. Phelps, Clerk
Florida Capitol, 402 S. Monroe St., Tallahassee, FL
32399-1300
(850) 488-1157; *Fax:* (850) 488-9707

Florida Judiciary

Supreme Court Bldg.
500 S. Duval St.
Tallahassee, FL 32399-1927
http://www.flcourts.org

Supreme Court
http://www.flcourts.org/pubinfo/sct.htm

Debbie Causseaux, Clerk (Acting)
Supreme Court Bldg., 500 S. Duval St., Tallahassee,
FL 32399-1927
(850) 488-0125

Justices
Composition: 7 justices
Selection Method: nonpartisan election;
  vacancies filled by governor; appointees must
  stand for retention in the first general election
  held at least a year after appointment
Length of term: 6 years

Major B. Harding, Chief Justice, (850) 488-2361
Harry Lee Anstead, Justice, (850) 488-2281
Fred R. Lewis, Justice, (850) 488-0007
Barbara J. Pariente, Justice, (850) 488-8421
Peggy A. Quince, Judge, (850) 922-5624
Leander J. Shaw Jr., Justice, (850) 488-0208
Charles T. Wells, Justice, (850) 921-1096

Office of the State Courts Administrator
http://www.flcourts.org/osca/divisions/index.html
Main phone: (850) 922-5081
Main fax: (850) 488-0156
General e-mail: osca@flcourts.org

Kenneth Palmer, State Courts Administrator
Supreme Court Bldg., 500 S. Duval St., Tallahassee,
FL 32399-1900

Supreme Court Library
Main phone: (850) 922-5520
Main fax: (850) 922-5219

Joan Cannon, Librarian
Supreme Court Bldg., 500 S. Duval St., Tallahassee,
FL 32399-1926

Legislative and Political Party Information Resources

House membership: http://www.leg.state.fl.us/house/members/index.html
Senate membership: http://www.leg.state.fl.us/senate/members/index.html
Committees: Senate: http://www.leg.state.fl.us/senate/committees/index.html; *House:* http://
  www.leg.state.fl.us/house/committees/index.html
Legislative process: http://www.leg.state.fl.us/citizen/documents/Howibl.pdf
Current session information: http://www.leg.state.fl.us/session/caljournal.html
Florida Democratic Party: http://www.florida-democrats.org
  P.O. Box 1758, Tallahassee, FL 32302; *Phone:* (850) 222-3411; *Fax:* (850) 222-0916
Florida Republican Party: http://www.rpof.org
  P.O. Box 311, Tallahassee, FL 32302; *Phone:* (850) 222-7920; *Fax:* (850) 681-0184; *E-mail:*
  info@rpof.org

Georgia

State Capitol
Atlanta, GA 30334
Public information: (404) 656-2000
Fax: (404) 657-7332
http://www.state.ga.us

Office of the Governor
http://www.gagovernor.org
Main phone: (404) 656-1776
Main fax: (404) 657-7332
TTY: (404) 651-7700

Roy E. Barnes (D), Governor
State Capitol, #203, Atlanta, GA 30334

Bobby Kahn, Chief of Staff
State Capitol, #201, Atlanta, GA 30334
(404) 651-7715; *Fax:* (404) 656-5948
E-mail: bobby@gov.state.ga.us

Joselyn Butler, Press Secretary
State Capitol, #203, Atlanta, GA 30334
(404) 656-1776; *Fax:* (404) 657-7332

Office of the Lieutenant Governor
http://www.ganet.org/ltgov
Main phone: (404) 656-5030
Main fax: (404) 656-6739

Mark Taylor (D), Lieutenant Governor
State Capitol, #240, Atlanta, GA 30334

Constituent Services
Main phone: (404) 656-5030
Main fax: (404) 656-6739

Sid Linton, Director
240 State Capitol, Atlanta, GA 30334
E-mail: slinton@legis.state.ga.us

Office of the Secretary of State
http://www.sos.state.ga.us/
General e-mail: sosweb@sos.state.ga.us
Main phone: (404) 656-2881
Main fax: (404) 656-0513

Cathy Cox (D), Secretary of State
State Capitol, #214, Atlanta, GA 30334

Office of the Attorney General
http://www.ganet.org/ago/
Main phone: (404) 656-3300
Main fax: (404) 657-8733

Thurbert E. Baker (D), Attorney General
40 Capitol Square S.W., Atlanta, GA 30334-1300

State of Georgia

Capital: Atlanta, since 1868
Founded: 1732, as British colony
Statehood: January 2, 1788 (4th state)
Constitution adopted: 1977
Area: 57,919 sq. mi. (ranks 21st)
Population: 7,642,207 (1998 est.; ranks 10th)
Largest cities: (1998 est.) Atlanta (403,819); Augusta (187,689); Columbus (182,828); Savannah (131,674); Macon (114,336)
Counties: 159, Most populous: (1998 est.) Fulton (739,367); De Kalb (593,850); Cobb (566,203); Gwinnett (522,095); Chatham (225,543)
U.S. Congress: Max Cleland (D), Paul Coverdell (R); 11 Representatives
Nickname(s): Peach State, Empire State of the South
Motto: Wisdom, justice, and moderation
Song: "Georgia on My Mind"
Bird: Brown thrasher
Tree: Live oak
Flower: Cherokee rose
State fair: at Macon, mid-Oct.
Former capital(s): Savannah, Augusta, Louisville, Milledgeville

Office of the Treasury and Fiscal Services Office
http://www2.state.ga.us/otfs/index.htm
Main phone: (404) 656-2168
Main fax: (404) 656-9048

W. Daniel Ebersole, Director
200 Piedmont Ave., 1202 W. Tower, #7028, Atlanta, GA 30334

Office of the State Auditor
http://www2.state.ga.us/Departments/AUDIT/
Main phone: (404) 656-2180
Main fax: (404) 651-9448

Russell W. Hinton, State Auditor
254 Washington St., #214, Atlanta, GA 30334-8400
(404) 656-2174
E-mail: hintonrw@mail.audits.state.ga.us

Agencies

Adminstrative Services Dept.
http://www.doas.state.ga.us
Main phone: (404) 656-2000
Main fax: (404) 651-9595

Dana R. Russell, Commissioner
200 Piedmont Ave., #1804, Atlanta, GA 30334
(404) 656-5514

Agriculture Dept.
http://www.agr.state.ga.us/
General e-mail: info@agr.state.ga.us
Main phone: (404) 656-3645
Main fax: (404) 656-9380
TTY: (404) 657-8387

Thomas T. Irvin (D), Commissioner
Agriculture Bldg., Capitol Square, #204, Atlanta, GA 30334
(404) 656-3600; *Fax:* (404) 651-8206

Architects Board
http://www.sos.state.ga.us/ebd
Main phone: (912) 207-1400
Main fax: (912) 207-1410

Barbara Kitchens, Executive Director
237 Coliseum Dr., Macon, GA 31217

Archives and History Dept.
http://www.sos.state.ga.us/archives/
Main phone: (404) 656-2393
Main fax: (404) 657-8427

Edward Weldon, Director
330 Capitol Ave S.E., Atlanta, GA 30334
(404) 656-2358

Arts Council
http://www.ganet.org/georgia-arts/
Main phone: (404) 685-2787
Main fax: (404) 685-2788
TTY: (404) 685-2799

Vacant, Director
260 14th St. N.W., #401, Atlanta, GA 30318
(404) 685-2785

Banking and Finance Dept.
http://www.state.ga.us/dbf/
Main phone: (770) 986-1633
Main fax: (770) 986-1654

Steven D. Bridges, Commissioner
2990 Brandywine Rd., #200, Atlanta, GA 30341-5565

Community Affairs Dept.
http://www.dca.state.ga.us
Main phone: (404) 679-4940
Main fax: (404) 679-0589
Toll free: (800) 359-4663

Jim Higdon, Commissioner
60 Executive Park South, Atlanta, GA 30329-2231
E-mail: jhigdon@dca.state.ga.us

Housing Finance Division
http://www.dca.state.ga.us/housing/index.html
Main phone: (404) 679-0607
Main fax: (404) 679-4844

Robin Meyer, Director
60 Executive Park South, Atlanta, GA 30329-2231
E-mail: rmeyer@dca.state.ga.us

Community Health Dept.
http://www.state.ga.us/gch
Main phone: (404) 656-4507
Main fax: (404) 651-6880

Russell Toad, Commissioner
2 Peachtree St. N.W., 40th Fl., Atlanta, GA 30303
Fax: (404) 657-5238

Medical Assistance Division
Main phone: (404) 656-7645
Main fax: (404) 656-6880

Gary B. Redding, Director
2 Peachtree St. N.W., 40th Fl., Atlanta, GA 30303
E-mail: gredding@dma.state.ga.us

Consumer Affairs Office
http://www2.state.ga.us/GaOCA/
Main phone: (404) 651-8600
Main fax: (404) 651-9018
Toll free: (800) 869-1123

Barry W. Reid, Administrator
2 Martin Luther King Jr. Dr. S.E., #356, Atlanta, GA 30334

Corrections Dept.
http://www.dcor.state.ga.us/
Main phone: (404) 656-4593
Main fax: (404) 656-6818
TTY: (404) 656-5467

Jim Wetherington, Commissioner
East Tower, 2 Martin Luther King Dr. S.E., #756, Atlanta, GA 30334-4900
(404) 656-6002

Criminal Justice Coordinating Council
http://www.ganet.org/cjcc
Main phone: (404) 559-4949
Main fax: (404) 559-4960
TTY: (404) 559-4177

Martha M. Gilland, Director
503 Oak Pl., #540, Atlanta, GA 30349

Defense Dept.

http://www.dod.state.ga.us/
General e-mail: webmaster@dod.state.ga.us
Main phone: (404) 624-6000
Main fax: (404) 624-6097
Mailing address: P.O. Box 17965, Atlanta, GA 30316-0965

David Poythress Jr., Adjutant General
935 E. Confederate Ave. S.E., Atlanta, GA 30316-0965
(404) 624-6001

Developmental Disabilities Council

http://www.ga-ddcouncil.org/
Main phone: (404) 657-2126
Main fax: (404) 657-2132
Toll free: (888) 275-4233
TTY: (404) 657-2133

Eric E. Jacobson, Executive Director
2 Peachtree St. N.W., #3-210, Atlanta, GA 30303-3142
E-mail: eej@ga-ddcouncil.org

Education Dept.

http://www.doe.k12.ga.us
General e-mail: webmaster@www.doe.k12.ga.us
Main phone: (404) 656-2800
Main fax: (404) 651-8737
TTY: (800) 255-0056

Linda C. Schrenko (R), State Superintendent of Schools
Twin Towers East, 205 Butler St. S.E., #2066, Atlanta, GA 30334-5001

Emergency Management Agency (GEMA)

http://www.state.ga.us/GEMA/
General e-mail: vbartlett@gema.state.ga.us
Main phone: (404) 635-7000
Main fax: (404) 635-7205
Toll free: (800) TRY-GEMA
Mailing address: P.O. Box 18055, Atlanta, GA 30316-0055

Gary McConnel, Director
935 E. Confederate Ave. S.E., Atlanta, GA 30316-0055

Employees Retirement System

General e-mail: dbthaxto@ers.state.ga.us
Main phone: (404) 352-6400
Main fax: (404) 352-6431
Toll free: (800) 805-4609

Rudolph Johnson, Director
Beta Bldg., 2 Northside 75 N.W., #300, Atlanta, GA 30318-7778
(404) 352-6411

Environmental Facilities Authority (GEFA)

http://www.gefa.org
General e-mail: gefa@mindspring.com

Main phone: (404) 656-0938
Main fax: (404) 656-6416

Paul Burks, Executive Director
100 Peachtree St. N.W., #2090, Atlanta, GA 30303
E-mail: pburks@gefa.org

Ethics Commission

http://rampages.onramp.net/~gaethics/
General e-mail: gaethics@onramp.net
Main phone: (770) 920-4385
Main fax: (770) 920-4395

C. Theodore Lee, Executive Secretary
8440 Courthouse Square East, Douglasville, GA 30134

Financing and Investment Commission

http://ganet.org/gsfic
Main phone: (404) 656-3400
Main fax: (404) 656-6009

John R. Butler Jr., Executive Secretary
West Tower, 2 Martin Luther King Dr. S.E., #1002, Atlanta, GA 30334
(404) 656-3401
E-mail: jrbutler@gsfic.state.ga.us

Forestry Commission

http://www.gfc.state.ga.us/
General e-mail: gastfor@gfc.state.ga.us
Main phone: (912) 751-3500
Main fax: (912) 751-3465
Toll free: (800) GATREES
Mailing address: P.O. Box 819, Macon, GA 31202-0819

J. Frederick Allen, Director
5645 Riggins Mills Rd., Dry Branch, GA 31202-9699
(912) 751-3480
E-mail: fallen@gfc.state.ga.us

Health Planning Agency

http://www.ganet.org/gch/shpa/
Main phone: (404) 656-0655
Main fax: (404) 656-0654

Pamela Sturdivant Stephenson, Executive Director
2 Peachtree St. N.W., 1 Park Tower, #34-262, Atlanta, GA 30303-3142
(404) 656-0710
E-mail: Pam@shpa.state.ga.us

Human Resources Dept.

http://www.dhr.state.ag.us
Main phone: (404) 656-5680
Main fax: (404) 651-8669
TTY: (404) 656-5757

Audrey W. Horne, Commissioner
2 Peachtree St. N.W., #29-250, Atlanta, GA
   30303-3142
(404) 651-6314
E-mail: awhorne@dhr.state.ga.us
Aging Division
http://www2.state.ga.us/departments/dhr/
   aging.html

Main phone: (404) 657-5258
Main fax: (404) 657-5285

Jeffrey A. Minor, Director
2 Peachtree St. N.W., #36-385, Atlanta, GA
   30303-3142
(404) 657-5252
E-mail: jaminor@dhr.state.ga.us

Higher Educational Institutions

Albany State College
http://argus.asurams.edu/asu/
   504 College Dr., Albany, GA 31705
   Main phone: (912) 430-4600

Armstrong Atlantic State University
http://www.armstrong.edu
   11935 Abercorn St., Savannah, GA 31419-1997
   Main phone: (912) 927-5277

Augusta State University
http://www.aug.edu
   Walton Way, Augusta, GA 30904
   Main phone: (800) 341-4373

Clayton College and State University
http://www.clayton.edu
   5900 N. Lee St., Morrow, GA 30260
   Main phone: (770) 961-3500

Columbus State University
http://www.colstate.edu
   4225 University Ave., Columbus, GA 31907-5645
   Main phone: (706) 568-2001

Fort Valley State University
http://www.fvsu.edu
   1005 State University Dr., Fort Valley, GA 31030-
   3298
   Main phone: (912) 825-6307

Georgia College and State University
http://www.gcsu.edu
   Campus Box 97, Milledgeville, GA 31061-0490
   Main phone: (912) 445-5004

Georgia Institute of Technology
http://www.gatech.edu
   225 North Ave. N.W., Atlanta, GA 30332-0320
   Main phone: (404) 894-2000

Georgia Southern University
http://www.gasou.edu
   P.O. Box 8024, Statesboro, GA 30460
   Main phone: (912) 681-5532

Georgia Southwestern State University
http://www.gsw.edu
   800 Wheatley St., Americus, GA 31709
   Main phone: (912) 928-1273

Georgia State University
http://www.gsu.edu
   University Plaza, Atlanta, GA 30303
   Main phone: (404) 651-2000

Kennesaw State University
http://www.kennesaw.edu
   1000 Chastain Rd., Kennesaw, GA 30144
   Main phone: (770) 423-6300

Macon State College
http://www.mc.peachnet.edu/
   100 College Station Dr., Macon, GA 31206-5144
   Main phone: (912) 471-2800

Medical College of Georgia
http://www.mcg.edu
   1120 15th St., Augusta, GA 30912
   Main phone: (706) 721-0211

North Georgia College and State University
http://www.ngc.peachnet.edu
   Dahlonega, GA 30533
   Main phone: (706) 864-1800

Savannah State University
http://www.savstate.edu
   P.O. Box 20209, Savannah, GA 31404
   Main phone: (800) 788-0478

Southern Polytechnic State University
http://www.sct.edu
   1100 S. Marietta Pkwy., Marietta, GA 30060
   Main phone: (770) 528-7222

State University of West Georgia
http://www.westga.edu
   1600 Maple St., Carrollton, GA 30118
   Main phone: (770) 836-6416

University of Georgia
http://www.uga.edu
   Athens, GA 30602
   Main phone: (706) 542-3000

Valdosta State University
http://www.valdosta.peachnet.edu
   1500 N. Patterson St., Valdosta, GA 31698
   Main phone: (800) 618-1878

Mental Health, Mental Retardation, and Substance Abuse Division
http://www2.state.ga.us/departments/dhr/
  mhmrsa.html
Main phone: (404) 657-2252
Main fax: (404) 657-1137

Joann Colwell Jr., Director (Acting)
2 Peachtree St. N.W., #22.224, Atlanta, GA
30303-3171

Industry, Trade, and Tourism Dept.
http://www.georgia.org/
Main phone: (404) 656-3545
Main fax: (404) 656-3567

Randolph B. Cardoza, Commissioner
285 Peachtree Center Ave. N.E., #1100, Atlanta, GA
30303
(404) 656-3556; *Fax:* (404) 651-8579
E-mail: rcardoza@georgia.org

Insurance and Fire Safety Commissioner Office
http://www.inscomm.state.ga.us/
Main phone: (404) 656-2056
Main fax: (404) 656-4030
TTY: (404) 656-4031

**John Oxendine (R), Insurance and Fire Safety
Commissioner**
West Tower, Floyd Bldg., 2 Martin Luther King Dr.
S.E., #704, Atlanta, GA 30334

Fire Marshal
http://www.inscomm.state.ga.us/
  inside.firemarshal.html
Main phone: (404) 656-2064
Main fax: (404) 657-6971

L. C. Cole, State Fire Marshal
2 Martin Luther King Jr. Dr. S.E., West Tower, 7th
Fl., Atlanta, GA 30334

Juvenile Justice Dept.
http://www.djj.state.ga.us
Main phone: (404) 657-2410
Main fax: (404) 657-2473

Orlando L. Martinez, Commissioner
2 Peachtree St. N.W., 5th Fl., Atlanta, GA 30303-3142
(404) 657-2400
E-mail: orlandomartinez@djj.state.ga.us

Labor Dept.
http://www.dol.state.ga.us/
Main phone: (404) 656-3011
Main fax: (404) 656-2683

Michael L. Thurmond (D), Commissioner
148 International Blvd. N.E., #600, Atlanta, GA
30303-1751
E-mail: commissioner@dol.state.ga.us

Lottery
http://www.galottery.com/
Main phone: (770) GA-LUCKY
Toll free: (800) GALUCKY
TTY: (800) 255-0056

Rebecca Paul, President
250 Williams St., INFORUM, #3000, Atlanta, GA
30303

Medical Examiners Board
http://www.state.ga.us/gcb/
Main phone: (404) 656-3913
Main fax: (404) 656-3723

Karen Mason, Director
2 Peachtree St. N.W., 6th Fl., Atlanta, GA 30303

Merit System of Personnel Administration
http://www.gms.state.ga.us
General e-mail: info@gms.state.ga.us
Main phone: (404) 656-2705
Main fax: (404) 656-5979
TTY: (404) 656-2922

Marjorie H. Young, Commissioner
West Tower, 200 Piedmont Ave., #502, Atlanta, GA
30334-5100

Natural Resources Dept.
http://www.ganet.org/dnr/
Main phone: (404) 656-3500
Main fax: (404) 656-0770

Lonice C. Barrett, Commissioner
205 Butler St. S.E., #1252, Atlanta, GA 30334
E-mail: lonice_barrett@mail.dnr.state.ga.us

Environmental Protection Division
http://www.ganet.org/dnr/environ/
Main phone: (404) 656-4713
Main fax: (404) 651-5778

Harold Reheis, Director
205 Butler St. S.E., #1152, Atlanta, GA 30334

Geological Survey
http://www.mail.dnr.state.ga.us/epd
Main phone: (404) 656-3214
Main fax: (404) 657-8379

William H. McLemore, State Geologist
19 Martin Luther King Jr. Dr., #400, Atlanta, GA
30334
E-mail: billmclemore@mail.dnr.state.ga.us/epd

Historic Preservation Division
http://www.ganet.org/dnr/histpres/
Main phone: (404) 656-2840
Main fax: (404) 651-8739

Frequently Called Numbers

Tourism: (404) 656-3545; 1-800-VISITGA;
http://www.georgia.org/
Library: (404) 982-3560;
http://www.public.lib.ga.us/
Board of Education: (404) 657-7410
Vital Statistics: (404) 656-4750;
http://www.ph.dhr.state.ga.us/org/
vitalrecords.faq.html
Tax/Revenue: (404) 656-4071;
http://www.state.ga.us/Departments/DOR
Motor Vehicles: (404) 362-6440;
http://www.ganet.org/dps/divisions.html
State Police/Highway Patrol: (404) 657-9300;
http://www.ganet.org/dps/statepat.html
Unemployment: (404) 656-3045;
http://www.dol.state.ga.us/ui/
General Election Information: (404)
656-2871; http://www.sos.state.ga.us/
elections/
Consumer Affairs: (404) 651-8600;
http://www2.state.ga.us/GaOCA/
Hazardous Materials: (404) 656-4713

Ray Luce, Director
500 The Healey Bldg., 57 Forsyth St. N.W.,
Atlanta, GA 30303
(404) 651-5061
E-mail: ray_luce@mail.dnr.state.ga.us

Parks, Recreation, and Historic Sites Division
http://www.ganet.org/dnr/parks/
Main phone: (404) 656-3530
Main fax: (404) 651-5871
Toll free: (800) 869-8420
TTY: (770) 389-7404

Burt Weerts, Director
205 Butler St. S.E., #1352-E, Atlanta, GA 30334
(404) 656-2770
E-mail: bweerts@mail.dnr.state.ga.us

Water Resources Branch
General e-mail: edp@mail.dnr.state.ga.us
Main phone: (404) 656-6328
Main fax: (404) 657-5002

Nolton G. Johnson, Chief
1166 East Floyd Tower, 205 Butler St. S.E., #1058,
Atlanta, GA 30334
(404) 651-5168; *Fax:* (404) 463-6432
E-mail: nolton_johnson@mail.dnr.state.ga.us

Wildlife Resources Division
http://www.ganet.org/dnr/wild/
Main phone: (770) 918-6400
Main fax: (706) 557-3030

David Waller, Director
2070 US Hwy. 278 S.E., Social Circle, GA
30025-4711
(770) 918-6401
E-mail: david_waller@mail.dnr.state.ga.us

Pardons and Parole Board
http://www.pap.state.ga.us
Main phone: (404) 656-2808
Main fax: (404) 651-8502

Walter S. Ray, Chair
East Tower, 2 Martin Luther King Dr. S.E., #458,
Atlanta, GA 30334
(404) 657-9451

Prosecuting Attorneys Council
http://www.ganet.org/pacg/
Main phone: (770) 438-2550
Main fax: (770) 438-6121

Joseph L. Chambers, Director
3200 Highlands Pkwy., #420, Smyrna, GA
30032-5192
E-mail: jchambers@ganet.org

Public Library Services
http://www.public.lib.ga.us/
General e-mail: webmaster@public.lib.ga.us
Main phone: (404) 982-3560
Main fax: (404) 982-3563

Roger Slater, Assistant Commissioner
1800 Century Plaza, #150, Atlanta, GA 30345
(404) 679-1606; *Fax:* (404) 679-1610
E-mail: rslater@dtae.org

Public Safety Dept.
http://www.ganet.org/dps
Main phone: (404) 657-9300
Mailing address: P.O. Box 1456, Atlanta, GA
30371-2303

Robert E. Hightower, Commissioner
959 E. Confederate Ave. S.E., Atlanta, GA 30371-2303
(404) 624-7710

Drivers License Division
http://www.ganet.org/dps/divisions.html
Main phone: (404) 624-7896
Mailing address: P.O. Box 1456, Atlanta, GA
30371-2303

Johnny Grimes, Director
959 E. Confederate Ave. S.E., Atlanta, GA 30371

State Patrol
http://www.ganet.org/dps/statepat.html
Main phone: (404) 657-9300

C. W. Starley, Adjutant
959 E. Confederate Ave. S.E., Atlanta, GA 30316

Public Service Commission
http://www.psc.state.ga.us
General e-mail: gpsc@psc.state.ga.us
Main phone: (404) 656-4501
Main fax: (404) 656-2341

Deborah K. Flannagan, Executive Director
47 Trinity Ave., Atlanta, GA 30334-5701

Public Television
http://www.gpb.org/gptv/gptv.htm
General e-mail: viewerservices@gpb.org
Main phone: (404) 685-2400
Main fax: (404) 685-2417
Toll free: (800) 222-6006

Claude Vickers, Executive Director
260 14th St. N.W., Atlanta, GA 30318
(404) 685-2410

Revenue Dept.
http://www.state.ga.us/Departments/DOR
Main phone: (404) 656-4071
Main fax: (404) 651-9490
TTY: (404) 656-3441

T. Jerry Jackson, Commissioner
270 Washington St. S.W., #410, Atlanta, GA 30334
(404) 656-4015
E-mail: jjackson@gw.rev.state.ga.us

Alcohol and Tobacco Tax Division
General e-mail: atdiv@rev.state.ga.us
Main phone: (404) 656-4252
Main fax: (404) 657-9690
Mailing address: P.O. Box 38368, Atlanta, GA 30334

Chet Bryant, Director
270 Washington St. S.W., #317, Atlanta, GA 30334
E-mail: cbryant@gw.rev.state.ga.us

Motor Vehicle Division
Main phone: (404) 362-6440
Main fax: (404) 362-6463
Mailing address: P.O. Box 740381, Atlanta, GA 30374-0381

Milt Dufford, Deputy Commissioner
270 Washington St. S.W., Atlanta, GA 30334

Soil and Water Conservation Commission
http://www.ganet.org/gswcc/
Main phone: (706) 542-3065
Main fax: (706) 542-4242

Mailing address: P.O. Box 8024, Athens, GA 30603

F. Graham Liles Jr., Executive Director
4310 Lexington Rd., Athens, GA 30605
E-mail: fliles@gwins.campuscwix.net

State Fair
http://www.mylink.net/~gsf/
General e-mail: sjscroggins@mindspring.com
Main phone: (912) 746-7184
Main fax: (912) 741-7232

Allen G. Freeman, Central City Park, Macon, GA 31208-4105
E-mail: gsf@mylink.net

Transportation Dept.
http://www.dot.state.ga.us/
General e-mail: webmaster@dot.state.ga.us
Main phone: (404) 656-5267
Main fax: (404) 656-3507

Wayne Shackelford, Commissioner
2 Capitol Square, Atlanta, GA 30334-1002
(404) 656-5206
E-mail: wayne.shakelfor@dot.state.ga.us

Air Transportation
Main phone: (404) 699-4483
Main fax: (404) 699-4486

David Carmichael, Director
4175 S. Airport Rd. S.W., Atlanta, GA 30336

University System of Georgia Board of Regents
http://www.peachnet.edu/
General e-mail:
chancellor@mail.regents.peachnet.edu
Main phone: (404) 656-2250
Main fax: (404) 651-9301

Kenneth W. Cannestra, Chair
270 Washington St. S.W., #7028, Atlanta, GA 30334
(404) 656-2022

Boards and Licensing

Accountancy, (912) 207-1400
Architects, (912) 207-1400
Child Care, (404) 657-5562
Contractors, (912) 207-1416
Cosmetology, (912) 207-1430
Engineers and Land Surveyors, (912) 207-1450
Medical Examiners, (404) 656-3913
Nursing, (912) 207-1440
Pharmacy, (912) 207-1686
Real Estate Appraisers, (404) 656-3916

Veterans Service Dept.
http://www.doas.state.ga.us/Departments/Veterans/
General e-mail: ga.vet.svc@mindspring.com
Main phone: (404) 656-2300
Main fax: (404) 656-7006

Pete Wheeler, Commissioner
Floyd Veterans Memorial Bldg., #E-970, Atlanta, GA
30334

Workers' Compensation Board
http://www.ganet.org/sbwc/
Main phone: (404) 656-3875
Main fax: (404) 651-7768
Toll free: (800) 533-0682

Carolyn C. Hall, Chair
270 Peachtree St. N.W., Atlanta, GA 30303-1299
(404) 656-2034

Georgia Legislature

State Capitol
Atlanta, GA 30334
General information: (404) 656-5000
http://www2.state.ga.us/Legis

Senate
General information: (404) 656-0028
Toll free: (800) 282-5803
Bill status: (404) 656-5040

Mark Taylor (D), President
State Capitol, #240, Atlanta, GA 30334
(404) 656-5030; *Fax:* (404) 656-6739
http://www2.state.ga.us/Legis/ltgov

Terrell Starr (D), President Pro Tempore
State Capitol, #321, Atlanta, GA 30334
(404) 656-7586; *Fax:* (404) 463-7781
http://www2.state.ga.us/Legis/1999_00/senate/
gass44.htm

Charles W. Walker (D), Majority Leader
State Capitol, #236, Atlanta, GA 30334
(404) 656-0400; *Fax:* (404) 651-5588
http://www2.state.ga.us/Legis/1999_00/senate/
gass22.htm

Richard O. Marable (D), Majority Whip
State Capitol, #420-C, Atlanta, GA 30334
(404) 656-5120; *Fax:* (404) 657-9728
http://www2.state.ga.us/Legis/1999_00/senate/
gass52.htm

Eric Johnson (R), Minority Leader
State Capitol, #121-B, Atlanta, GA 30334
(404) 656-5109; *Fax:* (404) 657-9887
E-mail: ejohnson@legis.state.ga.us

Laws

Sales tax: 4%
Income tax: 6%
State minimum wage:
Marriage age: 18
First-cousin marriage: Permitted
Drinking age: 21
State control of liquor sales: No
Blood alcohol for DWI: 0.10%
Driving age: 18
Speed limit: 70 mph
Permit to buy handguns: No
Minimum age to possess handguns: 18
Minimum age to possess rifles, shotguns:
    None
State lottery: Yes
Casinos: No
Pari-mutuel betting: No
Death penalty: Yes
3 strikes minimum sentence: Life, no parole
    (2nd serious violent felony)
Hate crimes law: No
Gay employment non-discrimination: No
Official language(s): English
Term limits: None

*State laws are complex and subject to
change; this information is not intended as
legal advice. For an explanation of this
information, see p. x.*

---

http://www2.state.ga.us/Legis/1999_00/senate/
gass01.htm

Frank Eldridge Jr., Secretary
State Capitol, Atlanta, GA 30334
(404) 656-5040; *Fax:* (404) 656-5043

House
General information: (404) 656-5082
Toll free: (800) 282-5800
Bill status: (404) 656-5015

Thomas B. Murphy (D), Speaker of the House
State Capitol, #332, Atlanta, GA 30334
(404) 656-5020
http://www2.state.ga.us/Legis/1999_00/house/
gash018.htm

Jack Connell (D), Speaker Pro Tempore
State Capitol, #340, Atlanta, GA 30334
(404) 656-5072
http://www2.state.ga.us/Legis/1999_00/house/
gash115.htm

Larry Walker (D), Majority Leader
State Capitol, #415, Atlanta, GA 30334
(404) 656-5024
http://www2.state.ga.us/Legis/1999_00/house/
   gash141.htm

Jimmy Skipper (D), Majority Whip
State Capitol, #415, Atlanta, GA 30334
(404) 656-5024
E-mail: jskipper@americus.americus.net
http://www2.state.ga.us/Legis/1999_00/house/
   gash137.htm

Robert (Bob) Irvin (R), Minority Leader
Legislative Office Bldg., #408, Atlanta, GA 30334
(404) 656-5058
http://www2.state.ga.us/Legis/1999_00/house/
   gash045.htm

Earl Ehrhart (R), Minority Whip
Legislative Office Bldg., #408, Atlanta, GA 30334
(404) 656-5058
E-mail: EAEH@FacilityGroup.com
http://www2.state.ga.us/Legis/1999_00/house/
   gash036.htm

Robert E. Rivers, Clerk
State Capitol, Atlanta, GA 30334
(404) 656-5015; *Fax:* (404) 651-6412

Georgia Judiciary

State Judicial Bldg.
244 Washington St. S.W.
Atlanta, GA 30334-5900

Supreme Court
http://www2.state.ga.us/courts/supreme/

Sherie M. Welch, Clerk
State Judicial Bldg., 244 Washington St. S.W., Atlanta,
   GA 30334-5900
(404) 656-3470; *Fax:* (404) 656-2253
E-mail: welchs@mindspring.com

Justices
Composition: 7 justices
Selection Method: nonpartisan election;
   vacancies filled by governor, but justice must
   stand for retention vote in next general election
Length of term: 6 years

Robert Benham, Chief Justice, (404) 656-3476
Norman S. Fletcher, Presiding Justice, (404) 656-3477
George H. Carley, Associate Justice, (404) 656-3471
P. Harris Hines, Associate Justice, (404) 656-3473
Carol W. Hunstein, Associate Justice, (404) 656-3475
Leah Ward Sears, Associate Justice, (404) 656-3474
Hugh P. Thompson, Associate Justice, (404) 656-3472

Administrative Office of the Courts
http://www2.state.ga.us/courts/aoc/
Main phone: (404) 656-5171
Main fax: (404) 651-6449

> **George Lange III, Director**
> State Judicial Bldg., 244 Washington St. S.W., Atlanta,
>   GA 30334-5900

State Law Library
Main phone: (404) 656-5171
Main fax: (404) 651-6449

> **Philleatra Gaylor, State Law Librarian**
> State Judicial Bldg., 244 Washington St. S.W., Atlanta,
>   GA 30334-5900

Hawaii

State Capitol
415 S. Beretania St.
Honolulu, HI 96813
Public information: (808) 586-2211
Fax: (808) 586-6006
http://www.state.hi.us

Office of the Governor
http://gov.state.hi.us
General e-mail: gov@gov.state.hi.us
Main phone: (808) 586-0034
Main fax: (808) 586-0006
TTY: (808) 586-0217

Benjamin J. Cayetano (D), Governor
State Capitol, 415 S. Beretania St., Honolulu, HI
96813

Paula Yoshioka, Chief of Staff
State Capitol, 415 S. Beretania St., 5th Fl., Honolulu,
HI 96813
(808) 586-0255; *Fax:* (808) 586-0231
E-mail: paula_yoshioka@exec.state.hi.us

Kathleen Racuya-Markrich, Press Secretary
State Capitol, 415 S. Beretania St., 5th Fl., Honolulu,
HI 96813
(808) 586-0034; *Fax:* (808) 586-0006

Vacant, Constituent Services
State Capitol, 415 S. Beretania St., Honolulu, HI
96813
(808) 586-0102; *Fax:* (808) 586-0006

Office of the Lieutenant Governor
http://www.state.hi.us/ltgov/index.html
General e-mail: ltgov@exec.state.hi.us
Main phone: (808) 586-0255
Main fax: (808) 586-0231

Mazie K. Hirono (D), Lieutenant Governor
State Capitol, 415 S. Beretania St., Honolulu, HI
96813

Office of the Attorney General
http://www.state.hi.us/ag/
Main phone: (808) 586-1500
Main fax: (808) 586-1239

Earl I. Anzai, Attorney General (Acting)
425 Queen St., Honolulu, HI 96813
(808) 586-1282

State of Hawaii

Capital: Honolulu, since 1845
Founded: 1898, U.S. annexation of formerly independent Kingdom of Hawaii; 1900, Hawaii Territory created
Statehood: August 21, 1959 (50th state)
Constitution adopted: n/a
Area: 6,423 sq. mi. (ranks 47th)
Population: 1,193,001 (1998 est.; ranks 41st)
Largest cities: (1998 est.) Honolulu (395,789)
Counties: 5, Most populous: (1998 est.) Honolulu (872,478); Hawaii (143,135); Maui (120,711); Kauai (56,603); Kalawao (74)
U.S. Congress: Daniel K. Akaka (D), Daniel K. Inouye (D); 2 Representatives
Nickname(s): Aloha State
Motto: The life of the land is perpetuated in righteousness
Song: "Hawaii Ponoi (Hawaii's Own)"
Bird: Nene (Hawaiian goose)
Tree: Kukui (candlenut)
Flower: Hibiscus
State fair: at Oahu, late June
Former capital(s): None

Agencies

Accounting and General Services Dept.
http://www.state.hi.us/icsd/dags/dags.html
Main phone: (808) 586-0400
Main fax: (808) 586-0775
Mailing address: P.O. Box 119, Honolulu, HI 96810-0119

Raymond H. Sato, Comptroller
1151 Punchbowl St., Honolulu, HI 96815

Archives Division
http://www.state.hi.us/dags/archives/
Main phone: (808) 586-0329
Main fax: (808) 586-0330
Toll free: (800) 468-4644

Jolyn G. Tamura, State Archivist
Kekauluohi Bldg., Iolani Palace Grounds,
Honolulu, HI 96813
(808) 586-0310

Audit Division
Main phone: (808) 586-0358
Main fax: (808) 586-0738

James T. Yamamura, Audit Administrator
1151 Punchbowl St., #230, Honolulu, HI 96813

Agriculture Dept.
http://www.hawaiiag.org/
General e-mail:
tomnann@elele.peacesat.hawaii.edu
Main phone: (808) 973-9600
Main fax: (808) 973-9613
Mailing address: P.O. Box 22159, Honolulu, HI
96823-2159

James J. Nakatani, Chair
1428 S. King St., Honolulu, HI 96814-2512
(808) 973-9550
E-mail: hdoa_chair@hawaiiag.org

Budget and Finance Dept.
http://www.state.hi.us/budget/index.htm
General e-mail:
HI_BudgetandFinance@exec.state.hi.us
Main phone: (808) 586-1518
Main fax: (808) 586-1976
Mailing address: P.O. Box 150, Honolulu, HI
96810-0150

Neal Miyahira, Director
1 Capitol District Bldg., 250 S. Hotel St., #305,
Honolulu, HI 96813
(808) 586-1518

Employees Retirement System
Main phone: (808) 586-1735
Main fax: (808) 586-1677

David Shimabukuro, Administrator
201 Merchant St., #1400, Honolulu, HI 96813-2929
(808) 586-1700

Public Defender's Office
Main phone: (808) 586-2200
Main fax: (808) 586-2222

Richard W. Pollack, State Public Defender
1130 N. Nimitz Hwy., #A-135, Honolulu, HI
96817

Public Utilities Commission
General e-mail: hipuc@lava.net
Main phone: (808) 586-2020
Main fax: (808) 568-2066

Dennis Yamada, Chair
465 S. King St., #103, Honolulu, HI 96813

Business, Economic Development, and Tourism Dept.
http://www.state.hi.us/dbedt/
Main phone: (808) 586-2423
Main fax: (808) 586-2377
Mailing address: P.O. Box 2359, Honolulu, HI
96804

Seiji F. Naya, Director
1 Capitol District Bldg., 250 S. Hotel St., Honolulu, HI
96813
(808) 586-2355
E-mail: snaya@dbedt.hawaii.gov

Commerce and Consumer Affairs Dept.
http://www.state.hi.us/dcca/
Main phone: (808) 586-2830
Main fax: (808) 586-2877
Mailing address: P.O. Box 541, Honolulu, HI
96809

Kathryn S. Matayoshi, Director
1010 Richards St., Honolulu, HI 96813
(808) 586-2850; *Fax:* (808) 586-2856
E-mail: kmatayos@dcca.state.hi.us

Consumer Protection Office
http://www.state.hi.us/dcca/ocp
General e-mail: ocp@dcca.state.hi.us
Main phone: (808) 586-2630
Main fax: (808) 586-2640
Mailing address: P.O. Box 3767, Honolulu, HI
96812

Stephen H. Levins, Executive Director
235 S. Beretania St., #801, Honolulu, HI 96813
(808) 586-2636
E-mail: slevins@dcca.state.hi.us

Financial Institutions Division
Main phone: (808) 586-2820

Professional and Vocational Licensing Division
(808) 586-3000

Accountancy, (808) 586-2696
Architects, (808) 586-2702
Child Care, (808) 587-5266
Contractors, (808) 586-2700
Cosmetology, (808) 586-2699
Engineers and Land Surveyors,
  (808) 586-2702
Medical Examiners, (808) 586-2708
Nursing, (808) 586-2695
Pharmacy, (808) 586-2694
Real Estate Appraisers, (808) 586-2704

Main fax: (808) 586-2818
Mailing address: P.O. Box 2054, Honolulu, HI 96805

Lynn Y. Wakatsuki, Commissioner
1010 Richards St., #602-A, Honolulu, HI 96813

Insurance Division
http://www.state.hi.us/insurance/
Main phone: (808) 586-2790

Wayne Metcalf, Commissioner
250 S. King St., 5th Fl., Honolulu, HI 96813

Professional and Vocational Licensing Division
Main phone: (808) 586-3000
Main fax: (808) 586-2689
Mailing address: P.O. Box 3469, Honolulu, HI 96801

Noe Noe Tom, Administrator
1010 Ricahrds St., Honolulu, HI 96813
(808) 586-2690

Criminal Justice Data Center
http://www.state.hi.us/ag/acjdc
Main phone: (808) 587-3100
Main fax: (808) 587-3109

Liane M. Moriyama, Administrator
Kekuanao'a Bldg., 465 S. King St., #101, Honolulu, HI 96813
(808) 587-3110

Culture and the Arts State Foundation
http://www.state.hi.us/sfca
General e-mail: sfca@sfca.state.hi.us
Main phone: (808) 586-0300
Main fax: (808) 586-0308
TTY: (808) 586-6740
Mailing address: P.O. Box 2359, Honolulu, HI 96804

Holly Richards, Director
44 Merchant St., Honolulu, HI 96813

Defense Dept.
http://www.dod.state.hi.us
General e-mail: webmaster@dod.state.hi.us
Main phone: (808) 733-4258
Main fax: (808) 733-4236

Edward V. Richardson, Adjutant General
3949 Diamond Head Rd., Honolulu, HI 96816-4495
(808) 733-4246; *Fax:* (808) 733-4238
E-mail: erichardson@hihik.ang.af.mil

Veterans Services Office
http://www.dod.state.hi.us/ovs
General e-mail: ovs@dod.state.hi.us
Main phone: (808) 433-0420
Main fax: (808) 433-0385

Walter Ozawa, Director
919 Aia Moana Blvd., #100, Honolulu, HI 96814
(808) 433-0422

Education Dept.
http://www.k12.hi.us
General e-mail: supt_doe@notes.k12.hi.us
Main phone: (808) 586-3230
Main fax: (808) 586-3234
TTY: (808) 586-3232
Mailing address: P.O. Box 2360, Honolulu, HI 96804

Paul G. LeMahieu, Superintendent
Queen Liliuokalani Bldg., 1390 Miller St., Honolulu, HI 96813
(808) 586-3310

Board of Education
http://www.doe.k12.hi.us
General e-mail: supt_doe@notes.k12.hi.us
Main phone: (808) 586-3334
Main fax: (808) 586-3433
Toll free: (800) 468-4644
TTY: (808) 586-3232
Mailing address: P.O. Box 2360, Honolulu, HI 96804

Mitsugi Nakashima, Chair
1390 Miller St., #405, Honolulu, HI 96813
(808) 586-3349

Ethics Commission
http://www.state.hi.us/ethics/index.html
General e-mail: ethics@ethics.mindwind.com
Main phone: (808) 587-0460
Main fax: (808) 587-0470
Mailing address: P.O. Box 616, Honolulu, HI 96809

Daniel J. Mollway, Executive Director
1001 Bishop St., Pacific Tower, #970, Honolulu, HI
96813

Health Dept.
http://www.state.hi.us/doh/
Main phone: (808) 586-4400
Main fax: (808) 586-4444
TTY: (808) 586-4408

Bruce Anderson, Director
1250 Punchbowl St., Honolulu, HI 96813
(808) 586-4410
E-mail: b.sanders@health.state.hi.us

Aging Executive Office
http://www.hawaii.gov.health/eoa
General e-mail: eoa@mail.health.state.hi.us
Main phone: (808) 586-0100
Main fax: (808) 586-0185

Marilyn Seely, Executive Director
1 Capitol District Bldg., 250 Hotel St., #109,
Honolulu, HI 96813-2831
E-mail: mrseely@mail.health.state.hi.us

Behavioral Health Services Administration
Main phone: (808) 586-4410
Main fax: (808) 586-4444

Anita Swanson, Deputy Director
1250 Punchbowl St., 3rd Fl., Honolulu, HI 96813

Health Planning and Development Agency
http://www.hawaii.gov/health/shpda.htm
General e-mail: shpda@health.state.hi.us
Main phone: (808) 587-0788
Main fax: (808) 587-0783
TTY: (808) 587-0854

Marilyn A. Matsunaga, Administrator
1177 Alakea St., #402, Honolulu, HI 96813

Health Resources Administration: Developmental Disabilities Division
Main phone: (808) 586-5840
Main fax: (808) 586-5844
TTY: (808) 586-5840
Mailing address: P.O. Box 3378, Honolulu, HI
96801

Vacant, Chief
1250 Punchbowl St., #258, Honolulu, HI 96813
(808) 586-5843

Housing and Community Development Corporation
http://www.hcdch.state.hi.us/
Main phone: (808) 587-3545
Main fax: (808) 587-0600
Toll free: (800) 587-0641
TTY: (808) 832-6083

Donald K.W. Lau, Executive Director
677 Queen St., #300, Honolulu, HI 96817-2908
(808) 587-0680; Fax: (808) 587-3146
E-mail: hcdch@hcdch.state.hi.us

Human Resources and Development Dept.
http://www.state.hi.us/hrd/
General e-mail: soh_hrd@hotmail.com
Main phone: (808) 587-1100
Main fax: (808) 587-1106
TTY: (808) 587-1148

Mike McCartney, Director
Leiopapa A. Kamehameha Bldg., 235 S. Beretania St.,
#1400, Honolulu, HI 96813-2437
E-mail: mikem_hrd@hotmail.com

Human Services Dept.
http://www.state.hi.us/dhs/
Main phone: (808) 586-4997
Main fax: (808) 586-4890
Mailing address: P.O. Box 339, Honolulu, HI
96809-0339

Susan M. Chandler, Director
1390 Miller St., #209, Honolulu, HI 96813

Youth Services
General e-mail: oys@pixi.com
Main phone: (808) 587-5700
Main fax: (808) 587-5734

Bert Y. Matsuoka, Executive Director
Haseko Ctr., 820 Mililani, #817, Honolulu, HI
96813
(808) 587-5706

Labor and Industrial Relations Dept.
http://www.aloha.net/~edpso/
General e-mail: edpso@aloha.net
Main phone: (808) 586-8842
Main fax: (808) 586-9099
TTY: (808) 586-8847

Lorraine H. Akiba, Director
830 Punchbowl St., Honolulu, HI 96813
(808) 586-8844

State Fire Council
http://www.cchnl.oceanic.com/fire
Main phone: (808) 831-7771
Main fax: (808) 831-7780

Attilio Leonardi Jr., Fire Chief
3375 Coapaka St., #H-425, Honolulu, HI 96819
(808) 831-7777
E-mail: aleonardi@co.honolulu.hi.us

Land and Natural Resources Dept.
http://www.state.hi.us/dlnr/
General e-mail: dlnr@pixi.com

Main phone: (808) 587-0406
Main fax: (808) 587-0404

Timothy E. Johns, Chair
Kalanimoku Bldg., 1151 Punchbowl St., #130,
Honolulu, HI 96813
(808) 587-0400; *Fax:* (808) 587-0390

Forestry and Wildlife Division
Main phone: (808) 587-0166

Michael Buck, Administrator
Kalanimoku Bldg., 1151 Punchbowl St., #325,
Honolulu, HI 96813
(808) 587-4181
E-mail: Michael_G_Buck@exec.state.hi.us

Historic Preservation Division
http://www.state.hi.us/dlnr/hpd/~hpgreeting.htm
General e-mail: dlnr@pixi.com
Main phone: (808) 692-8015
Main fax: (808) 692-8020

Don Hibbard, Administrator
Kakuhihewa Bldg., 601 Kamokila Blvd., #555,
Honolulu, HI 96707

State Parks
http://www.state.hi.us/dlnr/dsp/dsp.html
General e-mail: hiparks@pixi.com
Main phone: (808) 587-0290
Main fax: (808) 587-0311
Mailing address: P.O. Box 621, Honolulu, HI
96809

Ralston Nagata, Administrator
1151 Punchbowl St., #310, Honolulu, HI 96813

Water Resources Management Commission
http://www.hawaii.gov.dlnr/dwrm/dwrm.html
General e-mail: dwrm@pixi.com
Main phone: (808) 587-0214
Main fax: (808) 587-0219
Mailing address: P.O. Box 621, Honolulu, HI
96809

Linnel T. Nishioka, Deputy Director
Kalanimoku Bldg., 1151 Punchbowl St., #227,
Honolulu, HI 96813

Motor Vehicles and Licensing Division
http://www.co.honolulu.hi.us/Depts/fin/mvr
Main phone: (808) 532-7700
Main fax: (808) 532-7722
Mailing address: P.O. Box 30330, Honolulu, HI
96820

Dennis Kamimura, Licensing Administrator
1041 Nuuanu Ave., Honolulu, HI 96817

Frequently Called Numbers

Tourism: (808) 586-2550; 1-800-464-2924;
http://www.state.hi.us/tourism/rc.html
Library: (808) 586-3704;
http://www.hcc.hawaii.edu/hspls/
Board of Education: (808) 586-3334;
http://www.doe.k12.hi.us
Vital Statistics: (808) 586-4533;
http://www.state.hi.us/doh/records/index.html
Tax/Revenue: (808) 587-1510;
http://www.state.hi.us/tax/tax.html
Motor Vehicles: (808) 532-7700;
http://www.co.honolulu.hi.us/Depts/fin/mvr
State Police/Highway Patrol: (808) 587-1256
Unemployment: (808) 586-8970
General Election Information: (808) 453-
8683; http://www.state.hi.us/elections/
Consumer Affairs: (808) 586-2630;
http://www.state.hi.us/dcca/ocp
Hazardous Materials: (808) 586-4226

Public Broadcasting Authority
http://www.khet.org/
General e-mail: e_mail@khet.pbs.org
Main phone: (808) 973-1000
Main fax: (808) 973-1090

Don Robbs, General Manager
2350 Dole St., Honolulu, HI 96822
E-mail: don_robbs@khet.pbs.org

Public Library
http://www.hcc.hawaii.edu/hspls/
General e-mail: stlib@lib.state.hi.us
Main phone: (808) 586-3704
Main fax: (808) 586-3715

Virginia Lowell, State Librarian
KeKuanao'a Bldg., 465 S. King, #B-1, Honolulu, HI
96813

Public Safety Dept.
http://www.state.hi.us/icsd/psd/psd.html
Main phone: (808) 587-1350
Main fax: (808) 587-1282
Toll free: (800) 468-4644

Ted Sakai, Director
919 Ala Moana Blvd., 4th Fl., Honolulu, HI 96814

Law Enforcement
Main phone: (808) 587-1256
Main fax: (808) 587-1220

Sidney Hayakawa, Deputy Director
919 Ala Moana Blvd., 4th Fl., Honolulu, HI 96814

Paroling Authority
Main phone: (808) 587-1290

Alfred K. Beaver, Chair
Capitol Center, 1177 Alakea St., Honolulu, HI
96813

Regents Board
Main phone: (808) 956-8213
Main fax: (808) 956-5156

Donald C. W. Kim, Chair
Bachman Hall, 2444 Dole St., #209, Honolulu, HI
96822

Taxation Dept.
http://www.state.hi.us/tax/tax.html
Main phone: (808) 587-1510
Main fax: (808) 587-1560
Mailing address: P.O. Box 259, Honolulu, HI
96809

Ray K. Kamikawa, Director
830 Punchbowl St., #221, Honolulu, HI 96813

Tourism Resource Center
http://www.state.hi.us/tourism/rc.html
Main phone: (808) 586-2550
Main fax: (808) 586-2549
Mailing address: P.O. Box 2359, Honolulu, HI
96804

Diane S. Quitiquit, Chair
1 Capitol District Bldg., 250 S. Hotel St., 4th Fl.,
Honolulu, HI 96813

Transportation Dept.
http://www.hawaii.gov/dot
General e-mail: makli@hula.net
Main phone: (808) 587-2160
Main fax: (808) 587-2313
TTY: (808) 587-2257

Kazu Hayashida, Director
869 Punchbowl St., Honolulu, HI 96813
(808) 587-2150; *Fax:* (808) 587-2167
E-mail: kazu_hayashida@exec.state.hi.us

Airports Division
http://www.state.hi.us/dot/airhaw.html
Main phone: (808) 836-6411
Main fax: (808) 838-8750
Mailing address: 400 Rodgers Blvd., #700,
Honolulu, HI 96819

Jerry Matsuda, Airports Administrator
Honolulu International Airport, Interisland
Terminal Bldg., Honolulu, HI 96819-1898
(808) 838-8601
E-mail: Jerry_Matsuda@exec.state.hi.us

Women's Commission
http://www.state.hi.us/hscsw
General e-mail: hscsw@pixi.com
Main phone: (808) 586-5757
Main fax: (808) 586-5756

Allicyn Hikida Tasaka, Executive Director
State Office Tower, 235 S. Beretania St., #407,
Honolulu, HI 96813
(808) 586-5758

Hawaii Legislature
State Capitol
415 S. Beretania St.
Honolulu, HI 96813
General information: (808) 587-0666
Bill status: (808) 587-0478
http://www.capitol.hawaii.gov

Senate
General information: (808) 586-6720
Fax: (808) 586-6719

Norman Mizuguchi (D), President
Hawaii State Capitol, 415 S. Beretania St., #003,
Honolulu, HI 96813
(808) 586-6870; *Fax:* (808) 586-6819
E-mail: senmizuguchi@capitol.hawaii.gov
http://www.capitol.hawaii.gov/site1/senate/members/
sen15.asp?press1=senate&press2=members

Avery B. Chumbley (D), Vice President
Hawaii State Capitol, 415 S. Beretania St., #230,
Honolulu, HI 96813
(808) 586-6030; *Fax:* (808) 586-6031
E-mail: abc@aloha.net
http://www.capitol.hawaii.gov/site1/senate/members/
sen6.asp?press1=senate&press2=members

Les Ihara Jr. (D), Majority Leader
Hawaii State Capitol, 415 S. Beretania St., #214,
Honolulu, HI 96813
(808) 586-6250; *Fax:* (808) 586-6251
E-mail: SenIhara@capitol.hawaii.gov
http://www.capitol.hawaii.gov/site1/senate/members/
sen10.asp?press1=senate&press2=member

Jonathan Chun (D), Majority Floor Leader
Hawaii State Capitol, 415 S. Beretania St., #206,
Honolulu, HI 96813
(808) 586-7344; *Fax:* (808) 586-7348
E-mail: senchun@capitol.hawaii.gov
http://www.capitol.hawaii.gov/site1/senate/members/
sen7.asp?press1=senate&press2=members

Whitney Anderson (R), Minority Leader
Hawaii State Capitol, 415 S. Beretania St., #221,
Honolulu, HI 96813

(808) 586-6840; *Fax:* (808) 586-6839
E-mail: senanderson@capitol.hawaii.gov
http://www.capitol.hawaii.gov/site1/senate/members/
   sen25.asp?press1=senate&press2=members

Sam Slom (R), Minority Floor Leader
Hawaii State Capitol, 415 S. Beretania St., #208,
   Honolulu, HI 96813
(808) 586-8420; *Fax:* (808) 586-8426
E-mail: senslom@capitol.hawaii.gov
http://www.capitol.hawaii.gov/site1/senate/members/
   sen8.asp?press1=senate&press2=members

Paul T. Kawaguchi, Chief Clerk
Hawaii State Capitol, 415 S. Beretania St., Honolulu,
   HI 96813
(808) 586-6720; *Fax:* (808) 586-6719

House
General information: (808) 586-6400
Fax: (808) 586-6401

Calvin Say (D), Speaker of the House
Hawaii State Capitol, 415 S. Beretania St., #431,
   Honolulu, HI 96813
(808) 586-6100; *Fax:* (808) 586-6101
E-mail: repsay@capitol.hawaii.gov
http://www.capitol.hawaii.gov/site1/house/members/
   rep18.asp?press1=house&press2=members

Marcus Oshiro (D), Vice Speaker
Hawaii State Capitol, 415 S. Beretania St., #404,
   Honolulu, HI 96813
(808) 586-8505; *Fax:* (808) 586-8509
E-mail: repmoshiro@capitol.hawaii.gov
http://www.capitol.hawaii.gov/site1/house/members/
   rep40.asp?press1=house&press2=members

Ed Case (D), Majority Leader
Hawaii State Capitol, 415 S. Beretania St., #439,
   Honolulu, HI 96813
(808) 586-8475; *Fax:* (808) 586-8479
E-mail: repcase@capitol.hawaii.gov
http://www.capitol.hawaii.gov/site1/house/members/
   rep28.asp?press1=house&press2=members

Noboru Yonamine (D), Majority Floor Leader
Hawaii State Capitol, 415 S. Beretania St., #403,
   Honolulu, HI 96813
(808) 586-6520; *Fax:* (808) 586-6521
E-mail: repyonamine@capitol.hawaii.gov
http://www.capitol.hawaii.gov/site1/house/members/
   rep35.asp?press1=house&press2=members

Barbara Marumoto (R), Minority Leader
Hawaii State Capitol, 415 S. Beretania St., #313,
   Honolulu, HI 96813
(808) 586-6310; *Fax:* (808) 586-6311
E-mail: repmarumoto@capitol.hawaii.gov

Laws

Sales tax: None
Income tax: 10%
State minimum wage: $5.25 (Federal is $5.15)
Marriage age: 19
First-cousin marriage: Permitted
Drinking age: 21
State control of liquor sales: No
Blood alcohol for DWI: 0.08%
Driving age: 16 (effective 2001)
Speed limit: 55 mph
Permit to buy handguns: Yes, 15 days to
   acquire
Minimum age to possess handguns: 21
Minimum age to possess rifles, shotguns: 16
State lottery: No
Casinos: No
Pari-mutuel betting: No
Death penalty: No
3 strikes minimum sentence: None
Hate crimes law: No
Gay employment non-discrimination: Yes
Official language(s): English, Hawaiian
Term limits: None

*State laws are complex and subject to
change; this information is not intended as
legal advice. For an explanation of this
information, see p. x.*

---

http://www.capitol.hawaii.gov/site1/house/members/
   rep17.asp?press1=house&press2=members

David A. Pendleton (R), Minority Floor Leader
Hawaii State Capitol, 415 S. Beretania St., #442,
   Honolulu, HI 96813
(808) 586-9490; *Fax:* (808) 586-9496
E-mail: reppendleton@capitol.hawaii.gov
http://www.capitol.hawaii.gov/site1/house/members/
   rep50.asp?press1=house&press2=members

Patricia A. Mau-Shimizu, Chief Clerk
Hawaii State Capitol, 415 S. Beretania St., Honolulu,
   HI 96813
(808) 586-6400; *Fax:* (808) 586-6401

Hawaii Judiciary
Ali'iolani Hale
417 S. King St.
Honolulu, HI 96813-2914
http://www.hawaii.gov/jud/

Supreme Court
http://www.hawaii.gov/jud/SC.HTM

Darrell N. Phillips, Chief Clerk
Ali'iolani Hale, 417 S. King St., Honolulu, HI
96813-2914
(808) 539-4919; *Fax:* (808) 539-4928

Justices
Composition: 5 justices
Selection Method: appointed by governor with
consent of state senate
Length of term: 10 years

Ronald T. Y. Moon, Chief Justice, (808) 539-4700

Robert Gordon Klein, Associate Justice, (808) 539-4725

Steven H. Levinson, Associate Justice, (808) 539-4735

Paula A. Nakayama, Associate Justice, (808) 539-4720

Mario R. Ramil, Associate Justice, (808) 539-4715

Administrative Office of the Courts
http://www.hawaii.gov/jud/adm.htm
Main phone: (808) 539-4900
Main fax: (808) 539-4985

Michael F. Broderick, Administrative Director
Ali'iolani Hale, 417 S. King St., #206A, Honolulu, HI
96813-2914

Supreme Court Library
Main phone: (808) 539-4964
Main fax: (808) 539-4974

Ann S. Koto, Law Librarian
Ali'iolani Hale, 417 S. King St., Honolulu, HI
96813-2914

Legislative and Political Party Information Resources

Senate home page: http://www.capitol.hawaii.gov/site1/senate/senate.asp?press1=senate
House home page: http://www.capitol.hawaii.gov/site1/house/house.asp?press1=house
Committees: Senate: http://www.capitol.hawaii.gov/site1/senate/comm/
comm.asp?press1=senate&press2=comm; *House:* http://www.capitol.hawaii.gov/site1/house/comm/
comm.asp?press1=house&press2=comm
Legislative process: http://www.capitol.hawaii.gov/site1/info/guide/guide.asp?press1=info&press2=guide
Hawaii Democratic Party: http://www.hawaiidemocrats.org
404 Ward Ave., #201, Honolulu, HI 96814; *Phone:* (808) 596-2980; *Fax:* (808) 596-2985; *E-mail:*
info@hawaiidemocrats.org
Hawaii Republican Party
725 Kapiolani Blvd., #C-106, Honolulu, HI 96813; *Phone:* (808) 593-8180; *E-mail:*
GOPHawaii@aol.com

Idaho

State Capitol Bldg., West Wing
700 W. Jefferson St.
Boise, ID 83720-0034
Public information: (208) 334-2411
Fax: (208) 334-3454
http://www.state.id.us

Office of the Governor
http://www.state.id.us/gov/govhmpg.htm
General e-mail: governor@gov.state.id.us
Main phone: (208) 334-2100
Main fax: (208) 334-3454
TTY: (208) 334-2100 x 242
Mailing address: P.O. Box 83720, Boise, ID
83720-0034

Dirk Kempthorne (R), Governor
State Capitol Bldg., West Wing, 700 W. Jefferson St.,
2nd Fl., Boise, ID 83720-0034

Phil Reberger, Chief of Staff
State Capitol Bldg., West Wing, 700 W. Jefferson St.,
2nd Fl., Boise, ID 83720-0034
(208) 334-2100; *Fax:* (208) 334-3454

Mark Snider, Press Secretary
State Capitol Bldg., West Wing, 700 W. Jefferson St.,
2nd Fl., Boise, ID 83720-0034
(208) 334-2100; *Fax:* (208) 334-2175
E-mail: msnider@gov.state.id.us

Office of the Lieutenant Governor
http://www.state.id.us/gov/lgo/ltgov.htm
Main phone: (208) 334-2200
Main fax: (208) 334-3259
Mailing address: P.O. Box 83720, Boise, ID
83720-0057

C. L. (Butch) Otter (R), Lieutenant Governor
State Capitol Bldg., 700 W. Jefferson St., #225, Boise,
ID 83720-0057
E-mail: botter@lgo.state.id.us

Office of the Secretary of State
http://www.idsos.state.id.us
General e-mail: secstate@idsos.state.id.us
Main phone: (208) 334-2300
Main fax: (208) 334-2282
TTY: (208) 334-2366
Mailing address: P.O. Box 83720, Boise, ID
83720-0080

State of Idaho

Capital: Boise, since 1864
Founded: 1863, Idaho Territory created from Oregon Territory
Statehood: July 3, 1890 (43rd state)
Constitution adopted: 1890
Area: 82,751 sq. mi. (ranks 11th)
Population: 1,228,684 (1998 est.; ranks 40th)
Largest cities: (1998 est.) Boise City (157,452), Pocatello (53,074); Idaho Falls (48,122); Nampa (41,951); Twin Falls (33,296)
Counties: 44, Most populous: (1998 est.) Ada (275,687); Canyon (120,266); Kootenal (101,390); Bonneville (80,672); Bannock (74,886)
U.S. Congress: Larry E. Craig (R), Mike Crapo (R); 2 Representatives
Nickname(s): Gem State
Motto: It is forever
Song: "Here We Have Idaho"
Bird: Mountain bluebird
Tree: White pine
Flower: Syringa
State fair: Eastern Idaho at Blackfoot; western Idaho at Boise, late Aug.
Former capital(s): None

Pete T. Cenarrusa (R), Secretary of State
State Capitol Bldg., 700 W. Jefferson St., #203, Boise,
ID 83720-0080

Office of the Attorney General
http://www.state.id.us/ag
Main phone: (208) 334-2400
Main fax: (208) 334-2530
Mailing address: P.O. Box 83720, Boise, ID
83720-0010

Alan G. Lance (R), Attorney General
State Capitol Bldg., 700 W. Jefferson St., Boise, ID
83720-0010

Office of the State Treasurer
http://www.state.id.us/treasur/sto.htm
General e-mail: idahotreasurer@sto.state.id.us
Main phone: (208) 334-3200

Main fax: (208) 332-2960
Mailing address: P.O. Box 83720, Boise, ID 83720-0091

Ron G. Crane (R), State Treasurer
State Capitol Bldg., 700 W. Jefferson St., #102, Boise, ID 83720-0091

Office of the State Controller
http://www.sco.state.id.us/
General e-mail: scoinfo@sco.state.id.us
Main phone: (208) 334-3100
Main fax: (208) 334-2671
Mailing address: P.O. Box 83720, Boise, ID 83720-0011

J. D. Williams (D), State Controller
700 W. State St., Boise, ID 83720-0011
E-mail: jwilliam@sco.state.id.us

Military Division
http://www.state.id.us/mil/cover.htm
Main phone: (208) 422-5011
Main fax: (208) 422-6179
Toll free: (800) 543-6992
Mailing address: P.O. Box 45, Boise, ID 83707-5004

John F. Kane, Commanding General
Gowan Field, 4040 W. Guard St., Boise, ID 83707
(208) 422-5242
E-mail: kanej@id-ngnet.army.mil

Agencies

Accountancy Board
http://www.state.id.us/boa
General e-mail: isba@boa.state.id.us
Main phone: (208) 334-2490
Main fax: (208) 334-2615
Mailing address: P.O. Box 83720, Boise, ID 83720-0002

Barbara R. Porter, Executive Director
1109 Main St., #470, Boise, ID 83720-0002
E-mail: bporter@boa.state.id.us

Administration Dept.
http://www2.state.id.us/adm
General e-mail: dgarcia@adm.state.id.us
Main phone: (208) 332-1824
Main fax: (208) 334-2307
Mailing address: P.O. Box 83720, Boise, ID 83720-0003

Pamela I. Aherns, Director
650 W. State St., #100, Boise, ID 83720-0003
(208) 332-1825

Aging Commission
http://www.state.id.us/icoa/
Main phone: (208) 334-3833
Main fax: (208) 334-3033
Toll free: (800) 377-3529
Mailing address: P.O. Box 83720, Boise, ID 83720-0007

Lupe Wissel, Director
3380 Americana Terrace, #120, Boise, ID 83706
(208) 334-2423
E-mail: lwissel@icoa.state.id.us

Agriculture Dept.
http://www.agri.state.id.us
General e-mail: cjackson@agri.state.id.us
Main phone: (208) 332-8500
Main fax: (208) 334-2170
TTY: (800) 377-3529
Mailing address: P.O. Box 790, Boise, ID 83701-0790

Patrick A. Takasugi, Director
2270 Old Penitentiary Rd., Boise, ID 83712
(208) 332-8503
E-mail: ptakasug@agri.state.id.us

Architects Licensing Board
http://www.state.id.us/ibol/arc.htm
General e-mail: ibol@ibol.state.id.us
Main phone: (208) 334-3233
Main fax: (208) 334-3945

Thomas E. Limbaugh, Bureau Chief
1109 Main St., #220, Boise, ID 83702-5642
E-mail: tlimbaugh@ibol.state.id.us

Board of Education
http://www.sde.state.id.us/osbe.board.htm
General e-mail: board@osbe.state.id.us
Main phone: (208) 334-2270
Main fax: (208) 334-2632
Mailing address: P.O. Box 83720, Boise, ID 83720-0037

Gregory G. Fitch, Executive Director
650 W. State St., #307, Boise, ID 83702
E-mail: gfitch@osbe.state..id.us

Public Television
http://idahoptv.org
General e-mail: idptv@idptv.pbs.org
Main phone: (208) 373-7220
Main fax: (208) 373-7245

Peter Morrill, General Manager
1455 N. Orchard, Boise, ID 83706
E-mail: Peter_Morrill@idptv.pbs.org

Commerce Dept.
http://www.idoc.state.id.us/

Higher Educational Institutions

Boise State University
http://www.idbsu.edu
1910 University Dr., Boise, ID 83725
Main phone: (208) 426-1011

Idaho State University
http://www.isu.edu
Campus Box 8265, Pocatello, ID 83209
Main phone: (208) 236-2475

Lewis-Clark State College
http://www.lcsc.edu
500 8th Ave., Lewiston, ID 83501
Main phone: (208) 799-2210

University of Idaho
http://www.uidaho.edu
Moscow, ID 83844-4140
Main phone: (208) 885-6326

General e-mail: info@idoc.state.id.us
Main phone: (208) 334-2470
Main fax: (208) 334-2631
Mailing address: P.O. Box 83720, Boise, ID
83720-0093

Gary Mahn, Director
700 W. State St., Boise, ID 83702

Tourism Development
http://www.visitid.org/
General e-mail: tourism@idoc.state.id.us
Main phone: (208) 334-2470
Main fax: (208) 334-2631
Mailing address: P.O. Box 83720, Boise, ID
83720-0093

Carl Wilgus, Administrator
700 W. State St., Boise, ID 83720-0093

Consumer Protection Unit
Main phone: (208) 334-2424
Main fax: (208) 334-2830
Mailing address: P.O. Box 83720, Boise, ID
83720-0010

Brett DeLange, Deputy Attorney General
650 W. State St., Len B. Jordan Bldg., Boise, ID
83720
(208) 334-2424, ext. 3085
E-mail: bdelange@ag.state.id.us

Correction Board
http://www.corr.state.id.us/
General e-mail: chopson@corr.state.id.us
Main phone: (208) 658-2100

Main fax: (208) 327-7404
Mailing address: P.O. Box 500, Boise, ID 83720-
0018

Ralph Townsend, Chair
1299 N. Orchard St., #110, Boise, ID 83706
E-mail: jspalding@corr.state.id.us

Cosmetology Licensing Board
http://www.state.id.us/ibol/cos.htm
General e-mail: ibol@ibol.state.id.us
Main phone: (208) 334-3233
Main fax: (208) 334-3945

Helen Piippo, Secretary
1109 Main St., #220, Boise, ID 83702-5642
E-mail: hpiippo@ibol.state.id.us

Developmental Disabilities Council
http://www.state.id.us/icdd/index.htm
General e-mail: msword@icdd.state.id.us
Main phone: (208) 334-2178
Main fax: (208) 334-3417
Toll free: (800) 544-2433
TTY: (208) 334-2179
Mailing address: P.O. Box 83720, Boise, ID
83720-0280

Marilyn B. Sword, Executive Director
280 N. 8th St., #208, Boise, ID 83720-0280

Disaster Services Bureau
http://www.state.id.us/bds/bds.html
Main phone: (208) 334-3460
Main fax: (208) 334-2322

John Cline, State Director
4040 W. Guard Bldg. 600, Boise, ID 83705-5004
(208) 334-3460, ext. 305
E-mail: jcline@bds.state.id.us

Education Dept.
http://www.sde.state.id.us/Dept/
General e-mail: sde@state.id.us
Main phone: (208) 332-6800
Main fax: (208) 334-2228
Toll free: (800) 432-4601
TTY: (800) 377-3529
Mailing address: P.O. Box 83720, Boise, ID 83720

**Marilyn Howard (D), Superintendent of Public
Instruction**
650 W. State St., Boise, ID 83720
(208) 332-6811
E-mail: mhoward@sde.state.id.us

State Historical Society
http://www2.state.id.us/ishs/index.html
Main phone: (208) 334-2682
Main fax: (208) 334-2774

Steve Guerber, Director
1109 Main St., #250, Boise, ID 83702-5642
E-mail: Sguerber@ishs.state.id.us

State Historical Society: Library and Archives
http://www.state.id.us/ishs/LibArch.html
General e-mail: ishref@micron.net
Main phone: (208) 334-3356
Main fax: (208) 334-3198

Linda Morton-Keithly, Administrator
450 N. 4th St., Boise, ID 83702
E-mail: lindamk@micron.net

State Library
http://www.lili.org/isl/index.htm
Main phone: (208) 334-2150
Main fax: (208) 334-4016
Toll free: (800) 458-3271

Charles Bolles, State Librarian
325 W. State St., Boise, ID 83702
E-mail: cbolles@isl.state.id.us

Finance Dept.
http://www.state.id.us/finance/dof.htm
General e-mail: finance@fin.state.id.us
Main phone: (208) 332-8000
Main fax: (208) 332-8098
Toll free: (888) 346-3378
Mailing address: P.O. Box 83720, Boise, ID 83720-0031

Gavin M. Gee, Director
700 W. State St., 2nd Fl., Boise, ID 83720-0031
(208) 332-8010; *Fax:* (208) 332-8097

Financial Institutions Bureau
Main phone: (208) 332-8005
Main fax: (208) 332-8098
Toll free: (888) 346-3378
Mailing address: P.O. Box 83720, Boise, ID 83720-0031

Kelly P. Robison, Chief
700 W. State St., 2nd Fl., Boise, ID 83720-0031
(208) 332-8032
E-mail: krobison@fin.state.id.us

Fish and Game Dept.
http://www.state.id.us/fishgame/fishgame.html
General e-mail: idfginfo@idfg.state.id.us
Main phone: (208) 334-3700
Main fax: (208) 334-2114
Mailing address: P.O. Box 25, Boise, ID 83707

Jerry Mallet, Director (Interim)
600 S. Walnut St., Boise, ID 83707

(208) 334-5159
E-mail: jerrymallet@idfg.state.id.us

Forest Products Commission
http://www.idahoforests.org/
General e-mail: ifpc@micron.net
Main phone: (208) 334-3292
Main fax: (208) 334-3449
Toll free: (800) ID-WOODS
Mailing address: P.O. Box 855, Boise, ID 83701

Betty J. Munis, Director
350 North 9th St., #304, Boise, ID 83702

Forestry and Fire
Main phone: (208) 334-0200
Main fax: (208) 334-2339
Mailing address: P.O. Box 83720, Boise, ID 83720-0050

Winston A. Wiggins, Assistant Director
954 W. Jefferson St., Boise, ID 83720
E-mail: scooley@idl.state.id.us

Geological Survey
http://www.uidaho.edu/igs/igs.html
General e-mail: igs@uidaho.edu
Main phone: (208) 885-7991
Main fax: (208) 885-5826
Mailing address: P.O. Box 443014, Moscow, ID 83844-3014

Earl H. Bennett, Director
Morrill Hall, University of Idaho, #301, Moscow, ID 83844-3014

Health and Welfare Dept.
http://www2.state.id.us/dhw
General e-mail: osbornb@idhw.state.id.us
Main phone: (208) 334-5500
Main fax: (208) 334-6558
TTY: (208) 334-4921
Mailing address: P.O. Box 83720, Boise, ID 83720-0036

Karl Kurtz, Director
450 W. State St., 10th Fl., Boise, ID 83720-0036
(208) 334-5502
E-mail: kurtzk@idhw.state.id.us

Developmental Disabilities Bureau
Main phone: (208) 334-5512
Main fax: (208) 334-6664
Mailing address: P.O. Box 83720, Boise, ID 83720-0036

Paul A. Swatsenbarg, Chief
450 W. State St., Boise, ID 83720-0036

Frequently Called Numbers

Tourism: (208) 334-2470; 1-800-VISIT-ID; http://www.visitid.org/
Library: (208) 334-2150; http://www.lili.org/isl/index.htm
Board of Education: (208) 334-2270; http://www.sde.state.id.us/osbe.board.htm
Vital Statistics: (208) 334-5988
Tax/Revenue: (208) 334-7660; http://www.state.id.us/tax/index.html
Motor Vehicles: (208) 334-8606; http://www2.state.id.us/itd/dmv/dmv.htm
State Police/Highway Patrol: (208) 884-7000; http://www.state.id.us/dle/dle.htm
Unemployment: (208) 334-6280; http://www.labor.state.id.us/id-ui.htm
General Election Information: (208) 334-2852; http://www.idsos.state.id.us/elect/eleindex.htm
Consumer Affairs: (208) 334-2424
Hazardous Materials: (208) 334-3263; http://www.state.id.us/serc/index.html

Medicaid
http://www.state.id.us/dhw/Medicaid
Main phone: (208) 334-5747
Main fax: (208) 364-1811
Mailing address: P.O. Box 83720, Boise, ID 83720-0036

Joe Brunson, Administrator
3380 Americana Terrace, #230, Boise, ID 83706

Mental Health Bureau
Main phone: (208) 334-5528
Main fax: (208) 334-6699
Mailing address: P.O. Box 83720, Boise, ID 83720-0036

Roy Sargeant, Chief
450 W. State St., 5th Fl., Boise, ID 83720-0036
(208) 334-6500
E-mail: sargeantr@idhw.state.id.us

Veterans Services Division
http://www2.state.id.us/dhw/hwgd_www/vetserv/index.html
Main phone: (208) 334-5000
Main fax: (208) 334-2627
Mailing address: P.O. Box 7765, Boise, ID 83707

Gary Bermeosolo, Administrator
320 Collins Rd., Boise, ID 83702

Human Resources Division
http://www.dhr.state.id.us
Main phone: (208) 334-2263
Main fax: (208) 334-3182
TTY: (800) 542-5738
Mailing address: P.O. Box 83720, Boise, ID 83720-3182

Ann Heilman, Administrator
700 W. State St., Boise, ID 83720
(208) 334-3345
E-mail: aheilman@dhr.state.id.us

Human Rights Commission
http://www.state.id.us/ihrc/ihrchome.htm
General e-mail: inquiry@ihrc.state.id.us
Main phone: (208) 334-2873
Main fax: (208) 334-2664
Toll free: (888) 249-7025
TTY: (208) 334-4751
Mailing address: P.O. Box 83720, Boise, ID 83720-0400

Leslie R. Goddard, Director
1109 Main St., #400, Boise, ID 83720-0040
E-mail: Lgoddard@ihrc.state.id.us

Humanities Council
http://www2.state.id.us/ihc/
General e-mail: rickihc@micron.net
Main phone: (208) 345-5346
Main fax: (208) 345-5347
Toll free: (888) 345-5346

Rick Ardinger, Executive Director
217 W. State St., Boise, ID 83702
(208) 345-5346, ext. 202

Industrial Commission
http://www.state.id.us/iic/index.html
Main phone: (208) 334-6000
Main fax: (208) 334-2321
Toll free: (800) 950-2110
TTY: (800) 950-2110
Mailing address: P.O. Box 83720, Boise, ID 83720-0041

Rachel S. Gilbert, Chair
317 Main St., Boise, ID 83720-0041

Insurance Dept.
http://www.doi.state.id.us
Main phone: (208) 334-4250
Main fax: (208) 334-4398
Toll free: (800) 721-3272
Mailing address: P.O. Box 83720, Boise, ID 83720-0043

Mary Hartung, Director
700 W. State St., 3rd Fl., Boise, ID 83702

Fire Marshal
http://www.doi.state.id.us/firemars/firemars.htm
Main phone: (208) 334-4370
Main fax: (208) 334-4375
Mailing address: P.O. Box 83720, Boise, ID
83720-0043

Don McCoy, State Fire Marshal
700 W. State St., 3rd Fl., Boise, ID 83720
E-mail: dmccoy@doi.state.id.us

Juvenile Corrections Dept.
http://www.djc.state.id.us/
Main phone: (208) 334-5100
Main fax: (208) 334-5120
Mailing address: P.O. Box 83720, Boise, ID
83720-0285

Brent D. Reinke, Director
400 N. 10th St., 2nd Fl., Boise, ID 83720-0285
E-mail: breinke@djc.state.id.us

Labor Dept.
http://www.labor.state.id.us
Main phone: (208) 334-6100
Main fax: (208) 334-6430

Roger B. Madsen, Director
317 Main St., Boise, ID 83735-0001
(208) 334-6110
E-mail: rmadsen@labor.state.id.us

Law Enforcement Dept.
http://www.state.id.us/dle/dle.htm
Main phone: (208) 884-7000
Main fax: (208) 884-7090
Mailing address: P.O. Box 700, Meridian, ID
83680-0700

Ed Strickfaden, Director
700 S. Stratford Dr., Meridian, ID 83642
(208) 884-7003

Police Services Division: Alcohol Beverage Control Bureau
Main phone: (208) 884-7060
Main fax: (208) 884-7096
Toll free: (888) 222-1360
Mailing address: P.O. Box 700, Meridian, ID
83680-0700

Lonnie Gray, Chief
700 S. Stratford Dr., Meridian, ID 83680

Nursing Board
http://www2.state.id.us/ibn.ibnhome.htm
General e-mail: lcoley@ibn.state.id.us

Main phone: (208) 334-3110
Main fax: (208) 334-3262
TTY: (800) 377-3529
Mailing address: P.O. Box 83720, Boise, ID
83720-0061

Sandra Evans, Executive Director
280 N. 8th St., #210, Boise, ID 83720-0061
(208) 334-3110, ext. 21

Occupational Licenses Bureau
http://www.state.id.us/ibol/
General e-mail: ibol@ibol.state.id.us
Main phone: (208) 334-3233
Main fax: (208) 334-3945

Thomas F. Limbaugh, Bureau Chief
1109 Main St., #220, Boise, ID 83702
E-mail: tlimbaugh@ibol.state.id.us

Pardon and Parole Commission
General e-mail: jpage@corr.state.id.us
Main phone: (208) 334-2520
Main fax: (208) 334-3501
Mailing address: P.O. Box 83720, Boise, ID
83720-1807

Olivia Craven, Executive Director
3125 Shoshone St., Boise, ID 83720-1807
E-mail: ocraven@corr.state.id.us

Parks and Recreation Dept.
http://www.idahoparks.org/

Occupational Licenses Bureau

http://www.state.id.us/ibol/
(208) 334-3233

Accountancy, (208) 334-2490,
  http://www.state.id.us/boa
Architects, (208) 334-3233,
  http://www.state.id.us/ibol/arc.htm
Child Care, (208) 384-3710
Contractors, (208) 334-2966
Cosmetology, (208) 334-3233,
  http://www.state.id.us/ibol/cos.htm
Engineers and Land Surveyors, (208) 334-
  3860, http://www.state.id.us/ipels/index.htm
Nursing, (208) 334-3110,
  http://www2.state.id.us/ibn.ibnhome.htm
Pharmacy, (208) 334-2356
Real Estate Appraisers, (208) 334-3233,
  http://www.state.id.us/ibol/rea.htm

Main phone: (208) 334-4199
Main fax: (208) 334-3741
TTY: (800) 377-3529

Yvonne S. Ferrell, Director
5657 Warm Springs Ave., Boise, ID 83712
(208) 334-4180, ext. 302; *Fax:* (208) 334-5232
E-mail: yferrell@idpr.state.id.us

Personnel Commission
http://www.ipc.state.id.us/
Main phone: (208) 334-2263
Main fax: (208) 334-3182
Toll free: (800) 554-5627
TTY: (800) 542-5738
Mailing address: P.O. Box 83720, Boise, ID
83720-0066

Ann Heilman, Administrator
700 W. State St., Boise, ID 83720-0066
(208) 334-3345
E-mail: aheilman@dhr.state.id.us

Pharmacy Board
Main phone: (208) 334-2356
Main fax: (208) 334-3536
Mailing address: P.O. Box 83720, Boise, ID
83720-0067

Richard K. Markuson, Director
280 N. 8th St., #204, Boise, ID 83720-0067
E-mail: rmarkuson@bop.state.id.us

Professional Engineers and Land Surveyors Board
http://www.state.id.us/ipels/index.htm
Main phone: (208) 334-3860
Main fax: (208) 334-2008
TTY: (800) 377-3529

David L. Curtis, Executive Secretary
600 S. Orchard St., Boise, ID 83705
E-mail: dcurtis@ipels.state.id.us

Public Employees Retirement System
http://www.persi.state.id.us
Main phone: (208) 334-3365
Main fax: (208) 334-3804
Toll free: (800) 451-8228

Alan Winkle, Director
607 N. 8th, Boise, ID 83702
E-mail: awinkle@persi.state.id.us

Public Utilities Commission
http://www.puc.state.id.us/
General e-mail: ipuc@puc.state.id.us
Main phone: (208) 334-0300
Main fax: (208) 334-3762
Consumer complaint: (800) 554-5627

TTY: (208) 334-3151
Mailing address: P.O. Box 83720, Boise, ID
83720-0074

Dennis S. Hansen, President
472 W. Washington, Boise, ID 83702-5983
(208) 334-3427
E-mail: dhansen@puc.state.id.us

Real Estate Appraisers Board
http://www.state.id.us/ibol/rea.htm
Main phone: (208) 334-3233
Main fax: (208) 334-3945

Thomas E. Limbaugh, Bureau Chief
1109 Main St., #220, Boise, ID 83702-5642
E-mail: drandall@ibol.state.id.us

Soil Conservation Commission
http://www.scc.state.id.us/
Main phone: (208) 332-8650
Mailing address: P.O. Box 790, Boise, ID 83701-
0790

Jerry Nicolescu, Administrator
2270 Old Penitentiary Rd., Boise, ID 83712
(208) 332-8649
E-mail: jnicoles@agri.state.id.us

State Lottery
http://www.idaholottery.com/
General e-mail: info@idaho_lottery.com
Main phone: (208) 334-2600
Main fax: (208) 334-2610
Mailing address: P.O. Box 6537, Boise, ID 83707-
6537

Robert Ginkel, Executive Director (Acting)
1199 Shoreline Lane, #100, Boise, ID 83702
E-mail: bginkel@islc.state.id.us

Tax Commission
http://www.state.id.us/tax/index.html
Main phone: (208) 334-7660
Main fax: (208) 334-7846
Toll free: (800) 972-7660
TTY: (800) 377-3529
Mailing address: P.O. Box 36, Boise, ID 83712

R. Michael Southcombe, Chair
Plaza IV Bldg., 800 Park Blvd., Boise, ID 83722
(208) 334-7500; *Fax:* (208) 334-7844
E-mail: RSouthcombe@tax.state.id.us

Transportation Dept.
http://www.state.id.us/itd/hmpg.htm
Main phone: (208) 334-8000
Main fax: (208) 334-3858
TTY: (208) 334-4458

Mailing address: P.O. Box 7129, Boise, ID 83707-1129

Charles L. Winder, Board Chair
3311 W. State St., Boise, ID 83707-1129
(208) 334-8808; *Fax:* (208) 334-8195

Aeronautics Division
http://www.state.id.us/itd/aero/aerohome.htm
Main phone: (208) 334-8000
Main fax: (208) 334-8789
Toll free: (800) 426-4587
Mailing address: P.O. Box 7129, Boise, ID 83707-1129

William Parish, Chair
3483 Rickenbacker St., Boise, ID 83705
E-mail: parish@uidaho.edu

Motor Vehicles Division
http://www2.state.id.us/itd/dmv/dmv.htm
Main phone: (208) 334-8606
Main fax: (208) 334-8739
TTY: (208) 334-4458
Mailing address: P.O. Box 7129, Boise, ID 83707-1129

Morris Detmar, Administrator
3311 W. State St., #130, Boise, ID 83707-1129
E-mail: modetmar@itd.state.id.us

Water Resources Dept.
http://www.idwr.state.id.us/idwr.idwrhome.htm
General e-mail: dlarsen@idwr.state.id.us
Main phone: (208) 327-7900
Main fax: (208) 327-7866
Mailing address: P.O. Box 83720, Boise, ID 83720-0098

Karl J. Dreher, Director
1301 N. Orchard St., Boise, ID 83706-2237
(208) 327-7910
E-mail: kdreher@idwr.state.id.us

Women's Commission
http://www.state.id.us/women/
Main phone: (208) 334-4673
Main fax: (208) 334-4646
Toll free: (800) 643-7798
Mailing address: P.O. Box 83720, Boise, ID 83720-0036

Linda Hurlbutt, Executive Director
450 W. State St., 5th Fl., Boise, ID 83702
E-mail: lhurlbutt@women.state.id.us

Laws

Sales tax: 5%
Income tax: 8.2%
State minimum wage: $5.15 (Federal is $5.15)
Marriage age: 18
First-cousin marriage: Prohibited
Drinking age: 21
State control of liquor sales: Yes
Blood alcohol for DWI: 0.08%
Driving age: 16
Speed limit: 75 mph
Permit to buy handguns: No
Minimum age to possess handguns: 18
Minimum age to possess rifles, shotguns: None
State lottery: Yes; also Powerball
Casinos: No; but slot/video machines
Pari-mutuel betting: Horse and dog racing
Death penalty: Yes
3 strikes minimum sentence: 5 yrs. (3rd felony)
Hate crimes law: Yes
Gay employment non-discrimination: No
Official language(s): None
Term limits: Governor (8 yrs.); state legislators (8 yrs.)

State laws are complex and subject to change; this information is not intended as legal advice. For an explanation of this information, see p. x.

Idaho Legislature
State Capitol Bldg.
P.O. Box 83720
Boise, ID 83720
General information: (208) 332-1000
Fax: (208) 334-5397
TTY: (800) 626-0471
http://www.state.id.us/legislat/legislat.html

Senate
Address: State Capitol Bldg., P.O. Box 83720, Boise, ID 83720-0081
General information: (208) 332-1310
Fax: (208) 334-2320

C. L. (Butch) Otter (R), President
State Capitol Bldg., 700 W. Jefferson St., #225, Boise, ID 83720-0057

(208) 334-2200; *Fax:* (208) 334-3259
E-mail: botter@lgo.state.id.us
http://www.state.id.us/gov/lgo/ltgov.htm

Robert L. Geddes (R), President Pro Tempore
State Capitol Bldg., P.O. Box 83720, #351, Boise, ID 83720
(208) 332-1300

Jim Risch (R), Majority Leader
State Capitol Bldg., P.O. Box 83720, #339, Boise, ID 83720
(208) 332-1303

Clint Stennett (D), Democrat Leader
State Capitol Bldg., P.O. Box 83720, #356, Boise, ID 83720
(208) 332-1351

Jeannine Wood, Secretary
State Capitol Bldg., P.O. Box 83720, Boise, ID 83720
(208) 332-1310
E-mail: jwood@senate.state.id.us

House
Address: State Capitol Bldg., P.O. Box 83720, Boise, ID 83720-0038
General information: (208) 332-1140

Bruce Newcomb (R), Speaker of the House
State Capitol Bldg., P.O. Box 83720, #309, Boise, ID 83720
(208) 332-1111

Frank Bruneel (R), Majority Leader
State Capitol Bldg., P.O. Box 83720, #306, Boise, ID 83720
(208) 332-1120

Wendy Jaquet (D), Minority Leader
State Capitol Bldg., P.O. Box 83720, #322, Boise, ID 83720
(208) 332-1130

Pamm Juker, Chief Clerk
State Capitol Bldg., P.O. Box 83720, Boise, ID 83720
(208) 332-1140

Idaho Judiciary
451 W. State St.
Boise, ID 83720
http://www.state.id.us/judicial

Supreme Court
Frederick C. Lyon, Clerk
451 W. State St., Boise, ID 83702
(208) 334-2210; *Fax:* (208) 334-2616
E-mail: flyon@isc.state.id.us

Justices
Composition: 5 justices
Selection Method: nonpartisan election; vacancies filled by governor
Length of term: 6 years

Linda Copple Trout, Chief Justice, (208) 334-2207
Cathy R. Silak, Vice Chief Justice, (208) 334-3288
Wayne L. Kidwell, Associate Justice, (208) 334-3186
Gerald F. Schroeder, Associate Justice, (208) 334-3324
Jesse R. Walters Jr., Associate Justice, (208) 334-3464

Administrative Director of the Courts
Main phone: (208) 334-2246
Main fax: (208) 334-2146

Patricia Tobias, Administrative Director
451 W. State St., Boise, ID 83702
E-mail: ptobias@isc.state.id.us

State Law Library
http://www2.state.id.us/lawlib/lawlib.html
Main phone: (208) 334-3316
Main fax: (208) 334-4019
General e-mail: lawlib@isc.state.id.us

Elizabeth Peterson, Law Librarian
451 W. State St., Boise, ID 83702
E-mail: epeterso@isc.state.id.us

Legislative and Political Party Information Resources

Senate home page: http://www.state.id.us/legislat/sindex.html
House home page: http://www.state.id.us/legislat/hindex.html
Committees: Senate: http://www.state.id.us/legislat.scommit.html; *House:* http://www.state.id.us/legislat/hcommit.html
Legislative information: http://www.state.id.us/legislat/legtrack.html
Legislative process: http://www.state.id.us/legislat/billlaw.html
Current session information: http://www.state.id.us/legislat/agenda.html
Idaho Democratic Party: http://www.idaho-democrats.org
   710 W. Franklin, Boise, ID 83702; *Phone:* (208) 336-1815; *E-mail:* info@idaho_democrats.org
Idaho Republican Party: http://www.idgop.com
   1150 W. State St., #300, Boise, ID 83702; *Phone:* (208) 343-6405

Illinois

State House
Springfield, IL 62706
Public information: (217) 782-2000
http://www.state.il.us

Office of the Governor
http://www.state.il.us/gov/
General e-mail: governor@state.il.us
Main phone: (217) 782-6830
Main fax: (217) 782-1853
TTY: (217) 782-0244

George H. Ryan (R), Governor
State House, #207, Springfield, IL 62706

Robert H. Newtson, Chief of Staff
State House, #207, Springfield, IL 62706
(217) 782-3958; *Fax:* (217) 524-1675
E-mail: bob_newtson@gov.state.il.us

David Urbanek, Press Secretary
State House, Springfield, IL 62706
(217) 782-7355; *Fax:* (217) 782-1676

Bernie Robinson, Assistant to the Governor, Washington Office
444 N. Capitol St. N.W., #240, Washington, DC 20001
(202) 624-7776; *Fax:* (202) 724-0689
E-mail: Bernie_Robinson@gov.state.il.us

Office of the Lieutenant Governor
http://www.state.il.us/ltgov/
Main phone: (217) 782-7884
Main fax: (217) 524-6262
Toll free: (800) 843-5848

Corinne Wood (R), Lieutenant Governor
State House, #214, Springfield, IL 62706
E-mail: ltgov@gov.state.il.us

Office of the Secretary of State
http://www.sos.state.il.us/
Main phone: (217) 782-2201
Main fax: (217) 785-0358
Toll free: (800) 252-8980
TTY: (800) 252-2904

Jesse White (D), Secretary of State
State House, #213, Springfield, IL 62756
E-mail: jwhite@ccgate.sos.state.il.us

Office of the Attorney General
http://www.ag.state.il.us
General e-mail: attorney_general@state.il.us
Main phone: (217) 782-1090

State of Illinois

Capital: Springfield, since 1837
Founded: 1809, Illinois Territory created from Indiana Territory
Statehood: December 3, 1818 (21st state)
Constitution adopted: 1970
Area: 55,593 sq. mi. (ranks 24th)
Population: 12,045,326 (1998 est.; ranks 5th)
Largest cities: (1998 est.) Chicago (2,802,079); Rockford (143,656); Aurora (124,736); Springfield (117,098); Naperville (117,091)
Counties: 102, Most populous: (1998 est.) Cook (5,189,689); Du Page (880,491); Lake (605,116); Will (459,189); St. Clair (261,941)
U.S. Congress: Richard J. Durbin (D), Peter G. Fitzgerald (R); 20 Representatives
Nickname(s): Prairie State, Land of Lincoln
Motto: State sovereignty, national union
Song: "Illinois"
Bird: Cardinal
Tree: White oak
Flower: Native violet
State fair: at Springfield, mid-Aug.
Former capital(s): Kaskaskia, Vandalia

Main fax: (217) 782-7046
Toll free: (800) 243-0618
TTY: (217) 785-2771

Jim Ryan (R), Attorney General
500 S. 2nd St., Springfield, IL 62706
(217) 782-9000

Office of the State Treasurer
http://www.state.il.us/treas
General e-mail:
treasurer_webmaster@mail.state.il.us
Main phone: (217) 782-2211
Main fax: (217) 785-2777
TTY: (312) 814-3568

Judy Baar Topinka (R), State Treasurer
State House, #219, Springfield, IL 62706

Office of the Auditor General
http://www.state.il.us/auditor/audhome.htm

General e-mail: auditor@mail.state.il.us
Main phone: (217) 782-6046
Main fax: (217) 785-8222
TTY: (217) 524-4646

William G. Holland, Auditor General
Iles Park Plaza, 740 E. Ash St., Springfield, IL 62703
(217) 782-3536

Office of the Comptroller
http://www.comptroller.state.il.us
General e-mail: webmaster@mail.ioc.state.il.us
Main phone: (217) 782-6000
Main fax: (217) 782-7561
TTY: (217) 782-1308

Dan Hynes (D), Comptroller
State House, #201, Springfield, IL 62706

Military Affairs Dept.
http://www.il-arng.ngb.army.mil/default1.htm
General e-mail: doimil@il-arng.ngb.army.mil
Main phone: (217) 761-3702
Main fax: (217) 761-3712
TTY: (217) 761-3791

David Harris, Adjutant General
1301 N. MacArthur Blvd., Springfield, IL 62702-2399
(217) 761-3500; *Fax:* (217) 761-3736

Agencies

Aging Dept.
http://www.state.il.us/aging/
General e-mail: ilsenior@age084r1.state.il.us
Main phone: (217) 785-3356
Main fax: (217) 785-4477
Toll free: (800) 252-2966
TTY: (800) 252-8966

Margo E. Schreiber, Director
421 E. Capitol Ave., #100, Springfield, IL 62701-1789
(217) 785-2870
E-mail: mschreib@age084r1.state.il.us

Agriculture Dept.
http://www.agr.state.il.us/
Main phone: (217) 782-2172
Main fax: (217) 785-4505
TTY: (217) 524-6858
Mailing address: P.O. Box 19281, Springfield, IL
62794-9281

Joseph Hampton, Director
802 E. Sangamon Ave., Springfield, IL 62702
(217) 785-4789

Illinois State Fair Bureau
http://www.state.il.us/fair
Main phone: (217) 782-6661

Main fax: (217) 782-9115
Mailing address: P.O. Box 19427, Springfield,
IL 62794

Bud Ford, State Fair Manager
801 E. Sangamon, Springfield, IL 62702
(217) 782-6662
E-mail: bford@agr.state.il.us

Appellate Defender
http://www.state.il.us/defender/
Main phone: (217) 782-7203
Main fax: (217) 782-5385
TTY: (217) 782-5384
Mailing address: P.O. Box 5780, Springfield, IL
62705-5780

Theodore A. Gottfried, Appellate Defender
400 S. 9th St., #201, Springfield, IL 62705-5780

Archives and Records
http://www.sos.state.il.us/depts/archives/
arc_home.html
Main phone: (217) 782-3492
Main fax: (217) 524-3930

John Daly, Director
Margaret Cross Norton Bldg., Springfield, IL 62756
E-mail: jdaly@ccgate.sos.state.il.us

Arts Council
http://www.state.il.us/agency/iac
General e-mail: info@arts.state.il.us
Main phone: (312) 814-6750
Main fax: (312) 814-1471
Toll free: (800) 237-6994

Rhoda A. Pierce, Executive Director
James R. Thompson Center, 100 W. Randolph St.,
#10-500, Chicago, IL 60601-3298
(312) 814-6758

Banks and Real Estate Office
http://www.state.il.us/obr
General e-mail: obre_webmaster@mail.state.il.us
Main phone: (217) 782-3000
Main fax: (217) 524-5941
Toll free: (877) 793-3470
TTY: (217) 524-6644

William A. Darr, Commissioner
500 E. Monroe St., Springfield, IL 62701-1509
(312) 793-3000; *Fax:* (312) 793-7097

Board of Education
http://www.isbe.state.il.us/
Main phone: (217) 782-4321
Main fax: (217) 524-8585

Glenn W. McGee, State Superintendent
100 N. 1st St., Springfield, IL 62777-0001

Board of Higher Education

http://www.ibhe.state.il.us/
Main phone: (217) 782-2551
Main fax: (217) 782-8548
TTY: (217) 524-3494

Keith R. Sanders, Executive Director
431 E. Adams, 2nd Fl., Springfield, IL 62701-1418
(217) 557-7300
E-mail: sanders@ibhe.state.il.us

Central Management Services Dept.

http://www.state.il.us/cms
Main phone: (217) 782-2141
Main fax: (217) 524-1880
TTY: (217) 785-3979

Michael S. Schwartz, Director
715 William G. Stratton Bldg., Springfield, IL 62706

Personnel Agency Services Bureau

http://www.state.il.us/cms/persnl/
Main phone: (217) 782-3379
Main fax: (217) 524-1880

Dianne J. Hurrelbrink, Manager
715 William G. Stratton Bldg., Springfield, IL 62706
(217) 524-8773; *Fax:* (217) 524-0836

Commerce and Community Affairs Dept.

http://www.commerce.state.il.us
Main phone: (217) 782-7500
Main fax: (312) 814-7179
TTY: (217) 785-0211

Pam McDonough, Director
620 E. Adams St., Springfield, IL 62701
(217) 782-3233; *Fax:* (217) 524-0864

Tourism Bureau

http://www.enjoyillinois.com
General e-mail: tourism@state.il.us
Main phone: (312) 814-4735
Main fax: (312) 814-6175
Travel information: (800) 226-6632

Cathy Ritter, Deputy Director
100 W. Randolph St., #3-400, Chicago, IL 60601

Consumer Protection Division

Main phone: (312) 814-3749
Main fax: (312) 814-2593
Toll free: (800) 386-5438

Patricia Kelly, Chief
100 W. Randolph St., 12th Fl., Chicago, IL 60601

Corrections Dept.

http://www.idoc.state.il.us/
Main phone: (217) 522-2666
Main fax: (217) 522-8719

TTY: (800) 526-0844
Mailing address: P.O. Box 19277, Springfield, IL 62794-9277

Donald N. Snyder Jr., Director
1301 Concordia Court, Springfield, IL 62794-9277
(217) 522-2666, ext. 2015
E-mail: director@idoc.state.il

Criminal Justice Information Authority

http://www.icjia.org/public/index.cfm
Main phone: (312) 793-8550
Main fax: (312) 793-8422
TTY: (312) 793-4170

Candice Kane, Executive Director
120 S. Riverside Plaza, #1016, Chicago, IL 60606-3997

Development Finance Authority

http://www.idfa.com
Main phone: (312) 627-1434
Main fax: (312) 496-0578
TTY: (800) 526-0844

Michael Zavis, Chair
233 S. Wacker Dr., #4000, Chicago, IL 60606

Developmental Disabilities Planning Council

Main phone: (312) 814-2080
Main fax: (312) 814-7141
TTY: (312) 814-7151

Sheila Romano, Director
100 W. Randolph, #10-600, Chicago, IL 60601
E-mail: sramano@mail.state.il.us

Driver Services Dept.

Main phone: (217) 782-6212
Toll free: (800) 252-8980

Alan Woodson, Director
2701 S. Dirksen Pkwy., Springfield, IL 62723
(217) 785-4500

Emergency Management Agency

http://www.state.il.us/iema/
Main phone: (217) 782-7860
Main fax: (217) 782-2589
TTY: (217) 782-6023

Michael Chamness, Director
110 E. Adams St., Springfield, IL 62701
(217) 782-2700; *Fax:* (217) 524-7967
E-mail: mchamness@iema.state.il.us

Employees Retirement System

http://www.state.il.us/srs/sers/edefault.htm
General e-mail: ser@pop.state.il.us
Main phone: (217) 785-7444
Main fax: (217) 785-7019
TTY: (217) 785-7218

Higher Educational Institutions

Chicago State University
http://www.csu.edu
9501 S. M. L. King Dr., Chicago, IL 60628
Main phone: (773) 995-2000

Eastern Illinois University
http://www.eiu.edu
600 Lincoln Ave., Charleston, IL 61920-3099
Main phone: (217) 581-5000

Governors State University
http://www.govst.edu
University Park, IL 60466-0975
Main phone: (708) 534-4490

Illinois Institute of Art
http://www.ilia.aii.edu
350 N. Orleans St., #136, Chicago, IL 60654-1503
Main phone: (312) 280-3500, ext. 132
Branches: Schaumburg

Illinois State University
http://www.ilstu.edu
700 W. College Ave., Normal, IL 61790-9240
Main phone: (309) 438-2181

Northeastern Illinois University
http://www.neiu.edu
5500 N. St. Louis Ave., Chicago, IL 60625-4699
Main phone: (773) 583-4050

Northern Illinois University
http://www.niu.edu
DeKalb, IL 60115
Main phone: (815) 753-0446

Southern Illinois University
http://www.siu.edu
Box 1047, Edwardsville, IL 62026-0001
Main phone: (618) 650-3705
Branches: Carbondale, Edwardsville, IL; Niigata, Japan

University of Illinois
http://www.uillinois.edu
601 S. Morgan St., Chicago, IL 60607-7128
Main phone: (312) 996-4350
Branches: Chicago, Springfield, Urbana-Champaign

Western Illinois University
http://www.wiu.edu
1 University Circle, Malcomb, IL 61455-1390
Main phone: (309) 298-3157

Mailing address: P.O. Box 19255, Springfield, IL 62794-9255

Michael L. Mory, Executive Secretary
2101 S. Veterans Pkwy., Springfield, IL 62794-9255
(217) 785-7016

Environmental Protection Agency
http://www.epa.state.il.us/
Main phone: (217) 782-2829
Main fax: (217) 782-9039
TTY: (217) 782-9143
Mailing address: P.O. Box 19276, Springfield, IL 62794-9276

Thomas V. Skinner, Director
1021 N. Brand Ave. East, Springfield, IL 62794-9276
(217) 782-9540
E-mail: epa8181@epa.state.il.us

Ethics Commission
Main phone: (217) 524-5414
Main fax: (217) 524-6127

Tracy Winter, Executive Director
720 Stratton Office Bldg., 401 S. Spring St., #3-300, Springfield, IL 62706

Financial Institutions Dept.
http://www.state.il.us/dfi
General e-mail: dfi@mail.state.il.us
Main phone: (312) 814-2000
Main fax: (312) 814-5168
TTY: (312) 814-7138

Sarah D. Vega, Director
James R. Thompson Center, 100 W. Randolph St., #700-15, Chicago, IL 60601
(312) 814-2714

Fire Marshal
http://www.state.il.us/osfm
Main phone: (217) 785-0969
Main fax: (217) 782-1062

Thomas L. Armstead, State Fire Marshal
1035 Stevenson Dr., Springfield, IL 62703-4259
(217) 785-4143
E-mail: tarmstead@mail.state.il.us

Arson/Fire Prevention Division
General e-mail: jheminghous@mail.state.il.us
Main phone: (217) 785-0969
Main fax: (217) 782-1062

Jack (John) Ahern, Director
1035 Stevenson Dr., Springfield, IL 62703-4259
(217) 785-4714; *Fax:* (217) 782-6855

Health Care Cost Containment Council
http://www.state.il.us/agency/hcccc
Main phone: (217) 786-7001
Main fax: (217) 786-7179

Joseph A. Bonefeste, Executive Director
Springfield Regional Office Bldg., 4500 S. 6th St.,
#194, Springfield, IL 62703-5118

Historic Preservation Agency
http://www.state.il.us/HPA/ihpa/home/default.htm
Main phone: (217) 524-6977
Main fax: (217) 785-7937
TTY: (217) 524-7128

Susan Mogerman, Director
1 Old State Capitol Plaza, Springfield, IL 62701-1507
(217) 785-7930; *Fax:* (217) 785-7937

Housing Development Authority
http://www.idha.org
Main phone: (312) 836-5200
Main fax: (312) 832-2172
TTY: (312) 836-5222

Michael P. Rose, Executive Director (Acting)
401 N. Michigan Ave., #900, Chicago, IL 60611
(312) 836-5337; *Fax:* (312) 832-2170
E-mail: mrose@idha.org

Human Rights Dept.
http://www.state.il.us/dhr/
General e-mail:
  David_Espinoza@ccmailgw.state.il.us
Main phone: (312) 814-6200
Main fax: (312) 814-1436
TTY: (312) 263-1579

Carlos J. Salazar, Director
James R. Thompson Center, 100 W. Randolph St.,
#10-100, Chicago, IL 60601
(312) 814-6245
E-mail: Carlos_Salazar@ccMailgw.state.il.us

Human Services Dept.
http://www.state.il.us/agency/dhs/
General e-mail: llewis@dhs.state.il.us
Main phone: (217) 557-1601
Main fax: (217) 557-1647
TTY: (800) 447-6404

Howard A. Peters III, Secretary
100 S. Grand Ave. East, Springfield, IL 62762
E-mail: dhse015@dhs.state.il.us

Mental Health and Developmental Disability Services Division
Main phone: (847) 742-1040 x2954
Main fax: (847) 429-4910
TTY: (847) 429-5741

Nancy Staples, Administrator
Elgin Mental Health Center, 750 S. State St., Elgin,
IL 60123
(847) 742-1040, ext. 2010

Industrial Commission
http://www.state.il.us/agency/iic/
General e-mail: mis@mail.state.il.us
Main phone: (312) 814-6611
Main fax: (312) 814-6523
TTY: (312) 814-2959

John W. Hallock Jr., Chair
100 W. Randolph St., #8-200, Chicago, IL 60601
(312) 814-6500

Insurance Dept.
http://www.state.il.us/ins/
General e-mail: director@ins.state.il.us
Main phone: (217) 782-4515
Main fax: (217) 782-5020
TTY: (217) 524-4872

Nathaniel S. Shapo, Director
320 W. Washington St., 4th Fl., Springfield, IL 62767
(217) 785-0116

Labor Dept.
http://www.state.il.us/agency/idol
General e-mail: idol@pop.state.il.us
Main phone: (312) 793-2800
Main fax: (312) 793-5257
TTY: (312) 793-4463

Robert M. Healey, Director
160 N. La Salle St., #C-1300, Chicago, IL 60601
(312) 793-1808

Liquor Control Commission
http://www.state.il.us/lcc
General e-mail: lcc_webmaster@mail.state.il.us
Main phone: (312) 814-2206
Main fax: (312) 814-2241
TTY: (312) 814-1844

Leonard L. Branson, Chair
James R. Thompson Center, 100 W. Randolph St., #5-
300, Chicago, IL 60601
(312) 814-3930

Lottery Dept.
http://www.illinoislottery.com/
Main phone: (312) 793-3026
Main fax: (312) 951-7204
Toll free: (800) 252-1775
TTY: (312) 793-3038

Lori S. Montana, Director
676 St. Clair St., #2040, Chicago, IL 60611
(312) 793-1681; *Fax:* (312) 793-5514
E-mail: lori.montana@isl.state.il.us

Natural Resources Dept.
http://dnr.state.il.us/
Main phone: (217) 782-6302
Main fax: (217) 785-9236
TTY: (217) 782-9175

Frequently Called Numbers

Tourism: (312) 814-4735; 1-800-2-CONNECT; http://www.enjoyillinois.com

Library: (217) 782-2201; http://www.sos.state.il.us/depts/library/isl_home.html

Board of Education: (217) 782-4321; http://www.isbe.state.il.us/

Vital Statistics: (217) 782-6553; http://www.idph.state.il.us/vital/vitalhome.htm

Tax/Revenue: (217) 782-3336; http://www.revenue.state.il.us/

Motor Vehicles: (217) 782-6212

State Police/Highway Patrol: (217) 786-6677; http://www.state.il.us/isp/

Unemployment: (312) 793-7378, 888-337-7234; http://www.ides.state.il.us/html/worker.htm

General Election Information: (217) 782-4141; www.elections.state.il.us

Consumer Affairs: (312) 814-3749

Hazardous Materials: (217) 524-3300

Brent Manning, Director
Lincoln Tower Plaza, 524 S. 2nd St., Springfield, IL 62701-1787
E-mail: director@dnrmail.state.il.us

Land Management Office: State Parks
http://dnr.state.il.us/lands/landmgt/parks
Main phone: (217) 782-6752
Main fax: (217) 524-5612
Mailing address: 524 S. 2nd St., Lincoln Tower Plaza, Springfield, IL 62701

Jerry Beverlin, Director
600 N. Grand Ave. West, Springfield, IL 62706

Mines and Minerals Office: Oil and Gas Division
Main phone: (217) 782-7756
Main fax: (217) 524-4819
TTY: (217) 524-4626
Mailing address: 524 S. 2nd St., Lincoln Tower Plaza, Springfield, IL 62701

Larry Bengal, Manager
300 W. Jefferson, #300, Springfield, IL 62709
(217) 782-1689
E-mail: lbengal@dnrmail.state.il.us

Resource Conservation Office: Fisheries Resources Division
Main phone: (217) 782-6424

Main fax: (217) 785-8262
TTY: (217) 782-9175
Mailing address: 524 S. 2nd St., Lincoln Tower Plaza, Springfield, IL 62701-1787

Mike Conlin, Manager
600 N. Grand Ave. West, #5, Springfield, IL 62701
E-mail: MCONLIN@dnrmail.state.il.us

Resource Conservation Office: Forest Resources Division
Main phone: (217) 782-6384
Main fax: (217) 785-5517
TTY: (217) 782-9175
Mailing address: 524 S. 2nd St., Lincoln Tower Plaza, Springfield, IL 62701-1787

Stewart Pequignot, Chief
600 N. Grand Ave. West, #2, Springfield, IL 62701
(217) 782-2361

Resource Conservation Office: Wildlife Resources Division
Main phone: (217) 782-6384
Main fax: (217) 785-2438
TTY: (217) 782-9175
Mailing address: 524 S. 2nd St., Lincoln Tower Plaza, Springfield, IL 62701-1787

Jeff Ver Steeg, Manager
600 N. Grand Ave. West, #1, Springfield, IL 62701
E-mail: jwelch@dnrmail.state.il.us

Scientific Research and Analysis Office: State Geological Survey
http://www.isgs.uiuc.edu
Main phone: (217) 333-4747
Main fax: (217) 244-7004
TTY: (217) 785-0211

William W. Shilts, Chief
615 E. Peabody Dr., #121, Champaign, IL 61820
(217) 333-5111
E-mail: shilts@isgs.uiuc.edu

Water Resources Office
Main phone: (217) 782-2152
Main fax: (217) 785-5014
Mailing address: 524 S. 2nd St., Lincoln Tower Plaza, Springfield, IL 62701-1787

Donald R. Vonnahme, Director
3215 Executive Park Dr., Springfield, IL 62703
E-mail: dvonnahme@dnrmail.state.il.us

Professional Regulation Dept.
http://www.state.il.us/dpr
Main phone: (312) 814-4500
Main fax: (312) 814-1837
TTY: (217) 524-6735

Leonard A. Sherman, Director
100 W. Randolph St., #9-300, Chicago, IL 60601
(312) 814-4935

Public Health Dept.
http://www.idph.state.il.us/
Main phone: (217) 782-6187
Main fax: (217) 782-3987

John Lumpkin, Director
535 W. Jefferson St., Springfield, IL 62761
(217) 782-4977

Real Estate Professions
Main phone: (312) 793-3000
Main fax: (312) 793-7097

William A. Darr, Commissioner
310 S. Michigan Ave., #2130, Chicago, IL 60604-4278
(312) 793-1463

Revenue Dept.
http://www.revenue.state.il.us/
Main phone: (217) 782-3336
Main fax: (217) 782-4217
Toll free: (800) 732-8866
TTY: (800) 544-5304

Glen L. Bower, Director
101 W. Jefferson St., Springfield, IL 62794
(217) 785-7570; *Fax:* (217) 782-6337
E-mail: gbower@revenue.state.il.us

State Library
http://www.sos.state.il.us/depts/library/
   isl_home.html
Main phone: (217) 782-2201
Main fax: (217) 785-0358
Toll free: (800) 252-8980
TTY: (800) 252-2904

Jean E. Wilkins, Director
300 S. 2nd St., Springfield, IL 62701
(217) 782-2994; *Fax:* (217) 785-4326
E-mail: jwilkin@library.sos.state.il.us

State Police
http://www.state.il.us/isp/
General e-mail: isp_webmaster@state.il.us
Main phone: (217) 786-6677
Main fax: (217) 786-7191
TTY: (800) 255-3323
Mailing address: P.O. Box 19461, Springfield, IL
   62794-9461

Sam W. Nolan, Director
Armory Bldg., 125 E. Monroe St., #103, Springfield,
   IL 62794-9461
(217) 782-7263; *Fax:* (217) 785-2821
E-mail: director@isphost.state.il.us

State's Attorneys Appelate Prosecuter
http://www.state.il.us/prosecutor/
Main phone: (217) 782-1628
Main fax: (217) 782-6305

Norbert Goetten, Director
725 S. 2nd St., Springfield, IL 62704
E-mail: prosecutor@mail.state.il.us

Transportation Dept.
http://www.dot.state.il.us
Main phone: (217) 782-7820
Main fax: (217) 782-6828
TTY: (217) 524-4875

Kirk Brown, Secretary
2300 S. Dirksen Pkwy., #300, Springfield, IL 62764
(217) 782-5597

Aeronautics Division
Main phone: (217) 785-8515
Main fax: (217) 524-1022

Hugh E. Van Voorst, Director
1 Langhorne Bond Dr., Springfield, IL 62707
E-mail: vanvoorsthe@nt.dot.state.il.us

Veterans Affairs Dept.
http://www.state.il.us/agency/dva/
Main phone: (217) 782-6641
Main fax: (217) 524-0344
Toll free: (800) 437-9824
TTY: (217) 524-4645
Mailing address: P.O. Box 19432, Springfield, IL
   62794-9432

John W. Johnston, Director
833 S. Spring St., Springfield, IL 62794-9432
(217) 785-6642
E-mail: idva-dir@pop.state.il.us

Boards and Licensing

Accountancy, (217) 782-0458
Architects, (217) 782-0458
Child Care, (312) 793-8600
Cosmetology, (217) 782-0458
Engineers and Land Surveyors,
   (217) 782-0458
Medical Examiners, (217) 782-0458
Nursing, (217) 782-0458
Pharmacy, (217) 782-0458
Professional Regulation and Licensing,
   (217) 782-0458
Real Estate Appraisers, (217) 782-3000

Women's Commission
Main phone: (312) 944-4310
Main fax: (312) 814-3823

Judy Gold, Chair
100 W. Randolph St., #16-100, Chicago, IL 60601

Illinois Legislature
Springfield, IL 62706
General information: (217) 782-2000
Bill status: (217) 782-3944
http://www.state.il.us/legis/

Senate
Address: Capitol Bldg., Springfield, IL 62706
General information: (217) 782-4517

James (Pate) Philip (R), President
Capitol Bldg., #327, Springfield, IL 62706
(217) 782-3840
http://www.legis.state.il.us/homepages/senate/
philipja.html

Stanley Weaver (R), Majority Leader
Capitol Bldg., #329, Springfield, IL 62706
(217) 782-6904
http://www.legis.state.il.us/homepages/senate/
weaversb.html

Edward Petka (R), Majority Whip
Capitol Bldg., #122, Springfield, IL 62706
(217) 782-0422
http://www.legis.state.il.us/homepages/senate/
petkae.html

Emil Jones (D), Minority Leader
Capitol Bldg., #309-A, Springfield, IL 62706
(217) 782-2728; *Fax:* (217) 782-1967
http://www.legis.state.il.us/homepages/senate/
jonese.html

Debbie Halvorson (D), Minority Caucus Whip
Capitol Bldg., #105-E, Springfield, IL 62706
(217) 782-7419; *Fax:* (217) 782-5252
E-mail: halvorson@senatedem.state.il.us
http://www.legis.state.il.us/homepages/senate/
halvorsond.html

Jim Harry, Secretary
Capitol Bldg., Springfield, IL 62706
(217) 782-5715; *Fax:* (217) 782-0813

House
Address: State House, Springfield, IL 62706
General information: (217) 782-8223
Fax: (217) 782-3885

Laws

Sales tax: 6.25%
Income tax: 3%
State minimum wage: $5.15 (Federal is $5.15)
Marriage age: 18
First-cousin marriage: Prohibited
Drinking age: 21
State control of liquor sales: No
Blood alcohol for DWI: 0.08%
Driving age: 17
Speed limit: 65 mph
Permit to buy handguns: Yes, plus 3-day wait
Minimum age to possess handguns: 18
Minimum age to possess rifles, shotguns:
  None, with adult supervision
State lottery: Yes
Casinos: Yes (commercial)
Pari-mutuel betting: Horse racing
Death penalty: Yes
3 strikes minimum sentence: Life (3rd serious
  felony)
Hate crimes law: Yes
Gay employment non-discrimination: No
Official language(s): English
Term limits: None

*State laws are complex and subject to
change; this information is not intended as
legal advice. For an explanation of this
information, see p. x.*

Michael J. Madigan (D), Speaker of the House
State House, #300, Springfield, IL 62706
(217) 782-5350; *Fax:* (217) 524-1794
E-mail: mmadigan@housedem.state.il.us
http://www.legis.state.il.us/homepages/house/
madiganmj.html

Barbary Flynn Currie (D), Majority Leader
State House, #300, Springfield, IL 62706
(217) 782-8121; *Fax:* (217) 524-1794
E-mail: bcurrie@housedem.state.il.us
http://www.legis.state.il.us/homepages/house/
curriebf.html

Lee A. Daniels (R), Minority Leader
Capitol Bldg., #316, Springfield, IL 62706
(217) 782-4014
E-mail: cyberelm@wwa.com
http://www.legis.state.il.us/homepages/house/
danielsla.html

Anthony Ross, Chief Clerk
Capitol Bldg., Springfield, IL 62706
(217) 782-8223; *Fax:* (217) 782-3885

Illinois Judiciary

Supreme Court Bldg.
200 E. Capitol Ave.
Springfield, IL 62701
http://www.state.il.us/judicial/

Supreme Court

http://www.state.il.us/court/

Juleann Hornyak, Clerk
Supreme Court Bldg., 200 E. Capitol Ave., Springfield,
IL 62701
(217) 782-2035

Justices

Composition: 7 justices
Selection Method: partisan election
Length of term: 10 years

Moses W. Harrison, Chief Justice, (618) 624-3242
Michael A. Bilandic, Justice, (312) 793-5460
Charles E. Freeman, Justice, (312) 793-5480
James D. Heiple, Justice, (309) 671-3021
Mary Ann G. McMorrow, Justice, (312) 793-5470
Benjamin K. Miller, Justice, (217) 782-4154
S. Louis Rathje, Justice, (630) 513-3005

Administrative Office of the Courts

Main phone: (312) 793-3250
Main fax: (312) 793-1335

Joseph A. Schillaci, Director
222 N. LaSalle St., 13th Fl., Chicago, IL 60601

Supreme Court Library

Main phone: (217) 782-2424
Main fax: (217) 782-5287

Brenda Larison, Supreme Court Librarian
Supreme Court Bldg., 200 E. Capitol Ave., Springfield,
IL 62701
E-mail: blarison@mail.state.il.us

Legislative and Political Party Information Resources

Senate home page: http://www.state.il.us/legis/senate.htm
House home page: http://www.state.il.us/legis/house.htm
Committees: *Senate:* http://legis.state.il.us/schedules/senatesched.htm; *House:* http://legis.state.ilus/
    schedules/housesched.htm
Legislative process: http://www.legis.state.il.us/commission/lis/98bill_law.pdf
Illinois Democratic Party: http://www.ildems.org
    1104 S. Second St., Springfield, IL 62704; *Phone:* (217) 528-3471
Illinois Republican Party: http://www.ilgop.org
    P.O. Box 78, Springfield, IL 62705; *Phone:* (217) 525-0011; *Fax:* (217) 753-4712; *E-mail:*
    info@ilgop.org

Indiana

State House
200 W. Washington St.
Indianapolis, IN 46204
Public information: (317) 232-1000
Fax: (317) 232-3443
http://www.state.in.us

Office of the Governor
http://www.state.in.us/gov/
Main phone: (317) 232-4567
Main fax: (317) 232-3443

Frank L. O'Bannon (D), Governor
State House, 200 W. Washington St., #206,
Indianapolis, IN 46204
E-mail: fobannon@state.in.us

Margaret Burlingame, Chief of Staff
State House, 200 W. Washington St., #206,
Indianapolis, IN 46204
(317) 232-4567; *Fax:* (317) 232-3443

Phil Bremen, Press Secretary
State House, 200 W. Washington St., #206,
Indianapolis, IN 46204
(317) 232-4567; *Fax:* (317) 232-3443

Annette E. Craycroft, Special Assistant, Constituent Affairs
State House, 200 W. Washington St., #206,
Indianapolis, IN 46204
(317) 232-0668; *Fax:* (317) 232-3443
E-mail: acraycroft@gov.state.in.us

Jeff Viohl, Federal Liaison, Washington Office
444 N. Capitol St. N.W., #428, Washington, DC 20001
(202) 624-1474; *Fax:* (202) 624-1475

Office of the Lieutenant Governor
http://www.state.in.us/lgov/
Main phone: (317) 232-4545
Main fax: (317) 232-4788

Joseph E. Kernan (D), Lieutenant Governor
State House, 200 W. Washington St., #333,
Indianapolis, IN 46204-2790

Office of the Secretary of State
http://www.state.in.us/sos
Main phone: (317) 232-6531
Main fax: (317) 233-3283

Sue Anne Gilroy (R), Secretary of State
State House, 200 W. Washington St., #201,
Indianapolis, IN 46204
(317) 232-6536

State of Indiana

Capital: Indianapolis, since 1825
Founded: 1800, Indiana Territory created from Northwest Territory
Statehood: December 11, 1816 (19th state)
Constitution adopted: 1851
Area: 35,870 sq. mi. (ranks 38th)
Population: 5,899,195 (1998 est.; ranks 14th)
Largest cities: (1998 est.) Indianapolis (741,304); Fort Wayne (185,716); Evansville (122,779); Gary (108,469); South Bend (99,417)
Counties: 92, Most populous: (1998 est.) Marion (813,405); Lake (478,323); Allen (314,218); St. Joseph (258,088); Elkhart (172,310)
U.S. Congress: Evan Bayh (D), Richard G. Lugar (R); 10 Representatives
Nickname(s): Hoosier State
Motto: The crossroads of America
Song: "On the Banks of the Wabash, Far Away"
Bird: Cardinal
Tree: Tulip tree
Flower: Peony
State fair: at Indianapolis, mid-Aug.
Former capital(s): Vincennes, Corydon

Office of the Attorney General
http://www.state.in.us/hoosieradvocate/
Main phone: (317) 232-6201
Main fax: (317) 232-7979

Freeman-Wilson, Karen (D), Attorney General
Indiana Government Center South, 402 W. Washington St., 5th Fl., Indianapolis, IN 46204-2770

Office of the Treasurer
http://www.state.in.us/tos/
Main phone: (317) 232-6386
Main fax: (317) 233-1928

Tim Berry (R), Treasurer
State House, 200 W. Washington St., #242,
Indianapolis, IN 46204
E-mail: tberry@tos.state.in.us

Office of the State Auditor

http://www.state.in.us/auditor/
Main phone: (317) 232-3300
Main fax: (317) 233-2794
TTY: (317) 233-6220

Connie Kay Nass (R), State Auditor
State House, 200 W. Washington St., #240,
Indianapolis, IN 46204-2793
E-mail: nassck@audlan.state.in.us

Office of the Adjutant General

http://www.state.in.us/ing/
General e-mail: mdipa@source.isd.state.in.us
Main phone: (317) 247-3300
Main fax: (317) 247-3146

Robert J. Mitchell, Adjutant General
Military Department of Indiana, 2002 S. Holt Rd.,
Indianapolis, IN 46241-4839
(317) 247-3279

Agencies

Accounts Board

http://www.state.in.us/sboa
Main phone: (317) 232-2513
Main fax: (317) 232-4711

Charles Johnson III, State Examiner
Indiana Government Center South, 302 W. Washington
St., #E-418, Indianapolis, IN 46204
(317) 232-2524

Administration Dept.

http://www.ai.org/idoa
Main phone: (317) 232-4384
Main fax: (317) 233-5022

Betty Cockrum, Commissioner
Indiana Government Center South, 402 W. Washington
St., #W-479, Indianapolis, IN 46204
(317) 232-3115

Agriculture Commissioner

http://www.state.in.us/oca/
Main phone: (317) 232-4545
Main fax: (317) 232-4788

Joseph E. Kernan, Commissioner
State House, 200 W. Washington St., #333,
Indianapolis, IN 46204

Alcohol Beverage Commission

Main phone: (317) 232-2430
Main fax: (317) 233-6114

Glenn Lawrence, Chair
Indiana Government Center South, 302 W. Washington
St., #E-114, Indianapolis, IN 46204
(317) 232-2448

Arts Commission

http://www.state.in.us/iac/
General e-mail: arts@state.in.us
Main phone: (317) 232-1268
Main fax: (317) 232-5595
TTY: (317) 233-3001

Dorothy L. Ilgen, Executive Director
Indiana Government Center South, 402 W. Washington
St., #072, Indianapolis, IN 46204-2741
(317) 232-1288

Civil Rights Commission

http://www.state.in.us/icrc/
General e-mail: cjohnson@crc.state.in.us
Main phone: (317) 232-2600
Main fax: (317) 232-6580
Toll free: (800) 268-2909
TTY: (800) 743-3333

Sandra D. Leek, Executive Director
Indiana Government Center North, 100 N. Senate
Ave., #103, Indianapolis, IN 46204
E-mail: sleek@crc.state.in.us

Commerce Dept.

http://www.state.in.us/doc/
Main phone: (317) 232-8800
Main fax: (317) 232-4146
TTY: (317) 233-5977

Thomas F. McKenna, Executive Director
1 N. Capitol Ave., #700, Indianapolis, IN 46204-2288
(317) 232-8806
E-mail: tmckenna@commerce.state.in.us

Tourism Division

http://www.state.in.us/tourism/
Main phone: (317) 232-8864
Toll free: (800) 291-8844

John Goss, Director
1 N. Capitol Ave., #700, Indianapolis, IN 46204-2288

Correction Dept.

http://www.state.in.us/indcorrection/
Main phone: (317) 233-6984
Main fax: (317) 232-6798

Edward L. Cohn, Commissioner
Indiana Government Center South, 302 W. Washington
St., #E-334, Indianapolis, IN 46204
(317) 232-5711

Community Services/Programs: Parole Services

Main phone: (317) 232-5726
Main fax: (317) 232-5728

Higher Educational Institutions

Ball State University
http://www.bsu.edu/UP/cover.html
Muncie, IN 47306
Main phone: (800) 482-4278

Indiana State University
http://www-isu.indstate.edu
Tirey Hall, Terre Haute, IN 47809
Main phone: (812) 237-2121

Indiana University
http://www.indiana.edu
107 S. Indiana Ave., Bloomington, IN 47405-700
Main phone: (812) 855 4848
Branches: Bloomington, East, Fort Wayne, Indianapolis, Kokomo, Northwest, South Bend, Southeast

Purdue University
http://www.purdue.edu
Schleman Hall, West Lafayette, IN 47907-1080
Main phone: (765) 494-4600
Branches: Calumet, Columbus, Fort Wayne, Indianapolis, North Central

University of Southern Indiana
http://www.usi.edu
8600 University Blvd., Evansville, IN 47712-3596
Main phone: (812) 464-8600

David Ferguson, Director
Indiana Government Center South, 302 W. Washington St., #E-334, Indianapolis, IN 46204
E-mail: dferguson@coa.doc.state.in.us

Juvenile Services
Main phone: (317) 232-1746
Main fax: (317) 232-4948

Evelyn I. Ridley-Turner, Deputy Commissioner
Indiana Government Center South, 302 W. Washington St., #E-334, Indianapolis, IN 46204
(317) 232-5711; *Fax:* (317) 232-6798

Criminal Justice Institute
http://www.state.in.us/cji
Main phone: (317) 232-1233
Main fax: (317) 232-4979

Catherine O'Connor, Executive Director
Indiana Government Center South, 302 W. Washington St., #E-209, Indianapolis, IN 46204-2767

Development Finance Authority
http://www.state.in.us/idfa/
Main phone: (317) 233-4332
Main fax: (317) 232-6786

Courtney R. Tobin, Executive Director
1 N. Capitol Ave., #320, Indianapolis, IN 46204-2226
E-mail: ctobin@idfa.state.in.us

Disabilities Planning Council
http://www.state.in.us/gpcpd/
General e-mail: gpcpd@in.net
Main phone: (317) 232-7770
Main fax: (317) 233-3712
TTY: (317) 232-7771

Suellen Jackson-Boner, Executive Director
143 W. Market St., #404, Indianapolis, IN 46204

Education Dept.
http://www.doe.state.in.us
Main phone: (317) 232-6610
Main fax: (317) 232-9121
TTY: (317) 232-0570

Suellen Reed (R), Superintendent of Public Instruction
State House, 200 W. Washington St., #229, Indianapolis, IN 46204
(317) 232-6665; *Fax:* (317) 232-8004
E-mail: sreed@doe.state.in.us

Board of Education
http://www.board-of-education.state.in.us
Main phone: (317) 232-6610
Main fax: (317) 232-9121
TTY: (317) 232-0570

Suellen Reed, Chair
State House, 200 W. Washington St., #229, Indianapolis, IN 46204
(317) 232-6665; *Fax:* (317) 232-8004
E-mail: sreed@doe.state.in.us

Emergency Management Agency
http://www.state.in.us/sema/
Main phone: (317) 232-3980
Main fax: (317) 232-3895

Patrick R. Ralston, Executive Director
Indiana Government Center South, 302 W. Washington St., #E-208, Indianapolis, IN 46204-2760
(317) 232-6139

Environmental Management Dept.
http://www.state.in.us/idem/
Main phone: (317) 232-8603
Main fax: (317) 233-6647
Toll free: (800) 451-6027
Mailing address: P.O. Box 6015, Indianapolis, IN 46206-6015

Lori F. Kaplan, Commissioner
Indiana Government Center North, 100 N. Senate Ave., Indianapolis, IN 46204
(317) 232-8611
E-mail: lkaplan@dem.state.in.us

Ethics Commission

http://www.state.in.us/ethics
General e-mail: ethics@iquest.net
Main phone: (317) 232-3850
Main fax: (317) 232-0707

David Maidenberg, Director
Indiana Government Center South, 402 W. Washington St., #W-189, Indianapolis, IN 46204-2026

Family and Social Services Administration

http://www.state.in.us/fssa/
Main phone: (317) 233-4454
Main fax: (317) 233-4693
TTY: (317) 232-6478

Peter Andrew Sybinsky, Secretary
Indiana Government Center South, 402 W. Washington St., #W-461, Indianapolis, IN 46204-7083
(317) 233-4690; *Fax:* (317) 233-4693

Aging and Rehabilitative Services
Main phone: (317) 232-1147
Main fax: (317) 232-1240
Toll free: (800) 545-7763
TTY: (317) 232-1143

Debra M. Simmons Wilson, Director
Indiana Government Center South, 402 W. Washington St., #W-451, Indianapolis, IN 46204-7083
E-mail: dmwilson@fssa.state.in.us

Medicaid Policy and Planning
Main phone: (317) 233-4455
Main fax: (317) 232-7382

Kathleen D. Gifford, Assistant Secretary
Indiana Government Center South, 402 W. Washington St., #W-382, Indianapolis, IN 46204-7083

Mental Health Division
Main phone: (317) 232-7845
Main fax: (317) 233-3472
Toll free: (800) 901-1133
TTY: (317) 232-7844

Janet S. Corson, Director
Indiana Government Center South, 402 W. Washington St., #W-353, Indianapolis, IN 46204-7083
E-mail: jcorson@fssa.state.in.us

Financial Institutions Dept.

http://www.dfi.state.in.us
General e-mail: rbailey@dfi.state.in.us
Main phone: (317) 232-3955
Main fax: (317) 232-7655
Toll free: (800) 382-4880

Charles Phillips, Director
Indiana Government Center South, 402 W. Washington St., #W-066, Indianapolis, IN 46204
(317) 232-5854
E-mail: cphillips@dfi.state.in.us

Fire Marshal

http://www.state.in.us/sema/osfm.html
Main phone: (317) 232-2222
Main fax: (317) 233-0307
Toll free: (800) 423-0765

M. Tracy Boatwright, State Fire Marshal
Indiana Government Center South, 402 W. Washington St., #E-241, Indianapolis, IN 46204-2739
(317) 232-2226
E-mail: tboatwright@sema.state.in.us

Health Dept.

http://www.state.in.us/isdh/
Main phone: (317) 233-1325
Main fax: (317) 233-7387
TTY: (317) 233-7859

Richard D. Feldman, State Health Commissioner
2 N. Meridian St., #3-A, Indianapolis, IN 46204
(317) 233-7400

Special Institutions: School for the Blind

http://www.isb.butler.edu
Main phone: (317) 253-1481
Main fax: (317) 251-6511

Michael J. Bina, Superintendent
7725 N. College Ave., Indianapolis, IN 46240-2504
(317) 253-1481, ext. 141

Special Institutions: School for the Deaf

http://www.deafhoosiers.com
Main phone: (317) 924-8400
Main fax: (317) 923-2853

George Stailey, Superintendent
1200 E. 42nd St., Indianapolis, IN 46205-2099
E-mail: gstailey@isfd.state.in.us

Higher Education Commission

http://www.che.state.in.us/
Main phone: (317) 464-4400
Main fax: (317) 464-4410

Stanley G. Jones, Commissioner
101 W. Ohio St., #550, Indianapolis, IN 46204-1971
E-mail: sjones@che.state.in.us

Historical Bureau

http://www.statelib.lib.in.us/www/ihb/ihb.html
General e-mail: ihb@statelib.lib.in.us
Main phone: (317) 232-2535
Main fax: (317) 232-3728
TTY: (317) 232-7763

Pamela J. Bennett, Director
State Library Historical Bldg., 140 N. Senate Ave.,
   #408, Indianapolis, IN 46204-2296
(317) 232-2988
E-mail: pbennett@statelib.lib.in.us

Hoosier Lottery
http://www.state.in.us/hoosierlottery/
General e-mail: hoslot04@ai.org
Main phone: (317) 264-4800
Main fax: (317) 264-4908
TTY: (317) 264-4920

James F. Maguire, Executive Director
Pan Am Plaza, 201 S. Capitol Ave., #1100,
   Indianapolis, IN 46225
(317) 264-4698

Housing Finance Authority
http://www.indianahousing.org
Main phone: (317) 232-7777
Main fax: (317) 232-7778
Toll free: (800) 669-4432

Robert V. Welch Jr., Executive Director
115 W. Washington St., South Tower, #1350,
   Indianapolis, IN 46204

Human Resource Investment Council
Main phone: (317) 232-1980
Main fax: (317) 233-3091
Mailing address: 10 N. Serate Ave., Indianapolis,
   IN 46204

Timothy J. McGann, Executive Director
309 W. Washington St., 5th Fl., Indianapolis, IN 46204
E-mail: tmcgann@hric.state.in.us

Insurance Dept.
http://www.state.in.us/idoi/
Main phone: (317) 232-2385
Main fax: (317) 232-5251

Sally McCarty, Commissioner
311 W. Washington St., #300, Indianapolis, IN 46204-
   2787
(317) 232-3520

Labor Dept.
http://www.state.in.us/idoi/
Main phone: (317) 232-2655
Main fax: (317) 233-3790
TTY: (800) 743-3333

John Griffin, Commissioner
Indiana Government Center South, 402 W. Washington
   St., #W-195, Indianapolis, IN 46204
(317) 232-2378; *Fax:* (317) 232-5381

Medical Licensing Board
Main phone: (317) 232-2960
Main fax: (317) 233-4236
License verification: (888) 333-7515

Angela Smith-Jones, Director
Indiana Government Center South, 402 W. Washington
   St., #041, Indianapolis, IN 46204
(317) 233-4401
E-mail: ajones@hpb.state.in.us

Motor Vehicles Bureau
http://www.bmvexpress.org
Main phone: (317) 233-6000
Main fax: (317) 233-3135

Gary A. Gibson, Commissioner
Indiana Government Center North, 100 N. Senate
   Ave., #N-440, Indianapolis, IN 46204
(317) 232-2799

Natural Resources Dept.
http://www.state.in.us/dnr/
Main phone: (317) 232-4200
Main fax: (317) 233-6811

Larry D. Macklin, Director
Indiana Government Center South, 402 W. Washington
   St., #W-256, Indianapolis, IN 46204
(317) 232-4020; *Fax:* (317) 233-6811

Lands and Cultural Resources Bureau:
   Forestry Division
http://www.state.in.us/dnr/forestry/index.htm
Main phone: (317) 232-4105
Main fax: (317) 233-3863

Burnell Fischer, Director
Indiana Government Center South, 402 W.
Washington St., #W-296, Indianapolis, IN
46204
(317) 232-4107
E-mail: bfischer@dnr.state.in.us

Lands and Cultural Resources Bureau: State Parks and Reservoirs Division
Main phone: (317) 232-4124
Main fax: (317) 232-4132
Toll free: (800) 622-4931

Gerald J. Pagac, Director
Indiana Government Center South, 402 W.
Washington St., #W-298, Indianapolis, IN
46204
(317) 232-4136

Resource Management Bureau: Fish and Wildlife Division
http://www.state.in.us/dnr/fishwild/index.htm
Main phone: (317) 232-4080
Main fax: (317) 232-8150

Gary Doxtater, Director
Indiana Government Center South, 402 W.
Washington St., #W-273, Indianapolis, IN
46204

Resource Regulation Bureau: Oil and Gas Division
http://www.state.in.us/dnr/oil
Main phone: (317) 232-4055
Main fax: (317) 232-1550

Jim Slutz, Director
Indiana Government Center South, 402 W.
Washington St., #W-293, Indianapolis, IN
46204

Resource Regulation Bureau: Soil Conservation Division
Main phone: (317) 233-3870
Main fax: (317) 233-3882

Harry S. Nikides, Director
Indiana Government Center South, 402 W.
Washington St., #W-265, Indianapolis, IN
46204
(317) 233-3880
E-mail: hnikides@dnr.state.in.us

Resource Regulation Bureau: Water Division
http://www.ai.org/dnr/water
Main phone: (317) 232-4160
Main fax: (317) 233-4579
Toll free: (877) 928-3755

Mike Neyer, Director
Indiana Government Center South, 402 W.
Washington St., #W-264, Indianapolis, IN 46204
E-mail: mneyer@dnr.state.in.us

Nursing, Dietitians, and Health Facility Administrators Board
Main phone: (317) 232-2960
Main fax: (317) 233-4236
License verification: (888) 333-7515

Gina Voorhies, Director
Indiana Government Center South, 402 W. Washington
St., #041, Indianapolis, IN 46204
(317) 233-4405
E-mail: gvoorhies@hpb.state.in.us

Personnel Dept.
http://www.state.in.us/jobs/
Main phone: (317) 232-0200
Main fax: (317) 232-3089
TTY: (317) 232-4555

D. Sue Roberson, Director
Indiana Government Center South, 402 W. Washington
St., #W-161, Indianapolis, IN 46204
(317) 233-3777; *Fax:* (317) 233-1979

Pharmacy Board
Main phone: (317) 232-2960
Main fax: (317) 233-4236
License verification: (888) 333-7515

Kristen Burch, Director
Indiana Government Center South, 402 W. Washington
St., #041, Indianapolis, IN 46204
(317) 233-4403
E-mail: kburch@hpb.state.in.us

Professional Licensing Agency
http://www.state.in.us/pla/

Professional Licensing Agency
http://www.state.in.us/pla/
(317) 232-2980

Accountancy, (317) 232-2513,
http://www.state.in.us/sboa
Child Care, (317) 232-1144
Cosmetology, (317) 232-7215
Engineers and Land Surveyors,
(317) 232-3931
Medical Licensing, (317) 232-2960
*Nursing, Dietitians, and Health Facility
Administrators,* (317) 232-2960
Pharmacy, (317) 232-2960
Real Estate Appraisers, (317) 232-7209

Main phone: (317) 232-2980
Main fax: (317) 232-2312

Gerald H. Quigley, Executive Director
Indiana Government Center South, 302 W. Washington St., #E-034, Indianapolis, IN 46204
(317) 232-3997

Prosecuting Attorneys Council
http://www.state.in.us/ipac
Main phone: (317) 232-1836
Main fax: (317) 233-3599

Stephen J. Johnson, Executive Director
Indiana Government Center South, 302 W. Washington St., #E-205, Indianapolis, IN 46204

Public Defender
http://www.state.in.us/pdc/
General e-mail: spd@iquest.net
Main phone: (317) 232-2475
Main fax: (317) 232-2307

Susan K. Carpenter, Public Defender
1 N. Capitol Ave., #800, Indianapolis, IN 46204

Public Employees Retirement Fund
http://www.state.in.us/perf/
Main phone: (317) 233-4162
Main fax: (317) 232-1614
TTY: (317) 233-4160

E. William Butler, Executive Director
143 W. Market St., #500, Indianapolis, IN 46204
(317) 233-4133; *Fax:* (317) 233-1765
E-mail: wbutler@perf.state.in.us

Public Safety Training Institute
http://www.state.in.us/sema/psti.html
Main phone: (317) 233-6545
Main fax: (317) 233-0497
Toll free: (800) 666-7784

Patrick R. Ralston, Executive Director
Indiana Government Center South, 302 W. Washington St., #E-208, Indianapolis, IN 46204-2722
(317) 232-3980; *Fax:* (317) 232-3895
E-mail: pralston@sema.state.in.us

Revenue Dept.
http://www.ai.org/dor/index.html
Main phone: (317) 232-2240
Main fax: (317) 232-2103
TTY: (317) 233-5977

Kenneth L. Miller, Commissioner
Indiana Government Center North, 100 N. Senate Ave., #N-248, Indianapolis, IN 46204
(317) 232-8039

State Fair Commission
http://www.state.in.us/statefair/

Main phone: (317) 927-7500
Main fax: (317) 927-7695

William H. Stinson, Executive Director
State Fairgrounds Event Center, 1202 E. 38th St., Indianapolis, IN 46205
(317) 927-7501

State Library
http://www.statelib.lib.in.us
Main phone: (317) 232-3675
Main fax: (317) 232-3728
TTY: (317) 232-7763

C. Ray Ewick, Director
140 N. Senate Ave., #407, Indianapolis, IN 46204
(317) 232-3692; *Fax:* (317) 232-0002
E-mail: ewick@statelib.lib.in.us

State Police
http://www.state.in.us/isp
Main phone: (317) 232-8248
Main fax: (317) 232-0652

Melvin J. Carraway, Superintendent
Indiana Government Center North, 100 N. Senate Ave., 3rd Fl., Indianapolis, IN 46204
(317) 232-8241

Transportation Dept.
http://www.state.in.us/dot/
Main phone: (317) 232-5525
Main fax: (317) 232-0238

Cristine M. Klika, Commissioner
Indiana Government Center North, 100 N. Senate Ave., #N-755, Indianapolis, IN 46204-2217
(317) 232-5526
E-mail: cklika@indot.state.in.us

Utility Regulatory Commission
http://www.state.in.us/iurc
General e-mail: pbarnett@urc.state.in.us
Main phone: (317) 232-2701
Main fax: (317) 232-6758
Toll free: (800) 851-4268
TTY: (317) 232-8556

William D. McCarty, Chair
Indiana Government Center South, 302 W. Washington St., #E-306, Indianapolis, IN 46204

Veterans Affairs Dept.
http://www.state.in.us/veteran/
General e-mail: idva@dva.state.in.us
Main phone: (317) 232-3910
Main fax: (317) 232-7721
Toll free: (800) 827-1000

William D. Jackson, Director
Indiana Government Center South, 302 W. Washington St., #E-120, Indianapolis, IN 46204-2738
(317) 232-3923

Workers' Compensation Board
http://www.state.in.us/wkcomp
Main phone: (317) 232-3808
Main fax: (317) 233-5493
Toll free: (800) 824-2667

G. Terrence Coriden, Chair
Indiana Government Center South, 402 W. Washington
St., #W-196, Indianapolis, IN 46204
(317) 232-3809

Indiana Legislature

State House
200 W. Washington St.
Indianapolis, IN 46204
Fax: (317) 232-2554
TTY: (317) 232-0404
Bill status: (317) 232-9856
http://www.state.in.us/legislative

Senate
Address: State House, Senate Chambers, 3rd Fl.,
200 W. Washington St., Indianapolis, IN 46204-
2785
General information: (317) 232-9400
Toll free: (800) 382-9467

Joseph E. Kernan (R), President
State House, 200 W. Washington St., Indianapolis, IN
46204-2790
(317) 232-4545; *Fax:* (317) 232-4788
http://www.state.in.us/lgov/

Robert D. Garton (R), President Pro Tempore
State House, 200 W. Washington St., Indianapolis, IN
46204
(317) 232-9400
E-mail: s41@ai.org

Joseph W. Harrison (R), Majority Leader
State House, 200 W. Washington St., Indianapolis, IN
46204
(317) 232-9400
E-mail: s23@ai.org

Joseph C. Zakas (R), Majority Whip
State House, 200 W. Washington St., Indianapolis, IN
46204
(317) 232-9400
http://www.state.in.us/legislative/senate_republicans/
homepages/s11

Richard D. Young (D), Minority Leader
State House, 200 W. Washington St., Indianapolis, IN
46204
(317) 232-9400
E-mail: s47@ai.org

Laws

Sales tax: 5%
Income tax: 3.4%
State minimum wage: $5.15 (Federal is $5.15)
Marriage age: 18
First-cousin marriage: Prohibited
Drinking age: 21
State control of liquor sales: No
Blood alcohol for DWI: 0.10%
Driving age: 18
Speed limit: 65 mph
Permit to buy handguns: No
Minimum age to possess handguns: 18
Minimum age to possess rifles, shotguns:
  None
State lottery: Yes; also Powerball
Casinos: Yes (commercial)
Pari-mutuel betting: Horse racing
Death penalty: Yes
3 strikes minimum sentence: Life, no parole
  (3rd serious felony)
Hate crimes law: No
Gay employment non-discrimination: No
Official language(s): English
Term limits: None

*State laws are complex and subject to
change; this information is not intended as
legal advice. For an explanation of this
information, see p. x.*

Carolyn J. Tinkle, Secretary
State House, 200 W. Washington St., Indianapolis, IN
46204
(317) 232-9420

Lindel Hume (D), Minority Whip
State House, 200 W. Washington St., Indianapolis, IN
46204
(317) 232-9400

House
Address: State House, 200 W. Washington St.,
Indianapolis, IN 46204-2786
General information: (317) 232-9600
Fax: (317) 232-9679
Toll free: (800) 382-9842

John R. Gregg (D), Speaker of the House
State House, 200 W. Washington St., Indianapolis, IN
46204
(317) 232-9600
E-mail: H45@ai.org
http://www.state.in.us/legislative/homepages/R45

Chester F. Dobis (D), Speaker Pro Tempore
State House, 200 W. Washington St., Indianapolis, IN
  46204
(317) 232-9600
E-mail: H13@ai.org
http://www.state.in.us/legislative/homepages/R13
Mark Kruzan (D), Majority Leader
State House, 200 W. Washington St., Indianapolis, IN
  46204
(317) 232-9600
E-mail: H61@ai.org
http://www.state.in.us/legislative/homepages/R61
Paul J. Robertson (D), Majority Whip
State House, 200 W. Washington St., Indianapolis, IN
  46204
(317) 232-9600
E-mail: H70@ai.org
Paul S. Mannweiler (R), Minority Leader
State House, 200 W. Washington St., #3-7,
  Indianapolis, IN 46204
(317) 232-9604
E-mail: R87@ai.org
http://www.state.in.us/legislative/homepages/r87/
Sue W. Scholer (R), Minority Whip
State House, 200 W. Washington St., Indianapolis, IN
  46204
(317) 232-9600
E-mail: R26@ai.org
Lee A. Smith, Clerk
State House, 200 W. Washington St., Indianapolis, IN
  46204
(317) 232-9974

Indiana Judiciary
217 State House
200 W. Washington St.
Indianapolis, IN 46207
http://www.state.in.us/judiciary

Supreme Court
http://www.state.in.us/judiciary/supreme/
Brian Bishop, Clerk
217 State House, 200 W. Washington St., Indianapolis,
  IN 46207
(317) 232-1930; *Fax:* (317) 232-8365
E-mail: brianwb@iquest.net

Justices
Composition: 5 justices
Selection Method: gubernatorial appointment
  followed by retention ballot
Length of term: 2-year appointment; 10 years by
  retention ballot

Randall T. Shepard, Chief Justice, (317) 232-2550
Theodore R. Boehm, Associate Justice, (317) 232-2547
Brent E. Dickson, Associate Justice, (317) 232-2549
Myra C. Selby, Associate Justice, (317) 232-2544
Frank Sullivan Jr., Associate Justice, (317) 232-2548

Division of State Court Administration
http://www.state.in.us/judiciary/admin/
Main phone: (317) 232-2542
Main fax: (317) 233-6586
Lilia G. Judson, Executive Director
115 W. Washington St., #1080, Indianapolis, IN
  46204-3417
E-mail: ljudson@source.isd.state.in.us

Supreme Court Law Library
Main phone: (317) 232-2557
Main fax: (317) 232-8372
Rebecca Bethel, Supreme Court Law Librarian
200 W. Washington St., #316, Indianapolis, IN 46204
E-mail: bbethel@courts.state.in.us

Legislative and Political Party Information Resources

Membership: http://www.state.in.us/legislative/leg_staff.html
Committees: http://www.state.in.us/cgi-bin/legislative/bills/commlist.perl
Legislative process: http://www.state.in.us/legislative/billalaw.html
Current session information: http://www.state.in.us/legislative/session.html
Indiana Democratic Party: http://www.indems.org
  1 N. Capitol, #200, Indianapolis, IN 46204; *Phone:* (800) 223-3387; *Fax:* (317) 231-7129; *E-mail:*
  indems@indems.org
Indiana Republican Party: http://www.indgop.com
  200 S. Meridian St., #400, Indianapolis, IN 46225; *Fax:* (317) 632-8510; *Phone:* (800) 466-1087

Iowa

State Capitol Bldg.
Des Moines, IA 50319
Public information: (515) 281-5011
Fax: (515) 281-0009
http://www.state.ia.us

Office of the Governor
http://www.state.ia.us/government/governor/
index.htm
General e-mail: gen.office@igov.state.ia.us
Main phone: (515) 281-5011
Main fax: (515) 281-6611

Thomas J. Vilsack (D), Governor
State Capitol Bldg., Des Moines, IA 50319
(515) 281-5211

John Norris, Chief of Staff
State Capitol Bldg., Des Moines, IA 50319
(515) 281-0159; *Fax:* (515) 281-6611
E-mail: john.norris@igov.state.ia.us

Joe Shannahan, Communications Director
State Capitol Bldg., Des Moines, IA 50319
(515) 281-0173; *Fax:* (515) 281-6611
E-mail: joe.shanahan.@igov.state.ia.us

Cindy Jones, Constituent Caseworker Coordinator
State Capitol Bldg., Des Moines, IA 50319
(515) 281-0165; *Fax:* (515) 281-6611

Phil Buchanan, Director, Washington Office
Hall of the States, 444 N. Capitol St. N.W., #359,
Washington, DC 20001
(202) 624-5442; *Fax:* (202) 624-8189
E-mail: pbuchan@sos.org

Office of the Lieutenant Governor
http://www.state.ia.us/government/ltgov/
General e-mail: general.office@max.state.ia.us
Main phone: (515) 281-5211
Main fax: (515) 281-6611

Sally Pederson (D), Lieutenant Governor
State Capitol Bldg., Des Moines, IA 50319

Office of the Secretary of State
http://www.sos.state.ia.us/
General e-mail: sos@sos.state.ia.us
Main phone: (515) 281-5204
Main fax: (515) 242-5953
TTY: (515) 281-5865

State of Iowa

Capital: Des Moines,
  since 1857
Founded: 1838, Iowa Territory
  created from Wisconsin Territory
Statehood: December 28, 1846 (29th state)
Constitution adopted: 1857
Area: 55,875 sq. mi. (ranks 23rd)
Population: 2,862,447 (1998 est.; ranks 30th)
Largest cities: (1998 est.) Des Moines
  (191,293); Cedar Rapids (114,563);
  Davenport (96,842); Sioux City (82,697);
  Waterloo (63,703)
Counties: 99, Most populous: (1998 est.) Polk
  (359,826); Linn (182,651); Scott (158,591);
  Black Hawk (121,121); Johnson (102,724)
U.S. Congress: Chuck Grassley (R), Tom
  Harkin (D); 5 Representatives
Nickname(s): Hawkeye State
Motto: Our liberties we prize, and our rights
  we will maintain
Song: "Song of Iowa"
Bird: Eastern goldfinch
Tree: Oak
Flower: Wild rose
State fair: at Des Moines, mid-Aug.
Former capital(s): Burlington, Iowa City

Chester J. Culver (D), Secretary of State
State Capitol, Hoover Bldg., #105, Des Moines, IA
  50319
(515) 281-8993; *Fax:* (515) 242-5952

Office of the Attorney General
http://www.state.ia.us/government/ag/
General e-mail: iowaag@agmail.ag.state.ia.us
Main phone: (515) 281-5164
Main fax: (515) 281-4209

Thomas J. Miller (D), Attorney General
Hoover Bldg., 2nd Fl., Des Moines, IA 50319
(515) 281-8373

Office of the State Treasurer
http://www.treasurer.state.ia.us
General e-mail: treasurer@max.state.ia.us
Main phone: (515) 281-5368
Main fax: (515) 281-7562

Michael L. Fitzgerald (D), Treasurer
State Capitol Bldg., Des Moines, IA 50319
E-mail: mfitzgerald@max.state.ia.us

Office of the State Auditor
http://www.state.ia.us/government/auditor/
General e-mail: iowaaos@max.state.ia.us
Main phone: (515) 281-5834
Main fax: (515) 242-6134

Richard D. Johnson (R), State Auditor
State Capitol Bldg., Des Moines, IA 50319-0004
(515) 281-5835

Army National Guard
http://www.state.ia.us/government/dpd/
  dpd_text.html
Main phone: (515) 252-4242

Ron Dardis, Director
7700 N.W. Beaver Dr., Johnston, IA 50131-1902
(515) 252-4211; *Fax:* (515) 252-4787

Agencies

Accountancy Board
http://www.state.ia.us/iacc
General e-mail: IACC@max.state.ia.us
Main phone: (515) 281-4126
Main fax: (515) 281-7411

Bill Shroeder, Executive Secretary
1918 S.E. Hulsizer, Ankeny, IA 50021-3941

Agriculture and Land Stewardship Dept.
http://www2.state.ia.us/agriculture/
General e-mail: agri@idals.state.ia.us
Main phone: (515) 281-5321
Main fax: (515) 281-6236

Patty Judge (D), Secretary
Wallace Bldg., Des Moines, IA 50319
(515) 281-5322

Soil Conservation Division
Main phone: (515) 281-6146
Main fax: (515) 281-6170

James Gulliford, Director
Wallace Bldg., 2nd Fl., Des Moines, IA 50319
(515) 281-6153

Soil Conservation Division: Water Resources Bureau
Main phone: (515) 281-5321
Main fax: (515) 281-6236

Jim Gillespie, Chief
Wallace Bldg., 502 E. 9th St., Des Moines, IA
  50319
(515) 281-7043; *Fax:* (515) 281-6170
E-mail: jim.gillespie@idals.state.ia.us

Architectural Examiners Board
http://www.state.ia.us/iarch
General e-mail: iarch@max.state.ia.us
Main phone: (515) 281-4126
Main fax: (515) 281-7411

Glenda Loring, Executive Secretary
1918 S.E. Hulsizer, Ankeny, IA 50021-3941

Archives
http://www.culturalaffairs/iowahistory/archives/
Main phone: (515) 281-5111
Main fax: (515) 282-0502

Gordon O. Hendrickson, Director
600 E. Locust St., Des Moines, IA 50319-0290
(515) 281-8875
E-mail: ghendri@max.state.ia.us

Banking Division
http://www.idob.state.ia.us/
Main phone: (515) 281-4014
Main fax: (515) 281-4862

Holmes Foster, Superintendent
200 E. Grand Ave., #300, Des Moines, IA 50309

Blind Dept.
http://www.blind.state.ia.us
Main phone: (515) 281-1333
Main fax: (515) 281-1263
Toll free: (800) 362-2587
TTY: (505) 281-1355

R. Creig Slayton, Director
524 4th St., Des Moines, IA 50309-2364
(515) 281-1334
E-mail: slayton.creig@blind.state.ia.us

Commerce Dept.
http://www.state.ia.us/government/com/admin/
  admin.htm
General e-mail: shari.fett@comm1.state.ia.us
Main phone: (515) 281-7405
Main fax: (515) 242-5132

Roger A. Denton, Chief
324 E. Maple St., Des Moines, IA 50319
(515) 281-5596

Administrative Services Division
http://www.state.ia.us/government/com/admin/
  admin.htm
General e-mail: shari.fett@comm1.state.ia.us
Main phone: (515) 281-7364

Marty Deaton, Administrator
1918 S.E. Hulsizer, Ankeny, IA 50021

Alcoholic Beverages Division
http://www.state.ia.us/government/com/abd/
  abd.htm

Main phone: (515) 281-7407
Main fax: (515) 281-7385

Jack Nystrom, Administrator
1918 S.E. Hulsizer, Ankeny, IA 50021
E-mail: Jack.Nystrom@comm2.state.ia.us

Insurance Division
http://www.state.ia.us/government/com/ins/
   index.htm
General e-mail: insurance@comm6.state.ia.us
Main phone: (515) 281-5705
Main fax: (515) 281-3059

Therese Vaughan, Commissioner
330 Maple St., Des Moines, IA 50319-0065
(515) 281-5523; Fax: (515) 281-5692

Professional Licensing Division
http://www.state.ia.us/government/com/prof/
   pld.htm
General e-mail: proflic@max.state.ia.us
Main phone: (515) 281-3183
Main fax: (515) 281-7411

Kay Chapman, Administrator
1918 S.E. Hulsizer, Ankeny, IA 50021-3941
(515) 281-5596

Consumer Protection Division
http://www.state.ia.us/government/ag/
   consumer.html
General e-mail: consumer@max.state.ia.us
Main phone: (515) 281-5926
Main fax: (515) 281-6771

William Brauch, Director
Hoover Bldg., 1300 E. Walnut, 2nd Fl., Des Moines,
   IA 50319

Corrections Dept.
http://www.state.ia.us/government/doc
General e-mail: terry.boehlje@doc.state.ia.us
Main phone: (515) 242-5702
Main fax: (515) 281-7345

Walter L. Kautzky, Director
420 Keo Way, Des Moines, IA 50309
(515) 242-5703
E-mail: walter.kautzky@doc.state.ia.us

Cultural Affairs Dept.
http://www.state.ia.us/government/idca/
Main phone: (515) 281-7471
Main fax: (515) 242-6498

Doug Larche, Director
New Historical Bldg., 600 E. Locus St., Des Moines,
   IA 50319
E-mail: dlarche@max.state.ia.us

State Archives and Records Program
Main phone: (515) 281-8875
Main fax: (515) 282-0502

Gordon Hendrickson, State Archivist
600 E. Locus St., Des Moines, IA 50319

Economic Development Dept.
http://www.state.ia.us/ided
Main phone: (515) 242-4700
Main fax: (515) 242-4809

David J. Lyons, Director
200 E. Grand Ave., Des Moines, IA 50309
(515) 242-4814; Fax: (515) 242-4832
E-mail: dave.lyons@ided.state.ia.us

Tourism Division
http://www.traveliowa.com
General e-mail: tourism@ided.state.ia.us
Main phone: (515) 242-4705
Main fax: (515) 242-4718
Toll free: (888) 472-6035

Nancy Landess, Division Administrator
200 E. Grand Ave., Des Moines, IA 50309

Education Dept.
http://www.state.ia.us/educate/depteduc
Main phone: (515) 242-5294
Main fax: (515) 242-5988

Ted Stilwill, Director
Grimes State Office Bldg., Des Moines, IA 50319-
   0146
(515) 281-3436
E-mail: ted.stilwill@ed.state.ia.us

Board of Education
http://www.state.ia.us/educate/state_board/
   index.html
Main phone: (515) 281-5294
Main fax: (515) 242-5988

Corine A. Hadley, President
Grimes State Office Bldg., Des Moines, IA 50319-
   0146

Public Television
http://www.iptv.org
Main phone: (515) 242-3100
Main fax: (515) 242-4113
Toll free: (800) 532-1290
Mailing address: P.O. Box 6450, Johnston, IA
   50131

C. David Bolender, Executive Director
6450 Corporate Dr., Johnston, IA 50131
(515) 242-3150
E-mail: dbolender@iptv.org

Higher Educational Institutions

Iowa State University
http://www.iastate.edu
Alumni Hall, Ames, IA 50011
Main phone: (515) 294-3094

University of Iowa
http://www.uiowa.edu
107 Calvin Hall, Iowa City, IA 52242
Main phone: (319) 335-3847

University of Northern Iowa
http://www.uni.edu
1227 W. 27th St., Cedar Falls, IA 50514
Main phone: (319) 273-2311

Elder Affairs Dept.
http://www.state.ia.us/elderaffairs/
Main phone: (515) 281-5187
Main fax: (515) 281-4036
Toll free: (800) 532-3213

Judith A. Conlin, Executive Director
Clemens Bldg., 200 10th St., 3rd Fl., Des Moines, IA 50309
(515) 281-5288
E-mail: Judith.Conlin@dea.state.ia.us

Emergency Management Division
http://www.state.ia.us/emergencymanagement
General e-mail: david.miller@emd.state.ia.us
Main phone: (515) 281-3231
Main fax: (515) 281-7539

Ellen M. Gordon, Administrator
Hoover Bldg., A-Level, Des Moines, IA 50319

Engineers and Land Surveyors Board
http://www.state.ia.us/government/com/prof/engx/engx.htm
General e-mail: engls@max.state.ia.us
Main phone: (515) 281-5602
Main fax: (515) 281-7411

Susan M. Long, Chair
1918 S.E. Hulsizer, Ankeny, IA 50021-3941
(515) 472-8411; *Fax:* (515) 472-6211
E-mail: jsaalong@kbsi.net

Ethics and Campaign Disclosure Board
http://www.iowaccess.org/government/iecdb
Main phone: (515) 281-4028
Main fax: (515) 281-3701

Kay Williams, Executive Director
514 E. Locust St., #104, Des Moines, IA 50309
(515) 281-6841
E-mail: kwillia@max.state.ia.us

Fire Marshal
http://www.state.ia.us/government/dps/fm/isfm.html
Main phone: (515) 281-5821
Main fax: (515) 242-6299

Roy L. Marshall, State Fire Marshal
621 E. 2nd St., Des Moines, IA 50309-1831
E-mail: marshall@dps.state.ia.us

Historical Society
http://www.state.ia.us/government/dca/shsi/
Main phone: (515) 281-5111
Main fax: (515) 282-0502

Tom Morain, Administrator
State of Iowa Historical Bldg., 600 E. Locust, Des Moines, IA 50319-0290
(515) 281-8837; *Fax:* (515) 242-6498
E-mail: tmorain@max.state.ia.us

Human Rights Dept.
http://www.state.ia.us/government/dhr/
Main phone: (515) 281-7300
Main fax: (515) 242-6119
TTY: (515) 281-3164

Rose Vasquez, Director
Lucas State Office Bldg., Des Moines, IA 50319
E-mail: Rose.Vasquez@dhr.state.ia.us

Commission on the Status of Women
http://www.state.ia.us/government/dhr/index.html
General e-mail: dhr.icsw@dhr.state.ia.us
Main phone: (515) 281-4461
Main fax: (515) 242-6119
Toll free: (800) 558-4427

Charlotte Nelson, Executive Director
Lucas State Office Bldg., Des Moines, IA 50319

Criminal and Juvenile Justice Planning
http://www.state.ia.us/government/dhr/cjjp/index.html
Main phone: (515) 242-5823
Main fax: (515) 242-6119

Richard G. Moore, Administrator
321 E. 12th St., Lucas State Office Bldg., 1st Fl., Des Moines, IA 50319

Human Services Dept.
http://www.dhs.state.ia.us
General e-mail: tcrawfo@dhs.state.ia.us
Main phone: (515) 281-3147
Main fax: (515) 281-4597

Jessie Rasmussen, Director
Hoover Bldg., Des Moines, IA 50319-0114
(515) 281-5452

Medical Services Division

Main phone: (515) 281-8621
Main fax: (515) 281-4597

Donald Herman, Administrator
Hoover Bldg., 1305 E. Walnut, Des Moines, IA
50319-0114
(515) 281-8794
E-mail: dherman@dhs.state.ia.us

Mental Health/Developmental Disabilities Division

Main phone: (515) 281-5874
Main fax: (515) 281-4597

Linda Hinton, Administrator
Hoover Bldg., 1305 E. Walnut, Des Moines, IA
50319-0114
(515) 281-5126
E-mail: lhinton@dhs.state.ia.us

Medical Examiners Board

http://idph.state.ia.us/pa/pl/med_ex.htm
Main phone: (515) 281-6726
Main fax: (515) 281-4958
TTY: (800) 735-2942

Steven Gleason, Director
Lucas State Office Bldg., 321 E. 12th St., 5th Fl., Des
Moines, IA 50319-0075
(515) 281-5605
E-mail: sgleason@diph.state.ia.us

Natural Resources Dept.

http://www.state.ia.us/government/dnr/
Main phone: (515) 281-5145
Main fax: (515) 281-6794

Paul W. Johnson, Director
502 E. 9th St., Des Moines, IA 50319-0034
(515) 281-5385

Energy and Geological Resources Division: Geological Survey Bureau

http://www.igsb.uiowa.edu
Main phone: (319) 335-1575
Main fax: (319) 335-2754

Don Koch, Chief
109 Trowbridge Hall, Iowa City, IA 52242-1319
(319) 335-1573
E-mail: dkoch@igsb.uiowa.edu

Fish and Wildlife Division

Main phone: (515) 281-8681
Main fax: (515) 281-6794

Allen Farris, Administrator
Wallace Bldg., E. 9th and Grand, Des Moines, IA
50319-0034
(515) 242-5948

Frequently Called Numbers

Tourism: (515) 242-4705; 1-800-345-IOWA;
http://www.traveliowa.com
Library: (515) 281-4105;
http://www.silo.lib.ia.us/
Board of Education: (515) 281-5294;
http://www.state.ia.us/educate/state_board/
index.html
Vital Statistics: (515) 281-4944;
http://www.idph.state.ia.us/pa/vr.htm
Tax/Revenue: (515) 281-3135;
http://www.state.ia.us/tax
Motor Vehicles: (515) 244-1052
State Police/Highway Patrol: (515) 281-5824;
http://www.state.ia.us/government/dps/isp/
isp.html
Unemployment: (515) 281-4199;
http://www.state.ia.us/government/wd/ui/
index.html
General Election Information: (515)
281-5865, 888-SOS-VOTE; http://
www.sos.state.ia.us/elections/elections.html
Consumer Affairs: (515) 281-5926;
http://www.state.ia.us/government/ag/
consumer.html
Hazardous Materials: (515) 281-8927

Forests and Forestry Division

Main phone: (515) 281-8681
Main fax: (515) 281-6794

Michael Brandrup, Administrator
Wallace Bldg., E. 9th and Grand, Des Moines, IA
50319-0034
(515) 281-8657

Parks, Recreation, and Preservation Division

Main phone: (515) 281-5207
Main fax: (515) 281-6794

Michael Carrier, Administrator
Wallace Bldg., E. 9th and Grand, Des Moines, IA
50319-0034

Nursing Board

http://www.state.ia.us/nursing/
General e-mail: ibon@bon.state.ia.us
Main phone: (515) 281-3255
Main fax: (515) 281-4825

Lorinda Inman, Executive Director
Riverpoint Business Park, 400 S.W. 8th St., Des
Moines, IA 50306
(515) 281-3256

Parole Board

http://www.netins.net/showcase/jdwhite/ibop/cgi-bin/homepage.cgi
Main phone: (515) 242-5757
Main fax: (515) 242-5762

Charles W. Larson, Chair
Holmes-Murphy Bldg., 420 Keoway, Des Moines, IA 50309
(515) 242-5700

Personnel Dept.

http://www.state.ia.us/idop
Main phone: (515) 281-3087
Main fax: (515) 242-6450
TTY: (515) 281-7825

Mollie K. Anderson, Director
Grimes Bldg., Des Moines, IA 50319-0150
(515) 281-3351
E-mail: mollie.anderson@idop.state.ia.us

Public Defense Dept.

http://www.state.ia.us/government/dpd/index.html
General e-mail: moranf@ia-arng.ngb.arng.mil
Main phone: (515) 252-4000
Main fax: (515) 252-4787

Ron Dardis, Adjutant General
Camp Dodge Office, 7700 N.W. Beaver Dr., Johnston, IA 50131-1902
(515) 252-4211
E-mail: dardisr@ia-arng.ngb.arng.mil

Boards and Licensing

Accountancy, (515) 281-4126,
  http://www.state.ia.us/iacc
Architects, (515) 281-5596,
  http://www.state.ia.us/iarch
Child Care, (515) 242-5994
Contractors, (515) 242-5871
Cosmetology, (515) 281-4416
Engineers and Land Surveyors,
  (515) 281-5602,
  http://www.state.ia.us/government/com/prof/
  engx/engx.htm
Medical Examiners, (515) 281-6726,
  http://idph.state.ia.us/pa/pl/med_ex.htm
Nursing, (515) 281-3255,
  http://www.state.ia.us/nursing/
Pharmacy, (515) 281-5944
Real Estate Appraisers, (515) 281-7393,
  http://www.state.ia.us/government/com/prof/
  realappr/realappr.htm

Public Employees Retirement System

http://www.state.ia.us/government/idop/RetirementHome.html
General e-mail: info@ipers.state.ia.us
Main phone: (515) 281-0020
Main fax: (515) 281-0053
Toll free: (800) 622-3849
Mailing address: P.O. Box 9117, Des Moines, IA 50306-9117

Greg Cusack, Chief Benefits Officer
600 E. Court Ave., Des Moines, IA 50306-9117
E-mail: greg.cusack@idop.state.ia.us

Public Health Dept.

http://www.idph.state.ia.us/
General e-mail: webmaster@idph.state.ia.us
Main phone: (515) 281-5787
Main fax: (515) 281-4958
TTY: (800) 735-2942

Stephen C. Gleason, Director
Lucas State Office Bldg., 321 E. 12th St., Des Moines, IA 50319-0075
(515) 281-5605
E-mail: sgleason@idph.state.ia.us

Public Safety Dept.

http://www.state.ia.us/government/dps/
Main phone: (515) 281-3211
Main fax: (515) 242-6136

E. A. (Penny) Westfall, Commissioner
Wallace State Office Bldg., Des Moines, IA 50319-0040
(515) 281-5261

State Patrol Division

http://www.state.ia.us/government/dps/isp/isp.html
Main phone: (515) 281-5824
Main fax: (515) 242-6305

Jon Wilson, Chief
Wallace Bldg., E. 9th and Grand, Des Moines, IA 50319-0040
(515) 281-7304
E-mail: garrison@dps.state.ia.us

Public Television

http://www.iptv.org/
General e-mail: webcomm2@iptv.org
Main phone: (515) 242-3100
Toll free: (800) 532-1290
Mailing address: Box 6450, Johnston, IA 50131-6450

C. David Bolender, Executive Director
6450 Corporate Dr., Johnston, IA 50131

Real Estate Appraisers Board

http://www.state.ia.us/government/com/prof/
realappr/realappr.htm
General e-mail: iapp@max.state.ia.us
Main phone: (515) 281-7393
Main fax: (515) 281-7411

Gary J. Johnson, Chair
1918 S.E. Hulsizer, Ankeny, IA 50021-3941

Regents Board

http://www2.state.ia.us/regents/
Main phone: (515) 281-3934
Main fax: (515) 281-6420

Frank Stork, Executive Director
100 Court Ave., #203, Des Moines, IA 50319
E-mail: fstork@iastate.edu

Revenue and Finance Dept.

http://www.state.ia.us/tax
Main phone: (515) 281-3135
Main fax: (515) 242-6040
TTY: (515) 242-5942

Gerald D. Bair, Director
Hoover Bldg., Des Moines, IA 50319
(515) 281-3204; *Fax:* (515) 242-6156
E-mail: Gerald.Bair@irdf.state.ia.us

State Fair Authority

http://www.iowastatefair.org
General e-mail: info@iowastatefair.org
Main phone: (515) 262-3111
Main fax: (515) 262-6906
Toll free: (800) 545-3247
TTY: (515) 262-2029

Marion Lucas, Manager
400 E. 14th St., Des Moines, IA 50319-0210

State Library

http://www.silo.lib.ia.us/
Main phone: (515) 281-4105
Main fax: (515) 281-6191
Toll free: (800) 248-4483

Sharman Smith, State Librarian
1112 E. Grand Ave., Des Moines, IA 50319
E-mail: ssmith@mail.lib.state.ia.us

State Lottery

http://www.ialottery.com/
General e-mail: webmaster@ilot.state.ia.us
Main phone: (515) 281-7900
Main fax: (515) 281-7905

Ed Stanek, Commissioner
2015 Grand Ave., Des Moines, IA 50312-4999
Fax: (515) 281-7882

Transportation Dept.

http://www.dot.state.ia.us
Main phone: (515) 239-1101
Main fax: (515) 239-1639
TTY: (515) 239-1514

Mark F. Wandro, Director
800 Lincoln Way, Ames, IA 50010
(515) 239-1111; *Fax:* (515) 239-1120
E-mail: mwandro@max.state.ia.us

Motor Vehicle Division

Main phone: (515) 244-1052
Main fax: (515) 237-3355
Toll free: (800) 532-1121

Shirley Andre, Director
Park Fair Mall, 100 Euclid Ave., Des Moines,
IA 50313
E-mail: sandre@max.state.ia.us

Veterans Affairs Commission

Main phone: (515) 242-5331
Main fax: (515) 242-5659
Toll free: (800) 838-4692

Brian B. Bales, Executive Director
Camp Dodge, Bldg. A6A, 7700 N.W. Beaver Dr.,
Johnston, IA 50131-1902
(515) 242-5333
E-mail: brian.bales@icva.state.ia.us

Iowa Legislature

State Capitol
Des Moines, IA 50319
General information: (515) 281-5129
http://www.legis.state.ia.us

Senate

General information: (515) 281-3371
Fax: (515) 242-6108
TTY: (515) 281-3789

Mary E. Kramer (R), President
State Capitol, Des Moines, IA 50319
(515) 281-3811
E-mail: mary_kramer@legis.state.ia.us
http://www2.legis.state.ia.us/GA/78GA/Senate/
Members/MaryE-Kramer.html

Donald B. Redfern (R), President Pro Tempore
State Capitol, Des Moines, IA 50319
(515) 281-7694
E-mail: don_redfern@legis.state.ia.us
http://www2.legis.state.ia.us/GA/78GA/Senate/
Members/DonaldB-Redfern.html

Stewart E. Iverson Jr. (R), Majority Leader
State Capitol, Des Moines, IA 50319
(515) 281-3560
E-mail: stewart_iverson@legis.state.ia.us
http://www2.legis.state.ia.us/GA/78GA/Senate/
   Members/StewartE-Iverson.html

Michael E. Gronstal (D), Minority Leader
State Capitol, Des Moines, IA 50319
(515) 281-3901
E-mail: michael_gronstal@legis.state.ia.us
http://www2.legis.state.ia.us/GA/78GA/Senate/
   Members/Michael-Gronstal.html

Michael Marshall, Secretary
State Capitol, Des Moines, IA 50319
(515) 281-3371

House
General information: (515) 281-3221
TTY: (515) 281-8455

Laws

Sales tax: 6%
Income tax: 6%
State minimum wage: $5.15 (Federal is $5.15)
Marriage age: 18
First-cousin marriage: Prohibited
Drinking age: 21
State control of liquor sales: Yes
Blood alcohol for DWI: 0.10%
Driving age: 17
Speed limit: 65 mph
Permit to buy handguns: Yes, 3 days to
   acquire
Minimum age to possess handguns: 21
Minimum age to possess rifles, shotguns: 18
State lottery: Yes; also Powerball
Casinos: Yes (commercial, tribal); also slot/
   video machines
Pari-mutuel betting: Horse and dog racing
Death penalty: No
3 strikes minimum sentence: None
Hate crimes law: Yes
Gay employment non-discrimination: No
Official language(s): None
Term limits: None

*State laws are complex and subject to
change; this information is not intended as
legal advice. For an explanation of this
information, see p. x.*

Brent Siegrist (R), Speaker of the House
State Capitol, Des Moines, IA 50319
(515) 281-3054
E-mail: brent_siegrist@legis.state.ia.us
http://www2.legis.state.ia.us/GA/78GA/House/
   Members/Brent-Siegrist.html

Steve Sukup (R), Speaker Pro Tempore
State Capitol, Des Moines, IA 50319
(515) 281-5887
E-mail: steve_sukup@legis.state.ia.us
http://www2.legis.state.ia.us/GA/78GA/House/
   Members/Steve-Sukup.html

Christopher Rants (R), Majority Leader
State Capitol, Des Moines, IA 50319
(515) 281-3030
E-mail: christopher_rants@legis.state.ia.us
http://www2.legis.state.ia.us/GA/78GA/House/
   Members/Christopher-Rants.html

Elizabeth (Libby) Jacobs (R), Majority Whip
State Capitol, Des Moines, IA 50319
(515) 281-3465
E-mail: libby_jacobs@legis.state.ia.us
http://www2.legis.state.ia.us/GA/78GA/House/
   Members/Libby-Jacobs.html

David F. Schrader (D), Minority Leader
State Capitol, Des Moines, IA 50319
(515) 281-3521
E-mail: david_schrader@legis.state.ia.us
http://www2.legis.state.ia.us/GA/78GA/House/
   Members/David-Schrader.html

Richard E. (Dick) Myers (D), Minority Whip
State Capitol, Des Moines, IA 50319
(515) 281-3066
E-mail: richard_myers@legis.state.ia.us
http://www2.legis.state.ia.us/GA/78GA/House/
   Members/Dick-Myers.html

Elizabeth A. Isuarson, Chief Clerk
State Capitol, Des Moines, IA 50319
(515) 281-5381

Iowa Judiciary
State House
Des Moines, IA 50319
http://www.judicial.state.ia.us/

Supreme Court
Keith Richardson, Clerk
State House, #3, Des Moines, IA 50319
(515) 281-5911; *Fax:* (515) 242-6164

Justices

Composition: 8 justices

Selection Method: appointed by governor; must stand for retention in first general election one year after appointment

Length of term: 8 years

Arthur A. McGiverin, Chief Justice, (515) 682-3635

Mark S. Cady, Associate Justice, (515) 281-5174

James H. Carter, Associate Justice, (319) 398-3920

Jerry L. Larson, Associate Justice, (712) 755-2366

Louis A. Lavorato, Associate Justice, (515) 281-3952

Linda K. Neuman, Associate Justice, (319) 326-8668

Bruce M. Snell Jr., Associate Justice, (515) 281-5174

Marsha K. Ternus, Associate Justice, (515) 281-3953

Office of Court Administration

http://www.judicial.state.ia.us/courtadmin

Main phone: (515) 281-5241

Main fax: (515) 242-0014

William J. O'Brien, State Court Administrator

State House, Des Moines, IA 50319

State Law Library

http://www.judicial.state.ia.us/

Main phone: (515) 281-5124

Main fax: (515) 281-5405

Linda Robertson, Law Librarian

1007 E. Grand, State Capitol Bldg., Des Moines, IA 50319

Legislative and Political Party Information Resources

Membership: http://www.legis.state.ia.us/Members/78GA-members.html

Committees: Senate: http://www.legis.state.ia.us/GA/78GA/Senate/Comm/;
   House: http://www.legis.state.ia.us/GA/78GA/House/Comm/

Legislative process: http://www.legis.state.ia.us/Education.html

Current session information: http://www.legis.state.ia.us/Legislation.html

Iowa Democratic Party: http://www.iowademocrats.org
   5661 Fleur Dr., Des Moines, IA 50321; *Phone:* (515) 244-7292; *Fax:* (515) 244-5051; *E-mail:* idp@iowademocrats.org

Iowa Republican Party: http://www.iowagop.org
   521 E. Locust St., #200, Des Moines, IA 50309; *Phone:* (515) 282-8105; *Fax:* (515) 282-9019; *E-mail:* iowagop@iowagop.org

Kansas

State Capitol
Topeka, KS 66612-1590
Public information: (785) 296-0111
Fax: (785) 296-7973
http://www.state.ks.us

Office of the Governor
http://www.ink.org/public/governor/
General e-mail: rdugger@hr.state.ks.us
Main phone: (785) 296-3232
Main fax: (785) 296-7973
Toll free: (800) 748-4408

Bill Graves (R), Governor
State Capitol, #212-S, Topeka, KS 66612-1590
E-mail: governor@ink.org

Joyce Glasscock, Chief of Staff
State Capitol, #212-S, Topeka, KS 66612-1590
(785) 296-4052; *Fax:* (785) 296-7973

Don Brown, Communications Director
State Capitol, #212-S, Topeka, KS 66612-1590
(785) 291-3206; *Fax:* (785) 296-7973

Ed O'Malley, Constituent Services Director
State Capitol, 2nd Fl., Topeka, KS 66612-1590
(785) 296-6240; *Fax:* (785) 296-7973
E-mail: Omalley@state.ks.us

Office of the Lieutenant Governor
http://www.ink.org/public/ltgov/
General e-mail: ltgovernor@state.ks.us
Main phone: (785) 296-2213
Main fax: (785) 296-5669

Gary Sherrer (R), Lieutenant Governor
State Capitol, #222-S, Topeka, KS 66612-1504

Office of the Secretary of State
http://www.kssos.org/
General e-mail: kssos@ssmail.wpo.state.ks.us
Main phone: (785) 296-4564
Main fax: (785) 296-4570

Ron Thornburgh (R), Secretary of State
Memorial Hall, 120 S.W. 10th St., 1st Fl., Topeka, KS
66612-1594

Office of the Attorney General
http://www.ink.org/public/ksag/
General e-mail: general@ksag.org
Main phone: (785) 296-2215
Main fax: (785) 296-6296
TTY: (785) 291-3767

State of Kansas

Capital: Topeka, since 1861
Founded: 1854, Kansas Territory created
Statehood: January 29, 1861 (34th state)
Constitution adopted: 1859
Area: 81,823 sq. mi. (ranks 13th)
Population: 2,629,067 (1998 est.; ranks 32nd)
Largest cities: (1998 est.) Wichita (329,211);
Kansas City (141,297); Overland Park
(139,685); Topeka (118,977); Olathe
(85,035)
Counties: 105, Most populous: (1998 est.)
Sedgwick (448,050); Johnson (429,563);
Shawnee (165,348); Wyandotte (152,355);
Douglas (93,137)
U.S. Congress: Sam Brownback (R), Pat
Roberts (R); 4 Representatives
Nickname(s): Sunflower State, Jayhawk State,
Breadbasket of America
Motto: To the stars through difficulties
Song: "Home on the Range"
Bird: Western meadowlark
Tree: Cottonwood
Flower: Native sunflower
State fair: at Hutchinson, mid-Sept.
Former capital(s): Pawnee, Shawnee Mission,
Lecompton

Carla J. Stovall (R), Attorney General
127 S.W. 10th St., 2nd Fl., Topeka, KS 66612-1597

Office of the State Treasurer
http://www.kansastreasurer.com
General e-mail: public@treasurer.state.ks.us
Main phone: (785) 296-3171
Main fax: (785) 296-7950

Tim Shallenburger (R), State Treasurer
Landon State Office Bldg., 900 S.W. Jackson St.,
#201, Topeka, KS 66612-1235
E-mail: tim@treasurer.state.ks.us

Adjutant General Dept.
http://www.skyways.lib.ks.us/kansas/adjutant
Main phone: (785) 274-1000
Main fax: (785) 274-1650

Gregory B. Gardner, Adjutant General
2800 S.W. Topeka Blvd., Topeka, KS 66611-1287
(785) 274-1001

Agencies

Accountancy Board
http://www.ink.org/public/ksboa/
General e-mail: ksboa@ink.org
Main phone: (785) 296-2162
Main fax: (785) 291-3501
TTY: (800) 766-3777

Susan L. Somers, Executive Director
Landon State Office Bldg., 900 S.W. Jackson St.,
#556-S, Topeka, KS 66612-1239

Administration Dept.
http://da.state.ks.us/
General e-mail: delberta.pfeifer@state.ks.us
Main phone: (785) 296-3011
Main fax: (785) 296-2702

Daniel R. Stanley, Secretary
Capitol Bldg., #263-E, Topeka, KS 66612-1572

Personnel Services Division
http://da.state.ks.us/ps/
Main phone: (785) 296-4278

William B. McGlasson, Director
Landon State Office Bldg., 900 S.W. Jackson,
Topeka, KS 66612-1251

Public Broadcasting Commission
Main phone: (785) 296-3443
Main fax: (785) 296-1168

Elna Ensley, Administrator
263-E Statehouse, 900 S.W. Jackson St., #751-S,
Topeka, KS 66612
(785) 296-3463

Aging Dept.
http://www.k4s.org/kdoa/default.htm
General e-mail: Juanita1@aging.wpo.state.ks.us
Main phone: (785) 296-4986
Main fax: (785) 296-0256
Toll free: (800) 432-3535

Connie Hubbell, Secretary
503 S. Kansas, New England Bldg., #150, Topeka, KS
60003-3404

Agriculture Dept.
http://www.ink.org/public/kda/
Main phone: (785) 296-3556
Main fax: (785) 296-8389

Jamie Clover Adams, Secretary
109 S.W. 9th St., 4th Fl., Topeka, KS 66612-1280
(785) 296-3558

Arts Commission
Main phone: (785) 296-3335
Main fax: (785) 296-4989

David M. Wilson, Executive Director
Jayhawk Tower, 700 S.W. Jackson St., #1004, Topeka,
KS 66603-3758
E-mail: dave@arts.state.ks.us

Bank Commissioner's Office
http://www.ink.org/public/osbc/
General e-mail: bankcomm@ink.org
Main phone: (785) 296-2266
Main fax: (785) 296-0168

Judi M. Stork, Bank Commissioner (Acting)
Jayhawk Tower, 700 S.W. Jackson St., #300, Topeka,
KS 66612-3714
E-mail: Judi.Stork@state.ks.us

Commerce and Housing Dept.
http://www.kansascommerce.com
General e-mail: admin@kdoch.state.ks.us
Main phone: (785) 296-3481
Main fax: (785) 296-5055
TTY: (785) 296-3487

Gary Sherrer, Secretary
700 S.W. Harrison St., #1300, Topeka, KS 66603-3712
(785) 296-2741; *Fax:* (785) 296-3665

Travel and Tourism Development Division
http://www.kansascommerce.com/
0400travel.html
General e-mail: travtour@kdoh.state.ks.us
Main phone: (785) 296-7091
Main fax: (785) 296-6988
TTY: (785) 296-3487

Claudia Larkin, Director
700 S.W. Harrison St., #1300, Topeka, KS 66603-
3712
(785) 296-2741; *Fax:* (785) 296-3665

Conservation Commission
http://www.ink.org/public/kscc
Main phone: (785) 296-3600
Main fax: (785) 296-6172

Tracy D. Streeter, Executive Director
109 S.W. 9th St., #500, Topeka, KS 66612-1299
E-mail: tstreeter@scc.state.ks.us

Consumer Protection Division
http://www.ink.org/public/ksag
General e-mail: cprotect@01po.wpo.state.ks.us
Main phone: (785) 296-3751
Main fax: (785) 291-3699

Higher Educational Institutions

Emporia State University
http://www.emporia.edu
1200 Commercial St., Emporia, KS 66801-5087
Main phone: (316) 341-1200

Fort Hays State University
http://www.fhsu.edu
600 Park St., Hays, KS 67601-4099
Main phone: (785) 628-1000

Kansas State University
http://www.ksu.edu
119 Anderson Hall, Manhattan, KS 66506
Main phone: (785) 532-6250
Branches: Salina

Pittsburg State University
http://www.pittstate.edu
1701 S. Broadway, Pittsburg, KS 66762
Main phone: (316) 235-4251

University of Kansas
http://www.ukans.edu
1502 Iowa St., Lawrence, KS 66045-1910
Main phone: (785) 864-3911
Branches: Kansas City, Overland Park

Washburn University
http://www.washburn.edu
1700 S.W. College, Topeka, KS 66621
Main phone: (785) 231-1010

Wichita State University
http://www.wichita.edu
1845 Fairmount, Wichita, KS 67260
Main phone: (316) 978-3045

Toll free: (800) 432-2310
TTY: (785) 291-3767

C. Steven Rarrick, Deputy Attorney General
Kansas Judicial Center, 120 S.W. 10th St., 2nd Fl.,
Topeka, KS 66612-1597

Corrections Dept.
http://www.ink.org/public/kdoc/
Main phone: (785) 296-3317
Main fax: (785) 296-0014

Charles E. Simmons, Secretary
Landon State Office Bldg., 900 S.W. Jackson St.,
#401-N, Topeka, KS 66612-1284
(785) 296-3310

Cosmetology Board
Main phone: (785) 296-3155
Main fax: (785) 296-3002

Mary Lou Davis, Administrative Officer
2708 N.W. Topeka Blvd., Topeka, KS 66617-1139

Development Finance Authority
http://www.kdfa.org/
General e-mail: kdfa@kdfa.org
Main phone: (785) 296-6747
Main fax: (785) 296-6810
TTY: (800) 766-3777

Cheri L. Kern, Public Service Administrator
Jayhawk Tower, 700 S.W. Jackson St., #1000, Topeka,
KS 66603
Fax: (785) 296-6810
E-mail: cherik@kdfa.org

Education Dept.
http://www.ksbe.state.ks.us/
Main phone: (785) 296-3201
Main fax: (785) 296-7933
TTY: (785) 296-8170

Andy Tompkins, Commissioner
120 S.E. 10th Ave., Topeka, KS 66612-1182
(785) 296-0286; *Fax:* (785) 291-3791
E-mail: atompkins@ksbe.state.ks.us

Board of Education
http://www.ksbe.state.ks.us/commiss/board.html
General e-mail: pplamann@ksbe.state.ks.us
Main phone: (785) 296-3201
Main fax: (785) 296-7933

Andy Tompkins, Commissioner
120 S.E. 10th Ave., Topeka, KS 66612-1182
(785) 296-3202; *Fax:* (785) 291-3791
E-mail: atompkins@ksbe.state.ks.us

Emergency Management Division
http://www.ink.org/public/kdem/
Main phone: (785) 274-1409
Main fax: (785) 274-1426

Frank Moussa, Administrator
2800 S.W. Topeka Blvd., Topeka, KS 66611-1287
(785) 274-1408
E-mail: fhmoussa@agtop.state.ks.us

Fire Marshal
Main phone: (785) 296-3401
Main fax: (785) 296-0151

Gale Haag, Fire Marshal
Jayhawk Tower, 700 S.W. Jackson St., #600, Topeka,
KS 66603-3714

Forest Service
http://www.oznet.ksu.edu/dp_kfs/
General e-mail: KFS@lists.oznet.ksu.edu
Main phone: (785) 532-3300
Main fax: (785) 532-3305

Robert Atchison, Rural Forestry Coordinator
2610 Claflin Rd., Manhattan, KS 66502-2798
E-mail: ratchiso@oznet.ksu.edu

Geological Survey
http://www.kgs.ukans.edu/
General e-mail: douglass@kgs.ukans.edu
Main phone: (785) 864-3965
Main fax: (785) 864-5317

M. Lee Allison, State Geologist
Campus West, 1930 Constant Ave., Lawrence, KS 66047-3726
E-mail: lallison@kgs.ukans.edu

Health and Environment Dept.
http://www.kdhe.state.ks.us/
Main phone: (785) 296-0461
Main fax: (785) 296-6247

Clyde D. Graeber, Secretary (Acting)
400 S.W. 8th Ave., 900 S.W. Jackson St., #200, Topeka, KS 66603-3930

Highway Patrol
http://www.inc.org/public/khp
General e-mail: trafferty@mail.khp.state.ks
Main phone: (785) 296-6800
Main fax: (785) 296-5956

Donald W. Brownlee, Superintendent
122 S.W. 7th St., Topeka, KS 66603-3847
Fax: (785) 296-3049
E-mail: dbrownlee@mail.khp.state.ks

Historical Society
http://www.kshs.org
General e-mail: referenc@hspo.wpo.state.ks.us
Main phone: (785) 272-8681
Main fax: (785) 272-8682

Ramon Powers, Executive Director
6425 S.W. 6th Ave., Topeka, KS 66615-1099
(785) 272-8681, ext. 205
E-mail: rpowers@kshs.org

Human Resources Dept.
http://www.hr.state.ks.us
General e-mail: webmaster@hr.state.ks.us
Main phone: (785) 296-5000
Main fax: (785) 296-0179
TTY: (785) 296-5044

Richard E. Beyer, Secretary
401 S.W. Topeka Blvd., Topeka, KS 66603-3182
(785) 296-7474

Workers Compensation Division
http://www.hr.state.ks.us
General e-mail: workerscomp@hr.state.ks.us
Main phone : (785) 296-4000
Main fax: (785) 296-0839
Toll free: (800) 332-0353

Philip Harness, Director
800 S.W. Jackson St., #600, Topeka, KS 66612-1227
Fax: (785) 296-0025

Human Rights Commission
http://www.ink.org/public/khrc/
Main phone: (785) 296-3206
Main fax: (785) 296-0589
Toll free: (888) 793-6874
TTY: (785) 296-0245

William V. Minner, Executive Director
Landon State Office Bldg., 900 S.W. Jackson St., #851-S, Topeka, KS 66612-1258

Insurance Dept.
http://www.ksinsurance.org
Main phone: (785) 296-3071
Main fax: (785) 296-2283
Toll free: (800) 432-2484

Kathleen Sebelius (D), Commissioner
420 S.W. 9th St., Topeka, KS 66612-1678
(785) 296-7801; *Fax:* (785) 296-7805
E-mail: ksebelius@ins.wpo.state.ks.us

Juvenile Justice Authority
http://www.ink.org/public/kjja/
General e-mail: jja@jjaco.wpo.state.ks.us
Main phone: (785) 296-4213
Main fax: (785) 296-1412

Albert Murray, Commissioner
Jayhawk Walk, 714 S.W. Jackson St., #300, Topeka, KS 66603

Nursing Board
http://www.ink.org/public/ksbn/
General e-mail: ksbn0@ink.org
Main phone: (785) 296-4929
Main fax: (785) 296-3929

Mary Blubaugh, Executive Administrator
Landon State Office Bldg., 900 S.W. Jackson St., #551-S, Topeka, KS 66612-1230

Pharmacy Board
http://www.ink.org/public/pharmacy/
General e-mail: pharmacy@ink.org
Main phone: (785) 296-4056
Main fax: (785) 296-8420
Consumer hotline: (888) 792-6273

Larry Froelich, Executive Secretary
900 S.W. Jackson, #513, Topeka, KS 66612-1231

Public Employees Retirement System
http://www.kpers.com/kpers/index.html
General e-mail: kpers@kpers.org

Frequently Called Numbers

Tourism: (785) 296-7091; 1-800-2KANSAS;
http://www.kansascommerce.com/
0400travel.html
Library: (785) 296-3296;
http://skyways.lib.ks.us/kansas/
Board of Education: (785) 296-3201; http://
www.ksbe.state.ks.us/commiss/board.html
Vital Statistics: (785) 296-1400;
http://www.kdhe.state.ks.us/vital/
Tax/Revenue: (785) 296-3909;
http://www.ink.org/public/kdor/
Motor Vehicles: (785) 296-3601; http://
www.ink.org/public/kdor/kdorvehicle.html
State Police/Highway Patrol: (785) 296-6800;
http://www.inc.org/public/khp
Unemployment: (785) 296-5025;
http://www.hr.state.ks.us/ui/html/EnUI.htm
General Election Information: (785) 296-
4559; www.kssos.org/elewelc.html
Consumer Affairs: (785) 296-3751;
http://www.ink.org/public/ksag
Hazardous Materials: (785) 296-1600;
http://www.kdhe.state.ks.us/waste/

Main phone: (785) 296-6666
Main fax: (785) 296-2422
Toll free: (888) 275-5737

Meredith Williams, Executive Secretary
611 S. Kansas Ave., #100, Topeka, KS 66603-3803
E-mail: mwilliams@kpers.org

Real Estate Appraisers Board
http://www.ink.org/public/kreab
Main phone: (785) 296-0706
Main fax: (785) 296-1934

Michael Haynes, Director
Columbian Title Bldg., 820 S.E. Quincy St., #314,
Topeka, KS 66612

Regents Board
http://www.kansasregents.org
Main phone: (785) 296-3421
Main fax: (785) 296-0983

Kim Wilcox, Executive Director (Interim)
700 S.W. Harrison St., #1410, Topeka, KS 66603-3760
E-mail: kim@kbor.state.ks.us

Revenue Dept.
http://www.ink.org/public/kdor/
General e-mail: kdor46@ink.org

Main phone: (785) 296-3909
Main fax: (785) 296-7928
TTY: (785) 296-6461

Karla Pierce, Secretary
Docking State Office Bldg., 915 S.W. Harrison St.,
#230, Topeka, KS 66612-1588
(785) 296-3042

Alcoholic Beverage Control Division
http://www.ink.org/public/kdor
Main phone: (785) 296-7015
Main fax: (785) 296-1729

Jim Conant, Director
Townsite Plaza #4, 200 S.E. 6th St., #210, Topeka,
KS 66603
E-mail: jconant@kdor.state.ks.us

Motor Vehicles Division
http://www.ink.org/public/kdor/kdorvehicle.html
Main phone: (785) 296-3601
Main fax: (785) 296-3755

Sheila Walker, Director
915 S.W. Harrison St., Topeka, KS 66626-0001

Social and Rehabilitative Services Dept.
http://www.ink.org/public/srs/
General e-mail: libby@srskansas.org
Main phone: (785) 296-3959
Main fax: (785) 296-2173

Janet Schalansky, Secretary
915 Harrison St., Docking State Office Bldg., 6th Fl.,
Topeka, KS 66612
(785) 296-3271; *Fax:* (785) 296-4685

Adult and Medical Services: Medicaid Operations
http://www.ink.org/public/srs
Main phone: (785) 296-2500
Main fax: (785) 296-5937

Robena M. Farrell, Director
235 S. Kansas Ave., 6th Fl., Topeka, KS 66603
(785) 296-2502; *Fax:* (785) 296-5895

Substance Abuse, Mental Health, and Developmental Disabilities Services
http://www.ink.org/public/srs
Main phone: (785) 296-3471
Main fax: (785) 296-6142

Laurie Howard, Assistant Secretary
Docking State Office Bldg., 915 S.W. Harrison St.,
6th Fl., Topeka, KS 66612
(785) 296-3773
E-mail: lkzh@srskansas.org

State Fair
http://www.kansasstatefair.com/

General e-mail: ksfair@southwind.net
Main phone: (316) 669-3600
Toll free: (800) 362-3247

Bill Ogg, General Manager
2000 N. Poplar, Hutchinson, KS 67502-5598
E-mail: billogg@southwind.net

State Library
http://skyways.lib.ks.us/kansas/
Main phone: (785) 296-3296
Main fax: (785) 296-6650
Toll free: (800) 432-3919
TTY: (785) 296-2149

Duane Johnson, State Librarian
State Capitol, 300 S.W. 10th St., #343-N, Topeka, KS 66612-1593
(785) 296-5466
E-mail: duanej@ink.org

State Lottery
http://www.kslottery.com/
Main phone: (785) 296-5700

James W. Cates, Chair
128 N. Kansas Ave., Topeka, KS 66603

Transportation Dept.
http://www.ink.org/public/kdot
General e-mail: publicinfo@ksdot.org
Main phone: (785) 296-3566
Main fax: (785) 296-1095
TTY: (785) 296-3585

E. Dean Carlson, Secretary
Docking State Office Bldg., 915 S.W. Harrison St., Topeka, KS 66612
(785) 296-3461

Boards and Licensing

Accountancy, (785) 296-2162,
  http://www.ink.org/public/ksboa/
Architects, (785) 296-8899
Child Care, (785) 296-1270
Contractors, (785) 296-3168
Cosmetology, (785) 296-3155
Engineers and Land Surveyors,
  (785) 296-3053
Medical Examiners, (785) 296-7413
Nursing, (785) 296-4929,
  http://www.ink.org/public/ksbn/
Pharmacy, (785) 296-4056,
  http://www.ink.org/public/pharmacy/
Real Estate Appraisers, (785) 296-0706,
  http://www.ink.org/public/kreab

Veterans Affairs Commission
Main phone: (785) 296-3976
Main fax: (785) 296-1462

Don A. Myer, Executive Director
Jayhawk Tower, 700 S.W. Jackson St., Topeka, KS 66603

Water Office
http://www.kwo.org/
Main phone: (785) 296-3185
Main fax: (785) 296-0878
TTY: (785) 296-6604

Al LeDoux, Director
Mills Bldg., 901 Kansas, Topeka, KS 66612-1249

Wildlife and Parks Dept.
http://www.kdwp.state.ks.us
Main phone: (785) 296-2281
Main fax: (785) 296-6953

Steven A. Williams, Secretary
Landon State Office Bldg., 900 S.W. Jackson St., #502, Topeka, KS 66612-1233

Fish and Wildlife Division
http://www.kdwp.state.ks.us
Main phone: (316) 672-5911
Main fax: (316) 672-6020

Joe Kramer, Director
512 S.E. 25th Ave., Pratt, KS 67124-8174
(316) 672-0790
E-mail: joek@wp.state.ks.us

Kansas Legislature

State House
300 S.W. 10th Ave.
Topeka, KS 66612-1504
General information: (785) 296-2391
Fax: (785) 296-1153
Bill status: (785) 296-2149
http://www.ink.org/public/legislative/
main.html

Senate
General information: (785) 296-2456
Fax: (785) 296-6718

Dick Bond (R), President
State House, 300 S.W. 10th Ave., #359-E, Topeka, KS 66612-1504
(785) 296-2914
E-mail: bond@senate.state.ks.us
http://www.ink.org/public/legislative/senators/
bond_dick.html

Laws

Sales tax: 4.9%
Income tax: 7.8%
State minimum wage: $2.65 (Federal is $5.15)
Marriage age: 18
First-cousin marriage: Prohibited
Drinking age: 21
State control of liquor sales: No
Blood alcohol for DWI: 0.08%
Driving age: 16
Speed limit: 70 mph
Permit to buy handguns: In some areas
Minimum age to possess handguns: 18
Minimum age to possess rifles, shotguns:
  None
State lottery: Yes; also Powerball
Casinos: No
Pari-mutuel betting: Horse and dog racing
Death penalty: Yes
3 strikes minimum sentence: Court can double
  or triple term for 2nd, 3rd felony
Hate crimes law: No
Gay employment non-discrimination: No
Official language(s): None
Term limits: None

*State laws are complex and subject to
change; this information is not intended as
legal advice. For an explanation of this
information, see p. x.*

Alicia L. Salisbury (R), Vice President
State House, 300 S.W. 10th Ave., #120-S, Topeka, KS
  66612-1504
(785) 296-7374
E-mail: salisbury@senate.state.ks.us
http://www.ink.org/public/legislative/senators/
  salisbury_alicia.html

Tim Emert (R), Majority Leader
State House, 300 S.W. 10th Ave., #356-E, Topeka, KS
  66612-1504
(785) 296-2497
E-mail: emert@senate.state.ks.us
http://www.ink.org/public/legislative/senators/
  emert_tim.html

Pat Ranson (R), Majority Leader Whip
State House, 300 S.W. 10th Ave., #449-E, Topeka, KS
  66612-1504
(785) 296-7391
E-mail: ranson@senate.state.ks.us

http://www.ink.org/public/legislative/senators/
  ranson_pat.html

Anthony Hensley (D), Minority Leader
State House, 300 S.W. 10th Ave., #347-N, Topeka, KS
  66612-1504
(785) 296-3245
E-mail: hensley@senate.state.ks.us
http://www.ink.org/public/legislative/senators/
  hensley_anthony.html

Christine Downey (D), Minority Whip
State House, 300 S.W. 10th Ave., #126-S, Topeka, KS
  66612-1504
(785) 296-7377
E-mail: downey@senate.state.ks.us
http://www.ink.org/public/legislative/senators/
  downey_christine.html

Pat Saville, Secretary
State House, 300 S.W. 10th Ave., #360E, Topeka, KS
  66612-1504
(785) 296-2456 *Fax:* (785) 296-6718
E-mail: pats@senate.state.ks.us
http://www.ink.org/public/senate_secretary/

House
General information: (785) 296-7633
Fax: (785) 296-1153

Robin Jennison (R), Speaker of the House
State House, 300 S.W. 10th Ave., #380-W, Topeka, KS
  66612-1504
(785) 296-2302; *Fax:* (785) 296-1154
E-mail: jennison@house.state.ks.us
http://www.ink.org/public/legislative/representatives/
  jennison_robin.html

Doug Mays (R), Speaker Pro Tempore
State House, 300 S.W. 10th Ave., #330-N, Topeka, KS
  66612-1504
(785) 296-7668
E-mail: mays@house.state.ks.us
http://www.ink.org/public/legislative/representatives/
  mays_doug.html

Kent Glasscock (R), Majority Leader
State House, 300 S.W. 10th Ave., #381-W, Topeka, KS
  66612-1504
(785) 296-7662
E-mail: kentglass@house.state.ks.us
http://www.ink.org/public/legislative/representatives/
  glasscock_kent.html

Clark Shultz (R), Majority Whip
State House, 300 S.W. 10th Ave., #183-W, Topeka, KS
  66612-1504
(785) 296-7501
E-mail: shultz@house.state.ks.us
http://www.ink.org/public/legislative/representatives/
  shultz_clark.html

Jim D. Garner (D), Minority Leader
State House, 300 S.W. 10th Ave., #327-S, Topeka, KS
  66612-1504
(785) 296-7630
E-mail: garner@house.state.ks.us
http://www.ink.org/public/legislative/representatives/
  garner_jim.html

Richard Alldritt (D), Minority Whip
State House, 300 S.W. 10th Ave., #302-S, Topeka, KS
  66612-1504
(785) 296-7686
E-mail: alldritt@house.state.ks.us
http://www.ink.org/public/legislative/representatives/
  alldritt_richard.html

Janet E. Jones, Chief Clerk
State House, 300 S.W. 10th Ave., #477-W, Topeka, KS
  66612-1504
(785) 296-7633
E-mail: janetj@house.state.ks.us
http://www.ink.org/public/house_secretary/

Kansas Judiciary

Judicial Center
301 W. 10th Ave.
Topeka, KS 66612-1507
http://www.kscourts.org/

Supreme Court
http://www.kscourts.org/spct/

Carol Gilliam Green, Clerk
Judicial Center, 301 W. 10th Ave., Topeka, KS 66612-
1507

(785) 296-3229; *Fax:* (785) 296-1028
E-mail: greenc@kscourts.org

Justices
Composition: 7 justices
Selection Method: appointed by governor; must
  stand for retention in first general election one
  year after appointment
Length of term: 6 years

Kay McFarland, Chief Justice, (785) 296-5322
Bob Abbott, Justice, (785) 296-5348
Donald L. Allegrucci, Justice, (785) 296-3807
Robert E. Davis, Justice, (785) 296-5128
Edward Larson, Justice, (785) 296-4898
Tyler C. Lockett, Justice, (785) 296-4900
Fred N. Six, Justice, (785) 296-5364

Office of Court Administration
Main phone: (785) 296-2256
Main fax: (785) 296-7076

Howard P. Schwartz, Judicial Administrator
Judicial Center, 301 W. 10th Ave., Topeka, KS
  66612-1507
(785) 296-4873

Supreme Court Law Library
http://www.kscourts.org/ctlib/
Main phone: (785) 296-3257
Main fax: (785) 296-1863
General e-mail: oja06@ink.org

Fred Knecht, Director
Judicial Center, 301 W. 10th Ave., Topeka, KS
  66612-1507

Legislative and Political Party Information Resources

Committees: Senate: http://www.ink.org/public/legislative/senatecomm.html;
  House: http://www.ink.org/public/legislative/1998/housecomm.html
Legislative process: http://skyways.lib.ks.us/ksleg/KLRD/klrd.html
Current session information: http://www.ink.org/public/legislative/status/status.cgi
Kansas Democratic Party: http://www.ksdp.org
  P.O. Box 1914, Topeka, KS 66601-1914; *Phone:* (785) 234-0425; *E-mail:* kdp@ksdp.org
Kansas Republican Party: http://www.ksgop.org
  2025 S.W. Gage Blvd., Topeka, KS 66604; *Phone:* (785) 234-3456; *E-mail:* info@ksgop.org

Kentucky

State Capitol
Frankfort, KY 40601
Public information: (502) 564-3130
Fax: (502) 564-2517
http://www.state.ky.us

Office of the Governor
http://www.state.ky.us/agencies/gov/
Main phone: (502) 564-2611
Main fax: (502) 564-2517

Paul E. Patton (D), Governor
State Capitol, 700 Capitol Ave., #100, Frankfort, KY
40601
Fax: (502) 564-8154
E-mail: governor@mail.state.ky.us

Andrew (Skipper) Martin, Chief of Staff
State Capitol, 700 Capitol Ave., #102, Frankfort, KY
40601
(502) 564-2611; *Fax:* (502) 564-2517
E-mail: smartin2@mail.state.ky.us

**Melissa Forsythe, Press Secretary/Communications
Director**
State Capitol, 700 Capitol Ave., #112, Frankfort, KY
40601
(502) 564-2611; *Fax:* (502) 564-8154
E-mail: mforsythe@mail.state.ky.us

Jody A. Lassiter, Director, Constituent Affairs
State Capitol, 700 Capitol Ave., #142, Frankfort, KY
40601
(502) 564-2611; *Fax:* (502) 564-7379
E-mail: jlassiter@mail.state.ky.us

Office of the Lieutenant Governor
http://www.state.ky.us/agencies/gov/henrtxt3.htm
Main phone: (502) 564-2611
Main fax: (502) 564-2849

Stephen L. Henry (D), Lieutenant Governor
State Capitol, 700 Capitol Ave., #100, Frankfort, KY
40601
(502) 564-2611, ext. 375
E-mail: shenry@mail.state.ky.us

Office of the Secretary of State
http://www.sos.state.ky.us
Main phone: (502) 564-3490
Main fax: (502) 564-5687

John Y. Brown III (D), Secretary of State
State Capitol, 700 Capital Ave., #152, Frankfort, KY
40601
E-mail: jbrown@mail.state.ky.us

State of Kentucky

Capital: Frankfort,
 since 1792
Founded: 1783, Kentucky
 District of Virginia created
Statehood: June 1, 1792 (15th state)
Constitution adopted: 1891
Area: 39,732 sq. mi. (ranks 36th)
Population: 3,936,499 (1998 est.; ranks 25th)
Largest cities: (1998 est.) Louisville
 (255,045); Lexington (241,749); Owensboro
 (54,041); Bowling Green (44,822);
 Covington (40,389)
Counties: 120, Most populous: (1998 est.)
 Jefferson (672,104); Fayette (241,749);
 Kenton (146,732); Hardin (91,462); Daviess
 (91,139)
U.S. Congress: Jim Bunning (R), Mitch
 McConnell (R); 6 Representatives
Nickname(s): Bluegrass State
Motto: United we stand, divided we fall
Song: "My Old Kentucky Home"
Bird: Kentucky cardinal
Tree: Tulip poplar
Flower: Goldenrod
State fair: at Louisville, mid-late Aug.
Former capital(s): Danville

Office of the Attorney General
http://www.law.state.ky.us
Main phone: (502) 696-5300
Main fax: (502) 564-8310
TTY: (502) 696-5300

Albert B. Chandler III (D), Attorney General
State Capitol, 700 Capitol Ave., #118, Frankfort, KY
40601

Office of the State Treasurer
http://www.state.ky.us/agencies/treasury/
 homepage.htm
Main phone: (502) 564-4722
Main fax: (502) 564-6545

Jonathan Miller (D), State Treasurer
State Capitol Annex, West Wing, #183, Frankfort, KY
40601

Auditor of Public Accounts
http://www.kyauditor.net
Main phone: (502) 564-5841
Main fax: (502) 564-2912

Edward Bryan Hatchett Jr., Auditor of Public Accounts
State Capitol Annex, #144, Frankfort, KY 40601-3448
(502) 564-5841; *Fax:* (502) 564-2912
E-mail: hatchett@kyauditor.net

Adjutant General Office
http://www.military.state.ky.us
General e-mail: tagky@ky-arng.ngb.army.mil
Main phone: (502) 607-1600
Main fax: (502) 607-1614

John R. Groves Jr., Adjutant General
Boone National Guard Center, 100 Minuteman Pkwy., Frankfort, KY 40601-6168
(502) 607-1558; *Fax:* (502) 607-1271
E-mail: jgroves@ky-arng.ngb.army.mil

Agencies

Accountancy Board
http://www.state.ky.us/agencies/boa
Main phone: (502) 595-3037
Main fax: (502) 595-4500

Susan G. Stopher, Executive Director
332 W. Broadway, #310, Louisville, KY 40202
(502) 595-3037, ext. 26

Administration Dept.
http://www.state.ky.us/agencies/finance/descript/deptaddm.htm
Main phone: (502) 564-2317
Main fax: (502) 564-4279

Donald R. Speer, Commissioner
Capitol Annex, #362, Frankfort, KY 40601
E-mail: don.speer@mail.state.ky.us

Agriculture Dept.
http://www.kyagr.com
Main phone: (502) 564-5126
Main fax: (502) 564-5016
TTY: (502) 564-2075

Billy Ray Smith (D), Commissioner
State Capitol Annex, #188, Frankfort, KY 40601
E-mail: billyray.smith@kyagr.com

Architects Board
http://www.ky.bera.com
General e-mail: kybera@iglou.com
Main phone: (606) 246-2069
Main fax: (606) 246-2431

Jerry W. Herndon, Executive Director
841 Corporate Dr., #200-B, Lexington, KY 40503

Community-Based Services Dept.
Main phone: (502) 564-3703
Main fax: (606) 564-5002

Dietra Paris, Commissioner
275 E. Main St., #3W-A, Frankfort, KY 40621
Fax: (502) 564-6907
E-mail: dietra.paris@mail.state.ky.us

Consumer Protection Division
http://www.law.state.ky.us/cp/default.htm
Main phone: (502) 696-5389
Main fax: (502) 573-8317
Toll free: (888) 432-9527

Todd Leatherman, Director
1024 Capital Center Dr., Frankfort, KY 40601
(502) 696-5389, ext. 5387
E-mail: todd.leather@law.state.ky.us

Economic Development Cabinet
http://www.thinkkentucky.com
General e-mail: econdev@mail.state.ky.us
Main phone: (502) 564-7140
Main fax: (502) 564-3256
Toll free: (800) 626-2930

Marvin E. Strong Jr., Secretary
Capital Plaza Tower, 500 Mero St., Frankfort, KY 40601
(502) 564-7670; *Fax:* (502) 564-7697

Education, Arts, and Humanities Cabinet
http://www.kyeah.org
General e-mail: mclark@mail.state.ky.us
Main phone: (502) 564-0372
Main fax: (502) 564-5959

Marlene M. Helm, Secretary
300 W. Broadway, Old Capitol Annex, Frankfort, KY 40601
E-mail: marlene.helm@mail.state.ky.us

Education Dept.
http://www.state.ky.us/agencies/eah
Main phone: (502) 564-4770
Main fax: (502) 564-5680

Wilmer S. Cody, Commissioner
Capital Plaza Tower, 500 Mero St., Frankfort, KY 40601
(502) 564-3141
E-mail: wcody@kde.state.ky.us

Education Dept.: Board of Education
http://www.kde.state.ky.us/commiss/kbe/
Main phone: (502) 564-3141

Higher Educational Institutions

Eastern Kentucky University
http://www.eku.edu
521 Lancaster Ave., Richmond, KY 40475-3102
Main phone: (606) 622-1000

Kentucky State University
http://www.kysu.edu
400 E. Main St., Frankfort, KY 40601
Main phone: (502) 227-6000

Morehead State University
http://www.morehead-st.edu
150 University Blvd., Morehead, KY 40351
Main phone: (800) 585-6781

Murray State University
http://www.mursuky.edu
P.O. Box 9, Murray, KY 42071
Main phone: (800) 272-4678

Northern Kentucky University
http://www.nku.edu
Nunn Dr., Highland Heights, KY 41099
Main phone: (606) 572-5220

University of Kentucky
http://www.uky.edu
Lexington, KY 40506
Main phone: (606) 257-2000

University of Louisville
http://www.louisville.edu
2211 S. Brook, Louisville, KY 40208
Main phone: (502) 852-6531

Western Kentucky University
http://www.wku.edu
1 Big Red Way, Bowling Green, KY 42101-3576
Main phone: (270) 745-0111

Mary Ann Miller, Policy Coordinator
Capital Plaza Tower, 500 Mero St., Frankfort, KY 40601
E-mail: mmiller@kde.state.ky.us

Educational Television
http://www.KET.org
Main phone: (606) 258-7000
Main fax: (606) 258-7399
Toll free: (800) 432-0951

Virginia G. Fox, Executive Director
600 Cooper Dr., Lexington, KY 40502
E-mail: gfox@KET.org

Kentucky Heritage Council
http://www.state.ky.us/agencies/khc/
khchome.htm
Main phone: (606) 564-7005

David L. Morgan, Executive Director
300 Washington St., Frankfort, KY 40601

Kentucky School for the Blind
http://www.ksb.k12.ky.us
Main phone: (502) 897-1583
Main fax: (502) 897-2994
TTY: (502) 564-2929

Ralph Bartley, Superintendent
1867 Frankfort Ave., Louisville, KY 40206
(502) 897-1583, ext. 253
E-mail: rbartley@ksb.k12.ky.us

Kentucky School for the Deaf
Main phone: (606) 239-7017
Main fax: (606) 239-7007

Harvey Corson, Superintendent
S. 2nd St., Danville, KY 40423-0027
(606) 239-7017, ext. 2001
E-mail: ltcorson@ksd.k12.ky.us

Libraries and Archives Dept.
http://www.kdla.state.ky.us
Main phone: (502) 564-8300
Main fax: (502) 564-5773
Mailing address: P.O. Box 537, Frankfort, KY 40602-0537

James A. Nelson, State Librarian
300 Coffee Tree Rd., Frankfort, KY 40602-0537

Ethics Commission Executive Branch
http://www.state.ky.us/agencies/ethics/ethics.htm
Main phone: (606) 564-7954
Main fax: (606) 564-2686
Toll free: (800) 664-7954

Jill LeMaster, Executive Director
Capitol Annex, 702 Capital Ave., #258, Frankfort, KY 40601
E-mail: jlemaster@ofmca.f.state.ky.us

Finance and Administration Cabinet
http://www.state.ky.us/agencies/finance
Main phone: (502) 564-4240
Main fax: (502) 564-6785

John P. McCarty, Secretary
State Capitol Annex, #383, Frankfort, KY 40601
E-mail: john.mccartey@mail.state.ky.us

Adminstration Dept.: Occupations and Professions Division
http://www.state.ky.us/agencies/finance/
occupations
Main phone: (502) 564-3296
Main fax: (502) 564-4818
Mailing address: P.O. Box 1360, Frankfort, KY 40602

Nancy L. Black, Executive Director
Berry Hill Annex, 700 Louisville Rd., Frankfort, KY 40601
(502) 564-3296, ext. 224
E-mail: nancyl.black@mail.state.ky.us

Financial Institutions Dept.
http://www.dfi.state.ky.us
Main phone: (606) 573-3390
Main fax: (606) 573-8787
Toll free: (800) 223-2579

Ella D. Robinson, Commissioner
1025 Capital Center Dr., #200, Frankfort, KY 40601
(606) 573-3390; *Fax:* (606) 573-8787

Geological Survey
http://www.uky.edu/kgs
Main phone: (606) 257-5500
Main fax: (606) 257-1147

James C. Cobb, State Geologist and Director
Mining and Mineral Resources Bldg., University of Kentucky, #228, Lexington, KY 40506-0107
(606) 257-5500, ext. 110
E-mail: cobb@kgs.mm.uky.edu

Health Services Cabinet
http://cfc-chs.chr.state.ky.us
Main phone: (502) 564-7130
Main fax: (502) 564-3866

Jimmy D. Helton, Secretary
275 E. Main St., 4th Fl., Frankfort, KY 40621
(502) 564-7130, ext. 3268
E-mail: Jimmy.Helton@mail.state.ky.us

Medicaid Services
http://cfc-chs.chr.state.ky.us/chs/dms
Main phone: (502) 564-4321
Main fax: (502) 564-0509

Dennis Boyd, Commissioner
275 E. Main St., 6th Fl., Frankfort, KY 40621
E-mail: dennis.boyd@mail.state.ky.us

Mental Health and Mental Retardation Services
http://dmhmrs.chr.state.ky.us
Main phone: (606) 564-4527
Main fax: (606) 564-5478
TTY: (502) 564-4527

Margaret A. Pennington, Commissioner
100 Fair Oak Ln., 4E-B, Frankfort, KY 40621
E-mail: mapennington@mail.state.ky.us

Public Health Dept.
http://cfc-chs.chr.state.ky.us/ph.htm
Main phone: (502) 564-3970
Main fax: (502) 564-6533

Rice C. Leach, Commissioner
275 E. Main St., Frankfort, KY 40621

Housing Corporation
http://www.kyhousing.org
Main phone: (502) 564-7630
Main fax: (502) 564-5708

Lynn Luallen, Chief Executive Officer
1231 Louisville Rd., Frankfort, KY 40601
E-mail: lluallen@kyhousing.org

Human Rights Commission
General e-mail: kchr.mail@mail.state.ky.us
Main phone: (502) 595-4024
Main fax: (502) 595-4801
Toll free: (800) 292-5566
TTY: (502) 595-4084

Beverly L. Watts, Executive Director
Heyburn Bldg., 332 W. Broadway, #700, Louisville, KY 40202
(502) 595-4024, ext. 240; *Fax:* (502) 595-4801
E-mail: beverly.watts@mail.state.ky.us

Insurance Dept.
http://www.doi.state.ky.us
General e-mail: bonni.carpenter@mail.state.ky.us
Main phone: (502) 564-3630
Main fax: (502) 564-6090
Toll free: (800) 595-6053
Mailing address: P.O. Box 517, Frankfort, KY 40602

George Nichols III, Commissioner
215 W. Main St., Frankfort, KY 40601
(502) 564-6139
E-mail: george.nichols@mail.state.ky.us

Justice Cabinet
http://www.jus.state.ky.us
General e-mail: justice@mail.state.ky.us
Main phone: (502) 564-7554
Main fax: (502) 564-4840

Robert F. Stephens, Secretary
Bush Bldg., 403 Wapping St., 2nd Fl., Frankfort, KY 40601-2638

Corrections Dept.
http://www.state.ky.us/agencies.ksp/ksphome
Main phone: (502) 564-4726
Main fax: (502) 564-5037
Toll free: (800) 221-5991

Doug Sapp, Commissioner
275 E. Main St., Ground Fl., Frankfort, KY 40601
E-mail: doug.sapp@mail.state.ky.us

Juvenile Justice Dept.
http://www.djj.state.ky.us/directory/agencyn.htm

General e-mail: djjinfo@mail.state.ky.us
Main phone: (502) 573-2738
Main fax: (502) 573-4308

Ralph E. Kelly, Commissioner
1025 Capital Center Dr., 3rd Fl., Frankfort, KY
40601
(502) 573-2738; *Fax:* (502) 573-4308

Parole Board

http://www.state.ky.us/agencies/ksp/ksphome
Main phone: (502) 564-3620
Main fax: (502) 564-8995
Toll free: (800) 221-5991

Linda F. Frank, Chair
275 E. Main St., Ground Fl., Frankfort, KY 40601
(502) 564-3620, ext. 25

State Police Dept.

http://www.state.ky.us/agencies/ksp/
  ksphome.thm
General e-mail: kpayne@mail.state.ky.us
Main phone: (502) 695-6303
Main fax: (502) 573-1479
Toll free: (800) 221-5991
TTY: (502) 685-6300

Robert S. Stephens, Commissioner (Acting)
919 Versailles Rd., 5th Fl., Frankfort, KY 40601
E-mail: robert.stephens@mail.state.ky.us

Labor Cabinet

http://www.state.ky.us/agencies/laborhome.htm
Main phone: (502) 564-3070
Main fax: (502) 564-5387

Joe Norsworthy, Secretary
1047 U.S. Hwy. 127 South, #4, Frankfort, KY 40601

Lottery Corporation

http://www.kylottery.com
Main phone: (502) 560-1500
Main fax: (502) 473-2230
TTY: (800) 648-6056

Arthur L. Gleason Jr., President
1011 W. Main St., Louisville, KY 40202
(502) 560-1550; *Fax:* (502) 560-1532
E-mail: exagleas@ntr.net

Medical Licensure Board

http://www.state.ky.us/agencies/kbml
General e-mail: kbml@mail.state.ky.us
Main phone: (502) 429-8046
Main fax: (606) 429-9923

C. William Schmidt, Director
310 Whittington Pkwy., 1-B, Louisville, KY 40222

Motor Vehicle Commission

Main phone: (502) 564-3750
Main fax: (502) 564-5487

David Garnett, Executive Director
114 W. Clinton St., Frankfort, KY 40622
(502) 564-3750; *Fax:* (502) 564-5487
E-mail: dgarnett@mail.state.ky.us

Natural Resources and Environmental Protection Cabinet

http://www.nr.state.ky.us/nrhome.htm
Main phone: (502) 564-3350
Main fax: (502) 564-3354

James E. Bickford, Secretary
Capital Plaza Tower, 500 Mero St., 5th Fl., Frankfort,
  KY 40601
E-mail: james.bickford@mail.state.ky.us

Environmental Protection Dept.

http://www.nr.state.ky.us/nrepc/dep/dep2.htm
Main phone: (502) 564-2150
Main fax: (502) 564-4245
Toll free: (800) 926-8111

Robert W. Logan, Commissioner
14 Reilly Rd., Frankfort, KY 40601
E-mail: robert.logan@mail.state.ky.us

Forestry Division

http://www.nr.state.ky.us/nrepc/dnr/forestry/
  dnrdof.html

Main phone: (502) 564-4496
Main fax: (502) 564-6553

Mark Matuszewski, Director
627 Comanche Trail, Frankfort, KY 40601
(502) 564-4496; *Fax:* (502) 564-6553
E-mail: Mark.Matuszewski@mail.state.ky.us

Waste Management Division
Main phone: (502) 564-6716
Main fax: (502) 564-4049

Robert H. Daniell, Director
14 Reilly Rd., Frankfort, KY 40601

Nursing Board
http://www.kbn.state.ky.us
General e-mail: kbn@state.ky.us
Main phone: (502) 329-7006
Main fax: (502) 329-7011
Toll free: (800) 305-2042

Sharon M. Weisenbeck, Executive Director
312 Whittington Pkwy., #300, Louisville, KY 40222-5172
E-mail: sharon.weisenbeck@mail.state.ky.us

Personnel Cabinet
http://www.state.ky.us/agencies/personnel/pershome.htm
General e-mail:
personnel.cabinet@mail.state.ky.us
Main phone: (606) 564-4460
Main fax: (606) 564-7603

Carol Palmore, Secretary
200 Fair Oaks Ln., #516, Frankfort, KY 40601
E-mail: carol.palmore@mail.state.ky.us

Pharmacy Board
Main phone: (606) 573-1580
Main fax: (606) 573-1582

Michael A. Mone, Executive Director
1024 Capital Center Dr., #210, Frankfort, KY 40601-8204

Postsecondary Education Council
http://www.cpe.state.ky.us
General e-mail: cpe@mail.state.ky.us
Main phone: (502) 573-1555
Main fax: (502) 573-1535

Gordon R. Davies, President
1024 Capital Center Dr., #320, Frankfort, KY 40601
(502) 573-1555; *Fax:* (502) 573-1537
E-mail: gordon.davies@mail.state.ky.us

Professional Engineers and Land Surveyors Licensure Board
http://kyboels.state.ky.us
Main phone: (502) 573-2680

Main fax: (502) 573-6687
Toll free: (800) 573-2680

Larry S. Perkins, Executive Director
Kentucky Engineering Center, 160 Democrat Dr., Frankfort, KY 40601
(502) 573-2680, ext. 227
E-mail: larry.perkins@mail.state.ky.us

Prosecutor's Advisory Council Services Division
Main phone: (502) 696-5500
Main fax: (502) 696-5532

David H. MacKnight, Director (Acting)
700 Capital Ave., Frankfort, KY 40601
(502) 696-5300; *Fax:* (502) 564-8310
E-mail: david.macknight@law.state.ky.us

Public Protection and Regulation Cabinet
http://www.state.ky.us/agencies/ppc/Sec.htm
Main phone: (502) 564-7760
Main fax: (502) 564-3969
TTY: (800) 372-2988

Ronald B. McCloud, Secretary
90 Airport Rd., Louisville Rd., Frankfort, KY 40601
E-mail: ronald.mccloud@mail.state.ky.us

Alcoholic Beverage Control
Main phone: (502) 564-4850
Main fax: (502) 564-1442

Richard N. Johnstone, Commissioner
1003 Twilight Trail, #A-2, Frankfort, KY 40601
(502) 564-4850, ext. 247
E-mail: rick.johnstone@mail.state.ky.us

Boards and Licensing

Accountancy, (502) 595-3037,
http://www.state.ky.us/agencies/boa
Architects, (606) 246-2069,
http://www.ky.bera.com
Child Care, (502) 564-2800
Contractors, (502) 564-3490
Cosmetology, (502) 564-4262
Engineers and Land Surveyors, (502) 573-2680, http://kyboels.state.ky.us
Medical Licensing, (502) 429-8046,
http://www.state.ky.us/agencies/kbml
Nursing, (502) 329-7006, http://www.kbn.state.ky.us
Pharmacy, (606) 573-1580
Real Estate Appraisers, (502) 573-0091

Housing, Building, and Construction Dept.: Fire Marshal Division
http://www.state.ky.us/agencies/housing/ divfire.htm
General e-mail: charlene.slump@mail.state.ky.us
Main phone: (502) 564-3626
Main fax: (502) 564-6799

Dave L. Manley, Director
1047 U.S. Hwy. 127 South, #1, Frankfort, KY 40601-4337
E-mail: dave.manley@mail.state.ky.us

Mines and Minerals Dept.: Oil and Gas Division
http://www.caer.uky.edu/kdmm/ong.htm
Main phone: (502) 573-0140
Main fax: (502) 573-0152
Mailing address: P.O. Box 2244, Frankfort, KY 40602-2244

John R. (Rick) Bender, Director
1025 Capital Center Dr., 3rd Fl., Frankfort, KY 40601
E-mail: rick.bender@mail.state.ky.us

Public Service Commission
http://www.psc.mail.state.ky.us
Main phone: (502) 564-3940
Main fax: (502) 564-3460
Toll free: (800) 772-4636
Mailing address: P.O. Box 615, Frankfort, KY 40602

Helen C. Helton, Executive Director
211 Sower Blvd., 1st Fl., Frankfort, KY 40602
(502) 564-3940, ext. 210
E-mail: hc.helton@mail.state.ky.us

Real Estate Appraisers Board
Main phone: (502) 573-0091
Main fax: (502) 573-0093

Sam E. Blackburn, Executive Director
1025 Capital Center Dr., #100, Frankfort, KY 40601
E-mail: sam.blackburn@mail.state.ky.us

Retirement Systems
http://www.state.kyret.com
General e-mail: krsmail@kyret.com
Main phone: (502) 564-4646
Main fax: (502) 564-5656
Toll free: (800) 928-4646

Pamela S. Johnson, General Manager
Perimeter Park West, 1260 Louisville Rd., Frankfort, KY 40601-6124

Revenue Cabinet
http://www.state.ky.us/agencies/revenue/ revhome.htm

Main phone: (502) 564-4581
Main fax: (502) 564-3875
TTY: (502) 564-3058
Mailing address: P.O. Box 930, Frankfort, KY 40602-0930

F. Michael Haydon, Secretary
200 Fair Oaks Lane, Bldg. 2, Frankfort, KY 40602
(502) 564-3226
E-mail: mike.haydon@mail.state.ky.us

Tourism Development Cabinet
http://www.kentuckytourism.com
Main phone: (502) 564-4270
Main fax: (502) 564-1512

Ann R. Latta, Secretary
Capital Plaza Tower, 500 Mero St., #2400, Frankfort, KY 40601
Fax: (502) 564-1512
E-mail: ann.latta@mail.state.ky.us

Fish and Wildlife Resources
http://www.state.ky.us/agencies/fw/kdfwr.htm
Main phone: (502) 564-3400
Main fax: (502) 564-6508

Tom Bennett, Commissioner
Arnold Mitchell Bldg., 1 Game Farm Rd., Frankfort, KY 40601
Fax: (502) 564-0506

Parks Dept.
http://www.state.ky.us/agencies/parks/ parkhome.htm
Main phone: (502) 564-2172
Main fax: (502) 564-6100
Toll free: (800) 255-7275

Kenny Rapier, Commissioner
Capital Plaza Tower, 500 Mero St., 10th Fl., Frankfort, KY 40601
(502) 564-2172, ext. 205; *Fax:* (502) 564-9015
E-mail: kenny.rapier@mail.state.ky.us

State Fair Board
http://www.kyfairexpo.org
Main phone: (502) 367-5000
Main fax: (502) 367-5258
TTY: (502) 367-5131
Mailing address: P.O. Box 37130, Louisville, KY 40233-7130

Harold Workman, President
937 Phillips Lane, Louisville, KY 40209-1398
(502) 367-5114; *Fax:* (502) 367-5109
E-mail: harold.workman@mail.state.ky.us

Transportation Cabinet
http://www.kytc.state.ky.us
General e-mail: tonysmith@mail.kytc.state.ky.us

Main phone: (502) 564-6927
Main fax: (502) 564-4809

James C. Codell III, Secretary
State Office Bldg., 501 High St., #1002, Frankfort, KY 40622
(502) 564-4890; *Fax:* (502) 564-9540
E-mail: jcodell@kytc.state.ky.us

Intermodal Programs Office: Aeronautics Division
Main phone: (502) 564-4480
Main fax: (502) 564-7953

Arthur Pace, Director
125 Home St., 3rd Fl., Frankfort, KY 40622
E-mail: arthur.pace@mail.state.ky.us

Veterans Affairs Dept.
http://www.kydva.org
Main phone: (502) 564-1864
Main fax: (502) 564-1866
Toll free: (800) 572-6245

Leslie E. Beavers, Commssioner
1111 Louisville Rd., Frankfort, KY 40601
E-mail: les.beavers@mail.state.ky.us

Workforce Development Cabinet
http://www.state.ky.us/agencies/wforce/
Main phone: (502) 564-6606
Main fax: (502) 564-7967

Allen D. Rose, Secretary
Capital Plaza Tower, 500 Mero St., 2nd Fl., Frankfort, KY 40601
(502) 564-6606; *Fax:* (502) 564-2289

Kentucky Legislature
State Capitol
Frankfort, KY 40601
General information: (502) 564-8100
Bill status: (800) 809-0020
http://www.lrc.state.ky.us

Senate
General information: (502) 564-2840
Fax: (502) 564-6543

Larry Saunders (D), President
State Capitol, #324, Frankfort, KY 40601
(503) 564-3120
E-mail: larry.saunders@lrc.state.ky.us
http://www.lrc.state.ky.us/Whoswho/99GA/Jefferso/
saunders.htm

Joey Pendleton (D), President Pro Tempore
State Capitol, #328, Frankfort, KY 40601

(503) 564-2840
E-mail: joey.pendleton@lrc.state.ky.us

David K. Karem (D), Majority Leader
State Capitol, #330, Frankfort, KY 40601
(503) 564-2470
E-mail: david.karem@lrc.state.ky.us
http://www.lrc.state.ky.us/Whoswho/99GA/Jefferso/
karem.htm

David L. Williams (R), Minority Leader
State Capitol, #319, Frankfort, KY 40601
(503) 564-2450
E-mail: david.williams@lrc.state.ky.us
http://www.lrc.state.ky.us/Whoswho/99GA/Cumberla/
williams.htm

Walter Blevins Jr. (D), Majority Whip
State Capitol, #330, Frankfort, KY 40601
(503) 564-2470
E-mail: walter.blevins@lrc.state.ky.us
http://www.lrc.state.ky.us/Whoswho/99GA/Morgan/
blevins.htm

Elizabeth Tori (R), Minority Whip
State Capitol, #319, Frankfort, KY 40601
(503) 564-2450

Laws

Sales tax: 6%
Income tax: 6%
State minimum wage: $5.15 (Federal is $5.15)
Marriage age: 18
First-cousin marriage: Prohibited
Drinking age: 21
State control of liquor sales: No
Blood alcohol for DWI: 0.10%
Driving age: 16, 6 mos.
Speed limit: 65 mph
Permit to buy handguns: No
Minimum age to possess handguns: 18
Minimum age to possess rifles, shotguns: None
State lottery: Yes; also Powerball
Casinos: No
Pari-mutuel betting: Horse racing
Death penalty: Yes
3 strikes minimum sentence: None
Hate crimes law: Yes
Gay employment non-discrimination: No
Official language(s): English
Term limits: None

State laws are complex and subject to change; this information is not intended as legal advice. For an explanation of this information, see p. x.

E-mail: elizabeth.tori@lrc.state.ky.us

http://www.lrc.state.ky.us/Whoswho/99GA/Hardin/tori.htm

Barbara Ferguson, Chief Clerk
State Capitol, Frankfort, KY 40601
(503) 564-5320

House

General information: (502) 564-3366
Fax: (502) 564-7178

Jody Richards (D), Speaker of the House
State Capitol, #309, Frankfort, KY 40601
(503) 564-3366
E-mail: jody.richards@lrc.state.ky.us
http://www.lrc.state.ky.us/Whoswho/99GA/Warren/richards.htm

Larry Clark (D), Speaker Pro Tempore
State Capitol, #305, Frankfort, KY 40601
(503) 564-7520
E-mail: larry.clark@lrc.state.ky.us
http://www.lrc.state.ky.us/Whoswho/99GA/Jefferso/lclark.htm

Gregory D. Stumbo (D), Majority Leader
State Capitol, #304, Frankfort, KY 40601
(503) 564-7460

Danny R. Ford (R), Minority Leader
State Capitol, #314, Frankfort, KY 40601
(503) 564-5391
E-mail: danny.ford@lrc.state.ky.us

Joe Barrows (D), Majority Whip
State Capitol, #305, Frankfort, KY 40601
(503) 564-7756
E-mail: joe.barrows@lrc.state.ky.us

Woody Allen (R), Minority Whip
State Capitol, #316-A, Frankfort, KY 40601
(503) 564-2995

Lois Pulliam, Chief Clerk
State Capitol, Frankfort, KY 40601
(503) 564-3900

Kentucky Judiciary

700 Capitol Ave.
Frankfort, KY 40601
http://www.aoc.state.ky.us

Supreme Court
http://www.aoc.state.ky.us/supreme

Susan Stokley Clary, Court Administrator and Clerk
700 Capitol Ave., Frankfort, KY 40601
(502) 564-4176; *Fax:* (502) 564-2665

Justices
Composition: 7 justices
Selection Method: nonpartisan election; vacancies filled by temporary gubernatorial appointment
Length of term: 8 years

Joseph E. Lambert, Chief Justice, (502) 564-4162
William S. Cooper, Associate Justice, (502) 766-5179
J. William Graves, Associate Justice, (502) 564-4164
James E. Keller, Associate Justice, (606) 246-2220
Martin E. Johnstone, Associate Justice, (502) 595-3199
Janet L. Stumbo, Associate Justice, (606) 886-9288
Donald C. Wintersheimer, Associate Justice, (502) 564-4166

Administrative Office of the Courts
http://www.aoc.state.ky.us/aoc
Main phone: (502) 573-2350
Main fax: (502) 695-1759

Cicely J. Lambert, Director
100 Millcreek Park, Frankfort, KY 40601
E-mail: cicelyl@mail.aoc.state.ky.us

State Law Library
Main phone: (502) 564-4848
Main fax: (502) 564-5041

Marge Jones, Law Librarian (Acting)
700 Capitol Ave., #200, Frankfort, KY 40601

Legislative and Political Party Information Resources

Senate Home Page: http://www.lrc.state.ky.us/Senate/senate2.htm
House Home Page: http://www.lrc.state.ky.us/House/house2.htm
Committees: http://www.lrc.state.ky.us/Org_Adm/commite/comminfo.htm
Legislative process: http://www.lrc.state.ky.us/legproc/legproc2.htm
Current session information: http://www.lrc.state.ky.us/sch_vist/emailcal.htm
Kentucky Democratic Party: http://www.kydemocrat.com
   190 Democrat Dr., P.O. Box 694, Frankfort, KY 40602; *Phone:* (502) 695-4828
Kentucky Republican Party: http://www.rpk.org
   105 W. 3rd St., Frankfort, KY 40602; *Phone:* (502) 875-5130; *E-mail:* rpk@rpk.org

Louisiana

State Capitol
Baton Rouge, LA 70804-9004
Public information: (225) 342-6600
Fax: (225) 342-7099
http://www.state.la.us

Office of the Governor
http://www.gov.state.la.us
Main phone: (225) 342-7015
Main fax: (225) 342-7099
Mailing address: P.O. Box 94004, Baton Rouge,
LA 70804-9004

Murphy J. (Mike) Foster Jr. (R), Governor
State Capitol, 900 3rd St., Baton Rouge, LA 70804-
9004

J. Stephen Perry, Chief of Staff
State Capitol, 900 3rd St., Baton Rouge, LA 70802
(225) 342-1626; *Fax:* (225) 342-0002

Marsanne Golsby, Press Secretary
State Capitol, 900 N. 3rd St., Baton Rouge, LA 70804-
9004
(225) 342-9037; *Fax:* (225) 342-6003

Julie Strong Talbot, Constituent Services Director
State Capitol, Baton Rouge, LA 70804-9004
(225) 342-7015; *Fax:* (225) 342-7099

Office of the Lieutenant Governor
http://www.crt.state.la.us/crt/ltgov/ltgov.htm
Main phone: (225) 342-7009
Main fax: (225) 342-1949
Mailing address: P.O. Box 44243, Baton Rouge,
LA 70804

**Kathleen Babineaux Blanco (D), Lieutenant
Governor**
900 N. 3rd St., Pentagon Barracks, Bldg. C, 2nd Fl.,
Baton Rouge, LA 70802
E-mail: kblanco@crt.state.la.us

Office of the Secretary of State
http://www.sec.state.la.us/
Main phone: (225) 922-1000
Main fax: (225) 922-0002
TTY: (225) 342-4491
Mailing address: P.O. Box 94125, Baton Rouge,
LA 70804-9125

Walter Fox McKeithen (R), Secretary of State
Capitol Bldg., 800 N. 3rd St., 20th Fl., Baton Rouge,
LA 70802
(225) 342-4479; *Fax:* (225) 342-5577
E-mail: wmckeithen@sec.state.la.us

State of Louisiana

Capital: Baton Rouge, since 1882
Founded: 1803, Louisiana purchased from France; 1804, separate Territory of Orleans created
Statehood: April 30, 1812 (18th state)
Constitution adopted: 1974
Area: 43,566 sq. mi. (ranks 33rd)
Population: 4,368,967 (1998 est.; ranks 22nd)
Largest cities: (1998 est.) New Orleans (465,538); Baton Rouge (211,511); Shreveport (188,319); Lafayette (113,615); Bossier City (56,637)
Counties: 64, Most populous: (1998 est.) Orleans (465,538); Jefferson (450,933); East Baton Rouge (394,714); Caddo (242,471); St. Tammany (188,936)
U.S. Congress: John E. Breaux (D), Mary Landrieu (D); 7 Representatives
Nickname(s): Pelican State, Sportsman's Paradise, Creole State, Sugar State
Motto: Union, justice, and confidence
Song: "Give Me Louisiana," "You Are My Sunshine"
Bird: Pelican
Tree: Bald cypress
Flower: Magnolia
State fair: at Baton Rouge, mid-late Oct.
Former capital(s): New Orleans, Donaldsonville, Opelousas, Alexandria, Shreveport

Office of the Attorney General
http://www.laag.com/
Main phone: (225) 342-7013
Main fax: (225) 342-7335
Mailing address: P.O. Box 94005, Baton Rouge,
LA 70804-9005

Richard P. Ieyoub (D), Attorney General
State Capitol, 300 Capitol Dr., 22nd Fl., Baton Rouge,
LA 70804
(225) 339-5190; *Fax:* (225) 342-8703
E-mail: rieyoub@ag.state.la.us

Office of the State Treasurer
http://www.treasury.state.la.us

General e-mail: temp1@treasury.state.la.us
Main phone: (225) 342-0010
Main fax: (225) 342-0046
Mailing address: P.O. Box 44154, Baton Rouge, LA 70804-4154

John Kennedy (D), Treasurer
State Capitol, 900 N. 3rd St., 3rd Fl., Baton Rouge, LA 70802

Office of the State Auditor
http://www.lla.state.la.us/
Main phone: (225) 339-3800
Main fax: (225) 339-3870
Mailing address: P.O. Box 94397, Baton Rouge, LA 70804

Daniel G. Kyle, Legislative Auditor
1600 N. 3rd St., Baton Rouge, LA 70804
E-mail: dkyle@lla.state.la.us

Military Dept.
http://www.lan.ngb.army.mil
Main phone: (504) 271-6262
Main fax: (504) 278-7325
Toll free: (800) 233-6796

Bennett C. Landreneau, Adjutant General
Jackson Barracks, Bldg. 1, New Orleans, LA 70146-0330
(504) 278-8211; *Fax:* (504) 278-6554
E-mail: landreneb@la-arng.ngb.army.mil

Agencies

Administration Division
http://www.state.la.us/doa/doa.htm
Main phone: (225) 342-7000
Main fax: (225) 342-1057
Mailing address: P.O. Box 94095, Baton Rouge, LA 70804-9095

Mark C. Drennen, Commissioner of Administration
1051 N. 3rd St., Capitol Annex Bldg., #229, Baton Rouge, LA 70802
(225) 342-7086; *Fax:* (225) 342-1057
E-mail: commissioner@doa.state.la.us

Finance
http://www.state.la.us/dbc
General e-mail: kpatterson@doa.state.la.us
Main phone: (225) 342-7000
Main fax: (225) 342-1057
Mailing address: P.O. Box 94095, Baton Rouge, LA 70804-9095

Whitman Kling, Deputy Undersecretary
1051 N. 3rd St., #229, Baton Rouge, LA 70802
(225) 342-7058
E-mail: wkling@doa.state.la.us

Personnel Office
http://www.opswebpg/ops.htm
Main phone: (225) 342-6060
Main fax: (225) 342-0019
Mailing address: P.O. Box 94095, Baton Rouge, LA 70804-9095

Ann Graham, Director
1051 N. 3rd St., #125, Baton Rouge, LA 70804
E-mail: agraham@doa.state.la.us

Agriculture and Forestry Dept.
http://www.ldaf.state.la.us/
Main phone: (225) 922-1234
Main fax: (225) 922-1253
Mailing address: P.O. Box 631, Baton Rouge, LA 70821-0631

Robert F. Odom (D), Commissioner
5825 Florida Blvd., Baton Rouge, LA 70806
(225) 922-1233
E-mail: melanie@ldaf.state.la.us

Soil and Water Conservation Office
http://www.ldaf.state.la.us/soilwater/index.htm
Main phone: (225) 922-1269
Main fax: (225) 922-2577
Mailing address: P.O. Box 3554, Baton Rouge, LA 70821-3554

Bradley Spicer, Assistant Commissioner
5825 Florida Blvd., #1070, Baton Rouge, LA 70806
E-mail: brad_s@ldaf.state.la.us

Architectural Examiners Board
http://www.lastbdarchs.com
General e-mail: lastbdarchs@eatel.net
Main phone: (225) 925-4802
Main fax: (225) 925-4804

Teeny Simmons, Executive Director
8017 Jefferson Hwy., #B-2, Baton Rouge, LA 70809
(225) 925-4802; *Fax:* (225) 925-4804

Archives and Records Division
http://www.sec.state.la.us/arch-1.htm
Main phone: (225) 922-1200
Main fax: (225) 922-0433
Mailing address: P.O. Box 94125, Baton Rouge, LA 70804-9125

Donald J. Lemieux, Director
3851 Esson Lane, Baton Rouge, LA 70809

Board of Regents
http://www.regents.state.la.us
Main phone: (225) 342-4253
Main fax: (225) 342-9318

E. Joseph Savoie, Commissioner, Higher Education
150 3rd St., #129, Baton Rouge, LA 70801-1389
(225) 342-4253, ext. 211
E-mail: commish@regents.state.la.us

Civil Service Dept.

http://www.dscs.state.la.us
Main phone: (225) 342-8083
Main fax: (225) 342-6074
Mailing address: P.O. Box 94111, Baton Rouge, LA 70804-9111

Allen H. Reynolds, Director
1201 Capitol Access Rd., DOTD Annex Bldg., Baton Rouge, LA 70802
(225) 342-8272

Culture, Recreation, and Tourism Dept.

http://www.crt.state.la.us/
Main phone: (225) 342-8115
Main fax: (225) 342-3207
Toll free: (800) 334-8626
Mailing address: P.O. Box 94361, Baton Rouge, LA 70804-9361

Kathleen Babineaux Blanco, Commissioner
Capitol Annex, 1051 N. 3rd St., 3rd Fl., Baton Rouge, LA 70802
(225) 342-7009; *Fax:* (225) 342-8390
E-mail: kblanco@crt.state.la.us

Cultural Development Office: Arts Division

http://www.crt.state.la.us/arts/index.htm
General e-mail: cwhunt@crt.state.la.us
Main phone: (225) 342-8180
Main fax: (225) 342-8173
Mailing address: P.O. Box 44247, Baton Rouge, LA 70804-4247

James B. Borders, Director
Capitol Annex Bldg., 1051 N. 3rd St., #419, Baton Rouge, LA 70801
(225) 342-8172

Cultural Development Office: Historic Preservation Division

http://www.crt.state.la.us/crt/ocd/hp/ocdhp.htm
Main phone: (225) 342-8160
Main fax: (225) 342-8173
Mailing address: P.O. Box 44247, Baton Rouge, LA 70804-4247

Jonathan Fricker, Director
1051 N. 3rd St., Capitol Annex, 4th Fl., Baton Rouge, LA 70804

State Parks Office

http://www.crt.state.la.us/crt/parks/default.htm
General e-mail: cw@crt.state.la.us
Main phone: (225) 342-8111
Main fax: (225) 342-8107
Toll free: (888) 677-1400
Mailing address: P.O. Box 44426, Baton Rouge, LA 70804-4426

Dwight Landreneau, Assistant Secretary
1051 N. 3rd St., #300, Baton Rouge, LA 70802
E-mail: dlandreneau@crt.state.la.us

Day Care Licensing Bureau

Main phone: (225) 922-0015
Main fax: (225) 922-0014
Mailing address: P.O. Box 3078, Baton Rouge, LA 70821

Theresa Anzalone, Director
2751 Wooddale Blvd., #330, Baton Rouge, LA 70821

Economic Development Dept.

http://www.lded.state.la.us
General e-mail: mktg@lded.state.la.us
Main phone: (225) 342-3000
Main fax: (225) 342-5389
Mailing address: P.O. Box 94185, Baton Rouge, LA 70804-9185

Kevin P. Reilly Sr., Secretary
101 France St., 1 Maritime Plaza, #306, Baton Rouge, LA 70802
(225) 342-5388; *Fax:* (225) 342-9095
E-mail: reilly@lded.state.la.us

Financial Institutions Office

http://www.ofi.state.la.us
Main phone: (225) 925-4660
Main fax: (225) 925-4548
Mailing address: P.O. Box 94095, Baton Rouge, LA 70804-9095

Doris B. Gunn, Commissioner (Acting)
8660 United Plaza Blvd., 2nd Fl., Baton Rouge, LA 70809-7024
E-mail: dgunn@ofi.state.la.us

Racing Commission

http://www.state.la.us/new/lrc/lremain.htm
Main phone: (504) 483-4000
Main fax: (504) 483-4898

Albert M. Stall, Chair
320 N. Carrollton Ave., #2-B, New Orleans, LA 70119-5100
(504) 838-5659; *Fax:* (504) 833-4636

Education Dept.

http://www.doe.state.la.us
Main phone: (225) 342-5840
Main fax: (225) 342-7316
Mailing address: P.O. Box 94064, Baton Rouge, LA 70804-9064

Cecil J. Picard, State Superintendent
626 N. 4th St., 12th Fl., Baton Rouge, LA 70802
(225) 342-3602
E-mail: cpicard@mail.doe.state.la.us

Board of Education

Main phone: (225) 342-5840
Main fax: (225) 342-5843

Educational Institutions

Grambling State University
http://www.gram.edu
P.O. Box 607, Grambling, LA 71245
Main phone: (318) 274-3395

Louisiana State University
http://www.lsu.edu
110 Thomas Boyd Hall, Baton Rouge, LA 70803
Main phone: (225) 388-1175
Branches: Eunice, Medical Center, Shreveport

Louisiana Tech University
http://www.latech.edu
P.O. Box 3178, Ruston, LA 71271
Main phone: (318) 257-3036

McNeese State University
http://www.mcneese.edu
4205 Ryan St., Lake Charles, LA 70609
Main phone: (318) 475-5000

Nicholls State University
http://www.nich.edu
P.O. Box 2004-NSU, Thibodaux, LA 70310
Main phone: (504) 448-4507

Northwestern State University
http://www.nsula.edu
Roy Hall, #101, Natchitoches, LA 71497
Main phone: (318) 357-4503

Southeastern Louisiana University
http://www.selu.edu
SLU 10752, Hammond, LA 70402
Main phone: (504) 549-2000

Southern University and A&M College
http://www.subr.edu
P.O. Box 9901, Baton Rouge, LA 70813
Main phone: (225) 771-4500
Branches: New Orleans, Shreveport-Bossier City

University of Louisiana
http://www.louisiana.edu
104 University Circle, P.O. Box 42651,
Lafayette, LA 70504
Main phone: (337) 482-1000
Branches: Monroe (formerly Northeast Louisiana
University)

University of New Orleans
http://www.uno.edu
Lakefront, New Orleans, LA 70148
Main phone: (504) 280-6000

Mailing address: P.O. Box 94064, Capitol
Station, Baton Rouge, LA 70804-9064

Mary L. (Weegie) Peabody, Executive Director
626 N. 4th St., #104, Baton Rouge, LA 70802
(225) 342-5848
E-mail: mpeabody@mail.doe.state.la.us

Elderly Affairs Office
Main phone: (225) 342-7100
Main fax: (225) 342-7133
Toll free: (800) 256-4277
Mailing address: P.O. Box 80374, Baton Rouge,
LA 70890-0374

P. F. (Pete) Arceneaux, Director
412 N. 4th St., 3rd Fl., Baton Rouge, LA 70802

Elections and Registration Dept.
http://www.laelections.org/
Main phone: (225) 925-7885
Main fax: (225) 925-1841
Mailing address: P.O. Box 14179, Baton Rouge,
LA 70804-4179

Suzanne Haik Terrell (R), Commissioner
4888 Constitution Ave., Baton Rouge, LA 70808
E-mail: sterrell@laelections.org

Emergency Preparedness
http://www.loep.state.la.us/
General e-mail: sburr@loep.state.la.us
Main phone: (225) 342-5470
Main fax: (225) 342-5471
Toll free: (800) 256-7036
Mailing address: P.O. Box 44217, Baton Rouge,
LA 70804

Mike Brown, Assistant Director
625 N. 4th St. Basement, Baton Rouge, LA 70802
(225) 342-1583
E-mail: mbrown@loep.state.la.us

Employees Retirement System
http://www.lasers.state.la.us/
Main phone: (800) 922-0600
Main fax: (225) 922-0614
Toll free: (800) 256-3000
Mailing address: P.O. Box 44213, Baton Rouge,
LA 70804-4213

Glenda Chambers, Executive Director
8401 United Plaza Blvd., #100, Baton Rouge, LA
70809
(225) 922-0604

Engineers and Land Surveyors Board
http://www.lapels.com/
Main phone: (225) 925-6291
Main fax: (225) 925-6292

Merlin A. Pistorius, Chair
9643 Brookline Ave., #121, Baton Rouge, LA 70809-
1443

Environmental Quality Dept.
http://www.deq.state.la.us/
General e-mail: webmaster@deq.state.la.us
Main phone: (225) 765-0741
Main fax: (225) 765-0746
Toll free: (888) 763-5424
TTY: (800) 947-5277

Mailing address: P.O. Box 82263, Baton Rouge, LA 70804-2263

John Dale Givens, Secretary
7290 Blue Bonnet Rd., 6th Fl., Baton Rouge, LA 70810
(225) 765-0741
E-mail: dale_g@deq.state.la.us

Health and Hospitals Dept.
http://www.dhh.state.la.us
Main phone: (225) 342-9500
Main fax: (225) 342-9508
Mailing address: P.O. Box 629, Baton Rouge, LA 70804-0629

David W. Hood, Secretary
1201 Capitol Access Rd., 3rd Fl., Baton Rouge, LA 70802
(225) 342-9509; *Fax:* (225) 342-5568

Citizens with Developmental Disabilities Office
Main phone: (225) 342-0095
Main fax: (225) 342-8823
Mailing address: P.O. Box 3117, Bin 21, Baton Rouge, LA 70821-3117

Bruce C. Blaney, Assistant Secretary
1201 Capitol Access Rd., DOTD Annex, 4th Fl., Baton Rouge, LA 70802
E-mail: bblaney@dhhmail.dhh.state.la.us

Mental Health Office
Main phone: (225) 342-9238
Main fax: (225) 342-5066
Mailing address: P.O. Box 4049, Bin 12, Baton Rouge, LA 70821-4049

Richard C. Lippincott, Assistant Secretary
1201 Capitol Access Rd., DOTD Annex, 4th Fl., Baton Rouge, LA 70802
E-mail: rlippinc@dhh.state.la.us

Housing Finance Agency
http://www.lhfa.state.la.us
General e-mail: webmaster@lhfa.state.la.us
Main phone: (225) 342-1320
Main fax: (225) 342-1310

V. Jean Butler, President
200 Lafayette St., #300, Baton Rouge, LA 70801
(225) 342-1320, ext. 216; *Fax:* (225) 342-9386
E-mail: jbutler@lhfa.state.la.us

Insurance Dept.
http://wwwldi.ldi.state.la.us/
General e-mail: public@ldi.state.la.us
Main phone: (225) 342-5900
Main fax: (225) 342-8622
Toll free: (800) 259-5301

Mailing address: P.O. Box 94214, Baton Rouge, LA 70804-9214

James H. Brown Jr. (D), Commissioner
950 N. 5th St., 7th Fl., Baton Rouge, LA 70802
(225) 342-5423; *Fax:* (225) 342-1993

Labor Dept.
http://www.ldol.state.la.us/
General e-mail: webmaster@ldol.state.la.us
Main phone: (225) 342-3111
Main fax: (225) 342-3778
Toll free: (877) LAWORKS
TTY: (225) 342-3025
Mailing address: P.O. Box 94094, Baton Rouge, LA 70804-9094

Garey J. Forster, Secretary
1001 N. 23rd St., 1st Fl., Baton Rouge, LA 70804
(225) 342-3011
E-mail: gforster@ldol.state.la.us

Lottery Corporation
http://www.louisianalottery.com
General e-mail: lalott@bellsouth.com
Main phone: (225) 297-2000
Main fax: (225) 297-2005
Toll free: (800) 735-5825
Mailing address: P.O. Box 90008/70879, Baton Rouge, LA 70809

Charles R. Davis, President
11200 Industriplex Blvd., #190, Baton Rouge, LA 70809
(225) 297-2002

Natural Resources Dept.
http://www.dnr.state.la.us
Main phone: (225) 342-4500
Main fax: (225) 342-2707
Mailing address: P.O. Box 94396, Baton Rouge, LA 70804-9396

Jack C. Caldwell, Secretary
625 N. 4th St., Baton Rouge, LA 70802
(225) 342-4503; *Fax:* (225) 342-5861
E-mail: jackc@dnr.state.la.us

Conservation Office: Geological Oil and Gas Division
http://www.dnr.state.la.us/cons/conserv/Conserve.ssi
Main phone: (225) 342-5510
Main fax: (225) 342-4438
Mailing address: P.O. Box 94275, Baton Rouge, LA 70804-9275

Michael Killeen, Director
625 N. 4th St., Geological Section, Baton Rouge, LA 70802
(225) 342-5525
E-mail: michaelk@dnr.state.la.us

Public Broadcasting
http://www.lpb.org

Frequently Called Numbers

Tourism: (225) 342-8115; 1-800-677-4082;
http://www.crt.state.la.us/
Library: (225) 342-4913;
http://pelican.state.lib.la.us/
Board of Education: (225) 342-5840
Vital Statistics: (504) 568-5152;
http://www.dhh.state.la.us/oph/vital/
index.htm
Tax/Revenue: (225) 925-7532;
http://www.rev.state.la.us
Motor Vehicles: (225) 922-2807
State Police/Highway Patrol: (225) 925-6006;
http://www.lsp.org/
Unemployment: (225) 922-0042
General Election Information:
(225) 925-7885;
http://www.laelections.org
Consumer Affairs: (225) 342-7186
Hazardous Materials: (225) 765-2682

Main phone: (225) 767-5660
Main fax: (225) 767-4421

Beth Courtney, President
7733 Perkins Rd., Baton Rouge, LA 70810
Fax: (225) 767-4421
E-mail: bcourtney@lpb.org

Public Facilities Authority
http://www.lpfa.com
General e-mail: info@lpfa.com
Main phone: (225) 923-0020
Main fax: (225) 923-0021
Toll free: (800) 228-4755

James W. Parks II, President
2237 S. Acadian Thruway, #650, Baton Rouge, LA
70808
E-mail: parks@lpfa.com

Public Safety and Corrections Dept.
http://www.dps.state.la.us/
Main phone: (225) 342-6740
Main fax: (225) 342-3095
Mailing address: P.O. Box 94304, Baton Rouge,
LA 708049304

Richard L. Stalder, Secretary
Capitol Station, Baton Rouge, LA 70804-9304
(225) 342-6741

Corrections Dept.: Juvenile Services
Main phone: (225) 342-6001
Main fax: (225) 342-4441
Mailing address: P.O. Box 94304, Baton
Rouge, LA 70804-9304

B. R. Travis, Assistant Secretary
504 Mayflower St., Bldg. 6, 3rd Fl., Baton Rouge,
LA 70802
(225) 342-8678; *Fax:* (225) 342-5110

Corrections Dept.: Parole Board
Main phone: (225) 342-6622
Main fax: (225) 342-3701
Mailing address: P.O. Box 94304, Baton
Rouge, LA 70804-9304

Fred Y. Clark, Chair
504 Mayflower St., Bldg. 2, 1st Fl., Baton Rouge,
LA 70802
(225) 342-3701
E-mail: llandry@oyd01.corrections.state.la.us

Liquefied Petroleum Gas Commission
Main phone: (225) 925-4895
Main fax: (225) 925-4898
Mailing address: P.O. Box 66209, Baton
Rouge, LA 70896

Charles M. Fuller, Executive Director
1723 Dallas, Baton Rouge, LA 70806

Public Safety Dept: Fire Marshal's Office
http://www.dps.state.la.us/sfm
Main phone: (225) 925-4911
Main fax: (225) 925-4241
Toll free: (800) 256-5452

V. J. Bella, Fire Marshal
5150 Florida Blvd., Baton Rouge, LA 70806
(225) 925-3647
E-mail: vbella@dpsmail.dps.state.la.us

Public Safety Dept: Motor Vehicles Office
Main phone: (225) 922-2807
Main fax: (225) 925-1838
Toll free: (800) DMV-LINE
Mailing address: P.O. Box 64886, Baton
Rouge, LA 70896

Kay Covington, Assistant Secretary
109 S. Foster, Baton Rouge, LA 70806
(225) 925-6335
E-mail: kcovingt@dps.state.la.us

Public Service Commission
http://www.lpsc.org
General e-mail: joanh@lpsc.org
Main phone: (225) 342-4404
Main fax: (225) 342-2831
Toll free: (800) 256-2397
Mailing address: P.O. Box 91154, Baton Rouge,
LA 70821-9154

Lawrence C. St. Blanc, Executive Secretary
1 American Pl., #1630, Baton Rouge, LA 70825
(225) 342-4427; *Fax:* (225) 342-4087

Revenue and Taxation Dept.
http://www.rev.state.la.us
Main phone: (225) 925-7532

Main fax: (225) 925-3855
TTY: (225) 925-7533
Mailing address: P.O. Box 201, Baton Rouge, LA
70821-0201

Brett Crawford, Secretary (Acting)
330 N. Ardenwood Dr., 2nd Fl., Baton Rouge, LA
70806
(225) 925-7680; Fax: (225) 925-6797
E-mail: bcrawford@rev.state.la.us

Alcohol and Tobacco Control Office
http://www.atcla.com
Main phone: (225) 925-4054
Main fax: (225) 925-3975
Mailing address: P.O. Box 66404, Baton
Rouge, LA 70896

Murphy J. Painter, Assistant Secretary
1885 Wooddale Blvd., 6th Fl., Baton Rouge, LA
70806

Securities Commission
Main phone: (504) 846-6970

Harry Stansbury, Deputy Commissioner
3445 N. Causeway Blvd., #509, Metairie, LA 70002

Social Services Dept.
http://www.dss.state.la.us
Main phone: (225) 342-6729
Main fax: (225) 342-8636
Mailing address: P.O. Box 3776, Baton Rouge, LA
70821-3776

J. Renea Austin-Duffin, Secretary
755 3rd St., 2nd Fl., Baton Rouge, LA 70802
(225) 342-0286
E-mail: raustin@dss.state.la.us

Civil Rights
Main phone: (225) 342-2700
Main fax: (225) 342-8636
Mailing address: P.O. Box 3776, Baton Rouge,
LA 70821

Paula Braxton, Director
755 N. 3rd St., 4th Fl., Baton Rouge, LA 70821

State Fair
http://www.gbrsf.com
General e-mail: gbrsf@catel.net
Main phone: (225) 775-FAIR
Main fax: (225) 273-0997
Mailing address: P.O. Box 15010, Baton Rouge,
LA 70895

J. H. Martin, Chief Executive Officer
16072 Airline Hwy., Baton Rouge, LA 70817

State Library
http://pelican.state.lib.la.us/
Main phone: (225) 342-4913
Main fax: (225) 219-4725
Mailing address: P.O. Box 131, Baton Rouge, LA
70821

Thomas F. Jaques, State Librarian
701 N. 4th St., Baton Rouge, LA 70802
(225) 342-4923; Fax: (225) 219-4804
E-mail: TJaques@pelican.state.lib.la.us

State Police
http://www.lsp.org/
General e-mail: lspweb@dpsmail.dps.state.la.us
Main phone: (225) 925-6006
Main fax: (225) 925-3742
Mailing address: P.O. Box 66614, Baton Rouge,
LA 70896-6614

W.R. Whittington, Superintendent
265 S. Foster Dr., Executive Wing, 1st Fl., Baton
Rouge, LA 70806
(225) 925-6117
E-mail: deputy_secretary@dps.state.la.us

Teachers Retirement System
http://www.trsl.state.la.us
General e-mail: debbie@trsl.state.la.us
Main phone: (225) 925-6446
Main fax: (225) 925-6366
TTY: (225) 925-3653
Mailing address: P.O. Box 94123, Baton Rouge,
LA 70804-9123

James P. Hadley Jr., Director
8401 United Plaza Blvd., 3rd Fl., Baton Rouge, LA
70809
(225) 925-6454; Fax: (225) 925-3944
E-mail: james@trsl.state.la.us

Transportation and Development Dept.
http://www.dotd.state.la.us/
General e-mail:
webadmin@dotdmail.dotd.state.la.us
Main phone: (225) 379-1100
Main fax: (225) 379-1856
Toll free: (800) 259-4929
Mailing address: P.O. Box 94245, Baton Rouge,
LA 70804-9245

Boards and Licensing

Accountancy, (504) 566-1244
Architects, (225) 925-4802,
    http://www.lastbdarchs.com
Child Care, (225) 922-0015
Contractors, (225) 765-2301
Child Care, (225) 922-0015
Engineers and Land Surveyors,
    (225) 925-6291,
    http://www.lapels.com/
Medical Examiners, (504) 524-6763
Nursing, (504) 838-5332
Pharmacy, (225) 925-6469
Real Estate Appraisers, (225) 925-4771

Kam K. Movassaghi, Secretary
1201 Capitol Access Rd., 2nd Fl., Baton Rouge, LA
70804-9245
(225) 379-1200; *Fax:* (225) 379-1851

Public Works and Intermodal Transportation Office: Aviation
Main phone: (225) 379-1603
Main fax: (225) 379-1961
Mailing address: P.O. Box 94245, Baton
Rouge, LA 70804-9245

Anthony M. Culp, Director
8900 Jimmy Wedell St., #123, Baton Rouge, LA
70807
(225) 274-4112; *Fax:* (225) 274-4181
E-mail: tculp@dotdmail.state.la.us

Veterans Affairs Dept.
http://www.gov.state.la.us/depts/veteraaffairs.htm
Main phone: (225) 922-0500
Main fax: (225) 922-0511
Mailing address: P.O. Box 94095, Capitol Station,
Baton Rouge, LA 70804-9095

Joey Strickland, Executive Director
1885 Woodale Blvd., 10th Fl., Baton Rouge, LA
70806
(225) 922-0502
E-mail: strickland2@juno.com

Wildlife and Fisheries Dept.
http://www.wlf.state.la.us/
General e-mail: vaughan_ap@wlf.state.la.us
Main phone: (225) 765-2800
Main fax: (225) 765-2892
Toll free: (888) 765-2602

James H. Jenkins Jr., Secretary
2000 Quail Dr., #453, Baton Rouge, LA 70808
(225) 765-2623; *Fax:* (225) 765-2607

Women's Services
http://www.gov.state.la.us/depts/ows.htm
General e-mail: owsbradm@ows.state.la.us
Main phone: (225) 922-0960
Main fax: (225) 922-0959
Mailing address: P.O. Box 94095, Baton Rouge,
LA 70804-9095

Vera Clay, Executive Director
1885 Wooddale Blvd., 9th Fl., Baton Rouge, LA
70806
(225) 922-0962; *Fax:* (225) 922-0959
E-mail: vera@ows.state.la.us

Workers' Compensation Administration
http://www.laworks.net
Main phone: (225) 342-3111
Main fax: (225) 342-5665
Mailing address: P.O. Box 94040, Baton Rouge,
LA 70802

Dan Boudreaux, Assistant Secretary/Director
1001 N. 23rd St., Baton Rouge, LA 70802
(225) 342-7561; *Fax:* (225) 342-5665
E-mail: dboudreaux@ldol.state.la.us

Laws

Sales tax: 4%
Income tax: 3.6%
State minimum wage: None (Federal is $5.15)
Marriage age: 18
First-cousin marriage: Prohibited
Drinking age: 21
State control of liquor sales: No
Blood alcohol for DWI: 0.10%
Driving age: 17
Speed limit: 70 mph
Permit to buy handguns: No
Minimum age to possess handguns: None
Minimum age to possess rifles, shotguns:
None
State lottery: Yes; also Powerball
Casinos: Yes (commercial, tribal); also slot/
video machines
Pari-mutuel betting: Horse racing
Death penalty: Yes
3 strikes minimum sentence: Life, no parole
(3rd violent felony)
Hate crimes law: Yes
Gay employment non-discrimination: No
Official language(s): English
Term limits: State legislators (12 yrs.)

*State laws are complex and subject to
change; this information is not intended as
legal advice. For an explanation of this
information, see p. x.*

Louisiana Legislature

State Capitol
Baton Rouge, LA 70804
Fax: (225) 342-0617
Bill status: (225) 342-2456
http://www.legis.state.la.us/welcome.htm

Senate
Address: P.O. Box 94183, Baton Rouge, LA 70804
General information: (225) 342-2040
E-mail: websen@legis.state.la.us

John J. Hainkel Jr. (R), President
State Capitol, P.O. Box 94183, Baton Rouge, LA
70804
(225) 342-2040
E-mail: hainkelj@legis.state.la.us
http://senate.legis.state.la.us/Hainkel/

Louis J. Lambert (D), President Pro Tempore
State Capitol, P.O. Box 94183, Baton Rouge, LA 70804
(225) 342-2040
http://senate.legis.state.la.us/Lambert/

Michael S. Baer III, Secretary
State Capitol, P.O. Box 94183, Baton Rouge, LA 70804
(225) 342-0629; *Fax:* (225) 342-4399
E-mail: baerm@legis.state.la.us

House

Address: P.O. Box 94062, Baton Rouge, LA 70804-9062
General information: (225) 342-7263
Fax: (225) 342-8336
E-mail: webreps@legis.state.la.us

Charlie DeWitt (D), Speaker of the House
State Capitol, P.O. Box 94062, Baton Rouge, LA 70804-9062
(225) 342-7263

C. Emile (Peppi) Bruneau Jr. (R), Speaker Pro Tempore
State Capitol, P.O. Box 94062, Baton Rouge, LA 70804-9062
(225) 342-7263

Alfred W. Speer, Clerk
State Capitol Bldg., P.O. Box 44281, #G-106, Baton Rouge, LA 70804
(225) 342-7259; *Fax:* (225) 342-5045

Louisiana Judiciary

Supreme Court Bldg.
301 Loyola Ave.
New Orleans, LA 70112
http://www.state.la.us/state/judicial.htm

Supreme Court
http://www.lasc.org

John Tarlton Olivier, Clerk
Supreme Court Bldg., 301 Loyola Ave., New Orleans, LA 70112
(504) 568-5707; *Fax:* (504) 568-2846

Justices
Composition: 8 justices
Selection Method: nonpartisan election; vacancies filled by special election
Length of term: 10 years

Pascal F. Calogero Jr., Chief Justice, (504) 568-5727
Bernette Joshua Johnson, Justice, (504) 568-8062
Catherine D. Kimball, Justice, (504) 568-7757
Jeannette Theriot Knoll, Justice, (504) 568-5720
Harry T. Lemmon, Justice, (504) 568-5723
Walter F. Marcus Jr., Justice, (504) 568-5730
Chet D. Traylor, Justice, (504) 568-5744
Jeffrey P. Victory, Justice, (504) 568-5733

Office of the Judicial Administrator
http://www.lajao.org
Main phone: (504) 568-5747
Main fax: (504) 568-5687

Hugh M. Collins, Judicial Administrator
1555 Poydras St., #1540, New Orleans, LA 70112
E-mail: HMC@lajao.org

State Law Library
http://www.lasc.org/lawlib/lawlib.html
Main phone: (504) 568-5705
Main fax: (504) 568-5069

Carol D. Billings, Director
Supreme Court Bldg, 301 Loyola Ave., New Orleans, LA 70112

Legislative and Political Party Information Resources

Senate home page: http://senate.legis.state.la.us
House home page: http://house.legis.state.la.us
Committees: Senate: http://senate.legis.state.la.us/committees; *House:* http://house.legis.state.la.us/members/committees/committees1.htm
Legislative process: http://www.legis.state.la.us/howbill.htm
Current session information: http://www.legis.state.la.us/SessionInfo/current_session_information.htm
Louisiana Democratic Party: http://www.lademo.org
263 N. 3rd St., #102, Baton Rouge, LA 70801; *Phone:* (225) 336-4155; *Fax:* (225) 336-0046; *E-mail:* lademo@eatel.net
Louisiana Republican Party: http://www.lagop.com
7916 Wrenwood Blvd., Suite E, Baton Rouge, LA 70809; *Phone:* (225) 928-2998; *E-mail:* info@lagop.com

Maine

State Capitol
Augusta, ME 04333-0001
Public information: (207) 624-9494
Fax: (207) 287-1034
http://www.state.me.us

Office of the Governor
http://www.state.me.us/governor/govhome.htm
Main phone: (207) 287-3531
Main fax: (207) 287-1034
TTY: (207) 287-6548

Angus S. King Jr. (I), Governor
1 State House Station, Augusta, ME 04333-0001
E-mail: governor@state.me.us

Kay Rand, Chief of Staff
1 State House Station, #236, Augusta, ME 04333-0001
(207) 287-3531; *Fax:* (207) 287-1034
E-mail: kay.rand@state.me.us

Dennis Bailey, Communications Director
1 State House Station, Augusta, ME 04333-0001
(207) 287-2531; *Fax:* (207) 287-2532

Susan Crawford, Constituent Services
1 State House Station, Augusta, ME 04333-0001
(207) 287-3531; *Fax:* (207) 287-1034

Office of the Secretary of State
http://www.state.me.us/sos/sos.htm
General e-mail: sos.office@state.me.us
Main phone: (207) 626-8400
Main fax: (207) 287-8598
TTY: (207) 287-4476

Dan A. Gwadosky (D), Secretary of State
Nash Bldg., 148 State House Station, Augusta, ME 04333-0148
(207) 626-8400; *Fax:* (207) 287-8598
E-mail: Dan.Gwadosky@state.me.us

Office of the Attorney General
http://www.state.me.us/ag/homepage.htm
General e-mail: attorney.general@state.me.us
Main phone: (207) 626-8800
Main fax: (207) 287-3145
TTY: (207) 626-8865

Andrew Ketterer (D), Attorney General
6 State House Station, Augusta, ME 04333-0006

Office of the State Treasurer
http://www.state.me.us/treasurer/homepage.htm

State of Maine

Capital: Augusta, since 1831
Founded: 1691, as district of Massachusetts; earlier British settlements
Statehood: March 15, 1820 (23rd state)
Constitution adopted: 1820
Area: 30,865 sq. mi. (ranks 39th)
Population: 1,244,250 (1998 est.; ranks 39th)
Largest cities: (1998 est.) Portland (62,786); Lewiston (36,186); Bangor (30,508); South Portland (22,810); Auburn (22,617)
Counties: 16, Most populous: (1998 est.) Cumberland (253,582); York (175,165); Penobscot (142,323); Kennebec (115,207); Androscoggin (101,280)
U.S. Congress: Susan Collins (R), Olympia J. Snowe (R); 2 Representatives
Nickname(s): Pine Tree State
Motto: I direct
Song: "State of Maine Song"
Bird: Chickadee
Tree: White pine tree
Flower: White pine cone and tassel
State fair: at Bangor; Skowhegan
Former capital(s): Portland

Main phone: (207) 287-2771
Main fax: (207) 287-2367

Dale McCormick (D), State Treasurer
39 State House Station, Augusta, ME 04333-0039
E-mail: dale.mccormick@state.me.us

Office of the State Auditor
http://www.state.me.us/audit/Auditor.htm
Main phone: (207) 624-6250
Main fax: (207) 624-6273

Gail M. Chase, State Auditor
66 State House Station, Augusta, ME 04333-0066

Defense, Veterans, and Emergency Management Dept.
http://www.state.me.us/va/defense/dvs.htm
Main phone: (207) 626-4271
Main fax: (207) 626-4509

Earl L. Adams, Adjutant General and Commissioner
Camp Keyes, Augusta, ME 04333-0033

Agencies

Administrative and Financial Services Dept.
http://janus.state.me.us/dafs
General e-mail: sandra.j.tiacy@state.me.us
Main phone: (207) 287-4547
Main fax: (207) 287-4548
TTY: (207) 287-4537
Mailing address: 78 State House Station, Augusta, ME 04333-0078

Janet E. Waldron, Commissioner
40 Western Ave., Augusta, ME 04330
E-mail: janet.e.waldron@state.me.us

Accounts and Control Bureau
http://janus.state.me.us/bac/BAC.Home.Page/cover3.htm
Main phone: (207) 287-4600
Main fax: (207) 287-4601
Mailing address: 14 State House Station, Augusta, ME 04333-0014

Carol Whitney, State Controller
AMHI Complex, Tyson Bldg., Augusta, ME 04333
E-mail: carol.f.whitney@state.me.us

Alcoholic Beverages and Lottery Bureau
http://janus.state.me.us/bablo/
General e-mail: dolores.brown@state.me.us
Main phone: (207) 287-3721
Main fax: (207) 287-4049

Eben B. Marsh, Director
8 State House Station, Augusta, ME 04333
(207) 287-3432; *Fax:* (207) 287-4049
E-mail: eben.b.marsh@state.me.us

Financial and Personnel Division
Main phone: (207) 287-6632
Main fax: (207) 287-4032
TTY: (207) 287-4537
Mailing address: 78 State House Station, Augusta, ME 04333-0078

Edward Karass, Director
AMHI Complex, Tyson Bldg., Augusta, ME 04333
E-mail: Edward.a.Karass@state.me.us

Human Resources Bureau
http://janus.state.me.us/bhr/
General e-mail: Gerald.L.Rogers@state.me.us
Main phone: (207) 287-3761
Main fax: (207) 287-4414
TTY: (207) 287-4537
Mailing address: 4 State House Station, Augusta, ME 04333-0004

Donald A. Wills, Director
161 Capitol St., Augusta, ME 04333
(207) 287-4413

Revenue Services
http://janus.state.me.us/revenue/
General e-mail: main.revenue@state.me.us
Main phone: (207) 287-2076
Main fax: (207) 624-9694
Mailing address: 24 State House Station, Augusta, ME 04333-0024

Anthony J. Neves, Executive Director
Muskie Bldg., Sewall St. and Western Ave., Augusta, ME 04333
E-mail: anthony.j.neves@state.me.us

Agriculture, Food, and Rural Resources Dept.
http://www.state.me.us/agriculture/homepage.htm
Main phone: (207) 287-3871
Main fax: (207) 287-7548
TTY: (207) 287-4470

Robert W. Spear, Commissioner
28 State House Station, Augusta, ME 04333-0028
(207) 287-3419

Archives
http://www.state.me.us/sos/arc/general/admin/mawww001.htm
General e-mail: jeffrey.brown@state.me.us
Main phone: (207) 287-5790
Main fax: (207) 287-5739

James S. Henderson, State Archivist
84 State House Station, Augusta, ME 04333-0084
(207) 287-5793
E-mail: james.henderson@state.me.us

Arts Commission
http://www.mainearts.com
General e-mail: jan.poulin@state.me.us
Main phone: (207) 287-2724
Main fax: (207) 287-2335
TTY: (207) 287-2360
Mailing address: 25 State House Station, Augusta, ME 04333-0025

Alden C. Wilson, Director
55 Capitol St., Augusta, ME 04333
(207) 287-2720
E-mail: alden.wilson@state.me.us

Conservation Dept.
http://www.state.me.us/doc/dochome.htm
Main phone: (207) 287-2211
Main fax: (207) 287-2400
TTY: (207) 287-2213
Mailing address: 22 State House Station, Augusta, ME 04333-0022

Ronald B. Lovaglio, Commissioner
Harlow Bldg., Hospital St., Augusta, ME 04333
E-mail: doccommish@state.me.us

Higher Educational Institutions

Maine Maritime Academy
http://www.mainemaritime.edu
Pleasant St., Castine, ME 04420
Main phone: (800) 227-8465

University of Maine System
http://www.maine.edu
5713 Chadbourne Hall, Orono, ME 04469-5713
Main phone: (207) 581-1578
Branches: Augusta, Farmington, Fort Kent, Machias,
Presque Isle, Southern Maine

Forest Service
http://www.state.me.us/doc/mfs/mfshome.htm
Main phone: (207) 287-2791
Main fax: (207) 287-8422
Toll free: (800) 367-0223
TTY: (207) 287-2213

Thomas Doak, Director
22 State House Station, Augusta, ME 04333-0022
E-mail: Tom.Doak@state.me.us

Geological Survey
http://www.state.me.us/doc/nrimc/mgs/mgs.htm
General e-mail: nrimc@state.me.us
Main phone: (207) 287-2801
TTY: (207) 287-2213
Mailing address: 22 State House Station,
Augusta, ME 04333-0022

Robert G. Marvinney, Director
AMHI Complex, Hospital St., Augusta, ME 04333
E-mail: robert.g.marvinney@state.me.us

Parks and Lands Bureau
http://www.state.me.us/doc/prkslnds/
prkslnds.htm
Main phone: (207) 287-3821
Main fax: (207) 287-3823
Mailing address: Station 22, Augusta, ME
04333

Thomas Morrison, Director
22 State House Station, Augusta, ME 04330-0022
(207) 287-4717
E-mail: Tom.Morrison@state.me.us

Corrections Dept.
http://janus.state.me.us/corrections/homepage.htm
Main phone: (207) 287-2711
Main fax: (207) 287-4370
TTY: (207) 287-4472
Mailing address: 111 State House Station,
Augusta, ME 04333-0111

Martin A. Magnusson, Commissioner
Tyson Bldg./AMHI Complex, Hospital St., Augusta,
ME 04333-0111
(207) 287-4360
E-mail: martin.a.magnusson@state.me.us

Juvenile Services Bureau
Main pone: (207) 287-2711
Main fax: (207) 287-4370
Mailing address: 111 State House Station,
Augusta, ME 04333-0111

Mary Ann Saar, Associate Commissioner for Juvenile Services
AMHI Complex, Elkins Bldg., Augusta, ME 04333
(207) 287-4365
E-mail: mary.ann.saar@state.me.us

Parole Board
Main phone: (207) 287-2711
Main fax: (207) 287-4370
TTY: (207) 287-4472
Mailing address: 111 State House Station,
Augusta, ME 04333

Nancy Downs, Executive Secretary
AMHI Complex, Elkins Bldg., Augusta, ME 04333
(207) 783-5382
E-mail: nancy.downs@state.me.us

Economic and Community Development Dept.
http://www.econdevmaine.com/
General e-mail: biz.growth@state.me.us
Main phone: (207) 287-2656
Main fax: (207) 287-2861
Mailing address: 59 State House Station, Augusta,
ME 04333

Steven H. Levesque, Commissioner
33 Stone St., Augusta, ME 04333
(207) 287-6835
E-mail: steven.h.levesque@state.mo.us

Education Dept.
http://www.state.me.us
Main phone: (207) 287-5800
Main fax: (207) 287-5802
Mailing address: 23 State House Station, Augusta,
ME 04333

J. Duke Albanese, Commissioner
State Capitol St., Augusta, ME 04333
(207) 287-5114
E-mail: duke.albanese@state.me.us

Governor Baxter School for the Deaf
Main phone: (207) 781-3165
Main fax: (207) 781-6296
Mailing address: P.O. Box 799, Portland, ME
04104-0799

Roy Bishop, Superintendent
Mackworth Island, Falmouth, ME 04105
E-mail: roy.bishop@fc.baxter.pvt.k12.me.us

Environmental Protection Dept.
http://www.state.me.us/dep/mdephome.htm
Main phone: (207) 287-7688
Main fax: (207) 287-2814
Toll free: (800) 452-1942
Mailing address: 17 State House Station, Augusta, ME 04333-0017

Martha G. Kirkpatrick, Commissioner
Roy Bldg./AMHI Complex, Augusta, ME 04333
(207) 287-2812
E-mail: martha.g.kirkpatrick@state.me.us

Land and Water Quality Bureau: Water Resource Regulation Division
Main phone: (207) 287-3901
Main fax: (207) 287-7191
Toll free: (800) 452-1942
Mailing address: 17 State House Station, Augusta, ME 04333-0017

Michael Barden, Director
AMHI Complex, Ray Bldg., Augusta, ME 04333
(207) 287-7700
E-mail: michael.t.barden@state.me.us

Finance Authority
http://www.famemaine.com/
General e-mail: info@famemaine.com
Main phone: (800) 228-3734
Main fax: (207) 623-0095
TTY: (207) 626-2717
Mailing address: P.O. Box 949, Augusta, ME 04332-0949

Charlie Spies, Chief Executive Officer (Acting)
5 Community Dr., Augusta, ME 04330
(207) 623-3263
E-mail: charlie@famemaine.com

Health and Higher Educational Facilities Authority
http://www.mainebondbank.com
Main phone: (207) 622-1958
Main fax: (207) 623-5359
Toll free: (800) 821-1113
Mailing address: P.O. Box 2268, Augusta, ME 04338

Robert O. Lenna, Executive Director
45 University Dr., Augusta, ME 04330

Historic Preservation Commission
http://www.state.me.us/mhpc/homepag1.htm
Main phone: (207) 287-2132
Main fax: (207) 287-2335

Earle G. Shettleworth Jr., Director
65 State House Station, Augusta, ME 04333-0065

Housing Authority
http://www.mainehousing.org
General e-mail: msha@maine.com
Main phone: (207) 626-4600
Main fax: (207) 626-4678
Toll free: (800) 452-4668
TTY: (800) 452-4603

Dana Totman, Director (Acting)
353 Water St., Augusta, ME 04330
(207) 626-4611; *Fax:* (207) 624-5702
E-mail: dtotman@mainehousing.org

Human Rights Commission
http://www.state.me.us/mhrc
Main phone: (207) 624-6050
Main fax: (207) 624-6063
TTY: (207) 624-6064
Mailing address: 51 State House Station, Augusta, ME 04333-0051

Patricia Ryan, Executive Director
State House Annex, Winthrop Hill, Cleveland Bldg., Hallowell, ME 04347

Human Services Dept.
http://janus.state.me.us/dhs/welcome.htm
Main phone: (207) 287-3707
Main fax: (207) 287-3005
TTY: (207) 287-4479
Mailing address: 11 State House Station, Augusta, ME 04333-0011

Kevin W. Concannon, Commissioner
221 State St., Augusta, ME 04333-0011
(207) 287-2736
E-mail: kevin.w.concannon@state.me.us

Elder and Adult Services Bureau
http://janus.state.me.us/dhs/beas/
General e-mail: webmaster_beas@state.me.us
Main phone: (207) 624-5335
Main fax: (207) 624-5361
Toll free: (800) 262-2232
TTY: (207) 624-5442

Christine Gianopoulos, Director
11 State House Station, 35 Anthony Ave., Augusta, ME 04333

Health Bureau
http://janus.state.me.us/dhs/boh/txtwelco.htm
Main phone: (207) 287-8016
Main fax: (207) 287-9058
TTY: (207) 287-8066
Mailing address: 11 State House Station, Augusta, ME 04333-0011

Dora Anne Mills, Director
157 Capitol St., Augusta, ME 04333

Medical Services Bureau: Medicaid Policy and Program Division
http://www.state.me.us/bms/policy/hppo/pro.htm
Main phone: (207) 624-5521
Main fax: (207) 624-5524
TTY: (800) 423-4331
Mailing address: 11 State House Station,
Augusta, ME 04333

Marianne Ringel, Director
35 Anthony Ave., Augusta, ME 04333
E-mail: marianne.ringel@state.me.us

Inland Fisheries and Wildlife Dept.
http://janus.state.me.us/ifw/homepage.htm
General e-mail: ifw@state.me.us
Main phone: (207) 287-8000
Main fax: (207) 287-6395
TTY: (207) 287-4471
Mailing address: 41 State House Station, Augusta,
ME 04333-0041

Lee E. Perry, Commissioner
284 State St., Augusta, ME 04333
(207) 287-5202

Labor Dept.
http://janus.state.me.us/labor/

Main phone: (207) 287-3788
Main fax: (207) 287-5292
TTY: (800) 794-1110

Valerie R. Landry, Commissioner
20 Union St., 54 State House Station, Augusta, ME
04333-0054

Marine Resources Dept.
http://janus.state.me.us/dmr
Main phone: (207) 624-6550
Main fax: (207) 624-6024
TTY: (207) 287-4474
Mailing address: 21 State House Station, Augusta,
ME 04333-0021

George Lapointe, Commissioner
Baker Bldg., Winthrop St., Hallowell, ME 04347
(207) 624-6553
E-mail: george.lapointe@state.me.us

Mental Health, Mental Retardation, and Substance Abuse Services Dept.
http://www.state.me.us/dmhmrsa/
General e-mail: mhmrsa@state.me.us
Main phone: (207) 287-4200
Main fax: (207) 287-1022
TTY: (207) 287-2000

Lynn F. Duby, Commissioner
40 State House Station, Augusta, ME 04333-0040
(207) 287-4223; *Fax:* (207) 287-4268
E-mail: Lynn.F.Duby@state.me.us

Motor Vehicle Bureau
http://www.state.me.us/sos/bmv/bmv.htm
Main phone: (207) 624-9000
Main fax: (207) 624-9013

Peter C. Brazier, Deputy Secretary of State
29 State House Station, Augusta, ME 04333-0029

Municipal Bond Bank
http://mainebondbank.com
Main phone: (207) 622-9386
Main fax: (207) 623-5359
Mailing address: P.O. Box 2268, Augusta, ME
04338

Robert O. Lenna, Executive Director
3 University Dr., Augusta, ME 04338
(207) 622-9386
E-mail: rol@mainebondbank.com

Professional and Financial Regulation Dept.
http://www.state.me.us/pfr/pfrhome.htm
Main phone: (207) 624-8500
Main fax: (207) 624-8690
Mailing address: 35 State House Station, Augusta,
ME 04333

S. Catherine Longley, Commissioner
122 Northern Ave., Gardiner, ME 04345
(207) 624-8511; *Fax:* (207) 624-8545

Banking Bureau
http://www.MaineBankingReg.org
Main phone: (207) 624-8570
Main fax: (207) 624-8590
Mailing address: 36 State House Station,
Augusta, ME 04333-0036

Howard R. Gray Jr., Superintendent
122 Northern Ave., Gardiner, ME 04345
(207) 624-8575
E-mail: Howard.R.Gray.Jr@state.me.us

Insurance Bureau
http://www.maineinsurancereg.org
Main phone: (207) 624-8475
Main fax: (207) 624-8599
Toll free: (800) 300-5000
TTY: (207) 624-8563
Mailing address: 34 State House Station,
Augusta, ME 04333-0034

Alessandro A. Iuppa, Superintendent
124 Northern Ave., Augusta, ME 04345
E-mail: alessandro.a.iuppa@state.me.us

Licensing and Registration Office
http://www.state.me.us/pfr/led/ledhome2.htm
Main phone: (207) 624-8603
Main fax: (207) 624-8637
TTY: (207) 624-8563

Anne L. Head, Director
35 State House Station, Augusta, ME 04333-0035
(207) 624-8633; *Fax:* (207) 624-8637
E-mail: anne.l.head@state.me.us

Property Tax Review Board
Main phone: (207) 287-4031
Main fax: (207) 287-4032
TTY: (207) 287-4537
Mailing address: 49 State House Station, Augusta,
ME 04333-0049

Guy F. Chapman, Chair
Tyson Bldg., AMHI Complex/Hospital St., Augusta,
ME 04333-0049

Public Advocate's Office
http://janus.state.me.us/meopa/
Main phone: (207) 287-2445
Main fax: (207) 287-4317
Mailing address: 112 State House Station,
Augusta, ME 04333-0112

Stephen G. Ward, Public Advocate
193 State St., Augusta, ME 04333-0112
E-mail: stepehen.g.ward@state.me.us

Public Safety Dept.
http://janus.state.me.us/dps/homepage.htm
Main phone: (207) 624-7000
Main fax: (207) 624-7088
TTY: (207) 287-4478

Michael F. Kelly, Commissioner
36 Hospital St., 42 State House Station, Augusta, ME
04333-0042
(207) 624-7074
E-mail: michael.kelly@state.me.us

State Police
http://janus.state.me.us/dps/msp/home.htm
Main phone: (207) 624-7068
Main fax: (207) 624-7088
TTY: (207) 287-4478
Mailing address: 42 State House Station,
Augusta, ME 04333-0042

Michael R. Sperry, Chief of State Police
36 Hospital St., Augusta, ME 04333
E-mail: michael.sperry@state.me.us

Public Utilities Commission
http://www.state.me.us/mpuc/homepage.htm
General e-mail: Maine.puc@state.me.us
Main phone: (207) 287-3831
Main fax: (207) 287-1039
TTY: (800) 437-1220

Thomas Welch, Chair
242 State St., 18 State House Station, Augusta, ME
04333-0018
E-mail: thomas.welch@state.me.us

Retirement System
http://janus.state.me.us/employee/msrs/
Main phone: (207) 287-3461
Main fax: (207) 287-1032
Toll free: (800) 451-9800
TTY: (207) 287-8446

Licensing and Registration
(207) 624-8603

Accountancy, (207) 624-8603
Architects, (207) 624-8603
Child Care, (207) 287-5060
Contractors, (207) 624-8603
Cosmetology, (207) 624-8603
Engineers and Land Surveyors,
   (207) 287-3236
Medical Examiners, (207) 624-8603
Nursing, (207) 287-1133
Pharmacy, (207) 624-8603
Real Estate Appraisers, (207) 624-8603

Kay R. H. Evans, Executive Director
46 State House Station, Augusta, ME 04333-0046

State Library
http://www.state.me.msl
Main phone: (207) 287-5600
Main fax: (207) 287-5615
TTY: (207) 287-5622
Mailing address: 64 State House Station, Augusta,
ME 04333-0064

J. Gary Nichols, State Librarian
State St., Augusta, ME 04333
E-mail: gary.nichols@state.me.us

State Museum
General e-mail: museum@state.me.us
Main phone: (207) 287-2301
Main fax: (207) 287-6633
TTY: (207) 287-5622

Joseph R. Phillips, Director
83 State House Station, Augusta, ME 04333-0083
(207) 287-2303
E-mail: mmjphil@state.me.us

Transportation Dept.
http://www.state.me.us/mdot/homepage.htm
General e-mail: mdot@state.me.us
Main phone: (207) 287-2551
Main fax: (207) 287-2896
TTY: (207) 287-3392

John G. Melrose, Commissioner
16 State House Station, Augusta, ME 04333

Workers' Compensation Board
http://janus.state.me.us/wcb
General e-mail: anne.poulin@state.me.us
Main phone: (207) 287-3751
Main fax: (207) 287-7198
TTY: (207) 287-6119

Paul R. Dionne, Executive Director
AMHI Complex-Deering Bldg., 27 State House
Station, Augusta, ME 04333-0027
(207) 287-7086

Maine Legislature
Augusta, ME 04333
General information: (207) 287-1692
TTY: (207) 287-4469
http://janus.state.me.us/legis

Senate
Address: 3 State House Station, Augusta, ME
04333-0003
General information: (207) 287-1540
Fax: (207) 287-1900
TTY: (207) 287-1583

Mark W. Lawrence (D), President
3 State House Station, Augusta, ME 04333
(207) 287-1500
E-mail: Mark.Lawrence@state.me.us
http://www.state.me.us/legis/senate/about/offices/pres/
pres.htm

Chellie Pingree (D), Majority Leader
3 State House Station, Augusta, ME 04333
(207) 287-1515
E-mail: pingree@midcoast.com

Jane A. Amero (R), Minority Leader
3 State House Station, Augusta, ME 04333
(207) 287-1505
E-mail: Jane.Amero@state.me.us

Laws

Sales tax: 5.5%
Income tax: 8.5%
State minimum wage: $5.15 (Federal is $5.15)
Marriage age: 18
First-cousin marriage: Prohibited
Drinking age: 21
State control of liquor sales: Yes
Blood alcohol for DWI: 0.08%
Driving age: 16
Speed limit: 65 mph
Permit to buy handguns: No
Minimum age to possess handguns: None
Minimum age to possess rifles, shotguns:
None
State lottery: Yes; also Tri-State Lottery (with
NH, VT)
Casinos: No
Pari-mutuel betting: Horse racing
Death penalty: No
3 strikes minimum sentence: None
Hate crimes law: Yes
Gay employment non-discrimination: No
Official language(s): None
Term limits: Governor (8 yrs.); state legislators
(8 yrs.)

*State laws are complex and subject to
change; this information is not intended as
legal advice. For an explanation of this
information, see p. x.*

Joy J. O'Brien, Secretary
3 State House Station, Augusta, ME 04333
(207) 287-1540
E-mail: Joy.Obrien@state.me.us

House
Address: 2 State House Station, Augusta, ME
04333-0002
General information: (207) 287-1400
Fax: (207) 287-1456
TTY: (207) 287-4469

G. Steven Rowe (D), Speaker of the House
2 State House Station, Augusta, ME 04333-0002
(207) 287-1300
http://janus.state.me.us/house/hsebios/rowegs.htm

Michael V. Saxl (D), Majority Leader
2 State House Station, House Majority Office,
  Augusta, ME 04333-0002
(207) 287-1430
E-mail: RepMichael.Saxl@state.me.us
http://janus.state.me.us/house/hsebios/saxlmv.htm

David C. Shiah (D), Majority Whip
2 State House Station, House Majority Office,
  Augusta, ME 04333-0002
(207) 287-1430
E-mail: dshiah@horton.col.k12.me.us
http://janus.state.me.us/house/hsebios/shiadc.htm

Thomas W. Murphy Jr. (R), Minority Leader
2 State House Station, House Minority Office,
  Augusta, ME 04333-0002
(207) 287-1440
E-mail: murphy@cybertours.com
http://janus.state.me.us/house/hsebios/murptw.htm

Joseph W. Mayo, Clerk
2 State House Station, Augusta, ME 04333-0002
(207) 287-1400
E-mail: joseph.mayo@state.me.us

Maine Judiciary
142 Federal St.
Portland, ME 04101
http://www.courts.state.me.us/

Supreme Judicial Court
http://www.courts.state.me.us/supremecourt.html

James C. Chute, Clerk
142 Federal St., Portland, ME 04101
(207) 822-4146

Justices
Composition: 7 justices
Selection Method: appointed by governor with
  consent of legislature
Length of term: 7 years

Daniel E. Wathen, Chief Justice, (207) 287-6950
Donald G. Alexander, Associate Justice,
  (207) 822-4100
Susan W. Calkins, Associate Justice, (207) 822-4135
Robert W. Clifford, Associate Justice, (207) 783-5425
Howard H. Dana Jr., Associate Justice, (207) 822-4175
Paul L. Rudman, Associate Justice, (207) 947-5248
Leigh I. Saufley, Associate Justice, (207) 822-4286

Administrative Office of the Courts
http://www.courts.state.me.us/admin.html
Main phone: (207) 822-0792
Main fax: (207) 822-0781

James T. Glessner, State Court Administrator
62 Elm St., 2nd Fl., Portland, ME 04101

State Law Library
Main phone: (207) 287-1600
Main fax: (207) 287-6467

Lynn Randall, State Law Librarian
43 State House Station, Capitol and State Sts.,
  Augusta, ME 04333-0043

Legislative and Political Party Information Resources

Senate home page: http://janus.state.me.us/legis/senate
House home page: http://janus.state.me.us/legis/house
Committees: Senate: http://www.state.me.us/legis/senate/senators/committee/standing.htm;
  House: http://janus.state.me.us/house.commit.htm
Legislative process: http://www.state.me.us/legis/path/path1.htm
Current session information: http://www.state.me.us/legis/session
Maine Democratic Party: http://www.mainedems.org
  12 Spruce St., P.O. Box 5258, Augusta, ME 04332-5258; *Fax:* (207) 622-2657;
  Phone: (207) 622-6233; *E-mail:* dems@powerlink.net
Maine Republican Party: http://www.mainegop.com
  100 Water St., Hallowell, ME 04347-1313; *Fax:* (207) 623-5322; *Phone:* (207) 622-6247;
  E-mail: megop@ime.net

Maryland

State House
Annapolis, MD 21401
Public information: (410) 974-3901
Fax: (410) 974-3275
http://www.state.md.us

Office of the Governor
http://www.gov.state.md.us
General e-mail: governor@gov.state.md.us
Main phone: (410) 974-3901
Main fax: (410) 974-3275
Toll free: (800) 811-8336
TTY: (410) 333-3098

Parris N. Glendening (D), Governor
State House, 100 State Circle, Annapolis, MD 21401

Major F. Riddick Jr., Chief of Staff
State House, 100 State Circle, #210, Annapolis, MD
21401
(410) 974-3570; *Fax:* (410) 974-5735
E-mail: mriddick@gov.state.md.us

Mike Morrill, Press Secretary
State House, 100 State Circle, Annapolis, MD 21401
(410) 974-2316; *Fax:* (410) 974-3275

**Karen J. Simpson, Administration and Constituent
Services Director**
State House, 100 State Circle, Annapolis, MD 21401
(410) 974-5258; *Fax:* (410) 974-3275

**Elizabeth Pyke, Federal Relations Director,
Washington Office**
444 N. Capitol St. N.W., #311, Washington, DC 20001
(202) 624-1430; *Fax:* (202) 783-3061

Office of the Lieutenant Governor
http://www.mdarchives.state.md.us/msa/mdmanual/
08conoff/html/msa12084.html
Main phone: (410) 974-2804
Main fax: (410) 974-5882
TTY: (410) 333-3098

**Kathleen Kennedy Townsend (D), Lieutenant
Governor**
State House, 100 State Circle, Annapolis, MD 21401
E-mail: ktownsend@gov.state.md.us

Office of the Secretary of State
http://www.sos.state.md.us/
Main phone: (410) 974-5521
Main fax: (410) 974-5190
Toll free: (888) 874-0013

State of Maryland

Capital: Annapolis,
since 1694
Founded: 1632, as British colony
Statehood: April 28, 1788 (7th state)
Constitution adopted: 1867
Area: 9,775 sq. mi. (ranks 42nd)
Population: 5,134,808 (1998 est.; ranks 19th)
Largest cities: (1998 est.) Baltimore
(645,593); Frederick (47,468); Gaithersburg
(46,980); Rockville (46,788); Bowie (40,704)
Counties: 23, Most populous: (1998 est.)
Montgomery (840,879); Prince George's
(777,811); Baltimore (721,874); Anne
Arundel (476,060); Howard (236,388)
U.S. Congress: Barbara A. Mikulski (D), Paul
S. Sarbanes (D); 8 Representatives
Nickname(s): Free State, Old Line State
Motto: Manly deeds, womanly words
Song: "Maryland! My Maryland!"
Bird: Baltimore oriole
Tree: White oak
Flower: Black-eyed Susan
State fair: at Timonium, late Aug.-early Sept.
Former capital(s): St. Mary's City

John T. Willis (D), Secretary of State
Jeffrey Bldg., 16 Francis St., Annapolis, MD 21401
(410) 974-5521, ext. 470; *Fax:* (410) 974-5190

Office of the Attorney General
http://www.mdarchives.state.md.us/msa/mdmanual/
08conoff/html/msa01493.html
General e-mail: oag@oag.state.md.us
Main phone: (410) 576-6300
Main fax: (410) 576-6404
TTY: (410) 576-6372

J. Joseph Curran Jr. (D), Attorney General
200 St. Paul Pl., Baltimore, MD 21202-2021

Office of the State Treasurer
http://www.treasurer.state.md.us
General e-mail: treasurer@treasurer.state.md.us
Main phone: (410) 260-7533
Main fax: (410) 974-3530
Toll free: (800) 974-0468
TTY: (800) 735-2258

Richard N. Dixon, State Treasurer
Louis L. Goldstein Treasury Bldg., 80 Calvert St.,
#109, Annapolis, MD 21401
(410) 260-7160

Office of the Comptroller of the Treasury
http://www.comp.state.md.us/
General e-mail: taxhelp@comp.state.md.us
Main phone: (410) 260-7801
Main fax: (410) 974-3808
TTY: (410) 260-7157
Mailing address: P.O. Box 466, Annapolis, MD
21404-0466

William Donald Schaefer (D), Comptroller
Louis L. Goldstein Treasury Bldg., 80 Calvert St.,
Annapolis, MD 21401
E-mail: wdschaefer@comp.state.md.us

Military Dept.
http://www.marylandguard.com/
General e-mail: owingsdg@md-arng.ngb.army.mil
Main phone: (410) 576-6000
Main fax: (410) 576-6079

James F. Fretterd, Adjutant General
5th Regiment Armory, 29th Division St., Baltimore,
MD 21201-2288
(410) 576-6097
E-mail: fretterdjf@md-arng.ngb.army.mil

Agencies

Accountancy Board
Main phone: (410) 230-6262
Main fax: (410) 333-0021
Toll free: (888) 218-5925
TTY: (800) 735-2258

Mary E. Mays, Director
500 N. Calvert St., #308, Baltimore, MD 21202
(410) 230-6300
E-mail: mmays@dllr.state.md.us

Administrative Board of Election Laws
http://www.elections.state.md.us
General e-mail: 76427.2706@compuserv.com
Main phone: (800) 222-8683
Main fax: (410) 974-2019
TTY: (800) 735-2258
Mailing address: P.O. Box 6486, Annapolis, MD
21401

Linda H. Lamone, Administrator
151 West St., #200, Annapolis, MD 21401
(800) 222-8683, ext. 2852
E-mail: llamone@elections.state.md.us

Aging Dept.
http://www.inform.umd.edu:8080/UMS+State/
MD_Resources/OOA/index.html
General e-mail: ptc@mail.ooa.state.md.us
Main phone: (410) 767-1100
Main fax: (410) 333-7943
TTY: (410) 767-1083

Sue F. Ward, Director
301 W. Preston St., #1007, Baltimore, MD 21201
(410) 767-1102

Agriculture Dept.
http://www.mda.state.md.us/
General e-mail: janukme@mda.state.md.us
Main phone: (410) 841-5700
Main fax: (410) 841-5914
TTY: (800) 735-2258

Henry A. Virts, Secretary
50 Harry S Truman Pkwy., Annapolis, MD 21401
(410) 841-5880

Alcohol and Tobacco Tax Division
Main phone: (410) 260-7314
Main fax: (410) 974-3201
Toll free: (888) 784-0145
TTY: (410) 260-7157
Mailing address: P.O. Box 2999, Annapolis, MD
21404-2999

Charles Ehart, Director
Louis L. Goldstein Treasury Bldg., 80 Calvert St.,
Annapolis, MD 21401
(410) 260-7311
E-mail: ehart@comp.state.md.us

Architects Board
Main phone: (410) 230-6322
Main fax: (410) 333-0021
Toll free: (888) 218-5925
TTY: (800) 735-2258

Mary Mays, Executive Director
500 N. Calvert St., #308, Baltimore, MD 21202
(410) 230-6262
E-mail: mmays@dllr.state.md.us

Archives
http://www.mdarchives.state.md.us
General e-mail: archives@mdarchives.state.md.us
Main phone: (410) 260-6400
Main fax: (410) 974-3895
Toll free: (800) 235-4045
TTY: (800) 735-2258

**Edward C. Papenfuse, State Archivist and
Commissioner of Land Patents**

Higher Educational Institutions

Bowie State University
http://www.bowiestate.edu
14000 Jericho Park Rd., Bowie, MD 20715-9465
Main phone: (301) 464-3000

Coppin State College
http://www.coppin.umd.edu
2500 W. North Ave., Baltimore, MD 21216
Main phone: (410) 383-5400

Morgan State University
http://www.morgan.edu
1700 E. Cold Spring Ln., Baltimore, MD 21251
Main phone: (443) 885-3333

Salisbury State University
http://www.ssu.edu
1101 Camden Ave., Salisbury, MD 21801-6862
Main phone: (410) 543-0148

St. Mary's College of Maryland
http://www.smcm.edu
18952 E. Fisher Rd., St. Mary's City, MD 20686-3001
Main phone: (301) 862-0200

Towson State University
http://www.towson.edu
8000 York Rd., Towson, MD 21252-0001
Main phone: (410) 830-2000

Uniformed Services University of the Health Sciences
http://www.usuhs.mil
4301 Jones Bridge Rd., Bethesda, MD 20814
Main phone: (301) 295-3101

United States Naval Academy
http://www.nadn.navy.mil
121 Blake Rd., Annapolis, MD 21402-5000
Main phone: (410) 293-4361

University of Baltimore
http://www.ubalt.edu
1420 N. Charles St., Baltimore, MD 21201
Main phone: (410) 837-4200

University of Maryland
http://www.umd.edu
University Blvd. at Adelphi Rd., College Park, MD 20742-1600
Main phone: (301) 985-7000
Branches: Baltimore, Baltimore County, Eastern Shore, Frostburg

Hall of Records, 350 Rowe Blvd., #222, Annapolis, MD 21401-1686
(410) 260-6401
E-mail: edp@mdarchives.state.md.us

Assessments and Taxation Dept.
http://www.dat.state.md.us/
General e-mail: webmaster@dat.state.md.us
Main phone: (410) 767-1340
Main fax: (410) 333-7087
Toll free: (888) 246-5941
TTY: (800) 735-2258

Ronald W. Wineholt, Director
301 W. Preston St., Baltimore, MD 21201
(410) 767-1184; *Fax:* (410) 333-5873

Attorney Grievance Commission
http://www.courts.state.md.us
General e-mail: AGCM@erols.com
Main phone: (410) 514-7051

Melvin Hirshman, Bar Counsel
100 Community Pl., #3301, Crownsville, MD 21032-2027
(410) 514-7051

Automobile Insurance Fund
http://www.emaif.com
Main phone: (410) 269-1680
Main fax: (410) 269-4344
TTY: (301) 269-4355

David Trageser, Executive Director
1750 Forest Dr., Annapolis, MD 21401
(410) 269-8609; *Fax:* (410) 269-4344
E-mail: dtrageser@emaif.com

Blind Industries and Services of Maryland
http://www.bism.com
General e-mail: bism@bism.com
Main phone: (888) 322-4567
Main fax: (410) 233-0544
Toll free: (888) 322-4567
TTY: (800) 735-2258

Frederick J. Puente, President
2901 Strickland St., Baltimore, MD 21223-2796
(410) 233-4567
E-mail: fpuente@bism.com

Board of Contract Appeals
http://www.msbca.state.md.us/
General e-mail: msbca@state.md.us
Main phone: (410) 767-8228
Main fax: (410) 333-0890

Robert B. Harrison III, Chair
6 St. Paul St., William Donald Schaefer Tower, #601,
    Baltimore, MD 21202-1608
(410) 767-8228; Fax: (410) 333-0890

Budget and Management Dept.
http://www.dbm.state.md.us/
General e-mail: galbab@dbm.state.md.us
Main phone: (410) 260-7059
Main fax: (410) 974-5613
Toll free: (800) 705-3493
TTY: (800) 735-2258

Frederick W. Puddester, Secretary
45 Calvert St., #110, Annapolis, MD 21401
(410) 260-7041; Fax: (410) 974-2585
E-mail: fpudd@dbm.state.md.us

Finance and Administration Division
http://www.dbm.state.md.us/html/
    office_of_administration.html
General e-mail: galbab@dbm.state.md.us
Main phone: (410) 260-7059

John J. Pirro Jr., Executive Director
45 Calvert St., Annapolis, MD 21401
E-mail: jpirro@dbm.state.md.us

Personnel Services and Benefits Office
http://dop.state.md.us
General e-mail: dswanson@dbm.state.md.us
Main phone: (410) 767-4715
Main fax: (410) 333-5262
Toll free: (800) 705-3493
TTY: (800) 735-2258

Andrea Fulton Jr., Executive Director
301 W. Preston St., #609, Baltimore, MD 21201
E-mail: afulton@dbm.state.md.us

Business and Economic Development Dept.
http://www.choosemaryland.com
Main phone: (800) 541-8549
Main fax: (410) 333-6911
TTY: (410) 333-6926

Richard C. (Mike) Lewin, Secretary
217 E. Redwood St., #2300, Baltimore, MD 21202-
    3316
(410) 767-6300; Fax: (410) 333-8628
E-mail: mlewin@mdbusiness.state.md.us

Arts Council
http://www.msac.org/
Main phone: (410) 767-6555
Main fax: (410) 333-1062
TTY: (410) 333-4519

James Backas, Executive Director
175 W. Ostend St., Baltimore, MD 21230

Tourism Development
http://www.mdisfun.org
Main phone: (410) 767-6299
Main fax: (410) 333-6643
Toll free: (800) 543-1036

George Williams, Director
217 E. Redwood St., Baltimore, MD 21202-3316
(410) 767-6299; Fax: (410) 333-6643
E-mail: gwilliams@mdbusiness.state.md.us

Chesapeake Bay Commission
http://www.mdarchives.state.md.us//msa/
    mdmanual/38inters/html/04chesb.html
General e-mail: cbc@ari.net
Main phone: (410) 263-3420
Main fax: (410) 263-9338

Ann Pesiri Swanson, Executive Director
60 West St., #200, Annapolis, MD 21401

Child Care Board
http://www.boardofchildcare.org
Main phone: (410) 922-2100
Main fax: (410) 922-4830

Thomas L. Curcio, Executive Director
333 Gaither Rd., Baltimore, MD 21244

Cosmetology Board
Main phone: (410) 230-6320
Main fax: (410) 333-6314
Toll free: (888) 218-5925
TTY: (800) 735-2258

Kathleen A. Harryman, Director
500 N. Calvert St., #307, Baltimore, MD 21202

Developmental Disabilities Council
http://www.mdarchives.state.md.us/msa/mdmanual/
    26excom/html/12dis.html
General e-mail: mddc@erols.com
Main phone: (410) 305-6441
Main fax: (410) 333-3686
Toll free: (800) 305-6441

Mindy Morell, Executive Director
300 W. Lexington St., Box 10, Baltimore, MD 21201
(410) 333-3688

Education Dept.
http://www.msde.state.md.us/
Main phone: (410) 767-0100
Main fax: (410) 333-2226
TTY: (410) 333-6442

Frequently Called Numbers

Tourism: (410) 767-6299; 1-800-543-1036;
http://www.mdisfun.org
Library: (410) 767-0434;
http://www.sailor.lib.md.us
Board of Education: (410) 767-0100;
http://www.msde.state.md.us/stateboard/
default.htm
Vital Statistics: (410) 764-2962;
http://www.mdarchives.state.md.us/msa/
refserv/html/vitalrec.html
Tax/Revenue: (410) 767-1340;
http://www.dat.state.md.us/
Motor Vehicles: (301) 729-4550;
http://www.mva.state.md.us
State Police/Highway Patrol:
(410) 486-3101; http://www.info.umd.edu/
md-sp
Unemployment: (410) 767-3246;
http://www.dllr.state.md.us/employment/
unemployment.html
General Election Information: (410)
269-2840; http://www.elections.state.md.us
Consumer Affairs: (410) 528-8662
Hazardous Materials: (410) 631-3343

Nancy S. Grasmick, State Superintendent
200 W. Baltimore St., Baltimore, MD 21201
(410) 767-0462

Board of Education
http://www.msde.state.md.us/stateboard/
default.htm
General e-mail: tsouth@msde.state.md.us
Main phone: (410) 767-0100
Main fax: (410) 333-2226
TTY: (410) 333-6442

Walter Sondheim Jr., President
200 W. Baltimore St., Baltimore, MD 21201
(410) 767-0467

Library Development and Services Division
http://www.sailor.lib.md.us
Main phone: (410) 767-0434
Main fax: (410) 333-2507
TTY: (410) 333-6442

J. Maurice Travillian, Assistant State Superintendent
200 W. Baltimore St., #619, Baltimore, MD 21201
(410) 767-0435
E-mail: jmtravillian@msde.state.md.us

Employees Credit Union
http://www.secumd.org
Main phone: (410) 296-7328
Main fax: (410) 821-3600
Toll free: (800) TRY-SECU
TTY: (410) 821-3709
Mailing address: P.O. Box 17024, Baltimore, MD
21297-0411

Teresa A. Halleck, President
8503 LaSalle Rd., Baltimore, MD 21286
(410) 494-8030, ext. 2000; *Fax:* (410) 821-3606

Engineers and Land Surveyors Board
Main phone: (410) 230-6322
Main fax: (410) 333-0021
Toll free: (888) 218-5925
TTY: (800) 735-2258

Mary Mays, Director
500 N. Calvert St., #308, Baltimore, MD 21202
(301) 230-6262
E-mail: mmays@dllr.state.md.us

Environment Dept.
http://www.mde.state.md.us
Main phone: (410) 631-3000
Main fax: (410) 631-3888
TTY: (410) 631-3009

Jane T. Nishida, Secretary
2500 Broening Hwy., Baltimore, MD 21224
(410) 631-3084

Water Management Administration
http://www.mde.state.md.us/wma/index.html
Main phone: (410) 631-3567
Main fax: (410) 631-4894

J. L. Hearn, Director
2500 Broening Hwy., Baltimore, MD 21224
E-mail: jhearn@mde.state.md.us

Ethics Commission
http://www.op.state.md.us/ethics
Main phone: (410) 321-3636
Main fax: (410) 321-2388

John O'Donnell, Executive Director
300 E. Joppa Rd., #301, Towson, MD 21286-3004

Food Center Authority
http://www.mfca.state.md.us/
General e-mail: mfca@mail.state.md.us
Main phone: (410) 379-5760
Main fax: (410) 379-5773
TTY: (800) 735-2258

Donald J. Darnall, Executive Director
7801 Oceano Ave., Jessup, MD 20794

General Services Dept.
http://www.dgs.state.md.us/
General e-mail: pdethea@dgs.state.md.us
Main phone: (410) 767-4960
Main fax: (410) 333-5480
Toll free: (800) 449-4347

Peta N. Richkus, Secretary
301 W. Preston St., #1401, Baltimore, MD 21201
E-mail: prichkus@dgs.state.md.us

Health and Higher Educational Facilities Authority
http://www.mhhefa.org
Main phone: (410) 837-6220
Main fax: (410) 685-1611

Annette Anselmi, Executive Director
36 S. Charles St., #1500, Baltimore, MD 21201
E-mail: aanselmi@mhhefa.org

Health and Mental Hygiene Dept.
http://www.dhmh.state.md.us/
General e-mail: hammc@dhmh.state.md.us
Main phone: (410) 767-6860
Main fax: (410) 767-6489
TTY: (410) 383-7555

Georges C. Benjamin, Secretary
201 W. Preston St., 5th Fl., Baltimore, MD 21201
(410) 767-6500; *Fax:* (410) 767-6489

Medicaid Program
Main phone: (410) 767-4664
Main fax: (410) 333-7687

Debbie I. Chang, Deputy Secretary for Health Care
201 W. Preston St., Baltimore, MD 21201

Health Care Commission
http://www.mhcc.state.md.us
General e-mail: webmaster@mhcc.state.md.us
Main phone: (410) 764-3460
Main fax: (410) 358-1236

Donald E. Wilson, Chair
4201 Patterson Ave., 5th Fl., Baltimore, MD 21215

Health Services Cost Review Commission
http://www.hscrc.state.md.us
Main phone: (410) 764-2605
Main fax: (410) 358-6217
Toll free: (800) 735-2258

Robert Murray, Executive Director
4201 Patterson Ave., 2nd Fl., Baltimore, MD 21215
E-mail: b.murray@erols.com

Higher Education Commission
http://www.mhec.state.md.us/
General e-mail: ssamail@mhec.state.md.us
Main phone: (410) 974-2971
Main fax: (410) 974-3513
Toll free: (800) 974-0203
TTY: (800) 735-2258

Patricia S. Florestano, Secretary
Jeffrey Bldg., 16 Francis St., Annapolis, MD 21401-1781
(410) 974-2463; *Fax:* (410) 974-3513
E-mail: pflorest@mhec.state.md.us

Housing and Community Development Dept.
http://www.dhcd.state.md.us
General e-mail: webmaster@dhcd.state.md.us
Main phone: (410) 514-7206
Main fax: (410) 987-4070
Toll free: (800) 756-0119
TTY: (410) 514-7531

Raymond A. Skinner, Secretary
100 Community Pl., Crownsville, MD 21032
(410) 514-7001; *Fax:* (410) 987-4070
E-mail: skinner@dhcd.state.md.us

Historical and Cultural Programs Division
http://www.2ri.net/mdshpo
Main phone: (410) 514-7601
Main fax: (410) 987-4071

J. Rodney Little, Director
100 Community Pl., #3114, Crownsville, MD 21032
E-mail: Little@dhcd.state.md.us

Labor, Licensing, and Regulation Dept.
http://www.dllr.state.md.us/
(410) 230-6001

Accountancy, (410) 230-6262
Architects, (410) 230-6322
Child Care, (410) 922-2100,
  http://www.boardofchildcare.org
Cosmetology, (410) 230-6320
Engineers and Land Surveyors,
  (410) 230-6322
Medical Examiners, (410) 764-4777
Nursing, (410) 585-1900,
  http://www.mbon.org
Pharmacy, (410) 764-4755
Real Estate Appraisers, (410) 230-6322

Human Relations Commission

http://www.mchr.state.md.us/
General e-mail: mchr@mail.mchr.state.md.us
Main phone: (410) 767-8600
Main fax: (410) 333-1841
Toll free: (800) 637-6247
TTY: (410) 333-1737

Henry B. Ford, Executive Director
6 St. Paul St., William Donald Schaefer Tower, 9th Fl.,
   Baltimore, MD 21202-1631
(410) 767-8561; *Fax:* (410) 333-1841
E-mail: hford@mail.meltr.state.md.us

Human Resources Dept.

http://www.dhr.state.md.us/
General e-mail: dhrhelp@dhr.state.md.us
Main phone: (410) 767-7000
Main fax: (410) 333-0099
Toll free: (800) 332-6347
TTY: (800) 925-4434

Lynda G. Fox, Secretary
311 W. Saratoga St., #1045, Baltimore, MD 21201
(410) 767-7109; *Fax:* (410) 333-0099
E-mail: lfox@dhr.state.md.us

Women's Commission
http://www.dhr.sailorsite.net/mcw/
Main phone: (410) 767-7137
Main fax: (410) 333-0256
TTY: (410) 333-0017

Carol Silberg, Executive Director
311 W. Saratoga St., #232, Baltimore, MD 21201
(410) 767-7556
E-mail: csilberg@dhr.state.md.us

Insurance Administration

http://www.mia.state.md.us/
General e-mail: miaweb@mia.state.md.us
Main phone: (410) 468-2000
Main fax: (410) 468-2020
Toll free: (800) 492-6116
TTY: (800) 735-2258

Steven B. Larsen, Commissioner
525 St. Paul Pl., Baltimore, MD 21202-2272
(410) 468-2000

Juvenile Justice Dept.

http://www.djj.state.md.us/
General e-mail: PIO@djj.state.md.us
Main phone: (410) 230-3333
Main fax: (410) 333-4198
Toll free: (888) 639-7499
TTY: (800) 945-5798

Gilberto DeJesus, Secretary
120 W. Fayette St., Baltimore, MD 21201
(410) 230-3100
E-mail: dejesusg@djj.state.md.us

Labor, Licensing, and Regulation Dept.

http://www.dllr.state.md.us/
General e-mail: mddllr@dllr.state.md.us
Main phone: (410) 230-6001
Main fax: (410) 333-0853
TTY: (800) 735-2258

John P. O'Connor, Secretary
500 N. Calvert St., 4th Fl., Baltimore, MD 21202
(410) 230-6020; *Fax:* (410) 333-0853

Lottery Agency

http://www.mdlottery.com
General e-mail: paffairs@msla.state.md.us
Main phone: (410) 318-6200
Main fax: (410) 764-4263
TTY: (800) 735-2258

Buddy Roogow, Director
Plaza Office Center, 6776 Reisterstown Rd., #204,
   Baltimore, MD 21215-2345
(410) 318-6370

Natural Resources Dept.

http://www.dnr.state.md.us/
General e-mail: aburrows@dnr.state.md.us
Main phone: (410) 260-8021
Main fax: (410) 260-8024
Toll free: (877) 620-8367
TTY: (800) 735-2258

Sarah Taylor-Rogers, Secretary
Tawes State Office Bldg., 580 Taylor Ave., Annapolis,
   MD 21401
(410) 260-8101; *Fax:* (410) 260-8111
E-mail: staylor-rogers@dnr.state.md.us

Fisheries Service
http://www.dnr.state.md.us/fisheries
General e-mail: mlgary@dnr.state.md.us
Main phone: (410) 260-8280
Toll free: (877) 688-FINS
TTY: (410) 260-8835

Eric Schwabb, Director
Tawes State Office Bldg., 580 Taylor Ave.,
   Annapolis, MD 21401

Forest Service Division
http://www.dnr.state.md.us/forests/
Main phone: (410) 260-8531
Main fax: (410) 260-8595

Toll free: (877) 620-8367
TTY: (410) 260-8835

Jim Mallow, State Forester
Tawes State Office Bldg., 580 Taylor Ave., #E-1,
Annapolis, MD 21401
(410) 260-8501
E-mail: jmallow@dnr.state.md.us

Geological Survey
http://www.mgs.dnr.md.gov
Main phone: (410) 554-5500
Main fax: (410) 554-5502

Emery T. Cleaves, Director
2300 St. Paul St., Baltimore, MD 21218
(410) 554-5503; Fax: (410) 554-5502
E-mail: ecleaves@mgs.dnr.md.gov

Land and Water Conservation Office
General e-mail: staylor@dnr.state.md.us
Main phone: (410) 260-8401
Main fax: (410) 260-8404
Toll free: (877) 260-8DNR
TTY: (410) 260-8835

Michael J. Nelson, Director
Tawes State Office Bldg., 580 Taylor Ave., #E-4,
Annapolis, MD 21401
(410) 260-8446
E-mail: mnelson@dnr.state.md.us

State Parks and Forest Service
http://www.dnr.state.md.us/publiclands
Main phone: (410) 260-8186
Toll free: (800) 830-3974

Rick Barton, Superintendent
Tawes State Office Bldg., Annapolis, MD 21401
E-mail: tellrickbarton@dnr.state.md.us

Wildlife and Heritage Division
http://www.dnr.state.md.us/wildlife
Main phone: (410) 260-8540

Michael Slattery, Director
Tawes State Office Bldg., 580 Taylor Ave., #E-1,
Annapolis, MD 21401

Nursing Board
http://www.mbon.org
General e-mail: lkarkmbn@erols.com
Main phone: (410) 585-1900
Main fax: (410) 358-3530
Toll free: (888) 202-9861

Donna N. Dorsey, Director
4140 Patterson AVe., Baltimore, MD 21215
(410) 585-1900, ext. 1923

Public Defender's Office
http://www.opd.state.md.us/
Main phone: (410) 767-8460
Main fax: (410) 333-8496

Stephen E. Harris, Public Defender
6 St. Paul St., #1400, Baltimore, MD 21202
(410) 767-8479

People's Counsel Office
http://www.opc.state.md.us/
General e-mail: mdopc@mail.state.md.us
Main phone: (410) 767-8150
Main fax: (410) 333-3616
Toll free: (800) 207-4055

Michael J. Travieso, People's Counsel
6 St. Paul St., #2102, Baltimore, MD 21202
E-mail: MikeT@opc.state.md.us

Planning Office
http://www.op.state.md.us
Main phone: (410) 767-4500
Main fax: (410) 767-4480
TTY: (877) 767-6272

Ronald M. Kreitner, Director
301 W. Preston St., #1101, Baltimore, MD 21201-2365
(410) 767-4510
E-mail: rkreitner@mail.op.state.md.us

Property Tax Assessment Appeal Board
http://www.mdarchives.state.md.us/msa/mdmanual/
25ind/html/57prop.html
Main phone: (410) 974-2087
Main fax: (410) 974-5595

Craig C. Biggs, Administrator
60 West St., #210, Annapolis, MD 21401
(410) 974-2087; Fax: (410) 974-5595

Public Safety and Correctional Services Dept.
http://www.dpscs.state.md.us
General e-mail: franklra@ns1.dpscs.state.md.us
Main phone: (410) 339-5000
Main fax: (410) 339-5076
TTY: (800) 735-2258

Stuart O. Simms, Secretary
300 E. Joppa Rd., #1000, Towson, MD 21286-3020
(410) 339-5004; Fax: (410) 339-4243
E-mail: simmsso@ns1.dpscs.state.md.us

Parole and Probation Division
http://www.dpscs.state.md.us/pnp
Main phone: (410) 764-4274
Main fax: (410) 764-4091
Toll free: (877) 227-8031

Thomas H. Williams, Director
6776 Reisterstown Rd., #305, Baltimore, MD
   21215-2314
(410) 764-4276; *Fax:* (410) 764-4091
E-mail: twillia435@aol.com

Public Service Commission
http://www.psc.state.md.us/psc
General e-mail: mpsc@psc.state.md.us
Main phone: (410) 767-8000
Main fax: (410) 333-6086
Toll free: (800) 492-0474

Gregory V. Carmean, Executive Director
William Donald Schaeffer Tower, 6 St. Paul St., 17th
   Fl., Baltimore, MD 21202
(410) 767-8010
E-mail: gcarmean@psc.state.md.us

Public Television
http://www.mpt.org/
General e-mail: comments@mpt.org
Main phone: (410) 356-5600
Main fax: (410) 581-4338

Robert J. Shuman, President
11767 Owings Mills Blvd., Owings Mills, MD 21117
(410) 581-4141

Public Works Board
http://www.bpw.state.md.us/
General e-mail: bpw@comp.state.md.us
Main phone: (410) 260-7335
Main fax: (410) 974-5240

Sheila C. McDonald, Executive Secretary
Louis L. Goldstein Treasury Bldg., 80 Calvert St.,
   #213, Annapolis, MD 21401
E-mail: smcdonald@comp.state.md.us

Real Estate Board
Main phone: (410) 230-6322
Main fax: (410) 333-0021
Toll free: (888) 218-2258
TTY: (800) 735-2258

Elizabeth (Betty) Beggs, Director
500 N. Calvert St., 3rd Fl., Baltimore, MD 21202
(410) 230-6198
E-mail: b.beggs@dllr.state.md.us

School for the Deaf
http://www.msd.edu/
General e-mail: msdsupt@msd.edu
Main phone: (301) 360-2000
Main fax: (301) 360-1400
TTY: (301) 360-2001

Mailing address: P.O. Box 250, Frederick, MD
   21705-0250

James E. Tucker, Superintendent
101 Clarke Pl., Frederick, MD 21705-0250
(301) 360-2005; *Fax:* (301) 360-1400

Special Projects Office
Main phone: (410) 767-4712
Main fax: (410) 767-6967

Jody Albright, Director
300 W. Preston St., #400, Baltimore, MD 21201

State Fair and Agricultural Society
http://www.marylandstatefair.com
General e-mail: msfair@msn.com
Main phone: (410) 252-0200
Main fax: (410) 561-5610
Mailing address: P.O. Box 188, Timonium, MD
   21094-0188

F. Grove Miller, President
2200 York Rd., Timonium, MD 21093
(410) 252-0200, ext. 223

State Police Dept.
http://www.info.umd.edu/md-sp
General e-mail: pauinfo@qis.net
Main phone: (410) 486-3101
Main fax: (410) 653-4269
Toll free: (800) 525-5555
TTY: (410) 486-0677

David B. Mitchell, Superintendent
1201 Reisterstown Rd., Executive Bldg., Pikesville,
   MD 21208
(410) 653-4219; *Fax:* (410) 653-9651

Fire Prevention Commission
http://ns1.dpscs.state.md.us/fmc/fmcomm.htm
General e-mail: osfmowro@earthlink.net
Main phone: (301) 791-4758
Main fax: (301) 739-8785
Toll free: (877) 890-0199

Edward P. Sherlock Jr., Chair
33 W. Washington St., #305, Hagerstown, MD
   21740

State Fire Marshal
http://www.dpscs.state.md.us/fmo/
Main phone: (410) 339-4200
Toll free: (800) 525-3124

Rocco J. Gabriele, State Fire Marshal
300 E. Joppa Rd., #1002, Towson, MD 21286-
   3020

State Prosecutor's Office

http://www.osp.sailorsite.net/
Main phone: (410) 695-4058
Main fax: (410) 321-3851
Toll free: (800) 695-4058
TTY: (800) 735-2258

Stephen Montanarelli, State Prosecutor
Investment Bldg., 1 Investment Pl., #308, Towson, MD 21204-4120
(410) 321-4067

State Retirement and Pension System of Maryland

http://www.sra.state.md.us/sra/
General e-mail: msra@smart.net
Main phone: (410) 767-4030
Main fax: (410) 333-7557
Toll free: (800) 492-5909
TTY: (800) 735-2258

Peter Vaughn, Executive Director
301 W. Preston St., #700, Baltimore, MD 21201
(410) 767-4051; Fax: (410) 333-7557
E-mail: pvaughn@smart.net

Transportation Dept.

http://www.mdot.state.md.us/
General e-mail: oca@mdot.state.md.us
Main phone: (410) 865-1142
Main fax: (410) 865-1339
Toll free: (888) 713-1414
TTY: (410) 865-1342
Mailing address: P.O. Box 8755, BWI Airport, MD 21240-0755

John D. Porcari, Secretary
10 Elm Rd., BWI Airport, MD 21240-0755
(410) 865-1000; Fax: (410) 865-1334
E-mail: j.porcari@mdot.state.md.us

Aviation Administration

http://www.mdot.state.md.us/maa/index.html
General e-mail: webmaster@lighthouse-studios.com
Main phone: (410) 859-7111
Main fax: (410) 854-7763
Toll free: (800) 435-9294
TTY: (410) 859-7227
Mailing address: P.O. Box 8766, BWI Airport, MD 21240-0766

David L. Blackshear, Executive Director
BWI Terminal Bldg., 3rd Fl., BWI Airport, MD 21240
(410) 859-7060; Fax: (410) 850-4729
E-mail: d.blackshear@mdot.state.md.us

Motor Vehicle Administration

http://www.mva.state.md.us
General e-mail: MVACS@mdot.state.md.us
Main phone: (301) 729-4550
Main fax: (410) 768-7506
Toll free: (800) 950-1MVA
TTY: (800) 492-4575

Anne S. Ferro, Administrator
6601 Ritchie Hwy. N.E., #200, Glen Burnie, MD 21062
(410) 768-7274; Fax: (410) 768-0166

Veterans Affairs Dept.

http://www.gov.state.md.us/mvc/
General e-mail: md.veterans@erols.com
Main phone: (410) 333-4428
Main fax: (410) 333-1071
Toll free: (800) 446-4926

Thomas E. Bratten Jr., Secretary
Federal Bldg., 31 Hopkins Plaza, #110, Baltimore, MD 21201
(410) 333-4429, ext. 16

Waste Disposal Authority (Northeast Maryland)

http://www.nmwda.org/
General e-mail: authority@nmwda.org
Main phone: (410) 333-2730
Main fax: (410) 333-2721

Robin B. Davidov, Executive Director
25 S. Charles St., #2105, Baltimore, MD 21201-3330

Workers' Compensation Commission

http://www.charm.net/~wcc/
General e-mail: wcc@charm.net
Main phone: (410) 767-0900
Main fax: (410) 333-8122
Toll free: (800) 492-0749

Thomas Patrick O'Reilly, Chair
6 N. Liberty St., Baltimore, MD 21201-3785
(410) 767-0829; Fax: (410) 333-0229

Maryland Legislature

State House
Annapolis, MD 21401
General information: (410) 841-3000
Fax: (410) 841-3850
TTY: (410) 841-3814
Bill status: (410) 946-5100 (Baltimore area);
301-970-5400 (D.C. area)
http://www.mlis.state.md.us

Senate

Address: James Senate Office Bldg., 110 College Ave., Annapolis, MD 21401-1991

Thomas V. Mike Miller Jr. (D), President
State House, #H-107, Annapolis, MD 21401-1991
(410) 841-3700; *Fax:* (410) 841-3910
E-mail: thomas_v_mike_miller@senate.state.md.us
http://www.mdarchives.state.md.us/msa/mdmanual/
05sen/html/msa01619.html

Ida G. Ruben (D), President Pro Tempore
James Senate Office Bldg., 110 College Ave., #110,
Annapolis, MD 21401-1991
(410) 841-3634; *Fax:* (410) 841-3166
E-mail: ida_ruben@senate.state.md.us
http://www.mdarchives.state.md.us/msa/mdmanual/
05sen/html/msa12157.html

Clarence W. Blount (D), Majority Leader
James Senate Office Bldg., 110 College Ave., #201,
Annapolis, MD 21401-1991
(410) 841-3697; *Fax:* (410) 841-3850
http://www.mdarchives.state.md.us/msa/mdmanual/
05sen/html/msa02219.html

Paula C. Hollinger (D), Majority Whip
James Senate Office Bldg., 110 College Ave., #206,
Annapolis, MD 21401-1991
(410) 841-3131; *Fax:* (410) 841-3850
E-mail: paula_colodny_hollinger@senate.state.md.us
http://www.mdarchives.state.md.us/msa/mdmanual/
05sen/html/msa12150.html

Martin G. Madden (R), Minority Leader
James Senate Office Bldg., 110 College Ave., #407,
Annapolis, MD 21401-1991
(410) 841-3572; *Fax:* (410) 841-3455
E-mail: martin_madden@senate.state.md.us
http://www.mdarchives.state.md.us/msa/mdmanual/
05sen/html/msa12171.html

J. Lowell Stoltzfus (R), Minority Whip
James Senate Office Bldg., 110 College Ave., #410,
Annapolis, MD 21401-1991
(410) 841-3645; *Fax:* (410) 841-3569
E-mail: lowell_stoltzfus@senate.state.md.us
http://www.mdarchives.state.md.us/msa/mdmanual/
05sen/html/msa12158.html

William B. C. Addison Jr., Secretary
James Senate Office Bldg., 110 College Ave.,
Annapolis, MD 21401-1991
(410) 841-3908; *Fax:* (410) 841-3910

House

Address: Lowe House Office Bldg., 6 Governor
Bladen Blvd., Annapolis, MD 21401-1991

Casper R. Taylor Jr. (D), Speaker of the House
State House, #101, Annapolis, MD 21401-1991

Laws

Sales tax: 5%
Income tax: 5%
State minimum wage: $5.15 (Federal is $5.15)
Marriage age: 18
First-cousin marriage: Permitted
Drinking age: 21
State control of liquor sales: No
Blood alcohol for DWI: 0.10%
Driving age: 17, 7 mos.
Speed limit: 65 mph
Permit to buy handguns: No, but 7-day wait;
permit for repeat purchase within 30 days
Minimum age to possess handguns: 21
Minimum age to possess rifles, shotguns: 21
State lottery: Yes
Casinos: No
Pari-mutuel betting: Horse racing
Death penalty: Yes
3 strikes minimum sentence: 25 yrs. (3rd
crime of violence)
Hate crimes law: Yes
Gay employment non-discrimination: No
Official language(s): None
Term limits: None

*State laws are complex and subject to
change; this information is not intended as
legal advice. For an explanation of this
information, see p. x.*

---

(410) 841-3800; *Fax:* (410) 841-1138
E-mail: casper_taylor@house.state.md.us
http://www.mdarchives.state.md.us/msa/mdmanual/
06hse/html/msa12312.html

Thomas E. Dewberry (D), Speaker Pro Tempore
Lowe House Office Bldg., 84 College Ave., #312,
Annapolis, MD 21401-1991
(410) 841-3391; *Fax:* (410) 841-3157
E-mail: thomas_dewberry@house.state.md.us
http://www.mdarchives.state.md.us/msa/mdmanual/
06hse/html/msa12211.html

John Adams Hurson (D), Majority Leader
Lowe House Office Bldg., 84 College Ave., #313,
Annapolis, MD 21401-1991
(410) 841-3464; *Fax:* (410) 841-3850
E-mail: jhurson@aol.com
http://www.mdarchives.state.md.us/msa/mdmanual/
06hse/html/msa12247.html

George W. Owings III (D), Majority Whip
Lowe House Office Bldg., 84 College Ave., #219,
Annapolis, MD 21401-1991

(410) 841-3231; *Fax:* (410) 841-3252
E-mail: george_owings@house.state.md.us
http://www.mdarchives.state.md.us/msa/mdmanual/
    06hse/html/msa12286.html

Robert H. Kittleman (R), Minority Leader
Lowe House Office Bldg., 84 College Ave., #411,
    Annapolis, MD 21401-1991
(410) 841-3401; *Fax:* (410) 841-3395
E-mail: robert_kittleman@house.state.md.us
http://www.mdhousegop.org/kittlema.htm

Robert L. Flanagan (R), Minority Whip
Lowe House Office Bldg., 84 College Ave., #405,
    Annapolis, MD 21401-1991
(410) 841-3200; *Fax:* (410) 841-3850
E-mail: robert_flanagan@house.state.md.us
http://www.mdarchives.state.md.us/msa/mdmanual/
    06hse/html/msa12222.html

Mary K. Monahan, Chief Clerk
Lowe House Office Bldg., 84 College Ave., Annapolis,
    MD 21401-1991
(410) 841-3999

Maryland Judiciary

Robert C. Murphy Courts of Appeal Bldg.
361 Rowe Blvd.
Annapolis, MD 21401
http://www.courts.state.md.us/

Court of Appeals

Alexander L. Cummings, Clerk
Robert C. Murphy Courts of Appeal Bldg., 361 Rowe
    Blvd., Annapolis, MD 21401
(410) 260-1500

Justices
Composition: 7 judges
Selection Method: appointed by governor with
    consent of state senate; appointees must
    stand for retention ballot in general election
    one year after appointment
Length of term: 10 years, after retention ballot

Robert M. Bell, Chief Judge, (410) 333-6396
Dale R. Cathell, Judge, (410) 543-6014
John C. Eldridge, Judge, (410) 260-1515
Glenn T. Harrell Jr., Judge, (301) 952-2716
Irma S. Raker, Judge, (240) 777-9330
Lawrence F. Rodowsky, Judge, (410) 333-4374
Alan M. Wilner, Judge, (410) 887-2677

Administrative Office of the Courts
http://www.courts.state.md.us/aochq.html
Main phone: (410) 260-1400
Main fax: (410) 974-2169

**Frank Broccolina, State Court Administrator
(Acting)**
Robert C. Murphy Courts of Appeal Bldg., 361 Rowe
    Blvd., Annapolis, MD 21401
(410) 260-1290
E-mail: frank.broccolina@courts.state.md.us

State Law Library
Main phone: (410) 260-1430
Main fax: (410) 974-2063
General e-mail: mdlaw.library@courts.state.md.us

Michael S. Miller, Director
Robert C. Murphy Courts of Appeal Bldg., 361 Rowe
    Blvd., Annapolis, MD 21401
(410) 260-1432
E-mail: michael.miller@courts.state.md.us

Legislative and Political Party Information Resources

Senate home page: http://www.mdarchives.state.md.us/msa/mdmanual/05sen/html/sen.html
House home page: http://www.mdarchives.state.md.us/msa/mdmanual/06hse/html/hse.html
Committees: Senate: http://www.mdarchives.state.md.us/msa/mdmanual/05sencom.html;
    House: http://www.mdarchives.state.md.us/msa/mdmanual/06hse/html/hsecom.html
Legislative process: http://www.mdarchives.state.md.us/msa/mdmanual/07leg/html/proc.html
Budget: http://www.mdarchives.state.md.us/msa/mdmanual/07leg/html/gab.html
Maryland Democratic Party: http://www.clark.net/pub/mddem
    188 Main St., #1, Annapolis, MD 21401; *Phone:* (410) 280-8818; *Fax:* (410) 280-8882;
    E-mail: mddem@clark.net
Maryland Republican Party: http://www.mdgop.org
    15 West St., Annapolis, MD 21401; *Phone:* (410) 269-0113

Massachusetts

State House
Boston, MA 02133
Public information: (617) 727-3600
Fax: (617) 727-9725
http://www.state.ma.us

Office of the Governor
http://www.state.ma.us/gov/gov.htm
General e-mail: goffice@state.ma.us
Main phone: (617) 727-3600
Main fax: (617) 727-9725
TTY: (617) 727-3666

Argeo Paul Cellucci (R), Governor
Executive Office, State House, #360, Boston, MA
02133

Stephen O'Neill, Chief of Staff
Executive Office, State House, #360, Boston, MA
02133
(617) 727-9173; *Fax:* (617) 727-9725
E-mail: stephen.oneill@state.ma.us

John Birtwell, Press Secretary
Executive Office, State House, #265, Boston, MA
02133
(617) 727-2759; *Fax:* (617) 727-9416
E-mail: john.birtwell@state.ma.us

**Barbara Burke, Constituent Affairs/External
Relations Director**
Executive Office, State House, #111, Boston, MA
02133
(617) 727-6250; *Fax:* (617) 727-9725
E-mail: barbara.burke@state.ma.us

Anne Gavin, Director, Washington Office
444 N. Capitol St. N.W., #400, Washington, DC 20001
(202) 624-7713; *Fax:* (617) 624-7714

Office of the Lieutenant Governor
http://www.state.ma.us/gov/
Main phone: (617) 727-3600
Main fax: (617) 727-9725
TTY: (617) 727-3666

Jane M. Swift (R), Lieutenant Governor
State House, #360, Boston, MA 02133

Secretary of the Commonwealth
http://www.state.ma.us/sec/
General e-mail: cis@sec.state.ma.us
Main phone: (617) 727-7030
Main fax: (617) 742-4722
Toll free: (800) 392-6090

State of Massachusetts

Capital: Boston, since 1632
Founded: 1620, as Plymouth
   colony; 1629, as Massachusetts Bay
   colony; colonies merged 1691
Statehood: February 6, 1788 (6th state)
Constitution adopted: 1780
Area: 7,838 sq. mi. (ranks 45th)
Population: 6,147,132 (1998 est.; ranks 13th)
Largest cities: (1998 est.) Boston (555,447);
   Worcester (166,535); Springfield (148,144);
   Lowell (101,075); Fall River (90,654)
Counties: 14, Most populous: (1998 est.)
   Middlesex (1,424,116); Worcester (731,881);
   Essex (698,806); Norfolk (642,705); Suffolk
   (641,715)
U.S. Congress: Edward M. Kennedy (D), John
   F. Kerry (D); 10 Representatives
Nickname(s): Bay State, Old Colony State
Motto: By the sword we seek peace, but peace
   only under liberty
Song: "All Hail to Massachusetts"
Bird: Chickadee
Tree: American elm
Flower: Mayflower
State fair: Topsfield, early Oct.
Former capital(s): None

William Francis Galvin (D), Secretary
State House, #337, Boston, MA 02133
(617) 727-9180
E-mail: william.galvin@state.ma.us

Office of the Attorney General
http://www.state.ma.us/ago
Main phone: (617) 727-2200
Main fax: (617) 727-5768
TTY: (617) 727-4765

Thomas F. Reilly (D), Attorney General
1 Ashburton Pl., #2010, Boston, MA 02108-1698
(617) 727-2200, ext. 2042

Office of the Treasurer and Receiver General
http://www.state.ma.us/treasury
Main phone: (617) 367-3900
Main fax: (617) 227-1622

**Shannon P. O'Brien (D), State Treasurer and
Receiver General**
State House, #227, Boston, MA 02133
(617) 367-6900; *Fax:* (617) 248-0372

Office of the State Auditor
http://www.state.ma.us/sao/
Main phone: (617) 727-6200
Main fax: (617) 727-7192
TTY: (617) 727-7440

A. Joseph DeNucci (D), State Auditor
24 Beacon St., State House, #230, Boston, MA 02133
(617) 727-2075; *Fax:* (617) 727-2383

Office of the State Comptroller
http://www.state.ma.us/osc/overview.htm
Main phone: (617) 727-5000
Main fax: (617) 727-2163

Martin J. Benison, Comptroller
1 Ashburton Pl., 9th Fl., Boston, MA 02108
(617) 973-2315
E-mail: martin.benison@state.ma.us

Agencies

Administration and Finance
http://www.state.ma.us/eoaf/
Main phone: (617) 727-2040
Main fax: (617) 727-2779

Andrew S. Natsios, Secretary
State House, #373, Boston, MA 02133

Archives
http://www.state.ma.us/sec/arc/
Main phone: (617) 727-2816
Main fax: (617) 288-4505

John D. Warner, State Archivist
220 Morrissey Blvd., Boston, MA 02125
(617) 727-2816
E-mail: jwarner@sec.state.ma.us

Banks Division
http://www.state.ma.us/dob/
General e-mail:
bernard.n.waxman@state.ma.us
Main phone: (617) 956-1500
Main fax: (617) 956-1599
Toll free: (800) 495-2265

Thomas J. Curry, Commissioner
1 S. Station, 3rd Fl., Boston, MA 02110
(617) 956-1510, ext. 510; *Fax:* (617) 956-1599

Ethics Commission
http://www.state.ma.us/ethics/
Main phone: (617) 727-0060

Main fax: (617) 723-5851
Toll free: (888) 485-4766

Stephanie S. Lovell, Executive Director
John W. McCormack Bldg., 1 Ashburton Pl., #619,
Boston, MA 02108
(617) 727-0060; *Fax:* (617) 723-5851

Human Resources Division
http://www.state.ma.us/hrd/
Main phone: (617) 727-1556
Main fax: (617) 727-1175

James J. Hartnett Jr., Administrator
1 Ashburton Pl., 3rd Fl., Boston, MA 02108
(617) 727-3555, ext. 201
E-mail: james.hartnett@state.ma.us

State Library
http://www.state.ma.us/lib/
Main phone: (617) 727-2590
Main fax: (617) 727-5189

Stephen A. Fulchino, State Librarian
George Fingold Library, State House, #341,
Boston, MA 02133
(617) 727-2592
E-mail: Stephen.Fulchino@state.ma.us

Veterans Services Dept.
http://www.state.ma.us/vet
Main phone: (617) 727-3578
Main fax: (617) 727-5903

Thomas G. Kelley, Commissioner
239 Causeway St., #100, Boston, MA 02114
(617) 727-3578, ext. 101

Architects Board
http://www.state.ma.us/reg/boards/ar/default.htm
General e-mail: amy.m.missick@state.ma.us
Main phone: (617) 727-3074
Main fax: (617) 727-2197

Peter Steffian, Chair
239 Causeway St., 5th Fl., Boston, MA 02114
(617) 727-3072

Board of Higher Education
http://www.mass.edu/
General e-mail: bhestaff@bhe.mass.edu
Main phone: (617) 727-7785
Main fax: (617) 727-6397

Stanley Z. Koplik, Chancellor
1 Ashburton Pl., #1401, Boston, MA 02108-1696

Campaign and Political Finance Office
http://www.state.ma.us/ocpf
General e-mail: ocpf@cpf.state.ma.us
Main phone: (617) 727-8352

Higher Educational Institutions

Bridgewater State College
http://www.bridgew.edu
Bridgewater, MA 02325
Main phone: (508) 697-1200

Framingham State College
http://www.framingham.edu
100 State St., P.O. Box 9101, Framingham, MA
01701-9101
Main phone: (508) 620-1220

Massachusetts College of Art
http://www.massart.edu
621 Huntington Ave., Boston, MA 02115
Main phone: (617) 232-1555

Massachusetts College of Liberal Arts
http://www.mcla.mass.edu
375 Church St., North Adams, MA 01247-4100
Main phone: (413) 662-5000

Massachusetts Maritime Academy
http://ww2.mma.mass.edu/ie30.html
101 Academy Dr., Buzzards Bay, Cape Cod, MA
02532
Main phone: (800) 544-3411

Salem State College
http://www.salem.mass.edu
352 Lafayette St., Salem, MA 01970
Main phone: (978) 542-6000

University of Massachusetts
http://www.umassp.edu
1 Beacon St., 26th Fl., Boston, MA 02108
Main phone: (617) 287-7000
Branches: Amherst, Boston, Dartmouth, Lowell,
Worcester

Westfield State College
http://www.wsc.mass.edu
Westfield, MA 01086
Main phone: (413) 572-5218

Worcester State College
http://www.worc.mass.edu
486 Chandler St., Worcester, MA 01602-2597
Main phone: (508) 929-8000

Main fax: (617) 727-6549
Toll free: (800) 462-OCPF

Michael J. Sullivan, Director
1 Ashburton Pl., #411, Boston, MA 02108
(617) 727-8352; *Fax:* (617) 727-6549
E-mail: msullivan@cpf.state.ma.us

Civil Rights and Civil Liberties Division
Main phone: (617) 727-2200
Main fax: (617) 727-5768

Richard Cole, Chief (Acting)
1 Ashburton Pl., #2010, Boston, MA 02108
(617) 727-2200, ext. 2928
E-mail: Richard.Cole@state.ma.us

Consumer Affairs and Business Regulation Office
http://www.state.ma.us/consumer/
General e-mail: ask@consumer.com
Main phone: (617) 727-7780
Main fax: (617) 227-6094
Toll free: (888) 283-3757
TTY: (617) 727-1729

Jennifer Davis Carey, Director
1 Ashburton Pl., #1411, Boston, MA 02108
(617) 727-7755

Alcoholic Beverage Control Commission
Main phone: (617) 727-3040
Main fax: (617) 727-1258

Peter J. Connelly Jr., Executive Secretary
239 Causeway St., #200, Boston, MA 02114
(617) 727-3040, ext. 309

Consumer Protection and Anit-Trust Division
General e-mail: webmaster@state.ma.us.ag
Main phone: (617) 727-2200
Main fax: (617) 727-5765

Freda Fishman, Chief
1 Ashburton Pl., #2010, Boston, MA 02108
(617) 727-2200, ext. 2903
E-mail: Freda.Fishman@state.ma.us

Corrections Dept.
http://www.state.ma.us/doc/
General e-mail: docinfo@doc.state.ma.us
Main phone: (508) 422-3300
Main fax: (508) 422-3386

Michael T. Maloney, Commissioner
50 Maple St., #3, Milford, MA 01757
(508) 422-3339

Cosmetologists Board
http://www.state.ma.us/reg/boards/hd/default.htm
Main phone: (617) 727-3067
Main fax: (617) 727-1627

Helen Peveri, Executive Director
239 Causeway St., 5th Fl., Boston, MA 02114
(617) 727-9940

Cultural Council
http://www.massculturalcouncil.org
General e-mail: web@arts.state.ma.us
Main phone: (617) 727-3668
Main fax: (617) 727-0044
Toll free: (800) 232-0960
TTY: (617) 338-9153

Mary Kelley, Executive Director
120 Boylston St., 2nd Fl., Boston, MA 02116-4600
(617) 727-3668, ext. 304
E-mail: mary.kelley@arts.state.ma.us

Disability Office
http://www.state.ma.us/mod/
Main phone: (617) 727-7440
Main fax: (617) 727-0965
Toll free: (800) 322-2020
TTY: (800) 322-2020

Lorraine Greiff, Acting Director
1 Ashburton Pl., #1305, Boston, MA 02108

Economic Development Dept.
http://www.state.ma.us/econ/
General e-mail: susan.saia@state.ma.us
Main phone: (617) 727-8380
Main fax: (617) 727-4426

Carolyn E. Boviard, Director
1 Ashburton Pl., 21st Fl., Boston, MA 02108
E-mail: carolyn.boviard@state.ma.us

Travel and Tourism Office
http://www.massvacation.com
Main phone: (617) 973-8500
Main fax: (617) 973-8525
Toll free: (800) 227-MASS

Mary Jane McKenna, Director
10 Park Plaza, #4510, Boston, MA 02116
E-mail: mmkenna@state.ma.us

Education Dept.
http://www.doe.mass.edu
Main phone: (781) 388-3300
Main fax: (781) 397-0770
TTY: (800) 439-2370

David P. Driscoll, Commissioner
350 Main St., Malden, MA 02148-5023
(781) 388-3111; *Fax:* (781) 338-3392
E-mail: david.driscoll@doe.mass.edu

Board of Education
http://www.doe.mass.edu/orginfo/edboard.html
Main phone: (781) 998-9000
Main fax: (781) 338-3392

David P. Driscoll, Secretary
350 Main St., Malden, MA 02148
(781) 388-3111
E-mail: david.driscoll@doe.mass.edu

Educational Financing Authority
http://www.mefa.org
General e-mail: info@mefa.org
Main phone: (800) 842-1531
Main fax: (617) 261-9765

Thomas Graf, Executive Director
125 Summer St., 14th Fl., Boston, MA 02110
(617) 261-9760; *Fax:* (617) 261-9765
E-mail: tgraf@mefa.org

Elder Affairs Executive Office
http://www.state.ma.us/elder/
General e-mail: elder.affairs@state.ma.us
Main phone: (800) 882-2003
Main fax: (617) 727-9368
TTY: (800) 872-0166

Lillian Glickman, Secretary
1 Ashburton Pl., McCormack Bldg., 5th Fl., Boston, MA 02108
(617) 727-7750; *Fax:* (617) 727-6944

Engineers and Land Surveyors Board
http://www.state.ma.us/reg/boards/en/default.htm
General e-mail: marie.e.deveau@state.ma.us
Main phone: (617) 727-3074
Main fax: (617) 727-2197

H. William Flood, Chair
239 Causeway St., 5th Fl., Boston, MA 02114
(617) 727-9956

Environmental Affairs Executive Office
http://www.state.ma.us/envir
Main phone: (617) 626-1100
Main fax: (617) 626-1181

Bob Durand, Secretary
100 Cambridge St., #2000, Boston, MA 02202
E-mail: bobdurand@state.ma.us

Environmental Management Dept.
http://www.state.ma.us/dem/
General e-mail: mass.parks@state.ma.us
Main phone: (617) 626-1250
Main fax: (617) 626-1449

Peter C. Webber, Commissioner
100 Cambridge St., 19th Fl., Boston, MA 02202
(617) 626-1300

Forests and Parks Division
http://www.state.ma.us/dem/forparks.htm
General e-mail: mass.parks@state.ma.us
Main phone: (617) 626-1250
Main fax: (617) 626-1449

Todd A. Frederick, Director
100 Cambridge St., 19th Fl., Boston, MA 02202
(617) 626-1450
E-mail: Todd.Frederick@state.ma.us

Fisheries, Wildlife, and Environmental Law Enforcement Dept.
http://www.state.ma.us/dfwele/
Main phone: (617) 626-1500

Main fax: (617) 626-1505

David M. Peters, Commissioner
100 Cambridge St., #1901, Boston, MA 02202
(617) 626-1500; *Fax:* (617) 626-1505
E-mail: David.Peters@state.ma.us

Food and Agriculture Dept.
http://www.massdfa.org/
Main phone: (617) 626-1700
Main fax: (617) 626-1850

Jonathan Healy, Commissioner
100 Cambridge St., #2103, Boston, MA 02202
(817) 626-1701
E-mail: jhealy_dfa_boston@state.ma.us

Health and Educational Facilities Authority
http://www.mhefa.state.ma.us
Main phone: (617) 737-8377
Main fax: (617) 737-8366
Toll free: (888) 662-4332

Robert J. Ciolek, Executive Director
99 Summer St., #1000, Boston, MA 02110-1240
E-mail: bob@mhefa.state.ma.us

Health and Human Services Executive Office
http://www.state.ma.us/eohhs/

Main phone: (617) 727-7600
Main fax: (617) 727-1396
TTY: (617) 695-7834

William D. O'Leary, Secretary
McCormack Bldg., 1 Ashburton Pl., #1109, Boston,
   MA 02108
(617) 727-0077; *Fax:* (617) 727-5134
E-mail: william.oleary@ehs.state.ma.us

Medical Assistance Division
http://www.state.ma.us/dma
Main phone: (617) 210-5000
Main fax: (617) 210-5003
Toll free: (800) 841-2900
TTY: (617) 210-5004

Mark Reynolds, Commissioner (Acting)
600 Washington St., 5th Fl., Boston, MA 02111
(617) 210-5000, ext. 5669
E-mail: Mark.Reynolds@state.ma.us

Historical Commission
http://www.state.ma.us/sec/mhc/
Main phone: (617) 727-8470
Main fax: (617) 727-5128
Toll free: (800) 392-6090
TTY: (800) 392-6090

Judith McDonough, Executive Director
220 Morrissey Blvd., Boston, MA 02125
E-mail: judith.mcdonough@sec.state.ma.us

Housing and Community Development Dept.
http://www.magnet.state.ma.us/dhcd
Main phone: (617) 727-7765
Main fax: (617) 727-5060

Jane Wallace Gumble, Director
1 Congress St., 10th Fl., Boston, MA 02114
(617) 727-7765, ext. 111
E-mail: jane.gumble@state.ma.us

Housing Finance Agency
http://www.mhfa.com
General e-mail: info@mhfa.com
Main phone: (617) 854-1000
Main fax: (617) 854-1029
TTY: (617) 854-1025

Steven D. Pierce, Executive Director
1 Beacon St., Boston, MA 02108
(617) 854-1850; *Fax:* (617) 854-1029

Insurance Division
http://www.state.ma.us/doi/
Main phone: (617) 521-7794
Main fax: (617) 521-7772
TTY: (617) 521-7490

Linda Ruthardt, Commissioner
1 S. Station, 5th Fl., Boston, MA 02110

Juvenile Court
http://www.state.ma.us/courts/TrialC/TriaDept/
juvenile.htm
Main phone: (617) 788-6550
Main fax: (617) 788-8965
Mailing address: P.O. Box 9664, Boston, MA
02114-9664

Jane Strickland, Court Administrator
24 New Chardon St., #6.500, Boston, MA 02114

Labor and Workforce Development Dept.
Main phone: (617) 727-6573
Main fax: (617) 727-1090

Angelo R. Buonopane, Director
1 Ashburton Pl., 21st Fl., Boston, MA 02108
(617) 727-6573, ext. 100
E-mail: angelo.buonopane@state.ma.us

MassDevelopment
http://www.massdevelopment.com
Main phone: (617) 451-2477
Main fax: (617) 451-3429
Toll free: (800) 445-8030

Michael P. Hogan, Executive Director
75 Federal St., 10th Fl., Boston, MA 02110
E-mail: michael.hogan@state.ma.us

Medicine Board Registration
http://www.massmedboard.org
Main phone: (617) 727-3086
Main fax: (617) 451-9568

Nancy Achin Sullivan, Executive Director
10 West St., 3rd Fl., Boston, MA 02111
(617) 727-3086, ext. 319

Mental Health Legal Advisors Committee
http://www.state.ma.us/mhlac/
General e-mail: mhlac@email.mhl.state.ma.us
Main phone: (617) 338-2345
Main fax: (617) 338-2347
Toll free: (800) 342-9092

Frank J. Laski, Executive Director
294 Washington St., #320, Boston, MA 02108
(617) 338-2345, ext. 23; *Fax:* (617) 338-2347
E-mail: flaski@email.mhl.state.ma.us

Nursing Board
http://www.state.ma.us/reg/boards/rn/default.htm
General e-mail: elizabeth.lindberg@state.ma.us
Main phone: (617) 727-3074
Main fax: (617) 727-2197

Theresa Bonanno, Executive Director
239 Causeway St., 5th Fl., Boston, MA 02114
(617) 727-9961

Pharmacy Board
http://www.state.ma.us/reg/boards/ph/default.htm

Main phone: (617) 727-3074
Main fax: (617) 727-2197

Charles Young, Executive Director
239 Causeway St., #500, Boston, MA 02114
(617) 727-9953; *Fax:* (617) 727-2366
E-mail: Charles.R.Young@state.ma.us

Probation Commissioner's Office
http://www.state.ma.us/courts/trialC/TriaDept/
probcomm.htm
Main phone: (617) 727-5300
Main fax: (617) 727-5006
TTY: (617) 727-6746

John J. O'Brien, Commissioner
1 Ashburton Pl., #405, Boston, MA 02108
(617) 727-5300, ext. 258; *Fax:* (617) 727-0316
E-mail: john.obrien@state.ma.us

Public Accountancy Board
http://www.state.ma.us/reg/boards/pa/default.htm
Main phone: (617) 727-3074
Main fax: (617) 727-2197

Leo Bonarrigo, Executive Director
239 Causeway St., #450, Boston, MA 02114
(617) 727-1806; *Fax:* (617) 727-0139

Public Counsel Services Committee
http://www.state.ma.us/cpcs
Main phone: (617) 482-6212
Main fax: (617) 988-8495

Boards and Licensing

Accountancy, (617) 727-3074, http://
www.state.ma.us/reg/boards/pa/default.htm
Architects, (617) 727-3074, http://
www.state.ma.us/reg/boards/ar/default.htm
Cosmetology, (617) 727-3067, http://
www.state.ma.us/reg/boards/hd/default.htm
Engineers and Land Surveyors, (617)
727-3074, http://www.state.ma.us/reg/boards/
en/default.htm
Medical Licensing, (617) 727-3086,
http://www.massmedboard.org
Nursing, (617) 727-3074, http://
www.state.ma.us/reg/boards/rn/default.htm
Pharmacy, (617) 727-3074, http://
www.state.ma.us/reg/boards/ph/default.htm
Real Estate Appraisers, (617) 727-3074,
http://www.state.ma.us/reg/
Registration Division, (617) 727-3074,
http://www.state.ma.us/reg/

William J. Leahy, Chief Counsel
470 Atlantic Ave., #700, Boston, MA 02210
(617) 988-8311
E-mail: wjl@cpcs1.cpc.state.ma.us

Public Safety Executive Office
http://www.state.ma.us/eops/
Main phone: (617) 727-7775
Main fax: (617) 727-4764

Jane Perlov, Secretary
1 Ashburton Pl., #2133, Boston, MA 02108
(617) 727-7775

Emergency Management Agency
http://www.magnet.state.ma.us/mema/
  homepage.htm
Main phone: (508) 820-2000
Main fax: (508) 820-2030
Toll free: (800) 982-6846
Mailing address: P.O. Box 1496, Framingham,
  MA 01701

Stephen McGrail, Executive Director
400 Worcester Rd., Framingham, MA 01701
(508) 820-2010
E-mail: Stephen.Mcgrail@state.ma.us

Fire Services Dept.
Main phone: (978) 567-3100
Main fax: (978) 567-3121
Mailing address: P.O. Box 1025, Stowe, MA
  01775

Stephen D. Coan, State Fire Marshal
State Road, 2nd Fl., Stowe, MA 01775
(978) 567-3100, ext. 3118
E-mail: Stephen.Coan@state.ma.us

Military Division
http://www.magnet.state.ma.us/guard
Main phone: (508) 233-6590
Main fax: (508) 233-6527
Toll free: (888) 301-3103

George W. Keefe, Adjudant General (Interim)
50 Maple St., Milford, MA 01757
(508) 233-6552; *Fax:* (508) 233-6554
E-mail: george.keefe@ma.ngb.army.mil

Motor Vehicles Registry
http://www.state.ma.us/rmv
Main phone: (617) 351-4500
Toll free: (800) 858-3926
Mailing address: P.O. Box 199100, Boston, MA
  02119

Daniel A. Grabauskas, Registrar
630 Washington St., Boston, MA 02120
(617) 351-2700; *Fax:* (617) 351-9971
E-mail: daniel.grabauskas@state.ma.us

Parole Board
Main phone: (617) 727-3271
Main fax: (617) 727-2753

Natalie Hardy, Executive Director
27-43 Wormwood St., #300, Boston, MA 02210

Real Estate Appraisers Board
http://www.state.ma.us/reg/
Main phone: (617) 727-3074
Main fax: (617) 727-2669

William Pastuszek, Chair
239 Causeway St., Boston, MA 02114
(617) 727-3055

Registration Division
http://www.state.ma.us/reg/
Main phone: (617) 727-3074
Main fax: (617) 727-2197

William G. Wood, Director
239 Causeway St., Boston, MA 02114

Retirement Board
http://www.state.ma.us/treasury/srb
Main phone: (617) 367-7770
Main fax: (617) 723-1438
Toll free: (800) 392-6014

Ellen Philbin, Executive Director
1 Ashburton Pl., 12th Fl., Boston, MA 02108
(617) 367-7770, ext. 302
E-mail: Ellen.Philbin@state.ma.us

Revenue Dept.
http://www.state.ma.us/dor/
General e-mail: dortsd@shore.net
Main phone: (617) 887-6367
Main fax: (617) 626-2299
Toll free: (800) 392-6089
TTY: (617) 887-6140
Mailing address: P.O. Box 9494, Boston, MA
  02204

Frederick A. Laskey, Commissioner
51 Sleeper St., 8th Fl., Boston, MA 02205
(617) 626-2201
E-mail: frederick.laskey@dor.state.ma.us

Social Services Dept.
http://www.state.ma.us/dss/
General e-mail: dss-info@state.ma.us
Main phone: (617) 748-2000
Main fax: (617) 439-4482
Toll free: (800) 548-8402
TTY: (617) 261-7440

Jeffrey Locke, Interim Commissioner
24 Farnsworth St., Boston, MA 02210
(617) 748-2325
E-mail: jeffrey.locke@state.ma.us

State College Building Authority
Main phone: (617) 542-1081
Main fax: (617) 542-2303

Linda L. Snyder, Executive Director
136 Lincoln St., Boston, MA 02111
Fax: (617) 542-2303
E-mail: lsnyder@mscba.org

State Lottery
http://www.masslottery.com/
General e-mail: webmaster@masslottery.com
Main phone: (781) 848-7755
Main fax: (781) 849-5546
TTY: (617) 849-5678

Jay Mitchell, Executive Director
60 Columbian St., Braintree, MA 02184
(781) 849-5500
E-mail: jay.mitchell@masslottery.com

State Police Dept.
http://www.state.ma.us/msp/
General e-mail: msp.webmaster@pol.state.ma.us
Main phone: (508) 820-2300

John DiFava, Superintendent
470 Worcester Rd., Framingham, MA 01702
(508) 820-2352

Telecommunications and Energy Dept.
http://www.state.ma.us/dpu/
Main phone: (617) 305-3500

Janet Gail Besser, Commissioner
1 South Station, Boston, MA 02110

Transportation and Construction Executive Office
http://www.eotc.org/
Main phone: (617) 973-7000
Main fax: (617) 523-6454

Kevin J. Sullivan, Secretary
10 Park Plaza, #3170, Boston, MA 02116-3969
(617) 973-8080
E-mail: Kevin.J.Sullivan@state.ma.us

Aeronautics Commission
Main phone: (617) 973-8881
Main fax: (617) 973-8889

Stephen R. Muench, Executive Director
10 Park Plaza, #6620, Boston, MA 02116-3966
E-mail: steve.muench@state.ma.us

University of Massachusetts Building Authority
Main phone: (617) 263-0444
Main fax: (617) 287-7167

Joseph G. Brady, Executive Director
75 Park Plaza, Box 5, Boston, MA 02116

Water Resources Authority
http://www.mwra.com
Main phone: (617) 788-1170
Main fax: (617) 788-4894
TTY: (617) 788-4880

Bob Durand, Chair
Charlestown Navy Yard, 100 1st Ave., Boston, MA 02129
(617) 242-6000

Workers' Compensation Advisory Council
http://www.state.ma.us/wcac/
General e-mail: denisel@dia.state.ma.us
Main phone: (617) 727-4900, ext. 378
Main fax: (617) 727-7122

Denise A. Lucciola, Executive Director
600 Washington St., Boston, MA 02111
(617) 727-4900, ext. 378
E-mail: denisel@dia.state.ma.us

Massachussetts Legislature
State House
Boston, MA 02133
General information: (617) 722-2520
TTY: (617) 722-2539
http://www.state.ma.us/legis/legis.htm

Senate
General information: (617) 722-1455
Fax: (617) 722-2845

Thomas F. Birmingham (D), President
State House, #332, Boston, MA 02133
(617) 722-1500
E-mail: Tbirming@sen.state.ma.us
http://www.state.ma.us/legis/member/tfb0.htm

Linda J. Melconian (D), Majority Leader
State House, #333, Boston, MA 02133
(617) 722-1660
http://www.state.ma.us/legis/member/ljm0.htm

Robert E. Travaglini (D), Second Assistant Majority Leader and Majority Whip
State House, #511-B, Boston, MA 02133
(617) 722-1634
E-mail: RTravagl@senate.state.ma.us
http://www.state.ma.us/legis/member/ret0.htm

Brian P. Lees (R), Minority Leader
State House, #308, Boston, MA 02133
(617) 722-1291; *Fax:* (617) 722-1014
E-mail: BLees@senate.state.md.us
http://www.state.ma.us/legis/member/bpl0.htm

Laws

Sales tax: 5%
Income tax: 6%
State minimum wage: $6.00; $6.75 from 2001 (Federal is $5.15)
Marriage age: 18
First-cousin marriage: Permitted
Drinking age: 21
State control of liquor sales: No
Blood alcohol for DWI: 0.08%
Driving age: 18
Speed limit: 65 mph
Permit to buy handguns: Yes, 30 days to acquire. 7-day wait
Minimum age to possess handguns: 18, with Firearm ID Card
Minimum age to possess rifles, shotguns: 18, with Firearm ID Card
State lottery: Yes
Casinos: No
Pari-mutuel betting: Horse and dog racing
Death penalty: No
3 strikes minimum sentence: None
Hate crimes law: Yes
Gay employment non-discrimination: Yes
Official language(s): English
Term limits: Governor (8 yrs.); state legislators (8 yrs.)

State laws are complex and subject to change; this information is not intended as legal advice. For an explanation of this information, see p. x.

Michael R. Knapik (R), Second Assistant Minority Leader and Minority Whip
State House, #309, Boston, MA 02133
(617) 722-1415
E-mail: MKnapik@senate.state.ma.us
http://www.state.ma.us/legis/member/mrk0.htm

Patrick F. Scanlan, Clerk
State House, Boston, MA 02133
(617) 722-1276

House

General information: (617) 722-2000
Fax: (617) 722-2897

Thomas M. Finneran (D), Speaker of the House
State House, #356, Boston, MA 02133
(617) 722-2500
http://www.state.ma.us/legis/member/tmf1.htm

William P. Nagle Jr. (D), Majority Leader
State House, #343, Boston, MA 02133
(617) 722-2600
E-mail: Rep.WilliamNagle@state.ma.us
http://www.state.ma.us/legis/member/wpn1.htm

Barbara Gardner (D), Majority Whip
State House, #370, Boston, MA 02133
(617) 722-2300
E-mail: Rep.BarbaraGardner@state.ma.us
http://www.state.ma.us/legis/member/b_g1.htm

Francis L. Marini (R), Minority Leader
State House, #124, Boston, MA 02133
(617) 722-2100
E-mail: Rep.FrancisMarini@state.ma.us
http://www.state.ma.us/legis/member/flm1.htm

Bradley H. Jones (R), Minority Whip
State House, #443, Boston, MA 02133
(617) 722-2460
E-mail: Rep.BradleyJones@state.ma.us
http://www.state.ma.us/legis/member/bhj1.htm

Steven James, Clerk
State House, Boston, MA 02133
(617) 722-2356

Massachusetts Judiciary

New Court House
Pemberton Square
Boston, MA 02108
http://www.magnet.state.ma.us/courts/

Supreme Judicial Court

http://www.magnet.state.ma.us/courts/SJC/supreme.htm

Susan Mellen, Clerk
New Court House, Pemberton Square, Boston, MA 02108
(617) 557-1020; *Fax:* (617) 557-1145

Justices

Composition: 7 justices
Selection Method: appointed by governor with consent of the Executive Council
Length of term: until age 70

Margaret H. Marshall, Chief Justice, (617) 557-1000
Ruth I. Abrams, Associate Justice, (617) 557-1000
Judith A. Cowin, Associate Justice, (617) 557-1000
John M. Greaney, Associate Justice, (617) 557-1000
Roderick L. Ireland, Associate Justice, (617) 557-1000
Neil L. Lynch, Associate Justice, (617) 557-1000
Francis X. Spina, Associate Justice, (617) 557-1000

Administrative Office of the Courts
Main phone: (617) 557-1194
Main fax: (617) 557-1052
> **Marie Mossaides, Administrative Assistant to the Justices**
> 1400 New Court House, Pemberton Square, Boston, MA 02108

Legislative and Political Party Information Resources

Senate home page: http://www.state.ma.us/legis/memmenus.htm
House home page: http://www.state.ma.us/legis.memmenuh.htm
Committees: http://www.state.ma.us/legis/commenu.htm
Legislative process: http://www.state.ma.us/legis/lawmkng.htm
Massachussetts Democratic Party: http://www.massdems.org
   129 Portland St., Boston, MA 02114; *Phone:* (617) 742-6770; *Fax:* (617) 742-6598
Massachussetts Republican Party: http://www.massgop.com
   21 Milk St., 4th Fl., Boston, MA 02109-2402; *Phone:* (617) 357-1999; *Fax:* (617) 357-1975

Michigan

State Capitol
Lansing, MI 48933
Public information: (517) 373-1837
Fax: (517) 335-6863
http://www.state.mi.us

Office of the Governor

http://www.migov.state.mi.us
General e-mail: migov@mail.mi.us
Main phone: (517) 373-3400
Main fax: (517) 335-6863
TTY: (517) 335-3137
Mailing address: P.O. Box 30013, Lansing, MI
48909

John Engler (R), Governor
George W. Romney Bldg., 111 S. Capitol, Lansing, MI
48933

Sharon Rothwell, Chief of Staff
George W. Romney Bldg., 111 S. Capitol, Lansing, MI
48933
(517) 335-7863; *Fax:* (517) 335-6949

John Truscott, Communications Director
George W. Romney Bldg., 111 S. Capitol, Lansing, MI
48933
(517) 335-6397; *Fax:* (517) 335-6863
E-mail: Truscottj@exec.state.mi.us

Tom Davis, Constituent Services Manager
George W. Romney Bldg., 111 S. Capitol, 3rd Fl.,
Lansing, MI 48933
(517) 335-7858; *Fax:* (517) 335-6863
E-mail: davist@exec.state.mi.us

LeAnne Wilson, Director, Washington Office
444 N. Capitol St. N.W., #411, Washington, DC 20001
(202) 624-5840; *Fax:* (202) 624-5841

Office of the Lieutenant Governor

http://www.state.mi.us/migov/ltgov
Main phone: (517) 373-6800
Main fax: (517) 335-6763
Mailing address: P.O. Box 30026, Lansing, MI
48909

Dick Posthumus (R), Lieutenant Governor
State Capitol Bldg., George W. Romney Bldg., #S-215,
Lansing, MI 48909

Office of the Secretary of State

http://www.sos.state.mi.us/
General e-mail: webmaster@sos.state.mi.us
Main phone: (517) 322-1460

State of Michigan

Capital: Lansing,
since 1847
Founded: 1805, Michigan
Territory created from Indiana Territory
Statehood: January 26, 1837 (26th state)
Constitution adopted: April 1, 1963
Area: 56,809 sq. mi. (ranks 22nd)
Population: 9,817,242 (1998 est.; ranks 8th)
Largest cities: (1998 est.) Detroit (970,196);
Grand Rapids (185,437); Warren (142,455);
Flint (131,668); Lansing (127,825)
Counties: 83, Most populous: (1998 est.)
Wayne (2,118,129); Oakland (1,176,488);
Macomb (787,698); Kent (545,166); Genesee
(436,084)
U.S. Congress: Spencer Abraham (R), Carl
Levin (D); 16 Representatives
Nickname(s): Wolverine State
Motto: If you seek a pleasant peninsula, look
around you
Song: None
Bird: Robin
Tree: White pine
Flower: Apple blossom
State fair: at Detroit, late Aug.-early Sept.;
Upper Peninsula, mid-Aug.
Former capital(s): Detroit

Main fax: (517) 322-1968
TTY: (517) 322-1477

Candice S. Miller (R), Secretary of State
Treasury Bldg., 430 W. Allegan St., 1st Fl., Lansing,
MI 48918-9900
(517) 373-2510; *Fax:* (517) 241-3442
E-mail: millerc@state.mi.us

Office of the Attorney General

http://www.ag.state.mi.us/
Main phone: (517) 373-1110
Main fax: (517) 241-1850
Mailing address: P.O. Box 30212, Lansing, MI
48909

Jennifer Granholm (D), Attorney General
Williams Bldg., Lansing, MI 48909

Office of the State Treasurer

http://www.treasury.state.mi.us/
Main phone: (517) 373-3200
Main fax: (517) 373-4968

Mark A. Murray, State Treasurer
Treasury Bldg., 430 W. Allegan St., Lansing, MI 48922
(517) 373-3223
E-mail: MIStateTreasurer@state.mi.us

Office of the Auditor General

http://www.state.mi.us/audgen
Main phone: (517) 334-8050
Main fax: (517) 334-8079

Thomas H. McTavish, Auditor General
Victor Office Center, 201 N. Washington Square, #600, Lansing, MI 48913
E-mail: mctavist@state.mi.us

Military and Veterans Affairs Dept.

http://www.state.mi.us/dmva/index.htm
General e-mail: dma@state.mi.us
Main phone: (517) 483-5500
Main fax: (517) 483-5822

E. Gordan Stump, Adjutant General and Director
2500 S. Washington Ave., 1st Fl., Lansing, MI 48913-5101
(517) 483-5507; *Fax:* (517) 482-0356
E-mail: stumpg@state.mi.us

Agencies

Agriculture Dept.

http://www.mda.state.mi.us
General e-mail: mdainfo@state.mi.us
Main phone: (517) 373-1104
Main fax: (517) 373-9146

Dan Wyant, Director
Ottawa Bldg., 4th Fl., Lansing, MI 48909
(517) 373-1052; *Fax:* (517) 335-1423

Upper Peninsula State Fair
Main phone: (906) 786-4011
Main fax: (906) 786-4196
TTY: (906) 786-4011

Grant Larsen, Manager
Fair Grounds, 2401 12th Ave. North, Escanaba, MI 49829

Child Day Care Licensing Division

http://www.cis.state.mi.us/brs/cdc
Main phone: (517) 373-8300
Main fax: (517) 335-6121
Mailing address: P.O. Box 30650, Lansing, MI 48909-8150

Theodore J. deWolf, Director
7109 W. Saginaw, 2nd Fl., Lansing, MI 48909-8150

Civil Rights Dept.

http://www.mdcr.com/
General e-mail: mdcrdirector@state.mi.us
Main phone: (800) 482-3604
Main fax: (517) 241-0546
TTY: (313) 961-1552

Nanette Lee Reynolds, Director
Victor Office Center, 201 N. Washington Square, #700, Lansing, MI 48913
(517) 335-3165

Community Health Dept.

http://www.mdch.state.mi.us
Main phone: (517) 373-3500
Main fax: (517) 335-3090
TTY: (517) 373-3573

James K. Haveman Jr., Director
Lewis Cass Bldg., 320 S. Walnut St., 6th Fl., Lansing, MI 48933
(517) 335-0267; *Fax:* (517) 373-4288

Aging Services Division

http://www.mdch.state.mi.us/mass/masshome.html
Main phone: (517) 373-8230
Main fax: (517) 373-4092
TTY: (517) 373-4096
Mailing address: P.O. Box 30676, Lansing, MI 48909-8176

Lynn Alexander, Director
611 W. Ottawa, 3rd Fl., Lansing, MI 48933
E-mail: alexanderl@state.mi.us

Medical Services Administration
Main phone: (517) 335-5001
Main fax: (517) 335-5007
Mailing address: P.O. Box 30479, Lansing, MI 48909

Robert Smedes, Deputy Director
Capitol Commons Bldg., 400 S. Pine, Lansing, MI 48933
E-mail: smedesb@state.mi.us

Mental Health and Substance Abuse Services
Main phone: (517) 335-0196
Main fax: (517) 335-3090

Jeff Patton, Deputy Director (Acting)
Lewis Cass Bldg., 320 S. Walnut St., Lansing, MI 48913

Consumer and Industry Services Dept.

http://www.cis.state.mi.us/

Main phone: (517) 373-1820
Main fax: (517) 373-2129
TTY: (517) 373-7489
Mailing address: P.O. Box 30004, Lansing, MI
48909

Kathleen M. Wilbur, Director
G. Mennen Williams Bldg., 525 W. Ottawa, 4th Fl.,
Lansing, MI 48909
(517) 373-3034; Fax: (517) 373-2129

Arts and Cultural Affairs Council
http://www.cis.state.mi.us/arts/
General e-mail: artsinfo@cis.state.mi.us
Main phone: (517) 241-4011
Main fax: (517) 241-3979
Mailing address: P.O. Box 30705, Lansing, MI
48909

Betty Boone, Executive Director
525 W. Ottawa, Lansing, MI 48909

Financial Institutions Bureau
http://www.cis.state.mi.us/fib
Main phone: (517) 373-3460
Main fax: (517) 335-0908
Mailing address: P.O. Box 30224, Lansing, MI
48909

Gary K. Mielock, Commissioner (Acting)
333 S. Capitol Ave., Lansing, MI 48933
Fax: (517) 335-1109

Fire Safety Office
http://www.cis.state.mi.us/fire/
Main phone: (517) 322-1123
Main fax: (517) 322-1356
Mailing address: P.O. Box 30700, Lansing, MI
48909-8200

Tony Sanfilippo, Director
Gneral Office Bldg., 7150 Harris Dr., 2nd Fl.,
Lansing, MI 48913
(517) 322-5331

Higher Educational Institutions

Central Michigan University
http://www.cmich.edu
Mount Pleasant, MI 48859
Main phone: (517) 774-4000

Eastern Michigan University
http://www.emich.edu
Ypsilanti, MI 48197
Main phone: (734) 487-3060

Ferris State University
http://www.ferris.edu
901 S. State St., Big Rapids, MI 49307
Main phone: (231) 591-2000

Grand Valley State University
http://www.gvsu.edu
1 Campus Dr., Allendale, MI 49401-9403
Main phone: (616) 895-6611

Lake Superior State University
http://www.lssu.edu
650 W. Easterday Ave., Sault Ste. Marie, MI 49783
Main phone: (888) 800-5778

Michigan State University
http://www.msu.edu
E. Lansing, MI 48824-1020
Main phone: (517) 355-8332

Michigan Technological University
http://www.mtu.edu
1400 Townsend Dr., Houghton, MI 49931-1295
Main phone: (906) 487-1885

Northern Michigan University
http://www.nmu.edu
1401 Presque Isle Ave., Marquette, MI 49855
Main phone: (800) 682-9797

Northwestern Michigan College
http://www.nmc.edu
1701 E. Front, Traverse City, MI 49686
Main phone: (800) 748-0566
Branches: Cadillac

Oakland University
http://ou.sv3.com/finalsite/mainframe.htm
101 N. Foundation Hall, Rochester, MI 48309-4475
Main phone: (248) 370-3360

Saginaw Valley State University
http://tardis.svsu.edu
7400 Bay Rd., University Center, MI 48710-0001
Main phone: (517) 790-4000

University of Michigan
http://www.umich.edu
Ann Arbor, MI 48109-1316
Main phone: (734) 764-7433
Branches: Dearborn, Flint

Wayne State University
http://www.wayne.edu
3 E. HNJ, Detroit, MI 48202
Main phone: (313) 577-3577

Western Michigan University
http://www.wmich.edu
1201 Oliver St., Kalamazoo, MI 49008-5720
Main phone: (616) 387-2000

Housing Development Authority

http://www.mshda.org
Main phone: (517) 373-8370
Main fax: (517) 334-4797
TTY: (800) 382-4568
Mailing address: P.O. Box 30044, Lansing, MI 48909

James L. Logue III, Executive Director
401 S. Washington Square, Lansing, MI 48909
(517) 373-6022; *Fax:* (517) 373-7657

Insurance Bureau

http://www.cis.state.mi.us/ins/
Main phone: (517) 373-9273
Main fax: (517) 335-4978
Toll free: (877) 999-6442
Mailing address: P.O. Box 30220, Lansing, MI 48909-7720

Frank M. Fitzgerald, Commissioner
611 W. Ottawa, 2nd Fl., Lansing, MI 48933

Liquor Control Commission

http://www.cis.state.mi.us/lcc/
General e-mail: lccinfo@cis.state.mi.us
Main phone: (517) 322-1345
Main fax: (517) 322-5188
Mailing address: P.O. Box 30005, Lansing, MI 48909

Jacquelyn Stewart, Chair
Secondary Complex, 7150 Harris Dr., Lansing, MI 48909-7505
(517) 322-1353
E-mail: jackie.stewart@cis.state.mi.us

Public Service Commission

http://cis.state.mi.us/mpsc
Main phone: (517) 241-6180
Main fax: (517) 241-6181
Toll free: (800) 292-9555
Mailing address: P.O. Box 30221, Lansing, MI 48909

John Strand, Chair
6545 Mercantile Way, #7, Lansing, MI 48909
Fax: (517) 241-6189

Workers Disability Compensation Bureau

http://www.cis.state.mi.us/wkrcomp
Main phone: (517) 322-1296
Main fax: (517) 322-1808
Toll free: (888) 396-5041
TTY: (517) 322-5987
Mailing address: P.O. Box 30016, Lansing, MI 48909

Jack F. Wheatley, Director
State Secondary Complex, 7150 Harris Dr., Lansing, MI 48821

Corrections Dept.

http://www.state.mi.us/mdoc/
Main phone: (517) 335-1426
Main fax: (517) 373-2628
TTY: (517) 335-3972
Mailing address: P.O. Box 30003, Lansing, MI 48909

Bill Martin, Director
Grandview Plaza, 206 E. Michigan Ave., 4th Fl., Lansing, MI 48933
(517) 373-0720; *Fax:* (517) 373-6883
E-mail: martinb@state.mi.us

Parole Board

Main phone: (517) 373-0270
Main fax: (517) 373-2628
TTY: (517) 335-0039
Mailing address: P.O. Box 30003, Lansing, MI 48909

Stephen Marschke, Chair
Grandview Plaza, 206 E. Michigan Ave., Lansing, MI 48909

Driver and Vehicle Dept.

http://www.sos.state.mi.us/dv/index.html
Main phone: (517) 322-1460
Main fax: (517) 322-1960

Heidi Weber-Reed, Director
7064 Crowner Dr., Lansing, MI 48918

Education Dept.

http://www.mde.state.mi.us
Main phone: (517) 373-3324
Main fax: (517) 335-4565
Mailing address: P.O. Box 30008, Lansing, MI 48933

Arthur Ellis, Superintendent
608 W. Allegan St., Hannah Bldg., Lansing, MI 48933
(517) 373-9235; *Fax:* (517) 335-4565
E-mail: EllisAE@state.mi.us

Board of Education

http://www.mde.state.mi.us/off/board/
General e-mail:
stateboard@mdenet.mde.state.mi.us
Main phone: (517) 373-3324
Main fax: (517) 335-4575
TTY: (517) 373-4035
Mailing address: P.O. Box 30008, Lansing, MI 48909

Dorothy Beardmore, President
608 W. Allegan, John Hannah Bldg., 4th Fl., Lansing, MI 48933
(517) 373-3900
E-mail: beardmored@state.mi.us

Schools for the Deaf and Blind
http://www.msdb.k12.mi.us
Main phone: (810) 257-1460
Main fax: (810) 238-1220
TTY: (800) 622-6730

Alex Davlantes, Executive Director
1667 Miller Rd., Flint, MI 48503
E-mail: davlantesa@state.mi.us

Environmental Quality Dept.
http://www.deq.state.mi.us
Main phone: (800) 373-7917
Main fax: (517) 241-7401
Toll free: (800) 662-9278
Mailing address: P.O. Box 30473, Lansing, MI
48909-7973

Russell J. Harding, Director
106 W. Allegan St., Hollister Bldg., 6th Fl., Lansing,
MI 48933
E-mail: hardingr@state.mi.us

Geological Survey Division
http://www.deq.state.mi.us/gsd
Main phone: (517) 334-6907
Main fax: (517) 334-6038
Toll free: (800) 662-9270

Mailing address: P.O. Box 30256, Lansing, MI
48909

**Harold Fitch, Chief, State Geologist, Assistant
Supervisor of Wells, and Supervisor of
Mineral Wells**
35 E. Hazel St., Lansing, MI 48912
E-mail: fitchh@state.mi.us

Library of Michigan
http://www.libofmich.lib.mi.us/
General e-mail: lmrefdsk@libofmich.lib.mi.us
Main phone: (517) 373-5400
Main fax: (517) 373-5853
TTY: (517) 373-8937
Mailing address: P.O. Box 30007, Lansing, MI
48909

Vacant, State Librarian
717 W. Allegan St., Lansing, MI 48915
(517) 373-5504; *Fax:* (517) 373-4480

Management and Budget Dept.
http://www.state.mi.us/dmb/index.htm
General e-mail: dmbdir@state.mi.us
Main phone: (517) 373-1004
Main fax: (517) 373-7268

Janet E. Phipps, Director
320 S. Walnut, 1st Fl., Lansing, MI 48933

Administrative Services Office
http://www.state.mi.us/dmb/oas/
Main phone: (517) 373-0219
Main fax: (517) 373-1071
Mailing address: P.O. Box 30026, Lansing, MI
48909

Rose Wilson, Director
320 S. Walnut, 2nd Fl., Lansing, MI 48909
E-mail: Wilsonr@state.mi.us

Financial Management Office
http://www.state.mi.us/dmb/ofm/
Main phone: (517) 373-1010
Main fax: (517) 373-6458
Mailing address: P.O. Box 30026, Lansing, MI
48909

Leon E. Hank, Director
530 W. Allegan, Lansing, MI 48909

Retirement Services Office
http://www.state.mi.us/dmb/ors/
General e-mail:
ORSCustomerService@state.mi.us
Main phone: (517) 322-5103
Main fax: (517) 322-6145
Toll free: (800) 381-5111
Mailing address: P.O. Box 30171, Lansing, MI
48909-7671

Chris DeRose, Director
State Secondary Complex/General Office Bldg.,
7150 Harris Dr., Diamonddale, MI 48821
(517) 322-6235
E-mail: derosec@state.mi.us

Natural Resources Dept.
http://www.dnr.state.mi.us
Main phone: (517) 373-2329
Main fax: (517) 335-4242
TTY: (517) 335-4623
Mailing address: P.O. Box 30028, Lansing, MI
48909-7528

K. L. Cool, Director
Stevens T. Mason Bldg., Lansing, MI 48909-7528
(517) 373-2329; *Fax:* (517) 335-4242

Resource Management Bureau: Fisheries Division
Main phone: (517) 373-1280
Main fax: (517) 373-6705
Mailing address: P.O. Box 30028, Lansing, MI
48909

Kelley Smith, Chief
530 W. Allegan, Lansing, MI 48909

Resource Management Bureau: Forest Management Division
Main phone: (517) 373-1275
Main fax: (517) 373-1275
TTY: (517) 241-2683
Mailing address: P.O. Box 30452, Lansing, MI
48909-5792

John Robertson, Chief
530 W. Allegan, Lansing, MI 48933

Resource Management Bureau: Parks and Recreation Division
Main phone: (517) 373-9900
Mailing address: P.O. Box 30257, Lansing, MI
48909

Rodney Stokes, Chief
309 N. Washington Square, #12, Lansing, MI
48933
(517) 335-4827; *Fax:* (517) 373-4625
E-mail: stokesra@dnr.sc.dnr.prd

Resource Management Bureau: Wildlife Division
Main phone: (517) 373-1263
Mailing address: P.O. Box 30028, Lansing, MI
48909

Becky Humphries, Chief
530 W. Allegan, Lansing, MI 48909

Prosecuting Attorneys Appellate Service Division
Main phone: (517) 334-7147
Main fax: (517) 334-7109
Mailing address: P.O. Box 30212, Lansing, MI
48909

Charles D. Hackney, Assistant-in-Charge
116 W. Allegan, Samuel Ingham Bldg., #600, Lansing,
MI 48933
E-mail: hackneyc@ag.state.mi.us

South Central Power Agency
http://www.mspca.net
Main phone: (517) 542-2346
Main fax: (517) 542-3049
Mailing address: P.O. Box 62, Litchfield, MI 49252

J. P. Bierl, General Manager
720 Herring Rd., Litchfield, MI 49252
E-mail: bierlj@mscpa.net

State Lottery
http://www.state.mi.us/msl/index.htm
General e-mail: milottery@state.mi.us
Main phone: (517) 335-5640
Main fax: (517) 241-9120
Toll free: (800) 822-8888
TTY: (517) 335-5645
Mailing address: P.O. Box 30023, Lansing, MI
48909

Don Gilmer, Commissioner
101 E. Hillsdale, Lansing, MI 48913
(517) 335-5608; *Fax:* (517) 335-5651
E-mail: gilmerd@state.mi.us

State Police Dept.
http://www.msp.state.mi.us/
General e-mail: BaileyL@state.mi.us
Main phone: (517) 332-2521

Boards and Licensing

Accountancy, (517) 241-9249
Architects, (517) 241-9253
Child Day Care Licensing Division, (517)
373-8300, http://www.cis.state.mi.us/brs/cdc
Commercial Services Bureau, (517) 241-9223
Cosmetology, (517) 241-9201
Engineers and Land Surveyors, (517) 241-
9253
Medical Licensing, (517) 373-6873
Nursing, (517) 373-6873
Pharmacy, (517) 373-6873
Real Estate Appraisers, (517) 241-9201

Main fax: (517) 336-6255
TTY: (517) 333-2756

Michael D. Robinson, Director
714 S. Harrison Rd., East Lansing, MI 48823
(517) 336-6157

Administrative and Information Services Bureau: Emergency Management Division
http://www.mspemd.org
Main phone: (517) 333-5042
Main fax: (517) 333-4987
Mailing address: P.O. Box 30636, Lansing, MI
48909-8136

Ed Buikema, Commanding Officer
4000 Collins Rd., Lansing, MI 48909
E-mail: buikemae@state.mi.us

Investigative Services Bureau: Fire Marshal Division
http://www.mspfmd.org
Main phone: (517) 322-5454
Main fax: (517) 322-2908

Edmund K. Burke, Commanding Officer
7150 Harris Dr., East Lansing, MI 48913

Transportation Commission
http://www.mdot.state.mi.us
Main phone: (517) 373-2110
Main fax: (517) 373-2687
TTY: (517) 373-0012
Mailing address: P.O. Box 30050, Lansing, MI
48909

Barton LaBelle, Chair
425 W. Ottawa, 4th Fl., Lansing, MI 48933

Transportation Dept.
http://www.mdot.state.mi.us/mdotmain.htm
Main phone: (517) 373-2090
Main fax: (517) 373-0167
TTY: (517) 373-0012
Mailing address: P.O. Box 30050, Lansing, MI
48909

James R. DeSana, Director
425 W. Ottawa, 4th Fl., Lansing, MI 48933
(517) 373-2114; Fax: (517) 373-6457

Aeronautics Bureau
Main phone: (517) 335-9283
Main fax: (517) 321-6422

William E. Gehman, Deputy Director
2700 E. Airport Service Dr., Lansing, MI 48906
(517) 335-9943; Fax: (517) 321-6522

Treasury Dept.
http://www.treas.state.mi.us

Main phone: (517) 373-3223
Main fax: (517) 335-1785

Mark A. Murray, State Treasurer
Treasury Bldg., 430 W. Allegan St., Lansing, MI
48922

Tax Administration and Oversight: Revenue Bureau
Main phone: (517) 373-3196
Main fax: (517) 373-4023

June Summers Haas, Commissioner (Acting)
Treasury Bldg., 430 W. Allegan St., Lansing, MI
48922

Unemployment Agency
http://www.miun.com
Main phone: (313) 876-5000
Main fax: (313) 876-5587

Jack Wheatley, Director
7310 Woodward Ave., Detroit, MI 48202
(313) 876-5901

Michigan Legislature

State Capitol
Lansing, MI 48909
General information: (517) 373-0170
Fax: (517) 373-0171
TTY: (517) 373-0543
Bill status: (517) 373-0630
http://www.michiganlegislature.org

Senate
Address: State Capitol, P.O. Box 30036, Lansing,
MI 48909-7536
General information: (517) 373-2400
Fax: (517) 373-9635

Dick Posthumus, President
Capitol Bldg., #S-215, Lansing, MI 48909
(517) 373-6800; Fax: (517) 335-6763
http://www.state.mi.us/migov/ltgov

John Schwarz (R), President Pro Tempore
State Capitol, P.O. Box 30036, Lansing, MI 48909-
7536
(517) 373-3447; Fax: (517) 373-5849
E-mail: senjschwarz@senate.state.mi.us
http://www.gop.senate.state.mi.us/senator/schwarz/
callvisit.html

Dan L. DeGrow (R), Majority Leader
State Capitol, P.O. Box 30036, Lansing, MI 48909-
7536

(517) 373-7708; *Fax:* (517) 373-1450
E-mail: SenDDeGrow@senate.state.mi.us
http://www.gop.senate.state.mi.us/senator/degrow/

William Van Regenmorter (R), Majority Caucus Whip
State Capitol, P.O. Box 30036, Lansing, MI 48909-7536
(517) 373-6920; *Fax:* (517) 373-2751
E-mail: SenWVanReg@senate.state.mi.us
http://www.gop.senate.state.mi.us/senator/vanregenmorter/callvisit.html

John D. Cherry (D), Minority Leader
State Capitol, P.O. Box 30036, Lansing, MI 48909-7536
(517) 373-1636; *Fax:* (517) 373-1453
E-mail: SenJCherry@senate.state.mi.us
http://www.state.mi.us/senate/dem/sd28/sd28info.html

Raymond W. Murphy (D), Minority Whip
State Capitol, P.O. Box 30036, Lansing, MI 48909-7536
(517) 373-0990; *Fax:* (517) 373-2773
E-mail: SenRMurphy@senate.state.mi.us
http://www.state.mi.us/senate/dem/ds03/sd03info.html

Carol Morey Viventi, Secretary
State Capitol, P.O. Box 30036, Lansing, MI 48909-7536
(517) 373-2400; *Fax:* (517) 373-9635
E-mail: sensecretary@senate.state.mi.us

House
Address: State Capitol, P.O. Box 30014, Lansing, MI 48909-7514
General information: (517) 373-0135
Fax: (517) 373-5930

Charles Perricone (R), Speaker of the House
State Capitol, P.O. Box 30014, Lansing, MI 48909-7514
(517) 373-1774
E-mail: cperric@house.state.mi.us

Patricia Birkholz (R), Speaker Pro Tempore
State Capitol, P.O. Box 30014, Lansing, MI 48909-7514
(517) 373-0836
E-mail: pbirkho@house.state.mi.us

Andrew Raczkowski (R), Majority Leader
State Capitol, P.O. Box 30014, Lansing, MI 48909-7514

Laws

Sales tax: 6%
Income tax: 4.4%
State minimum wage: $5.15 (Federal is $5.15)
Marriage age: 18
First-cousin marriage: Prohibited
Drinking age: 21
State control of liquor sales: Yes
Blood alcohol for DWI: 0.10%
Driving age: 17
Speed limit: 70 mph
Permit to buy handguns: Yes, wait for permit varies
Minimum age to possess handguns: 18
Minimum age to possess rifles, shotguns: 18
State lottery: Yes
Casinos: Yes (tribal)
Pari-mutuel betting: Horse racing
Death penalty: No
3 strikes minimum sentence: None
Hate crimes law: Yes
Gay employment non-discrimination: No
Official language(s): None
Term limits: Governor (8 yrs.); state senate (8 yrs.), house (6 yrs.)

State laws are complex and subject to change; this information is not intended as legal advice. For an explanation of this information, see p. x.

(517) 373-1793
E-mail: araczko@house.state.mi.us

Paul N. DeWeese (R), Majority Whip
State Capitol, P.O. Box 30014, Lansing, MI 48909-7514
(517) 373-0587
E-mail: pdeweese@house.state.mi.us

Michael Hanley (D), Democratic Leader
State Capitol, P.O. Box 30014, Lansing, MI 48909-7514
(517) 373-0152
E-mail: mhanley@house.state.mi.us

Gary L. Randall, Clerk
State Capitol, P.O. Box 30014, Lansing, MI 48909-7514
(517) 373-0135; *Fax:* (517) 373-5130
E-mail: clerka@house.state.mi.us

Michigan Judiciary

525 W. Ottawa St.
Lansing, MI 48933
http://www.migov.state.mi.us/
GovernmentBranches_Judicial.shtm

Supreme Court
http://www.supremecourt.state.mi.us

Corbin R. Davis, Clerk
525 W. Ottawa St., 2nd Fl., Lansing, MI 48933
(517) 373-0120

Justices
Composition: 7 justices
Selection Method: nonpartisan election;
nominees are chosen by political parties
Length of term: 8 years

Elizabeth A. Weaver, Chief Justice, (231) 929-3700
Michael F. Cavanagh, Justice, (517) 373-8683
Maura D. Corrigan, Justice, (313) 256-9628
Marilyn Kelly, Justice, (313) 256-9134
Stephen J. Markman, Justice, (517) 373-9449
Clifford W. Taylor, Justice, (517) 373-8635
Robert P. Young Jr., Justice, (313) 256-9145

State Court Administrative Office
http://www.supremecourt.state.mi.us/scao.htm
Main phone: (517) 373-0130
Main fax: (517) 373-2112

John D. Ferry Jr., State Court Administrator
309 N. Washington Square, Lansing, MI 48933
E-mail: ferryj@jud.state.mi.us

State Law Library
Main phone: (517) 373-0630
Main fax: (517) 373-3915

Sue Adamczak, Director
525 W. Ottawa St., 2nd Fl., Lansing, MI 48933

Legislative and Political Party Information Resources

Senate home page: http://www.state.mi.us/senate/index.htm
House home page: http://www.house.state.mi.us/index.htm
Legislative process: http://www.michiganlegislature.org/Howbill.asp
Michigan Democratic Party: http://www.mi-democrats.com
606 Townsend, Lansing, MI 48933; *Phone:* (517) 371-5410; *Fax:* (517) 371-2056;
E-mail: midemparty@aol.com
Michigan Republican Party: http://www.michgop.org
2121 E. Grand River, Lansing, MI 48912; *Toll free:* (877) 644-6700; *Fax:* (517) 487-0090;
E-mail: elephant_ear@migop.org

Minnesota

State Capitol
St. Paul, MN 55155
Public information: (651) 296-6013
Fax: (651) 296-2089
http://www.state.mn.us

Office of the Governor
http://www.state.mn.us/ebranch/governor
General e-mail: governor@state.mn.us
Main phone: (651) 296-3391
Main fax: (651) 296-2089
Toll free: (800) 657-3717
TTY: (651) 296-0075

Jesse Ventura (REF), Governor
State Capitol, 75 Constitution Ave., #130, St. Paul,
MN 55155
E-mail: jesse.ventura@state.mn.us

**Steven Bosacker, Executive Assistant to the Governor
and Chief of Staff**
State Capitol, 75 Constitution Ave., #130, St. Paul,
MN 55155
(651) 296-0059; *Fax:* (651) 296-2089

John Wodele, Communications Director
130 State Capitol, 75 Constitution Ave., #130, St. Paul,
MN 55155
(651) 296-0001; *Fax:* (651) 296-0056

Rachel Wobschall, Citizen Outreach Director
State Capitol, #130, St. Paul, MN 55155
(651) 296-0028; *Fax:* (651) 296-2089
E-mail: rachel.wobschall@state.mn.us

Amy Gromer, Co-Director, Washington Office
444 N. Capitol St. N.W., #365, Washington, DC 20001
(202) 624-3642; *Fax:* (202) 624-5425

Ms. Bill Ranger, Co-Director, Washington Office
(202) 624-3641

Office of the Lieutenant Governor
http://www.mainserver.state.mn.us/governor/
General e-mail: ltgov@state.mn.us
Main phone: (651) 296-3391
Main fax: (651) 296-0674
TTY: (651) 296-0075

Mae Schunk (REF), Lieutenant Governor
130 State Capitol, #130, St. Paul, MN 55155
(651) 296-0041
E-mail: mae.schunk@state.mn.us

Office of the Secretary of State
http://www.sos.state.mn.us/

State of Minnesota

Capital: St. Paul, since 1849
Founded: 1849, Minnesota Territory created
Statehood: May 11, 1858 (32nd state)
Constitution adopted: 1858
Area: 79,617 sq. mi. (ranks 14th)
Population: 4,725,419 (1998 est.; ranks 20th)
Largest cities: (1998 est.) Minneapolis (351,731); St. Paul (257,284); Bloomington (86,186); Duluth (81,228); Rochester (78,173)
Counties: 87, Most populous: (1998 est.) Hennepin (1,059,669); Ramsey (485,636); Dakota (342,528); Anoka (292,181); Washington (196,486)
U.S. Congress: Rod Grams (R), Paul Wellstone (D); 8 Representatives
Nickname(s): North Star State, Gopher State, Land of 10,000 Lakes
Motto: The North Star
Song: "Hail Minnesota"
Bird: Common loon
Tree: Red (Norway) pine
Flower: Pink and white lady's slipper
State fair: at St. Paul, late Aug.
Former capital(s): None

General e-mail: secretary.state@state.mn.us
Main phone: (651) 296-2803
Main fax: (651) 215-0682
Toll free: (877) 600-VOTE
TTY: (800) 627-3529

Mary Kiffmeyer (R), Secretary of State
State Office Bldg., 100 Constitution Ave., #180, St.
Paul, MN 55155-1299
(651) 296-2079

Office of the Attorney General
http://www.ag.state.mn.us/
General e-mail: attorney.general@state.mn.us
Main phone: (651) 296-6196
Main fax: (651) 297-4193
TTY: (651) 297-7206

Mike Hatch (D), Attorney General
State Capitol, #102, St. Paul, MN 55155

Office of the State Treasurer

http://www.treasurer.state.mn.us/
General e-mail: state.treasurer@state.mn.us
Main phone: (651) 296-7091
Main fax: (651) 296-8615
TTY: (651) 297-5353

Carol C. Johnson (D), Treasurer
Administration Bldg., 50 Sherburne Ave., #303, St. Paul, MN 55155
(651) 282-5032

Office of the State Auditor

http://www.osa.state.mn.us/
General e-mail: stateauditor@osa.state.mn.us
Main phone: (651) 296-2551
Main fax: (651) 296-4755
TTY: (800) 627-3529

Judith H. Dutcher (D), State Auditor
525 Park St., #400, St. Paul, MN 55103
(651) 296-2524

Military Affairs Dept.

http://www.dma.state.mn.us/
General e-mail: buszstad@mn-arng.ngb.army.mil
Main phone: (651) 282-4662
Main fax: (651) 282-4504

Eugene R. Andreotti, Adjutant General
20 W. 12th St., St. Paul, MN 55155-2098
(651) 282-4666; *Fax:* (651) 282-4541

Agencies

Accountancy Board

Main phone: (651) 296-7937
Main fax: (651) 282-2644

Dennis J. Poppenhagen, Executive Secretary
85 E. 7th Pl., #125, St. Paul, MN 55101

Administration Dept.

http://www.admin.state.mn.us/
Main phone: (651) 296-6013
Main fax: (651) 297-7909
TTY: (651) 297-4357

David F. Fisher, Commissioner
Administration Bldg., 50 Sherburne Ave., #200, St. Paul, MN 55155
(651) 296-1424

Administrative Hearings Office

http://www.oah.state.mn.us
General e-mail: oah.apa@state.mn.us
Main phone: (612) 341-7600
Main fax: (612) 349-2665
TTY: (612) 341-7646

Kenneth A. Nickolai, Chief Administrative Law Judge
100 Washington Square, #1700, Minneapolis, MN 55401-2138
(612) 341-7640
E-mail: ken.nickolai@state.mn.us

Agriculture Dept.

http://www.mda.state.mn.us/
General e-mail: webinfo@mda.state.mn.us
Main phone: (651) 297-2200
Main fax: (651) 297-7868
TTY: (651) 297-5353

Eugene (Gene) Hugoson, Commissioner
90 W. Plato Blvd., St. Paul, MN 55107
(651) 297-3219; *Fax:* (651) 257-5522

Animal Health Board

Main phone: (651) 296-2942
Main fax: (651) 296-7417

Thomas J. Hagerty, Executive Director
90 W. Plato Blvd., #119, St. Paul, MN 55107
(651) 296-2942, ext. 16
E-mail: thomas.hagerty@state.mn.us

Architects, Engineers, and Land Surveyors Board

http://www.aelslagid.state.mn.us
Main phone: (651) 296-2388
Main fax: (651) 297-5310
TTY: (800) 627-3529

Doreen B. Frost, Director
85 E. 7th Pl., #160, St. Paul, MN 55101
(651) 297-3096
E-mail: doreen.b.frost@state.mn.us

Arts Board

http://www.arts.state.mn.us/
General e-mail: msab@state.mn.us
Main phone: (651) 215-1600
Main fax: (651) 215-1602
Toll free: (800) 866-2787
TTY: (651) 215-6235

Robert C. Booker, Executive Director
Park Square Court, 400 Sibley St., #200, St. Paul, MN 55101-1928

Campaign Finance and Public Disclosure Board

http://www.cfboard.state.mn.us
General e-mail: cf.board.info@state.mn.us
Main phone: (651) 296-5148
Main fax: (651) 296-1722
Toll free: (800) 657-3889
TTY: (800) 627-3529

Jeanne Olson, Executive Director
Centennial Bldg., 658 Cedar St., #190, St. Paul, MN
 55155-1603
(651) 296-1721

Children, Families, and Learning Dept.
http://cfl.state.mn.us/
General e-mail: cfl@state.mn.us
Main phone: (651) 582-8200
Main fax: (651) 582-8202

Christine Jax, Commissioner
Capitol Square Bldg., 1500 Highway 36 West,
 Roseville, MN 55113-4266
(651) 582-8204

Board of Education
http://cfl.state.mn.us/STATEbrd/statebrd.htm
General e-mail: state.board@state.mn.us
Main phone: (651) 582-8200
Main fax: (651) 582-8202
TTY: (651) 582-8201

Marsha Gronseth, Executive Director
1500 Hwy. 36 West, Roseville, MN 55113-4266
(651) 582-8787

Library Development and Services
http://cfl.state.mn.us/LIBRY/libdev.htm
General e-mail: cfl.library@state.mn.us
Main phone: (651) 582-8722
Main fax: (651) 582-8797

Joyce C. Swonger, Director
1500 Hwy. 36 West, Roseville, MN 55113
E-mail: joyce.swonger@state.mn.us

Commerce Dept.
http://www.commerce.state.mn.us/
General e-mail:
 commerce.commissioner@state.mn.us
Main phone: (651) 296-4026
Main fax: (651) 296-4328
TTY: (651) 296-2860

Steve Minn, Commissioner
133 E. 7th St., St. Paul, MN 55101
(651) 296-6025

Financial Institutions Division
http://www.commerce.state.mn.us/mainfe.htm
General e-mail: insurance@state.mn.us
Main phone: (651) 296-2135

Kevin H. Murphy, Assistant Commissioner
133 E. 7th St., St. Paul, MN 55101

Insurance Division
http://www.commerce.state.mn.us/mainin.htm
General e-mail: insurance@state.mn.us
Main phone: (651) 297-7161

Higher Educational Institutions

Duluth Business University
http://www.dbumn.com
 412 W. Superior St., Duluth, MN 55802
 Main phone: (218) 722-3361

Metropolitan State University
http://www.metrostate.edu
 700 E. 7th St., St. Paul, MN 55106-5000
 Main phone: (651) 772-7600
 Branches: Midway, Minneapolis

Minneapolis College of Art and Design
http://www.mcad.edu
 2501 Stevens Ave. South, Minneapolis, MN 55404
 Main phone: (612) 874-3700

Minnesota State University System
http://www.msus.edu
 P.O. Box 8400, MSU 55, Mankato, MN 56002-8400
 Main phone: (800) 722-0544
 Branches: Bemidji, Mankato, Moorhead, Southwest,
 Winona

St. Cloud State University
http://www.stcloudstate.edu
 720 4th Ave. South, St. Cloud, MN 56301-4498
 Main phone: (320) 255-0121

University of Minnesota
http://www.umn.edu
 220 Morrill Hall, 100 Church St., Minneapolis, MN
 55455
 Main phone: (612) 625-6300
 Branches: Crookston, Duluth, Morris, Twin Cities

Main fax: (651) 296-9434
TTY: (651) 296-2860

Jackie Gardner, Chief Examiner
133 E. 7th St., St. Paul, MN 55101
(651) 297-7030

Licensing Division
http://www.commerce.state.mn.us/
 MainLicensing.htm
General e-mail: licensing@state.mn.us
Main phone: (651) 296-6319
Toll free: (800) 657-3978

Vacant, Director
133 E. 7th St., St. Paul, MN 55101

Tourism Office
http://www.exploreminnesota.com
General e-mail: explore@state.mn.us
Main phone: (651) 296-5029
Toll free: (800) 657-3700

Steve Markuson, Director
500 Metro Square, 120 7th Pl. East, St. Paul, MN
55101-2146

Consumer Protection Division
http://www.ag.state.mn.us/home/consumer/
  default.shtml
Main phone: (651) 296-3353
Main fax: (651) 296-9663
Toll free: (800) 657-3787
TTY: (800) 366-4812

Charles Ferguson, Director
1400 NCL Tower, 445 Minnesota St., #1400, St. Paul,
  MN 55101
(651) 296-6196

Contractors Board
Main phone: (651) 296-6694
Main fax: (651) 296-2029
Toll free: (800) 657-3602
TTY: (651) 296-2860

Jim Allen, Director
133 E. 7th St., St. Paul, MN 55101
(651) 284-3860; *Fax:* (651) 297-3238

Corrections Dept.
http://www.corr.state.mn.us
Main phone: (651) 642-0200
Main fax: (651) 642-0223
TTY: (651) 643-3589

Sheryl Ramstad Hvass, Commissioner
1450 Energy Park Dr., #200, St. Paul, MN 55108-5219
(651) 642-0282; *Fax:* (651) 642-0414
E-mail: sramstadhvass@co.doc.state.mn.us

Community and Juvenile Services Division
http://www.corr.state.mn.us/dccomm.htm
Main phone: (651) 642-0288
Main fax: (651) 603-6768
TTY: (651) 643-3589

Mark Carey, Deputy Commissioner
1450 Energy Park Dr., #200, St. Paul, MN 55108-
  5219
E-mail: mark.carey@co.doc.state.mn.us

Pardons Board
Main phone: (651) 642-0284
Main fax: (651) 603-0148

Jeff Shorba, Secretary
1450 Energy Park Dr., St. Paul, MN 55108
(651) 642-0297
E-mail: jshorba@doc.state.mn.us

Corrections Ombudsman
Main phone: (651) 643-3656
Main fax: (651) 643-2148
TTY: (800) 627-3529

Dave Larson, Ombudsman
1885 University Ave. West, #395, St. Paul, MN 55104

Disability Council
http://www.disability.state.mn.us/
General e-mail: council.disability@state.mn.us
Main phone: (651) 296-6785
Main fax: (651) 296-5935
Toll free: (800) 945-8913

Clell Hemphill, Executive Director
121 E. 7th Pl., #107, St. Paul, MN 55101-2114
(651) 296-1743

Economic Security Dept.
http://www.des.state.mn.us
Main phone: (651) 296-2919
Main fax: (651) 296-0994
TTY: (651) 282-5909

Earl Wilson, Commissioner
390 N. Robert St., St. Paul, MN 55101
(651) 296-3711

Economic Status of Women Commission
http://www.commissions.leg.state.mn.us/lcesw
General e-mail:
  lcesw@commissions.leg.state.mn.us
Main phone: (800) 657-3949
Main fax: (651) 297-3697
Toll free: (800) 657-3949

Aviva Breen, Executive Director
State Office Bldg., #85, St. Paul, MN 55155
(651) 296-8590

Employee Relations Dept.
http://www.doer.state.mn.us/
General e-mail: jobinfo@state.mn.us
Main phone: (651) 297-1184
Main fax: (651) 282-5353
TTY: (651) 215-0175

Wayne Sinomeau, Commissioner Acting
200 Centennial Bldg., 658 Cedar St., 2nd Fl., St. Paul,
  MN 55155
(651) 296-3095; *Fax:* (651) 296-1990
E-mail: wayne.simoneau@state.mn.us

Administrative Services
General e-mail: admin.serv.der@state.mn.us
Main phone: (651) 296-7956

Chris Goodwell, Manager Acting
200 Centennial Bldg., 658 Cedar St., St. Paul, MN
  55155-1603

Environmental Assistance Office
http://www.moea.state.mn.us/
Main phone: (651) 296-3417
Main fax: (651) 215-0246
Toll free: (800) 657-3843

Sherry Enzler, Director
520 Lafayette Rd. North, 2nd Fl., St. Paul, MN 55155-4100
(651) 215-0263
E-mail: sherry.enzler@moea.state.mn.us

Finance Dept.
http://www.finance.state.mn.us
Main phone: (651) 296-5900
Main fax: (651) 296-8685
TTY: (800) 627-3529

Pamela Wheelock, Commissioner
Centennial Office Bldg., 658 Cedar St., #400, St. Paul, MN 55155
(651) 296-5900; *Fax:* (651) 296-8685
E-mail: Pam.Wheelock@state.mn.us

Gambling Control Board
http://www.gcb.state.mn.us/
Main phone: (651) 639-4000
Main fax: (651) 639-4032
TTY: (651) 639-4074

Harold Baltzer, Director
1711 W. Country Rd. B, #300-S, Roseville, MN 55113

Geological Survey
http://160.94.61.144/mgs/
General e-mail: mgs@gold.tc.umn.edu
Main phone: (612) 627-4780
Main fax: (612) 627-4778

David L. Southwick, Director
University of Minnesota, 2642 University Ave. West, St. Paul, MN 55114-1057
(612) 627-4780, ext. 224; *Fax:* (612) 627-4778
E-mail: south002@tc.umn.edu

Health Dept.
http://www.health.state.mn.us/
General e-mail: health@state.mn.us
Main phone: (651) 215-5800
Main fax: (651) 215-5801
TTY: (651) 215-8980
Mailing address: P.O. Box 64882, St. Paul, MN 55164-0882

Jan Malcom, Commissioner
Golden Rule Bldg., 85 E. 7th Pl., #400, St. Paul, MN 55164-0975
(651) 215-5806

Higher Education Facilities Authority
Main phone: (651) 296-4690
Main fax: (651) 297-5751

Vacant, Executive Director
175 E. 5th St., #450, St. Paul, MN 55101-2905

Frequently Called Numbers

Tourism: (651) 296-5029; 1-800-657-3700;
http://www.exploreminnesota.com
Library: (651) 582-8722; http://cfl.state.mn.us/LIBRY/libdev.htm
Board of Education: (651) 582-8200;
http://cfl.state.mn.us/STATEbrd/statebrd.htm
Vital Statistics: (651) 676-5120
Tax/Revenue: (651) 296-3781;
http://www.taxes.state.mn.us
Motor Vehicles: (651) 296-6911;
http://www.dps.state.mn.us/dvs/index.html
State Police/Highway Patrol: (651) 297-3936;
http://www.dps.state.mn.us/patrol/patrol.html
Unemployment: (651) 634-5002;
http://www.des.state.mn.us/ui/
General Election Information: (651) 215-1440, 877-600-8683;
http://www.sos.state.mn.us/election/
Consumer Affairs: (651) 296-3353;
http://www.ag.state.mn.us/home/consumer/default.shtml
Hazardous Materials: (651) 297-8675

Higher Education Services Office
http://www.heso.state.mn.us/
General e-mail: info@heso.state.mn.us
Main phone: (651) 642-0567
Main fax: (651) 642-0675
Toll free: (800) 657-3866

Robert K. Poch, Director
1450 Energy Park Dr., #350, St. Paul, MN 55108
(651) 642-0502; *Fax:* (651) 642-0675
E-mail: poch@heso.state.mn.us

Historical Society
http://www.mnhs.org/
Main phone: (651) 296-6126
Main fax: (651) 297-3343
Toll free: (800) 657-3773
TTY: (651) 282-5201

Nina M. Archabal, Director
345 Kellogg Blvd. West, St. Paul, MN 55102-1906
(651) 296-2747
E-mail: director@mnhs.org

Archives
http://www.mnhs.org/preserve/records/
General e-mail: archives@mnhs.org
Main phone: (651) 297-4502
Main fax: (651) 296-9961

Robert Horton, State Archivist
345 Kellogg Blvd. West, St. Paul, MN 55102-1906
(651) 215-5866; *Fax:* (651) 296-9961
E-mail: robert.horton@mnhs.org

Housing Finance Agency
http://www.mhfa.state.mn.us/
General e-mail: mhfa@state.mn.us
Main phone: (651) 296-7608
Main fax: (651) 296-8139
TTY: (651) 297-2361

Katherine G. (Kit) Hadley, Commissioner
Park Square Court, 400 Sibley St., #300, St. Paul, MN 55101

Human Rights Dept.
http://www.humanrights.state.mn.us
Main phone: (651) 296-5663
Main fax: (651) 296-9042
TTY: (651) 296-1283

Janeen Rosas, Commissioner
Army Corps of Engineers Centre, 190 E. 5th St., #700, St. Paul, MN 55101
(651) 296-5665; *Fax:* (651) 296-9064
E-mail: janeen.rosas@state.mn.us

Human Services Dept.
http://www.dhs.state.mn.us/
Main phone: (651) 296-6117
Main fax: (651) 296-6244
TTY: (651) 296-5705

Michael O'Keefe, Commissioner
Human Services Bldg., 444 Lafayette Rd., St. Paul, MN 55155
(651) 296-2701; *Fax:* (651) 296-5864

Aging Initiative
http://www.dhs.state.mn.us/agingint/default.htm

Boards and Licensing

Accountancy, (651) 296-7937
Architects, Engineers, and Land Surveyors, (651) 296-2388,
http://www.aelslagid.state.mn.us
Child Care, (651) 296-3971
Contractors, (651) 296-6694
Cosmetology, (651) 642-0489
Medical Examiners, (612) 617-2130,
http://www.bmp.state.mn.us
Nursing, (612) 617-2270,
http://www.nursingboard.state.mn.us
Pharmacy, (612) 617-2201,
http://www.phcybrd.state.mn.us
Real Estate Appraisers, (800) 657-3978

General e-mail: dhs.webmaster@state.mn.us
Main phone: (651) 296-2544
Main fax: (651) 296-6244
TTY: (651) 296-5705

Maria Gomez, Assistant Commissioner
Human Services Bldg., 444 Lafayette Rd., 4-S, St. Paul, MN 55155
(651) 297-3209; *Fax:* (651) 296-2052
E-mail: Maria.Gomez@state.mn.us

Health Care Division
http://www.dhs.state.mn.us/hlthcare/default.htm
Main phone: (651) 282-9921

Mary B. Kennedy, Assistant Commissioner/ Medicaid Director
444 Lafayette Rd., St. Paul, MN 55155
(651) 297-4122

Indian Affairs Council
http://www.indians.state.mn.us/
General e-mail: miac@mail.paulbunyan.net
Main phone: (218) 755-3825
Main fax: (218) 755-3739

Joseph B. Day, Executive Director
1819 Bemidji Ave., Bemidji, MN 56601

Investment Board
http://www.sbi.state.mn.us
Main phone: (651) 296-3328
Main fax: (651) 296-9572

Howard J. Bicker, Executive Director
Capitol Office Bldg., 590 Park St., #200, St. Paul, MN 55103
E-mail: howard.bicker@state.mn.us

Iron Range Resources and Rehabilitation Board
http://www.irrrb.org/
General e-mail: apery@irrrb.org
Main phone: (218) 744-7400
Main fax: (218) 744-7401
Toll free: (800) 765-5043
Mailing address: P.O. Box 441, Eveleth, MN 55734

John Swift, Commissioner
1006 Hwy. 53 South, Eveleth, MN 55734
(218) 744-7400; *Fax:* (218) 744-7401
E-mail: jswift@irrrb.org

Labor and Industry Dept.
http://www.doli.state.mn.us/
General e-mail: dli.commissioner@state.mn.us
Main phone: (651) 296-6107
Main fax: (651) 282-5405
Toll free: (800) 342-5354
TTY: (651) 297-4198

Gretchen Maglich, Commissioner
443 Lafayette Rd. North, St. Paul, MN 55155
(651) 296-2342; *Fax:* (651) 282-5405

Workers Compensation Division

http://www.doli.state.mn.us/workcomp.html
General e-mail: DLI.workcomp@state.mn.us
Main phone: (651) 297-4377
Main fax: (651) 296-9634
Toll free: (800) 342-5354
TTY: (651) 297-4198

Carolyn Ganz, Assistant Commissioner
443 Lafayette Rd. North, St. Paul, MN 55155
(651) 296-6490; *Fax:* (651) 282-5293

Mediation Services Bureau

http://www.bms.state.mn.us/
General e-mail: sdefoe@mediation.state.mn.us
Main phone: (651) 649-5421
Main fax: (651) 643-3013
TTY: (800) 627-3529

Lance Teachworth, Commissioner
1380 Energy Lane, #2, St. Paul, MN 55108
(651) 649-5433
E-mail: lteachworth@mediation.state.mn.us

Medical Examiners Board

http://www.bmp.state.mn.us
Main phone: (612) 617-2130
Main fax: (612) 617-2166
Toll free: (800) 627-3529

Robert Leach, Executive Director
2829 University Ave. S.E., #400, Minneapolis, MN
55414-3246

Natural Resources Dept.

http://www.dnr.state.mn.us
General e-mail: info@dnr.state.mn.us
Main phone: (651) 296-6157
Main fax: (651) 297-3618
Toll free: (888) 646-6367
TTY: (651) 296-5484
Mailing address: P.O. Box 40, St. Paul, MN 55155-
4001

Allen Garber, Commissioner
500 Lafayette Rd., St. Paul, MN 55155-4001
(651) 296-2549; *Fax:* (651) 297-4799
E-mail: allen.garber@dnr.state.mn.us

Fish and Wildlife Division

http://www.dnr.state.mn.us/fish_and_wildlife/
Main phone: (651) 297-1308
Main fax: (651) 297-7272

Roger Holmes, Director
500 Lafayette Rd., St. Paul, MN 55155

Forestry Division

http://www.dnr.state.mn.us/forestry
Main phone: (651) 296-4484
Main fax: (651) 296-5954

Gerald A. Rose, Director
550 Lafayette Rd., St. Paul, MN 55155

Parks and Recreation Division

http://www.dnr.state.mn.us/
parks_and_recreation/
Main phone: (651) 296-9223
Main fax: (651) 297-1157

William Morrissey, Director
550 Lafayette Rd., St. Paul, MN 55155

Waters Central Office

Main phone: (651) 296-4800
Toll free: (888) 646-6367
TTY: (800) 657-3929
Mailing address: Box 32, St. Paul, MN 55155-
4032

Kent Lokkesmoe, Director
500 Lafayette Rd., St. Paul, MN 55155-4032
(651) 296-4810; *Fax:* (651) 296-0445
E-mail: kent.lokkesmoe@dnr.state.mn.us

Nursing Board

http://www.nursingboard.state.mn.us
General e-mail: nursing.board@state.mn.us
Main phone: (612) 617-2270
Main fax: (612) 617-2190
Toll free: (888) 234-2690

Shirley A. Brekken, Executive Director
2829 University Ave. S.E., #500, Minneapolis, MN
55414
(612) 617-2296
E-mail: shirley.brekken@state.mn.us

Pharmacy Board

http://www.phcybrd.state.mn.us
General e-mail: pharmacy.board@state.mn.us
Main phone: (612) 617-2201
Main fax: (612) 617-2212
TTY: (800) 627-3529

David Holmstrom, Director
2829 University Ave. S.E., #530, Minneapolis, MN
55414

Planning Dept., Municipal Boundary Adjustments

General e-mail:
municpal.board@mnplan.state.mn.us
Main phone: (651) 284-3383
Main fax: (651) 284-3545
TTY: (800) 627-3529

Christine M. Scotillo, Executive Director
300 Centennial Office Bldg., 658 Cedar St., St. Paul,
MN 55155
E-mail: christine.scotillo@mnplan.state.mn.us

Pollution Control Agency
http://www.pca.state.mn.us/netscape.shtml
General e-mail: askpca@pca.state.mn.us
Main phone: (651) 296-6300
Main fax: (651) 296-7923
Toll free: (800) 657-3864
TTY: (651) 282-5332

Karen Studders, Commissioner
520 Lafayette Rd. North, 6th Fl., St. Paul, MN 55155-4194
(651) 296-7301; *Fax:* (651) 296-6334
E-mail: karen.studders@pca.state.mn.us

Public Defender's Office
http://www.pubdef.state.mn.us
Main phone: (612) 627-6980
Main fax: (612) 627-7979

John M. Stuart, State Public Defender
2829 University Ave. S.E., #600, Minneapolis, MN 55414
(612) 349-2565; *Fax:* (612) 349-2568

Public Employees Retirement Association
http://www.mnpera.org/
General e-mail: custservice@mnpera.org
Main phone: (651) 296-7460
Main fax: (651) 297-2547
Toll free: (800) 652-9026
TTY: (800) 652-9026

Mary Most Vanek, Executive Director
514 St. Peter St., #200, St. Paul, MN 55102
(651) 296-7489

Public Safety Dept.
http://www.dps.state.mn.us/
Main phone: (651) 296-6642
Main fax: (651) 297-5728
TTY: (651) 282-6555

Charles R. Weaver Jr., Commissioner
North Central Life Tower, 445 Minnesota St., #1000, St. Paul, MN 55101-2156

Alcohol and Gambling Enforcement Division: Alcohol Enforcement Section
http://www.dps.state.mn.us/alcgamb/alcenf/alcenf.html
General e-mail: jenny.richie@state.mn.us
Main phone: (651) 215-6209
Main fax: (651) 297-5259
TTY: (651) 282-6555

Norman Pint, Director (Acting)
444 Cedar St., #133, St. Paul, MN 55101

Driver and Vehicle Services Office
http://www.dps.state.mn.us/dvs/index.html
General e-mail: motor.vehicles@state.mn.us

Main phone: (651) 296-6911
Main fax: (651) 296-3141
TTY: (651) 282-6555

Brian Lamb, Director
445 Minnesota St., #195, St. Paul, MN 55101-5195
(651) 296-4544
E-mail: brian.lamb@state.mn.us

Emergency Management Division
http://www.dem.state.mn.us
General e-mail: dem@state.mn.us
Main phone: (651) 296-2233
Main fax: (651) 296-0459
TTY: (651) 282-6555

Kevin Leuer, Director
444 Cedar St., #223, St. Paul, MN 55101-6223
(651) 296-0450; *Fax:* (651) 296-0459
E-mail: kevin.leuer@state.mn.us

State Fire Marshal Division
http://www.dps.state.mn.us/fmarshal/fmarshal.html
Main phone: (651) 215-0500
Main fax: (651) 215-0541
TTY: (651) 282-6555

Thomas R. Bruce, State Fire Marshal
444 Cedar St., #145, St. Paul, MN 55101

State Patrol Division
http://www.dps.state.mn.us/patrol/patrol.html
Main phone: (651) 297-3936
Main fax: (651) 296-5937

Anne Beers, Chief
N. Central Life Tower, 444 Cedar St., #130, St. Paul, MN 55101
(651) 296-5936

Public Services Dept.
http://www.dpsv.state.mn.us/
Main phone: (651) 296-5120
Main fax: (651) 297-1959
TTY: (651) 297-3067

Steve Minn, Commissioner
Metro Square Office Bldg., 121 E. 7th Pl., #200, St. Paul, MN 55101-2145
(651) 296-6025

Public Utilities Commission
http://www.state.mn.us/ebranch/puc
Main phone: (651) 296-7124
Main fax: (651) 297-7073
Toll free: (800) 657-3782
TTY: (651) 297-1200

Greg Scott, Chair
121 E. 7th Pl., #350, St. Paul, MN 55101-2147
(651) 296-7124

Racing Commission
http://www.mnrace.commission.state.mn.us/
Main phone: (612) 496-7950
Main fax: (612) 496-7954
TTY: (800) 627-3529
Mailing address: P.O. Box 630, Shakopee, MN 55379

Richard Krueger, Executive Director
1100 Canterbury Rd., Shakopee, MN 55379
E-mail: richard.krueger@state.mn.us

Revenue Dept.
http://www.taxes.state.mn.us
Main phone: (651) 296-3781
Main fax: (651) 297-5309
TTY: (651) 297-2196

Matthew G. Smith, Commissioner
600 N. Robert St., St. Paul, MN 55146-7100
(651) 296-3403

State Colleges and Universities
http://www.mnscu.edu
General e-mail: darla.senn@so.mnscu.edu
Main phone: (651) 296-8012
Main fax: (651) 297-2024
Toll free: (888) MNSCU4U
TTY: (651) 282-2660

Morris Anderson, Chancellor
World Trade Center, 30 E. 7th St., #500, St. Paul, MN 55101
(651) 296-7971; *Fax:* (651) 296-3312
E-mail: morris.anderson@so.mnscu.edu

State Fair
http://www.mnstatefair.org/
General e-mail: fairinfo@statefair.gen.mn.us
Main phone: (651) 642-2200
Main fax: (651) 642-2440
TTY: (651) 642-2372

Jerry Hammer, Executive Vice President
1265 Snelling Ave. North, St. Paul, MN 55108
(651) 642-2212; *Fax:* (651) 642-2440
E-mail: jerry.hammer@mnstatefair.org

State Lottery
http://www.lottery.state.mn.us
Main phone: (651) 635-8100
Main fax: (651) 297-7496
TTY: (651) 635-8268

George R. Andersen, Director
2645 Long Lake Rd., Roseville, MN 55113

State Retirement System
http://www.msrs.state.mn.us
General e-mail: msrs@state.mn.us

Main phone: (651) 296-2761
Main fax: (651) 297-5238
Toll free: (800) 657-5757
TTY: (800) 627-3529

David Bergstrom, Executive Director
175 W. Lafayette Rd., #300, St. Paul, MN 55107-1425
(651) 296-1510
E-mail: dave.bergstrom@state.mn.us

Strategic and Long-Range Planning Office
http://www.mnplan.state.mn.us
Main phone: (651) 296-3985
Main fax: (651) 296-3698
TTY: (800) 627-3529

Dean Barkley, Director
Centennial Bldg., 658 Cedar St., #300, St. Paul, MN 55155
(651) 297-2325

Teachers Retirement Association
http://www.tra.state.mn.us/
Main phone: (800) 657-3669
Main fax: (651) 297-5999
TTY: (800) 627-3529

Gary Austin, Executive Director
Gallery Bldg., 17 W. Exchange St., #500, St. Paul, MN 55102
(651) 296-2409

Trade and Economic Development Dept.
http://www.dted.state.mn.us/
General e-mail: dted@state.mn.us
Main phone: (651) 297-1291
Main fax: (651) 296-4772
Toll free: (800) 366-2906
TTY: (651) 282-6142

Gerald Carlson, Commissioner
Metro Square Office Bldg., 121 E. 7th Pl., #500, St. Paul, MN 55101-2146
(651) 296-6424

Transportation Dept.
http://www.dot.state.mn.us/
Main phone: (651) 296-3000
Main fax: (651) 297-3160
TTY: (651) 296-9930

Elwyn Tinklenberg, Commissioner
395 John Ireland Blvd., St. Paul, MN 55155
(651) 297-2930

Aeronautics Office
http://www.dot.state.mn.us/aeronautics/mdot.html
Main phone: (651) 296-8202
Main fax: (651) 297-5643
Toll free: (800) 657-3922

Laws

Sales tax: 6.5%
Income tax: 8.5%
State minimum wage: $5.15; $4.90 for small employers (Federal is $5.15)
Marriage age: 18
First-cousin marriage: Prohibited
Drinking age: 21
State control of liquor sales: No
Blood alcohol for DWI: 0.10%
Driving age: 17
Speed limit: 70 mph
Minimum age to possess handguns: 18
Minimum age to possess rifles, shotguns: None
State lottery: Yes; also Powerball
Casinos: Yes (tribal)
Pari-mutuel betting: Horse racing
Death penalty: No
3 strikes minimum sentence: Life (3rd violent crime) proposed
Hate crimes law: Yes
Gay employment non-discrimination: Yes
Official language(s): None
Term limits: None
Permit to buy handguns: Yes, 7 days to acquire

State laws are complex and subject to change; this information is not intended as legal advice. For an explanation of this information, see p. x.

Raymond J. Rought, Director
222 E. Plato Blvd., St. Paul, MN 55107-1618
(651) 296-8046; *Fax:* (651) 297-5643
E-mail: raymond.rought@dot.state.mn.us

Veterans Affairs Dept.
http://www.mdva.state.mn.us/
Main phone: (651) 296-2562
Main fax: (651) 296-3954

Bernard Russell Melter, Commissioner
Veterans Services Bldg., 2nd Fl., St. Paul, MN 55155
(651) 296-2783
E-mail: bmelter@mdva.state.mn.us

Water and Soil Resources Board
http://www.bwsr.state.mn.us/
Main phone: (651) 296-3767
Main fax: (651) 297-5615
TTY: (800) 627-3529

Kathleen Roer, Chair
1 W. Water St., #200, St. Paul, MN 55107

Minnesota Legislature
State Capitol
St. Paul, MN 55155
General information: (651) 296-8338
http://www.leg.state.mn.us

Senate
Address: State Capitol, 75 Constitution Ave., St. Paul, MN 55155-1606
General information: (651) 296-0504
Fax: (651) 296-6511
TTY: (651) 296-0250
Bill status: (651) 296-2887

Allan H. Spear (DFL), President
State Capitol, 75 Constitution Ave., #120, St. Paul, MN 55155-1606
(651) 296-4191
E-mail: sen.allan.spear@senate.leg.state.mn.us
http://www.senate.leg.state.mn.us/members/sendis60.htm

Roger D. Moe (DFL), Majority Leader
State Capitol, 75 Constitution Ave., #208, St. Paul, MN 55155-1606
(651) 296-2577
E-mail: sen.roger.moe@senate.leg.state.mn.us
http://www.senate.leg.state.mn.us/members/sendis02.htm

Carol Flynn (DFL), Majority Whip
State Capitol, 75 Constitution Ave., #120, St. Paul, MN 55155-1606
(651) 296-4274
E-mail: sen.carol.flynn@senate.leg.state.mn.us
http://www.senate.leg.state.mn.us/members/sendis62.htm

Dick Day (R), Minority Leader
State Office Bldg., 100 Constitution Ave., #147, St. Paul, MN 55155-1606
(651) 296-9457
E-mail: sen.dick.day@senate.leg.state.mn.us
http://www.senate.leg.state.mn.us/members/sendis28.htm

Patrick E. Flahaven, Secretary
State Capitol, 75 Constitution Ave., St. Paul, MN 55155-1606
(651) 296-0271

House
Address: State Office Bldg., 100 Constitution Ave., St. Paul, MN 55155
General information: (651) 296-2146

Fax: (651) 296-1563
TTY: (651) 296-9896
Bill status: (651) 296-6646

Steven A. Sviggum (R), Speaker of the House
State Office Bldg., 100 Constitution Ave., #463, St.
  Paul, MN 55155
(651) 296-2273
E-mail: rep.Steven.Sviggum@house.leg.state.mn.us
http://www.house.leg.state.mn.us/members/28B/
  28B.htm

Tim Pawlenty (R), Majority Leader
State Office Bldg., 100 Constitution Ave., #459, St.
  Paul, MN 55155
(651) 296-4128
E-mail: rep.Tim.Pawlenty@house.leg.state.mn.us
http://www.house.leg.state.mn.us/members/38B/
  38B.htm

Thomas Pugh (DFL), Minority Leader
State Office Bldg., 100 Constitution Ave., #267, St.
  Paul, MN 55155
(651) 296-6828
E-mail: rep.Thomas.Pugh@house.leg.state.mn.us
http://www.house.leg.state.mn.us/members/39A/
  39A.htm

Edward A. Burdick, Chief Clerk
State Office Bldg., 100 Constitution Ave., St. Paul,
  MN 55155
(651) 296-2314

Minnesota Judiciary

Minnesota Judicial Center
25 Constitution Ave.
St. Paul, MN 55155-1500
http://www.courts.state.mn.us

Supreme Court

**Frederick K. Grittner, Clerk of the Appellate Courts
  and Supreme Court Administrator**
Minnesota Judicial Center, 25 Constitution Ave., St.
  Paul, MN 55155-1500
(651) 296-2581; *Fax:* (651) 297-4149

Justices
Composition: 7 justices
Selection Method: nonpartisan election;
  vacancies filled by governor; appointees may
  run for the seat in general election at least one
  year after appointment
Length of term: 6 years

Kathleen Blatz, Chief Justice, (651) 296-3380
Paul H. Anderson, Associate Justice, (651) 296-3314
Russell Anderson, Associate Justice, (651) 296-2484
James H. Gilbert, Associate Justice, (651) 297-5454
Joan Erickson Lancaster, Associate Justice, (651) 296-
  2285
Alan C. Page, Associate Justice, (651) 296-6615
Edward C. Stringer, Associate Justice, (651) 296-4033

Office of Court Administration
Main phone: (651) 296-2474
Main fax: (651) 297-5636

Sue K. Dosal, State Court Administrator
Minnesota Judicial Center, 25 Constitution Ave., St.
  Paul, MN 55155-1500
E-mail: sue.dosal@courts.state.mn.us

State Law Library
http://www.courts.state.mn.us/library/index.html
Main phone: (651) 296-2775
Main fax: (651) 296-6740

Marvin R. Anderson, State Law Librarian
Minnesota Judicial Center, 25 Constitution Ave., St.
  Paul, MN 55155-1500
(651) 297-2084

Legislative and Political Party Information Resources

Senate home page: http://www.senate.leg.state.mn.us
House home page: http://www.house.leg.state.mn.us
Committees: Senate: http://www.senate.leg.state.mn.us/committee/index.htm;
  House: http://www.house.leg.state.mn.us/hinfo/hcomm.htm
Legislative process: http://www.leg.state.mn.us/leg/howbill/htm
Legislative information: http://www.leg.state.mn.us/leg/legis.htm
Minnesota Democratic-Farmer Labor Party: http://www.dfl.org
  352 Wacouta St., St. Paul, MN 55101; *Phone:* (651) 293-1200; *Fax:* (651) 293-0706;
  E-mail: dfl@dfl.org
Minnesota Republican Party: http://www.mngop.com
  480 Cedar St., #560, St. Paul, MN 55101; *Phone:* (651) 222-0022; *Fax:* (651) 224-4122;
  E-mail: info@mngop.com
Minnesota Reform Party: http://www.minnesota.reformparty.org
  113 Monroe Ave., N. Mankato, MN 56003; *Phone:* (507) 387-2657; *Fax:* (507) 387-5089

Mississippi

State Capitol
Jackson, MS 39201
Public information: (601) 359-1000
Fax: (601) 359-3741
http://www.state.ms.us

Office of the Governor
http://www.govoff.state.ms.us/
General e-mail: governor@govoff.state.ms.us
Main phone: (601) 359-3100
Main fax: (601) 359-3741
Toll free: (800) 832-6123
Mailing address: P.O. Box 139, Jackson, MS
39205

Ronnie Musgrove (D), Governor
Walter Sillers Bldg., 550 High St., Jackson, MS 39201
(601) 359-2488
E-mail: mhenry@govoff.state.ms.us

Mark Henry, Chief of Staff
Walter Sillers Bldg., 550 High St., Jackson, MS 39201
(601) 359-3100; *Fax:* (601) 359-3741

**Robbie Wilbur, Communications Director and Press
Secretary**
Walter Sillers Bldg., 550 High St., Jackson, MS 39201
(601) 359-3100; *Fax:* (601) 359-3741

Debra Stone, Constituent Services Director
Walter Sillers Bldg., 555 High St., Jackson, MS 39201
(601) 359-3150; *Fax:* (601) 359-3741

Office of the Lieutenant Governor
http://www.ls.state.ms.us/ltgov/index.htm
General e-mail: ltgov@mail.senate.state.ms.us
Main phone: (601) 359-3200
Main fax: (601) 359-3935
Mailing address: P.O. Box 1018, Jackson, MS
39215-1018

Amy Tuck (D), Lieutenant Governor
New Capitol Bldg., 400 High St., 3rd Fl., Jackson, MS
39201
E-mail: atuck@mail.senate.state.ms.us

Office of the Secretary of State
http://www.sos.state.ms.us/
General e-mail: admin@sos.state.ms.us
Main phone: (601) 359-1350
Main fax: (601) 359-1499
Toll free: (800) 256-3494
Mailing address: P.O. Box 136, Jackson, MS
39205

State of Mississippi

Capital: Jackson,
  since 1821
Founded: 1798, Mississippi
  Territory created from Southwest Territory
Statehood: December 10, 1817 (20th state)
Constitution adopted: 1890
Area: 46,914 sq. mi. (ranks 31st)
Population: 2,752,092 (1998 est.; ranks 31st)
Largest cities: (1998 est.) Jackson (188,419);
  Gulfport (64,762); Hattiesburg (48,806);
  Biloxi (47,316); Greenville (42,042)
Counties: 82, Most populous: (1998 est.)
  Hinds (247,144); Harrison (177,981);
  Jackson (130,910); Rankin (109,613); De
  Soto (96,897)
U.S. Congress: Thad Cochran (R), Trent Lott
  (R); 5 Representatives
Nickname(s): Magnolia State
Motto: By valor and arms
Song: "Go, Mississippi"
Bird: Mockingbird
Tree: Magnolia
Flower: Magnolia
State fair: at Jackson, early to mid-Oct.
Former capital(s): Natchez, Washington

Eric C. Clark (D), Secretary of State
401 Mississippi St., Jackson, MS 39205-0136
(601) 359-6338

Office of the Attorney General
http://www.ago.state.ms.us/
General e-mail: msago1@ago.state.ms.us
Main phone: (601) 359-3680
Main fax: (601) 359-3796
Toll free: (800) 281-4418
Mailing address: P.O. Box 220, Jackson, MS
39205

Mike Moore (D), Attorney General
450 High St., Jackson, MS 39201
(601) 359-3692; *Fax:* (601) 359-4441

Office of the State Treasurer
http://www.treasury.state.ms.us
Main phone: (601) 359-3600
Main fax: (601) 359-2001

Mailing address: P.O. Box 138, Jackson, MS 39205

Marshall G. Bennett (D), State Treasurer
550 High St., #404, Jackson, MS 39201
E-mail: mbennett@treas.state.ms.us

Office of the State Auditor
http://www.osa.state.ms.us
General e-mail: auditor@osa.state.ms.us
Main phone: (601) 364-2888
Main fax: (601) 364-2828
Toll free: (800) 321-1275
Mailing address: P.O. Box 956, Jackson, MS 39205-0956

Phil Bryant (R), State Auditor
3750 I-55 N. Frontage Rd., Jackson, MS 39211

Agencies

Agriculture and Commerce Dept.
http://www.mdac.state.ms.us
Main phone: (601) 359-1100
Main fax: (601) 354-6290
Toll free: (800) 551-1830

Lester Spell Jr., Commissioner
121 N. Jackson St., Jackson, MS 39201
Fax: (601) 354-7710

Architecture Board
http://www.archbd.state.ms.us/
General e-mail: msboa@archbd.state.ms.us
Main phone: (888) 272-2627
Main fax: (601) 359-6011

Karen L. Owen, Executive Director
239 N. Lamar St., #502, Jackson, MS 39201-1311
(601) 359-6020

Archives and History Dept.
http://www.mdah.state.ms.us
Main phone: (601) 359-6850
Main fax: (601) 359-6975
Mailing address: P.O. Box 571, Jackson, MS 39205

Elbert Riley Hilliard, Director
100 S. State St., Jackson, MS 39201

Historic Preservation Office
http://www.mdah.state.ms.us/hpres/
  hprestxt.html
Main phone: (601) 359-6940
Main fax: (601) 359-6955
Mailing address: P.O. Box 571, Jackson, MS 39205

Kenneth H. P'Pool, Director
618 E. Pearl St., Depot Bldg., Jackson, MS 39201

Army and Air National Guard
http://www.ngms.state.ms.us/
Main phone: (601) 313-6271
Main fax: (601) 313-6251
Mailing address: P.O. Box 5027, Jackson, MS 39296-5027

James Hobart Garner, Adjutant General
1410 Riverside Dr., Jackson, MS 39216
(601) 313-6232
E-mail: garnerj@ms-arng.ngb.army.mil

Arts Commission
http://www.arts.state.ms.us
Main phone: (601) 359-6030
Main fax: (601) 359-6008
TTY: (800) 582-2233

Betsy Bradley, Executive Director
239 N. Lamar St., #207, Jackson, MS 39201
E-mail: bradley@arts.state.ms.us

Banking and Consumer Finance Dept.
http://www.dbcf.state.ms.us
Main phone: (601) 359-1031
Main fax: (601) 359-3557
Toll free: (800) 844-2499
Mailing address: P.O. Drawer 23729, Jackson, MS 39255-3729

Ronald G. Parham, Commissioner
550 High St., #304, Jackson, MS 39202
E-mail: rparham@dbcf.state.ms.us

Child Care Board
Main phone: (601) 576-7613
Main fax: (601) 576-7813
Mailing address: P.O. Box 1700, Jackson, MS 39215

Diane Herring, Director
2423 N. State St., Jackson, MS 39215

Community and Economic Development Dept.
http://www.mississippi.org/
Main phone: (601) 359-3797
Main fax: (601) 359-2832
Toll free: (800) 340-3323
Mailing address: P.O. Box 849, Jackson, MS 39205-0849

James Heidel, Director
550 High St., Walter Sillers Bldg., #12, Jackson, MS 39201

Tourism Development Division
http://www.visitmississippi.org
General e-mail: tinquiry@mississippi.org
Main phone: (601) 359-3297
Main fax: (601) 359-5757
Toll free: (800) WARMEST

Higher Educational Institutions

Alcorn State University
http://www.alcorn.edu
1000 ASU Dr., Alcorn State, MS 39096-7500
Main phone: (601) 877-6147

Delta State University
http://www.deltast.edu
Kethley 107, Cleveland, MS 38733-0001
Main phone: (601) 846-4018

Jackson State University
http://www.jsums.edu
1400 Lynch St., Jackson, MS 39217
Main phone: (800) 848-6817

Mississippi State University
http://www.msstate.edu
P.O. Box 5325, Mississippi State, MS 39762
Main phone: (662) 325-2323

Mississippi University for Women
http://www.muw.edu
P.O. Box 1613, Columbus, MS 39701-9998
Main phone: (667) 329-7106

University of Mississippi
http://www.olemiss.edu
University, MS 38677-9702
Main phone: (662) 915-7226
Branches: Jackson, Southaven, Tulepo

University of Southern Mississippi
http://www.usm.edu
Box 5166, Hattiesburg, MS 39406-5166
Main phone: (601) 266-5000
Branches: Gulf Coast, Marine Sciences Institute, Stennis Space Center

---

Mailing address: P.O. Box 849, Jackson, MS 39205-0849

George Milam, Director
550 High St., Walter Sillers Bldg., #1100, Jackson, MS 39201

Community and Junior Colleges Board
http://www.sbcjc.cc.ms.us/
General e-mail: info@sbcjc.cc.ms.us
Main phone: (601) 982-6518
Main fax: (601) 982-6363

Olon E. Ray, Executive Director
3825 Ridgewood Rd., #630, Jackson, MS 39211
(601) 982-6684; *Fax:* (601) 982-6363

Consumer Protection
http://www.ago.state.ms.us/consprot.htm
Main phone: (601) 359-4230
Main fax: (601) 359-4231

Toll free: (800) 281-4418
Mailing address: P.O. Box 22947, Jackson, MS 39225-2947

Mike Moore, Attorney General
802 N. State St., #303, Jackson, MS 39202
(601) 359-3692; *Fax:* (601) 359-3441

Contractors Board
http://www.msboc.com
Main phone: (601) 354-6161
Main fax: (601) 354-6161
Toll free: (800) 880-6161

Norman Brooks, Executive Director
2001 Airport Rd., #101, Jackson, MS 39208
E-mail: norman@mail.msboc.state.ms

Corrections Dept.
http://www.mdoc.state.ms.us
Main phone: (601) 359-5608
Main fax: (601) 359-5624

James Anderson, Commissioner
723 N. President St., 2nd Fl., Jackson, MS 39202-3097
(601) 359-5680

Cosmetology Board
Main phone: (601) 987-6837
Main fax: (601) 987-6840

Nelda Luckett, Executive Director
3000 Old Canton Rd., #112, Jackson, MS 39296
(601) 987-6837, ext. 112

Developmental Disabilities Council
Main phone: (601) 359-1270
Main fax: (601) 359-5330

Edwin Butler, Executive Director
Robert E. Lee Bldg., 239 N. Lamar St., #1101, Jackson, MS 39201

Economic and Community Development Dept.
http://www.mississippi.org/
Main phone: (601) 359-3449
Main fax: (601) 359-3613
Mailing address: P.O. Box 849, Jackson, MS 39205

James B. Heidel, Executive Director
Walter Sillers Bldg., Jackson, MS 39205
E-mail: heidel@mississippi.org

Education Dept.
http://www.mde.k12.ms.us/
General e-mail: mdek12@state.ms.us
Main phone: (601) 359-3513
Main fax: (601) 359-2326
Mailing address: P.O. Box 771, Jackson, MS 39205

Richard Thompson, State Superintendent
359 North West St., #365, Jackson, MS 39201
(601) 359-1750; *Fax:* (601) 359-3242
E-mail: rthompson@mde.k12.ms.us

Board of Education
http://www.mde.k12.ms.us/sbe.htm
Main phone: (601) 948-6882
Main fax: (601) 948-6902
Mailing address: P.O. Box 16526, Jackson, MS 39236

Rowan Taylor, Chair
359 North West St., Jackson, MS 39201

School for the Blind
http://www.mde.k12.ms.us/odss
Main phone: (601) 984-8203
TTY: (601) 984-8200

Rosie Thompson, Superintendent
1252 Eastover Dr., Jackson, MS 39211

School for the Deaf
http://www2.mde.k12.ms.us/msd
Main phone: (601) 984-8000
Main fax: (601) 984-8063
TTY: (601) 984-3934

John P. Keith, Superintendent
1253 Eastover Dr., #5, Jackson, MS 39211
(601) 984-8001
E-mail: jkeith@mde.k12.ms.us

Educational Network
http://etv.state.ms.us
Main phone: (601) 982-6565
Main fax: (601) 982-6746

Larry Miller, Executive Director
3825 Ridgewood Rd., Jackson, MS 39211
E-mail: lmiller@etv.state.ms.us

Emergency Management Agency
http://www.memaorg.com
Main phone: (601) 352-9100
Main fax: (601) 352-8314
Toll free: (800) 445-6362
TTY: (800) 445-6362
Mailing address: P.O. Box 4501, Jackson, MS 39296-4501

J. E. Maher, Executive Director
1410 Riverside Dr., Jackson, MS 39202
E-mail: maher@memaorg.com

Employment Security Commission
http://www.mesc.state.ms.us
General e-mail: webmaster@mesc.state.ms.us
Main phone: (601) 354-8711
Main fax: (601) 961-7405

Mailing address: P.O. Box 1699, Jackson, MS 39215-1699

Thomas E. Lord, Executive Director
1520 W. Capitol St., Jackson, MS 39203
(601) 961-7400
E-mail: tlord@mesc.state.ms.us

Engineers and Land Surveyors Board
http://www.pepls.state.ms.us
General e-mail: information@pepls.state.ms.us
Main phone: (601) 359-6160
Main fax: (601) 359-6159
Mailing address: P.O. Box 3, Jackson, MS 39205

Rosemary Brister, Executive Director
239 N. Lamar St., #501, Jackson, MS 39201

Environmental Quality Dept.
http://www.deq.state.ms.us
General e-mail: kent_young@deq.state.ms.us
Main phone: (601) 961-5650
Main fax: (601) 354-6965

Charles Chisolm, Executive Director (Acting)
Hwy. 80, Jackson, MS 39289
(601) 961-5000; *Fax:* (601) 961-5794
E-mail: charles_chisolm.deq.state.ms.us

Geology Office
http://www.deq.state.ms.us/mewweb/
   homepages.nsf
Main phone: (601) 961-5500
Main fax: (601) 961-5521
Mailing address: P.O. Box 20307, Jackson, MS 39289-1307

S. Cragin Knox, State Geologist
Southport Center, 2380 Hwy. 80 West, Jackson, MS 39204
(601) 961-5502
E-mail: cragin_knox@deq.state.ms.us

Pollution Control Office
http://www.deq.state.ms.us/newweb/
   homepages.nsf
Main phone: (601) 961-5171
Main fax: (601) 354-6612
Mailing address: P.O. Box 10385, Jackson, MS 39289-0385

Charles Chisolm, Chief
2380 Hwy. 80 West, Jackson, MS 39204
(601) 961-5100
E-mail: Charles_Chisolm@deq.state.ms.us

Ethics Commission
http://www.ethics.state.ms.us
General e-mail: cherylh@ethics.state.ms.us
Main phone: (601) 359-1285
Main fax: (601) 354-6253

Mailing address: P.O. Box 22746, Jackson, MS
39225-2746

Ronald E. Crowe, Executive Director
146 E. Amite St., #103, Jackson, MS 39201
E-mail: rcrowe@ethics.state.ms.us

Finance and Administration Dept.
http://www.dfa.state.ms.us/
Main phone: (601) 359-3402
Main fax: (601) 359-2405
Mailing address: P.O. Box 267, Jackson, MS
39205

**Edward L. Ranck, Executive Director and State
Comptroller**
550 High St., Jackson, MS 39205

Forestry Commission
http://www.mfc.state.ms.us
Main phone: (601) 359-1386
Main fax: (601) 359-1349

James L. Sledge Jr., State Forester
301 N. Lamar St., #300, Jackson, MS 39201
(601) 359-2801; *Fax:* (601) 359-1349

Gaming Commission
http://www.msgaming.com/
Main phone: (601) 351-2800
Main fax: (601) 351-2810

Toll free: (800) 504-7529
Mailing address: P.O. Box 23577, Jackson, MS
39225

Charles Patton, Executive Director
202 E. Pearl St., Jackson, MS 39201

Health Dept.
http://www.msdh.state.ms.us/
Main phone: (601) 576-7400
Main fax: (601) 576-7364
Mailing address: P.O. Box 1700, Jackson, MS
39215-1700

Ed Thompson, State Health Officer
2423 N. State St., #121, Jackson, MS 39216
(601) 576-7634; *Fax:* (601) 576-7931

Highway Patrol
http://www.dps.state.ms.us/mhp/mhp.html
Main phone: (601) 987-1500
Main fax: (601) 987-1498

Tom Ward, Director
1900 E. Woodrow Wilson, Jackson, MS 39216

Home Corporation
Main phone: (601) 354-6062
Main fax: (601) 354-7076
Toll free: (800) 544-6960
Mailing address: P.O. Box 23369, Jackson, MS
39225-3369

Dianne Bolen, Executive Officer
840 E. River Pl., #605, Jackson, MS 39201
(601) 354-6311

Human Services Dept.
http://www.mdhs.state.ms.us/
Main phone: (601) 359-4500
Main fax: (601) 359-4477
Mailing address: P.O. Box 352, Jackson, MS
39205-0352

Donald R. Taylor, Executive Director
750 N. State St., Jackson, MS 39205-0352
(601) 359-4480

Aging and Adult Services Division
http://www.mdhs.state.ms.us/aas.html
Main phone: (601) 359-4929
Main fax: (601) 359-4370
Toll free: (800) 948-3090

Eddie L. Anderson, Director
750 N. State St., #607, Jackson, MS 39202
(601) 359-4925
E-mail: elanderson@mdhs.state.ms.us

Youth Services Division
http://www.mdhs.state.ms.us/dys.html
Main phone: (601) 359-4972

Main fax: (601) 359-4970
Toll free: (800) 345-6347
Mailing address: P.O. Box 352, Jackson, MS
39202

James Cullider Jr., Director
750 N. State St., Jackson, MS 39202
E-mail: jcullider@mdhs.state.ms.us

Information Technology Services Dept.
http://www.its.state.ms.us/
Main phone: (601) 359-1395
Main fax: (601) 354-6016

David Litchliter, Executive Director
301 N. Lamar St., #508, Jackson, MS 39201-1495
E-mail: litchliter@its.state.ms.us

Insurance Dept.
http://www.doi.state.ms.us
Main phone: (601) 359-3569
Main fax: (601) 359-2474
Mailing address: P.O. Box 79, Jackson, MS
39205-0079

George Dale (D), Commissioner
1804 Walter Sillers Bldg., Jackson, MS 39205-0079
E-mail: georgedale@mid.state.ms.us

State Fire Marshal
http://www.doi.state.ms.us/marsha.html
General e-mail: firemarshal@mid.state.md.us
Main phone: (601) 359-1061
Main fax: (601) 359-1076
Toll free: (888) 648-0877
Mailing address: P.O. Box 79, Jackson, MS
39205

**Millard Mackey, Chief Deputy and Fire
Marshal**
550 High St., #706, Jackson, MS 39201
(601) 359-3569

Library Commission
http://www.mlc.lib.ms.us/
General e-mail: reference@mlc.lib.ms.us
Main phone: (601) 961-4111
Main fax: (601) 354-4181
Toll free: (800) 647-7542
TTY: (601) 354-7081
Mailing address: P.O. Box 10700, Jackson, MS
39289-0700

John A. Pritchard, Executive Director
1221 Ellis Ave., Jackson, MS 39289-0700
(601) 961-4038; *Fax:* (601) 354-6713
E-mail: japritchard@mlc.lib.ms.us

Medicaid Division
http://www.dom.state.ms.us
General e-mail: webmaster@medicaid.state.ms.us

Main phone: (601) 359-6050
Main fax: (601) 359-6048
Toll free: (800) 421-2408

Anna Marie Barnes, Director
239 N. Lamar St., #801, Jackson, MS 39201-1399
(601) 359-6056

Medical Licensure Board
http://www.msbml.state.ms.us/
General e-mail: mboard@msbml.state.ms.us
Main phone: (601) 987-3079
Main fax: (601) 987-4159
Mailing address: P.O. Box 9268, Jackson, MS
39286-9268

W. Joseph Burnett, Director
2600 Insurance Center Dr., #200-B, Jackson, MS
39216

Mental Health Dept.
http://www.dmh.state.ms.us/
Main phone: (601) 359-1288
Main fax: (601) 359-6295
Toll free: (877) 210-8513
TTY: (601) 359-6230

Albert Randel Hendrix, Executive Director
Robert E. Lee Bldg., 239 N. Lamar St., #1101,
Jackson, MS 39201

Mississippi State University Extension Service
http://www.ext.ms.statedu
Main phone: (601) 325-3036
Main fax: (601) 325-8407

Ronald A. Brown, Director
201 Bost Extension Center, University Blvd., #201,
Mississippi State, MS 39762
E-mail: brown@ext.msstate.edu

Motor Vehicle Commission
http://www.mmvc.state.ms.us
Main phone: (601) 987-3995
Main fax: (601) 987-3997
Mailing address: P.O. Box 16873, Jackson, MS
39236

H. Eagle Day, Executive Director
1755 Lelah Dr., #200, Jackson, MS 39216
(601) 987-4378
E-mail: day@mmvc.state.ms.us

Nursing Board
Main phone: (601) 987-4188
Main fax: (601) 364-4352

Marcia Rachel, Executive Director
1935 Lakeland Dr., Jackson, MS 39216

Oil and Gas Board
http://www.ogb.state.ms.us/

Main phone: (601) 354-7142
Main fax: (601) 354-6873

Walter L. Boone Jr., Director
500 Greymont Ave., Jackson, MS 39202
(601) 354-7114
E-mail: wboone@ogb.state.ms.us

Parole Board
Main phone: (601) 354-7716
Main fax: (601) 354-7725

Lydia Chassaniol, Chair
201 W. Capitol St., #800, Jackson, MS 39201

Personnel Board
http://www.spb.state.ms.us/
Main phone: (601) 359-2702
Main fax: (601) 359-2729

J. K. Stringer Jr., Director
301 N. Lamar St., #100, Jackson, MS 39201
Fax: (601) 359-2702

Pharmacy Board
http://www.mbp.state.ms.us
Main phone: (601) 354-6750
Main fax: (601) 354-6071
Mailing address: P.O. Box 24507, Jackson, MS 39225-4507

William L. Stevens, Executive Director
625 N. State St., Jackson, MS 39202
E-mail: bstevens@mpb.state.ms.us

Port Authority
http://www.gulfcoast.org/mspa/index.htm
Main phone: (228) 865-4300
Main fax: (228) 865-4307

Boards and Licensing

Accountancy, (601) 354-7320,
http://www.msbpa.state.ms.us
Architects, (888) 272-2627,
http://www.archbd.state.ms.us/
Child Care, (601) 576-7613
Contractors, (601) 354-6161,
http://www.msboc.com
Cosmetology, (601) 987-6837
Engineers and Land Surveyors,
(601) 359-6160, http://www.pepls.state.ms.us
Medical Licensing, (601) 987-3079,
http://www.msbml.state.ms.us/
Nursing, (601) 987-4188
Pharmacy, (601) 354-6750,
http://www.mbp.state.ms.us
Real Estate Appraisers, (601) 987-3969

Mailing address: P.O. Box 40, Gulfport, MS 39502

John K. Rester, President
2310 14th St., #1401, Gulfport, MS 39501

Public Accountancy Board
http://www.msbpa.state.ms.us
General e-mail: email@msbpa.state.ms.us
Main phone: (601) 354-7320
Main fax: (601) 354-7290

David C. Pippin, Chair
653 N. State St., Jackson, MS 39202
(601) 842-6475

Public Employees Retirement System
http://www.pers.state.ms.us/
Main phone: (601) 359-3589
Main fax: (601) 359-2285
Toll free: (800) 444-7377

Frank Ready, Executive Director
429 Mississippi St., Jackson, MS 39201-1005

Public Safety Dept.
http://www.dps.state.ms.us/
Main phone: (601) 987-1212
Main fax: (601) 987-1498
Mailing address: P.O. Box 958, Jackson, MS 39205-0958

Jim Ingram, Commissioner
1900 E. Woodrow Wilson, Jackson, MS 39216
(601) 987-1490

Criminal Information Center
Main phone: (601) 933-2600
Main fax: (601) 933-2676
Mailing address: P.O. Box 958, Jackson, MS 39205-0958

Will Span, Director
3891 Hwy. 468 West, Pearl, MS 39205-0958

Public Service Commission
http://www.mslawyer.com/mpsc/mpsc.html
General e-mail: shirley.bounds@psc.state.ms.us
Main phone: (601) 961-5434
Main fax: (601) 961-5469
Toll free: (800) 356-6428
Mailing address: P.O. Box 1174, Jackson, MS 39215-1174

Nielsen Cochran, Commissioner
Walter Sillers State Office Bldg., 550 High St., 19th
Fl., Jackson, MS 39215
(601) 961-5450; *Fax:* (601) 961-5476

Real Estate Commission
General e-mail: mrec@state.ms.us
Main phone: (601) 987-3969
Main fax: (601) 987-4984

Mailing address: P.O. Box 12685, Jackson, MS 39236-2685

Robert E. Praytor, Administrator
5176 Keele St., Jackson, MS 39206

Rehabilitation Services Dept.
Main phone: (601) 853-5100
Main fax: (601) 853-5205
Mailing address: P.O. Box 1698, Jackson, MS 39215

H. S. McMillan, Executive Director
1281 Hwy. 51 North, Madison, MS 39110
(601) 853-5203

Soil and Water Conservation Commission
Main phone: (601) 354-7645
Main fax: (601) 354-6628
Mailing address: P.O. Box 23005, Jackson, MS 39225

Gale Martin, Executive Director
680 Monroe St., Jackson, MS 39225-3005

State Fair
http://www.mdnc.state.ms.us
Main phone: (601) 961-4000
Main fax: (601) 354-6545
Mailing address: P.O. Box 892, Jackson, MS 39205

Wayne Smith, Director
1207 Mississippi St., Jackson, MS 39202

Tax Commission
http://www.mstc.state.ms.us/
General e-mail: clong@mstc.state.ms.us
Main phone: (601) 923-7000
Main fax: (601) 923-7404
Mailing address: P.O. Box 22828, Jackson, MS 39225

Ed Buelow Jr., Chair and Commissioner
1577 Springridge Rd., Raymond, MS 39154-9602
(601) 923-7400; *Fax:* (601) 923-7423

Alcoholic Beverage Control
http://www.mstc.state.ms.us/index2.htm
Main phone: (601) 856-1301
Main fax: (601) 856-1300
Mailing address: P.O. Box 540, Madison, MS 39110-0540

James Sullivan, Director
1286 Gluckstadt Rd., Madison, MS 39110

Transportation Dept.
http://www.mdot.state.ms.us/
General e-mail: ccox@mdot.state.ms.us
Main phone: (601) 359-7002
Main fax: (601) 359-7110

Mailing address: P.O. Box 1850, Jackson, MS 39215-1850

Kenneth I. Warren, Executive Director
401 North West St., 10th Fl., Jackson, MS 39210
Fax: (601) 359-7050
E-mail: kwarren@mdot.state.ms.us

Intermodal Planning: Aeronautics Division
http://www.mdot.state.ms.us/facts/orgchart/planning_office.htm
General e-mail: ejay@mdot.state.ms.us
Main phone: (601) 359-7850
Main fax: (601) 359-7855
Mailing address: P.O. Box 1850, Jackson, MS 39215-1850

Elton E. Jay, Director
401 North West St., Jackson, MS 39201

Veterans Affairs Board
http://www.vab.state.ms.us/
Main phone: (601) 354-7377
Main fax: (601) 354-7386

Jack Stephens, Executive Director
Standard Life Bldg., 206 W. Pearl St., #1100, Jackson, MS 39201
E-mail: jstephens@vab.state.ms.us

Wildlife, Fisheries, and Parks Dept.
http://www.mdwfp.com/
Main phone: (601) 362-9212
Main fax: (601) 364-2125

Sam Polles, Executive Director
1505 Eastover Dr., Jackson, MS 39211
(601) 432-2400

Parks and Recreation Division
http://www.mdwfp.com/parks.asp
Main phone: (601) 364-2010
Main fax: (601) 364-2147
Toll free: (800) GO-PARKS
Mailing address: P.O. Box 451, Jackson, MS 39205

Latrelle Ashley, Director
2106 N. State St., Jackson, MS 39216
(601) 364-2000; *Fax:* (601) 364-2008

Workers' Compensation Commission
http://www.mwcc.state.ms.us/
Main phone: (601) 987-4200
Main fax: (601) 987-4233
Mailing address: P.O. Box 5300, Jackson, MS 39296-5300

Mike Marsh, Chair
1428 Lakeland Dr., Jackson, MS 39216
(601) 987-4258

Laws

Sales tax: 7%
Income tax: 5%
State minimum wage: None (Federal is $5.15)
Marriage age: 21
First-cousin marriage: Prohibited
Drinking age: 21
State control of liquor sales: Yes
Blood alcohol for DWI: 0.10%
Driving age: 16
Speed limit: 70 mph
Permit to buy handguns: No
Minimum age to possess handguns: None
Minimum age to possess rifles, shotguns: None
State lottery: No
Casinos: Yes (commercial, tribal)
Pari-mutuel betting: No
Death penalty: Yes
3 strikes minimum sentence: Life, no parole (3rd felony, if any was violent)
Hate crimes law: Yes
Gay employment non-discrimination: No
Official language(s): English
Term limits: None

State laws are complex and subject to change; this information is not intended as legal advice. For an explanation of this information, see p. x.

Mississippi Legislature

New Capitol
Jackson, MS 39215-1018
General information: (601) 359-3770
http://www.ls.state.ms.us

Senate

General information: (601) 359-3267
Fax: (601) 359-3935
Bill status: (601) 359-3719

Amy Tuck (D), President
New Capitol Bldg., 400 High St., 3rd Fl., Jackson, MS 39201
(601) 359-3200; *Fax:* (601) 359-3935
E-mail: atuck@mail.senate.state.ms.us
http://www.ls.state.ms.us/ltgov/index.htm

Thomas Arlin (Tommy) Gollott (D), President Pro Tempore
New Capitol, P.O. Box 1018, #307-NC, Jackson, MS 39215-1018
(601) 359-3209
E-mail: tgollott@mail.senate.state.ms.us
http://www.ls.state.ms.us/senate/gollott.htm

Amy Tuck, Secretary
New Capitol, P.O. Box 1018, Jackson, MS 39215-1018
(601) 359-3202

House

General information: (601) 359-3358
Fax: (601) 359-3728

Timothy Alan (Tim) Ford (D), Speaker of the House
New Capitol, P.O. Box 1018, #306, Jackson, MS 39215-1018
(601) 359-3300; *Fax:* (601) 359-2969
http://www.ls.state.ms.us/house/ford.htm

Robert G. Clark Jr. (Independent), Speaker Pro Tempore
New Capitol, P.O. Box 1018, #302-A, Jackson, MS 39215-1018
(601) 359-3304; *Fax:* (601) 359-3728
http://www.ls.state.ms.us/house/clark.htm

Charles J. Jackson Jr., Clerk
New Capitol, P.O. Box 1018, Jackson, MS 39215-1018
(601) 359-3360

Mississippi Judiciary

Carroll Gartin Justice Bldg.
450 High St.
Jackson, MS 39201

Supreme Court

http://www.mssc.state.ms.us

Charlotte Williams, Clerk
Carroll Gartin Justice Bldg., 450 High St., Jackson, MS 39201
(601) 359-3694; *Fax:* (601) 359-2407
E-mail: sctclerk@mssc.state.ms.us

Justices

Composition: 9 justices
Selection Method: general election; vacancies filled by gubernatorial appointment; appointees can run for seat in first general election held more than 9 months after appointment
Length of term: 8 years

Lenore L. Prather, Chief Justice, (601) 359-3697
Edwin Lloyd Pittman, Presiding Justice, (601) 359-3697

Michael Sullivan, Presiding Justice, (601) 359-3697
Fred L. Banks Jr., Associate Justice, (601) 359-3697
Kay B. Cobb, Associate Justice, (601) 359-3697
Chuck R. McRae, Associate Justice, (601) 359-2184
Michael P. Mills, Associate Justice, (601) 359-2102
James W. Smith Jr., Associate Justice, (601) 359-3697
William L. Waller Jr., Associate Justice, (601) 359-2139

Administrative Office of Courts
http://www.mssc.state.ms.us/AOC/default.asp
Main phone: (601) 359-2182
Main fax: (601) 359-2443

Stephen J. Kirchmayr Jr., Supreme Court Administrator
Carroll Gartin Justice Bldg., 450 High St., Jackson, MS 39201
E-mail: skirchmayr@mssc.state.ms.us

State Law Library
Main phone: (601) 359-3672
Main fax: (601) 359-2912

Charlie Pearce, State Law Librarian
Carroll Gartin Justice Bldg., 450 High St., Jackson, MS 39201
E-mail: cpearce@mssc.state.ms.us

Legislative and Political Party Information Resources

Senate home page: http://www.ls.state.ms.us/senate.htm
House home page: http://www.ls.state.ms.us/house.htm
Committees: Senate: http://billstatus.ls.state.ms.us/2000/s_cmtmemb.htm;
  House: http://billstatus.ls.state.ms.us/2000/h_cmtmemb.htm
Legislative process: http://www.ls.state.ms.us/htms/billlaw/htm
Current session information: http://billstatus.ls.state.ms.us/default.htm
Mississippi Democratic Party
  832 N. Congress St., P.O. Box 1583, Jackson, MS 39215; *Phone:* (601) 969-2913;
  E-mail: msdemparty@aol.com
Mississippi Republican Party: http://www.msgop.org
  415 Yazoo St., P.O. Box 60, Jackson, MS 39205-0060; *Phone:* (601) 948-5191;
  E-mail: party@msgop.org

Missouri

State Capitol
Jefferson City, MO 65102
Public information: (573) 751-2000
Fax: (573) 751-1495
http://www.state.mo.us

Office of the Governor
http://www.gov.state.mo.us
General e-mail: constit@mail.state.mo.us
Main phone: (573) 751-3222
Main fax: (573) 751-1495
Mailing address: P.O. Box 720, Jefferson City, MO 65102

Mel Carnahan (D), Governor
State Capitol, #216, Jefferson City, MO 65102

Chris Sifford, Chief of Staff
State Capitol, #216, Jefferson City, MO 65102
(573) 751-4971; *Fax:* (573) 751-4458
E-mail: siffoc@mail.gov.state.mo.us

Jerry Nachtigal, Communications Director
State Capitol, 201 W. Capitol, #216, Jefferson City, MO 65101
(573) 751-3222; *Fax:* (573) 751-4458

Skip Schrock, Constituent Services Director
State Capitol, #216, Jefferson City, MO 65102
(573) 751-3222; *Fax:* (573) 751-8099
E-mail: schros@mail.gov.state.mo.us

Susan Harris, Director, Washington Office
400 N. Capital St. N.W., #376, Washington, DC 20001
(202) 624-7720; *Fax:* (202) 624-5855
E-mail: sharris@sso.org

Office of the Lieutenant Governor
http://www.ltgov.state.mo.us/homepg.htm
Main phone: (573) 751-4727
Main fax: (573) 751-9422

Roger B. Wilson (D), Lieutenant Governor
State Capitol, #121, Jefferson City, MO 65101
E-mail: wilson@mail.state.mo.us

Office of the Secretary of State
http://mosl.sos.state.mo.us
General e-mail: sosmain@mail.sos.state.mo.us
Main phone: (573) 751-4936
Main fax: (573) 526-4903
Mailing address: P.O. Box 1767, Jefferson City, MO 65102

Rebecca McDowell Cook (D), Secretary of State
600 W. Main St., Jefferson City, MO 65102
(573) 751-4595

State of Missouri

Capital: Jefferson City, since 1826
Founded: 1812, Missouri Territory created from Louisiana Territory
Statehood: August 10, 1821 (24th state)
Constitution adopted: 1945
Area: 68,898 sq. mi. (ranks 18th)
Population: 5,438,559 (1998 est.; ranks 16th)
Largest cities: (1998 est.) Kansas City (441,574); St. Louis (339,316); Springfield (142,898); Independence (116,832); Columbia (78,915)
Counties: 114, Most populous: (1998 est.) St. Louis (998,696); Jackson (654,986); St. Charles (272,353); Greene (226,758); Jefferson (195,675)
U.S. Congress: John Ashcroft (R), Christopher S. Bond (R); 9 Representatives
Nickname(s): Show-me State
Motto: The welfare of the people shall be the supreme law
Song: "Missouri Waltz"
Bird: Bluebird
Tree: Flowering dogwood
Flower: Hawthorn
State fair: at Sedalia, mid-Aug.
Former capital(s): St. Louis, St. Charles

Office of the Attorney General
http://www.ago.state.mo.us/index.htm
Main phone: (573) 751-3321
Main fax: (573) 751-0774
Toll free: (800) 392-8222
TTY: (800) 729-8668
Mailing address: P.O. Box 899, Jefferson City, MO 65102

Jeremiah W. (Jay) Nixon (D), Attorney General
Supreme Court Bldg., 207 W. High St., Jefferson City, MO 65101

Office of the State Treasurer
http://www.sto.state.mo.us/
Main phone: (573) 751-2411
Main fax: (573) 751-9443

Mailing address: P.O. Box 210, Jefferson City, MO 65102

Bob Holden (D), State Treasurer
State Capitol, #229, Jefferson City, MO 65102
(573) 751-4123

Office of the State Auditor
http://www.auditor.state.mo.us
General e-mail: moaudit@mail.auditor.state.mo.us
Main phone: (573) 751-4824
Main fax: (573) 751-6539
TTY: (800) 374-8597
Mailing address: P.O. Box 869, Jefferson City, MO 65102

Claire C. McCaskill (D), State Auditor
State Capitol, #224, Jefferson City, MO 65102
E-mail: claire@mail.auditor.state.mo.us

Adjutant General's Office (National Guard)
http://www.mong.org
Main phone: (573) 638-9500
Main fax: (573) 638-9929
Toll free: (800) 526-6664

John Havens, Adjutant General
2302 Militia Dr., Jefferson City, MO 65101-1203

Agencies

Accountancy Board
http://www.ecodev.state.mo.us/pr/account
General e-mail: BOA@mail.state.mo.us
Main phone: (573) 751-0012
Main fax: (573) 751-0890
Mailing address: P.O. Box 613, Jefferson City, MO 65101

Ken L. Bishop III, Executive Director
3605 Missouri Blvd., #340, Jefferson City, MO 65101
E-mail: kbishop@mail.state.mo.us

Administration Office
http://www.oa.state.mo.us/
General e-mail: murraj@mail.oa.state.mo.us
Main phone: (573) 751-3311
Main fax: (573) 751-1212
TTY: (800) 735-2966
Mailing address: P.O. Box 809, Jefferson City, MO 65102

Richard A. Hanson, Commissioner
State Capitol, #125, Jefferson City, MO 65102
(573) 751-1851; *Fax:* (573) 751-1212
E-mail: hanson@mail.oa.state.mo.us

Ethics Commission
http://www.moethics.state.mo.us

Main phone: (573) 751-2020
Main fax: (573) 526-4506
Toll free: (800) 392-8660
Mailing address: P.O. Box 1254, Jefferson City, MO 65102

Charles G. Lamb, Executive Director
221 Metro Dr., Jefferson City, MO 65109

Personnel Division
http://www.gov.state.mo.us/boards/cgi/boards.cgi
General e-mail: Persmail@mail.state.mo.us
Main phone: (573) 751-4162
Main fax: (573) 751-8641
TTY: (573) 526-4488
Mailing address: P.O. Box 388, Jefferson City, MO 65102-0388

H. Lee Capps, Director
430 Truman Bldg., 301 W. High St., Jefferson City, MO 65101
(573) 751-3053; *Fax:* (573) 522-8462

Agriculture Dept.
http://www.mda.state.mo.us
General e-mail: sklein@mail.state.mo.us
Main phone: (573) 751-4211
Main fax: (573) 751-1784
Mailing address: P.O. Box 630, Jefferson City, MO 65102

John L. Saunders, Director
1616 Missouri Blvd., Jefferson City, MO 65102
(573) 751-3359

Architects, Engineers, and Land Surveyors Board
http://www.gov.state.mo.us/pr/moapels
General e-mail: moapels@mail.state.mo.us
Main phone: (573) 751-0047
Main fax: (573) 751-8046
Mailing address: P.O. Box 184, Jefferson City, MO 65102

Brenda Crain, Executive Director
3605 Missouri Blvd., #380, Jefferson City, MO 65102
(573) 751-0800
E-mail: bcrain@mail.state.mo.us

Archives
http://www.mosl.sos.state.mo.us/rec-man/arch.html
Main phone: (573) 751-4717
Main fax: (573) 526-7333
Mailing address: P.O. Box 1747, Jefferson City, MO 65102

Kenneth H. Winn, Director
600 W. Main St., Jefferson City, MO 65101
E-mail: kwinn1@sos.mail.state.mo.us

Higher Educational Institutions

Central Missouri State University
http://www.cmsu.edu
Administration Bldg. 104, Warrensburg, MO 64093
Main phone: (800) 956-0177

Lincoln University
http://www.lincolnu.edu
820 Chestnut St., Jefferson City, MO 65101
Main phone: (573) 681-5599

Missouri Southern State College
http://www.mssc.edu
3950 E. Newman Rd., Joplin, MO 64801-1595
Main phone: (417) 782-6772

Missouri Western State College
http://www.mwsc.edu
4525 Downs Dr., St. Joseph, MO 64507
Main phone: (800) 662-7041

Northwest Missouri State University
http://www.nwmissouri.edu
800 University Dr., Maryville, MO 64468-6001
Main phone: (660) 562-1562

Southeast Missouri State University
http://www.semo.edu
1 University Plaza, Cape Girardeau, MO 63701
Main phone: (573) 651-2000

Southwest Missouri State University
http://www.smsu.edu
901 S. National Ave., Springfield, MO 65804
Main phone: (417) 836-5517
Branches: Mountain Grove, West Plains

Truman State University
http://www.truman.edu
100 E. Normal St., Kirksville, MO 63501
Main phone: (660) 785-4000

University of Missouri
http://www.system.missouri.edu
225 Jesse Hall, Columbia, MO 65211
Main phone: (573) 882-7786
Branches: Columbia, Kansas City, Rolla, St. Louis

Conservation Dept.
http://www.conservation.state.mo.us
General e-mail:
internet@mail.conservation.state.mo.us
Main phone: (573) 751-4115
Main fax: (573) 751-4467
TTY: (800) 735-2966
Mailing address: P.O. Box 180, Jefferson City, MO 65102-0180

Jerry M. Conley, Director
2901 W. Truman Blvd., Jefferson City, MO 65102-0180
(573) 751-4115, ext. 212

Fisheries Division
Main phone: (573) 751-4115, ext. 159
Main fax: (573) 526-4047
Toll free: (800) 669-3787
TTY: (800) 735-2966
Mailing address: P.O. Box 180, Jefferson City, MO 65102-0180

> **Norman P. Stucky, Administrator**
> 2901 W. Truman Blvd., Jefferson City, MO 65109
> *E-mail:* stuckn@mail.conservation.state.mo.us

Forestry Division
Main phone: (573) 751-4115, ext. 116
Main fax: (573) 526-6670
Toll free: (800) 669-3787
TTY: (800) 735-2966
Mailing address: P.O. Box 180, Jefferson City, MO 65102-0180

> **Robert Krepps, Administrator**
> 2901 W. Truman Blvd., Jefferson City, MO 65109
> *E-mail:* kreppr@mail.conservation.state.mo.us

Wildlife Division
Main phone: (573) 751-4115, ext. 149
Main fax: (573) 526-4663
Mailing address: P.O. Box 180, Jefferson City, MO 65102-0180

> **Oliver A. Torgerson, Administrator**
> 2901 W. Truman Blvd., Jefferson City, MO 65109
> *E-mail:* torgeo@mail.conservation.state.mo.us

Consumer Protection Division
http://www.agocp.moago.org
Main phone: (573) 751-3321
Main fax: (573) 751-0774
Toll free: (800) 392-8222
TTY: (800) 729-8668
Mailing address: P.O. Box 899, Jefferson City, MO 65102

> **Douglas Ommen, Chief Counsel**
> Supreme Court Bldg., 1530 Rax Court, Jefferson City, MO 65109

Corrections Dept.
http://www.corrections.state.mo.us/
Main phone: (573) 751-2389
Main fax: (573) 751-4099
TTY: (573) 751-5984
Mailing address: P.O. Box 236, Jefferson City, MO 65102

Dora B. Schriro, Director
2729 Plaza Dr., Jefferson City, MO 65109
(573) 526-6607

Probation and Parole Board
General e-mail: boards@mail.state.mo.us
Main phone: (573) 751-8488
Main fax: (573) 751-8501

Cranston J. Mitchell, Director
1511 Christy Dr., Jefferson City, MO 65101

Cosmetology Board
General e-mail: cosmo@mail.state.mo.us
Main phone: (573) 751-1052
Main fax: (573) 751-8167
Mailing address: P.O. Box 1062, Jefferson City,
MO 65102

Pam Hoelscher, Executive Director
3605 Missouri Blvd., Jefferson City, MO 65102

Economic Development Dept.
http://www.ecodev.state.mo.us/ded/
General e-mail: ecodev@mail.state.mo.us
Main phone: (573) 751-4962
Main fax: (573) 751-7258
Mailing address: P.O. Box 1157, Jefferson City,
MO 65102

Joseph L. Driskell, Director
301 West High St., #680, Jefferson City, MO 65101
(573) 751-3946; *Fax:* (573) 526-7700

Arts Council
http://www.missouriartscouncil.org
General e-mail: moarts@mail.state.mo.us
Main phone: (314) 340-6845
Main fax: (314) 340-7215

Flora Maria Garcia, Executive Director
Wainwright State Office Complex, 111 N. 7th St.,
#105, St. Louis, MO 63101
E-mail: fgarcia@mail.state.mo.us

Finance Division: Banking Board
http://www.ecodev.state.mo.us/finance
General e-mail: finance@mail.state.mo.us
Main phone: (573) 751-3242
Main fax: (573) 751-9192
Mailing address: P.O. Box 716, Jefferson City,
MO 65102

Ramona Tomka, Secretary
301 West High St., #630, Jefferson City, MO
65101
(573) 751-2545
E-mail: rtomka@mail.state.mo.us

Housing Development Commission
http://www.mhdc.com

General e-mail: info@MHDC.com
Main phone: (816) 759-6600
Main fax: (816) 759-6828

Richard G. Grose, Executive Director
3435 Broadway, Kansas City, MO 64111-2403

Humanities Council
http://www.mohumanities.org
General e-mail: mail@mohumanities.org
Main phone: (314) 781-9660
Main fax: (314) 781-9681
Toll free: (800) 357-0909

Michael Bouman, Director
593 Hanley Industrial Ct., #201, St. Louis, MO
63144-1905
E-mail: mbouman@mohumanities.org

Professional Registration
http://www.ecodev.state.mo.us/pr/
General e-mail: profreg@mail.state.mo.us
Main phone: (573) 751-0293
Main fax: (573) 751-4176
Mailing address: P.O. Box 1335, Jefferson City,
MO 65102

Randy Singer, Director
3605 Missouri Blvd., Jefferson City, MO 65102
E-mail: rsinger@mail.state.mo.us

Public Service Commission
http://www.ecodev.state.mo.us/psc
General e-mail: pscinfo@mail.state.mo.us
Main phone: (573) 751-3234
Main fax: (573) 751-1847
Toll free: (800) 392-4211
Mailing address: P.O. Box 360, Jefferson City,
MO 65102

Gordon Persinger, Executive Director
Truman State Office Bldg., 301 W. High St., 5th
Fl., Jefferson City, MO 65102
(573) 751-7491; *Fax:* (573) 751-0429
E-mail: gpersing@mail.state.mo.us

Tourism Division
http://missouritourism.com
General e-mail: tourism@mail.state.mo.us
Main phone: (573) 751-4133
Main fax: (573) 751-5160
Toll free: (800) 877-1234
Mailing address: P.O. Box 1055, Jefferson City,
MO 65102

Chris Jennings, Director
301 W. High St., #290, Jefferson City, MO 65101
(573) 751-3051

Women's Council
http://www.womenscouncil.org

Frequently Called Numbers

Tourism: (573) 751-4133; 1-888-925-3875, ext. 124; http://missouritourism.com
Library: (573) 751-3615; http://www.mosl.sos.state.mo.us/lib-ser/libser.html
Vital Statistics: (573) 751-6387; http://www.health.state.mo.us/BirthAndDeathRecords/BirthAndDeathRecords.html
Tax/Revenue: (573) 751-4450; http://www.dor.state.mo.us
Motor Vehicles: (573) 751-5398
State Police/Highway Patrol: (573) 751-3313; http://www.mshp.state.mo.us
Unemployment: (573) 751-3648; http://www.dolir.state.mo.us/es/dolir4b.htm
General Election Information: (573) 751-2301; http://mosl.sos.state.mo.us/sos-elec/soselec.html
Consumer Affairs: (573) 751-3321; http://www.agocp.moago.org
Hazardous Materials: (573) 526-9122

General e-mail: wcouncil@mail.state.mo.us
Main phone: (573) 751-0810
Main fax: (573) 751-8835
Mailing address: P.O. Box 1684, Jefferson City, MO 65102

Gale Kessler, Executive Director
421 E. Dunklin, Jefferson City, MO 65101

Elementary and Secondary Education Dept.
http://www.dese.state.mo.us/
General e-mail: pubinfo@mail.dese.state.mo.us
Main phone: (573) 751-4212
Main fax: (573) 751-8613
TTY: (800) 735-2966
Mailing address: P.O. Box 480, Jefferson City, MO 65102-0480

Robert E. Bartman, Commissioner
205 Jefferson St., Jefferson City, MO 65101

School for the Deaf
http://www.msd.k12.mo.us
Main phone: (573) 592-4000
Main fax: (573) 592-2570

Peter H. Ripley, Superintendent
505 E. 5th St., Fulton, MO 65251
E-mail: pripley@msd.k12.mo.us

Gaming Commission
http://www.gov.state.mo.us/boards/cgi/boards.cgi
Main phone: (314) 340-4400
Main fax: (314) 340-4404

Julian Seerberman Sr., Chair
11775 Borman Dr., #104, St. Louis, MO 63146

Health Dept.
http://www.health.state.mo.us/
Main phone: (573) 751-6400
Main fax: (573) 751-6010
Mailing address: P.O. Box 570, Jefferson City, MO 65102

Maureen E. Dempsey, Director
920 Wildwood St., Jefferson City, MO 65109
(573) 751-6001; *Fax:* (573) 751-6041

Higher Education Dept.
http://www.mocbhe.gov
Main phone: (573) 751-2361
Main fax: (573) 751-6635
TTY: (800) 735-2966

Kala M. Stoup, Commissioner
3515 Amazonas Dr., Jefferson City, MO 65109-5717

Highway and Transportation Commission
http://www.modot.state.mo.us/
Main phone: (573) 751-2824
Main fax: (573) 526-5419
Toll free: (800) 726-7390
Mailing address: P.O. Box 270, Jefferson City, MO 65102

S. Lee Kling, Chair
105 W. Capitol Ave., Jefferson City, MO 65101

Insurance Dept.
http://www.insurance.state.mo.us
Main phone: (573) 751-4126
Main fax: (573) 751-1165
Toll free: (800) 726-7390
TTY: (573) 526-4536

Keith Wenzel, Director (Acting)
301 W. High St., #630, Jefferson City, MO 65101

Labor and Industrial Relations Dept.
http://www.dolir.state.mo.us/
General e-mail: dolir@state.mo.us
Main phone: (573) 751-9691
Main fax: (573) 751-4135
Mailing address: P.O. Box 504, Jefferson City, MO 65102

Karla M. McLucas, Director
3315 W. Truman Blvd., Jefferson City, MO 65101

Disability Council
http://www.dolir.state.mo.us/gcd
General e-mail: gcd@dolir.state.mo.us
Main phone: (573) 751-2600
Main fax: (573) 526-4109
Toll free: (800) 877-8249
TTY: (573) 751-2600
Mailing address: P.O. Box 1668, Jefferson City,
MO 65102-1668

Vacant, Executive Director
3315 W. Truman Blvd., #132, Jefferson City, MO
65102-1668

Human Rights Commission
http://www.gov.state.mo.us/boards/cgi/
boards.cgi
General e-mail: aland01@mail.state.mo.us
Main phone: (573) 751-3325
Main fax: (573) 751-2905
Mailing address: P.O. Box 1129, Jefferson City,
MO 65102-1129

Donna Cavitte, Executive Director
3315 W. Truman Blvd., Jefferson City, MO 65102

Workers Compensation Division
http://www.dolir.state.mo.us/wc/index.htm
General e-mail: weblord@dolir.state.mo.us
Main phone: (573) 751-4231
Main fax: (573) 526-4960
Toll free: (800) 775-2667
TTY: (573) 522-5927
Mailing address: P.O. Box 58, Jefferson City,
MO 65102-0058

Jo Ann Karll, Director
3315 W. Truman Blvd., Jefferson City, MO 65102-
0058
(573) 751-4231
E-mail: jkarll@doildecmail.dolir.state.mo.us

Mental Health Dept.
http://www.modmh.state.mo.us
Main phone: (573) 751-4122
Main fax: (573) 751-8224
Toll free: (800) 364-9687
TTY: (573) 526-1201
Mailing address: P.O. Box 667, Jefferson City, MO
65102

Roy C. Wilson, Director
1706 E. Elm St., Jefferson City, MO 65102
(573) 751-3070; *Fax:* (573) 526-7926
E-mail: mzwilsr@mail.state.dmh.state.md.us

Natural Resources Dept.
http://www.dnr.state.mo.us/homednr.htm
Main phone: (573) 751-3443
Main fax: (573) 751-7449
Toll free: (800) 334-6946
Mailing address: P.O. Box 176, Jefferson City, MO
65102

Stephen M. Mahfood, Director
205 Jefferson St., Jefferson City, MO 65101
Fax: (573) 751-7627

Geology and Land Survey Division
http://www.dnr.state.mo.us/dgls
Main phone: (573) 368-2100
Main fax: (573) 368-2111
Toll free: (800) 334-6946
Mailing address: P.O. Box 250, Rolla, MO
65402

**James Hadley Williams, Director and State
Geologist**
111 Fairgrounds Rd., Rolla, MO 65401
(573) 368-2101
E-mail: nrwillj@mail.dnr.state.mo.us

Historic Preservation
http://www.dnr.state.mo.us/histpres.htm
Main phone: (573) 751-7858
Main fax: (573) 526-2852
Toll free: (800) 334-6946
Mailing address: P.O. Box 176, Jefferson City,
MO 65102

Claire Blackwell, Deputy
100 E. High St., Jefferson City, MO 65101

Oil and Gas Unit
http://www.gov.state.mo.us/boards/cgi/
boards.cgi
Main phone: (573) 368-2100
Main fax: (573) 368-2111
Mailing address: P.O. Box 250, Rolla, MO
65402

Evan Kifer, Chief
111 Fairgrounds Rd., Rolla, MO 65404
(573) 368-2170
E-mail: nrkifee@mail.dnr.state.mo.us

Soil and Water Districts Commission
http://www.gov.state.mo.us/boards/cgi/
boards.cgi
General e-mail: nrfasts@mail.dnr.state.mo.us
Main phone: (573) 751-4932
Main fax: (573) 526-3508
Mailing address: P.O. Box 176, Jefferson City,
MO 65102

**Sarah E. Fast, Director, Soil and Water
Conservation Program**

1738 E. Elm St., Jefferson City, MO 65101
E-mail: nrfasts@mail.dnr.state.mo.us

State Parks Board
http://www.dnr.state.mo.us/parks.htm
General e-mail: moparks@mail.dnr.state.mo.us
Main phone: (573) 751-8560
Main fax: (573) 751-8656
Toll free: (800) 334-6946
Mailing address: P.O. Box 176, Jefferson City, MO 65102

Douglas K. Eiken, Director
1739 E. Elm St., Jefferson City, MO 65102
(573) 751-9392

Nursing Board
http://www.gov.state.mo.us/boards/cgi/boards.cgi
General e-mail: nursing@mail.state.mo.us
Main phone: (573) 751-0681
Main fax: (573) 751-0075
Mailing address: P.O. Box 656, Jefferson City, MO 65102

Calvina Thomas, Executive Director
3605 Missouri Blvd., Jefferson City, MO 65109

Pharmacy Board
http://www.gov.state.mo.us/boards/cgi/boards.cgi
General e-mail: pharmacy@mail.state.mo.us
Main phone: (573) 751-0091
Main fax: (573) 526-3464
Mailing address: P.O. Box 625, Jefferson City, MO 65102

Kevin Kinkade, Executive Director
3605 Missouri Blvd., #220, Jefferson City, MO 65109
(573) 751-0093

Professional Registration
(573) 751-0293

Accountancy, (573) 751-0012,
http://www.ecodev.state.mo.us/pr/account
Architects, Engineers, and Land Surveyors,
(573) 751-0047, http://www.gov.state.mo.us/
pr/moapels
Child Care, (573) 751-2450
Contractors, (573) 751-0047
Cosmetology, (573) 751-1052
Medical Licensing, (573) 751-0098
Nursing, (573) 751-0681,
http://www.gov.state.mo.us/boards/cgi/
boards.cgi
Pharmacy, (573) 751-0091, http://
www.gov.state.mo.us/boards/cgi/boards.cgi
Real Estate, (573) 751-0038

Prosecutions Services Division
Main phone: (573) 751-0619
Main fax: (573) 751-1171
Mailing address: P.O. Box 899, Jefferson City, MO 65102

Elizabeth Ziegler, Director
Supreme Court Bldg., 221 W. High St., Jefferson City, MO 65101

Public Defender Commission
http://www.gov.state.mo.us/boards/cgi/boards.cgi
Main phone: (573) 526-5210
Main fax: (573) 526-5213

J. Marty Robinson, Public Defender
231 E. Capitol Ave., Jefferson City, MO 65101
E-mail: mrobinso@mspd.state.mo.us

Public Safety Dept.
http://www.dps.state.mo.us
General e-mail: dps001@mail.state.mo.us
Main phone: (573) 751-4905
Main fax: (573) 751-5399
Mailing address: P.O. Box 749, Jefferson City, MO 65102-0749

Gary B. Kempker, Director
Harry S. Truman Bldg., Jefferson City, MO 65102-0749

Emergency Response Commission
http://www.cema.state.mo.us/mercc
General e-mail: mosema@mail.state.mo.us
Main phone: (573) 526-9237
Main fax: (573) 526-9261
Toll free: (800) 780-1014
Mailing address: P.O. Box 3133, Jefferson City, MO 65102

Bob Dopp, Executive Director
2302 Militia Dr., Jefferson City, MO 65102
E-mail: bdopp01@mail.state.mo.us

Fire Safety Board
http://www.dps.state.mo.us/dps/msfs
General e-mail: firesafe@mail.state.mo.us
Main phone: (573) 751-2930
Main fax: (573) 751-1744
Toll free: (800) 877-5688
Mailing address: P.O. Box 844, Jefferson City, MO 65102

Bill Farr, State Fire Marshal
1709 Industrial Dr., Jefferson City, MO 65109

Juvenile Justice Advisory Group
http://www.gov.state.mo.us/boards/cgi/
boards.cgi

General e-mail: sandy@mail.state.mo.us
Main phone: (573) 751-2771
Main fax: (573) 751-5399
Toll free: (888) SYI-MDPS
Mailing address: P.O. Box 749, Jefferson City, MO 65101

> **Sandy Rempe, Juvenile Justice Specialist**
> Truman State Office Bldg., 301 W. High, #870, Jefferson City, MO 65101
> *E-mail:* sandy@dps.state.mo.us

Liquor Control Division
Main phone: (573) 751-2333
Main fax: (573) 526-4540
Mailing address: P.O. Box 837, Jefferson City, MO 65102

> **Hope Whitehead, Supervisor**
> 301 W. High St., #860, Jefferson City, MO 65101

State Highway Patrol
http://www.mshp.state.mo.us
General e-mail: mshppied@mail.state.mo.us
Main phone: (573) 751-3313
Main fax: (573) 751-9419
TTY: (573) 751-3313
Mailing address: P.O. Box 568, Jefferson City, MO 65102

> **Weldon L. Wilhoit, Superintendent**
> 1510 E. Elm, Jefferson City, MO 65101
> (573) 526-6120; *Fax:* (573) 526-1111

Veterans Commission
http://www.dps.state.mo.us/dps/mvc
Main phone: (573) 751-3779
Main fax: (573) 751-6836
TTY: (573) 522-1411
Mailing address: P.O. Drawer 147, Jefferson City, MO 65102

> **Robert R. Buckner, Executive Director**
> 1719 Southridge Dr., Jefferson City, MO 65102

Real Estate Appraisers Commission
http://www.ecodev.state.mo.us/pr/rea
General e-mail: reacom@mail.state.mo.us
Main phone: (573) 751-0038
Main fax: (573) 526-3489
TTY: (800) 735-2466
Mailing address: P.O. Box 1335, Jefferson City, MO 65102

> **Judy Kolb, Executive Director**
> 3605 Missouri Blvd., Jefferson City, MO 65109

Revenue Dept.
http://www.dor.state.mo.us

General e-mail: dormail@mail.dor.state.mo.us
Main phone: (573) 751-4450
Main fax: (573) 751-7150
TTY: (800) 735-2966
Mailing address: P.O. Box 311, Jefferson City, MO 65105-0311

> **Quentin Wilson, Director**
> 301 W. High St., Jefferson City, MO 65101
> (573) 751-5671

Motor Vehicles and Driver Licensing Division
Main phone: (573) 751-5398
Main fax: (573) 526-4774
Mailing address: P.O. Box 629, Jefferson City, MO 65105

> **Raymond Hune, Director**
> 301 W. High St., Jefferson City, MO 65105

State Lottery
http://www.gov.state.mo.us/boards/cgi/boards.cgi
Main phone: (573) 751-4050
Main fax: (573) 751-5188
Mailing address: P.O. Box 1603, Jefferson City, MO 65102-1603

> **James R. Scroggins, Executive Director**
> 1823 Southridge Dr., Jefferson City, MO 65102-1603

Social Services Dept.
http://www.dss.state.mo.us
Main phone: (573) 751-4815
Main fax: (573) 751-3203
TTY: (800) 735-2966
Mailing address: P.O. Box 1527, Jefferson City, MO 65101

> **Gary J. Stangler, Director**
> 221 W. High St., Jefferson City, MO 65102

Aging Council
http://www.gov.state.mo.us/boards/cgi/boards.cgi
General e-mail: dpullam@mail.state.mo.us
Main phone: (573) 751-3082
Main fax: (573) 751-8687
Toll free: (800) 235-5503
Mailing address: P.O. Box 1337, Jefferson City, MO 65102

> **Andrea Routh, Director**
> 615 Howerton Ct., Jefferson City, MO 65109

Medical Services Division
http://www.gov.state.mo.us/boards/cgi/

General e-mail: dpullam@mail.state.mo.us
Main phone: (573) 751-3425
Main fax: (573) 751-6564
Mailing address: P.O. Box 1337, Jefferson City,
MO 65102

Greg Vadner, Director
615 Howerton Ct., Jefferson City, MO 65102-6506

State Employees Retirement System
http://www.mosers.org
General e-mail: mosers@mosers.org
Main phone: (573) 632-6100
Main fax: (573) 632-6101
Toll free: (800) 827-1063
TTY: (800) 735-2466
Mailing address: P.O. Box 209, Jefferson City, MO
65109

Gary Findlay, Executive Director
907 Wildwood Dr., Jefferson City, MO 65109

State Fair
http://www.mostatefair.com/
Main phone: (660) 530-5600
Main fax: (660) 530-5609
Toll free: (800) 422-3247
TTY: (800) 735-2966

Gary D. Slater, Director
2503 W. 16th St., Sedalia, MO 65301

State Library
http://www.mosl.sos.state.mo.us/lib-ser/libser.html
Main phone: (573) 751-3615
Main fax: (573) 526-1142
TTY: (800) 735-2966
Mailing address: P.O. Box 387, Jefferson City, MO
65102-0387

Sara Parker, State Librarian
600 W. Main St., Jefferson City, MO 65101
E-mail: parks@sosmail.state.mo.us

Transportation Dept.
http://www.modot.state.mo.us/
Main phone: (573) 751-2551
Main fax: (573) 751-6555
Mailing address: P.O. Box 270, Jefferson City, MO
65101

Henry Hungerbeeler, Director
105 W. Capitol Ave., Jefferson City, MO 65101
(573) 751-4622; Fax: (573) 526-5419
E-mail: hungeh@mail.modot.state.mo.us

Laws

Sales tax: 4.225%
Income tax: 6%
State minimum wage: $5.15 (Federal is $5.15)
Marriage age: 18
First-cousin marriage: Prohibited
Drinking age: 21
State control of liquor sales: No
Blood alcohol for DWI: 0.10%
Driving age: 18 (effective 2001)
Speed limit: 70 mph
Permit to buy handguns: Yes, 7 days to
acquire
Minimum age to possess handguns: 21
Minimum age to possess rifles, shotguns:
None
State lottery: Yes; also Powerball
Casinos: Yes (commercial)
Pari-mutuel betting: No
Death penalty: Yes
3 strikes minimum sentence: None
Hate crimes law: Yes
Gay employment non-discrimination: No
Official language(s): English
Term limits: State legislators (8 yrs.)

*State laws are complex and subject to
change; this information is not intended as
legal advice. For an explanation of this
information, see p. x.*

Missouri Legislature
State Capitol
Jefferson City, MO 65101
General information: (573) 751-3824
TTY: (573) 751-3969
Bill status: (573) 751-4633
http://www.moga.state.mo.us

Senate
General information: (573) 751-3766
Fax: (573) 751-2745

Roger B. Wilson (D), President
State Capitol, #121, Jefferson City, MO 65101
(573) 751-4727; Fax: (573) 751-9422
E-mail: wilson@mail.state.mo.us
http://www.ltgov.state.mo.us/homepg.htm

Edward E. Quick (D), President Pro Tempore
State Capitol Bldg., #326, Jefferson City, MO 65101

(573) 751-4524; *Fax:* (573) 751-2745
E-mail: equick@services.state.mo.us
http://www.senate.state.mos.us/members/mem17.htm

Ronnie DePasco (D), Majority Leader
State Capitol Bldg., #321, Jefferson City, MO 65101
(573) 751-3074; *Fax:* (573) 751-2745
E-mail: rdepasco@services.state.mo.us
http://www.senate.state.mo.us/members/mem11.htm

Steve E. Ehlmann (R), Minority Leader
State Capitol Bldg., #428, Jefferson City, MO 65101
(573) 751-8635; *Fax:* (573) 751-2745
E-mail: sehlmann@services.state.mo.us
http://www.senate.state.mo.us/members/mem23.htm

Peter D. Kinder (R), Minority Caucus Whip
State Capitol Bldg., #431, Jefferson City, MO 65101
(573) 751-2455; *Fax:* (573) 751-2902
E-mail: pkinder@services.state.mo.us
http://www.senate.state.mo.us/members/mem27.htm

Terry L. Spieler, Secretary
State Capitol Bldg., Jefferson City, MO 65101
(573) 751-3766

House
General information: (573) 751-3659
Fax: (573) 751-0940
TTY: (573) 751-6911

Steve Gaw (D), Speaker of the House
State Capitol Bldg., 201 W. Capitol Ave., #308,
  Jefferson City, MO 65101
(573) 751-2700; *Fax:* (573) 751-5988
E-mail: sgaw01@services.state.mo.us
http://www.house.state.mo.us/bills99/member99/
  MEM022.htm

Jim Kreider (D), Speaker Pro Tempore
State Capitol Bldg., 201 W. Capitol Ave., #301,
  Jefferson City, MO 65101
(573) 751-2956; *Fax:* (573) 526-0507
E-mail: jkreider@services.state.mo.us
http://www.house.state.mo.us/bills99/member99/
  MEM142.htm

Wayne F. Crump (D), Majority Leader
State Capitol Bldg., 201 W. Capitol Ave., #309,
  Jefferson City, MO 65101
(573) 751-2101; *Fax:* (573) 526-1865
E-mail: wcrump@services.state.mo.us
http://www.house.state.mo.us/bills99/member99/
  MEM152.htm

Rita D. Days (D), Majority Whip
State Capitol Bldg., 201 W. Capitol Ave., #313,
  Jefferson City, MO 65101

(573) 751-4468; *Fax:* (573) 526-1239
E-mail: rdays01@services.state.mo.us
http://www.house.state.mo.us/bills99/member99/
  MEM071.htm

Delbert Scott (R), Minority Leader
State Capitol Bldg., 201 W. Capitol Ave., #204,
  Jefferson City, MO 65101
(573) 751-8793; *Fax:* (573) 526-8793
E-mail: dscott@services.state.mo.us
http://www.house.state.mo.us/bills99/member99/
  MEM119.htm

Charles W. Shields (R), Minority Whip
State Capitol Bldg., 201 W. Capitol Ave., #101-E,
  Jefferson City, MO 65101
(573) 751-9476; *Fax:* (573) 526-4765
E-mail: cshields@services.state.mo.us
http://www.house.statc.mo.us/bills99/member99/
  MEM028.htm

Anne C. Walker, Chief Clerk
State Capitol Bldg., 201 W. Capitol Ave., Jefferson
  City, MO 65101
(573) 751-3829

Missouri Judiciary
Supreme Court Bldg.
207 W. High St.
Jefferson City, MO 65101
http://www.osca.state.mo.us

Supreme Court
http://www.osca.state.mo.us/sup/index.nsf

Thomas F. Simon, Clerk
Supreme Court Bldg., 207 W. High St., Jefferson City,
  MO 65101
(573) 751-4144; *Fax:* (573) 751-7514
E-mail: thomas_f_simon@osca.state.mo.us

Justices
Composition: 7 judges
Selection Method: appointed by governor; must
  stand for retention in first general election after
  one year of service
Length of term: 12 years, after retention vote
William Ray Price Jr., Chief Justice, (573) 751-4513
Duane Benton, Judge, (573) 751-6880
Ann K. Covington, Judge, (573) 751-3570
John C. Holstein, Judge, (573) 751-1004
Stephen N. Limbaugh Jr., Judge, (573) 751-4375
Ronnie L. White, Judge, (573) 751-9652
Michael A. Wolff, Judge, (573) 751-4410

Office of State Courts Administrator
http://www.osca.state.mo.us/osca/index.nsf
Main phone: (573) 751-4377
Main fax: (573) 751-5540

Ronald L. Larkin, State Courts Administrator
2112 Industrial Blvd., Jefferson City, MO 65109
(573) 751-3585

State Law Library
Main phone: (573) 751-2636
Main fax: (573) 751-2573

Tyronne Allen, Supreme Court Librarian
Supreme Court Bldg., 207 W. High St., Jefferson
  City, MO 65101
E-mail: tyronne_allen@osca.state.mo.us

Legislative and Political Party Information Resources

Senate home page: http://www.senate.state.mo.us
House home page: http://www.house.state.mo.us
Committees: Senate: http://www.senate.state.mo.us/com_info.htm;
  House: http://www.house.state.mo.us/bills99/commit99/commlst.htm
Legislative process: http://www.senate.state.mo.us/bill-law.htm
Current session information: Senate: http://www.senate.state.mo.us/daily.htm;
  House: http://www.house.state.mo.us/bills99/dlyact.htm
Missouri Democratic Party: http://www.missouridems.org
  P.O. Box 719, Jefferson City, MO 65102; *Phone:* (573) 636-5241; *Fax:* (573) 634-8176
Missouri Republican Party: http://www.mogop.org
  204 E. Dunklin St., P.O. Box 73, Jefferson City, MO 65102; *Phone:* (573) 636-3146;
  Fax: (573) 636-3273

Montana

State Capitol
Helena, MT 59620
Public information: (406) 444-2511
Fax: (406) 444-4151
http://www.state.mt.us

Office of the Governor
http://www.mt.gov/governor/governor.htm
Main phone: (406) 444-3111
Main fax: (406) 444-5529
TTY: (406) 444-4339

Marc Racicot (R), Governor
State Capitol, 1625 11th Ave., Helena, MT 59620
Fax: (406) 444-4151

Mick Robinson, Chief of Staff
State Capitol, 1625 11th Ave., Helena, MT 59620
(406) 444-3111; *Fax:* (406) 444-4151

Anastasia Burton, Press Secretary
State Capitol, 1625 11th Ave., Helena, MT 59620
(406) 444-3111; *Fax:* (406) 444-4151

Myrna Omholt-Mason, Citizens Advocate
State Capitol, 1625 11th Ave., Helena, MT 59620-
0801
(406) 444-3468; *Fax:* (406) 444-4151

Office of the Lieutenant Governor
http://www.state.mt.us/governor/stff/ltgov.htm
Main phone: (406) 444-5551
Main fax: (406) 444-4648

Judy Martz (R), Lieutenant Governor
Capitol Station, 1625 11th Ave., Helena, MT 59620

Office of the Secretary of State
http://www.state.mt.us/sos/index.htm
Main phone: (406) 444-2034
Main fax: (406) 444-3976
TTY: (406) 444-4732
Mailing address: P.O. Box 202801, Helena, MT
59620-2801

Mike R. Cooney (D), Secretary of State
State Capitol, #225, Helena, MT 59620-2801
E-mail: sos@mt.gov

Office of the Attorney General
http://www.doj.state.mt.us/
General e-mail: mtattgen@counsel.com
Main phone: (406) 444-2026
Main fax: (406) 444-3549

State of Montana

Capital: Helena,
since 1875
Founded: 1864, Montana
Territory created from Idaho Territory
Statehood: November 8, 1889 (41st state)
Constitution adopted: 1972
Area: 145,556 sq. mi. (ranks 4th)
Population: 880,453 (1998 est.; ranks 44th)
Largest cities: (1998 est.) Billings (91,750);
Great Falls (56,395); Missoula (52,239);
Butte (33,994); Helena (28,306)
Counties: 56, Most populous: (1998 est.)
Yellowstone (126,158); Missoula (88,989);
Cascade (78,983); Flathead (71,831);
Gallatin (62,545)
U.S. Congress: Max Baucus (D), Conrad R.
Burns (R); 1 Representative
Nickname(s): Treasure State
Motto: Gold and silver
Song: "Montana"
Bird: Western meadowlark
Tree: Ponderosa pine
Flower: Bitterroot
State fair: at Great Falls, late July-early Aug.
Former capital(s): Bannack, Virginia City

Mailing address: P.O. Box 201401, Helena, MT
59620-1401

Joseph P. Mazurek (D), Attorney General
Justice Bldg., 215 N. Sanders St., Helena, MT 59601

Office of the State Auditor
http://www.state.mt.us/sao/index.html
Main phone: (406) 444-2040
Main fax: (406) 444-3497
Toll free: (800) 332-6148
TTY: (406) 444-3246
Mailing address: P.O. Box 4009, Helena, MT
59604-4009

Mark D. O'Keefe (D), State Auditor
Sam W. Mitchell Bldg., #270, Helena, MT 59604-4009
E-mail: okeefe@mt.gov

Military Affairs Dept.
http://www.state.mt.us/dma/

General e-mail: tagmt@mt-ngnnet.army.mil
Main phone: (406) 841-3000
Main fax: (406) 841-3145
Mailing address: P.O. Box 4789, Helena, MT
59604-4789

John E. Prendergast, Adjutant General
100 N. Main St., Helena, MT 59601
Fax: (406) 841-3011
E-mail: Prendergastje@MT-ARNG.ngb.army.mil

Agencies

Administration Dept.
http://www.state.mt.us/doa/
General e-mail: hvoderberg@state.mt.us
Main phone: (406) 444-2032
Main fax: (406) 444-2812
TTY: (406) 444-1241

Lois A. Menzies, Director
Sam W. Mitchell Bldg., #155, Helena, MT 59620
(406) 444-3033
E-mail: lmenzies@state.mt.us

Accounting and Management Support Division: Treasury Bureau
Main phone: (406) 444-2624
Main fax: (406) 444-2812
Mailing address: P.O. Box 200102, Helena, MT
59620-0102

Kathy Muri, Administrator
Sam W. Mitchell Bldg., 125 Roberts St., #176,
Helena, MT 59620-0102

Personnel Division
http://www.state.mt.us/doa/spd/spdmain.htm
Main phone: (406) 444-3871
Main fax: (406) 444-0544

John McEwen, Administrator
Sam W. Mitchell Bldg., 125 Roberts St., #130,
Helena, MT 59620
(406) 444-3894

Agriculture Dept.
http://www.agr.state.mt.us/
General e-mail: agr@state.mt.us
Main phone: (406) 444-3144
Main fax: (406) 444-5409
TTY: (406) 444-4687
Mailing address: P.O. Box 200201, Helena, MT
59620-0201

W. Ralph Peck, Director
Agriculture and Livestock Bldg., Helena, MT 59620-
0201
Fax: (406) 444-5409

Architects Board
http://www.com.state.mt.us/License/POL/index.htm
General e-mail: compolarc@state.mt.us
Main phone: (406) 444-3745
Main fax: (406) 444-1667
Mailing address: P.O. Box 200513, Helena, MT
59620-0513

Sharon McCullough, Program Manager
111 N. Jackson, Arcade Bldg., Lower Level, Helena,
MT 59620

Arts Council
http://www.art.state.mt.us
General e-mail: mac@state.mt.us
Main phone: (406) 444-6430
Main fax: (406) 444-6548
Toll free: (800) 282-3092
Mailing address: P.O. Box 202201, Helena, MT
59620-2201

Arlynn Fishbaugh, Director
316 N. Park Ave., #252, Helena, MT 59620

Board of Public Education
http://www.montana.edu/~wwwbpe/
General e-mail: MTBPC@bpe.montana.edu
Main phone: (406) 444-6576
Main fax: (406) 444-0847
Mailing address: P.O. Box 200601, Helena, MT
59620-0601

Wayne Buchanan, Executive Secretary
2500 Broadway, Helena, MT 59620-0601
(406) 444-6576; Fax: (406) 444-0847
E-mail: wbuchanan@bpe.montana.edu

School for the Deaf and Blind
Main phone: (406) 771-6000
Main fax: (406) 771-6164
Toll free: (800) 882-6732
TTY: (406) 771-6030

John Kinna, Superintendent
3911 Central Ave., Great Falls, MT 59405
E-mail: jkinna@sbd.state.mt.us

Board of Regents of Higher Education
http://www.montana.edu/wwwbor/docs/
borpage.html
General e-mail: srisette@oche.montana.edu
Main phone: (406) 444-6570
Main fax: (406) 444-1469
Mailing address: P.O. Box 203101, Helena, MT
59620-3101

Richard A. Crofts, Commissioner
2500 Broadway, Helena, MT 59620-3101
(406) 444-0311
E-mail: rcrofts@oche.montana.edu

Commerce Dept.
http://com.mt.gov
Main phone: (406) 444-3494
Main fax: (406) 444-2903
TTY: (406) 444-2978
Mailing address: P.O. Box 200501, Helena, MT
59620-0501

Peter S. Blouke, Director
1424 9th Ave., Helena, MT 59620-0501
(406) 444-3797

Housing Division
http://www.commerce.state.mt.us/housing/
index.html
Main phone: (406) 444-3040
Main fax: (406) 444-4688

Maureen Rude, Administrator
836 Front St., Helena, MT 59620

Lottery
http://www.montanalottery.com
Main phone: (406) 444-5825
Main fax: (406) 444-5830
TTY: (406) 444-2511

Gerald J. LaChere, Director
2525 N. Montana Ave., Helena, MT 59601-0598
E-mail: jlachere@state.mt.us

Professional and Occupational Licensing Division
http://www.com.state.mt.us/License/POL/
index.htm
Main phone: (406) 444-3737
Main fax: (406) 444-1667
TTY: (406) 444-2978
Mailing address: P.O. Box 200513, Helena, MT
59620-0513

Steve Meloy, Administrator
111 N. Jackson, Helena, MT 59620
(406) 444-1488; *Fax:* (406) 444-1667
E-mail: smeloy@state.mt.us

Commissioner of Political Practices
http://www.state.mt.us/cpp
Main phone: (406) 444-2942
Main fax: (406) 444-1643
Mailing address: P.O. Box 202401, Helena, MT
59620-2401

Linda L. Vaughey, Commissioner
1205 8th Ave., Helena, MT 59620-2401
E-mail: lvaughey@mt.state.us

Corrections Dept.
http://www.state.mt.us/cor/
General e-mail: jbouchee@state.mt.us
Main phone: (406) 444-3930

Higher Educational Institutions

Montana State University
http://www.msubillings.edu
1500 N. 30th St., Billings, MT 59101-0298
Main phone: (406) 657-2011
Branches: Bozeman, Northern

University of Montana
http://www.umt.edu
Missoula, MT 59812-0002
Main phone: (406) 243-6266
Branches: Montana Tech, Western Montana College

Main fax: (406) 444-4920
Mailing address: P.O. Box 201301, Helena, MT
59620-1301

Richard N. (Rick) Day, Director
1539 11th Ave., Helena, MT 59620-1301
(406) 444-3901

Cosmetologist Board
http://www.com.state.mt.us/License/POL/index.htm
General e-mail: compolcos@state.mt.us
Main phone: (406) 444-4288
Main fax: (406) 444-1667
Mailing address: P.O. Box 200513, Helena, MT
59620-0513

Jeanne Worsech, Administrator
111 N. Jackson, Arcade Bldg., Lower Level, Helena,
MT 59620

Disaster and Emergency Services Division
http://state.mt.us/dma/des/index.shtml
Main phone: (406) 841-3911
Main fax: (406) 841-3965
Mailing address: P.O. Box 4789, Helena, MT
59604-4789

James Greene, Administrator
National Guard Armory, 1100 N. Main, Helena, MT
59604-4789
E-mail: jigreene@state.mt.us

Environmental Quality Dept.
http://www.deq.state.mt.us/
General e-mail: drapkoch@state.mt.us
Main phone: (406) 444-2544
Main fax: (406) 444-4386
TTY: (406) 444-9526
Mailing address: P.O. Box 200901, Helena, MT
59620-0901

Mark Simonich, Director
1520 E. 6th Ave., Helena, MT 59620-0901

Fire Marshal Bureau
http://www.doj.state.mt.us/les/firmarsh.htm
General e-mail: drapkoch@state.mt.us
Main phone: (406) 444-2050
Mailing address: P.O. Box 201415, Helena, MT 59620-1415

Mark Simonich, Director
1310 Lockey Ave., Helena, MT 59620-1415

Fish, Wildlife, and Parks Dept.
http://www.fwp.state.mt.us/
Main phone: (406) 444-2535
Main fax: (406) 444-4952
TTY: (406) 444-1200
Mailing address: P.O. Box 200701, Helena, MT 59620-0701

Patrick J. Graham, Director
1420 E. 6th Ave., Helena, MT 59620-0701
(406) 444-3186; *Fax:* (406) 444-4952
E-mail: pagraham@state.mt.us

Highway Patrol Division
http://www.doj.state.mt.us/mhp
General e-mail: sdriscoll@state.mt.us
Main phone: (406) 444-3780
Main fax: (406) 444-4169
TTY: (406) 444-1205
Mailing address: P.O. Box 201419, Helena, MT 59620-1401

Bert J. Obert, Administrator
2550 Prospect Ave., Helena, MT 59620-1419

Historical Society
http://www.his.mt.gov
Main phone: (406) 444-2694
Main fax: (406) 444-2696
Toll free: (800) 243-9900
Mailing address: P.O. Box 201201, Helena, MT 59620-1201

Arnold Olsen, Director
225 N. Roberts St., Helena, MT 59620
(406) 444-4706

State Archivist
http://www.his.state.mt.us
General e-mail: archives@state.mt.us
Main phone: (406) 444-4774
Main fax: (406) 444-2696
Mailing address: P.O. Box 201201, Helena, MT 59620-1201

Kathryn Otto, State Archivist
225 N. Roberts St., Helena, MT 59620
(406) 444-4775
E-mail: archives@men.net

Insurance Dept.
Main phone: (406) 444-2997

Main fax: (406) 444-2040
Toll free: (800) 332-6148
TTY: (406) 444-3246
Mailing address: P.O. Box 4009, Helena, MT 59604-4009

Peter Funk, Deputy Commissioner
Sam W. Mitchell Bldg., #270, Helena, MT 59604-4009

Labor and Industry Dept.
http://dli.state.mt.us/
Main phone: (406) 444-3555
Main fax: (406) 444-1394
TTY: (406) 444-0532
Mailing address: P.O. Box 1728, Helena, MT 59624-1728

Patricia Haffey, Commissioner
1327 Lockey, Helena, MT 59624-1728
(406) 444-9091
E-mail: phaffey@state.mt.us

Livestock Board
http://www.liv.state.mt.us/
Main phone: (406) 444-2023
Main fax: (406) 444-1929
Mailing address: P.O. Box 202001, Helena, MT 59620-2001

Marc Bridges, Executive Officer
Capitol Station, 301 N. Roberts, Helena, MT 59620
(406) 444-7323
E-mail: mbridges@state.mt.us

Medical Examiners Board
http://www.com.state.mt.us/License/POL/
pol_boards/med_board/board_page.htm
General e-mail: compolmed@mt.gov
Main phone: (406) 444-4284
Main fax: (406) 444-9396
Mailing address: P.O. Box 200513, Helena, MT 59620-0513

Patricia England, Executive Secretary
111 N. Jackson, #4-B, Helena, MT 59620-0513
(406) 444-6435; *Fax:* (406) 444-9396

Motor Vehicle Division
Main phone: (406) 444-4536
Main fax: (406) 444-1631
Mailing address: P.O. Box 201430, Helena, MT 59620-1430

Dean Roberts, Administrator
Justice Bldg., 303 N. Roberts, Helena, MT 59620-1430
E-mail: droberts@state.mt.us

Natural Resources and Conservation Dept.
http://www.dnrc.state.mt.us/
General e-mail: pgreene@state.mt.us

Main phone: (406) 444-2074
Main fax: (406) 444-2684
TTY: (406) 444-2074
Mailing address: P.O. Box 201601, Helena, MT
59620-1601

Arthur R. Clinch, Director
1625 11th Ave., Helena, MT 59620-1601

Forestry Division
Main phone: (406) 542-4300
Main fax: (406) 542-4217

Don Artley, Administrator
2705 Spurgin Rd., Missoula, MT 59804
E-mail: dartley@state.mt.us

Oil and Gas Conservation Board
http://www.dnrc.state.mt.us/oilgas
Main phone: (406) 656-0040
Main fax: (406) 657-1604

Thomas T. Richmond, Administrator/Petroleum
Engineer
2535 St. John's Ave., Billings, MT 59102

Water Resources Division
http://www.dnrc.mt.gov/wrd/home.htm
Main phone: (406) 444-6601
Main fax: (406) 444-5918
Mailing address: P.O. Box 201601, Helena, MT
59620-1601

Jack Stults, Administrator
1625 11th Ave., Helena, MT 59620-1601
E-mail: jstults@state.mt.us

Nursing Board
http://www.com.state.mt.us/License/POL/
  pol_boards/nur_board/board_page.htm
General e-mail: compolnur@state.mt.us
Main phone: (406) 444-2071
Main fax: (406) 444-7759
Mailing address: P.O. Box 200513, Helena, MT
59620-0513

Jill Caldwell, Acting Executive Director
111 N. Jackson, Arcade Bldg., Lower Level, #4C,
  Helena, MT 59620
E-mail: jcaldwell@state.mt.us

Pharmacy Board
http://www.com.state.mt.us/License/POL/
  pol_boards/pha_board/contacts.htm
General e-mail: compolpha@state.mt.us
Main phone: (406) 444-1698
Main fax: (406) 444-1667
Mailing address: P.O. Box 200513, Helena, MT
59620-0513

Frequently Called Numbers

Tourism: (800) VISITMT; http://travel.mt.gov
Library: (406) 444-3004;
  http://msl.state.mt.us/
Board of Education: (406) 444-6576
Vital Statistics: (406) 444-4228
Tax/Revenue: (406) 444-6900;
  http://www.state.mt.us/revenue/
Motor Vehicles: (406) 444-4536
State Police/Highway Patrol: (406) 444-3780;
  http://www.doj.state.mt.us/mhp
Unemployment: (406) 444-2723;
  http://uid.dli.state.mt.us
General Election Information:
  (406) 444-4732, 888-884-VOTE;
  http://www.state.mt.us/sos/election.htm
Consumer Affairs: (406) 444-4312
Hazardous Materials: (406) 444-4643

Cami Robson, Program Manager
111 N. Jackson, Arcade Bldg., Lower Level, Helena,
  MT 59620
(406) 444-1698; *Fax:* (406) 444-1667
E-mail: compharmacy@mt.state.us

Professional Engineers and Land Surveyors Board
http://www.com.state.mt.us/License/POL/
  pol_boards/pel_board/board_page.htm
General e-mail: compolpel@state.mt.us
Main phone: (406) 444-4285
Main fax: (406) 444-1667
Mailing address: P.O. Box 200513, Helena, MT
59620-0513

Mary Hainlin, Program Manager
111 N. Jackson, Arcade Bldg., Lower Level, Helena,
  MT 59620
E-mail: mhainlin@state.mt.us

Public Accountants Board
http://www.com.state.mt.us/license/pol/index.htm
General e-mail: compolpac@state.mt.us
Main phone: (406) 444-3739
Main fax: (406) 444-1667
Mailing address: P.O. Box 200513, Helena, MT
59620-0513

Susanne Criswell, Administrator
111 N. Jackson, Arcade Bldg., Lower Level, Helena,
  MT 59620-0513

Public Employees Retirement Board
http://www.state.mt.us/doa/perb/perb.htm

General e-mail: perb@state.mt.us
Main phone: (406) 444-3154
Main fax: (406) 444-5428
Toll free: (877) 275-7372
Mailing address: P.O. Box 200131, Helena, MT
59620-0131

Michael O'Connor, Executive Director
1712 9th Ave., Helena, MT 59601
E-mail: moconnor@state.mt.us

Political Practices Commission
Main phone: (406) 444-2942
Main fax: (406) 444-1693
Mailing address: P.O. Box 202401, Helena, MT
59620-2401

Linda Vaughey, Commissioner
1205 8th Ave., Helena, MT 59620-2401

Professional and Occupational Licensing Division
(406) 444-3737

Accountancy, (406) 444-3739,
http://www.com.state.mt.us/license/pol/
index.htm
Architects, (406) 444-3745,
http://www.com.state.mt.us/License/POL/
index.htm
Child Care, (406) 444-7770,
http://www.com.state.mt.us/License/POL/
index.htm
Contractors, (406) 444-7734,
http://www.com.state.mt.us/License/POL/
index.htm
Cosmetology, (406) 444-4288,
http://www.com.state.mt.us/License/POL/
index.htm
Engineers and Land Surveyors, (406) 444-
4285, http://www.com.state.mt.us/License/
POL/pol_boards/pel_board/board_page.htm
Medical Examiners, (406) 444-4284,
http://www.com.state.mt.us/License/POL/
pol_boards/med_board/board_page.htm
Nursing, (406) 444-2071,
http://www.com.state.mt.us/License/POL/
pol_boards/nur_board/board_page.htm
Pharmacy, (406) 444-1698,
http://www.com.state.mt.us/License/POL/
pol_boards/pha_board/contacts.htm
Real Estate Appraisers, (406) 444-3561,
http://www.com.state.mt.us/License/POL/
pol_boards/rea_board/contacts.htm

Public Health and Human Services Dept.
http://www.dphhs.state.mt.us/
Main phone: (406) 444-5622
Main fax: (406) 444-1970
TTY: (406) 444-2590

Laurie Ekanger, Director
111 N. Sanders, #301/308, Helena, MT 59604
E-mail: lekanger@mt.gov

Addictive and Mental Disorders Division
Main phone: (406) 444-3964
Main fax: (406) 444-4435
Mailing address: P.O. Box 202951, Helena, MT
59620-2951

Dan Anderson, Administrator
1400 Broadway, #C-118, Helena, MT 59620
(406) 444-3969
E-mail: daanderson@state.mt.us

Disability Services Division
Main phone: (406) 444-2590
Main fax: (406) 444-3632
Mailing address: P.O. Box 4210, Helena, MT
59604

Joe Matthews, Administrator
111 Sanders St., Helena, MT 59620

Medicaid Services Bureau
Main phone: (406) 444-4540
Main fax: (406) 444-1861
Mailing address: P.O. Box 202951, Helena, MT
59620-2951

Mary Dalton, Chief
1400 Broadway, Helena, MT 59620-2951

Senior and Long Term Care Division
http://www.dphhs.state.mt.us/sltc
Main phone: (406) 444-4077
Main fax: (406) 444-7743
TTY: (800) 253-4091
Mailing address: P.O. Box 4210, Helena, MT
59604-4210

Mike Hanshew, Administrator
111 Sanders St., #210, Helena, MT 59604
(406) 444-4209

Public Instruction Office
http://www.metnet.state.mt.us
Main phone: (406) 444-3095
Main fax: (406) 444-2893
TTY: (406) 444-1812
Mailing address: P.O. Box 202501, Helena, MT
59620-2501

Nancy Keenan (D), State Superintendent
1227 11th Ave., Helena, MT 59601

(406) 444-7362; *Fax:* (406) 444-9299
E-mail: nkeenan@state.mt.us

Public Service Commission
http://www.psc.state.mt.us
Main phone: (406) 444-6199
Main fax: (406) 444-7618
TTY: (406) 444-6199
Mailing address: P.O. Box 202601, Helena, MT
59620-2601

Dave Fisher (D), Chair
1701 Prospect Ave., Helena, MT 59620-2601
(406) 444-6168
E-mail: dfisher@state.mt.us

Real Estate Appraisers Board
http://www.com.state.mt.us/License/POL/
pol_boards/rea_board/contacts.htm
General e-mail: compolrea@state.mt.us
Main phone: (406) 444-3561
Main fax: (406) 444-1667
Mailing address: P.O. Box 200513, Helena, MT
59620-0513

Becky Salminen, Administrator
111 N. Jackson, Arcade Bldg., Lower Level, Helena,
MT 59620-0513

Revenue Dept.
http://www.state.mt.us/revenue/
General e-mail: slang@state.mt.us
Main phone: (406) 444-6900
Main fax: (406) 444-3696
TTY: (406) 444-2830
Mailing address: P.O. Box 202701, Helena, MT
59620-2701

Mary Bryson, Director
Sam W. Mitchell Bldg., 125 N. Roberts St., #455,
Helena, MT 59620
(406) 444-2762

State Library
http://msl.state.mt.us/
General e-mail: msl@msl.state.mt.us
Main phone: (406) 444-3004
Main fax: (406) 444-5612
TTY: (406) 444-3005
Mailing address: P.O. Box 201800, Helena, MT
59620-1800

Karen Strege, State Librarian
1515 E. 6th Ave., Helena, MT 59620-1800
(406) 444-3115
E-mail: kstrege@msl.state.mt.us

Travel Montana
http://travel.state.mt.us/

Laws

Sales tax: None
Income tax: 6.6%
State minimum wage: $5.15, $4.00 for small
employers (Federal is $5.15)
Marriage age: 18
First-cousin marriage: Prohibited
Drinking age: 21
State control of liquor sales: Yes
Blood alcohol for DWI: 0.10%
Driving age: 15
Speed limit: 75 mph
Permit to buy handguns: No
Minimum age to possess handguns: 14
Minimum age to possess rifles, shotguns: 14
State lottery: Yes; also Powerball
Casinos: Yes (tribal); also slot/video machines
Pari-mutuel betting: Horse racing
Death penalty: Yes
3 strikes minimum sentence: 10 yrs. (3rd
felony)
Hate crimes law: Yes
Gay employment non-discrimination: No
Official language(s): English
Term limits: Governor (8 yrs.); state legislators
(8 yrs.)

*State laws are complex and subject to
change; this information is not intended as
legal advice. For an explanation of this
information, see p. x.*

General e-mail: http://travel.state.mt.us/feedback/
Main phone: (406) 444-2654
Main fax: (406) 444-1800
Toll free: (800) 847-4868
Mailing address: P.O. Box 200533, Helena, MT
59620-0053

Vacant, Director
1424 9th Ave., Helena, MT 59620-0533

Transportation Dept.
http://www.mdt.state.mt.us/
General e-mail: mdtwebadmin@state.mt.us
Main phone: (406) 444-6200
Main fax: (406) 444-7643
Toll free: (800) 335-7592
TTY: (406) 444-7696
Mailing address: P.O. Box 201001, Helena, MT
59620-1001

Marvin W. Dye, Director
2701 Prospect Ave., Helena, MT 59620-1001
(406) 444-6201; *Fax:* (406) 444-7643

Aeronautics Division
http://www.mdt.state.mt.us/aeronautics
Main phone: (406) 444-2506
Main fax: (406) 444-2519
Mailing address: P.O. Box 5178, Helena, MT
59604-5178

Michael Ferguson, Administrator
2630 Airport Rd., Helena, MT 59601
E-mail: mferguson@state.mt.us

Veterans Affairs Division
Main phone: (406) 841-3740
Mailing address: P.O. Box 5715, Helena, MT
59604

James F. Jacobsen, Administrator
National Guard Armory, 1100 N. Last Chance Gulch,
Helena, MT 59604
(406) 841-3741

Workers' Compensation Court
http://wcc.dli.state.mt.us/
General e-mail: pkessner@state.mt.us
Main phone: (406) 444-7794
Main fax: (406) 444-7798
Mailing address: P.O. Box 537, Helena, MT
59624-0537

Mike McCarter, Judge
1625 11th Ave., Helena, MT 59624

Montana Legislature

Capitol Station
Helena, MT 59620-1706
General information: (406) 444-3064
Fax: (406) 444-3036
TTY: (800) 832-0283
http://leg.state.mt.us

Senate
General information: (406) 444-4844
Fax: (406) 444-4875
E-mail: senate@state.mt.us

Bruce D. Crippen (R), President
Capitol Station, P.O. Box 20176, Helena, MT 59620-
1706
(406) 444-4800

Thomas A. Beck (R), President Pro Tempore

Capitol Station, P.O. Box 20176, Helena, MT 59620-
1706
(406) 444-4844
http://laws.leg.state.mt.us:8000/law/plsql/
LAW0260W$LGTR.QueryView?P_ENTY_ID_SEQ5=4

John G. Harp (R), Majority Leader
Capitol Station, P.O. Box 20176, Helena, MT 59620-
1706
(406) 444-4807

Don Hargrove (R), Majority Whip
Capitol Station, P.O. Box 20176, Helena, MT 59620-
1706
(406) 444-4844
E-mail: DonHSD16@aol.com
http://laws.leg.state.mt.us:8000/law/plsql/
LAW0260W$LGTR.QueryView?P_ENTY_ID_SEQ5=150

Steve Doherty (D), Minority Leader
Capitol Station, P.O. Box 20176, Helena, MT 59620-
1706
(406) 444-4364

Linda Nelson (D), Minority Whip
Capitol Station, P.O. Box 20176, Helena, MT 59620-
1706
(406) 444-4364

Rosana Skelton, Secretary
Capitol Station, P.O. Box 20176, Helena, MT 59620-
1706
(406) 444-4844
E-mail: rskelton@state.mt.us

House
General information: (406) 444-4822
E-mail: house@state.mt.us

John A. Mercer (R), Speaker of the House
Capitol Station, P.O. Box 20176, Helena, MT 59620-
1706
(406) 444-4815
http://laws.leg.state.mt.us:8000/law/plsql/
LAW0260W$LGTR.QueryView?P_ENTY_ID_SEQ5=432

Douglas Mood (R), Speaker Pro Tempore
Capitol Station, P.O. Box 20176, Helena, MT 59620-
1706
(406) 444-1507

Larry Hal Grinde (R), Majority Leader
Capitol Station, P.O. Box 20176, Helena, MT 59620-
1706
(406) 444-4368

Karl Ohs (R), Majority Whip
Capitol Station, P.O. Box 20176, Helena, MT 59620-
1706
(406) 444-4825
http://laws.leg.state.mt.us:8000/law/plsql/
LAW0260W$LGTR.QueryView?P_ENTY_ID_SEQ5=171

Emily Swanson (D), Minority Leader
Capitol Station, P.O. Box 20176, Helena, MT 59620-1706
(406) 444-4822
E-mail: emstony@aol.com
http://laws.leg.state.mt.us:8000/law/plsql/
LAW0260W$LGTR.QueryView?P_ENTY_ID_SEQ5=398

Dan W. Harrington (D), Minority Whip
Capitol Station, P.O. Box 20176, Helena, MT 59620-1706
(406) 444-4822
http://laws.leg.state.mt.us:8000/law/plsql/
LAW0260W$LGTR.QueryView?P_ENTY_ID_SEQ5=186

Marilyn Miller, Chief Clerk
Capitol Station, P.O. Box 20176, Helena, MT 59620-1706
(406) 444-4822

Montana Judiciary
Justice Bldg.
215 N. Sanders St., #414
Helena, MT 59620-3003

Supreme Court
http://www.lawlibrary.state.mt.us/mtlegal.htm

Ed Smith, Clerk
Justice Bldg., 215 N. Sanders St., #323, Helena, MT 59620-3003
(406) 444-3858; *Fax:* (406) 444-5705

Justices
Composition: 7 justices
Selection Method: nonpartisan election; vacancies filled by governor with consent of state senate
Length of term: 8 years

Jean A. Turnage, Chief Justice, (406) 444-5490
Karla M. Gray, Justice, (406) 444-5573
William E. Hunt Sr., Justice, (406) 444-5570
W. William Leaphart, Justice, (406) 444-2862
James C. Nelson, Justice, (406) 444-5570
James Regnier, Justice, (406) 444-5494
Terry N. Trieweiler, Justice, (406) 444-5494

Office of Court Administration
Main phone: (406) 444-2621
Main fax: (406) 444-0834

Patrick A. Chenovick, State Court Administrator
Justice Bldg., 215 N. Sanders St., #315, Helena, MT 59620-3002

State Law Library
http://www.lawlibrary.state.mt.us/
Main phone: (406) 444-3660
Main fax: (406) 444-3603

Judith Meadows, State Law Librarian
Justice Bldg., 215 N. Sanders St., #315, Helena, MT 59620-3004

Legislative and Political Party Information Resources

Senate home page: http://leg.state.mt.us/Senate/senate.htm
House home page: http://leg.state.mt.us/House/House.htm
Committees: http://leg.state.mt.us/interim_committees/int_com_1999-2000.htm
Montana Democratic Party: http://www.mtdemocrats.org
P.O. Box 802, Helena, MT 59624; *Phone:* (406) 442-9520; *Fax:* (406) 442-9534;
E-mail: mtdemocrats@mcn.net
Montana Republican Party: http://www.montanagop.org
1419B Helena Ave., Helena, MT 59601; *Phone:* (406) 442-6469; *Fax:* (406) 442-3293;
E-mail: exec@mtgop.org

Nebraska

State Capitol
Lincoln, NE 68509-4848
Public information: (402) 471-2311
Fax: (402) 472-0987
http://www.state.ne.us

State of Nebraska

Capital: Lincoln, since 1867
Founded: 1854, Nebraska Territory created
Statehood: March 1, 1867 (37th state)
Constitution adopted: October 20, 1875 (amended 1919-20)
Area: 76,878 sq. mi. (ranks 15th)
Population: 1,662,719 (1998 est.; ranks 38th)
Largest cities: (1998 est.) Omaha (371,291); Lincoln (213,088); Bellevue (44,047); Grand Island (41,392); Kearney (27,968)
Counties: 93, Most populous: (1998 est.) Douglas (443,794); Lancaster (235,589); Sarpy (120,785); Hall (51,851); Buffalo (40,596)
U.S. Congress: Chuck Hagel (R), J. Robert Kerrey (D); 3 Representatives
Nickname(s): Cornhusker State, Beef State, Tree Planter State
Motto: Equality before the law
Song: "Beautiful Nebraska"
Bird: Western meadowlark
Tree: Cottonwood
Flower: Goldenrod
State fair: at Lincoln, late Aug.-early Sept.
Former capital(s): Omaha

Office of the Governor
http://www.gov.nol.org
Main phone: (402) 471-2244
Main fax: (402) 471-6031
TTY: (402) 471-2414
Mailing address: P.O. Box 94848, Lincoln, NE 68509-4848

Mike Johanns (R), Governor
State Capitol, 1425 K St., Lincoln, NE 68509
E-mail: mjohanns@notes.state.ne.us

Larry Bare, Chief of Staff
State Capitol, 1425 K St., Lincoln, NE 68509-4848
(402) 471-2244; *Fax:* (402) 471-6031
E-mail: lbare@notes.state.ne.us

Chris Peterson, Media Relations/Press Secretary
State Capitol, 1425 K St., Lincoln, NE 68509-4848
(402) 471-2244; *Fax:* (402) 471-6031
E-mail: cpeterso@notes.state.ne.us

Office of the Lieutenant Governor
http://www.nol.org/home/LtGov/
Main phone: (402) 471-2256
Main fax: (402) 471-6031
Mailing address: P.O. Box 94863, Lincoln, NE 68509-4863

David I. Maurstad (R), Lieutenant Governor
State Capitol, #2315, Lincoln, NE 68509-4863
E-mail: dmaursta@notes.state.ne.us

Office of the Secretary of State
http://www.nol.org/home/SOS/
General e-mail: sosadmin@sos.state.ne.us
Main phone: (402) 471-2554
Main fax: (402) 471-3237
Mailing address: P.O. Box 94608, Lincoln, NE 68509-4608

Scott Moore (R), Secretary of State
State Capitol, #2300, Lincoln, NE 68509-4608

Office of the Attorney General
http://www.nol.org/home/ago/
Main phone: (402) 471-2682
Main fax: (402) 471-3297
Mailing address: P.O. Box 98920, Lincoln, NE 68509-8920

Donald Stenberg (R), Attorney General
2115 State Capitol, Lincoln, NE 68508

Office of the State Treasurer
http://www.nebraska.treasurer.org/
Main phone: (402) 471-2455
Main fax: (402) 471-4390
Mailing address: P.O. Box 94788, Lincoln, NE 68509-4788

David E. Heineman (R), Treasurer
State Capitol, #2003, Lincoln, NE 68509-4788
E-mail: heineman@treasurer.org

Office of the Auditor of Public Accounts
http://www.nol.org/home/auditor/index.html
Main phone: (402) 471-2111
Main fax: (402) 471-3301
Mailing address: P.O. Box 98917, Lincoln, NE
68509-8917

Kate Witek (R), State Auditor
State Capitol, #2303, Lincoln, NE 68509
E-mail: kwitek05@nol.org

Office of the Comptroller of Currency
Main phone: (402) 493-0654
Main fax: (402) 493-0329
Mailing address: P.O. Box 129, Grand Island, NE
68802

Eugene Koenig, Assistant Deputy Comptroller
11606 Nicholas St., #201, Omaha, NE 68154

Mr. William Glover, Assistant Deputy Comptroller

Office of the Adjutant General
General e-mail: tagne@ne-arng.ngb.army.mil
Main phone: (402) 471-3241
Main fax: (402) 471-7171

Stanley M. Heng, Adjutant General
1300 Military Rd., Lincoln, NE 68508-1090
(402) 471-7114

Agencies

Accountability and Disclosure Commission
http://nadc.nol.org
Main phone: (402) 471-2522
Main fax: (402) 471-6599
Mailing address: P.O. Box 95086, Lincoln, NE
68509-5086

Frank J. Daley Jr., Executive Director
1445 K St., 11th Fl., Lincoln, NE 68509-5086

Accountancy Board
http://www.nol.org/home/BPA/
General e-mail: nbpa01@nol.org
Main phone: (402) 471-3595
Main fax: (402) 471-4484
Mailing address: P.O. Box 94725, Lincoln, NE
68509-4725

Annette L. Harmon, Executive Director
140 N. 8th St., #290, Lincoln, NE 68509

Administrative Services Dept.
http://www.das.state.ne.us/
Main phone: (402) 471-2331
Main fax: (402) 471-4157

Lori McClurg, Director
State Capitol, #1315, Lincoln, NE 68509-4664

Employee Relations Division
http://www.das.state.ne.us/das_der/
erhome1.htm
Main phone: (402) 471-4106
Main fax: (402) 471-3394
Mailing address: P.O. Box 95061, Lincoln, NE
68509-5061

William J. Wood, Administrator
301 Centennial Mall South, Lincoln, NE 68509
E-mail: wwood@notes.state.ne.us

Personnel Division
http://www.wrk4neb.org
Main phone: (402) 471-2075
Main fax: (402) 471-3754
Mailing address: P.O. Box 94905, Lincoln, NE
68509-4905

Mike McCrory, Director
State Capitol, Lincoln, NE 68509-4905
(402) 471-2833
E-mail: mmccrory@notes.state.ne.us

Aeronautics Dept.
http://www.nol.org/home/NDOA/
General e-mail: NDADirect@aol.com
Main phone: (402) 471-2371
Main fax: (402) 471-2906
Mailing address: P.O. Box 82088, Lincoln, NE
68501-2088

Kenneth L. Penney Jr., Director
3431 Aviatio Rd., #150, Lincoln, NE 68524
(402) 471-7922
E-mail: kpenney@mail.state.ne.us

Agriculture and Natural Resources Institute
http://www.ianr.unl.edu/cgi/home.pl
Main phone: (402) 471-2871
Main fax: (402) 472-5854

Irv T. Omtvedt, Vice Chancellor
202 Ag Hall, Lincoln, NE 68583-0708
E-mail: iomtvedt1@unl.edu

Conservation and Survey Division
http://csd.unl.edu
Main phone: (402) 472-3471
Main fax: (402) 472-4608

Mark S. Kuzila, Director
113 Nebraska Hall, University of Nebraska-
Lincoln, Lincoln, NE 68588-0517
(402) 472-7537
E-mail: mkuzila1@unl.edu

Agriculture Dept.
http://www.agr.state.ne.us
Main phone: (402) 471-2341
Main fax: (402) 471-2759

Higher Educational Institutions

Chadron State College
http://www.csc.edu
1000 Main St., Chadron, NE 69337
Main phone: (800) 242-3766

Peru State College
http://pscosf.peru.edu
P.O. Box 10, Peru, NE 68421-0010
Main phone: (800) 742-4412

University of Nebraska
http://www.uneb.edu
1410 Q St., Lincoln, NE 68583-0417
Main phone: (402) 472-2030
Branches: Kearney, Medical Center, Omaha,
Technical Agriculture College

Wayne State College
http://www.wsc.edu
1111 Main St., Wayne, NE 68787
Main phone: (402) 375-7239

Toll free: (800) 831-0550
Mailing address: P.O. Box 94947, Lincoln, NE
68509-4947

Merlyn Carlson, Director
301 Centennial Mall South, Lincoln, NE 68509

Alcohol and Drug Abuse Prevention Center
General e-mail: npcada1@unl.edu
Main phone: (402) 472-6046
Main fax: (402) 472-4305
TTY: (800) 833-7352

Ian M. Newman, Director
257 Mabel Lee Hall, University of Nebraska-Lincoln,
Lincoln, NE 68588-0229
E-mail: inewman1@unl.edu

Arts Council
http://www.gps.k12.ne.us/nac_web_site/nac.htm
General e-mail: nacart@synergy.net
Main phone: (402) 595-2122
Main fax: (402) 595-2334

Jennifer Severin Clark, Executive Director
Joslyn Castle Carriage House, 3838 Davenport St.,
Omaha, NE 68131-2329

Banking and Finance Dept.
http://www.ndbf.org/
Main phone: (402) 471-2171
Main fax: (402) 471-3062
Mailing address: P.O. Box 95006, Lincoln, NE
68509-5006

Samuel P. Baird, Director
1200 N St., The Atrium, #311, Lincoln, NE 68508

Consumer Protection Division
Main phone: (402) 471-2682
Main fax: (402) 471-0006
Toll free: (800) 727-6432

Jason Hayes, Assitant Attorney General
2115 State Capitol, Lincoln, NE 68509

Corn Board
http://linux1.nrc.state.ne.us/cornstalk
General e-mail: petersen@nrcdec.nrc.state.ne.us
Main phone: (402) 471-2676
Main fax: (402) 471-3345
Toll free: (800) 632-6791
Mailing address: P.O. Box 95107, Lincoln, NE
68509-5107

Don Hutchens, Executive Director
301 Centennial Mall South, 4th Fl., Lincoln, NE 68508
E-mail: hutchens@nrcdec.nrc.state.ne.us

Correctional Services Dept.
http://www.corrections.state.ne.us/
Main phone: (402) 471-2654
Main fax: (402) 479-5119
Toll free: (888) 769-2359
TTY: (402) 479-5608
Mailing address: P.O. Box 94661, Linoln, NE
68509-4661

Harold W. Clarke, Director
Folsom and W. Prospect Pl., Lincoln, NE 68509-4661
Fax: (402) 479-5623

Economic Development Dept.
http://www.ded.state.ne.us
Main phone: (402) 471-3111
Main fax: (402) 471-3778
Toll free: (800) 426-6505
TTY: (402) 471-3441
Mailing address: P.O. Box 94666, Lincoln, NE
68508-4666

Al Wenstrand, Director
301 Centennial Mall South, 4th Fl., Lincoln, NE 68508
(402) 471-3747

Tourism Office
http://www.visitnebraska.org
General e-mail: tourism@ded2.ded.state.ne.us
Main phone: (402) 471-3791
Main fax: (402) 471-3026
Toll free: (800) 228-4307
TTY: (402) 471-3441
Mailing address: P.O. Box 98907, Dept. 9INT,
Lincoln, NE 68509-8907

Duane E. Miller, Director
700 S. 16th St., Lincoln, NE 68509
(402) 471-3796
E-mail: davem@visitnebraska.org

Education Dept.
http://www.nde.state.ne.us
Main phone: (402) 471-2295
Main fax: (402) 471-0117
Mailing address: P.O. Box 94987, Lincoln, NE 68509-4987

Douglas D. Christensen, Commissioner
301 Centennial Mall South, 6th Fl., Lincoln, NE 68509-4987
(402) 471-5020; *Fax:* (402) 471-4433
E-mail: doug_ch@nde4.nde.state.ne.us

Board of Education
http://www.edneb.org/IPS/StateBoard.html
Main phone: (402) 471-2295
Main fax: (402) 471-0117
Mailing address: P.O. Box 84987, Lincoln, NE 68509-4987

Beverly Peterson, President
301 Centennial Mall South, 6th Fl., Lincoln, NE 68509-4987
E-mail: bjp@edneb.org

Educational Lands and Funds Board
General e-mail: nebrbelf@mail.state.ne.us
Main phone: (402) 471-2014
Main fax: (402) 471-3599

L. Jay Gildersleeve, Deputy Director
555 N. Cotner Blvd., Lincoln, NE 68505

Educational Telecommunications Commission
http://net.unl.edu/
General e-mail: net@unlinfo.unl.edu
Main phone: (402) 472-3611
Main fax: (402) 472-1785
TTY: (402) 472-6839
Mailing address: P.O. Box 83111, Lincoln, NE 68501-3111

Arlene Nelson, Chair
1800 N. 33rd St., Lincoln, NE 68501-3111

Electrical Division
Main phone: (402) 471-3550
Main fax: (402) 471-4297
Mailing address: P.O. Box 95066, Lincoln, NE 68509-5066

Terry Carlson, Executive Director
800 S. 13th St., #109, Lincoln, NE 68509-5066

Emergency Management Agency
http://www.nebema.org

Main phone: (402) 471-7430
Main fax: (402) 471-7433

Stanley M. Heng, Director
1300 Military Rd., Lincoln, NE 68508-1090

Engineers and Architects Board of Examiners
http://www.nol.org/home/NBOP/index.htm
Main phone: (402) 471-2021
Main fax: (402) 471-0787
Mailing address: P.O. Box 94751, Lincoln, NE 68509-4751

Charles G. Nelson, Executive Director
301 Centennial Mall South, Lincoln, NE 68508
E-mail: execdir@nol.org

Environmental Quality Dept.
http://www.deq.state.ne.us/
General e-mail: deqstaff@doc.state.ne.us
Main phone: (402) 471-2186
Main fax: (402) 471-2909

Michael Linder, Director
Atrium Bldg., 1200 N St., #400, Lincoln, NE 68509-8922
(402) 471-4231

Equal Opportunity Commission
http://tc.unl.edu/neoc/
Main phone: (402) 471-2024
Main fax: (402) 471-4059
Toll free: (800) 642-6112
TTY: (800) 833-7352
Mailing address: P.O. Box 94934, Lincoln, NE 68509-4934

Alfonza Whitaker, Executive Director
301 Centennial Mall South, 5th Fl., Lincoln, NE 68509-4934
(402) 471-4060
E-mail: whitaker@neoc.state.ne.us

Ethanol Board
http://www.ne-ethanol.org
Main phone: (402) 471-2941
Main fax: (402) 471-2470
Mailing address: P.O. Box 94922, Lincoln, NE 68509-4922

Todd C. Sneller, Administrator
301 Centennial Mall South, Lincoln, NE 68509-4922
E-mail: sneller@nrcdec.nrc.state.ne.us

Fire Marshal's Office
http://vmhost.cdp.state.ne.us:97/~sfmweb/sfmhome.html
Main phone: (402) 471-2027
Main fax: (402) 471-3118

Ken Winters, State Fire Marshal
246 S. 14th St., Lincoln, NE 68508-1804

Tourism: (402) 471-3791, 1-800-228-4307;
http://www.visitnebraska.org
Library: (402) 471-4785; http://
www.nebraskahistory.org/lib-arch/index.htm
Board of Education: (402) 471-2295;
http://www.edneb.org/IPS/StateBoard.html
Vital Statistics: (402) 471-2871; http://
www.hhs.state.ne.us/ced/cedindex.htm
Tax/Revenue: (402) 471-2971,
1-800-742-5740; http://www.nol.org/revenue
Motor Vehicles: (402) 471-2281;
http://www.nol.org/home/DMV/
State Police/Highway Patrol: (402) 471-4545,
1-800-525-5555; http://www.nebraska-state-
patrol.org/
Unemployment: (402) 471-9979;
http://www.dol.state.ne.us/uihome.htm
General Election Information:
(402) 471-3229; http://www.nol.org/home/
SOS/Elections/election.htm
Consumer Affairs: (402) 471-2682,
1-800-727-6432
Hazardous Materials: (402) 471-4217

(402) 471-9478; *Fax:* (402) 471-3118
E-mail: kwinters@sfm.state.ne.us

Forest Service

http://www.ianr.unl.edu/nfs
Main phone: (402) 472-2944
Main fax: (402) 472-2964

Gary Hergenrader, State Forester
103 Plant Industry, University of Nebraksa-Lincoln,
Lincoln, NE 68583-0815
(402) 472-1467
E-mail: ghergenrader1@unl.edu

Game and Parks Commission

http://www.ngpc.state.ne.us
Main phone: (402) 471-0641
Main fax: (402) 471-5528
Mailing address: P.O. Box 30370, Lincoln, NE
68503-0370

Rex Amack, Director
2200 N. 33rd St., Lincoln, NE 68503-0370
(402) 471-5539

Grain Sorghum Board

General e-mail: sorghum@srcdec.nrc.state.ne.us
Main phone: (402) 471-4276
Main fax: (402) 471-3040

Mailing address: P.O. Box 94982, Lincoln, NE
68509-4982

Barbara Kliment, Executive Director
301 Centennial Mall South, Lincoln, NE 68509-4982

Health and Human Services System

http://www.hhs.state.ne.us
General e-mail: hhsinfo@http://
www.hhs.state.ne.us
Main phone: (402) 471-9105
TTY: (402) 471-9570
Mailing address: P.O. Box 95044, Lincoln, NE
68509-5044

Ron Ross, Director
301 Centennial Mall South, Lincoln, NE 68509
(402) 471-9106

Aging Services Division

http://www.hhs.state.ne.us/ags/agsindex.htm
Main phone: (402) 471-2307
Main fax: (402) 471-4619
Toll free: (800) 942-7830
Mailing address: P.O. Box 95044, Lincoln, NE
68509-5044

Mark Intermill, Administrator
301 Centennial Mall South, 5th Fl., Lincoln, NE
68509
(402) 471-4617
E-mail: intermill@age1.ndoa.state.ne.us

Behavioral Health Division

http://www.hhs.state.ne.us/beh.behindex.htm
Main phone: (402) 471-2851
Main fax: (402) 479-5162

Vacant, Director
301 Centennial Mall South, Lincoln, NE 68509

Developmental Disability System

http://www.hhs.state.ne.us/dip/dipindex.htm
Main phone: (402) 479-5110
Main fax: (402) 479-5094
Toll free: (800) 254-4202
TTY: (402) 471-9570
Mailing address: P.O. Box 94728, Lincoln, NE
68509-4728

Roger Stortenbecker, Director
801 W. Prospetor, Lincoln, NE 68522

Juvenile Services

http://www.hhs.state.ne.us/jus/jusindex.htm
Main phone: (402) 471-8410
Main fax: (402) 471-9034
Mailing address: P.O. Box 95044, Lincoln, NE
68509-5044

Mark Martin, Administrator
2345 N. 60th, Lincoln, NE 68507
E-mail: Mark.Martin@hhss.state.ne.us

Medicaid and Managed Care Division
http://www.hhs.state.ne.us/med/medindex.htm
Main phone: (402) 471-9147
Main fax: (402) 471-9092
Toll free: (800) 430-3244
TTY: (800) 833-7352
Mailing address: P.O. Box 95026, Lincoln, NE 68509-5026

Cecil A. Brady, Director (Acting)
301 Centennial Mall South, Lincoln, NE 68509-5026

Historical Society
http://www.nebraskhistory.org
General e-mail: nshs@nebraskahistory.org
Main phone: (402) 471-3270
Main fax: (402) 471-3100
Mailing address: P.O. Box 82554, Lincoln, NE 68501-2554

Lawrence J. Sommer, Director
1500 R St., Lincoln, NE 68501-2554
(402) 471-4745

Library/Archives Division
http://www.nebraskahistory.org/lib-arch/index.htm
Main phone: (402) 471-4785
Main fax: (402) 471-3100
Mailing address: P.O. Box 82554, Lincoln, NE 68501-2554

Andrea Faling, Associate Director
1500 R St., Lincoln, NE 68508

Housing and Urban Development Dept.
Main phone: (402) 492-3100
Mailing address: P.O. Box 82554, Lincoln, NE 68501-2554

Terry Gratz, State Coordinator
10909 Mill Valley Rd., Omaha, NE 68154-3955

Industrial Relations Commission
http://www.nol.org/home/NCIR/
General e-mail: ncir04@nol.org
Main phone: (402) 471-2934
Main fax: (402) 471-6597
TTY: (800) 833-7352
Mailing address: P.O. Box 94864, Lincoln, NE 68509-4864

Annette Hord, Clerk/Administrator
301 Centennial Mall South, Lincoln, NE 68509-4864
(402) 471-2935

Insurance Dept.
http://www.nol.org/home/ndoi
Main phone: (402) 471-2201
Main fax: (402) 471-4610
Toll free: (877) 564-7323
TTY: (800) 833-7352

L. Tim Wagner, Director
941 O St., #400, Lincoln, NE 68508
E-mail: twagner@doi.state.ne.us

Investment Council
Main phone: (402) 471-2043
Main fax: (402) 471-2498

Rex W. Holsapple, State Investment Officer
Terminal Bldg., 941 O St., #500, Lincoln, NE 68508

Investment Finance Authority
http://www.nifa.org
Main phone: (402) 434-3900
Main fax: (402) 434-3921
Toll free: (800) 204-6432

Timothy R. Kenny, Executive Director
200 Commerce Court, 1230 O St., #200, Lincoln, NE 68508
E-mail: timkenny@nifa.org

Labor Dept.
http://www.dol.state.ne.us/
General e-mail: lharvey@dol.state.ne.us
Main phone: (402) 471-9000
Main fax: (402) 471-2318
TTY: (402) 471-9924

Boards and Licensing

Accountancy, (402) 471-3595,
  http://www.nol.org/home/BPA/
Child Care, (402) 471-9238
Contractors, (402) 595-3189
Cosmetology, (402) 471-2051
Engineers and Architects, (402) 471-2021,
  http://www.nol.org/home/NBOP/index.htm
Land Surveyors, (402) 471-2566,
  http://www.sso.state.ne.us
Medical, (402) 471-8566,
  http://www.sso.state.ne.us
Nursing, (402) 471-8566,
  http://www.sso.state.ne.us
Pharmacy, (402) 471-8566,
  http://www.sso.state.ne.us
Real Estate, (402) 471-9015,
  http://www.dbdec.nrc.state.ne.us/appraiser

Mailing address: P.O. Box 94600, Lincoln, NE 68509-4600

Fernando (Butch) Lecuona, Commissioner
550 S. 16th St., Lincoln, NE 68509
(402) 471-9792
E-mail: flecuona@dol.state.ne.us

Land Surveyors Board
http://www.sso.state.ne.us
Main phone: (402) 471-2566
Main fax: (402) 471-3057

James L. Brown, Director
555 N. Cotmer Blvd., Lincoln, NE 68505

Law Enforcement and Criminal Justice Commission
Main phone: (402) 471-2194
Mailing address: P.O. Box 94946, Lincoln, NE 68509-4946

Curtis Allen, Executive Director
301 Centennial Mall South, 5th Fl., Lincoln, NE 68509-4946

Library Commission
http://www.nlc.state.ne.us
General e-mail: ready@neon.nlc.state.ne.us
Main phone: (402) 471-2045
Main fax: (402) 471-2083
TTY: (402) 471-4014

Rod G. Wagner, Director
Atrium Bldg., 1200 N. St., #120, Lincoln, NE 68508-2023
(402) 471-4001; *Fax:* (402) 471-2083
E-mail: rwagner@neon.nlc.state.ne.us

Liquor Control Commission
http://www.nol.org/home/NLCC/index.htm
General e-mail: nlcc01@nol.org
Main phone: (402) 471-2571
Main fax: (402) 471-2814
Mailing address: P.O. Box 95046, Lincoln, NE 68509-5046

Richard (Dick) Coyne, Chair
301 Centennial Mall South, Lincoln, NE 68509-5046

Motor Vehicles Dept.
http://www.nol.org/home/DMV/
Main phone: (402) 471-2281
Main fax: (402) 471-2281
TTY: (402) 471-4154

Beverly Neth, Director
301 Centennial Mall South, 1st Fl., Lincoln, NE 68509-4876

Natural Resources Commission
http://www.nrc.state.ne.us

Main phone: (402) 471-2081
Main fax: (402) 471-3132
Mailing address: P.O. Box 94876, Lincoln, NE 68509-4876

Dayle E. Williamson, Director
301 Centennial Mall South, Lincoln, NE 68509-4876
(402) 471-3927
E-mail: daylew@nrcdec.nrc.state.ne.us

Oil and Gas Conservation Commission
Main phone: (308) 254-6919
Main fax: (308) 254-6922
Mailing address: P.O. Box 399, Sidney, NE 69162-0399

William H. Sydow, Director
922 Illinois St., Sidney, NE 69162-0399

Parole Board
Main phone: (402) 471-2156
Main fax: (402) 471-2453
Mailing address: P.O. Box 94754, Lincoln, NE 68509-4754

Linda Krutz, Chair
Folsum and W. Prospector, Bldg. 15, Lincoln, NE 68522

Policy Research Office
Main phone: (402) 471-2414
Main fax: (402) 471-2528
Mailing address: P.O. Box 94601, Lincoln, NE 68509-4601

Lauren Hill, Director
State Capitol, #1319, Lincoln, NE 68509-4601

Postsecondary Education Coordinating Commission
http://www.nol.org/NEpostsecondaryed
General e-mail: staff@ccpe.state.ne.us
Main phone: (402) 471-2847
Main fax: (402) 471-2886
Mailing address: P.O. Box 95005, Lincoln, NE 68509-5005

David R. Powers, Executive Director
140 N. 8th St., #300, Lincoln, NE 68509
E-mail: dpowers@ccpe.state.ne.us

Power Review Board
Main phone: (402) 471-2301
Main fax: (402) 471-3715
Mailing address: P.O. Box 94713, Lincoln, NE 68509-4713

Timothy J. Texel, Executive Director
301 Centennial Mall South, 5th Fl., Lincoln, NE 68509-4713
E-mail: tjtexel@nrcdec.nrc.state.ne.us

Probation Administration Office

Main phone: (402) 471-4140
Main fax: (402) 471-2197
Mailing address: P.O. Box 98910, Lincoln, NE 68509-8910

Edward C. Birkel, Administrator

1445 K St., Lincoln, NE 68509-8910
(402) 471-4928
E-mail: ebirkel@nsc.state.ne.us

Public Advocacy Commission

http://www.nol.org/home/ncpa
General e-mail: advocate@ncpa.state.ne.us
Main phone: (402) 471-7774
Main fax: (402) 471-8087

Susan Jacobs, Chair

Apothecary Bldg., 140 N. 8th St., #270, Lincoln, NE 68509-8932

Public Employees Retirement Systems

http://www.nol.org/home/pers/
General e-mail: dgress@ret.state.ne.us
Main phone: (402) 471-2053
Main fax: (402) 471-9493
Toll free: (800) 245-5712
Mailing address: P.O. Box 94816, Lincoln, NE 68509-4816

Anna J. Sullivan, Director

301 Centennial Mall South, Lincoln, NE 68509-4816

Public Service Commission

http://www.nol.org/home/NPSC/
General e-mail: rlogsdon@navix.net
Main phone: (402) 471-3101
Main fax: (402) 471-0254
Toll free: (800) 526-0017
TTY: (402) 471-0213
Mailing address: P.O. Box 94927, Lincoln, NE 68509-4927

Robert R. Logsdon, Executive Director

300 The Atrium, 1200 N St., Lincoln, NE 68508
E-mail: rlogsdon@navix.net

Racing Commission

Main phone: (402) 471-4155
Main fax: (402) 471-2339
Mailing address: P.O. Box 95014, Lincoln, NE 68509-5014

Dennis Oeschlager, Director

301 Centennial Mall South, 4th Fl., Lincoln, NE 68508-2707
(402) 471-3543

Real Estate Appraiser Board

http://www.dbdec.nrc.state.ne.us/appraiser
Main phone: (402) 471-9015
Main fax: (402) 471-9017
Mailing address: P.O. Box 94963, Lincoln, NE 68509-4963

Marilyn Hasselbalch, Chair

301 Centennial Mall South, 5th Fl., Lincoln, NE 68509-4963
E-mail: mjhass@nrcdec.nrc.state.ne.us

Real Estate Commission

http://www.nol.org/home/nrec
General e-mail: infoTech@nrec.state.ne.us
Main phone: (402) 471-2004
Main fax: (402) 471-4492
Mailing address: P.O. Box 94667, Lincoln, NE 68509-4666

Les Tyrrell, Director

1200 N St., #402, Lincoln, NE 68509

Revenue Dept.

http://www.nol.org/revenue
Main phone: (402) 471-2971
Main fax: (402) 471-5608
Toll free: (800) 742-7474
TTY: (402) 471-5740
Mailing address: P.O. Box 94818, Lincoln, NE 68509-4818

Mary Jane Egr, Tax Commissioner

301 Centennial Mall South, Lincoln, NE 68509-4818
(402) 471-5604

State Lottery

http://www.nelottery.com
Main phone: (402) 471-6101
Main fax: (402) 471-6108
Toll free: (800) 587-5200
Mailing address: P.O. Box 98901, Lincoln, NE 68509-8901

James Quinn, Director

301 Centennial Mall South, Lincoln, NE 68509
E-mail: jquinn@notes.state.ne.us

Risk Management, Benefits, and State Claims Board

Main phone: (402) 471-2551
Main fax: (402) 471-2800

Leslie Donley, Risk Manager

521 S. 14th St., #230, Lincoln, NE 68508-2707
(402) 471-3543
E-mail: ldonley@das.state.ne.us

Roads Dept.
http://www.dor.state.ne.us/
General e-mail: droberts@dor.state.ne.us
Main phone: (402) 471-4567
Main fax: (402) 479-4325
TTY: (402) 479-3834
Mailing address: P.O. Box 94759, Lincoln, NE 68509-4759

John L. Craig, Director
1500 Hwy. 2, Lincoln, NE 68502
(402) 479-4615

Soybean Board
General e-mail: NS44557@navix.net
Main phone: (402) 441-3240
Main fax: (402) 441-3238
Toll free: (800) 852-2326

Victor Bohuslavsky, Executive Director (Acting)
1610 S. 70th St., #200, Lincoln, NE 68506-1565

State College System
http://www.nscs.edu/
Main phone: (402) 471-2505
Main fax: (402) 471-2669
Mailing address: P.O. Box 94605, Lincoln, NE 68509-4605

Carrol F. Krause, Executive Director
State Capitol, Lincoln, NE 68509-4605
E-mail: ckrause@library.nscs.edu

State Fair
http://www.statefair.org/
General e-mail: nestatefair@statefair.org
Main phone: (402) 474-4109
Main fax: (402) 473-4114
Mailing address: P.O. Box 81223, Lincoln, NE 68501-1223

John Skold, General Manager
State Fair Office, Lincoln, NE 68501-1223
(402) 473-4110
E-mail: jskold@statefair.org

State Library
http://court.nol.org/library/lawlibindex.htm
General e-mail: nsc_lawlib@nsc.state.ne.us
Main phone: (402) 471-3189

Marie Wiechman, Librarian
15th and K Sts., Lincoln, NE 68509

State Patrol
http://www.nebraska-state-patrol.org/
Main phone: (402) 471-4545
Main fax: (402) 479-4002

Toll free: (800) 525-5555
Mailing address: P.O. Box 94907, Lincoln, NE 68509-4907

Thomas Nesbitt, Superintendent
1600 Nebraska Hwy. 2, Lincoln, NE 68502

Veterans Affairs Dept.
Main phone: (402) 471-2458
Main fax: (402) 471-2491
Mailing address: P.O. Box 95083, Lincoln, NE 68509-5083

Keith E. Fickenscher, Director
State Office Bldg., Lincoln, NE 68509-5083
E-mail: fickens@mail.state.ne.us

Water Resources Dept.
http://www.nol.org/home/dwr/
Main phone: (402) 471-2363
Main fax: (402) 471-2900
Mailing address: P.O. Box 94676, Lincoln, NE 68509-4676

Roger Patterson, Director
301 Centennial Mall South, Lincoln, NE 68509-4676

Wheat Board
Main phone: (402) 471-2358
Main fax: (402) 471-3446
Mailing address: P.O. Box 94912, Lincoln, NE 68509-4912

Ron Maas, Executive Director
301 Centennial Mall South, Lincoln, NE 68509-4912
E-mail: rmaas@nrcdec.nrc.state.ne.us

Women's Commission
http://www.ncsw.org/
General e-mail: ncswmail@mail.state.ne.us
Main phone: (402) 471-2039
Main fax: (402) 471-5655
Mailing address: P.O. Box 94985, Lincoln, NE 68509-4985

Joni Gray, Executive Director
301 Centennial Mall South, Lincoln, NE 68509-4985

Workers' Compensation Court
http://www.nol.org/workcomp
General e-mail: nwecc@wcc.state.ne.us
Main phone: (402) 471-6468
Toll free: (800) 599-5155
Mailing address: P.O. Box 98908, Lincoln, NE 68509-8908

Glen W. Morton, Director
525 Bldg., 12th and 13th Fls., Lincoln, NE 68509-8908

Laws

Sales tax: 6.5%
Income tax: 6.7%
State minimum wage: $5.15 (Federal is $5.15)
Marriage age: 19
First-cousin marriage: Prohibited
Drinking age: 21
State control of liquor sales: No
Blood alcohol for DWI: 0.10%
Driving age: 17
Speed limit: 75 mph
Permit to buy handguns: Yes, 2 days to acquire
Minimum age to possess handguns: 18
Minimum age to possess rifles, shotguns: None
State lottery: Yes; also Powerball
Casinos: No
Pari-mutuel betting: Horse racing
Death penalty: Yes
3 strikes minimum sentence: 10 yrs. (3rd felony)
Hate crimes law: Yes
Gay employment non-discrimination: No
Official language(s): English
Term limits: None

State laws are complex and subject to change; this information is not intended as legal advice. For an explanation of this information, see p. x.

Nebraska Legislature

State Capitol
Lincoln, NE 68509-4604
General information: (402) 471-2271
Fax: (402) 471-2126
Bill status: (402) 471-2709
http://www.unicam.state.ne.us

Legislature

David I. Maurstad (R), President
State Capitol, P.O. Box 94604, #2103, Lincoln, NE 68509-4604
(402) 471-2256; *Fax:* (402) 471-6031
E-mail: dmaursta@notes.state.ne.us
http://www.nol.org/home/LtGov/

Douglas A. Kristensen (I), Speaker of the Legislature
State Capitol, P.O. Box 94604, #2103, Lincoln, NE 68509-4604
(402) 471-2726
E-mail: dkristensen@unicam.state.ne.us
http://www.unicam.state.ne.us/senators/D37.htm

Patrick J. O'Donnell, Clerk of the Legislature
State Capitol, P.O. Box 94604, #2018, Lincoln, NE 68509-4604
(402) 471-2271; *Fax:* (402) 471-2126
E-mail: podonnell@unicam.state.ne.us
http://www.unicam.state.ne.us/clerk.htm

Nebraska Judiciary

State Capitol Bldg.
1445 K St.
Lincoln, NE 68509
http://court.nol.org

Supreme Court
http://court.nol.org/courts.htm

Lanet S. Asmussen, Clerk
State Capitol Bldg., 1445 K St., #2143, Lincoln, NE 68509-8910
(402) 471-3731; *Fax:* (402) 471-3480

Justices
Composition: 7 justices
Selection Method: appointed by governor; must stand for retention in first general election more than 3 years after appointment
Length of term: 6 years

John V. Hendry, Chief Justice, (402) 471-3738
William M. Connolly, Associate Justice, (402) 471-3733
John M. Gerrard, Associate Justice, (402) 471-3736
Michael McCormack, Associate Justice, (402) 471-4345
Lindsey Miller-Lerman, Associate Justice, (402) 471-3734
Kenneth C. Stephan, Associate Justice, (402) 471-3737
John F. Wright, Associate Justice, (402) 471-3735

Office of Court Administration
Main phone: (402) 471-3730
Main fax: (402) 471-2197

Joseph C. Steele, State Court Administrator
State Capitol Bldg., 1445 K St., #1220, Lincoln, NE
68509-8910

Supreme Court Law Library
http://court.nol.org/library/lawlibindex.htm

Main phone: (402) 471-3189
Main fax: (402) 471-1011

Marie Wiechman, State Law Librarian
State Capitol Bldg., 1445 K St., #1220, Lincoln, NE
68509-8910

Legislative and Political Party Information Resources

Committees: http://www.unicam.state.ne.us/committe.htm
Legislative process: http://www.unicam.state.ne.us/process.htm
Current Session Information: http://www.unicam.state.ne.us/calendar/session.pdf
Nebraska Democratic Party: http://www.nebraskademocrats.org
   985 S. 27th St., Lincoln, NE 68510; *Phone:* (402) 434-2180; *Fax:* (402) 434-2188;
   E-mail: NebraskaDemocrats@nebraskademocrats.org
Nebraska Republican Party: http://www.negop.org
   421 S. 9th St., #233, Lincoln, NE 68508; *Phone:* (402) 475-2122; *Fax:* (402) 475-3541;
   E-mail: info@NEgop.org

Nevada

State Capitol
Carson City, NV 89710
Public information: (775) 684-1000
Fax: (775) 684-5846
http://www.state.nv.us

Office of the Governor
http://www.governor.state.nv.us
Main phone: (775) 684-5670
Main fax: (775) 684-5683

Kenny Guinn (R), Governor
101 N. Carson St., Carson City, NV 89710
E-mail: governor@govmail.state.nv.us

Scott Scherer, Chief of Staff
Executive Chambers, Capitol Complex, Carson City,
NV 89710
(775) 684-5670; *Fax:* (775) 684-5683
E-mail: sscherer@govmail.state.nv.us

Jack Finn, Press Secretary
Executive Chambers, 101 N. Carson St., Carson City,
NV 89701
(775) 684-5670; *Fax:* (775) 684-5689

Brian Catlett, Constituent Services Director
Executive Chambers, Capitol Complex, Carson City,
NV 89710
(775) 684-5670; *Fax:* (775) 684-5683

Michael Pieper, Director, Washington Office
444 N. Capitol St. N.W., #209, Washington, DC 20001
(202) 624-5405; *Fax:* (202) 624-8181
E-mail: mpieper@sso.org

Office of the Lieutenant Governor
http://www.state.nv.us/ltgovernor/
General e-mail: nvltgov@govmail.state.nv.us
Main phone: (702) 486-2400
Main fax: (702) 486-2404
Mailing address: 555 E. Washington, #5500, Las
Vegas, NV 89101

Lorraine T. Hunt (R), Lieutenant Governor
State Capitol Bldg., 101 N. Carson St., #2, Carson
City, NV 89701
(775) 684-5637; *Fax:* (775) 684-5782

Office of the Secretary of State
http://sos.state.nv.us
General e-mail: sosmail@govmail.state.nv.us
Main phone: (775) 684-5708
Main fax: (775) 684-5725
Toll free: (800) 992-0900

State of Nevada

Capital: Carson City, since 1861
Founded: 1861, Nevada Territory created from Utah Territory
Statehood: October 31, 1864 (36th state)
Constitution adopted: 1864
Area: 109,806 sq. mi. (ranks 7th)
Population: 1,746,898 (1998 est.; ranks 36th)
Largest cities: (1998 est.) Las Vegas (404,288); Reno (163,334); Henderson (152,717); Sparks (62,432); Carson City (49,301)
Counties: 16, Most populous: (1998 est.) Clark (1,162,129); Washoe (313,660); Elko (46,084); Lyon (30,072); Nye (28,799)
U.S. Congress: Richard Bryan (D), Harry Reid (D); 2 Representatives
Nickname(s): Sagebrush State, Silver State, Battle-born State
Motto: All for our country
Song: "Home Means Nevada"
Bird: Moutain bluebird
Tree: Bristlecone pine
Flower: Sagebrush
State fair: at Reno, late Aug.
Former capital(s): None

Dean Heller (R), Secretary of State
Capitol Complex, 101 N. Carson St., #3, Carson City,
NV 89701-4786

Office of the Attorney General
http://www.state.nv.us/ag/
General e-mail: aginfo@govmail.state.nv.us
Main phone: (775) 684-1100
Main fax: (775) 684-1108
Toll free: (800) 767-7381
TTY: (775) 687-1382

Frankie Sue Del Papa (D), Attorney General
Capitol Complex, 100 N. Carson St., Carson City, NV
89701-4717
(775) 684-1112

Office of the State Treasurer
http://treasurer.state.nv.us/
General e-mail: treasury@treasurer.state.nv.us

Main phone: (775) 684-5600
Main fax: (775) 684-5623

Brian K. Krolicki (R), State Treasurer
Capitol Bldg., 101 N. Carson St., #4, Carson City, NV 89701-4786

Office of the Controller
http://www.state.nv.us/controller/
Main phone: (775) 684-5750
Main fax: (775) 684-5650

Kathy Augustine (R), State Controller
Capitol Bldg., 101 N. Carson St., #5, Carson City, NV 89701
(775) 684-5777; *Fax:* (775) 684-5696
E-mail: kaugust@govmail.state.nv.us

Military Office
Main phone: (775) 887-7302
Main fax: (775) 887-7246

Drennan Anthony Clark, Adjutant General
2525 S. Carson St., Carson City, NV 89701

Agencies

Accountancy Board
http://www.state.nv.us/accountancy/
General e-mail: nvcpabd@govmail.state.nv.us
Main phone: (775) 786-0231
Main fax: (775) 786-0234

N. Johanna Bravo, Executive Director
200 S. Virginia St., #670, Reno, NV 89509

Administration Dept.
http://www.state.nv.us/budget/
General e-mail: dduck@govmail.state.nv.us
Main phone: (775) 684-0222
Main fax: (775) 684-0260

John Perry Comeaux, Director
209 E. Musser, #200, Carson City, NV 89710

Agriculture Dept.
http://www.state.nv.us/b&i/ad/
General e-mail: josborne@govmail.state.nv.us
Main phone: (775) 688-1180
Main fax: (775) 688-1178

Paul Iverson, Director
350 Capitol Hill Ave., Reno, NV 89502-2923
(775) 688-1182, ext. 222
E-mail: piverson@govmail.state.nv.us

Architecture and Design Board
http://www.state.nv.us/nsbaidrd
General e-mail: nsbaidrd@govmail.state.nv.us
Main phone: (702) 486-7300
Main fax: (702) 486-7304

Derrell Parker, Chair
2080 E. Flamingo Rd., #225, Las Vegas, NV 89119

Business and Industry Dept.
http://www.state.nv.us/b&i/
General e-mail: biinfo@govmail.state.nv.us
Main phone: (702) 486-2750
Main fax: (702) 486-2758
TTY: (702) 486-4393

Sydney Wickliffe, Director
Grant Sawyer Bldg., 555 E. Washington Ave., #4900, Las Vegas, NV 89101
E-mail: director@govmail.state.nv.us

Financial Institutions
http://www.state.nv.us/b&i/fi
Main phone: (775) 687-4259
Main fax: (775) 687-6909

L. Scott Walshaw, Commissioner
406 E. 2nd St., #3, Carson City, NV 89710-4758
E-mail: swalshaw@govmail.state.nv.us

Insurance Division
http://doi.state.nv.us
Main phone: (775) 687-4270
Main fax: (775) 687-3937

Alice Molasky-Arman, Commissioner
788 Fairview Dr., Carson City, NV 89701
(775) 687-7668
E-mail: icommish@doi.state.nv.us

Colorado River Commission
http://www.state.nv.us/colorado_river
Main phone: (702) 486-2670
Main fax: (702) 486-2695
TTY: (702) 486-2698

Richard W. Bunker, Lead Commissioner
Grant Sawyer Bldg., 555 E. Washington Ave., #3100, Las Vegas, NV 89101

Conservation and Natural Resources Dept.
http://www.state.nv.us/cnr/
Main phone: (775) 687-4360
Main fax: (775) 687-6122

Peter G. Morros, Director
123 W. Nye Lane, #230, Carson City, NV 89706-0818

Forestry Division
Main phone: (775) 684-2500
Main fax: (775) 687-4244

Roy W. Trenoweth, State Forester
1201 Johnson, Carson City, NV 89706

State Parks Division
http://www.state.nv.us/stparks

General e-mail: stparks@govmail.state.nv.us
Main phone: (775) 687-4370
Main fax: (775) 687-4117
TTY: (775) 684-3400

Wayne Perock, Administrator
1300 S. Curry St., #230, Carson City, NV 89703-5202
(775) 687-4384

Water Resources Division
Main phone: (775) 687-4380
Main fax: (775) 687-6972

R. Michael Turnipseed, State Engineer
123 W. Nye Lane, #246, Carson City, NV 89706-0818

Consumer Protection Bureau
Main phone: (775) 687-6300
Main fax: (775) 687-6304

Fred Schmidt, Deputy Attorney General
1000 E. Willaim St., #200, Carson City, NV 89701-3117

Economic Development Commission
http://www.state.nv.us/businessop/
General e-mail: bizinfo@bizopp.state.nv.us
Main phone: (775) 687-4325
Main fax: (775) 687-4450
Toll free: (800) 336-1600

Robert E. Shriver, Executive Director
108 E. Proctor St., Carson City, NV 89701-4240
E-mail: bobs@bizzop.state.nv.us

Education Dept.
http://www.nsn.k12.nv.us/nvdoe/
Main phone: (775) 687-9200
Main fax: (775) 687-9101

Mary L. Peterson, Superintendent
700 E. 5th St., Carson City, NV 89701-5096
(775) 687-9217; Fax: (775) 687-9202
E-mail: peterson@nsn.k12.nv.us

Emergency Management Office
General e-mail: nvdem@govmail.state.nv.us
Main phone: (775) 687-4240
Main fax: (775) 678-5584

Frank Siracusa, Chief
2525 S. Carson St., Carson City, NV 89710

Employment, Training, and Rehabilitation Dept.
http://www.state.nv.us/detr/
General e-mail: detrinfo@govmail.state.nv.us
Main phone: (775) 684-3849
Main fax: (775) 684-3850
TTY: (775) 687-5353

Higher Educational Institutions

University and Community College System
http://www.nevada.edu
2601 Enterprise Rd., Reno, NV 89512
Main phone: (775) 784-4905
Branches: Las Vegas, Reno

Carol A. Jackson, Director
500 E. 3rd St., #200, Carson City, NV 89713
(775) 684-3911; Fax: (775) 684-3908
E-mail: cjackson@govmail.state.nv.us

Engineers and Land Surveyors Board
http://www.state.nv.us/boe
General e-mail: nevengsur@natinfo.net
Main phone: (775) 688-1231
Main fax: (775) 688-2991
Toll free: (800) 728-2632

Noni Johnson, Executive Director
1775 E. Plumb Ln., #135, Reno, NV 89502

Ethics Commission
Main phone: (775) 687-5469
Main fax: (775) 687-1279

Kenneth A. Rohrs, Executive Director
3476 Executive Pointe Way, #10, Carson City, NV 89706

Gaming Commission
http://www.state.nv.us/gaming/
Main phone: (775) 687-6530
Main fax: (775) 687-5817
Mailing address: P.O. Box 8003, Carson City, NV 89702-8003

Brian Sandoval, Chair
1919 E. College Pkwy., Carson City, NV 89706

Gaming Control Board
http://www.state.nv.us/gaming/
Main phone: (775) 687-6500
Main fax: (775) 687-5817
Mailing address: P.O. Box 8003, Carson City, NV 89702-8003

Steve DuCharme, Chair
1919 E. College Pkwy., Carson City, NV 89702
(775) 687-6525

Human Resources Dept.
http://www.state.nv.us/hr/
Main phone: (775) 684-4000
Main fax: (775) 684-4010

Charlotte Crawford, Director
505 E. King St., #600, Carson City, NV 89701-3708

Aging Services Administrator
http://www.nvaging.net
General e-mail: dascc@govmail.state.nv.us
Main phone: (775) 687-4210
Main fax: (775) 687-4264

Mary Liveratti, Administrator
3416 Goni Rd., Bldg. D, #132, Carson City, NV
89706

Mental Hygiene/Developmental Services
General e-mail: mhds@govmail.state.nv.us
Main phone: (775) 684-5943
Main fax: (775) 684-5966

Carlos Brandenburg, Administrator
505 E. King St., #600, Carson City, NV 89710

State Public Defender's Office
Main phone: (775) 687-4880
Main fax: (775) 687-4993
Toll free: (800) 992-0900, ext. 4880

Steven G. McGuire, Public Defender
511 E. Robinson St., Carson City, NV 89701

Information Technology Dept.
http://www.state.nv.us/doit/
General e-mail: doitinfo@doit.state.nv.us
Main phone: (775) 684-5800
Main fax: (775) 684-5846

Marlene Lockard, Director
505 E. King St., #403, Carson City, NV 89701
(775) 684-5801
E-mail: mlockard@doit.state.nv.us

Frequently Called Numbers

Tourism: (775) 687-4322, 1-800-877-2000;
  http://www.travelnevada.com
Library: (775) 687-3315; 1-800-922-2880;
  http://dmla.clan.lib.nv.us
Vital Statistics: (775) 684-4280
Tax/Revenue: (775) 687-4892, 1-800-992-
  0900; http://www.state.nv.us/taxation/
Motor Vehicles: (775) 684-4549;
  http://www.state.nv.us/dmv_ps/
State Police/Highway Patrol: (775) 687-5300
Unemployment: (775) 684-3909;
  http://www.state.nv.us/detr/es/index.htm
General Election Information: (775)
  684-5705; http://sos.state.nv.us/nvelection/
Consumer Affairs: (775) 687-6300
Hazardous Materials: (702) 687-6973;
  http://www.state.nv.us/dmv_ps/serc.htm

Liquefied Petroleum Gas Board
http://www.state.nv.us/lpg/
General e-mail: lpgasbd@govmail.state.nv.us
Main phone: (775) 687-4890
Main fax: (775) 687-3956
Toll free: (800) 992-0900, ext. 4890
Mailing address: P.O. Box 338, Carson City, NV
89702-0338

Richard Forant, Chair
106 E. Adams, #216, Carson City, NV 89703

Medical Examiners Board
http://www.state.nv.us/medical/
General e-mail: nsbme@govmail.state.nv.us
Main phone: (775) 688-2559
Main fax: (775) 688-2321
Mailing address: P.O. Box 7238, Reno, NV 89510

Larry D. Lessly, Executive Director
1105 Terminal Way, #301, Reno, NV 89502

Motor Vehicles and Public Safety Dept.
http://www.state.nv.us/dmv_ps/
General e-mail: dmvinfo@govmail.state.nv.us
Main phone: (775) 684-4549
Main fax: (775) 684-4692

John Drew, Director (Acting)
555 Wright Way, Carson City, NV 89711-0900
(775) 684-4549

Public Safety: Highway Patrol Division
Main phone: (775) 687-5300
Main fax: (775) 684-4879

Michael Hood, Chief
555 Wright Way, #211, Carson City, NV 89711-
0900
(775) 684-4867

Public Safety: Parole and Probation Division
http://www.state.nv.us/dmv_ps/pphone.html
Main phone: (775) 684-2605
Main fax: (775) 687-5402

Carlos Concha, Chief
1445 Hot Springs Rd., #104, Carson City, NV
89711

Public Safety: State Fire Marshal
http://www.state.nv.us/dmv-ps/firemar.htm
General e-mail: hoster@govmail.state.nv.us
Main phone: (775) 687-4290
Main fax: (775) 687-5122

Marvin Carr, State Fire Marshal
Stewart Facility, 107 Jacobsen Way, Carson City,
NV 89710

Museums, Library, and Arts Dept.
http://dmla.clan.lib.nv.us/

General e-mail: webmstr@clan.liv.nv.us
Main phone: (775) 687-8393
Main fax: (775) 684-5446
TTY: (775) 687-8338

Michael D. Hillerby, Director (Acting)
708 N. Curry St., Carson City, NV 89703-3915
(775) 684-5444
E-mail: mhiller@clan.lib.nv.us

Arts Council
Main phone: (775) 687-6680
Main fax: (775) 687-6688

Susan Boskoff, Director
602 N. Curry St., Carson City, NV 89703-3914
(775) 687-6690

Historic Preservation Office
http://www.clan.lib.nv.us
General e-mail: blprudic@clan.lib.nv.us
Main phone: (775) 684-3440
Main fax: (775) 684-3442

Ron James, State Historic Preservation Officer
100 N. Stewart St., Carson City, NV 89701
(775) 684-3440; *Fax:* (775) 684-3442

State Library and Archives
http://dmla.clan.lib.nv.us
General e-mail: http://dmla.clan.lib.nv.us/docs/
email/webmaster.htm
Main phone: (775) 687-3315
Main fax: (775) 684-3311
Toll free: (800) 922-2880
TTY: (775) 687-8338

Monteria Hightower, Director
100 N. Stewart St., Carson City, NV 89701-4285
(775) 684-3315
E-mail: mhightow@clan.lib.nv.us

Nursing Board
http://nursingboard.state.nv.us
General e-mail: nsbnreno@govmail.state.nv.us
Main phone: (775) 688-2620
Main fax: (775) 688-2628

Kathy Apple, Executive Director
1755 E. Plumb Ln., #260, Reno, NV 89502

Personnel Dept.
http://www.state.nv.us/personnel/
Main phone: (775) 684-0150
Main fax: (775) 684-0124
TTY: (800) 326-6888

Jeanne Greene, Director (Acting)
209 E. Musser St., #101, Carson City, NV 89701-4204

Pharmacy Board
http://www.state.nv.us/pharmacy/

Boards and Licensing

Accountancy, (775) 786-0231,
http://www.state.nv.us/accountancy/
Architecture and Design, (702) 486-7300,
http://www.state.nv.us/nsbaidrd
Child Care, (775) 684-4421
Contractors, (702) 486-3500
Cosmetology, (702) 486-6542
Engineers and Land Surveyors, (775)
688-1231, http://www.state.nv.us/boe
Medical Examiners, (775) 688-2559,
http://www.state.nv.us/medical/
Nursing, (775) 688-2620,
http://nursingboard.state.nv.us
Pharmacy, (775) 850-1440,
http://www.state.nv.us/pharmacy/
Real Estate, (702) 486-40333

General e-mail: pharmacy@govmail.state.nv.us
Main phone: (775) 850-1440
Main fax: (775) 850-1444
Toll free: (800) 364-2081

Keith W. MacDonald, Executive Secretary
555 Double Eagle Court, #1100, Reno, NV 89511-8991

Prisons Dept.
Main phone: (775) 887-3285
Main fax: (775) 687-6715
Mailing address: P.O. Box 7011, Carson City, NV 89702

Robert Bayer, Director
5500 Snyder Ave., Carson City, NV 89701
(775) 887-3216

Public Employees Retirement System
http://www.nvpers.org/
Main phone: (775) 687-4200
Main fax: (775) 687-5131
Toll free: (800) 992-0900, ext. 4200
TTY: (775) 687-6326

George Pyne, Executive Officer
693 W. Nye Lane, Carson City, NV 89703-1599
(775) 687-4200, ext. 254
E-mail: gpyne@nvpers.org

Public Utilities Commission
http://www.state.nv.us/puc/
Main phone: (775) 687-6001
Main fax: (775) 687-8726
Toll free: (800) 992-0900, ext. 87-6001

Donald Soderberg, Chair
1150 E. William St., Carson City, NV 89701
(775) 687-6007

State Fair
http://www.nevadastatefair.org/
General e-mail: nvstatefair@inetworld.com
Main phone: (775) 688-5767
Main fax: (775) 688-5763

Gary Lubra, Executive Director
1350-A N. Wells Ave., Reno, NV 89512

Taxation Dept.
http://www.state.nv.us/taxation/
Main phone: (775) 687-4892
Main fax: (775) 687-5981
Toll free: (800) 992-0900

David P. Pursell, Executive Director
1550 E. College Pkwy., Carson City, NV 89706

Tourism Commission
http://www.travelnevada.com
General e-mail: ncot@travelnevada.com
Main phone: (775) 687-4322
Main fax: (775) 687-6779
Toll free: (800) 877-2000

Thomas G. Tait, Executive Director
401 N. Carson St., Carson City, NV 89701

Transportation Dept.
http://www.nevadadot.com/
General e-mail: info@nevadadot.com
Main phone: (775) 888-7000
Main fax: (775) 888-7115

Thomas E. Stephens, Director
1263 S. Stewart St., Carson City, NV 89712
(775) 888-7440; *Fax:* (775) 888-7201

University and Community College System
http://www.nevada.edu
Main phone: (775) 784-4901
Main fax: (775) 784-1127

Thomas Anderes, Chancellor (Interim)
2601 Enterprise Rd., Reno, NV 89512
(775) 784-4905, ext. 223

Veterans Affairs Commission
http://www.state.nv.us/veterans/
General e-mail: namvet71@aol.com
Main phone: (775) 688-1653
Main fax: (775) 688-1656

Wendell R. Alcom, Executive Director
1201 Terminal Way, #221, Reno, NV 89520

Nevada Legislature
401 S. Carson St.
Carson City, NV 89701-4747
General information: (775) 687-6800
Toll free: (800) 992-0973
Bill status: (775) 687-5545
http://www.leg.state.nv.us

Senate
General information: (775) 687-5742
Fax: (775) 687-8206
E-mail: senate@lcb.state.nv.us

Lorraine T. Hunt (R), President
State Capitol Bldg., 101 N. Carson St., #2, Carson
City, NV 89701
(775) 684-5637; *Fax:* (775) 684-5782

Laws

Sales tax: 7%
Income tax: None
State minimum wage: $5.15 (Federal is $5.15)
Marriage age: 18
First-cousin marriage: Prohibited
Drinking age: 21
State control of liquor sales: No
Blood alcohol for DWI: 0.10%
Driving age: 16
Speed limit: 75 mph
Permit to buy handguns: In some areas
Minimum age to possess handguns: 14
Minimum age to possess rifles, shotguns: 14
State lottery: No
Casinos: Yes (commercial, tribal); also slot/
    video machines
Pari-mutuel betting: Horse racing
Death penalty: Yes
3 strikes minimum sentence: Life (violent
    felony after 3 prior felonies)
Hate crimes law: Yes
Gay employment non-discrimination: Yes
Official language(s): None
Term limits: Governor (8 yrs.); state legislators
    (12 yrs.)

*State laws are complex and subject to
change; this information is not intended as
legal advice. For an explanation of this
information, see p. x.*

E-mail: nvltgov@govmail.state.nv.us
http://www.state.nv.us/ltgovernor/

Lawrence E. Jacobsen (R), President Pro Tempore
401 S. Carson St., Carson City, NV 87701-4747
(775) 687-8125
E-mail: ljacobsen@sen.state.nv.us
http://www.leg.state.nv.us/70th/Legislators/Senators/
Jacobsen.htm

William J. Raggio (R), Majority Leader
401 S. Carson St., Carson City, NV 87701-4747
(775) 687-3557
E-mail: wraggio@sen.state.nv.us
http://www.leg.state.nv.us/70th/Legislators/Senators/
Raggio.htm

Maurice E. Washington (R), Majority Whip
401 S. Carson St., Carson City, NV 87701-4747
(775) 687-3652
E-mail: mwashington@sen.state.nv.us
http://www.leg.state.nv.us/70th/Legislators/Senators/
Washington.htm

Alice Costadina (Dina) Titus (D), Minority Leader
401 S. Carson St., Carson City, NV 87701-4747
(775) 687-8123
E-mail: dtitus@sen.state.nv.us
http://www.leg.state.nv.us/70th/Legislators/Senators/
Titus.htm

Bernice Mathews (D), Minority Whip
401 S. Carson St., Carson City, NV 87701-4747
(775) 687-3658
E-mail: bmathews@sen.state.nv.us
http://www.leg.state.nv.us/70th/Legislators/Senators/
Mathews.htm

Janice L. Thomas, Secretary
401 S. Carson St., Carson City, NV 87701-4747
(775) 687-5742
E-mail: thomas@lcb.state.nv.us

House
General information: (775) 687-5739
Fax: (775) 687-4007
E-mail: assembly@lcb.state.nv.us

Joseph E. (Joe) Dini Jr. (D), Speaker of the House
401 S. Carson St., Carson City, NV 87701-4747
(775) 684-8503
E-mail: jdini@asm.state.nv.us
http://www.leg.state.nv.us/70th/Legislators/Assembly/
Dini.htm

Jan Evans (D), Speaker Pro Tempore
401 S. Carson St., Carson City, NV 87701-4747
(775) 684-8505

E-mail: jevans@asm.state.nv.us
http://www.leg.state.nv.us/70th/Legislators/Assembly/
evans.htm

Richard D. (Rick) Perkins (D), Majority Leader
401 S. Carson St., Carson City, NV 87701-4747
(775) 684-8537
E-mail: rperkins@asm.state.nv.us
http://www.leg.state.nv.us/70th/Legislators/Assembly/
Perkins.htm

Wendell P. Williams (D), Majority Whip
401 S. Carson St., Carson City, NV 87701-4747
(775) 684-8545
E-mail: wwilliams@asm.state.nv.us
http://www.leg.state.nv.us/70th/Legislators/Assembly/
williams.htm

Lynn C. Hettrick (R), Minority Leader
401 S. Carson St., Carson City, NV 87701-4747
(775) 684-8843
E-mail: lhettrick@asm.state.nv.us
http://www.leg.state.nv.us/70th/Legislators/Assembly/
Hettrick.htm

Dennis Nolan (R), Minority Whip
401 S. Carson St., Carson City, NV 87701-4747
(775) 684-8853
E-mail: dnolan@asm.state.nv.us
http://www.leg.state.nv.us/70th/Legislators/Assembly/
nolan.htm

Jacqueline Sneddon, Chief Clerk of the Assembly
401 S. Carson St., Carson City, NV 87701-4747
(775) 687-5739; *Fax:* (775) 687-4007

Nevada Judiciary
Supreme Court Bldg.
201 S. Carson St.
Carson City, NV 89701-4702

Supreme Court
http://www.state.nv.us/elec_judicial.html

Janette M. Bloom, Clerk
Supreme Court Bldg., 201 S. Carson St., Carson City,
NV 89701-4702
(775) 684-1600; *Fax:* (775) 684-1601

Justices
Composition: 7 justices
Selection Method: nonpartisan election;
vacancies filled by gubernatorial appointment;
appointees serve until next general election
Length of term: 6 years

Robert E. Rose, Chief Justice, (775) 687-5170
C. Clifton Young, Vice Chief Justice, (775) 687-5195
Deborah A. Agosti, Associate Justice, (775) 687-5190
Nancy A. Boecker, Associate Justice, (702) 486-3205
Myron E. Leavitt, Associate Justice, (702) 486-3225
A. William Maupin, Associate Justice, (775) 687-5188
Miriam Shearing, Associate Justice, (775) 687-5198

Administrative Office of the Courts
Main phone: (775) 684-1700
Main fax: (775) 684-1723

Karen Kavanau, State Court Administrator
Supreme Court Bldg., 201 S. Carson St., Carson City,
  NV 89701-4702
(775) 684-1717
E-mail: kkavanau@nvcourts.state.nv.us

Supreme Court Library
Main phone: (775) 684-1640
Main fax: (775) 684-1662

Susan A. Southwick, Law Librarian
Supreme Court Bldg., 201 S. Carson St., #100, Carson
  City, NV 89701-4702

Legislative and Political Party Information Resources

Senate home page: http://www.leg.state.nv.us/70th/Legislators/Senators/index.htm
House home page: http://www.leg.state.nv.us/70th/Legislators/Assembly/index.htm
Legislative process: http://www.leg.state.nv.us/General/im_just_a_bill.htm
Legislative information: http://www.leg.state.nv.us/US/Bills/Bills.htm
Current session information: http://www.leg.state.nv.us/70th/Interim
Nevada Democratic Party: http://www.nvdems.com
  1785 E. Sahara, #496, Las Vegas, NV 89104; *Phone:* (702) 737-8683; *Fax:* (702) 735-2700
Nevada Republican Party: http://www.nevadagop.com
  528 S. Decatur, Las Vegas, NV 89107; *Phone:* (702) 258-9182; *Fax:* (702) 258-9186

New Hampshire

State House
Concord, NH 03301
Public information: (603) 271-1110
Fax: (603) 271-6998
http://www.state.nh.us

Office of the Governor
http://www.state.nh.us/governor/index.html
Main phone: (603) 271-2121
Main fax: (603) 271-6998
TTY: (800) 735-2964

Jeanne Shaheen (D), Governor
State House, 107 N. Main St., #208-214, Concord, NH
03301

Richard Sigel, Chief of Staff
State House, Concord, NH 03301
(603) 271-2121; *Fax:* (603) 271-6998

Pamela Walsh, Press Secretary
State House, Concord, NH 03301
(603) 271-2121; *Fax:* (603) 271-6998

Ted Walsh, Citizen Affairs Director
State House, Concord, NH 03301
(603) 271-2121; *Fax:* (603) 271-6998

Office of the Secretary of State
http://www.state.nh.us/sos/
General e-mail: elections@state.nh.us
Main phone: (603) 271-3242
Main fax: (603) 271-6316
TTY: (603) 225-4033

William M. Gardner (D), Secretary of State
State House, 107 N. Main St., #204, Concord, NH
03301

Office of the Attorney General
http://www.state.nh.us/nhdoj
General e-mail: webmaster@doj.state.nh.us
Main phone: (603) 271-3658
Main fax: (603) 271-2110
TTY: (800) 735-2964

Philip Thomas McLaughlin (D), Attorney General
33 Capitol St., Concord, NH 03301-6397
(603) 271-3655; *Fax:* (603) 271-6815

Office of the State Treasurer
http://www.state.nh.us/treasury
General e-mail: treasury@treasury.state.nh.us
Main phone: (603) 271-2621
Main fax: (603) 271-3922

State of New Hampshire

Capital: Concord, since 1808
Founded: 1629, as British colony
Statehood: June 21, 1788 (9th state)
Constitution adopted: 1784
Area: 8,969 sq. mi. (ranks 44th)
Population: 1,185,048 (1998 est.; ranks 42nd)
Largest cities: (1998 est.) Manchester
(102,524); Nashua (82,169); Concord
(37,444); Derry (31,871); Rochester (27,869)
Counties: 10, Most populous: (1998 est.)
Hillsborough (363,031); Rockingham
(271,152); Merrimack (127,381); Stratford
(108,650); Grafton (78,277)
U.S. Congress: Judd Gregg (R), Bob Smith
(R); 2 Representatives
Nickname(s): Granite State
Motto: Live free or die
Song: "Old New Hampshire," "New
Hampshire, My New Hampshire"
Bird: Purple finch
Tree: White birch
Flower: Purple lilac
State fair: at Hopkinton, early Sept.
Former capital(s): Portsmouth, Exeter

Georgie A. Thomas (R), State Treasurer
State House Annex, 25 Capitol St., #121, Concord, NH
03301

Office of the Adjutant General
http://www.nhguard.org/
Main phone: (603) 228-1135
Main fax: (603) 225-1257
TTY: (800) 735-2964

John E. Blair, Adjutant General
State Military Reservation, 4 Pembroke Rd., Concord,
NH 03301-5652
(603) 225-1200

Agencies

Accountancy Board
http://www.state.nh.us/accountancy

General e-mail: lcollier@boa.state.nh.us
Main phone: (603) 271-3286

Kevin Howe, Chair
57 Regional Dr., Concord, NH 03301-8506

Administrative Services Dept.
http://www.state.nh.us/das/index.html
Main phone: (603) 271-3201
Main fax: (603) 271-6600
TTY: (603) 225-4033

Donald Hill, Commissioner
State House Annex, 25 Capitol St., #120, Concord, NH 03301

Accounting Services Division
http://www.state.nh.us/das/index.htm
Main phone: (603) 271-3372
Main fax: (603) 271-6666

Thomas E. Martin, State Comptroller
25 Capitol St., #413, Concord, NH 03301-6312
(603) 271-3373

Personnel Division
http://www.state.nh.us/das/personnel/index.html
Main phone: (603) 271-3261
Main fax: (603) 271-1422

Thomas F. Manning, Director
State House Annex, 25 Capitol St., #1, Concord, NH 03301-6395
E-mail: tmannin@admin.state.nh.us

Agriculture, Markets, and Food Dept.
http://www.state.nh.us/agric/aghome.html
General e-mail: marketbulletin@compuserve.com
Main phone: (603) 271-3551
Main fax: (603) 271-1109
TTY: (800) 735-2964

Stephen H. Taylor, Commissioner
25 Capitol St., Concord, NH 03301
(603) 271-3686

Architects, Engineers, and Land Surveyors Board
http://www.state.nh.us/jtboard/home.htm
Main phone: (603) 271-2219
Main fax: (603) 271-6990

Louise Laverty, Board Administrator
57 Regional Dr., Concord, NH 03301

Archives and Records Managment
http://www.state.nh.us/state/archives.htm
Main phone: (603) 271-2236

Frank Mevers, Executive Director
71 S. Fruit St., Concord, NH 03301-2410

Arts Council
http://www.state.nh.us/nharts
Main phone: (603) 271-2789
Main fax: (603) 271-3584
TTY: (800) 735-2964

Rebecca L. Lawrence, Director
40 N. Main St., Concord, NH 03301-4974
E-mail: rlawrence@narts.state.nh.us

Banking Dept.
http://www.state.nh.us/banking/
Main phone: (603) 271-3561
Main fax: (603) 271-1090

A. Roland Roberge, Commissioner
56 Old Suncook Rd., Concord, NH 03301

Business Finance Authority
http://www.state.nh.us/bfa/bfa.htm
Main phone: (603) 271-2391
Main fax: (603) 271-2396
TTY: (800) 735-2964

Jack Donovan, Executive Director
14 Dixon Ave., #101, Concord, NH 03301-4954
(603) 271-6457
E-mail: JackD@nhbfa.com

Child Care Licensing Bureau
http://www.state.nh.us/gencourt/ols/rules/he-C4000.html
Main phone: (603) 271-4624
Main fax: (603) 271-4782
Toll free: (800) 852-3345, ext. 4624

Wendy Kessler, Chief
Brown Bldg., 129 Pleasant St., Concord, NH 03301-3857

Christa McAuliffe Planetarium
http://www.starhop.com/
Main phone: (603) 271-7831
Main fax: (603) 271-7832

Jeanne T. Gerluskis, Director
3 Institute Dr., Concord, NH 03301-8520
E-mail: jgeruls@starhop.com

Consumer Protection Bureau
Main phone: (603) 271-3641
Main fax: (603) 271-2110

Walter L. Maroney, Director
33 Capitol St., Concord, NH 03301-6397

Corrections Dept.
http://www.state.nh.us/doc/nhdoc.html
General e-mail: nhdoccommr@aol.com
Main phone: (603) 271-5600
Main fax: (603) 271-5643
TTY: (603) 735-2964

Mailing address: P.O. Box 1806, Concord, NH 03302-1806

Edda Cantor, Assistant Commissioner
105 Pleasant St., Concord, NH 03302-1806
(603) 271-5606

Cosmetology, Barbering, and Esthetics Board
http://www.state.nh.us/cosmet
Main phone: (603) 271-3608
Main fax: (603) 271-8889

Sally A. Wells, Chair
2 Industrial Park Dr., Concord, NH 03301

Cultural Resources Dept.
http://www.state.nh.us/nhculture
Main phone: (603) 271-2144
Main fax: (603) 271-2205
TTY: (800) 735-2964

Van McLeod, Commissioner
20 Park St., Concord, NH 03301-6314
(603) 271-2540; *Fax:* (603) 271-6826
E-mail: vmcleod@finch.nhsl.lib.nh.us

Historical Resources Division
http://www.state.nh.us/nhdhr
General e-mail:
  preservation@nhdhr.state.nh.us
Main phone: (603) 271-3483
Main fax: (603) 271-3433
Mailing address: P.O. Box 2043, Concord, NH 03301-2043

Nancy Dutton, Director
19 Pillsbury St., Concord, NH 03301
(603) 271-3483; *Fax:* (603) 271-3433
E-mail: ndutton@nhdhr.state.nh.us

State Library
http://www.state.nh.us/nhsl/index.html
Main phone: (603) 271-2144
Main fax: (603) 271-6826
Toll free: (800) 499-1232
TTY: (800) 735-2964

Michael York, State Librarian
20 Park St., Concord, NH 03301-6314
(603) 271-2397
E-mail: myork@finch.nhsl.lib.nh.us

Education Dept.
http://www.state.nh.us/doe/education.html
Main phone: (603) 271-3494
Main fax: (603) 271-1953
Toll free: (800) 339-9900
TTY: (800) 735-2964

Elizabeth M. Twomey, Commissioner
101 Pleasant St., Concord, NH 03301

Higher Educational Institutions

University System of New Hampshire
http://usnh.unh.edu
25 Concord Rd., Durham, NH 03824
Main phone: (603) 862-1360
Branches: Keene State College, Plymouth State College, University of New Hampshire-Durham, University of New Hampshire-Manchester

---

(603) 271-3144
E-mail: etwomey@ed.state.nh.us

Board of Education
http://www.state.nh.us/doe/StateBoard/state.htm
Main phone: (603) 271-3144
Main fax: (603) 271-1953
Toll free: (800) 339-9900
TTY: (800) 735-2964

John Lewis, Chair
101 Pleasant St., Concord, NH 03301
(603) 431-3500; *Fax:* (603) 430-9920

Emergency Management Office
http://www.nhoem.state.nh.us/
Main phone: (603) 271-2231
Main fax: (603) 225-7341
TTY: (800) 735-2964

Woodbury P. Fogg, Director
State Office Park South, 107 Pleasant St., Concord, NH 03301-3809

Employment Security
http://www.nhes.state.nh.us
Main phone: (603) 224-3311
Main fax: (603) 228-4145
Toll free: (800) 852-3400

John J. Ratoff, Commissioner
32 S. Main St., Concord, NH 03301-4857
(603) 228-4000

Energy and Community Services Office
http://www.state.nh.us/governor/energycom
Main phone: (603) 271-2611
Main fax: (603) 271-2615

Deborah Schachter, Director
57 Regional Dr., #3, Concord, NH 03301-8519
E-mail: dschach@gov.state.nh.us

Environmental Protection Bureau
Main phone: (603) 271-3679
Main fax: (603) 271-2110

Michael J. Wells, Director
33 Capitol St., Concord, NH 03301-6397
(603) 271-3658

Environmental Services Dept.
http://www.des.state.nh.us/
General e-mail: pip@des.state.nh.us
Main phone: (603) 271-3503
Main fax: (603) 271-2867
TTY: (800) 735-2964

Robert W. Varney, Commissioner
6 Hazen Dr., Concord, NH 03301
(603) 271-3449
E-mail: rvarney@des.state.nh.us

Water Division
Main phone: (603) 271-3503
Main fax: (603) 271-2869
Mailing address: P.O. Box 95, Concord, NH 03302-0095

Harry T. Stewart, Director
6 Hazen Dr., Concord, NH 03301-6509

Fish and Game Dept.
http://wildlife.state.nh.us/
General e-mail: info@wildlife.state.nh.us
Main phone: (603) 271-3421
Main fax: (603) 271-1438
TTY: (800) 735-2964

Wayne E. Vetter, Executive Director
2 Hazen Dr., #206, Concord, NH 03301
(603) 271-3511
E-mail: director@wildlife.state.nh.us

Frequently Called Numbers

Tourism: (603) 271-2665;
  http://www.visitnh.gov/index.php3
Library: (603) 271-2144, 1-800-499-1232;
  http://www.state.nh.us/nhsl/index.html
Board of Education: (603) 271-3144; http://
  www.state.nh.us/doe/StateBoard/state.htm
Vital Statistics: (603) 271-4651
Tax/Revenue: (603) 271-2191;
  http://www.state.nh.us/revenue
Motor Vehicles: (603) 271-2251;
  http://www.state.nh.us/dmv
State Police/Highway Patrol: (603) 271-3636;
  http://www.state.nh.us/nhsp
Unemployment: (603) 228-4031;
  http://www.nhworks.state.nh.us/ucpage.htm
General Election Information:
  (603) 271-3242; http://www.state.nh.us/sos/
  elections.htm
Consumer Affairs: (603) 271-3641
Hazardous Materials: (603) 271-3644;
  http://www.des.state.nh.us/hwrb

Health and Human Services Dept.
http://www.dhhs.state.nh.us/
Main phone: (603) 271-4685
Main fax: (603) 271-4912
TTY: (800) 735-2964

Donald L Shumway, Commissioner
129 Pleasant St., Concord, NH 03301
(603) 271-4331

Behavioral Health Division
General e-mail: kfreese@dhhs.state.nh.us
Main phone: (603) 271-5000
Main fax: (603) 271-5058

Paul Gorman, Director
105 Pleasant St., Concord, NH 03301
(603) 271-5007

Children, Youth, and Family Division: Juvenile Justice
Main phone: (603) 271-4451
Main fax: (603) 271-4729
Toll free: (800) 852-3345
TTY: (800) 735-2964

John McDermott, Administrator
129 Pleasant St., 4th Fl., Concord, NH 03301
(603) 271-2175
E-mail: jmcdermo@dhhs.state.nh.us

Developmental Disabilities Council
General e-mail: nhddcncl@aol.com
Main phone: (603) 271-3236
Main fax: (603) 271-1156
Toll free: (800) 852-3345 ext3236

Alan Robichaud, Director
10 Ferry St., #315, Concord, NH 03301-5081

Elderly and Adult Services Division
Main phone: (603) 271-4680
Main fax: (603) 271-4643
Toll free: (800) 351-1888

Catherine Keane, Director
129 Pleasant St., Concord, NH 03301
(603) 271-4394
E-mail: ckeane@dhhs.state.nh.us

Health Care Services Division: Medical Care and Cost Containment
Main phone: (603) 271-4796
Main fax: (603) 271-4376
Toll free: (800) 852-3345
TTY: (800) 735-2964

Katie Dunn, Director (Acting)
6 Hazen Dr., Concord, NH 03301-6527
(603) 271-5998

Higher Educational and Health Facilities Authority
http://www.nhhehfa.com
General e-mail: nhhehfa@compuserve.com
Main phone: (603) 224-0696
Main fax: (603) 224-3058
Mailing address: P.O. Box 2110, Concord, NH 03302-2110

David C. Bliss, Executive Director
54 South State St., Concord, NH 03302-2110

Highway Safety Agency
http://www.state.nh.us/hsafety/
General e-mail: hwysafety@nhhsa.state.nh.us
Main phone: (603) 271-2131
Main fax: (603) 271-3790
TTY: (800) 735-2964

Peter M. Thomson, Coordinator
117 Manchester St., Pine Inn Plaza, Concord, NH 03301-5101

Housing Finance Authority
http://www.nhhfa.org
Main phone: (603) 472-8623
Main fax: (603) 472-8501
Toll free: (800) 640-7239
TTY: (603) 472-2089
Mailing address: P.O. Box 5087, Manchester, NH 03108-5087

Claira P. Monier, Executive Director
32 Constitution Dr., Bedford, NH 03110
(603) 472-8623, ext. 202

Human Rights Commission
http://www.state.nh.us/hrc/index.html
General e-mail: humanrights@nhsa.state.nh.us
Main phone: (603) 271-2767
Main fax: (603) 271-6339
TTY: (800) 735-2964

Raymond S. Perry Jr., Executive Director
2 Chenell Dr., Concord, NH 03301-8509
(603) 271-2050

Insurance Dept.
http://www.state.nh.us/insurance/depart.htm
Main phone: (603) 271-2261
Main fax: (603) 271-1406
TTY: (800) 735-2964

Paula T. Rogers, Commissioner
56 Old Suncook Rd., Concord, NH 03301

Judicial Council
Main phone: (603) 271-3592
Main fax: (603) 271-1112
TTY: (800) 735-2964

Nina C. Gardner, Executive Director
25 Capitol St., #424, Concord, NH 03301

Labor Dept.
http://www.state.nh.us/dol/index.htm
General e-mail: srivard@nhsa.state.nh.us
Main phone: (603) 271-3176
Main fax: (603) 271-6149
Toll free: (800) 272-4353

James D. Casey, Commissioner
State Office Park South, 95 Pleasant St., #405, Concord, NH 03301
(603) 271-3171; *Fax:* (603) 271-6852
E-mail: jcasey@nhsa.state.nh.us

Workers Compensation Division
http://www.state.nh.us/dol/dol-wc/index.html
Main phone: (603) 271-3176
Toll free: (800) 272-4353

Kathryn Barger, Director
95 Pleasant St., Concord, NH 03301
(603) 271-3599; *Fax:* (603) 271-6149

Liquor Commission
http://www.state.nh.us/liquor/index.html
General e-mail: commission@liquor.state.nh.us
Main phone: (603) 271-3134
Main fax: (603) 271-1107
TTY: (800) 735-2964
Mailing address: P.O. Box 503, Concord, NH 03302-0503

John W. Byrne, Chair
Storrs St., Concord, NH 03302-0503
(603) 271-3132

Lottery
http://www.state.nh.us/lottery/nhlotto.htm
Main phone: (603) 271-3391
Main fax: (603) 271-1160
Toll free: (800) 852-3324
Mailing address: P.O. Box 1208, Concord, NH 03302-1208

Rick A. Wisler, Executive Director
14 Integra Dr., Concord, NH 03302-1208

Medical Services/Medicaid Member Services
Main phone: (603) 271-4353
Main fax: (603) 271-4376
Toll free: (800) 852-3345
TTY: (800) 735-2964

Katie Dunn, Director (Acting)
6 Hazen Dr., 3rd Fl., Concord, NH 03301
(800) 852-3345, ext. 4796; *Fax:* (603) 271-4827
E-mail: kdunn@dhhs.state.nh.us

Medicine Board

http://www.state.nh.us/medicine
Main phone: (603) 271-1203
Main fax: (603) 271-6702

Lawrence W. O'Connell, President
2 Industrial Park Dr., #8, Concord, NH 03301

New Hampshire Public Television

http://nhptv.org
General e-mail: themailbox@nhptv.unh.edu
Main phone: (603) 868-1100
Main fax: (603) 868-7552

Peter A. Frid, Chief Executive Officer
268 Mast Rd., Durham, NH 03824
(603) 868-1100; *Fax:* (603) 868-7552

Nursing Board

http://www.state.nh.us/nursing
Main phone: (603) 271-6599
Main fax: (603) 271-4969
Mailing address: P.O. Box 3898, Concord, NH
03302-3898

Stanley J. Plodzik Jr., Director
78 Regional Dr., Bldg. B, Concord, NH 03302-3898

Pari-Mutuel Commission

http://www.state.nh.us/nhpmc
Main phone: (603) 271-2158
Main fax: (603) 271-3381

Paul M. Kelley, Director
Carrigain Commons, 244 N. Main St., 3rd Fl.,
Concord, NH 03301-5041
E-mail: pkelley@nhpmc.state.nh.us

Boards and Licensing

Accountancy, (603) 271-3286,
http://www.state.nh.us/accountancy
Architects, Engineers, and Land Surveyors,
(603) 271-2219, http://www.state.nh.us/
jtboard/home.htm
Child Care, (603) 271-4624,
http://www.state.nh.us/gencourt/ols/rules/
he-C4000.html
Cosmetology, (603) 271-3608,
http://www.state.nh.us/cosmet
Medical Licensing, (603) 271-1203,
http://www.state.nh.us/medicine
Nursing, (603) 271-6599,
http://www.state.nh.us/nursing
Pharmacy, (603) 271-2350,
http://www.state.nh.us/pharmacy
Real Estate, (603) 271-1039

Parole Board

Main phone: (603) 271-2569
Main fax: (603) 271-6179
Mailing address: P.O. Box 14, Concord, NH 03302

Thomas D. Winn, Chair
281 N. State St., Concord, NH 03301-3250
E-mail: twinn@nhdoc.state.nh.us

Pharmacy Board

http://www.state.nh.us/pharmacy
General e-mail: nhpharmacy@nhfa.state.nh.us
Main phone: (603) 271-2350
Main fax: (603) 271-2850

Paul G. Bouisseau, Executive Director
57 Regional Dr., Concord, NH 03301

Port Authority

http://www.state.nh.us/nhport/index.html
Main phone: (603) 436-8500
Main fax: (603) 436-2780
TTY: (800) 735-2964
Mailing address: P.O. Box 506, Portsmouth, NH
03802-0369

Thomas Orfe, Director
555 Market St., Portsmouth, NH 03802-0369
E-mail: tom.orfe@rscs.net

Postsecondary Education Commission

http://www.state.nh.us/postsecondary/index.html
Main phone: (603) 271-2555
Main fax: (603) 271-2696
TTY: (800) 735-2964

James A. Busselle, Executive Director
2 Industrial Park Dr., Concord, NH 03301-8512
E-mail: jbusselle@nhsa.state.nh.us

Public Defender

Main phone: (603) 224-1236
Main fax: (603) 226-4299
Toll free: (800) 464-0652

Michael K. Skibbie, Executive Director
117 N. State St., Concord, NH 03301-4493

Public Employee Labor Relations Board

http://www.state.nh.us/pelrb/
Main phone: (603) 271-2588
Main fax: (603) 271-2587
TTY: (603) 225-4033

Parker A. Denaco, Executive Director
153 Manchester St., Concord, NH 03301-5143
(603) 271-2587
E-mail: skenney@pelrb.state.nh.us

Public Utilities Commission

http://www.puc.state.nh.us
General e-mail: puc@puc.state.nh.us

Main phone: (603) 271-2431
Main fax: (603) 271-3878
TTY: (603) 225-4033

Douglas L. Patch, Chair
8 Old Suncook Rd., Concord, NH 03301-7319
(603) 271-2442

Real Estate Commission
http://www.state.nh.us/nhrec/
Main phone: (603) 271-2701
Main fax: (603) 271-1039
TTY: (603) 225-4033

Beth A. Emmons, Executive Director
State House Annex, 25 Capitol St., #435, Concord, NH
03301

Regional Community-Technical College System
http://www.nhctcs.tec.nh.us
General e-mail: system@tec.nh.us
Main phone: (603) 271-2722
Main fax: (603) 271-2725
TTY: (800) 735-2964

Glenn DuBois, Commissioner
5 Institute Dr., Concord, NH 03301
(603) 271-2739
E-mail: gdubois@tec.nh.us

Resources and Economic Development Dept.
http://www.dred.state.nh.us/
General e-mail: dedinfo@dred.state.nh.us
Main phone: (603) 271-2411
Main fax: (603) 271-2629
TTY: (800) 735-2964
Mailing address: P.O. Box 1856, Concord, NH
03302-1856

George M. Bald, Commissioner
172 Pembroke Rd., Concord, NH 03302-1856
E-mail: g_bald@dred.state.nh.us

Economic Development Division
Main phone: (603) 271-2411
Main fax: (603) 271-6784
Mailing address: P.O. Box 1856, Concord, NH
03302-1856

Stewart Arnett, Director
172 Pembroke Rd., Concord, NH 03302
(603) 271-2341

Forests and Land Division
http://www.dred.state.nh.us/forlands
Main phone: (603) 271-2214
Mailing address: P.O. Box 1856, Concord, NH
03302-1856

Philip Bryce, Director
172 Pembroke Rd., Concord, NH 03302-1856

Parks and Recreation Division
http://nhparks.state.nh.us
General e-mail: nhparks@dred.state.nh.us
Main phone: (603) 271-3556
Main fax: (603) 271-2629
Mailing address: P.O. Box 1856, Concord, NH
03302-1856

Richard McLeod, Director
172 Pembroke Rd., Concord, NH 03302

Travel and Tourism Division
http://www.visitnh.gov/index.php3
General e-mail: travel@dred.state.nh.us
Main phone: (603) 271-2665
Main fax: (603) 271-6784
Mailing address: P.O. Box 1856, Concord, NH
03302-1856

Lauri Ostrander Klefos, Director
172 Pembroke Rd., Concord, NH 03302

Retirement System
http://www.state.nh.us/retirement/
Main phone: (603) 271-3351
Main fax: (603) 271-6806
TTY: (603) 225-4033

Vacant, Executive Secretary
4 Chenell Dr., Concord, NH 03301-8509
(603) 271-3351, ext. 253

Revenue Administration Dept.
http://www.state.nh.us/revenue
General e-mail: advocate@totalnetnh.net
Main phone: (603) 271-2191
Main fax: (603) 271-6121
TTY: (800) 735-2964
Mailing address: P.O. Box 457, Concord, NH
03302-0457

Stanley R. Arnold, Commissioner
45 Chenell Dr., Concord, NH 03301
(603) 271-2318
E-mail: sarnold@nhsa.state.nh.us

Safety Dept.
http://www.state.nh.us/safety/safety.htm
Main phone: (603) 271-2251
Main fax: (603) 271-3903
TTY: (800) 735-2964

Richard M. Flynn, Commissioner
10 Hazen Dr., Concord, NH 03305
(603) 271-2791

Fire Safety Division
http://www.state.nh.us/safety/fire.htm
Main phone: (603) 271-3294
Main fax: (603) 271-1091

Mailing address: 10 Hazen Dr., Concord, NH
03305

Donald P. Bliss, Director
Richard M. Flynn Fire Academy, 222 Sheep Davis
Rd., Concord, NH 03301-8523

Motor Vehicles Division
http://www.state.nh.us/dmv
Main phone: (603) 271-2251
Main fax: (603) 271-3903

Virginia C. Beecher, Director
10 Hazen Dr., James H. Hayes Bldg., Concord, NH
03305-0002
(603) 271-2484

State Police
http://www.state.nh.us/nhsp
Main phone: (603) 271-3636
Main fax: (603) 271-1153

Gary M. Sloper, Director
10 Hazen Dr., Concord, NH 03301
(603) 271-2575; *Fax:* (603) 271-2527

State Fair
http://www.hsfair.org/
General e-mail: info@hsfair.org
Main phone: (603) 746-4191

Alan H. Hardy, General Manager
Fair Grounds, Contoocook, NH 03229-0700

Tax and Land Appeals Board
http://www.state.nh.us/btla/
General e-mail: btla@nh.ultranet.com
Main phone: (603) 271-2588
Main fax: (603) 271-2587
TTY: (603) 225-4033

Paul B. Franklin, Chair
State Office Park South, 107 Pleasant St., Concord,
NH 03301

Transportation Dept.
http://www.state.nh.us/dot/
Main phone: (603) 271-3734
Main fax: (603) 271-3914

Leon S. Kenison, Commissioner
1 Hazen Dr., Concord, NH 03302

Aeronautics Division
General e-mail: n64@dot.state.nh.us
Main phone: (603) 271-2551
Main fax: (603) 271-1689
TTY: (800) 735-2964
Mailing address: P.O. Box 483, Concord, NH
03301-0483

Jack Ferns, Director
65 Airport Rd., Terminal Bldg., Concord, NH
03301-5298
E-mail: j.ferns@dot.state.nh.us

Veterans Council
http://www.state.nh.us/nhveterans/index.html
Main phone: (603) 624-9230
Main fax: (603) 624-9236
Toll free: (800) 622-9230
TTY: (800) 735-2964

Dennis J. Viola, Director
275 Chestnut St., #321, Manchester, NH 03101
E-mail: nhviola@vba.va.gov

Women's Commission
http://www.state.nh.us/csw
Main phone: (603) 271-2660
Main fax: (603) 271-2361
TTY: (800) 735-2964

Molly Kelly, Chair
State House Annex, 25 Capitol St., #334, Concord, NH
03301

New Hampshire Legislature

State House
107 N. State St.
Concord, NH 03301
General information: (603) 271-1110
Bill status: (603) 271-2239
http://www.state.nh.us/gencourt/
gencourt.htm

Senate
General information: (603) 271-2111

Beverly A. Hollingworth (D), President
State House, #120, Concord, NH 03301
(603) 271-3073
E-mail: beverly.hollingworth@leg.state.nh.us
http://www.state.nh.us/gencourt/senate/shomepage/
senate23.htm

Sylvia Larsen (D), President Pro Tempore
State House, #302, Concord, NH 03301
(603) 271-2106
http://www.state.nh.us/gencourt/senate/shomepage/
senate15.htm

Burton J. (Burt) Cohen (D), Majority Leader
State House, #302, Concord, NH 03301
(603) 271-3042
E-mail: burtc@nh.ultranet.com
http://www.state.nh.us/gencourt/senate/shomepage/
senate24.htm

Laws

Sales tax: None
Income tax: None
State minimum wage: $5.15 (Federal is $5.15)
Marriage age: 18
First-cousin marriage: Prohibited
Drinking age: 21
State control of liquor sales: Yes
Blood alcohol for DWI: 0.08%
Driving age: 18
Speed limit: 65 mph
Permit to buy handguns: No
Minimum age to possess handguns: None
Minimum age to possess rifles, shotguns:
  None
State lottery: Yes; also Powerball, Tri-State
  Lottery (with ME, VT)
Casinos: No
Pari-mutuel betting: Horse and dog racing
Death penalty: Yes
3 strikes minimum sentence: 10 yrs. (3rd
  felony)
Hate crimes law: Yes
Gay employment non-discrimination: Yes
Official language(s): English
Term limits: None

*State laws are complex and subject to
change; this information is not intended as
legal advice. For an explanation of this
information, see p. x.*

Rick A. Trombly (D), Majority Whip
State House, #302, Concord, NH 03301
(603) 271-3043
http://www.state.nh.us/gencourt/senate/shomepage/
  senate7.htm

Carl R. Johnson (R), Republican Leader
State House, #9, Concord, NH 03301
(603) 271-3081
E-mail: carljean@worldpath.net
http://www.state.nh.us/gencourt/senate/shomepage/
  senate3.htm

Gary R. Francoeur (R), Republican Whip
State House, #101, Concord, NH 03301
(603) 271-2708
http://www.state.nh.us/gencourt/senate/shomepage/
  senate14.htm

Gloria Randlett, Clerk
State House, Senate Chamber, 107 N. Main St.,
  Concord, NH 03301

(603) 271-3420; *Fax:* (603) 271-2105
E-mail: gloria.randlett@leg.state.nh.us
http://www.state.nh.us/gencourt/senate/senateclerk/
  senclerk.htm

House
General information: (603) 271-3661
Fax: (603) 271-2361

Donna Sytek (R), Speaker of the House
State House, Concord, NH 03301
(603) 271-3661; *Fax:* (603) 271-3309
E-mail: donnasytek@aol.com

Alf E. Jacobson (R), Speaker Pro Tempore
State House, Concord, NH 03301
(603) 271-3184

Gene G. Chandler (R), Majority Leader
State House, Concord, NH 03301
(603) 271-3125; *Fax:* (603) 271-3309

Michael D. Whalley (R), Majority Whip
State House, Concord, NH 03301
(603) 271-3063; *Fax:* (603) 271-3309
E-mail: w03304@aol.com

Peter H. Burling (D), Democratic Leader
State House, Concord, NH 03301
(603) 271-3063

Raymond C. Buckley (D), Democratic Whip
State House, Concord, NH 03301
(603) 271-3661
E-mail: rcb2nh@aol.com

Karen O. Wadsworth, Clerk
State House, Concord, NH 03301
(603) 271-2548

New Hampshire Judiciary
Supreme Court Bldg.
1 Noble Dr.
Concord, NH 03301-6160
http://www.state.nh.us/courts

Supreme Court
http://www.state.nh.us/courts/supreme.htm

Howard J. Zibel, Clerk and Reporter of Decisions
Supreme Court Bldg., 1 Noble Dr., Concord, NH
  03301-6160
(603) 271-2646
E-mail: zibel@aol.com

Justices
Composition: 5 justices
Selection Method: appointed by governor with
  consent of Executive Council
Length of term: until age 70
David A. Brock, Chief Justice, (603) 271-2149

John T. Broderick Jr., Associate Justice, (603) 271-3751

Sherman D. Horton Jr., Associate Justice, (603) 271-3660

W. Stephen Thayer III, Associate Justice, (603) 271-3415

Vacant, Associate Justice, (603) 271-3279

Administrative Office of the Courts
http://www.state.nh.us/courts/aoc.htm
Main phone: (603) 271-2521
Main fax: (603) 271-3977

Donald D. Goodnow, State Court Administrator
2 Noble Dr., Concord, NH 03301-6179
E-mail: 75517.1771@compuserve.com

State Law Library
http://www.state.nh.us/courts/lawlib.htm
Main phone: (603) 271-3777
Main fax: (603) 271-2168

Christine Swan, Library Director
Supreme Court Bldg., 1 Noble Dr., Concord, NH 03301-6160

Legislative and Political Party Information Resources

Senate home page: http://www.state.nh.us/gencourt/senate/shomepage/nhsenate.htm
House home page: http://www.state.nh.us/gencourt/house/hhomepage/index.html
Budget: http://www.state.nh.us/lba/indexbudget.html
New Hampshire Democratic Party: http://www.nh-democrats.org
   43 Centre St., Concord, NH 03301; *Phone:* (603) 225-6899; *E-mail:* office@nh-democrats.org
New Hampshire Republican Party: http://www.nhgop.org
   134 N. Main St., Concord, NH 03301; *Phone:* (603) 225-9341; *Fax:* (603) 225-7498;
   E-mail: info@nhgop.org

New Jersey

State House
Trenton, NJ 08625-0001
Public information: (609) 292-2121
Fax: (609) 292-3454
http://www.state.nj.us

Office of the Governor
http://www.state.nj.us/governor/govoffice.htm
General e-mail:
ncs@capitol.statehouse.state.nj.us
Main phone: (609) 292-6000
Main fax: (609) 292-3454
Mailing address: P.O. Box 001

Christine Todd Whitman (R), Governor
State House, 125 W. State St., Trenton, NJ 08625-0001
(609) 777-2200

Michael Torpey, Chief of Staff
State House, 125 W. State St., Trenton, NJ 08625
(609) 777-2200; *Fax:* (609) 292-3454

Jayne O'Connor, Press Secretary
State House, 125 West State St., Trenton, NJ 08625
(609) 777-2600; *Fax:* (609) 292-9079
E-mail: jpo@gov.state.nj.us

Noel McGuire, Constituent Relations, Director
State House, Trenton, NJ 08625
(609) 777-2500; *Fax:* (609) 292-3454

Susan Spencer, Director, Washington Office
444 N. Capitol St. N.W., #201, Washington, DC 20001
(202) 638-0631; *Fax:* (202) 638-2296

Office of the Secretary of State
http://www.state.nj.us/state
Main phone: (609) 984-1900
Main fax: (609) 292-7665
Mailing address: P.O. Box 300, Trenton, NJ
08625-0300

DeForest B. Soaries Jr. (I), Secretary of State
125 W. State St., Trenton, NJ 08625-0300
(609) 777-0884

Attorney General's Office (Law and Public Safety Dept.)
http://www.state.nj.us/lps
Main phone: (609) 292-4925
Main fax: (609) 292-3508
Mailing address: P.O. Box 080, Trenton, NJ
08625-0080

John J. Farmer Jr., Attorney General
Justice Complex, West Wing, 8th Fl., Trenton, NJ
08625

State of New Jersey

Capital: Trenton,
since 1790
Founded: 1664, as British colony
Statehood: December 18, 1787 (3rd state)
Constitution adopted: 1947
Area: 7,419 sq. mi. (ranks 46th)
Population: 8,115,011 (1998 est.; ranks 9th)
Largest cities: (1998 est.) Newark (267,823);
Jersey City (232,429); Paterson (148,212);
Elizabeth (110,661); Camden (83,546)
Counties: 21, Most populous: (1998 est.)
Bergen (858,529); Essex (750,273);
Monmouth (603,434); Hudson (557,159);
Camden (505,204)
U.S. Congress: Robert Torricelli (D), Frank R.
Lautenberg (D); 13 Representatives
Nickname(s): Garden State
Motto: Liberty and prosperity
Song: None
Bird: Eastern goldfinch
Tree: Red oak
Flower: Purple violet
State fair: at Cherry Hill, late July-early Aug.
Former capital(s): Perth Amboy and
Burlington (co-capitals of East and
West Jersey)

Office of the State Treasurer
Main phone: (609) 292-5031
Main fax: (609) 292-6145
Mailing address: P.O. Box 002, Trenton, NJ
08625-0002

Roland A. Machold Jr., State Treasurer
State House, 225 W. State St., Trenton, NJ 08625
(609) 984-5131

Military and Veterans Affairs Dept.
http://www.state.nj.us/military
Main phone: (609) 530-4600
Main fax: (609) 530-7100
TTY: (609) 530-6966
Mailing address: P.O. Box 340, Trenton, NJ
08625-0340

Paul J. Glazar, Adjutant General

101 Eggert Crossing Rd., Lawrenceville, NJ 08648-2805
(609) 530-6957
E-mail: glazer@njdmava.state.nj.us

Agencies

Accountancy Board
Main phone: (973) 504-6380
Main fax: (973) 648-2855
Mailing address: P.O. Box 45000, Newark, NJ 07101

Kevin B. Earle, Executive Director
124 Halsey St., Newark, NJ 07102
(973) 504-6380

Agriculture Dept.
http://www.state.nj.us/agriculture
Main phone: (609) 292-8896
Main fax: (609) 292-3978
Mailing address: P.O. Box 330, Trenton, NJ 08625-0330

Arthur R. Brown Jr., Secretary
John Fitch Plaza, #304, Trenton, NJ 08625
(609) 292-3976
E-mail: agabrow@ag.state.nj.us

Alcoholic Beverage Control
http://www.state.nj.us/lps/abc/index.html
Main phone: (609) 984-2830
Main fax: (609) 633-6078
Mailing address: P.O. Box 087, Trenton, NJ 08625-0087

Alfred E. Ramey Jr., Assistant Attorney General In Charge
140 E. Front St., Trenton, NJ 08625

Archives and Records Management Division
http://www.state.nj.us/state/darm/darm.html
General e-mail: director@darm.sos.state.nj.us
Main phone: (609) 530-3200
Main fax: (609) 530-6121
Mailing address: P.O. Box 307, Trenton, NJ 08625-0307

Karl J. Niederer, Division Director
2300 Stuyvesant Ave., Trenton, NJ 08625-0307
(609) 530-3205; *Fax:* (609) 530-6121
E-mail: kniedere@darm.sos.state.nj.us

Arts Council
http://www.artswire.org/Artswire/njsca/
General e-mail: njsca@arts.sos.state.nj.us
Main phone: (609) 292-6130
Main fax: (609) 989-1440
TTY: (609) 633-1186

Mailing address: P.O. Box 306, Trenton, NJ 08625-0306

Barbara Russo, Executive Director
225 W. State St., Trenton, NJ 08625

Banking and Insurance Dept.
http://www.naic.org/mj/njhomepg.html
Main phone: (609) 341-2512
Main fax: (609) 984-5273
Mailing address: P.O. Box 325, Trenton, NJ 08625-0325

Jaynee LaVecchia, Commissioner
20 W. State St., Trenton, NJ 08625-0325
(609) 341-2511

Building Authority
http://www.state.nj.us/njba/
Main phone: (609) 633-7618
Main fax: (609) 292-6160
Mailing address: P.O. Box 219, Trenton, NJ 08625-0219

Charles Chianese, Executive Director
50 W. State St., Trenton, NJ 08625-0219

Capital Budgeting and Planning Commission
Main phone: (609) 292-9022
Main fax: (609) 984-8498
Mailing address: P.O. Box 221, Trenton, NJ 08625-0221

John Geniesse, Executive Director (Acting)
33 W. State St., Trenton, NJ 08625
E-mail: geniesse_j@tre.state.nj.us

Civil Rights Division
http://www.state.nj.us/lps/dcr/
General e-mail: dcr@smtp.lps.state.nj.us
Main phone: (609) 292-4605
Main fax: (609) 984-3812
TTY: (609) 292-1785
Mailing address: P.O. Box 090, Trenton, NJ 08625-0090

O. Lisa Dabreu, Acting Director
140 E. Front St., Trenton, NJ 08625-0090

Commerce and Economic Development Dept.
http://www.state.nj.us/commerce
Main phone: (609) 777-0885
Main fax: (609) 777-4097
Mailing address: P.O. Box 820, Trenton, NJ 08625-0820

Gualberto Medina, Secretary
20 W. State St., Trenton, NJ 08625

Travel and Tourism
http://www.state.nj.us/travel/index.html
General e-mail: email@commerce.state.nj.us

Main phone: (609) 292-2470
Main fax: (609) 633-7418
Toll free: (800) VISITNJ
Mailing address: P.O. Box 820, Trenton, NJ
08625-0820

Vacant, Director
20 W. State St., Trenton, NJ 08625-0820

Community Affairs Dept.
http://www.state.nj.us/dca/dcahome.htm
Main phone: (609) 292-6055
Main fax: (609) 984-6696
TTY: (609) 278-0175
Mailing address: P.O. Box 800, Trenton, NJ
08625-0800

Jane M. Kenny, Commissioner
101 S. Broad St., Trenton, NJ 08625-0800
(609) 292-6420

Fire Safety Division
http://www.state.nj.us/dca/dfs
Main phone: (609) 633-6106

Main fax: (609) 633-6134
Mailing address: P.O. Box 809, Trenton, NJ
08625-0809

William Cane, Director
101 S. Broad St., Trenton, NJ 08625-0809

Women's Division
Main phone: (609) 292-8840
Main fax: (609) 633-6821
Mailing address: P.O. Box 801, Trenton, NJ
08625-0801

Linda Bowker, Director
101 S. Broad St., Trenton, NJ 08625-0800

Consumer Affairs Division
General e-mail:
AskConsumerAffairs@oag.lps.state.nj.us
Main phone: (973) 504-6200
Main fax: (973) 648-3538
TTY: (973) 504-6588

Mark S. Herr, Director
124 Halsey St., 7th Fl., Newark, NJ 07102
(973) 504-6320; Fax: (973) 648-3538

Higher Educational Institutions

College of New Jersey
http://www.tcnj.edu
2000 Pennington Rd., P.O. Box 7718, Ewing, NJ
08628-0718
Main phone: (609) 771-1855

Kean University
http://www.kean.edu
1000 Morris Ave., Union, NJ 07083
Main phone: (908) 527-2000

Montclair State University
http://www.montclair.edu
1 Normal Ave., Upper Montclair, NJ 07043
Main phone: (973) 655-4000

New Jersey Institute of Technology
http://www.njit.edu
University Heights, Newark, NJ 07102
Main phone: (973) 596-3000

Ramapo College of New Jersey
http://www.ramapo.edu
505 Ramapo Valley Rd., Mahwah, NJ 07430-1680
Main phone: (201) 684-7500

Richard Stockton College
http://www2.stockton.edu
P.O. Box 105, Pomona, NJ 08240
Main phone: (800) 852-1770

Rowan University
http://www.rowan.edu

201 Mullica Hill Rd., Glassboro, NJ 08028-1701
Main phone: (856) 256-4000

Rutgers University
http://www.rutgers.edu
14 College Ave., Miller Hall, New Brunswick, NJ
08903
Main phone: (732) 932-7276
Branches: Camden, New Brunswick, Newark

Thomas Edison State College
http://www.tesc.edu
101 W. State St., Trenton, NJ 08608-1176
Main phone: (609) 984-1150

University of Medicine and Dentistry of New Jersey
http://www.umdnj.edu/homeweb/new/index.htm
65 Bergen St., Newark, NJ 07017
Main phone: (973) 972-5000
Branches: Biomedical Sciences Graduate School,
Health Related Professions School, New Jersey
Dental School, New Jersey Medical School, Robert
Wood Johnson Medical School, School of Nursing,
School of Osteopathic Medicine, School of Public
Health, University Behavioral Health Care, University
Hospital

William Paterson University
http://ww2.wpunj.edu
300 Pompton Rd., Wayne, NJ 07470
Main phone: (973) 720-2000

Corrections Dept.
http://www.state.nj.us/corrections
General e-mail: publicinfo@doc.state.nj.us
Main phone: (609) 292-4036
Main fax: (609) 777-0445
Mailing address: P.O. Box 863, Trenton, NJ 08625-0863

Jack Terhune, Commissioner
Whittlesey Rd., Trenton, NJ 08625-0863
Fax: (609) 292-9083

Economic Development Authority
General e-mail: njeda@njeda.com
Main phone: (609) 292-1800
Main fax: (609) 292-5722
Mailing address: P.O. Box 990, Trenton, NJ 08625-0990

Caren S. Franzini, Executive Director
36 W. State St., Trenton, NJ 08625-0990
(609) 977-4471

Education Dept.
http://www.state.nj.us/education
Main phone: (609) 292-4469
Main fax: (609) 984-6756
Mailing address: P.O. Box 500, Trenton, NJ 08635-0500

David C. Hespe, Commissioner
Bldg. 100, Riverview Executive Plaza, Trenton, NJ 08625-0500
(609) 292-4450; *Fax:* (609) 777-4099

Educational Facilities Authority
General e-mail: njefa@aol.com
Main phone: (609) 987-0880
Main fax: (609) 987-0850

Victor Cantillo, Executive Director
101 College Rd. East, Princeton, NJ 08540-6601

Environmental Protection Dept.
http://www.state.nj.us/dep
Main phone: (609) 777-3373
Main fax: (609) 292-7695
Mailing address: P.O. Box 402, Trenton, NJ 08625-0402

Robert C. Shinn Jr., Commissioner
401 E. State St., Trenton, NJ 08625-0402
(609) 292-2885
E-mail: rshinn@dep.state.nj.us

Fish, Game, and Wildlife
http://www.state.nj.us/dep/fgw/
General e-mail: njdivfgw@eclipse.net
Main phone: (609) 292-2965
Toll free: (877) 927-6337

Mailing address: P.O. Box 400, Trenton, NJ 08625-0400

Bob McDowell, Director
501 E. State St., 3rd Fl., Trenton, NJ 08625-0400

Forest Service
http://www.state.nj.us/dep/forestry/community/
General e-mail: mderrico@gis.dep.state.nj.us
Main phone: (609) 292-2532
Main fax: (609) 984-0378
Mailing address: P.O. Box 404, Trenton, NJ 08625-0404

G. Lester Alpaugh, State Forester
501 E. State St., Trenton, NJ 08625
(908) 984-3865

Geological Survey
http://www.state.nj.us/dep/njgs/index.html
General e-mail:
   webmaster@njgs.dep.state.nj.us
Main phone: (609) 292-1185
Main fax: (609) 633-1004
Mailing address: P.O. Box 427, Trenton, NJ 08625-0427

Haig F. Kasabach, State Geologist
29 Arctic Pkwy., Trenton, NJ 08625-0427

Natural and Historic Resources
Main phone: (609) 292-3541
Main fax: (609) 984-0836
Mailing address: P.O. Box 404, Trenton, NJ 08625-0404

Cari J. Wild, Assistant Commissioner
501 E. State St., Trenton, NJ 08625

Natural and Historic Resources: Parks and Forestry Division
Main phone: (609) 292-2733
Main fax: (609) 984-0503
Toll free: (800) 843-6420
Mailing address: P.O. Box 404, Trenton, NJ 08625-0404

Gregory Marshall, Director
501 E. State St., Trenton, NJ 08625

Ethical Standards Executive Commission
http://www.state.nj.us/lps/ethics/
General e-mail: ethics@eces.state.nj.us
Main phone: (609) 292-1892
Main fax: (609) 633-9252
Mailing address: P.O. Box 082, Trenton, NJ 08625-0082

Rita L. Strmensky, Executive Director
28 W. State St., #1407, Trenton, NJ 08625

Health and Senior Services Dept.

http://www.state.nj.us/health
Main phone: (609) 292-7837
Main fax: (609) 984-5474
Toll free: (800) 367-6534
Mailing address: P.O. Box 360, Trenton, NJ
08625-0360

Christine Grant, Commissioner
Health and Agriculture Bldg., Trenton, NJ 08625-0360

Health Planning and Regulation
Main phone: (609) 984-3939
Main fax: (609) 292-5333
Mailing address: P.O. Box 360, Trenton, NJ
08625-0360

Marilyn Dahl, Senior Assistant Commisioner (Acting)
Health and Agriculture Bldg., Trenton, NJ 08625-0360

Health Care Facilities Financing Authority

http://www.njhcffa.com
Main phone: (609) 292-8585
Main fax: (609) 633-7778
Mailing address: P.O. Box 366, Trenton, NJ
08625-0366

Edith F. Behr, Executive Director
Station Plaza 4, 22 S. Clinton Ave., 4th Fl., Trenton, NJ 08609-1212
(609) 292-8585, ext. 23

Higher Education Commission

http://www.state.nj.us/highereducation
General e-mail: nj_che@che.state.nj.us
Main phone: (609) 292-4310
Main fax: (609) 292-7225
Mailing address: P.O. Box 542, Trenton, NJ
08625-0542

James E. Sulton Jr., Executive Director
20 W. State St., Trenton, NJ 08625-0542
E-mail: jsulton@che.state.nj.us

Historical Commission

http://www.state.nj.us/state/history/hisidx.html
General e-mail: feedback@sos.state.nj.us
Main phone: (609) 292-6062
Main fax: (609) 633-8168
Mailing address: P.O. Box 305, Trenton, NJ
08625-0305

Mary Murrin, Director (Acting)
20 W. State St., Trenton, NJ 08625

Housing and Mortgage Finance Agency

http://www.state.nj.us/dca/hmfa

Frequently Called Numbers

Tourism: (609) 292-2470, 1-800-VISITNJ;
http://www.state.nj.us/travel/index.html
Library: (609) 292-6220;
http://www.njstatelib.org
Vital Statistics: (609) 292-4087;
http://www.state.nj.us/health/vital/vital.htm
Tax/Revenue: (609) 633-6734;
http://www.state.nj.us/treasury/revenue/
Motor Vehicles: (609) 292-4570;
http://www.state.nj.us/mvs
State Police/Highway Patrol: (609) 882-2000,
ext. 6311; 1-800-437-7839;
http://www.state.nj.us/lps/njsp/
Unemployment: (609) 292-2460;
http://www.state.nj.us/labor/uiex/main2.htm
General Election Information: (609) 292-
3760; http://www.state.nj.us/lps/elections/
Consumer Affairs: (973) 504-6200
Hazardous Materials: (609) 984-6880;
http://www.state.nj.us/dep/dshw

Main phone: (609) 278-7400
Main fax: (609) 278-1754
Mailing address: P.O. Box 18550, Trenton, NJ
08625-2085

Deborah De Santis, Executive Director
637 S. Clinton Ave., Trenton, NJ 08611
(609) 278-7440
E-mail: ddesantis@njhmfa.state.nj.us

Human Services Dept.

http://www.state.nj.us/humanservices
General e-mail: ddaniels@dhs.state.nj.us
Main phone: (609) 292-3703
Main fax: (609) 393-4846
Mailing address: P.O. Box 700, Trenton, NJ
08625-0700

Michele K. Guhl, Commissioner
240 W. State St., Trenton, NJ 08625-0700
(609) 292-3717

Developmental Disabilities Division
Main phone: (609) 292-7260
Main fax: (609) 292-6610
TTY: (609) 777-0842
Mailing address: P.O. Box 726, Trenton, NJ
08625-0726

Deborah Trub Wehrlen, Director
50 E. State St., Capitol Center, 4th Fl., Trenton, NJ 08625

Medical Assistance and Health Services Division
Main phone: (609) 588-2600
Main fax: (609) 588-3583
TTY: (609) 588-2607
Mailing address: P.O. Box 712, Trenton, NJ 08625-0712

Margaret A. Murray, Director
7 Quakerbridge Plaza, Trenton, NJ 08625

Mental Health Services Division
Main phone: (609) 777-0700
Main fax: (609) 777-0835
TTY: (609) 777-0714
Mailing address: P.O. Box 727, Trenton, NJ 08625-0727

Alan Kaufman, Director
50 E. State St., Trenton, NJ 08625-0727
Fax: (609) 777-0662

Juvenile Justice Commission
Main phone: (609) 530-5200
Main fax: (609) 530-2576
Mailing address: P.O. Box 107, Trenton, NJ 08625-0107

Bruce D. Stout, Executive Director
840 Bear Tavern Rd., 2nd Fl, Trenton, NJ 08625
(609) 530-5454; *Fax:* (609) 530-5037
E-mail: jjastou@smtp.lps.state.nj.us

Labor Dept.
http://www.state.nj.us/labor
General e-mail: cmycoff@dol.state.nj.us
Main phone: (609) 292-2323
Main fax: (609) 633-9271
TTY: (800) 852-7899
Mailing address: P.O. Box 110, Trenton, NJ 08625-0110

Melvin L. Galade, Commissioner
John Fitch Plaza, Trenton, NJ 08625
E-mail: mgelade@dol.state.nj.us

Boards and Licensing

Accountancy, (973) 504-6380
Architects, (973) 504-6460
Child Care, (609) 292-9220
Cosmetology, (973) 504-6400
Engineers and Land Surveyors,
  (973) 504-6460
Medical Licensing, (609) 826-7100
Nursing, (973) 504-6586
Pharmacy, (973) 504-6450
Real Estate, (973) 504-6480

Workers Compensation Division
http://www.state.nj.us/labor/wc/Default.htm
General e-mail: skosnik@dol.state.nj.us
Main phone: (609) 292-2515
Main fax: (609) 984-2515
Mailing address: P.O. Box 381, Trenton, NJ 08625-0381

Paul A. Kapalko, Director and Chief Judge
John Fitch Plaza, 6th Fl., Trenton, NJ 08625
(609) 292-2414
E-mail: pkapalko@dol.state.nj.us

Lottery
http://www.state.nj.us/lottery/
General e-mail: publicinfo@lottery.state.nj.us
Main phone: (609) 599-5800
Main fax: (609) 599-5935
Mailing address: P.O. Box 041, Trenton, NJ 08625-0041

Virginia E. Haines, Executive Director
One Lawrence Park Complex, Lawrenceville, NJ 08648
(609) 599-5900

Management and Budget Office
http://www.state.nj.us/treasury/omb/index.html
Main phone: (609) 292-6746
Main fax: (609) 984-8498
Mailing address: P.O. Box 221, Trenton, NJ 08625-0221

Charlene M. Holzbaur, Director and Comptroller
33 W. State St., Trenton, NJ 08625-0221
Fax: (609) 633-8179
E-mail: holzbauer_c@tre.state.nj.us

Personnel Dept.
http://www.state.nj.us/personnel
Main phone: (609) 292-4144
Main fax: (609) 984-1064
Mailing address: P.O. Box 317, Trenton, NJ 08625-0317

Janice Mitchell Mintz, Commissioner
Station Plaza 3, 44 S. Clinton Ave., 5th Fl., Trenton, NJ 08625-0317
(609) 292-4145; *Fax:* (609) 984-3631
E-mail: csbmint@dop.state.nj.us

Port Authority of New York and New Jersey
http://www.panynj.gov
Main phone: (212) 435-7000
Main fax: (212) 435-2706

Lewis M. Eisenberg, Chair
1 World Trade Center, #67-W, New York, NY 10048
(212) 435-4173

Public Defender's Office

Main phone: (609) 292-7087
Main fax: (609) 777-1795
Mailing address: P.O. Box 850, Trenton, NJ 08625-0850

Ivelisse Torres, Public Defender

25 Market St., Trenton, NJ 08625

Public Employment Relations Commission

http://www.state.nj.us/perc
Main phone: (609) 292-9830
Main fax: (609) 777-0089
Mailing address: P.O. Box 429, Trenton, NJ 08625-0429

Millicent A. Wasell, Chair

495 W. State St., Trenton, NJ 08625-0429

Public Utilities Board

http://www.bpu.state.nj.us
Main phone: (973) 648-2026
Main fax: (973) 648-4195

Herbert H. Tate, President

2 Gateway Center, Newark, NJ 07102
(973) 648-2013
E-mail: tate@orion.bpu.state.nj.us

Revenue Division

http://www.state.nj.us/treasury/revenue/
General e-mail: tkorchic@revenue.state.nj.us
Main phone: (609) 633-6734
Main fax: (609) 984-8460
Mailing address: P.O. Box 628, Trenton, NJ 08646-0628

Patricia A. Chiacchio, Director

160 S. Broad St., Trenton, NJ 08646

State Police Division

http://www.state.nj.us/lps/njsp/
Main phone: (609) 882-2000, ext. 6311
Main fax: (609) 882-6523
Toll free: (800) 437-7839
TTY: (800) 855-1155
Mailing address: P.O. Box 7068, Trenton, NJ 08628-0068

Carson J. Dunbar, Superintendent

Trooper Dr., West Trenton, NJ 08628-0068

Transportation Dept.

http://www.state.nj.us/transportation
Main phone: (609) 530-2000
Main fax: (609) 530-8294
Mailing address: P.O. Box 602, Trenton, NJ 08625-0602

James Weinstein, Commissioner

1035 Pkwy. Ave., Trenton, NJ 08625
(609) 530-3536; *Fax:* (609) 530-3894

Aeronautics and Freight Systems

Main phone: (609) 530-2080
Main fax: (609) 530-4549
Mailing address: P.O. Box 610, Trenton, NJ 08625-0610

Theodore (Ted) Matthews, Executive Director (Acting)

1035 Parkway Ave., Trenton, NJ 08625

Motor Vehicle Services

http://www.state.nj.us/mvs
Main phone: (609) 292-4570
Main fax: (609) 777-4171
Toll free: (888) 486-3339
Mailing address: P.O. Box 160, Trenton, NJ 08625-0160

C. Richard Kamin, Director

225 E. State St., #9-W, Trenton, NJ 08666

New Jersey Legislature

State House Annex
Trenton, NJ 08625-0068
General information: (609) 292-4840
Fax: (609) 777-2440
TTY: (609) 777-2744
http://www.njleg.state.nj.us

Senate

Address: State House, P.O. Box 099, Trenton, NJ 08625-0099
General information: (609) 292-6828

Donald T. DiFrancesco (R), President

State House, P.O. Box 099, Trenton, NJ 08625-0099
(609) 259-5199
E-mail: SenDiFrancesco@njleg.state.nj.us
http://www.njleg.state.nj.us/html98/difranc.htm

Joseph A. Palaia (R), President Pro Tempore

State House, P.O. Box 099, Trenton, NJ 08625-0099
(609) 292-5199
E-mail: SenPalaia@njleg.state.nj.us
http://www.njleg.state.nj.us/html98/palaia.htm

John O. Bennett (R), Majority Leader

State House, P.O. Box 099, Trenton, NJ 08625-0099
(609) 292-5199
E-mail: SenBennett@njleg.state.nj.us
http://www.njleg.state.nj.us/html98/bennett.htm

<table>
<tr><th colspan="2" style="text-align:center">Laws</th></tr>
</table>

Laws

Sales tax: 6%
Income tax: 6.4%
State minimum wage: $5.15 (Federal is $5.15)
Marriage age: 18
First-cousin marriage: Permitted
Drinking age: 21
State control of liquor sales: No
Blood alcohol for DWI: 0.10%
Driving age: 17, 6 mos. (effective 2001)
Speed limit: 65 mph
Permit to buy handguns: Yes, 30 days to acquire
Minimum age to possess handguns: 18
Minimum age to possess rifles, shotguns: 18
State lottery: Yes
Casinos: Yes (commercial)
Pari-mutuel betting: Horse racing
Death penalty: Yes
3 strikes minimum sentence: Life, no parole (3rd violent felony)
Hate crimes law: Yes
Gay employment non-discrimination: Yes
Official language(s): None
Term limits: None

State laws are complex and subject to change; this information is not intended as legal advice. For an explanation of this information, see p. x.

Diane B. Allen (R), Majority Whip
State House, P.O. Box 099, Trenton, NJ 08625-0099
(609) 292-5199
E-mail: SenAllen@njleg.state.nj.us
http://www.njleg.state.nj.us/html98/allen.htm

Richard J. Codey (D), Minority Leader
State House, P.O. Box 099, Trenton, NJ 08625-0099
(609) 292-5388
E-mail: SenCodey@njleg.state.nj.us
http://www.njleg.state.nj.us/html98/codey.htm

Edward T. O'Connor Jr. (D), Minority Whip
State House, P.O. Box 099, Trenton, NJ 08625-0099
(609) 292-5388
E-mail: SenOConnor@njleg.state.nj.us
http://www.njleg.state.nj.us/html98/oconno

Dolores A. Kirk, Secretary
State House, P.O. Box 099, #115, Trenton, NJ 08625-0099

(609) 292-6828; *Fax:* (609) 984-8148
http://www.njleg.state.nj.us/html98/kirk.htm

House
Address: State House, P.O. Box 098, Trenton, NJ 08625-0098
General information: (609) 292-5222

Jack Collins (R), Speaker of the Assembly
State House, P.O. Box 098, Trenton, NJ 08625-0098
(609) 292-5339
E-mail: AsmCollins@njleg.state.nj.us
http://www.njleg.state.nj.us/html98/collins.htm

Nicholas R. Felice (R), Speaker Pro Tempore
State House, P.O. Box 098, Trenton, NJ 08625-0098
(609) 292-5339
E-mail: AsmFelice@njleg.state.nj.us
http://www.njleg.state.nj.us/html98/felice.htm

Paul DiGaetano (R), Majority Leader
State House, P.O. Box 098, Trenton, NJ 08625-0098
(609) 292-5339
E-mail: AsmDiGaetano@njleg.state.nj.us
http://www.njleg.state.nj.us/html98/digaeta.htm

Kenneth C. LeFevre (R), Majority Whip
State House, P.O. Box 098, Trenton, NJ 08625-0098
(609) 292-5339
E-mail: AsmLeFevre@njleg.state.nj.us
http://www.njleg.state.nj.us/html/lefevre.htm

Joseph V. Doria Jr. (D), Minority Leader
State House, P.O. Box 098, Trenton, NJ 08625-0098
(609) 292-7065
http://www.njleg.state.nj.us/html98/doria.htm

Nia H. Gill (D), Minority Whip
State House, P.O. Box 098, Trenton, NJ 08625-0098
(609) 292-7065
http://www.njleg.state.nj.us/html98/gill.htm

Linda Metzger, Clerk of the General Assembly
State House, P.O. Box 098, #214, Trenton, NJ 08625-0098
(609) 292-5222; *Fax:* (609) 392-2073
http://www.njleg.state.nj.us/html98/Metzger.htm

New Jersey Judiciary
Richard J. Hughes Justice Complex
25 Market St.
Trenton, NJ 08625
http://www.judiciary.state.nj.us

Supreme Court
http://www.judiciary.state.nj.us/supreme/index.htm

Stephen W. Townsend, Clerk
Richard J. Hughes Justice Complex, 25 Market St.,
  Trenton, NJ 08625
(609) 292-4837; *Fax:* (609) 396-9056

Justices
Composition: 7 justices
Selection Method: appointed by governor with
  consent of state senate; may serve until age
  70 if reappointed
Length of term: 7 years upon appointment; until
  age 70 if reappointed

Deborah T. Poritz, Chief Justice, (609) 292-2448
James H. Coleman Jr., Associate Justice, (908) 769-
  9011
Marie L. Garibaldi, Associate Justice, (201) 659-6600
Virginia A. Long, Associate Justice, (609) 292-8090

Daniel J. O'Hern, Associate Justice, (732) 530-7854
Gary S. Stein, Associate Justice, (201) 996-8020
Peter G. Verniero, Associate Justice, (973) 631-6391

Administrative Office of the Courts
http://www.judiciary.state.nj.us/admin.htm
Main phone: (609) 984-0275
Main fax: (609) 984-6968

Richard J. Williams, Administrative Director
Richard J. Hughes Justice Complex, 25 Market St.,
  Trenton, NJ 08625

State Law Library
Main phone: (609) 292-6230
Main fax: (609) 984-7901

Marjorie Garwig, Director
185 W. State St., Trenton, NJ 08625-0520

Legislative and Political Party Information Resources

Committees: http://www.njleg.state.nj.us/html/commite.htm
Legislative information: http://www.njleg.state.nj.us/html/our.htm
Legislative process: http://www.njleg.state.nj.us/html/how.htm
Budget: http://www.njleg.state.nj.us/html/budget.htm
New Jersey Democratic Party: http://www.njdems.org
  150 W. State St., 3rd Fl., Trenton, NJ 08608; *Phone:* (609) 392-3367; *Fax:* (609) 396-4778
New Jersey Rebublican Party: http://www.njgop.org
  28 W. State St., #305, Trenton, NJ 08608; *Phone:* (609) 989-7300; *Fax:* (609) 989-8685

New Mexico

State Capitol
Santa Fe, NM 87503
Public information: (505) 827-9632
Fax: (505) 827-3026
http://www.state.nm.us

Office of the Governor
http://www.gov.state.nm.us
General e-mail: gov@gov.state.nm.us
Main phone: (505) 827-3000
Main fax: (505) 827-3026
Toll free: (800) 432-4406

Gary E. Johnson (R), Governor
State Capitol Bldg., #400, Santa Fe, NM 87503

Lou Gallegos, Chief of Staff
State Capitol Bldg., #400, Santa Fe, NM 87503
(505) 827-3000; *Fax:* (505) 827-3026

Diane Kinderwater, Press Secretary
State Capitol Bldg., #400, Santa Fe, NM 87503
(505) 827-3000; *Fax:* (505) 827-3026

Leon Duran, Constituent Affairs
State Capitol Bldg., #400, Santa Fe, NM 87503
(505) 827-3041; *Fax:* (505) 827-3026

Office of the Lieutenant Governor
http://164.64.43.1/structur/ltgovdir.htm
General e-mail: mlewis@gov.state.nm.us
Main phone: (505) 827-3050
Main fax: (505) 827-3057
Toll free: (800) 432-4406

Walter D. Bradley (R), Lieutenant Governor
State Capitol Bldg., #417, Santa Fe, NM 87503

Office of the Secretary of State
http://www.sos.state.nm.us
General e-mail: 73160.1711@compuserve.com
Main phone: (505) 827-3600
Main fax: (505) 827-3634
Toll free: (800) 477-3632
TTY: (505) 827-3926

Rebecca Vigil-Giron (D), Secretary of State
325 Don Gaspar, #300, Santa Fe, NM 87503
Fax: (505) 827-8081
E-mail: rebecca.vigil-giron@state.nm.us

Office of the Attorney General
http://www.ago.state.nm.us/
Main phone: (505) 827-6000
Main fax: (505) 827-5826

State of New Mexico

Capital: Santa Fe, since 1610
Founded: 1598, as province of Spain; 1850, New Mexico Territory created
Statehood: January 6, 1912 (47th state)
Constitution adopted: 1911
Area: 121,364 sq. mi. (ranks 5th)
Population: 1,736,931 (1998 est.; ranks 37th)
Largest cities: (1998 est.) Albuquerque (419,311); Las Cruces (76,102); Santa Fe (67,879); Rio Rancho (50,041); Farmington (39,028)
Counties: 33, Most populous: (1998 est.) Bernalillo (525,958); Dona Ana (169,165); Santa Fe (123,386); San Juan (106,020); Roosevelt (88,049)
U.S. Congress: Jeff Bingaman (D), Pete V. Domenici (R); 3 Representatives
Nickname(s): Land of Enchantment
Motto: It grows as it goes
Song: "O Fair New Mexico, Asi es Nuevo Mexico"
Bird: Roadrunner
Tree: Pinon
Flower: Yucca Flower
State fair: at Albuquerque, early to mid-Sept.
Former capital(s): None

Mailing address: P.O. Drawer 1508, Santa Fe, NM 85704-1508

Patricia Madrid (D), Attorney General
Bataan Memorial, 407 Galisteo St., #216, Santa Fe, NM 85701

Office of the State Treasurer
http://www.stonm.org
General e-mail: sto@newmexico.com
Main phone: (505) 827-6400
Main fax: (505) 827-6395
Mailing address: P.O. Box 608, Santa Fe, NM 85704-0608

Michael A. Montoya (D), State Treasurer
NEA Bldg., 130 S. Capitol, Santa Fe, NM 85704-0608

Office of the State Auditor

http://www.sao.nm.org
Main phone: (505) 827-3500
Main fax: (505) 827-3512
Toll free: (800) 432-5517

Domingo Martinez (D), State Auditor
2113 Warner Circle, Santa Fe, NM 87505-5499
E-mail: domingo.martinez@state.nm.us

Military Affairs Dept.

Main phone: (505) 474-1200
Main *Fax:* (505) 474-1289

Randall E. Horn, Adjutant General
47 Bataan Blvd., Santa Fe, NM 87505
(505) 474-1202; *Fax:* (505) 474-1355
E-mail: hornre@nm-arng.ngb.army.mil

Agencies

Adult Parole Board

Main phone: (505) 827-8892
Main fax: (505) 827-8933

Elizabeth Maestas, Chair
4351 State Rd. 14, Santa Fe, NM 87505
(505) 827-8825

Aging Agency

http://www.aoa.dhhs.gov
Main phone: (505) 827-7640
Main fax: (505) 827-7649
Toll free: (800) 432-2080

Michelle Lujan Grisham, Director
La Villa Rivera Bldg., 228 E. Palace Ave., Santa Fe,
NM 87501
E-mail: michelle.grisham@state.nm.us

Agriculture Dept.

http://www.nmdaweb.nmsu.edu
Main phone: (505) 646-3007
Main fax: (505) 646-8120
Mailing address: P.O. Box 30005, Las Cruces, NM
88003-8005

Frank A. DuBois, Director, Secretary
3190 Espina St., Las Cruces, NM 88003-8005

Architects Board

http://www.nmbea.org
Main phone: (505) 827-6375
Main fax: (505) 827-6373
Mailing address: P.O. Box 509, Santa Fe, NM
87503-0509

David J. Knauer, Director
491 Old Santa Fe Trail, Santa Fe, NM 87501
E-mail: dknauer@state.nm.us

Children, Youth, and Families Dept.

http://cyfabq.cyfd.state.nm.us/
Main phone: (505) 827-7610
Main fax: (505) 827-4053
Toll free: (800) 610-7610
Mailing address: P.O. Drawer 5160, Santa Fe, NM
87502-5160

Deborah Hartz, Cabinet Secretary
1120 Paseo de Peralta St., Santa Fe, NM 87502
(505) 827-7602

Juvenile Justice Division

Main phone: (505) 827-7629
Main fax: (505) 827-8408
Toll free: (800) 610-7610, ext. 7629
Mailing address: P.O. Drawer 5160, Santa Fe,
NM 87502-5160

Art Murphy, Director
1120 Paseo de Peralta St., Santa Fe, NM 87502

Commission for the Blind

http://www.state.nm.us/cftb/
Main phone: (505) 841-8844
Main fax: (505) 841-8850
Toll free: (888) 513-7958

Manuel Gonzales, Chair
2200 Yale Blvd. S.E., Albuquerque, NM 87106

Consumer Protection Division

Main phone: (505) 827-6094
Main fax: (505) 827-6685
Toll free: (800) 678-1508
Mailing address: P.O. Drawer 1508, Santa Fe, NM
87504-1508

Robert Reyna, Director
407 Galisteo St., Santa Fe, NM 87504
E-mail: rreyna@ago.state.ne.us

Corrections Dept.

http://www.state.nm.us/corrections
Main phone: (505) 827-8709
Main fax: (505) 827-8220
Mailing address: P.O. Box 27116, Santa Fe, NM
87502-0116

Robert J. Perry, Secretary
4337 State Rd. 18, Santa Fe, NM 87507
E-mail: corrections.secretary@state.nm.us

Cultural Affairs Office

http://www.nm.oca.org
Main phone: (505) 827-6364
Main fax: (505) 827-7308

J. Edson Way, Director
228 E. Palace Ave., Santa Fe, NM 87501
E-mail: eway@oca.state.nm.us

Higher Educational Institutions

Eastern New Mexico University
http://www.enmu.edu
Station #7 ENMU, Portales, NM 88130
Main phone: (800) 367-3668
Branches: Roswell, Ruidoso

New Mexico Highlands University
http://www.nmhu.edu
P.O. Box 9000, Las Vegas, NM 87701
Main phone: (505) 425-7511

New Mexico Institute of Mining and Technology
http://www.nmt.edu
801 Leroy Pl., Socorro, NM 87801
Main phone: (800) 428-8324

New Mexico State University
http://www.nmsu.edu
Box 30001, Las Cruces, NM 88003-8001
Main phone: (505) 646-3121
Branches: Alamogordo, Carlsbad, Dona Ana, Grants

University of New Mexico
http://www.unm.edu
Albuquerque, NM 87131-2046
Main phone: (800) 225-5866
Branches: Gallup, Los Alamos, Taos, Valencia

Western New Mexico University
http://www.wnmu.edu
100 W. College Ave., P.O. Box 680, Silver City, NM 88062

Historic Preservation Division
http://museums.state.nm.us/hpd
Main phone: (505) 827-6320
Main fax: (505) 827-6338

> **Dorothy Victor, Director** (Acting)
> 228 E. Palace Ave., 3rd Fl., Santa Fe, NM 87501

New Mexico Arts
http://www.artsnet.org/nma
Main phone: (505) 827-6490
Main fax: (505) 827-6043
Toll free: (800) 879-4278
TTY: (505) 827-6925
Mailing address: P.O. Box 1450, Santa Fe, NM 87504-1450

> **Margaret Brommelsick, Executive Director**
> 228 E. Palace Ave., Santa Fe, NM 87501

Economic Development Dept.
http://www.newmexicodevelopment.com
Main phone: (505) 827-0300
Main fax: (505) 827-0328
Toll free: (800) 374-3061

TTY: (505) 827-0248
Mailing address: P.O. Box 20003, Santa Fe, NM 87504-5003

> **John A. Garcia, Secretary**
> 1100 St. Francis Dr., Santa Fe, NM 87505
> (505) 827-0305
> *E-mail:* jgarcia@edd.state.nm.us

Education Dept.
http://www.sde.state.nm.us
Main phone: (505) 827-6516
Main fax: (505) 827-6696
TTY: (505) 827-6541

> **Michael J. Davis, State Superintendent of Public Instruction**
> Education Bldg., 300 Don Gaspar St., Santa Fe, NM 87503
> (505) 827-6520

Board of Education
Main phone: (505) 827-6516
Main fax: (505) 827-6696
TTY: (505) 827-6541

> **Mary Jo Bradley, Administrative Assistant**
> Education Bldg., 300 Don Gaspar St., #224, Santa Fe, NM 87501-2786
> (505) 827-6571
> *E-mail:* mbradley@sde.state.nm.us

Energy, Minerals, and Natural Resources Dept.
http://www.emnrd.state.nm.us
Main phone: (505) 827-5950
Main fax: (505) 827-1150
TTY: (505) 827-5970

> **Jennifer A. Salisbury, Secretary**
> 2040 S. Pacheco St., Santa Fe, NM 87505

Forestry Division
Main phone: (505) 827-5830
Main fax: (505) 827-3903
Mailing address: P.O. Box 1948, Santa Fe, NM 87504

> **Tobias A. Martinez, Director**
> 408 Galisteo St., Santa Fe, NM 87503
> (505) 827-7693
> *E-mail:* tamartinez@state.nm.us

State Parks Division
http://www.nmparks.com
Main phone: (505) 827-1193
Main fax: (505) 827-1376
Toll free: (888) 667-2757
Mailing address: P.O. Box 1147, Santa Fe, NM 87504-1147

> **Thomas P. Trujillo, Director**
> 2040 S. Pacheco, Santa Fe, NM 87505

Engineers and Land Surveyors Board

Main phone: (505) 827-7561
Main fax: (505) 827-7566

Elena Garcia, Executive Director
1010 Marquez Pl., Santa Fe, NM 87501
E-mail: Elena.Garcia@state.nm.us

Environment Dept.

http://www.nmenv.state.nm.us/
Main phone: (505) 827-2855
Main fax: (505) 827-2836
Toll free: (800) 219-6157
Mailing address: P.O. Box 26110, Santa Fe, NM 87502

Peter Maggiore, Secretary
1190 St. Francis Dr., Santa Fe, NM 87505

Ethics Administration

Main phone: (505) 827-3600
Main fax: (505) 827-3634
Toll free: (800) 477-3632

Denise Lamb, Administrator (Acting)
325 Don Gaspar, #300, Santa Fe, NM 87503
(505) 827-3622
E-mail: denise.lamb@state.nm.us

Finance and Administration Dept.

http://www.state.nm.us/clients/dfa/index.html
Main phone: (505) 827-4985
Main fax: (505) 827-4984

David W. Harris, Secretary
Bataan Memorial Bldg., #180, Santa Fe, NM 87501

Fire Marshal

Main phone: (505) 827-3721
Main fax: (505) 827-3778
Toll free: (800) 244-6708
Mailing address: P.O. Drawer 1269, Santa Fe, NM 87504-1269

George Chavez, Fire Marshal
142 W. Palace Ave., Santa Fe, NM 87504
E-mail: gchavez@state.nm.us

Game and Fish Dept.

http://www.gmfsh.state.nm.us
General e-mail: web_admin@gmfsh.state.nm.us
Main phone: (505) 827-7911
Main fax: (505) 827-7915
Toll free: (800) 862-9310
TTY: (505) 827-7822
Mailing address: P.O. Box 25112, Santa Fe, NM 87504-5112

Jerry Maracchini, Director
Villagra Bldg., 408 Galisteo, Santa Fe, NM 87503
(505) 827-7899

General Services Dept.

http://www.state.nm.us/gsd/gsd
Main phone: (505) 827-2000
Main fax: (505) 827-2041
Mailing address: P.O. Drawer 26110, Santa Fe, NM 87502-0110

Steven R. Beffort, Secretary
715 Alta Vista St., Santa Fe, NM 87505-4108
(505) 827-2000

Health Dept.

http://www.health.state.nm.us
Main phone: (505) 827-2613
Main fax: (505) 827-2530
TTY: (505) 827-7584
Mailing address: P.O. Box 26110, Santa Fe, NM 87502-6110

J. Alex Valdez, Secretary
1190 St. Francis Dr., Santa Fe, NM 87505
E-mail: avaldez@health.state.nm.us

Behavioral Health Services Division

Main phone: (505) 827-2658
Main fax: (505) 827-0097
Mailing address: P.O. Box 26110, Santa Fe, NM 87502-6110

Mary Schumacher, Director
1190 St. Francis Dr., #N-3300, Santa Fe, NM 87502-6110
E-mail: mschumac@health.state.nm.us

Higher Education Commission

http://www.nmche.org/
General e-mail: highered@che.state.nm.us
Main phone: (505) 827-7383
Main fax: (505) 827-7392

Bruce D. Hamlett, Executive Director
1068 Cerrillos Rd., Santa Fe, NM 87501

Highway and Transportation Dept.

http://www.nmshtd.state.nm.us/
Main phone: (505) 827-5100
Main fax: (505) 827-5469
Mailing address: P.O. Box 1149, Santa Fe, NM 87504-1149

Peter K. Rahn, Secretary
1120 Cerrillos Rd., Santa Fe, NM 87504-1149

Transportation: Aviation Division

Main phone: (505) 827-1525
Main fax: (505) 827-1531
Mailing address: P.O. Box 1149, Santa Fe, NM 87504-1149

Mike Rice, Director
1550 Pacheco St., Santa Fe, NM 87505

Frequently Called Numbers

Tourism: 1-800-545-2040;
http://www.newmexico.org/
Library: (505) 476-9700
Board of Education: (505) 827-6516
Vital Statistics: (505) 827-2338
Tax/Revenue: (505) 827-0700;
http://www.state.nm.us/tax/
Motor Vehicles: (505) 827-2294,
1-888-MVD-INFO; http://www.state.nm.us/
tax/mvd/mvd_home.htm
State Police/Highway Patrol: (505) 827-9000
Unemployment: (505) 841-8431;
http://www3.state.nm.us/dol/dol_quib.html
General Election Information:
(505) 827-3600, 1-800-477-3632;
http://www.sos.state.nm.us/elect.htm
Consumer Affairs: (505) 827-6094,
1-800-678-1508
Hazardous Materials: (505) 827-1557

Human Services Dept.
http://www.state.nm.us/hsd/home.html
Main phone: (505) 827-7750
Main fax: (505) 827-6286
Mailing address: P.O. Box 2348, Santa Fe, NM
87504-2348

Robin Dozie-Otten, Secretary
2009 S. Pacheco, Pellon Plaza, Santa Fe, NM 87504-
2348

Medical Assistance Division
Main phone: (505) 827-3106
Main fax: (505) 827-3185
Mailing address: P.O. Box 2348, Santa Fe, NM
87504-2348

Charles Milligan, Director
2020 S. Pacheco St., Santa Fe, NM 87505

Insurance Division
Main phone: (505) 827-4601
Main fax: (505) 827-4724
Toll free: (800) 947-4722
Mailing address: P.O. Drawer 1269, Santa Fe, NM
87504-1269

Don Letherer, Superintendent
1120 Paseo de Peralta St., Santa Fe, NM 87501

Labor Dept.
http://www.state.nm.us/dol/
Main phone: (505) 841-8518

Main fax: (505) 841-8491
Mailing address: P.O. Box 1928, Albuquerque, NM
87103-1928

Clinton D. Harden Jr., Secretary
401 Broadway N.E., Albuquerque, NM 87103
(505) 841-8409

Human Rights Division
Main phone: (505) 827-6838
Main fax: (505) 827-6878
Toll free: (800) 566-9471
Mailing address: P.O. Box 1928, Albuquerque,
NM 87505

Richard Galaz, Director
1596 Pacheco St., Santa Fe, NM 87505

Mortgage Finance Authority
http://www.nmmfa.org
Main phone: (505) 843-6880
Main fax: (505) 243-3289
Mailing address: P.O. Box 2047, Albuquerque, NM
87103-2047

James W. Stretz, Executive Director
344 4th St. S.W., Albuquerque, NM 87102
E-mail: jstretz@nmmfa.org

Nursing Board
Main phone: (505) 841-8340
Main fax: (505) 841-8347
TTY: (800) 659-8331

Debra Brady, Executive Director
4206 Louisiana Blvd. N.E., Albuquerque, NM 87109-
1807
(505) 841-8340, ext. 7

Oil and Gas Division
Main phone: (505) 827-5745
Main fax: (505) 827-4739
Mailing address: P.O. Box 1148, Santa Fe, NM
87504-1148

Jami Bailey, Director
310 Old Santa Fe Trail, Santa Fe, NM 87501

Personnel Office
http://www.state.nm.us/spo
Main phone: (505) 476-7777
Main fax: (505) 476-7806
TTY: (505) 476-7798
Mailing address: P.O. Box 26127, Santa Fe, NM
87505-0127

Rex Robberson, Director
2600 Cerrillos Rd., Santa Fe, NM 87505-0127
(505) 476-7805

Public Defender's Office
Main phone: (505) 827-3931

Main fax: (505) 827-3999
Toll free: (800) 296-8643

Phylis H. Subin, Chief Public Defender
301 N. Guadalupe St., #101, Santa Fe, NM 87501
(505) 827-3931, ext. 104
E-mail: psubin@nmpd.state.nm.us

Public Employees Retirement Association
http://www.state.nm.us/pera
Main phone: (505) 827-4700
Main fax: (505) 827-4670
Mailing address: P.O. Box 2123, Santa Fe, NM 87504-2123

Alice E. Herter, Executive Director
PERA Bldg., Santa Fe, NM 87504-2123
(505) 827-1232

Public Safety Dept.
http://www.dps.nm.org/
Main phone: (505) 827-9000
Main fax: (505) 827-3434
TTY: (505) 827-3413
Mailing address: P.O. Box 1628, Santa Fe, NM 87504-1628

Nicholas S. Bakas, Secretary (Interim)
4491 Cerrillos Rd., Santa Fe, NM 87503
(505) 827-3370
E-mail: dw@dps.state.nm.us

Public Regulation Commission
http://www.nmprc.state.nm.us/
Main phone: (505) 827-6940
Main fax: (505) 827-4068
Toll free: (800) 947-4722
TTY: (505) 827-6911
Mailing address: P.O. Box 1269, Sante Fe, NM 87504

Linda Lovejoy, Chair
Marian Hall, 224 E. Palace Ave., Santa Fe, NM 87501
(505) 827-8019; *Fax:* (505) 476-0472
E-mail: llovejoy@state.nm.us

Regulation and Licensing Dept.
http://www.rld.state.nm.us/
Main phone: (505) 827-7000
Main fax: (505) 827-1157

Kelly Ward, Superintendent
725 St. Michael's Dr., Santa Fe, NM 87505
(505) 827-7003

Financial Institutions Division
http://www.rld.state.nm.us/fid/index.htm
General e-mail: rldfid@state.nm.us
Main phone: (505) 827-7100
Main fax: (505) 827-7107

William (Bill) Verant, Director
725 St. Michael's Dr., Santa Fe, NM 87505
E-mail: william.verant@state.nm.us

State Records Center and Archives
http://www.state.nm.us/cpr
General e-mail: asd@rain.state.nm.us
Main phone: (505) 476-7900
Main fax: (505) 476-7901

L. Elaine Olah, State Records Administrator
1205 Camino Carlos Rey, Santa Fe, NM 87505
(505) 476-7902
E-mail: eolah@rain.state.nm.us

Taxation and Revenue Dept.
http://www.state.nm.us/tax/
Main phone: (505) 827-0700
Main fax: (505) 827-0469
Mailing address: P.O. Box 630, Santa Fe, NM 87504-0630

John Chavez, Secretary
1200 South St. Francis Dr., Santa Fe, NM 87504-0630
(505) 827-0341

Motor Vehicle Division
http://www.state.nm.us/tax/mvd/mvd_home.htm
General e-mail: jeanaf@state.nm.us
Main phone: (505) 827-2294
Main fax: (505) 827-2397
Toll free: (888) MVD-INFO
Mailing address: P.O. Box 1028, Santa Fe, NM 87504-1028

Gordon E. Eden Jr., Director
Joseph Montoya Bldg., #2107, Santa Fe, NM 87504

Regulation and Licensing Dept.

http://www.rld.state.nm.us/
(505) 827-7000

Accountancy, (505) 827-6375,
  http://www.nmbea.org
Architects, (505) 827-6375,
  http://www.nmbea.org
Child Care, (505) 827-3839
Contractors, (505) 982-9541
Engineers and Land Surveyors,
  (505) 827-7561
Medical, (505) 827-0522
Nursing, (505) 841-8340
Pharmacy, (505) 841-9102
Cosmetology, (505) 476-7117
Real Estate, (505) 841-9120

(505) 827-2296
E-mail: gordoned@state.nm.us

Tourism Dept.
http://www.newmexico.org/
General e-mail: enchantment@newmexico.org
Toll free: (800) 545-2040, ext. 751
Main fax: (505) 827-7402
TTY: (505) 827-0248

Janet L. Green, Secretary
491 Old Santa Fe Trail, Santa Fe, NM 87503
(505) 827-7449

State Fair Commission
http://www.nmstatefair.com
General e-mail: manager@nmstatefair.com
Main phone: (505) 265-1791
Main fax: (505) 266-7784
Mailing address: P.O. Box 8546, Albuquerque, NM 87198-8546

Kay Shollenbarger, Manager
State Fair Grounds, 300 San Pedro N.E., Albuquerque, NM 87108

Veterans Service Commission
http://www.state.nm.us/veterans
General e-mail: nmvsc@state.nm.us
Main phone: (505) 827-6300
Main fax: (505) 827-6372
Mailing address: P.O. Box 2324, Santa Fe, NM 87504-2324

Michael D'Arco, Director
401 Galisteo, Santa Fe, NM 87504

Women's Status Commission
General e-mail: johanna.akins@state.nm.us
Main phone: (505) 841-8920
Main fax: (505) 841-8926
Toll free: (800) 432-9168

Rebecca Jo Dakota, Executive Director
2401 12th St. N.W., Albuquerque, NM 87104-2302
(505) 841-8920, ext. 102

Workers' Compensation Administration
http://www.state.nm..us/wca
Main phone: (505) 841-6000
Main fax: (505) 841-6009
TTY: (505) 841-6814
Mailing address: P.O. Box 27198, Albuquerque, NM 87125-7198

Paul D. Barber, Director
2410 Centre Ave. S.E., Albuquerque, NM 87125-7198
(505) 841-6006

New Mexico Legislature
State Capitol
Santa Fe, NM 87501
General information: (505) 986-4600
Fax: (505) 986-4610
http://legis.state.nm.us

Senate
General information: (505) 986-4714
Fax: (505) 986-4280
E-mail: senate@state.nm.us

Walter D. Bradley (R), President
State Capitol Bldg., #417, Santa Fe, NM 87501
(505) 827-3050; *Fax:* (505) 827-3057

Manny M. Aragon (D), President Pro Tempore
State Capitol Bldg., #105, Santa Fe, NM 87503
(505) 986-4733

Laws

Sales tax: 5.8125%
Income tax: 8.5%
State minimum wage: $4.25 (Federal is $5.15)
Marriage age: 18
First-cousin marriage: Permitted
Drinking age: 21
State control of liquor sales: No
Blood alcohol for DWI: 0.08%
Driving age: 16, 6 mos.
Speed limit: 75 mph
Permit to buy handguns: No
Minimum age to possess handguns: 18
Minimum age to possess rifles, shotguns: 18
State lottery: Yes; also Powerball
Casinos: Yes (tribal)
Pari-mutuel betting: Horse racing
Death penalty: Yes
3 strikes minimum sentence: 30 yrs. (3rd violent felony)
Hate crimes law: No
Gay employment non-discrimination: No
Official language(s): English, Spanish
Term limits: None

State laws are complex and subject to change; this information is not intended as legal advice. For an explanation of this information, see p. x.

Timothy Z. Jennings (D), Majority Leader
State Capitol Bldg., #120, Santa Fe, NM 87503
(505) 986-4727
E-mail: tjennings@state.nm.us
Mary Jane M. Garcia (D), Majority Whip
State Capitol Bldg., #120, Santa Fe, NM 87503
(505) 986-4726
E-mail: mjgarcia@state.nm.us
L. Skip Vernon (R), Minority Leader
State Capitol Bldg., #109, Santa Fe, NM 87503
(505) 986-4701
Stuart Ingle (R), Minority Whip
State Capitol Bldg., #109, Santa Fe, NM 87503
(505) 986-4702
Margaret Larragoite, Chief Clerk
State Capitol Bldg., Santa Fe, NM 87503
(505) 986-4714; *Fax:* (505) 986-4280

House
General information: (505) 986-4751
Fax: (505) 986-4755
E-mail: house@state.nm.us
Raymond G. Sanchez (D), Speaker of the House
State Capitol Bldg., #104, Santa Fe, NM 87503
(505) 986-4782
Ben Lujan (D), Majority Leader
State Capitol Bldg., #134, Santa Fe, NM 87503
(505) 986-4777
Danice Picraux (D), Majority Whip
State Capitol Bldg., #134, Santa Fe, NM 87503
(505) 986-4775
E-mail: dpicraux@state.nm.us
Ted Hobbs (R), Minority Leader
State Capitol Bldg., #125, Santa Fe, NM 87503
(505) 986-4757
Earlene Roberts (R), Minority Whip
State Capitol Bldg., #125, Santa Fe, NM 87503
(505) 986-4758
Stephen R. Arias, Chief Clerk
State Capitol Bldg., Santa Fe, NM 87503
(505) 986-4751; *Fax:* (505) 986-4755

New Mexico Judiciary
Supreme Court Bldg.
237 Don Gaspar Ave.
Santa Fe, NM 87503
http://www.nmcourts.com

Supreme Court
Kathleen Jo Gibson, Chief Clerk
Supreme Court Bldg., 237 Don Gaspar Ave., Santa Fe, NM 87501
(505) 827-4860; *Fax:* (505) 827-4837
Justices
Composition: 5 justices
Selection Method: general election; vacancies filled by gubernatorial appointment; appointees serve until next general election
Length of term: 8 years
Pamela B. Minzner, Chief Justice, (505) 827-4889
Joseph F. Baca, Justice, (505) 827-4892
Gene E. Franchini, Justice, (505) 827-4880
Petra Jimenez Maes, Justice, (505) 827-4883
Patricio M. Serna, Justice, (505) 827-4886

Administrative Office of the Courts
http://www.nmcourts.com/aoc.htm
Main phone: (505) 827-4800
Main fax: (505) 827-4824
John M. Greacen, Director
Supreme Court Bldg., 237 Don Gaspar Ave., Santa Fe, NM 87501

Supreme Court Law Library
http://fscll.org/
Main phone: (505) 827-4850
Main fax: (505) 827-4852
General e-mail: libref@jidmail.nmcourts.com
Thaddeus P. Bejnar, Director
Supreme Court Bldg., 237 Don Gaspar Ave., Santa Fe, NM 87501

Legislative and Political Party Information Resources

Senate home page: http://legis.state.nm.us/scripts/senate_info.asp
House home page: http://legis.state.nm.us/scripts/house_info.asp
Committees: Senate: http://legis.state.nm.us/senate_agendas.asp
   House: http://legis.state.nm.us/house_agendas.asp
New Mexico Democratic Party: http://www.dpnm.org
   5317 Menaul Blvd. N.E., Albuquerque, NM 87110; *Phone:* (505) 830-3650;
   E-mail: headquarters@dpnm.org
New Mexico Republican Party: http://www.gopnm.org/gopnm
   2901 Juan Tabo N.E., #116, Albuquerque, NM 87112; *Phone:* (505) 998-5254; *Fax:* (505) 292-0755;
   E-mail: gopnm@aol.com

New York

State Capitol
Albany, NY 12224
Public information: (518) 474-2121
http://www.state.ny.us

Office of the Governor
http://www.state.ny.us/governor/
Main phone: (518) 474-8390

George E. Pataki (R), Governor
State Capitol, Albany, NY 12224
E-mail: gov.pataki@chamber.state.ny.us

Bradford J. Race Jr., Chief of Staff/Secretary to the Governor
State Capitol, Albany, NY 12224
(518) 474-4246

Zenia Mucha, Communications Director
Executive Chamber, State Capitol, #201, Albany, NY 12224
(518) 474-8418; *Fax:* (518) 473-7669

Cindee Berlin, Constituent Affairs
State Capitol, Albany, NY 12224
(518) 474-8390

James Mazzarella, Director, Washington Office
444 N. Capitol St. N.W., #301, Washington, DC 20001
(202) 434-7100; *Fax:* (202) 434-7110

Office of the Lieutenant Governor
http://www.state.ny.us/governor/ltgov/index.html
Main phone: (518) 474-4623
Main fax: (518) 486-4170

Mary O. Donohue (R), Lieutenant Governor
Executive Chamber, State Capitol, Albany, NY 12224

Office of the Secretary of State
http://www.dos.state.ny.us
General e-mail: info@dos.state.ny.us
Main phone: (518) 474-4750
Main fax: (518) 474-4765
TTY: (518) 474-4203

Alexander F. Treadwell (R), Secretary of State
41 State St., Albany, NY 12231
(518) 474-0050
E-mail: executive@dos.state.ny.us

Attorney General's Office
http://www.oag.state.ny.us

State of New York

Capital: Albany, since 1797
Founded: 1623, as Dutch colony of New Netherland; British from 1664
Statehood: July 26, 1788 (11th state)
Constitution adopted: 1777 (revised 1938)
Area: 47,224 sq. mi. (ranks 30th)
Population: 18,175,301 (1998 est.; ranks 3rd)
Largest cities: (1998 est.) New York (7,420,166); Buffalo (300,717); Rochester (216,887); Yonkers (190,153); Amherst (110,788)
Counties: 62, Most populous: (1998 est.) Kings (2,267,942); Queens (1,998,853); New York (1,550,649); Suffolk (1,371,269); Nassau (1,302,220)
U.S. Congress: Charles E. Schumer (D), Daniel P. Moynihan (D); 31 Representatives
Nickname(s): Empire State
Motto: Ever upward
Song: "I Love New York"
Bird: Bluebird
Tree: Sugar maple
Flower: Rose
State fair: at Syracuse, late Aug.-early Sept.
Former capital(s): New York, Kingston, Poughkeepsie

Main phone: (212) 416-8050
Main fax: (212) 416-8942
Toll free: (800) 771-7755
TTY: (800) 788-9898

Eliot Spitzer (D), Attorney General
120 Broadway, New York, NY 10271-0332

Office of the State Comptroller
http://www.osc.state.ny.us
General e-mail: comptroller@osc.state.ny.us
Main phone: (518) 474-4044
Main fax: (518) 473-3004

H. Carl McCall (D), State Comptroller
Governor Alfred E. Smith Bldg., 6th Fl., Albany, NY 12236
(518) 474-4040

Division of Military and Naval Affairs

http://www.dmna.state.ny.us
Main phone: (518) 786-4500
Main fax: (518) 786-4785

John H. Fenimore V, Adjutant General
333 Old Niskayuna Rd., Latham, NY 12110-2224
(518) 786-4502; *Fax:* (518) 786-4325
E-mail: FenimoreJ@ny-smtp.army.mil

Agencies

Accountancy Board

http://www.op.nysed.gov
General e-mail: cpabd@mail.nysced.gov
Main phone: (518) 474-3836
Main fax: (518) 473-6282

Daniel Dustin, Director
Cultural Education Center, #3013, Albany, NY 12230

Aging Office

http://www.aging.state.ny.us
Main phone: (518) 474-7158
Main fax: (518) 474-0608
Toll free: (800) 342-9871
TTY: (800) 342-9871

Walter G. Hoefer, Director
2 Empire State Plaza, 5th Fl., Albany, NY 12223-1251
(518) 474-4425; *Fax:* (518) 474-1398

Agriculture and Markets Dept.

http://www.agmkt.state.ny.us
General e-mail: nysagmk@nysnet.net
Main phone: (518) 457-3880
Main fax: (518) 457-3087
Toll free: (800) 554-4501
TTY: (518) 485-7784

Nathan L. Rudgers, Commissioner (Acting)
1 Winners Circle, Albany, NY 12235-0001
(518) 457-8876
E-mail: commnr@nysnet.net

Natural Resources and Environmental Programs: Soil and Water Conservation Committee

http://www.soilandwater.org
General e-mail: hoeffnel@nysnet.net
Main phone: (518) 457-3738
Main fax: (518) 457-3412

John Wildeman, Director
1 Winners Circle, Albany, NY 12235-0001
(518) 457-8886

State Fair

http://www.nysfair.org
General e-mail: nysfair@nysnet.net
Main phone: (315) 487-7711
Main fax: (315) 487-9260
Toll free: (800) 475-FAIR

Peter Cappuccilli Jr., Director
581 State Fair Blvd., Syracuse, NY 13209

Alcoholic Beverage Control Division

General e-mail: kobrien@abc.state.ny.us
Main phone: (518) 474-3114
Main fax: (518) 402-4015

Edward F. Kelly, Chair
State Liquor Authority, 84 Holland Ave., Albany, NY 12208
(518) 473-6559
E-mail: kobrien@abc.state.ny.us

Alcoholism and Substance Abuse Services Office

http://www.oasas.state.ny.us
General e-mail: webmaster@oasas.state.ny.us
Main phone: (518) 473-3460
Main fax: (518) 485-6014

Jean S. Miller, Commissioner
1450 Western Ave., Albany, NY 12203
(518) 457-2061
E-mail: leesharp@oasas.state.ny.us

Appearance Enhancement Board

General e-mail: info@dos.state.ny.us
Main phone: (518) 474-4429
Main fax: (518) 473-2730

Renato Donato Jr., Deputy Secretary
84 Holland Ave., Albany, NY 12208-3490

Architects Board

http://www.op.nysed.gov
General e-mail: archbd@mail.nysed.gov
Main phone: (518) 474-3930
Main fax: (518) 474-6375

Willliam Martin, Director
Cultural Education Center, Albany, NY 12230

Arts Council

http://www.nysca.org
Main phone: (212) 387-7000
Main fax: (212) 387-7164
TTY: (800) 895-9838

Richard J. Schwartz, Chair
915 Broadway, 8th Fl., New York, NY 10010
(212) 387-7003

Banking Dept.

http://www.banking.state.ny.us
Main phone: (212) 618-6642
Main fax: (212) 618-6948

Higher Educational Institutions

Berkeley College
http://www.berkeleycollege.edu
3 E. 43rd St., New York, NY 10017
Main phone: (212) 986-4343
Branches: Bergen, Garret Mountain, Middlesex, New York City, Westchester

Buffalo State College
http://www.buffalostate.edu
1300 Elmwood Ave., Buffalo, NY 14222
Main phone: (716) 878-4000

City University of New York (CUNY)
http://www.cuny.edu
535 E. 80 St., New York, NY 10021
Main phone: (212) 794-5555
Branches: Baruch College, Brooklyn College, City College, CUNY Medical School, CUNY School of Law, College of Staten Island, Hunter College, John Jay College of Criminal Justice, Lehman College, Medgar Evans College, Queens College, York College

D'Youville College
http://www.dyc.edu
320 Porter Ave., Buffalo, NY 14201-1084
Main phone: (716) 881-7600

State University of New York (SUNY)
http://www.suny.edu
State University Plaza, Albany, NY 12246
Main phone: (518) 443-5157
Branches: SUNY has University Centers in Albany, Binghamton, Buffalo, and Stony Brook. The main web page links to 61 other system campuses falling under the following categories: University Colleges, Health Science Centers, Colleges of Technology, Specialized Colleges, Statutory Colleges, and Community Colleges.

U.S. Merchant Marine Academy
http://www.usmma.edu
300 Steamboat Rd., Kings Point, NY 11024
Main phone: (516) 773-5000

U.S. Military Academy at West Point
http://www.usma.edu
606 Thayer Rd., West Point, NY 10996-1797
Main phone: (914) 938-4041

Elizabeth McCaul, Superintendent (Acting)
2 Rector St., New York, NY 10006-1894
(212) 618-6548

Budget Division
http://www.state.ny.us/dob/
Main phone: (518) 474-5312
Main fax: (518) 474-0132

Carole E. Stone, Director (Acting)
State Capitol, #113, Albany, NY 12224
(518) 474-2300; *Fax:* (518) 474-1969

Children and Family Services Office
Main phone: (518) 473-7793
Main fax: (518) 473-9131

John A. Johnson, Commissioner
52 Washington St., Rensselaer, NY 12144
(518) 473-8437

Civil Service Dept.
http://www.cs.state.ny.us
Main phone: (518) 457-2487
Main fax: (518) 457-6654

George C. Sinnott, President
State Office Bldg. 1, W. A. Harriman Campus, Albany, NY 12239
(518) 457-3701; *Fax:* (518) 457-7547

Consumer Protection Board
http://www.consumer.state.ny.us
General e-mail: webmaster@consumer.state.ny.us
Main phone: (518) 474-1471
Main fax: (518) 474-2474
Toll free: (800) 697-1220

Debra Martinez, Chair and Executive Director
5 Empire State Plaza, #2101, Albany, NY 12223-1556
(518) 474-3514

Correction Commission
http://www.scoc.state.ny.us
General e-mail: infoscoc@scoc.state.ny.us
Main phone: (518) 485-2346
Main fax: (518) 485-2467

Alan J. Croce, Chair
4 Tower Pl., Albany, NY 12203
E-mail: crocea@scoc.state.ny.us

Correctional Services Dept.
http://www.docs.state.ny.us
General e-mail: lfoglia@compuserve.com
Main phone: (518) 457-8126
Main fax: (518) 457-7070

Glenn S. Goord, Commissioner
Bldg. 2, W. A. Harriman Campus, 1220 Washington Ave., Albany, NY 12226

Crime Victims Board
http://www.cvb.state.ny.us
Main phone: (518) 457-8727
Main fax: (518) 457-8658
Toll free: (800) 247-8035
TTY: (518) 485-7953

Joan A. Cusack, Chair
270 Broadway, #200, New York, NY 10007
(212) 417-5136; *Fax:* (212) 417-5262

Criminal Justice Services Division
http://criminaljustice.state.ny.us/
Main phone: (518) 457-6113
Main fax: (518) 457-3089

Katherine N. Lapp, Commissioner and Director of Criminal Justice
4 Tower Pl., Albany, NY 12203
(518) 457-1260

Education Dept.
http://www.nysed.gov
Main phone: (518) 474-3852
Main fax: (518) 486-5631
TTY: (800) 622-1220

Richard P. Mills, Commissioner
Education Bldg., 89 Washington Ave., Albany, NY 12234
(518) 474-5891; *Fax:* (607) 732-3841
E-mail: chayden@zifflaw.com

Archives and Records Administration
http://www.sara.nysed.gov
General e-mail: sarainfo@mail.nysed.gov
Main phone: (518) 474-6926
Main fax: (518) 473-9985

V. Chapman Smith, Assistant Commissioner
Cultural Education Center, Empire State Plaza, #9C49, Albany, NY 12230
(518) 473-7058
E-mail: vchap.smi@mail.nysed.gov

Cultural Education Office: Educational Television and Public Broadcasting
http://www.oce.nysed.gov/etvpb
General e-mail: etvpbweb@mail.nysed.gov
Main phone: (518) 474-5862
Main fax: (518) 486-4850

Robert Reilly, Director
Cultural Education Center, Empire State Plaza, #10-A75, Albany, NY 12230
E-mail: rreilly@mail.nysed.gov

Professional Licensing Services
http://www.nysed.gov/prof
General e-mail: op4info@mail.nysed.gov
Main phone: (518) 474-3830
Main fax: (518) 473-0578
TTY: (518) 473-1426

Robert Bentley, Director
3029 Cultural Education Center, Albany, NY 12230
Fax: (518) 402-5265

State Library
http://www.nysl.nysed.gov

Main phone: (518) 474-5355
Main fax: (518) 474-5786

Janet Welch, Assistant Commissioner and State Librarian
Cultural Education Center, Empire State Plaza, #10-C34, Albany, NY 12230
(518) 474-5930

Election Board
http://www.elections.state.ny.us
Main phone: (518) 474-6220
Main fax: (518) 486-4068
Toll free: (800) 367-8683
TTY: (800) 533-8683

Thomas Wilkey, Executive Director
Core 1, Swan St. Bldg., 6 Empire State Pl., #201, Albany, NY 12223-1650
(518) 474-8113

Emergency Management Office
http://www.nysemo.state.ny.us
Main phone: (518) 457-2200
Main fax: (518) 457-9930

Edward F. Jacoby, Director
1220 Washington Ave., Bldg. 22, #101, Albany, NY 12226-2251
(518) 457-2222
E-mail: edward.jacoby@semo.state.ny.us

Empire State Development Corporation
http://www.empire.state.ny.us
Main phone: (212) 803-3100
Main fax: (212) 803-3735

Charles A. Gargano, Chair and Chief Executive Officer
633 3rd Ave., New York, NY 10017
(212) 803-3700

Employee Relations Office
http://www.goer.state.ny.us
General e-mail: info@goer.state.ny.us
Main phone: (518) 473-8766
Main fax: (518) 473-6795

Linda Angello, Director
2 Empire State Plaza, #1201, Albany, NY 12223-1250
(518) 474-6988

Energy Research and Development Authority
http://www.nyserda.org
General e-mail: tgc@nyserda.org
Main phone: (518) 862-1090
Main fax: (518) 862-1091

F. William Valentino, President
Corporate Plaza West, 286 Washington Ave. Extension, Albany, NY 12203-6399
(518) 862-1090, ext. 3237; *Fax:* (518) 862-2398

Engineers and Land Surveyors Board
http://www.op.nysed.gov
General e-mail: enginbd@mail.nysed.gov
Main phone: (518) 474-3846
Main fax: (518) 474-6375

Thomas King, Director
Cultural Education Center, Madison Ave., Albany, NY
12230

Environmental Conservation Dept.
http://www.dec.state.ny.us
Main phone: (518) 457-5400
Main fax: (518) 457-7744

John P. Cahill, Commissioner
50 Wolf Rd., Albany, NY 12233-1010
(518) 457-3446
E-mail: jcahill@gw.dec.state.ny.us

Fish, Wildlife, and Marine Resources Division
http://www.dec.state.ny.us/website/dfwmr/
index.html
General e-mail: fwinfo@gw.dec.state.ny.us
Main phone: (518) 457-5690
Main fax: (518) 457-0341

Gerald Barnhart, Director
50 Wolf Rd., Albany, NY 12233-4750

Land and Forests Division
http://www.dec.state.ny.ys/website/dlf/index.html
Main phone: (518) 457-2475

Frank Dunstan, Director
50 Wolf Rd., #410-C, Albany, NY 12233

Water Division
http://www.dec.state.ny.us/website/dow/
index.html
Main phone: (518) 457-7464
Main fax: (518) 485-7786

N. G. Kaul, Director
50 Wolf Rd., Albany, NY 12233

Environmental Facilities Corporation
http://www.nysefc.org
General e-mail: info@nysefc.org
Main phone: (518) 457-4100
Main fax: (518) 485-8773

Terry Agriss, President
50 Wolf Rd., #508, Albany, NY 12205-2603
(518) 457-4222

Ethics Commission
http://www.dos.state.ny.us/ethc/ethics.html
General e-mail: ethics@dos.state.ny.us
Main phone: (518) 432-8207
Main fax: (518) 432-8255
Toll free: (800) 873-8442

Donald P. Berens Jr., Executive Director
39 Columbia St., Albany, NY 12207-2717

Fire Prevention and Control Office
http://www.dos.state.ny.us/fire/fire/http://www.html
General e-mail: info@dos.state.ny.us
Main phone: (518) 474-6746
Main fax: (518) 474-3240

James A. Burns, State Fire Administrator
41 State St., Albany, NY 12231-0001
E-mail: jburns@dos.state.ny.us

General Services Office
http://www.ogs.state.ny.us
Main phone: (518) 474-3899
Main fax: (518) 474-1546

Joseph J. Seymour, Commissioner
Mayor Erastus Corning II Tower, 5 Empire State
Plaza, 41st Fl., Albany, NY 12242
(518) 474-5991

Health Dept.
http://www.health.state.ny.us
General e-mail: health@gopher.state.ny.us
Main phone: (518) 474-7354
Main fax: (518) 473-7071

Antonia C. Novello, Commissioner
Corning II Tower, Empire State Plaza, Albany, NY
12237-0001
(518) 474-2011

Medicaid Management Office
Main phone: (518) 474-3018
Main fax: (518) 486-6842

Kathryn Kuhmerker, Deputy Commissioner
Corning II Tower, Empire State Plaza, Albany, NY
12237

Higher Education Services Corporation
http://www.hesc.com
Main phone: (518) 474-8336
Main fax: (518) 474-2839

Peter J. Keitel, President
99 Washington Ave., Albany, NY 12255
(518) 474-5592; *Fax:* (518) 474-5593
E-mail: pkeitel@hesc.com

Housing and Community Renewal Division
http://www.dhcr.state.ny.us
General e-mail: dchrinfo@dchr.state.ny.us
Main phone: (518) 473-3247
Main fax: (518) 473-1907

Joseph B. Lynch, Commissioner
25 Beaver St., New York, NY 10004
(518) 473-8384; *Fax:* (518) 473-9462

Human Rights Division
http://www.nysdhr.com
Main phone: (212) 961-8400
Main fax: (212) 961-8552
TTY: (212) 961-8999

Jerome H. Blue, Commissioner
55 W. 125th St., New York, NY 10027
(212) 961-8790

Insurance Dept.
http://www.ins.state.ny.us/
Main phone: (518) 474-6600
Main fax: (518) 473-6814
Toll free: (800) 342-3736
Mailing address: Agency Bldg. 1, Empire State
Plaza, Albany, NY 12257

Neil D. Levin, Superintendent
25 Beaver St., New York, NY 10005
(212) 480-2284; *Fax:* (212) 480-2310

Labor Dept.
http://www.labor.state.ny.us
General e-mail: nysdol@labor.state.ny.us
Main phone: (518) 457-9000
Main fax: (518) 457-0620

James J. McGowan, Commissioner
Bldg. 12, W. A. Harriman Campus, #500, Albany, NY
12240
(518) 457-2741; *Fax:* (518) 457-6908

Lottery Division
http://www.nylottery.org
Main phone: (518) 388-3300
Main fax: (518) 388-3403
Mailing address: P.O. Box 7500, Schenectady, NY
12301-7500

Margaret R. DeFrancisco, Director (Acting)
1 Broadway Center, Schenectady, NY 12301-7500
(518) 388-3400
E-mail: yloucks@lottery.state.ny.us

Medical Examiners Board
http://www.op.nysed.gov
General e-mail: medbd@mail.nysed.gov
Main phone: (518) 474-3841
Main fax: (518) 486-4846

Thomas Monhan, Executive Secretary
Cultural Education Center, #3023, Albany, NY 12230

Mental Health Office
Main phone: (518) 474-6540
Main fax: (518) 473-3456
TTY: (518) 473-2714

James L. Stone, Commissioner
44 Holland Ave., Albany, NY 12229
(518) 474-4403

Mental Retardation and Developmental Disabilities Office
http://www.omr.state.ny.us
Main phone: (518) 473-9689
Main fax: (518) 474-1335
TTY: (518) 474-3694

Thomas A. Maul, Commissioner
44 Holland Ave., Albany, NY 12229
(518) 473-1997
E-mail: tom.maul@omr.state.ny.us

Mentally Disabled Commission
http://www.cqc.state.ny.us
Main phone: (518) 381-7000
Main fax: (518) 381-7045
Toll free: (800) 624-4143

Gary O'Brien, Chair
401 State St., Schenectady, NY 12305-2397
(518) 381-7102; *Fax:* (518) 381-7101
E-mail: garyo@cqc.state.ny.us

Metropolitan Transportation Authority
http://www.mta.nyc.ny.us/
Main phone: (212) 878-7200
Main fax: (212) 878-7030

Boards and Licensing

Accountancy, (518) 474-3836,
  http://www.op.nysed.gov
Architects, (518) 474-3930,
  http://www.op.nysed.gov
Child Care, (518) 486-7078
Cosmetology, (518) 474-4429
Engineers and Land Surveyors, (518) 474-
  3846, http://www.op.nysed.gov
Medical Examiners, (518) 474-3841,
  http://www.op.nysed.gov
Nursing, (518) 474-3843,
  http://www.op.nysed.gov
Pharmacy, (518) 474-3848,
  http://www.op.nysed.gov
Real Estate, (518) 474-2121

E. Virgil Conway, Chair and Chief Executive Officer
347 Madison Ave., New York, NY 10017-3706

Motor Vehicles Dept.
http://www.nysdmv.com
General e-mail: nydmv@dmv.state.ny.us
Main phone: (518) 473-5595
Main fax: (518) 474-9578
TTY: (800) 368-1186

Richard E. Jackson, Commissioner
6 Empire State Plaza, #510, Albany, NY 12228
(518) 474-0841

Nursing Board
http://www.op.nysed.gov
General e-mail: info@mail.nysed.gov
Main phone: (518) 474-3843
Main fax: (518) 474-3706

Miline Fowler, Director
Cultural Education Center, Albany, NY 12230
(518) 474-3845

Parks, Recreation, and Historic Preservation Office
http://www.nysparks.com
Main phone: (518) 474-0456
Main fax: (518) 486-2924
TTY: (518) 486-1899

Bernadette Castro, Commissioner
Bldg. 1, Empire State Plaza, 20th Fl., Albany, NY
  12238
(518) 474-0463; *Fax:* (518) 474-4492
E-mail: commissioner.castro@oprhp.state.ny.us

Parole Division
Main phone: (518) 473-9400
Main fax: (518) 473-6037

Brion D. Travis, Chair
97 Central Ave., Albany, NY 12206
(518) 473-9548

Pharmacy Board
http://www.op.nysed.gov
General e-mail: pharmbd@mail.nysed.gov
Main phone: (518) 474-3848
Main fax: (518) 473-6995

Lawrence H. Mokhiber, Executive Secretary
Cultural Education Center, #3035, Albany, NY 12230

Power Authority
http://www.nypa.gov/
Main phone: (518) 433-6700
Main fax: (518) 433-6782

Clarence D. Rappleyea, Chair and Chief Executive Officer
30 S. Pearl St., Albany, NY 12207-3425
(518) 433-6710
E-mail: rappleyeac@nypa.gov

Probation and Correctional Alternatives Division
http://dpca.state.ny.us
Main phone: (518) 485-2395
Main fax: (518) 485-5140

George L. Sanchez, State Director
4 Tower Pl., Stuyvesant Plaza, 3rd Fl., Albany, NY
  12203

Public Employment Relations Board
Main phone: (518) 457-2854
Main fax: (518) 457-2664

Michael R. Cuevas, Chair
80 Wolf Rd., Albany, NY 12205-2604
(518) 457-2578; *Fax:* (518) 485-9233
E-mail: cuevasm@perb.state.ny.us

Public Service Dept.
http://www.dps.state.ny.us
General e-mail: web@dps.state.ny.us
Main phone: (518) 474-7080
Main fax: (518) 474-0421
TTY: (212) 219-4292

Maureen O'Donnell Helmer, Chair
3 Empire State Plaza, Albany, NY 12223-1350
(518) 474-2523

Public Service Commission
http://www.dps.state.ny.us
Main phone: (518) 473-4544
Main fax: (518) 473-2838

Maureen O'Donnell Helmer, Chair
3 Empire State Plaza, Albany, NY 12223-1350

Racing and Wagering Board
http://www.racing.state.ny.us
General e-mail: wagering@racing.state.ny.us
Main phone: (518) 453-8460
Main fax: (518) 453-8490

Michael J. Hoblock Jr., Chair
1 Watervliet Ave. Extension, #2, Albany, NY 12206-1668

Real Estate Board
Main phone: (518) 474-2121
Main fax: (518) 473-2730

Renato Danato Jr., Deputy Secretary
84 Holland Ave., Albany, NY 12208-3490

Real Property Services Office
http://www.orps.state.ny.us
General e-mail: nysorps@orps.state.ny.us
Main phone: (518) 486-5446
Main fax: (518) 474-9276

Thomas G. Griffen, Executive Director
16 Sheridan Ave., Albany, NY 12210-2714
(518) 474-5711
E-mail: thomas.griffen@orps.state.ny.us

Regulatory Reform Office
http://www.gorr.state.ny.us
General e-mail: gorr@gorr.state.ny.us
Main phone: (518) 486-3292
Main fax: (518) 473-9342
Toll free: (800) 342-3464
Mailing address: P.O. Box 7027, Albany, NY 12225

David S. Bradley, Director (Acting)
Governor Alfred E. Smith Bldg., 17th Fl., Albany, NY 12225

State Police Divison
http://www.troopers.state.ny.us
Main phone: (518) 457-6811
Main fax: (518) 457-3207
TTY: (800) 342-4357

James W. McMahon, Superintendent
1220 Washington Ave., Bldg. 22, Albany, NY 12226-2252
(518) 457-6721
E-mail: superine@troopers.state.ny.us

Taxation and Finance Dept.
http://www.tax.state.ny.us
Main phone: (518) 457-7177
Main fax: (518) 457-2486
Toll free: (800) 225-5829
TTY: (800) 634-2110

Arthur J. Roth, Commissioner
W. A. Harriman Campus, Albany, NY 12227
(518) 457-2244

Teachers Retirement System
http://www.nystrs.state.ny.us
Toll free: (800) 348-7298
Main fax: (518) 447-2695

George M. Philip, Executive Director
10 Corporate Woods Dr., Albany, NY 12211-2395
(518) 447-2700
E-mail: execdir@nystrs.state.ny.us

Temporary and Disability Assistance Office
http://www.dfa.state.ny.us
Main phone: (518) 473-3170
Main fax: (518) 474-7870

Brian J. Wing, Commissioner
40 N. Pearl St., Albany, NY 12243
(518) 474-4152

Tourism Office
http://www.iloveny.state.ny.us
General e-mail: iloveny@empire.state.ny.us
Main phone: (518) 474-4116
Main fax: (518) 292-5802
Toll free: (800) CALL-NYS

Katherine C. Loucks, Deputy Commissioner
30 S. Pearl St., Albany, NY 12245

Transportation Dept.
http://www.dot.state.ny.us
Main phone: (518) 457-5100
Main fax: (518) 457-6506
TTY: (518) 457-8390

Joseph H. Boardman, Commissioner
Bldg.5, W. A. Harriman Campus, #506, Albany, NY 12232
(518) 457-4422; *Fax:* (518) 457-5583

Passenger Transportation Division: Aviation Services Bureau
http://www.dot.state.ny.us/pubtrans/airhome.html
Main phone: (518) 457-2821
Main fax: (518) 457-9779

Richard A. Chimera, Director
Bldg. 4-150, 1220 Washington Ave., Albany, NY 12232-0414
E-mail: rchimera@gw.dot.state.ny.us

Veterans Affairs Division
http://www.veterans.state.nv.us
Main phone: (518) 474-6784
Main fax: (518) 473-0379

George P. Basher, Director
Mayor Erastus Corning II Tower, 5 Empire State
  Plaza, #2836, Albany, NY 12223-1551
(518) 474-6114

Women's Division
http://www.women.state.ny.us
Main phone: (212) 681-4547
Main fax: (212) 681-7626

Elaine Wingate Conway, Director
633 3rd Ave., 38th Fl., New York, NY 10017

Workers' Compensation Board
http://www.wcb.state.ny.us
Main phone: (518) 474-6674
Main fax: (518) 473-1415
Toll free: (800) 580-6665

Robert R. Snashell, Chair
20 Park St., Albany, NY 12207
(518) 474-6670

Laws

Sales tax: 8.25%
Income tax: 6.8%
State minimum wage: $4.25 (Federal is $5.15)
Marriage age: 18
First-cousin marriage: Permitted
Drinking age: 21
State control of liquor sales: No
Blood alcohol for DWI: 0.10%
Driving age: 17
Speed limit: 65 mph
Permit to buy handguns: Yes, 6 mos. to
  acquire
Minimum age to possess handguns: 16
Minimum age to possess rifles, shotguns: 16
State lottery: Yes
Casinos: Yes (tribal)
Pari-mutuel betting: Horse racing
Death penalty: Yes
3 strikes minimum sentence: None
Hate crimes law: Yes
Gay employment non-discrimination: No
Official language(s): None
Term limits: None

*State laws are complex and subject to
change; this information is not intended as
legal advice. For an explanation of this
information, see p. x.*

New York Legislature

Legislative Office Bldg.
Albany, NY 12247
General information: (518) 455-2087
Bill status: (518) 455-7545

Senate
Address: Legislative Office Bldg., Albany, NY 12247
General information: (518) 455-2800
Fax: (518) 455-3332

Mary O. Donohue (R), President
Executive Chamber, State Capitol, Albany, NY 12224
(518) 474-4623; *Fax:* (518) 486-4170

Joseph L. Bruno (R), President Pro Tempore and
  Majority Leader
Legislative Office Bldg., #909, Albany, NY 12247
(518) 455-3191
E-mail: BRUNO@senate.state.ny.us

Hugh T. Farley (R), Majority Whip
Legislative Office Bldg., #412, Albany, NY 12247
(518) 455-2181
E-mail: FARLEY@senate.state.ny.us

Martin Connor (D), Minority Leader
Legislative Office Bldg., #907, Albany, NY 12247
(518) 455-2701
E-mail: CONNOR@senate.state.ny.us

Ada L. Smith (D), Minority Whip
Legislative Office Bldg., #304, Albany, NY 12247
(518) 455-3531
E-mail: SMITH@senate.state.ny.us

Steven M. Boggess, Secretary
Legislative Office Bldg., Albany, NY 12247
(518) 455-2051

House
Address: Legislative Office Bldg., Albany, NY 12248
General information: (518) 455-4100

Sheldon Silver (D), Speaker of the Assembly
Legislative Office Bldg., #932, Albany, NY 12248
(518) 455-3791
E-mail: speaker@assembly.state.ny.us
http://assembly.state.ny.us/Members/Directory/
  silvers.html

Elizabeth A. Connelly (D), Speaker Pro Tempore
Legislative Office Bldg., #645, Albany, NY 12248
(518) 455-4677
E-mail: connele@assembly.state.ny.us
http://assembly.state.ny.us/Members/Directory/
  connele.html

Michael J. Bragman (D), Majority Leader
Legislative Office Bldg., #926, Albany, NY 12248
(518) 455-4567

E-mail: bragman@assembly.state.ny.us
http://assembly.state.ny.us/Members/Directory/
  bragmam.html

Samuel Colman (D), Majority Whip
Legislative Office Bldg., #837, Albany, NY 12248
(518) 455-5118
E-mail: colmans@assembly.state.ny.us
http://assembly.state.ny.us/Members/Directory/
  colmans.html

John J. Faso (R), Minority Leader
Legislative Office Bldg., #933, Albany, NY 12248
(518) 455-3751
E-mail: fasoj@assembly.state.ny.us
http://assembly.state.ny.us/Members/Directory/
  fasoj.html

John Ravitz (R), Minority Whip
Legislative Office Bldg., #937, Albany, NY 12248
(518) 455-4794
E-mail: ravitzj@assembly.state.ny.us
http://assembly.state.ny.us/Members/Directory/
  ravitzj.html

Francine M. Misasi, Clerk
Legislative Office Bldg., Albany, NY 12248
(518) 455-4242; Fax: (518) 455-4935

New York Judiciary
Court of Appeals Hall
20 Eagle St.
Albany, NY 12207-1095
http://www.courts.state.ny.us/

Court of Appeals
http://www.courts.state.ny.us/ctapps/

Stuart M. Cohen, Clerk
Court of Appeals Hall, 20 Eagle St., Albany, NY
  12207-1095
(518) 455-7700

Justices
Composition: 7 judges
Selection Method: appointed by governor with
  consent of state senate
Length of term: 14 years

Judith S. Kaye, Chief Judge, (212) 661-6787

Joseph W. Bellacosa, Associate Judge, (212) 455-7730

Carmen Beauchamp Ciparick, Associate Judge, (518)
  455-7725

Howard A. Levine, Associate Judge, (518) 388-4497

Albert M. Rosenblatt, Associate Judge, (914) 486-6444

George Bundy Smith, Associate Judge, (212) 363-5990

Richard C. Wesley, Associate Judge, (716) 243-7910

Administrative Office of the Courts
http://usc.ljx.com/admindir.htm
Main phone: (212) 428-2100
Main fax: (212) 428-2188

Jonathan Lippman, Chief Administrative Judge
25 Beaver St., New York, NY 10004
E-mail: jlippman@courts.state.ny.us

Legislative and Political Party Information Resources

Senate home page: http://www.senate.state.ny.us
House home page: http://assembly.state.ny.us
Legislative process: http://assembly.state.ny.us/legproc.html
New York Democratic Party: http://www.nydems.org
  60 Madison Ave., New York, NY 10010; *Phone:* (212) 725-8825; *E-mail:* nydems@nydems.org
New York Republican Party: http://www.nygop.org/main.htm
  315 State St., Albany, NY 12210; *Phone:* (518) 462-2601; *Fax:* (518) 449-7443;
  E-mail: Republicans@nygop.org

North Carolina

State Capitol
Raleigh, NC 27603-8001
Public information: (919) 733-1110
Fax: (919) 733-2120
http://www.state.nc.us

Office of the Governor

http://www.governor.state.nc.us
Main phone: (919) 733-5811
Main fax: (919) 733-2120
TTY: (919) 733-2391
Mailing address: 20301 Mail Service Center,
Raleigh, NC 27699-0301

James B. Hunt Jr. (D), Governor
Capitol Square, State Capitol Bldg., Raleigh, NC
27603-8001
(919) 733-4240; *Fax:* (919) 715-3175

Franklin Freeman, Chief of Staff
1 E. Edenton St., Raleigh, NC 27601
(919) 733-4240; *Fax:* (919) 733-3175
E-mail: wayne_mcdevitt@gov.state.nc.us

Tad Boggs, Press Secretary
1 E. Edenton St., Raleigh, NC 27601
(919) 733-5612; *Fax:* (919) 733-2120
E-mail: tboggs@gov.state.nc.us

**Linda Povlich, Deputy Chief of Staff for
Administration and Citizen/Community Relations**
Capitol Square, State Capitol Bldg., Raleigh, NC
27603-8001
(919) 715-0963; *Fax:* (919) 733-2120
E-mail: lpovlich@gov.state.nc.us

Jim McCleskey, Director, Washington Office
444 N. Capitol St. N.W., #332, Washington, DC 20001
(202) 624-5830; *Fax:* (202) 624-5836
E-mail: jmcclesky@gov.state.nc.us

Office of the Lieutenant Governor

http://www.ltgov.state.nc.us
Main phone: (919) 733-7350
Main fax: (919) 733-6595
Mailing address: 20401 Mail Service Center,
Raleigh, NC 27699-0401

Dennis A. Wicker (D), Lieutenant Governor
State Capitol, Raleigh, NC 27699-0401
(919) 733-6248; *Fax:* (919) 715-4239
E-mail: dennis.wicker@ncmail.net

Office of the Secretary of State

http://www.secstate.state.nc.us/secstate/

State of North Carolina

Capital: Raleigh, since 1792
Founded: 1663, as part of British colony of
Carolina; separate from 1712
Statehood: November 21, 1789 (12th state)
Constitution adopted: 1971
Area: 48,718 sq. mi. (ranks 29th)
Population: 7,546,493 (1998 est.; ranks 11th)
Largest cities: (1998 est.) Charlotte (504,637);
Raleigh (259,423); Greensboro (197,910);
Winston-Salem (164,316); Durham (153,513)
Counties: 100, Most populous: (1998 est.)
Mecklenburg (630,848); Wake (570,615);
Guilford (387,722); Forsyth (287,701);
Cumberland (284,629)
U.S. Congress: John Edwards (D), Jesse
Helms (R); 12 Representatives
Nickname(s): Tar Heel State
Motto: To be rather than to seem
Song: "The Old North State"
Bird: Cardinal
Tree: Pine
Flower: Dogwood
State fair: at Raleigh, mid-Oct.
Former capital(s): New Bern

Main phone: (919) 733-4161
Main fax: (919) 733-1837
Mailing address: P.O. Box 29622, Raleigh, NC
27616-0622

Elaine F. Marshall (D), Secretary of State
300 N. Salisbury St., Raleigh, NC 27603
(919) 733-3705

Office of the Attorney General

http://www.jus.state.nc.us
General e-mail: agjus@mail.state.nc.us
Main phone: (919) 716-6400
Main fax: (919) 716-6750
TTY: (919) 716-6430
Mailing address: P.O. Box 629, Raleigh, NC 27602

Michael F. Easley (D), Attorney General
114 W. Edenton St., Raleigh, NC 27602

Office of the State Treasurer
Main phone: (919) 508-5176
Main fax: (919) 508-5167

Harlan E. Boyles, Treasurer
325 N. Salisbury St., Raleigh, NC 27603-1385

Office of the State Auditor
http://www.osa.state.nc.us/OSA/
Main phone: (919) 807-7500
Main fax: (919) 807-7647
Toll free: (800) 466-5209
Mailing address: 20601 Mail Service Center,
Raleigh, NC 27699-0601

Ralph Campbell Jr., State Auditor
2 S. Salisbury St., Raleigh, NC 27603
(919) 733-3217
E-mail: rcampbell@aud.osa.state.nc.us

Office of the State Controller
http://www.osc.state.nc.us/osc
Main phone: (919) 981-5454
Main fax: (919) 981-5567
Mailing address: 1410 Mail Service Center,
Raleigh, NC 27699-1410

Edward Renfrow, State Controller
3512 Bush St., Raleigh, NC 27609
(919) 981-5406
E-mail: erenfrow@controller.osc.state.nc.us

National Guard Division
http://www.ncguard.com
Main phone: (919) 664-6000
Main fax: (919) 666-6400
Toll free: (800) 621-4136

Gerald A. Rudisill Jr., Adjutant General
4105 Reedy Creek Rd., Raleigh, NC 27607-6410
E-mail: rudisillg@nc-arng.ngb.army.mil

Agencies

Administration Dept.
http://www.doa.state.nc.us/
General e-mail:
dianne_green@mail.doa.state.nc.us
Main phone: (919) 807-2425
Main fax: (919) 733-9571
Mailing address: 1301 Mail Service Center,
Raleigh, NC 27699-1301

Katie G. Dorsett, Secretary
Capitol Square, Raleigh, NC 27699-1301
E-mail: dianne.jordan@ncmail.net

Human Resources Management
http://www.doa.state.nc.us/doa/hrm/person1.htm
Main phone: (919) 733-4606

Main fax: (919) 715-7669
Mailing address: 1322 Mail Service Center,
Raleigh, NC 27699-1322

Linda Coleman, Director
116 W. Jones St., Raleigh, NC 27603-8003
E-mail: linda.coleman@ncmail.net

Veterans Affairs Division
http://www.doa.state.nc.us/vahome.htm
Main phone: (919) 733-3851
Main fax: (919) 733-2834
Mailing address: 1315 Mail Service Center,
Raleigh, NC 27699-1315

Charles F. Smith, Assistant Secretary
325 N. Salisbury St., #1065, Raleigh, NC 27603
E-mail: charlie.smith@ncmail.net

Women's Council
http://www.doa.state.nc.us/doa/cfw/cfw.htm
Main phone: (919) 733-2455
Main fax: (919) 733-2464
Mailing address: 1320 Mail Service Center,
Raleigh, NC 27699-1320

Juanita M. Bryant, Executive Director
Merrimon-Wynne House, 526 N. Wilmington St.,
Raleigh, NC 27604
E-mail: juanita.bryant@ncmail.net

Agriculture Dept.
http://www.agr.state.nc.us
Main phone: (919) 733-7125
Main fax: (919) 733-1141
Mailing address: P.O. Box 27647, Raleigh, NC
27611

James A. Graham (D), Commissioner
2 W. Edenton St., Raleigh, NC 27611
E-mail: james.graham@ncmail.net

State Fair Division
http://www.agr.state.nc.us/fair
Main phone: (919) 821-7400
Main fax: (919) 733-5079

Wesley V. Wyatt, Manager
1025 Blue Ridge Blvd., Raleigh, NC 27607
E-mail: wesley.wyatt@ncmail.net

Commerce Dept.
http://www.commerce.state.nc.us
Main phone: (919) 733-4151
Main fax: (919) 733-8356
TTY: (919) 733-4962
Mailing address: 4301 Mail Service Center,
Raleigh, NC 27699-4301

Rick Carlisle, Secretary
301 N. Wilmington St., Raleigh, NC 27626

Higher Educational Institutions

University of North Carolina
http://www.ga.unc.edu
910 Raleigh Rd., Chapel Hill, NC 27514
Main phone: (919) 962-1000
Branches: Appalachian State College; East Carolina University; Elizabeth City State University; Fayetteville State University; North Carolina Agricultural and Technical State University; North Carolina Central University; North Carolina School of the Arts; North Carolina State University; University of North Carolina at Asheville, Chapel Hill, Charlotte, Greensboro, Pembroke, and Wilmington; Western Carolina University; and Winston-Salem State University

Industrial Commission
http://www.comp.state.nc.us
Main phone: (919) 733-4820
Main fax: (919) 715-0282
Toll free: (800) 688-8349
Mailing address: 4319 Mail Service Center, Raleigh, NC 27699-4319

Buck Lattimore, Administrator
430 N. Salisbury St., Raleigh, NC 27611
E-mail: lattimob@iind.commerce.state.nc.us

Travel and Tourism Division
http://www.commerce.state.nc.us/tourism
General e-mail:
inquiry@travel.commerce.state.nc.us
Main phone: (919) 733-4171
Main fax: (919) 733-8582
Toll free: (800) VISIT-NC
Mailing address: P.O. Box 29571, Raleigh, NC 27826-0571

Gordan Clapp, Director
301 N. Wilmington St., Raleigh, NC 27611

Utilities Commission
http://www.ncuc.commerce.state.nc.us
Main phone: (919) 733-7328
Main fax: (919) 733-7300
Mailing address: P.O. Box 29510, Raleigh, NC 27626-0510

JoAnne Sanford, Chair
430 N. Salisbury St., Dobbs Bldg., Raleigh, NC 27603-5926
(919) 733-4249
E-mail: sanford@ncucmail.commerce.state.nc.us

Community College System
http://www.ncccs.cc.nc.us

Main phone: (919) 733-7051
Main fax: (919) 733-0680

H. Martin Lancaster, President
200 W. Jones St., Raleigh, NC 27603-1379
(919) 733-7051, ext. 709
E-mail: martinl@ncccs.cc.nc.us

Consumer Protection Office
http://www.jus.state.nc.us/Justice
Main phone: (919) 716-6000
Main fax: (919) 716-6050
Mailing address: P.O. Box 629, Raleigh, NC 27602-0629

Wanda Bryant, Senior Deputy
114 W. Edenton St., 2nd Fl., Raleigh, NC 27602
(919) 716-6780

Corrections Dept.
http://www.doc.state.nc.us
Main phone: (919) 733-4926
Main fax: (919) 733-4790
Mailing address: 4201 Mail Service Center, Raleigh, NC 27699-4201

Theodis Beck, Secretary
Shore Bldg., 214 W. Jones St., Raleigh, NC 27603-1337

Community Corrections Division
http://www.doc.state.nc.us/dcomcor/index.htm
Main phone: (919) 716-3100
Main fax: (919) 716-3996

Robert Guy, Director
2020 Yonkers Rd., Raleigh, NC 27604
(919) 716-3101
E-mail: grl08@doc.state.nc.us

Crime Control and Public Safety Dept.
http://www.nccrimecontrol.org
Main phone: (919) 733-2126
Main fax: (919) 733-0296
Mailing address: P.O. Box 29591, Raleigh, NC 27626-0591

David E. Kelly, Secretary
512 N. Salisbury St., Raleigh, NC 27626-0591
Fax: (919) 715-8477
E-mail: dkelly@nccrimecontrol.org

Alcohol Law Enforcement Division
http://www.ncale.org
General e-mail: stateale@ale.dcc.state.nc.us
Main phone: (919) 733-4060
Main fax: (919) 733-8002
Mailing address: 4704 Mail Service Center, Raleigh, NC 27699-4704

John D. Smith III, Director
430 N. Salisbury St., Dobbs Bldg., Raleigh, NC 27603

Emergency Management Division
http://www.ncem.org
Main phone: (919) 733-3867
Main fax: (919) 733-5406

Eric Tolbert, Director
116 W. Jones St., Raleigh, NC 27603-1335
E-mail: etolbert@ncem.org

State Highway Patrol Division
http://www.ncshp.org
General e-mail: webmaster@ncshp.org
Main phone: (919) 733-7952
Main fax: (919) 733-1189
Mailing address: 4702 Mail Service Center,
Raleigh, NC 27699-4702

Richard W. Holden, Commanding Officer
512 N. Salisbury St., Raleigh, NC 27699
E-mail: rholden@ncshp.org

Cultural Resources Dept.
http://web.dcr.state.nc.us
Main phone: (919) 715-3586
Main fax: (919) 715-8724
Mailing address: 4604 Mail Service Center,
Raleigh, NC 27699-4604

Betty Ray McCain, Secretary
109 E. Jones St., #315, Raleigh, NC 27601-2807
(919) 733-4867; *Fax:* (919) 733-1564

Archives and History Division
http://www.ah.dcr.state.nc.us
Main phone: (919) 733-7305
Main fax: (919) 733-8807
Mailing address: 4610 Mail Service Center,
Raleigh, NC 27699-4610

Jeffrey J. Crow, Director
109 E. Jones St., #305, Raleigh, NC 27699
E-mail: jcrow@ncsl.dcr.state.nc.us

State Library
http://statelibrary.dcr.state.nc.us/ncslhome.htm
Main phone: (919) 733-2570
Main fax: (919) 733-8748
Mailing address: 4640 Mail Service Center,
Raleigh, NC 27699-4640

Sandra Cooper, State Librarian
109 E. Jones St., Raleigh, NC 27601
E-mail: scooper@library.dcr.state.nc.us

Eastern Municipal Power Agency
http://www.electricities.com
Main phone: (919) 760-6000
Main fax: (919) 760-6050
Toll free: (800) 768-7697
Mailing address: P.O. Box 29513, Raleigh, NC
27626-0513

Jesse C. Tilton III, Chief Executive Officer
1427 Meadowwood Blvd., Raleigh, NC 27604
(919) 760-6330
E-mail: jesse.tilton@electricities.com

Elections Board
http://www.sboe.state.nc.us
Main phone: (919) 733-7173
Main fax: (919) 715-0135
TTY: (919) 715-0230
Mailing address: P.O. Box 2169, Raleigh, NC
27602-2169

Gary O. Bartlett, Executive Secretary/Director
133 Fayetteville St., #100, Raleigh, NC 27601
E-mail: gary.bartlett@ncmail.net

Environment and Natural Resources Dept.
http://www.ehnr.state.nc.us/EHNR/
Main phone: (919) 733-4984
Main fax: (919) 715-3060
Toll free: (877) 623-6748
Mailing address: 1601 Mail Service Center,
Raleigh, NC 27699-1601

Bill Holman, Secretary
512 N. Salisbury St., Raleigh, NC 27604
(919) 715-4101

Environmental Protection Division
Main phone: (919) 733-4984
Main fax: (919) 715-3060
Toll free: (877) 623-6748
Mailing address: 1601 Mail Service Center,
Raleigh, NC 27699-1601

Robin Smith, Assistant Secretary
512 N. Salisbury St., Raleigh, NC 27604
(919) 715-4141

Forest Resources Division
http://www.dfr.state.nc.us
Main phone: (919) 733-2162
Main fax: (919) 733-2835
Toll free: (888) 628-7337
Mailing address: P.O. Box 29581, Raleigh, NC
27626-0581

Stan Adams, Director
512 N. Salisbury St., Raleigh, NC 27604-1189
E-mail: stanford_adams@mail.enr.state.nc.us

Parks and Recreation Division
http://www.ncsparks.net
Main phone: (919) 733-4181
Main fax: (919) 715-3085
Mailing address: 1615 Mail Service Center,
Raleigh, NC 27699-1615

Phil McKnelly, Director
512 N. Salisbury St., Archdale Bldg., #732,
Raleigh, NC 27604

(919) 715-5422
E-mail: phil.mcknelly@ncmail.net

Soil and Water Conservation Commission
http://www.enr.state.nc.us/EHNR/DSWC
Main phone: (919) 733-2302
Main fax: (919) 715-3559
Mailing address: 1614 Mail Service Center,
Raleigh, NC 27699-1614

David S. Vogel, Director
512 N. Salisbury St., #504, Raleigh, NC 27604
(919) 715-6097
E-mail: David.Vogel@ncmail.net

Water Resources Division
http://www.dwr.ehnr.state.nc.us/home.htm
Main phone: (919) 733-4064
Main fax: (919) 733-3558
Mailing address: 1611 Mail Service Center,
Raleigh, NC 27699-1611

John Morris, Director
512 N. Salisbury St., Raleigh, NC 27604
(919) 715-5422
E-mail: john.morris@ncmail.net

Ethics Board
General e-mail: maureen.atta@ncmail.net

Main phone: (919) 733-2780
Main fax: (919) 733-2785

George F. Bason, Chair
116 W. Jones St., #2009-Q, Raleigh, NC 27699-1324

General Contractor's Licensing Board
http://www.nclbgc.net
Main phone: (919) 571-4183
Main fax: (919) 571-4703
Mailing address: P.O. Box 17187, Raleigh, NC
27619

Mark Selph, Secretary/Treasurer
3739 National Dr., #225, Raleigh, NC 27612

Health and Human Services Dept.
http://www.dhhs.state.nc.us
Main phone: (919) 733-4534
Main fax: (919) 733-7447
Toll free: (800) 662-7030
TTY: (919) 773-2963
Mailing address: 2001 Mail Service Center,
Raleigh, NC 27699-2001

H. David Bruton, Secretary
Adams Bldg., 101 Blair Dr., Raleigh, NC 27603
Fax: (919) 715-4645
E-mail: glenda.parker@ncmail.net

Aging Division
http://www.dhhs.state.nc.us/aging/index.htm
Main phone: (919) 733-3183
Main fax: (919) 733-0443
Mailing address: 2101 Mail Service Center,
Raleigh, NC 27699-2101

Karen E. Gottovi, Director
639 Palmer Dr., Raleigh, NC 27626
E-mail: karen.gottovi@ncmail.net

Developmental Disabilities Council
http://www.nc-ddc.org
Main phone: (919) 850-2833
Main fax: (919) 850-2895
Toll free: (800) 357-6916

Holly Riddle, Executive Director
1001 Navaho Dr., #GL-103, Raleigh, NC 27609
E-mail: holly.riddle@ncmail.net

Governor Morehead School
Main phone: (919) 733-6381
Main fax: (919) 715-7723
Mailing address: 2001 Mail Service Center,
Raleigh, NC 27699-2001

Robert Patterson, Director
301 Ashe Ave., Raleigh, NC 27606-2199
(919) 733-6651; *Fax:* (919) 715-0478
E-mail: robert.patterson@ncmail.net

Medical Assistance Division

http://www.dhhs.state.nc.us/docs/divinfo/
dma.htm
Main phone: (919) 857-4011
Main fax: (919) 733-6608
Mailing address: 2501 Mail Service Center,
Raleigh, NC 27699-2501

Dick Perruzzi, Director
Kirby Bldg., Dix Campus, 1985 Umstead Dr.,
Raleigh, NC 27626
E-mail: dick.perruzzi@ncmail.net

Mental Health, Developmental Disabilities, and Substance Abuse Services

http://www.dhhs.state.nc.us/docs/divinfo/
dmh.htm
Main phone: (919) 733-7011
Main fax: (919) 733-9455
Mailing address: 3001 Mail Service Center,
Raleigh, NC 27699-3001

John F. Baggett, Director
Albemarle Bldg., 325 N. Salisbury St., Raleigh,
NC 27603
E-mail: john.baggett@ncmail.net

Social Services Division

http://www.dhhs.state.nc.us/dss
Main phone: (919) 733-3055
Main fax: (919) 733-9386

Kevin FitzGerald, Director
Albemarle Bldg., 325 N. Salisbury St., Raleigh,
NC 27603

Housing Finance Agency

http://www.nchfa.com
Main phone: (919) 877-5700
Main fax: (919) 877-5701
Mailing address: P.O. Box 28066, Raleigh, NC
27611-8066

A. Robert Kucab, Executive Director
3508 Bush St., Raleigh, NC 27609
E-mail: ark@nchfa.com

Insurance Dept.

http://www.ncdoi.com
General e-mail: jcoan@ncdoi.net
Main phone: (919) 733-7343
Main fax: (919) 733-6495
Toll free: (800) 546-5664
Mailing address: P.O. Box 26387, Raleigh, NC
27611

James E. Long (D), Commissioner and State Fire Marshal
430 N. Salisbury St., #4140, Raleigh, NC 27611
(919) 733-3058
E-mail: jlong@ncdoi.net

State Fire Marshal's Dept.

http://www.ncdoi.com/ncfr
Main phone: (919) 733-3901
Mailing address: P.O. Box 26387, Raleigh, NC
27611

Tim Bradley, Senior Deputy Commissioner and Senior Deputy State Fire Marshal
430 N. Salisbury St., Raleigh, NC 27611
E-mail: TBradley@mail.doi.state.nc.us

Investment and Banking Division

http://www.treasurer.state.nc.us/frinvest.htm
Main phone: (919) 733-7282
Main fax: (919) 733-0075

C. Douglas Chappell, Director
325 N. Salisbury St., Raleigh, NC 27603
E-mail: doug_chappell@treasurer.state.nc.us

Judicial Standards Commission

Main phone: (919) 733-2690
Mailing address: P.O. Box 1122, Raleigh, NC
27602

Deborah R. Carrington, Executive Secretary
1 W. Morgan St., Raleigh, NC 27602

Labor Dept.

http://www.dol.state.nc.us/dol
General e-mail: mhowell@mail.dol.state.nc.us
Main phone: (919) 733-7166
Main fax: (919) 733-6197
Toll free: (800) LABOR-NC

Harry Eugene Payne Jr., Commissioner
Labor Bldg., 4 W. Edenton St., Raleigh, NC 27601
(919) 733-0359
E-mail: hpaynce@mail.dol.state.nc.us

Medical Care Commission

Main phone: (919) 733-2342
Main fax: (919) 733-2757

Boards and Licensing

Accountancy, (919) 733-4222
Architects, (919) 733-9544
Child Care, (919) 662-4527
Cosmetology, (919) 733-4117
Contractors, (919) 571-4183,
   http://www.nclbgc.net
Engineers and Land Surveyors,
   (919) 841-4000
Medical Examiners, (919) 828-1212
Nursing, (919) 733-5356
Pharmacy, (919) 942-4454
Real Estate, (919) 875-3700

Mailing address: 2701 Mail Service Center,
Raleigh, NC 27699-2701

Lucy H. Bode, Chair
701 Barbour Dr., Raleigh, NC 27603

Personnel Office
http://www.state.nc.us/osp
General e-mail:
ospweb@ospadmin.osp.state.nc.us
Main phone: (919) 733-7108
Main fax: (919) 733-0653
Mailing address: 1331 Mail Service Center,
Raleigh, NC 27699-1331

Ronald G. Penny, Director
116 W. Jones St., Raleigh, NC 27603
Fax: (919) 715-9750
E-mail: rpenny@ospadmin.osp.state.nc.us

Retirement Systems Division
http://www.treasurer.state.nc.us/frretire.htm
General e-mail: nc-
retirement@treasurer.state.nc.us
Main phone: (919) 508-5377
Main fax: (919) 508-5167

Jack W. Pruitt, Director
325 N. Salisbury St., Raleigh, NC 27603-1385
(919) 508-5303

Public Instruction Dept.
http://www.dpi.state.nc.us
Main phone: (919) 715-1000
Main fax: (919) 715-1253

**Michael E. Ward, Superintendent of Public
Instruction**
301 N. Wilmington St., Raleigh, NC 27601-2825
(919) 715-1299; *Fax:* (919) 715-1228

Board of Education
http://www.dpi.state.nc.us/about_dpi/
state_board/
Main phone: (919) 715-1318
Main fax: (919) 715-0764

Jane Worsham, Executive Director
Education Bldg., 301 N. Wilmington St., Raleigh,
NC 27601-2825
E-mail: jworsham@dpi.state.nc.us

Real Estate Commission
http://www.nrec.state.nc.us
General e-mail: exec@ncrec.state.nc.us

Main phone: (919) 875-3700
Main fax: (919) 872-0038

Phillip T. Fisher, Executive Director
1313 Navaho Dr., Raleigh, NC 27619-7100

Revenue Dept.
http://www.dor.state.nc.us/DOR/
Main phone: (919) 733-3991
Main fax: (919) 733-0023
Mailing address: P.O. Box 25000, Raleigh, NC
27640

Muriel K. Offerman, Secretary
501 N. Wilmington St., Raleigh, NC 27604
(919) 733-7211

State Education Assistance Authority
http://www.ncseaa.edu
General e-mail: information@ncseaa.edu
Main phone: (919) 549-8614
Main fax: (919) 549-8481
Mailing address: 14103 Research Triangle Park,
Chapel Hill, NC 27709

Steven E. Brooks, Executive Director
10 Alexander Dr., Chapel Hill, NC 27709

State Fair
http://www.agr.state.nc.us/fair/
General e-mail: wesley.wyatt@ncmail.net
Main phone: (919) 821-7400
Main fax: (919) 733-5079

Wesley Wyatt, Manager
1025 Blue Ridge Blvd., Raleigh, NC 27607

State Ports Authority
http://www.ncports.com
General e-mail: busdev@ncports.com
Main phone: (910) 763-1621
Main fax: (910) 763-6440
Mailing address: P.O. Box 9002, Wilmington, NC
28402

Erik Stromberg, Executive Director
2202 Burnett Blvd., Wilmington, NC 28401
E-mail: stromberg@ncports.com

Transportation Dept.
http://www.dot.state.nc.us
Main phone: (919) 733-2520
Main fax: (919) 733-9150
Mailing address: P.O. Box 25201, Raleigh, NC
27601

David T. McCoy, Secretary
Hwy. Bldg., 1 S. Wilmington St., Raleigh, NC 27611
E-mail: dmccoy@dot.state.nc.us

Aviation Division
http://www.dot.state.nc.us/transit/aviation/
Main phone: (919) 571-4904
Main fax: (919) 571-4908
Mailing address: P.O. Box 25201, Raleigh, NC 27611

William (Bill) H. Williams Jr., Director
6701 Aviation Pkwy., RDU Airport, NC 27623
E-mail: wwilliams@dot.state.nc.us

Motor Vehicles Division
http://www.dmv.state.nc.us
General e-mail: dmv-info@dot.state.nc.us
Main phone: (919) 861-3015
Main fax: (919) 733-0126

Janice Faulkner, Commissioner
Transportation Bldg., 1100 New Burn Ave., Raleigh, NC 27699

North Carolina Legislature
State Legislative Bldg.
Raleigh, NC 27603
General information: (919) 733-7928
Fax: (919) 733-2599
Bill status: (919) 733-7779
http://www.ncga.state.nc.us

Senate
Address: State Legislative Bldg., Raleigh, NC 27603-2808
General information: (919) 733-7761
Fax: (919) 715-2880

Dennis A. Wicker (D), President
State Capitol, Raleigh, NC 27699-0401
(919) 733-6248; *Fax:* (919) 715-4239
E-mail: dennis.wicker@ncmail.net
http://www.ltgov.state.nc.us

Marc Basnight (D), President Pro Tempore
Legislative Office Bldg., #2007, Raleigh, NC 27601-2808
(919) 733-6854
E-mail: Marcb@ms.ncga.state.nc.us

Laws

Sales tax: 6%
Income tax: 7.8%
State minimum wage: $5.15 (Federal is $5.15)
Marriage age: 18
First-cousin marriage: Permitted, except double first cousins
Drinking age: 21
State control of liquor sales: Yes
Blood alcohol for DWI: 0.08%
Driving age: 16, 6 mos.
Speed limit: 70 mph
Permit to buy handguns: Yes, 3 days to acquire
Minimum age to possess handguns: 18
Minimum age to possess rifles, shotguns: 12
State lottery: No
Casinos: Yes (tribal)
Pari-mutuel betting: No
Death penalty: Yes
3 strikes minimum sentence: Life (3rd violent felony)
Hate crimes law: Yes
Gay employment non-discrimination: No
Official language(s): English
Term limits: None

State laws are complex and subject to change; this information is not intended as legal advice. For an explanation of this information, see p. x.

http://www.ncga.state.nc.us/gascripts/members/senate/senator.pl?sUserID=38

Roy A. Cooper III (D), Majority Leader
Legislative Office Bldg., #2010, Raleigh, NC 27601-2808
(919) 733-5664
E-mail: Royc@ms.ncga.state.nc.us
http://www.ncga.state.nc.us/gascripts/members/senate/senator.pl?sUserID=46

Luther Henry Jordan Jr. (D), Majority Whip
Legislative Office Bldg., #407, Raleigh, NC 27601-2808
(919) 715-3034
E-mail: Lutherj@ms.ncga.state.nc.us
http://www.ncga.state.nc.us/gascripts/members/senate/senator.pl?sUserID=37

Patrick J. Ballantine (R), Minority Leader
Legislative Office Bldg., #1127, Raleigh, NC 27601-2808
(919) 715-2525
E-mail: Patrickb@ms.ncga.state.nc.us
http://www.ncga.state.nc.us/gascripts/members/senate/
senator.pl?sUserID=40

James S. Forrester (R), Minority Whip
Legislative Office Bldg., #1121, Raleigh, NC 27601-2808
(919) 733-5708
E-mail: Jamesf@ms.ncga.state.nc.us
http://www.ncga.state.nc.us/gascripts/members/senate/
senator.pl?sUserID=28

Janet B. Pruitt, Principal Clerk
Legislative Office Bldg., Raleigh, NC 27601-2808
(919) 733-7761; *Fax:* (919) 715-2880

House
Address: State Legislative Bldg., Raleigh, NC 27601-1096
General information: (919) 733-7760
Fax: (919) 715-2881

James B. Black (D), Speaker of the Assembly
Legislative Office Bldg., #2304, Raleigh, NC 27601-1096
(919) 733-3451
E-mail: Jimb@ms.ncga.state.nc.us
http://www.ncga.state.nc.us/gascripts/members/house/
representative.pl?sUserID=4

Joe Hackney (D), Speaker Pro Tempore
Legislative Office Bldg., #2207, Raleigh, NC 27601-1096
(919) 733-5752
E-mail: Joeh@ms.ncga.state.nc.us
http://www.ncga.state.nc.us/gascripts/members/house/
representative.pl?sUserID=45

Philip A. Baddour Jr. (D), Majority Leader
Legislative Office Bldg., #2301, Raleigh, NC 27601-1096
(919) 715-0850
E-mail: Philb@ms.ncga.state.nc.us
http://www.ncga.state.nc.us/gascripts/members/house/
representative.pl?sUserID=82

Andrew T. Dedmon (D), Majority Whip
Legislative Office Bldg., #2213, Raleigh, NC 27601-1096
(919) 733-5732

E-mail: Andrewd@ms.ncga.state.nc.us
http://www.ncga.state.nc.us/gascripts/members/house/
representative.pl?sUserID=54

Richard T. Morgan (R), Minority Leader
Legislative Office Bldg., #418-B, Raleigh, NC 27601-1096
(919) 715-3010
E-mail: Richardm@ms.ncga.state.nc.us
http://www.ncga.state.nc.us/gascripts/members/house/
representative.pl?sUserID=76

Julia C. Howard (R), Minority Whip
Legislative Office Bldg., #1023, Raleigh, NC 27601-1096
(919) 733-5904
E-mail: Juliah@ms.ncga.state.nc.us
http://www.ncga.state.nc.us/gascripts/members/house/
representative.pl?sUserID=53

Denise G. Weeks, Principal Clerk of the Assembly
Legislative Office Bldg., Raleigh, NC 27601-1096
(919) 733-7760; *Fax:* (919) 715-2881

North Carolina Judiciary
Justice Bldg.
2 E. Morgan St.
Raleigh, NC 27601
http://www.aoc.state.nc.us

Supreme Court
http://www.aoc.state.nc.us/http://www/public/html/
supreme_crt.html

Christie Speir Cameron, Clerk
Justice Bldg., 2 E. Morgan St., Raleigh, NC 27601
(919) 733-3723; *Fax:* (919) 733-0105

Justices
Composition: 7 justices
Selection Method: general election; vacancies filled by gubernatorial appointment
Length of term: 8 years

Henry E. Frye, Chief Justice, (919) 733-3717
Franklin E. Freeman Jr., Associate Justice, (919) 733-4840
I. Beverly Lake Jr., Associate Justice, (919) 733-3711
Mark D. Martin, Associate Justice, (919) 733-3714

Robert F. Orr, Associate Justice, (919) 733-3715

George L. Wainwright Jr., Associate Justice, (919) 733-3713

Sarah E. Parker, Associate Justice, (919) 733-3716

Administrative Office of the Courts

http://www.aoc.state.nc.us/http://www/public/html/aoc.htm

Main phone: (919) 733-7107

Main fax: (919) 715-5779

Thomas W. Ross, Director

Justice Bldg., 2 E. Morgan St., Raleigh, NC 27601

E-mail: thomas.ross@aoc.state.nc.us

Supreme Court Library

http://www.aoc.state.nc.us/http://www/public/html/sc_library.htm

Main phone: (919) 733-3425

Main fax: (919) 733-0105

General e-mail: tpd@sc.state.nc.us

Thomas P. Davis, Librarian

500 Justice Bldg., 2 E. Morgan St., Raleigh, NC 27601

Legislative and Political Party Information Resources

Senate home page: http://www.ncga.state.nc.us/html1999/senate/Senate.html

House home page: http://www.ncga.state.nc.us/html1999/house/House.htm

Legislative process: http://www.ncga.state.nc.us/html1999/NCInfo/Bill-Law/bill-law.html

North Carolina Democratic Party: http://www.ncdp.org
220 Hillsborough St., Raleigh, NC 27603; *Phone:* (919) 821-2777

North Carolina Republican Party: http://www.ncgop.org
1410 Hillsborough St., P.O. Box 12905, Raleigh, NC 12905; *Phone:* (919) 828-6423; *Fax:* (919) 899-3815

North Dakota

State Capitol
Bismarck, ND 58505-0001
Public information: (701) 328-2000
Fax: (701) 328-2205
http://www.state.nd.us

Office of the Governor
http://www.health.state.nd.us/gov
General e-mail: governor@state.nd.us
Main phone: (701) 328-2200
Main fax: (701) 328-2205
TTY: (701) 328-2887

Edward T. Schafer (R), Governor
600 E. Boulevard Ave., Dept. 101, Bismarck, ND
58505-0001

William Goetz, Chief of Staff
600 E. Boulevard Ave., Dept. 101, Bismarck, ND
58505-0001
(701) 328-2200; *Fax:* (701) 328-2205

Julie Liffrig, Communications Director
600 E. Boulevard Ave., Dept. 101, Bismarck, ND
58505-0001
(701) 328-2200; *Fax:* (701) 328-2205

Duane Houdek, Constituent Services Director
600 E. Boulevard Ave., Dept. 1, Bismarck, ND 58505-
0001
(701) 328-2200; *Fax:* (701) 328-2205

Craig Pattee, Director, Washington Office
400 N. Capitol St., #585, Washington, DC 20001-1512
(202) 347-6607; *Fax:* (202) 434-7110

Office of the Lieutenant Governor
http://www.health.state.nd.us/gov/ltgov/
General e-mail: governor@state.nd.us
Main phone: (701) 328-2200
Main fax: (701) 328-2205
TTY: (701) 328-2887

Rosemarie Myrdal (R), Lieutenant Governor
600 E. Boulevard Ave., Dept. 101, Bismarck, ND
58505-0001

Office of the Secretary of State
http://www.state.nd.us/sec
General e-mail: sos@state.nd.us
Main phone: (701) 328-2900
Main fax: (701) 328-2992
Toll free: (800) 352-0867

State of North Dakota

Capital: Bismarck, since 1883
Founded: 1861, as part of Dakota Territory; separated at statehood
Statehood: November 2, 1889 (39th state)
Constitution adopted: 1889
Area: 68,994 sq. mi. (ranks 17th)
Population: 638,244 (1998 est.; ranks 47th)
Largest cities: (1998 est.) Fargo (86,718); Bismarck (54,040); Grand Forks (47,327); Minot (35,286); Dickinson (16,221)
Counties: 53, Most populous: (1998 est.) Cass (116,832); Grand Forks (66,869); Burleigh (66,867); Ward (58,678); Morton (24,575)
U.S. Congress: Kent Conrad (D), Byron L. Dorgan (D); 1 Representative
Nickname(s): Sioux State, Flickertail State, Peace Garden State
Motto: Liberty and union, now and forever: one and inseparable
Song: "North Dakota Hymn"
Bird: Western meadowlark
Tree: American elm
Flower: Wild prairie rose
State fair: at Minot, July
Former capital(s): Yankton

Alvin A. Jaeger (R), Secretary of State
State Capitol, Dept. 108, 600 E. Boulevard Ave., Bismarck, ND 58505-0500

Office of the Attorney General
http://www.ag.state.nd.us/ndag
General e-mail: ndag@state.nd.us
Main phone: (701) 328-2210
Main fax: (701) 328-2226
TTY: (701) 328-3409

Heidi Heitkamp (D), Attorney General
State Capitol, Dept. 125, 600 E. Boulevard Ave., 1st Fl., Bismarck, ND 58505-0040

Office of the State Treasurer
http://www.state.nd.us/ndtreas
Main phone: (701) 328-2643
Main fax: (701) 328-3002

Kathi Gilmore (D), State Treasurer
State Capitol, Dept. 120, 600 E. Boulevard Ave.,
Bismarck, ND 58505-0600
E-mail: kgimore@pioneer.state.nd.us

Office of the State Auditor
http://www.state.nd.us/auditor
Main phone: (701) 328-2241
Main fax: (701) 328-1406

Robert R. Peterson (R), State Auditor
State Capitol, Dept. 117, 600 E. Boulevard Ave.,
Bismarck, ND 58505-0060
E-mail: rpeterson@state.nd.us

Office of the Adjutant General
http://www.guard.bismarck.nd.us
Main phone: (701) 224-5100
Main fax: (701) 224-5180
Mailing address: P.O. Box 5511, Bismarck, ND
58506-5511

Keith D. Bjerke, Adjutant General
Fraine Barracks Rd., Bldg. 30, Bismarck, ND 58504
(701) 224-5102
E-mail: kbjerke@nd-arng.ngb.army.mil

Agencies

Accountancy Board
http://www.state.nd.us/ndsba
General e-mail: ndsba@pioneer.statend.us
Main phone: (701) 775-7100
Main fax: (701) 775-7430
Toll free: (800) 532-5904

James Abbott, Executive Director
2701 S. Columbia Rd., Grand Fork, ND 58201-6029

Aeronautics Commission
http://www.state.nd.us/ndaero
General e-mail: ndaero@state.nd.us
Main phone: (701) 328-9650
Main fax: (701) 328-9656
Mailing address: P.O. Box 5020, Bismarck, ND
58502-5020

Robert J. Miller, Chair
2301 University Dr., Bismarck, ND 58504

Agricultural Products Utilization Commission
http://www.growingnd.com
General e-mail: rhanson@state.nd.us
Main phone: (701) 328-5350
Main fax: (701) 328-5320

Julie Mohler, Chair
1833 E. Bismarck Expressway, Bismarck, ND 58504

Agriculture Dept.
http://www.agdepartment.com
General e-mail: ndda@pioneer.state.nd.us
Main phone: (701) 328-2231
Main fax: (701) 328-4567
Toll free: (800) 242-7535

Roger Johnson (D), Commissioner
State Capitol, Dept. 602, 600 E. Boulevard Ave.,
Bismarck, ND 58505-0020
(701) 328-4754

Animal Health Board
Main phone: (701) 328-2655
Main fax: (701) 328-4567
Toll free: (800) 242-7535

**Larry Schuler, Executive Officer and State
Veterinarian**
State Capitol, Dept. 602, 600 E. Boulevard Ave., 6th
Fl., Bismarck, ND 58505-0020
E-mail: lschuler@state.nd.us

Arts Council
http://www.state.nd.us/arts/
Main phone: (701) 328-3954
Main fax: (701) 328-3963
TTY: (800) 366-6888

Daphne Ghorbani, Executive Director
418 E. Broadway, #70, Bismarck, ND 58501-4086
(701) 328-3956
E-mail: dghorbani@state.nd.us

Banking and Financial Institutions Dept.
http://www.state.nd.us/bank
General e-mail: banking@state.nd.us
Main phone: (701) 328-9933
Main fax: (701) 328-9955
TTY: (800) 366-6888

Gary D. Preszler, Commissioner
2000 Schafer St., #G, Bismarck, ND 58501-1204

Beef Commission
http://www.health.state.nd.us/gov/boards/
boards_query.asp?Board_ID=18
Main phone: (701) 328-5120
Main fax: (701) 328-5119

Nancy Jo Bateman, Executive Director
4023 State St., Bismarck, ND 58501

Consumer Protection Division
http://expedition.bismarck.ag.state.nd.us/ndag/cpat/
cpat.html
General e-mail: cpat@state.nd.us
Main phone: (701) 328-3404
Main fax: (701) 328-3535
Toll free: (800) 472-2600
TTY: (701) 328-3409

Higher Educational Institutions

North Dakota State College of Science
http://www.ndscs.nodak.edu
800 N. 6th St., Wahpeton, ND 58076-0002
Main phone: (800) 342-4325

North Dakota University System
http://www.ndus.nodak.edu
600 E. Boulevard Ave., Dept. 215, Bismarck, ND 58505-0230
Main phone: (701) 328-2960
Branches: Bismarck State College, Dickinson State University, Lake Region State College, Mayville State University, Minot State University, Minot State University at Bottineau, North Dakota State College of Science, North Dakota State University, University of North Dakota, Valley City State University, Williston State College

Parrell D. Grossman, Director
State Capitol, Dept. 125, 600 E. Boulevard Ave., Bismarck, ND 58505-0400

Contractors Licensing Division
General e-mail: sos@state.nd.us
Main phone: (701) 328-3665
Main fax: (701) 328-1690
Toll free: (800) 352-0867

Mary Feist, Director
State Capitol, 600 E. Boulevard Ave., Bismarck, ND 58505-0500

Corrections and Rehabilitation Dept.
http://www.state.nd.us/docr
General e-mail: vconklin@state.nd.us
Main phone: (701) 328-6390
Main fax: (701) 328-6651
TTY: (800) 366-6888
Mailing address: P.O. Box 1898, Bismarck, ND 58502-1898

Elaine Little, Director
3033 E. Main, Bismarck, ND 58502-1898

Juvenile Services Division
Main phone: (701) 328-6194
Main fax: (701) 328-6651
TTY: (800) 366-6888
Mailing address: P.O. Box 1898, Bismarck, ND 58502-1898

Al Lick, Director
3303 E. Main, Bismarck, ND 58502-1898

Cosmetology Board
General e-mail: cosmo@gcentral.com

Main phone: (701) 224-9800
Main fax: (701) 222-8756
Mailing address: P.O. Box 2177, Bismarck, ND 58502

Bert Knell, Director
1102 S. Washington St., #200, Bismarck, ND 58504

Economic Development and Finance Dept.
http://www.growingnd.com
General e-mail: ndedf@pioneer.state.nd.us
Main phone: (701) 328-5300
Main fax: (701) 328-5320
Toll free: (800) 366-6889
TTY: (800) 366-6888

Kevin Cramer, Director
1833 E. Bismarck Expressway, Bismarck, ND 58504

Emergency Management Division
http://www.state.nd.us/dem
General e-mail: nddem@state.nd.us
Main phone: (701) 328-8100
Main fax: (701) 328-8181
Toll free: (800) 773-3259
Mailing address: P.O. Box 5511, Bismarck, ND 58506-5511

Doug Friez, Director
Fraine Barracks, Bldg. 40, Bismarck, ND 58506-5511
E-mail: dfriez@state.nd.us

Engineers and Land Surveyors Board
General e-mail: drdofreg@btigate.com
Main phone: (701) 258-0786
Main fax: (701) 258-7471
Mailing address: P.O. Box 1357, Bismarck, ND 58502

Clifford E. Keller, Executive Secretary
721 W. Memorial Hwy., Bismarck, ND 58504

Fire Marshal Division
http://expedition.bismarck.ag.state.nd.us/ndag/firemarshal/FM.html
Main phone: (701) 328-5555
Main fax: (701) 328-5510
Mailing address: P.O. Box 1054, Bismarck, ND 58202-1054

Daniel Hoium, Fire Marshal
4205 State St., Bismarck, ND 58501
E-mail: dhoium@state.nd.us

Forest Service
http://www.state.nd.us/forest
General e-mail: forest@state.nd.us
Main phone: (701) 228-5422
Main fax: (701) 228-5448

Larry A. Kotchman, State Forester
307 1st St. East, Bottineau, ND 58318-1100
E-mail: lkotchma@badlands.nodak.edu

Game and Fish Dept.
http://www.state.nd.us/gnf
General e-mail: ndgf@state.nd.us
Main phone: (701) 328-6300
Main fax: (701) 328-6352

Dean C. Hildebrand, Director
100 N. Bismarck Expressway, Bismarck, ND 58501
(701) 328-6345
E-mail: dhildebr@state.nd.us

Geological Survey
http://www.state.nd.us/ndgs/
Main phone: (701) 328-8000
Main fax: (701) 328-8010

John P. Bluemle, State Geologist
State Capitol, Dept. 405, 600 E. Boulevard Ave.,
Bismarck, ND 58505-0840
(701) 328-8001
E-mail: bluemle@rival.ndgs.state.nd.us

Health Dept.
http://www.health.state.nd.us
Main phone: (701) 328-2372
Main fax: (701) 328-4727

Murray G. Sagsveen, State Health Officer
600 E. Boulevard Ave., Dept. 301, Bismarck, ND
58505-0200
E-mail: sagsveen@state.nd.us

Highway Patrol
http://www.state.nd.us/ndhp
General e-mail: ndhpinfo@state.nd.us
Main phone: (701) 328-2455
Main fax: (701) 328-1717
TTY: (800) 366-6888

James M. Hughes, Superintendent
State Capitol, Dept. 504, 600 E. Boulevard Ave.,
Bismarck, ND 58505-0240
E-mail: jhughes@state.nd.us

Historical Society
http://www.state.nd.us/hist
General e-mail: histsoc@state.nd.us
Main phone: (701) 328-2666
Main fax: (701) 328-3710
Mailing address: P.O. Box 1976, Bismarck, ND
58502-1976

Samuel J. Wegner, Superintendent
ND Heritage Center Bldg., 612 E. Boulevard Ave.,
Bismarck, ND 58505-0830
E-mail: swegner@state.nd.us

State Archives and Historical Research Library
http://www.state.nd.us/hist/sal.htm
General e-mail: archives@state.nd.us
Main phone: (701) 328-2666
Main fax: (701) 328-3710

Jerry Newborg, Director
North Dakota Heritage Center, 612 E. Boulevard Ave., Bismar
ND 58505-0830
(701) 328-2668
E-mail: gnewborg@state.nd.us

Housing Finance Agency
http://www.ndhfa.state.nd.us
General e-mail: info@ndhfa.state.nd.us
Main phone: (701) 328-8080
Main fax: (701) 328-8090
TTY: (800) 366-6888
Mailing address: P.O. Box 1535, Bismarck, ND 58502-1535

Pat S. Fricke, Executive Director
1600 E. Interstate Ave., Bismarck, ND 58501
(701) 328-8050

Human Services Dept.
http://www.state.nd.us/humanservices
Main phone: (701) 328-2310
Main fax: (701) 328-2359
Toll free: (800) 472-2622
TTY: (701) 328-3975

Carol K. Olson, Executive Director
State Capitol, Judicial Wing, 600 E. Boulevard Ave., Bismarck, N
58505
(701) 328-2538; *Fax:* (701) 328-1545
E-mail: socols@state.nd.us

Aging Services Division
http://lnotes.state.nd.us/dhsweb.nsf/servicepages/
agingservices
General e-mail: sosena@state.nd.us
Main pone: (701) 328-8910
Main fax: (701) 328-8989
Toll free: (800) 451-8693
TTY: (701) 328-8968

Linda Wright, Director
600 S. 2nd St., #1-C, Bismarck, ND 58504-5729

Disability Services Division
http://lnotes.state.nd.us/dhsweb.nsf/ServicePages/
DisabilityServices
General e-mail: sohysg@state.nd.us
Main phone: (701) 328-8930
Main fax: (701) 328-8969
Toll free: (800) 755-8529
TTY: (701) 328-8968

Gene Hysjulien, Director
600 S. 2nd St., #1-A, Bismarck, ND 58504-5729

Medical Services Division

http://lntoes.state.nd.us/dhsweb.nsf/
ServicePages//MedicalServices
Main phone: (701) 328-2321
Main fax: (701) 328-1544
Toll free: (800) 755-2604

David Zentner, Director
600 E. Boulevard Ave., Dept. 325, Bismarck, ND 58505
E-mail: sozend@state.nd.us

Mental Health and Substance Abuse Services Division

http://lnotes.state.nd.us/dhs/dhsweb.nsf/
ServicePages/
MentalHealthandSubstanceAbuseServices
Main phone: (701) 328-8940
Main fax: (701) 328-8969
Toll free: (800) 755-2719

Karen Larson, Director
600 S. 2nd St., #1-D, Bismarck, ND 58504
E-mail: solark@state.nd.us

Indian Affairs Commission

http://www.health.state.nd.us/ndiac
General e-mail: ndiac@state.nd.us
Main phone: (701) 328-2428
Main fax: (701) 328-1537

Cynthia Mala, Executive Director
State Capitol, Dept. 316, 600 E. Boulevard Ave.,
Bismarck, ND 58505
E-mail: cmala@state.nd.us

Industrial Commission

http://www.state.nd.us/ndic
Main phone: (701) 328-3726
Main fax: (701) 328-2820
TTY: (800) 366-6888

Edward T. Schafer, Chair
600 E. Boulevard Ave., Bismarck, ND 58505-0840
(701) 328-3722

Oil and Gas Division

http://www.explorer.ndic.state.nd.us
Main phone: (701) 328-8020
Main fax: (701) 328-8022

Lynn D. Helms, Director
600 E. Boulevard Ave., Dept. 405, Bismarck, ND 58505
E-mail: ldh@saturn.ndic.state.nd.us

Insurance Dept.

http://www.state.nd.us/ndins
General e-mail: insuranc@state.nd.us
Main phone: (701) 328-2440
Main fax: (701) 328-4880

Toll free: (800) 247-0560
TTY: (800) 366-6888

Glenn Pomeroy (D), Commissioner
State Capitol, Dept. 401, 600 E. Boulevard Ave., 5th
Fl., Bismarck, ND 58505-0320

Job Service

http://www.state.nd.us/jsnd
General e-mail: jsnd@state.nd.us
Main phone: (701) 328-2825
Main fax: (701) 328-4000
TTY: (800) 366-6888
Mailing address: P.O. Box 5507, Bismarck, ND
58506-5507

Jennifer L. Gladden, Executive Director
1000 E. Divide Ave., Bismarck, ND 58501
(701) 328-2836; *Fax:* (701) 328-1612
E-mail: jgladden@state.nd.us

Labor Dept.

http://www.state.nd.us/labor
General e-mail: labor@state.nd.us
Main phone: (701) 328-2660
Main fax: (701) 328-2031
Toll free: (800) 582-8032
TTY: (800) 366-6888

Tony Clark, Commissioner
State Capitol, Dept. 406, 600 E. Boulevard Ave., 13th
Fl., Bismarck, ND 58505-0340
E-mail: tclark@state.nd.us

Land Dept.

http://www.land.state.nd.us
Main phone: (701) 328-2800
Main fax: (701) 328-3650
Mailing address: P.O. Box 5523, Bismarck, ND
58506-5523

Robert J. Olheiser, Commissioner
1707 N. 9th St., Bismarck, ND 58506-5523
(701) 328-2806

Management and Budget Office

http://www.state.nd.us/omb
General e-mail: omb@state.nd.us
Main phone: (701) 328-4904
Main fax: (701) 328-3230

Rod A. Backman, Director
State Capitol, Dept. 110, 600 E. Boulevard Ave., 4th
Fl., Bismarck, ND 58505-0400
E-mail: rbackman@state.nd.us

Central Personnel Division

http://www.state.nd.us/cpers
Main phone: (701) 328-4735
Main fax: (701) 328-1475

Dan LeRoy, Director
State Capitol, 600 E. Boulevard Ave., 14th Fl.,
  Bismarck, ND 58505-0120
E-mail: dleroy@state.nd.us

Fiscal Management Division
http://www.state.nd.us/fiscal/Default.htm
Main phone: (701) 328-2680
Main fax: (701) 328-3230

Sheila Peterson, Director
State Capitol, Dept. 110, 600 E. Boulevard Ave.,
  Bismarck, ND 58505-0400
(701) 328-4905
E-mail: peterson@state.nd.us

Medical Examiners Board
General e-mail: bomex@tic.bisman.com
Main phone: (701) 328-6500
Main fax: (701) 328-6505

Rolf Sletten, Executive Secretary
418 E. Broadway, #12, Bismarck, ND 58501

Milk Marketing Board
Main phone: (701) 328-9588

John E. Weisgerber Jr., Director
410 E. Thayer Ave., Bismarck, ND 58501-4049

Municipal Bond Bank
General e-mail: ndmbb@state.nd.us
Main phone: (701) 328-3924
Main fax: (701) 328-3979
Toll free: (800) 526-3509

Tom Tudor, Executive Director
418 E. Broadway, #246, Bismarck, ND 58501
(701) 328-3981
E-mail: ttudor@state.nd.us

Natural Resources and Indian Affairs Division
Main phone: (701) 328-3640
Main fax: (701) 328-4300

Charles Carvell, Director
900 E. Boulevard Ave., Bismarck, ND 58505-0041
E-mail: ccarvell@state.nd.us

North Dakota University System
http://www.ndus.nodak.edu
General e-mail: ndus_office@ndus.nodak.edu
Main phone: (701) 328-2960
Main fax: (701) 328-2961

Larry A. Isaak, Chancellor
State Capitol, Dept. 215, 600 E. Boulevard Ave., 10th
  Fl., Bismarck, ND 58505-0230
(701) 328-2963

Nursing Board
http://www.ndbon.org

Frequently Called Numbers

Tourism: (701) 328-2525, 1-800-435-5663;
  http://www.ndtourism.com
Library: (701) 328-4622;
  http://ndsl.lib.state.nd.us
Vital Statistics: (701) 328-2360;
  http://www.health.state.nd.us/ndhd/
  admin/vital/
Tax/Revenue: (701) 328-2770;
  http://www.state.nd.us/taxdpt
Motor Vehicles: (701) 328-2581
State Police/Highway Patrol: (701) 328-2455;
  http://www.state.nd.us/ndhp
Unemployment: (701) 328-5011;
  http://www.state.nd.us/jsnd/ji.htm
General Election Information: (701)
  328-4146, 1-800-352-0867, ext. 8-4146;
  http://www.state.nd.us/sec/Elections/
  Elections.htm
Consumer Affairs: (701) 328-3404,
  1-800-472-2600;
  http://expedition.bismarck.ag.state.nd.us/
  ndag/cpat/cpat.html
Hazardous Materials: (701) 328-5555;
  http://expedition.bismarck.ag.state.nd.us/
  ndag/firemarshal/FM.html

Main phone: (701) 328-9777
Main fax: (701) 328-9785

Constance B. Kalanek, Executive Director
919 S. 7th St., #504, Bismarck, ND 58504-5881
(701) 328-9781
E-mail: executivedir@ndbon.org

Parks and Recreation Dept.
http://www.state.nd.us/ndparks
General e-mail: parkrec@state.nd.us
Main phone: (701) 328-5357
Main fax: (701) 328-5363

Douglass A. Prchal, Director
1835 E. Bismarck Expressway, Bismarck, ND 58504

Parole and Probation Dept.
Main phone: (701) 328-6190
Main fax: (701) 328-6186
Mailing address: P.O. Box 5521, Bismarck, ND
  58506-5521

Warren Emmer, Director
3303 E. Main St., Bismarck, ND 58506
E-mail: wemmer@state.nd.us

Pharmacy Board

Main phone: (701) 328-9535
Main fax: (701) 258-9312
Mailing address: P.O. Box 1354, Bismarck, ND
  58502-1354

Howard C. Anderson, Executive Director
1906 E. Broadway, Bismarck, ND 58502

Protection and Advocacy Project

http://www.ndcd.org/ndcpd.uapdis/pa.html
General e-mail: rrosenkr@state.nd.us
Main phone: (701) 328-2950
Main fax: (701) 328-3934
Toll free: (800) 472-2670
TTY: (800) 366-6888

Teresa Larsen, Executive Director
400 E. Broadway, #616, Bismarck, ND 58501

Public Employees Retirement System

http://www.state.nd.us/ndpers
General e-mail: ndpers@state.nd.us
Main phone: (701) 328-3900
Main fax: (701) 328-3920
Toll free: (800) 803-7377
TTY: (800) 366-6888
Mailing address: P.O. Box 1214, Bismarck, ND
  58502-1214

Sparb Collins, Director
400 E. Broadway, Bismarck, ND 58501

Public Instruction Dept.

http://www.dpi.state.nd.us/dpi/index.htm
Main phone: (701) 328-2260
Main fax: (701) 328-2461

Wayne G. Sanstead (D), State Superintendent
State Capitol, Dept. 201, 600 E. Boulevard Ave., 11th
  Fl., Bismarck, ND 58505
(701) 328-4572
E-mail: wsanstea@mail.dpi.state.nd.us

Boards and Licensing

Accountancy, (701) 775-7100,
  http://www.state.nd.us/ndsba
Architects, (218) 233-2062
Child Care, (701) 328-4809
Contractors, (701) 328-3665
Cosmetology, (701) 224-9800
Engineers and Land Surveyors, (701) 258-0786
Medical Examiners, (701) 328-6500
Nursing, (701) 328-9777, http://www.ndbon.org
Pharmacy, (701) 328-9535
Real Estate, (701) 328-9749

School for the Blind

http://www.ndsb.k12.nd.us
Main phone: (701) 795-2700
Main fax: (701) 795-2727
Toll free: (800) 421-1181

Carmen Grove Suminski, Superintendent
500 Stanford Rd., Grand Forks, ND 58203-2799
(701) 795-2708
E-mail: suminski@sendit.nodak.edu

School for the Deaf

http://www.ndsdeaf.k12.nd.us
Main phone: (701) 662-9000
Main fax: (701) 662-9009
Toll free: (800) 887-2980

**Rocklyn Cofer, Superintendent, Education
  Director**
1401 College Dr., Devils Lake, ND 58301-1596
E-mail: rcofer@sendit.nodak.edu

Public Service Commission

http://www.psc.state.nd.us
General e-mail:
  msmail.sab@oracle.psc.state.nd.us
Main phone: (701) 328-2400
Main fax: (701) 328-2410
TTY: (800) 366-6888

Bruce Hagen, President
State Capitol, Dept. 408, 600 E. Boulevard Ave.,
  Bismarck, ND 58505-0480

Public Utilities Division

http://www.psc.state.nd.us/psc/pud/pud.htm
General e-mail: sdh@oracle.psc.state.nd.us
Main phone: (701) 328-4076
Main fax: (701) 328-2410
TTY: (800) 366-6888

Illona Jeffcoat-Sacco, Director
State Capitol, Dept. 408, 600 E. Boulevard Ave.,
  Bismarck, ND 58505-0480

Radio Communications

Main phone: (701) 328-9921
Main fax: (701) 328-9926
Toll free: (800) 472-2121
Mailing address: P.O. Box 5511, Bismarck, ND
  58502-5511

Lyle V. Gallagher, Director
Fraine Barracks, EOC Bldg., Bismarck, ND 58502-
  5511
(701) 328-8150
E-mail: lgallagher@state.nd.us

Real Estate Commission

Main phone: (701) 328-9749
Main fax: (701) 328-9750

Mailing address: P.O. Box 727, Bismarck, ND 58502-0727

Dennis Schulz, Secretary/Treasurer
314 E. Thayer, Bismarck, ND 58502-0727
(701) 328-9737
E-mail: ddschulz@pioneer.state.nd.us

Retirement and Investment Office
http://www.state.nd.us/rio/
General e-mail: rio@state.nd.us
Main phone: (701) 328-9885
Main fax: (701) 328-9897
Toll free: (800) 952-2970
TTY: (800) 366-6888
Mailing address: P.O. Box 7100, Bismarck, ND 58507-7100

Steve Cochrane, Executive Director
1930 Burnt Boat Dr., Bismarck, ND 58501
(701) 328-9895

Securities Commissioner Office
http://www.state.nd.us/securities
General e-mail: seccom@pioneer.state.nd.us
Main phone: (701) 328-2910
Main fax: (701) 255-3113
Toll free: (800) 297-5124

Syver Vinje, Commissioner
State Capitol, Dept. 414, 600 E. Boulevard Ave., 5th
Fl., Bismarck, ND 58505

Small Business Development Center
http://bpa.und.nodak.edu/sbdc
General e-mail: ndsbdc@sage.und.nodak.edu
Main phone: (701) 777-3700
Main fax: (701) 777-3225
Toll free: (800) 445-7232
Mailing address: P.O. Box 7308, Grand Forks, ND
58202-7308

Wally Kearns, Director
118 Gamble Hall, Grand Forks, ND 58202
(701) 777-3700
E-mail: kearns@prairie.nodak.edu

Soil Conservation Committee
Main phone: (701) 328-5125
Main fax: (701) 328-5123

Scott Hochhalter, Soil Conservation Coordinator
4023 State St., #30, Bismarck, ND 58501-0620
E-mail: scohhal@ndsunext.nodak.edu

State Fair Association
http://www.ndstatefair.com
Main phone: (701) 857-7620
Main fax: (701) 857-7622
Mailing address: P.O. Box 1796, Minot, ND 58702-1796

Gerald Iverson, Manager
2005 Burdic Expressway East, Minot, ND 58702

State Library
http://ndsl.lib.state.nd.us
General e-mail: ndsladmn@state.nd.us
Main phone: (701) 328-4622
Main fax: (701) 328-2040
TTY: (701) 328-4923

Mike Jaugstetter, State Librarian
604 E. Boulevard Ave., Dept. 250, Bismarck, ND
58505-0800
(701) 328-2492

State Tax Commissioner Office
http://www.state.nd.us/taxdpt
General e-mail: taxinfo@state.nd.us
Main phone: (701) 328-2770
Main fax: (701) 328-3700
TTY: (800) 366-6888

**Richard (Rick) Clayburgh (R), State Tax
Commissioner**
State Capitol, Dept. 127, 600 E. Boulevard Ave.,
Bismarck, ND 58505-0599
E-mail: rclaybur@state.nd.us

Tourism Dept.
http://www.ndtourism.com
Main phone: (701) 328-2525
Main fax: (701) 328-4878
Toll free: (800) 435-5663

Robert W. Martinson, Director
604 E. Boulevard Ave., Bismarck, ND 58505
E-mail: bmartins@state.nd.us

Transportation Dept.
http://www.state.nd.us/dot/
Main phone: (701) 328-2500
Main fax: (701) 328-4545
TTY: (701) 328-4156

Marshall W. Moore, Director
608 E. Boulevard Ave., #321, Bismarck, ND 58505-0700
(701) 325-2581; *Fax:* (701) 328-1420
E-mail: mmoore@state.nd.us

Driver and Vehicle Services Office
Main phone: (701) 328-2581
Main fax: (701) 328-4545
TTY: (701) 328-4156

Keith C. Magnusson, Director
608 E. Boulevard Ave., Bismarck, ND 58505-0700
(701) 328-2727; *Fax:* (701) 328-1420
E-mail: kmagnuss@state.nd.us

Veterans Affairs Dept.
Main phone: (701) 239-7165
Main fax: (701) 239-7166
Mailing address: P.O. Box 9003, Fargo, ND 58106-9003

Ray Harkema, Commissioner
1411 32nd St. South, Fargo, ND 58106-9003

Vocational and Technical Education Board
General e-mail: sbvte@state.nd.us
Main phone: (701) 328-3180
Main fax: (701) 328-1255

Mel Olson, State Director and Executive Officer
State Capitol, Dept. 270, 600 E. Boulevard Ave., 15th Fl., Bismarck, ND 58505-0610
(701) 328-2259
E-mail: molson@state.nd.us

Water Commission
http://www.swc.state.nd.us
General e-mail: swc@water.swc.state.nd.us

Main phone: (701) 328-2750
Main fax: (701) 328-3696

David A. Sprynczynatyk, State Engineer and Secretary
900 E. Boulevard Ave., Bismarck, ND 58505-0187
(701) 328-4940
E-mail: dspry@water.swc.state.nd.us

Wheat Commission
http://www.ndwheat.com/
General e-mail: ndwheat@ndwheat.com
Main phone: (701) 328-5111
Main fax: (701) 328-5115

Neal Fisher, Administrator
4023 State St., Bismarck, ND 58501-0690

Women's Status Commission
Main phone: (701) 530-2059
Mailing address: P.O. Box 1913, Bismarck, ND 58501

Carol Reed, Chair
2917 Winnipeg Dr., Bismarck, ND 58501
(701) 530-2111

Workers' Compensation Bureau
Main phone: (701) 328-3800
Main fax: (701) 328-3820
Toll free: (800) 777-5033
TTY: (701) 328-3786

J. Patrick Traynor, Executive Director and Chief Executive Officer

500 E. Front Ave., Bismarck, ND 58504-5685

Laws

Sales tax: 6%
Income tax: 5.5%
State minimum wage: $5.15 (Federal is $5.15)
Marriage age: 18
First-cousin marriage: Prohibited
Drinking age: 21
State control of liquor sales: No
Blood alcohol for DWI: 0.10%
Driving age: 16
Speed limit: 70 mph
Permit to buy handguns: No
Minimum age to possess handguns: 18
Minimum age to possess rifles, shotguns: None
State lottery: No
Casinos: Yes (tribal)
Pari-mutuel betting: Horse racing
Death penalty: No
3 strikes minimum sentence: 10 yrs. (2nd felony)
Hate crimes law: Yes
Gay employment non-discrimination: No
Official language(s): English
Term limits: None

State laws are complex and subject to change; this information is not intended as legal advice. For an explanation of this information, see p. x.

North Dakota Legislature

State Capitol
600 E. Boulevard Ave.
Bismarck, ND 58505-0360
General information: (701) 328-2916
Fax: (701) 328-3615
Toll free: (800) NDLEGIS
http://www.state.nd.us/lr/

Senate

Rosemarie Myrdal (R), President
600 E. Boulevard Ave., Dept. 101, Bismarck, ND 58505-0001
(701) 328-2200; *Fax:* (701) 328-2205

Layton Freborg (R), President Pro Tempore
State Capitol, 600 E. Boulevard Ave., Bismarck, ND 58505-0360
http://www.state.nd.us/lr/senate/bios/freborg.html

Gary J. Nelson (R), Majority Leader
State Capitol, 600 E. Boulevard Ave., Bismarck, ND 58505-0360
E-mail: gnelson@state.nd.us
http://www.state.nd.us/lr/senate/bios/gnelson.html

Aaron Krauter (D), Minority Leader
State Capitol, 600 E. Boulevard Ave., Bismarck, ND 58505-0360
E-mail: akrauter@state.nd.us
http://www.state.nd.us/lr/senate/bios/krauter.html

William C. Parker, Secretary
State Capitol, 600 E. Boulevard Ave., Bismarck, ND 58505-0360
(701) 328-2916; *Fax:* (701) 328-3615

House

Francis J. Wald (R), Speaker of the House
State Capitol, 600 E. Boulevard Ave., Bismarck, ND 58505-0360
http://www.state.nd.us/lr/house/bios/wald.html

John Dorso (R), Majority Leader
State Capitol, 600 E. Boulevard Ave., Bismarck, ND 58505-0360
E-mail: jdorso@state.nd.usl

Merle Boucher (D), Minority Leader
State Capitol, 600 E. Boulevard Ave., Bismarck, ND 58505-0360
E-mail: mboucher@state.nd.us

Lance Hagen, Chief Clerk
State Capitol, 600 E. Boulevard Ave., Bismarck, ND 58505-0360
(701) 328-2916; *Fax:* (701) 328-3615

North Dakota Judiciary

State Capitol, Judicial Wing
600 E. Boulevard Ave., 1st Fl.
Bismarck, ND 58505

Supreme Court
http://www.court.state.nd.us

Penny Miller, Clerk
State Capitol, Judicial Wing, Dept. 180, 600 E. Boulevard Ave., 1st Fl., Bismarck, ND 58505
(701) 328-2221; *Fax:* (701) 328-4480
E-mail: pennym@court.state.nd.us

Justices
Composition: 5 justices
Selection Method: nonpartisan election; vacancies filled by gubernatorial appointment or special election; appointees serve until next general election
Length of term: 10 years

Gerald W. VandeWalle, Chief Justice, (701) 328-2221
Mary Muehlen Maring, Justice, (701) 328-4207
Carol Ronning Kapsner, Justice, (701) 328-4494
William A. Neumann, Justice, (701) 328-2221
Dale V. Sandstrom, Justice, (701) 328-2221

Office of the Court Administrator
Main phone: (701) 328-4216
Main fax: (701) 328-4480

Keithe E. Nelson, State Court Administrator
State Capitol, Judicial Wing, Dept. 180, 600 E. Boulevard Ave., Bismarck, ND 58505
E-mail: keithen@court.state.nd.us

Supreme Court Law Library
http://www.court.state.nd.us/LawLib/WWW6.HTM
Main phone: (701) 328-2227
Main fax: (701) 328-3609

Ted Smith, Librarian
State Capitol, Judicial Wing, Dept. 180, 600 E. Boulevard Ave., Bismarck, ND 58505
(701) 328-4594; *Fax:* (701) 328-4480
E-mail: TedS@court.state.nd.us

Legislative and Political Party Information Resources

Senate home page: http://www.state.nd.us/lr/senatecomp.html
House home page: http://www.state.nd.us/lr/housecomp.html
Committees: Senate: http://www.state.nd.us/lr/senate/committee/standing/html; *House:* http://www.state.nd.us/lr/house/committee/standing/html
Legislative process: http://www.state.nd.us/lr/billtolaw.html
North Dakota Democratic-NPL Party: http://www.demnpl.com
   Kennedy Memorial Center, 1962 E. Divide Ave., Bismarck, ND 58501; *Phone:* (701) 255-0460; *Fax:* (701) 258-7823; *E-mail:* people@demnpl.com
North Dakota Republican Party: http://www.tradecorridor.com/ndrepublicans
   101 E. Broadway Ave., P.O. Box 1917, Bismarck, ND 58502-1917; *Phone:* (701) 255-0030; *Fax:* (701) 255-7513; *E-mail:* ndgop@btigate.com

Ohio

Vern Riffe Center
Columbus, OH 43215
Public information: (614) 466-2000
Fax: (614) 466-8159
http://www.state.oh.us

Office of the Governor
http://www.state.oh.us/gov
Main phone: (614) 644-4357
Main fax: (614) 466-9354

Bob Taft II (R), Governor
Vern Riffe Center, 77 S. High St., 30th Fl., Columbus,
OH 43215
(614) 466-3555

Brian K. Hicks, Chief of Staff
77 S. High St., Columbus, OH 43215
(614) 644-0986; *Fax:* (614) 466-9354

Scott Milburn, Press Secretary
Vern Riffe Center, 77 S. High St., 30th Fl., Columbus,
OH 43215
(614) 644-0957; *Fax:* (614) 466-9354

Robert A. Paduchik, Constituent Services Director
Vern Riffe Center, 77 S. High St., 30th Fl., Columbus,
OH 43215-6117
(614) 728-5966; *Fax:* (614) 466-9354

June Garvin, Director, Washington Office
444 N. Capitol St. N.W., #546, Washington, DC 20001
(202) 624-5844; *Fax:* (202) 624-5847

Office of the Lieutenant Governor
http://www.state.oh.us/LtGov
General e-mail: webmaster@das.state.oh
Main phone: (614) 466-3396
Main fax: (614) 644-0575

Maureen O'Connor (R), Lieutenant Governor
Vern Riffe Center, 77 S. High St., 30th Fl., Columbus,
OH 43266

Office of the Secretary of State
http://www.state.oh.us/sos/
Main phone: (614) 466-2655
Main fax: (614) 644-0649
Toll free: (877) 767-6446
TTY: (614) 466-0562

J. Kenneth Blackwell (R), Secretary of State
180 E. Broad St., 15th Fl., Columbus, OH 43215
E-mail: blackwell@sos.state.oh.us

Office of the Attorney General
http://www.ag.state.oh.us

State of Ohio

Capital: Columbus, since 1816
Founded: 1800, Ohio Territory created from Northwest Territory
Statehood: March 1, 1803 (17th state)
Constitution adopted: 1851
Area: 40,953 sq. mi. (ranks 35th)
Population: 11,209,493 (1998 est.; ranks 7th)
Largest cities: (1998 est.) Columbus (670,234); Cleveland (495,817); Cincinnati (336,400); Toledo (312,174); Akron (215,712)
Counties: 88, Most populous: (1998 est.) Cuyahoga (1,380,696); Franklin (1,021,194); Hamilton (847,403); Montgomery (558,427); Summit (537,730)
U.S. Congress: Mike DeWine (R), George V. Voinovich (R); 19 Representatives
Nickname(s): Buckeye State
Motto: With God, all things are possible
Song: "Beautiful Ohio"
Bird: Cardinal
Tree: Buckeye
Flower: Scarlet carnation
State fair: at Columbus, early to mid-Aug.
Former capital(s): Chillicothe, Zanesville

General e-mail:
constituent_services@ag.state.oh.us
Main phone: (614) 466-4320
Main fax: (614) 466-5087

Betty D. Montgomery (R), Attorney General
30 E. Broad St., 17th Fl., Columbus, OH 43215-3428
(614) 466-3376; *Fax:* (614) 644-6135

Office of the State Treasurer
http://www.state.oh.us/treasurer
General e-mail: lara.mongelluzzo@tos.state.oh.us
Main phone: (614) 466-2160
Main fax: (614) 644-7313
Toll free: (800) 228-1102

Joseph T. Deters (R), State Treasurer
30 E. Broad St., 10th Fl., Columbus, OH 43266-0421

Office of the State Auditor
http://www.auditor.state.oh.us

Main phone: (614) 466-4514
Main fax: (614) 466-4490
Toll free: (800) 282-0370
TTY: (614) 466-8193

James M. Petro (R), State Auditor
88 E. Broad St., 5th Fl., Columbus, OH 43216-1140
E-mail: petro@auditor.state.oh.us

Office of the Adjutant General
General e-mail: tagoh@oh-arng.ngb.army.mil
Main phone: (614) 336-6000
Main fax: (614) 336-7074

John H. Smith, Adjutant General
2829 W. Dublin-Granville Rd., Columbus, OH 43235-2789
(614) 336-7070

Agencies

Accountancy Board
http://www.state.oh.us/acc
Main phone: (614) 466-4135
Main fax: (614) 466-2628

Ronald J. Rotaru, Executive Director
Vern Riffe Center, 77 S. High St., 18th Fl., Columbus, OH 43266-0301
(614) 925-0192; *Fax:* (614) 728-0429
E-mail: Ronald.Rotaru@acc.state.oh.us

Administrative Services Dept.
http://www.das.state.oh.us/das/
Main phone: (614) 752-9521
Main fax: (614) 728-0490

C. Scott Johnson, Director
30 E. Broad St., 40th Fl., Columbus, OH 43266-0401
(614) 466-6511; *Fax:* (614) 644-8151

Human Resources Division
http://www.state.oh.us/das/dhr/index.htm
General e-mail:
das.hrd.web.watchers@das.state.oh.us
Main phone: (614) 466-3455
Main fax: (614) 728-2785

Stephen V. Gulyassy, Deputy Director
30 E. Broad St., 28th Fl., Columbus, OH 43266-0405

Aging Dept.
http://www.state.oh.us/age
Main phone: (614) 466-5500
Main fax: (614) 466-5741
TTY: (614) 466-6191

James J. Lawrence, Director
50 W. Broad St., Columbus, OH 43215-3363
(614) 466-7246; *Fax:* (614) 995-1049

Agriculture Dept.
http://www.state.oh.us/agr
General e-mail: http://wwwagri@ohio.gov
Main phone: (614) 728-6200
Main fax: (614) 466-6124
TTY: (800) 750-0750

Fred L. Dailey, Director
8995 E. Main St., #344, Reynoldsburg, OH 43068
(614) 466-2732

Air Quality Development Authority
http://www.aqda.state.oh.us/air
Main phone: (614) 466-6825
Main fax: (614) 752-9188
Toll free: (800) 225-5051

Mark R. Shanahan, Executive Director
50 W. Broad St., #1901, Columbus, OH 43215
E-mail: mark.shanahan@aqda.state.oh.us

Alcohol and Drug Addiction Services Dept.
http://www.state.oh.us/ada.adada.htm
General e-mail: ada@ada.state.oh.us
Main phone: (614) 466-3445
Main fax: (614) 752-8645
TTY: (614) 644-9140

Luceille Fleming, Director
2 Nationwide Plaza, 280 N. High St., 12th Fl., Columbus, OH 43215-2537
E-mail: fleming@ada.state.oh.us

Architects and Landscape Architects Board
http://www.state.oh.us/arc
General e-mail: cmharch@aol.com
Main phone: (614) 466-2316
Main fax: (614) 644-9048

William N. Wilcox, Executive Director
Vern Riffe Center, 77 S. High St., 16th Fl., Columbus, OH 43266-0303

Arts Council
http://www.oac.state.oh.us
Main phone: (614) 466-2613
Main fax: (614) 466-4494
Toll free: (888) 243-8622

Barbara S. Robinson, Chair
727 E. Main St., Columbus, OH 43205-1796

Budget and Management Office
http://www.state.oh.us/obm
Main phone: (614) 466-4034
Main fax: (614) 466-3813

Thomas W. Johnson, Director
30 E. Broad St., 34th Fl., Columbus, OH 43266-0411

Building Authority
http://www.state.oh.us/oba

Higher Educational Institutions

Bowling Green State University
http://www.bgsu.edu
110 McFall Center, Bowling Green, OH 43403
Main phone: (419) 372-2086

Cleveland State University
http://www.csuohio.edu
1983 E. 24th St., Cleveland, OH 44115
Main phone: (216) 687-2000

Kent State University
http://www.kent.edu
P.O. Box 5190, Kent, OH 44242-0001
Main phone: (330) 672-2444

Miami University of Ohio
http://www.muohio.edu
Oxford, OH 45056
Main phone: (513) 529-2531
Branches: Middletown

Ohio State University
http://www.ohio-state.edu
Lincoln Tower, 3rd Fl., Columbus, OH 43210-1200
Main phone: (614) 292-6446
Branches: Lima, Mansfield, Marion, Newark

Ohio University
http://www.ohiou.edu
Chubb Hall 120, Athens, OH 45701-2979
Main phone: (740) 593-4100
Branches: Chillicothe, Eastern, Lancaster, Southern, Zanesville

Shawnee State University
http://www.shawnee.edu
940 2nd St., Portsmouth, OH 45662-4344
Main phone: (800) 959-2778

University of Akron
http://www.uakron.edu
302 E. Buchtel Mall, Akron, OH 44325
Main phone: (330) 972-7100

University of Cincinnati
http://www.uc.edu
2624 Clifton Ave., Cincinnati, OH 45221
Main phone: (513) 556-6000

University of Toledo
http://www.utoledo.edu
2801 W. Bancroft, Toledo, OH 43606-3398
Main phone: (419) 530-2077

Wright State University
http://www.wright.edu
3640 Colonel Glenn Hwy., Dayton, OH 45435-0001
Main phone: (937) 775-3333

Youngstown State University
http://www.ysu.edu
1 University Plaza, Youngstown, OH 44555
Main phone: (330) 742-3000

Main phone: (614) 466-5959
Main fax: (614) 644-6478

Paul E. Goggin, Director
30 E. Broad St., #4020, Columbus, OH 43215

Civil Rights Commission
http://ocrs.state.oh.us
General e-mail: ocrc@state.oh.us
Main phone: (614) 466-2785
Main fax: (614) 644-8776
Toll free: (888) 278-7101
TTY: (614) 466-9353

Melanie J. Mitchell, Executive Director
1111 E. Broad St., #301, Columbus, OH 43205-1379
(614) 466-6715
E-mail: mitchell@ocrc.state.oh.us

Commerce Dept.
http://www.com.state.oh.us
Main phone: (614) 466-3636
Main fax: (614) 644-8292

Gary C. Suhadolnik, Director
Vern Riffe Center, 77 S. High St., 23rd Fl., Columbus, OH 43266-0544
(614) 644-7053; *Fax:* (614) 466-5650

State Fire Marshal Division
http://www.com.state.oh.us/fire/
Main phone: (614) 752-8200
Main fax: (614) 752-7213

Robert Rielage, Fire Marshal
8895 E. Main St., Reynoldsburg, OH 43068
(614) 752-7161

Community Service Council
http://www.state.oh.us/ohiogcsc
Main phone: (614) 728-2916
Main fax: (614) 728-2921
Toll free: (888) 767-OHIO

Kitty Burcsu, Executive Director
51 N. High St., #481, Columbus, OH 43215
(614) 728-2917
E-mail: kitty.burcsu@gcsc.state.oh.us

Consumer Protection Division
http://www.ag.state.oh.us/consumer/consumer.htm
Main phone: (614) 466-1305
Main fax: (614) 466-8898
Toll free: (800) 282-0515
TTY: (614) 466-1393

Helen MacMurray, Chief
30 E. Broad St., 25th Fl., Columbus, OH 43215-3428
E-mail: hmacmurray@ag.state.oh.us

Cosmetology Board
http://www.state.oh.us/cos

Main phone: (614) 466-3834
Main fax: (614) 644-6880

LaVaughn Gearhart, Director of Operations
3700 S. High St., Columbus, OH 43207-4041
(614) 644-6099

Criminal Justice Services Office
http://www.ocjs.state.oh.us
General e-mail: info@dcjs.state.oh.us
Main phone: (614) 466-7782
Main fax: (614) 466-0308

John F. Bender, Director
400 E. Town St., #300, Columbus, OH 43215
(614) 466-7782, ext. 60286

Development Dept.
http://www.odod.state.oh.us
Main phone: (614) 466-2480
Main *Fax:* (614) 644-5167
Toll free: (800) 466-8552
Mailing address: P.O. Box 1001, Columbus, OH
43216-1001

C. Lee Johnson, Director
Vern Riffe Center, 77 S. High St., Columbus, OH
43215-6108
(614) 466-0990; *Fax:* (614) 644-0745
E-mail: cljohnson@odod.state.oh.us

Travel and Tourism Division
http://www.ohiotourism.com
General e-mail: ohiotourism@odod.state.oh.us
Main phone: (614) 466-8844
Main fax: (614) 466-6744
Toll free: (800) 282-5393
Mailing address: P.O. Box 1001, Columbus, OH
43216-1001

Jim Epperson, Deputy Director
Vern Riffe Center, Columbus, OH 43216
E-mail: jepperson@odod.state.nh.us

Education Dept.
http://www.ode.state.oh.us
Main phone: (614) 466-3641
Main fax: (614) 466-0599
Toll free: (877) 644-6338

Susan Tave Zelman, Superintendent of Public Instruction
65 S. Front St., Columbus, OH 43215-4183
(614) 466-7578
E-mail: sdeo-zelman@ode.state.oh.us

Board of Education
http://www.ode.state.oh.us/board/default.htm
General e-mail: br_trent@ode.state.oh.us
Main phone: (614) 466-4838
Main fax: (614) 466-0599

Martha W. Wise, President
65 S. Front St., #1005, Columbus, OH 43215-4183
E-mail: sbe_wise@ode.ohio.gov

Employment Services Bureau
http://www.obes.org
Main phone: (614) 466-4636
Main fax: (614) 466-5025

James J. Mermis, Administrator
145 S. Front St., Columbus, OH 43215
(614) 466-2100

Engineers and Land Surveyors Board
http://www.peps.state.oh.us/index.htm
Main phone: (614) 466-3650
Main fax: (614) 728-3059

Mark Jones, Executive Secretary
77 S. High St., 16th Fl., Columbus, OH 43266-0314
E-mail: mjones@mail.peps.state.oh.us

Environmental Protection Agency
http://www.epa.ohio.gov
Main phone: (614) 644-3020
Main fax: (614) 644-2329
TTY: (614) 644-2110
Mailing address: P.O. Box 1049, Columbus, OH
43216-1049

Christopher Jones, Director
Lazarus Government Center, 122 S. Front St.,
Columbus, OH 43215
(614) 644-2782; *Fax:* (614) 644-3184

Ethics Commission
http://www.ethics.state.oh.us
Main phone: (614) 466-7090
Main fax: (614) 466-8368

David E. Freel, Executive Director
Atlas Bldg., 8 E. Long St., 10th Fl., Columbus, OH
43215
(614) 466-7093
E-mail: David.Freel@ethics.state.oh.us

Health Dept.
http://www.odh.state.oh.us
Main phone: (614) 466-3543
Main fax: (614) 644-8526
Mailing address: P.O. Box 118, Columbus, OH
43266-0118

J. Nick Baird, Director
246 N. High St., Columbus, OH 43266-0118
(614) 466-2253; *Fax:* (614) 644-0085

Higher Education Facilities Commission
Main phone: (614) 466-7413
Main fax: (614) 466-5866

Thomas L. Needles, Chair
30 E. Broad St., 36th Fl., Columbus, OH 43266-0417

Historical Society
http://www.ohiohistory.org
Main phone: (614) 297-2300
Main fax: (614) 297-2411

Gary C. Ness, Director
1982 Velma Ave., Columbus, OH 43211-2497
(614) 297-2350; *Fax:* (614) 297-2352
E-mail: gness@ohiohistory.org

Human Services Dept.
http://www.state.oh.us/odhs
Main phone: (614) 466-6650
Main fax: (614) 466-2815
TTY: (614) 752-3951

Jacqueline Romer Sensky, Director
30 E. Broad St., 32nd Fl., Columbus, OH 43266-0423
(614) 466-6282

Medicaid Office
http://www.state.oh.us/odhs/medicaid
Main phone: (614) 644-0140
Main fax: (614) 752-3986

Barbara Coulter Edwards, Deputy Director
30 E. Broad St., 31st Fl., Columbus, OH 43266-0423

Industrial Commission
http://www.ic.state.oh.us
Main phone: (614) 466-3711
Main fax: (614) 752-6610
Toll free: (800) 507-4223
TTY: (614) 752-4782

William E. Thompson, Chair
30 W. Spring St., #L-30, Columbus, OH 43215-2233

Insurance Dept.
http://www.state.oh.us/ins
Main phone: (614) 644-2658
Main fax: (614) 644-3743

J. Lee Covington II, Director
2100 Stella Court, Columbus, OH 43215-1067
(614) 644-2651
E-mail: lee.covington@ins.state.oh.us

Lake Erie Commission
http://www.epa.state.oh.us/oleo
General e-mail: oleo@http://www.epa.state.oh.us
Main phone: (419) 245-2514
Main fax: (419) 245-2519
Mailing address: P.O. Box 1049, Columbus, OH 43216-1049

Christopher Jones, Chair
Lazarus Government Center, 122 S. Front St.,
Columbus, OH 43215
(614) 644-2782

Library Board
http://winslo.state.oh.us
Main phone: (614) 644-7061
Main fax: (614) 466-3584

Michael S. Lucas, State Librarian
65 S. Front St., 5th Fl., Columbus, OH 43215-4163

Lottery Commission
http://www.ohiolottery.com
General e-mail: olcwebmail@olc.state.oh.us
Main phone: (216) 787-3200
Main fax: (216) 787-3313
Toll free: (888) 882-3344

Mitchell J. Brown, Executive Director
State Office Bldg., 615 Superior Ave. N.W., Cleveland,
OH 44113-9885
(216) 787-3344

Medical Examiners Board
http://www.state.oh.us/med/
Main phone: (614) 466-3934
Main fax: (614) 728-5946
Toll free: (800) 554-7717

Ray Q. Bumgarner, Director
77 S. High St., 17th Fl., Columbus, OH 43266-0315
(614) 466-9304

Mental Health Dept.
http://www.mh.state.oh.us/
Main phone: (614) 466-2596
Main fax: (614) 752-9453
TTY: (614) 752-9696

Michael Hogan, Director
30 E. Broad St., 8th Fl., Columbus, OH 43266-0414
(614) 466-2337
E-mail: hoganm@mhmail.state.oh.us

Mental Retardation and Developmental Disabilities Dept.
http://www.dmr.state.oh.us
Main phone: (614) 466-6896
Main fax: (614) 644-5013
Toll free: (800) 231-5872
TTY: (614) 752-4688

Kenneth W. Ritchey, Director
1810 Sullivant Ave., Columbus, OH 43223-1239
(614) 466-5214
E-mail: ken.ritchey@dmr.state.oh.us

Natural Resources Dept.
http://www.dnr.state.oh.us
General e-mail: barb.buzard@dnr.state.oh.us
Main phone: (614) 265-6565
Main fax: (614) 261-9601

Samuel W. Speck, Director
Fountain Square, 1930 Belcher Dr., Columbus, OH
  43224-1387
(614) 265-6879

Forestry Division
http://www.hcs.ohio-state.edu/ODNR/
  forestry.htm
Main phone: (614) 265-6694
Main fax: (614) 447-9231

> **Ronald G. Abraham, Chief**
> 1855 Fountain Square Court, Bldg. H-1,
>   Columbus, OH 43224-1327

Geological Survey
http://www.dnr.state.oh.us/odnr/geo_survey/
General e-mail: geo.survey@dnr.state.oh.us
Main phone: (614) 265-6576
Main fax: (614) 447-1918

> **Thomas M. Berg, State Geologist and Chief**
> 4383 Fountain Square Dr., Columbus, OH 43224-
>   1362
> (614) 265-6988
> *E-mail:* thomas.berg@dnr.state.oh.us

Oil and Gas Division
http://www.dnr.state.oh.us/odnr/oil+gas/
General e-mail: dog@dnr.state.oh.us
Main phone: (614) 265-6922
Main fax: (614) 268-4316

> **Thomas G. Tugend, Chief**
> 4383 Fountain Square Dr., Bldg. B-3, Columbus,
>   OH 43224-1362
> (614) 265-6893
> *E-mail:* tom.tugend@dnr.state.oh.us

Parks and Recreation Division
http://www.dnr.state.oh.us/odnr/parks/
General e-mail: judi.love@dnr.state.oh.us
Main phone: (614) 265-6561
Main fax: (614) 261-8407

> **Dan West, Chief**
> 1952 Belcher Dr., Bldg. C-3, Columbus, OH 43224

Soil and Water Conservation Division
http://www.dnr.state.oh.us/odnr/soil+water/
  soil+water.html
Main phone: (614) 265-6610
Main fax: (614) 262-2064

> **Larry Vance, Chief**
> 1939 Fountain Square Dr., Columbus, OH 43224

Water Division
http://www.dnr.state.oh.us/odnr/water/
General e-mail: water@dnr.state.oh.us
Main phone: (614) 265-6717
Main fax: (614) 447-9503

Frequently Called Numbers

Tourism: (614) 466-8844, 1-800-282-5393;
  http://www.ohiotourism.com
Library: (614) 644-7061; 1-800-686-1531;
  http://winslo.state.oh.us
Board of Education: (614) 466-4838;
  http://www.ode.state.oh.us/board/default.htm
Vital Statistics: (614) 466-2531
Tax/Revenue: (614) 466-7606;
  http://www.state.oh.us/tax/
Motor Vehicles: (614) 752-7500;
  http://www.state.oh.us/odps/division/bmv
State Police/Highway Patrol: (614) 466-2660;
  http://www.state.oh.us/ohiostatepatrol
Unemployment: Benefits: (614) 466-9756, Tax:
  (614) 752-7995; http://www.state.oh.us/obes/
  html/Unemployment_compensation_faq_.htm
General Election Information: (614) 728-8361;
  http://www.state.oh.us/sos.elecpage.html
Consumer Affairs: (614) 466-1305, 1-800-
  282-0515; http://www.ag.state.oh.us/
  consumer/consumer.htm
Hazardous Materials: (614) 644-2917

> **Jim Morris, Chief**
> 1939 Fountain Square, Columbus, OH 43224-1336
> (614) 265-6712
> *E-mail:* jim.morris@dnr.state.oh.us

Wildlife Division
http://www.dnr.state.oh.us/odnr/wildlife/
  index.html
Main phone: (614) 265-6300
Toll free: (800) WILDLIFE

> **Mike Budzik, Chief**
> 1840 Belcher Dr., Columbus, OH 43224-1329

Nursing Board
http://www.state.oh.us/nur
Main phone: (614) 466-3947
Main fax: (614) 466-0388

> **Dorothy Fiorino, Executive Director**
> 17 S. High St., #400, Columbus, OH 43215-3413

Ohio Educational Telecommunications Network Commission
http://www.oet.edu
Main phone: (614) 644-1714
Main fax: (614) 644-3112

> **Dave Fornshell, Executive Director**
> 2470 North Star Rd., Columbus, OH 43221
> *E-mail:* fornshell@oet.state.oh.us

Pharmacy Board
http://www.state.oh.us/pharmacy
Main phone: (614) 466-4143
Main fax: (614) 752-4836

William T. Winsley, Director
77 S. High St., 17th Fl., Columbus, OH 43266-0320

Public Defender Commission
Main phone: (614) 466-5394
Main fax: (614) 644-9972

David H. Bodiker, State Public Defender
Atlas Bldg., 8 E. Long St., 11th Fl., Columbus, OH 43215

Public Employees Retirement System
http://www.opers.org
Main phone: (614) 466-2085
Main fax: (614) 728-0746
Toll free: (800) 222-7377

Richard E. Schumacher, Executive Director
277 E. Town St., Columbus, OH 43215
(614) 466-2822

Public Facilities Commission
Main phone: (614) 466-0691
Main fax: (614) 466-3813

Kurt Kauffman, Assistant Secretary
30 E. Broad St., 34th Fl., Columbus, OH 43266-0411
E-mail: kurt.kauffman@obm.state.oh.us

Public Safety Dept.
http://www.state.oh.us/odps/default.html
Main phone: (614) 466-2550
Main fax: (614) 466-0433
Mailing address: P.O. Box 182081, Columbus, OH 43218-2081

Maureen O'Connor, Director
1970 W. Broad St., Columbus, OH 43218-2081
(614) 466-3383

Emergency Management Agency
http://www.state.oh.us/odps/division/ema
Main phone: (614) 889-7150
Main fax: (614) 889-7183

James R. (Jim) Williams, Executive Director
2855 W. Dublin-Granville Rd., #206, Columbus, OH 43235-2206
E-mail: jwilliams@dps.state.oh.us

Motor Vehicles Bureau
http://www.state.oh.us/odps/division/bmv
Main phone: (614) 752-7500
TTY: (614) 752-7681

Franklin R. Caltrider, Registrar
1970 W. Broad St., #529, Columbus, OH 43223

Ohio State Patrol
http://www.state.oh.us/ohiostatepatrol
General e-mail: http://wwwohp@ohio.gov
Main phone: (614) 466-2660
Main fax: (614) 799-9249
Mailing address: P.O. Box 182074, Columbus, OH 43218

Kenneth B. Marshall, Superintendent
1970 W. Broad St., Columbus, OH 43223
(614) 466-2990; *Fax:* (614) 752-6409

Public Utilities Commission
http://www.puc.state.oh.us
Main phone: (614) 466-3016
Main fax: (614) 466-7366

Alan R. Schriber, Chair
180 E. Broad St., Columbus, OH 43215-3793
(614) 466-3204; *Fax:* (614) 995-3690
E-mail: alan.schriber@puc.state.oh.us

Racing Commission
Main phone: (614) 466-2757
Main fax: (614) 466-1900

Clifford A. Nelson II, Executive Director
Vern Riffe Center, 77 S. High St., 18th Fl., Columbus, OH 43266-0416
E-mail: can@osrc.state.oh.us

Rehabilitation and Corrections Dept.
http://www.drc.state.oh.us
General e-mail: linda.diroll@exchange.state.oh.us
Main phone: (614) 752-1159
Main fax: (614) 752-1086

Reginald Wilkinson, Director
1050 Freeway Dr. North, Columbus, OH 43229
(614) 752-1164; *Fax:* (614) 752-1171

Adult Parole Authority
http://www.drc.state.oh.us/web/apa.htm
Main phone: (614) 752-1254
Main fax: (614) 752-1251

John Kinkela, Chief
1050 Freeway Dr. North, Columbus, OH 43229

Rehabilitation Services Commission
http://www.state.oh.us/rsc
Main phone: (614) 438-1200
Main fax: (614) 438-1257
Toll free: (800) 282-4536
TTY: (800) 282-4536

Robert L. Rabe, Administrator
400 E. Campus View Blvd., Columbus, OH 43235-4604
(614) 438-1210

Rural Development Partnership
http://www.cpmra.muohio.edu/ordp

Main phone: (614) 466-5495
Main fax: (614) 466-4346
Toll free: (800) 282-1955

Randy Hunt, Executive Director
8995 E. Main St., Reynoldsburg, OH 43068
E-mail: hunt@odant.agri.state.oh.us

School Employees Retirement System
http://www.oh.sers.org
Main phone: (614) 222-5853
Main fax: (614) 222-5828
Toll free: (800) 878-5853

Thomas R. Anderson, Executive Director
45 N. 4th St., Columbus, OH 43215-3634
(614) 222-5801

School for the Blind
Main phone: (614) 752-1152
Main fax: (614) 752-1713

Louis A. Mazzoli, Superintendent
5220 N. High St., Columbus, OH 43214
(614) 752-1660

School for the Deaf
http://www.osd.ode.state.oh.us
Main phone: (614) 728-4030
TTY: (614) 728-4033

Edward E. Corbett Jr., Superintendent
500 Morse Rd., Columbus, OH 43214-1833
E-mail: corbett@osd.ode.state.oh.us

State Fair
http://www.ohioexpocenter.com
General e-mail: info@ohioexpocenter.com
Main phone: (614) 644-4000
Main fax: (614) 644-4031
Toll free: (888) OHO-EXPO

Rick Frenette, General Manager
Ohio Expo Center, 717 E. 17th Ave., Columbus, OH
43211
(614) 644-4070
E-mail: r.frenette@expo.state.oh.us

State Library
http://winslo.state.oh.us
Main phone: (614) 644-7061
Main fax: (614) 466-3584
Toll free: (800) 686-1531

Michael Lucas, State Librarian
65 S. Front St., 5th Fl., Columbus, OH 43215-4163
(614) 644-6843
E-mail: mlucas@winslo.state.oh.us

Tax Appeals Board
Main phone: (614) 466-6700
Main fax: (614) 644-5196

Kiehner Johnson, Chair
30 E. Broad St., 24th Fl., Columbus, OH 43266-0422

Taxation Dept.
http://www.state.oh.us/tax/
Main phone: (614) 466-7606
Main fax: (614) 466-8922
TTY: (800) 750-0750

Thomas M. Zaino, Tax Commissioner
30 E. Broad St., 22nd Fl., Columbus, OH 43215
(614) 466-2166; *Fax:* (614) 466-6401

Transportation Dept.
http://www.dot.state.oh.us
Main phone: (614) 466-7170
Main fax: (614) 644-8662
TTY: (614) 466-3174

Gordon D. Proctor, Director
1980 W. Broad St., Columbus, OH 43223
(614) 466-2335; *Fax:* (614) 644-0587

Aviation Office
http://www.dot.state.oh.us/Aviation
Main phone: (614) 793-5040
Main fax: (614) 793-8972

Robert (Rudy) Rudolph, Administrator
2829 W. Dublin-Granville Rd., Columbus, OH
43235-2786
(614) 793-5041
E-mail: rrudolph@dot.state.oh.us

Turnpike Commission
http://www.ohioturnpike.org

Boards and Licensing

Accountancy, (614) 466-4135,
 http://www.state.oh.us/acc
Architects, (614) 466-2316,
 http://www.state.oh.us/arc
Child Care, (614) 466-3822
Cosmetology, (614) 466-3834,
 http://www.state.oh.us/cos
Engineers and Land Surveyors, (614)
 466-3650, http://www.peps.state.oh.us/
 index.htm
Medical Examiners, (614) 466-3934,
 http://www.state.oh.us/med/
Nursing, (614) 466-3947,
 http://www.state.oh.us/nur
Pharmacy, (614) 466-4143,
 http://www.state.oh.us/pharmacy
Real Estate, (614) 466-4100

General e-mail: blesko@ohioturnpike.org
Main phone: (440) 234-2081
Main fax: (440) 234-4618
Toll free: (888) TURNPIKE

Gino Zompanelli, Executive Director
682 Prospect St., Berea, OH 44017
(440) 234-2081, ext. 203
E-mail: gzompanelli@ohioturnpike.org

Veterans Affairs Office
http://www.state.oh.us/gova
Main phone: (614) 644-0898
Main fax: (614) 728-9498

David E. Aldstadt, Director
77 S. High St., Columbus, OH 43266
(614) 644-0892

Water Development Authority
http://www.owda.org
Main phone: (614) 466-5822
Main fax: (614) 644-9964

Laws

Sales tax: 7%
Income tax: 7%
State minimum wage: $4.25 , $3.35 and $2.80
for small employers (Federal is $5.15)
Marriage age: 18
First-cousin marriage: Prohibited
Drinking age: 21
State control of liquor sales: Yes
Blood alcohol for DWI: 0.10%
Driving age: 17
Speed limit: 65 mph
Permit to buy handguns: In some areas
Minimum age to possess handguns: 18
Minimum age to possess rifles, shotguns: 18
State lottery: Yes
Casinos: No
Pari-mutuel betting: Horse racing
Death penalty: Yes
3 strikes minimum sentence: None
Hate crimes law: Yes
Gay employment non-discrimination: No
Official language(s): None
Term limits: Governor (8 yrs.); state legislators
(8 yrs.)

*State laws are complex and subject to
change; this information is not intended as
legal advice. For an explanation of this
information, see p. x.*

Steven J. Grossman, Executive Director
88 E. Broad St., #1300, Columbus, OH 43215-3516
(614) 466-0152
E-mail: steve@owda.org

Women's Policy and Research Commission
http://www.state.oh.us/wpr/vision.html
General e-mail:
womensvoices@owprc.state.oh.us
Main phone: (614) 466-5580
Main fax: (614) 466-5434
Toll free: (800) 282-3040

Sally Farran Bulford, Executive Director
77 S. High St., 24th Fl., Columbus, OH 43266-0920

Workers' Compensation Bureau
http://www.ohiobwc.com
Main phone: (614) 644-6292
Main fax: (614) 752-4732
Toll free: (800) 644-6292

James Conrad, Administrator
30 W. Spring St., Columbus, OH 43266
(614) 466-8751; Fax: (614) 752-8428

Youth Services Dept.
http://www.state.oh.us/oys
Main phone: (614) 466-4314
Main fax: (614) 752-9078

Geno Natalucci-Persichetti, Director
51 N. High St., Columbus, OH 43215
(614) 466-8783

Ohio Legislature
State Capitol
Colombus, OH 43215
General information: (614) 466-8842
Bill status: (614) 466-7434
http://www.state.oh.us/ohio/legislat.htm

Senate
Address: State House, Columbus, OH 43215
General information: (614) 466-4900
Fax: (614) 466-8261

Richard H. Finan (R), President
State House, #201, Columbus, OH 43215
(614) 466-9737
E-mail: SD07@mailr.sen.state.oh.us
http://www.senate.state.oh.us/senators/bios/finan.html

Robert R. Cupp (R), President Pro Tempore
State House, #138, Columbus, OH 43215
(614) 466-7584
E-mail: SD12@mailr.sen.state.oh.us
http://www.senate.state.oh.us/senators/bios/cupp.html

Bruce E. Johnson (R), Assistant President Pro Tempore and Majority Leader
State House, #137, Columbus, OH 43215
(614) 466-8064
E-mail: SD03@mailr.sen.state.oh.us
http://www.senate.state.oh.us/senators/bios/johnson_b.html

Merle Grace Kearns (R), Majority Whip
State House, #221, Columbus, OH 43215
(614) 466-3780
E-mail: SD10@mailr.sen.state.oh.us
http://www.senate.state.oh.us/senators/bios/kearns.html

Ben E. Espy (D), Minority Leader
State House, #303, Columbus, OH 43215
(614) 466-5131
E-mail: SD15@mailr.sen.state.oh.us
http://www.senate.state.oh.us/senators/bios/espy.html

Rhine L. McLin (D), Minority Whip
State House, #223, Columbus, OH 43215
(614) 466-6247
E-mail: SD05@mailr.sen.state.oh.us
http://www.senate.state.oh.us/senators/bios/mclin.html

Matthew T. Schuler, Clerk
State House, Columbus, OH 43215
(614) 466-4900; *Fax:* (614) 466-8261

House
Address: 77 High St., Columbus, OH 43266-0603
General information: (614) 466-3357
Fax: (614) 644-8744

Jo Ann Davidson (R), Speaker of the House
77 High St., 14th Fl., Columbus, OH 43266-0603
(614) 466-4847
http://www.house.state.oh.us/reps/bios/bio.cfm?DISTRICT=24

Randall Gardner (R), Speaker Pro Tempore
77 High St., 14th Fl., Columbus, OH 43266-0603
(614) 466-8104
http://www.house.state.oh.us/reps/bios/bio.cfm?DISTRICT=04

Patrick J. Tiberi (R), Majority Leader
77 High St., 14th Fl., Columbus, OH 43266-0603
(614) 644-6030
http://www.house.state.oh.us/reps/bios/bio.cfm?DISTRICT=26

Bill Harris (R), Majority Whip
77 High St., 14th Fl., Columbus, OH 43266-0603
(614) 466-1431
http://www.house.state.oh.us/reps/bios/bio.cfm?DISTRICT=93

Jack Ford (D), Minority Leader
77 High St., 14th Fl., Columbus, OH 43266-0603
(614) 466-1401
http://www.house.state.oh.us/reps/bios/bio.cfm?DISTRICT=49

Dan Metelsky (D), Minority Whip
77 High St., 14th Fl., Columbus, OH 43266-0603
(614) 466-5141
http://www.house.state.oh.us/reps/bios/bio.cfm?DISTRICT=61

Frederick E. Mills, Legislative Clerk
77 High St., Columbus, OH 43266-0603
(614) 466-3357; *Fax:* (614) 644-8744

Ohio Judiciary
30 E. Broad St.
Columbus, OH 43215

Supreme Court
http://www.sconet.ohio.gov

Marcia Mengel, Clerk
30 E. Broad St., Columbus, OH 43215
(614) 466-5201; *Fax:* (614) 752-4418
E-mail: mengelm@sconet.state.oh.us

Justices
Composition: 7 justices
Selection Method: nonpartisan election following party primaries; vacancies filled by gubernatorial appointment; appointees serve until general election
Length of term: 6 years

Thomas J. Moyer, Chief Justice, (614) 466-3627
Deborah L. Cook, Justice, (614) 466-3828
Andrew Douglas, Justice, (614) 466-4524
Paul E. Pfeifer, Justice, (614) 466-2523
Alice Robie Resnick, Justice, (614) 466-3578
Evelyn Lundberg Stratton, Justice, (614) 466-2926
Francis E. Sweeney Sr., Justice, (614) 466-4425

Office of Court Administration
Main phone: (614) 466-2653
Main fax: (614) 752-8736

Steven C. Hollon, Administrative Director
30 E. Broad St., Columbus, OH 43266-0419
E-mail: hollon@sconet.state.oh.us

State Law Library
http://www.sconet.ohio.gov/LawLibrary/
Main phone: (614) 466-4442

Main fax: (614) 466-1559
General e-mail: libref@sconet.state.oh.us

Paul S. Fu, Law Librarian
30 E. Broad St., 4th Fl., Columbus, OH 43266-0419
(614) 466-2044
E-mail: fup@sconet.state.oh.us

Legislative and Political Party Information Resources

Senate home page: http://www.senate.state.oh.us
House home page: http://www.house.state.oh.us
Committees: Senate: http://www.senate.state.oh.us/committees/;
   House: http://www.house.state.oh.us/committees/
Legislative process: http://www.house.state.oh.us/committees/bill.html
Current session information: http://www.legislature.state.oh.us/today.cfm
Budget: http://www.lbo.state.oh.us
Ohio Democratic Party: http://www.ohiodems.org
   271 E. State St., Columbus, OH 43215; *Phone:* (614) 221-6563; *Fax:* (614) 221-0721;
   E-mail: odpstaff@ohiodems.org
Ohio Republican Party: http://www.ohiogop.org
   211 S. 5th St., Columbus, OH 43215; *Phone:* (614) 228-2481; *Fax:* (614) 228-1093

Oklahoma

State Capitol
Oklahoma City, OK 73105
Public information: (405) 521-2011
Fax: (405) 521-3089
http://www.state.ok.us

Office of the Governor

http://governor.state.ok.us
General e-mail: governor@gov.state.ok.us
Main phone: (405) 521-2342
Main fax: (405) 521-3353

Frank Keating (R), Governor
State Capitol, 2300 N. Lincoln Blvd., #212, Oklahoma
City, OK 73105

Howard Barrett, Chief of Staff
State Capitol, 2300 N. Lincoln Blvd., #212, Oklahoma
City, OK 73105
(405) 521-2342; *Fax:* (405) 521-3353
E-mail: howard.barrett@gov.state.ok.us

Dan Mahoney, Communications Office Director
State Capitol, 2300 N. Lincoln Blvd., #212, Oklahoma
City, OK 73105
(405) 521-2342; *Fax:* (405) 521-3353
E-mail: dan.mahoney@gov.state.ok.us

Matt Ralls, Constituent Affairs
State Capitol, 2300 N. Lincoln Blvd., #212, Oklahoma
City, OK 73105
(405) 521-2342; *Fax:* (405) 521-3353
E-mail: matt.ralls@gov.state.ok.us

Office of the Lieutenant Governor

http://www.state.ok.us/~ltgov
General e-mail: ltgovernor@oklaosf.state.ok.us
Main phone: (405) 521-2161
Main fax: (405) 525-2702

Mary Fallin (R), Lieutenant Governor
State Capitol, 2300 N. Lincoln Blvd., #211, Oklahoma
City, OK 73105

Office of the Secretary of State

http://www.state.ok.us/~SOS
General e-mail: okla.treas@treas.state.ok.us
Main phone: (405) 521-3911
Main fax: (405) 521-3771

Mike Hunter (R), Secretary of State
State Capitol, 2300 N. Lincoln Blvd., #101, Oklahoma
City, OK 73105
(405) 521-3912

State of Oklahoma

Capital: Oklahoma City, since 1910
Founded: 1830, as Indian Territory; 1890, Oklahoma Territory created from part of Indian Territory
Statehood: November 16, 1907 (46th state)
Constitution adopted: 1907
Area: 68,679 sq. mi. (ranks 19th)
Population: 3,346,713 (1998 est.; ranks 27th)
Largest cities: (1998 est.) Oklahoma City (472,221); Tulsa (381,393); Norman (93,019); Lawton (81,107); Broken Arrow (72,564)
Counties: 77, Most populous: (1998 est.) Oklahoma (632,988); Tulsa (543,539); Cleveland (201,110); Comanche (113,508); Muskogee (70,004)
U.S. Congress: James M. Inhofe (R), Don Nickles (R); 6 Representatives
Nickname(s): Sooner State
Motto: Labor conquers all things
Song: "Oklahoma"
Bird: Scissor-tailed flycatcher
Tree: Redbud
Flower: Mistletoe
State fair: at Oklahoma City, mid-Sept.-early Oct.; at Tulsa, late Sept.-early Oct.
Former capital(s): Guthrie

Office of the Attorney General

http://www.oag.state.ok.us/oagweb.nsf
Main phone: (405) 521-3921
Main fax: (405) 521-6246

W. A. (Drew) Edmondson (D), Attorney General
State Capitol, 2300 N. Lincoln Blvd., #112, Oklahoma
City, OK 73105

Office of the State Treasurer

http://www.state.ok.us/~sto
General e-mail: treas@oklaosf.state.ok.us
Main phone: (405) 521-3191
Main fax: (405) 521-4994

Robert A. Butkin (D), Treasurer
State Capitol, 2300 N. Lincoln Blvd., #217, Oklahoma
City, OK 73105

Office of the State Auditor and Inspector
Main phone: (405) 521-3495
Main fax: (405) 521-3426

Clifton H. Scott (D), State Auditor and Inspector
State Capitol, 2300 N. Lincoln Blvd., #100, Oklahoma City, OK 73105

Military Dept.
http://www.omd.state.ok.us/
General e-mail: tagok@ok-ngnet.army.mil
Main phone: (405) 228-5000
Main fax: (405) 228-5524

Stephen P. Cortright, Adjutant General
3501 Military Circle, Oklahoma City, OK 73111-4398

Agencies

Accountancy Board
General e-mail: okaccybd@oklaosf.state.ok.us
Main phone: (405) 521-2397
Main fax: (405) 521-3118

Diana Collinsworth, Executive Director
4545 N. Lincoln Blvd., #165, Oklahoma City, OK 73105

Aeronautics Commission
http://www.okladot.state.ok.us/aeroinfo/index.htm
General e-mail:
 webinfo@fd9ns01.okladot.state.ok.us
Main phone: (405) 521-2377
Main fax: (405) 521-2379

Bill Boulton, Chair
200 N.E. 21st St., 1st Fl., Oklahoma City, OK 73105
(405) 478-1464
E-mail: ace5@flash.net

Agriculture Dept.
http://www.state.ok.us/osfdocs/aghp.html
Main phone: (405) 521-3864
Main fax: (405) 521-4912

Dennis Howard, Commissioner
2800 N. Lincoln Blvd., Oklahoma City, OK 73105-4298
(405) 521-3864, ext. 200

Forestry Services
http://www.oklaosf.state.ok.us/~okag/
 forhome.html
General e-mail:
 okforest@odagis.oklaosf.state.ok.us
Main phone: (405) 521-3864, ext. 2-6158
Main fax: (405) 522-4583

Roger Davis, Director
2800 N. Lincoln Blvd., Oklahoma City, OK 73105
E-mail: rogerd@odagis.oklaosf.state.ok.us

Alcoholic Beverage Laws Enforcement Commission
http://www.able.state.ok.us
General e-mail:
 ablecomm@mhs.oklaosf.state.ok.us
Main phone: (405) 521-3484
Main fax: (405) 521-6578

Bryan Close, Chair
4545 N. Lincoln Blvd., #270, Oklahoma City, OK 73105

Architects and Landscape Architects Board
Main phone: (405) 751-6512
Main fax: (405) 755-6391

Brian Dougherty, Chair
11212 N. May Ave., #110, Oklahoma City, OK 73120

Arts Council
http://www.state.ok.us/arts~
General e-mail: okarts@oklaosf.state.ok.us
Main phone: (405) 521-2931
Main fax: (405) 521-6418
Mailing address: P.O. Box 52001-2001, Oklahoma City, OK 73152-2001

Linda S. Frazier, Chair
2244 Terwilleger Blvd., #640, Tulsa, OK 7414-1318
E-mail: linda.frazier@utulsa.edu

Banking Dept.
http://www.state.ok.us/~osbd
Main phone: (405) 521-2782
Main fax: (405) 522-2993

Mick Thompson, Commissioner
4545 N. Lincoln Blvd., #164, Oklahoma City, OK 73105

Central Services Dept.
http://www.dcs.state.ok.us/OKDCS.nsf
Main phone: (405) 521-2121
Main fax: (405) 521-6403

Pamela M. Warren, Director
State Capitol, 2300 N. Lincoln Blvd., #104, Oklahoma City, OK 73105
(405) 521-4027

Civil Emergency Management
http://www.onenet.net/~odcem
Main phone: (405) 521-2481
Main fax: (405) 521-4053
Mailing address: P.O. Box 53365, Oklahoma City, OK 73152

Albert Ashwood, Director
2401 N. Lincoln Blvd., Oklahoma City, OK 73105
E-mail: albert.ashwood@oklaosf.state.ok.us

Commerce Dept.

http://www.locateok.com
Main phone: (405) 815-6552
Main fax: (405) 815-5199
Toll free: (800) 879-6552
Mailing address: P.O. Box 26980, Oklahoma City, OK 73126-0980

Russell Perry, Secretary
900 N. Stiles Ave., Oklahoma City, OK 73126-0980
(405) 815-5202; *Fax:* (405) 815-5290
E-mail: russell_perry@odoc.state.ok.us

Conservation Commission

http://www.okcc.state.ok.us
Main phone: (405) 521-2384
Main fax: (405) 521-6686

Mike Thralls, Executive Director
2800 N. Lincoln Blvd., #160, Oklahoma City, OK 73105-4210
(405) 521-4827

Consumer Credit Dept.

http://www.state.ok.us/~okdcc
Main phone: (800) 448-4904
Main fax: (405) 521-6740

Donald K. Hardin, Administrator
4545 N. Lincoln Blvd., #104, Oklahoma City, OK 73105
(405) 521-3653
E-mail: dhardin@okdcc.osf.state.ok.us

Corporation Commission

http://www.occ.state.ok.us
General e-mail:
webmaster@occmail.occ.state.ok.us
Main phone: (405) 521-2211
Main fax: (405) 521-6045
TTY: (405) 521-3513
Mailing address: P.O. Box 52000-2000, Oklahoma City, OK 73152-2000

Bob Anthony (R), Chair
Jim Thorpe Bldg., Oklahoma City, OK 73152-2000
(405) 521-2261

Consumer Services Division

Main phone: (405) 521-2211
Main fax: (405) 521-2087
Toll free: (800) 522-8154
TTY: (405) 521-3513
Mailing address: P.O. Box 52000-2000, Oklahoma City, OK 73152-2000

Bill Burnett, Director
2101 N. Lincoln Blvd., #260, Oklahoma City, OK 73105
(405) 521-3319

Higher Educational Institutions

Cameron University
http://www.cameron.edu
2800 W. Gore Blvd., Lawton, OK 73505-6377
Main phone: (580) 581-2289

East Central University
http://www.ecok.edu
Ada, OK 74820-6899
Main phone: (580) 332-8000

Langston University
http://www.lunet.edu
P.O. Box 838, Langston, OK 73050
Main phone: (405) 466-2231

Northeastern State University
http://www.nsuok.edu
600 N. Grand, Tahlequah, OK 74464
Main phone: (918) 456-5511
Branches: Broken Arrow, Muskogee, Tulsa

Northwestern Oklahoma State University
http://www.nwalva.edu
709 Oklahoma Blvd., Alva, OK 73717-2799
Main phone: (580) 327-8545

Oklahoma Panhandle State University
http://www.opsu.edu
P.O. Box 430, Goodwell, OK 73939
Main phone: (580) 349-2611

Oklahoma State University
http://osu.okstate.edu
210 Student Union, Stillwater, OK 74078-6046
Main phone: (405) 744-5358
Branches: College of Osteopathic Medicine, Oklahoma City, Okmulgee, Tulsa

Southwestern Oklahoma State University
http://www.swosu.edu
100 Campus Dr., Weatherford, OK 73094
Main phone: (580) 772-6611
Branches: Sayre

University of Central Oklahoma
http://www.ucok.edu
100 N. University Dr., Edmond, OK 73034
Main phone: (405) 974-2000

University of Oklahoma
http://www.ou.edu
1000 Asp Ave., Norman, OK 73019-4076
Main phone: (405) 325-2252
Branches: Health Sciences Center, Tulsa

Oil and Gas Conservation Division
http://www.occ.state.ok.us
Main phone: (405) 521-2302
Main fax: (405) 521-3099
TTY: (405) 521-3513
Mailing address: P.O. Box 52000-2000, Oklahoma City, OK 73152-2000

Michael S. Battles, Director
Jim Thorpe Bldg., Oklahoma City, OK 73152
E-mail: m.battles@occmail.occ.state.ok.us

Corrections Dept.
http://www.doc.state.ok.us
Main phone: (405) 425-2500
Main fax: (405) 425-2886
Mailing address: P.O. Box 11400, Oklahoma City, OK 73136-0400

James L. Saffle, Director
3400 Martin Luther King, Oklahoma City, OK 73111
(405) 425-2505; *Fax:* (405) 425-2578

Cosmetology Board
http://www.state.ok.us/~cosmo/
Main phone: (405) 521-2441
Main fax: (405) 528-8310

Betty Moore, Director
2200 Glassen Blvd., #1530, Oklahoma City, OK 73106
E-mail: bmoore@oklaosf.state.ok.us

Development Finance Authority
Main phone: (405) 842-1145
Main fax: (405) 848-3314

D. R. Shipley, Chair
5900 Classen Ct., Oklahoma City, OK 73118
(405) 848-9761

Education Dept.
http://www.sde.state.ok.us
Main phone: (405) 521-3301
Main fax: (405) 521-6205

Sandy Garrett (D), S⁷ ⸢ Superintendent
2500 N. Lincoln P⁷ ⸤., #116, Oklahoma City, OK 73105-4599
E-mail: sa⸍ ⸌-garrett@mail.state.ok.us

Boaʳ ⸍of Education
h⸍ ⸍.//www.state.ok.us/osfdocs/edhp.html
Main phone: (405) 521-3308
Main fax: (405) 521-6205

Brenda Deshazo, Chief Executive Secretary
2500 N. Lincoln Blvd., Oklahoma City, OK 73105-4599
E-mail: brenda_deshazo@mail.sde.state.ok.us

Educational Television Authority
http://www.oeta.onenet.net

General e-mail: info-oeta@onenet.net
Main phone: (405) 848-8501
Main fax: (405) 841-9216
Mailing address: P.O. Box 14190, Oklahoma City, OK 73113

Malcolm Wall, Executive Director
7403 N. Kelley Ave., Oklahoma City, OK 73113
E-mail: mac_wall@oeta.pbs.org

Election Board
Main phone: (405) 521-2391
Main fax: (405) 521-6457
TTY: (405) 521-3028

Glo Henley, Chair
2300 N. Lincoln Blvd., Oklahoma City, OK 73152-3156

Employment Security Commission
http://www.oesc.state.ok.us
General e-mail: webmaster@oesc.state.ok.us
Main phone: (405) 557-0200
Main fax: (405) 557-5375
TTY: (405) 557-5458
Mailing address: P.O. Box 52003, Oklahoma City, OK 73152

Jon Brock, Executive Director
2401 N. Lincoln Blvd., #504, Oklahoma City, OK 73105
(405) 557-7201

Engineers and Land Surveyors Board
http://www.okpels.com
General e-mail: okpels@okpels.org
Main phone: (405) 521-2874
Main fax: (405) 523-2135

Kathy Hart, Director
210 N.E. 27th St., #120, Oklahoma City, OK 73105-2788
E-mail: kathy@okpels.org

Environmental Quality Dept.
http://www.deq.state.ok.us
Main phone: (405) 702-1000
Main fax: (405) 702-1001
Toll free: (800) 869-1400
Mailing address: P.O. Box 1677, Oklahoma City, OK 73101-1677

Mark S. Coleman, Executive Director
707 N. Robinson, Oklahoma City, OK 73101-1677
(405) 702-7156; *Fax:* (405) 702-7101
E-mail: mark.coleman@deqmail.state.ok.us

Ethics Commission
http://www.state.ok.us/~ethics
Main phone: (405) 521-3451
Main fax: (405) 521-4905

Marilyn Hughes, Director
State Capitol Bldg., 2300 N. Lincoln Blvd., #B-5,
  Oklahoma City, OK 73105-4812
(405) 522-2515
E-mail: mhughes@mhs.oklaosf.state.ok.us

Finance Office
http://www.state.ok.us/osf.html
General e-mail: julie.dvorak@oklaosf.state.ok.us
Main phone: (405) 521-2141
Main fax: (405) 521-3902

Tom Daxon, Director
State Capitol, 2300 N. Lincoln Blvd., #122, Oklahoma
  City, OK 73105
(405) 521-2833
E-mail: tom.daxon@oklaosf.state.ok.us

State Comptroller
http://www.state.ok.us/osfdocs/comptrol.html
Main phone: (405) 521-2141

Mark Meadors, State Comptroller
State Capitol Bldg., 2300 N. Lincoln Blvd., #122,
  Oklahoma City, OK 73105
(405) 521-6162
E-mail: mark.meadors@oklaosf.state.ok.us

Fire Marshal Office
http://www.oklaosf.state.ok.us/~firemar/
Main phone: (405) 522-5005
Main fax: (405) 522-5028

Doug Blaine, Assistant State Fire Marshal
4545 N. Lincoln Blvd., #280, Oklahoma City, OK
  73105
E-mail: twilson855@aol.com

Geological Survey
http://www.ou.edu/special/ogs-pttc
General e-mail: cgsmith@ou.edu
Main phone: (405) 325-3031
Main fax: (405) 325-7069

Charles J. Mankin, Director
100 E. Boyd, #N-131, Norman, OK 73109-0628
E-mail: cjmankin@ou.edu

Grand River Dam Authority
http://www.grda.com
General e-mail: questions@grda.com
Main phone: (918) 256-5545
Main fax: (918) 256-5289
Mailing address: P.O. Box 409, Vinta, OK 74301-0409

**Ron Coker, General Manager and Chief Executive
  Officer**
226 W. Dwain Willis Ave., Vinta, OK 74301-0409
E-mail: rcoker@grda.com

Frequently Called Numbers

Tourism: (405) 521-2406, 1-800-652-6552;
  http://www.travelok.com
Library: (405) 521-2502;
  http://www.odl.state.ok.us
Board of Education: (405) 521-3308;
  http://www.state.ok.us/osfdocs/edhp.html
Vital Statistics: (405) 271-4040;
  http://www.health.state.ok.us/program/vital/
  index.html
Tax/Revenue: (405) 521-3160;
  http://www.oktax.state.ok.us
Motor Vehicles: (405) 425-2317;
  http://www.dps.state.ok.us/dls/
State Police/Highway Patrol: (405) 425-2003;http://www.dps.state.ok.us/ohp
Unemployment: (405) 557-7190;
  http://www.oesc.state.ok.us/ui/default.htm
General Election Information:
  (405) 521-2391
Consumer Affairs: (405) 521-2211,
  1-800-522-8154
Hazardous Materials: (405) 271-5338;
  http://www.deq.state.ok.us/waste/HW/
  hwmac.html

Health Care Authority
General e-mail: branstes@ohca.state.ok.us
Main phone: (405) 522-7300
Main fax: (405) 522-7417

**Mike Fogarty, Chief Executive Officer and
  Administrator**
4545 N. Lincoln Blvd., #124, Oklahoma City, OK
  73105
(405) 522-7471; *Fax:* (405) 522-7187

Health Dept.
http://www.health.state.ok.us
Main phone: (405) 271-5600
Main fax: (405) 271-3431

Jerry Raymond Nida, Commissioner
1000 N.E. 10th St., Oklahoma City, OK 73117-1299
(405) 271-4200
E-mail: nida@health.state.ok.us

Historical Society
http://www.ok-history.mus.ok.us
Main phone: (405) 521-2491
Main fax: (405) 521-2492

Bob L. Blackburn, Executive Director
Wiley Post Historical Bldg., 2100 N. Lincoln Blvd.,

Oklahoma City, OK 73105-4997
(405) 522-5202
E-mail: bblackburn@ok-history.mus.ok.us

Housing Finance Agency
http://www.state.ok.us/~ohfa
General e-mail: sherry.kast@oklaosf.state.ok.us
Main phone: (405) 848-1144
Main fax: (405) 840-1109
Toll free: (800) 256-1489
TTY: (405) 848-7471
Mailing address: P.O. Box 26720, Oklahoma City,
  OK 73126-0720

Dennis Shockley, Executive Director
1140 N.W. 63rd St., Box 26720, #200, Oklahoma City,
  OK 73116
(405) 848-1144, ext. 276
E-mail: dennis.shockley@oklaosf.state.ok.us

Human Rights Commission
http://www.onenet.net/~ohrc2
General e-mail: ohrc2@onenet.net
Main phone: (405) 521-2360
Main fax: (405) 522-3635
TTY: (405) 522-3993

Juanita Williams, Chair
2101 N. Lincoln Blvd., #480, Oklahoma City, OK
  73105
(405) 521-3441

Human Services Dept.
http://www.onenet.net/okdhs
Main phone: (405) 521-3646
Main fax: (405) 521-6816
TTY: (405) 521-2778
Mailing address: P.O. Box 25352, Oklahoma City,
  OK 73125

Howard H. Hendrick, Director
2400 N. Lincoln Blvd., Oklahoma City, OK 73105
Fax: (405) 521-6458
E-mail: howard.hendrick@okdhs.org

Aging Services Division
http://www.okdhs.org/iaging/index.htm
Main phone: (405) 521-2327
Main fax: (405) 521-2086
Mailing address: P.O. Box 25352, Oklahoma
  City, OK 73125

Roy R. Keen, Administrator
2400 N. Lincoln Blvd., Oklahoma City, OK 73125
E-mail: Roy.Keen@OKDHS.org

Developmental Disabilities Services Division
http://www.okdhs.org/officedivision/
  devdisabilities.htm
Main phone: (405) 521-6267

Main fax: (405) 522-3037
Mailing address: P.O. Box 25352, Oklahoma
City, OK 73125

James Nicholson, Administrator
2400 N. Lincoln Blvd., Oklahoma City, OK 73125
E-mail: james.nicholson@okdhs.org

Indian Affairs Commission
http://www.state.ok.us/~oiac
Main phone: (405) 521-3828
Main fax: (405) 522-4427

Tim Tall Chief, Chair
4545 N. Lincoln Blvd., #282, Oklahoma City, OK
  73105
(405) 271-3601; *Fax:* (405) 271-1155

Indigent Defense System
http://www.state.ok.us/~oids
General e-mail: duane@appellate.ou.nor.edu
Main phone: (405) 325-0802
Main fax: (405) 325-7567
Mailing address: P.O. Box 926, Norman, OK
  73070-0926

James Bednar, Executive Director
1660 Cross Center Dr., Norman, OK 73019
E-mail: jbednar@appellate.oids.ou.edu

Insurance Dept.
http://www.oid.state.ok.us
General e-mail: okinsdpt@telepath.com
Main phone: (405) 521-2828
Main fax: (405) 521-6652
TTY: (800) 522-0071
Mailing address: P.O. Box 53408, Oklahoma City,
  OK 73152-3408

Carroll Fisher, Commissioner
2401 N.W. 23rd St., #28, Oklahoma City, OK 73107
Fax: (405) 521-6635

Investigation Bureau
http://www.osbi.state.ok.us
Main phone: (405) 848-6724
Main fax: (405) 843-3804
Toll free: (800) 522-8017
TTY: (405) 843-7303

DeWade Langley, Director
6600 N. Harvey Ave., #300, Oklahoma City, OK
  73116
Fax: (405) 879-2574

Juvenile Affairs Office
http://www.state.ok.us/~oja
General e-mail: comments@oja.state.ok.us
Main phone: (405) 530-2800

Main fax: (405) 530-2890
Mailing address: P.O. Box 268812, Oklahoma City, OK 73126-8812

Jerry Regier, Director
3812 N. Santa Fe, #400, Oklahoma City, OK 73118-8509
E-mail: jerry.regier@oja.state.ok.us

Labor Dept.
http://www.state.ok.us/~okdol/
Main phone: (405) 528-1500
Main fax: (405) 528-5751

Brenda Reneau (R), Commissoner
4001 N. Lincoln Blvd., Oklahoma City, OK 73105
(405) 528-1500, ext. 200

Workers Compensation Division
http://www.state.ok.us/~okdol/workcomp/index.htm
Main phone: (405) 528-1500
Main fax: (405) 528-5751
Toll free: (888) 269-5353

Johnny Coleman, Director
4001 N. Lincoln Blvd., Oklahoma City, OK 73105
(405) 528-1500, ext. 259; *Fax:* (405) 525-0252

Libraries Dept.
http://www.odl.state.ok.us
Main phone: (405) 521-2502
Main fax: (405) 525-7804
Toll free: (800) 522-8116

Robert L. Clark, Director
200 N.E. 18th St., Oklahoma City, OK 73105-3298
(405) 522-3172
E-mail: bclark@oltn.odl.state.ok.us

Mr., Archives Administrator
E-mail: tkremm@oltn.odl.state.ok.us

Archives and Records Division
http://www.odl.state.ok.us/oar/index.htm
Main phone: (405) 521-2502, ext. 203
Main fax: (405) 525-7804

Gary Harrington, Archives Administrator
200 N.E. 18th St., Oklahoma City, OK 73105-3298
E-mail: gharrington@oltn.odl.state.ok.us

Liquefied Petroleum Gas Administration
Main phone: (405) 521-2458
Main fax: (405) 521-6037

W. A. (Bill) Glass, Administrator
2101 N. Lincoln Blvd., #B-45, Oklahoma City, OK 73105

Medical Examiners Board
http://www.osbmls.state.ok.us
Main phone: (405) 848-6841

Main fax: (405) 848-8240
Mailing address: P.O. Box 18256, Oklahoma City, OK 73154

Lyle Kelsey, Executive Director
5104 N. Francis, Suite C, Oklahoma City, OK 73118
(405) 848-6841, ext. 114

Mental Health and Substance Abuse Services Dept.
http://www.odmhsas.org
General e-mail: sharris@odmhsas.org
Main phone: (405) 522-3908
Main fax: (405) 522-3650
TTY: (405) 522-3851
Mailing address: P.O. Box 53277, Oklahoma City, OK 73152-3277

Sharron D. Boehler, Commissioner
1200 N.E. 13th St., Oklahoma City, OK 73117
(405) 522-3877; *Fax:* (405) 522-0637

Merit Protection Commission
Main phone: (405) 525-9144
Main fax: (405) 528-6245

James L. Howard, Executive Director
310 N.E. 28th St., #201, Oklahoma City, OK 73105

Mines Dept.
Main phone: (405) 521-3859
Main fax: (405) 427-9646

Mary Ann Pritchard, Director
4040 N. Lincoln Blvd., #107, Oklahoma City, OK 73105-5282

Narcotics and Dangerous Drugs Control Bureau
http://www.state.ok.us/~obndd
Main phone: (405) 521-2885
Main fax: (405) 524-7619
Toll free: (800) 522-8031

Boards and Licensing

Accountancy, (405) 521-2397
Architects, (405) 751-6512
Child Care, (405) 521-3561
Contractors, (405) 751-6512
Cosmetology, (405) 521-2441, http://www.state.ok.us/~cosmo/
Engineers and Land Surveyors, (405) 521-2874, http://www.okpels.com
Medical Examiners, (405) 848-6841, http://www.osbmls.state.ok.us
Nursing, (405) 962-1800
Pharmacy, (405) 521-3815, http://www.state.ok.us/~pharmacy/
Real Estate, (405) 521-3387

Malcom J. Atwood, Director
4545 N. Lincoln Blvd., #11, Oklahoma City, OK 73105
Fax: (405) 530-3189

Nursing Board
General e-mail: oklahoma@ncsbn.org
Main phone: (405) 962-1800
Main fax: (405) 962-1821

Kim Glazier, Executive Director
2915 N. Glassen, #524, Oklahoma City, OK 73106

Pardon and Parole Board
http://www.ppb.state.ok.us
Main phone: (405) 427-8601
Main fax: (405) 427-6648

Terry Jenks, Executive Director
4040 N. Lincoln Blvd., #219, Oklahoma City, OK 73105-5221

Personnel Management Office
http://www.state.ok.us/~opm
Main phone: (405) 521-2177
Main fax: (405) 524-6942
TTY: (405) 521-6314

Oscar B. Jackson Jr., Administrator and Human Resources Secretary
2101 N. Lincoln Blvd., #G-80, Oklahoma City, OK 73105-4904
(405) 521-6301
E-mail: ojackson@mhs.oklaosf.state.ok.us

Pharmacy Board
http://www.state.ok.us/~pharmacy/
General e-mail: pharmacy@oklaosf.state.ok.us
Main phone: (405) 521-3815
Main fax: (405) 521-3758

Bryan Potter, Executive Director
4545 N. Lincoln Blvd., #112, Oklahoma City, OK 73105

Public Employees Retirement System
http://www.opers.state.ok.us
Main phone: (405) 858-6737
Main fax: (405) 848-5967
Mailing address: P.O. Box 53007, Oklahoma City, OK 73152

Stephen C. Edmonds, Executive Director
6601 N. Broadway, #129, Oklahoma City, OK 73152
E-mail: sedmonds@oklaosf.state.ok.us

Public Safety Dept.
http://www.dps.state.ok.us
Main phone: (405) 425-2424
Main fax: (405) 425-2337
Mailing address: P.O. Box 11415, Oklahoma City, OK 73136-0415

Bob A. Ricks, Commissioner
3600 Martin Luther King Ave., Oklahoma City, OK 73111
(405) 425-2001

Drivers License Services
http://www.dps.state.ok.us/dls/
Main phone: (405) 425-2317
Main fax: (405) 425-2321
Mailing address: P.O. Box 11415, Oklahoma City, OK 73136-0415

Lonnie Jarman, Director
3600 N. Martin Luther King Blvd., Oklahoma City, OK 73111
E-mail: ljarman@dps.state.ok.us

Highway Patrol
http://www.dps.state.ok.us/ohp
Main phone: (405) 425-2003
Main fax: (405) 419-2028

Gary D. Adams, Chief
3600 N. Martin Luther King Blvd., Oklahoma City, OK 73111
E-mail: gadams@dps.state.ok.us

Public Utility Unit
Main phone: (405) 521-3921
Main fax: (405) 521-6246

Cece L. Coleman, Director
2300 N. Lincoln Blvd., #112, Oklahoma City, OK 73105-4894
E-mail: cece_coleman@oag.state.ok.us

Real Estate Commission
Main phone: (405) 521-3387
Main fax: (405) 521-1534

Norris Price, Executive Director
4040 N. Lincoln Blvd., #600, Oklahoma City, OK 73105

Regents for Higher Education
http://www.okhighered.org
Main phone: (405) 524-9100
Main fax: (405) 524-9230

Hans Brisch, Chancellor
500 Education Bldg., Oklahoma City, OK 73105-4503
Fax: (405) 524-9235
E-mail: hbrisch@osrhe.edu

Rehabilitation Services Dept.
http://www.onenet.net/~drspiowm
Main phone: (405) 951-3400
Main fax: (405) 951-3529
Toll free: (800) 845-8476
TTY: (800) 845-8476

Linda S. Parker, Director
3535 N.W. 58th St., #500, Oklahoma City, OK 73112-4815
(405) 951-3490

School for the Blind
http://www.onenet.net/~drspiowm/osb.htm
General e-mail: osb@azalea.net
Main phone: (918) 682-6641
Main fax: (918) 682-1651
Toll free: (877) 229-7136

Karen Kizzia, Superintendent (Acting)
3300 Gibson St., Muskogee, OK 74403

School for the Deaf
http://www.onenet/~drspiowm/osd.htm
Main phone: (580) 622-4900
Main fax: (580) 627-4950
TTY: (580) 622-4901

Linda Trice, Superintendent
1100 E. Oklahoma St., Oklahoma City, OK 73086-3108
(405) 622-4908

Securities Dept.
http://www.securities.state.ok.us
General e-mail: general@securities.state.ok.us
Main phone: (405) 280-7700
Main fax: (405) 280-7742

Irving Faught, Administrator
1st National Center, 120 N. Robinson, #860, Oklahoma City, OK 73102
(405) 280-7700, ext. 7706

State Fair
http://www.oklafair.org
General e-mail: oklafair@oklafair.org
Main phone: (405) 948-6700
Main fax: (405) 948-6828
Mailing address: P.O. Box 74943, Oklahoma City, OK 73147

Donald J. Hotz, President and General Manager
500 Land Rush St., Oklahoma City, OK 73147

Student Loan Authority
http://www.oslat.org
General e-mail: info@oslat.org
Main phone: (405) 556-9200
Main fax: (405) 556-9255
Toll free: (800) 456-6752
TTY: (405) 556-9230
Mailing address: P.O. Box 54530, Oklahoma City, OK 73154

Patrick Rooney, Chair
4545 N. Lincoln Blvd., #66, Oklahoma City, OK 73105
(405) 556-9210

Tax Commission
http://www.oktax.state.ok.us
General e-mail: helpmaster@oktax.state.ok.us
Main phone: (405) 521-3160
Main fax: (405) 521-3826

Robert E. (Bob) Anderson, Chair
2501 N. Lincoln Blvd., Oklahoma City, OK 73194
(405) 521-3115

Teachers Retirement System
http://www.state.ok.us/~okteachers
General e-mail: oktrs@oklaosf.state.ok.us
Main phone: (405) 521-2387
Main fax: (405) 521-3810
Mailing address: P.O. Box 53524, Oklahoma City, OK 73152

Tommy C. Beavers, Executive Secretary
2801 N. Lincoln Blvd., Oklahoma City, OK 73105
(405) 521-4745

Tourism and Recreation Dept.
http://www.travelok.com
General e-mail: information@travelok.com
Main phone: (405) 521-2406
Main fax: (405) 521-3992
Toll free: (800) 652-6552

Jane Jayroe, Executive Director
Colcord Bldg., 15 N. Robinson St., #100, Oklahoma City, OK 73102
(405) 521-2413; *Fax:* (405) 522-5354

Transportation Dept.
http://okladot.state.ok.us
Main phone: (405) 522-8000
Main fax: (405) 521-6528

Neal A. McCaleb, Secretary
200 N.E. 21st St., Oklahoma City, OK 73105-3204
(405) 521-2631

Veterans Affairs Dept.
http://www.odva.state.ok.us
Main phone: (405) 521-3684
Main fax: (405) 521-6533
Mailing address: P.O. Box 53067, Oklahoma City, OK 73152

Phillip C. Boatner, Director
2311 N. Central, Oklahoma City, OK 73105
E-mail: pboatner@adva.state.ok.us

Vocational and Technical Education Dept.
http://www.okvotech.org
Main phone: (405) 377-2000
Main fax: (405) 743-5541

Ann Benson, State Director
1500 W. 7th Ave., Stillwater, OK 74074-4364
(405) 743-5444
E-mail: abens@okvotech.org

Water Resources Board
http://www.state.ok.us/~owrb
Main phone: (405) 530-8800
Main fax: (405) 530-8900
TTY: (405) 530-8860

Duane A. Smith, Executive Director
3800 N. Classen Blvd., Oklahoma City, OK 73118

Wheat Commission
General e-mail: okwheat@iamerica.net
Main phone: (405) 521-2796
Main fax: (405) 848-0372

Bart Brorsen, Chair
800 N.E. 63rd St., Oklahoma City, OK 73105

Wildlife Conservation Dept.
http://www.state.ok.us/~odwc
Main phone: (405) 521-3851
Main fax: (405) 521-6535
TTY: (800) 522-8506
Mailing address: P.O. Box 53465, Oklahoma City, OK 73152

Greg D. Duffy, Director
1801 N. Lincoln, Oklahoma City, OK 73105
(405) 521-4660
E-mail: gduffy@odwc.state.ok.us

Oklahoma Legislature
State Capitol
2300 N. Lincoln Blvd.
Oklahoma City, OK 73105
http://www.lsb.state.ok.us

Senate
General information: (405) 524-0126
Fax: (405) 521-5507

Mary Fallin (R), President
State Capitol, 2300 N. Lincoln Blvd., #211, Oklahoma City, OK 73105
(405) 521-2161; *Fax:* (405) 525-2702
E-mail: ltgovernor@oklaosf.state.ok.us
http://www.state.ok.us/~ltgov

Stratton Taylor (D), President Pro Tempore
State Capitol, 2300 N. Lincoln Blvd., #422, Oklahoma City, OK 73105
(405) 521-5565
http://www.lsb.state.ok.us/senate/taylorbio.html

Billy Mickle (D), Majority Leader
State Capitol, 2300 N. Lincoln Blvd., #423, Oklahoma City, OK 73105
(405) 521-5586
E-mail: mickle@lsb.state.ok.us
http://www.lsb.state.ok.us/senate/micklebio.html

Gilmer Capps (D), Majority Whip

State Capitol, 2300 N. Lincoln Blvd., #424-A, Oklahoma City, OK 73105
(405) 521-5545
http://www.lsb.state.ok.us/senate/cappsbio.html

Mark Snyder (R), Minority Leader
State Capitol, 2300 N. Lincoln Blvd., #531, Oklahoma City, OK 73105
(405) 521-5622
http://www.lsb.state.ok.us/senate/snyderbio.html

Carol Martin (R), Minority Whip
State Capitol, 2300 N. Lincoln Blvd., #529-B, Oklahoma City, OK 73105
(405) 521-5569
E-mail: martin@lsb.state.ok.us
http://www.lsb.state.ok.us/senate/martinbio.html

Lance Ward, Secretary
State Capitol, 2300 N. Lincoln Blvd., Oklahoma City, OK 73105
(405) 524-0126; *Fax:* (405) 521-5507

House
General information: (405) 521-2711
Fax: (405) 557-7437

Laws

Sales tax: 8.375%
Income tax: 6%
State minimum wage: $5.15 , $2.00 for small employers (Federal is $5.15)
Marriage age: 18
First-cousin marriage: Prohibited
Drinking age: 21
State control of liquor sales: No
Blood alcohol for DWI: 0.10%
Driving age: 16
Speed limit: 75 mph
Permit to buy handguns: No
Minimum age to possess handguns: 18
Minimum age to possess rifles, shotguns: 18
State lottery: No
Casinos: No
Pari-mutuel betting: Horse racing
Death penalty: Yes
3 strikes minimum sentence: 20 yrs. (3rd felony)
Hate crimes law: Yes
Gay employment non-discrimination: No
Official language(s): None
Term limits: State legislators (12 yrs.)

State laws are complex and subject to change; this information is not intended as legal advice. For an explanation of this information, see p. x.

Loyd Benson (D), Speaker of the House
State Capitol, 2300 N. Lincoln Blvd., #401, Oklahoma
 City, OK 73105
(405) 557-7307; *Fax:* (405) 557-7445
E-mail: bensonlo@lsb.state.ok.us
http://www.lsb.state.ok.us/house/spkrpage.htm

Larry E. Adair (D), Speaker Pro Tempore
State Capitol, 2300 N. Lincoln Blvd., #442, Oklahoma
 City, OK 73105
(405) 557-7394
E-mail: adairla@lsb.state.ok.us
http://www.lsb.state.ok.us/house/hd86.htm

Tommy Thomas (D), Majority Leader
State Capitol, 2300 N. Lincoln Blvd., #411, Oklahoma
 City, OK 73105
(405) 557-7308
E-mail: thomasto@lsb.state.ok.us
http://www.lsb.state.ok.us/house/hd20.htm

Randy L. Beutler (D), Majority Whip
State Capitol, 2300 N. Lincoln Blvd., #328-B,
 Oklahoma City, OK 73105
(405) 557-7311
E-mail: beutlerra@lsb.state.ok.us
http://www.lsb.state.ok.us/house/hd60.htm

Fred Morgan (R), Minority Leader
State Capitol, 2300 N. Lincoln Blvd., #548, Oklahoma
 City, OK 73105
(405) 557-7409
E-mail: morganfr@lsb.state.ok.us
http://www.lsb.state.ok.us/house/hd83.htm

Tim Pope (R), Minority Whip
State Capitol, 2300 N. Lincoln Blvd., Oklahoma City,
 OK 73105
(405) 557-7362
E-mail: popet@lsb.state.ok.us

Larry Warden, Chief Clerk
State Capitol, 2300 N. Lincoln Blvd., Oklahoma City,
 OK 73105
(405) 557-7303
E-mail: wardenla@lsb.state.ok.us
http://www.lsb.state.ok.us/house/cco_page.htm

Oklahoma Judiciary
State Capitol Bldg.
2300 N. Lincoln Blvd., #B2
Oklahoma City, OK 73105
http://www.state.ok.us/osfdocs/judhp.html

Supreme Court
http://www.oscn.net
 James W. Patterson, Clerk
 State Capitol Bldg., 2300 N. Lincoln Blvd., #B2,
  Oklahoma City, OK 73105
 (405) 521-2163
Justices
Composition: 9 justices
Selection Method: nonpartisan election;
 vacancies filled by gubernatorial appointment
Length of term: 6 years
Hardy Summers, Chief Justice, (405) 521-3830
Daniel J. Boudreau, Justice, (405) 521-3843
Rudolph Hargrave, Justice, (405) 521-3847
Ralph B. Hodges, Justice, (405) 521-3844
Yvonne Kauger, Justice, (405) 521-3841
Robert E. Lavender, Justice, (405) 521-3846
Marian P. Opala, Justice, (405) 521-3839
Joseph M. Watt, Justice, (405) 521-3848

Administrative Office of the Courts
http://www.oscn.net
Main phone: (405) 521-2450
Main fax: (405) 521-6815
 Howard W. Conyers, Administrative Director
 1915 N. Stiles, #305, Oklahoma City, OK 73105
 E-mail: conyersh@oscn.net

State Law Library
Main phone: (405) 522-3213
Main fax: (405) 521-2753
 Marilyn Jacobs, Administrator
 200 N.E. 18th St., Oklahoma City, OK 73105-3298
General e-mail: arlene.b.meinzer@state.or.us
Main phone: (503) 378-4000
Main fax: (503) 373-1500

Legislative and Political Party Information Resources

Senate home page: http://www.lsb.state.ok.us/senate/welcome.html
House home page: http://www.lsb.state.ok.us/house/ohorpage.htm
Legislative information: http://www.lsb.state.ok.us/docs/legislative2.html
Legislative process: http://www.lsb.state.ok.us/house/idea.gif
Oklahoma Democratic Party: http://www.okdemocrats.org
 2726 N. Oklahoma Ave., Oklahoma City, OK 73105; *Phone:* (405) 239-2700
Oklahoma Republican Party: http://www.okgop.com
 4301 N. Lincoln Blvd., Oklahoma City, OK 73105; *Phone:* (405) 528-3501;
 Fax: (405) 521-9531; *E-mail:* okgop@okgop.com

Oregon

State Capitol
Salem, OR 97310-4001
Public information: (503) 378-6500
Fax: (503) 378-8333
http://www.state.or.us

Office of the Governor
http://www.governor.state.or.us
General e-mail: http://www.governor.state.or.us/
email.htm
Main phone: (503) 378-3111
Main fax: (503) 378-4863
TTY: (503) 378-4859

John A. Kitzhaber (D), Governor
State Capitol, #254, Salem, OR 97310-4001

Bill Wyatt, Chief of Staff
State Capitol, #254, Salem, OR 97310-4001
(503) 373-1565; *Fax:* (503) 378-4863

Bob Applegate, Communications Director
State Capitol, #254, Salem, OR 97310-4001
(503) 378-6496; *Fax:* (503) 378-4863

Annabelle Jaramillo, Citizens Representative
State Capitol, #254, Salem, OR 97310-4001
(503) 378-3111; *Fax:* (503) 378-4863

Kevin Smith, Director, Washington Office
444 N. Capitol St. N.W., Washington, DC 20001
(202) 624-3535

Office of the Secretary of State
http://www.sos.state.or.us/
General e-mail: executive-
office@sosinet.sos.state.or.us
Main phone: (503) 986-1500
Main fax: (503) 986-1616

Bill Bradbury (D), Secretary of State
State Capitol, #136, Salem, OR 97310
(503) 986-1523

Attorney General's Office
http://www.doj.state.or.us
Main phone: (503) 378-4400
Main fax: (503) 378-3784
TTY: (503) 378-5938

Hardy Myers (D), Attorney General
Justice Bldg., 1162 Court St. N.E., Salem, OR 97310
(503) 378-6002; *Fax:* (503) 378-4017
E-mail: hardy.myers@doj.state.or.us

Office of the State Treasurer
http://www.ost.state.or.us

State of Oregon

Capital: Salem,
since 1851
Founded: 1848, Oregon
Territory created from land also
claimed by Great Britain
Statehood: February 14, 1859 (33rd state)
Constitution adopted: 1859
Area: 96,002 sq. mi. (ranks 10th)
Population: 3,281,974 (1998 est.; ranks 28th)
Largest cities: (1998 est.) Portland (503,891);
Eugene (128,240); Salem (126,702);
Gresham (85,021); Beaverton (62,111)
Counties: 36, Most populous: (1998 est.)
Multnomah (631,082); Washington
(399,697); Clackamas (334,732); Lane
(314,068); Marion (268,541)
U.S. Congress: Gordon Smith (R), Ron Wyden
(D); 5 Representatives
Nickname(s): Beaver State
Motto: She flies with her own wings
Song: "Oregon, My Oregon"
Bird: Western meadowlark
Tree: Douglas fir
Flower: Oregon grape
State fair: at Salem, late Aug.-early Sept.
Former capital(s): Oregon City

General e-mail: arlene.b.meinzer@state.or.us
Main phone: (503) 378-4000
Main fax: (503) 373-1500
TTY: (503) 373-0947

Jim Hill (D), State Treasurer
350 Winter St. N.E., #100, Salem, OR 97301-3896
(503) 378-4329; *Fax:* (503) 373-7051

Military Dept.
http://www.oregonguard.com
Main phone: (503) 945-3980
Main fax: (503) 945-3962
Toll free: (800) 452-7500
Mailing address: P.O. Box 14350, Salem, OR
97309-5047

Alexander H. Burgin, Adjutant General
1776 Militia Way S.E., Salem, OR 97309-5047
(503) 945-3991
E-mail: burgina@or-ngnet.army.mil

Agencies

Accountancy Board
http://www.boa.state.or.us
Main phone: (503) 378-4181
Main fax: (503) 378-3575

Karen DeLorenzo, Administrator
Morrow Crane Bldg., 3218 Pringle Rd. S.E., #110,
Salem, OR 97310
E-mail: karen.delorenzo@state.or.us

Administrative Services Dept.
http://www.das.state.ar.us
General e-mail: oregon.info@state.or.us
Main phone: (503) 378-3106
Main fax: (503) 373-7643
TTY: (503) 378-4672

R. Jon Yunker, Director
155 Cottage St. N.E., Salem, OR 97310
(503) 378-3104

Human Resources Services Division
http://www.dashr.state.or.us
General e-mail: hrsd.information@state.or.us
Main phone: (503) 378-8344

Daniel Kennedy, Administrator
155 Cottage St. N.E., Salem, OR 97310

Agriculture Dept.
http://www.oda.state.or.us
Main phone: (503) 986-4550
Main fax: (503) 986-4747
TTY: (503) 986-4762

Phil Ward, Director
635 Capitol St. N.E., Salem, OR 97301-2532
(503) 986-4552; *Fax:* (503) 986-4750
E-mail: pward@oda.state.or.us

Appraiser Certification and Licensure Board
http://www.cbs.state.or.us/aclb
Main phone: (503) 373-1505
Main fax: (503) 378-6576
TTY: (503) 378-4100

Linda Riddell, Administrator
350 Winter St. N.E., #21, Salem, OR 97301-3878

Architect Examiners Board
http://www.architect-board.state.or.us
General e-mail: architect.board@state.or.us
Main phone: (503) 378-4270
Main fax: (503) 378-6091

Jeanette O. Bartel, Administrator
750 Front St. N.E., #260, Salem, OR 97310
E-mail: jeanette.o.bartel@state.or.us

Archives Division
http://arcweb.sos.state.or.us
Main phone: (503) 373-0701
Main fax: (503) 373-0953
TTY: (503) 378-3760

Roy Turnbaugh, State Archivist
800 Summer St. N.E., Salem, OR 97310

Commission for the Blind
Main phone: (503) 731-3221
Main fax: (503) 731-3230
TTY: (503) 731-3224

Charles E. Young, Administrator
535 S.E. 12th Ave., Portland, OR 97214-2488
(503) 731-3223

Construction Contractors Board and Landscape Contractors Board
http://www.ccb.state.or.us
Main phone: (503) 378-4621
Main fax: (503) 373-2007
Toll free: (888) 366-5635
TTY: (503) 373-2218

Kenneth K. Keudell, Administrator
700 Summer St. N.E., #300, Salem, OR 97301-1286
(503) 378-4621, ext. 4010
E-mail: kenneth.k.kuedell@state.or.us

Consumer and Business Services Dept.
http://www.cbs.state.or.us
General e-mail: dcbs.director@state.or.us
Main phone: (503) 378-4100
Main fax: (503) 378-6444

Michael Greenfield, Director
350 Winter St. N.E., Salem, OR 97301-3878

Insurance Division
http://www.cbs.state.or.us/external/ins/
index.html
General e-mail: DCBS.INSMail@state.or.us
Main phone: (503) 947-7980
Main fax: (503) 378-4351
TTY: (503) 947-7280

Charles Nicoloff, Adminstrator (Acting)
350 Winter St. N.E., #440, Salem, OR 97301-3883

Workers Compensation Division
http://www.cbs.state.or.us/wcd
Main phone: (503) 947-7810
Main fax: (503) 947-7630
Toll free: (800) 452-0288
TTY: (503) 947-7993

Mary Neidig, Administrator
350 Winter St. N.E., #27, Salem, OR 97301-3879
(503) 947-7500; *Fax:* (503) 967-7514

Corrections Dept.

http://www.doc.state.or.us/
Main phone: (503) 945-0920
Main fax: (503) 373-1173

David S. Cook, Director
2575 Center St. N.E., Salem, OR 97301-4667
E-mail: Dave.Cook@doc.state.or.us

Cosmetology Board

http://www.hdlp.hr.state.or.us/bhhome.htm
General e-mail: hdlp.mail@state.or.us
Main phone: (503) 378-8667
Main fax: (503) 585-9114

Susan Wilson, Administrator
700 Summer St. N.E., #320, Salem, OR 97301-1287

Criminal Justice Division

Main phone: (503) 378-6347
Main fax: (503) 373-1936
TTY: (503) 378-5938

Charles E. Pritchard, Chief Counsel and Assistant Attorney General
Justice Bldg., 1162 Court St. N.E., Salem, OR 97310
E-mail: charles.pritchard@state.or.us

Economic Development Dept.

http://www.econ.state.or.us
Main phone: (503) 986-0123
Main fax: (503) 581-5115
Toll free: (800) 233-3306

William C. Scott, Director
775 Summer St. N.E., Salem, OR 97310
(503) 986-0110
E-mail: william.c.scott@state.or.us

Arts Commission

http://art.econ.state.or.us
General e-mail: oregon.artscomm@state.or.us
Main phone: (503) 986-0088
Main fax: (503) 986-0260
Toll free: (800) 233-3306

Christine T. D'Arcy, Executive Director
775 Summer St. N.E., Salem, OR 97301-1284
(503) 986-0087

Education and Workforce Policy Office

Main phone: (503) 378-3921
Main fax: (503) 378-4789

Jean Thorne, Director
255 Capitol St. N.E., #126, Salem, OR 97310-1338
E-mail: jean.i.thorne@state.or.us

Education Dept.

http://www.ode.state.or.us
Main phone: (503) 378-3573

Main fax: (503) 373-7968
TTY: (503) 378-2892

Stan Bunn, Superintendent of Public Instruction
Public Service Bldg., 255 Capitol St. N.E., Salem, OR 97310-0203
(503) 378-3573, ext. 526
E-mail: stan.bunn@state.or.us

Board of Education

http://www.ode.state.or.us/admin/board/index.htm
Main phone: (503) 378-3573, ext. 289
Main fax: (503) 378-4772
TTY: (503) 378-2832

Clark Brody, Executive Secretary and Deputy Superintendent
255 Capitol St. N.E., Salem, OR 97310-0203

School for the Blind

Main phone: (503) 378-3820
Main fax: (503) 373-7537

Ann Hicks, Superintendent
700 Church St. S.E., Salem, OR 97301-3795
E-mail: ann.hicks@state.or.us

School for the Deaf

http://www.osd.k12.or.us
Main phone: (503) 378-3825
Main fax: (503) 373-7879

Jane Mulholland, Director
999 Locust St. N.E., Salem, OR 97303-5299
(503) 378-3826
E-mail: jane.mulholland@state.or.us

Employment Appeals Board

Main phone: (503) 947-1500
Main fax: (503) 947-1504
Toll free: (800) 237-3710, ext.71500

Renee Bryant, Chair
875 Union St. N.E., #305A, Salem, OR 97311

Employment Dept.

http://www.emp.state.or.us
Main phone: (503) 947-1394
Main fax: (503) 947-1472
TTY: (800) 237-3710

Virlena Crosley, Director
875 Union St. N.E., Salem, OR 97311
(503) 947-1475

Employment Relations Board

http://www.erb.state.or.us
General e-mail: emprel.board@state.or.us
Main phone: (503) 378-3807
Main fax: (503) 373-0021

David W. Stiteler, Chair
528 Cottage St. N.E., #400, Salem, OR 97301-3807
(503) 378-3807, ext. 230
E-mail: david.stiteler@state.or.us

Energy Dept.
http://www.energy.state.or.us
General e-mail: Michael.W.Grainey@state.or.us
Main phone: (503) 378-5489
Main fax: (503) 373-7806
Toll free: (800) 221-8035
TTY: (503) 328-4040

John F. Savage, Administrator
625 Marion St. N.E., Salem, OR 97301
(503) 378-4131
E-mail: John.F.Savage@state.or.us

Engineering Examiners and Land Surveying Board
http://www.osbeels.org
General e-mail: osbeels@osbeels.org
Main phone: (503) 362-2666
Main fax: (503) 362-5454

Edward B. Graham, Administrator/Executive Secretary
728 Hawthorne Ave. N.E., Salem, OR 97301

Environmental Quality Dept.
http://www.deq.state.or.us/
Main phone: (503) 229-5696
Main fax: (503) 229-6124
Toll free: (800) 452-4011
TTY: (503) 229-6993

J. Langdon Marsh, Director
811 S.W. 6th Ave., Portland, OR 97204-1390
(503) 229-5300

Fish and Wildlife Dept.
http://www.dfw.state.or.us
Main phone: (503) 872-5268
Main fax: (503) 872-5276
TTY: (503) 872-5259
Mailing address: P.O. Box 59, Portland, OR 97207

Jim Greer, Director
2501 S.W. 1st Ave., Portland, OR 97207
(503) 872-5272
E-mail: james.w.greer@state.or.us

Forestry Dept.
http://www.odf.state.or.us
General e-mail: rosemary.e.hardin@state.or.us
Main phone: (503) 945-7200
Main fax: (503) 945-7212
TTY: (503) 945-7213

James E. Brown, State Forester
2600 State St., Salem, OR 97310

Higher Educational Institutions

Eastern Oregon University
http://www.eou.edu
1 University Blvd., La Grande, OR 97850-2899
Main phone: (541) 962-3672

Oregon Health Sciences University
http://www.ohsu.edu
3181 S.W. Sam Jackson Park Rd., Portland, OR 97201-3098
Main phone: (503) 494-8311

Oregon Institute of Technology
http://www.oit.osshe.edu
3201 Campus Dr., Klamath Falls, OR 97601-8801
Main phone: (541) 885-1000
Branches: Portland

Oregon State University
http://www.orst.edu
150 Kerr Administration Bldg., Corvallis, OR 97331-2107
Main phone: (541) 737-2482

Portland State University
http://www.pdx.edu
P.O. Box 751, Portland, OR 97207
Main phone: (503) 725-3000

Southern Oregon University
http://www.sou.edu
1250 Siskiyou Blvd., Ashland, OR 97520
Main phone: (541) 552-7672

University of Oregon
http://www.uoregon.edu
Eugene, OR 97403
Main phone: (541) 346-3201

Western Oregon University
http://www.wosc.osshe.edu
345 N. Monmouth Ave., Monmouth, OR 97361
Main phone: (503) 838-8000

---

(503) 945-7211
E-mail: james.e.brown@state.or.us

Geologist Examiners Board
General e-mail: osbge@open.org
Main phone: (503) 566-2837
Main fax: (503) 362-6393

Susanna R. Knight, Administrator
707 13th St. N.E., #275, Salem, OR 97301

Geology and Mineral Industries Dept.
http://www.dogami.state.or.us
General e-mail: dogami@state.or.us
Main phone: (503) 731-4100
Main fax: (503) 731-4066

Frequently Called Numbers

Tourism: (503) 986-0000
Library: (503) 378-4243;
　http://www.osl.state.or.us/oshhome.htm
Board of Education: (503) 378-3573, ext. 289;
　http://www.ode.state.or.us/admin/board/
　index.htm
Vital Statistics: (503) 731-4095;
　http://www.ohd.hr.state.or.us/cdpe/chs/certif/
　certfaqs.htm
Tax/Revenue: (503) 378-4988;
　http://www.dor.state.us
Motor Vehicles: (503) 945-5000;
　http://www.odot.state.or.us/dmv/index.htm
State Police/Highway Patrol: (503) 378-3720;
　http://www.osp.state.or.us
Unemployment: (503) 947-1685;
　http://findit.emp.state.orus/uiinfo.cfm
General Election Information: (503) 986-
　1518; http://www.sos.state.or.us/elections/
　elechp.htm
Consumer Affairs: (503) 378-4100;
　http://www.cbs.state.or.us
Hazardous Materials: (541) 388-6146;
　http://www.deq.state.or.us/wmc/hw/hw.htm

John Beaulieu, State Geologist
State Office Bldg., 800 N.E. Oregon St., #965,
　Portland, OR 97232
(503) 731-4100, ext. 221
E-mail: john.beaulieu@state.or.us

Government Standards and Practices Commission
Main phone: (503) 378-5105
Main fax: (503) 373-1456

L. Patrick Hearn, Executive Director
100 High St. S.E., #220, Salem, OR 97310

Historical Society
http://www.ohs.org
General e-mail: orhist@ohs.org
Main phone: (503) 306-5200
Main fax: (503) 221-2035

Chet Orloff, Director
1200 S.W. Park Ave., Portland, OR 97205
E-mail: cheto@ohs.org

Housing and Community Services Dept.
http://www.hcs.state.or.us
General e-mail: info@hcs.state.or.us

Main phone: (503) 986-2000
Main fax: (503) 986-2020

Robert Repine, Director
1600 State St., Salem, OR 97310-0302
(503) 986-2005

Human Resources Dept.
http://www.hr.state.or.us/
General e-mail: dhr.info@state.or.us
Main phone: (503) 945-5944
Main fax: (503) 378-2897
TTY: (503) 945-6214

Gary K. Weeks, Director
Human Resources Bldg., 500 Summer St. N.E., Salem,
　OR 97301
E-mail: gary.k.weeks@state.or.us

Developmental Disabilites Services Office
http://oddsweb.mhd.hr.state.or.us
Main phone: (503) 945-9774
Main fax: (503) 373-7274
Mailing address: P.O. Box 14250, Salem, OR
　97309-0740

James Toews, Assistant Administrator
2575 Bittern St. N.E., Salem, OR 97310-0520

Health Division
http://www.ohd.hr.state.or.us
General e-mail: ohd.info@state.or.us
Main phone: (503) 731-4000
Main fax: (503) 731-4078
Toll free: (800) 422-6012
TTY: (503) 731-4031

Jono Hildner, Administrator (Acting)
800 N.E. Oregon St., Portland, OR 97232
E-mail: jono.hildner@state.or.us

Health Plan Policy and Research Office
http://www.ohppr.state.or.us
Main phone: (503) 378-2422
Main fax: (503) 378-5511

Bob DiPrete, Administrator (Acting)
255 Capitol St. N.E., Public Service Bldg., 5th Fl.,
　Salem, OR 97310
(503) 378-2422, ext. 402
E-mail: bob.diprete@state.or.us

Medical Assistance Programs Office
http://www.omap.hr.state.or.us
Main phone: (503) 945-5772
Main fax: (503) 373-7689
Toll free: (800) 527-5772
TTY: (800) 365-8135

Hersh Crawford, Director
500 Summer St. N.E., Salem, OR 97310-1014
E-mail: herschel.crawford@state.or.us

Mental Health Services Dept.
http://www.omhs.mhd.hr.state.or.us
Main phone: (503) 945-9700
Main fax: (503) 373-7327
Mailing address: P.O. Box 14250, Salem, OR 97309-0740

Madeline Olson, Assistant Administrator
2575 Bittern St. N.E., Salem, OR 97310-0520
(503) 945-9718
E-mail: olsonm@mail.mhd.hr.state.or.us

Senior and Disabled Services
http://www.sdsd.hr.state.or.us
Main phone: (503) 945-5811
Toll free: (800) 282-8096

Roger Auerbach, Administrator
500 Summer St. N.E., Salem, OR 97310-1015

Labor and Industries Bureau
http://www.boli.state.or.us
Main phone: (503) 731-4070
Main fax: (503) 731-4103
TTY: (503) 731-4106

Jack Roberts, Commissioner
State Office Bldg., 800 N.E. Oregon St., #1045, Portland, OR 97232

Land Conservation and Development Dept.
http://www.lcd.state.or.us
Main phone: (503) 373-0050
Main fax: (503) 378-5518
TTY: (800) 735-2900

Richard Benner, Director
635 Capitol St. N.E., #150, Salem, OR 97310
(503) 373-0050, ext. 222
E-mail: dick.benner@state.or.us

Liquor Control Commission
http://www.olcc.state.or.us
Main phone: (503) 872-5000
Main fax: (503) 872-5266
Toll free: (800) 452-6522
TTY: (503) 872-5013

Pamela Erickson, Administrator
9079 S.E. McLoughlin Blvd., Portland, OR 97222-7355
(503) 872-5062
E-mail: pamela.erickson@state.or.us

Marine Board
http://www.marinebd.osmb.state.or.us
General e-mail: marineboard@state.or.us
Main phone: (503) 378-8587
Main fax: (503) 378-4597

Paul E. Donheffner, Director
435 Commercial St. N.E., Salem, OR 97309

(503) 373-1405, ext. 244
E-mail: paul.donheffner@state.or.us

Medical Examiners Board
General e-mail: bme@state.or.us
Main phone: (503) 229-5770
Main fax: (503) 229-6543

Kathleen Haley, Executive Director
1500 S.W. 1st Ave., #620, Portland, OR 97201-5826

Nursing Board
http://www.osbn.state.or.us
General e-mail: oregon.bn.info@state.or.us
Main phone: (503) 731-4745
Main fax: (503) 731-4755
TTY: (800) 735-2900

Joan C. Bouchard, Executive Director
State Office Bldg., 800 N.E. Oregon St., #465, Portland, OR 97232
(503) 731-4754
E-mail: joan.bouchard@state.or.us

Pacific States Marine Fisheries Commission
http://www.psmfc.org
General e-mail: postmaster@psmfc.org
Main phone: (503) 650-5400
Main fax: (503) 650-5426

Randy Fisher, Executive Director
45 S.E. 82nd Dr., #100, Gladstone, OR 97027-2522

Parks and Recreation Dept.
http://www.prd.state.or.us
Main phone: (503) 378-6305
Main fax: (503) 378-6447
Toll free: (800) 551-6949

Robert L. Meinen, Director
1115 Commercial St. N.E., #1, Salem, OR 97301
(503) 378-5019; *Fax:* (503) 378-8936
E-mail: robert.meinen@state.or.us

Parole and Post-Prison Supervision Board
Main phone: (503) 945-0900
Main fax: (503) 373-7558

Diane M. Rea, Chair
2575 Center St. N.E., Salem, OR 97310
(503) 945-0904
E-mail: Diane.Rea@doc.state.or.us

Public Defender's Office
Main phone: (503) 378-3349
Main fax: (503) 375-9701

David E. Groom, Public Defender
1320 Capitol St. N.E., #200, Salem, OR 97303
(503) 378-3349, ext. 228
E-mail: dgroom@opd.state.or.us

Public Employees Retirement System
http://www.pers.state.or.us
Main phone: (503) 598-7377
Main fax: (503) 598-0561
Toll free: (888) 320-7377
TTY: (503) 603-7766
Mailing address: P.O. Box 23700, Tigard, OR 97281

David Bailey, Executive Director (Acting), Deputy Director
11410 S.W. 68th Pkwy., Tigard, OR 97223
(503) 603-7575; *Fax:* (503) 598-1218
E-mail: c.david.bailey@state.or.us

Public Utility Commission
http://www.puc.state.or.us
General e-mail: puc.commission@state.or.us
Main phone: (503) 373-7394
Main fax: (503) 378-6163
TTY: (800) 648-3458

Ron Eachus, Chair
550 Capitol St. N.E., #215, Salem, OR 97301-2551
(503) 378-6611; *Fax:* (503) 378-5505

Racing Commission
http://www.oregonvos.net/~orc
Main phone: (503) 731-4052
Main fax: (503) 731-4053

Steven Barham, Executive Director
State Office Bldg., 800 N.E. Oregon St. #11, #310, Portland, OR 97232
E-mail: sbarham@oregonvos.net

Real Estate Agency
http://bbs.chemek.cc.or.us/public/orea/orea.html
Main phone: (503) 378-4170
Main fax: (503) 373-7153

Scott W. Taylor, Commissioner
1177 Center St. N.E., Salem, OR 97301-2505
E-mail: scott.w.taylor@state.or.us

Revenue Dept.
http://www.dor.state.us
Main phone: (503) 378-4988
Main fax: (503) 945-8738
TTY: (503) 945-8617

Elizabeth Harchenko, Director
Revenue Bldg., 955 Cener St. N.E., Salem, OR 97310
(503) 945-8214; *Fax:* (503) 945-8888

State Fair and Exposition Center
http://www.fair.state.or.us
General e-mail: lin.wolfe@fair.state.or.us
Main phone: (503) 378-3247
Main fax: (503) 373-1788

Robert (Rusty) Vernon, Director
2330 17th St. N.E., Salem, OR 97303-3201
E-mail: robert.vernon@fair.state.or.us

State Lands Division
http://statelands.dsl.state.or.us
Main phone: (503) 378-3805
Main fax: (503) 378-4844
TTY: (503) 378-4615

Paul R. Cleary, Director
775 Summer St. N.E., Salem, OR 97301-1279
(503) 378-3805, ext. 224
E-mail: paul.cleary@dsl.state.or.us

State Library
http://www.osl.state.or.us/oshhome.htm
Main phone: (503) 378-4243
Main fax: (503) 588-7119
TTY: (503) 378-4276

Jim Scheppke, State Librarian
250 Winter St. N.E., Salem, OR 97301-3950
(503) 378-4367
E-mail: jim.b.scheppke@state.or.us

State Lottery
http://www.oregonlottery.org
General e-mail: lottery.webcenter@state.or.us
Main phone: (503) 540-1000
Main fax: (503) 540-1001
TTY: (503) 540-1068

Chris Lyons, Director
500 Airport Rd. S.E., Salem, OR 97310
(503) 540-1017; *Fax:* (503) 540-1009
E-mail: Chris.Lyons@state.or.us

State Police Dept.
http://www.osp.state.or.us
Main phone: (503) 378-3720
Main fax: (503) 363-5475
TTY: (503) 585-1452

Vacant, Superintendent
400 Public Service Bldg., 255 Capitol St. N.E., Salem, OR 97310
(503) 378-3720, ext. 4100

Intergovernmental Services Bureau: Emergency Management Office
http://www.osp.state.or.us/oem
Main phone: (503) 378-2911
Main fax: (503) 588-1378
TTY: (503) 373-7857

Myra T. Lee, Director
595 Cottage St. N.E., Salem, OR 97310
(503) 378-2911, ext. 225
E-mail: myra.t.lee@state.or.us

State Fire Marshal's Office

General e-mail: oregon.sfm@state.or.us
Main phone: (503) 378-3473
Main fax: (503) 373-1825
TTY: (503) 390-4661

Robert Panuccio, Director
4760 Portland Rd. N.E., Salem, OR 97305
(503) 373-1540, ext. 216
E-mail: robert.panuccio@state.or.us

Student Assistance Commission

http://www.osac.state.or.us
General e-mail:
general.information@oscc.state.or.us
Main phone: (541) 687-7400
Main fax: (541) 687-7419
TTY: (541) 687-7357

Patricia Aldworth, Executive Director
1500 Valley River Dr., #100, Eugene, OR 97401
(541) 687-7404
E-mail: patricia.j.aldworth@state.or.us

Teacher Standards and Practices Commission

http://www.ode.state.or.us/tspc
General e-mail: tspc@state.or.us
Main phone: (503) 378-3586
Main fax: (503) 378-4448
TTY: (503) 378-6961

David V. Myton, Executive Secretary
255 Capitol St. N.E., #105, Salem, OR 97310
(503) 378-6813
E-mail: david.myton@state.or.us

Transportation Dept.

http://www.odot.state.or.us
Main phone: (503) 986-3200
Main fax: (503) 986-3432

Grace Crunican, Director
355 Capitol St. N.E., #135, Salem, OR 97301-3871
E-mail: Grace.Crunican@odot.state.or.us

Aeronautics Division

http://www.odot.state.or.us/aero
Main phone: (503) 378-4880
Main fax: (503) 373-1688
Toll free: (800) 874-0102

Ann B. Crook, Manager (Interim)
3040 25th St. S.E., Salem, OR 97302-1125
(503) 378-8689, ext. 226
E-mail: ann.b.crook@dot.state.or.us

Driver and Motor Vehicle Services

http://www.odot.state.or.us/dmv/index.htm
Main phone: (503) 945-5000
Main fax: (503) 945-5254
TTY: (503) 945-5001

William Seely, Deputy
1905 Lana Ave. N.E., Salem, OR 97314
(503) 945-5100

Travel Information Council

Main phone: (503) 378-4508
Main fax: (503) 378-6282
Toll free: (800) 574-9397

Cheryl Gribskov, Director
229 Medrona Ave. S.E., Salem, OR 97302
(503) 373-1042
E-mail: cheryl@ncn.com

University System of Oregon

http://www.ous.edu
Main phone: (541) 346-5700
Main fax: (541) 346-5764
TTY: (541) 346-5741
Mailing address: P.O. Box 3175, Eugene, OR 97403

Joseph W. Cox, Chancellor
1431 Johnson Lane, Eugene, OR 97403
E-mail: joseph_cox@ous.edu

Veterans Affairs Dept.

http://www.odva.state.or.us
Main phone: (503) 373-2000
Main fax: (503) 373-2362
TTY: (503) 373-2217

Jon A. Mangis, Director
700 Summer St. N.E., Salem, OR 97310
(503) 373-2388
E-mail: mangisj@odva.state.or.us

Boards and Licensing

Accountancy, (503) 378-4181,
http://www.boa.state.or.us
Architects, (503) 378-4270,
http://www.architect-board.state.or.us
Child Care, (503) 947-1400
Construction and Landscape Contractors,
(503) 378-4621, http://www.ccb.state.or.us
Cosmetology, (503) 378-8667,
http://www.hdlp.hr.state.or.us/bhhome.htm
Engineers and Land Surveyors, (503) 362-2666, http://www.osbeels.org
Medical Examiners, (503) 229-5770
Nursing, (503) 731-4745,
http://www.osbn.state.or.us
Pharmacy, (503) 731-4032
Real Estate, (503) 373-1505,
http://www.cbs.state.or.us/aclb

Water Resources Dept.
http://www.wrd.state.or.us/
Main phone: (503) 378-3739
Main fax: (503) 378-2496

Martha O. Pagel, Director
Commerce Bldg., 158 12th St. N.E., Salem, OR 97310
(503) 378-2982

Women's Commission
Main phone: (503) 725-5889
Main fax: (503) 725-8152

Tracy Davies, Executive Director
Smith Center, Portland State University, #M-315,
Portland, OR 97207

Workers' Compensation Board
Main phone: (503) 378-3308
Main fax: (503) 373-1684

Maureen Bock, Chair
2601 25th St. S.E., #150, Salem, OR 97302-1282
E-mail: maureen.bock@state.or.us

Laws

Sales tax: None
Income tax: 9%
State minimum wage: $6.50 (Federal is $5.15)
Marriage age: 18
First-cousin marriage: Prohibited
Drinking age: 21
State control of liquor sales: Yes
Blood alcohol for DWI: 0.08%
Driving age: 17
Speed limit: 65 mph
Permit to buy handguns: No
Minimum age to possess handguns: 18
Minimum age to possess rifles, shotguns:
   None
State lottery: Yes; also Powerball
Casinos: Yes (tribal); also slot/video machines
Pari-mutuel betting: Horse and dog racing
Death penalty: Yes
3 strikes minimum sentence: None
Hate crimes law: Yes
Gay employment non-discrimination: No
Official language(s): None
Term limits: Governor (8 yrs.); state senate (8
   yrs.), house (6 yrs.)

*State laws are complex and subject to
change; this information is not intended as
legal advice. For an explanation of this
information, see p. x.*

Youth Authority
http://www.oya.state.or.us
General e-mail: oya.info@state.or.us
Main phone: (503) 373-7205

Rick Hill, Director
530 Center St. N.E., #200, Salem, OR 97301

Oregon Legislature

State Capitol
Salem, OR 97310
General information: (503) 986-1187
Fax: (503) 373-1527
Bill status: (503) 986-1180
http://www.leg.state.or.us

Senate
General information: (503) 986-1851
Fax: (503) 986-1132

Brady Adams (R), President
State Capitol, #S-203, Salem, OR 97310
(503) 986-1600
E-mail: brady.adams@state.or.us
http://landru.leg.state.or.us/senpres/

Randy Miller (R), President Pro Tempore
State Capitol, #S-211, Salem, OR 97310
(503) 986-1713
E-mail: rm13@teleport.com
http://www.leg.state.or.us/miller

Eugene (Gene) Derfler (R), Majority Leader
State Capitol, #S-223, Salem, OR 97310
(503) 986-1950
E-mail: senaterepublican@state.or.us
http://www.leg.state.or.us/derfler

**Eileen Qutub (R), Majority Whip and Assistant
   Majority Leader**
State Capitol, #S-210, Salem, OR 97310
(503) 986-1704
E-mail: qutub.sen@state.or.us
http://www.leg.state.or.us/qutub

Kate Brown (D), Democratic Leader
State Capitol, #S-323, Salem, OR 97310
(503) 986-1700
http://www.leg.state.or.us/brown

Tony Corcoran (D), Minority Whip
State Capitol, #S-314, Salem, OR 97310
(503) 986-1722
E-mail: tonycorcoran@compuserve.com
http://www.leg.state.or.us/corcoran

Judy Hall, Secretary
State Capitol, #233, Salem, OR 97310
(503) 986-1851; *Fax:* (503) 986-1132

E-mail: judy.m.hall@state.or.us
http://www.leg.state.or.us/secsen.htm

House
General information: (503) 986-1870
Fax: (503) 986-1876

Lynn Snodgrass (R), Speaker of the House
State Capitol, #269, Salem, OR 97310
(503) 986-1200; *Fax:* (503) 986-1201
E-mail: snodgrass.rep@state.or.us
http://www.leg.state.or.us/speaker.htm
Steve Harper (R), Majority Leader
State Capitol, #H-295, Salem, OR 97310
(503) 986-1400
E-mail: harper.rep@state.or.us
http://www.leg.state.or.us/majority.htm
Mark Simmons (R), Majority Whip
State Capitol, #H-292, Salem, OR 97310
(503) 986-1458; *Fax:* (503) 986-1347
E-mail: simmons.rep@state.or.us
http://www.leg.state.or.us/simmons/
Kitty Piercy (D), Democratic Leader
State Capitol, #H-395, Salem, OR 97310
(503) 986-1900
E-mail: RepPiercy@aol.com
http://www.leg.state.or.us/democrat.htm
Ramona Kenady, Chief Clerk
State Capitol, #H-271, Salem, OR 97310
(503) 986-1870; *Fax:* (503) 986-1876
E-mail: ramona.kenady@state.or.us
http://www.leg.state.or.us/clerk.htm

Oregon Judiciary
1163 State St.
Salem, OR 97310
http://www.publications.ojd.state.or.us

Supreme Court
http://www.publications.ojd.state.or.us/supreme.htm

Scott C. Crampton, Director, Management Services
1163 State St., Salem, OR 97310
(503) 986-5555; *Fax:* (503) 986-5560
E-mail: scott.c.crampton@state.or.us

Justices
Composition: 7 justices
Selection Method: nonpartisan election;
  vacancies filled by gubernatorial appointment;
  appointees serve until next general election
Length of term: 6 years

Wallace P. Carson Jr., Chief Justice, (503) 986-5700
Robert D. Durham, Justice, (503) 986-5725
W. Robert Gillette, Justice, (503) 986-5705
Theodore R. Kulongoski, Justice, (503) 986-5717
Susan M. Leeson, Justice, (503) 986-5713
R. William Riggs, Justice, (503) 986-5668
George Van Hoomissen, Justice, (503) 986-5709

State Court Administrator
Main phone: (503) 986-5900
Main fax: (503) 986-5503

Kingsley W. Click, State Court Administrator
1163 State St., Salem, OR 97310
E-mail: kingsley.click@ojd.state.or.us

Supreme Court Library
Main phone: (503) 986-5640
Main fax: (503) 986-5623

Joe Stephens, Librarian
1163 State St., Salem, OR 97310

Legislative and Political Party Information Resources

Senate home page: http://www.leg.state.or.us/senate.html
House home page: http://www.leg.state.or.us/house.html
Committees: http://www.leg.state.or.us/comm/comm.html
Legislative process: http://www.leg.state.or.us/process.html
Budget: http://www.leg.state.or.us/comm/budg_tax.htm
Oregon Democratic Party: http://www.dpo.org
  4445 S.W. Barbur Blvd., #105, Portland, OR 97201; *Phone:* (503) 224-8200; *Fax:* (503) 224-5335
Oregon Republican Party: http://www.orgop.org
  P.O. Box 789, Salem, OR 97308-0789; *Phone:* (503) 587-9233; *E-mail:* info@orgop.org

Pennsylvania

State Capitol
Harrisburg, PA 17120
Public information: (717) 787-2121
Fax: (717) 783-0584
http://www.state.pa.us

Office of the Governor
http://www.state.pa.us/PA_Exec/Governor/
  overview.html
General e-mail: governor@state.pa.us
Main phone: (717) 787-2500
Main fax: (717) 772-8284
Toll free: (800) 932-0784

Thomas J. Ridge (R), Governor
Main Capitol Bldg., #225, Harrisburg, PA 17120

Mark A. Holman, Chief of Staff
Main Capitol Bldg., #225, Harrisburg, PA 17120
(717) 787-2500; *Fax:* (717) 772-8284

**Tim Reeves, Press Secretary and Communications
  Director**
Main Capitol Bldg., #308, Harrisburg, PA 17120
(717) 783-1116; *Fax:* (717) 772-8462
E-mail: treeves@state.pa.us

Rebecca Halkias, Director, Washington Office
444 N. Capitol St. N.W., #700, Washington, DC 20001
(202) 624-7828; *Fax:* (202) 624-7831

Office of the Lieutenant Governor
http://www.state.pa.us/PA_Exec/
  Lieutenant_Governor/
General e-mail: lieutenant-governor@state.pa.us
Main phone: (717) 787-3300
Main fax: (717) 783-0150

Mark S. Schweiker (R), Lieutenant Governor
Main Capitol Bldg., #200, Harrisburg, PA 17120

Office of the Secretary of the Commonwealth
http://www.dos.state.pa.us/
Main phone: (717) 787-6458
Main fax: (717) 787-1734

Kim Pizzingrilli, Secretary of the Commonwealth
North Office Bldg., #302, Harrisburg, PA 17120

Office of the Attorney General
http://www.attorneygeneral.gov
Main phone: (717) 787-3391
Main fax: (717) 787-8242

D. Michael Fisher (R), Attorney General
Strawberry Square, 16th Fl., Harrisburg, PA 17120

State of Pennsylvania

Capital: Harrisburg,
  since 1812
Founded: 1681, as British colony
Statehood: December 12, 1787 (2nd state)
Constitution adopted: 1968
Area: 44,820 sq. mi. (ranks 32nd)
Population: 12,001,451 (1998 est.; ranks 6th)
Largest cities: (1998 est.) Philadelphia
  (1,436,287); Pittsburgh (340,520); Erie
  (102,640); Allentown (100,757); Scranton
  (74,683)
Counties: 67, Most populous: (1998 est.)
  Philadelphia (1,436,287); Allegheny
  (1,268,446); Montgomery (719,718); Bucks
  (587,942); Delaware (542,593)
U.S. Congress: Rick Santorum (R), Arlen
  Specter (R); 21 Representatives
Nickname(s): Keystone State
Motto: Virtue, liberty, and independence
Song: "Pennsylvania"
Bird: Ruffed grouse
Tree: Hemlock
Flower: Mountain laurel
State fair: at Harrisburg, mid-Jan.
Former capital(s): Philadelphia, Lancaster

Office of the Treasury
http://www.treasury.state.pa.us
General e-mail: patreas@libertynet.org
Main phone: (717) 787-2991
Main fax: (717) 772-4234
TTY: (800) 440-4000

Barbara Hafer (R), State Treasurer
Finance Bldg., #129, Harrisburg, PA 17120
(717) 787-2465
E-mail: bhafer@libertynet.org

Office of the Auditor General
http://www.auditorgen.state.pa.us
General e-mail:
  auditorgen@auditorgen.state.pa.us
Main phone: (717) 787-2543
Main fax: (717) 783-4407

Robert P. Casey Jr. (D), Auditor General
Finance Bldg., #229, Harrisburg, PA 17120-0018

Military Affairs Dept.

http://www.dmva.state.pa.us
General e-mail: tagpa@pa-arng.ngb.army.mil
Main phone: (717) 861-8572
Main fax: (717) 861-8481
TTY: (800) 645-8924

William B. Lynch, Adjutant General
Bldg. S-O-47, Fort Indiantown Gap, Annville, PA
17003-5002
(717) 861-8500
E-mail: lynchwb@pa-arng.ngb.army.mil

Agencies

Accountancy Board

http://www.dos.state.pa.us/bpoa/accbd.htm
General e-mail: accounta@pados.dos.state.pa.us
Main phone: (717) 783-1404
Main fax: (717) 705-5540
Mailing address: P.O. Box 2649, Harrisburg, PA
17105-2649

Thomas J. Baumgartner, Chair
124 Pine St., Harrisburg, PA 17101

Administration Office

http://www.oa.state.pa.us
Main phone: (717) 787-9945
Main fax: (717) 783-7374

Thomas G. Paese, Secretary
207 Finance Bldg., Harrisburg, PA 17120
E-mail: tpaese@state.pa.us

Personnel Bureau
Main phone: (717) 787-5545
Main fax: (717) 783-4429

Charles T. Sciotto, Director
517 Finance Bldg., Harrisburg, PA 17120
E-mail: c.sciotto@state.pa.us

Aging Dept.

http://www.aging.state.pa.us
Main phone: (717) 783-1550
Main fax: (717) 783-6842

Richard Browdie, Secretary
555 Walnut St., 5th Fl., Harrisburg, PA 17101-1919
Fax: (717) 772-3382
E-mail: rbrowdie@state.pa.us

Agriculture Dept.

http://www.pda.state.pa.us
General e-mail: skauffman@state.pa.us
Main phone: (717) 772-2853
Main fax: (717) 785-9709

Samuel E. Hayes Jr., Secretary
2301 N. Cameron St., Harrisburg, PA 17110

Architects Licensure Board

General e-mail: architec@pados.dos.state.pa.us
Main phone: (717) 783-3397
Main fax: (717) 705-5540
Mailing address: P.O. Box 2649, Harrisburg, PA
17105-2649

Robert J. Crowner, President
124 Pine St., Harrisburg, PA 17101

Arts Council

Main phone: (717) 787-3028

Philip Horn Jr., Executive Director
216 Finance Bldg., Harrisburg, PA 17120

Banking Dept.

http://www.banking.state.pa.us
General e-mail: pabanking@state.pa.us
Main phone: (717) 787-2665
Main fax: (717) 787-8773
Toll free: (800) PABanks
TTY: (800) 679-5070

David E. Zuern, Secretary
333 Market St., 16th Fl., Harrisburg, PA 17101-2290
(717) 787-6991
E-mail: dzuern@banking.state.pa.us

Board of Education

General e-mail: oostatbd@psupen.psu.edu
Main phone: (717) 787-3787
Main fax: (717) 787-7306
TTY: (717) 783-8445

Peter H. Garland, Executive Director
333 Market St., Harrisburg, PA 17126-0333

Budget Office

http://www.state.pa.us/PA_Exec/Budget
General e-mail: cmoyer@state.pa.us
Main phone: (717) 787-4472
Main fax: (717) 787-4590

Robert A. Bittenbender, Secretary
Main Capitol Bldg., #238, Harrisburg, PA 17120

Civil Rights Enforcement Section

http://www.attorneygeneral.gov/ppd/civilrights/
index.htm
General e-mail: civilrights@attorneygeneral.gov
Main phone: (717) 787-0822
Main fax: (717) 787-1190

Trent Hargrove, Chief Deputy Attorney General
Strawberry Square, 14th Fl., Harrisburg, PA 17120

Civil Service Commission

http://www.scsc.state.pa.us
Main phone: (717) 783-3058
Main fax: (717) 787-8650
TTY: (717) 772-2685

Mailing address: P.O. Box 569, Harrisburg, PA
17108-0569

Norma J. Gotwalt, Chair
320 Market St., 4th Fl., Harrisburg, PA 17108-0569
(717) 783-8806
E-mail: n.gotwalt@scsc.state.pa.us

Claims Board
http://www.boc.state.pa.us
General e-mail: webmaster@boc.state.pa.us
Main phone: (717) 787-3325
Main fax: (717) 787-0415

**David C. Clipper, Chair and Chief Administrative
Judge**
Fulton Bldg., 200 N. 3rd St., #700, Harrisburg, PA
17101-1501

Community and Economic Development Dept.
http://www.dced.state.pa.us
Main phone: (717) 787-3003
Main fax: (717) 787-6866
Toll free: (800) 379-7448

Samuel A. McCullough, Secretary
Forum Bldg., #433, Harrisburg, PA 17120
E-mail: sam_mccullough@dced.state.pa.us

Higher Educational Institutions

Bloomsburg University
http://www.bloomu.edu
400 E. 2nd St., Bloomsburg, PA 17815-1301
Main phone: (570) 389-4316

California University of Pennsylvanina
http://www.cup.edu
250 University Ave., California, PA 15419-1394
Main phone: (724) 938-4000

Clarion University of Pennsylvania
http://www.clarion.edu
840 Wood St., Clarion, PA 16214
Main phone: (814) 226-2306

East Stroudsburg University
http://www.esu.edu
200 Prospect St., E. Stroudsburg, PA 18301-2999
Main phone: (570) 422-3211

Edinboro University of Pennsylvania
http://www.edinboro.edu
Biggers House, Edinboro, PA 16444
Main phone: (814) 732-2761

Indiana University of Pennsylvania
http://www.iup.edu
201 Pratt Dr., Pratt Hall, Indiana, PA 15705-0001
Main phone: (724) 357-2230
Branches: Armstrong County Campus, Monroeville
Center for Graduate Studies, Punxsutawney Campus

Kutztown University
http://www.kutztown.edu
P.O. Box 730, Kutztown, PA 19530-0730
Main phone: (610) 683-4060, ext. 4053

Lincoln University
http://www.lincoln.edu
P.O. Box 179, Lincoln, PA 19352-0999
Main phone: (610) 932-8300

Lock Haven University of Pennsylvania
http://www.lhup.edu
N. Fairview St., Lock Haven, PA 17745-2390
Main phone: (570) 893-2011

Millersville University
http://www.millersv.edu
P.O. Box 1002, Millersville, PA 17551-0302
Main phone: (717) 872-3024

Pennsylvania State University
http://www.psu.edu
201 Old Main, University Park, PA 16802-1503
Main phone: (814) 863-0233
Branches: Abington, Altoona, Beaver, Berks, College
of Technology (Williamsport), Delaware County,
Dickinson School of Law (Carlisle), DuBois, Erie,
Fayette, Harrisburg, Harrisburg Downtown,
Harrisburg Eastgate, Hazleton, Lehigh Valley,
McKeesport, Mont Alto, New Kensington, Schuylkill,
Shenango, Wilkes-Barre, Worthington-Scranton, York

Shippensburg University
http://www.ship.edu
1871 Old Main Dr., Shippensburg, PA 17257
Main phone: (717) 477-9121

Slippery Rock University
http://www.sru.edu
Slippery Rock, PA 16057-1326
Main phone: (724) 738-2015

Temple University
http://www.temple.edu/temple
1801 N. Broad St., Philadelphia, PA 19122
Main phone: (215) 204-7000

University of Pittsburgh
http://www.pitt.edu
Bruce Hall, 2nd Fl., Pittsburgh, PA 15260
Main phone: (412) 624-4141
Branches: Bradford, Greensburg, Johnstown,
Titusville

West Chester University
http://www.wcupa.edu
100 W. Rosedale Ave., West Chester, PA 19383
Main phone: (610) 436-3411

Tourism and Marketing Council
http://www.visit.state.pa.us
General e-mail: decdtravel@dced.state.pc.us
Main phone: (717) 787-5453
Main fax: (717) 787-0687
Toll free: (800) 237-4363

Barbara Chaffee, Deputy Secretary
404 Forum Bldg., Harrisburg, PA 17120
E-mail: barbara_chaffee@dced.state.pa.us

Conservation and Natural Resources Dept.
http://www.dcnr.state.pa.us
General e-mail: askdcnr@dcnr.state.pa.us
Main phone: (717) 787-2869
Main fax: (717) 772-9106
Mailing address: P.O. Box 8767, Harrisburg, PA 17105-8767

John C. Oliver, Secretary
Rachel Carson State Office Bldg., Harrisburg, PA 17105-8767
Fax: (717) 705-2832

Forestry Bureau
http://www.dcnr.state.pa.us/forestry
Main phone: (717) 787-2703
Main fax: (717) 783-5109
Mailing address: P.O. Box 8552, Harrisburg, PA 17105-8552

James R. Grace, State Forester
Rachel Carson State Office Bldg., 400 Market St., 6th Fl., Harrisburg, PA 17101-2301

State Parks Bureau
http://www.dcnr.state.pa.us/stateparks/index.htm
Main phone: (717) 787-6640
Toll free: (888) PA-PARKS
Mailing address: P.O. Box 8551, Harrisburg, PA 17105

Roger Fickes, Director
Rachel Carson State Office Bldg., Harrisburg, PA 17105
E-mail: rfickes@dcnr.state.pa.us

Topographic and Geologic Survey Bureau
http://www.dcnr.state.pa.us/topogeo
Main phone: (717) 787-2169
Main fax: (717) 783-7267
Mailing address: P.O. Box 8453, Harrisburg, PA 17105

Donald Hoskins, Director
1500 N. 3rd St., 2nd Fl., Harrisburg, PA 17105
(717) 783-7251
E-mail: dhoskins@dcnr.state.pa.us

Consumer Protection Bureau
http://www.attorneygeneral.gov/ppd/bcp/index.htm

General e-mail: consumers@attorneygeneral.gov
Main phone: (717) 787-9707
Main fax: (717) 787-1190
Toll free: (800) 441-2555

Frank T. Donaghue, Director
Strawberry Square, 14th Fl., Harrisburg, PA 17120
E-mail: fdonaghue@attorneygeneral.gov

Corrections Dept.
http://www.cor.state.pa.us
Main phone: (717) 975-4860
Main fax: (717) 787-0132
Mailing address: P.O. Box 598, Camp Hill, PA 17001-0598

Martin F. Horn, Secretary
2520 Lisburn Rd., 3rd Fl., Camp Hill, PA 17001
(717) 975-4918
E-mail: mhorn@cor.state.pa.us

Cosmetology Board
http://www.dos.state.pa.us/bpoa/cosbd.htm
General e-mail: cosmetol@pados.dos.state.pa.us
Main phone: (717) 783-7130
Main fax: (717) 705-5540
Mailing address: P.O. Box 2649, Harrisburg, PA 17105-2649

Carol T. Micciche, Chair
124 Pine St., Harrisburg, PA 17101

Criminal Law Division
http://www.attorneygeneral.gov/cld/
Main phone: (717) 787-2100
Main fax: (717) 783-5431
Toll free: (800) 441-2555

William H. Ryan Jr., Executive Deputy Attorney General
Strawberry Square, 16th Fl., Harrisburg, PA 17120
E-mail: wryan@attorneygeneral.gov

Education Dept.
http://www.cas.psu.edu/pde.html
Main phone: (717) 783-6788
Main fax: (717) 783-9348
TTY: (717) 783-8445

Eugene W. Hickok, Secretary
333 Market St., 10th Fl., Harrisburg, PA 17126-0333
(717) 787-5820; *Fax:* (717) 787-7222
E-mail: 00SEC@psupen.psu.edu

Commonwealth Libraries: State Library
http://www.state.library.state.pa.us
General e-mail: ali@unix1.stlib.state.pa.us
Main phone: (717) 783-5968
Main fax: (717) 783-2070
TTY: (717) 772-2863

Mailing address: P.O. Box 1601, Harrisburg, PA 17105

Gary D. Wolfe, State Librarian
Forum Bldg., #200, Harrisburg, PA 17105
(717) 787-2646; *Fax:* (717) 772-3265

Emergency Management Agency
http://www.pema.state.pa.us
Main phone: (717) 651-2001
Main fax: (717) 651-2024
Toll free: (800) 424-7362
Mailing address: P.O. Box 3321, Harrisburg, PA 17105-3321

David L. Smith, Director
2605 Interstate Dr., 3rd Fl., Harrisburg, PA 17120
(717) 651-2007; *Fax:* (717) 651-2040
E-mail: davesmith@state.pa.us

State Fire Commissioner's Office
http://www.state.pa.us/PA_Exec/ofsc/index.htm
General e-mail: fire@pema.state.pa.us
Main phone: (717) 651-2201
Main fax: (717) 651-2210
Mailing address: P.O. Box 3321, Harrisburg, PA 17105

Vacant, State Fire Commissioner
2605 Interstate Dr., Harrisburg, PA 17110

Engineers, Land Surveyors, and Geologists
http://www.dos.state.pa.us/bpoa/engbd.htm
General e-mail: engineer@pados.dos.state.pa.us
Main phone: (717) 783-7049
Main fax: (717) 705-5540
Mailing address: P.O. Box 2649, Harrisburg, PA 17105-2649

Louis A. Guzzi, President-elect
124 Pine St., Harrisburg, PA 17101

Environmental Protection Dept.
http://www.dep.state.pa.us
General e-mail: depinfo@dep.state.pa.us
Main phone: (717) 783-2300
Main fax: (717) 705-4980
TTY: (800) 654-5984
Mailing address: P.O. Box 2063, Harrisburg, PA 17105-2063

James M. Seif, Secretary
Rachel Carson State Office Bldg., 400 Market St., Harrisburg, PA 17101-2301
(717) 787-2814
E-mail: seif.james@dep.state.pa.us

Mineral Resources Management Office: Oil and Gas Management Bureau
http://www.dep.state.pa.us/dep/deputate/minres/oilgas/oilgas.htm

Main phone: (717) 772-2199
Main fax: (717) 772-2291
Mailing address: P.O. Box 8765, Harrisburg, PA 17105

James Erb, Director
Rachel Carson State Office Bldg., 5th Fl., Harrisburg, PA 17105
E-mail: erb.james@dep.state.pa.us

Water Management Office
http://www.dep.state.pa.us/dep/deputate/watermgt/watermgt.htm
Main phone: (717) 783-4693
Main fax: (717) 705-4087

Lawrence Tropea Jr., Deputy Secretary
Rachel Carson State Office Bldg., 400 Market St., Harrisburg, PA 17105
(717) 787-4686
E-mail: tropeajr.lawrence@dep.state.pa.us

Ethics Commission
http://www.ethics.state.pa.us
General e-mail: ethics@state.pa.us
Main phone: (717) 783-1610
Main fax: (717) 787-0806
Toll free: (800) 932-0936
Mailing address: P.O. Box 11470, Harrisburg, PA 17108-1470

Daneen E. Reese, Chair
309 Finance Bldg., Harrisburg, PA 17120
E-mail: dreese@state.pa.us

Fish and Boat Commission
http://www.fish.state.pa.us
Main phone: (717) 657-4518
Main fax: (717) 657-4443
Mailing address: P.O. Box 67000, Harrisburg, PA 17106-7000

Peter A. Colangelo, Executive Director
3532 Walnut St., Harrisburg, PA 17109
(717) 657-4515; *Fax:* (717) 657-4033
E-mail: p.colangelo@fish.state.pa.us

Game Commission
http://www.pgc.state.pa.us
Main phone: (717) 787-4250
Main fax: (717) 772-0502
TTY: (800) 654-5984

Vernon R. Ross, Executive Director
2001 Elmerton Ave., Harrisburg, PA 17110-9797
(717) 787-3633

General Services Dept.
http://www.dgs.state.pa.us
General e-mail: mlorigan@exec.gsinc.state.pa.us
Main phone: (717) 787-5996

Main fax: (717) 772-2026
TTY: (800) 342-8040
Mailing address: P.O. Box 1365, Harrisburg, PA
  17105-1365

Gary E. Crowell, Secretary
North Office Bldg., #515, Harrisburg, PA 17120
E-mail: DGSSecretary@exec.gsinc.state.pa.us

Health Care Cost Containment Council
http://www.phc4.org
Main phone: (717) 232-6787
Main fax: (717) 232-3821

Marc Volavka, Executive Director
225 Market St., #400, Harrisburg, PA 17101
E-mail: mvolavka@phc4.org

Health Dept.
http://www.health.state.pa.us
General e-mail: webmaster@health.state.pa.us
Main phone: (717) 787-6436
Main fax: (717) 772-6959
TTY: (717) 783-6514
Mailing address: P.O. Box 90, Harrisburg, PA
  17108

Robert S. Zimmerman, Secretary (Acting)
7th and Forster St., Box 90, Harrisburg, PA 17108
Fax: (717) 787-0111
E-mail: r.zimmerm@health.state.pa.us

Higher Education Assistance Agency
http://www.pheaa.org
Main phone: (717) 720-2860
Main fax: (717) 720-3902
Toll free: (800) 692-7392
TTY: (717) 720-2366

**Michael H. Hershock, President and Chief Executive
Officer**
1200 N. 7th St., Harrisburg, PA 17102-1444
(717) 720-2867
E-mail: mherschoc@pheaa.org

Higher Educational Facilities Authority
Main phone: (717) 975-2200
Main fax: (717) 975-2215
Mailing address: P.O. Box 990, Camp Hill, PA
  17001-0990

Nicholas B. Moehlmann, Executive Director
1035 Mumma Rd., Wormleysburg, PA 17043
(717) 975-2201
E-mail: nmoehlma@spsba.org

Historical and Museum Commission
http://www.phmc.state.pa.us
Main phone: (717) 787-3362
Main fax: (717) 783-2839
Mailing address: Box 1026, Harrisburg, PA 17108-
  1026

Brent D. Glass, Executive Director
3rd and North Sts., Harrisburg, PA 17108
(717) 787-2891; *Fax:* (717) 705-0482
E-mail: b.glass@phmc.state.pa.us

Archives and History Bureau
http://www.state.pa.us/PA_Exec/
  Historical_Museum/bah.htm
Main phone: (717) 787-3051
Main fax: (717) 787-4822
TTY: (800) 654-5984
Mailing address: P.O. Box 1026, Harrisburg, PA
  17108

Frank Suran, Director
3rd and Foster Sts., Harrisburg, PA 17108
(717) 783-9872

Housing Finance Agency
http://www.phfa.org
General e-mail: bbailey@phfa.org
Main phone: (717) 780-3800
Main fax: (717) 780-3905
TTY: (800) 346-3597
Mailing address: P.O. Box 8029, Harrisburg, PA
  17105-8029

Frequently Called Numbers

Tourism: (717) 787-5453, 1-800-237-4363;
  http://www.visit.state.pa.us
Library: (717) 783-5968;
  http://www.state.library.state.pa.us
Board of Education: (717) 787-3787
Vital Statistics: (724) 656-3100;
  http://www.health.stte.pa.us/hpa/
Tax/Revenue: (717) 783-3682;
  http://www.revenue.state.pa.us
Motor Vehicles: (717) 391-6190, 1-800-932-
  4600; http://www.dmv.state.pa.us/home/
  index.asp
State Police/Highway Patrol: (717) 783-5558
Unemployment: (717) 787-3907; http://
  www.li.state.pa.us/ucb/bucba/index.html
General Election Information: (717)
  787-5280; http://www.dos.state.pa.us/
  election/election_night.htm
Consumer Affairs: (717) 787-9707,
  1-800-441-2555; http://
  www.attorneygeneral.gov/ppd/bcp/index.htm
Hazardous Materials: (717) 787-6239;
  http://www.dep.state.pa.us/dep/deputate/
  airwaste/wm/HW/HW.htm

William C. Bostic, Executive Director
Bldg. 2, 2101 N. Front St., Harrisburg, PA 17105-8029
(717) 780-3911
E-mail: wbostic@phfa.org

Human Relations Commission
Main phone: (717) 787-4412
Main fax: (717) 787-4087
TTY: (717) 783-9308
Mailing address: P.O. Box 3145, Harrisburg, PA
17105-3105

Homer C. Floyd, Executive Director
101 S. 2nd St., Box 3145, #300, Harrisburg, PA 17101
(717) 783-8266; *Fax:* (717) 787-0420

Inspector General
General e-mail: pafraud@oig.state.pa.us
Main phone: (717) 787-6835
Main fax: (717) 787-7291

Nicolette Parisi, Inspector General
333 Market St., 9th Fl., Harrisburg, PA 17126-0333
Fax: (717) 787-7923

Insurance Dept.
http://www.insurance.state.pa
Main phone: (717) 787-5173
Main fax: (717) 772-1969
Toll free: (877) 881-6388

M. Diane Koken, Commissioner
1326 Strawberry Square, Harrisburg, PA 17120
(717) 783-0442
E-mail: dkoken@ins.state.pa.us

Labor and Industry Dept.
http://www.li.state.pa.us
Main phone: (717) 787-5279
Main fax: (717) 787-8826

Johnny J. Butler, Secretary
Labor and Industry Bldg., 7th and Forster Sts., #1700,
Harrisburg, PA 17120
(717) 787-3756
E-mail: jbutler@dli.state.pa.us

Workers Compensation Bureau
http://www.li.state.pa.us/bwc/index.html
Main phone: (717) 783-5421
Toll free: (800) 482-2383
TTY: (800) 362-4228

Richard A. Himler, Director
1171 S. Cameron St., #324, Harrisburg, PA 17104-2501

Liquor Control Board
Main phone: (717) 783-7637
Main fax: (717) 772-3714
TTY: (717) 772-3725

John E. Jones III, Chair
Northwest Office Bldg., Harrisburg, PA 17124-0001
(717) 787-5230

Medicine Board
http://www.dos.state.pa.us/bpoa/medbd.htm
General e-mail: medicine@pados.dos.state.pa.us
Main phone: (717) 783-1400
Main fax: (717) 787-7769
Mailing address: P.O. Box 2649, Harrisburg, PA
17105-2649

Daniel B. Kimball Jr., Chair
124 Pine St., Harrisburg, PA 17101

Milk Marketing Board
http://www.state.pa.us/PA_Exec/Milk
General e-mail: mmb@sdl.pa.state.pa.us
Main phone: (717) 787-4194
Main fax: (717) 783-6492

Beverly R. Minor, Chair
Agriculture Bldg., 2301 N. Cameron St., #110,
Harrisburg, PA 17110-9408

Municipal Retirement System
General e-mail: staff@pmrs.state.pa.us
Main phone: (717) 787-2065
Main fax: (717) 783-8363
Toll free: (800) 622-7468
Mailing address: P.O. Box 1165, Harrisburg, PA
17108-1165

James B. Allen, Secretary
1010 N. 7th St., Eastgate Center, #301, Harrisburg, PA
17102
E-mail: jallen@pmrs.state.pa.us

Nursing Board
http://www.dos.state.pa.us/bpoa.nurbd.htm
General e-mail: nursing@pados.dos.state.pa.us
Main phone: (717) 783-7142
Main fax: (717) 783-0822
Mailing address: P.O. Box 2649, Harrisburg, PA
17105-2649

M. Christine Alichnie, Chair
124 Pine St., Harrisburg, PA 17101

Pharmacy Board
http://www.dos.state.pa.us/bpoa/phabd.htm
General e-mail: pharmacy@pados.dos.state.pa.us
Main phone: (717) 783-7156
Main fax: (717) 787-7769
Mailing address: P.O. Box 2649, Harrisburg, PA
17105-2649

Frank A. Rubino, Chair
124 Pine St., Harrisburg, PA 17101

Port of Pittsburgh Commission
http://www.port.pittsburgh.pa.us
Main phone: (412) 201-7330
Main fax: (412) 201-7337
Toll free: (877) 609-9870

James McCarville, Executive Director
425 6th Ave., #2990, Pittsburgh, PA 15219-1819
(412) 201-7335
E-mail: jim@port.pittsburgh.pa.us

Probation and Parole Board
Main phone: (717) 787-5699
Main fax: (717) 772-2156
TTY: (717) 772-3521

William F. Ward, Chair
1101 S. Front St., #5100, Harrisburg, PA 17104
(717) 787-5100

Professional and Occupational Affairs Bureau
http://www.dos.state.pa.us/bpoa/poa.htm
Main phone: (717) 787-8503
Main fax: (717) 783-7769
Mailing address: P.O. Box 2649, Harrisburg, PA
17105-2649

Dorothy Childress, Commissioner
124 Pine St., 6th Fl., Harrisburg, PA 17101
(717) 783-7192; *Fax:* (717) 783-0510

Public School Building Authority
http://www.spsba.org
Main phone: (717) 975-2200
Main fax: (717) 975-2215
Mailing address: P.O. Box 990, Camp Hill, PA
17001-0990

Nicholas B. Moehlmann, Executive Director
1035 Mumma Rd., 2nd Fl., Wormleysburg, PA 17043-1147
(717) 975-2201
E-mail: n.moehlma@spsba.org

Public School Employees' Retirement System
http://www.psers.state.pa.us
General e-mail: contact@psers.state.pa.us
Main phone: (717) 787-8540
Main fax: (717) 772-5372
Toll free: (888) 773-7748
TTY: (717) 772-5379
Mailing address: P.O. Box 125, Harrisburg, PA
17108-0125

Dale H. Everhart, Executive Director
5 N. State St., Harrisburg, PA 17108
(717) 720-4749
E-mail: everhartdh@psers.state.pa.us

Public Television Network Commission
http://www.pptn.org

Main phone: (717) 533-6011
Main fax: (717) 533-4236
Mailing address: P.O. Box 397, Hershey, PA 17033

Louis Pollock, General Manager
24 Northeast Dr., Hershey, PA 17033
E-mail: lpollock@pptn.org

Public Utility Commission
Main phone: (717) 783-1740
Main fax: (717) 787-3437
Toll free: (800) 782-1110
TTY: (800) 654-5988
Mailing address: P.O. Box 3265, Harrisburg, PA
17105-3265

Barbara Bruin, Executive Director
North Office Bldg., Harrisburg, PA 17105-3265
(717) 783-5331

Public Welfare Dept.
http://www.dpw.state.pa.us/
Main phone: (717) 787-3423
Main fax: (717) 772-2490
TTY: (717) 705-5040
Mailing address: P.O. Box 2675, Harrisburg, PA
17105

Feather O. Houstoun, Secretary
Health and Welfare Bldg., Harrisburg, PA 17105
(717) 787-2600

Children, Youth, and Families Division
http://www.dpw.state.pa.us/ocyf/dpwocyf.asp
Main phone: (717) 783-3856
Main fax: (717) 705-0364
Mailing address: P.O. Box 2675, Harrisburg, PA
17107

Boards and Licensing

Accountancy, (717) 783-1404,
   http://www.dos.state.pa.us/bpoa/accbd.htm
Architects, (717) 783-3397
Child Care, (717) 787-8691
Cosmetology, (717) 783-7130,
   http://www.dos.state.pa.us/bpoa/cosbd.htm
Engineers, (717) 783-7049
Land Surveyors, (717) 783-3398
Medical Licensing, (717) 783-1400,
   http://www.dos.state.pa.us/bpoa/medbd.htm
Nursing, (717) 783-7142,
   http://www.dos.state.pa.us/bpoa.nurbd.htm
Pharmacy, (717) 783-7156,
   http://www.dos.state.pa.us/bpoa/phabd.htm
Real Estate, (717) 783-4866,
   http://www.dos.state.pa.us/bpoa.creabd.htm

Jo Ann Lawer, Deputy Secretary
Health and Welfare Bldg., #131, Harrisburg, PA
17105-2675
(717) 787-4756; *Fax:* (717) 787-0414

Medical Assistance Programs Office
Main phone: (717) 787-1870
Mailing address: P.O. Box 2675, Harrisburg, PA
17105

Peg J. Dierkers, Deputy Secretary
Health and Welfare Bldg., #515, Harrisburg, PA
17105

Mental Health and Substance Abuse Services
Main phone: (717) 787-6443
Main fax: (717) 787-5394
Mailing address: P.O. Box 2675, Harrisburg, PA
17105

Charles G. Curie, Deputy Secretary
Health and Welfare Bldg., #502, Harrisburg, PA
17105

Mental Retardation Office
Main phone: (717) 787-3700
Main fax: (717) 787-6583
Mailing address: P.O. Box 2675, Harrisburg, PA
17105

Nancy Thaler, Deputy Secretary
Health and Welfare Bldg., #512, Harrisburg, PA
17105
E-mail: nancyt@dpw.state.pa.us

Social Programs Office: Community Services Program for Persons with Physical Disabilities
http://www.dpw.state.pa.us/osp/ospcspppd.asp
Main phone: (717) 787-3438
Main fax: (717) 772-2093
Mailing address: P.O. Box 2675, Harrisburg, PA
17105

Helen Powers, Program Manager
1401 N. 7th St., 2nd Fl., Harrisburg, PA 17102
(717) 772-2094

Real Estate Appraisers Board
http://www.dos.state.pa.us/bpoa.creabd.htm
General e-mail: appraise@pados.dos.state.pa.us
Main phone: (717) 783-4866
Main fax: (717) 705-5540
Mailing address: P.O. Box 2649, Harrisburg, PA
17105-2649

David J. King, Chair
124 Pine St., Harrisburg, PA 17101

Revenue Dept.
http://www.revenue.state.pa.us

General e-mail: parev@revenue.state.pa.us
Main phone: (717) 783-3682
Main fax: (717) 787-3990
Toll free: (888) PATAXES
TTY: (800) 447-3020

Robert A. Judge Sr., Secretary
1133 Strawberry Square, 11th Fl., Harrisburg, PA
17128-1100
(717) 783-3680
E-mail: rjudge@revenue.state.pa.us

State Lottery
http://www.palottery.com
General e-mail: comments@lottery.state.pa.us
Main phone: (717) 986-4759
Main fax: (717) 986-4767

Albert Taylor, Executive Director (Acting)
2850 Turnpike Industrial Dr., Middletown, PA
17057

Securities Commission
http://www.psc.state.pa.us
General e-mail: pscwebma@state.pa.us
Main phone: (717) 787-8061
Main fax: (717) 783-5122
Toll free: (800) 600-0007
TTY: (800) 654-5984

Robert M. Lam, Chair
1010 N. 7th St., 2nd Fl., Harrisburg, PA 17102-1410
(717) 787-6828
E-mail: rlam@psc.state.pa.us

State Employees Retirement System
http://www.sers.state.pa.us
Main phone: (717) 787-6293
Main fax: (717) 783-7300
Toll free: (800) 633-5461
Mailing address: P.O. Box 1147, Harrisburg, PA
17108-1147

John Brosius, Executive Director
30 N. 3rd St., Harrisburg, PA 17101
(717) 787-5759

State Police
Main phone: (717) 783-5558
Main fax: (717) 787-2948

Paul J. Evanko, Commissioner
1800 Elmerton Ave., Harrisburg, PA 17110
(717) 772-6924

State System of Higher Education
http://www.sshe.chan.edu
General e-mail: bmorabit@sshe.chan.edu
Main phone: (717) 720-4000
Main fax: (717) 720-4011
TTY: (717) 720-7040

James H. McCormick, Chancellor
Dixon University Center, 2986 N. 2nd St., Harrisburg,
PA 17110
(717) 720-4010

Tax Equalization Board
http://www.steb.state.pa.us
General e-mail: support@steb.state.pa.us
Main phone: (717) 787-5950
Main fax: (717) 787-3860
TTY: (800) 462-1610
Mailing address: P.O. Box 909, Harrisburg, PA
17108-0909

Martha Bell Schoeninger, Chair
Fulton Bank Bldg., 200 N. 3rd St., 5th Fl., Harrisburg,
PA 17101
(717) 787-3936
E-mail: mschoeninger@steb.state.pa.us

Transportation Dept.
http://www.dot.state.pa.us
General e-mail: webmaster@dot.state.pa.us
Main phone: (717) 787-2838
Main fax: (717) 787-1738
TTY: (800) 228-0676

Bradley L. Mallory, Secretary
Forum Pl., 555 Walnut St., Harrisburg, PA 17101-1900

Aviation Bureau
http://www.dot.state.pa.us/penndot/aviation.nsf/
aviation+intro?readform
General e-mail: Webmaster@dot.state.pa.us
Main phone: (717) 705-1260
Main fax: (717) 705-1255

Bill Shaffer, Director
Forum Pl., 555 Walnut St., 8th Fl., Harrisburg, PA
17101-1900
(717) 705-1200
E-mail: shaffwi@dot.state.pa.us

Driver and Vehicle Services
http://www.dmv.state.pa.us/home/index.asp
General e-mail: answerperson@divdata.com
Main phone: (717) 391-6190
Main fax: (717) 705-1046
Toll free: (800) 932-4600
TTY: (800) 228-0676

Betty L. Serian, Deputy Secretary
Riverfront Office Center, 1101 S. Front St.,
Harrisburg, PA 17104-2516
(717) 787-3928

Turnpike Commission
http://www.paturnpike.com
General e-mail: ptccustsrv@paturnpike.com
Main phone: (717) 939-9551
Main fax: (717) 986-8760

Toll free: (800) 331-3414
TTY: (800) 331-3414
Mailing address: P.O. Box 67676, Harrisburg, PA
17106-7676

James F. Malone III, Chair
176 Kost Rd., Carlysle, PA 17013
(717) 939-9551, ext. 6340; *Fax:* (717) 986-9686

Women's Commission
Main phone: (717) 787-8128

Loida Esbri, Executive Director
205 Finance Bldg., Harrisburg, PA 17120

Pennsylvania Legislature
Capitol Bldg.
Harrisburg, PA 17120
General information: (717) 787-2342
http://www.legis.state.pa.us

Senate
Address: Capitol Bldg., Senate Post Office,
Harrisburg, PA 17120
General information: (717) 787-5920
Fax: (717) 772-2344

Mark S. Schweiker (R), President
Capitol Bldg., Senate Box 203051, #200, Harrisburg,
PA 17120
(717) 787-3300
E-mail: mschweik@pasen.gov
http://www.pasen.gov/officers/schweiker.html

Robert C. Jubelirer (R), President Pro Tempore
Capitol Bldg., Senate Box 203030, #292, Harrisburg,
PA 17120-3030
(717) 787-5490
E-mail: rjubelirir@pasen.gov
http://www.pasen.gov/members/districts/sd30/sd30/
html

F. Joseph Loeper (R), Majority Leader
Captiol Bldg., Senate Box 203026, #362, Harrisburg,
PA 17120-3026
(717) 787-1350
E-mail: jloeper@pasen.gov
http://www.pasen.gov/members/districts/sd26/
sd26.html

David J. Brightbill (R), Majority Whip
Capitol Bldg., Senate Box 203048, #337, Harrisburg,
PA 17120-3048
(717) 787-5708
E-mail: dbrightbill@pasen.gov
http://www.pasen.gov/members/districts/sd48/
sd48.html

Robert J. Mellow (D), Minority Leader
Capitol Bldg., Senate Box 203022, #535, Harrisburg,
PA 17120-3022
(717) 787-6481
E-mail: mellow@dem.pasen.gov
http://www.pasen.gov/members/districts/sd22/
sd22.html

Leonard J. Bodack (D), Minority Whip
Capitol Bldg., Senate Box #230038, #535, Harrisburg,
PA 17120-3038
(717) 787-6123
E-mail: bodack@dem.pasen.gov
http://www.pasen.gov/members/districts/sd38/
sd38.html

Mark R. Corrigan, Secretary
Captiol Bldg., Senate Box 203053, #462, Harrisburg,
PA 17120-3053
(717) 787-5920; *Fax:* (717) 772-2344
E-mail: secretary@os.pasen.gov
http://www.pasen.gov/officers/corrigan.html

Laws

Sales tax: 6%
Income tax: 2.8%
State minimum wage: $5.15 (Federal is $5.15)
Marriage age: 18
First-cousin marriage: Prohibited
Drinking age: 21
State control of liquor sales: Yes
Blood alcohol for DWI: 0.10%
Driving age: 17
Speed limit: 65 mph
Permit to buy handguns: No, but 2-day wait
Minimum age to possess handguns: 18
Minimum age to possess rifles, shotguns: 18
State lottery: Yes
Casinos: No
Pari-mutuel betting: Horse racing
Death penalty: Yes
3 strikes minimum sentence: 25 yrs. (3rd
  violent felony)
Hate crimes law: Yes
Gay employment non-discrimination: No
Official language(s): None
Term limits: None

*State laws are complex and subject to
change; this information is not intended as
legal advice. For an explanation of this
information, see p. x.*

House
Address: Capitol Bldg., House Box 202020,
Harrisburg, PA 17120-2020
General information: (717) 787-2372
Fax: (717) 787-4990

Matthew J. Ryan (R), Speaker of the House
Capitol Bldg., House Box 202020, #139, Harrisburg,
PA 17120-2020
(717) 787-4610; *Fax:* (717) 787-9404
http://www.house.state.pa.us/members/districts/168/
168.htm

John Michael Perzel (R), Majority Leader
Capitol Bldg., House Box 202020, #110, Harrisburg,
PA 17120-2020
(717) 787-2016; *Fax:* (717) 783-7225
http://www.house.state.pa.us/members/districts/172/
172.htm

Donald William Snyder (R), Majority Whip
Capitol Bldg., House Box 202020, #128, Harrisburg,
PA 17120-2020
(717) 787-4145; *Fax:* (717) 783-8657
http://www.house.state.pa.us/members/districts/134/
134.htm

H. William DeWeese (D), Democratic Leader
Capitol Bldg., House Box 202020, #423, Harrisburg,
PA 17120-2020
(717) 783-3797; *Fax:* (717) 772-3605
http://www.house.state.pa.us/members/districts/018/
018.htm

Michael R. Veon (D), Democratic Whip
Capitol Bldg., House Box 202020, #428, Harrisburg,
PA 17120-2020
(717) 787-1290; *Fax:* (717) 772-3074
http://www.house.state.pa.us/members/districts/014/
014.htm

Ted Mazia, Chief Clerk
Capitol Bldg., House Box 202020, #129, Harrisburg,
PA 17120-2020
(717) 787-2372; *Fax:* (717) 787-4990
http://www.house.state.pa.us/officers/chief_clerk.htm

Pennsylvania Judiciary

City Hall
Philadelphia, PA 19107
http://www.aopc.org/index.htm

Supreme Court
http://www.aopc.org/Index/Supreme/
indexSupreme.htm

**Charles W. Johns, Prothonotary of the Supreme
Court**
City Hall, #468, Philadelphia, PA 19107
(215) 560-6370; *Fax:* (215) 560-5972

Justices

Composition: 7 justices

Selection Method: partisan election; vacancies filled by gubernatorial appointment with consent of state senate; until next general election

Length of term: 10 years

John P. Flaherty, Chief Justice, (412) 565-5545
Ralph J. Cappy, Justice, (412) 565-2700
Ronald D. Castille, Justice, (215) 560-5663

Sandra S. Newman, Justice, (610) 832-1700
Russell M. Nigro, Justice, (215) 560-3082
Thomas G. Saylor, Justice, (717) 772-1599
Stephen A. Zappala, Justice, (412) 565-7594

Administrative Office of Pennsylvania Courts

http://www.aopc.org/Index/Aopc/IndexAOPC.htm

Main phone: (215) 560-6300

Main fax: (215) 560-6315

Zygmont Tines, Court Administrator (Acting)
1515 Market St., #1414, Philadelphia, PA 19102

Legislative and Political Party Information Resources

Senate home page: http://www.pasen.gov
House home page: http://www.house.state.pa.us
Committees: Senate: http://www.pasen.gov/standing_committees.html;
       House: http://www.house.state.pa.us/members/lists/comm.htm
Current session information: http://www.legis.state.pa.us/WU01/sessinfo.htm
Pennsylvania Democratic Party: http://www.padems.com
       510 N. 3rd St., Harrisburg, PA 17101; *Phone:* (717) 238-0914
Pennsylvania Republican Party: http://www.pagop.org
       112 State St., Harrisburg, PA 17101; *Phone:* (717) 234-4901

Rhode Island

State Capitol
Providence, RI 02903
Public information: (401) 222-2000
Fax: (401) 222-4262
http://www.state.ri.us

State of Rhode Island and Providence Plantations

Capital: Providence, since 1636
Founded: 1636, as offshoot of Massachusetts Bay
Statehood: May 29, 1790 (13th state)
Constitution adopted: 1843
Area: 1,045 sq. mi. (ranks 50th)
Population: 988,480 (1998 est.; ranks 43rd)
Largest cities: (1998 est.) Providence (150,890); Warwick (84,094); Cranston (74,521); Pawtucket (68,169); East Providence (47,882)
Counties: 5, Most populous: (1998 est.) Providence (574,038); Kent (161,811); Washington (120,649); Newport (82,868); Bristol (49,114)
U.S. Congress: Jack Reed (D), Lincoln Chafee (R); 2 Representatives
Nickname(s): Ocean State
Motto: Hope
Song: "Rhode Island"
Bird: Rhode Island red
Tree: Red maple
Flower: Violet
State fair: at Richmond, mid-Aug.
Former capital(s): Newport (co-capital with Providence)

Office of the Governor
http://www.gov.state.ri.us
General e-mail: riedc@riedc.com
Main phone: (401) 222-2080
Main fax: (401) 273-5729

Lincoln C. Almond (R), Governor
State House, Providence, RI 02903
(401) 222-2080, ext. 603
E-mail: rigov@gov.state.ri.us

Michael DiBiase, Chief of Staff
State House, Providence, RI 02903
(401) 222-2080, ext. 603; *Fax:* (401) 273-5729

Lisa Pelosi, Communications Director
State House, Providence, RI 02903
(401) 222-2080, ext. 203; *Fax:* (401) 273-5729

Armeather Gibbs, Community Relations, Constituent Affairs, and Municipal Affairs Director
State House, #112, Providence, RI 02903
(401) 222-2080, ext. 299; *Fax:* (401) 273-5301

Samuel S. Reid, Director, Washington Office
444 N. Capitol St. N.W., #619, Washington, DC 20001
(202) 624-3605; *Fax:* (202) 624-3607

Office of the Lieutenant Governor
http://www.ltgov.state.ri.us
General e-mail: ltgov@state.ri.us
Main phone: (401) 222-2371
Main fax: (401) 222-2012

Charles J. Fogarty (D), Lieutenant Governor
State House, #116, Providence, RI 02903

Office of the Secretary of State
http://www.sec.state.ri.us
General e-mail: comments@sec.state.ri.us
Main phone: (401) 222-2357
Main fax: (401) 222-1356
TTY: (401) 222-2311

James R. Langevin (D), Secretary of State
State House, #220, Providence, RI 02903-1105
E-mail: jlangevin@sec.state.ri.us

Office of the Attorney General
http://www.riag.state.ri.us

General e-mail: contactus@riag.state.ri.us
Main phone: (401) 274-4400
Main fax: (401) 222-1331
Toll free: (800) 852-7776
TTY: (401) 453-0410

Sheldon Whitehouse (D), Attorney General
150 S. Main St., Providence, RI 02903-2856
(401) 274-4400, ext. 2339; *Fax:* (401) 222-1302

Office of the General Treasurer
http://www.state.ri.us/treas/treas.htm
General e-mail: treasury@treasury.state.ri.us
Main phone: (401) 222-2397
Main fax: (401) 222-6140

Paul J. Tavares (D), General Treasurer
State House, #102, Providence, RI 02903

Office of the Auditor General
Main phone: (401) 222-2435
Main fax: (401) 222-2111

Ernst A. Almonte, Auditor General
1145 Main St., Pawtucket, RI 02860-4807
E-mail: ealmonte@oag.state.ri.us

Office of the Adjutant General
http://www.ri.guard.com
General e-mail: tagri@ri-ngnet.army.mil
Main phone: (401) 457-4102
Main fax: (401) 457-4338

Reginald A. Centracchio, Adjutant General
645 New London Ave., Cranston, RI 02920-3097

Agencies

Administration Dept.
http://www.info.state.ri.us
Main phone: (401) 222-2000
TTY: (401) 222-1228

Robert L. Carl Jr., Director
1 Capitol Hill, Providence, RI 02908-5890
(401) 222-2280
E-mail: director@gw.doa.state.ri.us

Accounts and Control
Main phone: (401) 222-2271
Main fax: (401) 222-6437

Lawrence C. Franklin, State Controller
1 Capitol Hill, Providence, RI 02908
(401) 222-6731
E-mail: larryf@gw.doa.state.ri.us

Human Resources Division
Main phone: (401) 222-2200
Main fax: (401) 222-6391

Beverly A. Dwyer, Program Administrator
1 Capitol Hill, Providence, RI 02908
E-mail: bdwyer@doa.state.ri.us

Human Resources Division: Personnel Administration Office
Main phone: (401) 222-2160
Main fax: (401) 222-6391
TTY: (401) 222-6144

Anthony Bucci, Administrator
1 Capitol Hill, Providence, RI 02908

Taxation Division
Main phone: (401) 222-1111
Main fax: (401) 222-6006

R. Gary Clark, Executive Director and Tax Administrator
1 Capitol Hill, Providence, RI 02908

Water Resources Board
Main phone: (401) 222-2217
Main fax: (401) 222-4707

M. Paul Sams, General Manager
100 N. Main St., 5th Fl., Providence, RI 02903
E-mail: mpsams@wrb.state.ri.us

Workers Compensation Office
Main phone: (401) 222-6570
Main fax: (401) 222-6378

Frank Knight, Administrator
1 Capitol Hill, Providence, RI 02908
E-mail: frankk@doa.state.ri.us

Archives Division
http://www.state.ri.us/archives/
General e-mail: reference@archives.state.ri.us
Main phone: (401) 222-2353
Main fax: (401) 222-3199

Gwena Stearn, State Archivist
337 Westminster St., Providence, RI 02903

Arts Council
http://www.risca.state.ri.us
Main phone: (401) 222-3880
Main fax: (401) 521-1351
TTY: (401) 222-3880

Randall Rosenbaum, Executive Director
95 Cedar St., Providence, RI 02903-1062
E-mail: randy@risca.state.ri.us

Business Regulation Dept.
http://www.state.ri.us/manual/data/queries/
  stdept_.idc?id=19
Main phone: (401) 222-2246
Main fax: (401) 222-6098
TTY: (401) 222-2999

Tom Schumpert Jr., Director (Acting)
233 Richmond St., Providence, RI 02903

Children, Youth, and Families Dept.
Main phone: (401) 222-5212
Main fax: (401) 222-5300

Jay G. Lindgren Jr., Director
610 Mount Pleasant Ave., Providence, RI 02908-1935
(401) 222-5220; *Fax:* (401) 222-5230

Consumer Protection Unit
http://www.riag.state.ri.us/civil/consprot.html
Main phone: (401) 274-4400
Main fax: (401) 222-5110
Toll free: (800) 952-7776
TTY: (401) 453-0410

Ani Haroian, Director
150 S. Main St., Providence, RI 02903
E-mail: aharoian@riag.state.ri.us

Corrections Dept.
http://www.doc.state.ri.us
General e-mail: gvose@doc.state.ri.us
Main phone: (401) 462-1000
Main fax: (401) 462-2630
TTY: (401) 462-5180

Ashbel T. Wall Jr., Director (Interim)
40 Howard Ave., Cranston, RI 02920
(401) 462-2611

Parole Board
Main phone: (401) 222-3262
Main fax: (401) 222-1418

Lisa S. Farrell, Chair
1 Center Pl., Providence, RI 02903

Criminal Division
http://www.riag.state.ri.us/criminal/default.htm
Main phone: (401) 274-4400
Main fax: (401) 222-1331
TTY: (401) 453-0410

William J. Ferland, Assistant Attorney General, Chief
150 S. Main St., Providence, RI 02903

Developmental Disabilities Council
http://www.riddc.org
General e-mail: riddc@riddc.org
Main phone: (401) 462-3191
Main fax: (401) 462-3570
TTY: (401) 462-3191

Marie V. Citrone, Executive Director
14 Harrington Rd., Cranston, RI 02920

Economic Development Corporation
http://www.riedc.com
General e-mail: riedc@riedc.com
Main phone: (401) 222-2601
Main fax: (401) 222-2102
Toll free: (800) 631-0550

John Swen, Executive Director
1 W. Exchange St., Providence, RI 02903
Fax: (401) 274-1381
E-mail: jswen@riedc.com

Higher Educational Institutions

Rhode Island College
http://www.ric.edu
600 Mount Pleasant Ave., Providence, RI 02908-1924
Main phone: (401) 456-8000

University of Rhode Island
http://www.uri.edu
Green Hall, Kingston, RI 02881
Main phone: (401) 874-7000

Tourism Division
http://visitrhodeisland.com
Main phone: (401) 222-2601
Main fax: (401) 222-2102
Toll free: (800) 556-2484

David C. DePetrillo, Associate Director
1 W. Exchange St., Providence, RI 02903

Elderly Affairs Dept.
General e-mail: will@dea.state.ri.us
Main phone: (401) 222-2858
Main fax: (401) 222-1490
TTY: (401) 222-2880

Barbara A. Rayner, Director
160 Pine St., Providence, RI 02903
(401) 222-2894
E-mail: barbara@dea.state.ri.us

Elections Board
Main phone: (401) 222-2345
Main fax: (401) 621-3255
TTY: (401) 222-2239

Roger N. Begin, Chair
50 Branch Ave., Providence, RI 02904-2790

Elementary and Secondary Education Dept.
http://www.ride.ri.net
General e-mail: ride0001@ride.ri.net
Main phone: (401) 222-4600
Main fax: (401) 222-6178
TTY: (800) 745-6575

Peter McWalters, Commissioner
255 Westminster St., Providence, RI 02903-3400
(401) 222-4600, ext. 2001

Emergency Management Agency
http://www.state.ri.us/riema
General e-mail: scappaticcia@ri-arng.ngb.army.mil
Main phone: (401) 946-9996
Main fax: (401) 944-1891
Toll free: (800) 439-2990
TTY: (401) 751-7635

Reginald A. Centracchio, Director
645 New London Ave., Cranston, RI 02920-3097
(401) 457-4102

Environmental Management Dept.
http://www.state.ri.us/dem
General e-mail: sballard@dem.state.ri.us
Main phone: (401) 222-6800
Main fax: (401) 222-6802
Toll free: (800) 932-1000
TTY: (401) 831-5508

Jan H. Reitsma, Director
235 Promenade St., #425, Providence, RI 02908
(401) 222-2771

Environmental Protection Bureau

http://www.state.ri.us/dem/org/envprot/htm
Main phone: (401) 222-6677
Main fax: (401) 222-3162

Edward S. Szymanski, Associate Director
235 Promenade St., Providence, RI 02908-5767
(401) 222-6677, ext. 2404; *Fax:* (401) 222-6802
E-mail: eszymans@dem.state.ri.us

Natural Resources Bureau

http://www.state.ri.us/dem/org/natres/htm
Main phone: (401) 222-6605
Main fax: (401) 222-3162
Toll free: (800) 222-3070
TTY: (401) 831-5508

Malcom J. Grant, Associate Director
235 Promenade St., Providence, RI 02908-5767
E-mail: mgrant@dem.state.ri.us

Natural Resources Bureau: Fish and Wildlife Office

http://www.state.ri.us/dem/org/fish&w.htm
Main phone: (401) 789-3094
Main fax: (401) 783-4460
TTY: (401) 831-5508

John Stolgitis, Chief
4808 Tower Hill Rd., Wakefield, RI 02879

Natural Resources Bureau: Forest Environment Office

http://www.state.ri.us/dem/org/forest.htm
General e-mail: riforestry@edgenet.net
Main phone: (401) 647-3367
Main fax: (401) 647-3590

Thomas A. Dupree, Chief
1037 Hartford Pike, North Scituate, RI 02857

Parks and Recreation Division

http://www.riparks.com
General e-mail: riparks@earthlink.net
Main phone: (401) 222-2632
Main fax: (401) 934-0610

Larry Mouradjian, Chief
2321 Hartford Ave., Johnston, RI 02919-1719

Ethics Commission

http://www.state.ri.us/ethics/pg1.htm
General e-mail: ethics@ethics.state.ri.us
Main phone: (401) 222-3790
Main fax: (401) 272-6680
Toll free: (800) 752-8088

Martin F. Healey, Executive Director and Chief Prosecuter
40 Fountain St., Providence, RI 02903
E-mail: mhealey@ethics.state.ri.us

Frequently Called Numbers

Tourism: (401) 222-2601, 1-800-556-2484;
  http://visitrhodeisland.com
Library: (401) 222-2473;
  http://www.state.ri.us/library/web.htm
Board of Education:
Vital Statistics: (401) 222-2811
Tax/Revenue: (401) 222-1111
Motor Vehicles: (401) 588-3020;
  http://www.dmv.state.ri.us
State Police/Highway Patrol: (401) 444-1000;
  http://www.risp.state.ri.us
Unemployment: (401) 243-9191;
  http://www.dlt.state.ri.us/webdev/ui.html
General Election Information:
  (401) 222-2340; http://www.state.ri.us/
  submenus/rielclnk.htm
Consumer Affairs: (401) 274-4400;
  http://www.riag.state.ri.us/civil/consprot.html
Hazardous Materials: (401) 222-1360 or
  (401) 222-2797

Fire Marshal

Main phone: (401) 294-0861
Main fax: (401) 295-9092
TTY: (401) 295-9078

Irving J. Owens, Fire Marshal
24 Conway Ave., Quonset/Davisville Industrial Park,
North Kingstown, RI 02852

Health and Educational Building Corporation

Main phone: (401) 831-3770
Main fax: (401) 421-3910

James Salome, Chair
400 Westminster St., 2nd Fl., Providence, RI 02903

Health Dept.

http://www.health.state.ri.us
Main phone: (401) 222-2231
Main fax: (401) 222-6548
TTY: (401) 222-2506

Patricia A. Nolan, Director
Cannon Bldg., 3 Capitol Hill, Providence, RI 02908-5097

Higher Education Assistance Authority

http://www.riheaa.org
Main phone: (401) 736-1100
Main fax: (401) 732-3541
Toll free: (800) 922-9855
TTY: (401) 734-9481

William H. Hurry Jr., Executive Director
560 Jefferson Blvd., Warwick, RI 02886
(401) 736-1114
E-mail: whurrry@riheaa.org

Higher Education Office
http://www.uri.edu/ribog/
Main phone: (401) 222-6560
Main fax: (401) 222-2545
TTY: (401) 222-1350

Sally Dowling, Chair, Board of Governors
301 Promenade St., Providence, RI 02908
(401) 222-2088

Historical Preservation and Heritage Commission
General e-mail: rihphc@doa.state.ri.us
Main phone: (401) 222-2678
Main fax: (401) 222-2968
TTY: (401) 222-3700

Edward F. Sanderson, Executive Director
Old State House, 150 Benefit St., Providence, RI 02903
(401) 222-4130

Housing and Mortgage Finance Corporation
http://www.rihousing.com
General e-mail: ri_housing@ids.net
Main phone: (401) 751-5566
Main fax: (401) 457-1136
TTY: (401) 421-9799

Richard H. Godfrey, Executive Director
44 Washington St., Providence, RI 02903-1721

Human Rights Commission
General e-mail: gene.booth@hotmail.com
Main phone: (401) 222-2661
Main fax: (401) 222-2616
TTY: (401) 222-2664

Boards and Licensing

Accountancy, (401) 222-3185
Architects, Engineers, and Land Surveyors, (401) 222-2565
Child Care, (401) 222-4743
Contractors, (401) 222-1270
Cosmetology, (401) 222-2511
Nursing, (401) 222-2827
Real Estate, (401) 222-2262
Medical Examiners, (401) 222-3855, http://www.docboard.org/ri/main.htm
Pharmacy, (401) 222-2837

John B. Susa, Chair
Ten Abbot Park Pl., Providence, RI 02903-3768

Human Services Dept.
Main phone: (401) 462-5300
Main fax: (401) 462-3677
TTY: (401) 462-3363

Christine C. Ferguson, Director
600 New London Ave., Cranston, RI 02920
(401) 462-2121

Medical Services Division
Main phone: (401) 462-3575
Main fax: (401) 462-3677
TTY: (401) 462-6239

John Young, Associate Director
600 New London Ave., Cranston, RI 02920

Veterans Affairs Division
Main phone: (401) 254-9742
Main fax: (401) 254-1340
TTY: (401) 254-1345

David Foehr, Associate Director
490 Metacom Ave., Bristol, RI 02809
(401) 253-8000, ext. 220; *Fax:* (401) 253-2320
E-mail: dfoehr@gw.dhs.state.ri.us

Labor and Training Dept.
http://www.dlt.state.ri.us
Main phone: (401) 222-3600
Main fax: (401) 222-1473
TTY: (401) 222-3649

Lee H. Arnold, Director
101 Friendship St., Providence, RI 02903-3740
(401) 222-3732
E-mail: larnold@dlt.state.ri.us

Lottery Commission
http://www.ri.lot.com
Main phone: (401) 463-6500
Main fax: (401) 463-5669
TTY: (800) 745-5555

Gerald S. Aubin, Executive Director
1425 Pontiac Ave., Cranston, RI 02920
Fax: (401) 463-5008

Medical Examiners Board
http://www.docboard.org/ri/main.htm
Main phone: (401) 222-3855
Main fax: (401) 222-2158
TTY: (800) 745-5555

Milton Hamolsky, Chief Administrative Officer
3 Capitol Hill, #205, Providence, RI 02908

Mental Health, Retardation, and Hospitals Dept.
Main phone: (401) 462-1000
Main fax: (401) 462-3204

A. Kathryn Power, Director
14 Harrington Rd., Cranston, RI 02920
(401) 462-3201

Motor Vehicles Division
http://www.dmv.state.ri.us
Main phone: (401) 588-3020
Main fax: (401) 222-6052
TTY: (401) 722-0088

Thomas Harrington, Administrator
286 Main St., Pawtucket, RI 02860
(401) 588-3000; *Fax:* (401) 728-0810

Municipal Relations Office
Main phone: (401) 222-2080, ext. 209
Main fax: (401) 273-5301

Anthony Phillips, Deputy Director
State House, 82 Smith St., #143, Providence, RI 02903
E-mail: t.phillips@gov.state.ri.us

Pharmacy Board
Main phone: (401) 222-2837
Main fax: (401) 222-2158

Richard Yacino, Chief
3 Capitol Hill, #205, Providence, RI 02908

Public Defender
Main phone: (401) 222-3492
Main fax: (401) 222-3289
TTY: (401) 222-3492

Stephen P. Nugent, Public Defender
100 N. Main St., Providence, RI 02903

Public Telecommunications Authority
http://www.WSBE.org
Main phone: (401) 222-3636
Main fax: (401) 222-3407

Susan L. Farmer, President
50 Park Lane, Providence, RI 02907
E-mail: sfarmer@tv.wsbe.org

Public Utilities Commission
http://www.ripuc.org
Main phone: (401) 222-3500
Main fax: (401) 222-6805

James J. Malachowski, Chair
100 Orange St., Providence, RI 02903
(401) 222-3500, ext. 108

State Library
http://www.state.ri.us/library/web.htm
Main phone: (401) 222-2473
Main fax: (401) 331-6430

Thomas Evans, State Librarian
82 Smith St., State House, #208, Providence, RI 02903
E-mail: tevans@sec.state.ri.us

State Police
http://www.risp.state.ri.us
Main phone: (401) 444-1000
Main fax: (401) 444-1105
TTY: (401) 444-1144

Edmond S. Culhane Jr., Superintendent
311 Danielson Pike, North Scituate, RI 02857
(401) 444-1010

Transportation Dept.
http://www.dot.state.ri.us
Main phone: (401) 222-2481
Main fax: (401) 222-2086

William D. Ankner, Director
2 Capitol Hill, #210, Providence, RI 02903

Turnpike and Bridge Authority
Main phone: (401) 423-0800
Main fax: (401) 423-0830
Mailing address: P.O. Box 437, Jamestown, RI 02835

Kenneth M. Bidnchi Jr., Director
1 E. Shore Rd., Jamestown, RI 02835

Women's Commission
http://www.ricw.state.ri.us
Main phone: (401) 222-6105
Main fax: (401) 222-5638
TTY: (401) 222-6106

Toby D. Ayers, Director
260 W. Exchange St., #4, Providence, RI 02903
E-mail: tayers@doa.state.ri.us

Rhode Island Legislature
State House
Providence, RI 02903
General information: (401) 222-2466
Bill status: (401) 222-3580
http://www.rilin.state.ri.us

Senate
General information: (401) 222-6655
Fax: (401) 222-1306

Charles J. Fogarty (D), Presiding Officer
State House, Providence, RI 02903
(401) 222-2371; *Fax:* (401) 222-2012
E-mail: ltgov@state.ri.us

Charles D. Walton (D), President Pro Tempore
State House, Providence, RI 02903
(401) 222-6655
E-mail: sen-walton@rilin.state.ri.us

Paul S. Kelly (D), Majority Leader
State House, #318, Providence, RI 02903
(401) 222-6655
E-mail: sen-kelly@rilin.state.ri.us

William Enos (D), Majority Whip
State House, Providence, RI 02903
(401) 222-6655
E-mail: sen-enos@rilin.state.ri.us

Dennis L. Algiere (R), Minority Leader
State House, Providence, RI 02903
(401) 222-2708
E-mail: sen-algiere@rilin.state.ri.us

Leo R. Blais (R), Minority Whip
State House, Providence, RI 02903
(401) 222-2708
E-mail: sen-blais@rilin.state.ri.us

Raymond T. Hoyas Jr., Clerk
State House, Providence, RI 02903
(401) 222-6876

Laws

Sales tax: 7%
Income tax: 10.9%
State minimum wage: $5.65 (Federal is $5.15)
Marriage age: 18
First-cousin marriage: Permitted
Drinking age: 21
State control of liquor sales: No
Blood alcohol for DWI: 0.10%
Driving age: 17, 6 mos.
Speed limit: 65 mph
Permit to buy handguns: No, but 7-day wait
Minimum age to possess handguns: 18
Minimum age to possess rifles, shotguns: 18
State lottery: Yes; also Powerball
Casinos: No; but slot/video machines
Pari-mutuel betting: Dog racing; jai alai
Death penalty: No
3 strikes minimum sentence: court may add 25 yrs. (3rd felony)
Hate crimes law: Yes
Gay employment non-discrimination: Yes
Official language(s): None
Term limits: None

State laws are complex and subject to change; this information is not intended as legal advice. For an explanation of this information, see p. x.

House
General information: (401) 222-2466
Fax: (401) 222-1410

John B. Harwood (D), Speaker of the House
State House, #323, Providence, RI 02903
(401) 222-2466
E-mail: rep-harwood@rilin.state.ri.us

Mabel M. Anderson (D), Speaker Pro Tempore
State House, Providence, RI 02903
(401) 222-2466
E-mail: rep-manderson@rilin.state.ri.us

Gerard M. Martineau (D), Majority Leader
State House, Providence, RI 02903
(401) 222-2466
E-mail: rep-martineau@rilin.state.ri.us

Suzanne M. Henseler (D), Majority Whip
State House, #303, Providence, RI 02903
(401) 222-2466
E-mail: rep-henseler@rilin.state.ri.us

Robert A. Watson (R), Minority Leader
State House, Providence, RI 02903
(401) 222-2259
E-mail: rep-watson@rilin.state.ri.us

Christine H. Callahan (R), Minority Whip
State House, Providence, RI 02903
(401) 222-2259
E-mail: rep-callahan@rilin.state.ri.us

Louis D'Antuono, Reading Clerk
State House, Providence, RI 02903
(401) 222-1478
E-mail: dantuon@rilin.state.ri.us

Rhode Island Judiciary

Frank Licht Judicial Complex
250 Benefit St.
Providence, RI 02903
http://www.courts.state.ri.us

Supreme Court
http://www.courts.state.ri.us/supreme/index.html

Brian B. Burns, Clerk
Frank Licht Judicial Complex, 250 Benefit St., Providence, RI 02903
(401) 222-3272; *Fax:* (401) 222-3599

Justices
Composition: 5 justices
Selection Method: appointed by governor with consent of legislature
Length of term: life

Joseph R. Weisberger, Chief Justice, (401) 222-3290
John P. Bourcier, Justice, (401) 222-3285
Robert G. Flanders Jr., Justice, (401) 222-3775
Maureen McKenna Goldberg, Justice, (401) 222-3274
Victoria Lederberg, Justice, (401) 222-3943

Office of the Court Administrator
Main phone: (401) 222-3263
Main fax: (401) 222-5131

Robert C. Harrall, Court Administrator
Frank Licht Judicial Complex, 250 Benefit St., #709,
Providence, RI 02903

State Law Library
http://www.courts.state.ri.us/library/index.html
Main phone: (401) 222-3275
Main fax: (401) 222-3865

Kendall F. Svengalis, State Law Librarian
Frank Licht Judicial Complex, 250 Benefit St.,
Providence, RI 02903

Legislative and Political Party Information Resources

Senate home page: http://www.rilin.state.ri.us/senate.html
House home page: http://www.rilin.state.ri.us/hofrep.html
Committees: http://www.rilin.state.ri.us/gen_assembly/ComMembers/gencomm.html
Legislative process: http://www.rilin.state.ri.us/gen_assemby/GenMisc/genbilaw.html
Current session information: http://www.rilin.state.ri.us/gen_assembly/genmenu.html
Rhode Island Democratic Party
  P.O. Box 6004, Providence, RI 02940; *Phone:* (401) 721-9900
Rhode Island Republican Party
  551 S. Main St., Providence, RI 02903; *Phone:* (401) 453-4100

South Carolina

State Capitol
Columbia, SC 29211
Public information: (803) 896-0000
Fax: (803) 896-0094
http://www.state.sc.us

Office of the Governor
http://www.state.sc.us/governor
General e-mail: governor@state.sc.us
Main phone: (803) 734-9818
Main fax: (803) 734-9413
Mailing address: P.O. Box 11829, Columbia, SC
29211

Jim Hodges (D), Governor
State House, Columbia, SC 29211
(803) 734-9400; *Fax:* (803) 734-0396

Billy Boan, Chief of Staff
State House, Columbia, SC 29211
(803) 734-9400; *Fax:* (803) 734-9413

Nina Brook, Press Secretary
State House, Columbia, SC 29211
(803) 734-9400; *Fax:* (803) 734-9413

Wilbur Cave, Constituent Services Director
1205 Pendleton St., Columbia, SC 29201
(803) 734-0457; *Fax:* (803) 734-1560

Michael Tecklenburg, Director, Washington Office
444 N. Capitol St. N.W., #203, Washington, DC 20001
(202) 624-7784; *Fax:* (202) 624-7800
E-mail: mteckle@gov.state.sc.us

Office of the Lieutenant Governor
http://www.state.sc.us/ltgov/
Main phone: (803) 734-2080
Main fax: (803) 734-2082
Mailing address: P.O. Box 142, Columbia, SC
29202

Robert Lee (Bob) Peeler (R), Lieutenant Governor
1100 Gerbais St., Columbia, SC 29201
E-mail: bob@ltgov.state.sc.us

Office of the Secretary of State
http://www.scsos.com/
Main phone: (803) 734-2170
Main fax: (803) 734-1661
Mailing address: P.O. Box 11350, Columbia, SC
29211

James M. Miles (R), Secretary of State
1205 Pendleton St., #525, Columbia, SC 29201
(803) 734-2156

State of South Carolina

Capital: Columbia, since 1790
Founded: 1663, as part of British colony of
Carolina; separate from 1712
Statehood: May 23, 1788 (8th state)
Constitution adopted: 1895
Area: 30,111 sq. mi. (ranks 40th)
Population: 3,835,962 (1998 est.; ranks 26th)
Largest cities: (1998 est.) Columbia (110,840);
Charleston (87,044); North Charleston
(68,072); Rock Hill (46,218); Mount Pleasant
(41,330)
Counties: 46, Most populous: (1998 est.)
Greenville (353,845); Charleston (316,482);
Richland (307,056); Spartanburg (247,458);
Lexington (205,260)
U.S. Congress: Ernest Hollings (D), Strom
Thurmond (R); 6 Representatives
Nickname(s): Palmetto State
Motto: Prepared in mind and resources; While
I breathe, I hope
Song: "Carolina"
Bird: Carolina wren
Tree: Palmetto tree
Flower: Yellow jessamine
State fair: at Columbia, early to mid-Oct.
Former capital(s): Charleston

Office of the Attorney General
http://www.scattorneygeneral.com
General e-mail: contact@scattorneygeneral.org
Main phone: (803) 734-3970
Main fax: (803) 253-6283
TTY: (803) 734-4877
Mailing address: P.O. Box 11549, Columbia, SC
29211

Charles Molony Condon (R), Attorney General
1000 Assembly St., #501, Columbia, SC 29201

Office of the State Treasurer
http://www.state.sc.us/treas
General e-mail: Treasurer@sto.state.sc.us
Main phone: (803) 734-2101
Main fax: (803) 734-2039

Mailing address: P.O. Box 11778, Columbia, SC
29211

Grady L. Patterson Jr. (D), Treasurer
Wade Hampton Office Bldg., #118, Columbia, SC
29211
(803) 734-2101

Office of the State Auditor
http://www.osd.state.sc.us
General e-mail: sao@osa.sc.state.us
Main phone: (803) 253-4160
Main fax: (803) 343-0723

Thomas L. Wagner Jr., State Auditor
1401 Main St., #1200, Columbia, SC 29201
(803) 253-4160, ext. 2201
E-mail: twagner@osa.sc.state.us

Office of the Comptroller General
http://www.cg.state.sc.us/
General e-mail: nprice@cg.state.sc.us
Main phone: (803) 734-2121
Main fax: (803) 734-2064
Mailing address: P.O. Box 11228, Columbia, SC
29211

James A. Lander (D), Comptroller General
Wade Hampton Office Bldg., #305, Columbia, SC
29211

Office of the Adjutant General
General e-mail: tagsc@sc-arng.ngb.army.mil
Main phone: (803) 806-4200
Main fax: (803) 806-4468

Stanhope S. Spears, Adjutant General
1 National Guard Rd., Columbia, SC 29201
(803) 806-4217
E-mail: spearsss@sc-arng.ngb.army.mil

Agencies

Accountancy Board
http://www.llr.state.sc.us/bac.htm
Main phone: (803) 896-4492
Main fax: (803) 896-4554
Mailing address: P.O. Box 11329, Columbia, SC
29210

Robert W. (Robin) Wilkes Jr., Administrator
Koger Office Park, Kingstree Bldg., 110 Centerview
Dr., #104, Columbia, SC 29210

Agriculture Dept.
http://www.state.sc.us/scda
General e-mail: sinman@scda.state.sc.us
Main phone: (803) 734-2210
Main fax: (803) 734-2192

Mailing address: P.O. Box 11280, Columbia, SC
29211-1280

D. Leslie Tindal, Commissioner
1200 Senate St., Wade Hampton Bldg., 5th Fl.,
Columbia, SC 29201
(803) 734-2190
E-mail: tindal@scda.state.sc.us

Alcohol and Other Drug Abuse Services Dept.
http://www.daodas.state.sc.us
Main phone: (803) 734-9520
Main fax: (803) 734-9663

Rick C. Wade, Director
3700 Forest Dr., #300, Columbia, SC 29204
E-mail: rwade@daodas.state.sc.us

Archaeology and Anthropology Institute
http://www.cla.sc.edu/sciaa/sciaa.html
Main phone: (803) 799-1963
Main fax: (803) 254-1338

Bruce E. Rippeteau, Director and State Archaeologist
1321 Pendleton St., Columbia, SC 29208
(803) 734-0567
E-mail: rippeteau@sc.edu

Architectural Examiners Board
http://www.llr.state.sc.us/bae1.htm
General e-mail: debondea@mail.state.sc.us
Main phone: (803) 896-4408
Main fax: (803) 896-4410
Mailing address: P.O. Box 11419, Columbia, SC
29211

Jan Simpson, Administrator
Koger Office Park, Kingstree Bldg., 110 Centerview
Dr., #201, Columbia, SC 29210
E-mail: simpsonj@mail.llr.state.sc.us

Archives and History Dept.
http://www.state.sc.us/scdah
Main phone: (803) 896-6100
Main fax: (803) 896-6116

Rodger E. Stroup, Director
8301 Parklande Rd., Columbia, SC 29223-4905
(803) 896-6187

Arts Commission
http://www.state.sc.us/arts
General e-mail: mayken@arts.state.sc.us
Main phone: (803) 734-8696
Main fax: (803) 734-8526
TTY: (803) 734-8983

Suzette Surkamer, Executive Director
1800 Gervais St., Columbia, SC 29201
(803) 734-8688

Budget and Control Board

Main phone: (803) 734-2320
Main fax: (803) 734-2117
Mailing address: P.O. Box 12444, Columbia, SC 29211

Higher Educational Institutions

Clemson University
http://www.clemson.edu
105 Sikes Hall, Box 345124, Clemson, SC 29634-5124
Main phone: (864) 656-2287

Coastal Carolina University
http://www.coastal.edu
P.O. Box 261954, Conway, SC 29528-6054
Main phone: (843) 347-3161

College of Charleston
http://www.cofc.edu
66 George St., Charleston, SC 29424
Main phone: (843) 963-5507

Francis Marion University
http://www.fmarion.edu
P.O. Box 100547, Florence, SC 29501-0547
Main phone: (843) 661-1231

Lander University
http://www.lander.edu
320 Stanley Ave., Greenwood, SC 29649-2099
Main phone: (888) 452-6337

Medical University of South Carolina
http://www.musc.edu
171 Ashley Ave., Charleston, SC 29425
Main phone: (843) 792-2300

South Carolina State University
http://www.scsu.edu
300 College St. N.E., Orangeburg, SC 29117-0001
Main phone: (803) 536-7185, ext. 8407

The Citadel
http://www.citadel.edu
171 Moultrie St., Charleston, SC 29409
Main phone: (843) 953-5000

University of South Carolina
http://www.sc.edu
Columbia, SC 29208
Main phone: (803) 777-7700
Branches: Aiken, Spartanburg

Winthrop University
http://www.winthrop.edu
701 Oakland Ave., Rock Hill, SC 29733
Main phone: (803) 323-2191

Richard W. Kelly, Executive Director
612 Wade Hampton Office Bldg., Columbia, SC 29201
E-mail: kelly@oed.state.sc.us

Human Resources Office
http://www.state.sc.us/ohr
Main phone: (803) 737-0900
Main fax: (803) 737-3529

Donna G. Traywick, Director
1201 Main St., #1000, Columbia, SC 29201
E-mail: dtraywic@ohr.state.sc.us

Retirement Systems
http://www.scrs.state.sc.us
General e-mail: custservice@scrs.state.sc.us
Main phone: (803) 737-6800
Main fax: (803) 737-7594
Toll free: (800) 868-9002
Mailing address: P.O. Box 11960, Columbia, SC 29211

Robert Toomey, Executive Director
202 Arbor Lake Dr., Columbia, SC 29233
(803) 737-6934; *Fax:* (803) 737-6947
E-mail: rtoomey@scrs.state.tx.us

Carolina Capitol Investment Corporation
http://www.state.sc.us/ccic
Main phone: (803) 737-3817
Main fax: (803) 737-0016

Elliott E. Franks III, President and Chief Executive Officer
1201 Main St., #1750, Columbia, SC 29201
E-mail: efranks@ccic.state.sc.us

Commerce Dept.
http://www.teamsc.com
Main phone: (803) 737-0400
Main fax: (803) 737-0418
Mailing address: P.O. Box 927, Columbia, SC 29202

Charles S. Way Jr., Secretary
1201 Main St., 16th Fl., Columbia, SC 29201
(803) 737-0851

Aeronautics Division
http://www.callsouthcarolina.com/Aeronautics.dochome.htm
Main phone: (803) 896-6260
Main fax: (803) 896-6277
Toll free: (800) 922-0574
Mailing address: P.O. Box 280068, West Columbia, SC 29288-0068

Ira (Bud) Coward, Director
2553 Airport Blvd., W. Columbia, SC 29170
Fax: (803) 896-6266
E-mail: bcoward@aeronautics.state.sc.us

Commission for the Blind

Main phone: (803) 898-8700
Main fax: (803) 898-8800
Toll free: (800) 922-2222
TTY: (803) 734-7567
Mailing address: P.O. Box 79, Columbia, SC 29202-0079

Delbert H. Singleton Jr., Commissioner (Interim)
1430 Confederate Ave., Columbia, SC 29201
(803) 898-8822; *Fax:* (803) 898-8845

Consumer Affairs Dept.

http://www.state.sc.us/consumer/
Main phone: (803) 734-4200
Main fax: (803) 734-4286
Toll free: (800) 922-1594
Mailing address: P.O. Box 5757, Columbia, SC 29250-5757

Philip S. Porter, Administrator and Consumer Advocate
3600 Forest Dr., 3rd Fl., Columbia, SC 29204
(803) 734-9458

Contractors Licensing Board

http://www.llr.state.sc.us/contrctr/clb.htm
Main phone: (803) 896-4686
Main fax: (803) 896-4364
Mailing address: P.O. Box 11329, Columbia, SC 29210

Ronald E. Galloway, Administrator
Koger Office Park, Kingstree Bldg., 110 Centerview Dr., #104, Columbia, SC 29211

Corrections Dept.

http://www.state.sc.us/scdc/
General e-mail: corrections.info@doc.state.sc.us
Main phone: (803) 896-8500
Main fax: (803) 896-1220
Mailing address: P.O. Box 21787, Columbia, SC 29221-1787

William D. Catoe, Director
4444 Broad River Rd., Columbia, SC 29221-1787
(803) 896-8555

Cosmetology Board

http://www.llr.state.sc.us/boc.htm
Main phone: (803) 896-4494
Main fax: (803) 896-4484
Mailing address: P.O. Box 11329, Columbia, SC 29210

Eddie Jones, Administrator
Koger Office Park, Kingstree Bldg., 110 Centerview Dr., #104, Columbia, SC 29210
(803) 896-4540
E-mail: jonese@mail.llr.state.sc.us

Criminal Division

http://www.scattorneygeneral.com/office/criminal.html
General e-mail: info@scattorneygeneral.org
Main phone: (803) 734-3970
Main fax: (803) 734-6283
TTY: (803) 734-4877
Mailing address: P.O. Box 11549, Columbia, SC 29211

John McIntosh, Chief Deputy Attorney General
Rembert Dennis Bldg., 100 Assembly St., #501, Columbia, SC 29211

Disabilities and Special Needs Dept.

http://www.state.sc.us/ddsn
General e-mail: ddsn@ddsn.state.sc.us
Main phone: (803) 898-9600
Main fax: (803) 898-9653
Toll free: (888) DSN-INFO
Mailing address: P.O. Box 4706, Columbia, SC 29240

Stanley J. Butkus, State Director
3440 Harden St. Extension, Columbia, SC 29203
(803) 898-9769; *Fax:* (803) 898-9656

Education Dept.

http://www.state.sc.us/sde
General e-mail: bethrog@sde.state.sc.us
Main phone: (803) 734-8500
Main fax: (803) 734-3389

Inez Moore Tenenbaum, State Superintendent
1429 Senate St., #1006, Columbia, SC 29201
(803) 734-8492; *Fax:* (803) 734-8624
E-mail: itenenba@sde.state.sc.us

Board of Education

http://www.state.sc.us/sde/statebrd.sbindex.htm
Main phone: (803) 734-8492
Main fax: (803) 734-3389

Inez Moore Tenenbaum, Secretary
1429 Senate St., #1006, Columbia, SC 29201
E-mail: itenenba@sde.state.sc.us

Educational Television Network

http://www.scetv.org/
General e-mail: mail@scetv.org
Main phone: (803) 737-3200
Main fax: (803) 737-3417
Mailing address: P.O. Box 11000, Columbia, SC 29211

Paul Amos, President and General Manager
1101 George Rogers Blvd., Columbia, SC 29211
(803) 737-3240
E-mail: pamos@scetv.org

Election Commission
http://www.state.sc.us/scsec
General e-mail: hking@scsec.state.sc.us
Main phone: (803) 734-9060
Main fax: (803) 734-9366
Mailing address: P.O. Box 5897, Columbia, SC
29205

Samuel W. Howell IV, Chair
2221 Devine St., #105, Columbia, SC 29205

Emergency Preparedness Division
http://www.state.sc.us/epd/
Main phone: (803) 734-8020
Main fax: (803) 734-8062
TTY: (803) 734-8087

Stan M. McKinney, Director
1429 Senate St., Columbia, SC 29201
E-mail: smmckinn@strider.epd.state.sc.us

Employment Security Commission
http://www.sces.org
General e-mail: croberts@sces.org
Main phone: (803) 737-2400
Main fax: (803) 737-2642
TTY: (800) 206-8035
Mailing address: P.O. Box 995, Columbia, SC
29202

Joel T. Cassidy, Executive Director
1550 Gadsden St., Columbia, SC 29201
(803) 737-2652

Ethics Commission
http://www.state.sc.us/ethics
Main phone: (803) 253-4192
Main fax: (803) 253-7539
Mailing address: P.O. Box 11926, Columbia, SC
29211

Herbert R. Hayden Jr., Executive Director
5000 Thurmond Mall, #250, Columbia, SC 29201
E-mail: herb@ethics.state.sc.us

Financial Institutions Board
http://www.state.sc.us/treas
Main phone: (803) 734-2001
Main fax: (803) 734-2690
Mailing address: P.O. Box 11778, Columbia, SC
29211

Grady L. Patterson Jr., Chair
Capitol Complex, Columbia, SC 29211
(803) 734-2101; *Fax:* (803) 734-2013

Forestry Commission
http://www.state.sc.us/forest
General e-mail: scfc@forestry.state.sc.us
Main phone: (803) 896-8800
Main fax: (803) 798-8097

Mailing address: P.O. Box 21707, Columbia, SC
29221-1707

J. Hugh Ryan, State Forester
5500 Broad River Rd., Columbia, SC 29212

Health and Environmental Control Dept.
http://www.state.sc.us/dhec
Main phone: (803) 898-3432
Main fax: (803) 898-3323

Douglas E. Bryant, Commissioner
2600 Bull St., Columbia, SC 29201
(803) 898-3300
E-mail: bryantde@columb20.dhec.state.sc.us

Health and Human Services Dept.
http://www.dhhs.state.sc.us
General e-mail: askus@dhhs.state.sc.us
Main phone: (803) 898-2500
Main fax: (803) 898-4515
Mailing address: P.O. Box 8206, Columbia, SC
29202-8206

J. Samuel Griswold, Director
1801 Main St., Columbia, SC 29201
(803) 898-2504
E-mail: griswold@dhhs.state.sc.us

Senior and Long-Term Care Services
http://www.dhhs.state.sc.us
General e-mail: griswold@dhhs.state.sc.us
Main phone: (803) 898-2501
Main fax: (803) 898-4515
Mailing address: P.O. Box 8206, Columbia, SC
29202

Elizabeth M. Fuller, Deputy Director
1801 Main St., Columbia, SC 29202
(803) 899-2515
E-mail: fullerb@dhhs.state.sc.us

Higher Education Commission
Main phone: (803) 737-2260
Main fax: (803) 737-2275

Rayburn Barton, Executive Director
1333 Main St., #200, Columbia, SC 29201
Fax: (803) 737-2297
E-mail: rbarton@che400.state.sc.us

Historical Society
http://www.schistory.org
General e-mail: info@schistory.org
Main phone: (843) 723-3225
Main fax: (843) 723-8584

David O. Perry, Executive Director
100 Meeting St., Clarkston, SC 29401

Housing and Finance Development Authority
http://www.sha.state.sc.us

General e-mail: staff@sha.state.sc.us
Main phone: (803) 734-2000
Main fax: (803) 734-2356
TTY: (803) 734-2369

David M. Leopard, Executive Director
919 Bluff Rd., Columbia, SC 29201
(803) 734-2277
E-mail: leopd@sha.state.sc.us

Human Affairs Commission
http://www.schac.state.sc.us
Main phone: (803) 737-7825
Main fax: (803) 253-4191
Toll free: (800) 521-0725
TTY: (803) 253-4125
Mailing address: P.O. Box 4490, Columbia, SC
29240

Willis C. Ham, Commissioner
2611 Forest Dr., Columbia, SC 29240
(803) 737-7800
E-mail: willis@schac.state.sc.us

Insurance Dept.
http://www.state.sc.us/doi
General e-mail: scdi_mail@doi.state.sc.us
Main phone: (803) 737-6160
Main fax: (803) 737-6229
Toll free: (800) 768-3467
TTY: (803) 737-5769
Mailing address: P.O. Box 100105, Columbia, SC
29202-3105

Ernst N. Csiszar, Director
1612 Marion St., #428, Columbia, SC 29202-3105
(803) 737-6212
E-mail: ecsiszar@doi.state.sc.us

Jobs-Economic Development Authority
Main phone: (803) 737-0079
Main fax: (803) 737-0016

Elliott E. Franks III, Chief Executive Officer
1201 Main St., #1750, Columbia, SC 29201
E-mail: efranks@ccic.state.sc.us

Juvenile Justice Dept.
http://www.state.sc.us/djj
Main phone: (803) 896-9749
Main fax: (803) 896-9767
Mailing address: P.O. Box 21069, Columbia, SC
29221-1069

Gina Wood, Director
4900 Broad River Rd., Columbia, SC 29212
(803) 896-9791
E-mail: woodg@maindjj.state.sc.us

Labor, Licensing, and Regulation Dept.
http://www.llr.state.sc.us

Frequently Called Numbers

Tourism: (803) 734-0122;
  http://www.travelsc.com
Library: (803) 734-8666;
  http://www.state.sc.us/scsl/
Board of Education: (803) 734-8492;
  http://www.state.sc.us/sde/
  statebrd.sbindex.htm
Vital Statistics: (803) 898-3630;
  http://www.state.sc.us/dhec/biostats/
  vsbio.htm
Tax/Revenue: (803) 898-5000;
  http://www.dor.state.sc.us
Motor Vehicles: (803) 737-1767;
  http://www.state.sc.us/dps/dmv
State Police/Highway Patrol: (803) 896-7839;
  http://www.state.sc.us/dps/HP/
Unemployment: (803) 737-3089;
  http://www.sces.org/ui/index.htm
General Election Information: (803)
  734-9060; http://www.state.sc.us/scsec/
Consumer Affairs: (803) 734-4200,
  1-800-922-1594; /http://www.state.sc.us/
  consumer/
Hazardous Materials: (803) 896-4000

Main phone: (803) 896-4300
Main fax: (803) 896-4393
TTY: (803) 896-4553
Mailing address: Box 11329, Columbia, SC 29210

Rita M. McKinney, Director
110 Centerview Dr., Columbia, SC 29210
(803) 896-4390
E-mail: mckinneyr@mail.llr.state.sc.us

Liquefied Petroleum Gas Board
Main phone: (803) 896-9800
Main fax: (803) 896-9806

Pam Deweese, Administrative Coordinator
141 Monticello Trail, Columbia, SC 29203
(803) 896-9802

Professional and Occupational Licensing Division
http://www.llr.state.sc.us/boards.htm
Main phone: (803) 896-4300
Main fax: (803) 896-4719
Mailing address: P.O. Box 11329, Columbia,
SC 29211-1329

Marjorie Montgomery, Administrator
110 Centerview Dr., Columbia, SC 29210
(803) 896-4658

State Fire Marshal
http://www.llr.state.sc.us/fmarshal/marshal.htm
Main phone: (803) 896-9800
Main fax: (803) 896-9806
Toll free: (800) 896-1070

Lewis Lee, State Fire Marshal
141 Monticello Trail, Columbia, SC 29203
(803) 896-9802

Law Enforcement Division
http://www.sled.state.sc.us
Main phone: (803) 737-9000
Main fax: (803) 896-7041
Mailing address: P.O. Box 21398, Columbia, SC
29221-1398

Robert M. Stewart, Chief
4400 Broad River Rd., Columbia, SC 29221-1398
(803) 896-7136; *Fax:* (803) 896-7588

Medical Examiners Board
http://www.llr.state.sc.us/me.htm
General e-mail: medboard@mail.llr.state.sc.us
Main phone: (803) 896-4500
Main fax: (803) 896-4515
Mailing address: P.O. Box 11289, Columbia, SC
29210

Aaron J. Kozloski, Administrator
Koger Office Park, Kingstree Bldg., 110 Centerview
Dr., #202, Columbia, SC 29210

Labor, Licensing, and Regulation
http://www.llr.state.sc.us
(803) 896-4300

Accountancy, (803) 896-4492,
  http://www.llr.state.sc.us/bac.htm
Architects, (803) 896-4408,
  http://www.llr.state.sc.us/bae1.htm
Child Care, (803) 898-7513
Contractors, (803) 896-4686,
  http://www.llr.state.sc.us/contrctr/clb.htm
Cosmetology, (803) 896-4494,
  http://www.llr.state.sc.us/boc.htm
Engineers and Land Surveyors, (803)
  896-4422, http://www.llr.state.sc.us/bpe.htm
Medical Examiners, (803) 896-4500,
  http://www.llr.state.sc.us/me.htm
Nursing, (803) 896-4550,
  http://www.llr.state.sc.us/bon.htm
Pharmacy, (803) 896-4700,
  http://www.llr.state.sc.us/bop.htm
Real Estate, (803) 896-4400,
  http://www.llr.state.sc.us/reab.htm

Mental Health Dept.
http://www.state.sc.us/dmh
Main phone: (803) 898-8581
Main fax: (803) 898-8316
Toll free: (800) 763-1024
TTY: (803) 798-4936
Mailing address: P.O. Box 485, Columbia, SC
29202

Stephen M. Soltys, Director
2414 Bull St., Columbia, SC 29202
(803) 898-8319
E-mail: sms85@co.state.sc.us

Natural Resources Dept.
http://www.dnr.state.sc.us
Main phone: (803) 734-3888
Main fax: (803) 734-6310
Mailing address: P.O. Box 167, Columbia, SC
29202

Paul A. Sandifer, Director
Rembert C. Dennis Bldg., #330, Columbia, SC 29202
(803) 734-4007
E-mail: sandiferp@scdnr.state.sc.us

Geological Survey
http://www.dnr.state.sc.us/geology/geohome.htm
General e-mail: streeter@dnr.state.sc.us
Main phone: (803) 896-7708
Main fax: (803) 896-7695

C. W. Clendenin Jr., State Geologist
5 Geology Rd., Columbia, SC 29212
E-mail: clendenin@dnr.state.sc.us

Land, Resources, and Conservation Districts Division
http://www.dnr.state.sc.us/land/index.html
Main phone: (803) 734-9100
Main fax: (803) 734-9200

Alfred H. Vang, Deputy Director
2221 Devine St., #222, Columbia, SC 29205-2418
(803) 734-9101
E-mail: vang@water.dnr.state.sc.us

Water Resources Division
http://www.dnr.state.sc.us/water/index.html
Main phone: (803) 737-0800
Main fax: (803) 765-9080

Alfred H. Vang, Deputy Director
1201 Main St., #1100, Columbia, SC 29201
E-mail: vang@water.dnr.state.sc.us

Wildlife and Freshwater Fisheries Division
http://www.dnr.state.sc.us/wild/index.html
Main phone: (803) 734-3886
Main fax: (803) 734-6020
Mailing address: P.O. Box 167, Columbia, SC
20202

Billy McTeer, Deputy Director
1000 Assembly St., 2nd Fl., Columbia, SC 20202
(803) 734-3889
E-mail: mcteerb@scdnr.state.sc.us

Nursing Board
http://www.llr.state.sc.us/bon.htm
Main phone: (803) 896-4550
Main fax: (803) 896-4525
Mailing address: P.O. Box 12367, Columbia, SC
29211

Debbie Herman, Administrator
Koger Office Park, Kingstree Bldg., 110 Centerview
Dr., #202, Columbia, SC 29210
(803) 896-4533
E-mail: hermand@mail.llr.state.sc.us

Parks, Recreation, and Tourism Dept.
http://www.travelsc.com
Main phone: (803) 734-0122
Main fax: (803) 734-1409

William R. Jennings, Director
1205 Pendleton St., #248, Columbia, SC 29201
E-mail: bjennings@prt.state.sc.us

Pharmacy Board
http://www.llr.state.sc.us/bop.htm
General e-mail: funderbm2mail.llr.state.sc.us
Main phone: (803) 896-4700
Main fax: (803) 896-4596
Mailing address: P.O. Box 11927, Columbia, SC
29210

Cheryl A. Ruff, Administrator
Koger Office Park, Kingstree Bldg., 110 Centerview
Dr., #306, Columbia, SC 29210

Ports Authority
http://www.port-of-charleston.com
General e-mail: SCSPAinfo@scspa.com
Main phone: (843) 577-8121
Main fax: (843) 577-8626
Mailing address: P.O. Box 22287, Charleston, SC
29413

**Bernard S. Groseclose Jr., President and Chief
Executive Officer**
176 Concord St., Charleston, SC 29413
(843) 577-8600
E-mail: BGroseclose@scspa.com

Probation, Parole, and Pardon Services Dept.
http://www.state.sc.us/ppp/
Main phone: (803) 734-9220
Main fax: (803) 734-9440
Mailing address: P.O. Box 50666, Columbia, SC
29250

Stephen K. Benjamin, Director
2221 Devine St., #600, Columbia, SC 29250
(803) 734-9278

Professional Engineers and Land Surveyors Board
http://www.llr.state.sc.us/bpe.htm
General e-mail: engls@mail.llr.state.sc.us
Main phone: (803) 896-4422
Main fax: (803) 896-4427
Mailing address: P.O. Box 11597, Columbia, SC
29210

Jay Pitts, Administrator
Koger Office Park, Kingstree Bldg., 110 Centerview
Dr., #201, Columbia, SC 29210

Public Safety Dept.
http://www.state.sc.us/dps
Main phone: (803) 896-7839
Main fax: (803) 896-7881

B. Boykin Rose, Director
5410 Broad River Rd., Columbia, SC 29212
(803) 896-7932

Highway Patrol
http://www.state.sc.us/dps/HP/
Main phone: (803) 896-7839
Main fax: (803) 896-9683

Robert W. Luther, Superintendent
5410 Broad River Rd., Columbia, SC 29210
(803) 896-7894; *Fax:* (803) 896-7922

Motor Vehicles Division
http://www.state.sc.us/dps/dmv
Main phone: (803) 737-1767
Toll free: (800) 442-1DMV
Mailing address: P.O. Box 1498, Columbia, SC
29201

J. Glenn Beckham, Deputy Director
955 Park St., Columbia, SC 29201

Public Service Authority
http://www.santeecooper.com
Main phone: (843) 761-8000
Main fax: (843) 761-7060
Mailing address: P.O. Box 2946101, Moncks
Corner, SC 29461-2901

**T. Graham Edwards, President and Chief Executive
Officer**
1 Riverwood Dr., Moncks Corner, SC 29461-2901
(843) 761-7024; *Fax:* (843) 761-7037
E-mail: tgedward@santeecooper.com

Public Service Commission
http://www.psc.state.sc.us
General e-mail: psc@state.sc.us

Main phone: (803) 896-5100
Main fax: (803) 896-5199
Toll free: (800) 922-1531
Mailing address: P.O. Drawer 11649, Columbia, SC 29211

Phillip T. Bradley, Chair
101 Executive Center Dr., Saluda Bldg., Columbia, SC 29210
(803) 896-5220; Fax: (803) 896-5188

Real Estate Appraisers Board
http://www.llr.state.sc.us/reab.htm
Main phone: (803) 896-4400
Main fax: (803) 896-4404
Mailing address: P.O. Box 11847, Columbia, SC 29210

Robert Selman, Administrator
Koger Office Park, Kingstree Bldg., 110 Centerview Dr., #201, Columbia, SC 29210
E-mail: selmanr@mail.llr.state.sc.us

Revenue Dept.
http://www.dor.state.sc.us
Main phone: (803) 898-5000
Main fax: (803) 898-5020
TTY: (803) 898-5656
Mailing address: P.O. Box 125, Columbia, SC 29214

Elizabeth Carpentier, Director
301 Gervais St., Columbia, SC 29214
(803) 898-5040
E-mail: carpene@dor.state.sc.us

School for the Deaf and Blind
http://www.scsdb.k12.sc.us
Main phone: (864) 585-7711
Main fax: (864) 585-3555
TTY: (864) 585-7711

Sheila S. Breitweiser, President
355 Cedar Springs Rd., Spartanburg, SC 29302-4699
E-mail: sbreitweiser@scsdb.k12.sc.us

Social Services Dept.
http://www.state.sc.us/dss
Main phone: (803) 898-7601
Main fax: (803) 898-7277
Toll free: (800) 311-7220
TTY: (803) 898-7698
Mailing address: P.O. Box 1520, Columbia, SC 29202

Elizabeth Patterson, Director
1535 Confederate Ave. Extension, Columbia, SC 29202
(803) 898-7360

Family Preservation and Child Welfare Services: Child Day Care Licensing and Regulatory Services Division
http://www.state.sc.us/dss/cdclrs/index.html
Main phone: (803) 898-7345
Main fax: (803) 898-7179
Mailing address: P.O. Box 1520, Columbia, SC 29202

Helen Lebby, Director
1535 Confederate Ave., #520, Columbia, SC 29202

State Fair
http://www.scstatefair.org
Main phone: (803) 799-3387
Main fax: (803) 799-1760
Mailing address: P.O. Box 393, Columbia, SC 29202

Gary Goodman, Director
1200 Rosewood Dr., Columbia, SC 29201

State Library
http://www.state.sc.us/scsl/
General e-mail: reference@leo.scsl.state.sc.us
Main phone: (803) 734-8666
Main fax: (803) 734-8676
TTY: (803) 734-7298
Mailing address: P.O. Box 11469, Columbia, SC 29211

James B. Johnson Jr., Director
1500 Senate St., Columbia, SC 29211
E-mail: jim@leo.scsl.state.sc.us

State Museum
http://www.museum.state.sc.us
General e-mail: publicrelations@museum.state.sc.us
Main phone: (803) 898-4977
Main fax: (803) 898-4969
TTY: (803) 898-4486
Mailing address: P.O. Box 100107, Columbia, SC 29202-3107

Overton G. Ganong, Director
301 Gervais St., Columbia, SC 29201
(803) 898-4921
E-mail: ganong@museum.state.sc.us

Technical and Comprehensive Education Board
http://www.scteched.tec.sc.us
Main phone: (803) 896-5320
Main fax: (803) 896-5387

James L. Hudgins, Executive Director
111 Executive Center Dr., Columbia, SC 29210
(803) 896-5280; Fax: (803) 896-5281
E-mail: hudgins@sbt.tec.sc.us

Transportation Dept.
http://www.dot.state.sc.us/
Main phone: (803) 737-2314
Main fax: (803) 737-2038
TTY: (803) 737-3870
Mailing address: P.O. Box 191, Columbia, SC
29202

> **Elizabeth S. Mabry, Executive Director**
> 955 Park St., #309, Columbia, SC 29202
> (803) 737-1302

Tuition Grants Commission (Higher Education)
http://www.state.sc.us/tuitiongrants/
Main phone: (803) 734-1200
Main fax: (803) 734-1426
Mailing address: P.O. Box 12159, Columbia, SC
29211

> **Edward M. Shannon III, Executive Director**
> 1310 Lady St., Columbia, SC 29211
> *E-mail:* eshannon@usit.net

Veterans Affairs
Main phone: (803) 734-0200
Main fax: (803) 734-0197

> **Eugene Wages, Director**
> 1205 Pendleton St., #226, Columbia, SC 29201
> *E-mail:* swages@govoepp.state.sc.us

Vocational Rehabilitation Dept.
http://www.scvrd.net
Main phone: (803) 896-6500
Main fax: (803) 896-6529
TTY: (803) 896-6559
Mailing address: P.O. Box 15, West Columbia, SC
29171-0015

> **P. Charles LaRosa Jr., Commissioner**
> 1410 Boston Ave., W. Columbia, SC 29171-0015
> (803) 896-6504
> *E-mail:* clarosa@infoave.net

Women's Commission
Main phone: (803) 734-1609
Main fax: (803) 734-0241

> **Rebecca Collier, Director**
> 1205 Pendleton St., #366, Columbia, SC 29201

Workers' Compensation Commission
http://www.state.sc.us/wcc
General e-mail: aclawson@infoave.net
Main phone: (803) 737-5700
Main fax: (803) 737-5764
Mailing address: P.O. Box 1715, Columbia, SC
29202

> **Holly Saleeby Atkins, Chair**
> 1612 Marion St., Columbia, SC 29202
> (803) 737-5663

Laws

Sales tax: 6%
Income tax: 7%
State minimum wage: None (Federal is $5.15)
Marriage age: 18
First-cousin marriage: Permitted
Drinking age: 21
State control of liquor sales: No
Blood alcohol for DWI: 0.10%
Driving age: 16, 3 mos.
Speed limit: 70 mph
Permit to buy handguns: For repeat purchase within 30 days
Minimum age to possess handguns: 21
Minimum age to possess rifles, shotguns: None
State lottery: No
Casinos: No; but slot/video machines
Pari-mutuel betting: No
Death penalty: Yes
3 strikes minimum sentence: Life (3rd serious offense)
Hate crimes law: No
Gay employment non-discrimination: No
Official language(s): English
Term limits: None

State laws are complex and subject to change; this information is not intended as legal advice. For an explanation of this information, see p. x.

South Carolina Legislature

State Captiol
Columbia, SC 29202
General information: (803) 212-6720
http://www.state.sc.us/legislature.html

Senate
Address: Gressette Bldg., P.O. Box 142, Columbia,
SC 29202-0142
General information: (803) 212-6700
Fax: (803) 212-6299

> **Robert Lee (Bob) Peeler (R), President**
> 1100 Gerbais St., Columbia, SC 29201
> (803) 734-2080; *Fax:* (803) 734-2082
> *E-mail:* bob@ltgov.state.sc.us
> http://www.scstatehouse.net/ltgov.htm

John W. Drummond (D), President Pro Tempore
Gressette Bldg., P.O. Box 142, Columbia, SC 29202-0142
(803) 212-6640
E-mail: SFI@scsenate.org
http://www.scstatehouse.net/sdist10.htm

Frank B. Caggiano, Clerk and Director of Senate Research
Gressette Bldg., P.O. Box 142, Columbia, SC 29202-0142
(803) 212-6200
E-mail: scl@scsenate.org

House
Address: Blatt Bldg., P.O. Box 11867, Columbia, SC 29211-1867
General information: (803) 734-2010
Fax: (803) 734-2925

David H. Wilkins (R), Speaker of the House
Blatt Bldg., P.O. Box 11867, Columbia, SC 29211-1867
(803) 734-3125
E-mail: HSP@legis.lpitr.state.sc.us
http://www.lpitr.state.sc.us/hdist24.htm

Terry E. Haskins (R), Speaker Pro Tempore
Blatt Bldg., P.O. Box 11867, Columbia, SC 29211-1867
(803) 734-2701
E-mail: TEH@legis.lpitr.state.sc.us
http://www.lpitr.state.sc.us/hdist22.htm

Robert W. Harrell Jr. (R), Majority Leader
Blatt Bldg., P.O. Box 11867, Columbia, SC 29211-1867
(803) 734-3144
E-mail: RWH@legis.lpitr.state.sc.us
http://www.lpitr.state.sc.us/hdist114.htm

Gilda Cobb-Hunter (D), Minority Leader
Blatt Bldg., P.O. Box 11867, Columbia, SC 29211-1867
(803) 734-2809
E-mail: GCH@legis.lpitr.state.sc.us
http://www.lpitr.state.sc.us/hdist66.htm

Sandra K. McKinney, Clerk
Blatt Bldg., P.O. Box 11867, Columbia, SC 29211-1867
(803) 734-2010; *Fax:* (803) 734-2925
E-mail: hcl@legis.lpitr.state.sc.us

South Carolina Judiciary
1231 Gervais St.
Columbia, SC 29201
http://www.state.sc.us/judicial

Supreme Court
Daniel E. Shearouse, Clerk
1231 Gervais St., Columbia, SC 29201
(803) 734-1080; *Fax:* (803) 734-1499

Justices
Composition: 5 justices
Selection Method: elected by state general assembly; governor can fill vacancies in terms expiring in one year or less
Length of term: 10 years

Ernest A. Finney Jr., Chief Justice, (803) 436-2203
E. C. Burnett III, Associate Justice, (864) 596-2595
James E. Moore, Associate Justice, (864) 942-8565
Jean H. Toal, Associate Justice, (803) 734-1584
John H. Waller Jr., Associate Justice, (843) 423-8250

Court Administration
Main phone: (803) 734-1800
Main fax: (803) 734-1355

Rosalyn Woodson Frierson, Director
1015 Sumter St., 2nd Fl., Columbia, SC 29201
E-mail: rfrierson@scjd.state.sc.us

Supreme Court Law Library
Main phone: (803) 734-1080
Main fax: (803) 734-0519

Janet Meyer, Librarian
1231 Gervais St., Columbia, SC 29201
E-mail: jmeyer@scjd.state.sc.us

Legislative and Political Party Information Resources

Committees: Senate: http://www.scstatehouse.net/schair.htm; *House:* http://www.scstatehouse.net/hchair.htm
Current session information: http://www.scstatehouse.net/today.htm
Legislative information: http://www.leginfostate.sc.us
Budget: http://www.scstatehouse.net/budget.htm
South Carolina Democratic Party: http://www.scdp.org
    1517 Blanding St., P.O. Box 5965, Columbia, SC 29250; *Phone:* (803) 799-7798; *Fax:* (803) 765-1692
South Carolina Republican Party: http://www.scgop.com
    1508 Lady St., Columbia, SC 29201; *Phone:* (803) 988-8440; *Fax:* (803) 988-8444

South Dakota

State Capitol
Pierre, SD 57501-5070
Public information: (605) 773-3011
Fax: (605) 773-4711
http://www.state.sd.us

Office of the Governor
http://www.state.sd.us/state/govern.htm
General e-mail: sdgov@state.sd.us
Main phone: (605) 773-3212
Main fax: (605) 773-4711
TTY: (800) 877-1113

William J. Janklow (R), Governor
State Capitol, 500 E. Capitol Ave., Pierre, SD 57501-5070

Jim Soyer, Chief of Staff
State Capitol, 500 E. Capitol Ave., Pierre, SD 57501-5070
(605) 773-3212; *Fax:* (605) 773-4711
E-mail: jim.soyer@state.sd.us

Bob Mercer, Press Secretary
State Capitol, 500 E. Capitol Ave., Pierre, SD 57501-5070
(605) 773-3212; *Fax:* (605) 773-4711
E-mail: bob.mercer@state.sd.us

Susan Stoneback, Constituent Affairs
State Capitol, 500 E. Capitol Ave., Pierre, SD 57501-5070
(605) 773-5709; *Fax:* (605) 773-4711
E-mail: susan.stoneback@state.sd.us

Office of the Lieutenant Governor
http://www.state.sd.us/Lt.Gov/
Main phone: (605) 773-3661
Main fax: (605) 773-4711

Carole Hillard (R), Lieutenant Governor
State Capitol, 500 E. Capitol Ave., Pierre, SD 57501-5070
E-mail: carole.hillard@state.sd.us

Office of the Secretary of State
http://www.state.sd.us/sos/sos.htm
General e-mail: sdsos@state.sd.us
Main phone: (605) 773-3537
Main fax: (605) 773-6580
TTY: (605) 773-5010

Joyce Hazeltine (R), Secretary of State
State Capitol, 500 E. Capitol Ave., #204, Pierre, SD 57501-5070

State of South Dakota

Capital: Pierre, since 1889
Founded: 1861, as part of Dakota Territory; separated at statehood
Statehood: November 2, 1889 (40th state)
Constitution adopted: 1889
Area: 75,896 sq. mi. (ranks 16th)
Population: 738,171 (1998 est.; ranks 46th)
Largest cities: (1998 est.) Sioux Falls (116,762); Rapid City (57,513); Aberdeen (24,865); Watertown (19,909); Brookings (17,138)
Counties: 66, Most populous: (1998 est.) Minnehaha (143,011); Pennington (87,702); Brown (35,433); Brookings (25,989); Codington (25,456)
U.S. Congress: Thomas A. Daschle (D), Tim Johnson (D); 1 Representative
Nickname(s): Mount Rushmore State, Coyote State
Motto: Under God the people rule
Song: "Hail! South Dakota"
Bird: Ring-necked pheasant
Tree: Black Hills spruce
Flower: American pasqueflower
State fair: at Huron, late July-early Aug.
Former capital(s): Yankton, Bismarck

Office of the Attorney General
http://www.state.sd.us/attorney/attorney.html
General e-mail: help@atg.state.sd.us
Main phone: (605) 773-3215
Main fax: (605) 773-4106
TTY: (605) 773-6585

Mark Barnett (R), Attorney General
State Capitol, 500 E. Capitol Ave., Pierre, SD 57501-5070

Office of the State Treasurer
http://www.state.sd.us/treasurer/treasure.htm
Main phone: (605) 773-3378
Main fax: (605) 773-3115

Richard D. Butler (D), State Treasurer
State Capitol, 500 E. Capitol Ave., #212, Pierre, SD 57501-5070
E-mail: dickb@st-tres.state.sd.us

Office of the State Auditor
http://www.state.sd.us/state/executive/auditor/
auditor.htm
Main phone: (605) 773-3341
Main fax: (605) 773-5929

> **Vernon L. Larson (R), Auditor**
> State Capitol, 500 E. Capitol Ave., Pierre, SD 57501-5070
> *E-mail:* vern.larson@state.sd.us

Military and Veterans Affairs Dept.
http://www.state.sd.us/military/military.html
Main phone: (605) 737-6200
Main fax: (605) 399-6677

> **Philip G. Killey, Adjutant General**
> 2823 W. Main St., Rapid City, SD 57702-8186
> (605) 737-6702
> *E-mail:* phillip.killey@sd.ngb.army.mil

Agencies

Accountancy Board
http://www.state.sd.us/dcr/accountancy/
General e-mail: sdbdacct@dtgnet.com
Main phone: (605) 367-5770
Main fax: (605) 367-5773

> **Lynn Bethke, Executive Director**
> 301 E. 14th St., #200, Sioux Falls, SD 57104-5022

Administration Bureau
http://www.state.sd.us/boa/boa.html
General e-mail: info@boa.state.sd.us
Main phone: (605) 773-3688
Main fax: (605) 773-3887

> **Tom Geraets, Commissioner**
> State Capitol, 500 E. Capitol Ave., Pierre, SD 57501-5070

Agriculture Dept.
http://www.state.sd.us/doa/doa.html
General e-mail: leanneneuhauser@state.sd.us
Main phone: (605) 773-5425
Main fax: (605) 773-5926

> **Darrell Cruea, Secretary**
> Joe Foss Bldg., 523 E. Capitol Ave., Pierre, SD 57501-3182

Resource Conservation and Forestry
http://www.state.sd.us/doa/forestry/index2.htm
Main phone: (605) 773-3623
Main fax: (605) 773-4003

> **Raymond A. Sowers, Director and State Forester**
> Joe Foss Bldg., 523 E. Capitol Ave., Pierre, SD 57501-3182

(605) 773-4260
E-mail: ray.sowers@state.sd.us

Animal Industry Board
Main phone: (605) 773-3321
Main fax: (605) 773-5459

> **Sam D. Holland, Executive Secretary and State Veterinarian**
> 411 S. Fort St., Pierre, SD 57501
> *E-mail:* dr.holland@state.sd.us

Appraiser Certification Program
http://www.state.sd.us/dcr/appraisers
Main phone: (605) 773-4608
Main fax: (605) 773-5369

> **Sherry Bren, Administrator**
> 118 W. Capitol Ave., Pierre, SD 57501-2000
> *E-mail:* sherry.bren@state.sd.us

Child Care Services: Child Care Licensing
http://www.state.sd.us/social/CCS/liceninsg
General e-mail: ccs@dss.state.sd.us
Main phone: (605) 773-4766
Main fax: (605) 773-7294
Toll free: (800) 227-3020

> **Loila Hunking, Director**
> 700 Governor Dr., Pierre, SD 59501

Commerce and Regulation Dept.
http://www.state.sd.us/dcr
General e-mail: nancy.carroll@state.sd.us
Main phone: (605) 773-3178
Main fax: (605) 773-3018

> **David Volk, Secretary**
> 118 W. Capitol Ave., Pierre, SD 57501

Banking Division
http://www.state.sd.us/banking
General e-mail: dcrbank1@comm-bnk.state.sd.us
Main phone: (605) 773-3421
Main fax: (605) 773-5367

> **Richard Duncan, Director**
> 217 1/2 W. Missouri, Pierre, SD 57501-4590
> *E-mail:* dick.duncan@state.sd.us

Drivers Licensing Office
http://www.state.sd.us/dcr/dl/sddriver.htm
General e-mail: driverlic@crpr1.state.sd.us
Main phone: (605) 773-6883
Main fax: (605) 773-3018
Toll free: (800) 952-3696

> **Cynthia D. Gerber, Director**
> 118 W. Capitol Ave., Pierre, SD 57501-2000
> (605) 773-4846

Human Rights Division
http://www.state.sd.us/dcr/hr/HR_HOM.htm
Main phone: (605) 773-4493
Main fax: (605) 773-6893

Coral Assam, Director
118 W. Capitol Ave., Pierre, SD 57501

Insurance Division
http://www.state.sd.us/dcr/insurance/
Main phone: (605) 773-3563
Main fax: (605) 773-5369

Darla L. Lynch, Director
118 W. Capitol Ave., Pierre, SD 57501

Petroleum Release Compensation Fund
http://www.state.sd.us/dcr/prcf/prcfhome.htm
General e-mail: petro@crpr1.state.sd.us
Main phone: (605) 773-3769
Main fax: (605) 773-6048

Dennis Rounds, Director
445 E. Capitol Ave., #200, Pierre, SD 57501
E-mail: dennis.rounds@state.sd.us

Professional and Occupational Licensing Division
http://www.state.sd.us/dcr/boards.boardhom.htm
Main phone: (605) 773-3178
Main fax: (605) 773-3018

Wendy Kloeppner, Director
118 W. Capitol Ave., Pierre, SD 57501
E-mail: wendy.kloeppner@state.sd.us

State Fire Marshal's Office
http://www.state.sd.us/dcr/fire/FIRE_hom.htm
Main phone: (605) 773-3562
Main fax: (605) 773-6631

Dan Carlson, State Fire Marshal
118 W. Capitol Ave., Pierre, SD 57501

Consumer Protection Division
http://www.state.sd.us/atg/consumer/index.html
General e-mail: help@atg.state.sd.us
Main phone: (605) 773-4400
Main fax: (605) 773-7163
Toll free: (800) 300-1986
TTY: (605) 773-6585

Tim Bartlett, Director
500 E. Capitol Ave., Pierre, SD 57501

Corrections Dept.
http://www.state.sd.us/corrections/corrections.html
General e-mail: info@doc.state.sd.us
Main phone: (605) 773-3478
Main fax: (605) 773-3194
Mailing address: 500 E. Capitol Ave., Pierre, SD 57501-5070

Higher Educational Institutions

Black Hills State University
http://www.bhsu.edu
1200 University, Spearfish, SD 57799
Main phone: (800) 255-2478

Dakota State University
http://www.dsu.edu
820 N. Washington Ave., Madison, SD 57042-1799
Main phone: (888) 378-9988

Northern State University
http://www.northern.edu
1200 S. Jay St., Aberdeen, SD 57401
Main phone: (800) 678-5330

South Dakota School of Mines and Technology
http://www.sdsmt.edu
501 E. Saint Joseph St., Rapid City, SD 57701
Main phone: (605) 394-2400

South Dakota State University
http://www/sdstate.edu
Box 2201, Brookings, SD 57007
Main phone: (800) 952-3541

University of South Dakota
http://www.usd.edu
414 E. Clark St., Vermillion, SD 57069
Main phone: (605) 677-5011

Jeffrey Bloomberg, Secretary
3200 E. Hwy. 34, Pierre, SD 57501-5070

Juvenile Corrections and Facilities
http://www.state.sd.us/corrections/juvenile.htm
General e-mail: info@doc.state.sd.us
Main phone: (605) 773-3478
Main fax: (605) 773-3194
Mailing address: 500 E. Capitol Ave., Pierre, SD 57501

Kevin McLain, Director
3200 E. Hwy. 34, Pierre, SD 57501

Pardons and Parole Board
http://www.state.sd.us/corrections/board.htm
Main phone: (605) 367-5040
Main fax: (605) 367-5025
Mailing address: P.O. Box 5911, Sioux Falls, SD 57117

Kris Petersen, Executive Director
State Penitentiary, Sioux Falls, SD 57117

Cosmetology Commission
http://www.state.sd.us/dcr/cosmo/cosmo-ho.htm
General e-mail: sdcosmo@sd.cybernex.net

Main phone: (605) 773-6193
Main fax: (605) 773-7175
Mailing address: 500 E. Capitol Ave., Pierre, SD
57501

Susan Monge, Executive Secretary
111 E. Capitol Ave., Pierre, SD 57501

Economic Development Office
General e-mail: goedinfo@goed.state.sd.us
Main phone: (605) 773-5032
Main fax: (605) 773-3256
Toll free: (800) 872-6190
TTY: (800) 877-1113

Ron Wheeler, Commissioner
Capitol Lake Plaza, 711 E. Wells Ave., Pierre, SD
57501-3369

Education and Cultural Affairs Dept.
http://www.state.sd.us/state/deca/deca.htm
Main phone: (605) 773-3134
Main fax: (605) 773-6139
TTY: (605) 773-6302

Ray Christensen, Secretary
Kneip Bldg., 700 Governors Dr., Pierre, SD 57501-
2291
(605) 773-5669
E-mail: ray.christensen@state.sd.us

Board of Education
http://www.state.sd.us/deca/board/board.htm
Main phone: (605) 773-3426
Main fax: (605) 773-6159
TTY: (605) 773-6302

Ray Christensen, Secretary
700 Governors Dr., Pierre, SD 57501-2791
(605) 773-3426; Fax: (605) 773-6139
E-mail: ray.christensen@state.sd.us

Historical Society/History Office
http://www.state.sd.us/deca/cultural
Main phone: (605) 773-3458
Main fax: (605) 773-6041

Mary B. Edelen, Director
Cultural Heritage Center, 900 Governors Dr.,
Pierre, SD 57501-2217

State Archives
http://www.state.sd.us/state/executive/deca/
cultural/archives.htm
General e-mail: archref@state.sd.us
Main phone: (605) 773-3804
Main fax: (605) 773-6041

Richard Popp, Director
900 Governors Dr., Pierre, SD 57501-2217

State Library
http://www.state.sd.us/state/executive/deca/
st_lib/st_lib.htm
Main phone: (605) 773-3131
Main fax: (605) 773-4950
Toll free: (800) 423-6665

Suzanne Miller, State Librarian
Mercedes MacKay Bldg., 800 Governors Dr.,
Pierre, SD 57501-2294
Fax: (605) 773-6962
E-mail: suzanne.miller@state.sd.us

Emergency Management Division
http://www.state.sd.us/military/sddem.htm
Main phone: (605) 773-3231
Main fax: (605) 773-3580

John A. Berheim, Director
500 E. Capitol Ave., Pierre, SD 57501-5070

Environment and Natural Resources Dept.
http://www.state.sd.us/denr
General e-mail: denrinternet@state.sd.us
Main phone: (605) 773-3151
Main fax: (605) 773-6035

Nettie H. Myers, Secretary
Joe Foss Bldg., 523 E. Capitol Ave., Pierre, SD 57501-
3181
(605) 773-5559

Environmental Services Division: Minerals and Mining Program
http://www.state.sd.us/denr/DES/mining/
mineprg.htm
Main phone: (605) 773-4201

Bob Townsend, Administrator
523 E. Capitol Ave., Joe Foss Bldg., Pierre, SD
57501
E-mail: Bob.Townsend@state.sd.us

Financial and Technical Assistance Division: Geological Survey Program
http://www.sdgs.usd.edu
Main phone: (605) 677-5227
Main fax: (605) 677-5895

Derric Iles, State Geologist
414 E. Clark, Akeley Science Center, Vermillion,
SD 57069
E-mail: diles@usd.edu

Financial and Technical Assistance Division: Water Resources Assistance Program
http://www.state.sd.us/denr/DFTA/WRAP.htm
Main phone: (605) 773-4254
Main fax: (605) 773-4068

Jim Feeney, Administrator
Joe Foss Bldg., 523 E. Capitol Ave., Pierre, SD

57501-3181
E-mail: Jim.Feeney@state.sd.us

Finance and Management Bureau
http://www.state.sd.us/bfm
General e-mail:
bfm.accounting.system@state.sd.us
Main phone: (605) 773-3411
Main fax: (605) 773-4711

Curt A. Everson, Commissioner
State Capitol, 500 E. Capitol Ave., #A-216, Pierre, SD
57501-5070
E-mail: curt.everson@state.sd.us

Game, Fish, and Parks Dept.
http://www.state.sd.us/gfp/
Main phone: (605) 773-3485
Main fax: (605) 773-6245

John Cooper, Secretary
Joe Foss Bldg., 523 E. Capitol Ave., Pierre, SD 57501-3182
(605) 773-3718

Gaming Commission
http://www.state.sd.us/dcr/gaming/
Main phone: (605) 773-6050
Main fax: (605) 773-6053

Larry Eliason, Executive Secretary
118 W. Capitol Ave., Pierre, SD 57501

Health and Educational Facilities Authority
Main phone: (605) 224-9200
Main fax: (605) 224-7177
Mailing address: Box 846, Pierre, SD 57501

Jerry D. Fischer, Executive Director
330 S. Poplar Ave., Pierre, SD 57501
E-mail: fdhefajf@dtg.com

Health Dept.
http://www.state.sd.us/doh
Main phone: (605) 773-3361
Main fax: (605) 773-5683

Doneen B. Hollingsworth, Secretary
600 E. Capitol Ave., Pierre, SD 57501

Highway Patrol
http://www.state.sd.us/dcr/hp/page1sdh.htm
Main phone: (605) 773-3105
Main fax: (605) 773-6046

Gene G. Abdallah, Superintendent
500 E. Capitol Ave., Pierre, SD 57501-5070

Housing Development Authority
http://www.sdhda.org
Main phone: (605) 773-3181
Main fax: (605) 773-5154

Frequently Called Numbers

Tourism: (605) 773-3301, 1-800-732-5682;
http://www.travelsd.com
Library: (605) 773-3131;
http://www.state.sd.us/state/executive/deca/
st_lib/st_lib.htm
Board of Education: (605) 773-3426;
http://www.state.sd.us/deca/board/board.htm
Vital Statistics: (605) 773-4961; http://
www.state.sd.us/doh/VitalRec/index.htm
Tax/Revenue: (605) 773-3311;
http://www.state.sd.us/revenue
Motor Vehicles: Drivers Licensing: (605) 773-
6883; http://www.state.sd.us/dcr/dl/
sddriver.htm; *Motor Vehicles:* 773-3541;
http://www.state.sd.us/revenue/motorvcl.htm
State Police/Highway Patrol: (605) 773-3105;
http://www.state.sd.us/dcr/hp/page1sdh.htm
Unemployment: (605) 626-2312;
http://www.state.sd.us/dol/ui/ui-home.htm
General Election Information:
(605) 773-6580
Consumer Affairs: (605) 773-4400, 1-800-
300-1986; http://www.state.sd.us/atg/
consumer/index.html
Hazardous Materials: (605) 773-3153;
http://www.state.sd.us/denr/des/wastemgn/
HazWaste/HWpage1.htm

Toll free: (800) 540-4241
TTY: (605) 773-6107
Mailing address: P.O. Box 1237, Pierre, SD
57501-1237

Darlys J. Baum, Executive Director
221 S. Central Ave., Pierre, SD 57501-1237
E-mail: dar@sdhda.org

Human Services Dept.
http://www.state.sd.us/dhs/
General e-mail: infodhs@dhs.state.sd.us
Main phone: (605) 773-5990
Main fax: (605) 773-5483
Mailing address: 500 E. Capitol Ave., Pierre, SD
57501-5070

John N. Jones, Secretary
Hillsview Plaza, E. Hwy. 34, Pierre, SD 57501-5070

Developmental Disabilities Division
http://www.state.sd.us/dhs/dd/welcome.htm
General e-mail: infodd@dhs.state.sd.us
Main phone: (605) 773-3438

Main fax: (605) 773-5483
Toll free: (800) 265-9684
Mailing address: 500 E. Capitol Ave., Pierre, SD 57501

Kim Malsam-Rysdon, Director
Hillsview Plaza, E. Hwy. 34, Pierre, SD 57501

Mental Health Division
http://www.state.sd.us/dhs.dmh/index.htm
General e-mail: infomh@dhs.state.sd.us
Main phone: (605) 733-5991
Main fax: (605) 773-7076
Toll free: (800) 265-9684
TTY: (605) 773-5990
Mailing address: 500 E. Capitol Ave., Pierre, SD 57501

Betty Oldenkamp, Director
Hillsview Plaza, E. Hwy. 34, Pierre, SD 57501
E-mail: betty.oldenkamp@state.sd.us

Information and Telecommunications Bureau
http://www.state.sd.us/bit/index.htm
General e-mail: webmaster@state.sd.us
Main phone: (605) 773-5110
Main fax: (605) 773-6040

Boards and Licensing

Accountancy, (605) 367-5770,
   http://www.state.sd.us/dcr/accountancy/
Appraiser Certification Program, (605)
   773-4608, http://www.state.sd.us/dcr/
   appraisers
Architects, (605) 394-2510,
   http://www.state.sd.us/dcr/appraisers
Child Care, (605) 773-4766,
   http://www.state.sd.us/social/CCS/liceninsg
Contractors, (605) 394-2510,
   http://www.state.sd.us/social/CCS/liceninsg
Cosmetology, (605) 773-6193,
   http://www.state.sd.us/social/CCS/liceninsg
Engineers and Land Surveyors, (605)
   394-2510, http://www.state.sd.us/social/CCS/
   liceninsg
Medical and Osteopathic Examiners, (605)
   334-8343, http://www.state.sd.us/dcr/
   medical/med-hom.htm
Nursing, (605) 362-2760, http://
   www.state.sd.us/dcr/nursing/nurs-hom.htm
Pharmacy, (605) 362-2737,
   http://www.state.sd.us/dcr/pharmacy/pharm-
   ho.htm

Otto Doll, Commissioner
Kneip Bldg., 700 Governors Dr., Pierre, SD 57501
(605) 773-3416
E-mail: otto.doll@state.sd.us

Public Broadcasting Division
http://www.sdpb.org
General e-mail: admin@sdpb.org
Main phone: (605) 677-5861
Main fax: (605) 677-5010
Toll free: (800) 456-0766
Mailing address: P.O. Box 5000, Vermillion, SD 57069

Otto Doll, Executive Director (Acting)
Dakota and Cherry Sts., Vermillion, SD 57069

Investment Council
Main phone: (605) 362-2820

Stephen R. Myers, Investment Officer
4009 W. 49th St., #300, Sioux Falls, SD 57106-3784

Labor Dept.
http://www.state.sd.us/dol/dol.htm
General e-mail: labor@dol-pr.state.sd.us
Main phone: (605) 773-3101
Main fax: (605) 773-4211

Craig Johnson, Secretary
Kneip Bldg., 700 Governors Dr., Pierre, SD 57501-2291

Lottery
http://www.state.sd.us/lottery/lottery.html
General e-mail: lottery@lot.state.sd.us
Main phone: (605) 773-5770
Main fax: (605) 773-5786

Rodger Leonard, Executive Director
207 E. Capitol Ave., #200, Pierre, SD 57501
E-mail: rodger.leonard@state.sd.us

Medical and Osteopathic Examiners Board
http://www.state.sd.us/dcr/medical/med-hom.htm
Main phone: (605) 334-8343
Main fax: (605) 336-0270

L. Paul Jensen, Executive Secretary
1323 S. Minnesota Ave., Sioux Falls, SD 57105
E-mail: pjensen@sdsma.org

Nursing Board
http://www.state.sd.us/dcr/nursing/nurs-hom.htm
Main phone: (605) 362-2760
Main fax: (605) 362-2768

Diana Vander Woude, Executive Secretary
4300 S. Louise Ave., #C-1, Sioux Falls, SD 57106-3124
E-mail: Diana.VanderWoude@state.sd.us

Oahe Federal Credit Union
General e-mail: oahefcu@dtgnet.com
Main phone: (605) 224-6264
Main fax: (605) 224-7332
Toll free: (888) 461-6771
Mailing address: P.O. Box 818, Pierre, SD 57501

Marla Miller, Office Manager
124 S. Euclid, Pierre, SD 57501

Personnel Bureau
http://www.state.sd.us/bop/bop.htm
General e-mail: bopinfo@state.sd.us
Main phone: (605) 773-3148
Main fax: (605) 773-4344
TTY: (605) 773-6957

Sandra J. Zinter, Commissioner
State Capitol, 500 E. Capitol Ave., Pierre, SD 57501-5070
(605) 773-4918

Pharmacy Board
http://www.state.sd.us/dcr/pharmacy/pharm-ho.htm
Main phone: (605) 362-2737
Main fax: (605) 362-2738

Dennis M. Jones, Executive Secretary
4305 S. Louise Ave., #104, Sioux Falls, SD 57106-3115

Public Utilities Commission
http://www.state.sd.us/puc/puc.htm
Main phone: (605) 773-3201
Main fax: (605) 773-3809
Toll free: (800) 332-1782
TTY: (800) 877-1113

William Bullard Jr., Executive Director
Capitol Bldg., 500 E. Capitol Ave., 1st Fl., Pierre, SD 57501-5070
E-mail: bill.bullard@state.sd.us

Regents Board
http://www.ris.sdbor.edu/home.htm
General e-mail: info@ris.sdbor.edu
Main phone: (605) 773-3455
Main fax: (605) 773-5320

Robert T. Tad Perry, Executive Director
306 E. Capitol Ave., #200, Pierre, SD 57501-2409
E-mail: tadp@ris.sdbor.edu

School for the Deaf
http://www.ris.sdbor/sdsd/Main.htm
Main phone: (605) 367-5200
Main fax: (605) 367-5209

John Green, Superintendent
2001 E. 8th St., Sioux Falls, SD 57103-1899
E-mail: greenj@sdsd.sbor.edu

Retirement System
http://www.state.sd.us/sdrs
Main phone: (605) 773-3731
Main fax: (605) 773-3949
TTY: (605) 773-3958
Mailing address: P.O. Box 1098, Pierre, SD 57501

Elmer Brinkman, Chair
216 E. Capitol, Pierre, SD 57501

Revenue Dept.
http://www.state.sd.us/revenue
Main phone: (605) 773-3311
Main fax: (605) 773-6729

Gary Viken, Secretary
Anderson Bldg., 445 E. Capitol Ave., Pierre, SD 57501-3185
(605) 773-5131; *Fax:* (605) 773-5129
E-mail: Gary.Viken@state.sd.us

Motor Vehicles Division
http://www.state.sd.us/revenue/motorvcl.htm
General e-mail: motor@rev.state.sd.us
Main phone: (605) 773-3541
Main fax: (605) 773-5129

Debra Hillmer, Director
445 E. Capitol Ave., Anderson Bldg., Pierre, SD 57501-3100

School and Public Lands Office
http://www.state.sd.us/school/index.htm
Main phone: (605) 773-3303
Main fax: (605) 773-5520

Curt Johnson, Commissioner
State Capitol, 500 E. Capitol Ave., Pierre, SD 57501-5070
E-mail: curt.johnson@state.sd.us

Social Services Dept.
http://www.state.sd.us/state/executive/social/
General e-mail: info@dss.state.sd.us
Main phone: (605) 773-3165
Main fax: (605) 773-4855

James W. Ellenbecker, Secretary
700 Governors Dr., Pierre, SD 57501-2291
E-mail: James.Ellenbecker@state.sd.us

Adult Services and Aging Division
http://www.state.sd.us/social/ASA/asa.htm
General e-mail: ASAging@dss.state.sd.us
Main phone: (605) 773-3656
Main fax: (605) 773-6834

Gail Ferris, Administrator
700 Governors Dr., Pierre, SD 57501-2291

Medical Services Office
http://www.state.sd.us/social/medicaid/index.htm
General e-mail: medicaid@dss.state.sd.us
Main phone: (605) 773-3495
Main fax: (605) 773-5246
Toll free: (800) 452-7691

David Christensen, Administrator
700 Governors Dr., Pierre, SD 57501

State Fair
http://www.sdstatefair.com

Laws
Sales tax: 5%
Income tax: None
State minimum wage: $5.15 (Federal is $5.15)
Marriage age: 18
First-cousin marriage: Prohibited
Drinking age: 21
State control of liquor sales: No
Blood alcohol for DWI: 0.10%
Driving age: 16
Speed limit: 75 mph
Permit to buy handguns: No, but 2-day wait
Minimum age to possess handguns: 18
Minimum age to possess rifles, shotguns: None
State lottery: Yes; also Powerball
Casinos: Yes (commercial, tribal); also slot/ video machines
Pari-mutuel betting: Horse and dog racing
Death penalty: Yes
3 strikes minimum sentence: None
Hate crimes law: Yes
Gay employment non-discrimination: No
Official language(s): English
Term limits: Governor (8 yrs.); state legislators (8 yrs.)
State laws are complex and subject to change; this information is not intended as legal advice. For an explanation of this information, see p. x.

Main phone: (605) 353-7340
Main fax: (605) 353-7348
Toll free: (800) 529-0900
TTY: (800) 529-0900
Mailing address: P.O. Box 1275, Huron, SD 57350-1275

Craig Atkins, Manager
890 3rd St. S.W., Huron, SD 57350-1275
E-mail: craig.atkins@state.sd.us

Technical Professions Board
http://www.state.sd.us/dcr/engineer/eng-hom.htm
Main phone: (605) 394-2510
Main fax: (605) 394-2509

Ann Whipple, Executive Director
2040 W. Main St., #304, Rapid City, SD 57702-2447
E-mail: anwhipple@aol.com

Tourism Dept.
http://www.travelsd.com
General e-mail: sdinfo@state.sd.us
Main phone: (605) 773-3301
Main fax: (605) 773-3256
Toll free: (800) 732-5682
TTY: (800) 877-1113

Patricia Rahja Van Gerpen, Secretary
711 E. Wells Ave., Pierre, SD 57501-3369

Transportation Dept.
http://www.state.sd.us/dot/
Main phone: (605) 773-3265
Main fax: (605) 773-3921

Ronald W. Wheeler, Secretary
Transportaton Bldg., 700 E. Broadway Ave., #202, Pierre, SD 57501-2586

Tribal Government Relations
Main phone: (605) 773-3415
Main fax: (605) 773-6592

Webster Two Hawk Sr., Commissioner
Capitol Lake Plaza, 711 E. Wells Ave., #250, Pierre, SD 57501-3369
E-mail: webster@goed.statesd.us

South Dakota Legislature
Capitol Bldg.
Pierre, SD 57501-5070
General information: (605) 773-3251
Fax: (605) 773-6806
TTY: (605) 775-4305
http://www.state.sd.us/state/legis/lrc.htm

Senate

General information: (605) 773-3821

Carole Hillard (R), President
State Capitol, 500 E. Capitol Ave., Pierre, SD 57501-5070
(605) 773-3661; *Fax:* (605) 773-4711
E-mail: carole.hillard@state.sd.us

Harold Halverson (R), President Pro Tempore
Capitol Bldg., Pierre, SD 57501-5070
(605) 773-3824
http://www.state.sd.us/state/legis/lrc/lawstat/https/74/mbrdt12.htm

M. Michael Rounds (R), Majority Leader
Capitol Bldg., Pierre, SD 57501-5070
(605) 773-3828
http://www.state.sd.us/state/legis/lrc/lawstat/https/74/mbrdt31.htm

Dick Hainje (R), Majority Whip
Capitol Bldg., Pierre, SD 57501-5070
(605) 773-3821
http://www.state.sd.us/state/legis/lrc/lawstat/https/74/mbrdt141.htm

James K. (Jim) Hutmacher (D), Minority Leader
Capitol Bldg., Pierre, SD 57501-5070
(605) 773-4494
http://www.state.sd.us/state/legis/lrc/lawstat/https/74/mbrdt136.htm

Charles E. Flowers (D), Minority Whip
Capitol Bldg., Pierre, SD 57501-5070
(605) 773-4494
http://www.state.sd.us/state/legis/lrc/lawstat/https/74/mbrdt9.htm

Patricia Adam, Secretary
Capitol Bldg., Pierre, SD 57501-5070
(605) 773-3825; *Fax:* (605) 773-4576

House

General information: (605) 773-3851

Roger W. Hunt (R), Speaker of the House
Capitol Bldg., Pierre, SD 57501-5070
(605) 773-3830
E-mail: rep.hunt@state.sd.us
http://www.state.sd.us/state/legis/lrc/lawstat/https/74/mbrdt66.htm

Scott Eccarius (R), Speaker Pro Tempore
Capitol Bldg., Pierre, SD 57501-5070
(605) 773-4485
E-mail: NemoSD@aol.com
http://www.state.sd.us/state/legis/lrc/lawstat/https/74/mbrdt156.htm

Steve Cutler (R), Majority Leader
Capitol Bldg., Pierre, SD 57501-5070
(605) 773-3845
E-mail: rep.cutler@state.sd.us
http://www.state.sd.us/state/legis/lrc/lawstat/https/74/mbrdt50.htm

Jay L. Duenwald (R), Majority Whip
Capitol Bldg., Pierre, SD 57501-5070
(605) 773-5938
http://www.state.sd.us/state/legis/lrc/lawstat/https/74/mbrdt

Pat Haley (D), Minority Leader
Capitol Bldg., Pierre, SD 57501-5070
(605) 773-4484
http://www.state.sd.us/state/legis/lrc/lawstat/https/74/mbrdt62.htm

Deb Fischer-Clemens (D), Minority Whip
Capitol Bldg., Pierre, SD 57501-5070
(605) 773-4484
http://www.state.sd.us/state/legis/lrc/lawstat/https/74/mbrdt

Karen Gerdes, Chief Clerk
Capitol Bldg., Pierre, SD 57501-5070
(605) 773-3842; *Fax:* (605) 773-4576

South Dakota Judiciary

State Capitol
500 E. Capitol Ave.
Pierre, SD 57501-5070
http://www.state.sd.us/state/judicial/index.htm

Supreme Court

Dorothy A. Smith, Clerk
State Capitol, 500 E. Capitol Ave., Pierre, SD 57501-5070
(605) 773-3511; *Fax:* (605) 773-6128
E-mail: dorothys@ujs.state.sd.us

Justices
Composition: 5 justices
Selection Method: appointed by governor for 3-year term; subject to retention ballot in general election thereafter
Length of term: 3-year initial term; 8 years if retained in general election

Robert A. Miller, Chief Justice, (605) 773-6254
Robert A. Amundson, Justice, (605) 773-4886

David E. Gilbertson, Justice, (605) 773-4881
John K. Konenkamp, Justice, (605) 773-3511
Richard W. Sabers, Justice, (605) 773-4885

State Court Administrator
Main phone: (605) 773-3474
Main fax: (605) 773-5627

Michael L. Buenger, State Court Administrator

State Capitol, 500 E. Capitol Ave., Pierre, SD 57501-5070

Supreme Court Library
Main phone: (605) 773-4898
Main fax: (605) 773-6128

Sheridan Cash Anderson, Librarian
State Capitol, 500 E. Capitol Ave., Pierre, SD 57501-5070

Legislative and Political Party Information Resources

Senate home page: http://www.state.sd.us/state/legis/lrc/general/senrost.htm
House home page: http://www.state.sd.us/state/legis/lrc/general/hourost.htm
Committees: http://www.state.sd.us/state/legis/lrc/lawstat/https/74/comm.htm
Legislative process: http://www.state.sd.us/state.legis/lrc/general/bill2law.jpg
Current session information: http://www.state.sd.us/state/legis/lrc/lawstat/https/74/lrcmenu.htm
South Dakota Democratic Party
    401 E. 8th St., #221, Sioux Falls, SD 57104; *Phone:* (605) 335-7337; *Fax:* (605) 335-7401
South Dakota Republican Party
    P.O. Box 1099, Pierre, SD 57501; *Phone:* (605) 224-7347; *Fax:* (605) 224-7349

Tennessee

State Capitol
Nashville, TN 37243-0001
Public information: (615) 741-3011
Fax: (615) 532-6193
http://www.state.tn.us

Office of the Governor
http://www.state.tn.us/governor
Main phone: (615) 741-2001
Main fax: (615) 532-9711
TTY: (615) 741-0435

Don Sundquist (R), Governor
State Capitol, 1st Fl., Nashville, TN 37243-0001
E-mail: dsundquist@mail.state.tn.us

Wendell Moore, Deputy to the Governor/Chief of Staff
State Capitol, 1st Fl., Nashville, TN 37243-0001
(615) 532-8906; *Fax:* (615) 532-9711
E-mail: wmoore@mail.state.tn.us

Beth Fortune, Press Secretary
State Capitol, 600 Charlotte Ave., 1st Fl., Nashville, TN 37243-0001
(615) 741-1416; *Fax:* (615) 741-3763
E-mail: dsundquist@mail.state.tn.us

Vacant, Constituent Affairs
State Capitol, 1st Fl., Nashville, TN 37243-0001
(615) 741-2001; *Fax:* (615) 532-9711

Office of the Lieutenant Governor
Main phone: (615) 741-2368
Main fax: (615) 741-9349

John S. Wilder (D), Lieutenant Governor
1 Legislative Plaza, Nashville, TN 37243-0026
E-mail: lt.gov.john.wilder@legislature.state.tn.us

Office of the Secretary of State
http://www.state.tn.us/sos
Main phone: (615) 741-2819
Main fax: (615) 532-9547

Riley C. Darnell (D), Secretary of State
State Capitol, 1st Fl., Nashville, TN 37243-0305

Office of the Attorney General
http://www.attorneygeneral.state.tn.us
Main phone: (615) 741-3491
Main fax: (615) 741-2009

Paul G. Summers, Attorney General
425 5th Ave. North, Cordell Hull Bldg., Nashville, TN 37243

State of Tennessee

Capital: Nashville, since 1826
Founded: 1790, as Territory South of the River Ohio; formerly claimed by North Carolina
Statehood: June 1, 1796 (16th state)
Constitution adopted: 1870 (last amended 1978)
Area: 41,219 sq. mi. (ranks 34th)
Population: 5,430,621 (1998 est.; ranks 17th)
Largest cities: (1998 est.) Memphis (603,507); Nashville (510,274); Knoxville (165,540); Chattanooga (147,790); Clarksville (97,978)
Counties: 95, Most populous: (1998 est.) Shelby (868,825); Davidson (533,967); Knox (366,846); Hamilton (294,745); Rutherford (166,035)
U.S. Congress: William Frist (R), Fred Thompson (R); 9 Representatives
Nickname(s): Volunteer State
Motto: Agriculture and commerce
Song: "Tennessee Waltz"
Bird: Mockingbird
Tree: Tulip poplar
Flower: Iris
State fair: at Nashville, early to mid-Sept.
Former capital(s): Knoxville, Kingston, Murfreesboro

Office of the Comptroller
http://www.comptroller.state.tn.us
Main phone: (615) 741-2501
Main fax: (615) 741-7328

John G. Morgan (D), Comptroller
State Capitol, Nashville, TN 37243-0260
E-mail: jmorgan@mail.state.tn.us

Office of the Treasurer
http://www.treasury.state.tn.us
Main phone: (615) 741-2956
Main fax: (615) 253-1591

Steve Adams (D), Treasurer
State Capitol, 1st Fl., Nashville, TN 37243-0225
E-mail: sadams@mail.state.tn.us

Military Dept.
http://www.state.tn.us/military
General e-mail: rharris@mail.state.tn.us
Main phone: (615) 313-0633
Main fax: (615) 313-3129
Mailing address: P.O. Box 41502, Nashville, TN
37204-1502

Jackie D. Wood, Adjutant General
Houston Barracks, 3041 Sidco Dr., Nashville, TN
37204-1502
(615) 313-3001; *Fax:* (615) 313-3100

Agencies

Accountancy Board
http://www.state.tn.us/commerce/tnsba/index.htm
Main phone: (615) 741-2550
Main fax: (615) 532-8800
Toll free: (888) 453-6150

Darrel Tongate, Executive Director
Davy Crockett Tower, 500 James Robertson Pkwy.,
2nd Fl., Nashville, TN 37243-1143

Aging Commission
Main phone: (615) 741-2056
Main fax: (615) 741-3309
TTY: (800) 848-0298

James S. Whaley, Executive Director
Andrew Jackson Bldg., 500 Deaderick St., 9th Fl.,
Nashville, TN 37243-0860
E-mail: jwhaley@mail.state.tn.us

Agriculture Dept.
http://www.state.tn.us/agriculture
Main phone: (615) 837-5117
Main fax: (615) 837-5333
Mailing address: P.O. Box 40627, Nashville, TN
37204

Dan Wheeler, Commissioner
440 Hogan Rd., Nashville, TN 37220
(615) 837-5100
E-mail: dwheeler@mail.state.tn.us

Forestry Division
http://www.state.tn.us/agriculture/forestry/
forestry.html
Main phone: (615) 837-5520
Main fax: (615) 837-5003
Mailing address: P.O. Box 40627, Melrose
Station, Nashville, TN 37204

Ken Arney, State Forester
Ellington Agricultural Center, Bruer Bldg., 440
Hogan Rd., Nashville, TN 37220
(615) 837-5411
E-mail: karney@mail.state.tn.us

Alcoholic Beverage Commission
Main phone: (615) 741-1602
Main fax: (615) 741-0847

James L. Exum, Chair
226 Capitol Blvd., #300, Nashville, TN 37243-0755

Architects and Engineers Board
http://www.state.tn.us/commerce/ae.html
Main phone: (615) 741-3221
Main fax: (615) 532-9410
Toll free: (800) 256-5758

Barbara Bowling, Executive Director
Davy Crockett Tower, 500 James Robertson Pkwy.,
Nashville, TN 37243-0565
E-mail: bbowling@mail.state.tn.us

Arts Commission
http://www.arts.state.tn.us
Main phone: (615) 741-1701
Main fax: (615) 741-8559

Rich Boyd, Executive Director
401 Charlotte Ave., Nashville, TN 37243-0780
(615) 741-6396
E-mail: rboyd@mail.state.tn.us

Board of Education
http://www.state.tn.us/sbe/
Main phone: (615) 741-2966
Main fax: (615) 741-0371
Toll free: (800) 862-77923

J. V. Sailors, Executive Director
710 James Robertson Pkwy., Andrew Johnson Tower,
9th Fl., Nashville, TN 37243-1050
E-mail: jvsailors@mail.state.tn.us

Bureau of Investigation
http://www.tbi.state.tn.us
Main phone: (615) 741-0430
Main fax: (615) 741-4788

Larry D. Wallace, Director
1148 Foster Ave., Nashville, TN 37210-4406

Children and Youth Commission
http://www.state.tn.us/tccy
General e-mail: tccy@mail.state.tn.us
Main phone: (615) 741-2633
Main fax: (615) 741-5956

Linda O'Neal, Executive Director
Andrew Johnson Tower, 710 James Robertson Pkwy.,
9th Fl., Nashville, TN 37243-0800
E-mail: loneal2@mail.state.tn.us

Children's Services Dept.
http://www.state.tn.us/youth
General e-mail: gperry@mail.state.tn.us
Main phone: (615) 741-9699
Main fax: (615) 532-8079

George W. Hattaway, Commissioner
Cordell Hull Bldg., 436 6th Ave. North, 7th Fl.,
Nashville, TN 37243-2910
(615) 741-9701
E-mail: ghattaway@mail.state.tn.us

Commerce and Insurance Dept.
http://www.state.tn.us/commerce
General e-mail: dci@mail.state.tn.us
Main phone: (615) 741-2241
Main fax: (615) 532-6934

Anne B. Pope, Commissioner
Davy Crockett Tower, 500 James Robertson Pkwy.,
5th Fl., Nashville, TN 37243-0565
E-mail: apope@mail.state.tn.us

Consumer Affairs Division
http://www.state.tn.us/consumer
General e-mail: dca@mail.state.tn.us
Main phone: (615) 741-4737
Main fax: (615) 532-4994
Toll free: (800) 342-8385

Mark Williams, Director
500 James Roberston Pkwy., 5th Fl., Nashville, TN
37243-0600

Fire Prevention Division and State Fire Marshal's Office
http://www.state.tn.us/commerce/fpdiv.htm
Main phone: (615) 741-2981
Main fax: (615) 741-1583

W. Stuart Crine, Assistant Commissioner
Davy Crockett Tower, 500 James Robertson Pkwy.,
3rd Fl., Nashville, TN 37243
E-mail: scrine@mail.state.tn.us

Regulatory Boards Division
http://www.state.tn.us/commerce/regbrdiv.html
Main phone: (615) 741-3449
Main fax: (615) 741-6470

Stephanie H. Chivers, Assistant Commissioner
Davy Crockett Tower, 500 James Robertson Pkwy.,
Nashville, TN 37243-0572
E-mail: schivers@mail.state.tn.us

TennCare Division
http://www.state.tn.us/commerce/tncardiv.html
General e-mail: dci@mail.state.tn.us
Main phone: (615) 741-2677
Main fax: (615) 532-8872
Toll free: (800) 669-1851

Joseph P. Keane, Deputy Commissioner
Davy Crockett Tower, 500 James Robertson Pkwy.,
#750, Nashville, TN 37243-1169
E-mail: jpkeane2@mail.state.tn.us

Higher Educational Institutions

Austin Peay State University
http://www.apsu.edu
601 College St., Clarksville, TN 37044
Main phone: (931) 221-7011

East Tennessee State University
http://www.etsu.edu
P.O. Box 70731, Johnson City, TN 37614-0734
Main phone: (423) 439-6861

Middle Tennessee State University
http://www.mtsu.edu
1301 E. Main St., Murfreesboro, TN 37132-0001
Main phone: (615) 898-2300

Tennessee State University
http://www.tnstate.edu
3500 John A. Merritt Blvd., Nashville, TN 37209
Main phone: (615) 963-5000

Tennessee Technological University
http://www.tntech.edu
TTU Box 5006, Cookeville, TN 38505
Main phone: (931) 372-3888

University of Memphis
http://www.memphis.edu
Campus Box 526618, Memphis, TN 38152
Main phone: (901) 678-2169

University of Tennessee
http://www.utenn.edu
Knoxville, TN 37996
Main phone: (423) 974-2184
Branches: Chattanooga, Martin, Memphis

Community and Field Services: Child Care Services
http://www.state.tn.us/humanserv/childcare.htm
Main phone: (615) 313-4778
Main fax: (615) 532-9956

Brenda Ramsey, Director
400 Deaderick St., Nashville, TN 37248
(615) 313-4781

Contractors Board
Main phone: (615) 741-8307
Main fax: (615) 532-2868
Toll free: (800) 544-7693

Phyllis Blevins, Executive Director
Davy Crockett Tower, 500 James Robertson Pkwy.,
Nashville, TN 37243-1150
E-mail: pblevins@mail.state.tn.us

Correction Dept.
http://www.state.tn.us/correction

Main phone: (615) 741-1000
Main fax: (615) 532-8281
TTY: (615) 532-4423

Donald Campbell, Commissioner
Rachel Jackson Bldg., 320 6th Ave. North, 4th Fl.,
Nashville, TN 37243-0465

Cosmetology and Barber Board
http://www.state.tn.us/commerce/cosmo/index.htm
Main phone: (615) 741-2515
Main fax: (615) 741-1310

Evelyn Griffin, Administrative Director
Davy Crockett Tower, 500 James Robertson Pkwy., 1st
Fl., Nashville, TN 37243-1147
E-mail: egriffin@mail.state.tn.us

Economic and Community Development Dept.
http://www.state.tn.us/ecd
Main phone: (615) 741-1888
Main fax: (615) 741-7306

Bill Baxter, Commissioner
Rachel Jackson Bldg., 320 6th Ave. North, 8th Fl.,
Nashville, TN 37243-0405

Education Dept.
http://www.state.tn.us/education/
Main phone: (615) 741-2731
Main fax: (615) 741-6236

Vernon Coffey, Commissioner
Andrew Johnson Tower, 710 James Robertson Pkwy.,
Nashville, TN 37243-0375

Emergency Management Agency
http://www.tnema.org
General e-mail: dwilliams@tnema.org
Main phone: (615) 741-0001
Main fax: (615) 242-9635
Toll free: (800) 258-3300

John White Jr., Director
Houston Barracks, 3041 Sidco Dr., Nashville, TN
37204
(615) 741-4528; Fax: (615) 741-0006

Environment and Conservation Dept.
http://www.state.tn.us/environment
Main phone: (615) 532-0109
Main fax: (615) 532-0120

Milton H. Hamilton Jr., Commissioner
Life and Casualty Tower, 401 Church St., 21st Fl.,
Nashville, TN 37243-0435
(615) 532-0104

Geology Division
http://www.state.tn.us/environment/tdg/
index.html

General e-mail:
geology@langate.tnet.state.tn.us
Main phone: (615) 532-1500
Main fax: (615) 532-1517

Ron Zurawski, State Geologist
401 Church St., L & C Tower, 13th Fl., Nashville,
TN 37243-0445
(615) 532-1502
E-mail: rzurawski@mail.state.tn.us

Historical Commission
http://www.state.tn.us/environment/hist/hist.htm
Main phone: (615) 532-1550
Main fax: (615) 532-1549

Herbert Harper, Director
2941 Lebanon Rd., Nashville, TN 37243-0442

State Parks Division
http://www.state.tn.us/environment/parks/
index.html
Main phone: (615) 532-0001
Main fax: (615) 532-0732
Toll free: (888) 867-2757

Walter Butler, Director
L & C Tower, 401 Church St., 21st Fl., Nashville,
TN 37243

Water Resources Office
Main phone: (615) 837-4700

W. Scott Gain, District Chief
640 Grassmere Park, #100, Nashville, TN 37211

Finance and Administration Dept.
http://www.state.tn.us/finance/
Main phone: (615) 741-2401
Main fax: (615) 741-9872

John D. Ferguson, Commissioner
State Capitol, 1st Fl., Nashville, TN 37243-0285

Financial Institutions Dept.
http://www.state.tn.us/financialinst/
Main phone: (615) 741-2236
Main fax: (615) 741-2883

Bill C. Houston, Commissioner
John Sevier Bldg., 500 Charlotte Ave., 4th Fl.,
Nashville, TN 37243-0705

Fiscal Review Committee
Main phone: (615) 741-2564
Main fax: (615) 532-7393

James A. Davenport, Executive Director
War Memorial Bldg., 6th Ave. and Charotte, Nashville,
TN 37243-0057

General Services Dept.
http://www.state.tn.us/generalserv/

Main phone: (615) 741-9263
Main fax: (615) 532-8594

Larry Haynes, Commissioner
Tennessee Tower, 312 8th St. North, 24th Fl.,
Nashville, TN 37243-0530

Health Dept.
http://www.state.tn.us/health
General e-mail: ddenton@mail.state.tn.us
Main phone: (615) 741-3111
Main fax: (615) 741-2491

Fredia S. Wadley, Commissioner
425 5th Ave. North, 3rd Fl., Nashville, TN 37247-0101

Higher Education Commission
Main phone: (615) 741-3605
Main fax: (615) 741-6230

Richard G. Roda, Executive Director
Pkwy. Towers, 404 James Robertson Pkwy., #1900,
Nashville, TN 37243-0830
(615) 741-7561
E-mail: rroda@mail.state.tn.us

Housing Development Agency
http://www.state.tn.us/thda
Main phone: (615) 741-2400
Main fax: (615) 741-9634
Toll free: (800) 228-8432
TTY: (615) 741-6685

W. Jeff Reynolds, Executive Director
Pkwy. Towers, 404 James Robertson Pkwy., #1114,
Nashville, TN 37243-0900
(615) 741-2473
E-mail: jreynolds2@mail.state.tn.us

Human Rights Commission
Main phone: (615) 741-5825
Main fax: (615) 532-2197
Toll free: (800) 251-3589
TTY: (615) 741-2491

Julius Sloss, Executive Director
Cornerstone Square Bldg., 530 Church St., #400,
Nashville, TN 37243-0745
E-mail: J_O_Sloss@mail.state.tn.us

Human Services Dept.
http://www.state.tn.us/humanserv
Main phone: (615) 313-4700
Main fax: (615) 741-4165
TTY: (615) 259-2060

Natasha K. Metcalf, Commissioner
Citizens Plaza Bldg., 400 Deaderick St., Nashville, TN
37248
E-mail: nmetcalf@mail.state.tn.us

Rehabilitation Services
http://www.state.tn.us/humanserv

Frequently Called Numbers

Tourism: (615) 741-2159, 1-800-836-6200;
http://www.state.tn.us/tourdev
Library: (615) 741-2764; http://
www.state.tn.us/sos/statelib/tslahome.htm
Board of Education: (615) 741-2966; http://
www.state.tn.us/sbe/
Vital Statistics: (615) 741-1763; http://
www.state.tn.us/health/vr/
Tax/Revenue: (615) 741-2594, 1-800-342-
1003; http://www.state.tn.us/revenue
Motor Vehicles: (615) 741-3945; http://
www.state.tn.us/safety/listinfo.htm
State Police/Highway Patrol: (615) 251-5175;
http://www.state.tn.us/safety/thp.html
Unemployment: (615) 741-1948; http://
www.state.tn.us/labor-wfd/ui/ui.htm
General Election Information: (615) 862-
8800
Consumer Affairs: (615) 741-4737, 1-800-
342-8385; http://www.state.tn.us/consumer
Hazardous Materials: (615) 532-0780

Main phone: (615) 313-4714
TTY: (615) 313-4714

Carl Brown, Assistant Commissioner
400 Deaderick St., #1500, Nashville, TN 37248

Labor and Workforce Development Dept.
http://www.state.tn.us/labor-wfd/
Main phone: (615) 741-2131
Main fax: (615) 741-5078
TTY: (615) 532-2879

Michael Magill, Commissioner
Davy Crockett Tower, 710 James Robertson Pkwy.,
Nashville, TN 37423

Workers Compensation Divsion
http://www.state.tn.us/labor/wcomp.html
Main phone: (615) 532-4812
Main fax: (615) 532-1468
Toll free: (800) 332-2667
TTY: (800) 848-0299

James Farmer, Director
710 James Robertson Pkwy., Nashville, TN 37243-
0661

Land Surveyors Board
Main phone: (615) 741-3611
Main fax: (615) 741-5995

Donna Moulder, Director
Davy Crockett Tower, 500 James Robertson Pkwy.,
  Nashville, TN 37243-0565
Fax: (615) 741-6470
E-mail: dmoulder@mail.state.tn.us

Library and Archives Division
http://www.state.tn.us/sos/statelib/tslahome.htm
Main phone: (615) 741-2764
Main fax: (615) 741-6471

Edwin S. Gleaves, State Librarian and Archivist
403 7th Ave. North, #200, Nashville, TN 37243-0312
(615) 741-7996; *Fax:* (615) 532-9293
E-mail: egleaves@mail.state.tn.us

Medical Examiners Board
Main phone: (615) 532-3202, ext. 24384
Main fax: (615) 253-4484
Toll free: (888) 310-4650

Daniel Starnes, President
425 5th Ave. North, 1st Fl., Nashville, TN 37247-1010
(615) 222-6749

Mental Health and Mental Retardation Dept.
Main phone: (615) 532-6610
Main fax: (615) 532-6514
TTY: (615) 532-6612

Elizabeth Rukeyser, Commissioner
425 5th Ave. North, Nashville, TN 37243
(615) 532-6500

Nursing Board
Main phone: (615) 532-3202, ext. 25166
Main fax: (615) 741-7899
Toll free: (888) 310-4650

Boards and Licensing

Accountancy, (615) 741-2550, http://
  www.state.tn.us/commerce/tnsba/index.htm
Architects and Engineers, (615) 741-3221,
  http://www.state.tn.us/commerce/ae.html
Child Care, (615) 313-4778
Contractors, (615) 741-8307
Cosmetology, (615) 741-2515, http://
  www.state.tn.us/commerce/cosmo/index.htm
Land Surveyors, (615) 741-3611
Medical Examiners, (615) 532-3202,
  ext. 24384
Nursing, (615) 532-3202, ext. 25166
Pharmacy, (615) 741-2718
Real Estate, (615) 741-1831

Elizabeth Lund, Executive Director
425 5th Ave. North, 1st Fl., Nashville, TN 37247-1010

Parole Board
Main phone: (615) 741-1673

Donna Blackburn, Executive Director
404 James Robertson Pkwy., #1300, Nashville, TN
  37243-0850

Personnel Dept.
http://www.state.tn.us/personnel
Main phone: (615) 741-4841
Main fax: (615) 741-6985
Toll free: (800) 221-7345

Dorothy B. Shell, Commissioner
James K. Polk Bldg., 505 Deaderick St., 2nd Fl.,
  Nashville, TN 37243-0635
(615) 741-2958; *Fax:* (615) 532-0728

Pharmacy Board
Main phone: (615) 741-2718
Main fax: (615) 741-2722

Kendall Lynch, Director
Davy Crockett Tower, 500 James Robertson Pkwy.,
  Nashville, TN 37243-1149
E-mail: klynch@mail.state.tn.us

Real Estate Appraisers Board
Main phone: (615) 741-1831
Main fax: (615) 253-1692

Sandy Moore, Administrator
Davy Crockett Tower, 500 James Robertson Pkwy.,
  Nashville, TN 37243-1166
E-mail: smoore3@mail.state.tn.us

Regulatory Authority
http://www.state.tn.us/tra/index.htm
Main phone: (615) 741-2904
Main fax: (615) 741-5015
Toll free: (800) 342-8359

Melvin Malone, Chair
460 James Robertson Pkwy., Nashville, TN 37243-
  0505

Revenue Dept.
http://www.state.tn.us/revenue
General e-mail: tnrevenue@mail.state.tn.us
Main phone: (615) 741-2594
Main fax: (615) 741-1116
Toll free: (800) 342-1003
TTY: (615) 741-7398

Ruth E. Johnson, Commissioner
Andrew Jackson Bldg., 500 Deaderick St., #1200,
  Nashville, TN 37242-1099
(615) 741-2461; *Fax:* (615) 532-2285
E-mail: rjohnson@mail.state.tn.us

Safety Dept.

http://www.state.tn.us/safety
General e-mail: dkeeton@mail.state.tn.us
Main phone: (615) 741-3954
Main fax: (615) 253-2091

Mike Greene, Commissioner
1150 Foster Ave., Nashville, TN 37249-1000
(615) 251-5166
E-mail: mgreene@state.tn.us

Drivers License Issuance Division

http://www.state.tn.us/safety/listinfo.htm
General e-mail: safety@mail.state.tn.us
Main phone: (615) 741-3945
Main fax: (615) 253-2092
TTY: (615) 532-2281

Vona Lasater, Director
1150 Foster Ave., Nashville, TN 37249-1000
(615) 251-5310

Highway Patrol

http://www.state.tn.us/safety/thp.html
Main phone: (615) 251-5175
Main fax: (615) 532-1057

Jerry W. Scott, Deputy Commissioner
1150 Foster Ave., Nashville, TN 37249

Title and Registration Division

Main phone: (615) 741-3101
Mailing address: 44 Vantage Way, #160,
Nashville, TN 37273

Martha Irwin, Director
44 Vantage Way, Nashville, TN 37243-8000

State Fair

http://janis.nashville.org/tsf/st_fair.html
General e-mail: TSF@metro.nahsville.org
Main phone: (615) 862-8980
Main fax: (615) 862-8992
Mailing address: P.O. Box 40208, Melrose Station,
Nashville, TN 37204

Jennifer Hill, Director
625 Smith Ave., #200, Nashville, TN 37203

Tourist Development Dept.

http://www.state.tn.us/tourdev
General e-mail: mail@state.tn.us
Main phone: (615) 741-2159
Main fax: (615) 741-7225
Toll free: (800) 836-6200
TTY: (615) 741-0691

John A. Wade, Commissioner
Rachel Jackson Bldg., 320 6th Ave. North, 5th Fl.,
Nashville, TN 37243-0696
(615) 741-9001

Transportation Dept.

http://www.tdot.state.tn.us
General e-mail: transport@mail.state.tn.us
Main phone: (615) 741-2848
Main fax: (615) 741-2508
TTY: (615) 532-1603

J. Bruce Saltsman Sr., Commissioner
James K. Polk Bldg., 505 Deaderick St., #700,
Nashville, TN 37243-0349
(615) 741-2848

Aeronautics Commission

http://www.state.tn.us/transport/aeronautics-commission/index.htm
General e-mail: aeronautics@mail.state.tn.us
Main phone: (615) 741-3208
Main fax: (615) 741-4959
Mailing address: P.O. Box 17326, Nashville, TN
37217

John T. Baugh Jr., Chair
424 Knapp Blvd., Bldg. 4219, Nashville, TN
37217

Veterans Affairs Dept.

http://www.state.tn.us/veteran/
General e-mail: djohnson2@mail.state.tn.us
Main phone: (615) 741-2931
Main fax: (615) 741-5056
TTY: (800) 848-0298

Fred Tucker, Commissioner
215 8th Ave. North, Nashville, TN 37243-1010
(615) 741-6663; *Fax:* (615) 741-4785

Wildlife Resources Agency

http://www.state.tn.us/twra
General e-mail: jsmith7@mail.state.tn.us
Main phone: (615) 781-6500
Main fax: (615) 741-4606
Mailing address: P.O. Box 40747, Nashville, TN
37204

Gary Myers, Executive Director
Hogan Rd., Wildlife Bldg., Nashville, TN 37204
(615) 781-6552; *Fax:* (615) 781-6551

Tennessee Legislature

State Capitol
Nashville, TN 37243
General information: (615) 741-3511
Fax: (615) 532-6973
http://www.legislature.state.tn.us

Laws

Sales tax: 8.25%
Income tax: None
State minimum wage: None (Federal is $5.15)
Marriage age: 18
First-cousin marriage: Permitted
Drinking age: 21
State control of liquor sales: No
Blood alcohol for DWI: 0.10%
Driving age: 16
Speed limit: 70 mph
Permit to buy handguns: No
Minimum age to possess handguns: 18
Minimum age to possess rifles, shotguns: 18
State lottery: No
Casinos: No
Pari-mutuel betting: Horse racing
Death penalty: Yes
3 strikes minimum sentence: Life, no parole
(2nd violent conviction)
Hate crimes law: Yes
Gay employment non-discrimination: No
Official language(s): English
Term limits: None

State laws are complex and subject to change; this information is not intended as legal advice. For an explanation of this information, see p. x

Senate
General information: (615) 741-2730
Fax: (615) 532-6973
Toll free: (800) 449-8366

John S. Wilder (D), President
1 Legislative Plaza, Nashville, TN 37243-0026
(615) 741-2368; *Fax:* (615) 741-9349
E-mail: lt.gov.john.wilder@legislature.state.tn.us
http://www.legislature.state.tn.us/Senate/members/
s26.htm

Robert Rochelle (D), President Pro Tempore
4 Legislative Plaza, Nashville, TN 37243
(615) 741-4109
E-mail: sen.robert.rochelle@legislature.state.tn.us
http://www.legislature.state.tn.us/senate/members/
s17.htm

Ward Crutchfield (D), Majority Leader
13 Legislative Plaza, Nashville, TN 37243
(615) 741-6682
E-mail: sen.ward.crutchfield@legislature.state.tn.us
http://www.legislature.state.tn.us/senate/members/
s10.htm

Ben Atchley (R), Minority Leader
303 War Memorial Bldg., Nashville, TN 37243
(615) 741-3791
E-mail: sen.ben.atchley@legislature.state.tn.us
http://www.legislature.state.tn.us/senate/members/
s6.htm

Clyde W. McCullough Jr., Chief Clerk
State Capitol, 2nd Fl., Nashville, TN 37243
(615) 741-2730; *Fax:* (615) 532-6973
E-mail: clyde.mccullough@legislature.state.tn.us

House
General information: (615) 741-2901
Fax: (615) 532-6973

James O. (Jimmy) Naifeh (D), Speaker of the House
19 Legislative Plaza, Nashville, TN 37243-0181
(615) 741-3774
E-mail: speaker.jimmy.naifeh@legislature.state.tn.us
http://www.legislature.state.tn.us/house/members/
h81.htm

Lois M. Deberry (D), Speaker Pro Tempore
15 Legislative Plaza, Nashville, TN 37243-0191
(615) 741-3830
http://www.legislature.state.tn.us/house/members/
h91.htm

Jere L. Hargrove (D), Majority Leader
18A Legislative Plaza, Nashville, TN 37243-0142
(615) 741-1875
E-mail: rep.jere.hargrove@legislature.state.tn.us
http://www.legislature.state.tn.us/house/members/
h42.htm

Michael Ray (Mike) McDonald (D), Majority Whip
17 Legislative Plaza, Nashville, TN 37243-0144
(615) 741-1980
E-mail: rep.michael.mcdonald@legislature.state.tn.us
http://www.legislature.state.tn.us/house/members/
h44.htm

Steve McDaniel (R), Minority Leader
103 War Memorial Bldg., Nashville, TN 37243
(615) 741-0750
E-mail: rep.steve.mcdaniel@legislature.state.tn.us
http://www.legislature.state.tn.us/house/members/
h72.htm

Charles Michael Sargent (R), Minority Whip
214 War Memorial Bldg., Nashville, TN 37243-0161
(615) 741-6808
E-mail: rep.charles.sargent@legislature.state.tn.us
http://www.legislature.state.tn.us/house/members/
h61.htm

Burney T. Durham, Chief Clerk
State Capitol, 2nd Fl., Nashville, TN 37243
(615) 741-2901; *Fax:* (615) 532-6973
E-mail: burney.durham@legislature.state.tn.us
http://www.legislature.state.tn.us/staff/house/clerk/
clerk.htm

Tennessee Judiciary

Supreme Court Bldg.
401 7th Ave. North
Nashville, TN 37219-1407

Supreme Court
http://tscaoc.tsc.state.tn.us

Cecil Crowson Jr., Clerk
Supreme Court Bldg., 401 7th Ave. North, Nashville,
TN 37219-1407
(615) 741-2681; *Fax:* (615) 532-8757

Justices
Composition: 5 justices

Selection Method: partisan election
Length of term: 8 years

E. Riley Anderson, Chief Justice, (423) 594-6400
William M. Barker, Associate Justice, (423) 634-6146
Adolpho A. Birch Jr., Associate Justice, (615) 741-6750
Frank F. Drowota III, Associate Justice, (615) 741-2114
Janice M. Holder, Associate Justice, (901) 685-3949

Administrative Office of the Courts
http://tscaoc.tsc.state.tn.us/
Main phone: (615) 741-2687
Main fax: (615) 741-6285

Cornelia Clark, Acting Administrative Director
Nashville City Center, 511 Union St., Nashville, TN
37243-0607

Legislative and Political Party Information Resources

Senate home page: http://www.legislature.state.tn.us/senate/members/welcome.htm
House home page: http://www.legislature.state.tn.us/house/members/welcome.htm
Committees: Senate: http://www.legislature.state.tn.us/senate/Committees/Directory.htm
      House: http://www.legislature.state.tn.us/senate/house/Committees/Directory.htm
Legislative process: http://www.legislature.state.tn.us/Legislative/General/billtolaw.htm
Legislative information: http://www.legislature.state.tn.us/Legislative/Legislative.htm
Tennessee Democratic Party: http://www.tndemocrats.org
    1808 West End Ave., #515, Nashville, TN 37203; *Phone:* (615) 327-9779; *Fax:* (615) 327-9759
Tennessee Republican Party: http://www.tngop.org
    1922 W. End Ave., Nashville, TN 37203; *Phone:* (615) 329-9595; *Fax:* (615) 329-0595;
    E-mail: feedback@tngop.org

Texas

State Capitol
Austin, TX 78711
Public information: (512) 463-4630
Fax: (512) 936-6664
http://www.state.tx.us

Office of the Governor
http://www.governor.state.tx.us
Main phone: (512) 463-2000
Main fax: (512) 463-1849
Toll free: (800) 843-5789
TTY: (512) 463-5746
Mailing address: P.O. Box 12428, Austin, TX 78711

George W. Bush (R), Governor
State Capitol, 1100 San Jacinto, Austin, TX 78701

Clay Johnson, Chief of Staff
State Capitol, 1100 San Jacinto, Austin, TX 78701
(512) 463-2000; *Fax:* (512) 463-1849

Linda Edwards, Communications Director
State Capitol, #2S.2, Austin, TX 78711
(512) 463-1826; *Fax:* (512) 463-1847

Shirley Green, Constituent Affairs
State Capitol, 1100 San Jacinto, Austin, TX 78701
(512) 463-2000; *Fax:* (512) 463-1849

Laurie M. Rich, Executive Director, Office of State Federal Relations
122 C St. N.W., #200, Washington, DC 20001
(202) 638-3927; *Fax:* (202) 463-1984

Office of the Lieutenant Governor
http://www.senate.state.tx.us/75r/LtGov/LtGov.htm
Main phone: (512) 463-0001
Main fax: (512) 463-0039
TTY: (512) 475-3758
Mailing address: P.O. Box 12068, Austin, TX 78711-2068

Rick Perry (R), Lieutenant Governor
State Capitol, Austin, TX 78711-2068

Office of the Secretary of State
http://www.sos.state.tx.us/
Main phone: (512) 463-5701
Main fax: (512) 475-2761
TTY: (800) 735-2989
Mailing address: P.O. Box 12697, Austin, TX 78711

Elton Bomer, Secretary of State
State Capitol, #1E.8, Austin, TX 78711

State of Texas

Capital: Austin, since 1842
Founded: 1836, Mexican province becomes independent Republic of Texas; 1845, U.S. annexation
Statehood: December 29, 1845 (28th state)
Constitution adopted: 1876
Area: 261,914 sq. mi. (ranks 2nd)
Population: 19,759,614 (1998 est.; ranks 2nd)
Largest cities: (1998 est.) Houston (1,786,691); San Antonio (1,114,130); Dallas (1,075,894); Austin (552,434); Fort Worth (491,801)
Counties: 254, Most populous: (1998 est.) Harris (3,206,063); Dallas (2,050,865); Tarrant (1,355,273); Bexar (1,353,052); Travis (710,626)
U.S. Congress: Phil Gramm (R), Kay Bailey Hutchison (R); 30 Representatives
Nickname(s): Lone Star State
Motto: Friendship
Song: "Texas, Our Texas"
Bird: Mockingbird
Tree: Pecan
Flower: Bluebonnet
State fair: at Dallas, late Sept.-mid-Oct.
Former capital(s): San Antonio, Houston

Office of the Attorney General
http://www.oag.state.tx.us
General e-mail: cac@oag.state.tx.us
Main phone: (512) 463-2100
Main fax: (512) 476-2653
Toll free: (800) 252-8011
Mailing address: P.O. Box 12548, Austin, TX 78711-2548

John Cornyn (R), Attorney General
Price Daniel, Sr. Bldg., 8th Fl., Austin, TX 78711-2548
(512) 463-2191; *Fax:* (512) 936-1401
E-mail: john.cornyn@oag.state.tx.us

Comptroller of Public Accounts Office
http://www.cpa.state.tx.us
Main phone: (512) 463-4000
Main fax: (512) 475-0352

Carole Keeton Rylander (R), Comptroller
Lyndon B. Johnson State Office Bldg., 111 E. 17th St.,
Austin, TX 78774

Office of the State Auditor
http://www.sao.state.tx.us
General e-mail: auditor@sao.state.tx.us
Main phone: (512) 479-4700
Main fax: (512) 479-4884
Toll free: (800) RELAYTX
Mailing address: P.O. Box 12067, Austin, TX
78711-2067

Lawrence F. Alwin, State Auditor
206 E. 9th St., Austin, TX 78711-2067

Adjutant General Dept.
http://www.agd.state.tx.us
Main phone: (512) 465-5001
Main fax: (512) 465-5578
TTY: (800) 735-2988
Mailing address: P.O. Box 5218, Austin, TX 78763-
5218

Daniel James III, Adjutant General
Camp Mabry Bldg., 2210 W. 35th St., Austin, TX
78731-2210
(512) 465-5006
E-mail: jamesd@tx.ngb.army.mil

Agencies

Accountancy Board
http://www.tsbpa.state.tx.us
General e-mail: publicinfo@tsbpa.state.tx.us
Main phone: (512) 305-7800

William Treacy, Executive Director
Tower III, 333 Guadalupe St., #900, Austin, TX
78701-3900
(512) 305-7801
E-mail: executive@tsbpa.state.tx.us

Aerospace Commission
http://www.tac.state.tx.us
General e-mail: aerospace@tac.state.tx.us
Main phone: (512) 936-4822
Main fax: (512) 936-4823
Mailing address: P.O. Box 12088, Austin, TX
78711-2088

Thomas Moser, Director
Stephen F. Austin Bldg., 1700 N. Congress Ave., #B-
60, Austin, TX 78701

Aging Dept.
http://www.tdoa.state.tx.us
General e-mail: mail@tdoa.state.tx.us
Main phone: (512) 424-6840

Main fax: (512) 424-6890
Toll free: (800) 252-9240
Mailing address: P.O. Box 12786, Austin, TX
78751

Mary Sapp, Executive Director
4900 N. Lamar Blvd., 4th Fl., Austin, TX 78711
(512) 424-6845
E-mail: mary@tdoa.state.tx.us

Agriculture Dept.
http://www.agr.state.tx.us
General e-mail: contact@agr.state.tx.us
Main phone: (512) 463-7476
Main fax: (512) 463-1104
Toll free: (800) 835-5832
TTY: (800) 735-2989
Mailing address: P.O. Box 12847, Austin, TX
78711-2847

Susan Combs (R), Commissioner
1700 N. Congress Ave., 9th Fl., Austin, TX 78701
(512) 463-7854
E-mail: susanc@agr.state.tx.us

Alcohol and Drug Abuse Commission
http://www.tcada.state.tx.us
Main phone: (512) 349-6600
Main fax: (512) 837-9242
Toll free: (800) 832-9623
Mailing address: P.O. Box 80529, Austin, TX
78708

Jim McDade, Executive Director (Interim)
9001 N. Interstate Hwy. 35, #105, Austin, TX 78753
(512) 349-6601; *Fax:* (512) 837-4123

Alcoholic Beverage Commission
http://www.tabc.state.tx.us
General e-mail: questions@tabc.state.tx.us
Main phone: (512) 206-3333
Main fax: (512) 206-3350
TTY: (512) 206-3270
Mailing address: P.O. Box 13127, Austin, TX
78711

Doyne Bailey, Administrator
5806 Mesa Dr., Austin, TX 78703
(512) 206-3217

Animal Health Commission
http://www.tahc.state.tx.us
General e-mail: comments@tahc.state.tx.us
Main phone: (512) 719-0700
Main fax: (512) 719-0721
Mailing address: P.O. Box 12966, Austin, TX
78711-2966

Terry L. Beals, Executive Director
2105 Kramer Lane, Austin, TX 78758

Architectural Examiners Board
http://www.tbae.state.tx.us
General e-mail: trish.prehn@tbae.state.tx.us
Main phone: (512) 305-9000
Main fax: (512) 305-8900

Cathy L. Hendricks, Executive Director
333 Guadalupe St., #2-350, Austin, TX 78701-3942
(512) 305-8535

Arts Commission
http://www.arts.state.tx.us
Main phone: (512) 463-5535
Main fax: (512) 475-2699
Toll free: (800) 252-9415
TTY: (512) 475-3327

Mailing address: P.O. Box 13406, Austin, TX 78711-3406

John Paul Batiste, Executive Director
920 Colorado St., Austin, TX 78701
E-mail: jbatiste@arts.state.tx.us

Banking Dept.
http://www.banking.state.tx.us
Main phone: (512) 475-1300
Main fax: (512) 475-1313

Randall S. James, Banking Commissioner
2601 N. Lamar Blvd., Austin, TX 78705-4294

Commission for the Blind
http://www.tcb.state.tx.us

Higher Educational Institutions

Angelo State University
http://www.angelo.edu
Box 11014, San Angelo, TX 76909
Main phone: (915) 942-2041

Lamar University
http://www.lamar.edu
P.O. Box 10009, Beaumont, TX 77710
Main phone: (409) 880-7011

Midwestern State University
http://www.mwsu.edu
3410 Taft Blvd., Wichita Falls, TX 76308
Main phone: (940) 397-4000

Sam Houston State University
http://www.shsu.edu
1803 Ave. I, Huntsville, TX 77341
Main phone: (409) 294-1111

Southwest Texas State University
http://www.swt.edu
601 University Dr., San Marcos, TX 78666-4604
Main phone: (512) 245-2111

Stephen F. Austin State University
http://www.sfasu.edu
SFA Station, Nacogdoches, TX 75962
Main phone: (409) 468-2011

Sul Ross State University
http://www.sulross.edu
P.O. Box C-114, Alpine, TX 79832
Main phone: (915) 837-8011

Texas A&M University
http://tamusystem.tamu.edu
John B. Connally Bldg., 7th Fl., College Station, TX 77840-7896
Main phone: (409) 458-6000
Branches: Prairie View A&M University, Tarleton

State University, Texas A&M International University, TAMU-Commerce, TAMU-Corpus Christi, TAMU-Galveston, TAMU-Kingsville, TAMU-Texarkana, West Texas A&M University

Texas Southern University
http://www.tsu.edu
3100 Cleburne Ave., Houston, TX 77004
Main phone: (713) 313-7011

Texas Tech University
http://www.texastech.edu
Box 45005, Lubbock, TX 79409-5005
Main phone: (806) 742-1480
Branches: El Paso

Texas Woman's University
http://www4.twu.edu
P.O. Box 425589, Denton, TX 76204-5589
Main phone: (940) 898-3047
Branches: Dallas, Denton, Houston

University of Houston
http://www.uh.edu
4800 Calhoun Rd., Houston, TX 77204
Main phone: (713) 743-1000
Branches: Clear Lake, Downtown, Victoria

University of North Texas
http://www.unt.edu
Box 311277, Denton, TX 76203-9988
Main phone: (940) 565-2861

University of Texas
http://www.utsystem.edu
601 Colorado St., Austin, TX 78701
Main phone: (512) 499-4201
Branches: Arlington, Austin, Brownsville, Dallas, El Paso, Houston, Pan American, Permian Basin, San Antonio, Tyler

General e-mail: pio@tcb.state.tx.us
Main phone: (512) 377-0588
Main fax: (512) 377-0685
TTY: (512) 377-0697
Mailing address: P.O. Box 12866, Austin, TX
78711

Terrell I. Murphy, Executive Director
4800 N. Lamar St., Austin, TX 78756
(512) 377-0500

Commission for the Deaf and Hard of Hearing
http://www.tcdhh.state.tx.us
Main phone: (512) 407-3250
Main fax: (512) 451-9316
TTY: (512) 407-3251
Mailing address: P.O. Box 12904, Austin, TX
78711

David W. Myers, Executive Director
4800 N. Lamar St., #310, Austin, TX 78756
E-mail: dmyers@tcdhh.state.tx.us

Consumer Credit Commissioner Office
http://occc.state.tx.us
General e-mail: info@occc.state.tx.us
Main phone: (512) 936-7600
Main fax: (512) 936-7610
Toll free: (800) 538-1579

Leslie L. Pettijohn, Commissioner
2601 N. Lamar Blvd., 2nd Fl., Austin, TX 78705-4207
(512) 936-7640
E-mail: leslie.pettijohn@occc.state.tx.us

Cosmetology Commission
Main phone: (512) 454-4674
Main fax: (512) 454-0339
Mailing address: P.O. Box 26700, Austin, TX
78755-0700

Henry Holifield, Director
5717 Balcones Dr., Austin, TX 78731-4203
(512) 454-9970

Criminal Justice Dept.
http://www.tdcj.state.tx.us
General e-mail: webmaster@tdcj.state.tx.us
Main phone: (936) 437-2101
Main fax: (936) 437-2101
Mailing address: P.O. Box 99, Huntsville, TX
77340

Wayne Scott, Executive Director
Spur 59, off Hwy. 75 North, #205, Huntsville, TX
77340
E-mail: exec.director@tdcj.state.tx.us

Economic Development Dept.
http://www.tded.state.tx.us
Main phone: (512) 936-0101

Main fax: (512) 936-0193
TTY: (512) 936-0555
Mailing address: P.O. Box 12728, Austin, TX
78711-2728

Jeff Moseley, Executive Director
Stephen F. Austin Bldg., 1700 N. Congress Ave.,
Austin, TX 78701
(512) 936-0104; *Fax:* (512) 936-0306
E-mail: jmoseley@tded.state.tx.us

Tourism Division
Main phone: (512) 936-0091
Main fax: (512) 936-0088
Toll free: (800) 888-8TEX
Mailing address: P.O. Box 12728, Austin, TX
78711-2728

Tracye McDaniel, Director
1700 N. Congress Ave., #200, Austin, TX 789701

Economic Geology Bureau
http://www.utexas.edu/research/beg/
General e-mail: begmail@beg.utexas.edu
Main phone: (512) 471-1534
Main fax: (512) 471-0140
Toll free: (888) 839-4365
Mailing address: University Station, Box X, Austin,
TX 78713-8924

William Fisher, Director (Interim)
10100 Burnett Rd., Austin, TX 78758-4497

Education Agency
http://www.tea.state.tx.us
Main phone: (512) 463-9734
Main fax: (512) 463-9838
TTY: (512) 463-2994

Jim Nelson, Commissioner
1701 N. Congress Ave., Austin, TX 78701-1494
(512) 463-8985; *Fax:* (512) 463-9008

Board of Education
http://www.tea.state.tx.us/sboe
General e-mail: rjohnson@tmail.tea.state.tx.us
Main phone: (512) 463-9007
Main fax: (512) 463-9008

Chase Untermeyer, Chair
1701 N. Congress Ave., William B. Travis Bldg.,
Austin, TX 78701-1494

Employees Retirement System
http://www.ers.state.tx.us
Main phone: (512) 476-6431
Main fax: (512) 867-7334
Toll free: (800) 252-3645
Mailing address: P.O. Box 13207, Austin, TX
78701

Sheila W. Beckett, Executive Director
18th and Brazos Sts., #401, Austin, TX 78701
(512) 867-7174

Ethics Commission
http://www.ethics.state.tx.us
Main phone: (512) 463-5800
Main fax: (512) 463-5777
Toll free: (800) 325-8506
Mailing address: Box 12070, Austin, TX 78711

Tom Harrison, Executive Director
Sam Houston Bldg., 10th Fl., Austin, TX 78701

Finance Commission
http://www.banking.state.tx.us
Main phone: (512) 475-1300
Main fax: (512) 475-1313

W. D. (Dee) Hilton Jr., Chair
State Finance Commission Bldg., 2601 N. Lamar
Blvd., Austin, TX 78705

Fire Protection Commission
http://www.tcfp.state.tx.us
General e-mail: info@tcfp.state.tx.us
Main phone: (512) 239-4911
Main fax: (512) 239-4917
Mailing address: P.O. Box 2286, Austin, TX 78759

Gary L. Warren Sr., Executive Director
12015 Park 35 Circle, #570, Austin, TX 78753
(512) 239-4912
E-mail: gwarren@tcfp.state.tx.us

Forest Service
http://txforestservice.tamu.edu
General e-mail: tx-stateforester@tamu.edu
Main phone: (979) 458-6650
Main fax: (979) 458-6655

James B. Hull, State Forester
John B. Connally Bldg., 301 Tarrow, #364, College
Station, TX 77840-7896
(979) 458-6600; *Fax:* (979) 458-6610
E-mail: jim-hull@tamu.edu

General Land Office
http://www.glo.state.tx.us/
Main phone: (512) 463-5001
Main fax: (512) 475-1558
TTY: (512) 463-5330

David Dewhurst (R), Texas Land Commissioner
1700 N. Congress Ave., Austin, TX 78701-1495
E-mail: david.dewhurst@glo.state.tx.us

General Services Commission
http://www.gsc.state.tx.us
General e-mail: public.info@gsc.state.tx.us
Main phone: (512) 463-3035

Main fax: (512) 463-7966
Mailing address: P.O. Box 13047, Austin, TX
78701

Gene Shull, Chair
1711 San Jacinto, Austin, TX 78701
(512) 463-3446

Health and Human Services Commission
http://www.hhsc.state.tx.us
Main phone: (512) 424-6603
Main fax: (512) 424-6587
TTY: (512) 424-6597
Mailing address: P.O. Box 13247, Austin, TX
78711

Don A. Gilbert, Commissioner
4900 N. Lamar Blvd., Austin, TX 78751
(512) 424-6502
E-mail: don.gilbert@hhsc.state.tx.us

Health Dept.
http://www.tdh.state.tx.us
Main phone: (512) 458-7111
Main fax: (512) 458-7750
TTY: (512) 458-7708

William R. Archer II, Commissioner
1100 W. 49th St., Austin, TX 78756
(512) 458-7375; *Fax:* (512) 458-7477

Higher Education Authority
http://www.sthea.org
Main phone: (956) 682-6371
Main fax: (956) 971-3319
Toll free: (800) 949-6371

Robert F. Ziemski, Chief Executive Officer
Interplex Bldg., 1109 Nolana St., #201, McAllen, TX
78504-3201

Higher Education Coordinating Board
http://www.thecb.state.tx.us
General e-mail: kennedycy@thecb.state.tx.us
Main phone: (512) 483-6100
Main fax: (512) 483-6169
TTY: (800) 735-2988
Mailing address: P.O. Box 12788, Austin, TX
78711-2788

Don W. Brown, Commissioner
1200 E. Anderson Lane, Austin, TX 78752
(512) 483-6101; *Fax:* (512) 483-6127

Historical Commission
http://www.thc.state.tx.us
General e-mail: thc@thc.state.tx.us
Main phone: (512) 463-6100
Main fax: (512) 475-4872
Mailing address: P.O. Box 12276, Austin, TX
78711-2276

F. Lawrence Oaks, Executive Director
1511 Colorado St., Austin, TX 78701

Housing and Community Affairs Dept.
http://www.tdhca.state.tx.us
Main phone: (512) 475-3800
Main fax: (512) 469-9606
Mailing address: P.O. Box 13941, Austin, TX
78711-3941

Daisy Stiner, Executive Director
507 Sabine St., #400, Austin, TX 78711-3941
(512) 475-3934

Human Rights Commission
http://www.link.tsl.state.tx.us/tx/tchr
General e-mail: tchr.net@mail.capnet.state.tx.us
Main phone: (512) 437-3450
Main fax: (512) 437-3478
TTY: (800) 735-2989
Mailing address: P.O. Box 13493, Austin, TX
78711

William M. Hale, Executive Director
6330 Hwy. 290 East, #250, Austin, TX 78723

Human Services Dept.
http://www.dhs.state.tx.us
General e-mail: mail@dhs.state.tx.us
Main phone: (512) 438-3011
Main fax: (512) 438-4220
TTY: (512) 438-4313
Mailing address: P.O. Box 149030, Austin, TX
78714-9030

Eric M. Bost, Commissioner
701 W. 51st St., #W-619, Austin, TX 78714-9030
(512) 438-3030

Humanities Council
http://www.public-humanities.org
General e-mail: postmaster@public-
humanities.org
Main phone: (512) 440-1991
Main fax: (512) 440-0115

Monte K. Youngs, Executive Director
Banister Pl. A, 3809 S. 2nd St., Austin, TX 78704
(512) 440-1991, ext. 125
E-mail: myoungs@public-humanities.org

Incentive and Productivity Commission
http://www.tipc.state.tx.us
General e-mail: tipc@license.state.tx.us
Main phone: (512) 475-2393
Main fax: (512) 475-4813
TTY: (800) 735-2989
Mailing address: P.O. Box 12482, Austin, TX
78711-2482

Frequently Called Numbers

Tourism: (512) 936-0091, 1-800-936-0091
Library: (512) 463-5460;
http://www.tsl.state.tx.us
Board of Education: (512) 463-9007;
http://www.tea.state.tx.us/sboe
Vital Statistics: (512) 458-7111;
http://www.tdh.state.tx.us/bvs/default.htm
Tax/Revenue: (512) 463-4000
Motor Vehicles: (512) 424-2600;
http://www.txdps.state.tx.us/administration/
driver_licensing_control/dlindex.htm
State Police/Highway Patrol: (512) 424-2000
Unemployment: (512) 463-7234;
http://www.twc.state.tx.us/ui/bnfts/
uicihp.html
General Election Information: (512)
463-5650, 1-800-252-VOTE;
http://www.sos.state.tx.us/function/elec1/
index.html
Hazardous Materials: Permits: (512)
239-2334, Registration and Reporting:
(512) 239-6832

Vickers B. Meadows, Chair
E. O. Thompson Bldg., 920 Colorado St., #401,
Austin, TX 789701

Information Resources Dept.
http://www.dir.state.us
General e-mail: dirinfo@dir.state.tx.us
Main phone: (512) 475-4700
Main fax: (512) 475-4759
Mailing address: P.O. Box 13564, Austin, TX
78711

Carolyn Purcell, Executive Director
William P. Clements Bldg., 300 W. 15th St., #1300,
Austin, TX 78701
(512) 475-4720

Insurance Dept.
http://www.tdi.state.tx.us
General e-mail: pio@tdi.state.tx.us
Main phone: (512) 463-6169
Main fax: (512) 475-2005
Toll free: (800) 578-4677
TTY: (512) 322-4238
Mailing address: P.O. Box 149104, Austin, TX
78714-9104

Jose Montemayor, Commissioner
333 Guadalupe St., Austin, TX 78701
(512) 463-6464
E-mail: jose.montemayor@tdi.state.tx.us

Jail Standards Commission
http://link.tsl.state.tx.us/tx/TCJS
General e-mail: tcjs@mail.capnet.state.tx.us
Main phone: (512) 463-5505
Main fax: (512) 463-3185
Mailing address: P.O. Box 12985, Austin, TX
78711-2985

Jack E. Crump, Executive Director
300 W. 15th St., #503, Austin, TX 78711-2985

Land Surveying Board
http://www.txls.org
Main phone: (512) 452-9427

Vacant, Director
7701 N. Lamar Blvd., #400, Austin, TX 78752

Library and Archives Commission
http://www.tsl.state.tx.us
General e-mail: info@tsl.texas.gov
Main phone: (512) 463-5460
Main fax: (512) 463-5436
Mailing address: P.O. Box 12927, Austin, TX
78711

Peggy D. Rudd, Director/State Librarian
1201 Brazos, Austin, TX 78701

Licensing and Regulation Dept.
http://www.license.state.tx.us
Main phone: (512) 463-6599
Main fax: (512) 475-2974
Toll free: (800) 803-9202
Mailing address: P.O. Box 12157, Austin, TX
78711

Boards and Licensing

Accountancy, (512) 305-7800,
  http://www.tsbpa.state.tx.us
Architects, (512) 305-9000,
  http://www.tbae.state.tx.us
Child Care, (512) 538-9299
Cosmetology, (512) 454-4674
Land Surveyors, (512) 452-9427,
  http://www.txls.org
Medical Examiners, (512) 305-7010,
  http://www.tsbme.state.tx.us
Nursing, (512) 305-7400,
  http://www.bne.state.tx.us
Pharmacy, (512) 305-8000,
  http://www.tsbp.state.tx.us
Engineers, (512) 440-7723,
  http://www.main.org/peboard
Real Estate, (512) 530-6747

William N. Kuntz Jr., Executive Director
E. O. Thompson State Office Bldg., Austin, TX 78711
(512) 463-3173; *Fax:* (512) 475-2874

Lottery Commission
http://www.txlottery.org
General e-mail: txlotto@onr.com
Main phone: (512) 344-5000
Main fax: (512) 478-3682
Toll free: (800) 375-6886
TTY: (512) 344-5343
Mailing address: P.O. Box 16630, Austin, TX
78761-6630

Linda Cloud, Executive Director
611 E. 6th St., Austin, TX 78701
(512) 344-5350
E-mail: linda.cloud@mail.capnet.state.tx.us

Medical Examiners Board
http://www.tsbme.state.tx.us
Main phone: (512) 305-7010
Main fax: (512) 305-7006
Mailing address: P.O. Box 2018, Austin, TX 78768-
2018

Bruce A. Levy, Director
333 Guadalupe St., Tower III, #610, Austin, TX 78701
(512) 305-7017; *Fax:* (512) 305-7008

Mental Health and Mental Retardation Dept.
http://www.mhmr.state.tx.us
Main phone: (512) 454-3761
Main fax: (512) 206-4560
Toll free: (800) 252-8154
TTY: (512) 206-4716
Mailing address: P.O. Box 12668, Austin, TX
78711-2668

Karen F. Hale, Commissioner
909 W. 45th St., Austin, TX 78751
(512) 206-4588
E-mail: karen.hale@mhmr.state.tx.us

Municipal Power Agency
http://www.texasmpa.org
Main phone: (409) 873-1123
Main fax: (409) 873-1186
Mailing address: P.O. Box 7000, Bryan, TX 77805

Gary Parsons, General Manager (Acting)
FM 244, Carlos, TX 77830

Natural Resource Conservation Commission
http://www.tnrcc.state.tx.us
Main phone: (512) 239-1000
Main fax: (512) 239-5533
Mailing address: P.O. Box 13087, Austin, TX
78711-3087

Robert J. Huston, Chair
12100 Park 35 Circle, Bldg. F, #4214, Austin, TX 78753
(512) 239-5505
E-mail: rhuston@tnrcc.state.tx.us

Nurse Examiners Board
http://www.bne.state.tx.us
Main phone: (512) 305-7400
Main fax: (512) 305-7401
Mailing address: P.O. Box 430, Austin, TX 78767-0430

Katherine A. Thomas, Executive Director
333 Guadalupe St., #3-460, Austin, TX 78701-3942
E-mail: thomask@mail.state.tx.us

Pardons and Paroles Board
Main phone: (210) 226-6862
Main fax: (210) 226-1114
Mailing address: P.O. Box 13401, Austin, TX 78711

Gerald Garrett, Chair
Capitol Station, Price Daniel Bldg., 209 W. 14th St., #500, Austin, TX 78701

Parks and Wildlife Dept.
http://www.tpwd.state.tx.us
General e-mail: involved@tpwd.state.tx.us
Main phone: (512) 389-4800
Main fax: (512) 389-4814

Andrew H. Sansom, Executive Director
4200 Smith School Rd., Austin, TX 78744
(512) 389-4802

Pharmacy Board
http://www.tsbp.state.tx.us
Main phone: (512) 305-8000
Main fax: (512) 305-8075

Gay Dodson, Executive Director
William P. Hobby Bldg., 333 Guadalupe St., #600, Austin, TX 78701
E-mail: gaydodson@tsbp.state.tx.us

Planning Council for Developmental Disabilities
http://www.rehab.state.tx.us/tpcdd/index.htm
General e-mail: TXDDC@rehab.state.tx.us
Main phone: (512) 424-4080
Main fax: (512) 424-4097
TTY: (512) 424-4099

Roger A. Webb, Executive Director
4900 N. Lamar Blvd., Austin, TX 78751-2399
E-mail: roger.webb@rehab.state.tx.us

Professional Engineers Board
http://www.main.org/peboard
General e-mail: peboard@mail.capnet.state.tx.us
Main phone: (512) 440-7723

Main fax: (512) 442-1414
Mailing address: P.O. Drawer 18329, Austin, TX 78760

Jimmy Smith, Executive Director (Interim)
1917 Interstate Hwy. 35 South, Austin, TX 78741

Prosecuting Attorney
Main phone: (512) 463-1660
Main fax: (512) 463-5724
Mailing address: P.O. Box 12405, Austin, TX 78701

Vacant, Director
Price Daniel Sr. Bldg., 209 W. 14th St., #202, Austin, TX 78701

Protective and Regulatory Services Dept.
http://www.tdprs.state.tx.us
General e-mail: guzmanv@tdprs.state.tx.us
Main phone: (512) 438-4800
Main fax: (512) 438-3525
Mailing address: P.O. Box 149030, Austin, TX 78714-9030

James R. Hine, Executive Director
701 W. 51st St., #MC E-654, Austin, TX 78751
(512) 438-4870

Public Safety Dept.
http://www.txdps.state.tx.us
General e-mail: webmaster@txdps.state.tx.us
Main phone: (512) 424-2000
Main fax: (512) 424-5708
Mailing address: P.O. Box 4087, Austin, TX 78733-0001

Thomas Davis, Director
5805 N. Lamar Blvd., Box 4087, Austin, TX 78752

Driver License Division
http://www.txdps.state.tx.us/administration/driver_licensing_control/dlindex.htm
General e-mail: license.issuance@txdps.state.tx.us
Main phone: (512) 424-2600
Main fax: (512) 424-5233
Mailing address: P.O. Box 4087, Austin, TX 78773

Mike Anderson, Chief
5805 N. Lamar Blvd., Austin, TX 78773-0310
(512) 424-5232

Emergency Management Division
http://www.txdps.state.tx.us/dem
General e-mail: dem@txdps.state.tx.us
Main phone: (512) 424-2138
Main fax: (512) 424-2444
Mailing address: Box 4087, Austin, TX 78773-0220

Tom Millwee, State Coordinator
5805 N. Lamar Blvd., Austin, TX 78752
(512) 424-2443
E-mail: tom.millwee@txdps.state.tx.us

Public Utility Commission
http://www.puc.state.tx.us
General e-mail: webmaster@puc.state.tx.us
Main phone: (512) 936-7000
Main fax: (512) 936-7003
Toll free: (888) 782-8477
TTY: (512) 936-7136
Mailing address: P.O. Box 13326, Austin, TX
78711-3326

Patrick Wood III, Chair
William B. Travis Bldg., 1701 N. Congress Ave.,
Austin, TX 78701
(512) 936-7005

Racing Commission
http://www.txrc.state.tx.us
Main phone: (512) 833-6699
Main fax: (512) 833-6907
Mailing address: P.O. Box 12080, Austin, TX
78711-2080

Larry J. Christopher, Chair
8505 Cross Park Dr., #110, Austin, TX 78754-4594

Railroad Commission
http://www.rrc.state.tx.us
Main phone: (512) 463-7288
Main fax: (512) 463-7161
TTY: (512) 463-7284
Mailing address: P.O. Box 12967, Austin, TX
78711-2967

Tony Garza (R), Commissioner
1701 N. Congress Ave., Austin, TX 78711-2967
(512) 463-7131

Real Estate Commission
http://www.trec.state.tx.us
General e-mail: general.delivery@trec.state.tx.us
Main phone: (512) 459-6544
Main fax: (512) 465-3998
Toll free: (800) 250-8732
Mailing address: P.O. Box 12188, Austin, TX
78711-2188

Wayne Thorburn, Administrator
1101 Camino la Costa, Austin, TX 78752
(512) 465-3900; *Fax:* (512) 465-3910

Rehabilitation Commission
http://info.hhsc.texas.gov
Main phone: (512) 424-4000

Main fax: (512) 424-4012
TTY: (800) 628-5115

Max Arrell, Commissioner
4900 N. Lamar Blvd., Austin, TX 78751-2399
(512) 424-4001

Savings and Loan Dept.
http://www.tsld.state.tx.us
General e-mail: tsld@mail.capnet.state.tx.us
Main phone: (512) 475-1350
Main fax: (512) 475-1360

James L. Pledger, Commissioner
2601 N. Lamar Blvd., #201, Austin, TX 78705

School for the Blind and Visually Impaired
http://www.tsbvi.edu
Main phone: (512) 454-8631
Main fax: (512) 206-9450
Toll free: (800) 872-5273

Phil Hatlen, Superintendent
1100 W. 45th St., Austin, TX 78756
(512) 206-9133; *Fax:* (512) 206-9453
E-mail: hatlen_p@tsb1.tsbvi.edu

School for the Deaf
http://www.tsd.state.tx.us
Main phone: (512) 462-5353
Main fax: (512) 462-5313
Toll free: (800) DEAF-TSD
TTY: (512) 462-5352
Mailing address: P.O. Box 3538, Austin, TX 78704

Claire Bugen, Superintendent
1102 S. Congress, Austin, TX 78704
(512) 462-5300

Securities Board
http://www.ssb.state.tx.us
Main phone: (512) 305-8300
Main fax: (512) 305-8310
Mailing address: P.O. Box 13167, Austin, TX
78711-3167

Denise Voigt Crawford, Commissioner
208 E. 10th St., Austin, TX 78701

Soil and Water Conservation Board
Main phone: (512) 773-2250
Main fax: (512) 773-3311
Mailing address: P.O. Box 658, Temple, TX 76503-
0658

Robert G. Buckley, Executive Director
311 N. 5th St., Temple, TX 76503-0658
E-mail: bbuckley@tsswcb.state.tx.us

State Fair
http://www.texfair.com/
General e-mail: pr@greatstatefair.com

Main phone: (214) 565-9931
Mailing address: P.O. Box 150009, Dallas, TX 75315

Vacant, General Manager
Fair Park, Dallas, TX 75315

Teacher Retirement System
http://www.trs.state.tx.us
Main phone: (512) 397-6400
Main fax: (512) 370-0585
Toll free: (800) 223-8778
TTY: (800) 841-4497

Charles L. Dunlap, Executive Director
1000 Red River St., Austin, TX 78701-2698
(512) 397-6401

Transportation Dept.
http://www.state.tx.us/agency/601.html
General e-mail: admin@mailgw.dot.state.tx.us
Main phone: (512) 463-8585
Main fax: (512) 305-9567

Charles W. Heald, Executive Director
125 E. 11th St., Austin, TX 78701-2483
(512) 305-9512

Veterans Commission
http://www.tvc.state.tx.us
General e-mail:
texas.veterans.commission@tvc.state.tx.us
Main phone: (512) 463-5538
Main fax: (512) 475-2395
Mailing address: P.O. Box 12277, Austin, TX 78711-2277

Sue E. Turner, Chair
920 Colorado St., 6th Fl., Austin, TX 78701

Water Development Board
http://www.twdb.state.tx.us
General e-mail: info@twdb.state.tx.us
Main phone: (512) 463-7847
Main fax: (512) 475-2053
TTY: (800) 735-2989
Mailing address: P.O. Box 13231, Austin, TX 78711

Craig D. Pedersen, Executive Administrator
1700 N. Congress Ave., Austin, TX 78711

Women's Commission
http://www.governor.state.tx.us/women/
commission_index.html
General e-mail: llorenzi@governor.state.tx.us
Main phone: (512) 475-2615
Main fax: (512) 463-1832
Mailing address: P.O. Box 12428, Austin, TX 78711

Ashley Horton, Executive Director
100 San Jacinto, #3.100-A, Austin, TX 78701

Workers' Compensation Commission
http://www.twcc.state.tx.us
Main phone: (512) 804-4000
Main fax: (512) 804-4401

Leonard Riley, Executive Director
Southfield Bldg., 4000 S. Interstate Hwy. 35, Austin, TX 78794-7491
(512) 804-4400

Workforce and Economic Competitiveness Council
http://www.governor.state.tx.us./tcwec/index.html
General e-mail: dsantos@governor.state.tx.us
Main phone: (512) 936-8100
Main fax: (512) 936-8118

Cheryl Halliburtin, Director
1100 San Jacinto, #100, Austin, TX 78701
E-mail: challiburtin@governor.state.tx.us

Workforce Commission
http://www.twc.state.tx.us
General e-mail: ombudsman@twc.tx.us
Main phone: (512) 463-2222
Main fax: (512) 475-2321
Toll free: (800) 735-2988
TTY: (800) 735-2989

Mike Sheridan, Executive Director
101 E. 15th St., Austin, TX 78778
(512) 463-0735
E-mail: Mike.Sheridan@twc.state.tx.us

Youth Commission
http://www.tyc.state.tx.us
General e-mail: tyc@tyc.state.tx.us
Main phone: (512) 424-6000
Main fax: (512) 424-6010
TTY: (800) RELAYTX
Mailing address: P.O. Box 4260, Austin, TX 78765

Steve Robinson, Executive Director
4900 N. Lamar Blvd., Austin, TX 78751
(512) 424-6001
E-mail: steve.robinson@tyc.state.tx.us

Texas Legislature
State Capitol
Austin, TX 78711
General information: (512) 463-4630
Bill status: (512) 463-1252
http://www.capitol.state.tx.us

Laws

Sales tax: 8.25%
Income tax: None
State minimum wage: $3.35 (Federal is $5.15)
Marriage age: 18
First-cousin marriage: Permitted
Drinking age: 21
State control of liquor sales: No
Blood alcohol for DWI: 0.10%
Driving age: 16
Speed limit: 70 mph
Permit to buy handguns: No
Minimum age to possess handguns: None
Minimum age to possess rifles, shotguns:
  None
State lottery: Yes
Casinos: No
Pari-mutuel betting: Horse and dog racing
Death penalty: Yes
3 strikes minimum sentence: 25 yrs. (any 3rd felony)
Hate crimes law: Yes
Gay employment non-discrimination: No
Official language(s): None
Term limits: None

State laws are complex and subject to change; this information is not intended as legal advice. For an explanation of this information, see p. x.

Senate
Address: P.O. Box 12068, Austin, TX 78711
General information: (512) 463-0100
Fax: (512) 463-6034
TTY: (512) 475-3758

Rick Perry (R), President
State Capitol, Austin, TX 78711-2068
(512) 463-0001; *Fax:* (512) 463-0039
http://www.senate.state.tx.us

Rodney Ellis (D), President Pro Tempore
Capitol Station, P.O. Box 12068, Austin, TX 78711
(512) 463-0113
http://www.senate.state.tx.us/75r/Senate/members/
  dist13/dist13.htm#form

Betty King, Secretary
Capitol Station, P.O. Box 12068, Austin, TX 78711
(512) 463-0100; *Fax:* (512) 463-6034
http://www.senate.state.tx.us/75r/Senate/SoS.htm

House
Address: P.O. Box 12068, Austin, TX 78711
General information: (512) 463-0845
Fax: (512) 463-5896

James E. (Pete) Laney (D), Speaker of the House
Capitol Bldg., #2W.13, Austin, TX 78701
(512) 463-1000
http://www.house.state.tx.us/house/dist85/dist85.htm

D. R. (Tom) Uher (D), Speaker Pro Tempore
Capitol Bldg., #3N.5, Austin, TX 78701
(512) 463-0724
http://www.house.state.tx.us/house/dist29/dist29.htm

Sharon Carter, Chief Clerk
Capitol Bldg., P.O. Box 12068, Austin, TX 78711
(512) 463-0845; *Fax:* (512) 463-5896

Texas Judiciary
201 W. 14th St.
Austin, TX 78701
http://www.courts.state.tx.us

Supreme Court

John T. Adams, Clerk
201 W. 14th St., Austin, TX 78701
(512) 463-1312; *Fax:* (512) 463-1365

Justices
Composition: 9 justices
Selection Method: partisan election; vacancies filled by gubernatorial appointment with the consent of the state senate; appointees serve until next general election
Length of term: 6 years

Thomas R. Phillips, Chief Justice, (512) 463-1316
Greg Abbott, Justice, (512) 463-1328
James A. Baker, Justice, (512) 463-1336
Craig T. Enoch, Justice, (512) 463-1340
Alberto R. Gonzalez, Justice, (512) 463-7899
Deborah G. Hankinson, Justice, (512) 463-1332
Nathan L. Hecht, Justice, (512) 463-1348
Harriet O'Neill, Justice, (512) 463-1320
Priscilla R. Owen, Justice, (512) 463-1344

Office of Court Administration
Main phone: (512) 463-1625
Main fax: (512) 463-1648

Jerry Benedict, Administrative Director
Tom C. Clark Bldg., 205 W. 14th St., Austin, TX
  78701
E-mail: doug.rybacki@courts.state.tx.us

State Law Library
http://www.sll.courts.state.tx.us

Main phone: (512) 463-1722
Main fax: (512) 463-1728

Kay Schlueter, Director
Tom C. Clark Bldg., 205 W. 14th St., #G01, Austin,
  TX 78701

Legislative and Political Party Information Resources

Senate home page: http://www.senate.state.tx.us
House home page: http://www.house.state.tx.us
Committees: http://www.capitol.state.tx.us/tlo/cmte.htm
Legislative information: http://www.capitol.state.tx.us/capitol/leginfo.htm
Legislative process: http://www.capitol.state.tx.us/capitol/legproc/summary.htm
Budget: http://www.lbb.state.tx.us
Texas Democratic Party: http://www.txdemocrats.org
  919 Congress Ave., #600, Austin, TX 78705; *Phone:* (512) 478-9800; *Fax:* (512) 480-2500
Texas Republican Party: http://www.texasgop.org
  211 E. 7th St., #620, Austin, TX 78701; *Phone:* (512) 477-9620; *E-mail:* info@texasgop.org

Utah

State Capitol
Salt Lake City, UT 84114
Public information: (801) 538-3000
Fax: (801) 538-3561
http://www.state.ut.us

Office of the Governor
http://www.governor.state.ut.us
General e-mail: governor@state.ut.us
Main phone: (801) 538-1000
Main fax: (801) 538-1528
Toll free: (800) 705-2464
TTY: (801) 538-1734

Michael O. Leavitt (R), Governor
State Capitol, #210, Salt Lake City, UT 84114

Richard McKeown, Chief of Staff
State Capitol, #210, Salt Lake City, UT 84114
(801) 538-1000; *Fax:* (801) 538-1528

Vicki Varela, Press Secretary
State Capitol, #210, Salt Lake City, UT 84114
(801) 538-1000; *Fax:* (801) 538-1528

Linda Kedra, Constituent Affairs
State Capitol, #210, Salt Lake City, UT 84114
(801) 538-1000; *Fax:* (801) 538-1528

Joanne Snow Neumann, Director, Washington Office
400 N. Capitol St. N.W., #388, Washington, DC 20001
(202) 624-7704; *Fax:* (202) 624-7707
E-mail: jneumann@governor.state.ut.us

Office of the Lieutenant Governor
http://www.governor.state.ut.us/ltgov
Main phone: (801) 538-1000
Main fax: (801) 538-1557
TTY: (801) 538-1734

Olene S. Walker, Lieutenant Governor
State Capitol, #210, Salt Lake City, UT 84114
(801) 538-1520
E-mail: owalker@state.ut.us

Office of the Attorney General
http://www.attygen.state.ut.us/
Main phone: (801) 366-0260
Main fax: (801) 538-1121

Jan Graham (D), Attorney General
State Capitol, #236, Salt Lake City, UT 84114-0810
(801) 538-9600
E-mail: ATCAP01.jgraham@email.state.ut.us

Office of the State Treasurer
http://www.treasurer.state.ut.us

State of Utah

Capital: Salt Lake City, since 1856
Founded: 1847, Mormon settlement of Deseret; 1850, Utah Territory created from Mexican Cession
Statehood: January 4, 1896 (45th state)
Constitution adopted: 1896
Area: 82,168 sq. mi. (ranks 12th)
Population: 2,099,758 (1998 est.; ranks 34th)
Largest cities: (1998 est.) Salt Lake City (174,348); Provo (110,419); West Valley City (99,372); Sandy (99,186); Orem (78,937)
Counties: 29, Most populous: (1998 est.) Salt Lake (850,667); Utah (335,635); Davis (233,013); Weber (184,065); Washington (82,115)
U.S. Congress: Robert F. Bennett (R), Orrin G. Hatch (R); 3 Representatives
Nickname(s): Beehive State
Motto: Industry
Song: "Utah, We Love Thee"
Bird: California gull
Tree: Blue spruce
Flower: Sego lily
State fair: at Salt Lake City, early to mid-Sept.
Former capital(s): Fillmore

Main phone: (801) 538-1042
Main fax: (801) 538-1465
TTY: (801) 538-1042

Edward T. Alter (R), State Treasurer
State Capitol, #215, Salt Lake City, UT 84114
E-mail: stmain.ealter@st.ut.us

Office of the State Auditor
http://www.sao.state.ut.us/
Main phone: (801) 538-1025
Main fax: (801) 538-1383

Auston G. Johnson, State Auditor
State Capitol, #211, Salt Lake City, UT 84114
(801) 538-1360

National Guard
General e-mail: tagut@ut-arng.ngb.army.mil
Main phone: (801) 523-4400

Main fax: (801) 523-4677
Mailing address: P.O. Box 1776, Draper, UT 84020-1776

James M. Miller, Adjutant General
12953 S. Minuteman Dr., Draper, UT 84020-1776
(801) 523-4401

Agencies

Administrative Services Dept.
http://www.das.state.ut.us/
Main phone: (801) 538-3010
Main fax: (801) 538-3844
TTY: (801) 538-3340

Raylene G. Ireland, Executive Director
State Office Bldg., #3120, Salt Lake City, UT 84114

Agriculture and Food Dept.
http://www.ag.state.ut.us
General e-mail: agmain.jwinger@email.state.ut.us
Main phone: (801) 538-7100
Main fax: (801) 538-7126
Mailing address: P.O. Box 146500, Salt Lake City, UT 84114-6500

Cary G. Peterson, Commissioner
350 N. Redwood Rd., Salt Lake City, UT 84114
(801) 538-7101
E-mail: agmain.cpeters@state.ut.us

Alcoholic Beverage Control Dept.
Main phone: (801) 977-6800
Main fax: (801) 977-6888
Mailing address: P.O. Box 30408, Salt Lake City, UT 84114-0408

Kenneth F. Wynn, Director
1625 South, 1900 West, Salt Lake City, UT 84114

Archives
http://www.archives.state.ut.us
General e-mail: research@das.state.ut.us
Main phone: (801) 538-3012
Main fax: (801) 538-3354
Mailing address: P.O. Box 141021, Salt Lake City, UT 84114-1021

Jeffrey Johnson, Director
State Capitol, Archives Bldg., Salt Lake City, UT 84114
(801) 538-3191
E-mail: jjohnson@das.state.ut.us

Career Service Review Board
General e-mail: ejones@state.ut.us
Main phone: (801) 538-3048
Main fax: (801) 538-3139
TTY: (801) 538-3081

Robert N. White, Administrator
State Office Bldg., #1120, Salt Lake City, UT 84114-1561
(801) 538-3047
E-mail: pedhrm.rwhite@state.ut.us

Commerce Dept.
http://www.commerce.state.ut.us
Main phone: (801) 530-6701
Main fax: (801) 530-6001
TTY: (801) 530-6917
Mailing address: P.O. Box 146701, Salt Lake City, UT 84114-6701

Douglas C. Borba, Executive Director
160 East, 300 South, Salt Lake City, UT 84114-6701

Consumer Protection Division
http://www.commerce.state.ut.us/conpro/consprot.htm
Main phone: (801) 530-6601
Main fax: (801) 530-6001
Toll free: (800) 721-7233
Mailing address: Box 146704, Salt Lake City, UT 84114-6704

Francine Giani, Director
160 East, 300 South, Salt Lake City, UT 84114

Occupational and Professional Licensing
http://www.commerce.state.ut.us/DOPL/dopl1.htm
General e-mail: dblake@br.state.ut.us
Main phone: (801) 530-6628
Main fax: (801) 530-6511
Mailing address: P.O. Box 146741, Salt Lake City, UT 84114-6741

A. Gary Bowen, Director
160 East, 300 South, 4th Fl., Salt Lake City, UT 84114-6741
(801) 530-6039
E-mail: gbowen@br.state.ut.us

Public Utilities Division
http://www.commerce.state.ut.us/pubutls/dpuhp1.htm
Main phone: (801) 530-7622
Main fax: (801) 530-6512
Toll free: (800) 874-0904
Mailing address: Box 146751, Salt Lake City, UT 84114-6751

Ric Campbell, Director
160 East, 300 South, 4th Fl., Salt Lake City, UT 84114
E-mail: rcampbell@br.state.ut.us

Community and Economic Development Dept.
http://www.dced.state.ut.us

Higher Educational Institutions

Southern Utah University
http://www.suu.edu
351 W. Center St., Cedar City, UT 84720
Main phone: (435) 586-7700

University of Utah
http://www.utah.edu
250 S. Student Services Bldg., Salt Lake City, UT 84112
Main phone: (801) 581-8761

Utah State University
http://www.usu.edu
1600 Old Main Hill, Logan, UT 84322-1600
Main phone: (435) 797-1000

Utah Valley State College
http://www.uvsc.edu
800 W. University Pkwy., Orem, UT 84058-5999
Main phone: (801) 222-8000

Weber State University
http://www.weber.edu
1137 University Circle, Ogden, UT 84408-1137
Main phone: (801) 626-6050

General e-mail: dced@state.ut.us
Main phone: (801) 538-8700
Main fax: (801) 538-8888
Toll free: (877) 488-3233

David B. Winder, Executive Director
324 S. State St., #500, Salt Lake City, UT 84111
(801) 538-8708
E-mail: dwinder@dced.state.ut.us

Arts Council
http://www.dced.state.ut.us/arts
Main phone: (801) 236-7555
TTY: (800) 346-4128

Bonnie Stephens, Director
617 E. South Temple, Salt Lake City, UT 84102

Travel Council
Main phone: (801) 538-1900
Main fax: (801) 538-1399
Toll free: (800) 200-1160

Dean T. Reeder, Director
Council Hall-Capitol Hill, Salt Lake City, UT 84114
(801) 538-1370
E-mail: dean@utah.com

Corrections Dept.
http://www.cr.ex.state.ut.us
Main phone: (801) 265-5500
Main fax: (801) 265-5726

H. L. (Pete) Haun, Executive Director
6100 S. Fashion Blvd., #400, Murray, UT 84107

Education Office
http://www.usoe.k12.ut.us
Main phone: (801) 538-7500
Main fax: (801) 538-7521
TTY: (801) 538-7876

Steven O. Laing, State Superintendent of Public Instruction
250 E. 500 South, Salt Lake City, UT 84111
(801) 538-7510; *Fax:* (801) 538-7768

Board of Education
Main phone: (801) 538-7500
Main fax: (801) 538-7521
TTY: (801) 538-7876

Steven O. Laing, Superintendent
250 E. 500 South, Salt Lake City, UT 84111
(801) 538-7517; *Fax:* (801) 538-7768
E-mail: laing.steve@usde.k12.ut.us

Schools for the Deaf and Blind
http://www.usdb.k12.ut.us
Main phone: (801) 629-4700
Main fax: (801) 629-4896
Toll free: (800) 990-9328
TTY: (801) 629-4701

Lee Robinson, Superintendent
742 Harrison Blvd., Ogden, UT 84404
E-mail: lrobinso@usdb.state.ut.us

Environmental Quality Dept.
http://www.eq.state.ut.us
General e-mail: deqinfo@deq.state.ut.us
Main phone: (801) 536-4400
Main fax: (801) 536-0061
TTY: (801) 536-4414

Dianne R. Nielson, Executive Director
168 North, 1950 West, Salt Lake City, UT 84116
(801) 536-4404; *Fax:* (801) 536-4401
E-mail: drniels@deq.state.ut.us

Financial Institutions Dept.
http://www.dfi.state.ut.us
Main phone: (801) 538-8830
Main fax: (801) 538-8894
Mailing address: P.O. Box 89, Salt Lake City, UT 84110-0089

G. Edward Leary, Commissioner
324 S. State St., #201, Salt Lake City, UT 84110-0089
(801) 538-8854
E-mail: eleary@dfi.state.ut.us

Fire Marshal
http://www.fm.state.ut.us/

Main phone: (801) 284-6350
Main fax: (801) 284-6351

Gary A. Wise, State Fire Marshal
5272 S. College Dr., #302, Murray, UT 84123
E-mail: gwise@dps.state.ut.us

Geological Survey
http://www.ugs.state.ut.us/
General e-mail: nrugs@state.ut.us
Main phone: (801) 537-3300
Main fax: (801) 537-3400
Mailing address: P.O. Box 146100, Salt Lake City,
UT 84114-6100

Kimm M. Harty, Director (Acting)
1594 W. North Temple, #3110, Salt Lake City, UT
84116
E-mail: nrugs.kharty@state.ut.us

Health and Child Care Licensing
http://www.health.state.ut.us/hsi/hfl/
Main phone: (801) 538-9084
Main fax: (801) 538-6325
Toll free: (888) 287-3704
Mailing address: P.O. Box 142003, Salt Lake City,
UT 84114

Debra Wynkoop, Director
288 North, 1460 West, Salt Lake City, UT 84114
E-mail: dwynkoop@doh.state.ut.us

Health Dept.
http://www.dohnet.hl.state.ut.us
Main phone: (801) 538-6101
Main fax: (801) 538-6306
TTY: (801) 538-6622
Mailing address: P.O. Box 141000, Salt Lake City,
UT 84114-1000

Rod L. Betit, Executive Director
288 North, 1460 West, Salt Lake City, UT 84116
(801) 538-6111

Health Care Financing: Medical Assistance Program
Main phone: (801) 538-9984
Main fax: (801) 538-6952
Mailing address: P.O. Box 143107, Salt Lake
City, UT 84114-3107

Robert Knudson, Director
288 North, 1460 West, Salt Lake City, UT 84114-
3107
(801) 538-6416
E-mail: rknudson@doh.state.ut.us

Higher Education System
http://www.utahsbr.edu
Main phone: (801) 321-7101
Main fax: (801) 321-7156

Cecelia H. Foxley, Commissioner/Chief Executive Officer
3 Triad Center, 355 W. North Temple, #550, Salt Lake
City, UT 84158-1205
(801) 321-7103
E-mail: cfoxley@utahsbr.edu

Historical Society
http://www.history.utah.org
General e-mail: ushs@history.state.ut.us
Main phone: (801) 533-3500
Main fax: (801) 533-3503
TTY: (801) 533-3502

Max J. Evans, Director
300 S. Rio Grande St., Salt Lake City, UT 84101
(801) 533-3551
E-mail: mevans@history.state.ut.us

Housing Finance Agency
http://www.uhfa.org
General e-mail: cfinney@uhfa.state.ut.us
Main phone: (801) 521-6950
Main fax: (801) 359-1701
Toll free: (800) 284-6950
TTY: (801) 298-9484

William H. Erickson, Executive Director
554 South, 300 East, Salt Lake City, UT 84111
Fax: (801) 323-2660
E-mail: werickson@uhfa.state.ut.us

Human Resources Dept.
http://www.dhrm.state.ut.us
Main phone: (801) 538-3025
Main fax: (801) 538-3081
TTY: (801) 538-3696
Mailing address: P.O. Box 141531, Salt Lake City,
UT 84114-1531

Karen Suzuki-Okabe, Executive Director
State Office Bldg., #2120, Salt Lake City, UT 84114-
1531
(801) 538-3080

Human Services Dept.
http://www.dhs.state.ut.us
General e-mail: dirdhs@state.ut.us
Main phone: (801) 538-4171
Main fax: (801) 538-4016
TTY: (801) 538-3959
Mailing address: P.O. Box 45500, Salt Lake City,
UT 84145-0500

Robin Arnold-Williams, Executive Director
120 North, 200 West, Salt Lake City, UT 84145-0500
(801) 538-4001

Aging and Adult Services Division
http://www.hsdaas.state.ut.us

Frequently Called Numbers

Tourism: (801) 538-1030, 1-800-200-1160
Library: (801) 715-6777;
  http://www.state.lib.ut.us/
Board of Education: (801) 538-7500
Vital Statistics: (801) 538-6105;
  http://www.health.state.ut.us/bvr/
Tax/Revenue: (801) 297-2200, 1-800-662-
  4335; http://www.tax.ex.state.ut.us
Motor Vehicles: Drivers Licensing: (801)
  965-4437; http://www.dl.state.ut.us; Motor
  Vehicle: (801) 297-7780;
  http://www.dmv-utah.com/
State Police/Highway Patrol: (801)
  965-4518; http://www.uhp.state.ut.us/
Unemployment: (801) 526-4400,
  1-888-848-0688; http://ui.dws.state.ut.us
General Election Information: (801) 538-
  1041, 1-800-995-VOTE;
  http://www.governor.state.ut.us/menu/html/
  elections.html
Consumer Affairs: (801) 530-6601,
  1-800-721-7233;
  http://www.commerce.state.ut.us/conpro/
  consprot.htm
Hazardous Materials: (801) 538-6170;
  http://www.eq.state.ut.us/eqshw/dshe-1.htm

General e-mail: hsadm2.sbrown@state.ut.us
Main phone: (801) 538-3910
Main fax: (801) 538-4395
Mailing address: P.O. Box 45500, Salt Lake
  City, UT 84145-0500

> **Helen Goddard, Director**
> 120 North, 200 West, #325, Salt Lake City, UT
> 84103
> *E-mail:* hsadm2.hgoddard@state.ut.us

Mental Health Division
http://www.hsmh.state.ut.us/srvment.htm
General e-mail: hsadmin1.jchilton@state.ut.us
Main phone: (801) 538-4270
Main fax: (801) 538-4892

> **Meredith Alden, Director**
> 120 North, 200 West, #415, Salt Lake City, UT
> 84145
> *E-mail:* hsadmin1.malden@state.ut.us

People with Disabilities Council
http://www.gcpd.state.ut.us/

General e-mail:
  hsadmin.hsddcncl.knelson@state.ut.us
Main phone: (801) 533-4128
Main fax: (801) 533-5305
Toll free: (800) 333-8824

> **Catherine E. Chambless, Executive Director**
> 555 E. 300 South, #201, Salt Lake City, UT 84102

Youth Corrections
http://www.hsdyc.state.ut.us/srvyc.htm
General e-mail:
  hsadmin.hsadm2.dmaldona@email.state.ut.us
Main phone: (801) 538-4330
Main fax: (801) 538-4334
Mailing address: P.O. Box 45500, Salt Lake
  City, UT 84145-0500

> **Gary Dalton, Director**
> 120 North, 200 West, #419, Salt Lake City, UT
> 84103

Insurance Dept.
http://www.insurance.state.ut.us
Main phone: (801) 538-3800
Main fax: (801) 538-3829
Toll free: (800) 439-3805

> **Merwin U. Stewart, Commissioner**
> State Office Bldg., #3110, Salt Lake City, UT 84114
> (801) 538-3804

Labor Commission
http://www.labor.state.ut.us
General e-mail: icmain.bgerow@email.state.ut.us
Main phone: (801) 530-6800
Main fax: (801) 530-6390
Toll free: (800) 530-5090
TTY: (801) 530-7685
Mailing address: P.O. Box 146600, Salt Lake City,
  UT 84114-6600

> **R. Lee Ellertson, Commissioner**
> 160 East, 300 South, 3rd Fl., Salt Lake City, UT
> 84114-6600
> (801) 530-6848

Medical Examiners Board
http://hlunix.hl.state.ut.us/ome/
Main phone: (801) 584-8410
Main fax: (801) 584-8435

> **Todd C. Grey, Chief Medical Examiner**
> 48 N. Medical Dr., Salt Lake City, UT 84113
> *E-mail:* hldels.tgrey@state.ut.us

Motor Vehicle Division
http://www.dmv-utah.com/
Main phone: (801) 297-7780
Main fax: (801) 297-7697
Toll free: (800) DMV-UTAH

Viola Bodrero, Director
210 N. 1950 West, Salt Lake City, UT 84134

Natural Resources Dept.
http://www.nr.state.ut.us
Main phone: (801) 538-7200
Main fax: (801) 538-7315
TTY: (801) 538-7458

Kathleen Clarke, Executive Director
1594 W. North Temple, #3710, Salt Lake City, UT 84114-5610

Forestry, Fire, and State Lands Division
http://www.nr.state.ut.us/slf/slfhome.htm
Main phone: (801) 538-5555
Main fax: (801) 533-4111
Mailing address: P.O. Box 145703, Salt Lake City, UT 84114-5703

Art DuFault, State Forester and Director
1594 W. North Temple, #3520, Salt Lake City, UT 84114
E-mail: nrslf.adufault@state.ut.us

Oil, Gas, and Mining Division
http://dogm.nr.state.ut.us
Main phone: (801) 538-5340
Main fax: (801) 359-3940
Mailing address: P.O. Box 145801, Salt Lake City, UT 84114-5801

Lowell Braxton, Director
1594 W. North Temple, #1210, Salt Lake City, UT 84114-5801
(801) 538-5370
E-mail: lbraxton@state.vt.us

State Parks and Recreation
http://www.nr.state.ut.us/parks/utahstpk.htm
Main phone: (801) 538-7220
Main fax: (801) 538-7378
TTY: (801) 538-7458

Courtland Nelson, Director
1594 W. North Temple, #116, Salt Lake City, UT 84114
(801) 538-7201

Water Resources Division
http://www.nr.state.ut.us/wtrresc/wtrresc.htm
Main phone: (801) 538-7230
Mailing address: P.O. Box 146201, Salt Lake City, UT 84114-6201

D. Larry Anderson, Director
1594 W. North Temple, Salt Lake City, UT 84114-6201
E-mail: nrwres.landerso@state.ut.us

Wildlife Resources Division
http://www.nr.state.ut.us/dwr/!homeypg.htm

Main phone: (801) 538-4700
Main fax: (801) 538-4745

John Kimball, Director
1594 W. North Temple, #2110, Salt Lake City, UT 84114
E-mail: nrdwr.jkimball@state.ut.us

Pardons and Paroles Board
Main phone: (801) 261-6464
Main fax: (801) 261-6481

Michael R. Sibbett, Chair
448 East, 6400 South, #300, Murray, UT 84107

Public Safety Dept.
http://www.dps.state.ut.us/
Main phone: (801) 965-4461
Main fax: (801) 965-4756
Mailing address: P.O. Box 141775, Salt Lake City, UT 84114-1775

Craig L. Dearden, Commissioner
4501 South, 2700 West, Salt Lake City, UT 84114-1775

Comprehensive Emergency Management Division
http://www.cem.state.ut.us
General e-mail: pscem.frontdesk@state.ut.us
Main phone: (801) 538-3400
Main fax: (801) 538-3770
Toll free: (800) 753-2858

Earl R. Morris, Director
1110 State Office Bldg., Salt Lake City, UT 84114

Driver License Division Director
http://www.dl.state.ut.us
Main phone: (801) 965-4437
Main fax: (801) 964-4482

Occupational and Professional Licensing Division

(801) 530-6628

Accountancy, (801) 530-6163
Architects, Engineers, and Land Surveyors, (801) 530-6632
Contractors, (801) 530-6159
Cosmetology, (801) 530-6964
Medical, (801) 530-6623
Nursing, (801) 530-6733
Pharmacy, (801) 530-6623
Real Estate, (801) 530-6747
Health and Child Care, (801) 538-9084, http://www.health.state.ut.us/hsi/hfl/

Mailing address: P.O. Box 30560, Salt Lake City, UT 84119

David A. Beach, Director
4501 South, 2700 West, 3rd Fl., Salt Lake City, UT 84130-0560

Highway Patrol
http://www.uhp.state.ut.us/
Main phone: (801) 965-4518
Main fax: (801) 865-4716
Toll free: (800) 222-0038

Jim Utley, Assistant Superintendent
4501 South, 2700 West, Salt Lake City, UT 84114

Public Service Commission
http://www.psc.state.ut.us
General e-mail: jnelson1@state.ut.us
Main phone: (801) 530-6716
Main fax: (801) 530-6796
Mailing address: P.O. Box 45585, Salt Lake City, UT 84145

Stephen F. Mecham, Chair
Heber M. Wells Bldg., 160 East, 300 South, 4th Fl., Salt Lake City, UT 84111
E-mail: sfmecham@state.ut.us

Real Estate Division
http://www.commerce.state.ut.us/re/udre1.htm
General e-mail: realest@br.state.ut.us
Main phone: (801) 530-6747
Main fax: (801) 530-6749
Mailing address: P.O. Box 146711, Salt Lake City, UT 84114-6711

Theodore Boyer Jr., Director
160 East, 300 South, 2nd Fl., Salt Lake City, UT 84114-6711
E-mail: tboyer@br.state.ut.us

Retirement Office
http://www.urs.org
Main phone: (801) 366-7700
Main fax: (801) 328-7343

Robert V. Newman, Executive Director
540 East, 2nd South, Salt Lake City, UT 84102
(801) 366-7301
E-mail: robert.newman@urs.org

State Board of Regents
http://www.utahsbr.edu
Main phone: (801) 321-7101
Main fax: (801) 321-7199
TTY: (801) 321-7130

Charles E. Johnson, Chair
3 Triad Center, 355 W. North Temple, #550, Salt Lake City, UT 84180-1205
(801) 933-1940; *Fax:* (801) 355-3739
E-mail: CJohnson2@sisna.com

State Fair
www.utah-state-fair.com/
Main phone: (801) 538-8440
Main fax: (801) 538-8455

Donna Dahl, Director
155 North, 1000 West, Salt Lake City, UT 84116

State Library
http://www.state.lib.ut.us/
Main phone: (801) 715-6777
Main fax: (801) 715-6767

Amy Owen, Director
250 N. 1950 West, Suite A, Salt Lake City, UT 84116
(801) 715-6770

Tax Commission
http://www.tax.ex.state.ut.us
Main phone: (801) 297-2200
Main fax: (801) 297-3919
Toll free: (800) 662-4335
TTY: (801) 297-3819

Vacant, Chair
210 North, 1950 West, Salt Lake City, UT 84134
(801) 297-3901

Transportation Dept.
http://www.sr.ex.state.ut.us
Main phone: (801) 965-4113
Main fax: (801) 965-4338

Thomas R. Warne, Executive Director
4501 South, 2700 West, Salt Lake City, UT 84119
(801) 965-4113

Aeronautics
Main phone: (801) 715-2260
Main fax: (801) 715-2276

Robert P. Barrett, Director
135 North, 2400 West, Salt Lake City, UT 84116
(801) 715-2262

Veterans Affairs
http://www.dced.state.ut.us/veterans/welcome.htm
Main phone: (801) 524-6048
Main fax: (801) 359-9804

LaVonne Willis, Director
125 S. State St., #5223, Salt Lake City, UT 84147
E-mail: lwillis@dced.state.ut.us

Workers' Compensation Fund of Utah
http://www.wcf-utah.com
Main phone: (801) 288-8000
Main fax: (801) 288-8038
Toll free: (800) 530-5090
Mailing address: P.O. Box 57929, Murray, UT 84157-0929

Lane A. Summerhays, President and Chief Executive Officer
392 East 6400 South, Murray, UT 84107

Utah Legislature

State Capitol
Salt Lake City, UT 84114
General information: (801) 538-1032
http://www.le.state.ut.us/welcome.htm

Senate

Address: 319 State Capitol, Salt Lake City, UT 84114
General information: (801) 538-1035
Fax: (801) 538-1414
TTY: (801) 538-1457
E-mail: senate@le.state.ut.us

R. Lane Beattie (R), President
State Capitol, #319, Salt Lake City, UT 84114
(801) 538-1400

Lyle W. Hillyard (R), Majority Leader
State Capitol, #319, Salt Lake City, UT 84114
(801) 538-1532
E-mail: lhillyar@le.state.ut.us

Leonard M. Blackham (R), Majority Whip
State Capitol, #319, Salt Lake City, UT 84114
(801) 538-1402
E-mail: lblackha@le.state.ut.us

Scott N. Howell (D), Minority Leader
State Capitol, #319, Salt Lake City, UT 84114
(801) 538-1406; *Fax:* (801) 538-1449
E-mail: showell@le.state.ut.us

Paula F. Julander (D), Minority Whip
State Capitol, #319, Salt Lake City, UT 84114
(801) 538-1405
E-mail: prjuland@msn.com

Annette B. Moore, Secretary
State Capitol, #319, Salt Lake City, UT 84114
(801) 538-1458

House

Address: 318 State Capitol, Salt Lake City, UT 84114
General information: (801) 538-1029
Fax: (801) 538-1908
TTY: (801) 538-1016

Martin R. Stephens (R), Speaker of the House
State Capitol, #318, Salt Lake City, UT 84114
(801) 538-1612
E-mail: mstephen@le.state.ut.us
http://www.le.state.ut.us/house/Members/District/
district_6.htm

Bill Wright (R), Speaker Pro Tempore
State Capitol, #318, Salt Lake City, UT 84114
(801) 538-1254
E-mail: bwright@le.state.ut.us
http://www.le.state.ut.us/house/Members/District/
district_67.htm

Kevin S. Garn (R), Majority Leader
State Capitol, #318, Salt Lake City, UT 84114
(801) 538-1577
E-mail: kgarn@le.state.ut.us
http://www.le.state.ut.us/house/Members/District/
district_16.htm

David Ure (R), Majority Whip
State Capitol, #318, Salt Lake City, UT 84114
(801) 538-1576
E-mail: dure@le.state.ut.us
http://www.le.state.ut.us/house/Members/District/
district_53.htm

David M. Jones (D), Minority Leader
State Capitol, #318, Salt Lake City, UT 84114
(801) 538-1575

Laws

Sales tax: 5.875%
Income tax: 5.6%
State minimum wage: $5.15 (Federal is $5.15)
Marriage age: 18
First-cousin marriage: Prohibited
Drinking age: 21
State control of liquor sales: Yes
Blood alcohol for DWI: 0.08%
Driving age: 17
Speed limit: 75 mph
Permit to buy handguns: No
Minimum age to possess handguns: 18
Minimum age to possess rifles, shotguns: 18
State lottery: No
Casinos: No
Pari-mutuel betting: No
Death penalty: Yes
3 strikes minimum sentence: 5 yrs. (3rd serious felony)
Hate crimes law: Yes
Gay employment non-discrimination: No
Official language(s): None
Term limits: Governor (12 yrs.); state legislators (12 yrs.)

State laws are complex and subject to change; this information is not intended as legal advice. For an explanation of this information, see p. x.

E-mail: djones@le.state.ut.us
http://www.le.state.ut.us/house/Members/District/
district_25.htm

Ralph Becker (D), Minority Whip
State Capitol, #318, Salt Lake City, UT 84114
(801) 538-1581
E-mail: rbecker@le.state.ut.us
http://www.le.state.ut.us/house/Members/District/
district_24.htm

Carole E. Peterson, Chief Clerk
State Capitol, #318, Salt Lake City, UT 84114
(801) 538-1280
E-mail: cpeters@le.state.ut.us

Utah Judiciary

Scott M. Matheson Courthouse
450 S. State St.
Salt Lake City, UT 84111
http://www.state.ut.us/government/
judicial.html

Supreme Court
http://courtlink.utcourts.gov

Pat H. Bartholmew, Clerk
Scott M. Matheson Courthouse, 450 S. State St., Salt
Lake City, UT 84111
(801) 578-3900; *Fax:* (801) 578-3999

Justices
Composition: 5 justices
Selection Method: appointed by governor; but
must stand unopposed for retention at a
general election within 3 years of appointment
Length of term: 10 years

Richard C. Howe, Chief Justice, (801) 578-3900
Christine M. Durham, Associate Chief Justice, (801)
578-3900
Leonard H. Russon, Justice, (801) 578-3900
I. Daniel Stewart, Justice, (801) 238-7950
Michael D. Zimmerman, Justice, (801) 238-7937

Administrative Office of the Courts
Main phone: (801) 578-3800
Main fax: (801) 578-3843

Daniel J. Becker, State Court Administrator
Scott M. Matheson Courthouse, 450 S. State St., Salt
Lake City, UT 84111
E-mail: danb@email.utcourts.gov

State Law Library
Main phone: (801) 238-7989
Main fax: (801) 238-7980

Nancy Cheng, Supreme Court Law Librarian
Scott M. Matheson Courthouse, 450 S. State St., Salt
Lake City, UT 84114

Legislative and Political Party Information Resources

Senate home page: http://www.senate.le.state.ut.us
House home page: http://www.le.state.ut.us/house/house.htm
Committees: http://www.le.state.ut.us/lrgc/legcom.htm
Legislative process: http://www.le.state.ut.us/legproc.htm
Utah Democratic Party: http://www.utdemocrats.org
    455 South, 300 East, #102, Salt Lake City, UT 84111; *Phone:* (801) 328-1212;
    Fax: (801) 328-1238; *E-mail:* utdems@xmission.com
Utah Republican Party: http://www.utahgop.com
    117 E. South Temple, Salt Lake City, UT 84111; *Phone:* (801) 533-9777; *Fax:* (801) 533-0327;
    E-mail: mail@utahgop.com

Vermont

State Capitol
Montpelier, VT 05609
Public information: (802) 828-1110
Fax: (802) 828-3339
http://www.state.vt.us

Office of the Governor
http://www.state.vt.us/governor/index.htm
Main phone: (802) 828-3333
Main fax: (802) 828-3339
TTY: (800) 649-6825

Howard B. Dean (D), Governor
Pavilion Office Bldg., 109 State St., 5th Fl.,
Montpelier, VT 05609

Julie Peterson, Chief of Staff
Pavilion Office Bldg., 109 State St., Montpelier, VT
05609
(802) 828-3333; *Fax:* (802) 828-3339

Susan Allen, Press Secretary
Pavilion Office Bldg., 109 State St., Montpelier, VT
05609
(802) 828-3333; *Fax:* (802) 828-3339

Office of the Lieutenant Governor
http://www.leg.state.vt.us/ltgov/
General e-mail: ltgov@leg.state.vt.us
Main phone: (802) 828-2226
Main fax: (802) 828-3198

Douglas A. Racine (D), Lieutenant Governor
State House, Montpelier, VT 05633

Office of the Secretary of State
http://www.sec.state.vt.us/
Main phone: (802) 828-2363
Main fax: (802) 828-2496

Deborah L. Markowitz (D), Secretary of State
Pavilion Office Bldg., 109 State St., Montpelier, VT
05609-1101
(802) 828-2148
E-mail: dmarko@sec.state.vt.us

Office of the Attorney General
http://www.state.vt.us/atg
General e-mail: aginfo@atg.state.vt.us
Main phone: (802) 828-3171
Main fax: (802) 828-2154
TTY: (802) 828-3171

William H. Sorrell (D), Attorney General
Pavilion Office Bldg., 109 State St., Montpelier, VT
05609-1001
(802) 828-3173; *Fax:* (802) 828-3187

State of Vermont

Capital: Montpelier, since 1805
Founded: 1777, independent republic from lands claimed by New York and New Hampshire
Statehood: March 4, 1791 (14th state)
Constitution adopted: 1793
Area: 9,249 sq. mi. (ranks 43rd)
Population: 590,883 (1998 est.; ranks 49th)
Largest cities: (1998 est.) Burlington (38,453); Essex (18,076); Rutland (17,348); Colchester (16,275); Bennington (16,069)
Counties: 14, Most populous: (1998 est.) Chittenden (142,642); Rutland (62,524); Washington (56,308); Windsor (55,444); Franklin (44,017)
U.S. Congress: James M. Jeffords (R), Patrick Leahy (D); 1 Representative
Nickname(s): Green Mountain State
Motto: Vermont, freedom, and unity
Song: "Hail, Vermont"
Bird: Hermit thrush
Tree: Sugar maple
Flower: Red clover
State fair: at Rutland, early Sept.
Former capital(s): Windsor, Rutland

Office of the State Treasurer
http://www.state.vt.us/treasurer/
General e-mail: WebMaster@tre.state.vt.us
Main phone: (802) 828-2301
Main fax: (802) 828-2772

James H. Douglas (R), State Treasurer
133 State St., 2nd Fl., Montpelier, VT 05633-6200
E-mail: jdouglas@tre.state.vt.us

Auditor of Accounts Office
http://www.state.vt.us/sao/
General e-mail: auditor@pop.state.vt.us
Main phone: (802) 828-2281
Main fax: (802) 828-2198

Edward S. Flanagan (D), Auditor of Accounts
132 State St., Montpelier, VT 05633-5101
E-mail: eflanagan@sao.state.vt.us

Military Dept.
http://www.mil.state.vt.us/
Main phone: (802) 338-3124
Main fax: (802) 338-0425

Martha T. Rainville, Adjutant General
Camp Johnson, Green Mountain Armory, Colchester, VT 05446-3004

Agencies

Administration Agency
Main phone: (802) 828-3322
Main fax: (802) 828-3320

Kathleen C. Hoyt, Secretary
Pavilion Office Bldg., 109 State St., Montpelier, VT 05609-0201

Agriculture, Food, and Markets Dept.
http://www.state.vt.us/agric/index.htm
Main phone: (802) 828-2500
Main fax: (802) 828-2361
Mailing address: Drawer 20, Montpelier, VT 05620-2901

Leon C. Graves, Commissioner
116 State St., Montpelier, VT 05620-2901
(802) 828-2430
E-mail: lgraves@agr.state.vt.us

Archives
Main phone: (802) 828-2369
Main *Fax:* (802) 828-2465

D. Gregory Sanford, State Archivist
Redstone Bldg., 26 Terrace St., Montpelier, VT 05609-1101

Arts Council
http://www.state.vt.us/vermont-arts/
General e-mail: info@arts.vca.state.vt.us
Main phone: (802) 828-3291
Main fax: (802) 828-3363
TTY: (800) 253-0191
Mailing address: Drawer 33, Montpelier, VT 05633-6001

Alexander L. Aldrich, Executive Director
136 State St., Montpelier, VT 05633-6001
(802) 828-3293

Auctioneers, Land Surveyors, Real Estate, Funeral Services, and Appraisers Unit
Main phone: (802) 828-3256
Main fax: (802) 828-2368
Mailing address: Drawer 9, Montpelier, VT 05609-1106

Ted McKnight, Administrator
81 River St., Heritage Bldg., Montpelier, VT 05609-1106
E-mail: tmcknigh@heritage.sec.state.vt.us

Banking, Insurance, Securities, and Health Care Administration Dept.
http://www.state.vt.us/bis
Main phone: (802) 828-3301
Main fax: (802) 828-3306
Mailing address: Drawer 20, Montpelier, VT 05620-3101

Elizabeth R. Costle, Commissioner
89 Main St., Montpelier, VT 05620-3101

Civil Rights Unit
http://www.state.vt.us/atg/civilrights.htm
Main phone: (802) 828-5511
Main fax: (802) 828-2154
TTY: (802) 828-3665

Kate Hayes, Assistant Attorney General
Pavilion Office Bldg., 109 State St., Montpelier, VT 05609-1001

Commerce and Community Development Agency
http://www.state.vt.us/dca/
Main phone: (802) 828-3211
Main fax: (802) 828-3383
Toll free: (800) 622-4553
Mailing address: Drawer 20, Montpelier, VT 05620-0501

Molly Lambert, Secretary
National Life Bldg., Montpelier, VT 05620-0501
(802) 828-5204; *Fax:* (802) 828-5606

Tourism and Marketing Dept.
http://www.1-800-Vermont.com
Main phone: (802) 828-3237
Main fax: (802) 828-3233

Thomas Altemus, Commissioner
3 Baldwin St., Montpelier, VT 05633-1301
(802) 828-3649

Defender General Office
http://www.defgen.state.vt.us
Main phone: (802) 828-3168
Main fax: (802) 828-3163
TTY: (800) 253-0191

Robert Joseph Appel, Defender General
State Office Bldg., 120 State St., Montpelier, VT 05620-3301
E-mail: rappel@defgen.state.vt.us

Developmental and Mental Health Services Dept.
http://www.state.vt.us/dmh/

General e-mail: webmaster@ddmhs.state.vt.us
Main phone: (802) 241-2214
Main fax: (802) 241-1129

Rodney E. Copeland, Commissioner
103 S. Main St., Weeks Bldg., Waterbury, VT 05671-1601
(802) 241-2610
E-mail: rcopeland@ddmhs.state.vt.us

Economic Development Authority
http://www.state.vt.us/veda/
General e-mail: info@veda.state.vt.us
Main phone: (802) 828-5627
Main fax: (802) 828-5474

Roselea W. (Jo) Bradley, Manager
58 E. State St., #5, Montpelier, VT 05602
E-mail: jbradley@veda.state.vt.us

Education Dept.
http://www.state.vt.us/educ/
Main phone: (802) 828-3135
Main fax: (802) 828-3140

Marge Petit, Commissioner (Acting)
State Office Bldg., 120 State St., Montpelier, VT 05620-2501
(802) 828-5101
E-mail: mpetit@doe.state.vt.us

Board of Education
Main phone: (802) 650-7046
Main fax: (802) 650-2008

Frank McDougal, Chair (Acting)
120 State St., Montpelier, VT 05620-2501

Employment and Training Dept.
http://www.det.state.vt.us/
Main phone: (802) 828-4000
Main fax: (802) 828-4022
TTY: (802) 828-4203
Mailing address: P.O. Box 488, Montpelier, VT 05601-0488

Steven M. Gold, Commissioner
5 Green Mountain Dr., Montpelier, VT 05601
(802) 828-4301; *Fax:* (802) 828-4181
E-mail: sgold@pop.det.state.vt.us

Finance and Management Dept.
http://www.state.vt.us/fin/
Main phone: (802) 828-2376
Main fax: (802) 828-2428

Tom Pelham, Commissioner
109 State St., Montpelier, VT 05609-0401
E-mail: tom.pelham@state.vt.us

Health Dept.
http://www.state.vt.us/health/

Main phone: (802) 863-7200
Main fax: (802) 865-7754
Mailing address: P.O. Box 70, Burlington, VT 05402-0070

Jan K. Carney, Commissioner
108 Cherry St., Burlington, VT 05402-0070
(802) 863-7280
E-mail: jcarney@vdh.state.vt.us

Health Professions, Architecture, and Related Professions Unit
Main phone: (802) 828-2808
Main fax: (802) 828-2465
Toll free: (800) 439-8683

Rita Knapp, Administrator
Redstone Bldg., 26 Terrace St., Drawer 9, Montpelier, VT 05609-1101
E-mail: rknapp@sec.state.vt.us

Historical Society
http://www.state.vt.us/vhs
General e-mail: vhs@vhs.state.vt.us
Main phone: (802) 828-2291
Main fax: (802) 828-3638

Gainor Davis, Executive Director
109 State St., Montpelier, VT 05609-0901

Housing Finance Agency
http://www.vhfa.org/
Main phone: (802) 864-5743
Main fax: (802) 864-5746
Toll free: (800) 339-5866
TTY: (800) 586-5832
Mailing address: P.O. Box 408, Burlington, VT 05401-4364

Sarah Carpenter, Executive Director
164 St. Paul St., Burlington, VT 05401-4364

(802) 652-3421
E-mail: scarpenter@vhfa.org

Human Services Agency
http://www.ahs.state.vt.us/
Main phone: (802) 241-2220
Main fax: (802) 241-2979

Jane Kitchel, Secretary
State Complex, 103 S. Main St., Waterbury, VT
05671-0204

Aging and Disabilities Dept.
http://www.dad.state.vt.us/
General e-mail: danr@dad.state.vt.us
Main phone: (802) 241-2400
Main fax: (802) 241-2325

Vacant, Director
103 S. Main St., Waterbury, VT 05671

Corrections Dept.
http://www.doc.state.vt.us
General e-mail: rosej@doc.state.vt.us
Main phone: (802) 241-2442
Main fax: (802) 241-2565

John Gorczyk, Commissioner
State Complex, 103 S. Main St., Waterbury, VT
05671-1001

Social Welfare Dept.: Medicaid Division
Main phone: (802) 241-3985

Main fax: (802) 241-2897
TTY: (888) 834-7898

Paul Wallace-Brodur, Director
State Complex, 103 S. Main St., Waterbury, VT
05671-1021
E-mail: paulwb@wdgate1.ahs.state.vt.us

Labor and Industry Dept.
http://www.state.vt.us/labind/
Main phone: (802) 828-2288
Main fax: (802) 828-2195
Mailing address: Drawer 20, Montpelier, VT
05620-3401

Steve Janson, Commissioner
National Life Bldg., Montpelier, VT 05620-3401

Fire Prevention Division
Main phone: (802) 828-2106
Main fax: (808) 828-2195

Robert Howe, Director
National Life Bldg., Montpelier, VT 05620-3401
E-mail: robert.howe@labind.state.vt.us

Workers Compensation Division
http://www.state.vt.us/labind
Main phone: (802) 828-2286
Main fax: (802) 828-2195
Mailing address: Drawer 20, Montpelier, VT
05620-3401

Charles Bond, Director
National Life Bldg., Montpelier, VT 05620-3401
(802) 828-2990
E-mail: charles.bond@labind.state.vt.us

Labor Relations Board
http://www.state.vt.us/vlrb/
Main phone: (802) 828-2700
Main fax: (802) 828-2392

Catherine L. Frank, Chair
133 State St., Montpelier, VT 05633-6101

Libraries Dept.
http://dol.state.vt.us/
Main phone: (802) 828-3261
Main fax: (802) 828-2199

Sybil Brigham McShane, State Librarian
109 State St., Montpelier, VT 05609-0601
(802) 828-3265
E-mail: smcshane@dol.state.vt.us

Licensing and Professional Regulation Division
Main phone: (802) 828-2458

Thomas J. Lehner, Director
Redstone Bldg., 26 Terrace St., Montpelier, VT 05609-
1101

Liquor Control Dept.
http://www.state.vt.us/dlc
Main phone: (802) 828-2345
Main fax: (802) 828-2803
Mailing address: Drawer 20, Montpelier, VT
05620-4501

Michael J. Hogan, Commissioner
13 Green Mountain Dr., Montpelier, VT 05620-4501
(802) 828-4929
E-mail: mike@dlc.state.vt.us

Lottery Commission
http://www.vtlottery.com/
General e-mail: staff@vtlottery.com
Main phone: (802) 479-5686
Main fax: (802) 479-4294
Toll free: (800) 322-8800
Mailing address: P.O. Box 420, South Barre, VT
05670

Alan R. Yandow, Executive Director
379 S. Barre Rd., Rt. 14, South Barre, VT 05670

Medical Practice Board
http://www.docboard.org/vt/vermont.htm
Main phone: (802) 828-2673
Main fax: (802) 828-5450
Mailing address: 109 State St., Montpelier, VT
05609

Barbara Neuman, Director
1 Prospect St., Montpelier, VT 05602
E-mail: bneuman@medbd.state.vt.us

Motor Vehicles Dept.
http://www.aot.state.vt.us/dmv/dmvhp.htm
Main phone: (802) 828-2000
Main fax: (802) 828-2098
TTY: (800) 253-0191

Patricia A. McDonald, Commissioner
120 State St., Montpelier, VT 05603-0001
(802) 828-2011; *Fax:* (802) 828-2170
E-mail: patricia.mcdonald@state.vt.us

Municipal and State Employees' Retirement System
General e-mail: oholden@tre.state.vt.us
Main phone: (802) 828-2305
Main fax: (802) 828-5182
Toll free: (800) 642-3191

Cynthia L. Webster, Director
133 State St., Montpelier, VT 05633-6901

Natural Resources Agency
http://www.anr.state.vt.us/
Main phone: (802) 241-3600
Main fax: (802) 244-1102
TTY: (802) 253-0191

John Kassel, Secretary
State Complex, 103 S. Main St., Waterbury, VT
05671-0301

Environmental Conservation Dept.
http://anr.state.vt.us/dec/dec.htm
Main phone: (802) 241-3800
Main fax: (802) 244-5141

Canute Dalmasse, Commissioner
State Complex, 103 S. Main St., Waterbury, VT
05671

Environmental Conservation Dept.: Geological Survey
http://anr.state.vt.us/dec/geology
Main phone: (802) 241-3608

Larry Becker, State Geologist
State Complex, 103 S. Main St., Waterbury, VT
05671

Fish and Wildlife Dept.
http://anr.state.vt.us/fw/fwhome/index.htm
Main phone: (802) 241-3730
Main fax: (802) 241-3295

Ronald Regan, Commissioner
State Complex, 103 S. Main St., Waterbury, VT
05671

Forests, Parks, and Recreation Dept.
http://anr.state.vt.us/fpr/index.htm
Main phone: (802) 241-3670
Main fax: (802) 244-1481
TTY: (800) 253-0191

Conrad Motyka, Commissioner
State Complex, Bldg. 8 South, 103 S. Main St.,
Waterbury, VT 05671
E-mail: cmotyka@fpr.anr.state.vt.us

Licensing and Professional Regulation Division

http://www.vtprofessionals.org
(802) 828-2458

Accountancy, (802) 828-2191
Architects, (802) 828-2808
Cosmetology, (802) 828-2191
Land Surveyors, (802) 828-3256
Pharmacy, (802) 828-2808
Engineers, (802) 828-2808
Real Estate, (802) 828-3256
Health and Child Care, (802) 241-2158
Medical Licensing, (802) 828-2673,
http://www.docboard.org/vt/vermont.htm
Nursing, (802) 828-3180

Nursing Board Unit

Main phone: (802) 828-2396
Main fax: (802) 828-2484

Anita Ristau, Administrator
81 River St., Heritage Bldg., Montpelier, VT 05609-1101
E-mail: aristau@heritage.sec.state.ut.us

Personnel Dept.

http://www.state.vt.us/pers/
General e-mail: recruit@per.state.vt.us
Main phone: (802) 828-3491
Main fax: (802) 828-3409
TTY: (800) 253-0191

Eileen M. Boland, Commissioner
110 State St., Drawer 20, Montpelier, VT 05620
E-mail: eboland@per.state.vt.us

Public Power Supply Authority

Main phone: (802) 244-7678
Main fax: (802) 244-6889
Mailing address: P.O. Box 298, Waterbury Center, VT 05677-0298

William J. Gallagher, General Manager
5195 Waterbury-Stowe Rd., Waterbury Center, VT 05677-0298
E-mail: galleghe@vppsa.com

Public Safety Dept.

http://www.dps.state.vt.us/
Main phone: (802) 244-8727
Main fax: (802) 241-5552
Toll free: (800) 828-4894
TTY: (802) 244-5371

A. James Walton Jr., Commissioner
State Complex, 103 S. Main St., Waterbury, VT 05671-2101
(802) 244-8718; *Fax:* (802) 244-5551

Deputy Fire Marshal
Main phone: (802) 244-8781
Main fax: (802) 241-5551
TTY: (802) 244-5371

Nicholas Ruggiero, Deputy Fire Marshal
State Complex, 103 S. Main St., Waterbury, VT 05671
E-mail: nruggier@dps.state.vt.us

Emergency Management Office

http://www.dps.state.vt.us/vem
General e-mail: vem@dps.state.vt.us
Main phone: (802) 244-8721
Main fax: (802) 241-5556
Toll free: (800) 347-0488

Edward Von Turkovich, Director
State Complex, 103 S. Main St., Waterbury, VT 05676-0850
E-mail: evonturk@dps.state.vt.us

State Police

Main phone: (802) 244-7345
Main fax: (802) 241-5551
TTY: (802) 244-5371

Thomas A. Powlovich, Director
State Complex, 103 S. Main St., Waterbury, VT 05676-0850
E-mail: tpowlovi@dps.state.vt.us

Public Service Dept.

http://www.state.vt.us/psd/
General e-mail: vtdps@psd.state.vt.us
Main phone: (802) 828-2811
Main fax: (802) 828-2342
TTY: (800) 734-8390
Mailing address: Drawer 20, Montpelier, VT 05620-2701

Richard P. Sedano, Commissioner
112 State St., Montpelier, VT 05620-2601
(802) 828-2321

State Parks

http://www.vtstateparks.com/
General e-mail: parks@fpr.anr.state.vt.us
Main phone: (802) 241-3655
Main fax: (802) 244-1481
Toll free: (800) VERMONT
TTY: (800) 253-0191

Larry T. Simino, Director
103 S. Main St., Waterbury, VT 05671-0603
(802) 241-3664
E-mail: lsimino@fpr.anr.state.vt.us

Taxes Dept.

http://www.state.vt.us/tax/
General e-mail: vttaxdept@tax.state.vt.us
Main phone: (802) 828-2505
Main fax: (802) 828-2701
TTY: (802) 828-2574

Sean P. Campbell, Commissioner
109 State St., Montpelier, VT 05609-1401
E-mail: scampbell@tax.state.vt.us

Transportation Agency

http://www.aot.state.vt.us/
Main phone: (802) 828-2657
Main fax: (802) 828-3522
TTY: (800) 253-0191

Brian R. Searles, Secretary
National Life Bldg., Montpelier, VT 05633-5001

Veterans Affairs
http://www.visn1.org/wrj/
Main phone: (802) 828-3379
Main fax: (802) 828-5932

Mae E. Jennison, Supervisor
120 State St., Montpelier, VT 05620-4401
E-mail: mjennison@va.state.vt.us

Water Resources Board
http://www.state.vt.us/wtrboard/
General e-mail: jminadeo@envboard.state.vt.u
Main phone: (802) 828-3309
Mailing address: Drawer 20, Montpelier, VT 05620-3201

Gerry Gossens, Chair
National Life Records Center Bldg., Montpelier, VT 05620-3201

Women's Commission
http://www.women.state.vt.us
General e-mail: info@women.state.vt.us
Main phone: (802) 828-2851
Main fax: (802) 828-2930
Toll free: (800) 881-1561

Judith A. Sutphen, Executive Director
126 State St., Montpelier, VT 05633-6801
E-mail: jsutphen@women.state.vt.us

Vermont Legislature
State House
Montpelier, VT 05602
General information: (802) 828-2228
Fax: (802) 828-2424
Bill status: (802) 828-2231
http://www.leg.state.vt.us

Senate
General information: (802) 828-2241

Douglas A. Racine (D), President
State House, Montpelier, VT 05633
(802) 828-2226; *Fax:* (802) 828-3198
E-mail: ltgov@leg.state.vt.us

Peter E. Shumlin (D), President Pro Tempore
State House, Montpelier, VT 05633
(802) 828-3806

Richard J. McCormack (D), Majority Leader
State House, Montpelier, VT 05633
(802) 828-2241

John H. Bloomer Jr. (R), Minority Leader
State House, Montpelier, VT 05633
(802) 828-2241
E-mail: jbloomer@leg.state.vt.us

Robert H. Gibson, Secretary
State House, Montpelier, VT 05633
(802) 828-2241
E-mail: sensec@leg.state.vt.us

House
General information: (802) 828-2247

Michael J. Obuchowski (D), Speaker of the House
State House, Office of the Speaker, Montpelier, VT 05633
(802) 828-2245
E-mail: speaker@leg.state.vt.us
http://www.leg.state.vt.us/speaker/

John P. Tracy (D), Majority Leader
State House, Montpelier, VT 05633
(802) 828-2247
E-mail: jtracy@leg.state.vt.us

Walter E. Freed (R), Minority Leader
State House, Montpelier, VT 05633
(802) 828-2247

Laws

Sales tax: 5%
Income tax: 9.9%
State minimum wage: $5.75 (Federal is $5.15)
Marriage age: 18
First-cousin marriage: Permitted
Drinking age: 21
State control of liquor sales: Yes
Blood alcohol for DWI: 0.08%
Driving age: 16
Speed limit: 65 mph
Permit to buy handguns: No
Minimum age to possess handguns: 16
Minimum age to possess rifles, shotguns: None
State lottery: Yes; also Tri-State Lottery (with ME, NH)
Casinos: No
Pari-mutuel betting: Dog racing
Death penalty: None
3 strikes minimum sentence: Up to life optional (3rd serious felony)
Hate crimes law: Yes
Gay employment non-discrimination: Yes
Official language(s): No
Term limits: None

State laws are complex and subject to change; this information is not intended as legal advice. For an explanation of this information, see p. x.

John V. LaBarge (R), Minority Whip
State House, Montpelier, VT 05633
(802) 828-2247

Donald Milne, Clerk
State House, Montpelier, VT 05633
(802) 828-2247; *Fax:* (802) 828-2424
E-mail: hclerk@leg.state.vt.us

Vermont Judiciary

111 State St.
Montpelier, VT 05609-0801
http://www.state.vt.us/courts/

Supreme Court

Lee Suskin, Court Administrator and Clerk
111 State St., Montpelier, VT 05609-0801
(802) 828-3278; *Fax:* (802) 828-3457
E-mail: lee@supreme.crt.state.vt.us

Justices
Composition: 5 justices

Selection Method: appointed by governor with consent of state senate; each subsequent term subject to retention ballot at general election
Length of term: 6 years

Jeffrey Amestoy, Chief Justice, (802) 828-3278
John A. Dooley III, Associate Justice, (802) 828-3278
Denise R. Johnson, Associate Justice, (802) 828-3278
James L. Morse, Associate Justice, (802) 828-3278
Marilyn S. Skoglund, Associate Justice, (802) 828-3278

Office of the Court Administrator
http://www.state.vt.us/courts/admin.htm
Main phone: (802) 828-3278
Main fax: (802) 828-3457

Lee Suskin, Court Administrator and Clerk
111 State St., Montpelier, VT 05609-0801
E-mail: lee@supreme.crt.state.vt.us

State Law Library
Main phone: (802) 828-3268
Main fax: (802) 828-2199

Paul Donovan, Law Librarian
111 State St., Montpelier, VT 05609-0801

Legislative and Political Party Information Resources

Membership: Senate: http://www.leg.state.vt.us/legdir/legdir2.htm
Committees: Senate: http://www.leg.state.vt.us/legdir/scomms.htm; *House:* http://www.leg.state.vt.us/legdir/hcomms.htm
Budget: http://www.leg.state.vt.us/jfo/
Vermont Democratic Party: http://www.vtdemocrats.org
P.O. Box 1220, Montpelier, VT 05601-1220; *Phone:* (802) 229-1783; *Fax:* (802) 229-1784; *E-mail:* vtdems@vtdemocrats.org
Vermont Republican Party: http://www.vermontgop.org
P.O. Box 70, Montpelier, VT 05601; *Phone:* (802) 223-3411; *Fax:* (802) 229-1864; *E-mail:* vtgop@vermontgop.org

Virginia

State Capitol
Richmond, VA 23219
Public information: (804) 786-0000
Fax: (804) 786-4177
http://www.state.va.us

Office of the Governor
http://www.state.va.us/governor/
Main phone: (804) 786-2211
Main fax: (804) 371-0121
TTY: (804) 371-8015

James S. Gilmore III (R), Governor
State Capitol, Richmond, VA 23219
E-mail: governor@gov.state.va.us

M. Boyd Marcus Jr., Chief of Staff
State Capitol, Richmond, VA 23219
(804) 786-2211; *Fax:* (804) 692-0121
E-mail: mbmarcus@gov.state.va.us

Mark Miner, Press Secretary
State Capitol, Richmond, VA 23219
(804) 692-3110; *Fax:* (804) 692-0121
E-mail: mminer@gov.state.va.us

Carol Comstock, Constituent Services Director
State Capitol, 202 N. 9th St., Richmond, VA 23219
(804) 786-2211; *Fax:* (804) 371-6351
E-mail: ccomstack@gov.state.va.us

Michael McSherry, Director, Washington Office
444 N. Capitol St. N.W., #214, Washington, DC 20001
(202) 783-1769; *Fax:* (202) 783-7687
E-mail: mmcsherry@gov.state.va.us

Office of the Lieutenant Governor
http://www.state.va.us/ltgov/
General e-mail: ltgov@ltgov.state.va.us
Main phone: (804) 786-2078
Main fax: (804) 786-7514
TTY: (800) 828-1120

John H. Hager (R), Lieutenant Governor
900 E. Main St., #1400, Richmond, VA 23219-3523

Office of the Secretary of the Commonwealth
http://www.soc.vipnet.org
Main phone: (804) 786-2441
Main fax: (804) 371-0017
Mailing address: P.O. Box 2454, Richmond, VA 23219

Anne P. Petera, Secretary of the Commonwealth
1 Capitol Square, 830 E. Main St., 14th Fl., Richmond, VA 23219
E-mail: apetera@gov.state.va.us

State of Virginia

Capital: Richmond, since 1780
Founded: 1607, as British colony
Statehood: June 25, 1788 (10th state)
Constitution adopted: 1970
Area: 39,598 sq. mi. (ranks 37th)
Population: 6,791,345 (1998 est.; ranks 12th)
Largest cities: (1998 est.) Norfolk (215,215); Chesapeake (199,564); Richmond (194,173); Newport News (178,615); Arlington (177,275)
Counties: 95, Most populous: (1998 est.) Fairfax (929,239); Prince William (259,827); Henrico (246,052); Chesterfield (245,915); Arlington (177,275)
U.S. Congress: Charles Robb (D), John Warner (R); 11 Representatives
Nickname(s): Old Dominion, Mother of Presidents
Motto: Thus always to tyrants
Song: "Carry Me Back to Old Virginia"
Bird: Cardinal
Tree: Dogwood
Flower: Dogwood
State fair: at Richmond, late Sept.-early Oct.
Former capital(s): Jamestown, Williamsburg

Office of the Attorney General
http://www.vaag.com
General e-mail: mail@oag.state.va.us
Main phone: (804) 786-2071
Main fax: (804) 786-1991
TTY: (804) 371-8946

Mark L. Earley (R), Attorney General
900 E. Main St., Richmond, VA 23219

Office of the State Treasurer
http://www.trs.state.va.us/
General e-mail: web.master@trs.state.va.us
Main phone: (804) 225-2142
Main fax: (804) 225-3187
Mailing address: P.O. Box 1879, Richmond, VA 23219

Mary G. Morris, State Treasurer
101 N. 14th St., James Monroe Bldg., 3rd Fl.,
Richmond, VA 23219
E-mail: mmorris@trs.state.va.us

Agencies

Accountancy Board
http://www.state.va.us/dpor
General e-mail: accountancy@dpor.state.va.us
Main phone: (804) 367-8505
Main fax: (804) 367-2475
TTY: (804) 367-9753

David E. Dick, Administrator
3600 W. Broad St., 5th Fl., Richmond, VA 23230
(804) 367-2648

Administration Secretariat
http://www.soa.state.va.us/
General e-mail: soadministration@gov.state.va.us
Main phone: (804) 786-1201
Main fax: (804) 371-0038
TTY: (804) 786-1201
Mailing address: P.O. Box 1475, Richmond, VA
23218

G. Bryan Slater, Secretary
9th St. Office Bldg., 202 N. 9th St., #633, Richmond,
VA 23219

Aging Dept.
http://www.aging.state.va.us/
General e-mail: cslasor@vdh.state.va.us
Main phone: (804) 662-9333
Main fax: (804) 662-9354
Toll free: (800) 552-3402
TTY: (804) 662-9333

Ann Y. McGee, Commissioner
1600 Forest Ave., #102, Richmond, VA 23229
(804) 662-9312; *Fax:* (804) 662-7052
E-mail: amcgee@vdh.state.wa.us

Agriculture and Consumer Services Dept.
Main phone: (804) 786-3532
Main fax: (804) 371-2945

J. Carlton Courter III, Commissioner
1100 Bank St., Richmond, VA 23219

Alcohol Safety Action Program (VASAP) Commission
http://www.vasap.state.va.us
Main phone: (804) 786-5895
Main fax: (804) 786-6286
TTY: (804) 786-5895

William McCollum, Executive Director
701 E. Franklin St., #1110, Richmond, VA 23219
E-mail: wmcollum.vasap@state.va.us

Alcoholic Beverage Control
http://www.abc.state.va.us/
Main phone: (804) 213-4400
Main fax: (804) 213-4411
Toll free: (800) 552-3200
TTY: (804) 213-4687
Mailing address: P.O. Box 27491, Richmond, VA
23261

Clarence W. Roberts, Commissioner
2901 Hermitage Rd., Richmond, VA 23220
E-mail: cwrobes@abc.state.va.us

Architects, Professional Engineers, Land Survey, Interior Design, and Lanscape Architects Board
Main phone: (804) 367-8514
Main fax: (804) 367-9537

Mark Courtney, Administrator
3600 W. Broad St., Richmond, VA 23230

Arts Commission
http://www.artswire.org/~vacomm/
General e-mail: vacomm@artswire.org
Main phone: (804) 225-3132
Main fax: (804) 225-4327

Peggy J. Baggett, Executive Director
Lewis House, 223 Governor St., 2nd Fl., Richmond,
VA 23219-2010

Auditor of Public Accounts
http://www.apa.state.va.us/
Main phone: (804) 225-3350
Main fax: (804) 225-3357
Mailing address: P.O. Box 1295, Richmond, VA
23219

Walter J. Kucharski, Auditor of Public Accounts
101 N. 14th St., 8th Fl., Richmond, VA 23219
E-mail: wjkucharski@apa.state.va.us

Aviation Dept.
http://www.doav.state.va.us/
General e-mail: wilson@doav.state.va.us
Main phone: (804) 236-3625
Main fax: (804) 236-3635
Toll free: (800) 292-1034

Kenneth F. Wiegand, Director
5702 Gulfstream Rd., Richmond, VA 23250-2422
(804) 236-3625, ext. 108
E-mail: wiegand@doav.state.va.us

Chesapeake Bay Bridge and Tunnel District
http://www.cbbt.com
Main phone: (757) 331-2960
Main fax: (757) 331-4565
Mailing address: P.O. Box 111, Cape Charles, VA
23310

J. K. Brookshire Jr., Executive Director
32386 Lankfort Hwy., Cape Charles, VA 23310

Chesapeake Bay Commisson
http://www.chesbay.state.va.us
Main phone: (804) 786-4849
Main fax: (804) 371-0659
Mailing address: P.O. Box 406, Richmond, VA
23218

Russell W. Baxter, Director
General Assembly Bldg., 910 Capitol St., #502-B,
Richmond, VA 23219
E-mail: rbaxter@leg.state.va.us

Commerce and Trade Secretariat
http://www.vipnet.org/commerce/index.htm
Main phone: (804) 786-7831
Main fax: (804) 371-0250

Barry E. DuVal, Secretary
9th St. Office Bldg., 202 N. 9th St., #723, Richmond,
VA 23219
E-mail: bduval@gov.state.va.us

Mines, Minerals, and Energy Dept: Gas and Oil Division
http://www.mme.state.va.us
Main phone: (540) 676-5423
Main fax: (540) 676-5459
TTY: (800) 828-1120

B. R. Wilson, Director
230 Charwood Dr., Abingdon, VA 24212
E-mail: bxw@mme.state.va.us

Professional and Occupational Licensing Dept.
http://www.state.va.us/dpor

Higher Educational Institutions

Christopher Newport University
http://www.cnu.edu
1 University Pl., Newport News, VA 23606
Main phone: (757) 594-7100

College of William and Mary
http://www.wm.edu
P.O. Box 8795, Williamsburg, VA 23187-8795
Main phone: (757) 221-4000
Branches: Richard Bland College

George Mason University
http://www.gmu.edu
4400 University Dr., Fairfax, VA 22030-4444
Main phone: (703) 993-2400
Branches: Arlington, Fairfax, Prince William

James Madison University
http://www.jmu.edu
Sonner Hall, MSC 0101, Harrisonburg, VA 22807
Main phone: (540) 568-6147

Longwood College
http://www.lwc.edu
201 High St., Farmville, VA 23909
Main phone: (800) 281-4677

Mary Washington College
http://www.mwc.edu
1301 College Ave., Fredericksburg, VA 22401-5358
Main phone: (540) 654-1000

Norfolk State University
http://www.nsu.edu
700 Park Ave., Norfolk, VA 23504
Main phone: (757) 823-8600

Old Dominion University
http://web.odu.edu

Hampton Blvd., Norfolk, VA 23529
Main phone: (757) 683-3000

Radford University
http://www.runet.edu
E. Norwood St., Radford, VA 24142
Main phone: (540) 831-5000

Southern Virginia College
http://www.southernvirginia.edu
1 College Hill Dr., Buena Vista, VA 24416
Main phone: (540) 261-8421

University of Virginia
http://www.virginia.edu
P.O. Box 9017, Charlottesville, VA 22906
Main phone: (804) 924-0311
Branches: Wise

Virginia Commonwealth University
http://www.vcu.edu
821 W. Franklin St., Richmond, VA 23284
Main phone: (804) 828-0100

Virginia Military Institute
http://www.vmi.edu
Lexington, VA 24450
Main phone: (540) 464-7211

Virginia Polytechnic Institute and State University
http://www.vt.us
201 Burruss Hall, Blacksburg, VA 24061-0202
Main phone: (540) 231-6267

Virginia State University
http://www.vsu.edu
P.O. Box 9018, Petersburg, VA 23806-2096
Main phone: (804) 524-5902

Main phone: (804) 367-8500
Main fax: (804) 367-9537

Jack E. Kotvas, Director
3600 W. Broad St., Richmond, VA 23230
(804) 367-8519
E-mail: director@dpor.state.va.us

Contractors Board
Main phone: (804) 367-2785
Main fax: (804) 367-9537

Geralde Morgan, Administrator
3600 W. Broad St., Richmond, VA 23230

Corrections Dept.
http://www.cns.state.va.us/doc/
General e-mail: jonesjs@vadoc.state.va.us
Main phone: (804) 674-3000

Ron Angelone, Director
6900 Atmore Dr., Richmond, VA 23225

Cosmetology Board
http://www.state.va.us/dpor
General e-mail: dpor@state.va.us
Main phone: (804) 367-8590
Main fax: (804) 367-2474

Nancy Feldman, Administrator
3600 W. Broad St., Richmond, VA 23230

Criminal Justice Services Dept.
http://www.dcjs.state.va.us/
Main phone: (804) 786-4000
Main fax: (804) 371-8781

Joseph B. Benedetti, Director
805 E. Broad St., Richmond, VA 23219
(804) 786-8718; *Fax:* (804) 371-8981
E-mail: JBenedetti.dcjs@state.va.us

Education Dept.
http://www.seced.state.va.us
Main phone: (804) 786-1151
Main fax: (804) 371-0154
TTY: (804) 786-7765

Wilbert Bryant, Secretary of Education
9th St. Office Bldg., 202 N. 9th St., 5th Fl., Richmond, VA 23219

Board of Education
http://www.pen.k12.va.us/VDOE/VA.Board/home.shtml
Main phone: (804) 225-2023

Kirk Schroder, President
707 E. Main St., 11th Fl., Richmond, VA 23219

Emergency Services Dept.
http://www.vdes.state.va.us/
Main phone: (804) 897-6500

Main fax: (804) 897-6506
Toll free: (800) 468-8892

Michael Cline, State Coordinator
10501 Trade Ct., Richmond, VA 23236

Environmental Quality Dept.
http://www.deq.state.va.us/
General e-mail: webmaster@deq.state.va.us
Main phone: (804) 698-4000
Main fax: (804) 698-4019
Toll free: (800) 592-5482
Mailing address: P.O. Box 10009, Richmond, VA 23219

Dennis H. Treacy, Director
629 E. Main St., Richmond, VA 23219
E-mail: dhtreacy@deq.state.va.us

Water Quality Programs
Main phone: (804) 698-4000
Main fax: (804) 698-4019
Mailing address: P.O. Box 10009, Richmond, VA 23240

Alan Pollock, Director
629 E. Main St., Richmond, VA 23219
(804) 698-4002
E-mail: aepollock@deq.state.va.us

Finance Secretariat
http://www.state.va.us/sfin
Main phone: (804) 786-1148
Main fax: (804) 692-0676
TTY: (804) 786-7765
Mailing address: P.O. Box 1475, Richmond, VA 23218

Ronald L. Tillett, Secretary
9th St. Office Bldg., 202 N. 9th St., #636, Richmond, VA 23219

Accounts Dept.
http://www.state.va.us/doa
Main phone: (804) 225-3038
Main fax: (804) 371-8587
TTY: (804) 371-8588
Mailing address: P.O. Box 1971, Richmond, VA 23218-1971

William E. Landsidle, Comptroller
James Monroe Bldg., 101 N. 14th St., Richmond, VA 23219
(804) 225-2109

Taxation Dept.
Main phone: (804) 367-2062
Main fax: (804) 367-0971

Danny M. Payne, Tax Commissioner
2220 W. Broad St., Richmond, VA 23220-2008
(804) 367-8005

Forestry Dept.

http://www.dof.state.va.us
Main phone: (804) 977-6555
Main fax: (804) 296-2369
Mailing address: P.O. Box 3758, Charlottesville, VA 22903

James W. Garner, State Forester
Fontaine Research Park, 900 Natural Resources Dr., Charlottesville, VA 22903
E-mail: garnerj@hq.forestry.state.va.us

Health and Human Resources Secretariat

http://www.vipnet.org/shhr/
Main phone: (804) 786-7765
Main fax: (804) 371-6984
Mailing address: P.O. Box 1475, Richmond, VA 23219

Claude A. Allen, Secretary
9th St. Office Bldg., 202 N. 9th St., #622, Richmond, VA 23219

Medical Assistance Services Dept.

http://www.cns.state.va.us/dmas
Main phone: (804) 786-7933
Main fax: (804) 225-4512
Toll free: (800) 552-8627
TTY: (800) 343-0634

Dennis G. Smith, Director
600 E. Broad St., #1300, Richmond, VA 23219
(804) 786-8099; *Fax:* (804) 371-4981

Higher Education Council

http://www.schev.edu/
Main phone: (804) 225-2137
Main fax: (804) 225-2604
TTY: (804) 371-8017

Phyllis Palmiero, Director (Acting)
James Monroe Bldg., 101 N. 14th St., 9th Fl., Richmond, VA 23219
(804) 225-2600
E-mail: palmiero@schev.edu

Historic Resources Dept.

http://www.dhr.state.va.us
General e-mail: sdurham@dhr.state.va.us
Main phone: (804) 367-2323
Main fax: (804) 367-2391
TTY: (804) 367-2386

Alex Wise, Director
2801 Kensington Ave., Richmond, VA 23221

Housing and Community Development Dept.

http://www.dhcd.state.va.us/
General e-mail: scalhoun@dhcd.state.va.us
Main phone: (804) 371-7000
Main fax: (804) 371-7090

Frequently Called Numbers

Tourism: (804) 371-8100, 1-800-VISIT-VA; http://www.vatc.org/
Library: (804) 692-3500; http://www.lva.lib.va.us/:
Vital Statistics: (804) 225-5000; http://www.vdh.state.va.us/misc/f_08.htm
Tax/Revenue: (804) 367-2062
Motor Vehicles: (804) 367-0538; http://www.dmv.state.va.us/
State Police/Highway Patrol: (804) 674-2087; http://www.vsp.state.va.us/vsp.html
Unemployment: (804) 662-9596 or (804) 662-9614; http://www.vec.state.va.us/unins/insur.htm
General Election Information: (804) 786-6551; http://www.sbe.state.va.us
Consumer Affairs:
Hazardous Materials: (804) 698-4155; http://www.deq.state.va.us/waste/

William C. Shelton, Director
501 N. 2nd St., Jackson Center, Richmond, VA 23219
E-mail: bshelton@dhcd.state.va.us

Human Rights Council

http://www.chr.state.va.us/
Main phone: (804) 225-2292
Main fax: (804) 225-8294
Toll free: (800) 633-5510
Mailing address: P.O. Box 717, Richmond, VA 23206

Roxie Raines Kornegay, Director
Washington Bldg., 1100 Bank St., #1202, Richmond, VA 23219

Juvenile Justice Dept.

http://www.state.va.us/djj/
General e-mail: sehines@djj-state-va.com
Main phone: (804) 371-0700
Main fax: (804) 371-0725

Christine L. Turner, Director (Acting)
700 E. Franklin St., 4th Fl., Richmond, VA 23219

Labor and Industry Dept.

http://www.dli.state.va.us/
General e-mail: jap@doli.state.va.us
Main phone: (804) 371-2327
Main fax: (804) 371-2324
TTY: (804) 786-2376

John Mills Barr, Commissioner
Powers-Taylor Bldg., 13 S. 13th St., Richmond, VA 23219

Library of Virginia

http://www.lva.lib.va.us/
General e-mail: rschooff@vsla.edu
Main phone: (804) 692-3500
Main fax: (804) 692-3594
TTY: (804) 692-3976

Nolan T. Yelich, Librarian of Virginia
800 E. Broad St., Richmond, VA 23219-8000

Lottery Dept.

http://www.valottery.com
Main phone: (804) 692-7777
Main fax: (804) 692-7775
TTY: (804) 692-7115

Penelope Ward Kyle, Director
900 E. Main St., Richmond, VA 23219
(804) 692-7100
E-mail: pkyle@valottery.state.va.us

Mental Health, Mental Retardation, and Substance Abuse Dept.

http://www.dmhmrsas.state.va.us/
Main phone: (804) 786-3921
Main fax: (804) 371-0092

Richard E. Kellogg, Commissioner
109 Governor St., Richmond, VA 23219

Motor Vehicles Dept.

http://www.dmv.state.va.us/
Main phone: (804) 367-0538
Main fax: (804) 367-6631
TTY: (800) 272-9268
Mailing address: P.O. Box 27412, Richmond, VA 23219

Richard D. Holcomb, Commissioner
2300 W. Broad St., Richmond, VA 23220
(804) 367-6602
E-mail: commish@dmv.state.va.us

Natural Resources Secretariat

http://www.snr.vipnet.org
Main phone: (804) 786-0044
Main fax: (804) 371-8333
TTY: (804) 786-7765

John Paul Woodley Jr., Secretary
9th St. Office Bldg., 202 N. 9th St., #733, Richmond, VA 23219

Conservation and Recreation Dept.: Soil and Water Conservation Division

General e-mail: dcr@state.va.us
Main phone: (804) 786-2064
Main fax: (804) 786-1798

Jack E. Frye, Director
203 Governor St., Richmond, VA 23219
E-mail: jfrye@dcr.state.va.us

Conservation and Recreation Dept.: State Parks Division

Main phone: (804) 786-4377
Main fax: (804) 786-9294
TTY: (804) 786-2121

Joe Elton, Director
203 Governor St., Richmond, VA 23219
E-mail: joeelton@dcr.state.va.us

Game and Inland Fisheries Dept.

http://www.dgif.state.va.us
General e-mail: dgifweb@dgif.state.va.us
Main phone: (804) 367-9231
Main fax: (804) 367-0405
TTY: (804) 367-1000

William L. Woodfin Jr., Director
4010 W. Broad St., Richmond, VA 23230-1104
E-mail: bwoodfin@dgif.state.va.us

People with Disabilities Board

http://www.cns.state.va.us/vbpd/
Main phone: (804) 786-0016
Main fax: (804) 786-1118
Toll free: (800) 846-4464
TTY: (800) 846-4464

Brian S. Parsons, Director
202 N. 9th St., 9th Fl., Richmond, VA 23219
E-mail: parsonsbs@vbpd.state.va.us

Personnel and Training Dept.

http://www.dpt.state.va.us/
General e-mail: srwilson@dpt.state.va.us
Main phone: (804) 225-2237
Main fax: (804) 371-7401
TTY: (804) 371-7671

Sara Redding Wilson, Director
James Monroe Bldg., 101 N. 14th St., 12th Fl., Richmond, VA 23219

Public Safety Secretariat

http://publicsafety.state.va.us/
Main phone: (804) 786-5351
Main fax: (804) 371-6381
Mailing address: P.O. Box 1475, Richmond, VA 23218

Gary K. Aronhalt, Secretary
9th St. Office Bldg., 202 N. 9th St., #613, Richmond, VA 23219

Military Affairs Dept.

http://www.richmond.net/vaguard
General e-mail: webmgrva@va-arng.ngb.army.mil
Main phone: (804) 298-6100
Main fax: (804) 298-6338

Claude A. Williams, Adjudant General
Fort Pickett, Bldg. 316, Blackstone, VA 23824-6316
(804) 298-6102
E-mail: williamsc@va-arng.ngb.amry.mil

Virginia Parole Board
Main phone: (804) 674-3081
Main fax: (804) 674-3284
Toll free: (800) 467-4943
James L. Jenkins Jr., Chair
6900 Atmore Dr., Richmond, VA 23225

Real Estate Appraisers Board
Main phone: (804) 367-8552
Main fax: (804) 367-9537
Karen O'Neal, Administrator
3600 W. Broad St., Richmond, VA 23230

Retirement System
http://www.state.va.us/vrs/vrs
General e-mail: vrs@state.va.us
Main phone: (804) 649-8059
Main fax: (804) 786-1541
Toll free: (888) 827-3847
TTY: (804) 344-3190
Mailing address: P.O. Box 2500, Richmond, VA 23218-2500
William H. Leighty, Director
1200 E. Main St., Richmond, VA 23218-2500

Social Services Dept.
http://www.dss.state.va.us/
Main phone: (804) 692-1947
Main fax: (804) 692-1949
Toll free: (800) 230-6977
TTY: (800) 828-1120
Clarence Carter, Commissioner
730 E. Broad St., Richmond, VA 23219
E-mail: jcd2@email1.dss.state.va.us

State Corporation Commission
http://www.state.va.us/scc
Main phone: (804) 371-9141
Main fax: (804) 371-9211
Toll free: (800) 552-7945
TTY: (804) 371-9206
Mailing address: P.O. Box 1197, Richmond, VA 23218
Hullihen Williams Moore, Chair
Tyler Bldg., 1300 E. Main St., Richmond, VA 23219
(804) 371-9608

Financial Institutions Bureau
http://www.state.va.us/scc

Main phone: (804) 371-9659
Main fax: (804) 371-9416
Edward J. Face Jr., Commissioner
Tyler Bldg., 1300 E. Main St., 8th Fl., Richmond, VA 23218-1197
E-mail: jface@scc.state.va.us

Insurance Bureau
General e-mail: webmaster@scc.state.va.us
Main phone: (804) 371-9741
Main fax: (804) 371-9511
Toll free: (800) 552-7945
TTY: (804) 371-9206
Mailing address: P.O. Box 1157, Richmond, VA 23218
Alfred W. Gross, Commissioner
Tyler Bldg., 1300 E. Main St., Richmond, VA 23219
Fax: (804) 371-9873

State Fair
http://www.statefair.com/
General e-mail: mic@strawberryhill.com
Main phone: (804) 228-3200
Main fax: (804) 228-3252
Toll free: (800) 588-3247
Otis Brown, President
Earl Rd., Richmond, VA 23261-6805

State Police Dept.
http://www.vsp.state.va.us/vsp.html
General e-mail: cvaughan.vsp@state.va.us
Main phone: (804) 674-2087
Main fax: (804) 674-2132
Mailing address: P.O. Box 27472, Richmond, VA 23261-7472
M. Wayne Huggins, Superintendent
7700 Midlothian Turnpike, Richmond, VA 23235

Boards and Licensing

Accountancy, (804) 367-8505,
   http://www.state.va.us/dpor
Architects, Engineers, Land Survey, Interior Design, and Landscape Architects,
   (804) 367-8514
Child Care, (804) 692-1776
Contractors, (804) 367-2785
Cosmetology, (804) 367-8590,
   http://www.state.va.us/dpor
Medical, (804) 662-9900
Nursing, (804) 662-9900
Pharmacy, (804) 662-9900
Real Estate, (804) 367-8552

Technology Secretariat

http://www.sotech.state.va.us
General e-mail: sotech@gov.state.va.us
Main phone: (804) 786-9579
Main fax: (804) 786-9584
Mailing address: P.O. Box 1475, Richmond, VA 23219

Donald W. Upson, Secretary of Technology
9th St. Office Bldg., 202 N. 9th St., #506, Richmond, VA 23219

Tourism Corporation

http://www.vatc.org/
Main phone: (804) 371-8100
Main fax: (804) 786-1919
Toll free: (800) VISIT-VA
TTY: (804) 371-0327

Gayle Morgan Vail, President
901 E. Byrd St., Richmond, VA 23219
(804) 371-8175
E-mail: vail@vedp.state.va.us

Transportation Secretariat

http://www.sotrans.state.va.us/
General e-mail:
secretaryoftransportation@vdot.state.va.us
Main phone: (804) 786-8032
Main fax: (804) 786-6683

Shirley J. Ybarra, Secretary
1401 E. Broad St., Richmond, VA 23219
(804) 786-6675

Veterans Affairs Dept.

http://www.vdva.vipnet.org/
Main phone: (540) 857-7104
Main fax: (540) 857-7573

Don Duncan, Director
270 Franklin Rd. S.W., #503, Roanoke, VA 24011-2215

Workers' Compensation Commission

http://www.vwc.state.va.us/
General e-mail: vwc@compuserve.com
Main phone: (804) 367-8600
Main fax: (804) 367-9740

Virginia R. Diamond, Chair
1000 DMV Dr., Richmond, VA 23220
(804) 367-8657

Virginia Legislature

State Capitol
Richmond, VA 23218
General information: (804) 786-3591
http://legis.state.va.us

Laws

Sales tax: 4.5%
Income tax: 5.8%
State minimum wage: $5.15 (Federal is $5.15)
Marriage age: 18
First-cousin marriage: Permitted
Drinking age: 21
State control of liquor sales: Yes
Blood alcohol for DWI: 0.08%
Driving age: 16
Speed limit: 65 mph
Permit to buy handguns: In some areas, for repeat purchase within 30 days
Minimum age to possess handguns: 18
Minimum age to possess rifles, shotguns: None
State lottery: Yes
Casinos: No
Pari-mutuel betting: Horse racing
Death penalty: Yes
3 strikes minimum sentence: Life (3rd violent felony)
Hate crimes law: Yes
Gay employment non-discrimination: No
Official language(s): None
Term limits: None

State laws are complex and subject to change; this information is not intended as legal advice. For an explanation of this information, see p. x.

Senate

Address: General Assembly Bldg., P.O. Box 396, Richmond, VA 23218
General information: (804) 698-7410
Fax: (804) 698-7651
TTY: (804) 698-7419

John H. Hager (R), Presiding Officer
900 E. Main St., #1400, Richmond, VA 23219-3523
(804) 786-2078; *Fax:* (804) 786-7514
E-mail: ltgov@ltgov.state.va.us
http://www.state.va.us/ltgov/

John H. Chichester (R), President Pro Tempore
General Assembly Bldg., 910 Capitol St., #626, Richmond, VA 23219
(804) 698-7528
E-mail: Johnchich@aol.com
http://senate.state.va.us/s28bio.htm

Walter A. Stosch (R), Majority Leader
General Assembly Bldg., 910 Capitol St., #621, Richmond, VA 23219

---

(804) 698-7512
http://senate.state.va.us/s12bio.htm
Richard L. Saslaw (D), Minority Leader
General Assembly Bldg., 910 Capitol St., #613,
Richmond, VA 23219
(804) 698-7535
http://senate.state.va.us/s35bio.htm
Susan Clark Schaar, Clerk
General Assembly Bldg., 910 Capitol St., Richmond,
VA 23218
(804) 698-7400
E-mail: sschaar@sov.state.va.us

House
Address: State Capitol, P.O. Box 406, Richmond,
VA 23218
General information: (804) 698-1500
Fax: (804) 786-6310
TTY: (804) 786-2369
S. Vance Wilkins Jr. (R), Speaker of the House
General Assembly Bldg., P.O. Box 406, #635,
Richmond, VA 23218
(804) 698-1024
Morgan Griffith (R), Majority Leader
General Assembly Bldg., P.O. Box 406, #607,
Richmond, VA 23218
(804) 698-1014
Charles Richard Cranwell (D), Minority Leader
General Assembly Bldg., P.O. Box 406, #614,
Richmond, VA 23218
(804) 698-1088
Bruce F. Jamerson, Clerk
General Assembly Bldg., P.O. Box 406, Richmond, VA
23218
(804) 698-1619

Virginia Judiciary
Supreme Court Bldg.
100 N. 9th St.
Richmond, VA 23219
http://www.courts.state.va.us

Supreme Court
http://www.courts.state.va.us/scv/home.html
David B. Beach, Clerk
Supreme Court Bldg., 100 N. 9th St., Richmond, VA
23219
(804) 786-2251; *Fax:* (804) 786-6249
E-mail: dbeach@courts.state.va.us

Justices
Composition: 7 justices
Selection Method: elected by the General
Assembly
Length of term: 12 years

Harry L. Carrico, Chief Justice, (804) 786-2023
A. Christian Compton, Justice, (804) 786-7880
Leroy Rountree Hassell Sr., Justice, (804) 786-6404
Barbara Milano Keenan, Justice, (804) 786-2251
Cynthia D. Kinser, Justice, (540) 546-4563
Lawrence L. Koontz Jr., Justice, (540) 387-6082
Elizabeth B. Lacy, Justice, (804) 786-9980

Office of Court Administration
Main phone: (804) 786-6455
Main fax: (804) 786-4542
Robert N. Baldwin, Executive Secretary
Supreme Court Bldg., 100 N. 9th St., Richmond, VA
23219
E-mail: rbaldwin@courts.state.va.us

State Law Library
http://www.courts.state.va.us/library/library.htm
Main phone: (804) 786-2075
Main fax: (804) 786-4542

Gail Warren, State Law Librarian
Supreme Court Bldg., 100 N. 9th St., Richmond, VA
23219

Legislative and Political Party Information Resources

Senate home page: http://senate.state.va.us/welcome.htm
House home page: http://hod.state.va.us/welcome.htm
Legislative process: http://legis.state.va.us/vaonline/li5.htm
Legislative information: http://leg1.state.va.us
Virginia Democratic Party: http://www.vademocrats.org
   1108 E. Main St., 2nd Fl., Richmond, VA 23219; *Phone:* (804) 644-1966
Virginia Republican Party: http://www.rpv.org
   115 E. Grace St., Richmond, VA 23219; *Phone:* (804) 780-0111; *Fax:* (804) 343-1060;
   E-mail: rpva@concentric.net

Washington

State Capitol
Olympia, WA 98504-0002
Public information: (360) 902-4111
Fax: (360) 753-4110
http://www.state.wa.us

Office of the Governor
http://www.wa.gov/governor
Main phone: (360) 902-4111
Main fax: (360) 753-4110
TTY: (360) 753-6466
Mailing address: P.O. Box 40002, Olympia, WA
98504-0002

Gary Locke (D), Governor
Legislative Bldg., 2nd Fl., Olympia, WA 98504-0002
E-mail: governor.locke@governor.wa.gov

Joseph Dear, Chief of Staff
Legislative Bldg., 2nd Fl., Olympia, WA 98504-0002
(360) 902-4111; *Fax:* (360) 753-4110

Ed Penhale, Communications Director (Acting)
Legislative Bldg., 2nd Fl., Olympia, WA 98504-0002
(360) 902-4136; *Fax:* (360) 753-4110

Tim Kelley, Constituent Services Supervisor
Legislative Bldg., 2nd Fl., Olympia, WA 98504-0002
(360) 902-4111; *Fax:* (360) 753-4110

Jan Shinpoch, Director, Washington Office
444 N. Capitol St. N.W., #617, Washington, DC 20001
(202) 624-3680; *Fax:* (202) 624-3682

Office of the Lieutenant Governor
http://www.ltgov.wa.gov/brad/ltgov1.html
Main phone: (360) 786-7700
Main fax: (360) 786-7749
Mailing address: P.O. Box 40982, Olympia, WA
98504-0482

Bradley Scott Owen (D), Lieutenant Governor
Legislative Bldg., #304, Olympia, WA 98504-0482
E-mail: owen_br@leg.wa.gov

Office of the Secretary of State
http://www.secstate.wa.gov
General e-mail: mail@secstate.wa.gov
Main phone: (360) 902-4151
Main fax: (360) 586-5629
TTY: (800) 422-8683
Mailing address: P.O. Box 40220, Olympia, WA
98504-0220

Ralph Davies Munro (R), Secretary of State
Legislative Bldg., Olympia, WA 98504-0220

State of Washington

Capital: Olympia, since 1853
Founded: 1853, Washington Territory created from Oregon Territory
Statehood: November 11, 1889 (42nd state)
Constitution adopted: 1889
Area: 66,581 sq. mi. (ranks 20th)
Population: 5,689,263 (1998 est.; ranks 15th)
Largest cities: (1998 est.) Seattle (536,978); Spokane (184,058); Tacoma (179,814); Bellevue (104,052); Everett (88,625)
Counties: 39, Most populous: (1998 est.) King (1,654,876); Pierce (676,505); Snohomish (587,783); Spokane (408,669); Clark (326,943)
U.S. Congress: Slade Gorton (R), Patty Murray (D); 9 Representatives
Nickname(s): Evergreen State, Chinook State
Motto: by and by (Al-Ki)
Song: "Washington, My Home"
Bird: Willow goldfinch
Tree: Western hemlock
Flower: Western rhododendron
State fair: None
Former capital(s): None

Office of the Attorney General
http://www.wa.gov/ago
General e-mail: emailago@atg.wa.gov
Main phone: (360) 753-6200
Main fax: (360) 586-8474
Mailing address: P.O. Box 40100, Olympia, WA
98504-0100

Christine O. Gregoire (D), Attorney General
1125 Washington St. S.E., Olympia, WA 98504-0100

Office of the State Treasurer
http://www.wa.gov/tre
Main phone: (360) 902-9000
Main fax: (360) 902-9044
TTY: (360) 902-8963
Mailing address: P.O. Box 40200, Olympia, WA
98504-0200

Michael J. Murphy (D), State Treasurer
Legislative Bldg., #240, Olympia, WA 98504-0200
(360) 902-9003

Office of the State Auditor

http://www.sao.wa.gov
Main phone: (360) 902-0370
Main fax: (360) 753-0646
TTY: (360) 902-8963
Mailing address: P.O. Box 40021, Olympia, WA
98504-0021

Brian Sonntag (D), State Auditor
Legislative Bldg., Olympia, WA 98504-0021
(360) 902-0360
E-mail: sonntagb@sao.wa.gov

National Guard

http://www.cpmurray.army.mil
Main phone: (253) 512-8000
Main fax: (253) 512-8497

Timothy J. Lowenberg, Adjutant General
Camp Murray, #TA-20, Tacoma, WA 98430-5000
(253) 512-8201

Agencies

Accountancy Board

http://www.cpaboard.wa.gov
General e-mail: 103124.2013@compuserve.com
Main phone: (360) 753-2585
Main fax: (360) 664-9190
TTY: (800) 833-6388
Mailing address: P.O. Box 9131, Olympia, WA
98507-9131

Rufino Moraleja, Chair
210 E. Union Ave., Suite A, Olympia, WA 98507-9131

Agriculture Dept.

http://www.wa.gov/agr
Main phone: (360) 902-1800
Main fax: (360) 902-2092
TTY: (360) 902-1996
Mailing address: P.O. Box 42560, Olympia, WA
98504-2560

Jim Jesernig, Director
1111 Washington St. S.E., Olympia, WA 98504-2560
(360) 902-1801
E-mail: j.jesernig@arg.wa.gov

Apple Commission

http://www.bestapples.com
Main phone: (509) 663-9600
Main fax: (509) 662-5824
Mailing address: P.O. Box 18, Wenatchee, WA
98807

Steve Lutz, President and Chief Executive Officer
2900 Euclid Ave., Wenatchee, WA 98807

Architects Registration Board

http://www.wa.gov/dol/bpd/arcfront.htm
General e-mail: Architects@dol.wa.gov
Main phone: (360) 664-1388
Main fax: (360) 664-2551
Mailing address: P.O. Box 9045, Olympia, WA
98507-9045

Margaret Epting, Administrator
405 Black Lake Blvd., Olympia, WA 98502

Archives and Records Management Division

http://www.secstate.wa.gov/archives/
General e-mail: archives@secstate.wa.gov
Main phone: (360) 753-5485
Mailing address: P.O. Box 40238, Olympia, WA
98504-0238

Philip Coombs, State Archivist
1129 Washington St. S.E., Olympia, WA 98504
E-mail: pcoombs@secstate.wa.gov

Arts Commission

http://www.wa.gov/art
Main phone: (360) 753-3860
Main fax: (360) 586-5351
TTY: (800) 833-6388
Mailing address: P.O. Box 42675, Olympia, WA
98504-2675

Kris Tucker, Executive Director
234 E. 8th Ave., Olympia, WA 98504-2675
(360) 586-2423
E-mail: Krist@wsac.wa.gov

Board of Education

http://www.k12.wa.us/sbe/default.htm
Main phone: (360) 753-6715
Main fax: (360) 586-2357
TTY: (360) 664-3631
Mailing address: P.O. Box 47206, Olympia, WA
98504-7206

Linda Carpenter, President
600 S. Washington, Olympia, WA 98504-7206
E-mail: lindcarp@uswest.net

Building Code Council

http://www.sbcc.wa.gov
General e-mail: sbcc@cted.wa.gov
Main phone: (360) 753-5927
Main fax: (360) 586-5880
Mailing address: P.O. Box 48300, Olympia, WA
98504-8300

Ken Nogler, Managing Director
906 Columbia St. S.W., Olympia, WA 98504-8300
(360) 586-0486

Community, Trade, and Economic Development Dept.

http://www.cted.wa.gov
General e-mail: home@cted.wa.gov
Main phone: (360) 753-2200
Main fax: (360) 586-3582
TTY: (360) 586-4224
Mailing address: P.O. Box 48300, Olympia, WA 98504-8300

Martha Choe, Director
906 Columbia St. S.W., Olympia, WA 98504-8300
(360) 753-7426

Tourism Development Program

http://www.tourism.wa.gov
Main phone: (360) 753-5601
Main fax: (360) 753-4470
Toll free: (800) 544-1800
Mailing address: P.O. Box 48300, Olympia, WA 98504

Robin Dollard, Manager
101 General Administration Bldg., Olympia, WA 98504

Conservation Commission

http://www.conserver.org
Main phone: (360) 407-6200
Main fax: (360) 407-6215
Mailing address: P.O. Box 47721, Olympia, WA 98504-7721

Steven R. Meyer, Executive Director
303 Desmond Dr., Lacey, WA 98503
(360) 407-6201

Construction Compliance

http://www.wa.gov/lni/contractors/
General e-mail: berp235@lni.wa.gov
Main phone: (360) 902-5226
Main fax: (360) 902-5812
Toll free: (800) 647-0982
TTY: (360) 982-4666
Mailing address: P.O. Box 44450, Olympia, WA 98504-4450

Kevin Morris, Chief, Construction Compliance, Public Certification Programs
7273 Linderson Way S.W., Tumwater, WA 98501
(360) 902-5578; *Fax:* (360) 902-5292
E-mail: moke235@lni.wa.gov

Corrections Dept.

http://www.wa.gov/doc
Main phone: (360) 753-1573
Main fax: (360) 664-4056
TTY: (360) 664-9490
Mailing address: P.O. Box 41101, Olympia, WA 98504-1101

Joseph D. Lehman, Secretary
Capitol Center Bldg., Olympia, WA 98504-1101
(360) 753-2500
E-mail: jdlehman@doc1.wa.gov

Driver Services

http://www.wa.gov/dol/maintext.htm#Driver
Main phone: (360) 902-3900
Main fax: (360) 586-8351
TTY: (360) 664-8885
Mailing address: P.O. Box 9030, Olympia, WA 98504

Denise Movius, Assistant Director
Hwy.-Licenses Bldg., Olympia, WA 98504
(360) 902-3850

Ecology Dept.

http://www.wa.gov/ecology/
Main phone: (360) 407-6000
Main fax: (360) 407-6989
TTY: (360) 407-6006
Mailing address: P.O. Box 47600, Olympia, WA 98504-7600

Thomas C. Fitzsimmons, Director
300 Desmond Dr., Lacey, WA 98503
(360) 407-7001
E-mail: tfit461@ecy.wa.gov

Water Resources Program

http://www.wa.gov/ecology/
Main phone: (360) 407-6602
Main fax: (360) 407-7162
Mailing address: P.O. Box 47600, Olympia, WA 98504-7600

Keith Phillips, Manager
300 Desmond Dr., Lacey, WA 98503
E-mail: kphi461@ecy.wa.gov

Emergency Management Division

http://www.wa.gov/mil/wsem
General e-mail: mailroom@emd.wa.gov
Main phone: (253) 512-7000
Main fax: (253) 512-7200
Toll free: (800) 562-6108
TTY: (253) 512-7298

Glen L. Woodbury, Director
Camp Murray, Bldg. 20, Tacoma, WA 98430-5122

Employment Security Dept.

http://www.wa.gov/work
General e-mail: mwilson@esd.wa.gov
Main phone: (360) 902-9300
Main fax: (360) 902-9383
Mailing address: P.O. Box 9046, Olympia, WA 98504-9046

Carver Gayton, Commissioner
212 Maple Park, Olympia, WA 98504
(360) 902-9301

Energy Northwest
http://www.wnp2.com
Main phone: (509) 372-5860
Main fax: (509) 372-5328
Mailing address: P.O. Box 968, Richland, WA
99352-0968

> **J. V. Parrish, Chief Executive Officer**
> Plant 2 Warehouse, N. Powerplant Loop, Richland,
> WA 99352-0968
> *E-mail:* jvparrish@wnp2.com

Executive Ethics Board
http://www.wa.gov/ethics/
General e-mail: ethics@atg.wa.gov
Main phone: (360) 664-0871
Main fax: (360) 664-0229
Mailing address: P.O. Box 40100, Olympia, WA
98504

> **Margaret A. Grimaldi, Executive Secretary**
> 1125 Washington St. S.E., Olympia, WA 98504

Financial Institutions Dept.
http://www.wa.gov/dfi/home.htm
Main phone: (360) 902-8700
Main fax: (360) 586-5068
TTY: (360) 664-8126
Mailing address: P.O. Box 41200, Olympia, WA
98504

> **John L. Bley, Director**
> 210 11th Ave. S.W., #300, Olympia, WA 98504
> (360) 902-8707

Financial Management Office
http://www.ofm.wa.gov
General e-mail: The.Ear@ofm.wa.gov
Main phone: (360) 902-0555
Main fax: (360) 664-2832
TTY: (360) 902-0679
Mailing address: P.O. Box 43113, Olympia, WA
98504-3113

> **Marty Brown, Director**
> Insurance Bldg., #300, Olympia, WA 98504-3113
> (360) 902-0530

Fish and Wildlife Dept.
http://www.wa.gov/wdfw
Main phone: (360) 902-2200
Main fax: (360) 902-2947
TTY: (360) 902-2207

> **Jeffrey Koenings, Director**
> 600 Capitol Way North, Olympia, WA 98501-1091
> (360) 902-2225

Higher Educational Institutions

Central Washington University
http://www.cwu.edu
400 E. 8th Ave., Ellensburg, WA 98926-7550
Main phone: (509) 963-3001
Branches: University Centers in Lynnwood, Moses
Lake, SeaTac, Steilacoom, Wenatchee, and Yakima

Eastern Washington University
http://www.ewu.edu
526 5th St., Cheney, WA 99004-2431
Main phone: (509) 359-6692

Evergreen State College
http://www.evergreen.edu
2700 Evergreen Pkwy., Olympia, WA 98505
Main phone: (360) 866-6000, ext. 6170

University of Washington
http://www.washington.edu
Box 355840, Seattle, WA 98195-5840
Main phone: (206) 543-9686
Branches: Bothell, Tacoma

Washington State University
http://www.wsu.edu
1 S.E. Stadium Way, Pullman, WA 99164
Main phone: (509) 335-3564
Branches: Spokane, Tri-Cities, Vancouver

Western Washington University
http://www.wwu.edu
516 High St., Bellingham, WA 98225
Main phone: (360) 650-3440

Gambling Commission
http://www.wa.gov/gambling/wscg.htm
General e-mail: public-affairs@wscg.wa.gov
Main phone: (360) 438-7654
Main fax: (360) 438-8652
TTY: (360) 438-7638
Mailing address: P.O. Box 42400, Olympia, WA
98504-2400

> **Benjamin Bishop, Executive Director**
> 649 Woodland Square Loop S.E., Olympia, WA
> 98504-2400
> (360) 438-7640
> *E-mail:* benb@wsgc.wa.gov

General Administration Dept.
http://www.ga.wa.gov
Main phone: (360) 902-7300
Main fax: (360) 586-5898
TTY: (360) 664-3799
Mailing address: P.O. Box 41000, Olympia, WA
98504-1000

Marsha Tadano Long, Director
General Administration Bldg., #200, Olympia, WA
98504-1000
(360) 902-7200

Health Care Facilities Authority
http://www.olywa.net/whcfa
Main phone: (360) 753-6185
Main fax: (360) 586-9168
Mailing address: P.O. Box 40935, Olympia, WA
98504-0935

Jon Van Gorkom, Executive Director
410 11th Ave., #201, Olympia, WA 98504-0935
E-mail: johnvg@whcfa.wa.gov

Health Dept.
http://www.doh.wa.gov
Main phone: (360) 236-4501
Main fax: (360) 586-7424
Mailing address: P.O. Box 47890, Olympia, WA
98504-7890

Mary Selecky, Secretary
1112 S.E. Quince St., Olympia, WA 98504-7890
(360) 236-4015
E-mail: mary.selecky@doh.wa.gov

Health Professions Quality Assurance: Medical Quality Assurance Commission
http://www.doh.wa.gov/hsqa/hpqad/MQAC/
default.htm
Main phone: (360) 236-4789
Main fax: (360) 586-4573
Mailing address: P.O. Box 47866, Olympia, WA
98504-7866

Bonnie L. King, Executive Director
1300 Quince St. S.E., Olympia, WA 98504
E-mail: bonnie.king@doh.wa.gov

Health Professions Quality Assurance: Nursing Care Quality Assurance Commission
http://www.doh.wa.gov/hsqa/hpqad/Nursing/
default.htm
Main phone: (360) 236-4713
Main fax: (360) 236-4738
Mailing address: P.O. Box 47864, Olympia, WA
98504-7864

Paula Meyer, Executive Director
1300 Quince St. S.E., Olympia, WA 98504
E-mail: prm0303@doh.wa.gov

Higher Education Coordinating Board
http://www.hecb.wa.gov
Main phone: (360) 753-7800
Main fax: (360) 753-7808
TTY: (360) 753-7809

Mailing address: P.O. Box 43430, Olympia, WA
98504-3430

Marcus S. Gaspard, Executive Director
917 Lakeridge Way, Olympia, WA 98504-3430
(360) 753-7810
E-mail: marcg@hecb.wa.gov

Historical Society
http://www.wshs.org
Main phone: (253) 272-9747
Main fax: (253) 272-9518
Toll free: (888) 238-4373

David Nicandri, Executive Director
1911 Pacific Ave., Tacoma, WA 98402
E-mail: dnicandri@wshs.wa.gov

Horse Racing Commission
http://www.whrc.wa.gov
General e-mail: whrc@whrc.state.wa.us
Main phone: (360) 459-6462
Main fax: (360) 459-6461

Barbara Shinpoch, Chair
7912 Martin Way, Olympia, WA 98506

Housing Finance Commission
http://www.wshfc.org
Main phone: (206) 464-7139
Main fax: (206) 587-5113
Toll free: (800) 767-4663

Kim Herman, Executive Director
1000 2nd Ave., #2700, Seattle, WA 98104-1046
E-mail: kherman@wshfc.org

Human Rights Commission
Main phone: (360) 753-6770
Main fax: (360) 586-2282
Toll free: (800) 233-3247
TTY: (800) 300-7525
Mailing address: P.O. Box 42490, Olympia, WA
98504-2490

Susan J. Jordan, Executive Director
711 S. Capitol Way, #402, Olympia, WA 98504-2490
(360) 753-2558
E-mail: sjordan@hum.wa.gov

Industrial Insurance Appeals Board
http://www.wa.gov.biia
General e-mail: mathews@biia.wa.gov
Main phone: (360) 753-6823
Main fax: (360) 586-5611
Mailing address: P.O. Box 42401, Olympia, WA
98504-2401

Thomas E. Egan, Chair
2430 Chandler Court S.W., Olympia, WA 98504-2401
(360) 753-6824; *Fax:* (360) 664-9444

Information Services Dept.

http://www.wa.gov/dis/
Main phone: (360) 902-3560
Main fax: (360) 644-0733
Mailing address: P.O. Box 42445, Olympia, WA
98504-2445

Steve Kolodney, Director
1110 S.E. Jefferson St., Olympia, WA 98504-2445
(360) 902-3500
E-mail: stevek@dis.wa.gov

Insurance Commissioner

http://www.insurance.wa.gov
General e-mail: inscomr@aol.com
Main phone: (360) 753-7300
Main fax: (360) 586-3535
Toll free: (800) 562-6900
TTY: (360) 664-3154
Mailing address: P.O. Box 40255, Olympia, WA
98504-0255

Deborah Senn (D), Insurance Commissioner
Insurance Bldg., Olympia, WA 98504-0255
(360) 753-7301

Investment Board

http://www.wa.gov/sib
Main phone: (360) 664-8900
Main fax: (360) 664-8912
Mailing address: P.O. Box 40916, Olympia, WA
98504-0916

James F. Parker, Executive Director
2424 Heritage Court S.W., Olympia, WA 98502
(360) 664-8266
E-mail: jparker@sib.wa.gov

Labor and Industries Dept.

http://www.wa.gov/lni
Main phone: (360) 902-5800
Main fax: (360) 902-5798
Toll free: (800) 547-8367
TTY: (360) 902-5889
Mailing address: P.O. Box 44000, Olympia, WA
98504

Gary Moore, Director
7273 Linderson Way S.W., Tumwater, WA 98501
(360) 902-4203
E-mail: moga235@lni.wa.gov

Insurance Services Division

http://www.wa.gov/lni/insurance/
Main phone: (360) 902-4209
Main fax: (360) 902-4940
Toll free: (800) 547-8367
Mailing address: P.O. Box 44000, Olympia, WA
98504

Frequently Called Numbers

Tourism: (360) 753-5601, 1-800-544-1800;
  http://www.tourism.wa.gov
Library: (360) 753-5590;
  http://www.state.lib.wa.gov
Board of Education: (360) 753-6715;
  http://www.k12.wa.us/sbe/default.htm
Vital Statistics: (360) 236-4300
Tax/Revenue: (360) 647-7706;
  http://www.dor.wa.gov
Motor Vehicles: Driver Services: (360)
  902-3900; http://www.wa.gov/dol/
  maintext.htm#Driver; Vehicle Services:
  (360) 902-3820; http://www.wa.gov/dol/
  maintext.htm#Vehicle
State Police/Highway Patrol: (360) 753-6540;
  http://www.wa.gov/wsp/wsphome.htm
Unemployment: (360) 902-9303;
  http://www.wa.gov/esd/ui.htm
General Election Information: (360)
  902-4151, 1-800-448-4881; http://
  www.secstate.wa.gov/voting/default.htm
Consumer Affairs:
Hazardous Materials: (360) 753-0565;
  http://www.wa.gov/wsp/fire/hazmat.htm

Doug Connell, Assistant Director
7273 Linderson Way S.W., Olympia, WA 98504

Licensing Dept.

http://www.wa.gov/dol
Main phone: (360) 902-3600
Main fax: (360) 902-4042
TTY: (360) 664-8885
Mailing address: P.O. Box 9020, Olympia, WA
98504

Fred Stephens, Director
Hwy.-Licenses Bldg., Olympia, WA 98504
(360) 902-3600

Liquor Control Board

General e-mail: wslcb@liq.wa.gov
Main phone: (360) 664-1600
Main fax: (360) 586-3190
TTY: (360) 586-4727
Mailing address: P.O. Box 43076, Olympia, WA
98504-3076

Eugene A. Prince, Chair
3000 Pacific Ave. S.E., Olympia, WA 98504-3076
(360) 664-1711
E-mail: eap@liq.wa.gov

Natural Resources Dept.
http://www.wa.gov/dnr/
Main phone: (360) 902-1000
Main fax: (360) 902-1775
TTY: (360) 902-1125
Mailing address: P.O. Box 47001, Olympia, WA 98504-7001

Jennifer M. Belcher (D), Commissioner of Public Lands
1111 Washington St. S.E., Olympia, WA 98504-7001
(360) 902-1004

Geology and Earth Resources Division
General e-mail: geology@wadnr.gov
Main phone: (360) 902-1450
Main fax: (360) 902-1785
Mailing address: P.O. Box 47007, Olympia, WA 98504-7007

Ray Lasmanis, Manager
1111 Washington St. S.E., #148, Olympia, WA 98504

Personnel Dept.
http://www.wa.gov/dop
Main phone: (360) 664-1960
Main fax: (360) 664-2742
TTY: (360) 753-4107
Mailing address: P.O. Box 47500, Olympia, WA 98504-7500

Dennis Karras, Director
521 Capitol Way South, Olympia, WA 98504-7500
(360) 664-6349
E-mail: dennisk@dop.wa.gov

Pharmacy Board
General e-mail: dhw0303@hub.doh.wa.gov
Main phone: (360) 236-4825
Main fax: (360) 586-4359
TTY: (800) 833-6388
Mailing address: P.O. Box 47863, Olympia, WA 98504-7863

Donald H. Williams, Executive Director
1300 Quince St. S.E., Olympia, WA 98504

Printing Dept.
http://www_application1.wa.gov/printers
Main phone: (360) 753-6820
Main fax: (360) 586-8444
TTY: (360) 570-5069
Mailing address: P.O. Box 798, Olympia, WA 98507-0798

George Morton, Director
7850 New Market St. S.W., MS 4-7100, Tumwater, WA 98501
E-mail: george@prt.wa.gov

Professional Engineers and Land Surveyors Registration Board
http://www.wa.gov/dol/bpd/engfront.htm
General e-mail: Engineers@dol.wa.gov
Main phone: (360) 753-6966
Main fax: (360) 664-2551
Mailing address: P.O. Box 9649, Olympia, WA 98504

George Twiss, Executive Director
405 Black Lake Blvd., Olympia, WA 98502

Public Defense Office
http://www.opd.wa.gov
General e-mail: opd@opd.wa.gov
Main phone: (360) 956-2106
Main fax: (360) 956-2112
Mailing address: P.O. Box 40957, Olympia, WA 98504

Joanne I. Moore, Director
925 Plum St. S.E., Bldg. 4, Olympia, WA 98504

Public Disclosure Commission
http://www.pdc.wa.gov
General e-mail: pdc@pdc.wa.gov
Main phone: (360) 753-1111
Main fax: (360) 753-1112
Mailing address: P.O. Box 40908, Olympia, WA 98504-0908

Vacant, Executive Director
711 Capitol Way, #403, Olympia, WA 98504-0908
(360) 753-1980

Public Employment Relations Commission
General e-mail: perc@olywa.net
Main phone: (360) 753-3444
Main fax: (360) 586-7091
Mailing address: P.O. Box 40919, Olympia, WA 98504-0919

Marvin L. Schurke, Executive Director
Evergreen Plaza Bldg., #603, Olympia, WA 98504-0919

Public Instruction Dept.
http://www.K12.wa.us
General e-mail: kconway@ospi.wednet.edu
Main phone: (360) 753-6738
Main fax: (360) 753-6712
TTY: (360) 664-3631
Mailing address: P.O. Box 47200, Olympia, WA 98504-7200

Terry Bergeson (NP), State Superintendent of Public Instruction
Old Capitol Bldg., Olympia, WA 98504-7200
(360) 586-6904
E-mail: Bergeson@ospi.wednet.edu

Real Estate Appraiser Licensing Program
http://www.wa.gov/dol/bpd/appfront.htm
General e-mail: realestate@dol.wa.gov
Main phone: (360) 753-1062
Main fax: (360) 586-0998
Mailing address: P.O. Box 9015, Olympia, WA
98507-9015

Cleotis Borner Jr., Program Manager
2000 4th Ave. West, Olympia, WA 98504
E-mail: cborner@dol.wa.gov

Retirement Systems Dept.
http://www.wa.gov/DRS/drs.html
General e-mail: recep@drs.wa.gov
Main phone: (360) 664-7000
Main fax: (360) 753-3166
Toll free: (800) 547-6657
TTY: (360) 586-5450
Mailing address: P.O. Box 48380, Olympia, WA
98504-8380

John F. Charles, Director
Point Plaza West, 6835 Capitol Blvd., Tumwater, WA
98501
(360) 664-7312

Revenue Dept.
http://www.dor.wa.gov
Main phone: (800) 647-7706
Main fax: (360) 586-5543
TTY: (800) 451-7985
Mailing address: P.O. Box 47450, Olympia, WA
98504-7454

Frederick C. Kiga, Director
General Administration Bldg., #400, Olympia, WA
98504-7454
(360) 753-5574

School for the Deaf
http://www.wsdeaf.wednet.edu
Main phone: (360) 696-6525
Main fax: (360) 696-6291
TTY: (360) 418-4366

Leonard Aron, Superintendent
611 Grand Blvd., Vancouver, WA 98661
E-mail: laron@wsdeaf.wednet.edu

Services for the Blind Dept.
http://www.wa.gov/dsb
Main phone: (800) 552-7103
Main fax: (360) 586-7627
TTY: (360) 586-6437
Mailing address: P.O. Box 40933, Olympia, WA
98504-0933

Gary Haug, Director (Acting)
1400 S. Evergreen Park Dr., Olympia, WA 98504-0933

Social and Health Services Dept.
http://www.wa.gov/dshs/
General e-mail: askdshs@dshs.wa.gov
Main phone: (360) 902-8400
Main fax: (360) 902-7848
TTY: (360) 902-8000
Mailing address: P.O. Box 45010, Olympia, WA
98504

Lyle Quasim, Secretary
1115 Washington St. S.E., Olympia, WA 98504
(360) 902-7800

Aging and Adult Services Administration
http://www.aasa.dshs.wa.gov
Main phone: (360) 493-2500
Main fax: (360) 493-9484
Toll free: (800) 422-3263
TTY: (800) 737-7931
Mailing address: P.O. Box 45600, Olympia, WA
98504-5600

Ralph W. Smith, Assistant Secretary
1115 Washington St. S.E., Olympia, WA 98504

Health and Rehabilitative Services Administration: Developmental Disabilities Division
http://www.wa.gov/dshs/ddd.index.html
Main phone: (360) 902-8444
Main fax: (360) 902-8482
TTY: (360) 902-8455
Mailing address: P.O. Box 45310, Olympia, WA
98504

Tim Brown, Director
1115 Washington St. S.E., Olympia, WA 98504
(360) 902-8484
E-mail: browntr@dshs.wa.gov

Health and Rehabilitative Services Administration: Mental Health Division
Main phone: (360) 902-0790
Main fax: (360) 902-0809
Mailing address: P.O. Box 45320, Olympia, WA
98504

Pat Terry, Director (Acting)
12th and Franklin Sts., Olympia, WA 98504

Juvenile Rehabilitation Administration
http://www.wa.gov/dshs/jra/jra2hp.html
Main phone: (360) 407-7145
Main fax: (360) 407-7284
Mailing address: P.O. Box 45720, Olympia, WA
98504

Sid Sidorowicz, Assistant Secretary
14th and Jefferson Sts., #102, Olympia, WA 98504
(360) 902-8499; *Fax:* (360) 902-8108

Medical Assistance Administration
http://www.wa.gov/dshs/maa2/maa2hp.html
Main phone: (360) 902-7807
Main fax: (360) 902-7848
Toll free: (800) 562-3022
Mailing address: P.O. Box 45080, Olympia, WA 98504-5080

Tom Bedell, Assistant Secretary (Acting)
1115 Washington St. S.E., Olympia, WA 98504-5080

State Library
http://www.state.lib.wa.gov
Main phone: (360) 753-5590
Main fax: (360) 586-7575
TTY: (360) 753-3216
Mailing address: P.O. Box 42460, Olympia, WA 98504-2460

Nancy Zussy, State Librarian
State Library Bldg., 415 15th Ave. S.W., Olympia, WA 98504-2460
(360) 753-2915

State Lottery
http://www.wa.gov/lot/home.htm
Main phone: (360) 753-1412
Main fax: (360) 586-1039
TTY: (360) 586-0933
Mailing address: P.O. Box 43000, Olympia, WA 98504-3000

Merritt D. Long, Director
814 4th Ave., Olympia, WA 98504-3000
(360) 664-4800

Washington Licensing Dept.

http://www.wa.gov/dol
(360) 902-3600

Accountancy, (360) 753-2585,
 http://www.cpaboard.wa.gov
Architects, (360) 664-1388,
 http://www.wa.gov/dol/bpd/arcfront.htm
Child Care, (360) 902-8038
Contractors, (360) 664-1400
Cosmetology, (360) 753-3834
Engineers and Land Surveyors,
 (360) 753-6966, http://www.wa.gov/dol/bpd/
 engfront.htm
Medical, (360) 236-4800
Nursing, (360) 236-4703
Pharmacy, (360) 236-4825
Real Estate, (360) 753-1062,
 http://www.wa.gov/dol/bpd/appfront.htm

State Parks and Recreation Commission
http://www.parks.wa.gov
Main phone: (360) 902-8500
Main fax: (360) 664-8112
Toll free: (800) 233-0321
TTY: (360) 664-3133
Mailing address: P.O. Box 42650, Olympia, WA 98504-2650

Cleve Pinnix, Director
7150 Cleanwater Ln., Olympia, WA 98504-2650
(360) 902-8501

State Patrol
http://www.wa.gov/wsp/wsphome.htm
General e-mail: webmaster@wsp.wa.gov
Main phone: (360) 753-6540
Main fax: (360) 753-2492
TTY: (360) 407-0179
Mailing address: P.O. Box 42601, Olympia, WA 98504-2601

Annette M. Sandberg, Chief
General Administration Bldg., Olympia, WA 98504-2601

State Fire Marshal/Fire Protection Bureau
http://www.wa.gov/wsp/fire/firemars.htm
General e-mail: firemarsh@wsp.wa.gov
Main phone: (360) 753-6540
Main fax: (360) 753-0398
Mailing address: P.O. Box 42600, Olympia, WA 98504-2600

Mary Corso, State Fire Marshal
General Administration Bldg., Olympia, WA 98504-2600
(360) 753-0400

State School for the Blind
http://www.wssb.org
General e-mail: admin@wssb.org
Main phone: (360) 696-6321
Main fax: (360) 737-2120

Dean Stenehjem, Superintendent
2214 E. 13th St., #S-27, Vancouver, WA 98661
(360) 696-6321, ext. 130
E-mail: dstenehjem@wssb.org

Tax Appeals Board
http://bta.state.wa.us
General e-mail: bta@bta.state.wa.us
Main phone: (360) 753-5446
Main fax: (360) 586-9020
TTY: (360) 753-5446
Mailing address: P.O. Box 40915, Olympia, WA 98504-0915

Matthew J. Coyle, Chair
910 5th Ave. S.E., Olympia, WA 98504-0915

Traffic Safety Commission

http://www.wa.gov/wtsc
Main phone: (360) 753-6197
Main fax: (360) 586-6489
Mailing address: P.O. Box 40944, Olympia, WA 98504-0944

John Moffat, Director
1000 S. Cherry St., Olympia, WA 98504-0944
(360) 753-4018
E-mail: jmoffat@wtsc.wa.gov

Transportation Dept.

http://www.wsdot.wa.gov
General e-mail: info@wsdot.wa.gov
Main phone: (360) 705-7000
Main fax: (360) 705-6806
TTY: (800) 833-6388
Mailing address: P.O. Box 47300, Olympia, WA 98504-7300

Sid Morrison, Secretary
Transportation Bldg., 310 Maple Park Ave., Olympia, WA 98504
(360) 705-7054; *Fax:* (360) 705-6800

Aviation Division

http://www.wsdot.wa.gov/Aviation
Main phone: (206) 764-4131
Main fax: (206) 764-4001
Toll free: (800) 552-0666

Bill Brubaker, Director
8900 E. Marginal Way South, Seattle, WA 98108-4024
E-mail: brubakb@wsdot.wa.gov

Utilities and Transportation Commission

http://www.wutc.wa.gov
Main phone: (360) 664-1160
Main fax: (360) 586-1150
Toll free: (800) 562-6150
TTY: (360) 586-8203
Mailing address: P.O. Box 47250, Olympia, WA 98504-7250

Marilyn Showalter, Chair
1300 S. Evergreen Park Dr. S.W., Olympia, WA 98504-7250
(360) 664-1173
E-mail: mshowalt@wutc.wa.gov

Vehicle Services

http://www.wa.gov/dol/maintext.htm#Vehicle
Main phone: (360) 902-3820
Main fax: (360) 586-6703

Nancy Kelly, Assistant Director
Hwy.-Licenses Bldg., 1125 Washington St. S.E., Olympia, WA 98504

Veterans Affairs Dept.

http://www.wa.gov/dva/
General e-mail: Glenda@dva.wa.gov
Main phone: (360) 753-5586
Main fax: (360) 709-5266
TTY: (360) 709-5237
Mailing address: P.O. Box 41150, Olympia, WA 98504-1150

John M. King, Director
1011 Plum St., Olympia, WA 98504-1150
(360) 709-5230; *Fax:* (360) 586-4393

Workforce Training and Education Coordinating Board

http://www.wagov/wtb/
General e-mail: wtecb@wtb.wa.gov
Main phone: (360) 753-5662
Main fax: (360) 586-5862
Mailing address: P.O. Box 43105, Olympia, WA 98504-3105

Ellen O'Brien Saunders, Executive Director
Bldg. 17, Airdustrial Park, Olympia, WA 98504-3105
(360) 753-5660

Washington Legislature

State Capitol
Olympia, WA 98504
General information: (360) 786-7573
Fax: (360) 786-7520
TTY: (800) 635-9993
http://www.leg.wa.gov/wsladm/default.htm

Senate

Address: P.O. Box 40482, Olympia, WA 98504-0482
General information: (360) 786-7550
Fax: (360) 786-1999
Toll free: (800) 562-6000

Bradley Scott Owen (D), President
Legislative Bldg., P.O. Box 40982, #304, Olympia, WA 98504-0482
(360) 786-7700; *Fax:* (360) 786-7749
E-mail: owen_br@leg.wa.gov

R. Lorraine Wojahn (D), President Pro Tempore
Legislative Bldg., P.O. Box 40482, #309, Olympia, WA 98504-0482
(360) 786-7652; *Fax:* (360) 786-7520
E-mail: wojahn_lo@leg.wa.gov
http://www.leg.wa.gov/senate/members/senmem27.htm

Laws

Sales tax: 8.2%

Income tax: None

State minimum wage: $6.50; indexed rate from 2001 (Federal is $5.15)

Marriage age: 18

First-cousin marriage: Prohibited

Drinking age: 21

State control of liquor sales: Yes

Blood alcohol for DWI: 0.08%

Driving age: 16

Speed limit: 70 mph

Permit to buy handguns: No, but 5-day wait

Minimum age to possess handguns: 18

Minimum age to possess rifles, shotguns: 18

State lottery: Yes

Casinos: Yes (tribal)

Pari-mutuel betting: Horse racing

Death penalty: Yes

3 strikes minimum sentence: Life, no parole (3rd serious felony)

Hate crimes law: Yes

Gay employment non-discrimination: No

Official language(s): None

Term limits: Governor (8 yrs.); state senate (8 yrs.), house (6 yrs.)

State laws are complex and subject to change; this information is not intended as legal advice. For an explanation of this information, see p. x.

Sid Snyder (D), Democratic Majority Leader
Legislative Bldg., P.O. Box 40482, #311, Olympia, WA 98504-0482
(360) 786-7636; *Fax:* (360) 786-1999
http://www.leg.wa.gov/senate/members/senmem19.htm

Rosa Franklin (D), Majority Whip
Legislative Bldg., P.O. Box 40482, #410, Olympia, WA 98504-0482
(360) 786-7656; *Fax:* (360) 786-1999
E-mail: franklin_ro@leg.wa.gov
http://www.leg.wa.gov/senate/members/senmem29.htm

Dan McDonald (R), Republican Majority Leader
Irving R. Newhouse Bldg., P.O. Box 40482, #204, Olympia, WA 98504-0482
(360) 786-7694; *Fax:* (360) 786-7520
E-mail: mcdonald_da@leg.wa.gov
http://www.leg.wa.gov/senate/members/senmem48.htm

Alex Deccio (R), Republican Whip
Legislative Bldg., P.O. Box 40482, #407, Olympia, WA 98504-0482
(360) 786-7626; *Fax:* (360) 786-7524
E-mail: deccio_al@leg.wa.gov
http://www.leg.wa.gov/senate/members/senmem14.htm

Tony Cook, Secretary
Legislative Bldg., P.O. Box 40482, Olympia, WA 98504-0482
(360) 786-7550; *Fax:* (360) 786-1999

House

Address: P.O. Box 40600, Olympia, WA 98504-0600

General information: (360) 786-7573

Fax: (360) 786-7021

J. Clyde Ballard (R), Co-Speaker of the House
Legislative Bldg., P.O. Box 40600, Olympia, WA 98504-0600
(360) 786-7999
http://www.leg.wa.gov/house/members/d12_1.htm

Frank Chopp (D), Co-Speaker of the House
Legislative Bldg., P.O. Box 40600, 3rd Fl., Olympia, WA 98504-0600
(360) 786-7920
E-mail: chopp_fr@leg.wa.gov
http://www.leg.wa.gov/house/members/d43_2.htm

Val Ogden (D), Co-Speaker Pro Tempore
Legislative Bldg., P.O. Box 40600, #410, Olympia, WA 98504-0600
(360) 786-7872
E-mail: ogden_va@leg.wa.gov
http://www.leg.wa.gov/house/members/d49_2.htm

John E. Pennington (R), Co-Speaker Pro Tempore
Legislative Bldg., P.O. Box 40600, #402, Olympia, WA 98504-0600
(360) 786-7812
E-mail: penningt_jo@leg.wa.gov
http://www.leg.wa.gov/house/members/d18_2.htm

Lynn Kessler (D), Democratic Leader
Legislative Bldg., P.O. Box 40600, #409, Olympia, WA 98504-0600
(360) 786-7904
E-mail: kessler_ly@leg.wa.gov
http://www.leg.wa.gov/house/members/d24_2.htm

Cathy Wolfe (D), Democratic Whip
Legislative Bldg., P.O. Box 40600, #412, Olympia, WA 98504-0600
(360) 786-7992
E-mail: wolfe_ca@leg.wa.gov
http://www.leg.wa.gov/house/members/d22_2.htm

Barb Lisk (R), Republican Leader
Legislative Bldg., P.O. Box 40600, 3rd Fl., Olympia, WA 98504-0600
(360) 786-7874
http://www.leg.wa.gov/house/members/d15_2.htm

Mark Schoesler (R), Republican Whip
Legislative Bldg., P.O. Box 40600, #402, Olympia,
   WA 98504-0600
(360) 786-7844; *Fax:* (360) 786-1247
E-mail: schoesle_ma@leg.wa.gov
http://www.leg.wa.gov/house/members/d9_2.htm

Dean Foster, Chief Clerk
Legislative Bldg., P.O. Box 40600, Olympia, WA
   98504-0600
(360) 786-7750

Timothy A. Martin, Chief Clerk
Legislative Bldg., P.O. Box 40600, Olympia, WA
   98504-0600
(360) 786-7750

Washington Judiciary

Temple of Justice
Olympia, WA 98504
http://www.wa.gov/courts

Supreme Court
http://www.wa.gov/courts/crtinfo/supreme/
   home.htm

C. J. Merritt, Clerk
Temple of Justice, Olympia, WA 98504-0929
(360) 357-2077; *Fax:* (360) 357-2102

Justices
Composition: 9 justices
Selection Method: nonpartisan election;
   vacancies filled by gubernatorial appointment
   until next general election
Length of term: 6 years

Richard P. Guy, Chief Justice, (360) 357-2041
Gerry L. Alexander, Justice, (360) 357-2029
Bobbe Bridge, Justice, (360) 357-2050
Faith Ireland, Justice, (360) 357-2033
Charles W. Johnson, Justice, (360) 357-2020
Barbara A. Madsen, Justice, (360) 357-2037
Richard B. Sanders, Justice, (360) 357-2067
Charles Z. Smith, Justice, (360) 357-2053
Phil Talmadge, Justice, (360) 357-2045

Office of the Administrator for the Courts
Main phone: (360) 753-3365
Main fax: (360) 586-8869

Mary C. McQueen, Administrator
1206 Quince St., S.E., Olympia, WA 98510
(360) 357-2121; *Fax:* (360) 357-2127

State Law Library
http://www.wa.gov/courts/lawlib/home.htm
Main phone: (360) 357-2136
Main fax: (360) 357-2143

Deborah Norwood, Director
Temple of Justice, Olympia, WA 98504-0751

Legislative and Political Party Information Resources

Senate home page: http://www.leg.wa.gov/senate/default.htm
House home page: http://www.leg.wa.gov/house/default.htm
Committees: Senate: http://www.leg.wa.gov/senate/scs/; *House:* http://www.leg.wa.gov/house/opr/
   stcommpg.htm
Legislative process: http://www.leg.wa.gov/house/hadm/billlaw.htm
Current session information: http://www.leg.wa.gov/wsladm/ses.htm
Washington Democratic Party: http://www.wa-democrats.org
   P.O. Box 4027, Seattle, WA 98104; *Phone:* (206) 583-0664; *E-mail:* waparty@democrats.org
Washington Republican Party: http://www.wsrp.org
   16400 Southcenter Pkwy., #200, Seattle, WA 98188; *Phone:* (206) 575-2900;
   Washington*E-mail:* wsrp@seanet.com

West Virginia

State Capitol
Charleston, WV 25305
Public information: (304) 558-3456
Fax: (304) 558-8887
http://www.state.wv.us

Office of the Governor
http://www.state.wv.us/governor
General e-mail: governor@state.wv.us
Main phone: (304) 558-2000
Main fax: (304) 342-7025

Cecil H. Underwood (R), Governor
State Capitol Bldg., 1900 Kanawha Blvd. East,
Charleston, WV 25305

James W. Teets, Chief of Staff
State Capitol Bldg., Charleston, WV 25305
(304) 558-5430; *Fax:* (304) 342-7025
E-mail: jteets@governor.state.wv.us

Rod Blackstone, Press Secretary
State Capitol Bldg., Charleston, WV 25305
(304) 558-6343; *Fax:* (304) 558-2722
E-mail: rblackstone@governor.state.wv.us

Elizabeth Bowen, Director, Washington Office
4200 Massachusetts Ave. N.W., Washington, DC
20016
(202) 244-1194; *Fax:* (202) 244-2559
E-mail: weegee@gte.net

Office of the Secretary of State
http://www.state.wv.us/sos/
General e-mail: wvsos@secretary.state.wv.us
Main phone: (304) 558-6000
Main fax: (304) 558-0900

Ken Hechler (D), Secretary of State
1900 Kanawha Blvd. East, #157-K, Charleston, WV
25305-0770

Office of the Attorney General
http://www.state.wv.us/wvag/
Main phone: (304) 558-2021
Main fax: (304) 558-0140

Darrell V. McGraw Jr. (D), Attorney General
1900 Kanawha Blvd. East, #26-E, Charleston, WV
25305-0220

Office of the State Treasurer
http://www.wvtreasury.com
General e-mail: webmaster@wvtreasury.com
Main phone: (304) 558-5000

State of West Virginia

Capital: Charleston, since 1885
Founded: 1861, by secession from Virginia
Statehood: June 20, 1863 (35th state)
Constitution adopted: 1872
Area: 24,087 sq. mi. (ranks 41st)
Population: 1,811,156 (1998 est.; ranks 35th)
Largest cities: (1998 est.) Charleston (55,056);
Huntington (52,571); Wheeling (32,541);
Parkersburg (31,715); Morgantown (26,751)
Counties: 55, Most populous: (1998 est.)
Kanawha (202,011); Cabell (94,273); Wood
(86,768); Raleigh (79,066); Berkeley
(70,970)
U.S. Congress: Robert C. Byrd (D), John D.
(Jay) Rockefeller IV (D); 3 Representatives
Nickname(s): Mountain State
Motto: Mountaineers are always free
Song: "West Virginia, My Sweet Home,"
"West Virginia Hills," "This is My West
Virginia"
Bird: Cardinal
Tree: Sugar maple
Flower: Big rhododendron
State fair: at Lewisburg, mid-Aug.
Former capital(s): Wheeling

Main fax: (304) 558-4097
Toll free: (800) 422-7498
TTY: (800) 422-7498

John D. Perdue (D), State Treasurer
State Capitol Bldg., #E-145, Charleston, WV 25305
E-mail: rene@wvtreasury.com

Office of the Auditor
http://www.wvauditor.com
General e-mail: nancyp@wvauditor.com
Main phone: (304) 558-2251
Main fax: (304) 558-5200
Toll free: (877) 982-9148

Glen B. Gainer III (D), State Auditor
Bldg. 1, State Capitol Complex, 1900 Kanawha Blvd.
East, #W-100, Charleston, WV 25305

Office of the Adjutant General
Main phone: (304) 561-6316
Main fax: (304) 561-6327

> **Allen E. Tackett, Adjutant General**
> 1703 Coonskin Dr., Charleston, WV 25311-1085
> *E-mail:* tacketta@wv-arng.ngb.army.mil

Agencies

Administration Dept.
http://www.state.wv.us/admin/
Main phone: (304) 558-4331
Main fax: (304) 558-2999

> **Joseph F. Markus, Cabinet Secretary**
> Bldg. 1, State Capitol Complex, 1900 Kanawha Blvd.
> East, #E-119, Charleston, WV 25305-0120

Consolidated Public Retirement Board
http://www.state.wv.us/cprb
General e-mail: crpb@wvretirement.com
Main phone: (304) 558-3570
Main fax: (304) 558-6337
Toll free: (800) 654-4406

> **Betty S. Ireland, Executive Secretary**
> State Capitol Complex, Bldg. 5, 1900 Kanawha
> Blvd. East, #1000, Charleston, WV 25305-0720
> *E-mail:* bireland@wvretirement.com

Finance Division
http://www.state.wv.us/admin/finance/
General e-mail: LMartin@gwmail.state.wv.us
Main phone: (304) 558-6181
Main fax: (304) 558-4466
Mailing address: P.O. Box 50121, Charleston,
WV 25305

> **Bryan S. Michaels, Comptroller**
> 2019 Washington St. East, 2nd Fl., Charleston, WV
> 25305

Personnel Division
http://www.state.wv.us/admin/personel/
Main phone: (304) 558-3950
Main fax: (304) 558-1587

> **Joe E. Smith, Director (Acting)**
> 1900 Kanawha Blvd. East, State Capitol Complex,
> Bldg. 6, #416, Charleston, WV 25305
> *E-mail:* jsmith@gwmail.state.wv.us

Aeronautics Commission
http://www.state.wv.us/wvdot/dot/aero/aero.htm
Main phone: (304) 558-0330
Main fax: (304) 558-0333

> **Susan V. Chernenko, Director (Acting)**
> 1900 Kanawha Blvd. East, #A-512, Charleston, WV
> 25305-0330
> *E-mail:* schernenko@dot.state.wv.us

Agriculture Dept.
http://www.state.wv.us/agriculture
Main phone: (304) 558-3550
Main fax: (304) 558-2203

> **Gus R. Douglass (D), Commissioner**
> Bldg. 1, State Capitol Complex, 1900 Kanawha Blvd.
> East, #M-28, Charleston, WV 25305-0170
> (304) 558-2201; *Fax:* (304) 558-0451
> *E-mail:* douglass@ag.state.wv.us

Soil Conservation Agency
http://www.wvsca.org/
Main phone: (304) 558-2204
Main fax: (304) 340-4839

> **Lance Tabor, Executive Director**
> 1900 Kanawha Blvd. East, Charleston, WV 25305-
> 0193
> *E-mail:* ltabor@wvsca.org

Alcohol Beverage Control Commission
http://www.state.wv.us/abcc/
General e-mail: dstemple@abcc.state.wv.us
Main phone: (304) 558-2481
Main fax: (304) 558-0081
Toll free: (800) 642-8208

> **Donald L. Semple, Commissioner**
> 322 70th St. S.E., Charleston, WV 25304-2900
> *E-mail:* dsemple@abcc.state.wv.us

Archives and History Commission
http://www.wvculture.org
General e-mail: joe.geiger@wvculture.org
Main phone: (304) 558-0230
Main fax: (304) 558-2779

> **Fredrick H. Armstrong, Director**
> 1900 Kanawha Blvd. East, Charleston, WV 25305-
> 0300
> (304) 558-0230, ext. 164
> *E-mail:* fharmstrong@wvculture.org

Banking Division
http://www.wvdob.org
Main phone: (304) 558-2294
Main fax: (304) 558-0442

> **Sharon G. Bias, Commissioner**
> 1900 Kanawha Blvd. East, Bldg. 3, #311, Charleston,
> WV 25305-0240
> *E-mail:* sbias@wvdob.org

Civil Rights Division
Main phone: (304) 558-0546
Main fax: (304) 558-0649
Mailing address: P.O. Box 1789, Charleston, WV
25326-1789

> **Mary Kay Buchmelter, Deputy Attorney General**
> 812 Quarrier St., 5th Fl., Charleston, WV 25301

Higher Educational Institutions

Bluefield State College
http://www.bluefield.wvnet.edu
219 Rock St., Bluefield, WV 24701-2198
Main phone: (304) 327-4068

Concord College
http://www.concord.edu
P.O. Box 1000, Athens, WV 24712
Main phone: (888) 384-5249

Fairmont State College
http://www.fscvax.fairmont.wvnet.edu/
1201 Locust Ave., Fairmont, WV 26554
Main phone: (304) 367-4141

Glenville State College
http://www.glenville.wvnet.edu
200 High St., Glenville, WV 26351-1200
Main phone: (304) 462-4106

Marshall University
http://www.marshall.edu
400 Hal Greer Blvd., Huntington, WV 25755
Main phone: (304) 696-3160
Branches: South Charleston

Shepherd College
http://www.shepherd.wvnet.edu
King St., Shepherdstown, WV 25443-3210
Main phone: (304) 876-5212

West Liberty State College
http://www.wlsc.wvnet.edu
P.O. Box 295, West Liberty, WV 26074
Main phone: (304) 336-8078

West Virginia School of Osteopathic Medicine
http://www.wvsom.edu
400 N. Lee St., Lewisburg, WV 24901
Main phone: (800) 356-7836

West Virginia State College
http://www.wvsc.edu/index.html
P.O. Box 1000, Institute, WV 25112-1000
Main phone: (800) 987-2112

West Virginia University
http://www.wvu.edu
Box 6009, Morgantown, WV 26506
Main phone: (304) 293-2121, ext. 1511
Branches: Potomac State College, WVU Charleston
Division, WVU at Parkersburg

Commerce Bureau
http://www.state.wv.us/tourism
Main phone: (304) 558-2200
Main fax: (304) 558-2956

Robert A. Reintsema, Commissioner
Bldg. 17, State Capitol Complex, 2101 Washington St.
East, Charleston, WV 25305-0312
E-mail: breintsema@tourism.state.wv.us

Development Office
General e-mail: wvdo@wvdo.org
Main phone: (304) 558-2234
Main fax: (304) 558-0449
Toll free: (800) 982-3386

John Snider, Executive Director
Capitol Complex, Bldg. 6, 1900 Washington St.
East, #553, Charleston, WV 25305-0311
E-mail: jsnider@wvdo.org

Forestry Division
http://www.state.wv.us/forestry
General e-mail: wvforest@access.mountain.net
Main phone: (304) 558-2783
Main fax: (304) 558-0143

Charles R. (Randy) Dye, Director
Guthrie Agriculture Center, 1900 Kanawha Blvd.
East, Charleston, WV 25305-0180
(304) 558-3446

Geological and Economic Survey
http://www.wvgs.wvnet.edu/
Main phone: (304) 594-2331
Main fax: (304) 594-2575
Toll free: (800) 984-3656
Mailing address: P.O. Box 879, Morgantown,
WV 26507-0879

**Larry D. Woodfork, State Geologist and
Director**
Mount Chateau Research Center, Morgantown,
WV 26507-0879
Fax: (304) 594-2338
E-mail: woodfork@geosrv.wvnet.edu

Labor Division
Main phone: (304) 558-7890
Main fax: (304) 558-3797

Steven A. Allred, Commissioner
State Capitol Complex, Bldg. 3, 1900 Kanawha
Blvd. East, #319, Charleston, WV 25305

Natural Resources Division
http://www.dnr.state.wv.us/
General e-mail: wildlife@dnr.state.wv.us
Main phone: (304) 558-2754
Main fax: (304) 558-2768

John Rader, Director
1900 Kanawha Blvd. East, State Capitol Complex,
Bldg. 3, #669, Charleston, WV 25305-0060
(304) 558-2754

Natural Resources Division: State Parks and Forests
http://www.wvparks.com/

General e-mail: parks@westvirginia.com
Main phone: (304) 558-2764
Main fax: (304) 558-0077

Cordie Hudkins, Chief
1900 Kanawha Blvd. East, State Capitol Complex,
Bldg. 3, #714, Charleston, WV 25305

Natural Resources Division: Wildlife Resources
General e-mail: wildlife@dnr.state.wv.us
Main phone: (304) 558-2771
Main fax: (304) 558-2768

Bernard Dowler, Chief
State Capitol Complex, Bldg. 3, 1900 Kanawha
Blvd. East, #812, Charleston, WV 25305-0660
E-mail: bdowler@dnr.state.wv.us

Tourism Division
http://www.state.wv.us/tourism/
Main phone: (304) 558-2200
Main fax: (304) 558-2956
Toll free: (800) 225-5982

Robert A. Reintsema, Commissioner
2101 Washington St. East, State Capitol Complex,
Bldg. 17, Charleston, WV 25305-0312
E-mail: breintsema@tourism.state.wv.us

Consumer Protection/Antitrust Division
Main phone: (304) 558-8986
Main fax: (304) 558-0184
Mailing address: P.O. Box 1789, Charleston, WV
25312

Jill L. Miles, Deputy Attorney General
812 Quarrier St., 6th Fl., Charleston, WV 25301-2617

Corrections Division
http://www.state.wv.us/wvdoc/default.htm
General e-mail: cgraves1@mail.wvnet.edu
Main phone: (304) 558-2036
Main fax: (304) 558-5934

Paul W. Kirby, Commissioner
112 California Ave., Bldg. 4, #300, Charleston, WV
25305

Criminal Justice Services Division
http://www.wvdcjs.com/
General e-mail: wvdcjs@citynet.net
Main phone: (304) 558-8814
Main fax: (304) 558-0391

J. Norbert Federspiel, Executive Director
1204 Kanawha Blvd. East, Charleston, WV 25301
E-mail: n.federspiel@wvdcjs.org

Education and the Arts Dept.
http://www.wved-arts.wvnet.edu

Frequently Called Numbers

Tourism: (304) 558-2200, 1-800-225-5982;
http://www.state.wv.us/tourism/
Library: (304) 558-2041;
http://www.wvlc.lib.wv.us
Board of Education: (304) 558-3660;
wvde.state.wv.us/boe/
Vital Statistics: (304) 558-2931;
http://www.wvdhr.org/bph/oehp/
hschome.htm
Tax/Revenue: (304) 558-3333;
http://www.state.wv.us/taxrev/
Motor Vehicles: (304) 558-3900, 1-800-642-
9066; http://www.state.wv.us/dmv/
default.htm
State Police/Highway Patrol: (304) 746-2111;
http://www.wvstatepolice.com/
Unemployment: (304) 558-2624;
http://www.state.wv.us/bep/uc/default.htm
General Election Information: (304) 558-
6000; http://www.state.wv.us/sos/election/
Consumer Affairs: (304) 558-8986
Hazardous Materials: (304) 558-5393;
http://www.dep.state.wv.us/wm/index.html

Main phone: (304) 558-2440
Main fax: (304) 558-1311

David Ice, Secretary
Bldg. 5, State Capitol Complex, 1900 Kanawha Blvd.
East, #205, Charleston, WV 25305
E-mail: iced@mail.wvnet.edu

Library Commission
http://www.wvlc.lib.wv.us
Main phone: (304) 558-2041
Main fax: (304) 558-2044

David M. Price, Director
State Capitol Complex, Cultural Center, 1900
Kanawha Blvd. East, #205, Charleston, WV
25305
E-mail: priced@wvlc.lib.wv.us

Education Dept.
http://wvde.state.wv.us/
Main phone: (304) 558-2681
Main fax: (304) 558-0048
TTY: (304) 558-2696

Henry Marockie, State Superintendent of Schools
Bldg. 6, State Capitol Complex, 1900 Kanawha Blvd.
East, #358, Charleston, WV 25305-0330
E-mail: hrrockwv@access.k12.wv.us

Board of Education
http://wvde.state.wv.us/boe/
Main phone: (304) 558-3660
Main fax: (304) 558-0198

Cleo P. Mathews, President
Bldg. 6, State Capitol Complex, 1900 Kanawha
   Blvd. East, #351, Charleston, WV 25305-0330

Employment Programs Bureau
General e-mail: robinc@wvnvm.wvnet.edu
Main phone: (304) 558-2630
Main fax: (304) 558-5004

William F. Vieweg, Commissioner
112 California Ave., Charleston, WV 25305-0112
Fax: (304) 558-2992

Environment Bureau
Main phone: (304) 759-0515
Main fax: (304) 759-0526
TTY: (800) 637-5893

Michael C. Castle, Commissioner
10 McJunkin Rd., Nitro, WV 25143-2506
E-mail: mcastle@mail.dep.state.wv.us

Environmental Protection Division
http://www.dep.state.wv.us/
Main phone: (304) 759-0515
Main fax: (304) 759-0526

Michael C. Castle, Director
10 McJunkin Rd., Nitro, WV 25143-2506
E-mail: mcastle@mail.dep.state.wv.us

Environmental Protection Division: Oil and Gas Office
http://www.dep.state.wv.us/og/index.html
Main phone: (304) 759-0514
Main fax: (304) 759-0529
TTY: (800) 637-5893

Ava King, Chief
10 McJunkin Rd., Nitro, WV 25143
(304) 759-0517
E-mail: aking@mail.dep.state.wv.us

Environmental Protection Division: Water Resources
http://www.dep.state.wv.us/wr/index.html
Main phone: (304) 558-2107
Main fax: (304) 558-5905

Barbara S. Taylor, Chief
1201 Greenbrier St., Charleston, WV 25311

Fire Marshal
http://www.wvfiremarshal.org/
General e-mail: WVSFMO@xwv.net
Main phone: (304) 558-2191
Main fax: (304) 558-2537

Joe Leake, State Fire Marshal
1207 Quarrier St., 2nd Fl., Charleston, WV 25301

Health and Human Resources Dept.
http://www.wvdhhr.org
Main phone: (304) 558-0684
Main fax: (304) 558-1130

Joan E. Ohl, Secretary
Bldg. 3, State Capitol Complex, 1900 Kanawha Blvd.
   East, #206, Charleston, WV 25305
E-mail: joanohl@wvdhhr.org

Behavioral Health Services Office
Main phone: (304) 558-0627
Main fax: (304) 558-1008

John Bianconi, Director
350 Capitol St., #350, Charleston, WV 25301-3702

Behavioral Health Services Office: Developmental Disabilities Division
Main phone: (304) 558-0627
Main fax: (304) 558-1008

Frank Kirkland, Director (Acting)
350 Capitol St., 1900 Kanawha Blvd. East, #350,
   Charleston, WV 25301-3702
(304) 558-3296

Women's Commission
http://www.wvdhhr.org/womenscom
Main phone: (304) 558-0070
Main fax: (304) 558-5167

Joyce M. Stover, Executive Director
550 Capitol St., #721, Charleston, WV 25301-3700
E-mail: joycestover@wvdhhr.org

Human Rights Commission
http://www.state.wv.us/wvhrc/

General e-mail: wvhrc@wvhrc.state.wv.us
Main phone: (304) 558-2616
Main fax: (304) 558-0085
Toll free: (888) 676-5546
TTY: (304) 558-2976

Ivin B. Lee, Executive Director
1321 Plaza East, #108, Charleston, WV 25301
E-mail: leeib@wvhrc.state.wv.us

Insurance Commission
http://www.state.wv.us/insurance/
Main phone: (304) 558-3707
Main fax: (304) 558-0412
Toll free: (800) 642-9004
TTY: (304) 558-1296
Mailing address: P.O. Box 50540, Charleston, WV 25305

Hanley C. Clark, Commissioner
1124 Smith St., Charleston, WV 25305-0540

Military Affairs and Public Safety Dept.
Main phone: (304) 558-2930
Main fax: (304) 558-6221

Otis G. Cox Jr., Secretary
Bldg. 6, State Capitol Complex, 1900 Kanawha Blvd. East, #B-122, Charleston, WV 25305-0155

Emergency Services Office
Main phone: (304) 558-5380
Main fax: (304) 344-4538

John Pack, Director
State Capitol Complex, Bldg. 6, 1900 Kanawha Blvd. East, #EB80, Charleston, WV 25305
E-mail: jpacki@wvoes.state.wv.us

Juvenile Services Division
http://www.wvdjs.state.wv.us
General e-mail: mail@djs.state.wv.us
Main phone: (304) 558-6029
Main fax: (304) 558-6032

Manfred G. Holland, Director
1200 Quarrier St., 2nd Fl., Charleston, WV 25301
E-mail: mholland@djs.state.wv.us

Probation and Parole Board
Main phone: (304) 558-6366
Main fax: (304) 558-5678

Sandra M. Ilderton, Chair
112 California Ave., Bldg. 4, #307, Charleston, WV 25305
E-mail: ilders1@mail.wvnet.edu

Veterans Affairs Division
General e-mail: wvvetaff@aol.com
Main phone: (304) 558-3661
Main fax: (304) 558-3662
Toll free: (888) 838-2332

Gail L. Harper, Director
1321 Plaza East, #101, Charleston, WV 25301-1400

Public Broadcasting
http://www.wvptv.wvnet.edu/
General e-mail: tv@WSWP.pbs.org
Main phone: (304) 558-3400
Main fax: (304) 558-1561

Rita Ray, Executive Secretary
600 Capitol St., Charleston, WV 25301

Public Service Commission
http://www.state.wv.us/psc
General e-mail: info@psc.state.wv.us
Main phone: (304) 340-0300
Main fax: (304) 340-3758
Mailing address: P.O. Box 812, Charleston, WV 25323

Charlotte R. Lane, Chair
201 Brooks St., Charleston, WV 25323
(304) 340-0306
E-mail: clane@psc.state.wv.us

Real Estate Appraisers Board
http://www.state.wv.us/appraise/
Main phone: (304) 558-3919
Main fax: (304) 558-3983

Sharron L. Knotts, Executive Director
2110 Kanawha Blvd. East, Charleston, WV 25311
E-mail: knotts@wvnvm.wvnet.edu

Senior Services Bureau
Main phone: (304) 558-3317
Main fax: (304) 558-0004
Toll free: (877) 987-4463

Gaylene A. Miller, Commissioner
Holly Grove, Bldg. 10, 1900 Kanawha Blvd. East, Charleston, WV 25305-0160
Fax: (304) 558-5609
E-mail: gmiller@boss.state.wv.us

State Fair
http://www.wvstatefair.com/
General e-mail: publicrelations@wvstatefair.com
Main phone: (304) 645-1090
Main fax: (304) 645-6660
Mailing address: P.O. Drawer 986, Lewisburg, WV 24901

Ed Rock, General Manager
Rte. 219 S., Lewisburg, WV 24901

State Police
http://www.wvstatepolice.com/
General e-mail: troopers@wvstatepolice.com
Main phone: (304) 746-2111
Main fax: (304) 746-2246

Gary L. Edgell, Superintendent
725 Jefferson Rd. South, Charleston, WV 25309-1698
(304) 746-2111
E-mail: edgelg@mail.wvnet.edu

Tax and Revenue Dept.
http://www.state.wv.us/taxrev/
Main phone: (304) 558-3333
Main fax: (304) 558-2324
TTY: (800) 282-9833
Mailing address: P.O. Box 963, Charleston, WV
25305

Robin C. Capehart, Cabinet Secretary
State Capitol Bldg., #W-300, Charleston, WV 25305
(304) 558-0211

Lottery Commission
http://www.state.wv.us/lottery/
General e-mail: mail@wvlottery.com
Main phone: (304) 558-0500
Main fax: (304) 558-3321
Toll free: (800) 982-2274
Mailing address: P.O. Box 2067, Charleston,
WV 25327-2067

John C. Musgrave, Director
312 McCorkle Ave. S.E., Charleston, WV
25327-2067
E-mail: jmusgrave@wvlottery.com

Transportation Dept.
http://www.state.wv.us/wvdot/
Main phone: (304) 558-0444
Main fax: (304) 558-1004
TTY: (800) 724-6991

Samuel G. Bonasso, Secretary
Bldg. 5, State Capitol Complex, 1900 Kanawha Blvd.
East, #109, Charleston, WV 25305-0430
E-mail: sec.dot_q&a@dot.state.wv.us

Motor Vehicles Division
http://www.state.wv.us/dmv/default.htm
Main phone: (304) 558-3900
Main fax: (304) 558-1987
Toll free: (800) 642-9066

Joe E. Miller, Commissioner
1800 Kanawha Blvd. East, Charleston, WV 25317
(304) 558-2723
E-mail: jmiller@dot.state.wv.us

Workers' Compensation Board
http://www.state.wv.us/bep/wc/default.HTM
Main phone: (304) 926-5048
Main fax: (304) 926-5372
Mailing address: P.O. Box 3824, Charleston, WV
25338-3824

John E. Burdette, Executive Director
4700 MacCorkle Ave. S.E., Charleston, WV
25338-3824

West Virginia Legislature
State Capitol
Charleston, WV 25305
General information: (304) 347-4830
http://www.legis.state.wv.us

Senate
General information: (304) 357-7800
Fax: (304) 357-7829

Earl Ray Tomblin (D), President
State Capitol, 1900 Kanawha Blvd. East, #229-M,
Charleston, WV 25305
(304) 357-7801

William R. Sharpe Jr. (D), President Pro Tempore
State Capitol, 1900 Kanawha Blvd. East, #206-W,
Charleston, WV 25305
(304) 357-7845

H. Truman Chafin (D), Majority Leader
State Capitol, 1900 Kanawha Blvd. East, #223-M,
Charleston, WV 25305
(304) 357-7808

Billy Wayne Bailey Jr. (D), Majority Whip
State Capitol, 1900 Kanawha Blvd. East, #204-W,
Charleston, WV 25305
(304) 357-7807

Vic Sprouse (R), Minority Leader
State Capitol, 1900 Kanawha Blvd. East, #245-M,
Charleston, WV 25305
(304) 357-7901

R. Andy McKenzie (R), Minority Whip
State Capitol, 1900 Kanawha Blvd. East, #204-W,
Charleston, WV 25305
(304) 357-7984

Darrell E. Holmer, Clerk
State Capitol, 1900 Kanawha Blvd. East, Charleston,
WV 25305
(304) 357-7800; *Fax:* (304) 357-7829

House
General information: (304) 340-3200
Fax: (304) 347-4819
TTY: (304) 347-4901

Robert S. Kiss (D), Speaker of the House
State Capitol, 1900 Kanawha Blvd. East, #234-M,
Charleston, WV 25305
(304) 340-3210

John Pino (D), Speaker Pro Tempore
State Capitol, 1900 Kanawha Blvd. East, #242-M,
Charleston, WV 25305
(304) 340-3114

Laws

Sales tax: 6%
Income tax: 6.5%
State minimum wage: $5.15 (Federal is $5.15)
Marriage age: 18
First-cousin marriage: Prohibited
Drinking age: 21
State control of liquor sales: Yes
Blood alcohol for DWI: 0.10%
Driving age: 16
Speed limit: 70 mph
Permit to buy handguns: No
Minimum age to possess handguns: None
Minimum age to possess rifles, shotguns:
  None
State lottery: Yes; also Powerball
Casinos: No; but slot/video machines
Pari-mutuel betting: Horse and dog racing
Death penalty: No
3 strikes minimum sentence: Life (3rd felony)
Hate crimes law: Yes
Gay employment non-discrimination: No
Official language(s): None
Term limits: None

*State laws are complex and subject to
change; this information is not intended as
legal advice. For an explanation of this
information, see p. x.*

Joe Martin (D), Majority Leader
State Capitol, 1900 Kanawha Blvd. East, #228-M,
  Charleston, WV 25305
(304) 340-3220
Charles S. Trump IV (R), Minority Leader
State Capitol, 1900 Kanawha Blvd. East, #266-M,
  Charleston, WV 25305
(304) 340-3240
Gregory M. Gray, Clerk
State Capitol, 1900 Kanawha Blvd. East, Charleston,
  WV 25305
(304) 340-3200; *Fax:* (304) 347-4819

West Virginia Judiciary
State Capitol Complex
1900 Kanawha Blvd. East, #E-400
Charleston, WV 25305

Supreme Court of Appeals
http://www.state.wv.us/wvsca/

Deborah L. McHenry, Clerk and Chief Counsel
State Capitol Complex, 1900 Kanawha Blvd. East, #E-
  400, Charleston, WV 25305
(304) 558-6035; *Fax:* (304) 558-6045
E-mail: mchenryd@wvnvm.wvnet.edu

Justices
Composition: 5 justices
Selection Method: partisan election; vacancies
  filled by gubernatorial appointment until next
  general election
Length of term: 12 years

Elliott Maynard, Chief Justice, (304) 558-2606
Robin Jean Davis, Justice, (304) 558-4811
Warren R. McGraw, Justice, (304) 558-2602
George M. Scott, Justice, (304) 558-2605
Larry V. Starcher, Justice, (304) 558-2604

Administrative Office of the Courts
http://www.state.wv.us/wvsca/AO.htm
Main phone: (304) 558-0145
Main fax: (304) 558-1212

**James M. Albert, Administrative Director of the
  Courts**
State Capitol Complex, 1900 Kanawha Blvd. East, #E-
  100, Charleston, WV 25305
E-mail: alberj@mail.wvnef.edu

State Law Library
http://www.state.wv.us/wvsca/library/menu.htm
Main phone: (304) 558-2607
Main fax: (304) 558-3673

Michelle Mensore, Law Librarian
State Capitol Complex, 1900 Kanawha Blvd. East, #E-
  404, Charleston, WV 25305

West Virginia Legislative and Political Party Information Resources

Membership: http://www.legis.state.wv.us/general/memaddress.html
Current session information: http://www.legis.state.wv.us/general/legcalendar.html
West Virginia Democratic Party: http://www.wvdemocrats.com
405 Capitol St., #501, Charleston, WV 25301; *Phone:* (304) 342-8121; *Phone:* (304) 342-8122; *E-mail:*
  party@wvdemocrats.com
West Virginia Republican Party: http://www.wvgop.org; 1620 Kanawha Blvd. E., #4B, Charleston, WV
  25311; *Phone:* (304) 344-3446; *Fax:* (304) 344-3448

Wisconsin

State Capitol
Madison, WI 53707-7863
Public information: (608) 266-2211
Fax: (608) 262-0123
http://www.state.wi.us

Office of the Governor
http://www.wisgov.state.wi.us
General e-mail: wisgov@mail.state.wi.us
Main phone: (608) 266-1212
Main fax: (608) 267-8983
TTY: (608) 267-5163
Mailing address: P.O. Box 7863, Madison, WI
53707-7863

Tommy G. Thompson (R), Governor
State Capitol, #125-S, Madison, WI 53707-7863

Robert Wood, Chief of Staff
State Capitol, Madison, WI 53707-7863
(608) 266-1212; *Fax:* (608) 267-8983

Darrin Schmitz, Press Secretary
State Capitol, #125-S, Madison, WI 53703
(608) 266-1212; *Fax:* (608) 267-8983

Debbie Hochkammer, Constituent Affairs
State Capitol, #125-S, Madison, WI 53707-7863
(608) 266-1212; *Fax:* (608) 267-8983
E-mail: debbie.hochkammer@gov.state.wi.us

Schuyler Baab, Director, Washington Office
444 N. Capitol St. N.W., #613, Washington, DC 20001
(202) 624-5870; *Fax:* (202) 624-5871

Office of the Lieutenant Governor
http://badger.state.wi.us/agencies/ltgov
General e-mail: ltgov@ltgov.state.wi.us
Main phone: (608) 266-3516
Main fax: (608) 267-3571

Scott McCallum (R), Lieutenant Governor
1 S. Pinckney, #330, Madison, WI 53703

Office of the Secretary of State
http://badger.state.wi.us/agencies/sos
Main phone: (608) 266-8888
Main fax: (608) 266-3159
Mailing address: P.O. Box 7848, Madison, WI
53707-7848

Doug La Follette (D), Secretary of State
30 W. Mifflin St., 10th Fl., Madison, WI 53707-7848

Office of the Attorney General
http://www.doj.state.wi.us
General e-mail: wisag@doj.state.wi.us

State of Wisconsin

Capital: Madison,
  since 1836
Founded: 1836, Wisconsin
  Territory created from Michigan Territory
Statehood: May 29, 1848 (30th state)
Constitution adopted: 1848
Area: 54,314 sq. mi. (ranks 25th)
Population: 5,223,500 (1998 est.; ranks 18th)
Largest cities: (1998 est.) Milwaukee
  (578,364); Madison (209,306); Green Bay
  (97,789); Kenosha (87,849); Racine (81,095)
Counties: 72, Most populous: (1998 est.)
  Milwaukee (911,713); Dane (424,586);
  Waukesha (353,110); Brown (215,373);
  Racine (186,119)
U.S. Congress: Russell D. Feingold (D), Herb
  Kohl (D); 9 Representatives
Nickname(s): Badger State
Motto: Forward
Song: "On, Wisconsin!"
Bird: Robin
Tree: Sugar maple
Flower: Wood violet
State fair: at Milwaukee/West Allis, early to
  mid-Aug.
Former capital(s): Belmont

Main phone: (608) 244-4982
Main fax: (608) 267-2778
Mailing address: P.O. Box 7857, Madison, WI
53707-7857

James E. Doyle (D), Attorney General
123 W. Washington Ave., #117, Madison, WI 53707-7857

Office of the State Treasurer
http://badger.state.wi.us/agencies/ost
General e-mail: treasury@ost.state.wi.us
Main phone: (608) 264-6998
Main fax: (608) 266-2647
Toll free: (800) 462-2814
Mailing address: P.O. Box 7871, Madison, WI
53707

Jack Voight (R), Treasurer
1 S. Pinckney, #550, Madison, WI 53707
(608) 266-1714

Military Affairs Dept.

Main phone: (608) 242-3000
Main fax: (608) 242-3111
Mailing address: P.O. Box 2572, Madison, WI 53704-2572

James G. Blaney, Adjutant General
2400 Wright St., Madison, WI 53704-2572
(608) 242-3001

Agencies

Administration Dept.

http://www.doa.state.wi.us
Main phone: (608) 266-1741
Main fax: (608) 264-9500
TTY: (608) 267-9629
Mailing address: P.O. Box 7864, Madison, WI 53707-7864

George Lightbourn, Secretary (Acting)
101 E. Wilson St., Madison, WI 53702

Aging and Long-Term Care Board

Main phone: (608) 266-8944
Main fax: (608) 261-6570

George F. Potaracke, Executive Director
214 N. Hamilton St., Madison, WI 53703
(608) 266-8945
E-mail: gpotarac@mail.state.wi.us

Agriculture, Trade, and Consumer Protection Dept.

http://datcp.state.wi.us
General e-mail:
  datap_web@wheel.datcp.state.wi.us
Main phone: (608) 224-5012
Main fax: (608) 224-5045
TTY: (608) 224-5058
Mailing address: P.O. Box 8911, Madison, WI 53708-8911

Ben Brancel, Secretary
2811 Agriculture Dr., Madison, WI 53708-8911
E-mail: brancb@wheel.datcp.state.wi.us

Trade and Consumer Protection Division

http://datcp.state.wi.us/cp/
General e-mail:
  datcphotline@wheel.datcp.state.wi.us
Main phone: (608) 224-4953
Main fax: (608) 224-4939
Toll free: (800) 422-7128
TTY: (608) 224-5058
Mailing address: P.O. Box 8911, Madison, WI 53708-8911

William L. Oemichen, Administrator
2811 Agriculture Dr., Madison, WI 53708-8911
(608) 224-4920

Arts Board

http://www.arts.state.wi.us
General e-mail: artsboard@arts.state.wi.us
Main phone: (608) 266-0190
Main fax: (608) 267-0380
TTY: (608) 267-9629

George Tzougros, Executive Director
101 E. Wilson St., 1st Fl., Madison, WI 53702
E-mail: george.tzougros@arts.state.wi.us

Building Commission

Main phone: (608) 266-1855
Main fax: (608) 267-2710
TTY: (608) 267-9629
Mailing address: P.O. Box 7866, Madison, WI 53707

Tommy G. Thompson, Chair
101 E. Wilson, Madison, WI 53707
(608) 266-1212

Commerce Dept.

http://www.commerce.state.wi.us
Main phone: (608) 266-1018
Main fax: (608) 267-0436
TTY: (608) 264-8777
Mailing address: P.O. Box 7970, Madison, WI 53707-7970

Brenda Blanchard, Secretary
201 W. Washington Ave., Madison, WI 53707-7970
(608) 266-8976

Corrections Dept.

http://www.wi-doc.com
General e-mail: docweb@doc.state.wi.us
Main phone: (608) 266-2471
Main fax: (608) 267-3661
TTY: (608) 267-1746
Mailing address: P.O. Box 7925, Madison, WI 53707-7925

Jon E. Litscher, Secretary
149 E. Wilson St., Madison, WI 53707-7925
(608) 266-4548

Juvenile Corrections Division

http://www.wi-doc.com/index_juvenile.htm
Main phone: (608) 266-9342
Main fax: (608) 267-3693
Mailing address: P.O. Box 8930, Madison, WI 53708-8930

Eurial Jordan, Administrator
149 E. Wilson St., Madison, WI 53708-8930
(608) 267-3715; *Fax:* (608) 267-3661
E-mail: eurialjordan@doc.state.wi.us

Educational Communications Board

http://www.ecb.org

Higher Educational Institutions

University of Wisconsin System
http://www.uwsa.edu
Van Hise Hall, 1220 Linden Dr., Madison, WI 53706-1559
Main phone: (608) 262-3961
Branches: Eau Claire, Green Bay, La Crosse, Madison, Milwaukee, Oshkosh, Parkside, Platteville, River Falls, Stevens Point, Stout, Superior, and Whitewater.

Main phone: (608) 264-9600
Main fax: (608) 264-9664
TTY: (608) 264-9710

Thomas L. Fletemeyer, Executive Director
3319 W. Beltline Hwy., Madison, WI 53713-4296
(608) 264-9676

Elections Board
General e-mail: seb@seb.state.wi.us
Main phone: (608) 266-8005
Main fax: (608) 267-0500
Mailing address: P.O. Box 2973, Madison, WI 53701-2973

Kevin J. Kennedy, Executive Director
132 E. Wilson, Madison, WI 53701-2973

Employee Trust Funds Dept.
http://badger.state.wi.us/agencies/etf
Main phone: (608) 266-0407
Main fax: (608) 267-0633
TTY: (608) 267-0676
Mailing address: P.O. Box 7931, Madison, WI 53707-7931

Eric O. Stanchfield, Secretary
801 W. Badger Rd., Madison, WI 53702-2526

Retirement Division
Main phone: (608) 266-1071
Main fax: (608) 267-4549
Toll free: (800) 991-5540
TTY: (608) 267-0676
Mailing address: P.O. Box 7931, Madison, WI 53707-7931

David Stella, Administrator
801 W. Badger Rd., Madison, WI 53702
(608) 266-3285

Employment Relations Dept.
http://der.state.wi.us
General e-mail: derdas@mail.state.wi.us
Main phone: (608) 266-9820
Main fax: (608) 267-1020
TTY: (608) 267-1004

Mailing address: P.O. Box 7855, Madison, WI 53707-7855

Peter D. Fox, Secretary
345 W. Washington Ave., 2nd Fl., Madison, WI 53703

Ethics Board
http://ethics.state.wi.us
General e-mail: ethics@ethics.state.wi.us
Main phone: (608) 266-8123
Main fax: (608) 264-9319

Roth Judd, Director
44 E. Mifflin St., #601, Madison, WI 53703-2800

Financial Institutions Dept.
http://www.wdfi.org
Main phone: (608) 264-7800
Main fax: (608) 261-4334
Mailing address: P.O. Box 8861, Madison, WI 53708-8861

Richard L. Dean, Secretary
345 W. Washington Ave., 5th Fl., Madison, WI 53703

Banking Division
Main phone: (608) 266-0451
Main fax: (608) 267-6889
Mailing address: P.O. Box 7876, Madison, WI 53707-7876

Michael J. Mach, Administrator
345 W. Washington Ave., 4th Fl., Madison, WI 53703
(608) 266-1622

Credit Unions Office
Main phone: (608) 261-9543
Main fax: (608) 267-0479
Mailing address: P.O. Box 14137, Madison, WI 53714-0137

Ginger Larson, Director
345 W. Washington Ave., 3rd Fl., Madison, WI 53703
(608) 266-8893
E-mail: ginger.larson@dfi.state.wi.us

Gaming Division
Main phone: (608) 270-2555
Main fax: (608) 270-2564
Mailing address: P.O. Box 8979, Madison, WI 53708-8979

F. Scott Scepaniak, Administrator
2005 W. Beltine Hwy., #201, Madison, WI 53713

Geological and Natural History Survey
http://www.uwex.edu/wgnhs
Main phone: (608) 262-1705
Main fax: (608) 262-8086

James M. Robertson, Director
3817 Mineral Point Rd., Madison, WI 53705
(608) 263-7384
E-mail: jmrober1@facstaff.wisc.edu

Health and Family Services Dept.
http://www.dhfs.state.wi.us
Main phone: (608) 266-9622
Main fax: (608) 266-7882
TTY: (608) 266-3683
Mailing address: P.O. Box 7850, Madison, WI
53707

Joseph Leean, Secretary
1 W. Wilson St., Madison, WI 53702

Care and Treatment Facilities Division: Developmental Disabilities Services Program
Main phone: (608) 266-8740
Main fax: (608) 266-2579
Mailing address: P.O. Box 7851, Madison, WI
53707-7851

Mary Green, Manager
1 W. Wilson St., Madison, WI 53707
(608) 267-7803
E-mail: green.mk@dhfs.state.wi.us

Care and Treatment Facilities Division: Mental Health Services Program
Main phone: (608) 266-8740
Main fax: (608) 266-2579
Mailing address: P.O. Box 7851, Madison, WI
53707-7851

Tom Alt, Administrator
1 W. Wilson St., #850, Madison, WI 53707
(608) 267-7729

Health Care Financing Division
Main phone: (608) 266-2522
Main fax: (608) 266-1096
Mailing address: P.O. Box 309, Madison, WI
53701

Peggy Bartels, Administrator
1 W. Wilson St., #350, Madison, WI 53702

Management and Technology Division: Affirmative Action/Civil Rights
Main phone: (608) 266-3465
Main fax: (608) 267-6779
Mailing address: P.O. Box 7850, Madison, WI
53707-7850

Gladys Benavides, Officer
1 W. Wilson St., #672, Madison, WI 53702-0001
(608) 266-3356
E-mail: benavg@dhfs.state.wi.us

Supportive Living Division: Aging and Long Term Care Bureau
Main phone: (608) 266-2701
Main fax: (608) 267-3203
Mailing address: P.O. Box 7850, Madison, WI
53707-7850

Donna McDowell, Director
1 W. Wilson St., Madison, WI 53707
E-mail: mcdowdb@dhfs.state.wi.us

Higher Educational Aids Board
http://www.heab.state.wi.us
General e-mail: heabmail@heab.state.wi.us
Main phone: (608) 267-2206
Main fax: (608) 267-2808
Mailing address: P.O. Box 7885, Madison, WI
53707-7885

Jane Hojan-Clark, Executive Secretary
131 W. Wilson St., #902, Madison, WI 53707-7885
(608) 264-6181
E-mail: jane.hogan-clark@heab.state.wi.us

Historical Society
http://www.shsw.wisc.edu
Main phone: (608) 264-6400
Main fax: (608) 264-6404

George L. Vogt, Director
816 State St., Madison, WI 53706
Fax: (608) 264-6542

Housing and Economic Development Authority
http://www.wheda.com
General e-mail: info@wheda.com
Main phone: (608) 266-7884
Main fax: (608) 267-1099
TTY: (800) 943-9430
Mailing address: P.O. Box 1728, Madison, WI
53701-1728

Fritz Ruf, Executive Director
201 W. Washington Ave., #700, Madison, WI 53701-1728

Insurance Commission
http://badger.state.wi.us/agencies/oci/
oci_home.htm
General e-mail: information@oci.state.wi.us
Main phone: (608) 266-3585
Main fax: (608) 266-9935
Toll free: (800) 236-8517
TTY: (800) 947-3529
Mailing address: P.O. Box 7873, Madison, WI
53707-7873

Connie L. O'Connell, Commissioner
121 E. Wilson St., Madison, WI 53703
(608) 267-1233

Frequently Called Numbers

Tourism: (608) 266-2161, 1-800-372-2737;
  http://www.travelwisconsin.com
Library: (608) 264-6400
Vital Statistics: (608) 266-1371;
  http://www.dhfs.state.wi.us/VitalRecords/
  index.htm
Tax/Revenue: (608) 266-2772;
  http://www.dor.state.wi.us
Motor Vehicles: (608) 266-2233
State Police/Highway Patrol:
  (608) 266-3212; http://www.dot.state.wi.us/
  dsp
Unemployment: (608) 266-2103;
  http://www.dwd.state.wi.us/ui/
General Election Information: (608)
  266-8005; http://elections.state.wi.us
Consumer Affairs: (608) 224-4953,
  1-800-422-7128; http://datcp.state.wi.us/cp/
Hazardous Materials: (608) 267-6854;
  http://www.dnr.state.wi.us/org/aw/wm/
  hazard/

Investment Board
http://badger.state.wi.us/agencies.invbd
General e-mail: info@swib.state.wi.us
Main phone: (608) 266-2381
Main fax: (608) 266-2436
Toll free: (800) 424-7942
Mailing address: P.O. Box 7842, Madison, WI
  53707

Patricia Lipton, Executive Director
121 E. Wilson St., Madison, WI 53707
(608) 266-9451

Justice Dept. Crime Information Bureau
http://www.doj.state.wi.us/dles/cib/
General e-mail: wisag@doj.state.wi.us
Main phone: (608) 266-7314
Main fax: (608) 267-1338
TTY: (608) 267-8902
Mailing address: P.O. Box 2718, Madison, WI
  53701-2718

Michael Moschkau, Director
123 W. Washington Ave., Madison, WI 53701-2718

Labor and Industry Review Commission
http://www.dwd.state.wi.us/lirc/
Main phone: (608) 266-9850
Main fax: (608) 267-4409
Mailing address: P.O. Box 8126, Madison, WI
  53708-8126

David B. Falstad, Chair
3319 W. Beltline Hwy., Madison, WI 53713

Legislative Audit Bureau
http://www.legis.state.wi.us/lab
General e-mail: leg@legis.state.wi.us
Main phone: (608) 266-2818
Main fax: (608) 267-0410

Janice Mueller, State Auditor
22 E. Mifflin, Madison, WI 53703

Natural Resources Dept.
http://www.dnr.state.wi.us/
Main phone: (608) 266-2121
Main fax: (608) 266-6983
TTY: (608) 267-6897
Mailing address: P.O. Box 7921, Madison, WI
  53707-7921

George E. Meyer, Secretary
101 S. Webster St., Madison, WI 53702

Land Division: Forestry Division
Main phone: (608) 267-7494
Main fax: (608) 266-8576
Mailing address: P.O. Box 7921, Madison, WI
  53707

Gene Francisco, Director
101 S. Webster St., Madison, WI 53703
(608) 266-2694
E-mail: francg@dnr.state.wi.us

Land Division: Parks and Recreation Bureau
http://www.wiparks.net
General e-mail: wiparks@dnr.state.wi.us
Main phone: (608) 266-2185
Main fax: (608) 267-7474
Mailing address: P.O. Box 7921, Madison, WI
  53707

Sue Black, Director
101 S. Webster St., Madison, WI 53703

Land Division: Wildlife Management Bureau
Main phone: (608) 266-8204
Main fax: (608) 267-7857
Mailing address: P.O. Box 7921, Madison, WI
  53707

Thomas Hauge, Director
101 S. Webster St., Madison, WI 53707

Water Division
Main phone: (608) 266-2121
Main fax: (608) 266-6983
Mailing address: P.O. Box 7921, Madison, WI
  53707-7921

Susan Sylvester, Administrator
101 S. Webster St., Madison, WI 53707-7921
(608) 266-1099

Parole Commission

Main phone: (608) 266-2957
Main fax: (608) 261-7464
Mailing address: P.O. Box 7925, Madison, WI
53707-7925

Jerry E. Smith Jr., Chair
149 E. Wilson St., Madison, WI 53707
(608) 267-0921
E-mail: jerry.smithjr@doc.state.wi.us

Personnel Commission

Main phone: (608) 266-1995
Main fax: (608) 266-9608

Laurie R. McCallum, Chair
131 W. Wilson St., #1004, Madison, WI 53703
(608) 266-9571
E-mail: laurie.mccallum@pcm.state.wi.us

Public Defender's Office

http://www.spd.state.wi.us
Main phone: (608) 266-0087
Main fax: (608) 267-0584
Mailing address: P.O. Box 7923, Madison, WI
53707-7923

Nicholas L. Chiarkas, State Public Defender
315 N. Henry St., 2nd Fl., Madison, WI 53702

Public Instruction Dept.

http://www.dpi.state.wi.us
Main phone: (608) 266-3390
Main fax: (608) 267-1052
Toll free: (800) 441-4563
TTY: (608) 267-2427
Mailing address: P.O. Box 7841, Madison, WI
53707-7841

John T. Benson (NP), State Superintendent
125 S. Webster St., Madison, WI 53702
(608) 266-8687

School for the Deaf and Educational Services Center for the Deaf and Hard of Hearing

http://www.dpi.state.wi.us/dpi/disea/wsd/
index.html
Main phone: (262) 728-7120
Main fax: (262) 728-7160
Toll free: (877) 973-3323

Alex Slappey, Superintendent
309 W. Walworth Ave., Delavan, WI 53115-1099
E-mail: alex.slappey@dpi.state.wi.us

School for the Visually Handicapped and Educational Services Center for the Visually Impaired

Main phone: (608) 758-6100
Main fax: (608) 758-6116
Toll free: (800) 832-9784

Thomas Hanson, Superintendent
1700 W. State St., Janesville, WI 53546-5399
(608) 758-6120

Public Service Commission

http://www.psc.state.wi.us
General e-mail: pscrecs@psc.state.wi.us
Main phone: (608) 266-5481
Main fax: (608) 266-1401
TTY: (608) 267-1479
Mailing address: P.O. Box 7854, Madison, WI
53707-7854

Linda Dorr, Executive Secretary
610 N. Whitney Way, Madison, WI 53705-2729
(608) 267-7897; *Fax:* (608) 266-3957

Regulation and Licensing Dept.

http://badger.state.wi.us/agencies/drl/
Main phone: (608) 266-2112
Main fax: (608) 267-0644
TTY: (608) 267-2416
Mailing address: P.O. Box 8935, Madison, WI
53708-8935

Marlene A. Cummings, Secretary
1400 E. Washington Ave., Madison, WI 53703
(608) 266-8609

Revenue Dept.

http://www.dor.state.wi.us
Main phone: (608) 266-2772
Main fax: (608) 266-5718
TTY: (608) 266-1612
Mailing address: P.O. Box 8933, Madison, WI
53708-8933

Cate Zeuske, Secretary
125 S. Webster St., Madison, WI 53703
(608) 266-6466

Regulation and Licensing Dept.

http://badger.state.wi.us/agencies/drl/
(608) 266-2112

Accountancy, (608) 266-5111, ext. 42
Architects, (608) 266-5111, ext. 42
Child Care, (608) 266-9314
Contractors, (608) 261-8500
Cosmetology, (608) 266-5111, ext. 42
Engineers and Land Surveyors,
   (608) 266-5111, ext. 42
Medical, (608) 266-2811
Nursing, (608) 266-2811
Pharmacy, (608) 266-2811
Real Estate, (608) 266-5111, ext. 42

Lottery Division
http://www.wilottery.com
Main phone: (608) 266-7777
Mailing address: P.O. Box 8933, Madison, WI
53708-8933

Jerry Hoddinot, Administrator
1802 W. Beltline Hwy., Madison, WI 53713

State Fair
http://www.wsfp.state.wi.us/
General e-mail: wsfp@sfp.state.wi.us
Main phone: (414) 266-7000
Main fax: (414) 266-7007
Toll free: (800) 844-FAIR
Mailing address: P.O. Box 14990, West Allis, WI
53214-0990

Richard Bjorklund, Director
8100 W. Greenfield, W. Allis, WI 53214-0990
(414) 266-7020

State Patrol
http://www.dot.state.wi.us/dsp
Main phone: (608) 266-3212
Main fax: (608) 267-4495
Mailing address: P.O. Box 14990, West Allis, WI
53214-0990

David Schumacher, Superintendent
4802 Sheboygan Ave., Madison, WI 53077

Technical College System Board
http://www.board.tec.wi.us
General e-mail: wtcsb@board.tec.wi.us
Main phone: (608) 266-1207
Main fax: (608) 266-1690
TTY: (608) 267-2483
Mailing address: P.O. Box 7874, Madison, WI
53707-7874

Edward Chin, Director
310 Price Pl., Madison, WI 53707-7874
(608) 266-1770; *Fax:* (608) 266-1285
E-mail: chine@board.tec.wi.us

Tourism Dept.
http://www.travelwisconsin.com
General e-mail: tourinfo@tourism.state.wi.us
Main phone: (608) 266-2161
Main fax: (608) 266-3403
Toll free: (800) 372-2737
TTY: (608) 267-0756
Mailing address: P.O. Box 7976, Madison, WI
53707-7976

Richard (Moose) Speros, Secretary
201 W. Washington Ave., Madison, WI 53703
(608) 261-0339

Transportation Dept.
http://www.dot.state.wi.us

General e-mail: sec.exec@dot.state.wi.us
Main phone: (608) 266-1114
Main fax: (608) 266-9912
Mailing address: P.O. Box 7910, Madison, WI
53707-7910

Charles H. Thompson, Secretary
4802 Sheboygan Ave., Madison, WI 53702

Motor Vehicles Division
Main phone: (608) 266-2233
Main fax: (608) 267-6974
Mailing address: P.O. Box 7911, Madison, WI
53707-7911

Roger Cross, Administrator
4802 Sheboygan Ave., Madison, WI 53705

Veterans Affairs Dept.
http://badger.state.wi.us/agencies/dva
General e-mail: wdva@mail.state.wi.us
Main phone: (608) 266-1311
Main fax: (608) 267-0403
Mailing address: P.O. Box 7843, Madison, WI
53707-7843

Raymond G. Boland, Secretary
30 W. Mifflin, Madison, WI 53703
(608) 266-4838
E-mail: ray.boland@dva.state.wi.us

Women's Council
http://www.wwc.state.wi.us
Main phone: (608) 266-2219
Main fax: (608) 261-2432

Katie Mnuk, Executive Director
16 N. Carroll St., #720, Madison, WI 53703
E-mail: katie.mnuk@wwc.state.wi.us

Workforce Development Dept.
http://www.dwd.state.wi.us/
General e-mail: dwdsec@dwd.state.wi.us
Main phone: (608) 266-7552
Main fax: (608) 266-1784
TTY: (608) 267-0477
Mailing address: P.O. Box 7946, Madison, WI
53707-7946

Linda Stewart, Secretary
201 E. Washington Ave., Madison, WI 53702
(608) 267-9692

Workers Compensation Division
http://www.dwd.state.wi.us/wc
Main phone: (608) 266-6841
Main fax: (608) 267-0394
Mailing address: P.O. Box 7946, Madison, WI
53707

Judy Norman-Nunnery, Administrator
201 E. Washington Ave., #161, Madison, WI
53702

Wisconsin Legislature

State Capitol
Madison, WI 53707
General information: (608) 266-0341
http://www.legis.state.wi.us

Senate

Address: P.O. Box 7882, Madison, WI 53707-7882
General information: (608) 266-2517
Fax: (608) 266-7038
TTY: (800) 228-2115
Bill status: (608) 266-1803

Fred Risser (D), President
State Capitol, P.O. Box 7882, #220-S, Madison, WI 53707-7882
(608) 266-1627; *Fax:* (608) 266-1629
E-mail: Sen.Risser@legis.state.wi.us
http://www.legis.state.wi.us/senate/sen26/sen26.html

Gary R. George (D), President Pro Tempore
State Capitol, P.O. Box 7882, #118-S, Madison, WI 53707-7882
(608) 266-2500; *Fax:* (608) 266-7381
E-mail: Sen.George@legis.state.wi.us
http://www.legis.state.wi.us/senate/sen06/sen06.html

Chuck Chvala (D), Majority Leader
State Capitol, P.O. Box 7882, #211-S, Madison, WI 53707-7882
(608) 266-9170; *Fax:* (608) 266-5087
E-mail: Sen.Chvala@legis.state.wi.us
http://www.legis.state.wi.us/senate/sen16/sen16.html

Mary E. Panzer (R), Minority Leader
State Capitol, P.O. Box 7882, #202-S, Madison, WI 53707-7882
(608) 266-7513; *Fax:* (608) 267-0590
E-mail: Sen.Panzer@legis.state.wi.us
http://www.legis.state.wi.us/senate/sen20/sen20.html

Donald J. Schneider, Chief Clerk
State Capitol, P.O. Box 7882, Madison, WI 53707-7882
(608) 266-2517; *Fax:* (608) 266-7038
E-mail: don.schneider@legis.state.wi.us

House

Address: P.O. Box 8952, Madison, WI 53708
General information: (608) 266-1501
Fax: (608) 266-7038
Bill status: (608) 266-5550

Scott R. Jensen (R), Speaker of the House
State Capitol, P.O. Box 8952, #211-W, Madison, WI 53708
(608) 266-3387; *Fax:* (608) 266-7038

E-mail: Rep.Jensen@legis.state.wi.us
http://www.legis.state.wi.us/assembly/asm32/asm32.html

Stephen J. Freese (R), Speaker Pro Tempore
State Capitol, P.O. Box 8952, #115-W, Madison, WI 53708
(608) 266-7502; *Fax:* (608) 266-7038
E-mail: Rep.Freese@legis.state.wi.us
http://www.legis.state.wi.us/assembly/asm51/asm51.html

Steven M. Foti (R), Majority Leader
State Capitol, P.O. Box 8952, #215-W, Madison, WI 53708
(608) 266-2401; *Fax:* (608) 266-7038
http://www.legis.state.wi.us/assembly/asm38/asm38.html

Shirley Krug (D), Minority Leader
State Capitol, P.O. Box 8952, #201-W, Madison, WI 53708
(608) 266-5813; *Fax:* (608) 266-7038
E-mail: Rep.Krug@legis.state.wi.us

Laws

Sales tax: 5%
Income tax: 6.9%
State minimum wage: $5.15 (Federal is $5.15)
Marriage age: 18
First-cousin marriage: Prohibited
Drinking age: 21
State control of liquor sales: No
Blood alcohol for DWI: 0.10%
Driving age: 16
Speed limit: 65 mph
Permit to buy handguns: No, but 2-day wait
Minimum age to possess handguns: 16
Minimum age to possess rifles, shotguns: 16
State lottery: Yes; also Powerball
Casinos: Yes (tribal)
Pari-mutuel betting: Dog racing
Death penalty: No
3 strikes minimum sentence: Life, no parole (3rd serious felony)
Hate crimes law: Yes
Gay employment non-discrimination: Yes
Official language(s): None
Term limits: None

State laws are complex and subject to change; this information is not intended as legal advice. For an explanation of this information, see p. x.

http://www.legis.state.wi.us/assembly/asm12/
asm12.html

Charles R. Sanders, Chief Clerk of the Assembly
State Capitol, P.O. Box 8952, Madison, WI 53708
(608) 266-1501; *Fax:* (608) 266-5617
E-mail: charlie.sanders@legis.state.wi.us

Wisconsin Judiciary

110 E. Main St., #215
Madison, WI 53702
http://www.courts.state.wi.us

Supreme Court
http://www.courts.state.wi.us/WSC/sc.html

Marilyn L. Graves, Clerk
110 E. Main St., #215, Madison, WI 53702
(608) 266-1880; *Fax:* (608) 267-0640

Justices
Composition: 7 justices
Selection Method: nonpartisan election;
  vacancies filled by gubernatorial appointment
Length of term: 10 years

Shirley S. Abrahamson, Chief Justice, (608) 266-1885
William A. Bablitch, Justice, (608) 266-1888
Ann Walsh Bradley, Justice, (608) 266-1886
N. Patrick Crooks, Justice, (608) 266-1883
David T. Prosser Jr., Justice, (608) 266-1882
Donald W. Steinmetz, Justice, (608) 266-1884
Jon P. Wilcox, Justice, (608) 266-1881

Director of State Courts Office
Main phone: (608) 266-6828
Main fax: (608) 267-0980

J. Denis Moran, Director
119 Martin Luther King Jr. Blvd., #LL2, Madison, WI
  53703
E-mail: denis.moran@courts.state.wi.us

State Law Library
Main phone: (608) 266-1600
Main fax: (608) 267-2319

Vacant, Law Librarian
1 E. Main St., 2nd Fl., Madison, WI 53703
(608) 266-1424
E-mail: marcia.koslov2@courts.state.wi.us

Legislative and Political Party Information Resources

Senate home page: http://www.legis.state.wi.us/senate/senate.html
Assembly home page: http://www.legis.state.wi.us/assembly/assembly.html
Committees: Senate: http://www.legis.state.wi.us/senate/senco.html;
        Assembly: http://www.legis.state.wi.us/assembly/asmco.html
Budget: http://www.legis.state.wi.us/lfb.jfc.html
Wisconsin Democratic Party: http://www.execpc.com/democrat
    222 State St., #400, Madison, WI 53703; *Phone:* (608) 255-5172; *Fax:* (608) 255-8919
Wisconsin Republican Party: http://www.wisgop.org
    148 E. Johnson St., P.O. Box 31, Madison, WI 53701; *Phone:* (608) 257-4765; *Fax:* (608) 257-4141

Wyoming

State Capitol
Cheyenne, WY 82002-0010
Public information: (307) 777-7011
Fax: (307) 638-4898
http://www.state.wy.us/

Office of the Governor
http://www.state.wy.us/governor/
  governor_home.html
Main phone: (307) 777-7434
Main fax: (307) 632-3909

Jim Geringer (R), Governor
State Capitol, Cheyenne, WY 82002-0010
E-mail: governor@state.wy.us

Rita Meyer, Chief of Staff
State Capitol #124, Cheyenne, WY 82002

Eric Curry, Press Secretary
State Capitol #124, Cheyenne, WY 82002

Carolyn A. Teter, Constituent Services
State Capitol #124, Cheyenne, WY 82002

Office of the Secretary of State
http://soswy.state.wy.us
Main phone: (307) 777-7378
Main fax: (307) 777-6217

Joseph B. Meyer (R), Secretary of State
State Capitol Bldg., Cheyenne, WY 82002
E-mail: secofstate@state.wy.us

Office of the Attorney General
http://www.state.wy.us/~ag/index.html
Main phone: (307) 777-7841
Main fax: (307) 777-6869

Gay Woodhouse, Attorney General
123 Capitol Bldg., Cheyenne, WY 82002

Office of the Treasurer
http://www.state.wy.us/~sot/index.html
Main phone: (307) 777-7408
Main fax: (307) 777-5411

Cynthia Lummis (R), State Treasurer
200 W. 24th St., Cheyenne, WY 82002
E-mail: clummi@state.wy.us

Office of the Auditor
http://www.state.wy.us/~auditors/
Main phone: (307) 777-7831
Main fax: (307) 777-6983
Toll free: (800) 833-1065

Max Maxfield, State Auditor
Capitol Bldg., #114, Cheyenne, WY 82002
E-mail: mmaxfi@state.wy.us

State of Wyoming

Capital: Cheyenne, since 1868
Founded: 1868, Wyoming Territory created from Dakota, Idaho, and Utah territories
Statehood: July 10, 1890 (44th state)
Constitution adopted: 1890
Area: 97,105 sq. mi. (ranks 9th)
Population: 480,907 (1998 est.; ranks 51st)
Largest cities: (1998 est.) Cheyenne (53,640); Casper (48,283); Laramie (25,035); Gillette (19,463); Rock Springs (19,408)
Counties: 23, Most populous: (1998 est.) Laramie (78,872); Natrona (63,341); Sweetwater (39,780); Fremont (36,044); Campbell (32,465)
U.S. Congress: Michael B. Enzi (R), Craig Thomas (R); 1 Representative
Nickname(s): Equality State
Motto: Equal rights
Song: "Wyoming"
Bird: Meadowlark
Tree: Cottonwood
Flower: Indian paintbrush
State fair: at Douglas, late Aug.
Former capital(s): None

Agencies

Administration and Information Dept.
http://www.state.wy.us/ai/ai.html
Main phone: (307) 777-7201
Main fax: (307) 777-3633

Frank Galeotos, Director
Emerson Bldg., 2001 Capitol Ave., #104, Cheyenne, WY 82002-0060
E-mail: fgaleo@state.wy.us

Human Resources Division
http://personnel.state.wy.us/
Main phone: (307) 777-6713
Main fax: (307) 777-6562

Higher Educational Institutions

University of Wyoming
http://www.uwyo.edu
Box 3435, Laramie, WY 82071-3435
Main phone: (307) 766-5160

Darald Dykeman, Administrator
Emerson Bldg., 2001 Capitol Ave., Cheyenne, WY 82002
(307) 777-6740

Aeronautics Commission
http://www.state.wy.us/governor/boards/bdlist.html
Main phone: (307) 777-3952
Main fax: (307) 637-7352

Dick Spaeth, Director
5300 Bishop Blvd., Cheyenne, WY 82003-3340
E-mail: dspaet@state.wy.us

Agriculture Dept.
http://wyagric.state.wy.us/
Main phone: (307) 777-7321
Main fax: (307) 777-6598

Ron Micheli, Director
2219 Carey Ave., Cheyenne, WY 82002-0100
E-mail: rmiche@state.wy.us

State Fair
http://wyagric.state.wy.us/Fair/Fronttmp.htm
General e-mail: wystatefair@coffey.com
Main phone: (307) 358-2398
Main fax: (307) 358-6030
Mailing address: P.O. Drawer 10, Douglas, WY 82633

Barney Cosner, Director
400 W. Center, Douglas, WY 82633

Architects and Landscape Architects Board
http://soswy.state.wy.us/director/boards/arch.htm
Main phone: (307) 777-7788
Main fax: (307) 777-3508

Veronica Skoranski, Director
2020 Carey Ave., #201, Cheyenne, WY 82002
E-mail: vskora@state.wy.us

Arts Council
http://spacr.state.wy.us/cr/arts
Main phone: (307) 777-7473
Main fax: (307) 777-5499
TTY: (307) 777-5964

John G. Coe, Executive Director
2320 Capitol Ave., Cheyenne, WY 82002
E-mail: jcoe@missc.state.wy.us

Banking Board
http://www.state.wy.us/governor/boards/bdlist.html
General e-mail: banking@missc.state.wy.us
Main phone: (307) 777-7792
Main fax: (307) 777-3555

Marlene Aitchison, Projects Coordinator
Herschler Bldg., 122 W. 25th St., 3rd Fl., Cheyenne, WY 82002

Business Council
http://www.wyomingbusiness.org/
General e-mail: blinds@missc.state.wy.us
Main phone: (307) 777-2800
Main fax: (307) 777-2837

John Reardon, Chief Executive Officer
214 W. 15th St., Cheyenne, WY 82002
(307) 777-2802
E-mail: jreard@missc.state.wy.us

Certified Public Accountants Board
http://commerce.state.wy.us/B&C/CPA
Main phone: (307) 777-7551
Main fax: (307) 777-3796

Peggy Morgando, Director
2020 Carey Ave., #100, Cheyenne, WY 82001
E-mail: pmorgan@missc.state.wy.us

Child Care Certification Board
http://www.state.wy.us/governor/boards/bdlist.html
Main phone: (307) 777-6595
Main fax: (307) 777-3659

Glennda Lacey, Child Care Licensing Program Manager
2300 Capitol Ave., 3rd Fl., Cheyenne, WY 82002
E-mail: glacey@missc.state.wy.us

Consumer Affairs Division
http://www.state.wy.us/~ag/consumer.htm
Main phone: (307) 777-7874
Main fax: (307) 777-7956
Toll free: (800) 438-5799

Christopher Petrie, Assistant Attorney General
123 State Capitol, Cheyenne, WY 82002
(307) 777-5838
E-mail: cpetri@state.wy.us

Corrections Dept.
http://www.state.wy.us/~corr/corrections.html
Main phone: (307) 777-7208
Main fax: (307) 777-7479

Judith Uphoff, Director
700 W. 21st St., Cheyenne, WY 82002
E-mail: juphof@state.wy.us

Cosmetology Board
http://www.state.wy.us/governor/boards/bdlist.html

Main phone: (307) 777-3534
Main fax: (307) 777-3681

Betty Abernethy, Executive Director
Hansen Bldg., 2515 Warren Ave., #302, Cheyenne,
WY 82002
E-mail: babern@missc.state.wy.us

Education Dept.
http://www.k12.wy.us/
General e-mail: webmaster@www.k12.wy.us
Main phone: (307) 777-7690
Main fax: (307) 777-6234

Judy Catchpole, Superintendent
Hathaway Bldg., 2300 Capitol Ave., 2nd Fl.,
Cheyenne, WY 82002-0050
(307) 777-7675
E-mail: jcatch@educ.state.wy.us

Board of Education
http://www.state.wy.us/governor/boards/
bdlist.html
Main phone: (307) 777-7674
Main fax: (307) 777-6234

Debbie Jourgensen, Secretary
Hathaway Bldg., 2300 Capitol Ave., 2nd Fl.,
Cheyenne, WY 82002-0050

Emergency Management Agency
http://132.133.10.9/
General e-mail: wema@wy-arng.ngb.army.mil
Main phone: (307) 777-4900
Main fax: (307) 635-6017

Ed Boenisch, Director
5500 Bishop Blvd., Cheyenne, WY 82009-3320

Environmental Quality Dept.
http://deq.state.wy.us/
General e-mail: DEQWYO@missc.state.wy.us
Main phone: (307) 777-7937
Main fax: (307) 777-7682

Dennis Hemmer, Director
Herschler Bldg., 122 W. 25th St., 4th Fl., Cheyenne,
WY 82002
(307) 777-7938

Family Services Dept.
http://dfsweb.state.wy.us/
General e-mail: ttasse@state.wy.us
Main phone: (307) 777-7564
Main fax: (307) 777-7747
Toll free: (800) 457-3659

Kari Jo Gray, Director
Hathaway Bldg., 2300 Capitol Ave., 3rd Fl.,
Cheyenne, WY 82002-0490

Frequently Called Numbers

Tourism: (307) 777-7777
Library: (307) 777-7283;
  http://will.state.wy.us/
Board of Education: (307) 777-7674; http://
  www.state.wy.us/governor/boards/bdlist.html
Vital Statistics: (307) 777-7591
Tax/Revenue: (307) 777-7961;
  http://revenue.state.wy.us/
Motor Vehicles: Driver Services:
  (307) 777-4801; http://wydotweb.state.wy.us/
  licenses/DriverServices.html; Vehicle
  Services: (307) 777-4714
State Police/Highway Patrol: (307) 777-4301
Unemployment: (307) 777-3700;
  http://wydoe.state.wy.us/erd/ui/
General Election Information:
  (307) 777-7186; http://soswy.state.wy.us/
  election/election.htm
Consumer Affairs: (307) 777-7874,
  1-800-438-5799; http://www.state.wy.us/~ag/
  consumer.htm
Hazardous Materials: Cheyenne:
  (307) 777-7452, Lander: (307) 332-6924,
  Casper: (307) 473-3450; http://
  deq.state.wy.us/shwd.htm

Medicaid Eligibility Office
http://wdhfs.state.wy.us/WDH/medicaid.htm
Main phone: (307) 777-6079
Main fax: (307) 777-3693
Toll free: (800) 251-1269

Marianne Lee, Administrator
Hathaway Bldg., 2300 Captiol Ave., Cheyenne,
WY 82002

Fire Prevention and Electrical Safety (State Fire Marshal)
http://www.state.wy.us/~fire/default.htm
Main phone: (307) 777-7288
Main fax: (307) 777-2119

Jim Noel, State Fire Marshal and Director
Herschler Bldg., 122 W. 25th St., Cheyenne, WY
82002

Game and Fish Dept.
http://gf.state.wy.us/
Main phone: (307) 777-4600
Main fax: (307) 777-4699

John Baughman, Director
5400 Bishop Blvd., Cheyenne, WY 82006

Geological Survey
http://www.wsgsweb.uwyo.edu/
General e-mail: wsgs@wsgs.uwyo.edu
Main phone: (307) 766-2286
Main fax: (307) 766-2605
Mailing address: P.O. Box 3008, Laramie, WY
82071-3008

Lance Cook, State Geologist
University of Wyoming, Laramie, WY 82071-3008
E-mail: lcook@wsgs.uwyo.edu

Health Dept.
http://wdhfs.state.wy.us/WDH
General e-mail: wdh@missc.state.wy.us
Main phone: (307) 777-7656
Main fax: (307) 777-7439
TTY: (307) 777-5648

Garry L. McKee, Director
117 Hathaway Bldg., Cheyenne, WY 82002

Aging Division
http://wdhfs.state.wy.us/aging/index.html
General e-mail: cnoon@MISSC.state.wy.us
Main phone: (307) 777-7986
Main fax: (307) 777-5340
Toll free: (800) 442-2766

Wayne Milton, Administrator
6101 Yellowstone, #259-B, Cheyenne, WY 82002
(307) 777-6780
E-mail: wmilto@MISSC.state.wy.us

Developmental Disabilities Division
http://ddd.state.wy.us
Main phone: (307) 777-7115
Main fax: (307) 777-6047
Toll free: (800) 510-0280

Robert T. Clabby III, Administrator
117 Hathaway Bldg., 2300 Capitol Ave.,
Cheyenne, WY 82002
E-mail: rclabb@state.wy.us

Higher Education Assistance Authority
http://www.state.wy.us/governor/boards/bdlist.html
Main phone: (307) 382-3159
Main fax: (307) 362-3591

Grant Christensen, Director
1204 Hilltop Dr., #108, Rock Springs, WY 82901
E-mail: dentchild@fiw.net

Historic Preservation Office
http://commerce.state.wy.us/cr/shpo/staff.htm
Main phone: (307) 777-7697
Main fax: (307) 777-6421

Wendy Bredehoft, State Historic Preservation Officer
Barrett Bldg., 3rd Fl., Cheyenne, WY 82002
(307) 777-7637; Fax: (307) 777-5343
E-mail: wbrede@missc.state.wy.us

Juvenile Services Division
Main phone: (307) 777-7564
Main fax: (307) 777-3659

Kari Jo Gray, Director
Hathaway Bldg., 3rd Fl., Cheyenne, WY 82002-0490
Fax: (307) 777-7747

Medicine Board
http://www.state.wy.us/governor/boards/bdlist.html
General e-mail: WYOBOM@aol.com
Main phone: (307) 778-7053
Main fax: (307) 778-2069
Toll free: (800) 438-5784

Carole Shotwell, Director
211 W. 19th St., 2nd Fl., Cheyenne, WY 82002

Mental Health Planning Council
http://www.state.wy.us/governor/boards/bdlist.html
Main phone: (307) 777-6495
Main fax: (307) 777-5580

Carolyn Dennis, Mental Health Program Consultant
6101 Yellowstone Rd., #259-B, Cheyenne, WY 82002
E-mail: cdenni@missc.state.wy.us

Nursing Board
http://www.state.wy.us/governor/boards/bdlist.html
Main phone: (307) 777-6121
Main fax: (307) 777-3519

Cheryl Koski, Director
2020 Carey Ave., #110, Cheyenne, WY 82002
E-mail: ckoski@state.wy.us

Oil and Gas Conservation Commission
http://wogcc.state.wy.us
Main phone: (307) 234-7147
Main fax: (307) 234-5306
Mailing address: P.O. Box 2640, Casper, WY
82602

Don Likwartz, Director
777 W. 1st St., Casper, WY 82601
E-mail: dlikwa@missc.state.wy.us

Parks and Cultural Resources Dept.
http://commerce.state.wy.us/
Main phone: (307) 777-6303
Main fax: (307) 777-6005

John Keck, Director
2301 Central Ave., #450, Cheyenne, WY 82002
E-mail: JKeck@missc.state.wy.us

Cultural Resources Division: Archives Program
http://spacr.state.wy.us/cr/archives
General e-mail: wyarchive@state.wy.us
Main phone: (307) 777-7826
Main fax: (307) 777-7044

Tony Adams, Manager
2301 Central Ave., Cheyenne, WY 82002
E-mail: tadams@state.wy.us

Parks and Historic Sites
http://commerce.state.wy.us/sphs/
Main phone: (307) 777-6323
Main fax: (307) 777-6472

Bill Gentle, Director
Herschler Bldg., 122 W. 25th St., #1E-W, Cheyenne,
WY 82002
(307) 777-6324
E-mail: bgentl@state.wy.us

Parole Board
http://www.state.wy.us/governor/boards/bdlist.html
Main phone: (307) 777-7208
Main fax: (307) 777-7479

Steve Lindly, Liaison
700 W. 21st St., Cheyenne, WY 82002
E-mail: slindl@state.wy.us

Personnel Dept., Human Resources Division
http://personnel.state.wy.us/
General e-mail: stjobs@missc.state.wy.us
Main phone: (307) 777-6713
Main fax: (307) 777-6562

Darald Dykeman, Director
Emerson Bldg., 2001 Capitol Ave., Cheyenne, WY
82002-0060

Pharmacy Board
http://www.state.wy.us/governor/boards/bdlist.html
General e-mail: wypharmbd@wercs.com
Main phone: (307) 234-0294
Main fax: (307) 234-7226

James T. Carder, Director
1720 S. Poplar St., #4, Casper, WY 82601

Professional Engineers and Land Surveyors Board
http://www.wrds.uwyo.edu/wrds/borpe/borpe.html
Main phone: (307) 777-6155
Main fax: (307) 777-3403

Christine Turk, Executive Director
2424 Pioneer Ave., #400, Cheyenne, WY 82002
E-mail: cturk@wyoming.com

Public Service Commission
http://psc.state.wy.us/
Main phone: (307) 777-7427
Main fax: (307) 777-5700

Steve Oxley, Secretary and Chief Counsel
Hansen Bldg., 2515 Warren Ave., #300, Cheyenne,
WY 82002

Real Estate Appraisers Board
http://www.arello.org
Main phone: (307) 777-7141
Main fax: (307) 777-3796

Constance Anderson, Director
2020 Carey Ave., #1000, Cheyenne, WY 82002
E-mail: cander2@missc.state.wy.us

Revenue Dept.
http://revenue.state.wy.us/
General e-mail: dor@missc.state.wy.us
Main phone: (307) 777-7961
Main fax: (307) 777-7722

R. M. Burton, Director
Herschler Bldg., 122 W. 25th St., Cheyenne, WY
82002-0110
(307) 777-5287
E-mail: jburto1@missc.state.wy.us

Liquor Division
http://www.revenue.state.wy.us
Main phone: (307) 777-7120
Main fax: (307) 777-6255

Boards and Licensing

Accountancy, (307) 777-7551,
http://commerce.state.wy.us/B&C/CPA
Architects and Landscape Architects, (307)
777-7788, http://soswy.state.wy.us/director/
boards/arch.htm
Child Care, (307) 777-6595,
http://www.state.wy.us/governor/boards/
bdlist.html
Contractors, (307) 777-2843
Cosmetology, (307) 777-3534,
http://www.state.wy.us/governor/boards/
bdlist.html
Engineers and Land Surveyors,
(307) 777-6155, http://www.wrds.uwyo.edu/
wrds/borpe/borpe.html
Medical Licensing, (307) 778-7053,
http://www.state.wy.us/governor/boards/
bdlist.html
Nursing, (307) 777-6121,
http://www.state.wy.us/governor/boards/
bdlist.html
Pharmacy, (307) 234-0294,
http://www.state.wy.us/governor/boards/
bdlist.html
Real Estate, (307) 777-7141,
http://www.arello.org

Lisa K. Burgess, Administrator
1520 E. 5th St., Cheyenne, WY 82007
(307) 777-6448
E-mail: lburge@state.wy.us

State Lands and Investments Forestry Division
General e-mail: forestry@state.wy.us
Main phone: (307) 777-7586
Main fax: (307) 637-8726

Thomas Ostermann, State Forester
1100 W. 22nd St., Cheyenne, WY 82002
E-mail: toster@state.wy.us

State Library
http://will.state.wy.us/
Main phone: (307) 777-7283
Main fax: (307) 777-6289

Lesley Boughton, State Librarian
Supreme Court and State Library Bldg., 2301 Capitol
Ave., #G-7, Cheyenne, WY 82002
E-mail: lbough@missc.state.wy.us

Transportation Dept.
http://wydotweb.state.wy.us/
Main phone: (307) 777-4484
Main fax: (307) 777-4163

Gene Roccabruna, Director
5300 Bishop Blvd., Cheyenne, WY 82009-3340

Highway Patrol Division
Main phone: (307) 777-4301
Main fax: (307) 777-4282
Mailing address: P.O. Box 1708, Cheyenne,
WY 82009-3340

John Cox, Administrator
5300 Bishop Blvd., Cheyenne, WY 82009-3340
E-mail: jcox2@state.wy.us

Motor Vehicle Services
http://wydotweb.state.wy.us/licenses/
DriverServices.html
Main phone: (307) 777-4714
Main fax: (307) 777-4772
Mailing address: P.O. Box 1708, Cheyenne,
WY 82003-1708

Don Edington, Manager
5300 Bishop Blvd., Cheyenne, WY 82009
E-mail: deding@state.wy.us

Veterans Affairs Commission
http://www.state.wy.us/governor/boards/bdlist.html
General e-mail: wvac@trib.com

Main phone: (307) 265-7372
Main fax: (307) 265-7392
Toll free: (800) 833-5987

R. Stanley Lowe, Director
5905 CY Ave., Casper, WY 82604

Women's Issues Council
http://www.state.wy.us/governor/boards/bdlist.html
Main phone: (307) 332-9402

Amy McClure, Chair
Herschler Bldg., 122 W. 25th St., 2nd Fl., Cheyenne,
WY 82002

Workers' Compensation Medical Commission
http://www.state.wy.us/governor/boards/bdlist.html
Main phone: (307) 777-5422
Main fax: (307) 777-5201
Mailing address: P.O. Box 1207, Cheyenne, WY
82002

Scott Smith, Director
2020 Carey Ave., Cheyenne, WY 82002
E-mail: ssmith@state.wy.us

Wyoming Legislature
State Capitol
Cheyenne, WY 82002
General information: (307) 777-7881
Fax: (307) 777-5466
TTY: (307) 777-7860
Bill status: (800) 342-9570
http://legisweb.state.wy.us

Senate
General information: (307) 777-7711

James R. (Jim) Twiford (R), President
State Capitol, Cheyenne, WY 82002
(307) 777-7706
E-mail: jimjenne@aol.com
http://legisweb.state.wy.us/members/99/s2.htm

April Brimmer Kunz (R), Vice President
State Capitol, Cheyenne, WY 82002
(307) 777-5907
http://legisweb.state.wy.us/members/99/s4.htm

Henry H. R. (Hank) Coe (R), Majority Leader
State Capitol, Cheyenne, WY 82002
(307) 777-7773
http://legisweb.state.wy.us/members/99/s18.htm

Mark O. Harris (D), Minority Leader
State Capitol, Cheyenne, WY 82002
(307) 777-7212
http://legisweb.state.wy.us/members/99/s14.htm

Rich Cathcart (D), Minority Whip
State Capitol, Cheyenne, WY 82002
(307) 777-7711
http://legisweb.state.wy.us/members/99/s6.htm

Liv C. Hanes, Chief Clerk
State Capitol, Cheyenne, WY 82002
(307) 777-7733; *Fax:* (307) 777-5466

House
General information: (307) 777-7852

Eli D. Bebout (R), Speaker of the House
State Capitol, Cheyenne, WY 82002
(307) 777-7617
http://legisweb.state.wy.us/members/99/h41.htm

Harry B. Tipton (R), Speaker Pro Tempore
State Capitol, Cheyenne, WY 82002
(307) 777-5901
http://legisweb.state.wy.us/members/99/h33.htm

Rick Tempest (R), Majority Leader
State Capitol, Cheyenne, WY 82002
(307) 777-7223
http://legisweb.state.wy.us/members/99/h37.htm

Louise Ryckman (D), Minority Leader
State Capitol, Cheyenne, WY 82002
(307) 777-6384
E-mail: lryckman@house.wyoming.com
http://legisweb.state.wy.us/members/99/h60.htm

Mac McGraw (D), Minority Whip
State Capitol, Cheyenne, WY 82002
(307) 777-7754
E-mail: macmcgraw@aol.com
http://legisweb.state.wy.us/members/99/h41.htm

Marvin Helart, Chief Clerk
State Capitol, Cheyenne, WY 82002
(307) 777-7330; *Fax:* (307) 777-5466

Laws

Sales tax: 6%
Income tax: None
State minimum wage: $1.60 (Federal is $5.15)
Marriage age: 18
First-cousin marriage: Prohibited
Drinking age: 21
State control of liquor sales: Yes
Blood alcohol for DWI: 0.10%
Driving age: 16
Speed limit: 75 mph
Permit to buy handguns: No
Minimum age to possess handguns: None
Minimum age to possess rifles, shotguns:
  None
State lottery: No
Casinos: No
Pari-mutuel betting: Horse racing
Death penalty: Yes
3 strikes minimum sentence: 10 yrs. (violent
  felony after 2 prior felonies)
Hate crimes law: No
Gay employment non-discrimination: No
Official language(s): None
Term limits: Governor (8 yrs.); state legislators
  (12 yrs.)

*State laws are complex and subject to
change; this information is not intended as
legal advice. For an explanation of this
information, see p. x.*

Wyoming Judiciary
Supreme Court Bldg.
2301 Capitol Ave.
Cheyenne, WY 82002
http://www.courts.state.wy.us

Supreme Court
http://www.courts.state.wy.us

Judy Pacheco, Clerk
Supreme Court Bldg., 2301 Capitol Ave., Cheyenne,
  WY 82002
(307) 777-7316; *Fax:* (307) 777-6129
E-mail: jpacheco@courts.state.wy.us

Justices
Composition: 5 justices
Selection Method: appointed by governor;
  retention ballot after first year
Length of term: 8 years

Larry L. Lehman, Chief Justice, (307) 777-7557
Michael Golden, Justice, (307) 777-7421
William U. Hill, Justice, (307) 777-7571
Richard J. Macy, Justice, (307) 777-7422
Richard V. Thomas, Justice, (307) 777-7573

Court Administrator

Main phone: (307) 777-7480
Main fax: (307) 777-3447

Holly Hansen, Court Administrator
Supreme Court Bldg., 2301 Capitol Ave., Cheyenne,
WY 82002
E-mail: hhansen@courts.state.wy.us

State Law Library

http://www.courts.state.wy.us/lawlib.htm
Main phone: (307) 777-7509
Main fax: (307) 777-7240

Kathy Carlson, Librarian
Supreme Court Bldg., 2301 Capitol Ave., Cheyenne,
WY 82002
E-mail: kcarlson@state.wy.us

Legislative and Political Party Information Resources

Senate home page: http://legisweb.state.wy.us/members/99/sen99.htm
House home page: http://legisweb.state.wy.us/members/99/rep99.htm
Committees: http://legisweb.state.wy.us/sessions/activite.htm
Legislative information: http://legisweb.state.wy.us/leginfo/leginfo.htm
Current session information: http://legisweb.state.wy.us/sessions/legsess..htm
Budget: http://legisweb.state.wy.us/budget/budget.htm
Wyoming Democratic Party: http://members.aol.com/wyodem/dems.html
    254 N. Center St., #101, P.O. Box 1963, Casper, WY 82602; *Phone:* (307) 473-1457;
    Fax: (307) 473-1459; *E-mail:* wyodem@aol.com
Wyoming Republican Party: http://www.wygop.org
    400 E. 1st St., #314, P.O. Box 241, Casper, WY 82602; *Phone:* (307) 234-9166;
    Fax: (307) 473-8640; *E-mail:* wygop@coffey.com

Functional Index

Functional Index

Accounting

AL	Public Accountancy Board, 7	
AK	Public Accountancy Board, 17	
AZ	Accountancy Board, 21	
AR	Public Accountancy Board, 35	
CA	Accountancy Board, 39	
CO	Accountancy Board, 48	
CT	Accountancy Board, 57	
HI	Accounting and General Services Dept., 96	
ID	Accountancy Board, 105	
IN	Accounts Board, 123	
IA	Accountancy Board, 132	
KS	Accountancy Board, 141	
KY	Accountancy Board, 149	
ME	Accounts and Control Bureau, 167	
MD	Accountancy Board, 175	
MA	Public Accountancy Board, 191	
MN	Accountancy Board, 206	
MS	Public Accountancy Board, 222	
MO	Accountancy Board, 227	
MT	Public Accountants Board, 241	
NE	Accountancy Board, 247	
NV	Accountancy Board, 258	
NH	Accountancy Board, 265	
NH	Accounting Services Division, 266	
NJ	Accountancy Board, 276	
NY	Accountancy Board, 293	
ND	Accountancy Board, 313	
OH	Accountancy Board, 323	
OK	Accountancy Board, 334	
OR	Accountancy Board, 345	
PA	Accountancy Board, 355	
RI	Accounts and Control, 367	
SC	Accountancy Board, 375	
SD	Accountancy Board, 386	
TN	Accountancy Board, 396	
TX	Accountancy Board, 405	
VA	Accountancy Board, 434	
VA	Accounts Dept., 436	

WA Accountancy Board, 443
WY Certified Public Accountants Board, 472

Adjudant General/Military

AL Military Dept., 2
AK Military and Veteran's Affairs Dept., 11
AZ Army National Guard, Adjudant General's Office, 21
AR Military Dept., 30
CA Military Dept., 39
CO Military Affairs Dept., 47
CT Military Dept., 57
DE National Guard, 66
FL Military Affairs Dept., 80
GA Defense Dept., 89
HI Defense Dept., 98
ID Military Division, 105
IL Military Affairs Dept., 114
IN Office of the Adjutant General, 123
IA Army National Guard, 132
KS Adjutant General Dept., 140
KY Adjutant General Office, 149
LA Military Dept., 158
ME Defense, Veterans, and Emergency Management Dept., 166
MD Military Dept., 175
MA Military Division, 192
MI Military and Veterans Affairs Dept., 197
MN Military Affairs Dept., 206
MS Army and Air National Guard, 217
MO Adjutant General's Office (National Guard), 227
MT Military Affairs Dept., 237
NE Office of the Adjutant General, 247
NV Military Office, 258
NH Office of the Adjutant General, 265
NJ Military and Veterans Affairs Dept., 275
NM Military Affairs Dept., 285
NY Division of Military and Naval Affairs, 293
NC National Guard Division, 303
ND Office of the Adjutant General, 313
OH Office of the Adjutant General, 323
OK Military Dept., 334
OR Military Dept., 344
PA Military Affairs Dept., 355
RI Office of the Adjutant General, 367
SC Office of the Adjutant General, 375

Administration

Aeronautics

Aging

Agriculture

ND Agricultural Products Utilization Commission, 313
ND Agriculture Dept., 313
ND Milk Marketing Board, 317
ND Wheat Commission, 320
OH Agriculture Dept., 323
OK Agriculture Dept., 334
OK Wheat Commission, 342
OR Agriculture Dept., 345
PA Agriculture Dept., 355
PA Milk Marketing Board, 360
SC Agriculture Dept., 375
SD Agriculture Dept., 386
TN Agriculture Dept., 396
TX Agriculture Dept., 405
UT Agriculture and Food Dept., 417
VT Agriculture, Food, and Markets Dept., 426
VA Agriculture and Consumer Services Dept., 434
WA Agriculture Dept., 443
WA Apple Commission, 443
WV Agriculture Dept., 455
WI Agriculture, Trade, and Consumer Protection Dept.,
    463
WY Agriculture Dept., 472

Alcoholic Beverage Control

AL Alcoholic Beverage Control Board, 2
AK Alcoholic Beverage Control Board, 17
AZ Liquor Licences and Control Dept., 24
AR Alcoholic Beverage Control Administration, 32
CA Alcoholic Beverage Control, 39
CO Liquor Enforcement Division, 51
CT Liquor Control Division, 58
DE Alcoholic Beverage Control Division, 70
DC Alcohol and Beverage Control Board, 74
FL Alcoholic Beverages and Tobacco Divison, 80
GA Alcohol and Tobacco Tax Division, 93
ID Police Services Division: Alcohol Beverage Control
    Bureau, 109
IL Liquor Control Commission, 117
IN Alcohol Beverage Commission, 123
IA Alcoholic Beverages Division, 132
KS Alcoholic Beverage Control Division, 144
KY Alcoholic Beverage Control, 153
LA Alcohol and Tobacco Control Office, 163
ME Alcoholic Beverages and Lottery Bureau, 167
MD Alcohol and Tobacco Tax Division, 175
MA Alcoholic Beverage Control Commission, 188
MI Liquor Control Commission, 199
MN Alcohol and Gambling Enforcement Division: Alcohol
    Enforcement Section, 212
MS Alcoholic Beverage Control, 223
MO Liquor Control Division, 233
NE Liquor Control Commission, 252
NH Liquor Commission, 269
NJ Alcoholic Beverage Control, 276
NY Alcoholic Beverage Control Division, 293
NC Alcohol Law Enforcement Division, 304

OK Alcoholic Beverage Laws Enforcement Commission,
    334
OR Liquor Control Commission, 349
PA Liquor Control Board, 360
TN Alcoholic Beverage Commission, 396
TX Alcoholic Beverage Commission, 405
UT Alcoholic Beverage Control Dept., 417
VT Liquor Control Dept., 429
VA Alcohol Safety Action Program (VASAP)
    Commission, 434
VA Alcoholic Beverage Control, 434
WA Liquor Control Board, 447
WV Alcohol Beverage Control Commission, 455
WY Liquor Division, 475

Alcoholism

DE Alcoholism, Substance Abuse, and Mental Health
    Division, 68
NE Alcohol and Drug Abuse Prevention Center, 248
NY Alcoholism and Substance Abuse Services Office, 293
OH Alcohol and Drug Addiction Services Dept., 323
SC Alcohol and Other Drug Abuse Services Dept., 375
TX Alcohol and Drug Abuse Commission, 405

Animals

MN Animal Health Board, 206
ND Animal Health Board, 313
SD Animal Industry Board, 386
TX Animal Health Commission, 405

Archaeology and Anthropology

CO Archaeology and Historic Preservation, 48
SC Archaeology and Anthropology Institute, 375

Architects

AL Architects Registration Board, 2
AK Architects, Engineers, and Land Surveyors
    Occupational Licensing, 12
AR Architects State Board, 30
CA Architectural Examiners Board, 39
CO Architects Board of Examiners, 48
GA Architects Board, 88
ID Architects Licensing Board, 105
IA Architectural Examiners Board, 132
KY Architects Board, 149
LA Architectural Examiners Board, 158
MD Architects Board, 175
MA Architects Board, 187
MN Architects, Engineers, and Land Surveyors Board, 206
MS Architecture Board, 217
MO Architects, Engineers, and Land Surveyors Board, 227
MT Architects Board, 238
NE Engineers and Architects Board of Examiners, 249
NV Architecture and Design Board, 258
NH Architects, Engineers, and Land Surveyors Board, 266
NM Architects Board, 285

Attorney General

AL   Office of the Attorney General, 1
AK   Office of the Attorney General, 11
AZ   Office of the Attorney General, 20
AR   Office of the Attorney General, 29
CA   Office of the Attorney General, 38
CO   Office of the Attorney General, 47
CT   Office of the Attorney General, 57
DE   Office of the Attorney General, 65
FL   Office of the Attorney General, 79
GA   Office of the Attorney General, 87
HI   Office of the Attorney General, 96
ID   Office of the Attorney General, 104
IL   Office of the Attorney General, 113
IN   Office of the Attorney General, 122
IA   Office of the Attorney General, 131
KS   Office of the Attorney General, 140
KY   Office of the Attorney General, 148
LA   Office of the Attorney General, 157
ME   Office of the Attorney General, 166
MD   Office of the Attorney General, 174
MA   Office of the Attorney General, 186
MI   Office of the Attorney General, 196
MN   Office of the Attorney General, 205
MS   Office of the Attorney General, 216
MO   Office of the Attorney General, 226
MT   Office of the Attorney General, 237
NE   Office of the Attorney General, 246
NV   Office of the Attorney General, 257
NH   Office of the Attorney General, 265
NJ   Attorney General's Office (Law and Public Safety Dept.), 275
NM   Office of the Attorney General, 284
NY   Attorney General's Office, 292
NC   Office of the Attorney General, 302
ND   Office of the Attorney General, 312
OH   Office of the Attorney General, 322
OK   Office of the Attorney General, 333
OR   Attorney General's Office, 344
PA   Office of the Attorney General, 354
RI   Office of the Attorney General, 366
SC   Office of the Attorney General, 374
SD   Office of the Attorney General, 385
TN   Office of the Attorney General, 395
TX   Office of the Attorney General, 404
UT   Office of the Attorney General, 416
VT   Office of the Attorney General, 425
VA   Office of the Attorney General, 433
WA   Office of the Attorney General, 442
WV   Office of the Attorney General, 454
WI   Office of the Attorney General, 462
WY   Office of the Attorney General, 471

Auditor

AL   Office of the State Auditor, 2
AZ   Office of the Auditor General, 20
AR   Office of the Auditor of State, 30
CT   Auditors of Public Accounts Office, 57
DE   Auditor of Accounts Office, 66
DC   Auditor, 74
FL   Office of the Auditor General, 79
GA   Office of the State Auditor, 87
HI   Audit Division, 97
IL   Office of the Auditor General, 113
IN   Office of the State Auditor, 123
IA   Office of the State Auditor, 132
KY   Auditor of Public Accounts, 149
LA   Office of the State Auditor, 158
ME   Office of the State Auditor, 166
MA   Office of the State Auditor, 187
MI   Office of the Auditor General, 197
MN   Office of the State Auditor, 206
MS   Office of the State Auditor, 217
MO   Office of the State Auditor, 227
MT   Office of the State Auditor, 237
NE   Office of the Auditor of Public Accounts, 247
NM   Office of the State Auditor, 285
NC   Office of the State Auditor, 303
ND   Office of the State Auditor, 313
OH   Office of the State Auditor, 322
OK   Office of the State Auditor and Inspector, 334
PA   Office of the Auditor General, 354
RI   Office of the Auditor General, 367
SC   Office of the State Auditor, 375
SD   Office of the State Auditor, 386
TX   Office of the State Auditor, 405
UT   Office of the State Auditor, 416
VT   Auditor of Accounts Office, 425
VA   Auditor of Public Accounts, 434
WA   Office of the State Auditor, 443
WV   Office of the Auditor, 454
WI   Legislative Audit Bureau, 466
WY   Office of the Auditor, 471

Banking

AL   Banking Dept., 2
AK   Banking, Securities, and Corporations Division, 13
AZ   Banking Dept., 21
AR   Bank Dept., 30
CA   Financial Institutions Dept., 41
CO   Banking Division, 48
CT   Banking Dept., 57
DE   Bank Commissioner, 66
DC   Banking and Financial Institutions Office, 74
FL   Banking and Finance Dept., 80
GA   Banking and Finance Dept., 88
HI   Financial Institutions Division, 97
ID   Financial Institutions Bureau, 107
IL   Banks and Real Estate Office, 114
IL   Financial Institutions Dept., 116
IN   Financial Institutions Dept., 125
IA   Banking Division, 132
KS   Bank Commissioner's Office, 141
KY   Financial Institutions Dept., 151
LA   Financial Institutions Office, 159

Behavioral Health

Budget

Buildings

Business

Child Care/Day Care

Children and Youth Services

OR Youth Authority, 352
PA Children, Youth, and Families Division, 361
RI Children, Youth, and Families Dept., 367
TN Children and Youth Commission, 396
TN Children's Services Dept., 396
TX Youth Commission, 413
WY Juvenile Services Division, 474

Civil Rights

CO Civil Rights Commission, 48
FL Civil Rights Division, 80
IN Civil Rights Commission, 123
LA Civil Rights, 163
MA Civil Rights and Civil Liberties Division, 188
MI Civil Rights Dept., 197
NE Equal Opportunity Commission, 249
NJ Civil Rights Division, 276
OH Civil Rights Commission, 324
PA Civil Rights Enforcement Section, 355
VT Civil Rights Unit, 426
WV Civil Rights Division, 455
WI Management and Technology Division: Affirmative
    Action/Civil Rights, 465

Civil Service

LA Civil Service Dept., 159
NY Civil Service Dept., 294
PA Civil Service Commission, 355

Commerce

AZ Commerce Dept., 22
CA Trade and Commerce Agency, 44
HI Commerce and Consumer Affairs Dept., 97
ID Commerce Dept., 105
IL Commerce and Community Affairs Dept., 115
IN Commerce Dept., 123
IA Commerce Dept., 132
KS Commerce and Housing Dept., 141
MN Commerce Dept., 207
MS Agriculture and Commerce Dept., 217
MT Commerce Dept., 239
NJ Commerce and Economic Development Dept., 276
NC Commerce Dept., 303
NC Industrial Commission, 304
NE Housing and Urban Development Dept., 251
OH Commerce Dept., 324
OK Commerce Dept., 335
SC Commerce Dept., 376
SD Commerce and Regulation Dept., 386
TN Commerce and Insurance Dept., 397
TN Consumer Affairs Division, 397
UT Commerce Dept., 417
VT Commerce and Community Development Agency, 426
VA Commerce and Trade Secretariat, 435
WV Commerce Bureau, 456
WI Commerce Dept., 463

Community Affairs

GA Community Affairs Dept., 88
IL Commerce and Community Affairs Dept., 115
NJ Community Affairs Dept., 277
NY Housing and Community Renewal Division, 297
TX Housing and Community Affairs Dept., 409

Community Development

AK Community and Economic Development Dept., 13
CA Housing and Community Development, 39
CT Economic and Community Development Dept., 58
DC Committee to Promote Washington, 76
HI Housing and Community Development Corporation,
    99
ME Economic and Community Development Dept., 168
MD Housing and Community Development Dept., 179
MA Housing and Community Development Dept., 190
MS Community and Economic Development Dept., 217
MS Economic and Community Development Dept., 218
PA Community and Economic Development Dept., 356
TN Economic and Community Development Dept., 398
UT Community and Economic Development Dept., 417
VT Commerce and Community Development Agency, 426
VA Housing and Community Development Dept., 437
WA Community, Trade, and Economic Development Dept.,
    444

Comptroller

CT Office of the Comptroller, 57
IL Office of the Comptroller, 114
MD Office of the Comptroller of the Treasury, 175
MA Office of the State Comptroller, 187
NE Office of the Comptroller of Currency, 247
NY Office of the State Comptroller, 292
OK State Comptroller, 337
SC Office of the Comptroller General, 375
TN Office of the Comptroller, 395
TX Comptroller of Public Accounts Office, 404

Conservation

AL Conservation and Natural Resources Dept., 3
CA Conservation Dept., 40
IL Land Management Office: State Parks, 118
IN Lands and Cultural Resources Bureau: Forestry
    Division, 126
IN Lands and Cultural Resources Bureau: State Parks and
    Reservoirs Division, 127
KS Conservation Commission, 141
ME Conservation Dept., 167
ME Land and Water Quality Bureau: Water Resource
    Regulation Division, 169
MO Conservation Dept., 228
MT Natural Resources and Conservation Dept., 240
NE Conservation and Survey Division, 247
NV Conservation and Natural Resources Dept., 258
OK Conservation Commission, 335

Cosmetology

Court Administration

Criminal Justice

Cultural Affairs

Developmental Disabilities

NM	Commission for the Blind, 285
NY	Mental Retardation and Developmental Disabilities Office, 297
NY	Mentally Disabled Commission, 297
NC	Developmental Disabilities Council, 306
NC	Governor Morehead School, 306
NC	Mental Health, Developmental Disabilities, and Substance Abuse Services, 307
ND	Disability Services Division, 315
ND	Protection and Advocacy Project, 318
ND	School for the Blind, 318
ND	School for the Deaf, 318
OH	Mental Retardation and Developmental Disabilities Dept., 326
OH	School for the Blind, 329
OH	School for the Deaf, 329
OK	Developmental Disabilities Services Division, 338
OK	School for the Blind, 341
OK	School for the Deaf, 341
OR	Commission for the Blind, 345
OR	Developmental Disabilites Services Office, 348
OR	School for the Blind, 346
OR	School for the Deaf, 346
PA	Mental Retardation Office, 362
PA	Social Programs Office: Community Services Program for Persons with Physical Disabilities, 362
RI	Developmental Disabilities Council, 368
RI	Mental Health, Retardation, and Hospitals Dept., 370
SC	Commission for the Blind, 377
SC	Disabilities and Special Needs Dept., 377
SC	School for the Deaf and Blind, 382
SD	Developmental Disabilities Division, 389
SD	School for the Deaf, 391
TN	Mental Health and Mental Retardation Dept., 400
TX	Commission for the Blind, 406
TX	Commission for the Deaf and Hard of Hearing, 407
TX	Mental Health and Mental Retardation Dept., 410
TX	Planning Council for Developmental Disabilities, 411
TX	School for the Blind and Visually Impaired, 412
TX	School for the Deaf, 412
UT	People with Disabilities Council, 420
UT	Schools for the Deaf and Blind, 418
VT	Developmental and Mental Health Services Dept., 426
VA	Mental Health, Mental Retardation, and Substance Abuse Dept., 438
VA	People with Disabilities Board, 438
WA	Health and Rehabilitative Services Administration: Developmental Disabilities Division, 449
WA	School for the Deaf, 449
WA	Services for the Blind Dept., 449
WA	State School for the Blind, 450
WI	Care and Treatment Facilities Division: Developmental Disabilities Services Program, 465
WI	School for the Deaf and Educational Services Center for the Deaf and Hard of Hearing, 467
WI	School for the Visually Handicapped and Educational Services Center for the Visually Impaired, 467
WY	Developmental Disabilities Division, 474

Economic Development

AL	Development Office, 4
AK	Banking, Securities, and Corporations Division, 13
AK	Community and Economic Development Dept., 13
AR	Development Finance Authority, 31
AR	Economic Development Commission, 31
CO	Economic Development, 49
CT	Business and Housing Development, 58
CT	Economic and Community Development Dept., 58
DE	Economic Development Office, 67
HI	Business, Economic Development, and Tourism Dept., 97
IL	Development Finance Authority, 115
IN	Development Finance Authority, 124
IA	Economic Development Dept., 133
KS	Development Finance Authority, 142
KY	Economic Development Cabinet, 149
LA	Economic Development Dept., 159
ME	Economic and Community Development Dept., 168
MD	Business and Economic Development Dept., 177
MA	Economic Development Dept., 189
MA	MassDevelopment, 191
MN	Economic Security Dept., 208
MN	Trade and Economic Development Dept., 213
MS	Community and Economic Development Dept., 217
MS	Economic and Community Development Dept., 218
MO	Economic Development Dept., 229
NE	Economic Development Dept., 248
NV	Economic Development Commission, 259
NH	Economic Development Division, 271
NH	Resources and Economic Development Dept., 271
NJ	Commerce and Economic Development Dept., 276
NJ	Economic Development Authority, 278
NM	Economic Development Dept., 286
NY	Empire State Development Corporation, 295
ND	Economic Development and Finance Dept., 314
ND	Job Service, 316
ND	Small Business Development Center, 319
OH	Development Dept., 325
OH	Rural Development Partnership, 328
OK	Development Finance Authority, 336
OR	Economic Development Dept., 346
PA	Community and Economic Development Dept., 356
RI	Economic Development Corporation, 368
SC	Jobs-Economic Development Authority, 379
SD	Economic Development Office, 388
TN	Economic and Community Development Dept., 398
TX	Economic Development Dept., 407
TX	Incentive and Productivity Commission, 409
UT	Community and Economic Development Dept., 417
VT	Economic Development Authority, 427
WA	Community, Trade, and Economic Development Dept., 444
WV	Development Office, 456
WI	Housing and Economic Development Authority, 465

Education

Elections

Environmental Affairs

Ethics

Finance

Fire Safety

VT   Fire Prevention Division, 428
WA   State Fire Marshal/Fire Protection Bureau, 450
WV   Fire Marshal, 458
WY   Fire Prevention and Electrical Safety (State Fire
     Marshal), 473

Food

CA   Food and Agriculture Dept., 41
ME   Agriculture, Food, and Rural Resources Dept., 167
MD   Food Center Authority, 178
MA   Food and Agriculture Dept., 190
NH   Agriculture, Markets, and Food Dept., 266
UT   Agriculture and Food Dept., 417
VT   Agriculture, Food, and Markets Dept., 426

Forestry

AL   Forestry Commission, 5
AK   Forestry Division, 16
AZ   Forestry Management Division, 24
AR   Forestry Commission, 32
CA   Forestry and Fire Protection Dept., 41
CO   Forest Service, 50
DE   Forestry Administration, 66
FL   Forestry Division, 80
GA   Forestry Commission, 89
HI   Forestry and Wildlife Division, 100
ID   Forest Products Commission, 107
ID   Forestry and Fire, 107
IL   Resource Conservation Office: Forest Resources
     Division, 118
IN   Lands and Cultural Resources Bureau: Forestry
     Division, 126
IA   Forests and Forestry Division, 135
KS   Forest Service, 142
KY   Forestry Division, 152
LA   Agriculture and Forestry Dept., 158
ME   Forest Service, 168
MD   Forest Service Division, 180
MD   State Parks and Forest Service, 181
MA   Forests and Parks Division, 189
MI   Resource Management Bureau: Forest Management
     Division, 201
MI   Resource Management Bureau: Forest Management
     Division, 201
MN   Forestry Division, 211
MS   Forestry Commission, 220
MO   Forestry Division, 228
MT   Forestry Division, 241
NE   Forest Service, 250
NV   Forestry Division, 258
NH   Forests and Land Division, 271
NJ   Forest Service, 278
NJ   Natural and Historic Resources: Parks and Forestry
     Division, 278
NM   Forestry Division, 286
NY   Land and Forests Division, 296
NC   Forest Resources Division, 305

ND   Forest Service, 314
OH   Forestry Division, 327
OK   Forestry Services, 334
OR   Forestry Dept., 347
PA   Forestry Bureau, 357
RI   Natural Resources Bureau: Forest Environment Office,
     369
SC   Forestry Commission, 378
SD   Resource Conservation and Forestry, 386
TN   Forestry Division, 396
TX   Forest Service, 408
UT   Forestry, Fire, and State Lands Division, 421
VT   Forests, Parks, and Recreation Dept., 429
VA   Forestry Dept., 437
WV   Forestry Division, 456
WV   Natural Resources Division: State Parks and Forests,
     456
WI   Land Division: Forestry Division, 466
WY   Forestry Division, 476

Gaming/Gambling

LA   Racing Commission, 159
MN   Gambling Control Board, 209
MN   Racing Commission, 213
MS   Gaming Commission, 220
MO   Gaming Commission, 230
NE   Racing Commission, 253
NV   Gaming Commission, 259
NV   Gaming Control Board, 259
NH   Pari-Mutuel Commission, 270
NY   Racing and Wagering Board, 299
OH   Racing Commission, 328
OR   Racing Commission, 350
SD   Gaming Commission, 389
TX   Racing Commission, 412
WA   Gambling Commission, 445
WA   Horse Racing Commission, 446
WI   Gaming Division, 464

General Services

CA   General Services Dept., 42
HI   Accounting and General Services Dept., 96
MD   General Services Dept., 179
NM   General Services Dept., 287
NY   General Services Office, 296
PA   General Services Dept., 358
TN   General Services Dept., 398
TX   General Services Commission, 408

Geology

AL   Geological Survey of Alabama, 5
AK   Geological and Geophysical Surveys Division, 16
AZ   Geological Survey, 23
AR   Geology Commission, 32
CO   Geological Survey, 50
DE   Geological Survey, 68
GA   Geological Survey, 91

Governor

Health

History/Historic Preservation

AL Archives and History Dept., 2
AL Historical Commission, 5
AK Parks and Outdoor Recreation Division: Historical
       Commission, 16
AZ Historical Society, 23
AZ History and Archives Division, 24
AR Heritage Dept., 33
CA Historic Preservation Office, 42
CO Archaeology and Historic Preservation, 48
CT Historical Commission, 60
DE Historic Preservation Office, 68
FL Historical Resources Division, 82
GA Archives and History Dept., 88
GA Historic Preservation Division, 91
GA Parks, Recreation, and Historic Sites Division, 92
HI Historic Preservation Division, 100
ID State Historical Society, 106
IL Historic Preservation Agency, 117
IN Historical Bureau, 125
IA Historical Society, 134
IA Parks, Recreation, and Preservation Division, 135
KS Historical Society, 143
KY Kentucky Heritage Council, 150
LA Cultural Development Office: Historic Preservation
       Division, 159
ME Historic Preservation Commission, 169
MD Historical and Cultural Programs Division, 179
MA Historical Commission, 190
MN Historical Society, 209
MS Archives and History Dept., 217
MS Historic Preservation Office, 217
MO Historic Preservation, 231
MT Historical Society, 240
NE Historical Society, 251
NV Historic Preservation Office, 261
NH Historical Resources Division, 267
NJ Historical Commission, 279
NJ Natural and Historic Resources, 278
NM Historic Preservation Division, 286
NY Parks, Recreation, and Historic Preservation Office,
       298
ND Historical Society, 315
ND State Archives and Historical Research Library, 315
OH Historical Society, 326
OK Historical Society, 337
OR Historical Society, 348
PA Archives and History Bureau, 359
PA Historical and Museum Commission, 359
RI Historical Preservation and Heritage Commission, 370
SC Archives and History Dept., 375
SC Historical Society, 378
SD Historical Society/History Office, 388
TN Historical Commission, 398
TX Historical Commission, 408
UT Historical Society, 419
VT Historical Society, 427

VA Historic Resources Dept., 437
WA Historical Society, 446
WV Archives and History Commission, 455
WI Historical Society, 465
WY Historic Preservation Office, 474
WY Parks and Historic Sites, 475

Housing

AL Housing Finance Authority, 5
AK Housing Finance Corporation, 17
CA Business, Transportation, and Housing Agency, 39
CA Housing and Community Development, 39
CA Housing Finance Agency, 39
CO Housing and Finance Authority, 50
CT Business and Housing Development, 58
DE Housing Authority, 68
DC Housing and Community Development Dept., 77
DC Housing Authority, 76
DC Housing Finance Authority, 77
GA Housing Finance Division, 88
HI Housing and Community Development Corporation,
       99
IL Housing Development Authority, 117
IN Housing Finance Authority, 126
KS Commerce and Housing Dept., 141
KY Housing Corporation, 151
LA Housing Finance Agency, 161
ME Housing Authority, 169
MD Housing and Community Development Dept., 179
MA Housing and Community Development Dept., 190
MA Housing Finance Agency, 190
MI Housing Development Authority, 199
MN Housing Finance Agency, 210
MS Home Corporation, 220
MO Housing Development Commission, 229
MT Housing Division, 16
NE Housing and Urban Development Dept., 251
NH Housing Finance Authority, 269
NJ Housing and Mortgage Finance Agency, 279
NM Mortgage Finance Authority, 288
NY Housing and Community Renewal Division, 297
NC Housing Finance Agency, 307
ND Housing Finance Agency, 315
OK Housing Finance Agency, 338
OR Housing and Community Services Dept., 348
PA Housing Finance Agency, 359
RI Housing and Mortgage Finance Corporation, 370
SC Housing and Finance Development Authority, 378
SD Housing Development Authority, 389
TN Housing Development Agency, 399
TX Housing and Community Affairs Dept., 409
UT Housing Finance Agency, 419
VT Housing Finance Agency, 427
VA Housing and Community Development Dept., 437
WA Housing Finance Commission, 446
WI Housing and Economic Development Authority, 465

Human Resources

AL Human Resources Dept., 5
AZ Human Resources Division, 21
CA Human Resources Office, 42
CO Human Resource Services, 50
CT Human Resources, 57
GA Human Resources Dept., 89
HI Human Resources and Development Dept., 99
ID Human Resources Division, 108
IN Human Resource Investment Council, 126
KS Human Resources Dept., 143
ME Human Resources Bureau, 167
MD Human Resources Dept., 180
MA Human Resources Division, 187
NV Human Resources Dept., 259
NC Human Resources Management, 303
OH Human Resources Division, 323
OR Human Resources Dept., 348
OR Human Resources Services Division, 345
RI Human Resources Division, 367
RI Human Resources Division: Personnel Administration Office, 367
SC Human Resources Office, 376
UT Human Resources Dept., 419
VA Health and Human Resources Secretariat, 437
WV Health and Human Resources Dept., 458
WY Human Resources Division, 471
WY Human Resources Division, 475

Human Rights

AK Human Rights Commission, 15
CT Human Rights and Opportunities Commission, 60
DC Human Rights and Local Business Development Dept., 77
DC Human Rights Commission, 76
ID Human Rights Commission, 108
IL Human Rights Dept., 117
IA Human Rights Dept., 134
KS Human Rights Commission, 143
KY Human Rights Commission, 151
ME Human Rights Commission, 169
MN Human Rights Dept., 210
MO Human Rights Commission, 231
NH Human Rights Commission, 269
NM Human Rights Division, 288
NY Human Rights Division, 297
OK Human Rights Commission, 338
RI Human Rights Commission, 370
SD Human Rights Division, 387
TN Human Rights Commission, 399
TX Human Rights Commission, 409
VA Human Rights Council, 437
WA Human Rights Commission, 446
WV Human Rights Commission, 459

Human Services

AR Aging and Adult Services Division, 33
AR Developmental Disabilities Services Division, 33
AR Human Services Dept., 33
CO Aging Commission, 50
CO Human Services Dept., 50
DC Human Services Dept., 75
GA Aging Division, 90
HI Human Services Dept., 99
IL Human Services Dept., 117
IA Human Services Dept., 134
ME Elder and Adult Services Bureau, 169
ME Human Services Dept., 169
MA Health and Human Services Executive Office, 190
MI Aging Services Division, 197
MN Aging Initiative, 210
MN Human Services Dept., 210
MS Aging and Adult Services Division, 220
MS Human Services Dept., 220
MT Disability Services Division, 242
MT Public Health and Human Services Dept., 242
NE Aging Services Division, 250
NE Behavioral Health Division, 250
NE Developmental Disability System, 250
NE Health and Human Services System, 250
NE Juvenile Services, 250
NV Aging Services Administrator, 260
NH Behavioral Health Division, 268
NH Children, Youth, and Family Division: Juvenile Justice, 268
NH Developmental Disabilities Council, 268
NH Elderly and Adult Services Division, 268
NH Health and Human Services Dept., 268
NH Health Care Services Division: Medical Care and Cost Containment, 268
NJ Developmental Disabilities Division, 279
NJ Human Services Dept., 279
NM Human Services Dept., 288
NC Aging Division, 306
NC Developmental Disabilities Council, 306
NC Governor Morehead School, 306
NC Health and Human Services Dept., 306
ND Disability Services Division, 315
ND Human Services Dept., 315
OH Human Services Dept., 326
OK Aging Services Division, 338
OK Developmental Disabilities Services Division, 338
OK Human Services Dept., 338
OR Developmental Disabilites Services Office, 348
RI Human Services Dept., 370
SC Health and Human Services Dept., 378
SC Human Affairs Commission, 379
SD Developmental Disabilities Division, 389
SD Human Services Dept., 389
TN Human Services Dept., 399
TX Health and Human Services Commission, 408

TX Human Services Dept., 409
UT Aging and Adult Services Division, 419
UT Human Services Dept., 419
VT Aging and Disabilities Dept., 428
VT Human Services Agency, 428

Indian Affairs

MN Indian Affairs Council, 210
ND Indian Affairs Commission, 316
ND Natural Resources and Indian Affairs Division, 317
OK Indian Affairs Commission, 338
SD Tribal Government Relations, 392

Industrial Affairs

AL Agriculture and Industries Dept., 2
AL Industrial Relations Dept., 5
AZ Industrial Commission, 23
CA Industrial Relations Dept., 42
DE Industrial Affairs Division, 69
GA Industry, Trade, and Tourism Dept., 91
HI Labor and Industrial Relations Dept., 99
ID Industrial Commission, 108
IL Industrial Commission, 117
MI Consumer and Industry Services Dept., 197
MN Labor and Industry Dept., 210
MO Labor and Industrial Relations Dept., 230
MT Labor and Industry Dept., 240
NC Industrial Commission, 304
ND Industrial Commission, 316
NE Industrial Relations Commission, 251
NV Business and Industry Dept., 258
OH Industrial Commission, 326
OR Labor and Industries Bureau, 349
PA Labor and Industry Dept., 360
VA Labor and Industry Dept., 437
VT Fire Prevention Division, 428
VT Labor and Industry Dept., 428
WA Labor and Industries Dept., 447
WI Labor and Industry Review Commission, 466

Information Services

MS Information Technology Services Dept., 221
NV Information Technology Dept., 260
SD Information and Telecommunications Bureau, 390
TX Information Resources Dept., 409
VA Technology Secretariat, 440
WA Information Services Dept., 447

Insurance

AL Insurance Dept., 6
AK Insurance Division, 13
AZ Insurance Dept., 23
AR Insurance Dept., 34
CA Insurance Dept., 42
CT Insurance Dept., 60
DE Insurance Dept., 69

DC Insurance and Securites Regulation Dept., 76
FL Insurance Dept., 82
GA Fire Marshal, 91
GA Insurance and Fire Safety Commissioner Office, 91
HI Insurance Division, 98
ID Fire Marshal, 109
ID Insurance Dept., 108
IL Insurance Dept., 117
IN Insurance Dept., 126
IA Insurance Division, 133
KS Insurance Dept., 143
KY Insurance Dept., 151
LA Insurance Dept., 161
ME Insurance Bureau, 171
MD Automobile Insurance Fund, 176
MD Insurance Administration, 180
MA Insurance Division, 190
MI Insurance Bureau, 199
MN Insurance Division, 207
MS Insurance Dept., 221
MS State Fire Marshal, 221
MO Insurance Dept., 230
MT Insurance Dept., 240
NE Insurance Dept., 251
NV Insurance Division, 258
NH Insurance Dept., 269
NJ Banking and Insurance Dept., 276
NM Insurance Division, 288
NY Insurance Dept., 297
NC Insurance Dept., 307
ND Insurance Dept., 316
OH Insurance Dept., 326
OK Insurance Dept., 338
OR Insurance Division, 345
PA Insurance Dept., 360
SC Insurance Dept., 379
SD Insurance Division, 387
TN Commerce and Insurance Dept., 397
TN Consumer Affairs Division, 397
TN Fire Prevention and State Fire Marshal's Office, 397
TX Insurance Dept., 409
UT Insurance Dept., 420
VT Banking, Insurance, Securities, and Health Care Administration Dept., 426
VA Insurance Bureau, 439
WA Industrial Insurance Appeals Board, 446
WA Insurance Commissioner, 447
WA Insurance Services Division, 447
WV Insurance Commission, 459
WI Insurance Commission, 465

Investment

MN Investment Board, 210
NE Investment Council, 251
NE Investment Finance Authority, 251
SD Investment Council, 390
WA Investment Board, 447
WI Investment Board, 466

Judiciary

AL Alabama Judiciary, 10
AK Alaska Judiciary, 19
AZ Arizona Judiciary, 28
AR Arkansas Judiciary, 37
CA California Judiciary, 46
CO Colorado Judiciary, 55
CT Connecticut Judiciary, 63
DE Delaware Judiciary, 72
FL Florida Judiciary, 86
GA Georgia Judiciary, 95
HI Hawaii Judiciary, 102
ID Idaho Judiciary, 112
IL Illinois Judiciary, 121
IN Indiana Judiciary, 130
IA Iowa Judiciary, 138
KS Kansas Judiciary, 147
KY Kentucky Judiciary, 156
LA Louisiana Judiciary, 165
ME Maine Judiciary, 173
MD Maryland Judiciary, 185
MA Massachusetts Judiciary, 194
MI Michigan Judiciary, 204
MN Minnesota Judiciary, 215
MS Mississippi Judiciary, 224
MO Missouri Judiciary, 235
MT Montana Judiciary, 245
NE Nebraska Judiciary, 255
NV Nevada Judiciary, 263
NH New Hampshire Judiciary, 273
NJ New Jersey Judiciary, 282
NM New Mexico Judiciary, 291
NY New York Judiciary, 301
NC North Carolina Judiciary, 310
ND North Dakota Judiciary, 321
OH Ohio Judiciary, 331
OK Oklahoma Judiciary, 343
OR Oregon Judiciary, 353
PA Pennsylvania Judiciary, 364
RI Rhode Island Judiciary, 372
SC South Carolina Judiciary, 384
SD South Dakota Judiciary, 393
TN Tennessee Judiciary, 403
TX Texas Judiciary, 414
UT Utah Judiciary, 424
VT Vermont Judiciary, 432
VA Virginia Judiciary, 441
WA Washington Judiciary, 453
WV West Virginia Judiciary, 461
WI Wisconsin Judiciary, 470
WY Wyoming Judiciary, 477

Juvenile Justice

AL Youth Services Dept., 9
AZ Juvenile Corrections Dept., 24
CO Youth Corrections, 50
CT Juvenile Justice Bureau, 58

MD Youth Services Administration, 77
FL Juvenile Justice Dept., 82
GA Juvenile Justice Dept., 91
ID Juvenile Corrections Dept., 109
IN Juvenile Services, 124
KS Juvenile Justice Authority, 143
KY Juvenile Justice Dept., 151
ME Juvenile Services Bureau, 168
MD Juvenile Justice Dept., 180
MA Juvenile Court, 191
MO Juvenile Justice Advisory Group, 232
NE Juvenile Services, 250
NH Children, Youth, and Family Division: Juvenile
    Justice, 268
NJ Juvenile Justice Commission, 280
NM Juvenile Justice Division, 285
ND Juvenile Services Division, 314
OH Youth Services Dept., 330
OK Juvenile Affairs Office, 338
OR Youth Authority, 352
SC Juvenile Justice Dept., 379
SD Juvenile Corrections and Facilities, 387
TX Youth Commission, 413
UT Youth Corrections, 420
VA Juvenile Justice Dept., 437
WA Juvenile Rehabilitation Administration, 449
WV Juvenile Services Division, 459
WI Juvenile Corrections Division, 463

Labor

AL Labor Dept., 6
AK Labor and Workforce Development Dept., 16
AK Workers' Compensation Division, 16
AR Labor Dept., 34
CO Labor and Employment Dept., 51
CT Labor Dept., 60
DE Industrial Affairs Division, 69
DE Labor Dept., 69
FL Labor and Employment Security Dept., 83
GA Labor Dept., 91
HI Labor and Industrial Relations Dept., 99
ID Labor Dept., 109
IL Labor Dept., 117
IN Labor Dept., 126
KY Labor Cabinet, 152
LA Labor Dept., 161
ME Labor Dept., 170
MD Labor, Licensing, and Regulation Dept., 180
MA Labor and Workforce Development Dept., 191
MN Labor and Industry Dept., 210
MN Workers' Compensation Division, 211
MO Disability Council, 231
MO Labor and Industrial Relations Dept., 230
MO Workers' Compensation Division, 231
MT Labor and Industry Dept., 240
NE Labor Dept., 251
NH Labor Dept., 269
NJ Labor Dept., 280

Land

Land Surveyors

Law Library

Legislative

Library Services

VA   Library of Virginia, 438
WA   State Library, 450
WV   Library Commission, 457
WY   State Library, 476

Lieutenant Governor

AL   Office of the Lieutenant Governor, 1
AK   Office of the Lieutenant Governor, 11
AR   Office of the Lieutenant Governor, 29
CA   Office of the Lieutenant Governor, 38
CO   Office of the Lieutenant Governor, 47
CT   Office of the Lieutenant Governor, 56
DE   Office of the Lieutenant Governor, 65
FL   Office of the Lieutenant Governor, 79
GA   Office of the Lieutenant Governor, 87
HI   Office of the Lieutenant Governor, 96
ID   Office of the Lieutenant Governor, 104
IL   Office of the Lieutenant Governor, 113
IN   Office of the Lieutenant Governor, 122
IA   Office of the Lieutenant Governor, 131
KS   Office of the Lieutenant Governor, 140
KY   Office of the Lieutenant Governor, 148
LA   Office of the Lieutenant Governor, 157
MD   Office of the Lieutenant Governor, 174
MA   Office of the Lieutenant Governor, 186
MI   Office of the Lieutenant Governor, 196
MN   Office of the Lieutenant Governor, 205
MS   Office of the Lieutenant Governor, 216
MO   Office of the Lieutenant Governor, 226
MT   Office of the Lieutenant Governor, 237
NE   Office of the Lieutenant Governor, 246
NV   Office of the Lieutenant Governor, 257
NM   Office of the Lieutenant Governor, 284
NY   Office of the Lieutenant Governor, 292
NC   Office of the Lieutenant Governor, 302
ND   Office of the Lieutenant Governor, 312
OH   Office of the Lieutenant Governor, 322
OK   Office of the Lieutenant Governor, 333
PA   Office of the Lieutenant Governor, 354
RI   Office of the Lieutenant Governor, 366
SC   Office of the Lieutenant Governor, 374
SD   Office of the Lieutenant Governor, 385
TN   Office of the Lieutenant Governor, 395
TX   Office of the Lieutenant Governor, 404
UT   Office of the Lieutenant Governor, 416
VT   Office of the Lieutenant Governor, 425
VA   Office of the Lieutenant Governor, 433
WA   Office of the Lieutenant Governor, 442
WI   Office of the Lieutenant Governor, 462

Liquefied Petroleum Gas

AR   Liquefied Petroleum Gas Board, 34
FL   Liquefied Petroleum Gas Inspections Bureau, 80
LA   Liquefied Petroleum Gas Commission, 162
NV   Liquefied Petroleum Gas Board, 260
OK   Liquefied Petroleum Gas Administration, 339
SC   Liquefied Petroleum Gas Board, 379

Lottery

AZ   Lottery, 24
CA   Lottery Commission, 42
CO   Lottery Division, 53
DE   Lottery, 69
DC   Lottery and Charitable Games Control Board, 76
FL   Lottery Dept. , 83
GA   Lottery, 91
ID   State Lottery, 110
IL   Lottery Dept., 117
IN   Hoosier Lottery, 126
IA   State Lottery, 137
KS   State Lottery, 145
KY   Lottery Corporation, 152
LA   Lottery Corporation, 161
MD   Lottery Agency, 180
MA   State Lottery, 193
MI   State Lottery, 201
MN   State Lottery, 213
MO   State Lottery, 233
MT   Lottery, 239
NE   State Lottery, 253
NH   Lottery, 269
NJ   State Lottery, 280
NY   Lottery Division, 297
OH   Lottery Commission, 326
OR   State Lottery, 350
PA   State Lottery, 362
RI   Lottery Commission, 370
SD   Lottery, 390
TX   Lottery Commission, 410
VT   Lottery Commission, 429
VA   Lottery Dept., 438
WA   State Lottery, 450
WV   Lottery Commission, 460
WI   Lottery Division, 468

Management

IL   Central Management Services Dept., 115
MD   Budget and Management Dept., 177
MD   Personnel Services and Benefits Office, 177
MI   Financial Management Office, 200
MI   Management and Budget Dept., 200
NJ   Management and Budget Office, 280
ND   Central Personnel Division, 316
ND   Management and Budget Office, 316
OH   Budget and Management Office, 323
SD   Finance and Management Bureau, 389
VT   Finance and Management Dept., 427

Marine Resources

ME   Marine Resources Dept., 170
NY   Fish, Wildlife, and Marine Resources Division, 296
OR   Marine Board, 349
OR   Pacific States Marine Fisheries Commission, 349

Medicaid

AL   Medicaid Agency, 6
AK   Medical Assistance Division, 15
AR   Medical Services Division, 33
CO   Medical Assistance Office, 50
DC   Medical Assistance Administration, 76
GA   Medical Assistance Division, 88
ID   Medicaid, 108
IN   Medicaid Policy and Planning, 125
IA   Medical Services Division, 135
KS   Adult and Medical Services: Medicaid Operations, 144
KY   Medicaid Services, 151
ME   Medical Services Bureau: Medicaid Policy and
        Program Division, 170
MD   Medicaid Program, 179
MA   Medical Assistance Division, 190
MI   Medical Services Administration, 197
MS   Medicaid Division, 221
MO   Medical Services Division, 233
MT   Medicaid Services Bureau, 242
NE   Medicaid and Managed Care Division, 251
NH   Medical Services/Medicaid Member Services, 269
NJ   Medical Assistance and Health Services Division, 280
NM   Medical Assistance Division, 288
NY   Medicaid Management Office, 297
NC   Medical Assistance Division, 307
NC   Medical Care Commission, 307
ND   Medical Services Division, 316
OH   Medicaid Office, 326
OR   Medical Assistance Programs Office, 348
PA   Medical Assistance Programs Office, 362
RI   Medical Services Division, 370
SD   Medical Services Office, 392
TN   TennCare Division, 397
VT   Medical Practice Board, 429
VT   Social Welfare Dept.: Medicaid Division, 428
VA   Medical Assistance Services Dept., 437
WA   Medical Assistance Administration, 450
WY   Medicaid Eligibility Office, 473

Medical Examiners

AL   Medical Examiners Board, 6
AZ   Medical Examiners Board, 24
AR   Medical Board, 34
CA   Medical Board, 42
CO   Medical Examiners Board, 51
CT   Medical Examiner's Office, 60
DE   Medical Board, 69
GA   Medical Examiners Board, 91
IN   Medical Licensing Board, 126
IA   Medical Examiners Board, 135
KY   Medical Licensure Board, 152
MA   Medicine Board Registration, 191
MN   Medical Examiners Board, 211
MS   Medical Licensure Board, 221
MT   Medical Examiners Board, 240
NV   Medical Examiners Board, 260

NH   Medicine Board, 270
NY   Medical Examiners Board, 297
ND   Medical Examiners Board, 317
OH   Medical Examiners Board, 326
OK   Medical Examiners Board, 339
OR   Medical Examiners Board, 349
PA   Medicine Board, 360
RI   Medical Examiners Board, 370
SC   Medical Examiners Board, 380
SD   Medical and Osteopathic Examiners Board, 390
TN   Medical Examiners Board, 400
TX   Medical Examiners Board, 410
UT   Medical Examiners Board, 420
WY   Medicine Board, 474

Mental Health

AL   Mental Health and Mental Retardation Dept., 6
AK   Mental Health and Developmental Disabilities
        Division, 15
AR   Mental Health Services Division, 34
CA   Mental Health Dept., 43
CO   Mental Health Services, 51
CT   Mental Health and Addiction Services Dept., 60
DE   Alcoholism, Substance Abuse, and Mental Health
        Division, 68
FL   Mental Health Division, 80
GA   Mental Health, Mental Retardation, and Substance
        Abuse Division, 91
ID   Mental Health Bureau, 108
IL   Mental Health and Developmental Disability Services
        Division, 117
IN   Mental Health Division, 125
IA   Mental Health/Developmental Disabilities Division,
        135
KS   Substance Abuse, Mental Health, and Developmental
        Disabilities Services, 144
KY   Mental Health and Mental Retardation Services, 151
LA   Mental Health Office, 161
ME   Mental Health, Mental Retardation, and Substance
        Abuse Services Dept., 170
MD   Health and Mental Hygiene Dept., 179
MA   Mental Health Legal Advisors Committee, 191
MI   Mental Health and Substance Abuse Services, 197
MS   Mental Health Dept., 221
MO   Mental Health Dept., 231
MT   Addictive and Mental Disorders Division, 242
NV   Mental Hygiene/Developmental Services, 260
NJ   Mental Health Services Division, 280
NY   Mental Health Office, 297
NC   Mental Health, Developmental Disabilities, and
        Substance Abuse Services, 307
ND   Mental Health and Substance Abuse Services Division,
        316
OH   Mental Health Dept., 326
OK   Mental Health and Substance Abuse Services Dept.,
        339
OR   Mental Health Services Dept., 349
PA   Mental Health and Substance Abuse Services, 362

Mines

Motor Vehicles

Natural Resources

Nursing

Occupational and Professional Licensing

WA Licensing Dept., 447
WI Regulation and Licensing Dept., 467

Oil and Gas

AL Oil and Gas Board, 7
AK Oil and Gas Division, 16
AZ Oil and Gas Conservation Commission, 23
AR Oil and Gas Commission, 34
CA Oil and Gas Division, 43
CO Oil and Gas Conservation Commission, 52
IL Mines and Minerals Office: Oil and Gas Division, 118
IN Resource Regulation Bureau: Oil and Gas Division, 127
KY Mines and Minerals Dept.: Oil and Gas Division, 154
LA Conservation Office: Geological Oil and Gas Division, 161
MS Oil and Gas Board, 221
MO Oil and Gas Unit, 231
MT Oil and Gas Conservation Board, 241
NE Oil and Gas Conservation Commission, 252
NM Oil and Gas Division, 288
ND Oil and Gas Division, 316
OH Oil and Gas Division, 327
OK Oil and Gas Conservation Division, 336
PA Mineral Resources Management Office: Oil and Gas Management Bureau, 358
UT Oil, Gas, and Mining Division, 421
VA Mines, Minerals, and Energy Dept: Gas and Oil Division, 435
WV Environmental Protection Division: Oil and Gas Office, 458
WY Oil and Gas Conservation Commission, 474

Parks

AL State Parks Division, 3
AK Parks and Outdoor Recreation Division: State Parks, 16
AZ State Parks, 26
AR Parks and Tourism Dept., 34
CA Parks and Recreation, 43
CO Parks and Outdoor Recreation Division, 51
DE Parks and Recreation, 70
DC Recreation and Parks Dept., 75
FL Recreation and Parks Division, 81
GA Parks, Recreation, and Historic Sites Division, 92
HI State Parks, 100
ID Parks and Recreation Dept., 109
IL Land Management Office: State Parks, 118
IN Lands and Cultural Resources Bureau: State Parks and Reservoirs Division, 127
IA Parks, Recreation, and Preservation Division, 135
KS Wildlife and Parks Dept., 145
KY Parks Dept., 154
LA State Parks Office, 159
ME Parks and Lands Bureau, 168
MD State Parks and Forest Service, 181
MA Forests and Parks Division, 189

MI Resource Management Bureau: Parks and Recreation Division, 201
MN Parks and Recreation Division, 211
MS Parks and Recreation Division, 223
MS Wildlife, Fisheries, and Parks Dept., 223
MO State Parks Board, 232
NE Game and Parks Commission, 250
NV State Parks Division, 258
NH Parks and Recreation Division, 271
NJ Natural and Historic Resources: Parks and Forestry Division, 278
NM State Parks Division, 286
NY Parks, Recreation, and Historic Preservation Office, 298
NC Parks and Recreation Division, 305
ND Parks and Recreation Dept., 317
OH Parks and Recreation Division, 327
OR Parks and Recreation Dept., 349
PA State Parks Bureau, 357
RI Parks and Recreation Division, 369
SC Parks, Recreation, and Tourism Dept., 381
SD Game, Fish, and Parks Dept., 389
TN State Parks Division, 398
TX Parks and Wildlife Dept., 411
UT State Parks and Recreation, 421
VT Forests, Parks, and Recreation Dept., 429
VT State Parks, 430
VA Conservation and Recreation Dept.: State Parks Division, 438
WA State Parks and Recreation Commission, 450
WV Natural Resources Division: State Parks and Forests, 456
WI Land Division: Parks and Recreation Bureau, 466
WY Parks and Cultural Resources Dept., 474
WY Parks and Historic Sites, 475

Personnel

AL Personnel Dept., 7
AK Personnel Division, 12
AZ Personnel Board, 25
AR Management Services Division: Personnel Management Office, 32
CA Personnel Administration Dept., 43
CO Personnel/General Support Services Dept., 52
DE Personnel Office, 70
DC Personnel Dept., 77
GA Merit System of Personnel Administration, 91
ID Personnel Commission, 110
IL Personnel Agency Services Bureau, 115
IN Personnel Dept., 127
IA Personnel Dept., 136
KS Personnel Services Division, 141
KY Personnel Cabinet, 153
LA Personnel Office, 158
ME Financial and Personnel Division, 167
MD Personnel Services and Benefits Office, 177
MS Personnel Board, 222
MO Personnel Division, 227

Pharmacy

Police

Port

Probation and Parole

CA	Prison Terms Board, 45
CO	Parole Board, 52
CT	Parole Board, 61
DE	Parole Board, 70
DC	Parole Board, 77
FL	Parole Commission, 83
GA	Pardons and Parole Board, 92
HI	Paroling Authority, 101
ID	Pardon and Parole Commission, 109
IN	Community Services/Programs: Parole Services, 123
IA	Parole Board, 136
KY	Parole Board, 152
ME	Parole Board, 168
MD	Parole and Probation Division, 181
MA	Parole Board, 192
MA	Probation Commissioner's Office, 191
MI	Parole Board, 199
MN	Pardons Board, 208
MS	Parole Board, 222
MO	Probation and Parole Board, 229
NE	Parole Board, 252
NE	Probation Administration Office, 253
NV	Public Safety: Parole and Probation Division, 260
NH	Parole Board, 270
NM	Adult Parole Board, 285
NY	Parole Division, 298
NY	Probation and Correctional Alternatives Division, 298
ND	Parole and Probation Dept., 317
OH	Adult Parole Authority, 328
OK	Pardon and Parole Board, 340
OR	Parole and Post-Prison Supervision Board, 349
PA	Probation and Parole Board, 361
RI	Parole Board, 368
SC	Probation, Parole, and Pardon Services Dept., 381
SD	Pardons and Parole Board, 387
TN	Parole Board, 400
TX	Pardons and Paroles Board, 411
UT	Pardons and Paroles Board, 421
VA	Virginia Parole Board, 439
WV	Probation and Parole Board, 459
WI	Parole Commission, 467
WY	Parole Board, 475

Prosecuting Attorneys

AL	Prosecution Services Office, 7
DE	Prosecution Office, 70
FL	Prosecution Office, 83
GA	Prosecuting Attorneys Council, 92
IL	State's Attorneys Appelate Prosecuter, 119
IN	Prosecuting Attorneys Council, 128
KY	Prosecutor's Advisory Council Services Division, 153
MD	State Prosecutor's Office, 183
MI	Prosecuting Attorneys Appellate Service Division, 201
MO	Prosecutions Services Division, 232
TX	Prosecuting Attorney, 411

Public Advocacy

| ME | Public Advocate's Office, 171 |
| NE | Public Advocacy Commission, 253 |

Public Broadcasting

AL	Public Television, 8
AK	Public Broadcasting Commission, 12
AR	Educational Television Network, 31
GA	Public Television, 93
HI	Public Broadcasting Authority, 100
ID	Public Television, 105
IA	Public Television, 133
IA	Public Television, 136
KS	Public Broadcasting Commission, 141
KY	Educational Television, 150
LA	Public Broadcasting, 161
MD	Public Television, 182
MA	Telecommunications and Energy Dept., 193
MS	Educational Network, 219
NE	Educational Telecommunications Commission, 249
NH	New Hampshire Public Television, 270
NY	Cultural Education Office: Educational Television and Public Broadcasting, 295
ND	Radio Communications, 318
OH	Ohio Educational Telecommunications Network Commission, 327
OK	Educational Television Authority, 336
PA	Public Television Network Commission, 361
RI	Public Telecommunications Authority, 371
SC	Educational Television Network, 377
SD	Public Broadcasting Division, 390
WV	Public Broadcasting, 459

Public Defender

AK	Public Defender Agency, 12
AR	Public Defender Commission, 35
CA	Public Defender, 43
CO	Public Defender, 52
DE	Public Defender, 70
DC	Public Defender Service, 77
FL	Public Counsel's Office, 83
HI	Public Defender's Office, 97
IL	Appellate Defender, 114
IN	Public Defender, 128
IA	Public Defense Dept., 136
MD	People's Counsel Office, 181
MD	Public Defender's Office, 181
MA	Public Counsel Services Committee, 191
MN	Public Defender's Office, 212
MO	Public Defender Commission, 232
NV	State Public Defender's Office, 260
NH	Public Defender, 270
NJ	Public Defender's Office, 281
NM	Public Defender's Office, 288
OH	Public Defender Commission, 328
OK	Indigent Defense System, 338
OR	Public Defender's Office, 349

Retirement

Revenue

WI   Revenue Dept., 467
WY   Revenue Dept., 475

Secretary of State

AL   Office of the Secretary of State, 1
AZ   Office of the Secretary of State, 20
AR   Office of the Secretary of State, 29
CA   Office of the Secretary of State, 38
CO   Office of the Secretary of State, 47
CT   Office of the Secretary of State, 56
DE   Office of the Secretary of State, 65
DC   Office of the Secretary, 74
FL   Office of the Secretary of State, 79
GA   Office of the Secretary of State, 87
ID   Office of the Secretary of State, 104
IL   Office of the Secretary of State, 113
IN   Office of the Secretary of State, 122
IA   Office of the Secretary of State, 131
KS   Office of the Secretary of State, 140
KY   Office of the Secretary of State, 148
LA   Office of the Secretary of State, 157
ME   Office of the Secretary of State, 166
MD   Office of the Secretary of State, 174
MA   Secretary of the Commonwealth, 186
MI   Office of the Secretary of State, 196
MN   Office of the Secretary of State, 205
MS   Office of the Secretary of State, 216
MO   Office of the Secretary of State, 226
MT   Office of the Secretary of State, 237
NE   Office of the Secretary of State, 246
NV   Office of the Secretary of State, 257
NH   Office of the Secretary of State, 265
NJ   Office of the Secretary of State, 275
NM   Office of the Secretary of State, 284
NY   Office of the Secretary of State, 292
NC   Office of the Secretary of State, 302
ND   Office of the Secretary of State, 312
OH   Office of the Secretary of State, 322
OK   Office of the Secretary of State, 333
OR   Office of the Secretary of State, 344
PA   Office of the Secretary of the Commonwealth, 354
RI   Office of the Secretary of State, 366
SC   Office of the Secretary of State, 374
SD   Office of the Secretary of State, 385
TN   Office of the Secretary of State, 395
TX   Office of the Secretary of State, 404
VT   Office of the Secretary of State, 425
VA   Office of the Secretary of the Commonwealth, 433
WA   Office of the Secretary of State, 442
WV   Office of the Secretary of State, 454
WI   Office of the Secretary of State, 462
WY   Office of the Secretary of State, 471

Securities

DC   Insurance and Securites Regulation Dept., 76
LA   Securities Commission, 163
ND   Securities Commissioner Office, 319

OK   Securities Dept., 341
PA   Securities Commission, 362
TX   Securities Board, 412

Social Services

AK   Family and Youth Services Division, 15
AK   Health and Social Services Dept., 15
CA   Social Services Dept., 44
CT   Social Services Dept., 61
DE   Health and Social Services, 68
DE   Social Services Division, 68
IN   Aging and Rehabilitative Services, 125
IN   Family and Social Services Administration, 125
IN   Medicaid Policy and Planning, 125
IN   Mental Health Division, 125
KS   Adult and Medical Services: Medicaid Operations, 144
KS   Social and Rehabilitative Services Dept., 144
KY   Community-Based Services Dept., 149
KY   Public Protection and Regulation Cabinet, 153
LA   Social Services Dept., 163
MA   Social Services Dept., 192
MN   Mediation Services Bureau, 211
MO   Aging Council, 233
MO   Social Services Dept., 233
NC   Social Services Division, 307
OH   Community Service Council, 324
OK   Central Services Dept., 334
OR   Housing and Community Services Dept., 348
PA   Public Welfare Dept., 361
SC   Social Services Dept., 382
SD   Social Services Dept., 391
VA   Social Services Dept., 439
WA   Aging and Adult Services Administration, 449
WA   Juvenile Rehabilitation Administration, 449
WA   Social and Health Services Dept., 449
WY   Family Services Dept., 473

Soil and Water

AL   Soil and Water Conservation Committee, 8
AR   Soil and Water Conservation Commission, 35
CO   Soil Conservation Board, 53
CO   Soil Conservation Division, 51
DE   Soil and Water Conservation Division, 70
GA   Soil and Water Conservation Commission, 93
ID   Soil Conservation Commission, 110
IN   Resource Regulation Bureau: Soil Conservation
      Division, 127
IA   Soil Conservation Division, 132
IA   Soil Conservation Division: Water Resources Bureau,
      132
LA   Soil and Water Conservation Office, 158
MD   Land and Water Conservation Office, 181
MN   Water and Soil Resources Board, 214
MS   Soil and Water Conservation Commission, 223
MO   Soil and Water Districts Commission, 231
NY   Natural Resources and Environmental Programs: Soil
      and Water Conservation Committee, 293

NC Soil and Water Conservation Commission, 306
ND Soil Conservation Committee, 319
OH Soil and Water Conservation Division, 327
TX Soil and Water Conservation Board, 412
VA Conservation and Recreation Dept.: Soil and Water Conservation Division, 438
WV Environmental Protection Division: Water Resources, 458
WV Soil Conservation Agency, 455

State Fair

AL State Fair Facilities Management, 8
AK State Fair, 17
AZ State Fair and Exposition, 26
AR State Fair, 35
CO State Fair and Industrial Exposition, 53
DE State Fair, 71
FL State Fair, 84
GA State Fair, 93
IL Illinois State Fair Bureau, 114
IN State Fair Commission, 128
IA State Fair Authority, 137
KS State Fair, 144
KY State Fair Board, 154
LA State Fair, 163
MD State Fair and Agricultural Society, 182
MI Upper Peninsula State Fair, 197
MN State Fair, 213
MS State Fair, 223
MO State Fair, 234
NE State Fair, 254
NV State Fair, 262
NH State Fair, 272
NM State Fair Commission, 290
NY State Fair, 293
NC State Fair, 308
NC State Fair Division, 303
ND State Fair Association, 319
OH State Fair, 329
OK State Fair, 341
OR State Fair and Exposition Center, 350
SC State Fair, 382
SD State Fair, 392
TN State Fair, 401
TX State Fair, 412
UT State Fair, 422
VA State Fair, 439
WV State Fair, 459
WI State Fair, 468
WY State Fair, 472

Substance Abuse

CT Mental Health and Addiction Services Dept., 60
DE Alcoholism, Substance Abuse, and Mental Health Division, 68
GA Mental Health, Mental Retardation, and Substance Abuse Division, 91

KS Substance Abuse, Mental Health, and Developmental Disabilities Services, 144
ME Mental Health, Mental Retardation, and Substance Abuse Services Dept., 170
MI Mental Health and Substance Abuse Services, 197
MT Addictive and Mental Disorders Division, 242
NE Alcohol and Drug Abuse Prevention Center, 248
NY Alcoholism and Substance Abuse Services Office, 293
NC Mental Health, Developmental Disabilities, and Substance Abuse Services, 307
ND Mental Health and Substance Abuse Services Division, 316
OH Alcohol and Drug Addiction Services Dept., 323
OK Mental Health and Substance Abuse Services Dept., 339
OK Narcotics and Dangerous Drugs Control Bureau, 339
PA Mental Health and Substance Abuse Services, 362
SC Alcohol and Other Drug Abuse Services Dept., 375
TX Alcohol and Drug Abuse Commission, 405
VA Mental Health, Mental Retardation, and Substance Abuse Dept., 438

Supreme Court

AL Supreme Court, 10
AK Supreme Court, 19
AZ Supreme Court, 28
AR Supreme Court, 37
CA Supreme Court, 46
CO Supreme Court, 55
CT Supreme Court, 63
DE Supreme Court, 72
FL Supreme Court, 86
GA Supreme Court, 95
HI Supreme Court, 103
ID Supreme Court, 112
IL Supreme Court, 121
IN Supreme Court, 130
IA Supreme Court, 138
KS Supreme Court, 147
KY Supreme Court, 156
LA Supreme Court, 165
ME Supreme Judicial Court, 173
MD Court of Appeals, 185
MA Supreme Judicial Court, 194
MI Supreme Court, 204
MN Supreme Court, 215
MS Supreme Court, 224
MO Supreme Court, 235
MT Supreme Court, 245
NE Supreme Court, 255
NV Supreme Court, 263
NH Supreme Court, 273
NJ Supreme Court, 282
NM Supreme Court, 291
NY Court of Appeals, 301
NC Supreme Court, 310
ND Supreme Court, 321
OH Supreme Court, 331

Taxes

Tourism

Trade

Transportation

Treasurer

Veterans Affairs

MD Wildlife and Heritage Division, 181
MA Fisheries, Wildlife, and Environmental Law
      Enforcement Dept., 189
MI   Resource Management: Fisheries Division, 201
MI   Resource Management Bureau: Wildlife Division, 201
MN Fish and Wildlife Division, 211
MS Wildlife, Fisheries, and Parks Dept., 223
MO Fisheries Division, 228
MO Wildlife Division, 228
MT Fish, Wildlife, and Parks Dept., 240
NE   Game and Parks Commission, 250
NH   Fish and Game Dept., 268
NJ   Fish, Game, and Wildlife, 278
NM Game and Fish Dept., 287
NY   Fish, Wildlife, and Marine Resources Division, 296
ND   Game and Fish Dept., 315
OH   Wildlife Division, 327
OK   Wildlife Conservation Dept., 342
OR   Fish and Wildlife Dept., 347
RI   Natural Resources: Fish and Wildlife Office, 369
SC   Wildlife and Freshwater Fisheries Division, 380
SD   Game, Fish, and Parks Dept., 389
TN   Wildlife Resources Agency, 401
TX   Parks and Wildlife Dept., 411
UT   Wildlife Resources Division, 421
VT   Fish and Wildlife Dept., 429
VA   Game and Inland Fisheries Dept., 438
WA Fish and Wildlife Dept., 445
WV Natural Resources Division: Wildlife Resources, 457
WI   Land Division: Wildlife Management Bureau, 466
WY Game and Fish Dept., 473

Women

AZ   Women's Division, 26
CA   Women's Commission, 44
CT   Women's Commission, 62
DE   Women's Commission Office, 69
HI   Women's Commission, 101
ID   Women's Commission, 111
IL   Women's Commission, 120
IA   Commission on the Status of Women, 134
LA   Women's Services, 164
MD Women's Commission, 180
MN Economic Status of Women Commission, 208
MO Women's Council, 229
NE   Women's Commission, 254
NH   Women's Commission, 272
NJ   Women's Division, 277
NM Women's Status Commission, 290
NY   Women's Division, 300
NC   Women's Council, 303
ND   Women's Status Commission, 320
OH   Women's Policy and Research Commission, 330
OR   Women's Commission, 352
PA   Women's Commission, 363
RI   Women's Commission, 371
SC   Women's Commission, 383
TX   Women's Commission, 413

VT   Women's Commission, 431
WV Women's Commission, 458
WI   Women's Council, 468
WY Women's Issues Council, 476

Workers' Compensation

AK   Workers' Compensation Division, 16
AR   Workers' Compensation Commission, 36
CO   Workmen's Compensation/Pinnacol Assurance, 53
CT   Workers' Compensation Commission, 62
DE   Workers' Compensation Administration, 69
DC   Workers' Compensation Office, 77
FL   Workers' Compensation Division, 83
GA   Workers' Compensation Board, 94
IN   Workers' Compensation Board, 128
KS   Workers' Compensation Division, 143
LA   Workers' Compensation Administration, 164
ME   Workers' Compensation Board, 172
MD Workers' Compensation Commission, 183
MA Workers' Compensation Advisory Council, 193
MI   Workers Disability Compensation Bureau, 199
MN Workers' Compensation Division, 211
MS Workers' Compensation Commission, 223
MO Workers' Compensation Division, 231
MT Workers' Compensation Court, 244
NE   Workers' Compensation Court, 254
NH   Workers' Compensation Division, 269
NJ   Workers' Compensation Division, 280
NM Workers' Compensation Administration, 290
NY   Workers' Compensation Board, 300
ND   Workers' Compensation Bureau, 320
OH   Workers' Compensation Bureau, 330
OK   Workers' Compensation Division, 339
OR   Workers' Compensation Division, 345
OR   Workers' Compensation Board, 352
PA   Workers' Compensation Bureau, 360
RI   Workers' Compensation Office, 367
SC   Workers' Compensation Commission, 383
TN   Workers' Compensation Divsion, 399
TX   Workers' Compensation Commission, 413
UT   Workers' Compensation Fund of Utah, 422
VT   Workers' Compensation Division, 428
VA   Workers' Compensation Commission, 440
WV Workers' Compensation Board, 460
WI   Workers' Compensation Division, 468
WY Workers' Compensation Medical Commission, 476

Workforce Development

AK   Labor and Workforce Development Dept., 16
KY   Workforce Development Cabinet, 155
MA Labor and Workforce Development Dept., 191
TN   Labor and Workforce Development Dept., 399
TX   Workforce and Economic Competitiveness, 413
TX   Workforce Commission, 413
WA Workforce Training and Education Coordinating
      Board, 451
WI   Workforce Development Dept., 468

Name Index

Name Index

Alt, Tom (WI), (608) 267-7729 465

Altemus, Thomas (VT), (802) 828-3649 426

Alter, Edward T. (R-UT), (801) 538-1042 416

Alvarado, Tomas (CA), (916) 653-2158 44

Alwin, Lawrence F. (TX), (512) 479-4700 405

Amack, Rex (NE), (402) 471-5539 250

Amato, Anthony J. (DE), (302) 760-2160 71

Ambrose, Sharon (DC), (202) 724-8072 78

Ament, Don (CO), (303) 239-4104 48

Amero, Jane A. (R-ME), (207) 287-1505 172

Amestoy, Jeffrey (VT), (802) 828-3278 432

Amick, Steven H. (R-DE), (302) 739-4138 71

Amos, Paul (SC), (803) 737-3240 377

Amsterdam, Peggy (DE), (302) 577-8280 66

Amundson, Robert A. (SD), (605) 773-4886 393

Anable, Michael E. (AZ), (602) 542-4621 24

Anderes, Thomas (NV), (775) 784-4905 262

Andersen, George R. (MN), (651) 635-8100 213

Anderson, Bruce (HI), (808) 586-4410 99

Anderson, Constance (WY), (307) 777-7141 475

Anderson, D. Larry (UT), (801) 538-7230 421

Anderson, Dan (MT), (406) 444-3969 242

Anderson, E. Riley (TN), (423) 594-6400 403

Anderson, Eddie L. (MS), (601) 359-4925 220

Anderson, Howard C. (ND), (701) 328-9535 318

Anderson, James (MS), (601) 359-5680 218

Anderson, Mabel M. (D-RI), (401) 222-2466 372

Anderson, Marvin R. (MN), (651) 297-2084 215

Anderson, Mike (TX), (512) 424-5232 411

Anderson, Mollie K. (IA), (515) 281-3351 136

Anderson, Morris (MN), (651) 296-7971 213

Anderson, Paul H. (MN), (651) 296-3314 215

Anderson, Robert E. (Bob) (OK),
    (405) 521-3115 341

Anderson, Russell (MN), (651) 296-2484 215

Anderson, Sheridan Cash (SD), (605) 773-4898 ... 394

Anderson, Thomas R. (OH), (614) 222-5801 329

Anderson, Whitney (R-HI), (808) 586-6840 101

Andre, Shirley (IA), (515) 244-1052 137

Andreotti, Eugene R. (MN), (651) 282-4666 206

Angelides, Philip (D-CA), (916) 653-2995 38

Angello, Linda (NY), (518) 474-6988 295

Angelone, Ron (VA), (804) 674-3000 436

Ankner, William D. (RI), (401) 222-2481 371

Anselmi, Annette (MD), (410) 837-6220 179

Anson, Theodore R. (CT), (860) 713-5800 61

Anstead, Harry Lee (FL), (850) 488-2281 86

Anthony, Bob (R-OK), (405) 521-2261 335

Anzai, Earl I. (HI), (808) 586-1282 96

Anzalone, Theresa (LA), (225) 922-0015 159

Appel, Robert Joseph (VT), (802) 828-3168 426

Apple, Kathy (NV), (775) 688-2620 261

Applegate, Bob (OR), (503) 378-6496 344

Aragon, Manny M. (D-NM), (505) 986-4733 290

Arceneaux, P. F. (Pete) (LA), (225) 342-7100 160

Archabal, Nina M. (MN), (651) 296-2747 209

Archangelo, Elaine (DE), (302) 577-4400 68

Archer, William R., II (TX), (512) 458-7375 408

Ardinger, Rick (ID), (208) 345-5346 108

Areias, Rusty (CA), (916) 653-8380 43

Arias, Stephen R. (NM), (505) 986-4751 291

Armstead, Thomas L. (IL), (217) 785-4143 116

Armstrong, Fredrick H. (WV), (304) 558-0230 455

Armstrong, John J. (CT), (860) 692-7482 58

Armstrong, Peggy (DC), (202) 727-5011 74

Armstrong, Vickie (CO), (303) 620-4701 51

Arnett, Stewart (NH), (603) 271-2341 271

Arney, Ken (TN), (615) 837-5411 396

Arnold, Lee H. (RI), (401) 222-3732 370

Arnold, Stanley R. (NH), (603) 271-2318 271

Arnold, W. H. (Dub) (AR), (501) 682-6861 37

Arnold-Williams, Robin (UT), (801) 538-4001 419

Aron, Leonard (WA), (360) 696-6525 449

Aronhalt, Gary K. (VA), (804) 786-5351 438

Arrell, Max (TX), (512) 424-4001 412

Artley, Don (MT), (406) 542-4300 241

Ashbaker, Bill (FL), (850) 414-4500 84

Ashley, Latrelle (MS), (601) 364-2000 223

Ashwood, Albert (OK), (405) 521-2481 334

Asmussen, Lanet S. (NE), (402) 471-3731 255

Assam, Coral (SD), (605) 773-4493 387

Atchison, Robert (KS), (785) 532-3300 142

Atchley, Ben (R-TN), (615) 741-3791 402

Atkins, Craig (SD), (605) 353-7340 392

Atkins, Holly Saleeby (SC), (803) 737-5663 383

Atwood, Malcom J. (OK), (405) 521-2885 340

Aubin, Gerald S. (RI), (401) 463-6500 370

Auerbach, Roger (OR), (503) 945-5811 349

Augustine, Kathy (R-NV), (775) 684-5777 258

Austin, Gary (MN), (651) 296-2409 213

Austin, Michael P. (AZ), (602) 231-6219 22

Austin-Duffin, J. Renea (LA), (225) 342-0286 163

Ayers, Jim (AK), (907) 465-3500 11

Ayers, Toby D. (RI), (401) 222-6105 371

B

Baab, Schuyler (WI), (202) 624-5870 462

Bablitch, William A. (WI), (608) 266-1888 470

Baca, Joseph F. (NM), (505) 827-4892 291

Backas, James (MD), (410) 767-6555 177

Backman, Rod A. (ND), (701) 328-4904 316

Bacon, Nick D. (AR), (501) 370-3820 36

Baddour, Philip A., Jr. (D-NC), (919) 715-0850 ... 310

Baer, Michael S., III (LA), (225) 342-0629 165

Branson, Leonard L. (IL), (312) 814-3930 117
Bratten, Thomas E., Jr. (MD), (410) 333-4429 183
Brauch, William (IA), (515) 281-5926 133
Bravo, N. Johanna (NV), (775) 786-0231 258
Braxton, Lowell (UT), (801) 538-5370 421
Braxton, Paula (LA), (225) 342-2700 163
Brazier, Peter C. (ME), (207) 624-9000 170
Brazil, Harold (DC), (202) 724-8174 78
Bredehoft, Wendy (WY), (307) 777-7637 474
Breen, Aviva (MN), (651) 296-8590 208
Breitweiser, Sheila S. (SC), (864) 585-7711 382
Brekken, Shirley A. (MN), (612) 617-2296 211
Bremen, Phil (IN), (317) 232-4567 122
Bren, Sherry (SD), (605) 773-4608 386
Brett, Leslie (CT), (860) 240-8300 62
Bridge, Bobbe (WA), (360) 357-2050 453
Bridges, Edwin C. (AL), (334) 242-4441 2
Bridges, Marc (MT), (406) 444-7323 240
Bridges, Steven D. (GA), (770) 986-1633 88
Briggs, Mike (R-CA), (916) 319-2029 46
Brightbill, David J. (R-PA), (717) 787-5708 363
Brimner, Karl (AK), (907) 465-3166 15
Brink, Barbara (AK), (907) 264-4400 12
Brinkman, Elmer (SD), (605) 773-3731 391
Brisch, Hans (OK), (405) 524-9100 340
Brister, Rosemary (MS), (601) 359-6160 219
Broccolina, Frank, Jr. (MD), (410) 260-1290 185
Brock, David A. (NH), (603) 271-2149 273
Brock, Jon (OK), (405) 557-7201 336
Broderick, John T., Jr. (NH), (603) 271-3751 274
Broderick, Michael F. (HI), (808) 539-4900 103
Brody, Clark (OR), (503) 378-3573, ext. 289 346
Brogan, Frank T. (R-FL), (850) 488-4711 79
Brommelsick, Margaret (NM), (505) 827-6490 286
Bronner, David G. (AL), (334) 832-4140 8
Brook, Nina (SC), (803) 734-9400 374
Brooks, Bob (AR), (501) 324-9731 32
Brooks, Norman (MS), (601) 354-6161 218
Brooks, Robert G. (FL), (850) 487-2945 82
Brooks, Rudolph (CT), (860) 550-6654 58
Brooks, Steven E. (NC), (919) 549-8614 308
Brookshire, J. K., Jr. (VA), (757) 331-2960 435
Brorsen, Bart (OK), (405) 521-2796 342
Brosius, John (PA), (717) 787-5759 362
Browdie, Richard (PA), (717) 783-1550 355
Brown, Arthur R., Jr. (NJ), (609) 292-3976 276
Brown, Carl (TN), (615) 313-4714 399
Brown, Don (KS), (785) 291-3206 140
Brown, Don W. (TX), (512) 483-6101 408
Brown, Jack (D-AZ), (602) 542-4129 27
Brown, James E. (OR), (503) 945-7211 347
Brown, James H., Jr. (D-LA), (225) 342-5423 161

Brown, James L. (NE), (402) 471-2566 252
Brown, Janice R. (CA), (415) 865-7040 46
Brown, Jean Williams (AL), (334) 353-4244 10
Brown, John Y., III (D-KY), (502) 564-3490 148
Brown, Kate (D-OR), (503) 986-1700 352
Brown, Kirk (IL), (217) 782-5597 119
Brown, Marty (WA), (360) 902-0530 445
Brown, Michele D. (AK), (907) 465-5065 15
Brown, Mike (LA), (225) 342-1583 160
Brown, Mitchell J. (OH), (216) 787-3344 326
Brown, Otis (VA), (804) 228-3200 439
Brown, Robert L. (AR), (501) 682-6864 37
Brown, Ronald A. (MS), (601) 325-3036 221
Brown, Tim (WA), (360) 902-8484 449
Brownlee, Donald W. (KS), (785) 296-6800 143
Brubaker, Bill (WA), (206) 764-4131 451
Bruce, Thomas R. (MN), (651) 215-0500 212
Bruin, Barbara (PA), (717) 783-5331 361
Bruneau, C. Emile (Peppi), Jr. (R-LA),
   (225) 342-7263 165
Bruneel, Frank (R-ID), (208) 332-1120 112
Bruno, Joseph L. (R-NY), (518) 455-3191 300
Brunson, Joe (ID), (208) 334-5747 108
Bruton, H. David (NC), (919) 733-4534 306
Bryant, Chet (GA), (404) 656-4252 93
Bryant, Douglas E. (SC), (803) 898-3300 378
Bryant, John (FL), (850) 413-0936 80
Bryant, Juanita M. (NC), (919) 733-2455 303
Bryant, Phil (R-MS), (601) 364-2888 217
Bryant, Renee (OR), (503) 947-1500 346
Bryant, Wanda (NC), (919) 716-6780 304
Bryant, Wilbert (VA), (804) 786-1151 436
Bryce, Philip (NH), (603) 271-2214 271
Bryner, Alexander O. (AK), (907) 264-0632 19
Bryson, Mary (MT), (406) 444-2762 243
Bucci, Anthony (RI), (401) 222-2160 367
Buchanan, Phil (IA), (202) 624-5442 131
Buchanan, Wayne (MT), (406) 444-6576 238
Buchmelter, Mary Kay (WV), (304) 558-0546 455
Buck, Michael (HI), (808) 587-4181 100
Buckley, Raymond C. (D-NH), (603) 271-3661 ... 273
Buckley, Robert G. (TX), (512) 773-2250 412
Buckner, Adrienne (DC), (202) 673-7657 76
Buckner, Robert R. (MO), (573) 751-3779 233
Budzik, Mike (OH), (614) 265-6300 327
Buelow, Ed, Jr. (MS), (601) 923-7400 223
Buenger, Michael L. (SD), (605) 773-3474 394
Bugen, Claire (TX), (512) 462-5300 412
Buikema, Ed (MI), (517) 333-5042 202
Bulford, Sally Farran (OH), (614) 466-5580 330
Bullard, William, Jr. (SD), (605) 773-3201 391
Bullock, Jeff (DE), (302) 577-3210 65

C

Carney, Jan K. (VT), (802) 863-7280 427
Carney, John C., Jr. (DE), (302) 577-8980 67
Carpeneti, Walter L. (AK), (907) 463-4771 19
Carpenter, Linda (WA), (360) 753-6715 443
Carpenter, Sarah (VT), (802) 652-3421 427
Carpenter, Susan K. (IN), (317) 232-2475 128
Carpentier, Elizabeth (SC), (803) 898-5040 382
Carper, Thomas R. (D-DE), (302) 577-3210 65
Carr, Marvin (NV), (775) 687-4290 260
Carraway, Melvin J. (IN), (317) 232-8241 128
Carrico, Harry L. (VA), (804) 786-2023 441
Carrier, Michael (IA), (515) 281-5207 135
Carrington, Deborah R. (NC), (919) 733-2690 307
Carson, Wallace P., Jr. (OR), (503) 986-5700 353
Carter, Alvin (DC), (202) 727-1614 76
Carter, Clarence (VA), (804) 692-1947 439
Carter, James H. (IA), (319) 398-3920 139
Carter, Sharon (TX), (512) 463-0845 414
Carvell, Charles (ND), (701) 328-3640 317
Carver, H. Wayne, II (CT), (860) 679-3980 60
Case, Ed (D-HI), (808) 586-8475 102
Casey, James D. (NH), (603) 271-3171 269
Casey, Robert P., Jr. (D-PA), (717) 787-2543 354
Cassidy, Joel T. (SC), (803) 737-2652 378
Castille, Ronald D. (PA), (215) 560-5663 365
Castle, Michael C. (WV), (304) 759-0515 458
Castle, Michael C. (WV), (304) 759-0515 458
Castro, Bernadette (NY), (518) 474-0463 298
Catania, David A. (DC), (202) 724-7772 78
Catchpole, Judy (WY), (307) 777-7675 473
Cates, James W. (KS), (785) 296-5700 145
Cathcart, Rich (D-WY), (307) 777-7711 477
Cathell, Dale R. (MD), (410) 543-6014 185
Catlett, Brian (NV), (775) 684-5670 257
Catoe, William D. (SC), (803) 896-8555 377
Causseaux, Debbie (FL), (850) 488-0125 86
Cauthen, Stephen M. (AL), (334) 242-2620 8
Cavanagh, Michael F. (MI), (517) 373-8683 204
Cave, Wilbur (SC), (803) 734-0457 374
Cavitte, Donna (MO), (573) 751-3325 231
Cayetano, Benjamin J. (D-HI), (808) 586-0034 96
Cellucci, Argeo Paul (R-MA), (617) 727-3600 186
Cenarrusa, Pete T. (R-ID), (208) 334-2300 104
Centracchio, Reginald A. (RI),
  (401) 457-4102 .... 367, 368
Ceresko, Richard (CO), (303) 894-7474 50
Chaffee, Barbara (PA), (717) 787-5453 357
Chafin, H. Truman (D-WV), (304) 357-7808 460
Chambers, Glenda (LA), (225) 922-0604 160
Chambers, Joseph L. (GA), (770) 438-2550 92
Chambless, Catherine E. (UT), (801) 533-4128 420
Chamness, Michael (IL), (217) 782-2700 115

Chandler, Albert B., III (D-KY),
  (502) 696-5300 148
Chandler, Gene G. (R-NH), (603) 271-3125 273
Chandler, Susan M. (HI), (808) 586-4997 99
Chang, Debbie I. (MD), (410) 767-4664 179
Chapman, Guy F. (ME), (207) 287-4031 171
Chapman, Kay (IA), (515) 281-5596 133
Chappell, C. Douglas (NC), (919) 733-7282 307
Charles, John F. (WA), (360) 664-7312 449
Chase, Gail M. (ME), (207) 624-6250 166
Chassaniol, Lydia (MS), (601) 354-7716 222
Chavez, George (NM), (505) 827-3721 287
Chavez, John (NM), (505) 827-0341 289
Chavous, Kevin P. (DC), (202) 724-8068 78
Cheng, Nancy (UT), (801) 238-7989 424
Chenovick, Patrick A. (MT), (406) 444-2621 245
Chernenko, Susan V. (WV), (304) 558-0330 455
Cherry, John D. (D-MI), (517) 373-1636 203
Chiacchio, Patricia A. (NJ), (609) 633-6734 281
Chianese, Charles (NJ), (609) 633-7618 276
Chiarkas, Nicholas L. (WI), (608) 266-0087 467
Chichester, John H. (R-VA), (804) 698-7528 440
Childress, Dorothy (PA), (717) 783-7192 361
Chimera, Richard A. (NY), (518) 457-2821 299
Chin, Edward (WI), (608) 266-1770 468
Chin, Ming W. (CA), (415) 865-7050 46
Chisolm, Charles (MS), (601) 961-5000 219
Chivers, Stephanie H. (TN), (615) 741-3449 397
Choe, Martha (WA), (360) 753-7426 444
Chopp, Frank (D-WA), (360) 786-7920 452
Chorpenning, Patrick F. (AZ), (602) 255-3373 26
Christensen, David (SD), (605) 773-3495 392
Christensen, Douglas D. (NE), (402) 471-5020 249
Christensen, Grant (WY), (307) 382-3159 474
Christensen, Ray (SD), (605) 773-3426 388
Christenson, Cindi (CA), (916) 263-2222 41
Christopher, Larry J. (TX), (512) 833-6699 412
Chumbley, Avery B. (D-HI), (808) 586-6030 101
Chun, Jonathan (D-HI), (808) 586-7344 101
Chute, James C. (ME), (207) 822-4146 173
Chvala, Chuck (D-WI), (608) 266-9170 469
Ciolek, Robert J. (MA), (617) 737-8377 190
Ciparick, Carmen Beauchamp (NY), (518) 455-7725 . 301
Citrone, Marie V. (RI), (401) 462-3191 368
Clabby, Robert T., III (WY), (307) 777-7115 474
Clapp, Gordan (NC), (919) 733-4171 304
Clark, Charles (FL), (850) 922-3170 x3601 81
Clark, Cornelia (TN), (615) 741-2687 403
Clark, Drennan Anthony (NV), (775) 887-7302 ... 258
Clark, Eric C. (D-MS), (601) 359-6338 216
Clark, Fred Y. (LA), (225) 342-3701 162
Clark, Hanley C. (WV), (304) 558-3707 459

Cooke, Paul (CO), (303) 239-4463 50
Cooks, Clifford (DC), (202) 442-4320 76
Cool, K. L. (MI), (517) 373-2329 201
Cooley, Don (AL), (334) 242-3334 3
Coombs, Philip (WA), (360) 753-5485 443
Cooney, Mike R. (D-MT), (406) 444-2034 237
Cooper, Anthony S. (DC), (202) 645-8010 76
Cooper, John (SD), (605) 773-3718 389
Cooper, Roy A., III (D-NC), (919) 733-5664 309
Cooper, Sandra (NC), (919) 733-2570 305
Cooper, William S. (KY), (502) 766-5179 156
Copeland, Rodney E. (VT), (802) 241-2610 427
Corbett, Edward E., Jr. (OH), (614) 728-4030 329
Corbin, Donald L. (AR), (501) 682-6838 37
Corcoran, Tony (D-OR), (503) 986-1722 352
Coriden, G. Terrence (IN), (317) 232-3809 128
Cornwell, Ann (AR), (501) 682-5951 36
Cornyn, John (R-TX), (512) 463-2191 404
Corrigan, Mark R. (PA), (717) 787-5920 364
Corrigan, Maura D. (MI), (313) 256-9628 204
Corso, Mary (WA), (360) 753-0400 450
Corson, Harvey (KY), (606) 239-7017 150
Corson, Janet S. (IN), (317) 232-7845 125
Cortright, Stephen P. (OK), (405) 228-5000 334
Cosner, Barney (WY), (307) 358-2398 472
Costle, Elizabeth R. (VT), (802) 828-3301 426
Cottrell, Kent A. (CO), (719) 583-5800 52
Courter, J. Carlton, III (VA), (804) 786-3532 434
Courtney, Beth (LA), (225) 767-5660 162
Courtney, Mark (VA), (804) 367-8514 434
Covington, Ann K. (MO), (573) 751-3570 235
Covington, J. Lee, II (OH), (614) 644-2651 326
Covington, Kay (LA), (225) 925-6335 162
Coward, Ira (Bud) (SC), (803) 896-6260 376
Cowart, Vicki (CO), (303) 866-2611 50
Cowin, Judith A. (MA), (617) 557-1000 195
Cox, Cathy (D-GA), (404) 656-2881 87
Cox, John (WY), (307) 777-4301 476
Cox, Joseph W. (OR), (541) 346-5700 351
Cox, Otis G., Jr. (WV), (304) 558-2930 459
Coyle, Matthew J. (WA), (360) 753-5446 450
Coyne, Richard (Dick) (NE), (402) 471-2571 252
Craig, John L. (NE), (402) 479-4615 254
Crain, Brenda (MO), (573) 751-0800 227
Cramer, Kevin (ND), (701) 328-5300 314
Crampton, Scott C. (OR), (503) 986-5555 353
Crane, Karen (AK), (907) 465-2911 14
Crane, Ron G. (R-ID), (208) 334-3200 105
Cranwell, Charles Richard (D-VA), (804) 698-1014 441
Craven, Olivia (ID), (208) 334-2520 109
Crawford, Bob (D-FL), (850) 488-3022 80
Crawford, Brett (LA), (225) 925-7680 163

Crawford, Charlotte (NV), (775) 684-4000 259
Crawford, Denise Voigt (TX), (512) 305-8300 412
Crawford, Hersh (OR), (503) 945-5772 348
Crawford, Susan (ME), (207) 287-3531 166
Craycroft, Annette E. (IN), (317) 232-0668 122
Crine, W. Stuart (TN), (615) 741-2981 397
Crippen, Bruce D. (R-MT), (406) 444-4800 244
Criswell, Susanne (MT), (406) 444-3739 241
Croce, Alan J. (NY), (518) 485-2346 294
Crofts, Richard A. (MT), (406) 444-0311 238
Crook, Ann B. (OR), (503) 378-8689 351
Crooks, N. Patrick (WI), (608) 266-1883 470
Cropp, Linda W. (DC), (202) 724-8032 77
Crosley, Virlena (OR), (503) 947-1475 346
Cross, Roger (WI), (608) 266-2233 468
Crow, Jeffrey J. (NC), (919) 733-7305 305
Crowe, Ronald E. (MS), (601) 359-1285 220
Crowell, Gary E. (PA), (717) 787-5996 359
Crowner, Robert J. (PA), (717) 783-3397 355
Crowson, Cecil, Jr. (TN), (615) 741-2681 403
Cruea, Darrell (SD), (605) 773-5425 386
Crump, Jack E. (TX), (512) 463-5505 410
Crump, Wayne F. (D-MO), (573) 751-2101 235
Crunican, Grace (OR), (503) 986-3200 351
Crutchfield, Ward (D-TN), (615) 741-6682 402
Cryer, Peggy (AR), (501) 296-1802 34
Csiszar, Ernst N. (SC), (803) 737-6212 379
Cuevas, Michael R. (NY), (518) 457-2578 298
Cugno, William A. (CT), (860) 524-4991 57
Culhane, Edmond S., Jr. (RI), (401) 444-1010 371
Cullider, James, Jr. (MS), (601) 359-4972 221
Culp, Anthony M. (LA), (225) 274-4112 164
Culver, Chester J. (D-IA), (515) 281-8993 131
Cummings, Alexander L. (MD), (410) 260-1500 .. 185
Cummings, Marlene A. (WI), (608) 266-8609 467
Cupp, Robert R. (R-OH), (614) 466-7584 331
Curcio, Thomas L. (MD), (410) 922-2100 177
Curie, Charles G. (PA), (717) 787-6443 362
Curran, J. Joseph, Jr. (D-MD), (410) 576-6300 174
Currie, Barbary Flynn (D-IL), (217) 782-8121 120
Curry, Eric (WY), (307) 777-7434 471
Curry, Thomas J. (MA), (617) 956-1510.............. 187
Curtis, David L. (ID), (208) 334-3860 110
Cusack, Greg (IA), (515) 281-0020 136
Cusack, Joan A. (NY), (212) 417-5136 294
Cutillo, Louis S. (CT), (860) 594-2575 62
Cutler, Steve (R-SD), (605) 773-3845 393

D

D'Antuono, Louis (RI), (401) 222-1478 372
D'Arco, Michael (NM), (505) 827-6300 290
D'Arcy, Christine T. (OR), (503) 986-0087 346

DiFava, John (MA), (508) 820-2352 193
DiFrancesco, Donald T. (R-NJ),
(609) 259-5199 281
DiGaetano, Paul (R-NJ), (609) 292-5339 282
Dinger, Regina A. (AL), (334) 242-5021 4
Dini, Joseph E. (Joe), Jr. (D-NV),
(775) 684-8503 263
DiNinni, Louie (CA), (916) 445-1539 45
Dionne, Paul R. (ME), (207) 287-7086 172
Dipasquale, Nicholas A. (DE), (302) 739-4403 69
DiPrete, Bob (OR), (503) 378-2422 348
Dixon, Larry D. (AL), (334) 242-4116 6
Dixon, Richard N. (MD), (410) 260-7160 175
Doak, Thomas (ME), (207) 287-2791 168
Dobis, Chester F. (D-IN), (317) 232-9600 130
Dodson, Gay (TX), (512) 305-8000 411
Doherty, Steve (D-MT), (406) 444-4364 244
Doll, Otto (SD), (605) 677-5861 390
Dollard, Robin (WA), (360) 753-5601 444
Dombroskas, Edward (CT), (860) 270-8075 59
Donaghue, Frank T. (PA), (717) 787-9707 357
Donato, Renato, Jr. (NY), (518) 474-4429 293
Dong, Norman (DC), (202) 727-6053 76
Donheffner, Paul E. (OR), (503) 373-1405 349
Donley, Leslie (NE), (402) 471-3543 253
Donnelly, Kevin (DE), (302) 739-4860 70
Donohue, Mary O. (R-NY),
(518) 474-4623 .... 292, 300
Donovan, Jack (NH), (603) 271-6457 266
Donovan, Paul (VT), (802) 828-3268 432
Dooley, John A., III (VT), (802) 828-3278 432
Dopp, Bob (MO), (573) 526-9237 232
Doria, Joseph V., Jr. (D-NJ), (609) 292-7065 282
Dorr, Linda (WI), (608) 267-7897 467
Dorsett, Katie G. (NC), (919) 807-2425 303
Dorsey, Donna N. (MD), (410) 585-1900 181
Dorso, John (R-ND), (701) 293-6941 321
Dosal, Sue K. (MN), (651) 296-2474 215
Dougherty, Brian (OK), (405) 751-6512 334
Douglas, Andrew (OH), (614) 466-4524 331
Douglas, James H. (R-VT), (802) 828-2301 425
Douglas, John (AR), (501) 682-0190 35
Douglass, Gus R. (D-WV), (304) 558-2201 455
Dowdel, William (AZ), (602) 542-2657 24
Dowler, Bernard (WV), (304) 558-2771 457
Dowling, Sally (RI), (401) 222-2088 370
Downes, Donald W. (CT), (860) 827-2801 61
Downey, Christine (D-KS), (785) 296-7377 146
Downs, Nancy (ME), (207) 783-5382 168
Doxtater, Gary (IN), (317) 232-4080 127
Doyle, James E. (D-WI), (608) 244-4982 462
Dozie-Otten, Robin (NM), (505) 827-7750 288

Dreher, Karl J. (ID), (208) 327-7910 111
Drennen, Mark C. (LA), (225) 342-7086 158
Drew, John (NV), (775) 684-4549 260
Drew, Mimi (FL), (850) 487-1855 81
Driscoll, David P. (MA), (781) 388-3111 189
Driskell, Joseph L. (MO), (573) 751-3946 229
Drowota, Frank F., III (TN), (615) 741-2114 403
Drumm, Francis J., Jr. (CT), (860) 566-8160 63
Drummond, John W. (D-SC), (803) 212-6640 384
DuBois, Frank A. (NM), (505) 646-3007 285
DuBois, Glenn (NH), (603) 271-2739 271
Duby, Lynn F. (ME), (207) 287-4223 170
DuCharme, Steve (NV), (775) 687-6525 259
Duenwald, Jay L. (R-SD), (605) 773-5938 393
DuFault, Art (UT), (801) 538-5555 421
Dufford, Milt (GA), (404) 362-6440 93
Duffy, Greg D. (OK), (405) 521-4660 342
Dunbar, Carson J. (NJ),
(609) 882-2000, ext. 6311 281
Duncan, Don (VA), (540) 857-7104 440
Duncan, Richard (SD), (605) 773-3421 386
Dunlap, Charles L. (TX), (512) 397-6401 413
Dunn, Katie (NH), (603) 271-5998 .... 268, 269
Dunstan, Frank (NY), (518) 457-2475 296
Dupree, Thomas A. (RI), (401) 647-3367 369
Duran, Leon (NM), (505) 827-3041 284
Durand, Bob (MA), (617) 242-6000 .... 189, 193
Durden, Gregory (FL), (954) 712-4600 80
Durham, Burney T. (TN), (615) 741-2901 402
Durham, Christine M. (UT), (801) 578-3900 424
Durham, Robert D. (OR), (503) 986-5725 353
Dustin, Daniel (NY), (518) 474-3836 293
Dutcher, Judith H. (D-MN), (651) 296-2524 206
Dutton, Nancy (NH), (603) 271-3483 267
DuVal, Barry E. (VA), (804) 786-7831 435
Dwyer, Beverly A. (RI), (401) 222-2200 367
Dye, Charles R. (Randy) (WV), (304) 558-3446 .. 456
Dye, Marvin W. (MT), (406) 444-6201 244
Dyer, Buddy (D-FL), (850) 487-5190 85
Dykeman, Darald (WY), (307) 777-6713 ..... 472, 475

E

Eachus, Ron (OR), (503) 378-6611 350
Eads, M. Adela (R-CT), (860) 240-8800 62
Eagerton, John C. (AL), (334) 242-4480 2
Earle, Kevin B. (NJ), (973) 504-6380 276
Earley, Mark L. (R-VA), (804) 786-2071 433
Easley, Michael F. (D-NC), (919) 716-6400 302
Eastaugh, Robert L. (AK), (907) 264-0624 19
Eastin, Delaine A. (CA), (916) 657-4766 41
Eberdt, David (AR), (501) 682-2222 31
Ebersole, W. Daniel (GA), (404) 656-2168 87

Gray, Lonnie (ID), (208) 884-7060 109
Gray, Walter P. (CA), (916) 653-7715 39
Greacen, John M. (NM), (505) 827-4800 291
Greaney, John M. (MA), (617) 557-1000 195
Green, Carol Gilliam (KS), (785) 296-3229 147
Green, Charles L. (DC), (202) 576-7525 77
Green, Janet L. (NM), (505) 827-7449 290
Green, Joe (R-AK), (907) 465-4931 18
Green, John (SD), (605) 367-5200 391
Green, Mary (WI), (608) 267-7803 465
Green, Shirley (TX), (512) 463-2000 404
Greene, James (MT), (406) 841-3911 239
Greene, Jeanne (NV), (775) 684-0150 261
Greene, Mike (TN), (615) 251-5166 401
Greenfield, Michael (OR), (503) 378-4100 345
Greer, Jim (OR), (503) 872-5272 347
Gregg, Guy R. (R-NJ), (609) 292-5339 282
Gregg, John R. (D-IN), (317) 232-9600 129
Gregoire, Christine O. (D-WA), (360) 753-6200 .. 442
Gregory, Frank W. (AL), (334) 242-0366 10
Greiff, Lorraine (MA), (617) 727-7440 189
Grey, Todd C. (UT), (801) 584-8410 420
Gribskov, Cheryl (OR), (503) 373-1042 351
Griebling, Rich (CO), (303) 894-2100 52
Grier, Tom (CO), (303) 273-1622 49
Griffen, Thomas G. (NY), (518) 474-5711 299
Griffin, David (AR), (501) 682-8590 30
Griffin, David (FL), (850) 487-7728 83
Griffin, Douglas B. (AK), (907) 269-0351 17
Griffin, Evelyn (TN), (615) 741-2515 398
Griffin, John (IN), (317) 232-2378 126
Griffith, Daniel R. (DE), (302) 739-5313 68
Griffith, Morgan (R-VA), (804) 698-1088 441
Grimaldi, Margaret A. (WA), (360) 664-0871 445
Grimes, Frank J. (CA), (916) 324-9100 40
Grimes, Johnny (GA), (404) 624-7896 92
Grinde, Larry Hal (R-MT), (406) 444-4368 244
Grisham, Michelle Lujan (NM), (505) 827-7640 .. 285
Griswold, J. Samuel (SC), (803) 898-2504 378
Grittner, Frederick K. (MN), (651) 296-2581 215
Gromer, Amy (MN), (202) 624-3642 205
Gronseth, Marsha (MN), (651) 582-8787 207
Gronstal, Michael E. (D-IA), (515) 281-3901 138
Groom, David E. (OR), (503) 378-3349 349
Groscost, Jeff (R-AZ), (602) 542-5735 27
Grose, Richard G. (MO), (816) 759-6600 229
Groseclose, Bernard S., Jr. (SC), (843) 577-8600 . 381
Gross, Alfred W. (VA), (804) 371-9741 439
Grossi, Paul L. (AK), (907) 465-2790 16
Grossman, Parrell D. (ND), (701) 328-3404 314
Grossman, Steven J. (OH), (614) 466-0152 330
Groves, John R., Jr. (KY), (502) 607-1558 149

Guay, David (CT), (860) 509-6182 57
Guerard, William F., Jr. (CA), (916) 323-1777 43
Guerber, Steve (ID), (208) 334-2682 107
Guhl, Michele K. (NJ), (609) 292-3717 279
Guin, Ken (D-AL), (334) 242-7771 10
Guinn, Kenny (R-NV), (775) 684-5670 257
Gulliford, James (IA), (515) 281-6153 132
Gulyassy, Stephen V. (OH), (614) 466-3455 323
Gumble, Jane Wallace (MA), (617) 727-7765 190
Gunn, Doris B. (LA), (225) 925-4660 159
Guntharp, G. David (AR), (501) 682-9566 30
Guy, Richard P. (WA), (360) 357-2041 453
Guy, Robert (NC), (919) 716-3101 304
Guzzi, Louis A. (PA), (717) 783-7049 358
Gwadosky, Dan A. (D-ME), (207) 626-8400 166

H

Haag, Gale (KS), (785) 296-3401 142
Haas, June Summers (MI), (517) 373-3196 202
Hackney, Charles D. (MI), (517) 334-7147 201
Hackney, Joe (D-NC), (919) 733-5752 310
Hadley, Corine A. (IA), (515) 281-5294 133
Hadley, James P., Jr. (LA), (225) 925-6454 163
Hadley, Katherine G. (Kit) (MN),
  (651) 296-7608 210
Hafer, Barbara (R-PA), (717) 787-2465 354
Haffey, Patricia (MT), (406) 444-9091 240
Hagen, Bruce (ND), (701) 328-2400 318
Hagen, Lance (ND), (701) 328-2916 321
Hager, John H. (R-VA), (804) 786-2078 ...... 433, 440
Hagerty, Thomas J. (MN), (651) 296-2942 206
Haines, Virginia E. (NJ), (609) 599-5900 280
Hainje, Dick (R-SD), (605) 773-3821 393
Hainkel, John J., Jr. (R-LA), (225) 342-2040 164
Hainlin, Mary (MT), (406) 444-4285 241
Hale, Karen F. (TX), (512) 206-4588 410
Hale, William M. (TX), (512) 437-3450 409
Haley, Kathleen (OR), (503) 229-5770 349
Haley, Michael W. (AL), (334) 353-3883 4
Haley, Pat (D-SD), (605) 773-4484 393
Haley, Paula (AK), (907) 276-7474 16
Halkias, Rebecca (PA), (202) 624-7828 354
Hall, Carolyn C. (GA), (404) 656-2034 94
Hall, Eugene M. (DE), (302) 577-8600 68
Hall, Judy (OR), (503) 986-1851 352
Hall, William (DC), (202) 727-6055 75
Halleck, Teresa A. (MD), (410) 494-8030 178
Halliburtin, Cheryl (TX), (512) 936-8100 413
Hallock, John W., Jr. (IL), (312) 814-6500 117
Halverson, Harold (R-SD), (605) 773-3824 393
Halvorson, Debbie (D-IL), (217) 782-7419 120
Ham, Willis C. (SC), (803) 737-7800 379

Hodges, Jim (D-SC), (803) 734-9400 374
Hodges, Ralph B. (OK), (405) 521-3844 343
Hoefer, Walter G. (NY), (518) 474-4425 293
Hoelscher, Pam (MO), (573) 751-1052 229
Hogan, Michael (OH), (614) 466-2337 326
Hogan, Michael J. (VT), (802) 828-4929 429
Hogan, Michael P. (MA), (617) 451-2477 191
Hoium, Daniel (ND), (701) 328-5555 314
Hojan-Clark, Jane (WI), (608) 264-6181 465
Holbrook, Sidney J. (CT), (860) 566-4840 56
Holcomb, Richard D. (VA), (804) 367-6602 438
Holden, Bob (D-MO), (573) 751-4123 227
Holden, Fran (CO), (303) 894-2617 48
Holden, Richard W. (NC), (919) 733-7952 305
Holder, Janice M. (TN), (901) 685-3949 403
Holifield, Henry (TX), (512) 454-9970 407
Holland, Jim W., Jr. (AL), (334) 242-8748 8
Holland, Manfred G. (WV), (304) 558-6029 459
Holland, Randy J. (DE), (302) 856-5363 72
Holland, Sam D. (SD), (605) 773-3321 386
Holland, William G. (IL), (217) 782-3536 114
Hollinger, Paula C. (D-MD), (410) 841-3131 184
Hollingsworth, Doneen B. (SD),
   (605) 773-3361 389
Hollingworth, Beverly A. (D-NH),
   (603) 271-3073 272
Hollon, Steven C. (OH), (614) 466-2653 332
Holman, Bill (NC), (919) 715-4101 305
Holman, Mark A. (PA), (717) 787-2500 354
Holmer, Darrell E. (WV), (304) 357-7800 460
Holmes, Roger (MN), (651) 297-1308 211
Holmstrom, David (MN), (612) 617-2201 211
Holsapple, Rex W. (NE), (402) 471-2043 251
Holstein, John C. (MO), (573) 751-1004 235
Holthoff, Timothy N. (AR), (501) 682-2147 37
Holzbaur, Charlene M. (NJ), (609) 292-6746 280
Hood, David W. (LA), (225) 342-9509 161
Hood, Michael (NV), (775) 684-4867 260
Hooks, Mary B. (FL), (850) 922-7021 83
Hoomissen, George Van (OR), (503) 986-5709 353
Hooper, Perry O., Sr. (AL), (334) 242-4599 10
Hord, Annette (NE), (402) 471-2935 251
Horn, Martin F. (PA), (717) 975-4918 357
Horn, Philip, Jr. (PA), (717) 787-3028 355
Horn, Randall E. (NM), (505) 474-1202 285
Horne, Audrey W. (GA), (404) 651-6314 90
Hornyak, Juleann (IL), (217) 782-2035 121
Horton, Ashley (TX), (512) 475-2615 413
Horton, Robert (MN), (651) 215-5866 210
Horton, Sherman D., Jr. (NH), (603) 271-3660 274
Hoskins, Donald (PA), (717) 783-7251 357
Hotz, Donald J. (OK), (405) 948-6700 341

Houdek, Duane (ND), (701) 328-2200 312
Houseworth, Richard C. (AZ), (602) 255-4421 21
Houston, Bill C. (TN), (615) 741-2236 398
Houston, J. Gorman, Jr. (AL), (334) 242-4587 10
Houstoun, Feather O. (PA), (717) 787-2600 361
Howard, Cathy (DE), (302) 739-4155 72
Howard, Dennis (OK), (405) 521-3864 334
Howard, James L. (OK), (405) 525-9144 339
Howard, Julia C. (R-NC), (919) 733-5904 310
Howard, Laurie (KS), (785) 296-3773 144
Howard, Marilyn (D-ID), (208) 332-6811 106
Howarth, Helen (AK), (907) 269-6607 14
Howarth, Susan (AR), (501) 682-2386 32
Howe, Kevin (NH), (603) 271-3286 266
Howe, Richard C. (UT), (801) 578-3900 424
Howe, Robert (VT), (802) 828-2106 428
Howell, Samuel W., IV (SC), (803) 734-9060 378
Howell, Scott N. (D-UT), (801) 538-1406 423
Hoyas, Raymond T., Jr. (RI), (401) 222-6876 372
Hoyt, Kathleen C. (VT), (802) 828-3322 426
Hubbard, James (CO), (970) 491-6303 50
Hubbell, Connie (KS), (785) 296-4986 141
Huckabee, Mike (R-AR), (501) 682-2345 29
Hudgins, James L. (SC), (803) 896-5280 382
Hudkins, Cordie (WV), (304) 558-2764 457
Huggins, M. Wayne (VA), (804) 674-2087 439
Hughes, James M. (ND), (701) 328-2455 315
Hughes, John A. (DE), (302) 739-4411 70
Hughes, Marilyn (OK), (405) 522-2515 337
Hugoson, Eugene (Gene) (MN),
   (651) 297-3219 206
Hull, James B. (TX), (979) 458-6600 408
Hull, Jane Dee (R-AZ), (602) 542-4331 20
Hume, Lindel (D-IN), (317) 232-9400 128
Humphries, Becky (MI), (517) 373-1263 201
Hune, Raymond (MO), (573) 751-5398 233
Hungerbeeler, Henry (MO), (573) 751-4622 234
Hunking, Loila (SD), (605) 773-4766 386
Hunstein, Carol W. (GA), (404) 656-3475 95
Hunt, James B., Jr. (D-NC), (919) 733-4240 302
Hunt, Lorraine T. (R-NV), (775) 684-5637 ... 257, 262
Hunt, Randy (OH), (614) 466-5495 329
Hunt, Roger W. (R-SD), (605) 773-3830 393
Hunt, William E., Sr. (MT), (406) 444-5570 245
Hunter, Mike (R-OK), (405) 521-3912 333
Hurlbutt, Linda (ID), (208) 334-4673 111
Hurrelbrink, Dianne J. (IL), (217) 524-8773 115
Hurry, William H., Jr. (RI), (401) 736-1114 370
Hurson, John Adams (D-MD), (410) 841-3464 184
Hurst, Rodney (FL), (904) 727-3689 81
Huston, Robert J. (TX), (512) 239-5505 411
Hutchens, Don (NE), (402) 471-2676 248

I

J

Johnson, Duane (KS), (785) 296-5466 145
Johnson, Eric (R-GA), (404) 656-5109 94
Johnson, Gary E. (R-NM), (505) 827-3000 284
Johnson, Gary J. (IA), (515) 281-7393 137
Johnson, Grantland (CA), (916) 654-3345 42
Johnson, James B., Jr. (SC), (803) 734-8666 382
Johnson, Jeffrey (UT), (801) 538-3191 417
Johnson, John A. (NY), (518) 473-8437 294
Johnson, Kiehner (OH), (614) 466-6700 329
Johnson, Nolton G. (GA), (404) 651-5168 92
Johnson, Noni (NV), (775) 688-1231 259
Johnson, Pamela S. (KY), (502) 564-4646 154
Johnson, Paul W. (IA), (515) 281-5385 135
Johnson, Richard D. (R-IA), (515) 281-5835 132
Johnson, Roger (D-ND), (701) 328-4754 313
Johnson, Ross (R-CA), (916) 445-4961 45
Johnson, Rudolph (GA), (404) 352-6411 89
Johnson, Ruth E. (TN), (615) 741-2461 400
Johnson, Stephen J. (IN), (317) 232-1836 128
Johnson, Thomas W. (OH), (614) 466-4034 323
Johnston, John W. (IL), (217) 785-6642 119
Johnstone, Douglas Inge (AL), (334) 242-4597 10
Johnstone, Martin E. (KY), (502) 595-3199 156
Johnstone, Richard N. (KY), (502) 564-4850 153
Jolly, Jerry R. (CA), (916) 263-0722 43
Jones, Bill (R-CA), (916) 653-7244 38
Jones, Bradley H. (R-MA), (617) 722-2460 194
Jones, Charles E. (AZ), (520) 542-4534 28
Jones, Christopher (OH), (614) 644-2782 ..... 325, 326
Jones, Cindy (IA), (515) 281-0165 131
Jones, Dallas (CA), (916) 262-1816 41
Jones, David M. (D-UT), (801) 538-1575 423
Jones, Dennis L. (R-FL), (850) 488-9960 85
Jones, Dennis M. (SD), (605) 362-2737 391
Jones, Eddie (SC), (803) 896-4540 377
Jones, Emil (D-IL), (217) 782-2728 120
Jones, Janet E. (KS), (785) 296-7633 147
Jones, John E., III (PA), (717) 787-5230 360
Jones, John N. (SD), (605) 773-5990 389
Jones, Jonathan (DE), (202) 624-7724 65
Jones, Lawrence W. (AK), (907) 465-3384 14
Jones, Marge (KY), (502) 564-4848 156
Jones, Mark (CT), (860) 566-5650 62
Jones, Mark (OH), (614) 466-3650 325
Jones, Sheldon R. (AZ), (602) 542-0998 21
Jones, Stanley G. (IN), (317) 464-4400 125
Jordan, Eurial (WI), (608) 267-3715 463
Jordan, Lloyd J. (DC), (202) 442-8947 77
Jordan, Luther Henry, Jr. (D-NC),
   (919) 715-3034 309
Jordan, Robert R. (DE), (302) 831-2833 68
Jordan, Susan J. (WA), (360) 753-2558 446

Joseph, Ron (CA), (916) 263-2389 43
Joule, Reggie (D-AK), (907) 465-4833 18
Jourgensen, Debbie (WY), (307) 777-7674 473
Jubelirer, Robert C. (R-PA), (717) 787-5490 363
Judd, Roth (WI), (608) 266-8123 464
Judge, Patty (D-IA), (515) 281-5322 132
Judge, Robert A., Sr. (PA), (717) 783-3680 362
Judson, Lilia G. (IN), (317) 232-2542 130
Juker, Pamm (ID), (208) 332-1140 112
Julander, Paula F. (D-UT), (801) 538-1405 423

K

Kahn, Bobby (GA), (404) 651-7715 87
Kalanek, Constance B. (ND), (701) 328-9781 317
Kamikawa, Ray K. (HI), (808) 587-1510 101
Kamimura, Dennis (HI), (808) 532-7700 100
Kamin, C. Richard (NJ), (609) 292-4570 281
Kane, Candice (IL), (312) 793-8550 115
Kane, James (DE), (302) 577-5030 66
Kane, John F. (ID), (208) 422-5242 105
Kapalko, Paul A. (NJ), (609) 292-2414 280
Kaplan, Lori F. (IN), (317) 232-8611 124
Kapsner, Carol Ronning (ND), (701) 328-4494 321
Karass, Edward (ME), (207) 287-6632 167
Karem, David K. (D-KY), (503) 564-2470 155
Karll, Jo Ann (MO), (573) 751-4231 231
Karras, Dennis (WA), (360) 664-6349 448
Kasabach, Haig F. (NJ), (609) 292-1185 278
Kassel, John (VT), (802) 241-3600 429
Katz, Joette (CT), (860) 566-5641 64
Katz, John (AK), (202) 624-5858 11
Kauffman, Kurt (OH), (614) 466-0691 328
Kaufman, Alan (NJ), (609) 777-0700 280
Kaufman, Alison (CT), (202) 347-4535 56
Kaufman, William G. (Bill) (R-CO),
   (303) 866-2947 54
Kauger, Yvonne (OK), (405) 521-3841 343
Kaul, N. G. (NY), (518) 457-7464 296
Kautzky, Walter L. (IA), (515) 242-5703 133
Kavanau, Karen (NV), (775) 684-1717 264
Kawaguchi, Paul T. (HI), (808) 586-6720 102
Kaye, Judith S. (NY), (212) 661-6787 301
Keane, Catherine (NH), (603) 271-4394 268
Keane, Joseph P. (TN), (615) 741-2677 397
Kearns, Merle Grace (R-OH), (614) 466-3780 331
Kearns, Wally (ND), (701) 777-3700 319
Keating, Frank (R-OK), (405) 521-2342 333
Keck, John (WY), (307) 777-6303 474
Kedra, Linda (UT), (801) 538-1000 416
Keefe, George W. (MA), (508) 233-6552 192
Keegan, Lisa Graham (R-AZ), (602) 542-5460 22
Keeley, Fred (D-CA), (916) 319-2027 46

Little, Elaine (ND), (701) 328-6390 314
Little, J. Rodney (MD), (410) 514-7601 179
Liveratti, Mary (NV), (775) 687-4210 260
Lloyd, L. A. (AZ), (602) 255-5125 25
Lockard, Marlene (NV), (775) 684-5801 260
Locke, Gary (D-WA), (360) 902-4111 442
Locke, Jeffrey (MA), (617) 748-2325 192
Lockett, Tyler C. (KS), (785) 296-4900 147
Lockyer, Bill (D-CA), (916) 324-5437 38
Loeper, F. Joseph (R-PA), (717) 787-1350 363
Logan, Robert W. (KY), (502) 564-2150 152
Logsdon, Robert R. (NE), (402) 471-3101 253
Logue, James L., III (MI), (517) 373-6022 199
Lohr, Robert A. (AK), (907) 465-7900 13
Lokkesmoe, Kent (MN), (651) 296-4810............. 211
Long, James E. (D-NC), (919) 733-3058 307
Long, Marsha Tadano (WA), (360) 902-7200 446
Long, Merritt D. (WA), (360) 664-4800.............. 450
Long, Susan M. (IA), (515) 472-8411 134
Long, Virginia A. (NJ), (609) 292-8090 283
Longley, S. Catherine (ME), (207) 624-8511 171
Longway, Robert T. (CO), (303) 894-7794 48
Loots, James M. (DC), (202) 727-0656 76
Lord, Thomas E. (MS), (601) 961-7400 219
Loredo, John A. (D-AZ), (602) 542-5830 27
Loring, Glenda (IA), (515) 281-4126 132
Loucks, Katherine C. (NY), (518) 474-4116........ 299
Lovaglio, Ronald B. (ME), (207) 287-2211 167
Lovejoy, Linda (NM), (505) 827-8019 289
Lovell, Stephanie S. (MA), (617) 727-0060 187
Lowe, R. Stanley (WY), (307) 265-7372 476
Lowell, Howard (DE), (302) 739-5318 70
Lowell, Suzanne (AK), (907) 465-3725 18
Lowell, Virginia (HI), (808) 586-3704 100
Lowenberg, Timothy J. (WA), (253) 512-8201 443
Luallen, Lynn (KY), (502) 564-7630 151
Lubra, Gary (NV), (775) 688-5767 262
Lucas, Marion (IA), (515) 262-3111 137
Lucas, Michael S. (OH), (614) 644-6843 ...... 326, 329
Lucciola, Denise A. (MA), (617) 727-4900 193
Luce, Ray (GA), (404) 651-5061 92
Luckett, Nelda (MS), (601) 987-6837 218
Lujan, Ben (D-NM), (505) 986-4777 291
Lummis, Cynthia (R-WY), (307) 777-7408 471
Lumpkin, John (IL), (217) 782-4977 119
Lund, Elizabeth (TN),
  (615) 532-3202, ext. 25166.............................. 400
Luther, Robert W. (SC), (803) 896-7894 381
Lutz, Steve (WA), (509) 663-9600 443
Lynch, Darla L. (SD), (605) 773-3563 387
Lynch, Joseph B. (NY), (518) 473-8384 297
Lynch, Kendall (TN), (615) 741-2718 400

Lynch, Neil L. (MA), (617) 557-1000 195
Lynch, William B. (PA), (717) 861-8500 355
Lyon, Frederick C. (ID), (208) 334-2210 112
Lyons, Champ, Jr. (AL), (334) 242-4351 10
Lyons, Chris (OR), (503) 540-1017 350
Lyons, David J. (IA), (515) 242-4814 133
Lyons, Moira K. (D-CT), (860) 240-8500 63
Lyons, William (CA), (916) 654-0433 41

M

Maas, Ron (NE), (402) 471-2358 254
Mabry, Elizabeth S. (SC), (803) 737-1302 383
Mabry, Henry C., III (AL), (334) 242-7160 4
MacDonald, Keith W. (NV), (775) 850-1440........ 261
Mace, Frana Araujo (D-CO), (303) 866-2954 54
Mach, Michael J. (WI), (608) 266-1622 464
Machold, Roland A., Jr. (NJ), (609) 984-5131 275
Mackey, Millard (MS), (601) 359-3569 221
Mackie, Jerry (R-AK), (907) 465-4925 18
Macklin, Larry D. (IN), (317) 232-4020 126
MacKnight, David H. (KY), (502) 696-5300 153
MacMurray, Helen (OH), (614) 466-1305 324
Macy, Richard J. (WY), (307) 777-7422 477
Madden, Martin G. (R-MD), (410) 841-3572 184
Maddox, Alva Hugh (AL), (334) 242-4593 10
Madigan, Michael J. (D-IL), (217) 782-5350........ 120
Madrid, Patricia (D-NM), (505) 827-6000 284
Madsen, Barbara A. (WA), (360) 357-2037 453
Madsen, Roger B. (ID), (208) 334-6110 109
Maes, Petra Jimenez (NM), (505) 827-4883 291
Maestas, Elizabeth (NM), (505) 827-8825 285
Maggiore, Peter (NM), (505) 827-2855 287
Magill, Michael (TN), (615) 741-2131 399
Maglich, Gretchen (MN), (651) 296-2342 210
Magnusson, Keith C. (ND), (701) 328-2727 319
Magnusson, Martin A. (ME), (207) 287-4360 168
Maguire, James F. (IN), (317) 264-4698 126
Maher, J. E. (MS), (601) 352-9100 219
Mahfood, Stephen M. (MO), (573) 751-3443 231
Mahn, Gary (ID), (208) 334-2470 106
Mahone, Othello (DC), (202) 442-7210 77
Mahoney, Dan (OK), (405) 521-2342 333
Maidenberg, David (IN), (317) 232-3850 125
Mainella, Fran (FL), (850) 488-6131 81
Mala, Cynthia (ND), (701) 328-2428 316
Malachowski, James J. (RI), (401) 222-3500........ 371
Malcom, Jan (MN), (651) 215-5806 209
Mallet, Jerry (ID), (208) 334-5159 107
Mallory, Bradley L. (PA), (717) 787-2838 363
Mallow, Jim (MD), (410) 260-8501 181
Malone, James F., III (PA), (717) 939-9551 363
Malone, Melvin (TN), (615) 741-2904 400

McCarter, Mike (MT), (406) 444-7794 244
McCartney, Mike (HI), (808) 587-1100 99
McCarty, John P. (KY), (502) 564-4240 150
McCarty, Sally (IN), (317) 232-3520 126
McCarty, William D. (IN), (317) 232-2705 128
McCarville, James (PA), (412) 201-7335 361
McCaskill, Claire C. (D-MO), (573) 751-4824 227
McCaul, Elizabeth (NY), (212) 618-6548 294
McCleskey, Jim (NC), (202) 624-5830 302
McCloud, Ronald B. (KY), (502) 564-7760 153
McClure, Amy (WY), (307) 332-9402 476
McClurg, Lori (NE), (402) 471-2331 247
McCollum, William (VA), (804) 786-5895 434
McConnel, Gary (GA), (404) 635-7000 89
McCormack, Michael (NE), (402) 471-4345 255
McCormack, Richard J. (D-VT),
   (802) 828-2241 431
McCormick, Dale (D-ME), (207) 287-2771 166
McCormick, James H. (PA), (717) 720-4010 363
McCoy, David T. (NC), (919) 733-2520 309
McCoy, Don (ID), (208) 334-4370 109
McCrory, Mike (NE), (402) 471-2833 247
McCullough, Clyde W., Jr. (TN),
   (615) 741-2730 402
McCullough, Samuel A. (PA), (717) 787-3003 356
McCullough, Sharon (MT), (406) 444-3745 238
McDade, Jim (TX), (512) 349-6601 405
McDaniel, Steve (R-TN), (615) 741-0750 402
McDaniel, Tracye (TX), (512) 936-0091 407
McDermott, John (NH), (603) 271-2175 268
McDermott, Mark (AZ), (602) 248-1490 26
McDonald, Dan (R-WA), (360) 786-7694 452
McDonald, Francis M., Jr. (CT), (860) 566-1102 ... 64
McDonald, Judy (CA), (916) 322-5520 41
McDonald, Michael Ray (Mike) (D-TN),
   (615) 741-1980 402
McDonald, Patricia A. (VT), (802) 828-2011 429
McDonald, Sheila (AR), (501) 682-3649 35
McDonald, Sheila C. (MD), (410) 260-7335 182
McDonough, Judith (MA), (617) 727-8470 190
McDonough, Pam (IL), (217) 782-3233 115
McDougal, Frank (VT), (802) 650-7046 427
McDowell, Bob (NJ), (609) 292-2965 278
McDowell, Donna (WI), (608) 266-2701 465
McDowell, Harris B., II (D-DE), (302) 739-4147 .. 71
McElwain, Jenny (AK), (907) 465-2542 13
McEwen, John (MT), (406) 444-3894 238
McFarland, Kay (KS), (785) 296-5322 147
McGann, Timothy J. (IN), (317) 232-1980 126
McGee, Ann Y. (VA), (804) 662-9312 434
McGee, Glenn W. (IL), (217) 782-4321 114
McGiverin, Arthur A. (IA), (515) 682-3635 139

McGlasson, William B. (KS), (785) 296-4278 141
McGowan, James J. (NY), (518) 457-2741 297
McGrail, Stephen (MA), (508) 820-2010 192
McGraw, Darrell V., Jr. (D-WV),
   (304) 558-2021 454
McGraw, Mac (D-WY), (307) 777-7754 477
McGraw, Warren R. (WV), (304) 558-2602 461
McGregor, Ruth V. (AZ), (602) 542-5789 28
McGuire, Noel (NJ), (609) 777-2500 275
McGuire, Steven G. (NV), (775) 687-4880 260
McHenry, Deborah L. (WV), (304) 558-6035 461
McIntosh, John (SC), (803) 734-3970 377
McKee, Garry L. (WY), (307) 777-7656 474
McKeithen, Walter Fox (R-LA),
   (225) 342-4479 157
McKenna, Mary Jane (MA), (617) 973-8500 189
McKenna, Thomas F. (IN), (317) 232-8806 123
McKenzie, R. Andy (R-WV), (304) 357-7984 460
McKeown, Richard (UT), (801) 538-1000 416
McKinney, Alice D. (AL), (334) 242-8990 5
McKinney, Rita M. (SC), (803) 896-4390 379
McKinney, Sandra K. (SC), (803) 734-2010 384
McKinney, Stan M. (SC), (803) 734-8020 378
McKnelly, Phil (NC), (919) 715-5422 305
McKnight, Ted (VT), (802) 828-3256 426
McLain, Kevin (SD), (605) 773-3478 387
McLaughlin, Philip Thomas (D-NH),
   (603) 271-3655 265
McLemore, William H. (GA), (404) 656-3214 91
McLendon, Robert (D-AZ), (602) 542-4430 27
McLeod, Richard (NH), (603) 271-3556 271
McLeod, Van (NH), (603) 271-2540 267
McLin, Rhine L. (D-OH), (614) 466-6247 331
McLucas, Karla M. (MO), (573) 751-9691 231
McMahon, James W. (NY), (518) 457-6721 299
McMillan, H. S. (MS), (601) 853-5203 223
McMorrow, Mary Ann G. (IL), (312) 793-5470 ... 121
McMullian, A. J., III (FL), (850) 488-5540 84
McQueen, Mary C. (WA), (360) 357-2121 453
McRae, Chuck R. (MS), (601) 359-2184 225
McShane, Sybil Brigham (VT), (802) 828-3265 ... 428
McSherry, Michael (VA), (202) 783-1769 433
McTavish, Thomas H. (MI), (517) 334-8050 197
McTeer, Billy (SC), (803) 734-3889 381
McWalters, Peter (RI), (401) 222-4600 368
Meadors, Mark (OK), (405) 521-6162 337
Meadows, Judith (MT), (406) 444-3660 245
Meadows, Vickers B. (TX), (512) 475-2393 409
Means, Preston (AR), (501) 682-7025 32
Mecham, Stephen F. (UT), (801) 530-6716 422
Meconi, Vincent P. (DE), (302) 739-3611 66
Medina, Gualberto (NJ), (609) 777-0885 276

Molasky-Arman, Alice (NV), (775) 687-7668 258
Mollway, Daniel J. (HI), (808) 587-0460 99
Moloney, William J. (CO), (303) 866-6806 49
Monahan, Mary K. (MD), (410) 841-3999 185
Mone, Michael A. (KY), (606) 573-1580 153
Monge, Susan (SD), (605) 773-6193 388
Monhan, Thomas (NY), (518) 474-3841 297
Monier, Claira P. (NH), (603) 472-8623 269
Monroe, Paul D., Jr. (CA), (916) 854-3500 39
Monroe, William O. (FL), (850) 487-9175 80
Montana, Lori S. (IL), (312) 793-1681 117
Montanarelli, Stephen (MD), (410) 321-4067 183
Montemayor, Jose (TX), (512) 463-6464 409
Montgomery, Betty D. (R-OH), (614) 466-3376 .. 322
Montgomery, Gary D. (AZ), (602) 252-6771 26
Montgomery, Marjorie (SC), (803) 896-4658 379
Montoya, Michael A. (D-NM), (505) 827-6400 284
Mood, Douglas (R-MT), (406) 444-1507 244
Moon, Ronald T. Y. (HI), (808) 539-4700 103
Moore, Annette B. (UT), (801) 538-1458 423
Moore, Betty (OK), (405) 521-2441 336
Moore, Gary (WA), (360) 902-4203 447
Moore, Hullihen Williams (VA),
  (804) 371-9608 439
Moore, James E. (SC), (864) 942-8565 384
Moore, James T. (Tim) (FL), (850) 410-7001 83
Moore, Jerry (AL), (205) 967-0130 7
Moore, Joanne I. (WA), (360) 956-2106 448
Moore, Marshall W. (ND), (701) 325-2581 319
Moore, Michael W. (FL), (850) 488-7480 81
Moore, Mike (D-MS), (601) 359-3692 .... 216, 218
Moore, Norman (AZ), (602) 542-3032 27
Moore, Richard G. (IA), (515) 242-5823 134
Moore, Robert S., Jr. (AR), (501) 682-1105 32
Moore, Sandy (TN), (615) 741-1831 400
Moore, Scott (R-NE), (402) 471-2554 246
Moore, Wendell (TN), (615) 532-8906 395
Morain, Tom (IA), (515) 281-8837 134
Moraleja, Rufino (WA), (360) 753-2585 443
Moran, J. Denis (WI), (608) 266-6828 470
Morell, Mindy (MD), (410) 333-3688 177
Morgan, David L. (KY), (606) 564-7005 150
Morgan, Fred (R-OK), (405) 557-7409 343
Morgan, Geralde (VA), (804) 367-2785 436
Morgan, John G. (D-TN), (615) 741-2501 395
Morgan, Olivia (CA), (202) 624-5270 38
Morgan, Richard T. (R-NC), (919) 715-3010 310
Morgando, Peggy (WY), (307) 777-7551 472
Morgenstern, Marty (CA), (916) 322-5193 43
Moriyama, Liane M. (HI), (808) 587-3110 98
Morrill, Mike (MD), (410) 974-2316 174
Morrill, Peter (ID), (208) 373-7220 105

Morris, Earl R. (UT), (801) 538-3400 421
Morris, Jim (OH), (614) 265-6712 327
Morris, John (NC), (919) 715-5422 306
Morris, Kevin (WA), (360) 902-5578 444
Morris, Mary G. (VA), (804) 225-2142 434
Morrison, Sid (WA), (360) 705-7054 451
Morrison, Thomas (ME), (207) 287-4717 168
Morrissette, Jeffrey J. (CT), (860) 627-6363 59
Morrissey, William (MN), (651) 296-9223 211
Morros, Peter G. (NV), (775) 687-4360 258
Morrow, Don C. (AR), (501) 212-5100 30
Morse, James L. (VT), (802) 828-3278 432
Morton, George (WA), (360) 753-6820 448
Morton, Glen W. (NE), (402) 471-6468 254
Morton-Keithly, Linda (ID), (208) 334-3356 107
Mory, Michael L. (IL), (217) 785-7016 116
Moschkau, Michael (WI), (608) 266-7314 466
Moseley, Jeff (TX), (512) 936-0104 407
Moser, Thomas (TX), (512) 936-4822 405
Mosk, Stanley (CA), (415) 865-7090 461
Mossaides, Marie (MA), (617) 557-1194 195
Mott, Austin (FL), (850) 488-5607 85
Motyka, Conrad (VT), (802) 241-3670 429
Moulder, Donna (TN), (615) 741-3611 400
Mount, W. Kent (CO), (303) 894-7753 52
Mouradjian, Larry (RI), (401) 222-2632 369
Moussa, Frank (KS), (785) 274-1408 142
Movassaghi, Kam K. (LA), (225) 379-1200 164
Movius, Denise (WA), (360) 902-3850 444
Moyer, Thomas J. (OH), (614) 466-3627 331
Mucha, Zenia (NY), (518) 474-8418 292
Mueller, Janice (WI), (608) 266-2818 466
Muench, Stephen R. (MA), (617) 973-8881 193
Mulhern, John P. (DE), (302) 659-2240 67
Mulholland, Jane (OR), (503) 378-3826 346
Mullarkey, Mary J. (CO),
  (303) 861-1111, ext. 271 55
Mullen, Michael L. (CT), (860) 692-7402 61
Mumma, John (CO), (303) 291-7208 51
Munis, Betty J. (ID), (208) 334-3292 107
Munro, Ralph Davies (R-WA), (360) 902-4151 442
Muri, Kathy (MT), (406) 444-2624 238
Murphy, Art (NM), (505) 827-7629 285
Murphy, John A. "Pat", Jr. (AR),
  (501) 682-1526 35
Murphy, Kevin H. (MN), (651) 296-2135 207
Murphy, Michael J. (D-WA), (360) 902-9003 442
Murphy, Raymond W. (D-MI), (517) 373-0990 203
Murphy, Terrell I. (TX), (512) 377-0500 407
Murphy, Thomas B. (D-GA), (404) 656-5020 94
Murphy, Thomas W., Jr. (R-ME),
  (207) 287-1440 173

Rester, John K. (MS), (228) 865-4300 222
Reyna, Robert (NM), (505) 827-6094 285
Reynolds, Allen H. (LA), (225) 342-8272 159
Reynolds, Mark (MA), (617) 210-5000 190
Reynolds, Nanette Lee (MI), (517) 335-3165 197
Reynolds, W. Jeff (TN), (615) 741-2473 399
Rice, Mike (NM), (505) 827-1525 287
Rice, Nancy E. (CO), (303) 861-1111, ext. 266 55
Rich, Laurie M. (TX), (202) 638-3927 404
Richards, Holly (HI), (808) 586-0300 98
Richards, Jody (D-KY), (503) 564-3366 156
Richardson, Ed (AL), (334) 242-9700 4
Richardson, Edward V. (HI), (808) 733-4246 98
Richardson, Keith (IA), (515) 281-5911 138
Richardson, Peg (FL), (850) 487-2980 81
Richkus, Peta N. (MD), (410) 767-4960 179
Richmond, Thomas T. (MT), (406) 656-0040 241
Ricks, Bob A. (OK), (405) 425-2001 340
Riddell, Linda (OR), (503) 373-1505 345
Riddick, Major F., Jr. (MD), (410) 974-3570 174
Riddle, Gladys R. (AL), (334) 242-8700 7
Riddle, Holly (NC), (919) 850-2833 306
Ridenour, Joey (AZ), (602) 331-8111 24
Ridge, Thomas J. (R-PA), (717) 787-2500 354
Ridley-Turner, Evelyn I. (IN), (317) 232-5711 124
Rielage, Robert (OH), (614) 752-7161 324
Riggs, R. William (OR), (503) 986-5668 353
Rigsby, Russell (AR), (501) 682-8755 34
Riley, Leonard (TX), (512) 804-4400 413
Ringel, Marianne (ME), (207) 624-5521 170
Rios, Peter (D-AZ), (602) 542-5685 27
Ripley, Peter H. (MO), (573) 592-4000 230
Rippeteau, Bruce E. (SC), (803) 734-0567 375
Risch, Jim (R-ID), (208) 332-1303 112
Risser, Fred (D-WI), (608) 266-1627 469
Ristau, Anita (VT), (802) 828-2396 430
Ritchey, Kenneth W. (OH), (614) 466-5214 326
Ritter, Cathy (IL), (312) 814-4735 115
Rivers, Beverly D. (DC), (202) 727-6306 74
Rivers, Robert E. (GA), (404) 656-5015 95
Rizzuto, Jim (CO), (303) 866-2868 50
Robberson, Rex (NM), (505) 476-7805 288
Robbs, Don (HI), (808) 973-1000 100
Roberge, A. Roland (NH), (603) 271-3561 266
Roberson, D. Sue (IN), (317) 233-3777 127
Roberts, Clarence W. (VA), (804) 213-4400 434
Roberts, Dean (MT), (406) 444-4536 240
Roberts, Earlene (R-NM), (505) 986-4758 291
Roberts, G. Mack (AL), (334) 242-6311 8
Roberts, Jack (OR), (503) 731-4070 349
Robertson, James M. (WI), (608) 263-7384 465
Robertson, John (MI), (517) 373-1275 201

Robertson, Linda (IA), (515) 281-5124 139
Robertson, Paul J. (D-IN), (317) 232-9600 130
Robichaud, Alan (NH), (603) 271-3236 268
Robinson, Barbara S. (OH), (614) 466-2613 323
Robinson, Bernie (IL), (202) 624-7776 113
Robinson, Ella D. (KY), (606) 573-3390 151
Robinson, J. Marty (MO), (573) 526-5210 232
Robinson, Lee (UT), (801) 629-4700 418
Robinson, Michael D. (MI), (517) 336-6157 202
Robinson, Mick (MT), (406) 444-3111 237
Robinson, Steve (TX), (512) 424-6001 413
Robison, John S. (AL), (334) 241-4166 6
Robison, Kelly P. (ID), (208) 332-8032 107
Robson, Cami (MT), (406) 444-1698 241
Roccabruna, Gene (WY), (307) 777-4484 476
Rochelle, Robert (D-TN), (615) 741-4109 402
Rock, Ed (WV), (304) 645-1090 459
Rockefeller, Winthrop P. (R-AR),
   (501) 682-2144 .... 29, 36
Rocque, Arthur J., Jr. (CT), (860) 424-3001 59
Roda, Richard G. (TN), (615) 741-7561 399
Rodowsky, Lawrence F. (MD), (410) 333-4374 ... 185
Rodrigue, Judith M. (J.R.) (CO), (303) 866-2903 ... 54
Roer, Kathleen (MN), (651) 296-3767 214
Rogers, Joe (R-CO), (303) 866-2087 47
Rogers, Mike (R-AL), (334) 242-7749 10
Rogers, Paula T. (NH), (603) 271-2261 269
Rohrs, Kenneth A. (NV), (775) 687-5469 259
Romano, Sheila (IL), (312) 814-2080 115
Romero, Gloria (D-CA), (916) 319-2049 46
Roogow, Buddy (MD), (410) 318-6370 180
Rooney, Patrick (OK), (405) 556-9210 341
Rosas, Janeen (MN), (651) 296-5665 210
Rose, Allen D. (KY), (502) 564-6606 155
Rose, B. Boykin (SC), (803) 896-7932 381
Rose, Gerald A. (MN), (651) 296-4484 211
Rose, Michael P. (IL), (312) 836-5337 117
Rose, Robert E. (NV), (775) 687-5170 264
Rosenbaum, Randall (RI), (401) 222-3880 367
Rosenberg, David (CA), (916) 323-7095 42
Rosenblatt, Albert M. (NY), (914) 486-6444 301
Ross, Anthony (IL), (217) 782-8223 120
Ross, Ron (NE), (402) 471-9106 250
Ross, Thomas W. (NC), (919) 733-7107 311
Ross, Vernon R. (PA), (717) 787-3633 358
Rotaru, Ronald J. (OH), (614) 925-0192 323
Roth, Arthur J. (NY), (518) 457-2244 299
Rothwell, Sharon (MI), (517) 335-7863 196
Rought, Raymond J. (MN), (651) 296-8046 214
Rounds, Dennis (SD), (605) 773-3769 387
Rounds, M. Michael (R-SD), (605) 773-3828 393
Routh, Andrea (MO), (573) 751-3082 233

Schillaci, Joseph A. (IL), (312) 793-3250 121
Schlueter, Kay (TX), (512) 463-1722 415
Schmidt, C. William (KY), (502) 429-8046 152
Schmidt, Fred (NV), (775) 687-6300 259
Schmidt, Gregory P. (CA), (916) 445-4251 45
Schmitz, Darrin (WI), (608) 266-1212 462
Schneider, Donald J. (WI), (608) 266-2517 469
Schoeninger, Martha Bell (PA), (717) 787-3936 ... 363
Schoesler, Mark (R-WA), (360) 786-7844 453
Scholer, Sue W. (R-IN), (317) 232-9600 130
Schrader, David F. (D-IA), (515) 281-3521 138
Schreiber, Margo E. (IL), (217) 785-2870 114
Schrenko, Linda C. (R-GA), (404) 656-2800 89
Schriber, Alan R. (OH), (614) 466-3204 328
Schriro, Dora B. (MO), (573) 526-6607 229
Schrock, Skip (MO), (573) 751-3222 226
Schroder, Kirk (VA), (804) 225-2023 436
Schroeder, Gerald F. (ID), (208) 334-3324 112
Schuler, Larry (ND), (701) 328-2655 313
Schuler, Matthew T. (OH), (614) 466-4900 331
Schulz, Dennis (ND), (701) 328-9737 319
Schumacher, David (WI), (608) 266-3212 468
Schumacher, Mary (NM), (505) 827-2658 287
Schumacher, Richard E. (OH), (614) 466-2822 328
Schumpert, Tom, Jr. (RI), (401) 222-2246 367
Schunk, Mae (REF-MN), (651) 296-0041 205
Schurke, Marvin L. (WA), (360) 753-3444 448
Schwabb, Eric (MD), (410) 260-8280 180
Schwartz, Carol (DC), (202) 724-8105 78
Schwartz, Howard P. (KS), (785) 296-4873 147
Schwartz, Michael S. (IL), (217) 782-2141 115
Schwartz, Richard J. (NY), (212) 387-7003 293
Schwarz, John (R-MI), (517) 373-3447 202
Schweiker, Mark S. (R-PA),
  (717) 787-3300 .... 354, 363
Sciotto, Charles T. (PA), (717) 787-5545 355
Scotillo, Christine M. (MN), (651) 284-3383 211
Scott, Clifton H. (D-OK), (405) 521-3495 334
Scott, Delbert (R-MO), (573) 751-8793 235
Scott, George M. (WV), (304) 558-2605 461
Scott, Greg (MN), (651) 296-7124 212
Scott, Gregory Kellam (CO),
  (303) 861-1111, ext. 256 55
Scott, Jerry W. (TN), (615) 251-5175 401
Scott, Wayne (TX), (936) 437-2101 407
Scott, William C. (OR), (503) 986-0110 346
Scroggins, James R. (MO), (573) 751-4050 233
Scudder, Susan (AK), (907) 465-3500 11
Searles, Brian R. (VT), (802) 828-2657 430
Sears, Leah Ward (GA), (404) 656-3474 95
Sebelius, Kathleen (D-KS), (785) 296-7801 143
Sedano, Richard P. (VT), (802) 828-2321 430

Sedwick, Deborah B. (AK), (907) 465-2500 13
See, Harold F. (AL), (334) 242-1001 10
Seely, Marilyn (HI), (808) 586-0100 99
Seely, William (OR), (503) 945-5100 351
Seerberman, Julian, Sr. (MO), (314) 340-4400 230
Seif, James M. (PA), (717) 787-2814 358
Seiler, Peter J. (AR), (501) 324-9506 31
Selby, Myra C. (IN), (317) 232-2544 130
Selecky, Mary (WA), (360) 236-4015 446
Selman, Robert (SC), (803) 896-4400 382
Selph, Mark (NC), (919) 571-4183 306
Semple, Donald L. (WV), (304) 558-2481 455
Senn, Deborah (D-WA), (360) 753-7301 447
Sensky, Jacqueline Romer (OH),
  (614) 466-6282 326
Sergi, Theodore S. (CT), (860) 566-5061 59
Serian, Betty L. (PA), (717) 787-3928 363
Serna, Patricio M. (NM), (505) 827-4886 291
Seymour, Joseph J. (NY), (518) 474-5991 296
Shackelford, Wayne (GA), (404) 656-5206 93
Shaffer, Bill (PA), (717) 705-1200 363
Shahan, Michael D. (DE), (302) 744-2510 71
Shaheen, Jeanne (D-NH), (603) 271-2121 265
Shallenburger, Tim (R-KS), (785) 296-3171 140
Shanahan, Mark R. (OH), (614) 466-6825 323
Shannahan, Joe (IA), (515) 281-0173 131
Shannahan, John W. (CT), (860) 566-3005 60
Shannon, Edward M., III (SC), (803) 734-1200 383
Shannon, John T. (AR), (501) 296-1940 32
Shapo, Nathaniel S. (IL), (217) 785-0116 117
Sharp, Thomas B. (D-DE), (302) 739-4163 71
Sharpe, William R., Jr. (D-WV),
  (304) 357-7845 460
Shaw, Leander J., Jr. (FL), (850) 488-0208 86
Shearing, Miriam (NV), (775) 687-5198 264
Shearouse, Daniel E. (SC), (803) 734-1080 384
Shell, Dorothy B. (TN), (615) 741-2958 400
Shelley, Kevin (D-CA), (916) 319-2012 46
Shelton, William C. (VA), (804) 371-7000 437
Shepard, Randall T. (IN), (317) 232-2550 130
Sheridan, Mike (TX), (512) 463-0735 413
Sheridan, Thomas P. (CT), (860) 240-0500 63
Sherlock, Edward P., Jr. (MD),
  (301) 791-4758 182
Sherman, Leonard A. (IL), (312) 814-4935 119
Sherrer, Gary (R-KS), (785) 296-2741 .... 140, 141
Shettleworth, Earle G., Jr. (ME),
  (207) 287-2132 169
Shiah, David C. (D-ME), (207) 287-1430 173
Shields, Charles W. (R-MO), (573) 751-9476 235
Shilts, William W. (IL), (217) 333-5111 118
Shimabukuro, David (HI), (808) 586-1700 97

Smith, V. Chapman (NY), (518) 473-7058 295
Smith, Wayne (MS), (601) 961-4000 223
Smith, Wayne A. (R-DE), (302) 739-4120 72
Smith-Jones, Angela (IN), (317) 233-4401 126
Snashell, Robert R. (NY), (518) 474-6670........... 300
Sneddon, Jacqueline (NV), (775) 687-5739 263
Snell, Bruce M., Jr. (IA), (515) 281-5174 139
Sneller, Todd C. (NE), (402) 471-2941 249
Snider, John (WV), (304) 558-2234 456
Snider, Mark (ID), (208) 334-2100 104
Snodgrass, Lynn (R-OR), (503) 986-1200 353
Snyder, Donald N., Jr. (IL), (217) 522-2666 115
Snyder, Donald William (R-PA),
(717) 787-4145 364
Snyder, Ed (CA), (916) 657-7669 40
Snyder, Linda L. (MA), (617) 542-1081 193
Snyder, Mark (R-OK), (405) 521-5622 342
Snyder, Shawn (DE), (202) 577-3210 65
Snyder, Sid (D-WA), (360) 786-7636 452
Snyder, Steve (AK), (907) 465-2580 17
Soaries, DeForest B., Jr. (I-NJ),
(609) 777-0884 275
Soden, Margaret (AK), (907) 465-2589 17
Soderberg, Donald (NV), (775) 687-6007 262
Solin, David M. (CO), (303) 892-3840 49
Solnit, Albert J. (CT), (860) 418-6969 60
Soltys, Stephen M. (SC), (803) 898-8319 380
Somers, Susan L. (KS), (785) 296-2162 141
Sommer, Lawrence J. (NE), (402) 471-4745 251
Sondheim, Walter, Jr. (MD), (410) 767-0467 178
Sonntag, Brian (D-WA), (360) 902-0360 443
Sorrell, William H. (D-VT), (802) 828-3173 425
Sorrells, Tom W. (AL), (334) 242-4191 7
Southcombe, R. Michael (ID), (208) 334-7500 110
Southwick, David L. (MN), (612) 627-4780......... 209
Southwick, Susan A. (NV), (775) 684-1640 264
Sowers, Raymond A. (SD), (605) 773-4260 386
Soyer, Jim (SD), (605) 773-3212 385
Spaeth, Dick (WY), (307) 777-3952 472
Span, Will (MS), (601) 933-2600 222
Spear, Allan H. (DFL-MN), (651) 296-4191 214
Spear, Robert W. (ME), (207) 287-3419 167
Spears, Stanhope S. (SC), (803) 806-4217 375
Speck, Samuel W. (OH), (614) 265-6879 327
Speer, Alfred W. (LA), (225) 342-7259 165
Speer, Donald R. (KY), (502) 564-2317 149
Spell, Lester, Jr. (MS), (601) 359-1100 217
Spence, Terry R. (R-DE), (302) 739-4127 72
Spencer, Susan (NJ), (202) 638-0631 275
Speros, Richard (Moose) (WI), (608) 261-0339 ... 468
Sperry, Michael R. (ME), (207) 624-7068 171
Spicer, Bradley (LA), (225) 922-1269 158

Spieler, Terry L. (MO), (573) 751-3766 235
Spies, Charlie (ME), (207) 623-3263 169
Spina, Francis X. (MA), (617) 557-1000 195
Spitzer, Eliot (D-NY), (212) 416-8050 292
Springer, Carol (R-AZ), (602) 542-1463 20
Sprouse, Vic (R-WV), (304) 357-7901 460
Sprynczynatyk, David A. (ND), (701) 328-4940 .. 320
St. Blanc, Lawrence C. (LA), (225) 342-4427 162
Stailey, George (IN), (317) 924-8400 125
Stalder, Richard L. (LA), (225) 342-6741 162
Stall, Albert M. (LA), (504) 838-5659 159
Stanchfield, Eric O. (WI), (608) 266-0407 464
Stanek, Ed (IA), (515) 281-7900 137
Stangler, Gary J. (MO), (573) 751-4815 233
Stanley, Daniel R. (KS), (785) 296-3011 141
Stansbury, Harry (LA), (504) 846-6970 163
Stanton, Stacey (AZ), (602) 712-8152 26
Staples, Nancy (IL), (847) 742-1040 117
Starcher, Larry V. (WV), (304) 558-2604 461
Starley, C. W. (GA), (404) 657-9300 93
Starnes, Daniel (TN), (615) 222-6749 400
Starr, Kevin (CA), (916) 654-0174 44
Starr, Terrell (D-GA), (404) 656-7586 94
Stearn, Gwena (RI), (401) 222-2353 367
Steeg, Jeff Ver (IL), (217) 782-6384 118
Steele, Joseph C. (NE), (402) 471-3730 256
Steen, Leslie W. (AR), (501) 682-6849 37
Steffian, Peter (MA), (617) 727-3072 187
Stein, Gary S. (NJ), (201) 996-8020 283
Steinmetz, Donald W. (WI), (608) 266-1884 470
Stella, David (WI), (608) 266-3285 464
Stenberg, Donald (R-NE), (402) 471-2682 246
Stenehjem, Dean (WA), (360) 696-6321 450
Stennett, Clint (D-ID), (208) 332-1351 112
Stephan, Kenneth C. (NE), (402) 471-3737 255
Stephens, Bonnie (UT), (801) 236-7555 418
Stephens, Fred (WA), (360) 902-3600 447
Stephens, Jack (MS), (601) 354-7377 223
Stephens, Joe (OR), (503) 986-5640 353
Stephens, Martin R. (R-UT), (801) 538-1612 423
Stephens, Robert F. (KY), (502) 564-7554 151
Stephens, Robert S. (KY), (502) 695-6303 152
Stephens, Thomas E. (NV), (775) 888-7440 262
Stephenson, Pamela Sturdivant (GA),
(404) 656-0710 89
Stevens, William L. (MS), (601) 354-6750 222
Stewart, Harry T. (NH), (603) 271-3503 268
Stewart, I. Daniel (UT), (801) 238-7950 424
Stewart, Jacquelyn (MI), (517) 322-1353 199
Stewart, John (AK), (907) 465-2275 14
Stewart, Linda (WI), (608) 267-9692 468
Stewart, Merwin U. (UT), (801) 538-3804 420

Vertefeuille, Christine (CT), (860) 566-4104 64
Vetter, Wayne E. (NH), (603) 271-3511 268
Vickers, Claude (GA), (404) 685-2410 93
Vickrey, William C. (CA), (415) 865-4200 46
Victor, Dorothy (NM), (505) 827-6320 286
Victory, Jeffrey P. (LA), (504) 568-5733 165
Vieh, Jackie (AZ), (602) 280-1306 22
Vieweg, William F. (WV), (304) 558-2630 458
Vigil-Giron, Rebecca (D-NM), (505) 827-3600 284
Viken, Gary (SD), (605) 773-5131 391
Villaraigosa, Antonio R. (D-CA),
    (916) 445-0703 45
Vilsack, Thomas J. (D-IA), (515) 281-5211 131
Vinje, Syver (ND), (701) 328-2910 319
Viohl, Jeff (IN), (202) 624-1474 122
Viola, Dennis J. (NH), (603) 624-9230 272
Virts, Henry A. (MD), (410) 841-5880 175
Viventi, Carol Morey (MI), (517) 373-2400 203
Vogel, David S. (NC), (919) 715-6097 306
Vogt, George L. (WI), (608) 264-6400 465
Voight, Jack (R-WI), (608) 266-1714 462
Volavka, Marc (PA), (717) 232-6787 359
Volk, David (SD), (605) 773-3178 386
Von Turkovich, Edward (VT), (802) 244-8721 430
Vonnahme, Donald R. (IL), (217) 782-2152 118
Voorhies, Gina (IN), (317) 233-4405 127
Vymlatil, Rick (FL), (813) 627-FAIR 84

W

Wade, John A. (TN), (615) 741-9001 401
Wade, Rick C. (SC), (803) 734-9520 375
Wadhams, Dick (CO), (303) 866-6324 47
Wadley, Fredia S. (TN), (615) 741-3111 399
Wadsworth, Karen O. (NH), (603) 271-2548 273
Wages, Eugene (SC), (803) 734-0200 383
Waggoner, J. T. (R-AL), (334) 242-7892 9
Wagner, L. Tim (NE), (402) 471-2201 251
Wagner, R. Thomas, Jr. (R-DE), (302) 739-5055 66
Wagner, Rod G. (NE), (402) 471-4001 252
Wagner, Thomas L., Jr. (SC), (803) 253-4160 375
Wainwright, George L., Jr. (NC),
    (919) 733-3713 311
Wakatsuki, Lynn Y. (HI), (808) 586-2820 98
Walcher, Greg E. (CO), (303) 866-4902 51
Wald, Francis J. (R-ND), (701) 483-9104 321
Waldron, Janet E. (ME), (207) 287-4547 167
Walker, Anne C. (MO), (573) 751-3829 235
Walker, Charles W. (D-GA), (404) 656-0400 94
Walker, Larry (D-GA), (404) 656-5024 95
Walker, Olene S. (UT), (801) 538-1520 416
Walker, Sheila (KS), (785) 296-3601 144

Walks, Ivan C.A. (DC), (202) 442-5999 76
Wall, Ashbel T., Jr. (RI), (401) 462-2611 368
Wall, Malcolm (OK), (405) 848-8501 336
Wallace, Larry D. (TN), (615) 741-0430 396
Wallace-Brodur, Paul (VT), (802) 241-3985 428
Waller, David (GA), (770) 918-6401 92
Waller, John H., Jr. (SC), (843) 423-8250 384
Waller, William L., Jr. (MS), (601) 359-2139 225
Walley, W. Dale (AL), (334) 242-5000 6
Walsh, Joseph T. (DE), (302) 577-8690 72
Walsh, Pamela (NH), (603) 271-2121 265
Walsh, Ted (NH), (603) 271-2121 265
Walshaw, L. Scott (NV), (775) 687-4259 258
Walters, Bill (R-AR), (501) 682-6050 36
Walters, Jesse R., Jr. (ID), (208) 334-3464 112
Walton, A. James, Jr. (VT), (802) 244-8718 430
Walton, Charles D. (D-RI), (401) 222-6655 371
Wandro, Mark F. (IA), (515) 239-1111 137
Wandruff, Robert F. (CA), (415) 865-7000 46
Ward, Kelly (NM), (505) 827-7003 289
Ward, Lance (OK), (405) 524-0126 342
Ward, Michael E. (NC), (919) 715-1299 308
Ward, Phil (OR), (503) 986-4552 345
Ward, Robert M. (R-CT), (860) 240-8700 63
Ward, Stephen G. (ME), (207) 287-2445 171
Ward, Sue F. (MD), (410) 767-1102 175
Ward, Tom (MS), (601) 987-1500 220
Ward, William F. (PA), (717) 787-5100 361
Warden, Larry (OK), (405) 557-7303 343
Warne, Thomas R. (UT), (801) 965-4113 422
Warner, John D. (MA), (617) 727-2816 187
Warner, Lee (AL), (334) 242-3184 5
Warr, James W. (AL), (334) 271-7710 4
Warren, Gail (VA), (804) 786-2075 441
Warren, Gary L., Sr. (TX), (512) 239-4912 408
Warren, Keith E. (AL), (334) 242-1918 4
Warren, Kenneth I. (MS), (601) 359-7002 223
Warren, Pamela M. (OK), (405) 521-4027 334
Wasell, Millicent A. (NJ), (609) 292-9830 281
Washington, Maurice E. (R-NV),
    (775) 687-3652 263
Washington, Odie (DC), (202) 673-7316 75
Waters, Barbara A. (CT), (860) 713-5100 57
Wathen, Daniel E. (ME), (207) 287-6950 173
Watson, Robert A. (R-RI), (401) 222-2259 372
Watt, Joseph M. (OK), (405) 521-3848 343
Watts, Beverly L. (KY), (502) 595-4024 151
Watts-Elder, Cynthia (CT), (860) 541-3451 60
Way, Charles S., Jr. (SC), (803) 737-0851 376
Way, J. Edson (NM), (505) 827-6364 285
Weaver, Charles R., Jr. (MN), (651) 296-6642 212
Weaver, Elizabeth A. (MI), (231) 929-3700 204

Williams, Juanita (OK), (405) 521-3441 338
Williams, Kay (IA), (515) 281-6841 134
Williams, Mark (TN), (615) 741-4737 397
Williams, Meredith (KS), (785) 296-6666 144
Williams, Richard J. (NJ), (609) 984-0275 283
Williams, Steven A. (KS), (785) 296-2281 145
Williams, Thomas H. (MD), (410) 764-4276 182
Williams, Wendell P. (D-NV), (775) 684-8545 263
Williams, William (Bill) H., Jr. (NC),
   (919) 571-4904 309
Williamson, Dayle E. (NE), (402) 471-3927 252
Williamson, Donald Ellis (AL), (334) 206-5200 7
Willis, John T. (D-MD), (410) 974-5521 174
Willis, LaVonne (UT), (801) 524-6048 422
Wills, Donald A. (ME), (207) 287-4413 167
Wilner, Alan M. (MD), (410) 887-2677 185
Wilson, Alden C. (ME), (207) 287-2720 167
Wilson, B. R. (VA), (540) 676-5423 435
Wilson, Benjamin F. (DC), (202) 727-2525 75
Wilson, David M. (KS), (785) 296-3335 141
Wilson, Debra M. Simmons (IN),
   (317) 232-1147 125
Wilson, Donald E. (MD), (410) 764-3460 179
Wilson, E. Dotson (CA), (916) 319-2856 46
Wilson, Earl (MN), (651) 296-3711 208
Wilson, Jon (IA), (515) 281-7304 136
Wilson, LeAnne (MI), (202) 624-5840 196
Wilson, Quentin (MO), (573) 751-5671 233
Wilson, Roger B. (D-MO), (573) 751-4727 .. 226, 234
Wilson, Rose (MI), (517) 373-0219 200
Wilson, Roy C. (MO), (573) 751-3070 231
Wilson, Sara Redding (VA), (804) 225-2237 438
Wilson, Steve N. (AR), (501) 223-6305 32
Wilson, Susan (OR), (503) 378-8667 346
Wilson-Coker, Patricia (CT), (860) 424-5008 62
Wiltse, John T. (CT), (860) 566-3180 59
Wiltse, Milton A. (AK), (907) 451-5001 16
Winder, Charles L. (ID), (208) 334-8808 111
Winder, David B. (UT), (801) 538-8708 418
Windom, Steve (R-AL), (334) 242-7900 .... 1, 9
Wineholt, Ronald W. (MD), (410) 767-1184 176
Wing, Brian J. (NY), (518) 474-4152 299
Wingfield, Gus (D-AR), (501) 682-6030 30
Winkle, Alan (ID), (208) 334-3365 110
Winn, Kenneth H. (MO), (573) 751-4717 227
Winn, Thomas D. (NH), (603) 271-2569 270
Winsley, William T. (OH), (614) 466-4143 328
Winstead, Jean D. (DE), (302) 577-2437 73
Winter, Tracy (IL), (217) 524-5414 116
Winters, Ken (NE), (402) 471-9478 249
Wintersheimer, Donald C. (KY),
   (502) 564-4166 156

Wise, Alex (VA), (804) 367-2323 437
Wise, Gary A. (UT), (801) 284-6350 419
Wise, Martha W. (OH), (614) 466-4838 325
Wisler, Rick A. (NH), (603) 271-3391 269
Wissel, Lupe (ID), (208) 334-2423 105
Witek, Kate (R-NE), (402) 471-2111 247
Wobschall, Rachel (MN), (651) 296-0028 205
Wodele, John (MN), (651) 296-0001 205
Wojahn, R. Lorraine (D-WA), (360) 786-7652 451
Wolfe, Cathy (D-WA), (360) 786-7992 452
Wolfe, Gary D. (PA), (717) 787-2646 358
Wolfe, Nancy (CA), (916) 445-8174 41
Wolff, Michael A. (MO), (573) 751-4410 235
Wood, Corinne (R-IL), (217) 782-7884 113
Wood, Gina (SC), (803) 896-9791 379
Wood, J. Walter, Jr. (AL), (334) 215-3800 9
Wood, Jackie D. (TN), (615) 313-3001 396
Wood, Jeannine (ID), (208) 332-1310 112
Wood, Patrick, III (TX), (512) 936-7005 412
Wood, Robert (WI), (608) 266-1212 462
Wood, William G. (MA), (617) 727-3074 192
Wood, William J. (NE), (402) 471-4106 247
Woodbury, Glen L. (WA), (253) 512-7000 444
Woodfin, William L., Jr. (VA), (804) 367-9231 438
Woodfork, Larry D. (WV), (304) 594-2331 456
Woodhouse, Gay (WY), (307) 777-7841 471
Woodley, John Paul, Jr. (VA), (804) 786-0044 438
Woodruff, Valerie A. (DE), (302) 739-4601 67
Woodson, Alan (IL), (217) 785-4500 115
Woodson, Roderic L. (DC), (202) 442-4445 74
Workman, Harold (KY), (502) 367-5114 154
Worsech, Jeanne (MT), (406) 444-4288 239
Worsham, Jane (NC), (919) 715-1318 308
Woude, Diana Vander (SD), (605) 362-2760 391
Wright, Bill (R-UT), (801) 538-1254 423
Wright, Dennis M. (AL), (334) 242-7463 3
Wright, John F. (NE), (402) 471-3735 255
Wright, Larry (AL), (334) 242-4900 4
Wright, Linda (ND), (701) 328-8910 315
Wyant, Dan (MI), (517) 373-1052 197
Wyatt, Bill (OR), (503) 373-1565 344
Wyatt, Wesley (NC), (919) 821-7400 308
Wyman, Nancy (D-CT), (860) 702-3301 57
Wynkoop, Debra (UT), (801) 538-9084 419
Wynn, Kenneth F. (UT), (801) 977-6800 417

Y

Yacino, Richard (RI), (401) 222-2837 371
Yamada, Dennis (HI), (808) 586-2020 97
Yamamura, James T. (HI), (808) 586-0358 97
Yandow, Alan R. (VT), (802) 479-5686 429